Books
Are Fun®

Children's

Dictionary

The most
up-to-date
dictionary
available

Editorial Staff

Editor in Chief **Robert B. Costello**

Editorial Director **Jonathan P. Latimer**

Photography Coordinator **Martin W. Sandler**

Managing Editor **Karen Stray Nolting**

Editors **Linda Butler, Harold Niergarth, Joseph Patwell, Julia Penelope**

Copy Editors **Sharon Goldstein, Jennifer S. Goss, Judith Kaplan**

Proofreader **M. Madeleine Newell**

Advisors

Language Arts **Charles Temple, Hobart and William Smith Colleges, New York**

Pronunciation **Sharon Goldstein**

Etymology **Joseph M. Patwell**

Book design   **Watertown, MA**

Cover design **Paul Dronsfield**

Photo Credits appear on page 864
Gallaudent font of Manual Alphabet on page 679 © 1991 by David Rakowski
Maps on pages 850 to 861 © 1997 GeoSystems Global Corp.

Every effort has been made to ascertain the proper sources for the photographs in this book.
The inclusion or misattribution of ownership in this book without proper authorization is purely
accidental. Such mistakes will be rectified upon proper notification.

SIMON & SCHUSTER BOOKS FOR YOUNG READERS
An imprint of Simon & Schuster Children's Publishing Division
1230 Avenue of the Americas, New York, New York 10020

Library of Congress Cataloging-in-Publication Data
Books Are Fun dictionary for children
        p.   cm.
Summary: Includes 35,000 entries, with photographs, illustrations, and maps,
as well as word histories, spelling hints, and cultural- and gender-inclusive definitions.
ISBN 1-58209-827-1

Printed in China

Contents

Spelling Hints give key information at the beginning of each letter where you can find it easily.

SPELLING TIPS

The letter G has two sounds in English. Both of these sounds can be made in several ways:

The sound of G in words such as get, give, and go is often made by:
  gg in the middle or at the end of words such as egg and wriggle.

The sound of G in get is made less often by:
  gu as in guard.

The letter G also sounds like the letter J in words such as gem and page.

The letter G also appears silently in combinations with other letters such as:
  gh in laugh and though; ght as in light, sight, and thought.

Main Entries are easy to find.

g, G The seventh letter of the alphabet. **g, G** (jē) *noun, plural* **g's, G's.**

g An abbreviation for gram.

GA Postal abbreviation for Georgia.

Ga. An abbreviation for Georgia.

gable The part of an outside wall between the sides of a sloping roof. The gable is shaped like a triangle. **ga·ble** (gā'bəl) *noun, plural* **gables.**

Gabon A country in west-central Africa. **Ga·bon** (ga bōn') *noun.*

Words that sound alike are clearly indicated.

gadget A small, useful tool or device. **gad·get** (gaj'it) *noun, plural* **gadgets.**

Verb Forms.

gag 1. Something put in the mouth to keep a person from talking or shouting. 2. A joke. *Noun.*
  ○ 1. To keep someone from talking or shouting by using a gag. 2. To feel as if one were about to vomit; choke: *The dog gagged on a bone. Verb.*
gag (gag) *noun, plural* **gags;** *verb,* **gagged, gagging.**

Syllable Division.

gaiety Joy and fun; being merry: *the gaiety of a circus.* **gai·e·ty** (gā'i tē) *noun, plural* **gaieties.**

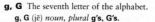

SYNONYMS

Synonym lists help you select the right words.

gaiety, glee, festivity, fun
The gaiety of the children at the party delighted all the grown ups. We laughed with glee at the monkey's tricks. The festivity of the carnival made up for the long trip we took to get there. The children couldn't stop talking about the fun they had in the amusement park on the boardwalk.

302

gaily In a gay manner; happily. **gai·ly** (gā'lē) *adverb.*

gain 1. To get or win: *You will gain experience by working at the store.* 2. To benefit in some way: *We all gained from the building of the new bridge.* 3. To get to; reach: *The ship gained the port before the storm. Verb.*
  ○ Something gained: *a gain of ten yards. Noun.*
gain (gān) *verb,* **gained, gaining;** *noun, plural* **gains.**

gait A way of walking or running: *The horse's gait changed from a trot to a gallop.*
Another word that sounds like this is **gate.**
gait (gāt) *noun, plural* **gaits.**

A zebra's gait allows it to move at a rapid pace.

gal. An abbreviation for gallon.

gala Festive; suitable for a celebration: *a gala banquet. Adjective.*
  ○ A festive occasion; celebration. *Noun.*
ga·la (gā'lə or gal'ə) *adjective; noun, plural* **galas.**

Abbreviations are included in alphabetical order.

More than 1,100 dazzling color photos illustrate and expand your understanding of words.

Full captions add interest and information.

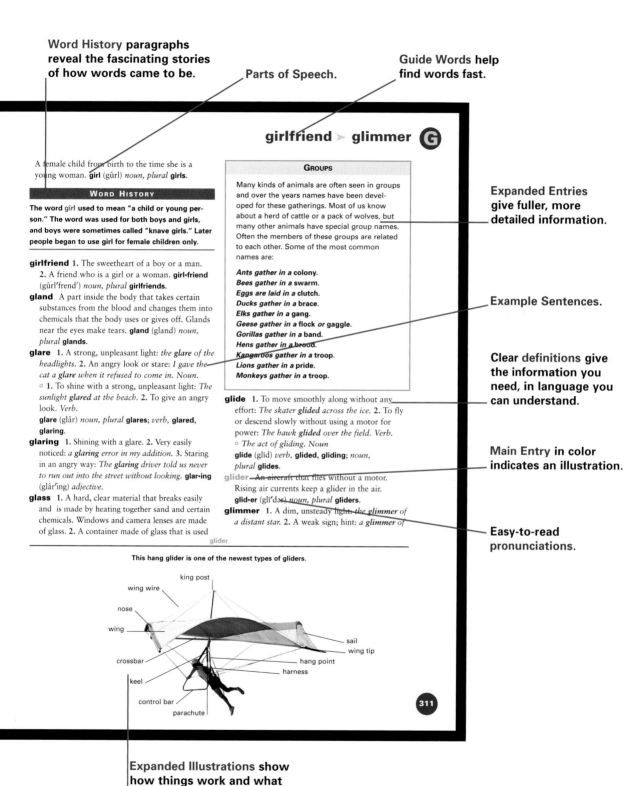

Word History paragraphs reveal the fascinating stories of how words came to be.

Parts of Speech.

A female child from birth to the time she is a young woman. **girl** (gûrl) *noun, plural* **girls.**

WORD HISTORY

The word girl used to mean "a child or young person." The word was used for both boys and girls, and boys were sometimes called "knave girls." Later people began to use girl for female children only.

girlfriend 1. The sweetheart of a boy or a man. 2. A friend who is a girl or a woman. **girl·friend** (gûrl′frend′) *noun, plural* **girlfriends.**

gland A part inside the body that takes certain substances from the blood and changes them into chemicals that the body uses or gives off. Glands near the eyes make tears. **gland** (gland) *noun, plural* **glands.**

glare 1. A strong, unpleasant light: *the glare of the headlights.* 2. An angry look or stare: *I gave the cat a glare when it refused to come in.* Noun. ○ 1. To shine with a strong, unpleasant light: *The sunlight glared at the beach.* 2. To give an angry look. Verb.
glare (glâr) *noun, plural* **glares;** *verb,* **glared, glaring.**

glaring 1. Shining with a glare. 2. Very easily noticed: *a glaring error in my addition.* 3. Staring in an angry way: *The glaring driver told us never to run out into the street without looking.* **glar·ing** (glâr′ing) *adjective.*

glass 1. A hard, clear material that breaks easily and is made by heating together sand and certain chemicals. Windows and camera lenses are made of glass. 2. A container made of glass that is used

GROUPS

Many kinds of animals are often seen in groups and over the years names have been developed for these gatherings. Most of us know about a herd of cattle or a pack of wolves, but many other animals have special group names. Often the members of these groups are related to each other. Some of the most common names are:

Ants gather in a colony.
Bees gather in a swarm.
Eggs are laid in a clutch.
Ducks gather in a brace.
Elks gather in a gang.
Geese gather in a flock or gaggle.
Gorillas gather in a band.
Hens gather in a brood.
Kangaroos gather in a troop.
Lions gather in a pride.
Monkeys gather in a troop.

glide 1. To move smoothly along without any effort: *The skater glided across the ice.* 2. To fly or descend slowly without using a motor for power: *The hawk glided over the field.* Verb. ○ *The act of gliding.* Noun
glide (glīd) *verb,* **glided, gliding;** *noun, plural* **glides.**

glider An aircraft that flies without a motor. Rising air currents keep a glider in the air. **glid·er** (glī′dər) *noun, plural* **gliders.**

glimmer 1. A dim, unsteady light: *the glimmer of a distant star.* 2. A weak sign; hint: *a glimmer of*

Expanded Entries give fuller, more detailed information.

Example Sentences.

Clear definitions give the information you need, in language you can understand.

Main Entry in color indicates an illustration.

Easy-to-read pronunciations.

glider

This hang glider is one of the newest types of gliders.

king post
wing wire
nose
wing
crossbar
keel
control bar
parachute
sail
wing tip
hang point
harness

311

Expanded Illustrations show how things work and what their parts are called.

How to Use Your Dictionary

Welcome to the *Books Are Fun Dictionary for Children*. All kinds of information about words is waiting for you in these pages. You can learn the meaning of words you read or hear. You can learn how to spell words, how to say them, and where they come from. But you can't make use of all this information unless you know how to find it and how to understand it.

Fortunately, learning how a dictionary works is easy. But this dictionary has some special things you need to know in order get the most out of it. The following sections show you how to use your dictionary.

How to Look Up Words

Because there are so many words in this dictionary, there would be no way that you could find the one you wanted if all the words were not arranged according to a system.

Main Entries The words you are looking for are printed in heavy black letters—**like this**. They are called *main entries*. You will find these words at the left-hand side of each column on the dictionary pages.

Alphabetical Order Main entries are organized in *alphabetical order*. This means that the words are arranged in a long list following the order of the alphabet. All the words that start with the letter **A**, like **admit**, **afternoon**, and **astronaut**, are found at the beginning of the book. They are followed by words that begin with **B**, then **C**, and so on through the rest of the alphabet to **Z**.

Under each letter of the alphabet, the words are also listed in alphabetical order. Since all the words in the **A** section start with the same letter, the second letter decides the order of words in the list. If the second letter of two words is the same, or even the third letter—as in **alligator** and **allow**—then a letter farther along in the word decides which comes first, as in this example.

acrobat	allow
add	asparagus
admit	aspen
afternoon	asphalt
alligator	astronaut

Guide Words Help You Find the Word You Are Looking For

Suppose you want to find the word **comet** in your dictionary. If you turn to where the C words are, you will find that they begin on page **107** and end on page **183**. But you do not have to hunt through every page of the C's to find **comet**. Instead, you can look at the top outside corner of each page. There you will find pairs of **guide words** that look like these:

combination ➤ comma

"Guide" means to show the way, and "guide words" show you the way to the word you are looking for. The first guide word tells you the first main entry on that page, on the upper left-hand corner. The second guide word tells you the last main entry on that page, on the lower right-hand corner. The word you want will be found between the guide words in its proper alphabetical place.

Because the word **comet** comes between **combination** and **comma**, you will know that it is on the page with those guide words.

Can you see that the sign for **hippopotamus** to the right is spelled wrong? If you look up **hipopotamus** in the dictionary, you will find that it is spelled **hippopotamus**, with two *p*'s, not one. Whenever you are not sure how to spell a word, look it up in your dictionary. It will be easy to find because it is printed in dark, heavy letters. If you want to write the word, you must spell it *exactly* as you see it in the dictionary. That way your spelling will always be correct.

Something is wrong with this sign.

How Can I Find a Word if I Don't Know How to Spell It?

Trying to figure out how a word is spelled in English can be very confusing. Many letters or combinations of letters can stand for the same sound or for more than one sound. Some letters can even be silent in certain words, such as the *b* in *comb* or the *p* in *pneumonia*.

Spelling Hints You can find a special feature on spelling at the beginning of each letter in this dictionary. This feature lists the various sounds each letter can have, and other letters or combinations of letters that give the same sound in English. You should be able to find the letter that gives the sound you need to spell in the word you are looking for in these *Spelling Hints*.

What Words Mean

This dictionary can answer many questions about words, but the one you will ask most often is "What does this word mean?" That is why the meaning of a word comes right after the word itself in your dictionary.

> **boa constrictor** A large snake that is found in Mexico and in Central and South America. A boa constrictor is not poisonous. It kills its prey by coiling around it and squeezing it to death.

The Definition of a Word The meaning of a word is also called its *definition*. As you can see from the example above, the definition of the word **boa constrictor** begins by telling you what it is—a large snake. Then as you read on, you can learn more things about a **boa constrictor**—that it is found in Mexico and Central and South America, that it is not poisonous, and that it kills its prey in a special way.

Sometimes part of a definition is just one word. This word is a *synonym*. A synonym is a word that has nearly the same meaning as another word. For example, the words **gather** and **collect** are synonyms.

> **gather** 1. To come or bring together: collect.

In some cases, several words share similar meanings. In this dictionary, many of these groups of words are presented in special notes, called **Synonyms**. A discussion of these notes appears on page **f14**.

Words With More Than One Meaning Many words have more than one meaning. The different meanings are listed separately and numbered. The meaning that is used most often is listed first. It is followed by the second most common meaning, and so on.

> **uncertain** 1. Not known for sure; not certain: *It is still **uncertain** whether our team will win the game.* 2. Not dependable; changing: *The weather was **uncertain**, so we canceled the picnic.*

Some words have more than one meaning because they can be used as more than one part of speech, as explained on page **f12**. For words like these, the meanings for each part of speech are listed separately. A change in the part of speech is indicated by an open dot (∘).

> **beach** The land along the edge of a body of water: *A **beach** is covered with sand or pebbles.* Noun.
> ∘ To run a boat onto a beach: *They **beached** the sailboat.* Verb.

How Words Are Used

After the definition of a word, you will usually find an example that shows you how the word is used. These examples appear in *italic* type after the definition, with the key word in **bold type**:

> **pamphlet** A small book that has a paper cover: *The board game came with a **pamphlet** of playing instructions.* **pam·phlet** (pam′flit) *noun*, *plural* **pamphlets**.

Such examples make a word's meaning clearer. Whenever you hear or read a new word, you get an idea of what the word means from the way it is used and the words it is used with. This dictionary lets you use that skill by giving you an example of how the word is used in a sentence.

Words that Do Not Mean What They Say

Suppose you were to read that several senators want more time "to make up their minds" before they vote on a new law. You know that they do not want more time to put makeup on their minds before voting. Instead, they want more time to decide. "To make up one's mind" means "to decide."

The phrase "to make up one's mind" means something different from what you would expect from the meanings of the individual words in it. Such a phrase is called an **idiom**.

Many idioms are defined in your dictionary. You can find them easily because each entry is introduced with a black dot (•). If you want to find the definition of an idiom, look at the entry for the most important word in the idiom. To locate the idiom **to make up one's mind**, for example, you would look up the entry **mind**.

> **mind** **1.** The part of a person that thinks, knows, learns, remembers, understands, and feels: *Keep your **mind** on what you're doing.* **2.** A wish or opinion: *I changed my **mind** about visiting when I heard you were sick.* Noun.
> ° **1.** To pay attention to or worry about: ***Mind** your manners.* **2.** To take care of: *A baby-sitter **minded** the children when their parents went out.* **3.** To dislike something; to object to: *Do you **mind** doing to the movies alone?* Verb.
> • **never mind.** To not worry or pay attention: ***Never mind** about the dirty dishes.*
> • **to make up one's mind.** To decide: *I **made up** my **mind** to leave.*

How Words Are Spoken

After the definition or definitions of a word have been given, the main-entry word is printed again in **bold** black letters. This marks the beginning of a block of information that tells you many useful and important things about the word.

> **ath·lete** (ath′lēt) *noun, plural* **athletes.**
> **grate** (grāt) *verb,* **grated, grating.**
> **raw** (rô) *adjective,* **rawer, rawest.**
> **tru·ly** (trü′lē) *adverb.*

Syllables   The word may be divided into smaller parts by black dots:

> **lar·yn·gi·tis**
> **ma·chine**
> **Cal·i·for·nia**

These smaller parts of a word are called *syllables.* Knowing how to divide a word into syllables can help you when you write. Suppose you were writing the word **California,** and you did not have room for the whole word at the end of a line. You could break the word wherever there is a black dot and put a hyphen (-) after the first part to show that there is more to come on the next line.

> My grandparents lived in Cal-
> ifornia all their lives.

If a word is not divided into smaller parts by black dots, the word has only one syllable. Such a word should never be broken. If it doesn't fit at the end of a line, move the whole word to the next line.

Pronouncing a Word   After the division of the word into syllables comes a special spelling of the word which is placed between parentheses. This special spelling, called the *pronunciation,* tells you how to say the word. It usually looks somewhat different from the regular spelling of the word because it uses special symbols that are not found in ordinary writing and printing.

> **care** (kâr)
> **dry-clean** (drī′klēn′)
> **eyebrow** (ī′brou′)
> **gaunt** (gônt)
> **know** (nō)
> **mother** (mu<u>th</u>′ər)
> **truce** (trüs)

The special symbols are needed to show all the different sounds we use when we speak. We use only the 26 letters in the regular alphabet when we write, but we use more than 40 different sounds when we speak. Think about the letter **e**. It is said one way in **me**, another way in **end**, and still another way in **taken**.

Stress or Accent Marks Also, when we say a word with more then one part or syllable, we say some syllables with a stronger tone than we do others. In the pronunciation, a heavy black mark (′) after a syllable shows that it is spoken the most loudly of any part of the word. A lighter mark (′) means that the syllable is spoken loudly but not as loudly as a syllable with a heavy black mark. These are called *stresses* or *accents*. If there is no mark at all, it means that the syllable is spoken with less emphasis than any syllable with a mark.

but·ter·fly (but′ər flī′)

You will find all the different sounds of the English language on the left column of the *Pronunciation Key* on page **f32**. On the right-hand columns, you will find different ways these sounds are spelled. But you usually do not have to turn to the *Pronunciation Key* to understand a pronunciation. Instead, you can look at the bottom of most right-hand pages in this dictionary. There you will find a shorter pronunciation key across the bottom of the page. It gives all the special symbols and spellings that are used to show sounds in the pronunciations. The short pronunciation key looks like this:

PRONUNCIATION KEY:

at	āpe	fär	câre	end	mē	it	īce	pierce	hot	ōld	sông	fôrk
oil	out	up	ūse	rüle	pûll	tûrn	chin	sing	shop	thin	this	

hw in white; zh in treasure. The symbol ə stands for the unstressed vowel sound in about, taken, pencil, lemon, and circus.

How Words Are Classified

The Parts of Speech The words we use when we speak or write are divided into different groups. These groups are called *parts of speech*. The part of speech of a word depends on the way the word is used. Some words can be used as more than one part of speech. The parts of speech are *noun, verb, adjective, adverb, pronoun, preposition, conjunction*, and *interjection*. In this dictionary a word's part of speech is shown right after the pronunciation.

> **mid·night** (mid′nīt′) *noun.*
> **stuck** (stuk) *verb.*

How Words Change

After the part of speech, there may be more special information about the word. Most words have several different forms in addition to the basic form that is given in the main entry.

Nouns If the word is a **noun,** this dictionary shows the form to use when you want to show the idea of more than one. This form is called the noun's *plural.*

> **class·mate** (klas′māt′) *noun, plural* **classmates.**
> **lar·va** (lär′və) *noun, plural* **larvae** (lär′vē).

Verbs For a **verb,** this dictionary shows the forms to use when talking or writing about an action or condition that was in the past, or that is or was continuing.

> **al·low** (ə lou′) *verb,* **allowed, allowing.**
> **grow** (grō) *verb,* **grew, grown, growing.**

Adjectives and Adverbs If an **adjective** or **adverb** has special forms that are used to show the idea of more or most, this dictionary also shows those forms.

> **crisp** (krisp) *adjective,* **crisper, crispest.**
> **good** (gu̇d) *adjective,* **better, best.**
> **lit·tle** (lit′əl) *adverb,* **less, least.**

If a word can be used as **more than one part of speech,** the dictionary shows the form for each part.

> **cam·paign** (kam pān′) *noun, plural* **campaigns;** *verb,*
> **campaigned, campaigning.**

Words that Sound Alike

Some words sound the same but are spelled differently. These words are called *homophones*. Words like **no** and **know, ate** and **eight,** or **sun** and **son** are examples of homophones. Words that sound alike can make our language tricky.

Suppose some friends were to describe their trip to the zoo and tell you about an animal you have never heard of. Its name sounds like the words **knew** and **new.** If you look up **knew** or **new,** you will not see anything about an animal. But this dictionary has a way to get you to the right place. At the end of the definitions for **new** you will find a sentence that is highlighted in green. That sentence will read "Other words that sound like this are **knew** and **gnu.**" The **gnu** is what you're hunting for!

> **gnu** A large African animal. A gnu is a kind of antelope but has a large head and a stocky build like an ox.
> Other words that sound like this are **knew** and **new.**
> **gnu** (nü *or* nū) *noun, plural* **gnus** *or* **gnu.**

Watch for a sentence highlighted in green at the end of an entry. It will tell you that there are other words that sound like the one you looked up.

Words that Look Alike

Two different words can also be spelled the same way. Suppose you were to read this sentence: "Many baseball bats are made of **ash.**" If you only know about the kind of ash that comes from burning something, a baseball bat made of ash might sound strange. Your dictionary can solve this puzzle. It has two different entries for **ash.**

> **ash**[1] A small amount of grayish white powder left after something has burned: *A pile of ashes was all that remained of the burned leaves.* **ash** (ash) *noun, plural* **ashes.**
> **ash**[2] A tree that has a strong wood. Ash is used in construction and in making baseball bats. **ash** (ash) *noun, plural* **ashes.**

Words such as these are called *homographs*. In this dictionary the main entries for words that are homographs have a small number after them. Some homographs, like **ash**[1] and **ash**[2], are both spelled and pronounced the same way. Other homographs are spelled the same but pronounced differently. For example, **bow**[2] (a weapon for shooting arrows) and **bow**[3] (the front end of a boat) look the same, but sound quite different.

Words with Similiar Meanings

Synonyms Some words are very close to each other in meaning, but also have slight differences from each other. When you are searching for just the right word, these differences can mean a lot. That is why this dictionary has special notes called *Synonyms*. These notes appear under a blue rule. They list words that have close meanings and give examples of how those words are used.

> ### SYNONYMS
>
> **gather, accumulate, assemble, collect**
> *The principal gathered all the teachers for a meeting.*
> *The snow kept accumulating on all the roads and*
> *sidewalks. The entire school assembled for the play.*
> *Our class collects over 3,000 cans in the drive every*
> *year.*

Learning about Words from Pictures

Even in a dictionary, which is a book of words, a picture can be very important. Sometimes a picture can help you understand something more clearly than a definition alone can. Read the following entry:

> **dam** A wall built across a stream or river to hold
>   back the water and form a lake or pond. Dams can
>   be used to prevent floods or generate electricity.
>   ° To hold back with a dam: *Beavers dam streams*
>   *with mud and sticks. Verb.*
>   **dam** (dam) *noun, plural* **dams**; *verb*, **dammed,**
>   **damming**.

What does a dam look like, and how does it hold back water? Look at the picture here, which appears in the dictionary with the entry for **dam**. It helps answer these questions.

This dictionary contains many pictures like this to help you understand the meanings of words. Read the following entry, and then look at the photograph. Does it help you understand the meaning of **gait**?

Picture Captions The pictures in this dictionary are accompanied by captions. These captions add information about the subject of the picture and the entry word it illustrates. For example, look again at the picture and caption for the word **gait**.

> **gait** A way of walking or running: *The horse's* **gait** *changed from a trot to a gallop.*
> Another word that sounds like this is **gate.**
> **gait** (gāt) *noun, plural* **gaits**.

A zebra's gait allows it to move at a rapid pace.

The caption not only helps explain the meaning of **gait**, it also tells you something interesting about zebras.

Expanded Illustrations Some of the words in this dictionary name complex objects that have many parts. Many of these have illustrations which contain labels that name the important parts of that object. All the words used in the labels in the expanded illustrations are also defined in the entry list of this dictionary. For example, here is the expanded illustration found with the entry for **volcano**.

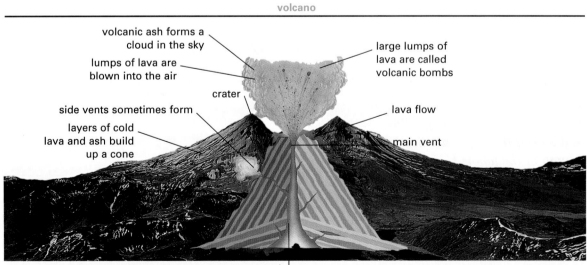

volcano

volcanic ash forms a cloud in the sky

lumps of lava are blown into the air

large lumps of lava are called volcanic bombs

crater

side vents sometimes form

layers of cold lava and ash build up a cone

lava flow

main vent

magma (molten rock) rises from beneath the earth

Where Words Come From

Many words have interesting stories to tell us. They may have been borrowed from a foreign language, or they may have changed their meaning greatly since they were first used. This dictionary presents these stories in special features, with the title **Word History**, which are printed beneath a red box below the word whose story they tell.

For example, did you know that the word **bankrupt** comes from two Italian words meaning "a broken bench"? Here is the Word History that appears below the entry for **bankrupt**:

WORD HISTORY

The word bankrupt comes from two Italian words that mean "broken bench." In the Middle Ages in Italy, bankers kept their money in benches. When a banker could not pay people what they were owed, the bench was broken.

The Names of the States There is a Word History for every state in the United States. Look up the entry for the state that you live in. What does the Word History tell you about the name of your state?

WORD HISTORY

Nebraska was an Indian name for the Platte River. It means "flat water." The river's name was changed, but the Indian name was kept for the state.

Information about the States At the entry for each state you will also find a map of the state showing its capital, followed by some interesting information about the state, including its nickname and its state flower and bird.

Additional information about each state can be found on pages 838 and 839 of the Reference Section. A map of the whole United States is located on page 855.

Michigan
U. S. Postal Abbreviation: **MI**
Capital: **Lansing**
Population: **9,200,000**
Area: **58,216 sq. mi./150,779 sq. km**
State Nickname: **Wolverine State**
State Bird: **Robin**
State Flower: **Apple Blossom**

Learning More about Words

A **Language Note** will help you use a word correctly. It appears in a blue box right after the entry for the word it discusses. Be sure to read the Language Note when you find one. It will help you to express yourself more clearly.

For example, do you know when to use the word **can** and when to use the word **may**? Here is the Language Note that appears after the entry for **can**:

> ### LANGUAGE NOTE
>
> **At one time people were careful to use the word can to mean only "to be able to" and to use the word may to mean "to have permission to." Many people still prefer to use these words carefully with different meanings, especially in writing.**

Adding to Your Knowledge about Words

In many places in this dictionary you will find **expanded entries** which give additional interesting information about an entry. For example, on the same page as the entry for **size** you will find this expanded entry:

> ### SIZE
>
> Animals come in all sizes, from the microscopic to the giant. The smallest is hard to choose because there are numerous one-celled animals. The records for the largest living animals are:
>
> **Largest animal:** the blue whale with a length of 110 feet and a weight of 209 tons.
> **Largest land animal:** the African elephant which weighs 8 tons.
> **Largest reptile:** the saltwater crocodile at 16 feet long and 1,150 pounds.
> **Largest fish:** the whale shark at 41 feet long.
> **Largest bird:** the ostrich which is 9 feet tall and weighs 345 pounds.
> **Largest insect:** the stick insect which is 15 inches long.

Similar expanded entries can be found throughout the book. For example, look up **alphabet, dinosaur, hurricane, money,** or **wonder.**

The Story of English

"This hamburger tastes great!" "What time does the next show start?" "I think it's going to rain." "Watch out for that car!" "You did a good job on your homework."

Look at the five sentences above. How are they the same? They tell about different things. They are arranged in different ways. Each one has a different number of words. They are made up of 30 different words in all. Yet in one important way all these sentences are the same. They are all written in one *language*—**English**. But just what *is* a "language" and what is "English"?

What is a Language?

When a lot of people live in the same place and talk the same way, the words they use are called a *language*. We use words all the time to tell other people what we are thinking, and we want to be sure that they can understand us. That is why we have languages. If each person had his or her own special words and own special way of talking, no one would be able to understand what anybody else was saying. Suppose you made up a word—*snizzel*—and decided that it meant "good." If you said "That is a *snizzel* book," nobody would know whether you meant that the book was *good, bad, big, new, funny, heavy*, or whatever. So you say "That is a *good* book," because *good* is a word other people know. We learn to agree on what a word means and how to use it so that we can understand each other.

Today there are more than 3,000 languages spoken and written in the world. They include **French, Spanish, German, Russian, Arabic, Chinese, Japanese, Vietnamese,** and the language in this book—**English.**

MAJOR LANGUAGES	
The native languages of the largest number of people are :	
Mandarin (Chinese)	930 million
Hindi	380 million
Spanish	375 million
English	350 million
Bengali	225 million
Arabic	220 million
Portuguese	200 million
Russian	180 million
Japanese	140 million

Humans seem to have a natural gift for language. You learned to speak when you were very young, probably without even knowing that you were learning anything. The language that you speak is the one you heard around you as you were growing up—the one your family and friends speak. If you were born in the United States, that language is probably English. If you were born somewhere else, you might have learned a different language—in some countries two, three, or even more languages are spoken. In fact, the country with the largest number of native languages is India, with over 840.

If you think about it, you can probably remember times when you have heard people speaking a different language. The way that you knew it was different was simple—you couldn't understand what was being said. And that is exactly what makes two languages different from each other—a person speaking one language can't understand a person speaking the other. If you and a friend both speak only English, you can understand each other even though both of you don't speak it in exactly the same way. But if you met a person who spoke only Chinese, you and that person could not understand each other's words at all.

How Language Started

Suppose that you found yourself in a situation where you spoke only English and you met someone who spoke only Chinese. How would you and that person talk with each other?

You would probably use the same kind of "language" that the first people who lived on earth probably used—*sign language*. To show you wanted something to eat, you might put your hand to your mouth and pretend to chew something, or you might point to your stomach and say "food." After a while, you and the other person would find some common words for basic things, like your names or food and water. This could be the beginning of a common language.

Writing Words The reason that we do not know very much about the first languages is that they were never written down. Once people had words, they could tell one another what they were thinking. But as soon as someone said something, that person's idea would be gone unless other people could remember what had been said. Then, about 5,000 years ago, people invented writing. This meant that a person's thoughts could be put down for others to see and remember, even when the person was not there.

Picture Writing The first kinds of writing did not use letters as we do today. Instead, each idea was shown by a picture that stood for the idea. For example, "fish" was shown by a picture of a fish.

People were much better off with "picture writing" than they had been when they had no writing at all, but there were certain things wrong with this system. First, people could only write down something that they could see—they could not draw a picture of words like *love*, *see*, *tired*, *true*, or *help*. Also, whoever drew a picture could never be sure that a person who saw it would know what was meant—did a picture of two men and three deer mean "two men saw three deer" or "two men chased three deer" or what?

The Alphabet Then, about 3,500 years ago, something very important happened. Someone—we do not know who that person was—invented the alphabet. Now, any word could be written down just as we write words today—by putting together letters that stand for the sound of the word. This made writing much easier to understand. The invention of "letter writing" brought language to the form in which we use it today

---

ECHOES OF THE PAST

Many of today's languages are part of what is called the *Indo-European* group. They have a common source and many of their basic words are similar. For example, here is a list of three common words in several Indo-European languages.

English	three	yes	no
Dutch	drie	ja	nee
French	trois	oui	non
German	drei	ja	nein
Greek	treis	ne	óhee
Icelandic	thrir	já	nei
Italian	tre	si	no
Norwegian	tre	ya	nej
Polish	trzy	tak	nie
Russian	tri	dah	nyet
Spanish	tres	si	no

Languages before English

We have said that there are many different languages spoken in the world. But more than half the people in the world today speak languages that come from a single old language called **Indo-European.**

The Indo-Europeans were a group of people who lived in the eastern part of the continent of Europe. There was not much food in the area where these people lived, and life was hard. So the Indo-European people began to leave their homes to live in other places. As they moved, they took their language with them. They settled down to live all over Europe and as far away as India.

As time went by, the Indo-European people who lived in different places began to speak in different ways. Over thousands of years, the original Indo-European language changed to become many different languages. Some of these are no longer spoken, but many still are, including **German, Spanish, French, Russian, Portuguese, Hindi, Bengali**—and **English.** We know that all these languages come from Indo-European because they all have similar words for certain things, such as mother, father, cow, house, wolf, and winter.

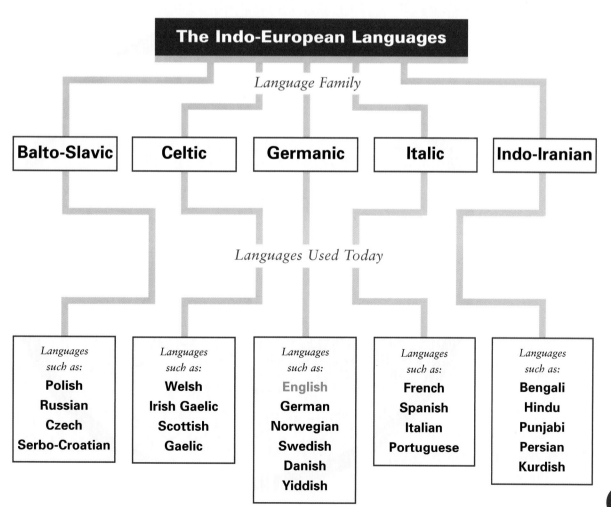

The Indo-European Languages

Language Family

| Balto-Slavic | Celtic | Germanic | Italic | Indo-Iranian |

Languages Used Today

Languages such as:	Languages such as:	Languages such as:	Languages such as:	Languages such as:
Polish	**Welsh**	**English**	**French**	**Bengali**
Russian	**Irish Gaelic**	**German**	**Spanish**	**Hindu**
Czech	**Scottish**	**Norwegian**	**Italian**	**Punjabi**
Serbo-Croatian	**Gaelic**	**Swedish**	**Portuguese**	**Persian**
		Danish		**Kurdish**
		Yiddish		

The Beginnings of English

England is part of a group of islands called the **British Isles**. Up until about 1,500 years ago, the people who lived in these islands did not speak English. They were called **Celts** and spoke a language called **Celtic**, which is very different from English, although it can also trace its roots to Indo-European.

Then, about the year 450, the land of the Celts was invaded by three tribes from a place that is now the country of **Germany**, in northern Europe. These tribes were named the **Angles**, the **Saxons**, and the **Jutes**. They fought a war with the Celtic people. The Celts lost the war, and they had to leave England and move to other parts of the British Isles. Today only a few people in the British Isles speak a Celtic language, and there are almost no words in English that come from Celtic.

The Angles, Saxons, and Jutes all spoke the same language, but in slightly different ways because they had lived in different parts of Germany. Once they had settled in one place—England—all the tribes began to speak the same way. The Angles were the most important of the three tribes, and they ruled the most land. Therefore this new language became known as **English**, after the name of the tribe called the **Angles**.

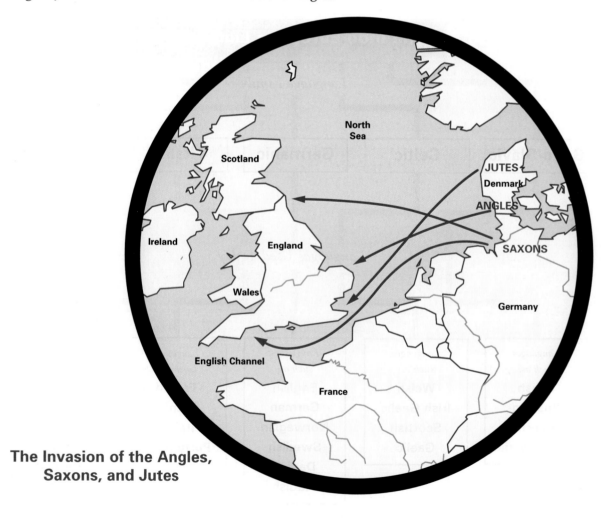

The Invasion of the Angles, Saxons, and Jutes

Old English

We have said that the Angles, Saxons, and Jutes spoke English. But it was not the same as the English that is spoken today. The form of English that they spoke is now called **Old English.**

There is no one alive today who speaks Old English in everyday life, but if you met someone who could, you would not be able to understand them. Although many of the words of Old English have been passed down to modern English, over the years they have changed greatly in what they mean and in the way they are spelled and pronounced. Old English sounded very different from modern English.

Even though Old English would sound strange if you heard it today, most of the common words that you use every day came from Old English. When we speak about the most important things in life, we use Old English words—words like *man, woman,* and *child; eat, drink,* and *sleep; morning, noon,* and *night; day, month,* and *year;* or *love, life,* and *death.*

When you learned to talk, the words you first used were probably from Old English, such as *eyes, nose, mouth, dog, cat, play, walk, house, go,* and *eat.* The names of the colors—*red, yellow,* and so on—come from Old English. So do the words we use when we count from one to a thousand. Old English also gives us the common words we use to put sentences together, like *at, in, by, out, from, of, to, a, an,* and *the.* In fact, if a word is short and simple and is used a lot, the chances are good that it comes from Old English.

The Angles, the Saxons, and the Jutes were not the only groups to come to England in early times. Other tribes, known as **Vikings,** also invaded England. The Vikings were also known as **Scandinavians,** because the area they came from was called **Scandinavia.** This area is now the countries of **Denmark, Norway** and **Sweden.** From about the year 800 to the year 1000, the Vikings fought many battles with the English people. Kings from Denmark ruled the northern part of England for a long period of time. The part of England that they ruled was called the *Danelaw.*

The Scandinavians were related to the Angles, Saxons, and Jutes who already lived in the country. Because of this, the language that they spoke was very similar to English. So the Scandinavians did not change English in any important way when they began to use it. The Scandinavians did, however, add many new words to the English language. Scandinavian words include such important ones as *they, them,* and *their; law, dirt, knife, sky,* and *egg; cut, scare, take,* and *get;* and *flat, low, tight,* and *wrong.*

The 'War' between English and French

England is separated from the continent of Europe by a small body of water called the English Channel. In the year 1066, another group of people invaded England, this time by sailing across the Channel. These people lived in an area just on the other side of the Channel, called **Normandy**, and they were known as **Normans**.

Like the other groups that invaded England, the Normans originally came from northern Europe. (The word *Norman* meant "north man.") They had first lived in Scandinavia and were related to the Vikings. But they did not speak the same language. After the Normans settled in Normandy, they had begun to speak the language already spoken by the people living there. This language was **French**, because Normandy was in an area that is now part of the country of **France**.

When the Normans invaded England, the English army marched out to fight them. At a place near the English Channel called Hastings, the Norman army and the English army fought a great battle. The Normans won, and Harold, the English king, was killed. The Norman king, known in history as William the Conqueror, became king of England.

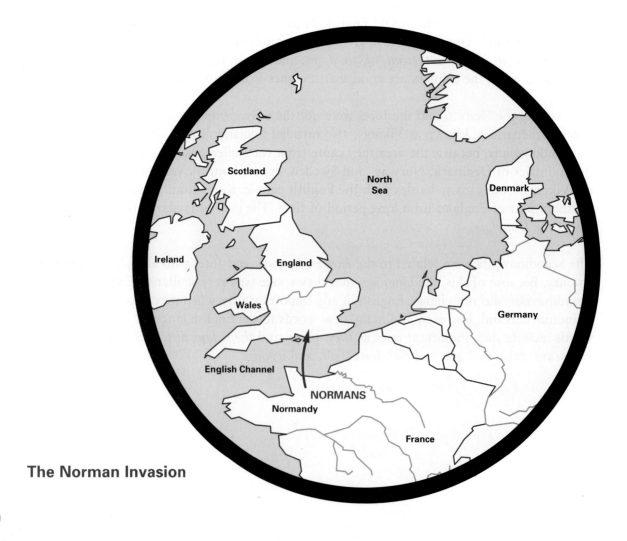

The Norman Invasion

The Normans brought about the most important changes in England since the English language was first spoken there. Because they ruled the country, their language—French—became the main language. All people who were rich or important spoke French. English was spoken only by poor country people.

The king and the people around him conducted the affairs of the government in French. People in the towns spoke French when they were buying or selling something or carrying on other kinds of business. Men who held high positions in the army, the navy, or the church also spoke French. Poems and other kinds of literature were written in French. For a time it seemed that people might stop speaking English altogether.

By the year 1362, however, English had again become the main language of the country. That was the first year that Parliament, the place where the laws of the country were made, passed a rule that people who spoke there had to use English rather than French. By the middle of the 1500s, French was not used at all in England.

There were several reasons why French "lost out" to English as the language of the country. First, the common people had continued to speak English and did not learn French. This meant that the only language everyone could understand was English. A court of law could not carry on its business in French if the person on trial spoke only English. Second, as time went on, the Normans began to think of themselves as English, not French. Normandy had come under the rule of the king of France, and England and France were now at war with each other. Finally, a disease called the Black Death killed thousands of people. After the Black Death, there were not enough French-speaking people to fill all the important jobs, and many of them were filled by English-speaking people.

French Words in English

Even though French did not become the permanent language of England, it did change the English language. Thousands of French words were added to English, including some of our most important words. The English people did not change the way they spoke or the way they put words together in a sentence because of French. But they now had many new words that were not in English before. This change in English created what is now known as Middle English. The new form of English was much more like modern English than Old English was.

Because the French-speaking Normans had ruled the country, many French words having to do with government came into English. These include *president, congress, mayor, constitution, city, state*, and *nation*. We can see the areas where French-speaking people were important from the words themselves, which came from French—*religion, art, poetry, court, medicine, army, navy, dance, fashion*, and *society*.

Most jobs done by English-speaking people were simple and involved working outdoors with the hands. *Farmer, woodsman, fisherman, hunter*, and *shepherd* are Old English words. The French-speaking people, on the other hand, often had indoor jobs that called for more education or training—*tailor, physician, attorney, carpenter*, and *plumber* all came from French.

French-speaking and English-speaking people lived in very different ways. This is shown by the words we get from each language. The English were farmers, so our words for farm animals come from Old English—*cow, calf, pig*, and *sheep*. But because the French were good at cooking, the words for these animals when they are cooked and served as food come from French—*beef, veal, pork*, and *mutton*.

Many of the French words in English were originally part of an older language called **Latin**. The French language comes from Latin, and words passed from Latin to French and then to English. Latin was spoken in ancient times by a group of people called the **Romans**. They went out from **Rome**, a large city in Italy, to live in France and many other parts of Europe, including England. But there are not many words that came straight from Latin into English. Before the Norman invasion, only a few Latin words, such as *camp, wine, bishop*, and *pope*, were added to English. The coming of the Normans changed this situation, and Latin has been important to English ever since.

Different Kinds of English

We have seen how language changes when people move. This is what happened when the different groups—the Angles, Saxons, Jutes, Vikings, Normans, and others—came to England. The next great change in English also happened because of people moving. But this time people did not come to England; they left it.

The first group of English-speaking people who came to live in North America and succeeded in staying here arrived in 1607. They were led by Captain John Smith, and they settled in what is now Virginia. As soon as they arrived, a new kind of language was born. It is called **American English.**

You might think that since those early settlers spoke English, they could have just gone on talking the same way that they had when they were back in England. But life in America was different. When people saw something they had never seen in England, they had to have a new word to talk about it.

In 1608, only one year after he came to America, Captain John Smith wrote about a kind of boat called a *canoe*. This word had never been used in England, because there were no canoes there. By the year 1620, there were already many new American English words, including *moose, raccoon*, and *opossum*. Where did these new words come from? Most of them came from the people who were already here when the English settlers came—the **Native Americans,** called "Indians" by the English settlers. When English people saw a North American plant or animal for the first time—such as a skunk—they would find out what the Native Americans called it and start using that word.

REPEATING YOURSELF

Did you ever think about how many times you use a word? We use some words over and over. The words used most often in English are:

In Writing	In Speaking
the	the
of	and
to	I
in	to
and	of
a	a
for	you
was	that
is	in
that	it
on	is

People from England went to live in other places besides North America; in fact, they settled all over the world. In each place they went, life was different from the life they were familiar with in England. So the way they spoke changed.

Several kinds of English grew up and were named after the places where the English people went to live. Besides American English, they include **Canadian English, South African English, Australian English,** and **Indian English** (the kind of English spoken in India). The kind of English spoken by the people who stayed in England is called **British English.**

Today British English and American English are not really that different. If you met people who came from England, you could tell from the way they said their words that they were not Americans. But you would probably not have much trouble understanding what they were saying.

The one real difference between British and American English is in the names of certain things. For example, what we call an *elevator*, they call a *lift*. What we call a *truck*, they call a *lorry*; what we call *gasoline*, they call *petrol*. The reason for these differences is simple: these things have been invented since the United States became independent from England.

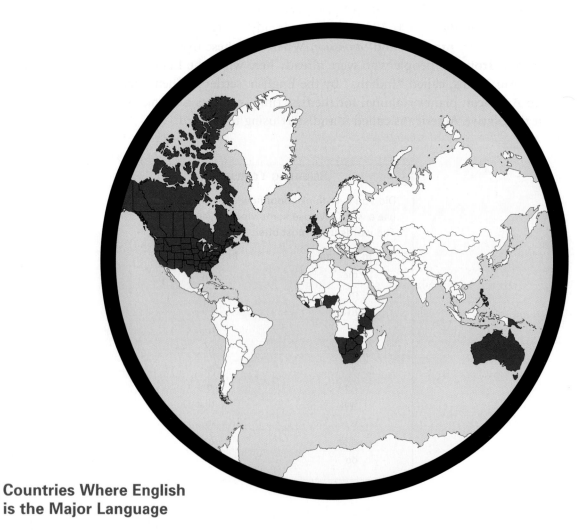

■ **Countries Where English is the Major Language**

Different Kinds of American English

Just as there are different kind of English spoken in different parts of the world, so there is a variety of different ways of speaking English in various parts of the United States. These differences are often due to the history of the area; who settled the region and what languages they spoke when they arrived.

Usually you can easily recognize that someone is from another part of the country by the way they pronounce certain words or by the words they use. The most widely recognized regional word is probably *you-all* from the South (which is often pronounced *y'all*). But most of us can also recognize a New England or a Midwestern accent where familiar words are pronounced differently from what we are used to hearing.

The differences in pronunciation from place to place are not the only clue to where a person is from. There are also differences in what things are called. For example, people settling in different areas gave the same animals different names. The largest member of the cat family native to North America is widely known as the *mountain lion*. But, depending on where you live, it may also be known as a *cougar*, a *painter*, a *panther*, a *puma*, or a *mountain cat*. A smaller animal that lives underground is often known as a *woodchuck*, but in some places it is called a *groundhog*.

An good example of different regional names for an insect is the *dragonfly*. In the South it is sometimes known as a *snake doctor* or a *mosquito hawk*. In the North it is sometimes called a *darning needle* or a *spindle*. In the far West in is sometimes called an *ear sewer*.

The names for certain foods also vary from place to place. When you want a refreshing drink on a hot day, you may ask for a *soda*. But if you live in the West, you may call it a *pop*. In the South, the same drink might be called a *cold drink*, while around Boston you might order a *tonic*.

If you wanted something to eat with your drink, you might order a huge sandwich made with sliced meat and cheese piled on a long roll. But what would you call it? In many places you would call it a *submarine*, a *sub*, or a *hero*. But in New York you might call it a *bomber*. In the area around Philadelphia you could order a *hoagie*, or in New England you would ask for a *grinder*. In New Orleans, the same sandwich would be called a *poor boy*, in Miami, a *Cuban sandwich*. Or, you might find it listed as an *Italian sandwich*. In any case, it would taste just as good.

English Words from Other Languages

Throughout the years, people who speak English have in one way or another known or learned about people from all over the world. In early times, this happened because people from many other countries came to England and brought their languages with them. Later, it happened because people left England to go to many other countries and brought back foreign words to add to English. When people from England came here, they borrowed words from the languages of the Native Americans. It would take up too much room to list all the words English has gotten from other languages, but a few are listed on these pages.

ITALY (LATIN)
author
aviation
bus
cereal
clock
congress
education
fossil
hospital
human
individual
insect
lava
liberty
map
muscle
notice
obey
president
pupil
reptile
republic
rotate
salary
senator
student
union
vaccine
vertebra
video

ITALY (ITALIAN)
balcony
baritone
duet
lagoon
macaroni
oboe
opera
piano
pizza
quarantine
sonata
umbrella

NATIVE AMERICAN
avocado
cashew
chili
chipmunk
chocolate
cocoa
condor
cougar
hickory
llama
moccasin
moose
opossum
pecan
petunia
poncho
raccoon
squash
toboggan
tomato

LATIN AMERICA (SPANISH)
alpaca
bronco
burrito
cafeteria
chaps
llama
mustang
salsa
stampede
taco

SPAIN
alligator
armadillo
cargo
castanets
corral
fiesta
hacienda
hammock
lariat
lasso
mesa
mosquito
patio
plaza
ranch
rodeo
sierra
silo
tornado
tuna
vanilla

GREECE
alphabet
ameba
astronaut
bacteria
Bible
church
clinic
comet
crocodile
diagonal
dinosaur
drama
electric
elephant
galaxy
govern
lantern
licorice
melon
meteorite
octopus
panic
planet
priest
rhinoceros
skeleton
telephone

SCANDINAVIAN COUNTRIES
anger
egg
flaw
get
geyser
guest
knife
loft
nickel
odd
outlaw
scare
sister
ski
skirt
skull
sky
take
tight
ugly
window
wrong

THE NETHERLANDS (DUTCH)
boss
cookie
cruise
easel
gruff
iceberg
pickle
skate
sled
slim
tub
waffle
wagon
yacht

FRANCE
amateur
baboon
barber
bribe
butcher
cafe
curfew
dandelion
faith
garage
grudge
joy
kerchief
lawn
parachute
plateau
restaurant
spaniel

GERMANY
delicatessen
fife
frankfurter
hamburger
hamster
noodle
poodle
pretzel
pumpernickel
waltz

CZECH REPUBLIC
pistol
polka
robot

HUNGARY
paprika
saber

RUSSIA
mammoth
parka
tundra

IRELAND
banshee
leprechaun

PORTUGAL
cobra
flamingo
jaguar
junk
mango
pagoda
teak
zebra

JAPAN
haiku
judo
karate
kimono
tsunami

CHINA
ketchup
kumquat
sampan
tea
typhoon

TURKEY
coffee
jackal
sherbet
turban
yogurt

IRAN (PERSIAN)
bazaar
candy
khaki
lemon
orange
shawl
spinach
tulip

INDIA (HINDUSTANI)
bandanna
bungalow
cot
pajamas
shampoo

INDONESIA (MALAY)
bamboo
camphor
cockatoo
gingham
gong
orangutan

AFRICA
banana
bongo
canary
gumbo
okra
yam

ISRAEL (HEBREW)
amen
Hanukkah
Jehovah
kosher
rabbi
Sabbath
schwa

ARABIC-SPEAKING COUNTRIES
admiral
algebra
cotton
giraffe
hazard
magazine
massage
mattress
satin
sugar
syrup
zero

f31

Pronunciation Key

Symbol	Sample Words		Symbol	Sample Words
a	at, bad		ō	old, oat, toe, low
ā	ape, pain, day, break		ô	coffee, all, taught, law, fought
ä	father, car, heart		ôr	order, fork, horse, story, pour
âr	care, pair, bear, their, where		oi	oil, toy
b	bat, above, job		ou	out, now
ch	chin, such, match		p	pail, repair, soap, happy
d	dear, soda, bad		r	ride, parent, more, marry
e	end, pet, said, heaven, friend		s	sit, pets, cent, pass
ē	equal, me, feet, team, piece, key		sh	shoe, fish, mission, nation
f	five, leaf, off, cough, elephant		t	tag, fat, button, dressed
g	game, ago, fog, egg		th	thin, panther, both
h	hat, ahead		th	this, mother, smooth
wh	white, whether, which		u	up, mud, love, double
i	it, big, English, him		ū	use, mule, cue, feud, few
ī	ice, fine, lie, my		ü	rule, true, food
îr	ear, deer, here, pierce		ù	put, would, should
j	joke, enjoy, gem, page, edge		ûr	burn, term, word, courage
k	kite, bakery, seek, tack, cat		v	very, favor, wave
l	lid, sailor, feel, ball, allow		w	wet, weather, reward
m	man, family, dream		y	yes, onion
n	not, final, pan, knife		z	zoo, jazz, rose, dogs, houses
ng	long, singer, pink		zh	vision, treasure, azure
o	odd, hot, watch		ə	about, taken, pencil, lemon, circus

Stress

A heavy (primary) stress mark or accent ′ comes right after a syllable that gets the most emphasis, as in **athlete** (ath′lēt).

A light (secondary) stress mark or accent ′ comes right after a syllable that gets less emphasis, as in **clambake** (klam′bāk′).

To help you recall these pronunciation symbols when you are using this dictionary, the following shorter pronunciation key appears at the bottom of most right handed pages of this dictionary.

PRONUNCIATION KEY:

at   āpe   fär   câre   end   mē   it   īce   pîerce   hot   ōld   sông   fôrk
oil   out   up   ūse   rüle   pùll   tûrn   chin   sing   shop   thin   this

hw in white; zh in treasure. The symbol ə stands for the unstressed vowel sound in about, taken, pencil, lemon, and circus.

f32

The letter A has three different sounds in English, all of which can also be given by other combinations of letters.

The sound of A in ask, bad, and hat is sometimes made by:
> ai in words such as plaid; al in half and calves; and au in laugh.

The sound of A in ate, cake, and page is commonly made by:
> ai in aid and rain; and ay in day, spray, and tray;

And less often made by:
> ei in veil and vein; ea in break; and ey in obey and they.

The sound of A in car, father, and swan is occasionally made by:
> ea as in heart; and er in sergeant.

The sound of the letter A combined with r in words such as care, compare, and dare can also be made by:
> air in words such as pair.

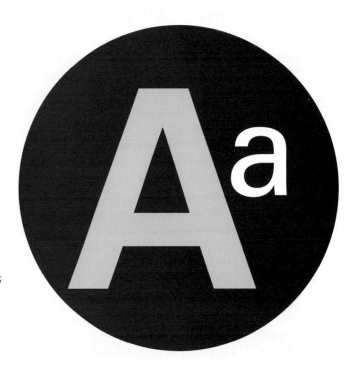

Once in a while this sound is also made by:
> ear in bear and pear.

In words such as about, annoy, and apart, the sound of the letter A is represented in the pronunciations in the dictionary by a schwa (ə).

A The first letter of the alphabet. **a, A** (ā) *noun,* *plural* **a's, A's.**

a 1. Any: *A dog would love that bone.* 2. One: *My cousin has a new bicycle.* 3. One kind of: *The orange is a fruit.* 4. In each; in every: *We wash our car once a week.* 5. For each; for every: *The meat was two dollars a pound.* **a** (ə *or* ā) *indefinite article.*

aardvark An African animal with a pointed snout, a long, sticky tongue that it uses to catch ants and termites, and sharp claws. **aard·vark** (ärd′värk′) *noun, plural* **aardvarks.**

AB Postal abbreviation for Alberta.

abacus A frame that has beads that slide on wires or in grooves and is used to do arithmetic. **ab·a·cus** (ab′ə kəs) *noun, plural* **abacuses.**

abalone A large sea snail that has a flat, pearly shell; its meat is used for food. **ab·a·lo·ne** (ab′ə lō′nē) *noun, plural* **abalones.**

abandon 1. To leave and not return; desert: *The sailors abandoned the sinking ship.* 2. To give up completely: *Because of heavy rain we abandoned our picnic.* **a·ban·don**

(ə ban′dən) *verb,* **abandoned, abandoning.**

abandoned Left behind; no longer used or lived in: *The porch of the abandoned house is overgrown with vines.* **a·ban·doned** (ə ban′dənd) *adjective.*

abate To make or become less in amount or intensity: *After an hour the storm abated.* **a·bate** (ə bāt′) *verb,* **abated, abating.**

abbey A building or buildings where monks or nuns live. **ab·bey** (ab′ē) *noun, plural* **abbeys.**

abbreviate To make shorter: *We abbreviate the words "United States of America" as "U.S.A."* **ab·bre·vi·ate** (ə brē′vē āt′) *verb,* **abbreviated, abbreviating.**

abbreviation A letter or group of letters that stand for a longer word or phrase: *"N.Y." is an abbreviation for "New York," "cm" is an abbreviation for "centimeter," "Jan." is an abbreviation for "January," and "Fri." is an abbreviation for "Friday."* **ab·bre·vi·a·tion** (ə brē′vē ā′shən) *noun, plural* **abbreviations.**

abdicate To give up power: *When the queen abdicated, her oldest son became king.* **ab·di·cate** (ab′di kāt′) *verb,* **abdicated, abdicating.**

abdomen 1. The part of the body between the chest and hips. It contains the stomach, intestines, kidneys, and liver. 2. The rear part of an insect's body. **ab·do·men** (ab′də mən *or* ab dō′mən) *noun, plural* **abdomens**.

abduct To carry off by force; kidnap: *In the movie, beings from another galaxy **abducted** people from Earth.* **ab·duct** (ab dukt′) *verb,* **abducted, abducting.**

abide 1. To put up with; bear; endure: *My parents cannot **abide** a messy room.* 2. To continue to live or dwell: *The family **abided** on a farm for many years.* This meaning is not used very often today.
  • **to abide by.** 1. To accept and obey: *A good citizen **abides** by the law.* 2. To be faithful to; carry out: *I was sure you would **abide** by your promise.* **a·bide** (ə bīd′) *verb,* **abided, abiding.**

ability 1. The power to do something; capability: *People are the only mammals that have the **ability** to speak.* 2. Talent or skill: *That singer also has great **ability** as a painter.* **a·bil·i·ty** (ə bil′i tē) *noun, plural* **abilities.**

SYNONYMS

ability, flair, skill, talent

A doctor has the ability to heal people. They have a flair for having fun. It takes skill to cook well. She has enough talent to become a rock star.

---

ablaze 1. On fire: *When the fire trucks arrived, the old building was **ablaze**.* 2. Very strong: *The freedom fighters were **ablaze** with passion for their cause.* **a·blaze** (ə blāz′) *adjective.*

able 1. Having the power to do something: *A deer is **able** to run very fast.* 2. Having more than usual ability or talent: *You are an **able** pianist.* **a·ble** (ā′bəl) *adjective,* **abler, ablest.**

-able A suffix that means: 1. Able to be; capable of being: *Mov**able** means able to be moved.* 2. Likely to; tending to: *Agree**able** means likely to agree.* 3. Worthy of being: *Lik**able** means worthy of being liked.*

abnormal Not normal, average, or usual: *It is **abnormal** for it to be so cold in July.* **ab·nor·mal** (ab nôr′məl) *adjective.*

aboard On or into a ship, train, or airplane. *The plane took off just after we got **aboard**. We had breakfast **aboard** the plane.* **a·board** (ə bôrd′) *adverb; preposition.*

abolish To end; stop: *That law will **abolish** the dumping of toxic waste into the ocean.* **a·bol·ish** (ə bol′ish) *verb,* **abolished, abolishing.**

abolition The act of abolishing: *The **abolition** of slavery in the United States occurred in 1865.* **ab·o·li·tion** (ab′ə lish′ən) *noun.*

abolitionist A person who was in favor of abolishing slavery in the United States before the Civil War. **a·bo·li·tion·ist** (ab′ə lish′ə nist) *noun, plural* **abolitionists.**

abominable 1. Causing hatred or disgust: *The bombing of the school was an **abominable** act.* 2. Very unpleasant; offensive: *You have **abominable** table manners.* **a·bom·i·na·ble** (ə bom′ə nə bəl) *adjective.*

aborigine One of the first people to live in a place: *The Inuit are among the **aborigines** of North America.* **ab·o·rig·i·ne** (ab′ə rij′ə nē) *noun, plural* **aborigines.**

abound To be present in great amounts; be plentiful: *Buffalo used to **abound** on the western plains of North America.* **a·bound** (ə bound′) *verb,* **abounded, abounding.**

about 1. Having to do with; concerning: *We are reading a book **about** the exploration of outer space.* 2. On every side of; around: *Look **about** you. Preposition.*
○ 1. Very close to; approximately: *There were **about** twenty people there.* 2. Nearly; almost: *Are you **about** ready to go?* 3. In several directions; all around: *I looked **about** to find my dog. Adverb.*
  • **about to.** Very near the time when something will happen or begin; ready to: *It is **about to** rain. We are **about to** leave.* **a·bout** (ə bout′) *preposition; adverb.*

above In or to a higher place; overhead: *Stars glittered **above**. Adverb.*
○ 1. Over or higher than: *The kite flew **above** the trees.* 2. Better than: *She is **above** average in math.* 3. Higher in rank: *A captain is **above** a lieutenant in the army.* 4. More than; over: *Don't*

As the moon rises above **the city, it casts its own special light.**

pay **above** ten dollars for the ticket. Preposition. **a•bove** (ə buv′) adverb; preposition.

aboveboard Honest: The traders were open and aboveboard in their business. **a•bove•board** (ə buv′bôrd′) adjective.

abrasive 1. Causing something to wear away by rubbing; rough: Sandpaper is an **abrasive** material. 2. Not pleasant; irritating: Your coach has an **abrasive** way of talking to people. **ab•ra•sive** (ə brā′siv) adjective.

abreast Next to each other; side by side: The students walked two **abreast**. **a•breast** (ə brest′) adverb; adjective.

abridge To make shorter by using fewer words: The book I am reading was **abridged** from a much longer book. **a•bridge** (ə brij′) verb, **abridged, abridging.**

abroad Outside of one's country: We went **abroad** to visit relatives in France. **a•broad** (ə brôd′) adverb.

abrupt 1. Without warning; sudden: The bus made an **abrupt** stop at the traffic light. 2. Not polite or gentle; blunt: The impatient clerk gave us an **abrupt** answer. **a•brupt** (ə brupt′) adjective.

abscess A collection of pus in some part of the body. It usually is caused by an infection. **ab•scess** (ab′ses) noun, plural **abscesses.**

absence 1. The condition of being away: In the teacher's **absence**, a substitute teacher taught our class. 2. A period of being away: After an **absence** of a year, my cousin came home from college. 3. The condition of being without; lack: The **absence** of rain caused the plants to wilt. **ab•sence** (ab′səns) noun, plural **absences.**

absent 1. Not present; away: My friend was **absent** from school because of a cold. 2. Not existing; missing: Leaves are **absent** on trees in winter. **ab•sent** (ab′sənt) adjective.

absentee A person who is absent from a place where he or she is supposed to be. **ab•sen•tee** (ab′sən tē′) noun, plural **absentees.**

absent-minded 1. Not paying attention to what is going on: The child stared out the window in an **absent-minded** way. 2. Forgetful: **Absent-minded** people often misplace things. **ab•sent-mind•ed** (ab′sənt mīn′did) adjective.

absolute 1. Complete; entire; whole: The witness told the **absolute** truth. 2. Not limited or restrict-

ed: Some rulers have **absolute** power. 3. Certain; convincing: The family had **absolute** proof that the land belonged to them. **ab•so•lute** (ab′sə lüt′) adjective.

absolutely 1. Completely: He is **absolutely** right about that. 2. Without any doubt; really: I was **absolutely** sure that I wanted to buy that shirt. **ab•so•lute•ly** (ab′sə lüt′lē or ab′sə lüt′lē) adverb.

absorb 1. To soak up or take in: A towel **absorbed** the spilled water. 2. To hold the interest of: The book about animals **absorbed** me. 3. To take in and hold without reflecting back: Thick draperies **absorb** sound. **ab•sorb** (ab sôrb′ or ab zôrb′) verb, **absorbed, absorbing.**

absorbent Able to soak up water or moisture: These towels are very **absorbent**. **ab•sorb•ent** (ab sôr′bənt or ab zôr′bənt) adjective.

absorption The act or process of absorbing: A sponge picks up water by **absorption**. **ab•sorp•tion** (ab sôrp′shən or ab zôrp′shən) noun.

abstain To keep oneself from doing something: I **abstained** from eating candy. **ab•stain** (ab stān′) verb, **abstained, abstaining.**

abstract 1. Expressing a quality of something that cannot be seen or touched, such as a feeling or idea. "Sourness" is an abstract word. "Lemon" is not an abstract word. 2. Hard to understand: This book on physics is too **abstract** for me. 3. Having to do with a style of art that does not show real objects, but uses lines, shapes, and colors to suggest an idea or feeling. **ab•stract** (ab′strakt or ab strakt′) adjective.

absurd Silly, foolish, or untrue: It is **absurd** to believe that the moon is made of green cheese. **ab•surd** (ab sûrd′ or ab zûrd′) adjective.

abundance A very large amount; a quantity that is more than enough: The farmer had an **abundance** of food. **a•bun•dance** (ə bun′dəns) noun.

The fall season brings an abundance of pumpkins.

PRONUNCIATION KEY:

| at | āpe | fär | câre | end | mē | it | īce | pierce | hot | ōld | sông | fôrk |
| oil | out | up | ūse | rüle | pull | tûrn | chin | sing | shop | thin | this | |

hw in white; zh in treasure. The symbol ə stands for the unstressed vowel sound in about, taken, pencil, lemon, and circus.

3

abundant More than enough; plentiful: *We have an* ***abundant*** *supply of wood for our campfire.* **a·bun·dant** (ə bun′dənt) *adjective.*

abuse 1. To use in a way that is bad or wrong; misuse: *We must not* ***abuse*** *our natural resources.* 2. To treat roughly or cruelly; harm: *In the story, the villain was punished for* ***abusing*** *the servants.* 3. To attack with harsh or insulting words. *Verb.* ○ 1. Bad or wrong use; misuse: *The ruler's* ***abuse*** *of power caused the people to revolt.* 2. Rough or cruel treatment: *During the trip on the old, bumpy road our car took a lot of* ***abuse.*** 3. Harsh or insulting words: *The audience hurled* ***abuse*** *at the clumsy performers. Noun.* **a·buse** (ə būz′ *for verb;* ə būs′ *for noun*) *verb,* **abused, abusing;** *noun, plural* **abuses.**

abyss A hole so deep that it seems impossible to measure. **a·byss** (ə bis′) *noun, plural* **abysses.**

academic Having to do with school and learning. **ac·a·dem·ic** (ak′ə dem′ik) *adjective.*

academy 1. A private high school. 2. A school that trains people in a special field or subject: *I take violin lessons at the music* ***academy.*** **a·cad·e·my** (ə kad′ə mē) *noun, plural* **academies.**

accelerate To move or cause to move faster: *The bicycle* ***accelerated*** *as it went down the hill.* **ac·cel·er·ate** (ak sel′ə rāt′) *verb,* **accelerated, accelerating.**

acceleration An increase in speed; moving faster: *The sudden* ***acceleration*** *of the car frightened the passengers.* **ac·cel·er·a·tion** (ak sel′ə rā′shən) *noun, plural* **accelerations.**

accent 1. The stress or stronger tone of voice given to a word or part of a word. In the word "happy," the accent is on the first syllable. In "forget," the accent is on the second syllable. 2. A mark used on a word to show which syllable is spoken with an accent. In this dictionary, the heavy mark ′ is used to show the syllable in the word spoken with the most stress. The lighter mark ′ is used to show a syllable with a weaker accent. In the word "abbreviation," we place the accents like this: ə brē′vē ā′shən. 3. A particular way in which people in one part of a country speak a language: *My cousins from Georgia have a Southern* ***accent.*** 4. A particular way in which people speak a language that is not their first language: *My grandparents from Holland speak English with a Dutch* ***accent.*** *Noun.*

○ To pronounce or mark a word or syllable with a stronger tone of voice. You accent the first syllable of the word "apple." *Verb.* **ac·cent** (ak′sent *for noun;* ak′sent *or* ak sent′ *for verb*) *noun, plural* **accents;** *verb,* **accented, accenting.**

accentuate To make something more obvious; draw attention to something: *That sweater* ***accentuates*** *the color of her eyes.* **ac·cen·tu·ate** (ak sen′chə wāt′) *verb,* **accentuating, accentuated.**

accept 1. To take something that is given: *I* ***accepted*** *the birthday gift from my cousin.* 2. To receive or admit, often with favor or approval: *Our class* ***accepted*** *the new teacher immediately.* 3. To agree to; answer "yes" to: *The author* ***accepted*** *the invitation to give a speech to our book club.* 4. To think of as true, satisfactory, or correct: *My parents* ***accepted*** *my reason for being late.* **ac·cept** (ak sept′) *verb,* **accepted, accepting.**

acceptable Good enough to be accepted; satisfactory: *Our plan for the bazaar was* ***acceptable*** *to everyone in the club.* **ac·cept·a·ble** (ak sep′tə bəl) *adjective.*

acceptance 1. The act of taking something given or offered: *Your* ***acceptance*** *of my invitation pleased me.* 2. A favorable reception; approval: *The new television series won immediate* ***acceptance.*** **ac·cept·ance** (ak sep′təns) *noun, plural* **acceptances.**

access 1. The right to approach, enter, or use: *Only the governor has* ***access*** *to the secret files.* 2. A way or means of approaching or entering:

The dock provides access to boats that tie up beside it.

The only **access** to the lake is through the woods. *Noun.*

○ To get something: *Can I **access** my bank account from this machine? Verb.* **ac·cess** (ak′ses) *noun, plural* **accesses**; *verb,* **accessed, accessing.**

accessory 1. Something that is added to a more important thing: *A modem is an **accessory** for a computer.* 2. A person who helps another person commit a crime: *Two suspects have been arrested as **accessories** to the theft.* 3. Something extra that goes with clothes: *That store sells belts and other **accessories**.* **ac·ces·so·ry** (ak ses′ə rē) *noun, plural* **accessories.**

accident 1. Something that happens for no apparent reason and is unexpected: *The discovery of oil on the farm was a happy **accident**.* 2. A sad event that is not expected and in which people may be hurt: *During the snowstorm there were many **accidents** on the highways.*

• **by accident.** In a way not planned; unexpectedly: *I found the missing watch **by accident** while looking for my comb.*

ac·ci·dent (ak′si dənt) *noun, plural* **accidents.**

accidental Not planned or expected; happening by chance: *We did not know we would see each other; our meeting was **accidental**.* **ac·ci·den·tal** (ak′si den′təl) *adjective.* **accidentally** *adverb.*

acclaim To welcome with praise: *The crowd **acclaimed** the astronauts. Verb.*

○ Enthusiastic praise: *The tennis champion was greeted with **acclaim**. Noun.*

ac·claim (ə klām′) *verb,* **acclaimed, acclaiming;** *noun, plural* **acclaims.**

accommodate 1. To have room for; hold: *That movie theater **accommodates** 600 people.* 2. To supply with a place to stay or sleep: *That motel **accommodates** about forty guests each night.* 3. To do a favor for; help out: *The police officer **accommodated** us when we asked for directions.* **ac·com·mo·date** (ə kom′ə dāt′) *verb,* **accommodated, accommodating.**

accommodations A place to stay or sleep, often one where food is served: *When we were traveling, we found good **accommodations**.*

ac·com·mo·da·tions (ə kom′ə dā′shənz) *plural noun.*

accompaniment Something that goes with something else: *Cranberry sauce is a delicious **accompaniment** to turkey.* 2. A musical part that is played as background for a main part: *The soloist performed with a piano **accompaniment**.* **ac·com·pa·ni·ment** (ə kum′pə ni mənt) *noun, plural* **accompaniments.**

accompany 1. To go together with: *One of my parents always **accompanies** me to the movies.* 2. To happen at the same time as: *Wind often **accompanies** rain.* 3. To play a musical accompaniment: *While I played the flute, my cousin **accompanied** me on the piano.* **ac·com·pa·ny** (ə kum′pə nē) *verb,* **accompanied, accompanying.**

accomplice A person who helps another person do something that is illegal or wrong. **ac·com·plice** (ə kom′plis′) *noun, plural* **accomplices.**

accomplish To do something successfully; complete: *We **accomplished** more work than we had planned.* **ac·com·plish** (ə kom′plish) *verb,* **accomplished, accomplishing.**

accomplishment 1. The act of finishing something successfully; completion: *The **accomplishment** of our goal will be very difficult.* 2. Something accomplished; achievement: *The first landing on the moon was a great **accomplishment**.* 3. A special skill or ability that is usually gained by training: *Practice has certainly increased your **accomplishment** as a pianist.* **ac·com·plish·ment** (ə kom′plish mənt) *noun, plural* **accomplishments.**

accord 1. Agreement; harmony: *A higher wage is in **accord** with the demands of the workers.* 2. An agreement made, such as a treaty between nations. *Noun.*

○ To agree or be in harmony: *Her opinions on politics **accord** with his. Verb.*

• **of one's own accord** or **on one's own accord.** With no influence or help; voluntarily or spontaneously: *The twins cleaned their room **of their own accord**.*

ac·cord (ə kôrd′) *noun, plural* **accords**; *verb,* **accorded, according.**

PRONUNCIATION KEY:											
at	āpe	fär	câre	end	mē	it	īce	pîerce	hot	ōld	sông	fôrk
oil	out	up	ūse	rüle	pùll	tûrn	chin	sing	shop	thin	this

hw in white; zh in treasure. The symbol ə stands for the unstressed vowel sound in about, taken, pencil, lemon, and circus.

5

accordance Agreement: *Thank you for acting in accordance with my request.* **ac·cord·ance** (ə kôr′dəns) *noun.*

according to **1.** As expected: *Everything went according to our plan.* **2.** On the basis of: *People were paid according to the amount of work they did.* **3.** As described or reported by: *According to the weather report, it will probably rain tomorrow.* **ac·cord·ing** (ə kôr′ding).

The keys on an accordion are similar to those on a piano.

accordion A musical instrument with keys and metal reeds that you squeeze in order to force air past the reeds to produce musical tones. **ac·cor·di·on** (ə kôr′dē ən) *noun, plural* **accordions.**

account **1.** A spoken or written statement; report: *There was an account of the baseball game in the newspaper.* **2.** A record of money spent or received: *Who takes care of the household accounts for your family?* **3.** A sum of money that a person allows a bank to hold until it is needed: *How much do you have in your savings account?* **4.** Importance or worth: *This old watch is of little account. Noun.*

 • **to account for. 1.** To explain: *How do you account for your lateness?* **2.** To be the reason for: *The heavy snow accounts for the closing of school today.* **3.** To explain what happened to or what was done with: *The police have accounted for everyone who was on the boat when it capsized.*

ac·count (ə kount′) *noun, plural* **accounts.**

accountant A person who takes care of money and financial records. **ac·count·ant** (ə koun′tənt) *noun, plural* **accountants.**

accumulate To gather or pile up; collect: *My cousin accumulated a number of books at college. The mail accumulated while we were on vacation.* **ac·cu·mu·late** (ə kū′myə lāt′) *verb,* **accumulated, accumulating.**

accumulation **1.** The act of accumulating; piling up: *The accumulation of snow during the blizzard created traffic problems.* **2.** An amount accumulated; collection; heap; mass: *There was an accumulation of dust under the bed.* **ac·cu·mu·la·tion** (ə kū′myə lā′shən) *noun, plural* **accumulations.**

accuracy Freedom from errors or mistakes; correctness: *Check the accuracy of your arithmetic answers. You can trust the accuracy of the scale in the doctor's office.* **ac·cu·ra·cy** (ak′yər ə sē) *noun.*

accurate Correct, exact, or precise: *The newspaper stories about the accident were not accurate.* **ac·cu·rate** (ak′yər it) *adjective.*

accusation A statement that a person has done something wrong or illegal; charge: *What is the accusation against the prisoner?* **ac·cu·sa·tion** (ak′yə zā′shən) *noun, plural* **accusations.**

accuse To say that a person has done something wrong or illegal: *The store manager accused the clerk of stealing.* **ac·cuse** (ə kūz′) *verb,* **accused, accusing.**

accustom To make familiar through experience or use; adjust: *You have to accustom yourself to a new school when your family moves.* **ac·cus·tom** (ə kus′təm) *verb,* **accustomed, accustoming.**

accustomed Usual: *The dog lay in its accustomed place by the fire.*

 • **accustomed to.** Familiar with; used to: *The police officer was accustomed to the noisy traffic.*

ac·cus·tomed (ə kus′təmd) *adjective.*

ace **1.** A playing card having one mark in the center. **2.** A person who is an expert at something: *You're an ace at bowling. Noun.*

 ○ Of the highest quality; expert: *It takes years to become an ace pitcher. Adjective.*

ace (ās) *noun, plural* **aces;** *adjective.*

ache **1.** To hurt with a dull or constant pain: *My whole body ached after I did those new exercises.* **2.** To want very much; be eager:

*After being away for a month, we **ached** to get back home. Verb.*
° A dull or constant pain: *I had an **ache** in my side from laughing. Noun.*
ache (āk) *verb,* **ached, aching;** *noun, plural* **aches.**

achieve 1. To do or carry out successfully; accomplish: *Did you **achieve** all that you had set out to do?* 2. To gain or to reach by one's own effort: *Marie and Pierre Curie **achieved** fame as scientists.*
a•chieve (ə chēv′) *verb,* **achieved, achieving.**

achievement 1. Something accomplished or achieved: *The invention of the telephone was a great **achievement.*** 2. The act of achieving something. **a•chieve•ment** (ə chēv′mənt) *noun, plural* **achievements.**

acid 1. Sour, sharp, or biting to the taste: *A lemon has an **acid** taste.* 2. Sharp or biting in actions or speech: *The **acid** remark hurt my feelings. Adjective.*
° A chemical compound that has a sour taste, dissolves in water, and turns blue litmus paper red. *Noun.*
ac•id (as′id) *adjective; noun, plural* **acids.**

acid rain Rain or snow full of poisonous chemicals. It does great harm to plants, water, and other parts of the environment.

acknowledge 1. To admit the existence or truth of; concede: *The scientists **acknowledged** the mistakes of their research.* 2. To recognize the ability or authority of: *The teacher **acknowledged** you as the best speller in the class.* 3. To let someone know that one has received something: *I **acknowledged** the invitation with a phone call.*
ac•knowl•edge (ak nol′ij) *verb,* **acknowledged, acknowledging.**

acknowledgment 1. The act of acknowledging: *My **acknowledgment** that I was wrong made me feel better.* 2. A response made to show that one has received something: *Have you sent an **acknowledgment** of your gift?*
ac•knowl•edg•ment (ak nol′ij mənt) *noun, plural* **acknowledgments.**

acne A skin disease in which pimples appear, especially on the face. It happens when the oil glands in the skin become blocked and inflamed.
ac•ne (ak′nē) *noun.*

acorn The nut of the oak tree. **a•corn** (ā′kôrn) *noun, plural* **acorns.**

acoustic *or* **acoustical** Having to do with

hearing or sound. **a•cous•tic** (ə kü′stik) *or* **a•cous•ti•cal** (ə kü′sti kəl) *adjective.*

acoustics The quality of producing good sound that can be clearly heard: *The **acoustics** in the auditorium were poor and made everything echo.* The word acoustics can be used with a singular or plural verb. **acoustics** (ə kü′stiks) *noun, plural* **acoustics.**

acquaint To make familiar. **ac•quaint** (ə kwānt′) *verb,* **acquainted, acquainting.**

acquaintance 1. A person one knows, but who is not a close friend. 2. Knowledge of something gained from experience: *I have an **acquaintance** with the game of chess.* **ac•quaint•ance** (ə kwān′təns) *noun, plural* **acquaintances.**

acquire To get or gain as one's own: *I **acquired** the ability to speak Spanish.* **ac•quire** (ə kwīr′) *verb,* **acquired, acquiring.**

acquit To free from a charge of a crime; declare not guilty: *The jury **acquitted** the person accused of the crime.* **ac•quit** (ə kwit′) *verb,* **acquitted, acquitting.**

acre A measure of land equal to 43,560 square feet. An acre is slightly smaller in size than a football field. **a•cre** (ā′kər) *noun, plural* **acres.**

acreage The number of acres in a piece of land. **a•cre•age** (ā′kər ij) *noun.*

acrobat A person who is skilled at performing stunts such as walking on a tightrope or swinging on a trapeze. **ac•ro•bat** (ak′rə bat′) *noun, plural* **acrobats.**

These performers are doing an acrobatic split in midair.

acrobatic Having to do with acrobats: *The team won a gold medal for their wonderful*

PRONUNCIATION KEY:
| at | āpe | fär | câre | end | mē | it | īce | pîerce | hot | ōld | sông | fôrk |
| oil | out | up | ūse | rüle | pùll | tûrn | chin | sing | shop | thin | this | |

hw in white; zh in treasure. The symbol ə stands for the unstressed vowel sound in about, taken, pencil, lemon, and circus.

7

acrobatic performance. **ac·ro·bat·ic** (ak rə ba′tik) *adjective.*

across 1. From one side of to the other; over: *We drove across the bridge.* 2. On the other side of; beyond: *They live across the street from me.* 3. In a direction that crosses: *The cat walked across our path.* 4. Into contact with, usually by accident: *I came across your old baseball cards yesterday. Preposition.*
○ From one side to the other: *We came across in a rowboat. Adverb.*
a·cross (ə krôs′) *preposition; adverb.*

acrylic A plastic used to make many things, such as paint and yarns. **a·cryl·ic** (ə kril′ik) *noun, plural* **acrylics.**

act 1. Something done; a deed: *Saving the child's life was an act of bravery.* 2. The process of doing something: *The thief was caught in the act of opening the safe.* 3. A law: *The United States can declare war only by an act of Congress.* 4. One of the main parts of a play, opera, or ballet: *Our school play this year has five acts.* 5. A short performance: *The magician's act follows the intermission.* 6. A showing of some emotion that one does not feel. *His anger is just an act. Noun.*
○ 1. To do something: *After the accident, the doctor acted quickly to help the victims.* 2. To be an actor; play a part: *Did you ever act in a play?* 3. To conduct oneself; behave: *They acted as though they had no manners.* 4. To have or produce an effect: *The medicine acted slowly. Verb.*
  • **to act on** *or* **to act upon.** 1. To behave according to; follow: *We will act upon your orders.* 2. To have an effect upon; influence: *This acid acts on metal.*
  • **to act up.** 1. To behave in a mischievous or playful way. 2. To cause discomfort: *My stomach acted up after dinner.*
  act (akt) *noun, plural* **acts;** *verb,* **acted, acting.**

action 1. The process of doing something: *Throwing a ball, jumping over a fence, and running down a hill are all actions.* 2. Something that is done; an act: *Helping a blind person across a street is a kind action.* 3. **actions.** Behavior; conduct: *We couldn't understand their strange actions at the party.* 4. A way of working or moving: *This washing machine has a very gentle action.* 5. Fighting in battles; combat: *wounded in action.*
  • **to take action.** To do something when it is very important.
  ac·tion (ak′shən) *noun, plural* **actions.**

action verb A verb that shows its subject performing an action. Take, write, cut, send, vote, run, and practice are some examples of action verbs.

activate To cause to work or operate: *Pushing the button activates the machine.* **ac·ti·vate** (ak′tə vāt′) *verb,* **activated, activating.**

active 1. Moving around or doing something much of the time; lively; busy: *Are you very active in your club?* 2. Doing something or capable of doing something; functioning; working: *Steam rose from the active volcano.* **ac·tive** (ak′tiv) *adjective.*

activity 1. The condition of doing something or moving around; action; movement: *There was a lot of activity during recess.* 2. A thing to do or to be done for pleasure: *I take part in many school activities.* **ac·tiv·i·ty** (ak tiv′i tē) *noun, plural* **activities.**

actor A person who plays a part in a play, movie, television program, or radio program. **ac·tor** (ak′tər) *noun, plural* **actors.**

An **actor** needs to display many different kinds of emotions.

actress A girl or woman who plays a part in a play, movie, television program, or radio program. **ac·tress** (ak′tris) *noun, plural* **actresses.**

actual Real; existing: *That book is about actual people, not imaginary ones.* **ac·tu·al** (ak′chü əl) *adjective.*

actually In fact; really: *Were you actually sick on the day you missed class?* **ac·tu·al·ly** (ak′chü ə lē) *adverb.*

acupuncture The practice of relieving pain or treating a disease by putting needles into the skin at certain points on the body. Acupuncture has been practiced in China for thousands of years. **ac·u·punc·ture** (ak′yü pungk′chər) *noun.*

acute **1.** Very keen or quick: *My vision became acute when I started wearing glasses.* **2.** Sharp and severe: *I got an acute pain in my side.* **3.** Very important; urgent; critical: *an acute water shortage.* **a·cute** (ə kūt′) *adjective.*

acute angle An angle that is less than 90 degrees.

acute angle

ad A short form of the word **advertisement.** Another word that sounds like this is **add.** **ad** (ad) *noun, plural* **ads.**

A.D. The abbreviation for the Latin words Anno Domini, meaning "in the year of the Lord." It is used in giving dates since the birth of Jesus. A.D. 1000 means 1,000 years after the birth of Jesus.

adage An old and familiar saying that is believed to be true; proverb. "The early bird catches the worm" is an adage. **ad·age** (ad′ij) *noun, plural* **adages.**

adapt **1.** To change in order to make suitable: *The authors adapted their play for television.* **2.** To make or become used to: *When the family moved to Florida, they had to adapt to the warm weather.* **a·dapt** (ə dapt′) *verb,* **adapted, adapting.**

add **1.** To find the sum of two or more numbers: *If you add 2 and 7, you get 9 because 2 + 7 = 9.* **2.** To put in or on as something extra: *I like to add fruit to my yogurt. We plan to add a porch to our house.* **3.** To say more about something one has just written or said: *I thanked them for the gift and added that it was just what I wanted.* Another word that sounds like this is **ad.** **add** (ad) *verb,* **added, adding.**

addend Any number to be added to another number: *In the problem 5 + 3 = 8, the addends*

are 5 and 3. **ad·dend** (ad′end *or* ə dend′) *noun, plural* **addends.**

In **2 + 3 = 5,** **2** **4** **1**
     4 + 7 = 11, or **+3** **+7** **+8**
     1 + 8 = 9 **5** **11** **9**

2 and **3**, **4** and **7**, and **1** and **8** are **addends.**

adder A small, poisonous snake found in Europe. The adder found in North America is not poisonous. **ad·der** (ad′ər) *noun, plural* **adders.**

addict **1.** A person who is unable to give up or stop doing something that is usually bad for them, as taking drugs. **2.** A person who really enjoys an activity: *a science fiction addict.* Noun.
○ To become so dependent on something, especially a drug, that one cannot do without it. *Verb.*
ad·dict (ad′ikt *for noun;* ə dikt′ *for verb*) *noun, plural* **addicts;** *verb,* **addicted, addicting.**

addiction The condition of needing something badly, especially a drug or something else that is not healthy. **ad·dic·tion** (ə dik′shən) *noun, plural* **addictions.**

addition **1.** The adding of two or more numbers: *9 + 2 + 5 = 16 is an example of addition.* **2.** The act of adding: *The addition of salt gave flavor to the soup.* **3.** Something that is added: *Our neighbors built an addition to their house.*
• **in addition** or **in addition to.** Besides: *In addition to checkers, we also play chess.* **ad·di·tion** (ə dish′ən) *noun, plural* **additions.**

additional More; extra: *You can get additional information for your report from the library.* **ad·di·tion·al** (ə dish′ə nəl) *adjective.*

additive A small amount of a substance added to another substance to change or improve it: *Some packaged foods have additives that keep the food from spoiling.* **ad·di·tive** (ad′i tiv) *noun, plural* **additives.**

address **1.** The place at which a person lives or an organization is located: *That store's address is 595 Main Street.* **2.** The writing printed on a piece of mail that tells where it is to be delivered. **3.** A formal speech: *the president's address to the nation. Noun.*

PRONUNCIATION KEY:

| at | āpe | fär | câre | end | mē | it | īce | pierce | hot | ōld | sông | fôrk |
| oil | out | up | ūse | rüle | pùll | tûrn | chin | sing | shop | thin | this | |

hw in white; zh in treasure. The symbol ə stands for the unstressed vowel sound in about, taken, pencil, lemon, and circus.

9

○ **1.** To speak or give a formal speech to: *The mayor addressed the audience in the town hall.* **2.** To put directions for delivery on: *Please address these envelopes. Verb.* **ad·dress** (ə dres′ or ad′res *for noun*; ə dres′ *for verb*) *noun, plural* **addresses**; *verb,* **addressed, addressing.**

adenoids Small masses of tissue that grow at the top of the throat in back of the nose. Adenoids can become swollen and make it hard to breathe and speak. **ad·e·noids** (ad′ə noidz′) *plural noun.*

adept Skillful; expert: *It takes practice to be an adept skater.* **a·dept** (ə dept′) *adjective.*

adequate **1.** As much as is needed; enough: *Those plants will not grow without adequate rain.* **2.** Satisfactory but not outstanding: *The actor's performance was no more than adequate.* **ad·e·quate** (ad′i kwit) *adjective.*

adhere **1.** To stick tightly; become attached: *The chewing gum adhered to my shoe.* **2.** To follow closely; be faithful: *They adhered to their beliefs even though it meant they would lose their jobs.* **ad·here** (ad hîr′) *verb,* **adhered, adhering.**

adhesive A substance that makes things stick together: *Glue and paste are adhesives. Noun.* ○ Having a sticky surface that will hold tight to other things: *An adhesive bandage will stick to your skin. Adjective.* **ad·he·sive** (ad hē′siv) *noun, plural* **adhesives**; *adjective.*

adios The Spanish word that means "good-bye." **a·di·os** (ä′dē ōs′) *interjection.*

In cities, buildings are often built adjacent to each other.

adjacent Next to or very near: *The garage is adjacent to the house.* **ad·ja·cent** (ə jā′sənt) *adjective.*

adjective A word that describes or modifies a noun or pronoun. In the sentence "The large suitcase is green," the words "large" and "green" are adjectives. **ad·jec·tive** (aj′ik tiv) *noun, plural* **adjectives.**

adjoin To be very close or next to: *Our football field adjoins the playground.* **ad·join** (ə join′) *verb,* **adjoined, adjoining.**

adjourn **1.** To bring to an end for a while: *The class president adjourned the meeting until next week.* **2.** To stop work: *The senate will adjourn for the summer.* **ad·journ** (ə jûrn′) *verb,* **adjourned, adjourning.**

adjust **1.** To change or regulate so as to correct or improve: *The mechanic had to adjust the brakes on the car.* **2.** To be used to; adapt: *We found it hard to adjust to our new schedule.* **ad·just** (ə just′) *verb,* **adjusted, adjusting.** —**adjustable** *adjective.*

adjustment **1.** The act of making a change to correct or improve something: *Adjustment of the thermostat took no time at all.* **2.** The act of becoming used to or comfortable in a situation: *Adjustment to their new home was difficult at first.* **ad·just·ment** (ə just′mənt) *noun, plural* **adjustments.**

ad-lib To do or say something that has not been planned or practiced, usually in public: *I forgot part of my speech, so I ad-libbed.* **ad-lib** (ad′lib′) *verb,* **ad-libbed, ad-libbing.**

administer **1.** To manage or direct something: *Who administers the company's sales department?* **2.** To give or provide something: *The nurse administered first aid.* **ad·min·is·ter** (ad min′ə stər) *verb,* **administered, administering.**

administration **1.** The control of the operations of a business or other organization: *Since you once ran a business with several employees, you have some experience in administration.* **2.** A group of people in charge of the operation of something: *The principal is the head of the school administration.* **3. the Administration:** The president of the United States, together with the cabinet and the other officials who make up the executive branch of the government. **4.** The period of time during which a government holds office: *American astronauts first traveled in space during the administration of President John F. Kennedy.* **ad·min·is·tra·tion** (ad min′ə strā′shən) *noun, plural* **administrations.**

admirable Deserving respect: *The senator has an admirable record.* **ad·mi·ra·ble** (ad′mər ə bəl) *adjective.*

admiral A naval officer of the highest rank. **ad·mi·ral** (ad′mər əl) *noun, plural* **admirals.**

admiration A feeling of approval or respect: *The astronauts have earned the admiration of the whole country.* **ad·mi·ra·tion** (ad′mə rā′shən) *noun.*

admire 1. To respect: *I admire a person who is always honest.* 2. To look at or speak of with appreciation and pleasure: *I admired my friend's new coat.* **ad·mire** (ad mīr′) *verb,* **admired, admiring.**

admission 1. The act of allowing to enter: *Who is in charge of the admission of patients to that hospital?* 2. The price a person must pay to enter: *The admission to the park was one dollar.* 3. The act of admitting that something is true; confession. **ad·mis·sion** (ad mish′ən) *noun, plural* **admissions.**

admit 1. To allow to enter; let in: *We were admitted to the club last week.* 2. To make known that something is true; confess: *They admitted that they had broken the lamp.* **ad·mit** (ad mit′) *verb,* **admitted, admitting.**

admittance The right or permission to enter: *This ticket gives you admittance to the movie theater.* **ad·mit·tance** (ad mit′əns) *noun.*

admonish To tell someone that he or she has done something wrong. **ad·mon·ish** (ad mon′ish) *verb,* **admonished, admonishing.**

These adobes once housed scores of **Native American families.**

adobe 1. A brick made of clay, that is sometimes mixed with straw, and dried in the sun. 2. A

building made with adobe bricks, popular in Mexico and the southwestern United States. **a·do·be** (ə dō′bē) *noun, plural* **adobes.**

adolescence The time in one's life when they change from a child into an adult. **ad·o·les·cence** (ad′ə les′əns) *noun.*

adolescent A person who is not a child anymore but is not yet an adult. **ad·o·les·cent** (ad′ə les′ənt) *noun, plural* **adolescents.**

adopt 1. To take a child into one's family according to the law and become its legal parent. 2. To take and use as one's own: *The English language has adopted many words from other languages.* 3. To accept or approve: *The people voted to adopt the plan.* **a·dopt** (ə dopt′) *verb,* **adopted, adopting.**

adoption The act of legally adopting a child. **a·dop·tion** (ə dop′shən) *noun, plural* **adoptions.**

adorable Cute; very sweet; lovable: *The fluffy kittens are really adorable.* **a·dor·a·ble** (ə dôr′ə bəl) *adjective.*

adore 1. To love and admire very much: *We adore our parents.* 2. To honor for being divine; worship: *Religious people adore God.* 3. To like very much: *I adore folk music.* **a·dore** (ə dôr′) *verb,* **adored, adoring.**

adorn To add something beautiful to; decorate: *We adorned the room with flowers.* **a·dorn** (ə dôrn′) *verb,* **adorned, adorning.**

adrift Moving freely with the wind or on water; drifting. **a·drift** (ə drift′) *adverb; adjective.*

adult 1. A person who is fully grown; grown-up. 2. A plant or animal that is fully grown. *Noun.* ○ Having grown to full size; mature: *An adult elephant is a huge animal. Adjective.* **a·dult** (ə dult′ *or* ad′ult) *noun, plural* **adults;** *adjective.*

adulthood The period of a person's life when he or she is an adult. **a·dult·hood** (ə dult′hůd) *noun, plural* **adulthoods.**

advance 1. To move forward: *The running back advanced the football enough for a first down.* 2. To help the progress or growth of; further: *The scientists hoped that their experiments would advance our knowledge.* 3. To offer; propose: *The club's president advanced a new plan for a fund drive.* 4. To get a better

Pronunciation Key:

| at | āpe | fär | câre | end | mē | it | īce | pîerce | hot | ōld | sông | fôrk |
| oil | out | up | ūse | rüle | půll | tûrn | chin | sing | shop | thin | this | |

hw in white; zh in treasure. The symbol ə stands for the unstressed vowel sound in about, taken, pencil, lemon, and circus.

11

or higher job; move up in position. **5.** To give before it is due: *My parents **advanced** me my allowance. Verb.*

○ **1.** A move forward: *The army made a steady **advance** toward the city.* **2.** Progress; improvement: *The development of the new medicine was an **advance** in treating serious illnesses.* **3.** A payment given before it is due: *Did you receive an **advance** on your allowance? Noun.*

> • **in advance.** Before the time when something is due to happen; ahead of time: *Order your tickets **in advance**.*

ad·vance (ad vans′) *verb,* **advanced, advancing;** *noun, plural* **advances.**

advanced 1. Beyond the level of others in development or progress: *The **advanced** civilization of ancient Egypt is known for the Pyramids and other achievements in architecture.* **2.** Beyond the beginning level; not elementary: *I'm taking a class in **advanced** algebra.* **3.** Very old: *My grandparents lived to an **advanced** age.* **ad·vanced** (ad vanst′) *adjective.*

advancement 1. A moving forward or ahead. **2.** A move up in position; promotion: *That job offers good opportunities for **advancement**.* **ad·vance·ment** (ad vans′mənt) *noun, plural* **advancements.**

advantage Something that is helpful or useful; benefit: *Being tall is an **advantage** for a basketball player.*

> • **to take advantage of. 1.** To use in a helpful or beneficial way; benefit by: *We **took advantage of** the opportunity to learn French.* **2.** To use or treat in an unfair or selfish way: *Don't **take advantage of** your friend's willingness to be helpful.*

ad·van·tage (ad van′tij) *noun, plural* **advantages.**

advantageous Giving an advantage; favorable; beneficial: *Capturing my opponent's queen put me in an **advantageous** position in the chess game.* **ad·van·ta·geous** (ad′vən tā′jəs) *adjective.*

adventure 1. Something a person does that is difficult and dangerous: *The astronauts' landing on the moon was a great **adventure**.* **2.** An exciting or unusual experience: *Their first trip by airplane was an **adventure** for the whole family.* **ad·ven·ture** (ad ven′chər) *noun, plural* **adventures.**

adventurous 1. Willing to risk danger in order to have exciting or unusual experiences; bold: *The **adventurous** campers hiked into the wilderness.* **2.** Full of danger or risks: *an **adventurous** trip down the river's rapids.* **ad·ven·tu·rous** (ad ven′chər əs) *adjective.*

Crossing a moving stream or river is often an adventurous experience.

adverb A word that describes or modifies a verb, an adjective, or another adverb. In the sentence "Two very large vans drove quite slowly down the street," the words "very," "quite," and "slowly" are adverbs. **ad·verb** (ad′vûrb′) *noun, plural* **adverbs.**

adversary A person or group that fights another person or enemy: *The American colonists and Great Britain were **adversaries** in the American Revolution.* **ad·ver·sar·y** (ad′vər ser′ē) *noun, plural* **adversaries.**

adverse 1. Not helpful to what is wanted; not favorable: *The football game was played under **adverse** conditions because of the heavy rain.* **2.** Unfriendly or hostile: *Your **adverse** remarks about the party hurt my feelings.* **ad·verse** (ad vûrs′ *or* ad′vûrs) *adjective.*

adversity A difficult time or situation; hardship: *The homeless people showed courage in the face of **adversity**.* **ad·ver·si·ty** (ad vûr′si tē) *noun, plural* **adversities.**

advertise 1. To make a product known to people so they will want to buy it: *That company **advertises** its toothpaste on television.* **2.** To tell people about something: *The school **advertised***

the play by putting up posters. **3.** To place an advertisement: *Our parents **advertised** for a baby-sitter in the town newspaper.*
ad·ver·tise (ad′vər tīz′) *verb,* **advertised, advertising.**

advertisement A public notice that tells people about a product, event, or something a person needs. **ad·ver·tise·ment** (ad′vər tīz′mənt) *noun, plural **advertisements**.*

Advertisements **for bicycles were common in the late 1800s.**

advice An idea about how to solve a problem or how to act in a certain situation; suggestion; opinion: *Our friends gave us **advice** about how to care for our new puppy.* **ad·vice** (ad vīs′) *noun.*

advisable Showing good sense; sensible; wise; recommended: *It is **advisable** to drive at a slower speed on wet roads.* **ad·vis·a·ble** (ad vī′zə bəl) *adjective.*

advise **1.** To give advice to: *The doctor **advised** us to exercise regularly.* **2.** To let know; notify: *The letter **advised** me that I had won first prize.* **ad·vise** (ad vīz′) *verb,* **advised, advising.**

adviser or **advisor** A person who gives advice: *High schools have **advisers** who help students decide what to study.* **ad·vis·er** (ad vī′zər) *noun, plural **advisers**.*

advocate To speak in favor of; urge; support: *The senator **advocated** honest government.* Verb. ○ A person who speaks in favor of someone or something: *My mother is an **advocate** for improving education.* Noun. **ad·vo·cate** (ad′və kāt′ *for verb;* ad′və kit *for noun) verb,* **advocated, advocating;** *noun, plural* **advocates.**

aerial **1.** Of or in the air: *Trapeze artists do **aerial** acrobatics.* **2.** About flying or aircraft: *That photographer takes a lot of **aerial** photographs of seacoasts. Adjective.* ○ A radio or television antenna. *Noun.* **aer·i·al** (âr′ē əl) *adjective; noun, plural **aerials**.*

aerobic Making the human body able to take in oxygen and use it better: *Running and dancing are **aerobic**.* **aer·o·bic** (â rō′ biks) *adjective.*

aerobics Exercises that help the body to take in and use more oxygen. If aerobics are done regularly, they can strengthen the heart and lungs: *Running, biking, and swimming are three kinds of **aerobics**.* **aer·o·bics** (â rō′biks) *plural noun.*

aerodynamic Designed to move through the air easily: *The bodies of airplanes and cars are **aerodynamic**.* **aer·o·dy·nam·ic** (âr′ō dī nam′ik) *adjective.*

aeronautics The science that deals with flight. Aeronautics is concerned with designing, building, and flying aircraft. The word aeronautics is used with a singular verb. **aer·o·nau·tics** (âr′ə nô tiks) *noun.*

aerosol Very fine solid or liquid particles suspended in a gas, sometimes under pressure. Smoke and fog are aerosols that occur in nature. Paints and deodorants are produced and sold as aerosols. **aer·o·sol** (âr′ə sôl) *noun, plural **aerosols**.*

aerospace **1.** The earth's atmosphere and outer space. The region in which aircraft and spacecraft operate is called aerospace. **2.** The science that deals with aerospace. **aer·o·space** (âr′ō spās′) *noun.*

aesthetic Of or having to do with art and beauty or with things that are beautiful: *The architect judged the building on both its **aesthetic** and practical merits.* **aes·thet·ic** (es thet′ik) *adjective.*

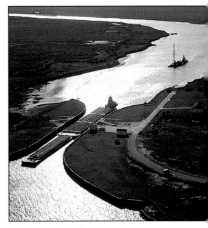

Most aerial **photographs provide wider views than pictures taken from the ground.**

PRONUNCIATION KEY:

| at | āpe | fär | câre | end | mē | it | īce | pierce | hot | ōld | sông | fôrk |
| oil | out | up | ūse | rüle | pull | tûrn | chin | sing | shop | thin | this | |

hw in white; zh in treasure. The symbol ə stands for the unstressed vowel sound in about, taken, pencil, lemon, and circus.

13

afar To a great distance away or at a distance; far away: *The explorers traveled* ***afar*** *to discover new lands.* **a·far** (ə färʹ) *adverb*.

affable Pleasant to be with and talk to; friendly. **af·fa·ble** (afʹə bəl) *adjective*.

affair 1. A thing that is done or has to be done: *Moving to the new home was a confusing* ***affair***. 2. An event; occasion: *The dance is going to be a formal* ***affair***. 3. **affairs**. Business matters: *A lawyer handles the company's* ***affairs***. **af·fair** (ə fârʹ) *noun, plural* **affairs**.

affect¹ 1. To make something happen to; have an effect on: *The lack of rain may* ***affect*** *the crops.* 2. To cause to feel sad; touch; move: *The photographs of the hungry children* ***affected*** *us.* Another word that sounds close to this is **effect**. **af·fect** (ə fektʹ) *verb*, **affected, affecting**.

affect² To pretend to have or feel: *They* ***affected*** *bravery, but they were really afraid.* Another word that sounds close to this is **effect**. **af·fect** (ə fektʹ) *verb*, **affected, affecting**.

affection A feeling of tenderness, fondness, or love: *I have deep* ***affection*** *for my sister.* **af·fec·tion** (ə fekʹshən) *noun, plural* **affections**.

affectionate Full of or showing affection; tender, fond, or loving: *The* ***affectionate*** *boy gave his baby sister a hug.* **af·fec·tion·ate** (ə fekʹshə nit) *adjective*.

affiliate To join or unite: *Our local television station is* ***affiliated*** *with a national network. Verb.* ○ A group connected with another, similar group. *Noun.* **af·fil·i·ate** (ə filʹē ātʹ *for verb;* ə filʹē ət *for noun*) *verb*, **affiliated, affiliating**; *noun, plural* **affiliates**.

affirm To state in a positive way; assert; declare: *My mother* ***affirmed*** *that I was going to school, no matter what.* **af·firm** (ə fûrmʹ) *verb*, **affirmed, affirming**.

affirmative Saying that something is true; saying "yes." *They gave an* ***affirmative*** *answer to my question by nodding their heads.* **af·firm·a·tive** (ə fûrʹmə tiv) *adjective*.

affirmative action A policy of providing educational and employment opportunities to certain people, such as minorities and women, who have not had proper opportunities in the past.

affix To attach or fasten: *I* ***affixed*** *labels to the packages. Verb.* ○ A syllable or group of syllables added to a word to change its meaning; a prefix or suffix. In the word unbreakable, un- and -able are affixes. *Noun.* **af·fix** (ə fiksʹ *for verb;* afʹiks *for noun*) *verb*, **affixed, affixing**; *noun, plural* **affixes**.

afflict To cause pain or trouble; make miserable: *The campers were* ***afflicted*** *by a rash caused by poison ivy.* **af·flict** (ə fliktʹ) *verb*, **afflicted, afflicting**.

affliction 1. The condition of being afflicted; pain or trouble: *The* ***affliction*** *of poverty affects many people.* 2. A cause of pain or trouble: *Influenza can be a severe* ***affliction***. **af·flic·tion** (ə flikʹshən) *noun, plural* **afflictions**.

affluent Having a large amount of money; rich; wealthy: *The jewelry store had many* ***affluent*** *customers.* **af·flu·ent** (afʹlü ənt) *adjective*.

afford 1. To have enough money to pay for: *Can you* ***afford*** *a new car?* 2. To be able to give or do: *They couldn't* ***afford*** *the time to help us.* 3. To be able to do without causing harm: *I can't* ***afford*** *to skip breakfast.* **af·ford** (ə fôrdʹ) *verb*, **afforded, affording**.

affront Something said or done that is purposely mean and insulting: *Your rude comment about my home was an* ***affront*** *to me. Noun.* ○ To insult deliberately and openly: *The audience* ***affronted*** *the speaker by booing. Verb.* **af·front** (ə fruntʹ) *noun, plural* **affronts**; *verb* **affronted, affronting**.

afghan A blanket that is knitted or crocheted. **af·ghan** (afʹgan) *noun, plural* **afghans**.

Afghanistan A country in south-central Asia. **Af·ghan·i·stan** (af ganʹə stanʹ) *noun*.

afield Off the right path; not near by: *His work takes him far* ***afield*** *during the week.* **afield** (ə fēldʹ) *adverb*.

afire On fire; burning. **a·fire** (ə fīrʹ) *adjective; adverb*.

afloat Floating on water or in the air: *The lifeboat was made to stay* ***afloat***.

The blacksmith has set the coals afire in his forge.

The dandelion seeds are **afloat** in the wind.
a·float (ə flōt′) adjective; adverb.

afoot **1.** By walking; on foot: I left my bicycle and
continued **afoot**. **2.** Going on; in progress: Plans
for the attack were **afoot**. **a·foot** (ə fut′) adverb;
adjective.

afraid **1.** Feeling fear; frightened: Are you **afraid**
of snakes? **2.** Feeling unhappy or sorry: I'm
afraid I can't play now. **a·fraid** (ə frād′) adjective.

afresh Once more; again: After the cat shredded
my homework, I had to begin **afresh**. **a·fresh**
(ə fresh′) adverb.

Africa A continent south of Europe and between the
Atlantic and Indian Oceans. **Af·ri·ca** (af′ri kə) noun.

African Of or having to do with Africa or its
people. Adjective.
◦ **1.** A person who was born or is living in Africa.
2. A person who is a citizen of an African country. Noun.
Af·ri·can (af′ri kən) adjective; noun, plural **Africans**.

**The man at the center of the poster is the great early
African-American leader Frederick Douglass.**

African-American A black American. Noun.
◦ Of or having to do with African-Americans:
This museum has **African-American** art.
Adjective.
African-American (af′ri kən ə mer′i kən) noun,
plural **African-Americans**; adjective.

Afro-American Another word for African-
American. Look up African-American for more
information. **Af·ro-A·mer·i·can** (af′rō ə mer′i kən)
noun, plural **Afro-Americans**; adjective.

after **1.** Following in place or order; behind:
My dog walked **after** me. **2.** With the purpose of

following, finding, or catching: The police went
after the thieves. **3.** Following in time; later than:
I arrived **after** dark. Preposition.
◦ **1.** Following in place; behind: Our parents
walked ahead, and we walked **after**. **2.** Following
in time; later: They left on Sunday, and I left
three days **after**. Adverb.
◦ Following the time that: It happened **after** you
left. Conjunction.
af·ter (af′tər) preposition; adverb; conjunction.

afternoon The part of the day between noon and
evening. **af·ter·noon** (af′tər nün′) noun, plural
afternoons.

afterward or **afterwards** At a later time: We
swam and **afterward** we rested. **af·ter·ward** or
af·ter·wards (af′tər wərd or af′tər wərdz) adverb.

again Once more; another time: I failed that test
once, but I took it **again** and passed. **a·gain**
(ə gen′) adverb.

against **1.** Not in favor of; opposed to: The senator voted **against** the bill. **2.** In the opposite direction to. The salmon swam **against** the current.
3. Next to; touching: We leaned our bicycles
against the building. **4.** So as to strike or come
into contact with: I threw the ball **against** the
wall. **5.** As a protection or defense from:
We covered the windows with plywood **against**
the hurricane. **a·gainst** (ə genst′) preposition.

agate **1.** A kind of quartz that has layers or masses of different colors. **2.** A marble used in games
that is made of agate
or a material that
looks like agate.
ag·ate (ag′it) noun,
plural **agates**.

age **1.** The amount of
time that a person,
animal, or thing has
lived or existed: My
age is eleven.
2. A particular time
of life: My grandpar-
ents are enjoying
their old **age**. **3.** The

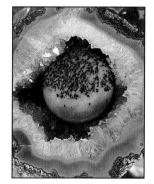

**Agate is often used in
jewelry or displayed as a
piece of art.**

latter part of life; old age: The judge has the
wisdom and experience of **age**. **4.** A particular
period of history: The second part of the

PRONUNCIATION KEY:

| at | āpe | fär | câre | end | mē | it | īce | pîerce | hot | ōld | sông | fôrk |
| oil | out | up | ūse | rüle | pull | tûrn | chin | sing | shop | thin | this | |

hw in white; zh in treasure. The symbol ə stands for the unstressed vowel sound in about, taken, pencil, lemon, and circus.

15

*twentieth century might be known as the **age** of the computer. Noun.*
○ **1.** To make or become old: *Having a hard life can **age** a person.* **2.** To become ready to be used: *Some cheese tastes better after it **ages**. Verb.* **age** (āj) *noun, plural* **ages;** *verb,* **aged, aging** *or* **ageing.**

AGE

Humans can look forward to a life span of 70 or 80 years, or more. But most animals don't live as long as humans. Here are the life spans of some common animals:

Mouse	**3 years**
Guinea Pig	**4 years**
Rabbit	**5 years**
Kangaroo	**7 years**
Squirrel	**10 years**
Giraffe	**10 years**
Dog	**12 years**
Cat	**12 years**
Lion	**15 years**
Gorilla	**20 years**
Horse	**20 years**
Asian elephant	**40 years**
Giant tortoise	**100 years**

The life span of a tortoise may seem long, but not when compared to some plants. The oldest living tree is believed to be a bristlecone pine in California. It is called Methuselah and it is over 4,700 years old.

---

aged **1.** Old; elderly: *The children take care of their **aged** grandparents.* **2.** Having the age of: *She had a brother **aged** three.* **a•ged** (ā′jid *for definition 1;* ājd *for definition 2*) *adjective.*

ageism Discrimination or prejudice against older people. **age•ism** (ā′jiz əm) *noun.*

agency **1.** A company or a person that does business for other companies or people: *That advertising **agency** prepares the advertisements for several large companies.* **2.** A special department of the government: *A federal **agency** set the safety rules followed in the factory.* **a•gen•cy** (ā′jən sē) *noun, plural* **agencies.**

agenda A list or plan of things to be talked about or done. **a•gen•da** (a gen′da) *noun, plural* **agendas.**

agent **1.** A person who acts for some other person or company: *The real estate **agent** sold the family a new house.* **2.** Something that produces a certain effect: *Soap is a cleaning **agent**.* **a•gent** (ā′jənt) *noun, plural* **agents.**

aggravate **1.** To make worse: *Being out in the rain **aggravated** my cold.* **2.** To irritate; bother; annoy: *Their constant complaining **aggravated** us.* **ag•gra•vate** (ag′rə vāt′) *verb,* **aggravated, aggravating.** —**aggravation** *noun.*

aggression **1.** An attack or warlike action, especially one that is not provoked: *A country that sends an army to take over the land of another country has committed an act of **aggression**.* **2.** Hostile or mean behavior. **ag•gres•sion** (ə gresh′ən) *noun, plural* **aggressions.**

aggressive **1.** Ready and eager to attack or start a fight: *The neighborhood bullies get into trouble because they are so **aggressive**.* **2.** Very forceful and bold: *An **aggressive** salesperson does not easily accept "no" for an answer.* **ag•gres•sive** (ə gres′iv) *adjective.*

aghast Feeling shocked or horrified: *We were **aghast** at the damage caused by the tornado.* **a•ghast** (ə gast′) *adjective.*

agile **1.** Able to move and react quickly and easily: *A cat is an **agile** animal.* **2.** Able to think quickly: *Astronauts need **agile** minds.* **ag•ile** (aj′əl) *adjective.*

agility The ability to move or think quickly and easily: *An acrobat must have **agility**.* **a•gil•i•ty** (ə jil′i tē) *noun.*

aging The process of growing older: *Losing the sense of hearing may be a sign of **aging**.* **ag•ing** (ā′jing) *noun.*

It takes a great deal of agility to walk along this rope.

agitate **1.** To stir up or shake: *The wind **agitated** the water and made waves.* **2.** To disturb the feelings of; excite: *The report that a hurricane was approaching **agitated** the people in the area.* **3.** To try to stir interest in the public: *A group of employees from the factory **agitated** for safer working*

conditions. **ag•i•tate** (aj′i tāt) *verb*, **agitated,**
agitating. —**agitation** *noun*.

aglow Bright with light or warmth; glowing:
*During the festival the park was **aglow** with
colored lights*. **a•glow** (ə glō′) *adjective; adverb*.

ago Before now: *They left ten minutes **ago***. *Dinosaurs lived long **ago***. **a•go** (ə gō′) *adjective; adverb*.

agony Great pain or suffering of the mind or
body: *I was in **agony** from the toothache.
We suffered **agony** at the death of our dog*.
ag•o•ny (ag′ə nē) *noun, plural* **agonies**.

agree **1.** To have the same opinion or feeling:
*My friends all **agreed** that it was a good movie*.
2. To say that one is willing; give permission: *Will
you **agree** to lend me your bicycle?* **3.** To come to
an understanding: *The car dealer and the customer
agreed on a price*. **4.** To be alike; correspond:
*Their stories about the car accident don't **agree***.

• **to agree with.** To be healthful or suitable for:
*Humid weather does not **agree with** me*.
a•gree (ə grē′) *verb*, **agreed, agreeing**.

agreeable **1.** Nice; pleasant: *Our new neighbors
are very **agreeable***. **2.** Willing to give permission:
*I will come to the party if my parents are **agreeable***. **a•gree•a•ble** (ə grē′ə bəl) *adjective*.

agreement **1.** An understanding between people
or groups: *The two nations signed a peace **agreement***. **2.** The condition of agreeing; harmony: *My
parents are in **agreement** about what color to
paint the house*. **a•gree•ment** (ə grē′mənt) *noun,
plural* **agreements**.

agricultural Having to do with farming or farms:

**Large farm machinery helped make the United States
a world agricultural leader.**

Because of their interest in farming, my cousins
went to an **agricultural** college*. **ag•ri•cul•tur•al**
(ag′ri kul′chər əl) *adjective*.

agriculture The science and business of raising
crops and farm animals; farming. **ag•ri•cul•ture**
(ag′ri kul′chər) *noun*.

ah A word used to show concern, hurt, joy, admiration, surprise, or other strong feelings: *Ah, now
I understand*. **ah** (ä) *interjection*.

aha A word used to show triumph, satisfaction,
discovery, or other feelings: *Aha! I caught you
sneaking up on me!* **a•ha** (ä hä′) *interjection*.

ahead **1.** In front: *At the end of the race I moved
ahead of the other runners*. **2.** In advance:
*We planned **ahead** for your visit*. **a•head**
(ə hed′) *adverb*.

ahoy An expression used by sailors as a greeting
or to attract attention. *When the sailors saw the
other ship, they yelled "Ship ahoy!"* **a•hoy** (ə hoi′)
interjection.

AI An abbreviation of artificial intelligence.

aid To give help or support: *We **aided** the farmers
in their search for the lost cattle*. *Verb*.
○ **1.** Help or support; assistance: *My friends came
to my **aid** when I climbed too high in the tree*.
2. A person or thing that is helpful: *A dictionary
is an **aid** in learning new words*. *Noun*.
Another word that sounds like this is **aide**.
aid (ād) *verb*, **aided, aiding**; *noun, plural* **aids**.

aide A person who helps or supports; assistant:
*During the summer, I worked as a nurse's **aide***.
Another word that sounds like this is **aid**.
aide (ād) *noun, plural* **aides**.

AIDS A very serious illness caused by a virus
that attacks the body's ability to protect itself.
AIDS stands for Acquired Immune Deficiency
Syndrome. **AIDS** (ādz) *noun*.

ail **1.** To cause illness or trouble for: *What **ails**
the twins?* **2.** To be ill; feel sick: *They have been
ailing for a month*.
Another word that sounds like this is **ale**.
ail (āl) *verb*, **ailed, ailing**.

ailment An illness; sickness: *My **ailment** was
cured by a long rest*. **ail•ment** (āl′mənt) *noun,
plural* **ailments**.

aim **1.** To direct or point a weapon or a blow:
*Take careful **aim**, then release the arrow*.

PRONUNCIATION KEY:
at   āpe   fär   câre   end   mē   it   īce   pîerce   hot   ōld   sông   fôrk
oil   out   up   ūse   rūle   pùll   tûrn   chin   sing   shop   thin   this
hw in white; zh in treasure. The symbol ə stands for the unstressed vowel sound in about, taken, pencil, lemon, and circus.

2. To intend for; direct toward. *I aimed my speech at the classmates who might vote for me in the election. Verb.*

○ **1.** The act of pointing or directing a weapon or blow: *The child's **aim** was not good enough to hit the target.* **2.** Goal. *My **aim** is to become a doctor. Noun.*

aim (ām) *verb,* **aimed, aiming;** *noun, plural* **aims.**

aimless Without purpose or aim: *They took an aimless walk through the fields.* **aim·less** (ām′lis) *adjective.*

ain't **1.** Am not. **2.** Is not; are not. **3.** Has not; have not. **ain't** (ānt).

LANGUAGE USAGE

Ain't is not considered to be good English. Because of this, careful speakers avoid using ain't if they wish to impress others.

---

air **1.** The mixture of gases that surrounds Earth and forms its atmosphere. Air is made up mainly of nitrogen and oxygen, with small amounts of other gases: *The **air** is fragrant with roses.* **2.** The open space above Earth; sky: *I threw the ball into the **air**.* **3.** Fresh air: *Please open the window and let in some **air**.* **4.** A look or manner: *The principal has a very serious **air**.* **5. airs.** Showy manners used to impress others: *Don't put on **airs**.* **6.** A melody or tune: *I whistled a cheerful **air** while I worked. Noun.*

○ **1.** To let air through; freshen: *Please open the windows and **air** the room.* **2.** To make known widely; express freely: *The workers **aired** their complaints. Verb.*

Other words that sound like this are **ere** and **heir**.

• **off the air.** Not broadcasting or being broadcast: *That program has been **off the air** for two years.*

• **on the air.** Broadcasting or being broadcast: *That program will be **on the air** at 6:30.*

air (âr) *noun, plural* **airs;** *verb,* **aired, airing.**

air bag A large bag that fills with air instantly to protect passengers in a car crash. **air bag** (âr′bag′) *noun.*

air conditioner A machine that cools air and removes dust and humidity from it. An air conditioner is used to move air around in an enclosed space, such as a room or automobile. **air con·di·tion·er** (air kən dish′ə nər).

air conditioning A system for cooling the insides of buildings and cars when the weather is very hot. **air con·di·tion·ing**

aircraft Any machine made to fly in the air: *Airplanes, helicopters, gliders, and balloons are all **aircraft**.* **air·craft** (âr′kraft′) *noun, plural* **aircraft.**

air force The branch of a country's armed forces trained to fight using aircraft. The words *air force* are often capitalized when they mean the air force of a particular country.

airline An organization or business that carries passengers and freight from one place to another by airplane. **air·line** (âr′līn′) *noun, plural* **airlines.**

airliner A large airplane that carries passengers. **air·lin·er** (âr′lī′nər) *noun, plural* **airliners.**

airmail **1.** A system for carrying mail by airplane. **2.** Mail carried by airplane. *Noun.*

○ To send by airmail. *Verb.*

○ Having to do with or sent by means of airmail: *Our cousin in Canada sent us an **airmail** letter. Adjective.*

○ By means of airmail: *Please send this package **airmail**. Adverb.*

air·mail (âr′māl′) *noun; verb,* **airmailed, airmailing;** *adjective; adverb.*

airplane A machine with wings that flies: *An airplane is heavier than air, and is driven by propellers or jet engines.* **air·plane** (âr′plān′) *noun, plural* **airplanes.**

airport A place where airplanes can take off and land: *An **airport** has buildings for sheltering and repairing airplanes and for receiving passengers and freight.* **air·port** (âr′pôrt′) *noun, plural* **airports.**

Huge airports can accommodate aircraft both large and small.

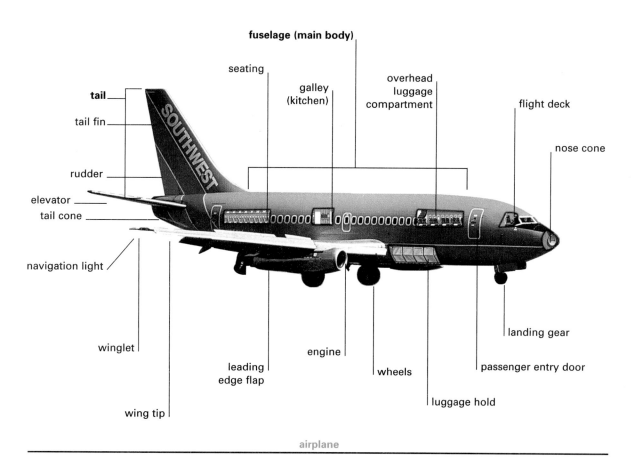

fuselage (main body)

seating

galley
(kitchen)

overhead
luggage
compartment

flight deck

tail

tail fin

nose cone

rudder

elevator

tail cone

navigation light

winglet

leading
edge flap

engine

wheels

luggage hold

landing gear

passenger entry door

wing tip

airplane

air pressure The force that air puts on things. Air pressure in the atmosphere is caused by the weight of the air high above the earth pressing down on the air that is below.

airship An aircraft that is filled with gas and is lighter than air. It is driven by a motor and can be steered: *A blimp is an airship.* **air·ship** (âr′ship′) *noun, plural* **airships**.

airsick Having nausea or feeling dizzy when flying in an aircraft. **air·sick** (âr′sik′) *adjective*.

airstrip A paved or cleared area where aircraft can take off and land. **air·strip** (âr′strip′) *noun, plural* **airstrips**.

airtight **1.** So tight that no air or gases can get in or out: *The jelly was packed in an airtight jar so that it would stay fresh.* **2.** Having no weak points that could be easily attacked: *The police had an airtight case against the car thieves.* **air·tight** (âr′tīt′) *adjective*.

airy **1.** Light as air; delicate: *The costume was*

made of an *airy* material. **2.** Open to the movement of air: *an airy, cool porch.* **air·y** (âr′ē) *adjective*, **airier, airiest**.

aisle The space between two rows or sections of something: *There are several aisles in the supermarket. I like to sit next to the aisle when I fly.* Other words that sound like this are **I'll** and **isle**. **aisle** (īl) *noun, plural* **aisles**.

ajar Partly open: *The front door was ajar.* **a·jar** (ə jär′) *adjective; adverb*.

AK Postal abbreviation for Alaska.

akimbo With the hands on the hips and the elbows turned outward. *She stood with her arms akimbo, waiting for us.* **a·kim·bo** (ə kim′bō) *adjective*.

akin **1.** Belonging to the same family; related: *My cousin and I are akin.* **2.** Like each other; similar: *Love and friendship are akin.* **a·kin** (ə kin′) *adjective*.

AL Postal abbreviation for Alabama.

PRONUNCIATION KEY:

| at | āpe | fär | câre | end | mē | it | īce | pîerce | hot | ōld | sông | fôrk |
| oil | out | up | ūse | rüle | pull | tûrn | chin | sing | shop | thin | this | |

hw in white; zh in treasure. The symbol ə stands for the unstressed vowel sound in about, taken, pencil, lemon, and circus.

19

Ala. An abbreviation for Alabama.

Alabama A state in the southeastern United States. Its capital is Montgomery. **Al·a·bam·a** (al'ə bam'ə) *noun.*

Alabama
U. S. Postal Abbreviation: **AL**
Capital: **Montgomery**
Population: **4,083,000**
Area: **51,609 sq. mi./133,667 sq. km**
State Nicknames: **Yellowhammer State; Heart of Dixie; Cotton State**
State Bird: **Yellowhammer**
State Flower: **Camellia**

WORD HISTORY

The name **Alabama** comes from two Indian words that mean "people who gather plants" or "people who clear land." The words were used first as the name of an Indian tribe that lived near the **Alabama** River. The tribe's name was used for the river, and the state of **Alabama** was later named for the river.

alabaster A smooth, white stone. It is used to make sculptures. *Noun.*
○ Having a smooth, pale appearance: *An alabaster complexion. Adjective.*
a·la·bas·ter (al'ə bas'tər) *noun; adjective.*

a la mode Served with ice cream: *I'll have pie a la mode for dessert.* **a la mode** (al ə mōd') *adjective.*

alarm 1. A bell, buzzer, or other device used to wake people up or to warn them of danger: *Set the alarm for seven o'clock. The bank has an alarm that alerts the police in case of a robbery.* 2. A sudden fear of danger: *The loud thunder filled the child with alarm.* 3. A warning of danger: *The radio broadcast spread the alarm that a hurricane was approaching. Noun.*
○ To make afraid; frighten: *The news that the river was rising alarmed us. Verb.*
a·larm (ə lärm') *noun, plural* **alarms**; *verb,* **alarmed, alarming.**

alarm clock A clock that can be set to ring, buzz, or make some other sound at a particular time. People use alarm clocks to wake them up in the morning.

alas A word used to express sorrow, regret, or disappointment. **a·las** (ə las') *interjection.*

Alas. An abbreviation for Alaska.

Alaska The largest state of the United States. It is located in the northwestern part of North America. The capital of Alaska is Juneau. **A·las·ka** (ə las'kə) *noun.*

Alaska
U. S. Postal Abbreviation: **AK**
Capital: **Juneau**
Population: **525,000**
Area: **586,412 sq. mi./1,518,800 sq. km**
State Nickname: **The Last Frontier**
State Bird: **Willow Ptarmigan**
State Flower: **Forget-Me-Not**

WORD HISTORY

The name **Alaska** comes from an Inuit word meaning "mainland." The Inuit who named **Alaska** lived on islands off of its coast.

Albania A country in southeastern Europe. **Al·ba·ni·a** (al bā'nē ə) *noun.*

albatross A large, black and white bird that has a long, hooked beak and webbed feet: *The albatross has very large wings and is able to fly great distances.* **al·ba·tross** (al'bə trôs) *noun, plural* **albatrosses.**

Alberta A province in western Canada. Its capital is Edmonton. **Al·ber·ta** (al bûr'tə) *noun.*

albino A person, animal, or plant that lacks normal coloring: *An albino rabbit has white fur* *and pink eyes.* **al•bi•no** (al bī′nō) *noun, plural* **albinos.**

album 1. A book with blank pages: *People use albums to hold things like photographs and stamps.* 2. A phonograph record or set of records in one container: *You have more jazz albums than anyone else I know.* **al•bum** (al′bəm) *noun, plural* **albums.**

alcohol A clear liquid that burns easily and evaporates quickly. It comes from certain grains and fruits, or it can be made in a laboratory. One kind of alcohol is found in drinks like whiskey, wine, and beer. Alcohol is also used in making medicines and chemicals. **al•co•hol** (al kə hôl) *noun, plural* **alcohols.**

alcoholic 1. Containing or caused by alcohol: *At the party the host served alcoholic drinks as well as soft drinks.* 2. Suffering from alcoholism. *Adjective.*
○ A person who suffers from alcoholism. *Noun.* **al•co•hol•ic** (al′kə hô′lik) *adjective; noun, plural* **alcoholics.**

alcoholism A disease in which a person has a very strong desire to drink alcoholic beverages and finds it hard to control the desire. **al•co•hol•ism** (al′kə hô liz′əm) *noun.*

alcove A small area of a room that opens out from a main area: *I study in an alcove off our living room.* **al•cove** (al′kōv) *noun, plural* **alcoves.**

alder A small tree or shrub that has rough bark and oval leaves with jagged edges. The alder is related to the birch tree and grows in cool, moist places. **al•der** (ôl′dər) *noun, plural* **alders.**

ale An alcoholic drink, similar to beer, that is made from malt and hops.
Another word that sounds like this is **ail**.
ale (āl) *noun, plural* **ales.**

alert 1. Watching carefully; attentive: *The rabbit was alert to the slightest movement.* 2. Quick to act or learn. *Adjective.*
○ 1. A signal that warns of possible danger; alarm: *A siren sounded the alert.* 2. The time that a warning lasts: *The storm alert lasted two hours. Noun.*
○ To warn: *The Coast Guard alerted the town about the coming hurricane. Verb.*
a•lert (ə lûrt′) *adjective; noun, plural* **alerts;** *verb,* **alerted, alerting.**

Aleut A member of a people living on the Aleutian Islands, a chain of islands that are part of Alaska. **Al•eut** (ə lüt′) *noun, plural* **Aleut** or **Aleuts.**

alfalfa A plant that has bluish purple flowers and groups of three leaflets like clover leaves, grown as a food for cattle and other livestock. **al•fal•fa** (al fal′fə) *noun.*

algae Simple living things that are composed of one or more cells. Most algae are plants that do not have roots or flowers. Some kinds of algae are neither plants nor animals. Seaweed and some other ocean plants are algae. **al•gae** (al′jē) *plural noun.*

algebra The branch of mathematics that deals with the relations between known and unknown numbers. In an algebra problem, letters are used to stand for unknown numbers. In the algebra problem $X + Y = 7$, if $X = 3$, then $Y = 4$. **al•ge•bra** (al′jə brə) *noun.*

Algeria A country in northern Africa. **Al•ge•ri•a** (al jîr′ē ə) *noun.*

alias A name used to hide one's real name: *The criminal had three aliases. Noun.*
○ Otherwise called; also known as: *Lee Hunter, alias Kim Tracey, was wanted by the police for questioning. Adverb.*
a•li•as (ā′lē əs) *noun, plural* **aliases;** *adverb.*

alibi 1. A claim or proof that one was somewhere else when a crime was committed: *The suspects in the robbery had good alibis.* 2. An excuse: *Do you have an alibi for being late?* **al•i•bi** (al′ə bī′) *noun, plural* **alibis.**

WORD HISTORY

The word alibi comes from a Latin word that means "somewhere else." Persons accused of a crime would try to prove that they were in another place at the time of the crime. The claim or proof that a person was somewhere else became known as an alibi.

---

alien 1. A person who is not a citizen of the country in which he or she lives; foreigner. 2. A being from some place outside of the earth or its atmosphere: *The movie was about aliens who tried to take over the earth. Noun.*
○ 1. Of or from another country: *This city has a large alien population.* 2. Not familiar; different:

PRONUNCIATION KEY:
at　āpe　fär　cāre　end　mē　it　īce　pierce　hot　ōld　sông　fôrk
oil　out　up　ūse　rüle　pull　tûrn　chin　sing　shop　thin　this
hw in white; zh in treasure. The symbol ə stands for the unstressed vowel sound in about, taken, pencil, lemon, and circus.

21

*The customs of those people are **alien** to me. Adjective.*
al·ien (āl′yən *or* āl′ē ən) *noun, plural* **aliens**; *adjective*.

alight¹ 1. To get down or get off: *The door of the plane opened, and the passengers alighted.* 2. To come down from the air; land: *The bee alighted on the flower.* **a·light** (ə līt′) *verb*, **alighted** *or* **alit** (ə lit′), **alighting**.

alight² 1. Lit up; glowing: *The child's face was alight with joy.* 2. On fire; burning: *Is the charcoal alight yet?* **a·light** (ə līt′) *adjective*.

align To put in a straight line: *The captain aligned the troops for the parade.* **a·lign** (ə līn′) *verb*, **aligned**, **aligning**.

alike In the same way; similarly: *The twins often dress alike. Adverb.*
○ Like one another; similar: *No two people have fingerprints that are exactly alike. Adjective.*
a·like (ə līk′) *adverb; adjective*.

alimentary canal
A long tube that carries food through the body. It includes the esophagus, stomach, small intestine, and large intestine. It is a part of the digestive system. **al·i·men·ta·ry canal** (al′ə men′tə rē *or* al′ə men′trē).

alimentary canal

alimony Money paid by a person to a spouse after they have been divorced or legally separated. **al·i·mo·ny** (al′ə mō′nē) *noun*.

alive 1. Having life; living: *These plants must be given water if you want them to stay alive.* 2. In existence or operation; active: *The results of the poll kept the candidate's hopes alive during the campaign.* 3. Full of life: *The child's eyes were alive with excitement.* **a·live** (ə līv′) *adjective*.

all 1. The whole of: *We ate all the ice cream.* 2. Every one: *Students from all the schools in town were in the swimming meet.* 3. Without anything else; only: *Sometimes life cannot be all fun. Adjective.*
○ The whole amount or number: *All of us are going to the party. All of the sugar is gone. Pronoun.*
○ Completely: *The work is all finished. Adverb.*
○ Everything that one has: *The team gave its all during the game and won. Noun.*
• **all over.** 1. Finished; ended: *School will soon be all over.* 2. Everywhere: *We looked all over for you yesterday.*
• **at all.** Not in the smallest amount; in any way: *I couldn't do any of the arithmetic problems at all.*
Another word that sounds like this is **awl**.
all (ôl) *adjective; pronoun; adverb; noun*.

Allah God, in the Muslim religion. **Al·lah** (al′ə) *noun*.

all-American 1. Made up entirely of Americans: *An all-American team of scientists working in Antarctica.* 2. Selected as one of the best college athletes in the US: *He is an all-American basketball player.* **all-A·mer·i·can** (ôl′ə mer′i kən) *adjective*.

all-around 1. Having talent, skill, or knowledge in many areas: *Some events in the Olympic games require all-around athletes, and others involve a particular skill.* 2. Wide in range; not limited; broad: *That school will give you an all-around education.* **all-a·round** (ôl′ə round′) *adjective*.

allege To say or declare positively but without final proof: *The villagers alleged that the sawmill caused the water pollution.* **al·lege** (ə lej′) *verb*, **alleged**, **alleging**.

allegiance Faithful support of a country, person, group, or cause. *Americans owe allegiance to the United States:* **al·le·giance** (ə lē′jəns) *noun*.

allergic 1. Having an allergy: *Are you sniffling because you're allergic to pollen?* 2. Of or caused by an allergy: *A rash is sometimes an allergic reaction.* **al·ler·gic** (ə lûr′jik) *adjective*.

allergy A condition that causes a person to have an unpleasant reaction to certain things that are harmless to most people. A person can have an allergy to pollen, dust, certain foods, and other substances. Rashes and sneezing are some of the reactions that allergies can cause. **al·ler·gy** (al′ər jē) *noun, plural* **allergies**.

alley 1. A narrow street or passageway between or behind buildings: *There is an alley behind those apartments where people can park their cars.* 2. A long, narrow lane down which bowling balls are rolled. The pins to be knocked down by the ball are at the far end of the alley. **al·ley** (al′ē) *noun, plural* **alleys**.

alliance An agreement between two or more countries, groups, or people to work together in doing something: *The two nations had an alliance in which each promised to defend the other.* **al·li·ance** (ə lī′əns) *noun, plural* **alliances**.

allied 1. Joined together by an alliance: *The allied countries fought on the same side during the war.* 2. Related or similar: *Drawing and painting are allied arts.* **al·lied** (ə līd *or* al′īd) *adjective*.

alligator An animal with a long head and tail and a thick, tough skin. Alligators are reptiles and live in rivers and swamps in the southeastern United States and in China. They are closely related to crocodiles. **al·li·ga·tor** (al′i gā′tər) *noun, plural* **alligators**.

Alligators **have shorter, wider heads than crocodiles.**

alliteration The repetition of the same sound at the beginning of several words in a phrase or sentence. "The bees buzzed in the birches in back of the barn" is an example of alliteration. **al·lit·er·a·tion** (ə lit′ə rā′shən) *noun, plural* **alliterations**.

allosaur A huge dinosaur that lived in North America in prehistoric times and resembled a tyrannosaur. *Noun.* This animal is also called *allosaurus.* **al·lo·saur** (al′ə sôr′) *noun, plural* **allosaurs**.

allot 1. To give out as a share: *The money raised at the bazaar was allotted to three charities. The chairperson allotted ten minutes to each speaker.* 2. To reserve for some use: *The city council allotted funds for a new library.* **al·lot** (ə lot′) *verb*, **allotted, allotting**.

allow 1. To give permission to or for; permit: *Will you allow me to use your bicycle?* 2. To provide for; assign: *We allowed an extra hour to make the trip in case of heavy traffic.*

• **to allow for.** To provide for some future need or possibility: *We allowed for medical expenses in preparing the household budget.* **al·low** (ə lou′) *verb*, **allowed, allowing**.

allowance 1. A sum of money or quantity of something given at regular times or set aside for a particular purpose: *How much is your weekly allowance?* 2. A reduction in price made for a special reason; discount: *We got an allowance of $600 when we traded in our old car for a new one.* **al·low·ance** (ə lou′əns) *noun, plural* **allowances**.

alloy A substance made by melting and mixing two or more metals or a metal and another substance. Brass is an alloy of copper and zinc. **al·loy** (al′oi *or* ə loi′) *noun, plural* **alloys**.

all right 1. Acceptable; good enough: *The book was not as good as I had hoped, but it was all right.* 2. Not hurt or ill; safe; well: *Our friend asked if we were all right after the accident. Adjective.*

○ Yes: *All right, I'll do it. Adverb.*

all-round The same as all-around. **all·round** (ôl′round′) *adjective*.

all-star Made up of the very best players or entertainers: *That movie had an all-star cast. Adjective.* ○ Someone who is a member of such a group. *Noun.*

all·star (ôl′ stär′) *adjective; noun, plural* **all-stars**.

allude To mention briefly or refer to indirectly: *The reporter alluded to the errors made by the shortstop.* **al·lude** (ə lüd′) *verb*, **alluded, alluding**.

ally To unite in order to do something: *Great Britain and the United States allied themselves during World War II. Verb.*

○ A person, group, or nation united with another in order to do something: *France was an ally of the American colonies during the Revolutionary War. Noun.*

al·ly (ə lī′ *for verb*; a′lī *or* ə lī′ *for noun*) *verb*, **allied, allying**; *noun, plural* **allies**.

almanac 1. A book that contains facts and figures on many different subjects: *Almanacs are pub-*

PRONUNCIATION KEY:

| at | āpe | fär | câre | end | mē | it | īce | pîerce | hot | ōld | sông | fôrk |
| oil | out | up | ūse | rüle | pùll | tûrn | chin | sing | shop | thin | <u>th</u>is | |

hw in white; zh in treasure. The symbol ə stands for the unstressed vowel sound in about, taken, pencil, lemon, and circus.

23

lished every year. **2.** A book that gives facts about the weather, the tides, and the rising and setting of the sun for each day of the year. **al·ma·nac** (ôl′mə nak′) *noun, plural* **almanacs.**

almighty Having complete power: *the almighty dollar. Adjective.*
  ○ *Almighty, the.* God. *Noun.*
  al·might·y (ôl mī′tē) *adjective; noun.*

almond An oval nut. It grows on a tree that is also called an almond. **al·mond** (ä′mənd *or* am′ənd) *noun, plural* **almonds.**

almost Very close to; nearly: *I am **almost** finished with my work.* **al·most** (ôl′mōst) *adverb.*

aloft Far above the ground; high up: *There were many kites **aloft** at the beach last weekend.* **a·loft** (ə lôft′) *adverb; adjective.*

aloha The Hawaiian word that means both "hello" and "good-bye." **a·lo·ha** (ə lō′ə *or* ä lō′hä) *noun, plural* **alohas;** *interjection.*

alone **1.** Apart from anyone or anything else: *We were **alone** all day on the beach.* **2.** With no other person, group, or thing; only: *The Supreme Court **alone** can declare a law unconstitutional. Adjective.*
  ○ **1.** Without anyone or anything else: *My cousin lives **alone**.* **2.** Without help or support: *Can you finish the job **alone**? Adverb.*
    • **To leave alone** *or* **to let alone.** To not bother, interrupt, or interfere with: *Please **leave** me **alone** for an hour so I can finish reading this book.*
  a·lone (ə lōn′) *adjective; adverb.*

along **1.** Over or following the length of: *We walked **along** the highway.* **2.** At some place on: *Can we stop **along** the way for lunch? Preposition.*
  ○ **1.** Toward what is ahead; farther on; onward; forward: *After we got through the traffic jam, we were able to drive **along** quickly.* **2.** With oneself: *Don't forget to bring **along** your umbrella. Adverb.*
    • **to get along. 1.** To manage successfully: *How are you **getting along** with your new business?* **2.** To be in harmony; agree: *The children **get along** well.*
  a·long (ə lông′) *preposition; adverb.*

alongside At, close to, or by the side: *Another car pulled up **alongside** and then passed us. Adverb.*
  ○ By or at the side of; beside: *The truck was*

parked **alongside** the curb. Preposition.
  a·long·side (ə lông′sīd′) *adverb; preposition.*

The raccoon and fox are lying alongside each other.

aloof **1.** Having or showing little or no concern or friendliness: *The queen and king had an **aloof** manner toward their subjects.* **2.** Not involved; apart: *When my friends argue, I always try to remain **aloof**.* **a·loof** (ə lüf′) *adjective.*

aloud Using the voice so as to be heard; out loud: *Students will read their reports **aloud** to the class.* **a·loud** (ə loud′) *adverb.*

alpaca An animal that lives in the mountains of South America and has long, silky wool. **al·pac·a** (al pak′ə) *noun, plural* **alpacas.**

alphabet The letters or characters that are used to write a language, arranged in their proper order. **al·pha·bet** (al′fə bet′) *noun, plural* **alphabets.**

WORD HISTORY

The word alphabet comes from alpha and beta, the names of the first two letters in the Greek alphabet.

---

alphabetical Arranged in the order of the letters of the alphabet: *The words in a dictionary are listed in **alphabetical** order.* **al·pha·bet·i·cal** (al′fə bet′i kəl) *adjective.*

alphabetize To put in alphabetical order: *The teacher asked me to **alphabetize** the names of all the students in my class.* **al·pha·bet·ize** (al′fə bə tīz′) *verb,* **alphabetized, alphabetizing.**

already By a certain time: *When we got to the bus station the bus had **already** left.* **al·read·y** (ôl red′ē) *adverb.*

also In addition; as well; too: *My cousin swims well and is **also** a good tennis player.* **al·so** (ôl′sō) *adverb.*

Alta. An abbreviation for Alberta.

ALPHABETS

Each of the 26 letters of our alphabet has a long history, often going back to the ancient Greeks and Phoenicians. By Roman times most of the letters we use were in a form you can recognize today. But the modern English alphabet is not the only one currently in use. The Hebrew alphabet is still uses the same characters it has for thousands of years, as does the Greek alphabet. The Russian Cyrillic alphabet is of more recent origin, invented by Saint Cyril in the 9th century. Even more recently, the Native American Sequoya created an alphabet for the language of his nation, Cherokee, in the early 1800s. It contained 82 symbols and was used for several decades, although it is no longer in use today.

Modern English		A	B	C	D	E	F	G
Greek	Form	A	B	Γ	Δ	E	Z	H
	Name	alpha	beta	gamma	delta	epsilon	zeta	eta
Hebrew	Form	א	ב	ג	ד	ה	ו	ז
	Name	aleph	beth	gimel	daleth	he	waw	zayin
Cyrillic (Russian)		А	Б	В	Г	Д	Е	Ж

Modern English		H	I	J	K	L	M	N
Greek	Form	Θ	I		K	Λ	M	N
	Name	theta	iota		kappa	lambda	mu	nu
Hebrew	Form	ח	ט	י	כ ך	ל	מ ם	נ ן
	Name	heth	teth	yod	kaph	lamed	mem	nun
Cyrillic (Russian)		З	И	Й	К	Л	М	Н

Modern English		O	P	Q	R	S	T	U
Greek	Form	Ξ	O	Π	P	Σ	T	Υ
	Name	xi	omicron	pi	rho	sigma	tau	upsilon
Hebrew	Form	ס	ע	פ ף	צ ץ	ק	ר	שׁ
	Name	samekh	ayin	pe	sadh	qoph	resh	sin
Cyrillic (Russian)		О	П	Р	С	Т	У	Ф

Modern English		V	W	X	Y	Z		
Greek	Form	Φ	X	Ψ	Ω			
	Name	phi	chi	psi	omega			
Hebrew	Form	שׁ	ת					
	Name	shin	taw					
Cyrillic (Russian)		Х	Ц	Ч	Ш	Щ	Ъ	Ы
Cyrillic (Russian)		Ь	Э	Ю	Я			

altar A table or a raised place that is used for religious services.
Another word that sounds like this is **alter**.
al·tar (ôltər) *noun*, plural **altars**.

alter To make or become different; change: *The tailor **altered** the coat to fit me. The new student's attitude has **altered** greatly since the beginning of the year.*
Another word that sounds like this is **altar**.
al·ter (ôl'tər) *verb*, **altered, altering**.

alternate 1. To take turns: *My brother and sister **alternate** washing the car each week.* 2. To happen or appear with one thing following another: *Red stripes **alternate** with white stripes on the American flag.* 3. To pass or change back and forth: *The act **alternated** between singing and dancing. Verb.*

○ 1. Happening or appearing one after another: *The dessert had **alternate** layers of cake and icing.* 2. First one, then the other; every other: *I have piano lessons on **alternate** Mondays.* 3. Taking the place of another; substitute: *Please*

PRONUNCIATION KEY:
at   āpe   fär   câre   end   mē   it   īce   pîerce   hot   ōld   sông   fôrk
oil   out   up   ūse   rüle   pull   tûrn   chin   sing   shop   thin   this
hw in white; zh in treasure. The symbol ə stands for the unstressed vowel sound in about, taken, pencil, lemon, and circus.

25

think of an **alternate** plan in case the first plan doesn't work. *Adjective.*

○ A person or thing that takes the place of another; substitute: *In case you cannot attend the meeting, can you send an* **alternate***? Noun.*
al·ter·nate (ôl′tər nāt *for verb;* ôl′tər nit *for adjective and noun*) *verb,* **alternated, alternating;** *adjective; noun, plural* **alternates.**

alternative **1.** A choice between two or more things: *We had the* **alternative** *of going to the beach with our friends or going on a picnic with our family.* **2.** One of two or more things that may be chosen: *We chose the first* **alternative***, and went to the beach. Noun.*

○ Being or giving a choice between two or more things: *We were offered the* **alternative** *plans of leaving that day or the next. Adjective.*
al·ter·na·tive (ôl tûr′nə tiv) *noun, plural* **alternatives;** *adjective.*

alternative energy Energy from sources other than coal, gas, or oil that do not harm the environment, such as the wind, sun, or water.

although **1.** In spite of the fact that; though: *Although I ate a big dinner, I was hungry again in an hour.* **2.** However; but: *Most students missed the field trip,* **although** *I was able to go.* **3.** Even if: *You will have other chances to take the test,* **although** *you fail the first time.*
al·though (ôl thō′) *conjunction.*

altimeter An instrument that shows how high something is above the ground or above sea level. An altimeter is used in an airplane to show the pilot how high the airplane is flying.
al·tim·e·ter (al tim′i tər *or* al′tə mē′tər) *noun, plural* **altimeters.**

altitude The height that something is above the ground or above sea level: *The pilot flew at an* **altitude** *of 8,000 feet. As we drove up the mountain we passed a sign that said the* **altitude** *was 4,000 feet above sea level.* **al·ti·tude** (al′ti tüd *or* al′ti tüd′) *noun, plural* **altitudes.**

alto **1.** The lowest female singing voice or the highest male singing voice. **2.** A singer who has such a voice. **3.** A musical instrument that has the range of an alto voice. **al·to** (al′tō) *noun, plural* **altos.**

altogether **1.** Completely; entirely; wholly: *The arrow missed the target* **altogether***.* **2.** With everyone or everything counted; in all: *There were twelve of us* **altogether** *at the party.* **3.** With everything considered; on the whole: *Altogether, I think the project was successful.* **al·to·geth·er** (ôl′tə geth′ər) *adverb.*

aluminum A light, soft, silver-white metal. Aluminum is the most abundant metal in the earth's crust. It conducts heat and electricity well and does not tarnish easily. It is used in making pots and pans, trucks, airplanes, and machines. It is also used as a building material. Aluminum is a chemical element. **a·lu·mi·num** (ə lü′mə nəm) *noun.*

always **1.** All the time; continuously: *There is* **always** *snow and ice at the North Pole.* **2.** Every time; at all times: *No matter when I schedule our meetings, you are* **always** *late.* **3.** For all time; forever: *I'll remember their kindness* **always***.* **al·ways** (ôl′wāz *or* ôl′wēz) *adverb.*

am A form of the present tense of **be** that is used with I: *I* **am** *happy that you can come to my party. I* **am** *going to the circus tomorrow:* Look up **be** for more information. **am** (am *or* əm) *verb.*

a.m. *or* **A.M.** An abbreviation used when referring to the time of day between midnight and noon.

WORD HISTORY

A.M. comes from the first letters of the Latin words "ante meridiem." Ante meridiem means "before noon."

---

amateur **1.** A person who does something for the pleasure of doing it, not for pay: *Her father was an* **amateur** *golfer before he became a pro.* **2.** A person who does something without much experience or skill: *The star of the play was a professional, but the rest of the performers were* **amateurs***. Noun.*

As one climbs into high altitudes, the temperature drops about two degrees fahrenheit every 500 feet.

○ Done by or made up of amateurs: *I will run the mile in the* **amateur** *track meet. Adjective.* **am·a·teur** (am′ə chər *or* am′ə tər) *noun, plural* **amateurs;** *adjective.*

amaze To surprise greatly; astonish: *The child's speed at solving mathematical problems* **amazed** *us.* **a·maze** (ə māz′) *verb,* **amazed, amazing.**

amazement Great surprise or wonder; astonishment: *The people watching the whales swim by were filled with* **amazement.** **a·maze·ment** (ə māz′mənt) *noun.*

Amazon The longest river in South America. It flows across Brazil to the Atlantic. **Am·a·zon** (a′mə′zôn) *noun.*

ambassador 1. An official of a government who is sent to represent his or her country in another country. 2. Any person who acts as a representative or messenger: *A group of high school athletes were sent as* **ambassadors** *of good will to European countries.* **am·bas·sa·dor** (am bas′ə dər) *noun, plural* **ambassadors.**

amber 1. A hard, yellowish to brownish material that is used to make jewelry. Amber is a fossil that is formed from the resin of pine trees that grew millions of years ago. 2. A yellowish to brownish color. **am·ber** (am′bər) *noun.*

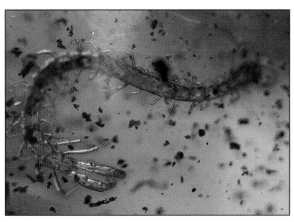

The fossil of a centipede is preserved within this amber.

ambidextrous Able to use both the right and left hands equally well. **am·bi·dex·trous** (am′ bi dek′ strəs) *adjective.*

ambiguous Having more than one possible meaning; not clear. The sentence "The Johnsons told the Browns that their dog had won the prize" is ambiguous. We cannot be sure to which family the dog belongs. **am·big·u·ous** (am big′ū əs) *adjective.*

ambition A strong desire to do or succeed at something: *My cousin's* **ambition** *is to become a sculptor.* **am·bi·tion** (am bish′ən) *noun, plural* **ambitions.**

ambitious 1. Having a strong desire to succeed at something; having ambition: *The* **ambitious** *clerk hoped to be president of the company someday.* 2. Requiring great ability or effort: *The governor proposed an* **ambitious** *plan to end water pollution in the state.* **am·bi·tious** (am bish′əs) *adjective.*

WORD HISTORY

The word ambitious goes back to a Latin word meaning "going around trying to get votes." In ancient Rome, men who wanted to be chosen for a government job would walk around the city in white robes to seek support for their election.

---

amble To walk or move at a slow pace: *We* **ambled** *through the town, looking for a restaurant.* **am·ble** (am′bəl) *verb,* **ambled, ambling.**

ambulance A special vehicle that is used to carry sick or injured people to a hospital. **am·bu·lance** (am′byə ləns) *noun, plural* **ambulances.**

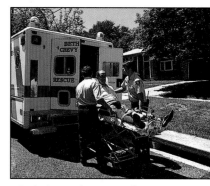

Ambulances **have saved the lives of millions of people around the world.**

ambush 1. A surprise attack made by people who are in a hidden place: *In the jungle the troops were always afraid of an* **ambush** *by the enemy.* 2. A hidden place from which people can make a surprise attack. *The bandits waited in* **ambush** *to hold up the stagecoach. Noun.*
○ To make a surprise attack from a hidden place: *The soldiers* **ambushed** *the enemy near the river. Verb.*
am·bush (am′bush) *noun, plural* **ambushes;** *verb,* **ambushed, ambushing.**

PRONUNCIATION KEY:
at ape far care end me it ice pierce hot old song fork
oil out up use rule pull turn chin sing shop thin this
hw in white; zh in treasure. The symbol ə stands for the unstressed vowel sound in about, taken, pencil, lemon, and circus.

27

ameba *or* **amoeba** A tiny living cell. An ameba is so small that it can be seen only through a microscope. It is always moving and changing shape. An ameba eats by wrapping itself around its food. **a•me•ba** (ə mē′bə) *noun, plural* **amebas**.

amen 1. A word said at the end of a prayer to mean "may it come true" *or* "may it be so." 2. A word used after a statement to show agreement or approval. **a•men** (ā′men′ *or* ä′men′) *interjection*.

amend To change formally, according to an official procedure: *It is a complicated procedure to amend the Constitution of the United States.* **a•mend** (ə mend′) *verb,* **amended, amending**.

amendment A formal change made according to official procedures: *In 1920, women were given the right to vote by an amendment to the Constitution.* **a•mend•ment** (ə mend′mənt) *noun, plural* **amendments**.

amends To make amends. To make up for a wrong. *I tried to make amends for my rude behavior by apologizing to the teacher after class.* **a•mends** (ə mendz′) *plural noun*.

Amer. An abbreviation for America or American.

America 1. Another name for the United States. 2. Another name for North America or South America. 3. Another name for the Western Hemisphere. Look up **Western Hemisphere** for more information. **A•mer•i•ca** (ə mer′i kə) *noun*.

WORD HISTORY

The name America comes from Amerigo Vespucci, an Italian explorer. Some people gave him credit for discovering the New World and put his name on early maps of those lands.

American 1. Of or having to do with the United States: *July 4, 1776 is an important date in American history.* 2. Of or having to do with North America, Central America, or South America: *The coyote is an American animal. Adjective.*
◦ 1. A person who was born in or is a citizen of the United States. 2. A person who was born in or is a citizen of a country in North America, Central America, or South America. *Noun.*
A•mer•i•can (ə mer′i kən) *adjective; noun, plural* **Americans**.

American English The variety of English that is used by most people who live in the United States.

American Indian 1. A person who was living in North America, Central America, South America, or the West Indies when European people first arrived. 2. A person who is descended from any of these peoples. American Indians are also called Native Americans or First Peoples. **American Indian**, *noun, plural* **American Indians**.

American Revolution The war between Great Britain and the thirteen American colonies that was fought from 1775 to 1783. It resulted in the Americans setting up a free and independent country. This war is also called the **Revolutionary War**.

amethyst Quartz that has a purple or bluish purple color. Amethyst is used as a gem. **am•e•thyst** (am′ə thist) *noun, plural* **amethysts**.

amiable Friendly and kind; good-natured: *The owners of the shop are an amiable couple who don't mind people coming in just to browse.* **a•mi•a•ble** (ā′mē ə bəl) *adjective*.

amid *or* **amidst** In the middle of: *The house stood amid a grove of pine trees.* **a•mid** *or* **a•midst** (ə mid′ *or* ə midst′) *preposition*.

amigo A Spanish word that means "friend." The word for a female friend is amiga. **a•mi•go** (ə mē′gō) *noun, plural* **amigos**.

amiss Not right; wrong: *I knew something was amiss when they said they didn't want to go to the baseball game.* **a•miss** (ə mis′) *adjective; adverb*.

amnesia A partial or total loss of memory. Amnesia is caused by injury to a person's brain or by sickness or shock. **am•ne•sia** (amnēzhə) *noun*.

amoeba A spelling sometimes used for the word ameba. Look up **ameba** for more information. **a•moe•ba** (ə mē′bə) *noun*.

among 1. In the middle of; surrounded by: *The campers pitched their tents among the trees.* 2. In the company of; in association with; with: *We spent last summer among friends in Canada.* 3. In the number, class, or group of; part of: *Elephants and whales are among the largest animals in the world.* 4. With a portion or share for each of: *The dessert was divided among the six children.* 5. To or through every part of; throughout: *The excitement quickly spread among the* *crowd outside the auditorium.* **a·mong** (ə mung′) *preposition.*

Among is only used when you write about more than two people or things: *The house stands* among *a group of tall trees.* The preposition between is usually used when you write about just two people or things: *Please sit here* between *my friend and me.*

amount **1.** The sum of two or more numbers or quantities: *What is the amount of money you spent this week?* **2.** Quantity: *No amount of hard work will keep me from going to college.* Noun.
∘ **1.** To be equal in number or quantity; add up: *The bill amounts to ten dollars.* **2.** To be equal; be the same: *Their story amounts to a big lie.* Verb.
a·mount (ə mount′) *noun, plural* **amounts;** *verb,* **amounted, amounting.**

ampersand A sign or symbol (&) that stands for the word *and:* *red & white.* **am·per·sand** (am′pər sand′) *noun, plural* **ampersands.**

Many amphibians have webbed feet.

amphibian **1.** Any of a group of cold-blooded animals with backbones that have moist skin without scales and usually live in or near water. Frogs and toads are amphibians. **2.** An airplane or other vehicle, such as a tank, that can travel on both land and water. **am·phib·i·an** (am fib′ē ən) *noun, plural* **amphibians.**

amphibious **1.** Able to live both on land and in water. Not all amphibious animals are amphibians. The seal and the frog are amphibious animals. **2.** Able to travel or operate both on land or in water: *The soldier drove an amphibious tank.* **am·phib·i·ous** (am fib′ē əs) *adjective.*

amphitheater A circular or oval building that is used for sports and other public events with seats rising in rows around a central open space. **am·phi·the·a·ter** (am′fə thē′ə tər) *noun, plural* **amphitheaters.**

ample **1.** More than enough; abundant: *We bought ample food for our camping trip.* **2.** Large in size or capacity; roomy: *Our house has an ample kitchen.* **am·ple** (am′pəl) *adjective,* **ampler, amplest.**

amplifier An electronic device that makes sounds louder. **am·pli·fi·er** (am′ plə fī′ ər) *noun, plural* **amplifiers.**

amplify **1.** To give more details about; explain more: *The teacher asked me to amplify my report by giving more details.* **2.** To make louder or stronger: *The microphone will amplify the speaker's voice so that everyone can hear.* **am·pli·fy** (am′plə fī′) *verb,* **amplified, amplifying.**

amputate To cut off an arm, leg, or finger, usually because it is diseased or damaged: *The doctor had to amputate the soldier's wounded leg.* **am·pu·tate** (am′pyə tāt) *verb,* **amputated, amputating.**

amt. An abbreviation for amount.

amuse **1.** To cause to laugh or smile: *The silly clowns amused the children.* **2.** To keep interested or busy in a way that gives pleasure; entertain: *I amused myself by reading an exciting book.* **a·muse** (ə mūz′) *verb,* **amused, amusing.**

amusement **1.** The condition of being amused and entertained: *The magician did tricks for our amusement.* **2.** Something that amuses or entertains: *Playing baseball is my favorite outdoor amusement.* **a·muse·ment** (ə mūz′mənt) *noun, plural* **amusements.**

amusement park A park where there are rides, games, and other kinds of entertainment.

an Another word for **a.** It is used before words that begin with the letters a, e, i, o, or u, and before words that begin with an h that is not pronounced: *I ate an ear of corn. The nurse checks patients once an hour.* **an** (an *or unstressed* ən) *indefinite article.*

anaconda A very large snake found in South America. The anaconda can kill another animal by wrapping itself around the animal so tightly that it cannot breathe. **an·a·con·da** (an′ə kon′də) *noun, plural* **anacondas.**

analog Using parts that point to information as it changes. An analog clock shows the time by using hour and minute hands. **an·a·log** (an′ ə lôg′) *adjective.*

analysis 1. Taking something apart in order to find out how it is put together: *In chemistry class we made analyses of several compounds.* 2. A careful examination and study of something: *An analysis of the play will show you why it remains popular.* **a·nal·y·sis** (ə nal′ə sis) *noun, plural* **analyses** (ə nal′ə sēz′).

analyze 1. To find out what something is made of by taking it apart. If we analyze air we find that it is made up mostly of nitrogen and oxygen. 2. To study something carefully: *The detective analyzed the evidence of the crime.* **an·a·lyze** (an′ə līz′) *verb,* **analyzed, analyzing.**

anarchy A situation in which there is no order or law: *The class was in a state of anarchy as soon as the teacher left the room.* **an·ar·chy** (an′ər kē) *noun.*

anatomy 1. A science that deals with the structure of animals or plants. 2. The structure of an animal or plant or one of its parts: *We are studying the anatomy of the frog in science class.* **a·nat·o·my** (ə nat′ə mē) *noun, plural* **anatomies.**

ancestor A person from whom one is descended: *Your grandparents and great-grandparents are among your ancestors.* **an·ces·tor** (an′ses tər) *noun, plural* **ancestors.**

anchor 1. A heavy metal device that is attached to a ship by a chain or cable: *When an anchor is dropped overboard, it digs into the ground below the water and keeps the ship from drifting.* 2. Anything that holds something steady or in place: *Friendship has been my anchor in hard times. Noun.*
○ 1. To hold something in place with an anchor: *We will anchor the boat while we fish.* 2. To fasten firmly. *Anchor the shelf to the wall. Verb.* **an·chor** (ang′kər) *noun, plural* **anchors;** *verb,* **anchored, anchoring.**

anchovy A small, silver fish that lives in salt water and is used for food. Anchovies are related to sardines. **an·cho·vy** (an′chō vē *or* an chō′vē) *noun, plural* anchovies.

ancient 1. Of or having to do with times very long ago: *The archaeologist found the ruins of an ancient city buried under the ashes.* 2. Very old: *I found a book of ancient stories in the library.* **an·cient** (ān′shənt) *adjective.*

and 1. As well as; in addition to; also: *The twins are tall and strong for their age.* 2. Added to; plus: *Two and two make four.* 3. Then as a result: *Treat us fairly, and we'll be fair with you.* 4. To: *Try and finish the work today.* **and** (and *or* ənd *or* ən) *conjunction.*

andiron Either of two metal supports that are used for holding wood in a fireplace. **and·i·ron** (and′ī′ərn) *noun, plural* **andirons.**

android A robot that has the form or appearance of a human being. **an·droid** (an′droid) *noun, plural* **androids.**

anecdote A short story about an interesting or funny event or incident: *The newscast on the election featured anecdotes about the candidates.* **an·ec·dote** (an′ik dōt′) *noun, plural* **anecdotes.**

anemia A condition in which the blood does not have enough red cells or when a person has lost blood. A person with anemia often feels tired and weak. **a·ne·mi·a** (ə nē′mē ə) *noun,* **a·ne·mic** *adjective.*

anemometer An instrument used to measure the speed of the wind. **an·e·mom·e·ter** (an′ə mom′i tər) *noun, plural* **anemometers.**

anemone A plant that has delicate white, red, pink, or purple flowers. **a·nem·o·ne** (ə nem′ə nē) *noun, plural* **anemones.**

anesthesia The loss of all feeling, especially pain. This loss of feeling may be in all or part of the

These anchors are housed in the bow of the ship.

body. Doctors give patients drugs that produce anesthesia before surgery. **an•es•the•sia** (an′əs thē′zhə) *noun.*

anesthetic A drug or other substance that causes a loss of feeling or consciousness: *The doctor gave me an* **anesthetic** *before setting my broken arm.* **an•es•thet•ic** (an′əs thet′ik) *noun, plural* **anesthetics.**

anew Once more; again: *I accidentally crumpled my sketch in art class, so I began* **anew.** **a•new** (ə nü′ *or* ə nū′) *adverb.*

angel **1.** In the Bible and other writings, a heavenly being who serves God as a helper and messenger. **2.** A kind, gentle person. **an•gel** (ān′jəl) *noun, plural* **angels.**

anger A strong feeling caused by a person or thing that opposes, displeases, or hurts one: *I had a fit of* **anger** *when the heavy traffic made me late for my appointment. Noun.*
○ To make or become angry. *The students' rudeness* **angered** *their teacher. My cousin* **angers** *easily. Verb.*
an•ger (ang′gər) *noun; verb,* **angered, angering.**

angle **1.** The figure formed by two lines or flat surfaces that extend from one point or line. **2.** The space between these lines or flat surfaces. **3.** A corner: *The sculpture has many* **angles** *and curves.* **4.** A way of thinking or feeling about something; point of view: *I was having trouble solving the problem, so I tried to look at it from another* **angle.** *Noun.*
○ To move or turn so as to form an angle: *The road* **angles** *to the right as it goes up the mountain. Verb.*
an•gle (ang′gəl) *noun, plural* **angles;** *verb,* **angled, angling.**

Angola A country in southwestern Africa. **An•go•la** (ang gō′lə) *noun.*

angora Yarn or cloth made from the long, silky hair of a kind of rabbit or goat. Angora feels soft and fluffy and is used to make sweaters and other clothing. **an•gor•a** (ang gôr′ə) *noun.*

angry **1.** Feeling or showing anger: *I was* **angry** *with my friends for breaking my model airplane. I gave them an* **angry** *look.* **2.** Giving a sign of something bad, dangerous, or harmful; threatening: *We were afraid to sail in the* **angry** *sea.*

3. Inflamed and painful: *I had an* **angry** *sore on my knee.* **an•gry** (ang′grē) *adjective,* **angrier, angriest.**

anguish Great suffering of the body or mind; agony: *The children were in* **anguish** *over the death of their dog.* **an•guish** (ang′gwish) *noun.*

animal **1.** A living thing that takes in food and moves about and that is made up of many cells. Unlike plants, most animals do not have to stay in one place, and they cannot make their own food. Jellyfish, worms, clams, insects, birds, fish, mammals, and human beings are all animals. **2.** Animals other than humans: *My aunt and uncle raise* **animals** *on their farm.* **an•i•mal** (an′ə məl) *noun, plural* **animals.**

Many animals, like these goats, get their nourishment from leaves.

animal rights A movement that argues that other animals deserve to live without being treated cruelly or killed for the convenience of humans.

animated cartoon A film made by photographing a series of drawings that show slight changes as the figures act and speak so that they seem to be alive.

animosity Deep hatred; hostility: *The* **animosity** *between the two countries led to war.* **an•i•mos•i•ty** (an′ə mos′i tē) *noun, plural* **animosities.**

ankle The joint that connects the foot and the leg. **an•kle** (ang′kəl) *noun, plural* **ankles.**

anklet A short sock that reaches just above the ankle. **an•klet** (ang′klit) *noun, plural* **anklets.**

annex To add or attach to something larger: *The United States* **annexed** *the independent*

PRONUNCIATION KEY:

| at | āpe | fär | câre | end | mē | it | īce | pîerce | hot | ōld | sông | fôrk |
| oil | out | up | ūse | rüle | pull | tûrn | chin | sing | shop | thin | this | |

hw in white; zh in treasure. The symbol ə stands for the unstressed vowel sound in about, taken, pencil, lemon, and circus.

31

republic of Texas and made it a state in 1845. *Verb.*

○ A wing added to a building or a separate building used as an addition to a main building: *The school needs an* **annex** *with extra classrooms. Noun.*
an·nex (ə neks′ *for verb*; an′eks *for noun*) *verb,* **annexed, annexing;** *noun, plural* **annexes.**

annihilate To destroy completely; wipe out: *The earthquake* **annihilated** *the town.* **an·ni·hi·late** (ə nī′ə lāt′) *verb,* **annihilated, annihilating.**

anniversary The date on which an event happened in the past or its celebration: *On February 15 the couple will celebrate the tenth* **anniversary** *of their wedding.* **an·ni·ver·sa·ry** (an′ə vûr′sə rē) *noun, plural* **anniversaries.**

announce 1. To make something known in an official or formal way: *The principal* **announced** *that the school would be closed because of the blizzard.* **an·nounce** (ə nouns′) *verb,* **announced, announcing.**

announcement 1. The act of making known officially or formally: ***Announcement*** *of the election results brought cheers from the audience.* 2. A public statement that makes something known. **an·nounce·ment** (ə nouns′mənt) *noun, plural* **announcements.**

announcer A person on radio or television who does such things as introduce programs, present advertisements, describe sports events, and read the news. **an·nounc·er** (ə noun′sər) *noun, plural* **announcers.**

annoy To bother or disturb: *The sound of that loud radio* **annoys** *me.* **an·noy** (ə noi′) *verb,* **annoyed, annoying.**

annoyance 1. A person or thing that annoys: *Their constant complaining was an* **annoyance** *to me.* 2. The condition of being annoyed. *Your* **annoyance** *at being teased was easy to understand.* **an·noy·ance** (ə noi′əns) *noun, plural* **annoyances.**

annual 1. Measured by the year. *The average annual rainfall in my state is 15 inches.* 2. Happening or returning once a year: *Thanksgiving is an* **annual** *holiday that we celebrate in November.* 3. Living its full life in one year or one growing season: *Corn is an* **annual** *plant. Adjective.*

○ A plant that lives only one year or growing season: *We plant* **annuals** *in our garden every spring. Noun.*
an·nu·al (an′ū əl) *adjective; noun, plural* **annuals.**

annual ring One of the rings of wood on the inside of the trunk of a tree.

Each of these annual rings represents one year of the tree's growth.

annually Once a year in every year: *We visit my grandparents* **annually.** **an·nu·al·ly** (an′ū ə le) *adverb.*

anoint To put oil on during a ceremony: *The archbishop* **anointed** *the king.* **a·noint** (ə noint′) *verb,* **anointed, anointing.**

anonymous 1. From or by someone whose name is not known or given: *The police got an* **anonymous** *phone call telling them where to find the robbers.* 2. With a name not known or given: *The person who donated the money wanted to remain* **anonymous.** **a·non·y·mous** (ə non′ə məs) *adjective.*

another 1. One more; an additional: *Do you want* **another** *apple?* 2. A different; some other: *I saw* **another** *coat that I liked better than the first one. Adjective.*

○ 1. One more; an additional one: *When you have read that book, I have* **another** *I think you'll like.* 2. A different person or thing: *That plan didn't work, so we'll use* **another.** *Pronoun.*
an·oth·er (ə nu<u>th</u>′ər) *adjective; pronoun.*

answer 1. Something said or written in reply: *I could not get an* **answer** *to my question. Did you get an* **answer** *to your letter?* 2. Something, such as an action or movement, done as a response: *The* *employer's* **answer** *to the workers' complaints was to raise their pay.* **3.** The solution to a problem: *To find the right* **answer,** *multiply by 12. Noun.*

○ **1.** To speak or write as a reply: *I* **answered** *my friend's long letter.* **2.** To do in response to: *I ran to* **answer** *the doorbell.* **3.** To agree with; match: *The suspect* **answers** *to the description of the person seen by witnesses. Verb.*
an•swer (an′sər) *noun, plural* **answers;** *verb,* **answered, answering.**

answering machine A device connected to a telephone that takes messages from people who call when someone is not at home or doesn't want to answer the phone.

ant A small insect related to bees and wasps: *Ants live together in large groups called colonies.* **ant** (ant) *noun, plural* **ants.**

antacid A substance people take when they have an upset stomach. **ant•ac•id** (ant as′id) *noun, plural* **antacids.**

antagonism A strong feeling against a person or thing: *After their quarrel, the children felt* **antagonism** *toward each other.* **an•tag•o•nism** (an tag′ə niz′əm) *noun, plural* **antagonisms.**

antagonize To cause dislike in; irritate: *The clerk's rude manner* **antagonized** *many customers.* **an•tag•o•nize** (an tag′ə nīz′) *verb,* **antagonized, antagonizing.**

antarctic Of or having to do with the South Pole or the region around the South Pole: *antarctic explorers. Adjective.*

○ **the Antarctic.** Another name for Antarctica. *Noun.*
ant•arc•tic (ant ärk′tik *or* ant är′tik) *adjective; noun.*

Antarctica The continent at the South Pole. Antarctica is almost completely covered with ice all year long. **Ant•arc•ti•ca** (ant ärk′ti kə *or* ant är′ti kə) *noun.*

Antarctic Ocean The water around Antarctica that includes the most southern parts of the Atlantic, Pacific, and Indian oceans. **Ant•arc•tic** (ant ärk′tik *or* ant ärt′ik).

anteater An animal with a long head, sticky tongue, and strong claws that it uses to dig ants, termites, and other insects out of their nests and eat them. Anteaters live in Central America and South America. **ant•eat•er** (ant′ē′tər) *noun, plural* **anteaters.**

antecedent The word or group of words in a sentence that a pronoun in the same sentence refers to. In the sentence "The secretary typed the letter and then mailed it," the antecedent of "it" is "the letter."
an•te•ced•ent (an′tə sē′dənt) *noun, plural* **antecedents.**

antelope A slender, swift animal, found in Africa and Asia, that has long horns without branches. **an•te•lope** (ant′ə lōp′) *noun, plural* **antelopes.**

Antelopes **are related to goats.**

antenna **1.** A metallic device, such as a rod or wire, used to send out or receive radio or television signals; aerial. **2.** One of a pair of long, thin body parts, such as that on the head of an insect or a lobster; feelers. Antennae are used to sense touch and smells. **an•ten•na** (an ten′ə) *noun, plural* **antennas** *for definition 1 or* **antennae** (an ten′ē) *for definition 2.*

anthem **1.** A song of gladness, praise, or patriotism: *The national* **anthem** *of the United States is "The Star-Spangled Banner."* **2.** A religious song, usually with words from the Bible. **an•them** (an′thəm) *noun, plural* **anthems.**

anther The upper part of the stamen of a flower. The anther contains the flower's pollen. **an•ther** (an′thər) *noun, plural* **anthers.**

anthill A mound of earth made by ants around the entrance to their underground nest. **ant•hill** (ant′hil′) *noun, plural* **anthills.**

anthology A book or other collection of writings, such as poems, stories, or articles. **an•thol•o•gy** (an thol′ə jē) *noun, plural* **anthologies.**

anthracite A very hard, shiny black coal that burns with a low flame and gives off little smoke;

PRONUNCIATION KEY:

| at | āpe | fär | câre | end | mē | it | īce | pierce | hot | ōld | sông | fôrk |
| oil | out | up | ūse | rüle | pu̇ll | tûrn | chin | sing | shop | thin | this | |

hw in white; zh in treasure. The symbol ə stands for the unstressed vowel sound in about, taken, pencil, lemon, and circus.

33

it is sometimes called hard coal. **an·thra·cite** (an′thrə sīt′) *noun*.

anthropology The study of human beings and their beliefs and ways of life. Anthropology deals with the development of these features of culture from prehistoric times to the present. **an·thro·pol·o·gy** (an′thrə pol′ə jē) *noun*.

anti- A prefix that means opposed to or against. Antifreeze means something that works against freezing. Antiwar means against a war.

antibiotic A drug that is used in medicine to kill or slow the growth of germs that cause disease. **an·ti·bi·ot·ic** (an′tē bī ot′ik) *noun*, *plural* **antibiotics**.

antibody A substance produced by the body's white blood cells to destroy or weaken germs. **an·ti·bod·y** (an′ti bod′ē) *noun*, *plural* **antibodies**.

anticipate 1. To look forward to; expect: *I anticipate their arrival at noon.* 2. To think of and do something about in advance: *We anticipated your objection to our plan and thought of another one that you might like.* **an·tic·i·pate** (an tis′ə pāt′) *verb*, **anticipated**, **anticipating**.

anticipation The act of anticipating; expectation: *In anticipation of a hot summer, we bought an air conditioner.* **an·tic·i·pa·tion** (an tis′ə pā′shən) *noun*, *plural* **anticipations**.

antidote A medicine that works against the effects of a poison: *The doctor prescribed an antidote for the child who accidentally swallowed poison.* **an·ti·dote** (an′ti dōt′) *noun*, *plural* **antidotes**.

antifreeze A substance that is added to a liquid to help keep the liquid from freezing. Antifreeze is added to the cooling liquid used in the radiators of cars and trucks. **an·ti·freeze** (an′ti frēz′) *noun*.

antique Of times long ago; very old: *We went to*

These antique cars date from early in the 20th century.

*an exhibit of **antique** carriages. Adjective.* ○ Something made very long ago. *The museum has **antiques** from the time of colonial America. Noun.* **an·tique** (an tēk′) *adjective*; *noun*, *plural* **antiques**.

antiseptic A substance that kills germs or stops their growth. Alcohol and iodine are antiseptics. **an·ti·sep·tic** (an′ti sep′tik) *noun*, *plural* **antiseptics**.

antitoxin A substance produced by the body that protects a person from a poison produced by a living thing. For example, the body makes antitoxins when stung by a bee. **an·ti·tox·in** (an′ti tok′sin) *noun*, *plural* **antitoxins**.

antler One of the two bony growths on the head of a deer and certain other animals. Antlers usually have branches. Animals with antlers shed them each year and grow new ones. **ant·ler** (ant′lər) *noun*, *plural* **antlers**.

antonym A word that has the opposite meaning of another word. "High" is the antonym of "low," and "hot" is the antonym of "cold." **an·to·nym** (an′tə nim) *noun*, *plural* **antonyms**.

LANGUAGE USAGE

Not every word has an antonym, but many do. You can improve your vocabulary by thinking of pairs of words that are opposite in meaning. Some subjects fascinate me, and others bore me. Elephants are gigantic, but ants are tiny. Can you think of others?

---

anvil An iron or steel block on which metals are hammered into shape. **an·vil** (an′vəl) *noun*, *plural* **anvils**.

anxiety A feeling of fearful worry or uneasiness about what may happen: *We were filled with anxiety about our boat capsizing in the stormy sea.* **anx·i·e·ty** (ang zī′i tē) *noun*, *plural* **anxieties**.

Metals are softened by heating before being placed on an anvil.

anxious 1. Nervous, worried, or fearful about what may happen: *My cousin was **anxious** about driving on the slippery mountain roads.* 2. Wanting very much; eager: *I was **anxious** to make friends at my new school.* **anx·ious** (angk′shəs) *adjective.*

any 1. One or some: *Sit in **any** chair. Did they eat **any** lunch?* 2. Every: ***Any** child can do this problem. Adjective.*
○ 1. Any one or ones: ***Any** of these books is sure to interest you. **Any** of you who are ready can leave now.* 2. Any quantity or part: *Did you finish **any** of your work? Pronoun.*
○ To any extent or degree: *Are you feeling **any** better? Adverb.*
an·y (en′ē) *adjective; pronoun; adverb.*

anybody Any person whatever; anyone: *Has **anybody** seen the teacher?* **an·y·bod·y** (en′ē bod′ē) *pronoun.*

anyhow 1. No matter what happens; in any case: *Maybe it won't rain, but we should be prepared **anyhow**.* 2. Without being stopped or prevented by that; in spite of that: *Our best player was hurt, but we won the game **anyhow**.* **an·y·how** (en′ē hou′) *adverb.*

anymore Now; nowadays: *Now that I can ride a bicycle I don't use my tricycle **anymore**.* **an·y·more** (en′ē môr′) *adverb.*

anyone Any person whatever; anybody: ***Anyone** who lives in this town can go swimming in the town pool.* **an·y·one** (en′ē wun′) *pronoun.*

anyplace In, at, or to any place; anywhere: *Take the car and drive **anyplace** you want.* **an·y·place** (en′ē plās) *adverb.*

anything Any thing whatever: *I'll do **anything** you ask. Pronoun.*
○ In any way; at all: *You aren't **anything** like your twin. Adverb.*
an·y·thing (en′ē thing′) *pronoun; adverb.*

anytime At any time: *You may leave **anytime** you want.* **an·y·time** (en′ē tīm′) *adverb.*

anyway No matter what happens; in any case: *The water is cold, but I want to go swimming **anyway**.* **an·y·way** (en′ē wā′) *adverb.*

anywhere In, at, or to any place: *Just put the books down **anywhere**.* **an·y·where** (en′ē hwâr′ *or* en′ē wâr′) *adverb.*

aorta The main artery of the body. The aorta carries blood from the left side of the heart to all parts of the body except the lungs. **a·or·ta** (ā ôr′tə) *noun,* plural **aortas.**

aorta

Apache 1. A member of a Native American tribe of the southwestern United States. 2. Any of several languages spoken by these people. **A·pach·e** (ə pach′ē) *noun, plural* **Apache** or **Apaches.**

apart 1. Away from each other in space or time: *The houses are 2 miles **apart**. The trains left three hours **apart**.* 2. In or into two or more parts or pieces: *In sewing class, we tore a coat **apart** at the seams and then sewed it back together.*
• **to take apart.** To separate into two or more parts or pieces: *The mechanic **took the engine apart** to find out what was wrong with it.*
a·part (ə pärt′) *adverb.*

apartheid The government policy of racial segregation that used to be followed in South Africa. **a·part·heid** (ə pär′tīd *or* ə pärt′hāt) *noun.*

WORD HISTORY

Apartheid is a word borrowed from Afrikaans, the form of Dutch that is spoken in South Africa. It means "being apart."

apartment A room or group of rooms used as a place to live. **a·part·ment** (ə pärt′mənt) *noun, plural* **apartments.**

apathy A lack of feeling, interest, or concern; indifference: ***Apathy** kept some people from voting in the election.* **ap·a·thy** (ap′ə thē) *noun.*

apatosaur Another name for brontosaur. This animal is also called *apatosaurus.* **a·pat·o·saur** (ə pat′ə sôr′) *noun,* **apatosaurs.**

PRONUNCIATION KEY:

| at | āpe | fär | câre | end | mē | it | īce | pîerce | hot | ōld | sông | fôrk |
| oil | out | up | ūse | rüle | pull | tûrn | chin | sing | shop | thin | this | |

hw in white; zh in treasure. The symbol ə stands for the unstressed vowel sound in about, taken, pencil, lemon, and circus.

35

ape A large animal with no tail that is able to stand and walk in an almost upright position. Chimpanzees, gorillas, gibbons, and orangutans are all types of apes. *Noun.*

○ To imitate; mimic: *My cousin likes to **ape** famous politicians. Verb.*

ape (āp) *noun, plural* **apes**; *verb,* **aped, aping.**

The gibbon is a member of the ape family.

aperture A small hole. Cameras have apertures that control the amount of light that shines on the film. **ap·er·ture** (ap′ət char) *noun, plural* **apertures.**

apex The highest point of anything; top. **a·pex** (ā′peks) *noun, plural* **apexes.**

aphid A small insect that lives by sucking juices from plants. **a·phid** (ā′fid *or* af′id) *noun, plural* **aphids.**

apiece For or to each one; each: *These red pencils are fifteen cents **apiece**. The store manager gave us five dollars **apiece** for our work.* **a·piece** (ə pēs′) *adverb.*

apologize To say one is sorry or embarrassed; make an apology: *I **apologized** to my parents for being rude.* **a·pol·o·gize** (ə pol′ə jīz′) *verb,* **apologized, apologizing.**

apology A statement that one is sorry or embarrassed about something, such as an offense or a mistake: *Please accept my **apology** for being late.* **a·pol·o·gy** (ə pol′ə jē) *noun, plural* **apologies.**

Apostle 1. One of the early Christian leaders, especially one of the twelve disciples chosen by Jesus. 2. A close follower of another person. **A·pos·tle** (ə pos′əl) *noun, plural* **Apostles.**

apostrophe A punctuation mark (') that is used in the following ways: **1.** To show that one or more letters or numbers have been left out. For example, "you're" means "you are," and '91 can mean 1991. **2.** To form a possessive noun or possessive pronoun that shows that something belongs to a person or thing. In the sentence "My cousin's bike is red" the word "cousin's" means that the bike belongs to my cousin. **3.** To form the plural of letters and numbers, for example, "I got three B's on my report card." **a·pos·tro·phe** (ə pos′trə fē) *noun, plural* **apostrophes.**

appall To fill with horror or terror; shock or terrify: *We were **appalled** by the news of the airplane crash.* **ap·pall** (ə pôl′) *verb,* **appalled, appalling.**

apparatus Anything that is used for a particular purpose. Gymnasium equipment, chemistry sets, tools, and machinery are all different kinds of apparatus. **ap·pa·rat·us** (ap′ə rat′əs *or* ap′ə rā′təs) *noun, plural* **apparatus** *or* **apparatuses.**

apparel Clothing; clothes: *That store sells children's **apparel**.* **ap·par·el** (ə par′əl) *noun.*

Selecting the right apparel is often a difficult decision.

apparent **1.** Easily seen or understood: *It's **apparent** that you did not comb your hair. It was **apparent** they were enjoying themselves.* **2.** Seeming real or true even though it may not be: *The **apparent** size of a star is much smaller than its real size.* **ap·par·ent** (ə par′ənt) *adjective.*

apparently As far as one can judge by the way things appear: ***Apparently**, it is going to rain.* **ap·par·ent·ly** (ə par′ənt lē) *adverb.*

appeal **1.** An earnest request for something needed or wanted: *Each year our church makes an **appeal** for money to aid poor people.* **2.** The power to interest or attract: *Sports have a great **appeal** to people of every age.* **3.** A request to have a legal case heard again by a higher court: *If they lose their case, the lawyer will certainly **appeal**. Noun.*

○ **1.** To make an earnest request: *The people of the town **appealed** to the governor for help after the flood.* **2.** To be attractive or interesting: *Camping out in the woods does not **appeal** to me.* **3.** To request to have a case heard again before a higher court of law. *Verb.* **ap·peal** (ə pēl′) *noun, plural* **appeals;** *verb,* **appealed, appealing.**

appear **1.** To come into sight; be seen: *The snowy mountain peaks **appeared** in the distance.* **2.** To give the impression of being; seem; look: *They **appeared** interested in the game, but they were really bored.* **3.** To come before the public: *That actor has often **appeared** on television.* **4.** To come before a court of law: *They were ordered to **appear** in the county court.* **ap·pear** (ə pîr′) *verb,* **appeared, appearing.**

appearance **1.** The act of appearing or coming into sight: *The sun made a sudden **appearance** through the clouds.* **2.** The way a person or thing looks; outward look: *I could tell from your **appearance** that you were disappointed.* **3.** The act of coming before the public: *That was the actor's first **appearance** in the movies.* **ap·pear·ance** (ə pîr′əns) *noun, plural* **appearances.**

appease **1.** To make content or calm: *The owner of the business **appeased** the striking workers by giving them more pay.* **2.** To supply with what is needed or wanted; satisfy: *The sandwich **appeased** my appetite.* **ap·pease** (ə pēz′) *verb,* **appeased, appeasing.**

appendicitis An inflammation of the appendix. It causes sharp pain on the lower right side of the abdomen. **ap·pen·di·ci·tis** (ə pen′də sī′tis) *noun.*

appendix **1.** A short, hollow pouch that is attached to the large intestine. **2.** A section at the end of a book or other piece of writing. An appendix gives more information about the subject of the book. **ap·pen·dix** (ə pen′diks) *noun, plural* **appendixes** *or* **appendices** (ə pen′də sēz′).

appetite **1.** A desire for food: *When I was sick I had no **appetite**.* **2.** Any strong desire: *Some people have no **appetite** for adventure and excitement.* **ap·pe·tite** (ap′i tīt′) *noun, plural* **appetites.**

appetizer A small snack or drink served before a meal. **ap·pe·tiz·er** (ap′ə ti′zər) *noun, plural* **appetizers.**

appetizing Pleasing or stimulating the appetite; tasty: *We made some **appetizing** sandwiches for our picnic.* **ap·pe·tiz·ing** (ap′i tī′zing) *adjective.*

applaud **1.** To show approval or enjoyment of something by clapping the hands: *The children **applauded** the clown's funny tricks.* **2.** To approve or praise: *The public **applauded** the mayor's plan for lower taxes.* **ap·plaud** (ə plôd′) *verb,* **applauded, applauding.**

applause **1.** Approval or enjoyment shown by clapping the hands: *Everyone joined in the **applause** at the end of the act.* **2.** Approval or praise: *The author's first novel received **applause** from the critics.* **ap·plause** (ə plôz′) *noun.*

Apples are used for eating, cooking, and for making cider.

apple A round fruit with red, yellow, or green skin. Apples have firm white flesh surrounding a core with small seeds. Apples grow on a tree that is also called an apple. **ap·ple** (ap′əl) *noun, plural* **apples.**

applesauce A food made from pieces of apple that have been sweetened with sugar and cooked in water until soft. **ap·ple·sauce** (ap′əl sôs′) *noun.*

appliance A device or small machine that has a particular use. Refrigerators, washing machines, toasters, and irons are household appliances. **ap·pli·ance** (ə plī′əns) *noun, plural* **appliances.**

applicant A person who makes a formal request for something, such as a job: *There were several*

PRONUNCIATION KEY:

| at | āpe | fär | câre | end | mē | it | īce | pierce | hot | ōld | sông | fôrk |
| oil | out | up | ūse | rüle | pull | tûrn | chin | sing | shop | thin | this | |

hw in white; zh in treasure. The symbol ə stands for the unstressed vowel sound in about, taken, pencil, lemon, and circus.

37

applicants for the position of school custodian.
ap·pli·cant (ap′li kənt) *noun, plural* **applicants**.

application **1.** The act of putting something to use: *The application of scientific knowledge has made space exploration possible.* **2.** The act of putting something on: *The application of paint made the old house look like new.* **3.** A way of being used: *Many scientific discoveries have practical applications.* **4.** A request: *I made an application for the job of gardener's assistant.* **5.** A computer program used for a special task, such as word processing. **ap·pli·ca·tion** (ap′li kā′shən) *noun, plural* **applications**.

apply **1.** To use: *You have to apply force to open the locked door.* **2.** To put on: *They applied two coats of paint to the wall.* **3.** To ask; make a request: *I applied for a summer job at the grocery store.* **4.** To devote oneself with effort: *We applied ourselves to the task of cleaning the basement.* **5.** To be suitable or have to do with: *The law against speeding applies to all drivers.* **ap·ply** (ə plī′) *verb,* **applied, applying**.

appoint **1.** To name or select for a position, office, or duty: *The president appointed Judge Smith to the Supreme Court.* **2.** To decide on; set; fix: *The judge appointed the date of the trial.* **ap·point** (ə point′) *verb,* **appointed, appointing**.

appointment **1.** The act of naming or selecting for a position, office, or duty: *The appointment of the new judge was announced in the newspaper.* **2.** A position or office to which one is appointed: *The doctor was offered an appointment on the staff of a major hospital.* **3.** An agreement to meet or see someone at a certain time and place: *I have an appointment with the dentist at ten o'clock.* **ap·point·ment** (ə point′mənt) *noun, plural* **appointments**.

appraise **1.** To estimate the value of; set a price for: *A real estate agent appraised our house.* **2.** To judge the quality, importance, or worth of: *The critic appraised the concert in a newspaper review.* **ap·praise** (ə prāz′) *verb,* **appraised, appraising**.

appreciate **1.** To understand the value of: *Everyone appreciates loyal friends.* **2.** To be grateful for something: *I appreciate your running these errands for me.* **3.** To be aware of; realize: *Do you appreciate the difficulties involved in that experiment?* **4.** To rise in value: *Real estate has appreciated in that town.*

ap·pre·ci·ate (ə prē′shē āt′) *verb,* **appreciated, appreciating**.

appreciation **1.** An understanding of the value of something: *After studying carpentry, I had a better appreciation of fine woodworking.* **2.** A feeling of being thankful; gratitude: *I want to show my appreciation for your help.* **3.** An increase in value: *The appreciation of our property has been very great.* **ap·pre·ci·a·tion** (ə prē′shē ā′shən) *noun.*

apprehend **1.** To capture and arrest: *The police apprehended the suspects.* **2.** To understand: *Did you fully apprehend the meaning of the speech?* **ap·pre·hend** (ap′ri hend′) *verb,* **apprehended, apprehending**.

apprehension **1.** A fear of what may happen: *The thought of going to the dentist filled me with apprehension.* **2.** Arrest or capture: *The chase ended with the apprehension of the suspects.* **3.** Understanding: *I have no apprehension of the way a computer works.* **ap·pre·hen·sion** (ap′ri hen′shən) *noun, plural* **apprehensions**.

apprehensive Fearful; worried: *We were apprehensive about taking the test.* **ap·pre·hen·sive** (ap′rē hen′siv) *adjective.*

apprentice A person who works for a skilled worker in order to learn a trade or art: *The students worked as apprentices in a woodworking shop. Noun.*
○ To take on or place as an apprentice: *When I was apprenticed to the tailor, I learned to sew and run the business. Verb.*
ap·pren·tice (ə pren′tis) *noun, plural* **apprentices**; *verb,* **apprenticed, apprenticing**.

approach **1.** To come near: *The plane approached the airport. The car approached at a high speed.* **2.** To go to with a plan or request: *I approached my parents with the hope of getting a higher allowance.* **3.** To begin to work on: *How should we approach the problem? Verb.*
○ **1.** The act of coming near: *I always look forward to the approach of summer.* **2.** A method of doing something: *My approach to training the dog was to be very patient.* **3.** A way of reaching a place or person: *The only approach to the town was blocked by snow. Noun.* **ap·proach** (ə prōch′) *verb,* **approached, ap-proaching**; *noun, plural* **approaches**.

approachable Easy to get close to; friendly. **ap·proach·a·ble** (ə prō′chə bəl) *adjective.*

appropriate Suitable; proper; correct: *Warm clothes are* **appropriate** *for a cold day. I began my letter to the ambassador with an* **appropriate** *greeting.* Adjective.
○ To reserve for a particular use: *Congress* **appropriated** *money to add land to the park system and to maintain campgrounds.* Verb. **ap•pro•pri•ate** (ə prō′prē it *for adjective;* ə prō′prē āt′ *for verb*) *adjective; verb,* **appropriated, appropriating.**

approval 1. Favorable opinion; acceptance: *The mayor's plan to attract businesses to the city had the* **approval** *of most of the people.* 2. Permission or consent: *I got my parents'* **approval** *to give a Halloween party.* **ap•pro•val** (ə prü′vəl) *noun,* plural **approvals.**

approve 1. To have or give a favorable opinion: *My parents don't* **approve** *of my staying up very late.* 2. To consent or agree to officially; authorize: *The town recently* **approved** *the construction of a public swimming pool.* **ap•prove** (ə prüv′) *verb,* **approved, approving.**

approximate Nearly correct or exact: *My* **approximate** *weight is 100 pounds.* Adjective.
○ To be nearly the same as; come close to: *Your estimate* **approximates** *the actual cost of the repairs.* Verb. **ap•prox•i•mate** (ə prok′sə mit *for adjective;* ə prok′sə māt′ *for verb*) *adjective; verb,* **approximated, approximating.**

approximately Nearly; about: *We had* **approximately** *4 inches of snow yesterday.* **ap•prox•i•mate•ly** (ə prok′sə mit lē) *adverb.*

Apr. An abbreviation for April.

apricot A round, yellowish orange fruit that looks like a small peach. Apricots grow in warm climates on a tree that is also called an apricot. **a•pri•cot** (ā′pri kot′ *or* ap′ri kot′) *noun,* plural **apricots.**

April The fourth month of the year. April has thirty days. **A•pril** (ā′prəl) *noun.*

WORD HISTORY

April goes back to the Latin name for this month. In Latin the month may have been named after Aphrodite, the Greek goddess of love.

April Fools' Day April 1, a day on which people often play friendly jokes on each other.

apron A garment worn over the front of the body to protect one's clothing: *The cook's* **apron** *was made of white cloth.* **a•pron** (ā′prən) *noun,* plural **aprons.**

In some jobs, rubber aprons are used to protect a worker's clothes.

apt 1. Likely; inclined: *You're* **apt** *to hurt yourself if you're not more careful.* 2. Appropriate; suitable: *My friend gave me some* **apt** *suggestions for my science project.* 3. Quick to learn: *You are an* **apt** *student in mathematics.* **apt** (apt) *adjective.*

apt. Abbreviation for apartment.

aptitude 1. A natural ability or talent: *The twins seem to have an* **aptitude** *for drawing.* 2. Quickness in learning: *There were many students with great* **aptitude** *in my class.* **ap•ti•tude** (ap′it üd′ *or* ap′ti tūd′) *noun,* plural **aptitudes.**

aquaculture The cultivation of animals and plants that live in water. **aq•ua•cul•ture** (ak′wâr′ē əm) *noun.*

Aqua-Lung A trademark for a device used by a person to breathe underwater. **Aq•ua-lung** (ak′wə kul′chər) *noun,* plural **aqualungs.**

People visit aquariums for pleasure or to study the animals or plants kept there.

aquarium 1. A tank, bowl, or similar container in which fish, other water animals, and water plants are kept. 2. A building used to display

PRONUNCIATION KEY:

| at | āpe | fär | câre | end | mē | it | īce | pîerce | hot | ōld | sông | fôrk |
| oil | out | up | ūse | rüle | pull | tûrn | chin | sing | shop | thin | this | |

hw in white; zh in treasure. The symbol ə stands for the unstressed vowel sound in about, taken, pencil, lemon, and circus.

39

collections of fish, other water animals, and water plants. **aq·uar·i·um** (ə kwâr′ē əm) *noun*, *plural* **aquariums**.

aquatic **1.** Growing or living in water: *Aquatic plants.* **2.** Done or performed in water: *Aquatic sports.* **a·quat·ic** (ə kwot′ik) *adjective*.

aqueduct **1.** A large pipe or other channel that carries water over a long distance. **2.** A structure like a bridge used to support such a pipe or channel. **aq·ue·duct** (ak′wi dukt′) *noun*, *plural* **aqueducts**.

aquifer A layer of rock, gravel, or sand that holds the water that supplies wells and springs. **aq·ui·fer** (ak′wə fər) *noun*, *plural* **aquifers**.

AR Postal abbreviation for Arkansas.

Arab **1.** A member of one of the Arabic-speaking peoples who live in southwestern Asia and northern Africa. **2.** A person who was born in or is a citizen of an Arabian country. *Noun.*
○ Of or having to do with the Arabs or Arabia. *Adjective.*
Ar·ab (ar′əb) *noun*, *plural* **Arabs**; *adjective*.

Arabia A peninsula in southwestern Asia. **A·ra·bi·a** (ə rā′bē ə) *noun*.

Arabian Of or having to do with Arabia or the people of Arabia. *Adjective.*
○ A person who was born in or is a citizen of an Arabian country. *Noun.*
A·ra·bi·an (ə rā′bē ən) *adjective*; *noun*, *plural* **Arabians**.

Arabic Of or having to do with the Arabs or their language. *Adjective.*
○ The language of the Arabs. *Noun.*
Ar·a·bic (ar′ə bik) *adjective*; *noun*.

Arabic numerals The number symbols 1, 2, 3, 4, 5, 6, 7, 8, 9, and 0.

arable Suitable for farming: *Irrigation can turn a desert into arable land.* **ar·a·ble** (ar′ə bəl) *adjective*.

arbitrary Based on personal opinions, feelings, or wishes rather than on reason or on a rule or law: *Judges may not make arbitrary decisions when they decide legal cases.* **ar·bi·trar·y** (är′bə trer′ē) *adjective*.

arbitrate **1.** To settle a dispute or disagreement: *The umpires arbitrated between the two teams.* **2.** To settle by or submit to arbitration: *The union and the company agreed to arbitrate their dispute.* **ar·bi·trate** (är′bi trāt′) *verb*, **arbitrated**, **arbitrating**. **ar·bi·tra·tion** (är′bi trā′shən) *noun*.

arbor A place that is covered and shaded by trees or shrubs or by vines growing on a frame. **ar·bor** (är′bər) *noun*, *plural* **arbors**.

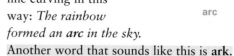

arc **1.** A curved line between two points on a circle. **2.** Any line curving in this way: *The rainbow formed an arc in the sky.* Another word that sounds like this is **ark**. **arc** (ärk) *noun*, *plural* **arcs**.

arcade **1.** A passageway that is covered by a curved roof: *Arcades often have a row of shops along each side.* **2.** A place with a selection of video games, for which a person pays to play. **ar·cade** (är kād′) *noun*, *plural* **arcades**.

arch **1.** A curved structure over an open space. An arch is usually built to support the weight of the material above it. **2.** A monument that contains an arch or arches. **3.** Anything like an arch in shape or use. The curved underside of the foot between the toes and the heel is called the arch. *Noun.*
○ To form into an arch; curve: *The cat arched its back. Verb.*
arch (ärch) *noun*, *plural* **arches**; *verb*, **arched**, **arching**.

A series of arches supports this ceiling.

archaeology The study of the way humans lived a long time ago. Archaeologists dig up the remains of ancient cities and towns and then study the tools, weapons, pottery, and other things they find. This word is also spelled **archeology**. **ar·chae·ol·o·gy** (är′kē ol′ə jē) *noun*.

archbishop A bishop of the highest rank. **arch·bish·op** (ärch′bish′əp) *noun, plural* **archbishops**.

archeology Another spelling for **archaeology**. **ar·che·ol·o·gy** (är′kē ol′ə jē) *noun*.

archer A person who shoots with a bow and arrow. **arch·er** (är′chər) *noun, plural* **archers**.

Archery is an Olympic sport.

archery The skill or sport of shooting with a bow and arrow. **arch·er·y** (är′chə rē) *noun*.

archipelago 1. A large group of islands. 2. A large body of water having many islands in it. **ar·chi·pel·a·go** (är′kə pel′i gō) *noun, plural* **archipelagoes** *or* **archipelagos**.

architect A person who designs buildings and supervises their construction: *The architect showed us the plans for our new house.* **ar·chi·tect** (är′ki tekt′) *noun, plural* **architects**.

architecture 1. The science, art, or profession of designing buildings. 2. A particular style or method of building: *We studied Greek architecture in art class.* **ar·chi·tec·ture** (är′ki tek′chər) *noun*.

arctic 1. Of or having to do with the North Pole or the region around the North Pole: *Reindeer live in the arctic wilderness.* 2. Very cold; freezing: *arctic weather.* **arc·tic** (ärk′tik *or* är′tik) *adjective*.

Arctic Ocean The ocean surrounding the North Pole.

ardent Very loyal or enthusiastic: *My sister is an ardent fan of the local volleyball team.* **ar·dent** (ard′nt) *adjective*.

are A form of the present tense of **be** that is used with you, we, they, or the plural form of a noun: *You are late. We are glad you could come. How are your friends?* **are** (är) *verb*.

area 1. The amount of surface within a given boundary: *The area of our yard is 400 square feet.* 2. A particular space, region, or section: *We moved from the city to a rural area.* 3. A field of interest, study, or activity: *What area will you specialize in at college?* **ar·e·a** (âr′ē ə) *noun, plural* **areas**.

area code A set of three numbers assigned to each area into which the United States and Canada are divided for telephone service. You dial these three numbers before the local number when you call especially from one area to another.

arena 1. A space that is used for contests or entertainment. In the arenas of ancient Rome, gladiators fought each other. Today, circuses and sports events take place in arenas. 2. A building with an arena. 3. An area or scene of activity or conflict: *My cousin is interested in getting into the political arena.* **a·re·na** (ə rē′nə) *noun, plural* **arenas**.

aren't Shortened form of "are not." *Why aren't you going with us?* **aren't** (ärnt *or* är′ənt) *contraction*.

Argentina A country in southern South America. **Ar·gen·ti·na** (är′jən tē′nə) *noun*.

argue 1. To express a difference of opinion; disagree: *My parents always argue about politics.* 2. To give reasons for or against something: *I argued against going to the beach because it looked like it might rain.* **ar·gue** (är′gū) *verb*, **argued, arguing**.

argument 1. A discussion of something by people who do not agree: *They had an argument about who was the better musician.* 2. An angry disagreement; quarrel: *I was unhappy after the argument with my best friend.* 3. A reason or reasons given for or against something: *The children's argument for getting new bicycles was that they needed them to deliver newspapers.* **ar·gu·ment** (är′gyə mənt) *noun, plural* **arguments**.

PRONUNCIATION KEY:

| at | āpe | fär | câre | end | mē | it | īce | pîerce | hot | ōld | sông | fôrk |
| oil | out | up | ūse | rüle | pull | tûrn | chin | sing | shop | thin | this | |

hw in white; zh in treasure. The symbol ə stands for the unstressed vowel sound in about, taken, pencil, lemon, and circus.

41

arid Getting very little rain; dry: *A desert is an* **arid** *region*. **ar·id** (ar′id) *adjective*.

arise 1. To rise from a sitting, kneeling, or lying position; get up. 2. To move upward; rise: *A mist slowly* **arises** *from the lake*. 3. To come into being; appear: *Questions often* **arise** *in our minds as we read about new things*. **a·rise** (ə rīz′) *verb*, **arose**, **arisen**, **arising**.

aristocracy 1. A class of people who are born into a high social position; nobility. Members of an aristocracy usually have more wealth and enjoy more privileges than the rest of society. 2. Any group of people who are thought to be outstanding because of wealth, intelligence, or ability. **ar·is·toc·ra·cy** (ar′ə stok′rə sē) *noun*, *plural* **aristocracies**.

aristocrat A person who belongs to an aristocracy. **a·ris·to·crat** (ə ris′tə krat′) *noun*, *plural* **aristocrats**. —**aristocratic** *adjective*.

arithmetic 1. The science and technique of figuring with numbers. Arithmetic deals with addition, subtraction, multiplication, and division. 2. The act of adding, subtracting, multiplying, or dividing: *You are good at* **arithmetic**. **a·rith·me·tic** (ə rith′mə tik′) *noun*.

Ariz. An abbreviation for Arizona.

Arizona
U. S. Postal Abbreviation: **AZ**
Capital: **Phoenix**
Population: **3,386,000**
Area: **113,909 sq. mi./295,023 sq. km**
State Nickname: **Grand Canyon State**
State Bird: **Cactus Wren**
State Flower: **Blossom of the Saguaro Cactus**

Arizona A state in the southwestern United States. Its capital is Phoenix. **Ar·i·zo·na** (ar′ə zō′nə) *noun*.

ark 1. In the Bible, the ship that Noah built to save himself, his family, and two of every kind of animal from the flood God sent to punish humanity. 2. A chest carried by the ancient Hebrews. It contained the two stone tablets on which the Ten Commandments were written. 3. A large, clumsy vessel or vehicle. Another word that sounds like this is **arc**. **ark** (ärk) *noun*.

Ark. An abbreviation for Arkansas.

Arkansas
U. S. Postal Abbreviation: **AR**
Capital: **Little Rock**
Population: **2,388,000**
Area: **53,104 sq. mi./137,539 sq. km**
State Nickname: **Land of Opportunity**
State Bird: **Mockingbird**
State Flower: **Apple Blossom**

Arkansas A state in the south-central United States. Its capital is Little Rock. **Ar·kan·sas** (är′kən sô′) *noun*.

arm¹ 1. The part of the body between the shoulder and the wrist. 2. Anything shaped or used like an arm: *The arms of the green chair are loose.* **arm** (ärm) *noun, plural* **arms.**

arm² Any weapon: *Guns and bombs are arms. Noun.*
  ○ 1. To supply with weapons: *The sheriff armed the deputies before they searched for the bandits.* 2. To supply with anything that protects or strengthens: *A porcupine is armed with quills. Verb.*
  arm (ärm) *noun, plural* **arms;** *verb,* **armed, arming.**

armada A large group of warships. **ar·ma·da** (är mä′də) *noun, plural* **armadas.**

The armadillo **is found in South America and parts of the southern United States.**

armadillo A small animal that has a hard bony shell, a long snout, sharp claws, and a long tail. The armadillo is a mammal. **ar·ma·dil·lo** (är′mə dil′ō) *noun, plural* **armadillos.**

armaments The military forces, weapons, equipment, and supplies of a country. **ar·ma·ments** (ärməmənts) *plural noun.*

armchair A chair with parts on both sides that support a person's arms or elbows. **arm·chair** (ärm′châr′) *noun, plural* **armchairs.**

armed forces All of a nation's military branches. The Army, Navy, Marine Corps, Air Force, and Coast Guard are the armed forces of the United States.

Armenia A country in southeastern Europe. **Ar·me·ni·a** (är mē′nē yə) *noun.* **Ar·men·i·an** (är mē′nē ən) *noun, adjective.*

armistice A temporary stop in fighting agreed on by those who are fighting; truce. **ar·mi·stice** (är′mə stis) *noun, plural* **armistices.**

armor 1. A covering for the body, usually made from metal. In former times it was worn for protection during battle. 2. Any protective covering. The metal plates on a tank or warship are armor. The hard shell of a turtle is armor. **ar·mor** (är′mər) *noun.*

armored Protected or equipped with armor: *The money was delivered to the bank in an armored car.* **ar·mored** (är′mərd) *adjective.*

armory 1. A place where weapons are kept. 2. A building in which a military unit is trained. **ar·mor·y** (är′mə rē) *noun, plural* **armories.**

armpit The hollow part under the arm at the shoulder. **arm·pit** (ärm′pit′) *noun, plural* **armpits.**

army 1. A large, organized group of soldiers who are armed and trained to fight on land. The word army is often capitalized when it means the branch of a country's armed forces that is trained to fight on land. In some nations, the Army also includes the Air Force: *A United States Army recruiting poster was on the wall.* 2. Any large group of people or things: *An army of teenagers came to the concert to hear the famous singing group.* **ar·my** (är′mē) *noun, plural* **armies.**

aroma A pleasant or agreeable smell; fragrance: *The bread we were baking gave off a delicious aroma.* **a·ro·ma** (ə rō′mə) *noun, plural* **aromas.**

arose Past tense of arise: *I arose at seven o'clock this morning.* **a·rose** (ə rōz′) *verb.*

This amusement park ride spins people around **at a rapid rate.**

around 1. In a circle or path that surrounds: *I wore a belt around my waist. We walked*

PRONUNCIATION KEY:
at   āpe   fär   câre   end   mē   it   īce   pierce   hot   ōld   sông   fôrk
oil   out   up   ūse   rüle   pull   tûrn   chin   sing   shop   thin   this
hw in white; zh in treasure. The symbol ə stands for the unstressed vowel sound in about, taken, pencil, lemon, and circus.

43

around the block. **2.** On all sides of: *Flowers were planted* **around** *the house.* **3.** Here and there in: *Tourists wandered* **around** *the city.* **4.** Somewhat near in place, time, or amount: *Please stay* **around** *the house. I'll meet you* **around** *noon. That watch is worth* **around** *ten dollars.* **5.** On or to the other side of: *Their house is* **around** *the corner. Preposition.*
○ **1.** In a circle: *The wheel spun* **around.** **2.** In circumference: *The column measures 3 feet* **around.** **3.** On all sides; in various directions; here and there: *We looked* **around** *but couldn't see anyone.* **4.** Somewhere near: *Why not stay* **around** *for a few minutes?* **5.** In or to the opposite direction: *I turned* **around** *quickly. Adverb.*
a•round (ə round′) *preposition; adverb.*

arouse **1.** To cause an action or strong feeling; excite; stir: *Your rudeness* **aroused** *everyone's anger.* **2.** To awaken: *The alarm clock* **aroused** *me in time for school.* **a•rouse** (ə rouz′) *verb,* **aroused, arousing.**

arrange **1.** To put in order or position: *The teacher* **arranged** *the names of the children in alphabetical order.* **2.** To prepare for; plan: *Who* **arranged** *this meeting?* **3.** To adapt a piece of music for instruments, voices, or a style of performance for which it was not originally written. **ar•range** (ə rānj′) *verb,* **arranged, arranging.**

arrangement **1.** The act of putting in order or position: *Arrangement of the books took two hours.* **2.** Something arranged: *They made a flower* **arrangement** *for the party.* **3.** arrangements. Plans or preparations: *We made* **arrangements** *for our class party.* **4.** A piece of music that has been arranged: *The band played a new* **arrangement** *of an old folk song.* **ar•range•ment** (ə rānj′mənt) *noun, plural* **arrangements.**

array **1.** An orderly grouping or arrangement: *The books in the shop window were in an attractive* **array.** **2.** A large or impressive group or display: *There was quite an* **array** *of food at the banquet.* **3.** Beautiful or splendid clothing: *The monarch appeared in royal* **array.** *Noun.*
○ **1.** To put in order or position: *We* **arrayed** *the family photographs on the shelf.* **2.** To dress beautifully or splendidly: *The couple were* **arrayed** *like a queen and king. Verb.*
ar•ray (ə rā′) *noun, plural* **arrays;** *verb,* **arrayed, arraying.**

arrest **1.** To seize and hold by authority of the law: *The police officer* **arrested** *the suspect.* **2.** To stop or hold: *We hope to* **arrest** *pollution in our country.* **3.** To catch and hold; attract and keep: *The commotion* **arrested** *our attention. Verb.*
○ The act of seizing by authority of the law: *The* **arrest** *of the suspects was reported on the morning newscast. Noun.*
ar•rest (ə rest′) *verb,* **arrested, arresting;** *noun, plural* **arrests.**

arrival **1.** The act of arriving: *The reporters were waiting for the* **arrival** *of the president.* **2.** A person or thing that arrives or has arrived. **ar•riv•al** (ə rī′vəl) *noun, plural* **arrivals.**

arrive **1.** To come to a place: *We will* **arrive** *in Florida at midnight.* **2.** To come: *The week of my cousin's visit has* **arrived.**
• **to arrive at.** To come to or reach: *Has the jury* **arrived at** *a decision yet?*
ar•rive (ə rīv′) *verb,* **arrived, arriving.**

arrogant Having or showing too much pride or feelings of superiority: *The* **arrogant** *visitors were surprised and upset when they lost the game to our school's team.* **ar•ro•gant** (ar′ə gənt) *adjective.*

arrow **1.** A straight, slender stick that has a sharp point at one end and feathers at the other: *An* **arrow** *is made to be shot from a bow.* **2.** Something that is like an arrow in shape: *The road sign had an* **arrow** *to show which way traffic should go.* **ar•row** (a′rō) *noun, plural* **arrows.**

**Most early arrowheads
were made of stone.**

arrowhead The pointed tip or head of an arrow. **ar•row•head** (ar′ō hed′) *noun, plural* **arrowheads.**

arroyo A ditch with steep sides that has been cut in the ground by the force of running water;

gully. Arroyos are dry most of the year. **ar·roy·o** (ə roi′ō) *noun, plural* **arroyos**.

arsenal A place for making or storing weapons and ammunition. **ar·se·nal** (är′sə nəl) *noun, plural* **arsenals**.

arsenic A gray, very poisonous substance that has no taste. Arsenic is used in rat, insect, and weed poisons. Arsenic is a chemical element. **ar·se·nic** (är′sə nik) *noun*.

arson The crime of deliberately setting fire to a building or other property. **ar·son** (är′sən) *noun*.

art **1.** An activity by which one creates a work that has beauty or special meaning. Painting, sculpture, composing music, and writing are forms of art. **2.** The works created by this kind of activity. Murals, ballets, and poems are examples of such works. **3.** A skill, craft, or occupation that requires study, practice, or experience: *You have an **art** for making people feel at ease. The **art** of cooking came easily to me.* **art** (ärt) *noun, plural* **arts**.

artery 1. One of the blood vessels that carry blood away from the heart. 2. A main road or channel: *This highway is the major **artery** between the two cities.* **ar·te·ry** (är′tə rē) *noun, plural* **arteries**.

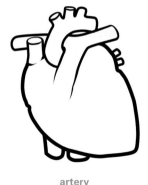
artery

arthritis A painful inflammation of a joint or joints of the body: *People who suffer from **arthritis** often find certain activities very painful.* **ar·thri·tis** (är thrī′tis) *noun*.

arthropod One of a large group of animals with legs that have several joints, a body divided into two or more parts, and no backbone. Lobsters, crabs, insects, and spiders are all arthropods. **ar·thro·pod** (är′thrə pod′) *noun, plural* **arthropods**.

artichoke A plant like a thistle, with large, coarse leaves and purple flowers. The immature greenish yellow flower head is cooked and eaten as a vegetable. **ar·ti·choke** (är′ti chōk′) *noun, plural* **artichokes**.

article **1.** A piece of writing published in a newspaper, magazine, or book: *The scientist wrote an **article** on space travel for the encyclopedia.* **2.** A thing or object; item: *Several **articles** were stolen from the house.* **3.** A separate section of a formal document. There are articles in treaties, constitutions, and contracts. **4.** Any one of the words *a*, *an*, or *the* used to modify a noun. *A* and *an* are indefinite articles. *The* is a definite article. **ar·ti·cle** (är′ti kəl) *noun, plural* **articles**.

articulate Able to speak or express oneself clearly: *The professor was **articulate** on the subject of mathematics. Adjective.*
○ To speak or express oneself clearly: *I was so upset that I could not **articulate** my feelings. Verb.*
ar·tic·u·late (är tik′yə lit *for adjective;* är tik′yə lāt′ *for verb*) *adjective; verb,* **articulated, articulating**.

artifact **1.** An old tool, weapon, or other thing made by people in the past. In order to last a long time, artifacts are usually made of a material that does not decay. **2.** Something left over from an earlier time: *Some customs are **artifacts** from a time when they were useful to people.* **ar·ti·fact** (är′ti fakt) *noun, plural* **artifacts**.

artificial **1.** Made by people, not by nature; not natural: *The **artificial** flowers were made of plastic.* **2.** Not sincere or true: *The actor's smile seemed cold and **artificial**.* **ar·ti·fi·cial** (är′tə fish′əl) *adjective*.

artificial intelligence The science of creating computers that can think like people.

artificial respiration The forcing of air into and out of the lungs of a person who has stopped breathing. This helps the person to start breathing normally again.

artillery **1.** Large firearms that are too heavy to carry. They are fixed on stationary bases, supported by wheels, or mounted on vehicles with wheels or tracks. **2.** The part of the army that uses such firearms. **ar·til·ler·y** (är til′ə rē) *noun*.

artisan A person who is skilled in a particular craft. Carpenters, plumbers, and electricians are artisans. **ar·ti·san** (är′tə zən) *noun, plural* **artisans**.

PRONUNCIATION KEY:
at āpe fär câre end mē it īce pierce hot ōld sông fôrk
oil out up ūse rüle pull tûrn chin sing shop thin this
hw in white; zh in treasure. The symbol ə stands for the unstressed vowel sound in about, taken, pencil, lemon, and circus.

45

artist 1. A person who is skilled in painting, music, literature, or any other form of art. 2. A person whose work shows talent or skill: *This restaurant's chef is an artist.* **ar•tist** (är′tist) *noun, plural* **artists**.

artistic 1. Of or having to do with art or artists: *My teacher has artistic interests.* 2. Having or showing talent or skill: *The dancer gave an artistic performance.* **ar•tis•tic** (är tis′tik) *adjective*.

as To the same amount or degree: *The first movie was exciting, but the second was not as good. Adverb.*

Artists often like to paint in outdoor light.

○ 1. To the same degree or extent that: *They were proud as they could be.* 2. In the same way or manner that: *Pronounce the word as I am pronouncing it.* 3. At the same time that; while or when: *My parents arrived as we were leaving.* 4. For the reason that; because; since: *As you are not ready, we will wait for you. Conjunction.*

○ In the manner, role, or function of: *I'm speaking to you as a friend. Preposition.*

• **as if** *or* **as though**. In the way it would be if: *The children behaved as if they had no manners.*

• **as of**. By or up to a certain time: *As of Wednesday, we had read four books for our English class.*

• **as yet**. Up to now; yet: *Our new television set hasn't arrived as yet.*

as (az) *adverb; conjunction; preposition*.

ASAP An abbreviation for "as soon as possible": *Please answer this letter ASAP.* This abbreviation is often used as shorthand in business but not in formal writing or speaking. **ASAP** (ā es ā pē′ *or* ā′sap).

asbestos A grayish mineral. Its fibers can be woven or pressed into a material that does not burn or conduct electricity, and they are very harmful if they enter the lungs. **as•bes•tos** (as bes′təs *or* az bes′təs) *noun*.

The climber is ascending the mountain to reach the top.

ascend To move or go up; rise or climb: *The elevator ascended to the twentieth floor.* The hikers ascended the hill. **as•cend** (ə send′) *verb*, **ascended, ascending**.

ascent 1. The act of moving or going up: *A heavy snowstorm made an ascent of the mountain impossible.* 2. A place or way where one ascends; upward slope: *Ahead of us there was a steep ascent.* **as•cent** (ə sent′) *noun, plural* **ascents**.

ascertain To find out definitely; determine: *The police quickly ascertained the whereabouts of the gang.* **as•cer•tain** (as′ər tān′) *verb*, **ascertained, ascertaining**.

ash¹ A small amount of grayish white powder left after something has burned: *A pile of ashes was all that remained of the burned leaves.* **ash** (ash) *noun, plural* **ashes**.

ash² A tree that has a strong wood. Ash is used in construction and in making baseball bats. **ash** (ash) *noun, plural* **ashes**.

ashamed 1. Feeling shame; upset or guilty because one has done something wrong or silly: *The student was ashamed for having failed the arithmetic test.* 2. Not wanting to do something because of fear or shame: *I was ashamed to admit that I had broken my friend's bicycle.* **a•shamed** (ə shāmd′) *adjective*.

ashore On or to the shore or land: *The children paddled the canoe ashore. Most of the ship's passengers are already ashore.* **a•shore** (ə shôr′) *adverb; adjective*.

Asia The largest continent. Asia lies between the Pacific Ocean and Europe and Africa. **A•sia** (ā′zhə) *noun*.

Asian Of or having to do with Asia or the people of Asia: *I am studying* **Asian** *history. Adjective.*
○ A person who was born or is living in Asia. *Noun.*
A·sian (ā′zhən) *adjective; noun, plural* **Asians**.

Asian-American A person born in the U.S. whose family can trace its history back to Asia.
Asian-American (ā′zhən əmerikan) *noun, plural* **Asian-Americans**; *adjective*.

aside **1.** On or to one side: *I turned my bike* **aside** *so the riders behind me could pass.* **2.** Out of one's thoughts or consideration: *Put your worries* **aside** *and have a good time!* **3.** So as to be available at some future time: *The librarian is keeping the book* **aside** *for me.* **a·side** (ə sīd′) *adverb.*

ask **1.** To put a question about something; inquire: *We* **asked** *how to get to town.* **2.** To call for an answer to: *Don't* **ask** *that question again.* **3.** To make a request: *May I* **ask** *for your help?* **4.** To invite. *We* **asked** *our friends to the party.*
• **to ask for.** To do or say something that will get you in trouble: *You'll be* **asking for** *it if you break another dish.*
ask (ask) *verb,* **asked, asking**.

askew At or to one side; crooked: *The picture hung* **askew**. **a·skew** (ə skū′) *adverb; adjective.*

asleep **1.** Not awake; sleeping: *Be quiet because the baby is* **asleep**. **2.** Without feeling; numb: *My foot is* **asleep**. **3.** Not paying attention: *You must have been* **asleep** *when the teacher gave us homework. Adjective.*
○ Into a condition of sleep: *The children fell* **asleep** *while they were watching television. Adverb.*
a·sleep (ə slēp′) *adjective; adverb.*

asparagus The young, green shoots of a garden plant, cooked and eaten as a vegetable. They are shaped like spears and have large, scaly leaves at the tip. **as·par·a·gus** (ə spar′ə gəs) *noun.*

A.S.P.C.A. *or* **ASPCA** Abbreviation for American Society for the Prevention of Cruelty to Animals.

aspect **1.** A particular feature or characteristic of something: *The mayor's committee considered every* **aspect** *of the traffic problem.* **2.** Look; appearance: *The deserted house had a gloomy* **aspect**. **as·pect** (as′pekt) *noun, plural* **aspects**.

aspen A tree whose leaves shake in the slightest breeze. Its wood is used to make pulp for paper. An aspen is a kind of poplar. **as·pen** (as′pən) *noun, plural* **aspens**.

Trembling leaves and white bark are easy ways to identify aspens.

asphalt A brown or black substance found in the ground or obtained when petroleum is refined. It is mixed with sand or gravel and is used to pave roads. **as·phalt** (as′fôlt) *noun.*

aspiration A strong hope or desire: *My* **aspiration** *is to become a scientist.* **as·pi·ra·tion** (as′pə rā shən) *noun, plural* **aspirations**.

aspire To want or try very strongly to achieve some goal; seek ambitiously: *My cousin* **aspires** *to a career in medicine.* **as·pire** (ə spīr′) *verb,* **aspired, aspiring**.

aspirin A kind of drug used to ease pain and reduce fevers. Some people take aspirin when they have a cold or a headache. **as·pi·rin** (as′pər in) *noun, plural* **aspirins**.

ass **1.** An animal that is closely related to the horse but is smaller and has longer ears; donkey. **2.** A stupid or silly person. **ass** (as) *noun, plural* **asses**.

assassin A person who murders someone important, such as a government leader. **as·sas·sin** (ə sas′in) *noun, plural* **assassins**.

assassinate To murder an important or famous person: *The plot to* **assassinate** *the ambassador was foiled by the police.* **as·sas·si·nate** (ə sas′ə nāt′) *verb,* **assassinated, assassinating**.
—**assassination** *noun.*

PRONUNCIATION KEY:

at   āpe   fär   câre   end   mē   it   īce   pîerce   hot   ōld   sông   fôrk
oil   out   up   ūse   rüle   püll   tûrn   chin   sing   shop   thin   this

hw in white; zh in treasure. The symbol ə stands for the unstressed vowel sound in about, taken, pencil, lemon, and circus.

47

assault 1. A sudden, violent attack: *The troops retreated under the assault of the enemy.* 2. An unlawful attempt or threat to do physical harm to someone: *The suspect was charged with assault.* Noun.
○ To make an assault on; attack: *The soldiers assaulted the fort.* Verb.
as•sault (ə sôlt′) *noun, plural* **assaults**; *verb,* **assaulted, assaulting.**

assemble 1. To come or bring together: *A crowd began to assemble for the rally. I have assembled a large shell collection.* 2. To put or fit together: *We had to assemble the parts of the bicycle.*
as•sem•ble (ə sem′bəl) *verb,* **assembled, assembling.**

assembly 1. A group of people gathered together for some purpose: *An assembly of school principals met to discuss new topics in education.* 2. A group of people who make laws. In some states of the United States, one of the houses of the legislature is called the **Assembly.** 3. The act of putting or fitting together: *Robots were used for the hazardous jobs in the assembly of the automobiles.* 4. A group of parts that fit or work together: *The plane was grounded when a crack in the wing assembly was discovered.* **as•sem•bly** (ə sem′blē) *noun, plural* **assemblies.**

assembly line A line of workers and machines used for putting together a product step by step in a factory. As the product is moved along an assembly line, a part is added or some other work is done until the product is finished.

assent To agree; consent: *The town council assented to changes in the budget.* Verb.
○ Approval, agreement, or consent: *The community gave its assent, and the new traffic light was added at the intersection.* Noun.
as•sent (ə sent′) *verb,* **assented, assenting,** *noun.*

assert 1. To state in a positive way: *The scientists asserted that their theory was correct.* 2. To insist on; claim: *As children mature, they feel a need to assert their independence.* **as•sert** (ə sûrt′) *verb,* **asserted, asserting.**

assess 1. To set the value of property for taxation: *That farm is assessed at $100,000.* 2. To set the amount of a fine or tax: *The judge assessed a fine of fifty dollars.* 3. To charge or tax: *The library assesses a person five cents for each day a book is overdue.* **as•sess** (ə ses′) *verb,* **assessed, assessing.**

asset 1. Something valuable or useful; advantage: *Being tall is a great asset for a basketball player.* 2. **assets.** Property and other things of value that belong to a person or organization: *Their assets include a house, a car, and a boat.* **as•set** (as′et) *noun, plural* **assets.**

assign 1. To give out as a task: *Our teacher will assign a different science project to each student.* 2. To appoint; designate: *The mayor assigned three people to the committee on education.* **as•sign** (ə sīn′) *verb,* **assigned, assigning.**

assignment 1. Something that is assigned: *My arithmetic assignment is to do ten multiplication problems.* 2. The act of assigning: *The company's president is responsible for the assignment of tasks to employees.* **as•sign•ment** (ə sīn′mənt) *noun, plural* **assignments.**

assist To help; aid: *All the people in the town got together to assist the family whose house had burned down.* **as•sist** (ə sist′) *verb,* **assisted, assisting.**

assistance The act of assisting; help; aid: *We will need some assistance in carrying the packages upstairs.* **as•sist•ance** (ə sis′təns) *noun.*

assistant A person who assists; helper; aide: *The manager's assistant helps to run the store.* Noun.
○ Acting to assist another person: *The head football coach has four assistant coaches.* Adjective.
as•sist•ant (ə sis′tənt) *noun, plural* **assistants;** *adjective.*

associate 1. To connect in one's mind: *I always associate summer with picnics at the beach.* 2. To join as a friend, companion, or partner: *At first the new student was too shy to associate with the rest of us.* Verb.
○ A friend, companion, or partner: *One of the associates in the business left to work for another company.* Noun.
○ 1. Closely connected with another or others in work, responsibility, or status: *The two associate judges went to the same law school.* 2. Having or giving some, but not all, rights and privileges: *My parents have an associate membership in the club.* Adjective.

as·so·ci·ate (ə sō′shē āt′ or ə sō′sē āt′ for verb; ə sō′shē it or ə sō′sē it for noun, adjective) verb, **associated, associating;** noun, plural **associates;** adjective.

association **1.** A group of people joined together for a common purpose: *My friends and I belong to an* **association** *that helps preserve forests.* **2.** The act of associating or the condition of being associated: *My friends and I are proud of our long* **association.** **3.** A thought or feeling one has in connection with a person, place, or thing: *This house has many happy* **associations** *for me.* **as·so·ci·a·tion** (ə sō′sē ā′shən or ə sō′shē ā′shən) noun, plural **associations.**

associative property A characteristic of addition and multiplication that allows you to add or multiply three or more numbers in any order and still get the same answer. For example, $(6 + 5) + 2$ gives the same answer as $5 + (6 + 2)$, and $(2 \times 3) \times 4$ gives the same answer as $3 \times (4 \times 2)$. **as·so·ci·a·tive property** (ə sō′shē ā′tiv or ə sō′sē ā′tiv).

Associative property in addition:
$(7 + 3) + 4$ is the same as $3 + (7 + 4)$.
They both equal 14.

Associative property in multiplication:
$(7 \times 3) \times 4$ is the same as $3 \times (7 \times 4)$.
They both equal 84.

assorted Of different kinds mixed together: *We have* **assorted** *snacks to eat.* **as·sort·ed** (ə sôr′təd) adjective.

assortment A collection of different kinds: *That store carries a large* **assortment** *of sports equipment.* **as·sort·ment** (ə sôrt′mənt) noun, plural **assortments.**

assume **1.** To take for granted; suppose: *I assume we will arrive on time.* **2.** To take upon oneself; undertake: *You will have to* **assume** *the responsibility of feeding the dog.* **3.** To take for oneself; seize: *The military leaders* **assumed** *control of the country.* **4.** To give a false impression of; pretend: *I* **assumed** *a lack of interest in the party because I had not been invited.* **as·sume** (ə süm′) verb, **assumed, assuming.**

assumption **1.** The act of taking for granted: *A member of a jury must make the* **assumption** *that a person is innocent until proven guilty.* **2.** Something that is taken for granted: *Your* **assumption** *turned out to be wrong.* **as·sump·tion** (ə sump′shən) noun, plural **assumptions.**

assurance **1.** A statement that is supposed to make a person certain or sure: *We had their* **assurance** *that they would help with our project.* **2.** Freedom from doubt; certainty: *The speaker had the* **assurance** *that comes from experience.* **as·sur·ance** (ə shùr′əns) noun, plural **assurances.**

assure **1.** To state positively: *I assure you that I won't be late.* **2.** To make certain or sure: *Their hard work* **assured** *the success of the project.* **3.** To give confidence to: *We* **assured** *the child that the dog was friendly.* **as·sure** (ə shùr′) verb, **assured, assuring.**

aster A flower like a daisy that has white, pink, purple, or yellow petals around a yellow center. Asters bloom in the fall. **as·ter** (as′tər) noun, plural **asters.**

asterisk A mark (*) shaped like a star that is used in printing or writing to tell the reader to look somewhere else on the page for more information. **as·ter·isk** (as′tə risk′) noun, plural **asterisks.**

asteroid Any of the thousands of small planets that revolve around the sun. Most of them are between the orbits of Mars and Jupiter. Some asteroids are less than 1 mile wide. Others are as big as 500 miles wide. **as·ter·oid** (as′tə roid′) noun, plural **asteroids.**

asthma A disease that makes it difficult to breathe and causes wheezing and coughing. Sometimes asthma is caused by an allergy. **asth·ma** (az′mə) noun.

astir In motion; active: *Very few people were* **astir** *at dawn.* **a·stir** (ə stûr′) adjective.

astonish To surprise very much; amaze: *The good news* **astonished** *me.* **as·ton·ish** (ə ston′ish) verb, **astonished, astonishing.**

astonishment Great surprise; amazement: *The child was filled with* **astonishment** *when the magician pulled a rabbit out of a hat.* **as·ton·ish·ment** (ə ston′ish mənt) noun.

PRONUNCIATION KEY:

| at | āpe | fär | câre | end | mē | it | īce | pîerce | hot | ōld | sông | fôrk |
| oil | out | up | ūse | rüle | pùll | tûrn | chin | sing | shop | thin | this | |

hw in white; zh in treasure. The symbol ə stands for the unstressed vowel sound in about, taken, pencil, lemon, and circus.

49

astound To surprise very much; amaze; astonish: *The first flight in outer space astounded the whole world.* **as·tound** (ə stound′) *verb*, **astounded, astounding**.

astray Off the right way or path: *The family was sad because their dog had gone astray and gotten lost.* **a·stray** (ə strā′) *adverb*.

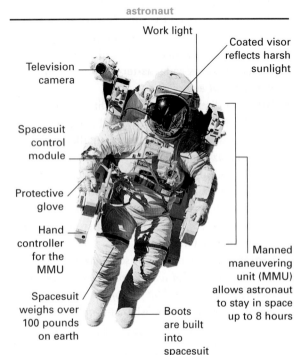

The cowboy sits astride his horse.

astride With one leg on each side of. **a·stride** (ə strīd′) *preposition*.

astrology The study of the influence that the stars and planets are supposed to have on people and events. **as·trol·o·gy** (ə strol′ə jē) *noun*.

astronaut A person trained to fly in a spacecraft: *The astronauts landed safely on the moon.* **as·tro·naut** (as′trə nôt′) *noun, plural* **astronauts**.

astronaut

Work light

Coated visor reflects harsh sunlight

Television camera

Spacesuit control module

Protective glove

Hand controller for the MMU

Spacesuit weighs over 100 pounds on earth

Boots are built into spacesuit

Manned maneuvering unit (MMU) allows astronaut to stay in space up to 8 hours

astronomer A person who works or specializes in astronomy. **as·tron·o·mer** (ə stron′ə mər) *noun, plural* **astronomers**.

astronomical 1. Of or having to do with astronomy: *The spacecraft radioed astronomical information to earth.* 2. Very great or large: *The cost of the yacht was astronomical.* **as·tro·nom·i·cal** (as′trə nom′i kəl) *adjective*.

astronomy The science that deals with the sun, moon, stars, planets, and other heavenly bodies. **as·tron·o·my** (ə stron′ə mē) *noun*.

asylum 1. A place where people who cannot care for themselves receive care: *People who are mentally ill may live in an asylum.* 2. A place of refuge or protection: *A church may be an asylum where criminals are safe from arrest.* 3. Protection given to a refugee: *Some people leave their own country to seek asylum in another country.* **a·sy·lum** (ə sī′ləm) *noun, plural* **asylums**.

at 1. In, on, or by: *I stood at my parents' side. The race started at the top of the hill.* 2. To or toward: *Look at this picture.* 3. In a place or condition of: *The children are at home. The nations were at war.* 4. On or near the time or age of: *We rise at dawn. Some people retire at sixty-five.* 5. In the amount of; for: *The car was sold at a low price.* **at** (at) *preposition*.

ate Past tense of **eat**: *We ate all the pie.* Another word that sounds like this is **eight**. **ate** (āt) *verb*.

atheist A person who does not believe that a god exists. **a·the·ist** (ā′thē ist) *noun, plural* **atheists**. —**atheism** *noun*.

athlete A person who is trained in sports or other exercises that take strength, skill, and speed. Baseball players, hockey players, swimmers, skiers, and runners are athletes. **ath·lete** (ath′lēt) *noun, plural* **athletes**.

athlete's foot An infection of the foot that is caused by a fungus and is marked by blisters that itch.

athletic 1. Of or having to do with an athlete or athletics: *Our school has just bought new athletic equipment.* 2. Active and strong: *My grandparents are very athletic; they love to swim and ice-skate.* **ath·let·ic** (ath let′ik) *adjective*.

athletics Athletic games, sports, or activities:

Athletics *are often an important part of a* *student's education.* **ath·let·ics** (ath let′iks) *plural noun.*

Atlantic The ocean that separates Europe and Africa from North America and South America. This is also called the *Atlantic Ocean. Noun.*
○ Of, on, near, or having to do with the Atlantic Ocean: *We sailed down the **Atlantic** coast of Florida. Adjective.*
At·lan·tic (at lan′tik) *noun; adjective.*

atlas A book of maps: *We took a road **atlas** along when we drove to Canada.* **at·las** (at′ləs) *noun, plural* **atlases.**

WORD HISTORY

In Greek mythology, Atlas was a giant who was made to hold the sky on his shoulders. In the front of early books of maps, there was often a picture of Atlas holding up the sky. So people began to call a book of this kind an atlas.

ATM A computerized banking machine that allows a user to withdraw money, make deposits, and do other tasks. ATM stands for automated teller machine or automatic teller machine. **ATM** *noun,* *plural* **ATMs.**

The **atmosphere** of Jupiter is
thousands of miles thick.

atmosphere 1. The layer of gases that surrounds the Earth. The atmosphere is made up of oxygen, nitrogen, carbon dioxide, and other gases. Outer space lies beyond the Earth's atmosphere. 2. The layer of gases that surrounds any heavenly body:

Scientists do not think people could live in the **atmosphere** *of Mars.* 3. The air in a particular place: *This attic has a hot, stuffy* **atmosphere.** 4. Character or mood: *Our house has a happy* **atmosphere** *at holiday time.* 5. Environment; surroundings: *We moved to the country because we wanted to live in a quiet* **atmosphere.** **at·mos·phere** (at′məs fîr) *noun, plural* **atmospheres.**

atmospheric Of, in, or having to do with the atmosphere: S*evere* **atmospheric** *disturbances were reported by the weather bureau.* **at·mos·pher·ic** (at′məs fer′ik) *adjective.*

atoll A coral island or string of coral islands that surrounds a lagoon. **at·oll** (at′ôl or ə tôl′) *noun, plural* **atolls.**

atom 1. The smallest particle of a chemical element that has all the properties of that element. An atom has a central nucleus of protons and neutrons that is surrounded by electrons. All matter in the universe is made up of atoms. 2. Any very small particle; tiny bit: *There was not an* **atom** *of sense in their solution to the problem.* **at·om** (at′əm) *noun, plural* **atoms.**

atomic 1. Of or having to do with an atom or atoms: *Those scientists are performing* **atomic** *research.* 2. Using atomic energy: *An* **atomic** *submarine can stay underwater for long periods of time.* **a·tom·ic** (ə tom′ik) *adjective.*

atomic bomb A very powerful bomb. Its great force and the radiation it produces come from the energy released by the splitting of atoms. This bomb is also called an *atom bomb.*

atomic energy A term that is sometimes used for **nuclear energy.**

atone To make up for a wrong; make amends: *I atoned for my rude behavior by apologizing to them.* **a·tone** (ə tōn′) *verb,* **atoned, atoning.**

atop On top of: *There were ten candles* **atop**

The butterfly is sipping
nectar from **atop**
the flower.

PRONUNCIATION KEY:
| at | āpe | fär | câre | end | mē | it | īce | pierce | hot | ōld | sông | fôrk |
| oil | out | up | ūse | rüle | pull | tûrn | chin | sing | shop | thin | this | |

hw in white; zh in treasure. The symbol ə stands for the unstressed vowel sound in about, taken, pencil, lemon, and circus.

51

my birthday cake.
a·top (ə top′) *preposition.*

atrium 1. An open
or glass-covered patio
or courtyard inside
a building. 2. One
of the two sections
of the heart that take
in blood from the
veins. **a·tri·um** (ā′trē əm) *noun, plural* **atriums**
or **atria.**

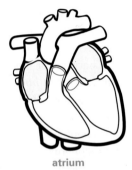
atrium

atrocious 1. Very bad or unpleasant: *Their man-ners are* **atrocious.** *What* **atrocious** *weather we've been having!* 2. Cruel, brutal, or wicked.
a·tro·cious (ə trō′shəs) *adjective.* **a·troc·i·ty** *noun.*

attach 1. To fasten: *You can* **attach** *the sign to the wall with nails.* 2. To add or include at the end: *They* **attached** *their signatures to the document.* 3. To bind by a strong feeling: *I am very* **attached** *to my family.* 4. To think of as belonging; assign: *We* **attach** *great importance to our parents' advice.* **at·tach** (ə tach′) *verb,* **attached, attaching.**

attachment 1. The act of attaching: *The* **attach-ment** *of the wrecked car to the tow truck was difficult.* 2. A strong feeling of affection or devo-tion: *The children had a great* **attachment** *to their dog.* 3. A part or device that is connected to a thing: *The camera has an* **attachment** *for winding the film automatically.* **at·tach·ment** (ə tach′mənt) *noun, plural* **attachments.**

attack 1. To begin to fight against with violence; assault: *The enemy troops* **attacked** *the town at dawn.* 2. To write or speak against: *The news-paper editorial* **attacked** *the mayor's speech.* 3. To begin to work on with energy. *We* **attacked** *the job of setting up the tent.* 4. To act harmfully on: *A plant disease* **attacked** *many of the trees in our yard. Verb.*
○ 1. The act of attacking: *The* **attack** *on the fort came without warning.* 2. A sudden occurrence of sickness or disease: *A doctor was called when my cousin had an* **attack** *of asthma. Noun.*
at·tack (ə tak′) *verb,* **attacked, attacking;** *noun, plural* **attacks.**

attain 1. To get by hard work; achieve: *I* **attained** *my ambition to work on the school newspaper.* 2. To arrive at; reach: *My grandparents have*

attained *the ages of ninety and ninety-one.*
at·tain (ə tān′) *verb,* **attained, attaining.**
—**attainment** *noun.*

attempt To make an effort; try: *The kitten* **attempted** *to follow the squirrel up the tree. Verb.*
○ 1. A try; effort: *We made an* **attempt** *to learn how to ski.* 2. An attack: *The traitor made an* **attempt** *on the monarch's life. Noun.*
at·tempt (ə tempt′) *verb,* **attempted, attempting;** *noun, plural* **attempts.**

attend 1. To be present at: *I have to* **attend** *a club meeting this afternoon.* 2. To be with as a helper or companion: *Three aides* **attended** *the ambas-sador.* 3. To take care of: *Doctors and nurses* **attended** *the victims of the accident.* 4. To listen carefully: **Attend** *to what the doctor tells you.* 5. To devote oneself: **Attend** *to your work.*
at·tend (ə tend′) *verb,* **attended, attending.**

attendance 1. The act of being present: *Your* **attendance** *at band practice was poor last year.* 2. The number of people present: *The* **attendance** *at the baseball game was over 500.* **at·ten·dance** (ə ten′dəns) *noun.*

attendant A person who takes care of someone or provides service to other people: *The* **atten-dant** *at the park showed us where we could rent a canoe.* **at·ten·dant** (ə ten′dənt) *noun, plural* **attendants.**

attention 1. The act or power of watching, listen-ing, or concentrating: *The magician had the chil-dren's* **attention.** *The noise called our* **attention** *to the airplane flying above us.* 2. Careful thought with the intention to act; consideration: *Pollution of our rivers and lakes requires immediate* **atten-tion.** 3. Care, kindness, and affection: *The chil-dren gave their grandparents much* **attention.** 4. **attentions.** Kind, polite, or affectionate acts: *The host's many* **attentions** *made every guest at the party feel welcome.* 5. A military position in which a person stands very straight, with arms at the sides, heels together, and eyes looking ahead: *The troops stood at* **attention** *while waiting for the parade to start.* **at·ten·tion** (ə ten′shən) *noun, plural* **attentions.**

attentive 1. Paying attention: *The audience was* **attentive** *throughout the concert.* 2. Considerate; thoughtful; courteous: *When you have a party, you try to be* **attentive** *to your guests.* **at·ten·tive** (ə ten′tiv) *adjective.*

attest To be the proof of; show clearly: *Your high grades **attest** your good study habits.* **at•test** (ə test′) *verb,* **attested, attesting.**

attic The space just below the roof of a house: *We use our **attic** to store trunks of old clothes.* **at•tic** (at′ik) *noun, plural* **attics.**

These young women are helping each other dress in formal attire.

attire Apparel; clothing: *The queen and king were clothed in royal **attire**. Noun.*
○ To dress; clothe: *The children were **attired** in their best clothes. Verb.*
at•tire (ə tīr′) *noun; verb,* **attired, attiring.**

attitude **1.** A way of thinking, acting, or feeling: *Your **attitude** toward school is more enthusiastic than mine.* **2.** A position of the body: *The body's **attitude** often shows the feelings or thoughts of a person.* **at•ti•tude** (at′i tüd′ *or* at′i tūd′) *noun, plural* **attitudes.**

attorney A lawyer: *An **attorney** presented the case to the judge and jury.* **at•tor•ney** (ə tûr′nē) *noun, plural* **attorneys.**

attract **1.** To cause to come near; draw by physical force: *A magnet will **attract** an iron bar.* **2.** To draw by gaining the attention or admiration of: *The beautiful scenery in these mountains **attracts** many tourists.* **at•tract** (ə trakt′) *verb,* **attracted, attracting.**

attraction **1.** The act or power of attracting: *The **attraction** of the magnet drew the nails across the table.* **2.** A person or thing that attracts: *The clowns were the main **attraction** at the circus.* **at•trac•tion** (ə trak′shən) *noun, plural* **attractions.**

attractive Having a quality that attracts people; appealing; pleasing: *Friendly people are naturally **attractive**.* **at•trac•tive** (ə trak′tiv) *adjective.*

attribute To think of as belonging to or being caused by: *We **attribute** stubbornness to mules. The coach **attributed** the team's victory to training and practice. Verb.*
○ A quality that is thought of as belonging to a person or thing; characteristic: *One of your greatest **attributes** is your kindness. Noun.*
at•trib•ute (ə tri′būt *for verb;* at′rə būt′ *for noun) verb,* **attributed, attributing;** *noun, plural* **attributes.**

auburn A reddish brown color. **au•burn** (ô′bərn) *noun.*

auction A public sale at which things are sold to the person who offers the most money: *My cousin bid five dollars for a rocking chair at the village **auction**. Noun.*
○ To sell at an auction: *We **auctioned** off our old furniture. Verb.*
auc•tion (ôk′shən) *noun, plural* **auctions;** *verb,* **auctioned, auctioning.**

At cattle auctions different types of livestock are sold.

audible Loud enough to be heard: *The music is barely **audible**.* **au•di•ble** (ô′də bəl) *adjective.*

audience **1.** A group of people gathered to hear or see something: *The **audience** applauded at the end of the play.* **2.** All the people who give attention to something: *That television program has a large **audience**.* **3.** A formal meeting with a person of very high rank: *The diplomat was granted*

PRONUNCIATION KEY:

| at | āpe | fär | câre | end | mē | it | īce | pierce | hot | ōld | sông | fôrk |
| oil | out | up | ūse | rüle | pull | tûrn | chin | sing | shop | thin | this | |

hw in white; zh in treasure. The symbol ə stands for the unstressed vowel sound in about, taken, pencil, lemon, and circus.

53

an audience with the king and queen. **au·di·ence** (ô′dē əns) *noun, plural* **audiences.**

audio Of or having to do with sound or how sound is recorded, sent, or received: *I bought new audio equipment because my old stereo no longer worked.* **au·di·o** (ô′dē ō′) *adjective.*

audiobook A recording on cassette tape of someone reading a book aloud. **au·di·o·book** (ô′dē ō bůk′) *noun.*

audiovisual Designed to teach something by means of both sound and pictures: *audiovisual equipment.* **au·di·o·vis·u·al** (ô′dē ō vizh′ü əl) *adjective.*

audition A short performance that demonstrates the ability of an actor, singer, or other performer. *Noun.*

○ To perform or test in an audition: *The young actor audituned for a small role in the play. The conductor auditioned three pianists this afternoon. Verb.*

au·di·tion (ô dish′ən) *noun, plural* **auditions;** *verb,* **auditioned, auditioning.**

Large auditoriums like this one can hold thousands of people.

auditorium A large room or building where people can gather: *The concert will be in the school auditorium.* **au·di·to·ri·um** (ô′di tôr′ē əm) *noun, plural* **auditoriums.**

auditory Having to do with hearing or the organs of hearing. **au·di·to·ry** (ô′di tôr′ē) *adjective.*

Aug. An abbreviation for August.

auger A tool for boring holes in wood. **au·ger** (ô′gər) *noun, plural* **augers.**

augment To make greater; increase: *Some people augment their incomes by working at two jobs.* **aug·ment** (ôg ment′) *verb,* **augmented, augmenting.**

August The eighth month of the year. August has thirty-one days. **Au·gust** (ô′gəst) *noun.*

auk Any of various diving birds that live along northern sea coasts. Auks have webbed feet, short wings that are used as paddles in swimming, and black and white feathers. **auk** (ôk) *noun, plural* **auks.**

aunt 1. The sister of one's mother or father. 2. The wife of one's uncle. **aunt** (ant *or* änt) *noun, plural* **aunts.**

auricle Either of the two upper chambers of the heart. The auricles receive blood from the veins and send it to the ventricles. **au·ri·cle** (ôr′i kəl) *noun, plural* **auricles.**

aurora borealis Shining bands of lights sometimes seen in the sky at night, especially in areas near the North Pole. The lights are caused by particles from the sun that strike the Earth's atmosphere. Another name for this is **northern lights. au·ro·ra bo·re·al·is** (ə rôr′ə bôr′ē al′is).

austere 1. Very stern in looks or behavior. 2. Very simple or plain: *A monk's austere room.* **aus·tere** (ô stîr′) *adjective.* —**austerity** *noun.*

Australia 1. A continent southeast of Asia, between the Indian Ocean and the Pacific Ocean. It is the smallest continent. 2. A country made up of this continent and the island of Tasmania. **Aus·tra·lia** (ô strāl′yə) *noun.*

Australian A person who was born in or is a citizen of Australia. *Noun.*

○ Of or having to do with Australia or its people. *Adjective.*
Aus·tra·lian (ô strāl′yən) *noun, plural*
Australians; *adjective.*

Austria A country in central Europe. **Aus·tri·a** (ôs′trē ə) *noun.*

Austrian A person who was born in or is a citizen of Austria. *Noun.*
○ Of or having to do with Austria or its people. *Adjective.*
Aus·tri·an (ôs′trē ən) *noun, plural* **Austrians;** *adjective.*

authentic **1.** Worthy of belief; reliable; true; correct: *This book gives an* **authentic** *account of the Civil War.* **2.** Being what it appears or claims to be; real; genuine: *These are* **authentic** *signatures of famous people.* **au·then·tic** (ô then′tik) *adjective.*

author A person who has written a book, story, play, article, or other work of literature. **au·thor** (ô′thər) *noun, plural* **authors.**

authoritative **1.** Worthy of belief; reliable: *No one believed the rumor because it did not come from an* **authoritative** *source.* **2.** Showing authority: *The principal has an* **authoritative** *manner.* **au·thor·i·ta·tive** (ə thôr′i tā′tiv) *adjective.*

authority **1.** The power or right to make decisions, command, act, or control: *The captain has* **authority** *over the sailors on a ship.* **2.** A person or group having this power or right: *We reported the car accident to the* **authorities.** **3.** A good source of information or facts: *That professor is an* **authority** *on the life of Abraham Lincoln.* **au·thor·i·ty** (ə thôr′i tē) *noun, plural* **authorities.**

authorize **1.** To give authority to: *My parents* **authorized** *the real estate agent to sell our house.* **2.** To approve officially: *The governor* **authorized** *the building of the new highway.* **au·thor·ize** (ô′thə rīz′) *verb,* **authorized, authorizing.**

auto A short form of the word automobile. **au·to** (ô′tō) *noun, plural* **autos.**

autobiography The story of a person's own life written by that person. **au·to·bi·og·ra·phy** (ô′tə bī og′rə fē) *noun, plural* **autobiographies.**

autograph A person's signature written in that person's own handwriting. *Noun.*

○ To write one's name in one's own handwriting: *Will you* **autograph** *a copy of your book for me? Verb.*
au·to·graph (ô′tə graf′) *noun, plural* **autographs;** *verb,* **autographed, autographing.**

automatic **1.** Operating by itself: *We have an* **automatic** *dishwasher.* **2.** Done without a person's control: *Digestion is an* **automatic** *action of the body.* **au·to·mat·ic** (ô′tə mat′ik) *adjective.*

automation The development and use of machines to do jobs that used to be done by people: *Automobiles are now built by* **automation.** **au·to·ma·tion** (ô′tə mā′shən) *noun.*

automobile A vehicle that usually has four wheels and is powered by an engine that uses gasoline; car. An automobile is used mainly to carry passengers. **au·to·mo·bile** (ô′tə mə bēl′) *noun, plural* **automobiles.**

autopsy A medical examination of a dead body to find the cause of death: **au·top·sy** (ô′top sē) *noun, plural* **autopsies.**

In autumn **the leaves of different trees change to various colors.**

autumn The season of the year coming between summer and winter; fall: *In* **autumn** *the leaves fell from the trees.* **au·tumn** (ô′təm) *noun, plural* **autumns.**

PRONUNCIATION KEY:

| at | āpe | fär | câre | end | mē | it | īce | pierce | hot | ōld | sông | fôrk |
| oil | out | up | ūse | rüle | pu̇ll | tûrn | chin | sing | shop | thin | this | |

hw in white; zh in treasure. The symbol ə stands for the unstressed vowel sound in about, taken, pencil, lemon, and circus.

55

auxiliary **1.** Giving aid or support: *This sailboat has an auxiliary engine in case there is no wind.* **2.** Additional; extra: *The mayor put auxiliary police on duty during the president's visit. Adjective.*
○ A person, group, or thing giving aid or support. *Our town has a firefighters' auxiliary. Noun.* **aux·il·ia·ry** (ôg zil′yə rē) *adjective; noun, plural* **auxiliaries.**

auxiliary verb A verb that helps a main verb to express an action or condition. *Be, have, do, can, must,* and *may* can be used as auxiliary verbs. In the sentence "They must have returned by now," the verbs "must" and "have" are used as auxiliary verbs. An auxiliary verb is also called a helping verb.

available **1.** Possible to get: *There are still a few seats available for the game. Strawberries become available in early summer.* **2.** Ready for use or service: *The telephone is now available.* **a·vail·a·ble** (ə vā′lə bəl) *adjective.*

avalanche The swift, sudden fall of a mass of snow, ice, earth, or rocks down a mountain slope: *The avalanche completely covered the village with mud.* **av·a·lanche** (av′ə lanch′) *noun, plural* **avalanches.**

Ave. An abbreviation for Avenue used in a written address.

avenue A street. Avenues are often wider than other streets. **av·e·nue** (av′ə nū′ *or* av′ə nü′) *noun, plural* **avenues.**

average **1.** A number found by adding two or more quantities together, and then dividing the sum by the number of quantities; mean: *The average of 2, 4, 6, and 8 is 5.* **2.** The usual amount or kind: *This year's rainfall came close to the average. Noun.*
○ **1.** Found by figuring an average: *The average grade on the test was 81.* **2.** Usual; typical; ordinary: *You are of average height and weight. Adjective.*
○ **1.** To find the average of. *I averaged my three bowling scores and got 126.* **2.** To have as an average: *That basketball player averages twenty points a game. Verb.*
av·er·age (av′ər ij *or* av′rij) *noun, plural* **averages;** *adjective; verb,* **averaged, averaging.**

avert **1.** To turn away or aside: *Avert your eyes from the glare of the sun.* **2.** To prevent; avoid:

The driver averted a crash by steering carefully to the side of the road. **a·vert** (ə vûrt′) *verb,* **averted, averting.**

aviation The science or techniques of flying aircraft. **a·vi·a·tion** (ā′vē ā′shən) *noun.*

Military **aviators** made their first appearance in World War I.

aviator A person who flies an airplane or other aircraft; pilot. **a·vi·a·tor** (ā′vē ā′tər) *noun, plural* **aviators.**

avid **1.** Very eager or enthusiastic: *I am an avid fan of mystery novels.* **2.** Having a great desire; greedy: *Some people are so avid for wealth that they commit crimes to get it.* **av·id** (av′id) *adjective.*

avocado A tropical fruit that is shaped like a pear. It has a dark green skin, a large seed, and yellowish green pulp. Avocados grow on trees. **av·o·ca·do** (av′ə kä′dō) *noun, plural* **avocados.**

avoid To keep away from: *We took a back road to avoid the heavy highway traffic.* **a·void** (ə void′) *verb,* **avoided, avoiding.**

await **1.** To wait for: *The parents had long await-ed the day of their children's graduation from college.* **2.** To be ready for; be in store for: *Many changes await you in your new school.* **a·wait** (ə wāt′) *verb,* **awaited, awaiting.**

awake To wake up: *The barking of the dog awoke everyone in the house. Verb.*
○ **1.** Not asleep: *We were awake most of the night because of the noise outside.* **2.** Alert; aware: *Are you awake to the risks in the plan? Adjective.*
a·wake (ə wāk′) *verb,* **awoke** or **awaked, awaking**; *adjective.*

awaken To wake up: *I awakened at dawn.* **a·wak·en** (ə wā′kən) *verb,* **awakened, awakening.**

These athletes have received the award for winning the basketball championship.

award **1.** To give after careful thought: *The judges awarded my dog first prize at the dog show.* **2.** To give because of a legal decision: *The jury awarded money to the people who had been injured in the accident. Verb.*
○ Something that is given after careful thought: *My cousin received the award for writing the best essay. Noun.*
a·ward (ə wôrd′) *verb,* **awarded, awarding**; *noun, plural* **awards.**

aware Knowing or realizing; conscious: *We were not aware that you were planning a party for us.* **a·ware** (ə wâr′) *adjective.*

away **1.** From this or that place: *The frightened rabbit hopped away.* **2.** At a distance: *They stood far away from us.* **3.** In another direction; aside: *I turned away to hide my tears.* **4.** From or out of one's possession or use: *Throw away that old coat.* **5.** At or to an end; out of existence: *The sound of footsteps faded away.* **6.** Without interruption; continuously: *I worked away at my typewriter for two hours. Adverb.*
○ **1.** Distant: *The town is 3 miles away.* **2.** Absent; gone: *My cousin has been away for three weeks. Adjective.*
a·way (ə wā′) *adverb; adjective.*

awe Great wonder, fear, and respect: *They read with awe the news of the astronauts' landing on the moon. Noun.*
○ To fill with awe: *We were awed by the violence of the thunderstorm. Verb.*
awe (ô) *noun; verb,* **awed, awing.**

awesome Causing wonder or fear: *The huge whale was an awesome sight.* **awe·some** (ô′səm) *adjective.*

awful **1.** Causing fear, dread, or awe; terrible: *The earthquake was an awful disaster.* **2.** Very bad: *I thought that movie was awful.* **3.** Very large; great. *A million dollars is an awful lot of money.* **aw·ful** (ô′fəl) *adjective.*

awfully **1.** Very much; badly; terribly: *My knee hurt awfully where I had scraped it.* **2.** Very: *I am awfully glad you won the prize.* **aw·ful·ly** (ô′fə lē or ô′flē) *adverb.*

awhile For a short time: *They rested awhile before playing another game of tennis.* **a·while** (ə hwīl′ or ə wīl′) *adverb.*

awkward **1.** Lacking grace or poise in movement or behavior; clumsy or uncomfortable: *The colt was awkward and had trouble standing up.* **2.** Difficult or embarrassing: *It was an awkward moment when the teacher found out that I hadn't done my homework.* **3.** Difficult to use or handle: *The piano was an awkward piece of furniture to move.* **awk·ward** (ôk′wərd) *adjective.*

PRONUNCIATION KEY:
at | āpe | fär | câre | end | mē | it | īce | pierce | hot | ōld | sông | fôrk
oil | out | up | ūse | rüle | pull | tûrn | chin | sing | shop | thin | this
hw in white; zh in treasure. The symbol ə stands for the unstressed vowel sound in about, taken, pencil, lemon, and circus.

57

awl A pointed tool used for making small holes in leather or wood.
Another word that sounds like this is **all**.
awl (ôl) *noun, plural* **awls**.

This awning provides shade
for shoppers.

awning A cover of canvas, metal, or other material that serves as a small roof over a door or window. An awning is used as a shelter from the sun or rain. **aw·ning** (ô′ning) *noun, plural* **awnings**.

awoke Past tense of awake: *I awoke at seven o'clock this morning.* **a·woke** (ə wōk′) *verb*.

awoken A past participle of awake. **a·wok·en** (ə wō′kən) *verb*.

ax *or* **axe** A tool that has a metal blade attached to a handle. An ax is used for cutting down trees and chopping wood. **ax** (aks) *noun, plural* **axes** (ak′siz).

axis A real or imaginary straight line through the center of an object, around which the object turns: *The earth rotates on its axis once every twenty-four hours.* **ax·is** (ak′sis) *noun, plural* **axes** (ak′sēz).

axle A bar or shaft on which a wheel or pair of wheels turns: *The front axle of our car is broken.* **ax·le** (ak′səl) *noun, plural* **axles**.

aye Yes: *All in favor of the plan say "aye."* *Adverb.*
○ A vote of yes or a person who votes yes. *Noun.*
Other words that sound like this are **eye** and **I**.
aye (ī) *adverb; noun, plural* **ayes**.

AZ Postal abbreviation for Arizona.

azalea A shrub with dark green leaves and clusters of pink, orange, or white flowers. **a·za·lea** (ə zāl′yə) *noun, plural* **azaleas**.

Several species of azaleas are found
in North America and Asia.

WORD HISTORY

The azalea takes its name from a Greek word meaning "dry." It was once thought that azaleas grow best in dry soil.

Aztec A member of a Native American people of central Mexico. The Aztec developed an advanced civilization and controlled an empire in the fourteenth and fifteenth centuries. **Az·tec** (az′tek) *noun, plural* **Aztec** *or* **Aztecs**.

azure A clear blue color; the color of a clear blue sky. *Noun.*
○ Having a clear blue color. *Adjective.*
az·ure (azh′ər) *noun, plural* **azures**; *adjective*.

The letter B has only one sound in English, as in bad and both, but it is sometimes doubled as in rabbit.

The letter B is also silent in some words such as climb, comb, or plumber.

b, B The second letter of the alphabet.
b, B (bē) *noun, plural* **b's, B's.**

baa The sound a sheep makes. *Noun.*
○ To make such a sound. *Verb.*
baa (bä) *noun, plural* **baas;** *verb,* **baaed, baaing.**

babble **1.** To make meaningless sounds: *Babies babble before they learn to talk.* **2.** To talk foolishly; chatter: *The children babbled during lunch.* **3.** To make a low, murmuring sound: *The brook babbled. Verb.*
○ **1.** Confused, meaningless, or unclear sounds. **2.** A low, murmuring sound. *Noun.*
bab·ble (bab'əl) *verb,* **babbled, babbling;** *noun, plural* **babbles.**

babe A baby. **babe** (bāb) *noun, plural* **babes.**

baboon A large monkey with a face like a dog's. Baboons live together in large groups, and they travel great distances in search of food. **ba·boon** (ba bün') *noun, plural* **baboons.**

Africa and the southwestern part of Arabia are home to baboons.

baby **1.** A very young child; infant. **2.** The youngest person in a group: *I am the baby of the family.* **3.** A childish person: *Don't be a baby when you don't get your way. Noun.*
○ **1.** Of or for a baby: *a baby carriage.* **2.** Very young: *Baby bears are called cubs. Adjective.*
○ To treat like a baby: *My parents babied me when I was sick. Verb.*
ba·by (bā'bē) *noun, plural* **babies;** *adjective; verb,* **babied, babying.**

baby boom A great increase in the number of babies born in a country, especially in the United States from 1946 to 1960. **—baby boomer** *noun.*

baby-sit To take care of children while their parents are away. **ba·by-sit** (bā'bē sit') *verb,* **baby-sat** (bā'bē sat'), **baby-sitting. —baby-sitter** *noun.*

baby tooth One of the first set of teeth of infants and baby mammals.

bachelor A man who has not married. **bach·e·lor** (bach'ə lər) *noun, plural* **bachelors.**

back **1.** The part of the human body behind the chest. **2.** The upper part of the body of an animal: *I petted the puppy on its back.* **3.** The part of anything opposite the front: *I signed my name on the back of the check. Noun.*
○ **1.** To move backward: *Back the car out of the garage.* **2.** To help or support: *I'll back you for class president. Verb.*
○ **1.** Behind the front part: *the back door.* **2.** Past; old: *back copies of magazines. Adjective.*
○ **1.** Toward the back; backward: *We moved back to let people on the bus.* **2.** In the place where something used to be: *Put the keys back in your purse.* **3.** In or to a time or place in the past: *That was a while back.* **4.** In reply or in return: *I gave you back your pen. Adverb.*
• **back and forth.** First in one direction and then in the other: *When we read, our eyes move back and forth across the page.*
• **behind one's back.** Without someone's knowledge or approval: *We planned the party behind your back.*

• **in back of.** At the rear of; behind: *There is a porch in back of the house.*

• **to back out** or **to back out of.** To not keep a promise or agreement: *Don't back out on your promise.*

• **to back up. 1.** To move backward in an automobile. **2.** To give support to; back: *Back up your opinions with facts.*
back (bak) *noun, plural* **backs;** *verb,* **backed, backing;** *adjective; adverb.*

backboard The board to which the basket is attached in basketball. **back·board** (bak′bôrd′) *noun, plural* **backboards.**

backbone The column of bones running down the center of the back; spine. People, dogs, birds, fish, frogs, and snakes all have backbones. **back·bone** (bak′bōn′) *noun, plural* **backbones.**

backfire A small but noisy explosion inside a gasoline engine. *Noun.*
○ **1.** To make such a noise: *My old car backfires a lot.* **2.** To go wrong: *Our practical joke backfired. Verb.*
back·fire (bak′fīr′) *noun, plural* **backfires;** *verb,* **backfired, backfiring.**

backgammon A game for two people, played on a special board. The players throw dice to see how they may move their pieces. **back·gam·mon** (bak′gam′ən) *noun.*

The large ship is in the background of this photograph.

background **1.** The part of a picture or scene that seems to be in the distance. **2.** In a design, the empty space around figures or objects: *a bedspread* with yellow flowers on a green **background.** **3.** A person's experience or learning: *Her background is in physics.* **back·ground** (bak′ground′) *noun, plural* **backgrounds.**

backhand A kind of stroke in tennis and other games, made with the back of the hand turned forward. **back·hand** (bak′hand′) *noun, plural* **backhands.**

backhoe A machine for digging that has a bucket with teeth that is pulled down and through the earth. **back·hoe** (bak′ hō′) *noun, plural* **backhoes.**

backpack A bag with straps for the shoulders, used for carrying things on the back. *Noun.*
○ To go hiking or camping while carrying a backpack: *We backpacked through the mountains for a week. Verb.*
back·pack (bak′pak′) *noun, plural* **backpacks;** *verb,* **backpacked, backpacking.**

backstroke A swimming stroke performed by the swimmer on his or her back. **back·stroke** (bak′ strōk′) *noun.*

backward **1.** Toward the back: *I looked backward toward the noise.* **2.** With the back first: *I was walking backward. Adverb.*
○ Toward the back: *a backward glance. Adjective.*
back·ward (bak′wərd) *adverb; adjective.*

backwards Another spelling of the adverb **backward. back·wards** (bak′wərdz) *adverb.*

backyard A yard behind a building. **back·yard** (bak′yärd′) *noun, plural* **backyards.**

bacon Meat from the back and sides of a hog. **ba·con** (bā′kən) *noun.*

bacteria Tiny living cells that can only be seen through a microscope. Some bacteria cause diseases, but others do useful things, like making soil richer. **bac·te·ri·a** (bak tîr′ē ə) *plural noun, singular* **bacterium. —bacterial** *adjective.*

bacterium The singular of bacteria. **bac·te·ri·um** (bak tîr′ē əm) *noun, plural* **bacteria.**

bad **1.** Having little quality or worth: *a bad movie.* **2.** Not good or moral; wrong; evil: *bad thoughts of revenge.* **3.** Having a harmful effect; damaging: *Candy is bad for your teeth.* **4.** Severe or violent: *a bad storm.* **5.** Having errors; incorrect: *bad spelling.* **6.** Not well or happy, especially because of regret; sorry: *I felt bad when my dog died.* **7.** Unpleasant; disagreeable: *bad news.* **8.** Rotten or spoiled: *Milk turns bad if it is not kept cool.*

• **not bad** or **not half bad** or **not so bad.** Fairly

good; acceptable: *This soup is not bad.* **bad** (bad) *adjective*, **worse**, **worst**.

badge Something worn to show that a person belongs to a certain group or has received an honor. **badge** (baj) *noun, plural* **badges**.

Organizations award various types of badges to their members.

badger A furry animal with short legs and long claws. Badgers hunt for food at night and live in holes in the ground, which they dig with their claws. *Noun.*
○ To bother with questions; pester: *I'll keep badgering you until you answer me. Verb.*
badg•er (baj′ər) *noun, plural* **badgers**; *verb*, **badgered**, **badgering**.

badly 1. In a bad way: *They played badly and lost.* 2. Very much: *You badly need new shoes.* **bad•ly** (bad′lē) *adverb*.

badminton A game for two or four players. The players use rackets to hit a small object, called a shuttlecock, back and forth over a high net. **bad•min•ton** (bad′min tən) *noun*.

WORD HISTORY

The game of badminton was named after an English duke's estate where the game was first played.

---

badmouth To say unkind things about someone or something, especially unfairly. **bad•mouth** (bad′mouth′) *verb*, **badmouthed**, **badmouthing**.

baffle To be too confusing for someone to solve or understand: *The message "EM TISIV EMOC" baffled me until I read it from right to left.* **baf•fle** (baf′əl) *verb*, **baffled**, **baffling**.

bag 1. Something made of paper or other soft material, used to hold things. 2. A handbag; purse. 3. A suitcase: *Have you packed your bags for the trip?* **bag** (bag) *noun, plural* **bags**.

bagel A round roll with a hard, shiny crust and a hole in the center. **ba•gel** (bā′gəl) *noun, plural* **bagels**.

baggage The suitcases, trunks, or bags a person takes on a trip. **bag•gage** (bag′ij) *noun*.

baggy Hanging loosely; sagging: *Baggy trousers make you look sloppy.* **bag•gy** (bag′ē) *adjective*, **baggier**, **baggiest**.

bagpipe A musical instrument made of a leather bag and pipes, often played in Scotland and Ireland. A person makes music by blowing air into the bag and then pressing the bag so that the air is forced out through the pipes. **bag•pipe** (bag′pīp′) *noun, plural* **bagpipes**. —**bagpiper** *noun*.

Bagpipes are included in many parades.

bail¹ 1. Money given to a court of law to allow an arrested person to remain out of jail until trial. The money is returned when the person appears for trial. *Noun.*
Another word that sounds like this is **bale**.
• **to bail out.** 1. To arrange for the temporary release of a person who has been arrested: *Who bailed them out of jail?* 2. To help or assist, as by giving money: *When my business failed, my family bailed me out.*
bail (bāl) *noun, plural* **bails**; *verb*, **bailed**, **bailing**.

bail² 1. To take water out of a boat with a scoop: *Bail water out of your boat or it will sink.*
Another word that sounds like this is **bale**.
• **to bail out.** To jump out of an airplane with a

PRONUNCIATION KEY:
at   āpe   fär   câre   end   mē   it   īce   pierce   hot   ōld   sông   fôrk
oil   out   up   ūse   rüle   pull   tûrn   chin   sing   shop   thin   this
hw in white; zh in treasure. The symbol ə stands for the unstressed vowel sound in about, taken, pencil, lemon, and circus.

61

parachute: *The pilot **bailed out** when the plane stalled.*
bail (bāl) *verb,* **bailed, bailing.**

bait **1.** Food put on a hook or in a trap to attract and catch fish or animals. **2.** Something that attracts: *Using the costumes as **bait**, we got the children to come out and play. Noun.*
○ **1.** To put bait on. *I **baited** the fishhook with a worm.* **2.** To tease again and again in a mean way: *The bully **baited** the smaller children by calling them names. Verb.*
bait (bāt) *noun, plural* **baits;** *verb,* **baited, baiting.**

bake **1.** To cook by dry heat in an oven. **2.** To harden or dry by heating: *People **bake** clay pots in ovens called kilns.* **bake** (bāk) *verb,* **baked, baking.** —**baker** *noun.* —**bakery** *noun.*

Many people enjoy baking at home.

baking powder A powder used in baking to make dough or batter rise.

baking soda A white powder used in cooking and as a medicine to soothe an upset stomach.

balance **1.** The condition in which opposite sides or parts are the same in weight, amount, or force: *The two kids kept the seesaw in **balance**.* **2.** A steady, secure position: *I lost my **balance** and fell.* **3.** A scale that looks like a small seesaw and is used for weighing things. The things to be weighed are placed in two flat pans hanging from an upright post: *The chemist weighed the powder on the **balance**.* **4.** The part left over; remainder: *We'll do most of the gardening today, and the **balance** tomorrow. Noun.*
○ **1.** To make equal in weight, amount, or force. *Try to **balance** the two sides of the scale.* **2.** To

put or keep in a steady position: *I can **balance** a book on my head. Verb.*
bal·ance (bal′əns) *noun, plural* **balances;** *verb,* **balanced, balancing.**

balanced diet A diet having all the different kinds of food the body needs to stay healthy and to grow. A balanced diet is made up of the proper amounts of these foods.

balcony **1.** A platform that juts out from the outside of a building and has a low wall or railing on three sides. **2.** An upper floor that juts out into a large room or auditorium: *Theaters often have **balconies** with seats.* **bal·co·ny** (bal′kə nē) *noun, plural* **balconies.**

bald **1.** Having little or no hair on the head. **2.** Without a natural covering: *The **bald** hilltop had no trees or shrubs.* **bald** (bôld) *adjective,* **balder, baldest.**

bald eagle A large eagle of North America. A fully grown bald eagle is brown with a white head, neck, and tail. The bald eagle is the national symbol of the United States.

bale A large bundle of things tied together tightly: *The farmer stored the **bales** of hay in the barn.* Another word that sounds like this is **bail.**
bale (bāl) *noun, plural* **bales.**

balk **1.** To stop short and refuse to go on: *The mule **balked** and would not move.* **2.** To keep from going on; hinder: *The guards **balked** the prisoners' plans to escape.* **balk** (bôk) *verb,* **balked, balking.**

ball¹ **1.** A round object. **2.** A roundish object used in various games: *Baseball and jacks are played with different **balls**.* **3.** A game played with a ball: *Let's play **ball** after school.* **4.** A pitch in baseball that the batter does not swing at and that does not pass over home plate in the area between the batter's knees and shoulders. Another word that sounds like this is **bawl.**
ball (bôl) *noun, plural* **balls.**

ball² A large, formal party for dancing: *My parents met at a costume **ball**.* Another word that sounds like this is **bawl.**
ball (bôl) *noun, plural* **balls.**

ballad A simple poem or song that tells a story: *The singer sang **ballads** about the old West.* **bal·lad** (bal′əd) *noun, plural* **ballads.**

ballast Something heavy carried in the bottom of a ship to keep it steady and balanced in the water.

Sand or rocks are used as ballast. **bal·last** (bal′əst) *noun, plural* **ballasts**.

ball bearing A bearing made up of a number of small metal balls in a groove. A moving part can slide easily on a ball bearing: *The wheels of my bike turn on* **ball bearings**.

ballerina A woman or girl who dances ballet. **bal·le·ri·na** (bal′ə rē′nə) *noun, plural* **ballerinas**.

These dancers are performing in a ballet.

ballet 1. A form of dance in which dancers use certain formal steps and movements. 2. A presentation by a dancer or dancers using ballet steps. A ballet usually tells a story: *In the* **ballet**, *a mechanical doll turned into a real person.* **bal·let** (balā′ or bal′ā) *noun, plural* **ballets**.

ball game A game played with a ball. Baseball is a ball game.

balloon A rubber or plastic bag filled with gas. Small balloons are used as children's toys or for decoration. Large balloons are filled with hot air

This hot air balloon **can carry passengers.**

or very light gas so that they rise and float. *Noun.*
○ To swell out or grow larger like a balloon: *The parachute* **ballooned** *when it opened. Verb.* **bal·loon** (bə lün′) *noun, plural* **balloons**; *verb,* **ballooned, ballooning**.

ballot 1. A printed form used in voting. A voter checks or writes down a choice on a paper ballot or on a ballot that appears on the face of a machine. Later the ballots are counted to see who has won the election. 2. The act or the right of voting *The United States granted women the* **ballot** *in 1920. Noun.*
○ To use a ballot for voting: *The students* **balloted** *to choose a class president. Verb.* **bal·lot** (bal′ət) *noun, plural* **ballots**; *verb,* **balloted, balloting**.

WORD HISTORY

The word ballot comes from an Italian word meaning "little ball." People would cast their votes by putting little balls into a voting box. A white ball meant a vote for the candidate, but a black ball meant a vote against.

ballpoint pen A pen whose point is a small metal ball that rolls the ink from a container inside the pen onto the paper. **ball·point pen** (bôl′point′).

ballroom A large room where dances and parties are given. **ball·room** (bôl′rüm′ *or* bôl′rùm′) *noun, plural* **ballrooms**.

balsa A strong, very light wood from a tropical American tree. Balsa is easy to cut and is used to make airplane and boat models. **bal·sa** (bôl′sə) *noun*.

balsam fir A fragrant evergreen tree that grows in North America. Wood from the balsam fir is used as lumber and to make boxes and pulp. **bal·sam** (bôl′səm).

bamboo A tall plant related to grass. The bamboo has woody stems used to make fishing poles, canes, and furniture. **bam·boo** (bam bü′) *noun, plural* **bamboos**.

ban An official order that forbids something: *a ban on smoking. Noun.*
○ To forbid by law; prohibit: *The government* **banned** *the hunting of deer. Verb.* **ban** (ban) *noun; verb* **banned, banning**.

banana A slightly curved fruit with a thick yellow skin. Bananas grow in bunches on a tree-like

PRONUNCIATION KEY:

| at | āpe | fär | câre | end | mē | it | īce | pierce | hot | ōld | sóng | fôrk |
| oil | out | up | ūse | rüle | pùll | tûrn | chin | sing | shop | thin | this | |

hw in white; zh in treasure. The symbol ə stands for the unstressed vowel sound in about, taken, pencil, lemon, and circus.

plant with very large leaves. **ba·na·na** (bə nan′ə) *noun, plural* **bananas.**

band¹ **1.** A group of people or animals. **2.** A group of musicians playing together. *Noun.*

○ To gather together in a group: *The neighbors banded together to clean up litter in the vacant lot. Verb.*

band (band) *noun, plural* **bands;** *verb,* **banded, banding.**

band² **1.** A strip of cloth or other material: *There were metal bands around the barrel.* **2.** A stripe of color: *The umbrella had wide bands of red and white.* **3.** A range of frequencies in radio broadcasting. *Noun.*

○ To put a band on: *Scientists banded the leg of the pigeon for identification. Verb.*

band (band) *noun, plural* **bands;** *verb,* **banded, banding.**

bandage A strip of cloth used to cover a wound or protect an injured part. *Noun.*

○ To cover or protect with a bandage: *The nurse bandaged my cut. Verb.*

band·age (ban′dij) *noun, plural* **bandages;** *verb,* **bandaged, bandaging.**

A bandanna tied across the face keeps dust out of one's mouth.

bandanna or **bandana** A large handkerchief with a bright pattern on it. **ban·dan·na** or **ban·dan·a** (ban dan′ə) *noun, plural* **bandannas** or **bandanas.**

bandit A robber or outlaw. **ban·dit** (ban′dit) *noun, plural* **bandits.**

bang A sudden, loud noise or blow. *Noun.*

○ **1.** To make a sudden, loud noise. **2.** To strike or hit noisily: *The chairwoman banged the table with a gavel. Verb.*

bang (bang) *noun, plural* **bangs;** *verb,* **banged, banging.**

Bangladesh A country in south-central Asia. **Ban·gla·desh** (bang′glə desh′) *noun.*

bangle A bracelet or anklet worn for decoration. **ban·gle** (bang′gəl) *noun, plural* **bangles.**

bangs Hair cut short and worn over the forehead. **bangs** (bangz) *plural noun.*

banish **1.** To punish someone by making him or her leave a country: *The government banished the enemy spy.* **2.** To send or drive away: *The children banished their friend from the game for cheating.* **ban·ish** (ban′ish) *verb,* **banished, banishing.** **—banishment** *noun.*

banister **1.** A railing along a staircase. **2.** The posts that support this railing. **ban·is·ter** (ban′ə stər) *noun, plural* **banisters.**

banjo A musical instrument with a round body, a long neck, and five strings. **ban·jo** (ban′jō) *noun, plural* **banjos** or **banjoes.**

A banjo is played by plucking the strings with fingers or with a pick.

bank¹ **1.** A long mound of rising ground along a river or lake: *A bank of earth protected the town from flood waters. Noun.*

○ To form into a bank; pile; heap: *The plow banked the snow along the side of the road. Verb.*

bank (bangk) *noun, plural* **banks;** *verb,* **banked, banking.**

bank² **1.** A small, strong container for storing money. **2.** A place of business where people store, borrow, and exchange money. **3.** A place for storing a reserve supply of something: *Hospitals keep blood banks for people who need transfusions. Noun.*

○ To do business with a bank: *We bank at the savings bank around the corner. Verb.*

bank (bangk) *noun, plural* **banks;** *verb,* **banked, banking.** **—banker** *noun.*

bankrupt Not able to pay what one owes: *When the business failed, its owners went bankrupt.* **bankrupt** (bangk′rupt) *adjective;*

verb, **bankrupted, bankrupting.** —**bankruptcy** *noun.*

WORD HISTORY

The word **bankrupt** comes from two Italian words that mean "broken bench." In the Middle Ages in Italy, bankers kept their money in benches. When a banker could not pay people what they were owed, the bench was broken.

Banners are used to decorate and to give messages.

banner A piece of cloth that has a design and sometimes writing on it. *Noun.*
○ Important; outstanding: *With the hedges and roadsides full of raspberries, it was a **banner** season for raspberry pickers. Adjective.*
ban·ner (ban′ər) *noun, plural* **banners**; *adjective.*

banquet A large formal dinner given for a special occasion. **ban·quet** (bang′kwit) *noun, plural* **banquets**.

banshee In Irish folklore, a female spirit that wails to foretell a person's death. **ban·shee** (ban′shē) *noun, plural* **banshees**.

banter Playful teasing or joking: *The interview was full of **banter** between the mayor and the reporters. Noun.*
○ To tease or make jokes in a playful way: *After the game we **bantered** about our mistakes. Verb.*
ban·ter (ban′tər) *noun; verb,* **bantered, bantering.**

baptism A religious ceremony for admitting a person into a Christian church. In this ceremony a person is dipped in water or sprinkled with water. **bap·tism** (bap′tiz əm) *noun, plural* **baptisms**.

baptize To perform the rite of baptism: *The minister **baptized** the baby.* **bap·tize** (bap tīz′ or bap′tīz) *verb,* **baptized, baptizing.**

bar **1.** A long, slender piece of metal, wood, soap, or other solid material: *a **bar** of soap.* **2.** Something that blocks the way: *My small size was a **bar** to becoming a football player.* **3.** A stripe or band of color: *a shirt with **bars** of blue and yellow on it.* **4.** In music, an upright line placed on a staff to mark the division between two equal measures of time. **5.** A unit of music between two bars; measure. **6.** The profession of a lawyer: *The young law student was admitted to the **bar**.* **7.** A place with a counter where foods and drinks are served. *Noun.*
○ **1.** To use a bar to fasten something: *We **barred** the door with a piece of wood.* **2.** To keep out: *Visitors are **barred** from the hospital in the morning. Verb.*
bar (bär) *noun, plural* **bars**; *verb,* **barred, barring.**

barb A sharp point that sticks out from something else: *The **barb** of the fishhook caught in the fish's mouth.* **barb** (bärb) *noun, plural* **barbs**.

barbarian A person who belongs to a tribe or a people that is savage or uncivilized. **bar·bar·i·an** (bär bâr′ē ən) *noun, plural* **barbarians**.

barbecue **1.** A meal cooked outdoors over an open fire. **2.** A grill or small fireplace that uses gas or charcoal for fuel. It is used for cooking food outdoors. *Noun.*
○ To cook a meal outdoors over an open fire. *Verb.*
bar·be·cue (bär′bi kū′) *noun, plural* **barbecues**; *verb,* **barbecued, barbecuing.**

barbed wire Wire with barbs attached. It is used in fences. **barbed wire** (bärbd).

barber A person whose work is cutting hair. **bar·ber** (bär′bər) *noun, plural* **barbers**.

bar code A band of thick and thin black bars on a white background, printed on items sold in a store. The bars are scanned

The barbed wire used for fencing in land was important in settling the West.

PRONUNCIATION KEY:

| at | āpe | fär | câre | end | mē | it | īce | pierce | hot | ōld | sông | fôrk |
| oil | out | up | ūse | rüle | pull | tûrn | chin | sing | shop | thin | this | |

hw in white; zh in treasure. The symbol ə stands for the unstressed vowel sound in about, taken, pencil, lemon, and circus.

65

by a computer that lists the price and other information about the item sold.

bare 1. Without covering or clothing; naked: *We went walking in our* **bare** *feet.* 2. Empty: *The refrigerator was* **bare**. 3. Just enough; mere: *The campers brought only the* **bare** *necessities on their trip. Adjective.*
○ To uncover: *The dog* **bared** *its teeth. Verb.*
Another word that sounds like this is **bear**.
bare (bâr) *adjective,* **barer**, **barest**; *verb,* **bared**, **baring**.

bareback On the back of a horse without a saddle. **bare·back** (bâr′bak′) *adjective; adverb.*

barefoot Having the feet bare. **bare·foot** (bâr′fŏt′) *adjective; adverb.*

barely Only just; scarcely: *There was* **barely** *enough food to go around.* **bare·ly** (bâr′lē) *adverb.*

bargain 1. Something offered for sale or bought at a low price. 2. An agreement: *We made a* **bargain** *that I would wash the dishes and you dry them. Noun.*
○ To talk over the price of a sale or the terms of an agreement: *I* **bargained** *with the salesperson to get a good price on the bicycle. Verb.*
bar·gain (bär′gin) *noun, plural* **bargains**; *verb,* **bargained**, **bargaining**.

Barges are used to carry freight on canals and rivers.

barge A boat with a flat bottom, used to carry freight on canals and rivers. **barge** (bärj) *noun, plural* **barges**.

bar graph A kind of graph that displays information by lengths of parallel rectangular bars.

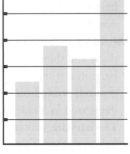
Bar graph

baritone 1. A man's singing voice that is lower than tenor and higher than bass. 2. A singer with such a voice. **bar·i·tone** (bar′i tōn′) *noun, plural* **baritones**.

WORD HISTORY

The word **baritone** comes from the Italian name for this singing voice. The Italian word comes from two Greek words meaning "deep" and "tone."

---

barium A soft, silver-colored metal. Barium is a chemical element. Some compounds of barium are used as white pigments for paints and ceramics. One compound of barium absorbs X rays. Doctors give this compound to patients whose digestive systems will be examined by X rays. **bar·i·um** (bar′ē əm) *noun.*

bark¹ The outer covering of the outside of a tree. Bark is usually rough and dark in color. *Noun.*
○ To scrape or rub the skin off: *If you climb that tree in shorts, you might* **bark** *your legs. Verb.*
bark (bärk) *noun, plural* **barks**; *verb,* **barked**, **barking**.

bark² The short, loud sound that a dog makes. *Noun.*
○ 1. To make this sound. 2. To speak loudly and sharply: *The sheriff* **barked** *"Hands up!" at the outlaw. Verb.*
bark (bärk) *noun, plural* **barks**; *verb,* **barked**, **barking**.

barley The grain of a plant that is like grass. Barley is used as animal feed, in cooking, and to make malt. **bar·ley** (bär′lē) *noun.*

bar mitzvah A religious ceremony and celebration taking place around an Jewish boy's 13th birthday and marking him as an adult Jew. **bar mitz·vah** (bär mits′və) *noun, plural* **bar mitzvahs**.

barn A building on a farm used to store hay and grain, and to house animals. **barn** (bärn) *noun, plural* **barns**.

barnacle Any of a group of small, saltwater shellfish. Barnacles attach themselves to animals, rocks, ship bottoms, and other objects in

Farm machinery is housed in a barn.

the water. Some barnacles can be eaten.
bar·na·cle (bär′nə kəl) *noun, plural* **barnacles**.

barnyard An area around a barn that is surrounded by a fence. **barn·yard** (bärn′yärd′) *noun, plural* **barnyards**.

barometer An instrument for measuring the pressure of the atmosphere, used to forecast changes in the weather. **ba·rom·e·ter** (bə rom′i tər) *noun, plural* **barometers**.

baron A nobleman of the lowest rank.
Another word that sounds like this is **barren**.
bar·on (bar′ən) *noun, plural* **barons**.

baroness A noblewoman of the lowest rank.
bar·on·ess (bar′ə nis) *noun, plural* **baronesses**.

barracks The building or buildings where soldiers live: *The barracks are inspected every week.* The word barracks may be used with a singular or plural verb. **bar·racks** (bar′əks) *plural noun*.

barracuda A fierce fish that lives in warm seas and has a long, narrow body and a large mouth with sharp teeth. **bar·ra·cu·da** (bar′ə kü′də) *noun, plural* **barracuda** *or* **barracudas**.

barrage A heavy amount of rocket or gun fire aimed at an area: *The barrage kept the enemy from the town.* **bar·rage** (bə räzh′) *noun, plural* **barrages**.

barrel 1. A large, round, wooden container with curved sides. 2. A metal tube in a gun that is the part through which the bullet passes when fired. **bar·rel** (bar′əl) *noun, plural* **barrels**.

The metal straps around a barrel helps it hold in a heavy load.

barren Not able to produce anything: *No plants could grow in the barren soil.*
Another word that sounds like this is **baron**.
bar·ren (bar′ən) *adjective;* **barrenness** *noun*.

barrette A small clasp used to hold hair in place. **bar·rette** (bə ret′) *noun, plural* **barrettes**.

barricade A structure put up quickly to block the way or for protection: *The police set up barricades along the street before the parade.*
○ To block the way with a barricade. *Verb.*
bar·ri·cade (bar′i kād′) *noun, plural* **barricades;** *verb,* **barricaded, barricading**.

barrier Something that blocks the way: *The fallen tree was a barrier to traffic on the road.* **bar·ri·er** (bar′ē ər) *noun, plural* **barriers**.

barrier island A long, narrow island that lies parallel and close to the mainland, such as Fire Island, off the coast of Long Island, NY, and Cape Hatteras National Seashore, off the coast of North Carolina.

barrio In a city of the United States, a district where Spanish is the main language spoken. **bar·ri·o** (bär′ē ō *or* bar′ē ō) *noun, plural* **barrios**.

barter To trade things for other things without using money: *The pioneers bartered grain for blankets with the natives. Verb.*
○ The trading of goods or services without the use of money: *Among early settlers in this country much business was carried on by barter. Noun.*
bar·ter (bär′tər) *verb,* **bartered, bartering;** *noun,* **barter**.

basalt A kind of volcanic rock that is hard, heavy, dark, and glassy in appearance. **ba·salt** (bə sôlt′ *or* bā′ sôlt′) *noun.* —**basaltic** *adjective.*

base[1] 1. The part that something stands on; the lowest part: *the base of a mountain.* 2. The main part of something: *The soup has a chicken base.* 3. A starting place: *The airplanes returned to base.* 4. One of the four corners of a baseball diamond: *The batter reached first base.* 5. A chemical that joins with an acid to form a salt, and will cause red litmus paper to turn blue. *Noun.*
○ To use something as a base for something else: *Writers often base stories on their own experiences. Verb.*
Another word that sounds like this is **bass**.
base (bās) *noun, plural* **bases** (bā′siz); *verb,* **based, basing**.

PRONUNCIATION KEY:
at āpe fär câre end mē it īce pierce hot ōld sông fôrk
oil out up ūse rüle pull tûrn chin sing shop thin this
hw in white; zh in treasure. The symbol ə stands for the unstressed vowel sound in about, taken, pencil, lemon, and circus.

67

base²   **1.** Not brave or honorable; cowardly or bad: *Telling lies was a **base** thing to do.* **2.** Low in value when compared with something else: *Iron is a **base** metal; gold is a precious metal.* Another word that sounds like this is **bass**. **base** (bās) *adjective*, **baser**, **basest**.

baseball   **1.** A game played with a ball and bat by two teams of nine players each. Baseball is played on a field with four bases that form a diamond. To score a run, a player on one team must reach home base by touching first, second, and third bases before that team is put out. Each team is allowed three outs in an inning, and a game is made up of nine innings. **2.** The ball used in this game. **base·ball** (bās′bôl′) *noun, plural* **baseballs**.

basement   The lowest floor of a building, below or partly below the ground. **base·ment** (bās′mənt) *noun, plural* **basements**.

bashful   Shy around people: *The **bashful** child hid behind the chair.* **bash·ful** (bash′fəl) *adjective*. —**bashfully** *adverb* —**bashfulness** *noun*.

basic   Forming the most important part; fundamental. **ba·sic** (bā′sik) *adjective.* —**basically** *adverb*.

BASIC   A computer language simple enough for beginners to use to write programs. **BA·SIC** (bā′sik) *noun*.

Boats are well protected inside a basin.

basin   **1.** A bowl for holding liquids: *Fill the **basin** with water.* **2.** An enclosed or sheltered area containing water: *The harbor has a boat **basin**.* **3.** All the land drained by a river and by all the streams flowing into the river: *Iowa, Missouri, and Illinois are all in the **basin** of the Mississippi River.* **ba·sin** (bā′sin) *noun, plural* **basins**.

basis   The part that something rests or depends on; foundation: *The idea that toads give you warts has no **basis** in fact.* **ba·sis** (bā′sis) *noun, plural* **bases** (bā′sēz).

bask   To lie in and enjoy a pleasant warmth: *The cat **basked** in the sun.* **bask** (bask) *verb*, **basked**, **basking**.

basket   **1.** A container woven from twigs, straw, or other material. **2.** A metal hoop with a net hanging from it, used in basketball. **bas·ket** (bas′kit) *noun, plural* **baskets**.

Weaving baskets is an ancient activity.

basketball   **1.** A game played with an inflated ball on a court by two teams of five players each. To score, a player must throw the ball through a raised basket at the opponent's end of the court. **2.** The ball used in this game. **bas·ket·ball** (bas′kit bôl′) *noun, plural* **basketballs**.

bass¹   **1.** The lowest man's singing voice. **2.** A singer who has such a voice. **3.** A musical instrument that has a similar range. Another word that sounds like this is **base**. **bass** (bās) *noun, plural* **basses**.

bass²   Any of a number of North American food fish found in streams and lakes, and in the sea. **bass** (bas) *noun, plural* **bass** or **basses**.

bass drum   A very large drum that gives a deep, booming sound when it is struck. **bass drum** (bās).

bass fiddle   Another name for a **bass viol**.

bassoon   A musical instrument that makes a low sound when it is played. The bassoon has a long, straight, wooden body attached to a smaller, curved, metal tube. It is played by blowing into the metal tube and pressing holes and keys on the body. **bas·soon** (bə sün′) *noun, plural* **bassoons**.

bass viol   The largest musical instrument that has strings. It gives a very low sound when played. The bass viol is shaped like a violin, but it is played standing upright on the floor. The musician plays a bass viol with a bow or by plucking with the fingers. **bass vi·ol** (bās vī′əl).

baste¹ To put melted butter or other liquid on food to keep it moist while it is roasting: *Use the brush to **baste** the chicken.* **baste** (bāst) *verb,* **basted, basting.**

baste² To sew with long, loose stitches: *Baste the seam of the dress in place before sewing it on the sewing machine.* **baste** (bāst) *verb,* **basted, basting.**

bat¹ A strong wooden stick or club, used to hit the ball in baseball and softball. *Noun.*
○ To hit the ball with a bat. *Verb.*
• **at bat.** Having a turn to hit the ball in a baseball or softball game: *The visiting team is **at bat** first.*
bat (bat) *noun, plural* **bats;** *verb,* **batted, batting.**

bat² A small, furry animal that flies. It has a body like a mouse and wings of thin skin. **bat** (bat) *noun, plural* **bats.**

batch A group of things prepared or gathered together: *a **batch** of muffins.* **batch** (bach) *noun, plural* **batches.**

bath 1. A washing of something in water: *We gave the dog a **bath**.* 2. The water used for bathing: *The **bath** is too hot.* 3. A place or room for bathing; bathroom: *The house has two bedrooms and one **bath**.* **bath** (bath) *noun, plural* **baths** (ba<u>th</u>z *or* baths).

bathe 1. To wash something in water: *I **bathe** every night.* 2. To go swimming: *The children liked to **bathe** in the lake.* 3. To seem to cover as if with a liquid: *Sunlight **bathes** our bedroom in the morning.* **bathe** (bā<u>th</u>) *verb,* **bathed, bathing.**

bathing suit A piece of clothing worn while swimming.

bathrobe A loose piece of clothing similar to a coat, worn before and after bathing or when relaxing. **bath•robe** (bath′rōb′) *noun, plural* **bathrobes.**

bathroom A room with a sink and a toilet, and often a bathtub or shower. **bath•room** (bath′rüm′ *or* bath′rŭm′) *noun, plural* **bathrooms.**

bathtub A large tub to bathe in. **bath•tub** (bath′tub′) *noun, plural* **bathtubs.**

bat mitzvah A religious ceremony and celebration taking place around a Jewish girl's 13th birthday and marking her as an adult Jew. **bat mitz•vah** (bôt mits′ və) *noun. plural* **bat mitzvahs.**

baton A stick or rod: *The conductor used a **baton** to direct the orchestra.* **ba•ton** (bə ton′) *noun, plural* **batons.**

A conductor keeps time to the music with his baton.

battalion A large section of an army, made up of several companies. **bat•tal•ion** (bə tal′yən) *noun, plural* **battalions.**

batter¹ To hit over and over again with heavy blows: *The high waves **battered** the small boat to pieces.* **bat•ter** (bat′ər) *verb,* **battered, battering.**

batter² A mixture of flour, milk or water, and other things. Batter is fried or baked to make pancakes, biscuits, or cakes. **bat•ter** (bat′ər) *noun, plural* **batters.**

batter³ A person whose turn it is to bat in a game of baseball or softball. **bat•ter** (bat′ər) *noun, plural* **batters.**

battering ram A heavy beam once used in war to batter down walls or gates.

battery 1. A device that produces an electric current by chemical changes in the materials inside it: *Batteries make flashlights work.* 2. A group of things that are alike or that work together: *A **battery** of microphones stood in front of the mayor.* **bat•ter•y** (bat′ə rē) *noun, plural* **batteries.**

battle 1. A fight between two armed persons or groups. Battles happen during wars: *The two armies fought a **battle**.* 2. A long, hard effort or contest; struggle: *Life in the Arctic is a constant **battle** against the cold. Noun.*
○ To fight or struggle: *The armies **battled** for control of the city. Verb.*

This painting shows soldiers engaged in a Civil War battle.

bat•tle (bat′əl) *noun, plural* **battles;** *verb,* **battled, battling.**

battlefield A place where a battle was fought or is being fought. **bat•tle•field** (bat′əl fēld′) *noun, plural* **battlefields.**

PRONUNCIATION KEY:
| at | āpe | fär | câre | end | mē | it | īce | pîerce | hot | ōld | sông | fôrk |
| oil | out | up | ūse | rüle | pull | tûrn | chin | sing | shop | thin | <u>th</u>is | |
hw in white; zh in treasure. The symbol ə stands for the unstressed vowel sound in about, taken, pencil, lemon, and circus.

69

battleground A battlefield. **bat·tle·ground**
(bat′əl ground′) *noun, plural* **battlegrounds**.

battlement A low wall along the top of a fort or
tower. A battlement has a series of openings for
soldiers to shoot through. **bat·tle·ment**
(bat′əl mənt) *noun, plural* **battlements**.

battleship A large warship with very powerful
guns and thick, heavy armor. **bat·tle·ship**
(bat′əl ship′) *noun, plural* **battleships**.

bawl To cry or shout loudly. *Verb.*
○ A loud cry or shout. *Noun.*
Another word that sounds like this is **ball**.
• **to bawl out**. To scold loudly: *Our neighbor
bawled us out for making so much noise.*
bawl (bôl) *verb*, **bawled, bawling**; *noun*.

Bays **are often used for
boating and fishing.**

bay¹ A part of an ocean or lake partly enclosed by
the coastline. **bay** (bā) *noun, plural* **bays**.

bay² The deep, long barking or howling of a
dog. **bay** (bā) *noun, plural* **bays**; *verb*, **bayed,
baying**.

bayonet A large knife that fits on the end of a
rifle, used to stab an opponent in close fighting.
bay·o·net (bā′ə nit *or* bā′ə net′) *noun, plural*
bayonets.

bayou A stream that flows slowly through a
swamp or marsh. Bayous are found in the southern United States. **bay·ou** (bī′ü *or* bī′ō) *noun,
plural* **bayous**.

bazaar 1. A market made up of rows of small
shops or stalls. 2. A sale of different things for
some special purpose: *We baked a carrot cake
for the church bazaar last week.* **ba·zaar** (bə zär′)
noun, plural **bazaars**.

BC Postal abbreviation for British Columbia.

B.C. An abbreviation for *before Christ*. It is
used in giving dates before the birth of Jesus
Christ. 100 *B.C.* means 100 years before the birth
of Jesus.

be 1. To have reality; exist: *There is one apple left.*
2. To take place; happen: *My birthday was last
week.* 3. To occupy a place or situation; lie:
A caterpillar was in the jar. 4. To come or go:
Have you ever been to California? 5. To stay or
continue: *I have been in the house all day.*
6. A linking verb used to join the subject of a sentence and a word or words that tell something
about the subject: *That house is the largest one in
town.* 7. An auxiliary verb used to form special
verb tenses. When *be* is used as an auxiliary
verb, the main verb is a present participle or a
past participle: *We are studying for a test.
The child was lifted high in the air.*
Another word that sounds like this is **bee**.
be (bē) *verb*.

beach The land along the edge of a body of water.
A beach is covered with sand or pebbles. *Noun.*
○ To run a boat onto a beach: *They beached the
sailboat. Verb.*
Another word that sounds like this is **beech**.
beach (bēch) *noun, plural* **beaches**; *verb*,
beached, beaching.

This beach **is located between the ocean
and sand dunes.**

beacon A light or other signal that warns or
guides ships or aircraft. **bea·con** (bē′kən) *noun,
plural* **beacons**.

bead 1. A small, round piece of glass, wood, or
plastic that has a hole through it. Beads are often
strung together on a wire or string. 2. Any small,
round thing: *beads of sweat. Noun.*
○ To decorate with beads. *Verb.*

bead (bēd) *noun, plural* **beads**; *verb,* **beaded, beading.**

WORD HISTORY

In Middle English, the word bead meant "a prayer." During the Middle Ages, people counted their prayers on small beads that were strung together. Later the word bead lost the meaning "prayer" and became the word used for these small rounded pieces of bone or wood.

---

beagle A small dog with short legs, a smooth coat, and drooping ears. Beagles are kept as pets and also are used to hunt small animals. **bea·gle** (bē′gəl) *noun, plural* **beagles.**

beak The hard, projecting mouth part of a bird or a turtle: *Hawks have sharp, hooked beaks.* **beak** (bēk) *noun, plural* **beaks.**

beaker A glass container with a lip shaped to make pouring easier, used in laboratories to hold liquids or chemicals. **beak·er** (bē′kər) *noun, plural* **beakers.**

beam **1.** A long, strong piece of wood or metal, used in building to support floors or ceilings. **2.** A narrow ray of light: *Beams of sunlight came through the window. Noun.*
○ **1.** To shine brightly: *The sun beamed down on the field.* **2.** To smile happily. *Verb.*
beam (bēm) *noun, plural* **beams**; *verb,* **beamed, beaming.**

bean **1.** A pod or seed eaten as a vegetable. There are many kinds of beans, including the lima bean, string bean, and kidney bean. **2.** Any seed that looks like a bean: *coffee beans. Noun.*
○ To hit on the head with something thrown, such as a pitched baseball: *I wasn't paying attention and I got beaned by the pop fly. Verb.*
bean (bēn) *noun, plural* **beans**; *verb,* **beaned, beaning.**

bear¹ **1.** To hold up; support or carry: *Don't climb that tree; its branches won't bear your weight.* **2.** To produce offspring: *The peach tree bears fruit.* **3.** To put up with patiently; stand: *I cannot bear being teased.* **4.** To have as a visible mark or feature; show: *You bear a resemblance to your father.* Another word that sounds like this is **bare.**

• **to bear down.** To press or weigh down.

• **to bear with.** To be patient toward; tolerate: *Please bear with me today if I seem in a bad mood.*
bear (bâr) *verb,* **bore, borne** *or* **born, bearing.**

bear² A large, heavy animal with thick, shaggy fur. A bear has sharp claws and a very short tail. There are many kinds of bears, including the black bear, brown bear, grizzly bear, and the polar bear. Another word that sounds like this is **bare.**
bear (bâr) *noun, plural* **bears.**

**Most bears have one cub;
this one has twins.**

beard **1.** The hair that grows on a man's face. **2.** A growth of hair that is like a beard: *That goat has a beard on its chin.* **beard** (bîrd) *noun, plural* **beards.**

bearing **1.** The way that a person walks, stands, or acts. **2.** Connection in thought: *That remark has no bearing on our conversation.* **3. bearings.** Knowledge of one's position or direction: *I lost my bearings in the woods.* **4.** A part of a machine that holds a moving part and allows it to move with less friction. **bear·ing** (bâr′ing) *noun, plural* **bearings.**

beast **1.** Any animal that has four feet: *At the zoo we saw tigers, elephants, and other beasts of the jungle.* **2.** A coarse or cruel person. **beast** (bēst) *noun, plural* **beasts.**

beat **1.** To hit again and again; pound. **2.** To do better than; defeat: *My friend beat me at checkers.* **3.** To thump or throb: *You could feel the kitten's heart beat.* **4.** To move up and down; flap: *The eagle beat its wings.* **5.** To stir or mix with force: *I beat three eggs for the omelet. Verb.*
○ **1.** A blow made over and over again: *the steady beat of the hammer.* **2.** A pounding sound, rhythm, or sensation: *The dance music had a*

PRONUNCIATION KEY:
at ape far câre end mē it īce pierce hot old song fôrk
oil out up ūse rūle pull tûrn chin sing shop thin this
hw in white; zh in treasure. The symbol ə stands for the unstressed vowel sound in about, taken, pencil, lemon, and circus.

71

loud *beat*. **3.** A regular route or round: *We saw a police officer patrolling the beat.* **4.** The basic unit of time in music: *There are three beats to a measure in this waltz. Noun.*

Another word that sounds like this is **beet**.
beat (bēt) *verb,* **beat, beaten** *or* **beat, beating;** *noun, plural* **beats.**

beaten Past participle of **beat.** *Verb.*
○ **1.** Worn by use: *a beaten path through the woods.* **2.** Defeated: *a sad and beaten football team. Adjective.* **beat·en** (bē′tən) *verb; adjective.*

beautiful Pleasing to look at, hear, or think about: *There are beautiful paintings at the museum. The band played some beautiful music. We had beautiful weather for the picnic.* **beau·ti·ful** (bū′tə fəl) *adjective.*

beautify To make beautiful: *We beautified the yard with flowers and shrubs.* **beautify** (bū′tē fī) *verb,* **beautified, beautifying.**

beauty **1.** A quality that makes a person or thing pleasing to look at, hear, or think about: *The garden is a place of beauty.* **2.** A person or thing that is beautiful: *That bicycle is a beauty.* **beau·ty** (bū′tē) *noun, plural* **beauties. beau·ti·ful** (bū′tə fəl) *adjective.* —**beautifully** *adverb.*

SYNONYMS

beautiful, handsome, lovely, pretty
The snow-capped mountains are a beautiful sight. The prince and princess make a handsome couple. She has a lovely, clear singing voice. Violets and daisies make a pretty bouquet.

---

beaver A furry, brown rodent with a broad, flat tail and webbed hind feet to help it swim. The beaver lives in or near the water in a house built of branches, stones, and mud. It can build dams from these same materials to keep the water around its house. Most beavers live in North America. **bea·ver** (bē′vər) *noun, plural* **beavers.**

became Past tense of **become. be·came** (bi kām′) *verb.*

because For the reason that: *You're cold because you did not wear your sweater.*
• **because of.** On account of: *They were late because of a flat tire.*
be·cause (bi kôz′) *conjunction.*

beckon To make a sign or signal by moving the hand or head: *I beckoned to my friends to come closer.* **beck·on** (bek′ən) *verb,* **beckoned, beckoning.**

become **1.** To grow to be; come to be: *Tadpoles become frogs.* **2.** To look good on; flatter; suit: *That blue shirt becomes you.*
• **to become of.** To happen to: *What has become of my pencil?*
be·come (bi kum′) *verb,* **became, become, becoming.**

becoming Looking good on; flattering: *Green is becoming to you.* **be·com·ing** (bi kum′ing) *adjective.*

bed **1.** Something used to sleep or rest on. **2.** A piece of ground used to grow plants in: *a flower bed.* **3.** The ground at the bottom of a river, lake, or other body of water: *The stream had a bed of sand and pebbles.* **4.** A foundation or support: *The road was built on a bed of gravel. Noun.*
○ To give a place to sleep to. *Verb.*
bed (bed) *noun, plural* **beds;** *verb,* **bedded, bedding.**

bedding Sheets, blankets, and other coverings used on a bed: *Extra bedding is kept in the hall closet.* **bed·ding** (bed′ing) *noun.*

bedpan A pan used as a toilet by a person who cannot get out of bed. **bed·pan** (bed′pan′) *noun, plural* **bedpans.**

bedraggled Wet, limp, and dirty: *We found a bedraggled kitten under the porch.* **be·drag·gled** (bi drag′əld) *adjective.*

bedrock Solid, unbroken rock beneath the soil or looser rock. **bed·rock** (bed′rok′) *noun.*

bedroom A room for sleeping. **bed·room** (bed′rüm′ *or* bed′rùm′) *noun, plural* **bedrooms.**

bedside The space beside a bed. **bed·side** (bed′sīd′) *noun, plural* **bedsides.**

bedspread A top cover for a bed. **bed·spread** (bed′spred′) *noun, plural* **bedspreads.**

bedtime The time at which a person goes to bed. **bed·time** (bed′tīm′) *noun, plural* **bedtimes.**

bee **1.** An insect that has a thick, hairy body, four wings, and sometimes a stinger. A bee feeds on nectar and pollen. Some bees live in colonies and make honey and beeswax. **2.** A gathering of people to work on something together or to have a contest: *a spelling bee.*
Another word that sounds like this is **be**.
bee (bē) *noun, plural* **bees.**

beech A tree that has smooth, light gray bark and small, sweet nuts.
Another word that sounds like this is **beach**.
beech (bēch) *noun, plural* **beeches.**

beef The meat of a steer, cow, or bull. **beef** (bēf) *noun.*

beefsteak A slice of beef to be broiled or fried. **beef·steak** (bēf'stāk') *noun, plural* **beefsteaks.**

Beehives in man-made frames like this hold a lot of honey.

beehive A nest or house that bees live in. **bee·hive** (bē'hīv') *noun, plural* **beehives.**

been Past participle of **be.**
Another word that sounds like this is **bin.**
been (bin) *verb.*

beep A short sound, as from a horn or an electronic device, that signals or warns. *Noun.*
beep (bēp) *noun, plural* **beeps;** *verb,* **beeped, beeping. —beep·er** *noun.*

beer An alcoholic drink made from specially treated grains, called *malt,* and the bud of a certain plant, called *hops.* **beer** (bîr) *noun, plural* **beers.**

beeswax The yellow wax given out by honeybees and used by them to make their honeycombs. **bees·wax** (bēz'waks') *noun.*

beet A plant with a thick, round, fleshy root. The leaves grow on long stalks from the top of the root. The leaves and roots are cooked and eaten as vegetables.
Another word that sounds like this is **beat.**
beet (bēt) *noun, plural* **beets.**

beetle An insect with hard front wings that cover the thin hind wings when they are folded. Beetles have chewing mouth parts. **bee·tle** (bē'təl) *noun, plural* **beetles.**

befall To happen to or happen: *We were sad that misfortune had befallen our friends.* **be·fall** (bi fôl') *verb,* **befell** (bi fel'), **befallen, befalling.**

before 1. In front of; ahead of: *We arrived before three o'clock.* 2. In the presence of: *The criminals stood before the judge. Preposition.*
○ 1. At an earlier time; previously: *I've seen them before.* 2. In front; in advance: *Some soldiers went on before to scout. Adverb.*
○ 1. Earlier than the time when: *It grew dark before the children finished the game.* 2. Rather than; sooner than: *I would beg before I would steal. Conjunction.*
be·fore (bi fôr') *preposition; adverb; conjunction.*

beforehand Ahead of time: *Let's find out beforehand what we're having for dinner.* **be·fore·hand** (bi fôr'hand') **adverb.**

befriend To become a friend to: *We befriended our new neighbors.* **be·friend** (bi frend') *verb,* **befriended, befriending.**

beg 1. To ask in a humble way: *The late guest begged to be excused.* 2. To ask in an eager or insisting way; plead: *The child begged to go to the rodeo.* 3. To ask for money or food as charity. **beg** (beg) *verb,* **begged, begging.**

began Past tense of **begin. be·gan** (bi gan') *verb.*

beggar A person who asks others for money, food, or clothes in order to live. **beg·gar** (beg'ər) *noun, plural* **beggars.**

begin 1. To do the first part of something; make a start: *Begin your homework now.* 2. To come into being; start: *Spring begins in March.* **be·gin** (bi gin') *verb,* **began, begun, beginning. —be·gin·ner** *noun.*

begonia A tropical plant with flowers that are white, yellow, red, purple, or pink. **be·gon·ia** (bi gōn'yə) *noun, plural* **begonias.**

begun Past participle of **begin. be·gun** (bi gun') *verb.*

behalf 1. In behalf of. For the benefit or good of; for: *The school held a fair in behalf of the town hospital.* 2. On behalf of. As a representative of: *The class president spoke on behalf of the whole class.* **be·half** (bi haf') *noun.*

behave 1. To do things in a certain way; act: *You behaved bravely after you hurt your knee.* 2. To act in a good way: *The children behaved*

PRONUNCIATION KEY:
at   āpe   fär   câre   end   mē   it   ice   pierce   hot   ōld   sông   fôrk
oil   out   up   ūse   rüle   pull   tûrn   chin   sing   shop   thin   this
hw in white; zh in treasure. The symbol ə stands for the unstressed vowel sound in about, taken, pencil, lemon, and circus.

73

themselves. **be·have** (bi hāv′) *verb,* **behaved,** **behaving.** —**behavior** *noun.*

behead To cut off someone's head: *Criminals were once executed by being beheaded.* **be·head** (bi hed′) *verb,* **beheaded, beheading.**

behind 1. At the back of: *I sit behind my best friend in school.* 2. Later than; after: *The second bus came ten minutes behind the first bus.* 3. Less advanced than; not as far or as high as: *I've been sick, so I'm behind the rest of the class.* 4. In support of; backing: *The whole town got behind the minister's plan.* Preposition.
○ 1. At the back: *I sneaked up on my friend from behind.* 2. In a place just left: *When the picnic was over, I stayed behind to clean up.* 3. Less advanced than most others; below a goal or standard: *They fell behind in their work.* Adverb.
be·hind (bi hīnd′) *preposition; adverb.*

behold To look at; see: *Behold the beauty of the stars!* **be·hold** (bi hōld′) *verb,* **beheld** (bi held′), **beholding.**

beige A pale brown color. *Noun.*
○ Having the color beige. *Adjective.*
beige (bāzh) *noun, plural* **beiges;** *adjective.*

being Present participle of **be.** *Verb.*
○ 1. The state of existing; existence: *That custom came into being years ago.* 2. A person or animal: *Platypuses are strange beings.* Noun.
be·ing (bē′ing) *verb; noun, plural* **beings.**

belated Late: *I received a belated birthday present a week after my birthday.* **be·la·ted** (bi lā′tid) *adjective.* —**belatedly** *adverb.*

belch 1. To let out gas from the stomach through the mouth; burp. 2. To throw out or be thrown out suddenly: *The chimney belched smoke.* Verb.
○ The act of belching. *The baby gave a quiet belch. Noun.*
belch (belch) *verb,* **belched, belching;** *noun, plural* **belches.**

belfry A tower or a room in a tower where bells are hung. Some churches have a belfry. **bel·fry** (bel′frē) *noun, plural* **belfries.**

Belgium A country in northwestern Europe. **Bel·gium** (bel′jəm) *noun.*

believe 1. To feel sure that something is true, real, or worthwhile: *I believe in getting regular exercise.* 2. To feel sure that someone is telling the truth: *They say they ran five miles, and I believe them.*

3. To think; suppose: *I believe peanuts grow underground, but I'm not sure.* **be·lieve** (bi lēv′) *verb,* **believed, believing. be·lief** (bi lēf′) *noun, plural* **beliefs.**

bell 1. A hollow metal object shaped like a cup. 2. Something that makes a ringing sound like a bell. **bell** (bel) *noun, plural* **bells.**

belligerent 1. Wanting to fight: *That belligerent child always picks on other students.* 2. Busy fighting; at war: *The two belligerent countries fought a long battle.* **bel·lig·er·ent** (bə lij′ər ənt) *adjective.*

A bell makes a ringing sound when struck.

bellow A loud, deep sound; roar. *Noun.*
○ To make this sound: *The bull bellowed in the pasture. Verb.*
bel·low (bel′ō) *noun, plural* **bellows;** *verb,* **bellowed, bellowing.**

bellows A bag between two handles that has an opening. It makes a strong current of air when it is pumped open and closed. The word *bellows* may be used with a singular or plural verb: *A bellows makes fires burn faster. Bellows produce sound in accordions and some other musical instruments.* **bel·lows** (bel′ōz) *plural noun.*

belly 1. The front part of the body below the chest and above the legs; abdomen. 2. The stomach. 3. The underside of the body of an animal: *A snake crawls on its belly.* 4. The under surface of something: *The airplane made an emergency landing on its belly.* **bel·ly** (bel′ē) *noun, plural* **bellies.**

bellybutton The round scar on the belly of humans and most other mammals; navel. **bel·ly·but·ton** (bel′ē but′ən) *noun, plural* **bellybuttons.**

belong 1. To have a special or right place: *The coat belongs in the closet, not on the floor.* 2. To be owned by someone: *That book belongs to me.* 3. To be a member of something: *Some stamp collectors belong to clubs.* **be·long** (bi lông′) *verb,* **belonged, belonging.**

belongings Things owned by a person; possessions. **be·long·ings** (bi lông′ingz) *plural noun.*

beloved Loved very much: *The dog was beloved by the whole neighborhood.* **be·lov·ed** (bi luv′id *or* bi luvd′) *adjective.*

below In or to a lower place: *From the roof we could see the street below. Adverb.*
○ 1. In a lower place than; beneath: *Our grandparents' apartment is below ours.* 2. Less than: *It was 5° below 0° this morning. Preposition.* **be·low** (bi lō′) *adverb; preposition.*

belt 1. A strip or band of cloth, leather, or other material. 2. A region or area: *We drove through the farm belt.* 3. A band that forms a loop and is wound around two wheels or pulleys. A belt transfers power or motion from one wheel or pulley to another. 4. An endless band in a factory that carries objects being worked on by a row of people. **belt** (belt) *noun, plural* **belts.**

bench 1. A long seat: *We sat on the park bench.* 2. A long table for doing work on: *I repaired the broken chair on a bench.* 3. The position or job of a judge in a court of law: *The lawyer was appointed to the bench. Noun.*
○ To keep a player from playing: *The coach benched the exhausted football player. Verb.* **bench** (bench) *noun, plural* **benches**; *verb,* **benched, benching.**

The river bends sharply as it makes its way through a canyon.

bend 1. To change in shape by becoming or causing to become curved or crooked. 2. To move the top part of the body forward and down; stoop;

bow: *Can you bend over and touch your toes? Verb.*
○ Something bent: *a bend in the trail. Noun.* **bend** (bend) *verb,* **bent, bending**; *noun, plural* **bends.**

beneath 1. Lower than; below; under: *The cellar is beneath the house.* 2. Unworthy of: *Telling a lie is beneath you. Preposition.*
○ In a lower place; below: *The house has an attic above and a basement beneath. Adverb.* **be·neath** (bi nēth′) *preposition; adverb.*

beneficial Having a good effect; tending to help: *Some insects are beneficial to plants.* **ben·e·fi·cial** (ben′ə fish′əl) *adjective.* —**beneficially** *adverb.*

benefit Something that helps a person or thing; advantage: *Plenty of sunshine is one of the benefits of living in Arizona. Noun.*
○ To help or be an advantage to. *Verb.* **ben·e·fit** (ben′ə fit) *noun, plural* **benefits**; *verb,* **benefited, benefiting.**

bent Past tense and past participle of bend. *Verb.*
○ 1. Curved or crooked. 2. Determined; set: *We were bent on going on vacation. Adjective.* **bent** (bent) *verb; adjective.*

beret A soft, round, flat cap. **be·ret** (bə rā′) *noun, plural* **berets.**

berry A small, juicy, fleshy fruit that has one or more seeds. Blueberries and grapes are berries that can be eaten.
Another word that sounds like this is **bury.** **ber·ry** (ber′ē) *noun, plural* **berries.**

berth 1. A bed or bunk on a train or ship. 2. A place for a ship to dock: *The freighter was in its berth in the harbor.*
Another word that sounds like this is **birth.** **berth** (bûrth) *noun, plural* **berths.**

beseech To ask someone in a pleading way; beg: *I beseech you to help me.* **be·seech** (bi sēch′) *verb,* **besought** (bi sôt′) *or* **beseeched, beseeching.**

beset To surround and attack: *The hunter and the dogs beset the bear.* **be·set** (bi set′) *verb,* **beset, besetting.**

beside 1. At the side of; next to: *Sit down beside me.* 2. Compared with: *This bicycle looks tiny beside that motorcycle.* 3. Not connected with: *What you just said is beside the point.* **be·side** (bi sīd′) *preposition.*

PRONUNCIATION KEY:
at   āpe   fär   câre   end   mē   it   īce   pîerce   hot   ōld   sông   fôrk
oil   out   up   ūse   rüle   pùll   tûrn   chin   sing   shop   thin   this
hw in white; zh in treasure. The symbol ə stands for the unstressed vowel sound in about, taken, pencil, lemon, and circus.

75

besides In addition; also: *I don't want to go; besides, I have work to do.* Adverb.
○ In addition to: *Besides you, no one else is coming to lunch.* Preposition.
be·sides (bi sīdz′) *adverb; preposition.*

besiege 1. To surround in order to capture: *The soldiers besieged the fort.* 2. To crowd around: *The fans besieged the singer.* **be·siege** (bi sēj′) *verb*, **besieged, besieging.**

best 1. Of the highest quality; better than all others: *My friend is the best pitcher on our team.* 2. Most preferred; most suitable: *What is the best way home from here?* 3. Largest: *The canoe trip took the best part of a day.* Adjective.
○ 1. With the most success or effectiveness: *I work best by myself.* 2. Most: *I like all fruits, but I like peaches best.* Adverb.
○ Something or someone of the highest quality: *I studied hard to do my best on the test.* Noun.
○ To do better than; defeat: *Our chess team bested the other team in a close match.* Verb.
best (best) *adjective; adverb; noun; verb*, **bested, besting.**

bestow To give: *The school bestowed a medal on the outstanding student.* **be·stow** (bi stō′) *verb*, **bestowed, bestowing.**

bet An agreement to pay money to another person if that person is right about something and you are wrong: *I made a bet with my friend that our team would win.* Noun.
○ 1. To make such an agreement. 2. To say with confidence; be certain: *I bet it won't rain tomorrow.* Verb.
bet (bet) *noun, plural* **bets**; *verb*, **bet** or **betted**, **betting.**

betray 1. To give help to the enemy of: *They betrayed their country to the invaders.* 2. To be unfaithful to: *You should not betray your friends by telling their secrets.* **be·tray** (bi trā′) *verb*, **betrayed, betraying.** —**betrayal** *noun.*

better 1. Of higher quality: *These are better pants than those.* 2. More preferred; more suitable: *A firm mattress is better for your back.* 3. Improved in health: *I was sick with the flu, but I'm better now.* 4. Larger; greater: *We spent the better part of Saturday cleaning the attic.* Adjective.
○ 1. With more success or effectiveness: *Cactuses grow better in dry soil.* 2. To a higher degree; more: *I like painting better than gardening.* Adverb.
○ Something or someone of higher quality: *Which is the better of these two books?* Noun.
○ 1. To make better; improve: *You can better your piano playing if you practice more.* 2. To do better than; outdo: *The runner bettered the school record for the 100-yard dash.* Verb.
• **better off.** In a better situation or condition: *We'll be better off staying here until the rain stops.*
• **had better.** Ought to: *You had better study if you want to do well on the test.*
bet·ter (bet′ər) *adjective; adverb; noun, plural* **betters**; *verb*, **bettered, bettering.**

between 1. In the space or time separating: *a rest period between classes.* 2. Joining; connecting: *There is a long bridge between the island and the mainland.* 3. Involving; among: *A quarrel broke out between two students.* 4. By the combined action of: *Between us, we can clean our room in an hour.* 5. By comparing: *You can choose between pancakes and oatmeal.* Preposition.

A plant is growing between these rocks.

○ In the space or time separating two things: *A sandwich is two pieces of bread with a filling between.* Adverb.
Look up **among** for a Language Note about this word.
be·tween (bi twēn′) *preposition; adverb.*

beverage A liquid for drinking, such as orange juice, milk, or cocoa. **bev·er·age** (bev′ər ij) *noun, plural* **beverages.**

beware To be on one's guard; be careful: *Beware of the traffic when you cross the street.* **be·ware** (bi wâr′) *verb.*

bewilder To confuse or puzzle; mix up: *The math problem bewildered me.* **be·wil·der** (bi wil′dər) *verb*, **bewildered, bewildering.**

bewitch 1. To cast a magic spell over someone: *In the story, the wicked fairy bewitched the prince and turned him into a frog.* 2. To charm:

*The child's smile **bewitched** everyone.* **be·witch** (bi wich′) *verb,* **bewitched, bewitching.**

beyond 1. On the far side of. 2. Later than: *I stayed awake well **beyond** my bedtime.* 3. Outside the reach or limits of; too advanced for: *The veterinarian told us that our old dog was **beyond** help. Preposition.*
○ Farther on: *Look **beyond**, and you'll see the mountains in the distance. Adverb.*
be·yond (bē ond′) *preposition; adverb.*

bi- A prefix that means "having or involving two." *Bilevel* means "having two levels."

bias A strong feeling for or against a person or thing that keeps someone from being fair: *A good judge never shows **bias** during a trial. Noun.*
○ To cause to have or show bias. *Verb.*
bi·as (bī′əs) *noun, plural* **biases;** *verb,* **biased, biasing.**

Bible 1. The sacred writings of the Christian religion, contained in the Old Testament and the New Testament. 2. The Old Testament alone, which is part of the sacred writings of the Jewish religion. **Bi·ble** (bī′bəl) *noun.*

biblical Found in the Bible; relating to the Bible: *The story of Noah's ark is a **biblical** story.* **bib·li·cal** (bib′li kəl) *adjective.*

bibliography A list of books about a subject: *This book on dinosaurs has a **bibliography** in the back.* **bib·li·og·ra·phy** (bib′lē og′rə fē) *noun, plural* **bibliographies.**

biceps The large muscle that runs down the front of the arm from the shoulder to the elbow. When it is contracted, the arm bends. **bi·ceps** (bī′seps) *noun, plural* **biceps** *or* **bicepses.**

bicker To quarrel noisily about something unimportant. **bick·er** (bik′ər) *verb,* **bickered, bickering.**

bicuspid A tooth with two points. A grown person has eight bicuspids. **bi·cus·pid** (bī kus′pid) *noun, plural* **bicuspids.**

bicycle A light vehicle with two wheels, one behind the other. It has a seat, handlebars to steer with, and two foot pedals to turn the wheels and make it go forward. *Noun.*
○ To ride a bicycle: *Sometimes I **bicycle** to school. Verb.*
bi·cy·cle (bī′si kəl) *noun, plural* **bicycles;** *verb,* **bicycled, bicycling.**

bid 1. To give an order to; command. 2. To say when meeting or leaving someone: *The children **bid** their friend good-bye.* 3. To offer to pay: *We **bid** thirty-five dollars for the old desk at the auction. Verb.*

bicycle

saddle · grip · crossbar · seat post · handlebars · brake lever · brakes · fork · safety reflector · rim · spokes · tire · gear cable · chain · pedal

PRONUNCIATION KEY:

at · āpe · fär · câre · end · mē · it · ice · pierce · hot · ōld · sông · fôrk
oil · out · up · ūse · rüle · pull · tûrn · chin · sing · shop · thin · this
hw in white; zh in treasure. The symbol ə stands for the unstressed vowel sound in about, taken, pencil, lemon, and circus.

77

○ An offer to pay money: *The rug was sold to the person who made the highest **bid**. Noun.*
bid (bid) *verb* **bid** *or* **bidden, bidding**; *noun, plural* **bids.**

bide To bide one's time. To wait for the right moment or chance: *I'm going to **bide** my time until I find a bicycle that I really want.* **bide** (bīd) *verb,* **bided, biding.**

biennial 1. Lasting or living for two years. 2. Happening every two years: *a **biennial** festival. Adjective.*
○ 1. An event that takes place every two years. 2. A plant with a two-year life cycle. *Noun*
bi·en·ni·al (bi en′ ē əl) *adjective; noun, plural* **biennials. —biennially** *adverb.*

big 1. Great in size or amount; large: *Chicago is a **big** city.* 2. Very important: *a **big** moment in my life.* 3. Proud and boasting: *Some people are **big** talkers.* **big** (big) *adjective,* **bigger, biggest.**

Big Dipper A group of seven bright stars that looks like a ladle in outline. It is found in the northern part of the sky.

bighorn A wild sheep that lives in the Rocky Mountains of North America. Bighorn have large, curled horns. **big·horn** (big′hôrn′) *noun, plural* **bighorn** *or* **bighorns.**

bike A bicycle. *Noun.*
○ To ride a bicycle. *Verb.*
bike (bīk) *noun, plural* **bikes** *verb,* **biked, biking.**

bile A bitter yellow or green liquid made in the liver. Bile helps the body to digest food. **bile** (bīl) *noun.*

bilingual 1. Speaking or writing two languages: *My Canadian friends are **bilingual**; they speak both French and English.* 2. Spoken or written in two languages. **bi·lin·gual** (bī ling′gwəl) *adjective.*

WORD HISTORY

Bilingual comes from a Latin word meaning "two tongues." The Latin word for "tongue" also means "language" or "speech." A bilingual person does not have two tongues but does speak two languages.

---

bill¹ 1. A notice of money owed for something bought or for work done: *Mom pays the telephone **bill** every month.* 2. A piece of paper money. 3. A poster or sign with an advertisement: *A **bill** on the wall advertised a sale.* 4. A suggest-

ed law: *The new tax **bill** was passed by Congress. Noun.*
○ To send a written notice of money owed to someone: *The store will **bill** us for the things we are buying today. Verb.*
bill (bil) *noun, plural* **bills**; *verb,* **billed, billing.**

bill² The hard, projecting mouth part of a bird or a turtle; beak. A duck has a broad, flat bill. **bill** (bil) *noun, plural* **bills.**

This bird's bill is shaped like a spoon.

billboard A large board placed outdoors for displaying signs or advertisements. Billboards are often seen along highways. **bill·board** (bil′bôrd′) *noun, plural* **billboards.**

billfold A folding case for paper money. Many billfolds also have places for a driver's license, cards, and other things. **bill·fold** (bil′fōld′) *noun, plural* **billfolds.**

billiards A game played with hard balls hit with a long stick called a cue. Billiards is played on a large, felt-covered table with a raised edge. **bil·liards** (bil′yərdz) *noun.*

billion One thousand times one million; 1,000,000,000. **bil·lion** (bil′yən) *noun, plural* **billions**; *adjective.*

billow A great swelling wave of something: *billows of smoke. Noun.*
○ To rise or swell in billows: *The sail of the boat **billowed** in the wind. Verb.*
bil·low (bil′ō) *noun, plural* **billows**; *verb,* **billowed, billowing.**

bin A closed place or box for holding or storing something: *Coal for the furnace is stored in a **bin**.* Another word that sounds like this is **been.** **bin** (bin) *noun, plural* **bins.**

binary system A system of numbers that uses only 0 and 1. In the binary system, any number can be expressed by 0, 1, or a combination of these. The ordinary decimal number 2 is the same as the binary number 10. Many electronic computers use the binary system of numbering. **bi·na·ry system** (bī′nə rē).

bind 1. To tie together; fasten: *The clerk **bound** the packages with string.* 2. To tie a bandage around: *The nurse will **bind** your sprained ankle.* 3. To fasten together between covers: *This machine **binds** the pages into a book.* 4. To force by a promise or an obligation; oblige: *The agreement **binds** me to work for the company for three years.* **bind** (bīnd) *verb,* **bound, binding.**

bingo A game in which each player covers numbers on a card as they are called out. The winner is the first player to cover a row of numbers or the whole card. **bin•go** (bing′gō) *noun.*

binoculars A device that makes distant objects look larger and closer. Binoculars are made up of two small telescopes joined together, so that a person can look at distant objects with both eyes. **bi•noc•u•lars** (bə nok′yə lərz) *plural noun.*

biodegradable Able to decay and to be absorbed by the environment. Food and paper are biodegradable. When they decay, they become part of the earth's natural resources. **bi•o•de•grad•a•ble** (bī′ō di grā′də bəl) *adjective.*

biography A true story of someone's life written by another person. **bi•og•ra•phy** (bī′og′rə fē) *noun, plural* **biographies.**

biology The study of living things. Biology deals with the way in which plants and animals and other living things live and grow, and where they are found. **bi•ol•o•gy** (bī ol′ə jē) *noun.* —**biologist** *noun.*

bioluminescence Visible light given off by certain living creatures such as fireflies and some fish and bacteria. **bi•o•lu•mi•nes•cence** (bī′ō lü′ mə nes′ əns) *noun.* —**bioluminescent** *adjective.*

biomass The total amount of all living things within a specific volume of environment. **bi•o•mass** (bī′ō mas′) *noun.*

bionic Having to do with mechanical or electronic devices that work like the things in nature from which they are copied. A bionic arm and a real arm are both worked by signals from the brain. **bi•on•ic** (bī on′ik) *adjective.*

birch Any of a large group of trees that have hard wood. One kind of birch has white bark. **birch** (bûrch) *noun, plural* **birches.**

bird An animal that has wings, two legs, and a body covered with feathers. Birds have a backbone, are warm-blooded, and lay eggs. Most birds can fly. **bird** (bûrd) *noun, plural* **birds.**

birth 1. The time when a person or animal first comes from its mother. 2. The start of something; beginning: *The **birth** of the United States took place in 1776.*
Another word that sounds like this is **berth.**
 • **to give birth to.** 1. To produce offspring: *Our beagle **gave birth to** four puppies.* 2. To produce or be the cause of something: *The artist's work **gave birth to** a new style of painting.* **birth** (bûrth) *noun, plural* **births.**

birthday 1. The day on which a person is born. 2. The return each year of this day. **birth•day** (bûrth′dā′) *noun, plural* **birthdays.**

A **birthday** is an important occasion in every person's life.

birthmark A mark on the skin that was there at birth. **birth•mark** (bûrth′märk′) *noun, plural* **birthmarks.**

birthplace The place where a person was born. **birth•place** (bûrth′plās′) *noun, plural* **birthplaces.**

birthright A right or possession a person is entitled to because of having been born into a certain family or at a certain time or place: *The right to vote is a **birthright** of anyone born in the United States.* **birth•right** (bûrth′rīt′) *noun, plural* **birthrights.**

biscuit 1. A small cake of baked dough. 2. A cracker. **bis•cuit** (bis′kit) *noun, plural* **biscuits.**

WORD HISTORY

Biscuit comes from an old French word meaning "baked twice." When dough was put in the oven twice, it became crisp and dry.

PRONUNCIATION KEY:
at āpe fär câre end mē it īce pîerce hot ōld sông fôrk
oil out up ūse rüle pùll tûrn chin sing shop thin this
hw in white; zh in treasure. The symbol ə stands for the unstressed vowel sound in about, taken, pencil, lemon, and circus.

79

bisect To divide into two equal parts. An angle is bisected when a straight line is drawn through the middle of it. **bi·sect** (bī sekt′ or bī′sekt) *verb*.

bishop 1. A Christian church official who has a high rank. 2. A piece in the game of chess. **bish·op** (bish′əp) *noun, plural* **bishops**.

WORD HISTORY

Centuries ago, English borrowed the word bishop from a Greek word meaning "a person who watches over." The bishop was the person who watched over the religious life of the people.

---

bison A large animal that has a big, shaggy head with short horns and a hump on its back; buffalo. Bison are found in North America. **bi·son** (bī′sən or bī′zən) *noun, plural* **bison**.

The prairie region of the United States was once filled with roaming herds of bison.

bit¹ 1. The metal piece of a bridle that goes into the horse's mouth. 2. The part of a drilling tool that makes holes in wood or other material. A bit fits into the part of a tool called the brace. **bit** (bit) *noun, plural* **bits**.

bit² 1. A small piece or part: *The glass fell and broke into bits.* 2. A short while: *Wait a bit.* • **a bit**. A little; slightly: *I am a bit tired.* **bit** (bit) *noun, plural* **bits**.

bit³ Past tense and a past participle of **bite**. **bit** (bit) *verb*.

bit⁴ The smallest unit of memory in a computer. A bit may be either 0 or 1. **bit** (bit) *noun, plural* **bits**.

bite 1. To seize, cut into, or pierce with the teeth. 2. To wound with teeth, fangs, or a stinger: *A mosquito bit me.* 3. To make something sting: *The icy wind will bite our cheeks.* 4. To take or swallow bait: *The fish are not biting today. Verb.* ○ 1. A seizing or cutting into something with the teeth. 2. A wound made by biting: *a mosquito bite.* 3. A piece bitten off: *a bite of an apple.* 4. A sharp sensation; sting: *the bite of the cold air. Noun.* **bite** (bīt) *verb*, **bit, bitten** *or* **bit, biting**; *noun, plural* **bites**.

bitten A past participle of **bite**. **bit·ten** (bit′ən) *verb*.

bitter 1. Having a biting, harsh, bad taste: *bitter cough medicine.* 2. Causing or showing sorrow or pain: *The children shivered in the bitter cold.* 3. Showing anger, resentment, or hatred: *bitter enemies.* **bit·ter** (bit′ər) *adjective*;

black 1. The darkest of all colors; the opposite of white. 2. A member of one of the major divisions of the human race; Negro: *Blacks often have dark skin. Noun.* ○ 1. Having the darkest of all colors. 2. Having no light; dark: *When the lights went out, the room became black.* 3. Of or being a member of one of the major divisions of the human race; Negro: *Both white and black families live in this neighborhood.* 4. Unhappy or gloomy: *When they lost all their money, their future looked black. Adjective.* **black** (blak) *noun, plural* **blacks**; *adjective*, **blacker, blackest**.

blackberry A sweet, juicy black fruit. Blackberries grow on a prickly bush. **black·ber·ry** (blak′ber′ē) *noun, plural* **blackberries**.

Blackberries **often grow wild.**

blackbird Any of various birds that are mostly black. Grackles, crows, and ravens are blackbirds. **black·bird** (blak′bûrd′) *noun, plural* **blackbirds**.

blackboard A hard, smooth board made of slate or other material, used for writing or drawing on with chalk. Some blackboards are black; others are green. **black·board** (blak′bôrd′) *noun, plural* **blackboards**.

blacken 1. To make or become black: *Smoke from the fireplace blackened the walls of the room.* 2. To do harm to: *Don't blacken your reputation by lying.* **black·en** (blak′ən) *verb*, **blackened, blackening**.

black eye A bruise on the skin around the eye, usually caused by a blow to the eye.

black hole An invisible object in space that has a pull of gravity so strong that nothing can escape from it, not even light.

blackmail The attempt to get money from a person by threatening to tell things that would harm the person's reputation. *Noun.*
○ To make such an attempt. *Verb.*
black·mail (blak′māl′) *noun; verb,* **blackmailed, blackmailing.**

blackout A sudden loss of electrical power in a large area: *I was in an elevator when the blackout began.* **black·out** (blak′out′) *noun, plural* **blackouts.**

blacksmith A person who makes and repairs iron objects. A blacksmith heats the iron in a forge and then hammers it into shape on an anvil. A blacksmith can make horseshoes. **black·smith** (blak′smith′) *noun, plural* **blacksmiths.**

blacktop A black material used for paving roads, playgrounds, and other surfaces. *Noun.*
○ To pave a surface with this material. *Verb.*
black·top (blak′top′) *noun; verb,* **blacktopped, blacktopping.**

black widow A black spider. The female black widow is poisonous and has a red mark on her body. The female black widow is larger than the male, and often eats the male after mating.

bladder A small balloon-like part in the body. The bladder stores urine from the kidneys. **blad·der** (blad′ər) *noun, plural* **bladders.**

blade 1. The sharp part of anything that cuts. 2. A leaf of grass. 3. The wide, flat part of something: *the blades of a fan.* 4. The runner of an ice skate. **blade** (blād) *noun, plural* **blades.**

blame 1. To find fault with: *I don't blame you for getting angry at me when I took your bike without asking.* 2. To hold responsible for something wrong or bad: *The neighbor blamed us for breaking the window.* *Verb.*
○ Responsibility for something wrong or bad: *The other driver took the blame for the accident. Noun.*
blame (blām) *verb,* **blamed, blaming;** *noun.*

blank 1. Without writing or printing; unmarked: *a blank page in the notebook.* 2. With empty spaces to be filled in: *Please fill in the blank order form.*
3. Without thought; vacant: *a blank stare. Adjective.*
○ 1. An empty space to be filled in: *Fill in the blank with your name.* 2. A paper with spaces to be filled in: *an application blank.* 3. A cartridge with gunpowder but no bullet. *Noun.*
blank (blangk) *adjective,* **blanker, blankest;** *noun, plural* **blanks.**

blanket 1. A covering made of wool, nylon, or other material. Blankets are used on beds to keep people warm while they sleep. 2. Anything that covers like a blanket: *a blanket of fog. Noun.*
○ To cover with or as if with a blanket. *Verb.*
blan·ket (blang′kit) *noun, plural* **blankets;** *verb,* **blanketed, blanketing.**

blare 1. To make a loud, harsh sound: *The car horns blared in the traffic jam.* 2. To send or be sent out with loud, harsh sounds: *The radio blared the news. Verb.*
○ A loud, harsh sound: *the blare of a horn. Noun.*
blare (blâr) *verb,* **blared, blaring;** *noun, plural* **blares.**

blast 1. A strong rush of wind or air: *a blast of cold air.* 2. A loud noise made by a horn: *the blast of trumpets.* 3. An explosion: *The blast of the explosion made the windows of our house rattle. Noun.*
○ 1. To blow up with explosives. 2. To ruin: *The rain blasted our hopes for a picnic. Verb.*
• **to blast off.** To take off into flight propelled by rockets.
blast (blast) *noun, plural* **blasts;** *verb,* **blasted, blasting.**

blast-off The launching of a rocket or space vehicle: *Blast-off is scheduled for noon.* **blast-off** (blast′ôf′) *noun, plural* **blast-offs.**

blaze¹ 1. A bright flame; a glowing fire: *the blaze of a burning building.* 2. A bright light: *the blaze of the sun.* 3. A bright dis-

The **blast-off** of a space shuttle is accompanied by noise and huge billows of smoke.

PRONUNCIATION KEY:
at   āpe   fär   câre   end   mē   it   īce   pîerce   hot   ōld   sông   fôrk
oil   out   up   ūse   rüle   pull   tûrn   chin   sing   shop   thin   this
hw in white; zh in treasure. The symbol ə stands for the unstressed vowel sound in about, taken, pencil, lemon, and circus.   **81**

play: *The parade was a **blaze** of color. Noun.*
○ **1.** To burn brightly: *The campfire **blazed** all night.* **2.** To shine brightly: *The tree **blazed** with lights on Christmas. Verb.*
blaze (blāz) *noun, plural* **blazes**; *verb,* **blazed, blazing.**

blaze² A mark made on a tree or rock to show a trail or boundary. A blaze is made with paint or by chipping off a piece of bark. *Noun.*
○ To show a trail or boundary with such a mark. *Verb.*
blaze (blāz) *noun, plural* **blazes**; *verb,* **blazed, blazing.**

bleach To make something white: *We will **bleach** these shirts when we wash them. Verb.*
○ A substance used for bleaching. *Noun.*
bleach (blēch) *verb,* **bleached, bleaching**; *noun, plural* **bleaches.**

People sit in bleachers to watch an event, such as a baseball game.

bleachers A group of seats or benches in rows placed one above and behind another. **bleach•ers** (blē′chərz) *plural noun.*

bleak **1.** Open and not protected from the wind; bare: *There were no trees growing on the **bleak** mountain top.* **2.** Cold and gloomy: *a **bleak** February day.* **bleak** (blēk) *adjective,* **bleaker, bleakest.**

bled Past tense and past participle of **bleed. bled** (bled) *verb.*

bleed **1.** To lose blood. **2.** To lose sap or other liquid: *The tree will **bleed** if you cut into its trunk.* **bleed** (blēd) *verb,* **bled, bleeding.**

blemish Something that spoils beauty or perfection; flaw: *The scar is a **blemish** on his face. Noun.*
○ To spoil the beauty or perfection of something. *Verb.*

blem·ish (blem′ish) *noun, plural* **blemishes**; *verb,* **blemished, blemishing.**

blend **1.** To mix together completely: ***Blend** the milk and eggs in a bowl.* **2.** To shade into each other: *The sea and sky seemed to **blend** on the horizon. Verb.*
○ A mixture: *This drink is a **blend** of fruit juices. Noun.*
blend (blend) *verb,* **blended, blending**; *noun, plural* **blends.**

bless **1.** To make holy by a religious ceremony: *The minister **blessed** the new chapel.* **2.** To ask God's help for: *The minister **blessed** everyone in the church.* **3.** To make happy or fortunate: *Our family is **blessed** with good health.* **bless** (bles) *verb,* **blessed** or **blest, blessing.**

blessing **1.** A prayer asking for God's favor, or giving thanks: *The priest gave a **blessing** at the end of Mass.* **2.** A person or thing that brings happiness: *The helpful child was a **blessing** to the disabled people in the building.* **3.** A wish for happiness or success; good wishes: *Our friends sent their **blessings** for a happy new year.*
bless·ing (bles′ing) *noun, plural* **blessings.**

blew Past tense of **blow.**
Another word that sounds like this is **blue.**
blew (blü) *verb.*

blight **1.** A disease of plants. Blight makes a plant wither and die. **2.** Something that spoils the looks or health of something else: *Those abandoned buildings are a **blight** on our city.* **blight** (blīt) *noun, plural* **blights.**

blimp An airship that does not have a rigid framework to form its shape. **blimp** (blimp) *noun, plural* **blimps.**

Television crews often use a blimp to show spectacular aerial views.

blind 1. Without sight; unable to see. 2. Not easily seen; hidden: *a blind driveway.* 3. Done with instruments only and not with the eyes: *The pilot of the airplane made a blind landing in the storm.* 4. Closed at one end: *a blind alley.* 5. Without thinking or using one's judgment: *a blind guess. Adjective.*
○ 1. To make unable to see. 2. To take away thought or good judgment: *Fear blinded the people in the theater when the fire broke out. Verb.*
○ Something that blocks a person's sight or keeps the light out: *window blinds. Noun.*
blind (blīnd) *adjective; verb,* **blinded, blinding;** *noun, plural* **blinds. —blindly** *adverb.*

blindfold To cover someone's eyes with a strip of cloth or a bandage. *Verb.*
○ A strip of cloth or other cover for the eyes. *Noun.*
blind·fold (blīnd′fōld′) *verb,* **blindfolded, blindfolding;** *noun, plural* **blindfolds.**

blink 1. To close and open the eyes quickly. 2. To flash on and off; twinkle: *Stars blinked in the sky.*
blink (blingk) *verb,* **blinked, blinking.**

bliss Great happiness: *We were filled with bliss at the thought of our vacation.* **bliss** (blis) *noun;* **blissful** *adjective.*

blister 1. A sore place that looks like a small bubble on the skin. A blister is filled with a liquid and is usually caused by rubbing or by a burn. 2. Any small bubble or swelling: *Blisters formed on the new coat of paint. Noun.*
○ To form a blister on; have blisters. *Verb.*
blis·ter (blis′tər) *noun, plural* **blisters;** *verb,* **blistered, blistering.**

**Blizzards leave behind
many inches of snow.**

blizzard A heavy snowstorm with very strong winds. **bliz·zard** (bliz′ərd) *noun, plural* **blizzards.**

bloat To make or become too full with a lot of liquid or gas; swell: *Eating too much bloated our stomachs.* **bloat** (blōt) *verb,* **bloated, bloating.**

blob A drop or small lump of something soft: *I got a blob of paint on my overalls.* **blob** (blob) *noun, plural* **blobs.**

block 1. A piece of something hard and solid, with flat surfaces: *a wall built with blocks of stone.* 2. An area in a town or city with four streets around it: *I walked my dog around the block.* 3. The length of one side of a block in a town or city: *I live three blocks from school.* 4. A number of things that are alike: *The teacher bought a block of theater tickets so our class could sit together.* 5. Something that stops or obstructs something else; obstacle: *The fallen tree was a block to traffic.* 6. A pulley in a frame. *Noun.*
○ To get in the way of; obstruct: *A tall building blocks the view from my window. Verb.*
block (blok) *noun, plural* **blocks;** *verb,* **blocked, blocking.**

blockade A shutting off of an area to keep people and supplies from going in or out. During a war, a country may use ships to set up a blockade around an enemy country. *Noun.*
○ To shut off with a blockade. *Verb.*
block·ade (blo kād′) *noun, plural* **blockades;** *verb,* **blockaded, blockading.**

blockhouse 1. A building of wooden timbers or logs, with holes in the walls to shoot weapons from. Blockhouses were formerly used as forts. 2. A strong building near the launch pad of a rocket. A blockhouse is used to protect people who are watching rockets launch. **block·house** (blok′hous′) *noun, plural* **blockhouses** (blok′hou′ziz).

blond 1. Light yellow: *blond hair.* 2. Having light yellow hair and usually light-colored eyes and skin: *Most of the members of that family are blond. Adjective.*
○ A person with light yellow hair and usually light-colored eyes and skin. *Noun.*
This word is also spelled *blonde* when the person is a girl or woman.
blond (blond) *adjective,* **blonder, blondest;** *noun, plural* **blonds.**

PRONUNCIATION KEY:
at   āpe   fär   câre   end   mē   it   īce   pierce   hot   ōld   sông   fôrk
oil   out   up   ūse   rüle   pull   tûrn   chin   sing   shop   thin   this
hw in white; zh in treasure. The symbol ə stands for the unstressed vowel sound in about, taken, pencil, lemon, and circus.

83

blood   1. The bright red liquid pumped by the heart. Blood circulates in the arteries and veins through all parts of the body. It carries oxygen and food to the body and takes away waste materials. **2.** Family relationship: *The cousins are related by blood because their mothers are sisters.* **3.** National origin; descent: *The doctor was of Indian blood.* **blood** (blud) *noun.*

blood bank   A place where blood is collected and stored until it is needed to replace the blood someone has lost in an operation or an injury.

bloodhound   A large dog with long, drooping ears and a wrinkled face. Bloodhounds have a good sense of smell and are used to track escaped criminals or find people who are lost. **blood·hound** (blud′hound′) *noun, plural* **bloodhounds.**

bloodshed   The loss of blood or life: *The soldiers won the battle without much bloodshed.* **blood·shed** (blud′shed′) *noun.*

bloodshot   Irritated and marked with reddish veins. When the eyes are tired, sometimes they become bloodshot. **blood·shot** (blud′shot′) *adjective.*

bloodstream   The blood flowing through the body. **blood·stream** (blud′strēm′) *noun, plural* **bloodstreams.**

bloodthirsty   Eager to cause bloodshed; cruel: *bloodthirsty pirates.* **blood·thirst·y** (blud′thûr′stē) *adjective.*

blood vessel   Any of the tubes in the body through which the blood flows. Arteries and veins are blood vessels.

bloody   1. Covered or stained with blood: *a bloody bandage.* **2.** Causing much bloodshed: *a bloody battle.* **blood·y** (blud′ē) *adjective,* **bloodier, bloodiest.**

bloom   1. The flower of a plant: *The forsythia branches were covered with yellow blooms.* **2.** The time of flowering: *The roses are in bloom. Noun.*
○ To have flowers; blossom: *Cherry trees bloom in the spring. Verb.*
bloom (blüm) *noun, plural* **blooms;** *verb,* **bloomed, blooming.**

blossom   1. The flower of a plant or tree, especially one that produces fruit: *We gathered blossoms from the apple trees.* **2.** The time of flowering: *The lilacs are in blossom. Noun.*
○ **1.** To have flowers or blossoms; bloom. **2.** To grow; develop: *As the artist worked, the sketch*

blossomed into a detailed portrait. Verb.
blos·som (blos′əm) *noun, plural* **blossoms;** *verb,* **blossomed, blossoming.**

In the South, peach blossoms are a sign of spring.

blot   1. A spot or stain: *The letter was neat, except for a blot at the end.* **2.** Something that spoils or mars: *Those billboards along the highway are a blot on the countryside. Noun.*
○ **1.** To spot or stain: *Spilled ink blotted my letter.* **2.** To soak up or dry with a blotter: *Blot your signature so the ink won't smear. Verb.*
blot (blot) *noun, plural* **blots;** *verb,* **blotted, blotting.**

blotch   A large spot or stain: *The rash covered my arms with red blotches. Noun.* **blotch** (bloch) *noun, plural* **blotches.**

blotter   A piece of soft, thick paper used to soak up or dry wet ink. **blot·ter** (blot′ər) *noun, plural* **blotters.**

blouse   A loose piece of clothing for the upper part of the body, worn with a skirt or pants. **blouse** (blous *or* blouz) *noun, plural* **blouses.**

blow¹   1. A hard hit or stroke. A blow may be made with the fist, a tool, or some other object: *a blow with a hammer.* **2.** A sudden event that causes great shock or unhappiness: *The death of their dog was a blow to the family.* **blow** (blō) *noun, plural* **blows.**

blow²   1. To move with speed or force: *A breeze blew the leaves across the yard.* **2.** To send out a current of air: *Blow on your hands to warm them.* **3.** To move by a current of air: *My hat blew off as I ran for the bus.* **4.** To form or shape by a current of air: *Children love to blow soap bubbles.* **5.** To sound by a blast of air: *When the whistle blows,* *the race will start.* **6.** To clear by forcing air through: *I blew my nose.* **7.** To break or destroy by an explosion: *The soldiers blew the enemy's bridge to pieces.* **8.** To burst because of being worn out, filled too much, or used too much.

　• **to blow out. 1.** To stop burning or stop from burning: *The lantern blew out during the storm.* **2.** To burst: *One of our tires blew out.*

　• **to blow up. 1.** To explode: *The gasoline truck blew up.* **2.** To fill with air or gas: *They blew up balloons for the party.* **3.** To lose one's temper: *I'll blow up if they are late again.* **4.** To start; arise: *A storm blew up during the night.*
blow (blō) *verb,* **blew, blown, blowing.**

blow hole **1.** A nostril on the top of the head of whales, dolphins, and porpoises. **2.** A hole in the ice where aquatic mammals such as seals come up to breathe. **3.** A vent or hole for air and gases to escape.

blown Past participle of **blow. blown** (blōn) *verb.*

The man is working on jewelry with a small blowtorch.

blowtorch A small torch that shoots out a very hot flame, used to melt metal and to burn off old paint. **blow·torch** (blō′tôrch′) *noun, plural* **blowtorches.**

blubber A layer of fat under the skin of whales, seals, and other sea animals. The oil made from whale blubber used to be burned in lamps. *Noun.*
○ To cry and sob noisily. *Verb.*
blub·ber (blub′ər) *noun, plural* **blubbers;** *verb,* **blubbered, blubbering.**

blue The color of the clear sky in the daytime. *Noun.*
○ **1.** Having the color blue. **2.** Unhappy; discouraged: *I felt blue during the first week at camp.* *Adjective.*
Another word that sounds like this is **blew.**

　• **out of the blue.** Suddenly and unexpectedly: *The announcement came out of the blue.*
blue (blü) *noun, plural* **blues;** *adjective,* **bluer, bluest.**

blueberry A small, dark blue, sweet berry with tiny seeds. Blueberries grow on a shrub.
blue·ber·ry (blü′ber′ē) *noun, plural* **blueberries.**

bluebird A small songbird of North America that has blue feathers on its back. **blue·bird** (blü′bûrd′) *noun, plural* **bluebirds.**

The bluebird **has a distinctive song.**

bluefish A blue or green saltwater fish that lives in coastal waters in various parts of the world. It is caught for sport or food. **blue·fish** (blü′fish′) *noun, plural* **bluefish** *or* **bluefishes.**

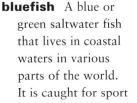

bluegrass A grass with bluish green stems, used as food for cattle and horses and for lawns.
blue·grass (blü′gras′) *noun, plural* **bluegrasses.**

blue jay A North American jay that has a crest on its head and blue feathers with black-and-white marks.

blue jeans Pants or overalls made of blue denim.

blueprint **1.** A paper printed with white lines on a blue background, used to show the plan for building something: *The construction workers looked at the blueprints as they built the house.* **2.** A detailed plan for how to do or make something: *The U.S. Constitution is a blueprint for democracy.*
blue·print (blü′print′) *noun, plural* **blueprints.**

blues **1.** Sadness; low spirits. **2.** Music that sounds sad and has a jazz rhythm. **blues** (blüz) *plural noun.*

blue whale A blue-gray whale, the largest mammal that has ever lived.

PRONUNCIATION KEY:
at　āpe　fär　câre　end　mē　it　īce　pierce　hot　ōld　sông　fôrk
oil　out　up　ūse　rüle　pull　tûrn　chin　sing　shop　thin　this
hw in white; zh in treasure. The symbol ə stands for the unstressed vowel sound in about, taken, pencil, lemon, and circus.

85

bluff¹ A high, steep bank or cliff. **bluff** (bluf) *noun, plural* **bluffs.**

The tall bluffs can be seen in the distance.

bluff² To try to fool people with a false show of courage, confidence, or knowledge. *Verb.*
○ A false show of courage, confidence, or knowledge put on to fool other people: *All your boasting about being able to speak French was a big bluff. Noun.*
bluff (bluf) *verb,* **bluffed, bluffing**; *noun, plural* **bluffs.**

blunder A careless or stupid mistake: *Forgetting my friend's birthday was a blunder. Noun.*
○ **1.** To make a careless or stupid mistake.
2. To move in a clumsy way: *The lost campers blundered through the woods. Verb.*
blun·der (blun′dər) *noun, plural* **blunders**; *verb,* **blundered, blundering.**

blunt 1. Having a dull edge or point; not sharp: *This pencil is blunt and needs to be sharpened.*
2. Outspoken and frank about what one thinks: *My friend's blunt criticism of my essay hurt my feelings. Adjective.*
○ To make less sharp; make dull. *Verb.*
blunt (blunt) *adjective,* **blunter, bluntest**; *verb,* **blunted, blunting.** —**bluntly** *adverb.*

blur To make dim or hard to see; make less clear: *Fog blurred the outline of the boat. Verb.*
○ Something dim or hard to see. *Noun.*
blur (blûr) *verb,* **blurred, blurring**; *noun, plural* **blurs.**

blurt To say suddenly or without thinking: *I was sorry after I blurted out the secret.* **blurt** (blûrt) *verb,* **blurted, blurting.**

blush To become red in the face. A person blushes when feeling ashamed, embarrassed, or confused. *Verb.*

○ A reddening of the face from shame, embarrassment, or confusion. *Noun.*
blush (blush) *verb,* **blushed, blushing**; *noun, plural* **blushes.**

bluster 1. To blow in a noisy or violent way: *The wind blustered through the trees.* **2.** To talk in a loud or threatening way: *The store manager told the angry customer to stop blustering and calm down. Verb.*
○ **1.** A noisy, violent blowing: *The bluster of the storm kept us awake all night.* **2.** Loud, threatening, or boastful talk. *Noun.*
blus·ter (blus′tər) *verb,* **blustered, blustering**; *noun.*

Blvd. An abbreviation for **Boulevard** used in a written address. 20 Riverside Blvd.

boa constrictor A large snake found in Mexico and in Central and South America. A boa constrictor is not poisonous. It kills its prey by coiling around it and squeezing it to death.
bo·a constrictor (bō′ə).

boar A wild pig that has bristles and a long snout. Boars live in forests in Europe and Asia. Another word that sounds like this is **bore.**
boar (bôr) *noun, plural* **boars.**

board 1. A long, flat piece of sawed wood, used in building houses and other things. **2.** A flat piece of wood or other material used for a special purpose: *Get the board and we'll play checkers.*
3. A group of people chosen to manage or direct something: *The school board helps to run the school.* **4.** Meals served daily to guests for pay: *The student found a good room with board near campus. Noun.*
○ **1.** To cover with boards: *I boarded up the broken window.* **2.** To get a room to sleep in and meals for pay: *I boarded with a family in France last summer.* **3.** To get on a ship, plane, or train: *We will board the plane in ten minutes. Verb.*
• **on board.** On, onto, or in a ship, plane, or train; aboard: *When the plane took off, there were seventy-five people on board.*
board (bôrd) *noun, plural* **boards**; *verb,* **boarded, boarding.**

boarding school A school that provides meals and a place to live for its students when the school is in session.

boast 1. To talk too much or with too much pride about oneself; brag: *They are always boasting of* *their grades.* **2.** To be proud of having: *Our town* **boasts** *a new arena. Verb.*

○ A statement in which one brags. *Noun.* **boast** (bōst) *verb,* **boasted, boasting;** *noun, plural* **boasts. —boastful** *adjective.*

boat **1.** A small vessel used for traveling on water, moved by oars, paddles, sails, or a motor: *Passengers in a* **boat** *usually sit in the open air.* **2.** A ship. An ocean liner is a boat. *Noun.*

○ To go in a boat: *We want to spend the morning* **boating.** *Verb.*

boat (bōt) *noun, plural* **boats;** *verb,* **boated, boating.**

The **boat** is making a large wake as it moves through the water.

boathouse A building for sheltering or storing boats. **boat·house** (bōt′hous′) *noun, plural* **boathouses** (bōt′hou′ziz).

bob¹ To move up and down or back and forth with a jerky motion: *The ball* **bobbed** *on the waves. Verb.*

○ A jerky motion: *The bus driver answered my question with a* **bob** *of the head. Noun.* **bob** (bob) *verb,* **bobbed, bobbing;** *noun, plural* **bobs.**

bob² **1.** A short haircut for a woman or child. **2.** A float or cork of a fishing line. *Noun.*

○ To cut hair short. *Verb.* **bob** (bob) *noun, plural* **bobs;** *verb,* **bobbed, bobbing.**

bobbin A spool around which yarn or thread is wound. A bobbin is used in weaving and in sewing on a sewing machine. **bob·bin** (bob′in) *noun, plural* **bobbins.**

bobcat A small wildcat of North America. A bobcat has reddish brown fur with dark stripes or spots and a short tail. **bob·cat** (bob′kat′) *noun, plural* **bobcats.**

bobolink A songbird of North and South America that lives in fields. **bob·o·link** (bob′ə lingk′) *noun, plural* **bobolinks.**

bobsled A long sled for racing. A bobsled has two sets of runners, a steering wheel, and brakes. **bob·sled** (bob′sled′) *noun, plural* **bobsleds.**

bobwhite A North American quail that has a reddish brown body with white, black, and tan markings. Its call sounds a little like its name. **bob·white** (bob′hwīt′ *or* bob′wīt′) *noun, plural* **bobwhites.**

bode To be a sign of: *Those dark clouds* **bode** *a storm.* **bode** (bōd) *verb,* **boded, boding.**

bodily Of the body: *They suffered no* **bodily** *harm.* **bod·i·ly** (bod′əlē) *adjective.*

body **1.** The whole physical structure that makes up a person, animal, or plant. **2.** The main part of a human being or animal, without the head, arms, and legs: *This bathing suit covers the* **body** *but leaves the limbs bare.* **3.** The main part of something: *The* **body** *of the new jet airplane is very large.* **4.** A group of persons or things: *the student* **body.** **5.** A separate mass: *The sun, the moon, and the stars are heavenly* **bodies.** **bod·y** (bod′ē) *noun, plural* **bodies.**

bodyguard A person or persons who protect someone from danger or attack. **bod·y·guard** (bod′ēgärd′) *noun, plural* **bodyguards.**

bog Wet, spongy ground; marsh; swamp: *Cranberries grow in* **bogs.** *Noun.*

○ To become stuck: *The car will* **bog** *down in the mud. Verb.* **bog** (bog) *noun, plural* **bogs;** *verb,* **bogged, bogging.**

Different types of insects live in **bogs** such as this one.

boil¹ **1.** To heat or be heated so that bubbles form and steam is given off: *Water* **boils** *at 212 degrees Fahrenheit.* **2.** To cook by boiling: *We* **boiled** *the potatoes for dinner. Verb.*

PRONUNCIATION KEY:

| at | āpe | fär | câre | end | mē | it | īce | pierce | hot | ōld | sông | fôrk |
| oil | out | up | ūse | rüle | pull | tûrn | chin | sing | shop | thin | this | |

hw in white; zh in treasure. The symbol ə stands for the unstressed vowel sound in about, taken, pencil, lemon, and circus.

87

○ The condition of boiling: *Bring the water to a boil. Noun.*
boil (boil) *verb,* **boiled, boiling;** *noun.*

boil² A painful red swelling beneath the skin that is caused by infection and is full of pus. **boil** (boil) *noun, plural* **boils.**

boiler **1.** A large tank in which water is heated and turned into steam. The steam made in a boiler is used to heat buildings and to run engines. **2.** A pan or pot in which something is heated or boiled: *We cooked the ears of corn in a large boiler.* **boil·er** (boi′lər) *noun, plural* **boilers.**

boiling point The temperature at which a liquid begins to boil. The boiling point of fresh water at sea level is 212 degrees on a Fahrenheit thermometer, or 100 degrees on a Centigrade thermometer.

bold **1.** Not afraid; brave: *A bold person is willing to do dangerous things. The firefighter made a bold rescue of the child from the burning roof.* **2.** Not polite; rude; fresh: *The bold child talked back to the teacher.* **3.** Very easy to see; standing out clearly: *The mountains make a bold outline against the sky.* **bold** (bōld) *adjective,* **bolder, boldest.** —**boldly** *adverb.* —**boldness** *noun.*

Bolivia A country in west-central South America. **Bo·liv·i·a** (bə liv′ē ə) *noun.*

boll The seed pod of a cotton or flax plant. Another word that sounds like this is **bowl.** **boll** (bōl) *noun, plural* **bolls.**

boll weevil A beetle that lays eggs in the seed pods of the cotton plant. Boll weevils cause a great deal of damage to cotton plants. **boll wee·vil** (wē′vəl).

bolster A long pillow or cushion. *Noun.*
○ To give support or strength to: *The sight of land bolstered the sailors' low spirits. Verb.* **bol·ster** (bōl′stər) *noun, plural* **bolsters;** *verb,* **bolstered, bolstering.**

bolt **1.** A rod used to hold things together. A bolt usually has a head at one end and screw threads for a nut at the other. **2.** A sliding bar for fastening a door: *I closed the door and slid the bolt shut.* **3.** The part of a lock moved by a key. **4.** A sudden spring or start: *The deer made a bolt for the woods.* **5.** A flash of lightning. **6.** A roll of cloth or paper. *Noun.*
○ **1.** To fasten with a bolt. **2.** To spring or move suddenly: *The child bolted out the door.* **3.** To swallow quickly or without chewing; gulp down: *Don't bolt your breakfast! Verb.*
bolt (bōlt) *noun, plural* **bolts;** *verb,* **bolted, bolting.**

bomb A hollow case filled with an explosive. It is used as a weapon and explodes when it strikes something or when it is set off by a fuse or a timing device. *Noun.*
○ To throw or drop a bomb on. *Verb.*
bomb (bom) *noun, plural* **bombs;** *verb,* **bombed, bombing.**

bombard **1.** To attack with bombs or heavy fire from big guns: *Cannons bombarded the fort.* **2.** To aim many questions or criticisms at: *The reporters bombarded the candidates with questions.* **bom·bard** (bom bärd′) *verb,* **bombarded, bombarding.**

bomber An airplane used to drop bombs. **bomb·er** (bom′ər) *noun, plural* **bombers.**

bond **1.** Something that fastens or holds together: *The prisoner's bonds were made of rope.* **2.** A feeling or understanding that holds people together; tie: *a bond of friendship between us.* **3.** A certificate given by a government or a business for a loan of money. A bond is a promise to pay back the money borrowed on a certain date with interest. **bond** (bond) *noun, plural* **bonds.**

bondage Slavery; lack of freedom: *Abraham Lincoln freed the slaves from bondage in 1863.* **bond·age** (bon′dij) *noun.*

bone One of the parts of the skeleton of an animal with a backbone. Bones are hard and firm. *Noun.*
○ To take out the bones of: *We boned the fish before cooking it. Verb.*
bone (bōn) *noun, plural* **bones;** *verb,* **boned, boning.**

bonfire A large fire built outdoors: *We sat around the bonfire at camp.* **bon·fire** (bon′fīr′) *noun, plural* **bonfires.**

bongo drums A pair of small drums played with the hands while being held between the knees. **bon·go drums** (bong′gō).

bonnet **1.** A covering for the head, usually tied under the chin by ribbons or strings. **2.** A covering for the head made of feathers, worn during ceremonies by North American Indians. **bon·net** (bon′it) *noun, plural* **bonnets.**

bonus Something extra given or paid in addition to what is usual: *At the end of the year, the workers received a bonus in addition to their wages.* **bo·nus** (bō′nəs) *noun, plural* **bonuses.**

bony 1. Made of bone: *The skeleton is a* **bony** *structure*. 2. Full of bones: *The fish we caught was so* **bony** *that it was hard to eat*. 3. Very thin: *a* **bony** *old dog*. **bon·y** (bō′nē) *adjective*, **bonier**, **boniest**.

boo A sound made to frighten or to show dislike: *I leaped out of the closet and yelled "Boo!"* *Interjection*.
○ To show that one does not like something by shouting "boo." *Verb*.
boo (bü) *interjection; verb*, **booed**, **booing**.

book 1. Sheets of paper fastened together between two covers. The pages of a book usually have writing or printing on them. 2. A section of a long printed work: *There are sixty-three* **books** *in my Bible. Noun*.
○ To arrange for ahead of time: *My parents* **booked** *rooms at the motel. Verb*.
book (bûk) *noun, plural* **books**; *verb*, **booked**, **booking**.

bookcase A set of shelves for holding books. **book·case** (bûk′kās′) *noun, plural* **bookcases**.

bookkeeper A person who keeps the records of a business: *The* **bookkeeper** *at the grocery store keeps a record of the store's sales*. **book·keep·er** (bûk′kē′pər) *noun, plural* **bookkeepers**.

booklet A small, thin book, usually with paper covers. **book·let** (bûk′lit) *noun, plural* **booklets**.

bookmark A piece of paper, a ribbon, or something similar placed in a book to show the page the reader wishes to return to. **book·mark** (bûk′märk′) *noun, plural* **bookmarks**.

bookmobile A truck or other vehicle that travels around with books that can be borrowed. **book·mo·bile** (bûk′mō bēl′) *noun, plural* **book·mobiles**.

boom¹ 1. A deep, hollow sound: *the* **boom** *of thunder*. 2. A time of fast growth: *There was a* **boom** *in the sale of overshoes after the heavy snowstorm. Noun*.
○ 1. To make a deep, hollow sound. 2. To grow suddenly and rapidly: *The number of people at baseball games* **booms** *as summer comes closer. Verb*.
boom (büm) *noun, plural* **booms**; *verb*, **boomed**, **booming**.

boom² 1. A long pole or beam used to stretch the bottom of a sail. 2. The long movable arm of a crane or derrick. The load being lifted hangs from the end of the boom. **boom** (büm) *noun, plural* **booms**.

boomerang A flat curved piece of wood that can be thrown so that it returns to the thrower. **boom·er·ang** (bü′mə rang′) *noun, plural* **boomerangs**.

The boomerang originated in Australia among the native peoples.

boon A help; benefit: *The rain was a* **boon** *to my vegetable garden after the dry weather*. **boon** (bün) *noun, plural* **boons**.

boost 1. A push or shove up: *a* **boost** *up the tree*. 2. Something that gives support or encouragement: *The teacher's praise gave me a* **boost**. *Noun*.
○ 1. To push or shove up. 2. To give support to; encourage. 3. To make greater; increase: *The factory* **boosted** *its production of cars. Verb*.
boost (büst) *noun, plural* **boosts**; *verb*, **boosted**, **boosting**.

booster shot An extra injection of a vaccine, given to continue the protection given by an earlier injection. **boost·er shot** (bü′stər).

boot A covering for the foot and lower part of the leg, usually made of leather or rubber. *Noun*.
○ 1. To kick: *The player* **booted** *the football*.
• **to boot up**. To start up a computer. *Verb*.
boot (büt) *noun, plural* **boots**; *verb*, **booted**, **booting**.

bootee A soft shoe for a baby: *We bought a pair of* **bootees** *for our neighbor's baby that were knitted from soft cotton*.
Another word that sounds like this is **booty**.
boot·ee (bü′tē) *noun, plural* **bootees**.

booth 1. A stall where things are sold or shown: *People crowded around the refreshment* **booth** *at the fair*. 2. A small closed place: *a telephone* **booth**. **booth** (büth) *noun, plural* **booths** (büthz or bü<u>th</u>s).

booty Things taken from people by force; plunder, loot: *The* **booty** *the pirates had included jewelry, coins, and silk*.

PRONUNCIATION KEY:
at   āpe   fär   câre   end   mē   it   īce   pierce   hot   ōld   sông   fôrk
oil   out   up   ūse   rüle   pùll   tûrn   chin   sing   shop   thin   <u>th</u>is
hw in white; zh in treasure. The symbol ə stands for the unstressed vowel sound in about, taken, pencil, lemon, and circus.

89

Another word that sounds like this is **bootee**. **boot·y** (bü′tē) *noun, plural* **booties**.

border **1.** A line where one country or other area ends and another begins; boundary. **2.** A strip along the edge of something: *This skirt has a pretty red* **border**. *Noun.*
○ **1.** To lie on the edge of: *California* **borders** *Oregon*. **2.** To put an edging on: *The handkerchief was* **bordered** *with lace. Verb.*
bor·der (bôr′dər) *noun, plural* **borders**; *verb*, **bordered, bordering**.

bore¹ **1.** To make by digging or drilling: *The road builders* **bored** *a tunnel through the mountain.* **2.** To make a hole in: *The carpenter* **bored** *the wood with a drill.*
Another word that sounds like this is **boar**.
bore (bôr) *verb*, **bored, boring**.

bore² To make tired or restless by being dull: *You can* **bore** *people by telling them the same jokes over and over again. Verb.*
○ A person or thing that is dull. *Noun.*
Another word that sounds like this is **boar**.
bore (bôr) *verb*, **bored, boring**; *noun, plural* **bores**.

bore³ Past tense of **bear**.
Another word that sounds like this is **boar**.
bore (bôr) *verb*.

boredom The condition of being bored: *Boredom with my job caused me to quit.* **bore·dom** (bôr′dəm) *noun.*

born **1.** Brought into life or being. **2.** By birth; natural: *a* **born** *athlete. Adjective.*
○ A past participle of **bear**: *I was* **born** *and raised on a farm. Verb.*
Another word that sounds like this is **borne**.
born (bôrn) *adjective; verb.*

borne A past participle of **bear**: *My friend has* **borne** *the pain bravely.*
Another word that sounds like this is **born**.
borne (bôrn) *verb.*

borough **1.** In some states of the United States, a town or village that governs itself. **2.** One of the five divisions of New York City.
Other words that sound like this are **burro** and **burrow**.
bor·ough (bûr′ō) *noun, plural* **boroughs**.

borrow **1.** To take something from another person with the understanding that it must be given back: *We* **borrow** *books from the library.* **2.** To take something and use it as one's own: *The word "chipmunk" was* **borrowed** *from*
Native Americans. **bor·row** (bôr′ō or bor′ō) *verb*, **borrowed, borrowing**.

bosom The upper, front part of the chest: *I hugged the kitten to my* **bosom**. *Noun.*
○ Close and dear: **bosom** *buddies. Adjective.*
bos·om (bùz′əm) *noun, plural* **bosoms**; *adjective.*

boss A person who watches over and plans the work of others. *Noun.*
○ To act like the boss of: *The older campers* **bossed** *us around. Verb.*
boss (bôs) *noun, plural* **bosses**; *verb*, **bossed, bossing**.

botany The study of plants. People who study botany learn about many kinds of plants and how they grow and where they grow. **bot·a·ny** (bot′ə nē) *noun.* —**botanist** *noun.*

both One and also the other; the two: *Both players are left-handed. Adjective.*
○ The one and also the other: *You need a pencil and paper, so bring* **both**. *Pronoun.*
○ Equally; as well: *That bowl you made is* **both** *beautiful and useful. Conjunction.*
both (bōth) *adjective; pronoun; conjunction.*

bother **1.** To give trouble to; annoy. **2.** To make concerned or worried: *It* **bothers** *me that my parents aren't home yet.* **3.** To take the trouble: *Don't* **bother** *to make lunch for me. Verb.*
○ A person or thing that troubles or annoys: *Making my bed is a* **bother**. *Noun.*
both·er (both′ər) *verb*, **bothered, bothering**; *noun, plural* **bothers**.

Botswana A country in south-central Africa. **Bot·swa·na** (bot swä′nə) *noun.*

bottle A container to hold liquids. A bottle has a narrow neck closed with a cap or stopper. Bottles are usually made of glass or plastic. *Noun.*
○ To put in bottles. *Verb.*
  • **to bottle up.** To hide or control; hold in: *I* **bottled** *up my anger at their rude behavior.*

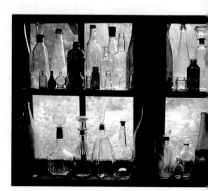

Like basket-weaving, the making of bottles is an ancient craft.

bot·tle (bot′əl) *noun, plural* **bottles**; *verb,* **bottled, bottling.**

bottom **1.** The lowest part: *the* **bottom** *of a hill.* **2.** The under or lower part: *the* **bottom** *of a rowboat.* **3.** The ground under a body of water: *the* **bottom** *of a pond.* **4.** The most important part; basis: *the* **bottom** *of a mystery. Noun.*
○ Lowest or last: *the* **bottom** *drawer of a bureau. Adjective.*
bot·tom (bot′əm) *noun, plural* **bottoms**; *adjective.*

bough A large branch of a tree.
Other words that sound like this are **bow**[1] and **bow**[3].
bough (bou) *noun, plural* **boughs.**

bought Past tense and past participle of **buy.**
bought (bôt) *verb.*

boulder A large, usually rounded rock. **boul·der** (bōl′dər) *noun, plural* **boulders.**

boulevard A wide city street, often with trees growing along its sides. **boul·e·vard** (búl′ə värd′) *noun, plural* **boulevards.**

bounce **1.** To spring back or up after hitting something: *The ball* **bounced** *off the wall.* **2.** To cause to spring back or up: *I* **bounced** *the basketball against the sidewalk. Verb.*
○ A spring; bound. *Noun.*
bounce (bouns) *verb,* **bounced, bouncing**; *noun, plural* **bounces.**

bound[1] **1.** Fastened; tied: *The bank robbers left the guard* **bound** *and gagged.* **2.** Certain; sure: *We are* **bound** *to lose if we don't practice.* **3.** Have an obligation; obliged: *I am* **bound** *to keep the secret. Adjective.*
○ Past tense and past participle of **bind.** *Verb.*
bound (bound) *adjective; verb.*

bound[2] **1.** To leap; spring; jump: *The rabbit* **bounded** *away into the woods.* **2.** To spring back after hitting something: *The ball* **bounded** *off the wall. Verb.*
○ A long or high leap. *Noun.*
bound (bound) *verb,* **bounded, bounding**; *noun, plural* **bounds.**

bound[3] A border; boundary: *We marked the* **bounds** *of the volleyball court with string. Noun.*
○ To form the boundary of: *A road* **bounds** *the farmer's land on the north. Verb.*
  • **out of bounds. 1.** Beyond the limits of a playing field or court: *The soccer ball rolled* **out of bounds. 2.** Not allowed: *Swimming in the pool is* **out of bounds** *after six o'clock.*
bound (bound) *noun, plural* **bounds**; *verb,* **bounded, bounding.**

bound[4] Going or intending to go; headed: *The train is* **bound** *for New York.* **bound** (bound) *adjective.*

boundary A line that marks the edge of a country, state, or other area; border: *The Rio Grande forms the* **boundary** *between Mexico and the United States.* **bound·a·ry** (bound′ə rē *or* boun′drē) *noun, plural* **boundaries.**

bountiful More than enough; abundant: *a* **bountiful** *harvest.* **boun·ti·ful** (boun′təfəl) *adjective.*

bounty **1.** A reward for killing a dangerous or destructive animal. **2.** Generosity; goodness: *Many poor people were helped by the rich family's* **bounty.** **boun·ty** (boun′tē) *noun, plural* **bounties.**

bouquet A bunch of flowers. **bou·quet** (bō kā′ *or* bü kā′) *noun, plural* **bouquets.**

bout **1.** A trial of skill; contest: *The two boxers will fight in the second* **bout. 2.** An attack or outburst; fit; spell: *a* **bout** *of coughing.* **bout** (bout) *noun, plural* **bouts.**

bow[1] **1.** To bend forward. People bow to show respect, to greet someone, or to accept the applause of an audience. **2.** To give in; submit: *I* **bowed** *to my parents' wishes. Verb.*
○ A bending forward of the head or body. *Noun.*
Another word that sounds like this is **bough.**
bow (bou) *verb,* **bowed, bowing**; *noun, plural* **bows.**

bow[2] **1.** A weapon for shooting arrows, made of a strip of wood bent by a string fastened to each end. **2.** A knot with two or more loops: *I'll tie a green* **bow** *on the package.* **3.** A long piece of wood with horsehairs stretched from one end to the other, used to play the violin and other stringed instruments. **bow** (bō) *noun, plural* **bows.**

A bow is as important to a violinist as his or her violin.

PRONUNCIATION KEY:

| at | āpe | fär | câre | end | mē | it | īce | pierce | hot | ōld | sông | fôrk |
| oil | out | up | ūse | rüle | púll | tûrn | chin | sing | shop | thin | this | |

hw in white; zh in treasure. The symbol ə stands for the unstressed vowel sound in about, taken, pencil, lemon, and circus.

91

bow³ The front end of a boat.
Another word that sounds like this is **bough.**
bow (bou) *noun, plural* **bows.**

bowels **1.** A long tube that forms the part of the digestive system below the stomach; intestines. **2.** The deepest part of something: *The coal mine was in the **bowels** of the earth.* **bow·els** (bou′əlz) *plural noun.*

bowl¹ **1.** A rounded dish that holds things. **2.** Something shaped like a bowl. The round end of a spoon is called a bowl. A football stadium is sometimes called a bowl.
Another word that sounds like this is **boll.**
bowl (bōl) *noun, plural* **bowls.**

bowl² A wooden ball used in a game. *Noun.*
○ **1.** To play the game of bowling. **2.** To roll a ball in bowling. *Verb.*
Another word that sounds like this is **boll.**
bowl (bōl) *noun, plural* **bowls**; *verb,* **bowled, bowling.**

bowlegged Having legs that curve outward at the knee when the ankles are together.
bow·leg·ged (bō′leg′id) *adjective.*

bowling A game you play by rolling a heavy ball to knock down wooden pins. The balls are rolled on a wooden alley or a smooth lawn.
bowl·ing (bō′ling) *noun.*

Bowling is a highly popular sport.

box¹ **1.** A stiff container, usually having four sides, a bottom, and a cover. A box is made of cardboard, wood, or other material. **2.** A closed-in area or place: *We sat in a **box** at the theater. Noun.*
○ To put in a box. *Verb.*
box (boks) *noun, plural* **boxes**; *verb,* **boxed, boxing.**

box² A blow made with the open hand or the fist: *In the old movie, the mad scientist woke the sleeping assistant with a **box** on the ear. Noun.*
○ **1.** To hit with the open hand or the fist. **2.** To fight someone with the fists as a sport. *Verb.*

box (boks) *noun, plural* **boxes**; *verb,* **boxed, boxing.**

boxcar A car of a railroad train used to carry freight, enclosed on all sides and loaded through a sliding door on the side. **box·car** (boks′kär′) *noun, plural* **boxcars.**

boxer **1.** A person who fights with the fists as a sport. **2.** A dog that has a wide face, short hair, and a tan or reddish-brown coat, sometimes with white markings. Boxers are related to bulldogs. **box·er** (bok′sər) *noun, plural* **boxers.**

boxing The sport of fighting with the fists. **box·ing** (bok′sing) *noun.*

Boxing Day A holiday observed the first weekday after Christmas in England, Canada, and some other countries.

boy A male child from birth to the time he is a young man. **boy** (boi) *noun, plural* **boys.**

boycott To join with others in refusing to buy from or deal with a person, nation, or business: *We **boycotted** the store to show support for the strike by its employees. Verb.*
○ A planned joining with others in refusing to buy from or deal with a person, nation, or business. *Noun.*
boy·cott (boi′kot) *verb,* **boycotted, boycotting**; *noun, plural* **boycotts.**

WORD HISTORY

Over one hundred years ago a man named Captain Charles **Boycott** collected rent from farmers in Ireland. The owner of the land was English, and the farmers thought they should own the land themselves, instead of someone from another country. So they refused to pay their rent to Captain Boycott. None of the people would talk to him. Captain Boycott finally had to give up his job and go back to England. Since then, the word **boycott** has been used in talking about actions of this kind.

boyfriend **1.** A man or boy who is one's sweetheart. **2.** A friend who is a man or boy. (boi′ frend′)

boyhood The time of being a boy. **boy·hood** (boi′hŏd′) *noun, plural* **boyhoods.**

boyish Of a boy; like a boy. **boy·ish** (boi′ish) *adjective.*

boy scout A member of the Boy Scouts.

Boy Scouts An organization for boys. The Boy Scouts teaches boys outdoor skills, physical fitness, and good citizenship.

brace **1.** Something that holds parts together or holds a thing steady: *The roof of the shed needs a brace to hold it up.* **2. braces**. Metal wires used to help teeth to grow straight. **3.** A tool that is like a handle, used to hold a drill or bit. **4.** A pair: *a brace of pistols. Noun.*
○ **1.** To hold steady; support. **2.** To prepare for a shock: *Brace yourself for some bad news.* **3.** To give energy to: *The cold air braced us. Verb.*
brace (brās) *noun, plural* **braces**; *verb,* **braced, bracing.**

bracelet A band or chain worn around the wrist as an ornament. **brace·let** (brās′lit) *noun, plural* **bracelets.**

bracket **1.** A piece of wood, metal, or stone fastened to a wall to support something: *The shelf was held up by brackets.* **2.** One of two marks, [ ], used to enclose words or numbers. **3.** Group: *books for children in the 8-to-11 age bracket. Noun.*
○ **1.** To put words or numbers in brackets. **2.** To group together: *The teacher will bracket the students according to their reading speeds. Verb.*
brack·et (brak′it) *noun, plural* **brackets**; *verb,* **bracketed, bracketing.**

brad A thin nail with a small head. **brad** (brad) *noun, plural* **brads.**

brag To speak with too much praise about what one does or owns; boast. **brag** (brag) *verb,* **bragged, bragging.**

braid A strip made by weaving together three or more long pieces of hair, straw, or cloth: *I wear my hair in braids. Noun.*
○ To weave together long pieces of hair, straw, or cloth. *Verb.*
braid (brād) *noun, plural* **braids**; *verb,* **braided, braiding.**

braille A system of printing for blind

The girl is wearing her hair in a braid.

people. The letters of the alphabet in braille are formed by raised dots. Blind people read braille by touching the dots with their fingers. **braille** (brāl) *noun.*

WORD HISTORY

The word braille comes from the name of the blind Frenchman, Louis Braille, who invented this way to read and write.

---

brain **1.** The large mass of nerve tissue inside the skull of persons and animals. The brain is the main part of the nervous system and controls the actions of the body. It is also the center of thought, memory, learning, and the emotions. **2. brains**. Intelligence: *It takes brains to figure out this puzzle. Noun.*
○ To hit on the head: *I got brained with a baseball. Verb.*
brain (brān) *noun, plural* **brains**; *verb,* **brained, braining.**

brainstorm A sudden, bright idea; inspiration. **brain·storm** (brān′stôrm′) *noun, plural* **brainstorms.**

brake A device used to stop or slow the movement of a vehicle. Many brakes work by pressing a pad against the moving wheel. *Noun.*
○ To cause something to stop or slow down by using a brake. *Verb.*
Another word that sounds like this is **break.**
brake (brāk) *noun, plural* **brakes**; *verb,* **braked, braking.**

bramble A bush with thorny stems. The blackberry plant is a kind of bramble. **bram·ble** (bram′bəl) *noun, plural* **brambles.**

bran The outer covering of wheat or other grains. The bran is separated from the flour by sifting and is used in breakfast cereals and other foods. **bran** (bran) *noun.*

branch **1.** A part of a tree or bush that grows out from the trunk. **2.** Something that goes out of or into a main part, like the branch of a tree: *The Missouri River is a branch of the Mississippi River.* **3.** A division, office, or part of a large thing: *a neighborhood branch of the city library. Noun.*
○ To divide into branches. *Verb.*
branch (branch) *noun, plural* **branches**; *verb,* **branched, branching.**

PRONUNCIATION KEY:

| at | āpe | fär | câre | end | mē | it | ice | pierce | hot | ōld | sông | fôrk |
| oil | out | up | ūse | rüle | pùll | tûrn | chin | sing | shop | thin | this | |

hw in white; zh in treasure. The symbol ə stands for the unstressed vowel sound in about, taken, pencil, lemon, and circus.

93

brand **1.** A kind or make of something: *I tried a new brand of soap.* **2.** A mark made on the skin of cattle or other animals. A brand is often made with a hot iron and shows who owns an animal. **3.** A mark of disgrace. In former times a brand was burned on the skin of criminals. *Noun.*
○ **1.** To mark with a brand: *They branded the steers.* **2.** To call by a bad or shameful name: *branded as a coward. Verb.*
brand (brand) *noun, plural* **brands;** *verb,* **branded, branding.**

Cowboys brand cattle so that they will
be returned if they go astray.

brand-new Completely new: *a brand-new car.*
brand-new (brand′nü′ *or* brand′nū′) *adjective.*

brandy An alcoholic drink made from fermented fruit juice or wine. **bran·dy** (bran′dē) *noun, plural* **brandies.**

brass **1.** A yellow metal that is a mixture of copper and zinc melted together. **2. brasses.** Wind instruments made of brass or other metal, such as trumpets, trombones, and French horns. **brass** (bras) *noun.*

This trombone is
a brass.

brat A child who misbehaves or has bad manners. **brat** (brat) *noun, plural* **brats.**

brave Having courage. A brave person can face danger or pain without being overcome by fear: *brave firefighters. Adjective.*
○ To face danger or pain without being overcome by fear. *Verb.*
brave (brāv) *adjective,* **braver, bravest;** *verb,* **braved, braving.** —**bravely** *adverb.*

bravery The ability to face danger or pain without

being overcome by fear; courage. **brav·er·y** (brā′və rē) *noun.*

Brazil A country in eastern South America. **Bra·zil** (brə zil′) *noun.*

breach A break made in something: *Water poured through the breach in the dam. Noun.*
○ To make a break in; break through. *Verb.*
breach (brēch) *noun, plural* **breaches;** *verb,* **breached, breaching.**

bread **1.** A food made by mixing flour or meal with water or milk, and then baking it in an oven. **2.** The food and other things needed for a person to live: *We earn our daily bread by working.* Another word that sounds like this is **bred.**
bread (bred) *noun, plural* **breads.**

From the earliest days, bread has been
one of the world's most basic foods.

breadth The wideness of something measured from one side to the other side; width. **breadth** (bredth) *noun.*

break **1.** To come apart or make something come apart by force. **2.** To crack a bone: *I broke my wrist in gym.* **3.** To open the surface of: *It's time to break ground for planting.* **4.** To make or become useless because of damage; ruin: *If you play roughly with that calculator, you might break it.* **5.** To stop; end: *It's hard to break a habit like smoking.* **6.** To fail to obey or fulfill: *Don't break the law.* **7.** To go beyond; surpass: *This heat could break a record.* **8.** To fill with sorrow: *The disappointment broke my heart.* **9.** To tell; reveal: *Break the news gently. Verb.*
○ **1.** A broken place; something broken: *a break in a fence.* **2.** A sudden rush; dash: *a break for the door.* **3.** A sudden change: *a break in the rainy weather.* **4.** A short rest period: *I took a break. Noun.*
Another word that sounds like this is **brake.**

• **to break down. 1.** To stop or stop working: *Our car broke down.* **2.** To become ill physically or mentally. **3.** To lose one's self-control; act in an emotional way: *I broke down and cried.* **4.** To separate into smaller or simpler parts: *The chemist broke down the substance into its elements.*

• **to break in. 1.** To make ready for use or wear: *I'm breaking in a new pair of sneakers.* **2.** To enter by force: *A thief broke in through the door.* **3.** To interrupt: *The student broke in with a question while the teacher was talking.*

• **to break off.** To stop suddenly: *The speaker broke off to take a drink of water.*

• **to break out. 1.** To start suddenly: *A fire broke out.* **2.** To become covered with a rash or pimples: *The poison ivy made my skin break out.* **3.** To escape: *Three prisoners broke out last night.*

• **to break up. 1.** To separate, scatter, or disperse: *The ice on the pond is breaking up.* **2.** To come or bring to an end: *The meeting broke up very late.*

break (brāk) *verb*, **broke, broken, breaking**; *noun*, *plural* **breaks.**

breakdown 1. A failing to work: *Because of the breakdown of the car, we had to walk.* **2.** A sudden loss of good health; collapse: *When people work too hard, they sometimes suffer a breakdown.* **break·down** (brāk′doun′) *noun*, *plural* **breakdowns.**

breaker A large wave that foams as it breaks on

Breakers often roll in one after another.

rocks or the shore. **break·er** (brā′kər) *noun*, *plural* **breakers.**

breakfast The first meal of the day. *Noun.*
○ To eat breakfast. *Verb.*
break·fast (brek′fəst) *noun*, *plural* **breakfasts**; *verb*, **breakfasted, breakfasting.**

WORD HISTORY

The word *fast* means "a time of eating little or no food." The morning meal breakfast was given its name because it is the meal that "breaks" the "fast" that lasts from after supper until waking up the next morning.

---

breast 1. The front part of the body, between the stomach and the neck; chest: *I pressed the baby to my breast.* **2.** Either of the two milk glands of women. **breast** (brest) *noun*, *plural* **breasts.**

breastbone The flat narrow bone in the center of the breast. The ribs are joined to the breastbone. **breast·bone** (brest′bōn) *noun*, *plural* **breastbones.**

breath 1. Air drawn into and forced out of the lungs when you breathe. **2.** The act of breathing; respiration: *The doctor asked me to take a deep breath.* **3.** The ability to breathe easily: *It took a few minutes for me to get my breath back after the race.* **4.** A slight flow of air: *There was not a breath of fresh air in the room.*

• **to catch one's breath.** To rest long enough to regain one's normal rhythm of breathing: *I had to sit down to catch my breath after the long climb.*
breath (breth) *noun*, *plural* **breaths.**

breathe 1. To draw air into the lungs and then release it. **2.** To whisper: *Don't breathe a word of the secret.* **breathe** (brēth) *verb*, **breathed, breathing.**

breathless 1. Out of breath: *I was breathless after running all the way.* **2.** Holding the breath because of excitement or fear: *The children were breathless as they watched the acrobats at the circus.* **breath·less** (breth′lis) *adjective*;

bred Past tense and past participle of **breed.** Another word that sounds like this is **bread. bred** (bred) *verb*.

PRONUNCIATION KEY:
at   āpe   fär   câre   end   mē   it   īce   pierce   hot   ōld   sông   fôrk
oil   out   up   ūse   rüle   pull   tûrn   chin   sing   shop   thin   this
hw in white; zh in treasure. The symbol ə stands for the unstressed vowel sound in about, taken, pencil, lemon, and circus.   **95**

breeches Pants that reach to or just below the knees, worn by men and boys in the past. **breech·es** (brich′iz) *plural noun.*

The young people in this parade are wearing breeches.

breed 1. To raise plants or animals: *They breed orchids in their greenhouse.* 2. To bring forth young. 3. To give rise to; produce: *War breeds misery. Verb.*
○ A particular kind of plant or animal: *Dachshunds and collies are breeds of dogs. Noun.*
breed (brēd) *verb,* **bred, breeding;** *noun, plural* **breeds.**

breeding 1. The raising or growing of animals or plants. 2. The way someone is brought up; training: *Good manners are a sign of good breeding.* **breed·ing** (brē′ding) *noun.*

breeze A mild, gentle wind. *Noun.*
○ To move or act in an easy or quick way: *We all breezed through the test. Verb.*
breeze (brēz) *noun, plural* **breezes;** *verb,* **breezed, breezing.**

brew 1. To make beer or ale. Beer and ale are brewed by soaking, boiling, and fermenting malt and hops. 2. To make by soaking in hot or boiling water: *I'll brew a pot of peppermint tea.* 3. To bring about; cause: *brewing mischief.* 4. To form; gather: *A storm is brewing. Verb.*
○ A drink made by brewing. *Noun.* **brew** (brü) *verb,* **brewed, brewing;** *noun, plural* **brews.**

briar *or* **brier** A thorny shrub. Look up **brier** for more information. **bri·ar** (brī′ər) *noun, plural,* **briars.**

bribe Money or gifts given to make a person do something wrong or something the person does not want to do. *Noun.*
○ To give a bribe to: *I bribed the child to stop crying by offering a toy. Verb.*

bribe (brīb) *noun, plural* **bribes;** *verb,* **bribed, bribing.**

brick A block of clay baked in a kiln or in the sun. **brick** (brik) *noun, plural* **bricks.**

bride A woman who has just married or is about to be married. **bride** (brīd) *noun, plural* **brides.**

bridegroom A man who has just married or is about to be married. **bride·groom** (brīd′grüm′ *or* brīd′grùm′) *noun, plural* **bridegrooms.**

Bricks are used in building.

bridge 1. A structure built across a river, road, or railroad track so that people can get from one side to the other. 2. The top, bony part of a person's nose. 3. A raised structure on the deck of a ship. The captain guides or runs the ship from the bridge. *Noun.*
○ To build a bridge across. *Verb.*
bridge (brij) *noun, plural* **bridges;** *verb,* **bridged, bridging.**

bridle The part of a horse's harness that fits over the animal's head, used to guide or control the horse. *Noun.*
○ 1. To put a bridle on. 2. To hold back; control: *You should bridle your bad temper. Verb.*
bri·dle (brī′dəl) *noun, plural* **bridles;** *verb,* **bridled, bridling.**

brief 1. Short in time: *a brief visit.* 2. Using few words: *a brief letter. Adjective.*
○ To give important details or facts to: *The commander briefed the pilots before the mission. Verb.*
brief (brēf) *adjective,* **briefer, briefest;** *verb,* **briefed, briefing. —briefly** *adverb.*

brier *or* **briar** A bushy plant with thorns. The raspberry plant and the blackberry plant are sometimes called briers. The thorns on these plants are also called briers. **bri·er** (brī′ər) *noun, plural* **briers.**

brig 1. A sailing ship with square sails on two masts. 2. A prison on a ship. **brig** (brig) *noun, plural* **brigs.**

brigade 1. A large part of an army, made up of two or more battalions. 2. A group of people organized for a purpose: *a fire brigade.* **bri·gade** (bri gād′) *noun, plural* **brigades.**

bright **1.** Giving much light; filled with light: *the bright light of the sun.* **2.** Clear; strong: *Let's paint the chair a bright red.* **3.** Smart; clever: *bright children.* **bright** (brīt) *adjective,* **brighter, brightest.**

brilliant **1.** Very bright; sparkling: *a brilliant light.* **2.** Very fine; splendid: *The fielder made a brilliant catch.* **3.** Very intelligent: *a brilliant scientist.* **bril·liant** (bril′yənt) *adjective;*

brim An edge or rim: *a glass filled to the brim.* *Noun.*
○ To be full to the brim: *The bathtub was brimming with water. Verb.*
brim (brim) *noun, plural* **brims;** *verb,* **brimmed, brimming.**

brine Water full of salt, used for pickling foods. **brine** (brīn) *noun.*

bring **1.** To cause something or someone to come with you. **2.** To cause something to come or happen: *The heavy rains will bring floods.* **3.** To cause to reach a certain condition: *Bring the water to a boil.* **4.** To be sold for: *The necklace brought a high price.*
• **to bring on.** To lead to; cause: *That chilly wind brought on my stiff neck.*
• **to bring out.** **1.** To make clear; show: *That shirt brings out the color of your eyes.* **2.** To offer to the public; present: *The producer is bringing out a new movie.*
• **to bring up.** **1.** To take care of during childhood; raise: *After their parents died, their grandparents brought them up.* **2.** To offer as a subject for discussion or consideration; mention: *I brought up what happened at the game.*
bring (bring) *verb,* **brought, bringing.**

brink **1.** The edge at the top of a steep place: *The old chief stood on the brink of the cliff to look down at the valley below.* **2.** The point just before something happens: *The baby is on the brink of tears.* **brink** (bringk) *noun, plural* **brinks.**

brisk **1.** Quick and lively: *a brisk pace.* **2.** Refreshing; keen; bracing: *brisk winter air.* **brisk** (brisk) *adjective,* **brisker, briskest.**

bristle A short, stiff hair. Hogs have bristles: *My toothbrush is made of bristles. Noun.*
○ **1.** To have the hairs on the neck or body rise: *The dog bristled when it saw the fox.* **2.** To stand up stiffly: *The porcupine's quills bristled. Verb.* **bris·tle** (bris′əl) *noun, plural* **bristles;** *verb,* **bristled, bristling.**

Brit. An abbreviation for Britain or British.

Britain The countries of England, Scotland, and Wales; Great Britain. **Brit·ain** (brit′ən) *noun.*

British Of Great Britain or the people of Great Britain. *Adjective.*
○ **the British.** The people of Great Britain. *Noun.* **Briti·sh** (brit′ish) *adjective; noun.*

British Columbia A province in southwestern Canada. Its capital is Victoria. **British Co·lum·bi·a** (kə lum′bē ə).

brittle Very easily broken: *The brittle icicles snapped in two when I touched them.* **brit·tle** (brit′əl) *adjective.*

broad **1.** Large from one side to the other side; wide. **2.** Wide in range; not limited: *a broad knowledge of history.* **3.** Clear and open: *broad daylight.* **broad** (brôd) *adjective,* **broader, broadest.**

broadcast **1.** To send out music, news, or other kinds of programs by radio or television. **2.** To make widely known: *Don't broadcast the secret to the whole school. Verb.*
○ Something broadcast; a radio or television program: *a news broadcast. Noun.* **broad·cast** (brôd′kast′) *verb,* **broadcast** *or* **broadcasted, broadcasting;** *noun, plural* **broadcasts.**

broaden To make or become broad or broader. **broad·en** (brô′dən) *verb,* **broadened, broadening.**

brocade A heavy cloth with patterns woven into it: *a robe of gold brocade.* **bro·cade** (brō kād′) *noun, plural* **brocades.**

broccoli A plant whose thick green stems and flower buds are eaten as a

Broccoli is a variety of cabbage.

PRONUNCIATION KEY:
at | āpe | fär | câre | end | mē | it | īce | pierce | hot | ōld | sông | fôrk
oil | out | up | ūse | rüle | pull | tûrn | chin | sing | shop | thin | this
hw in white; zh in treasure. The symbol ə stands for the unstressed vowel sound in about, taken, pencil, lemon, and circus.

97

vegetable. **broc•co•li** (brok′ə lē) *noun, plural* **broccoli.**

broil 1. To cook over an open fire or under the flame in the broiler of a stove. 2. To be or make very hot: *The hot sun broiled us.* **broil** (broil) *verb,* **broiled, broiling.**

broiler A pan, grill, or part of a stove that is used to broil food. **broil•er** (broi′lər) *noun, plural* **broilers.**

broke Past tense of **break.** *Verb.*
○ Having no money. *Adjective.*
broke (brōk) *verb; adjective.*

broken Past participle of **break.** *Verb.*
○ 1. In pieces: *a broken dish.* 2. Not kept: *a broken promise.* 3. Not working; damaged: *Our television is broken.* 4. Not spoken perfectly: *broken English. Adjective.*
bro•ken (brō′kən) *verb; adjective.*

bronchial tubes The branches of the windpipe. Air flows to and from the lungs through the bronchial tubes. **bron•chi•al tubes** (brong′kē əl).

bronchitis A sickness from an inflammation of the bronchial tubes. When you have bronchitis you have a bad cough. **bron•chi•tis** (brong kī′tis) *noun.*

bronco A small, partly wild horse of the western United States. Broncos are descendants of the horses first brought to the New World by the Spanish. **bron•co** (brong′kō) *noun, plural* **broncos.**

brontosaur A huge, plant-eating dinosaur with a long neck and tail and a small head. This dinosaur is also called *brontosaurus.* **bron•to•saur** (bron′tə sôr′) *noun, plural* **brontosaurs.**

bronze 1. A reddish brown metal made by melting together copper and tin. Bronze is made into dishes, jewelry, and statues. 2. A reddish brown color. *Noun.*
○ Reddish brown. *Adjective.*
○ To make reddish brown: *The sun had bronzed the lifeguard's back. Verb.*
bronze (bronz) *noun, plural* **bronzes;** *adjective;* *verb,* **bronzed, bronzing.**

brooch A pin worn as an ornament and fastened with a clasp. **brooch** (brōch *or* brüch) *noun, plural* **brooches.**

brood The young birds hatched from eggs at the same time. *Noun.*
○ 1. To sit on eggs to hatch them. Hens, robins, and other birds brood until the baby birds hatch from their eggs. 2. To think or worry about for a long time: *After I lost my new jacket, I brooded over it. Verb.*
brood (brüd) *noun, plural* **broods;** *verb,* **brooded, brooding.**

brook A small stream. **brook** (brŭk) *noun, plural* **brooks.**

broom A brush with a long handle, used for sweeping. **broom** (brüm *or* brŭm) *noun, plural* **brooms.**

broth A thin soup made by boiling meat, fish, or vegetables in water. **broth** (brôth) *noun, plural* **broths.**

The parts of these brooms used for sweeping are made of straw.

brother A boy or man having the same parents as another person. **broth•er** (bru<u>th</u>′ər) *noun, plural* **brothers.**

brotherhood 1. The close feeling between brothers or among a group of males. 2. A group of people united by interest or aims. Labor unions are sometimes called brotherhoods. **broth•er•hood** (bru<u>th</u>′ər hŭd′) *noun, plural* **brotherhoods.**

brother-in-law 1. The brother of one's husband or wife. 2. The husband of one's sister. **broth•er-in-law** (bru<u>th</u>′ər in lô′) *noun, plural* **brothers-in-law.**

brought Past tense and past participle of **bring.** **brought** (brôt) *verb.*

brow 1. The part of the face above the eyes; forehead. 2. The curved line of hair above the eye; eyebrow. 3. The edge of a steep place: *the brow of a hill.* **brow** (brou) *noun, plural* **brows.**

brown A dark color like that of chocolate or cocoa. *Noun.*
○ Having the color brown. *Adjective.*
○ To make or become brown: *Brown the onions in a frying pan. Verb.*
brown (broun) *noun, plural* **browns;** *adjective,* **browner, brownest;** *verb,* **browned, browning.**

brownie 1. An elf or goblin. Brownies are supposed to do good things for people. 2. A small, flat chocolate cake with nuts in it. 3. Brownie. A girl who belongs to the junior division of the Girl Scouts. **brown•ie** (brou′nē) *noun, plural* **brownies.**

brownout A lessening of the electric power supplied to an area. **brown•out** (broun′out′) *noun, plural* **brownouts.**

browse 1. To look through something in a casual way: *I like to browse in antique shops.* 2. To feed or nibble on the leaves or twigs of a tree or shrub: *The giraffe browsed on the tree.* **browse** (brouz) *verb*, **browsed, browsing.**

WORD HISTORY

Browse comes from a French word meaning "to feed on young shoots or sprouts." Browse was first used to describe the way some animals feed on the leaves of bushes and other plants. Later browse was used to describe the way people look around in a library or bookstore.

---

browser 1. An animal or person that browses. 2. A computer program that enables a person to explore the Internet. **brow•ser** (brou′zər)

bruise 1. An injury that does not break the skin but makes a bluish or blackish mark on it. A bruise is caused by a fall, blow, or bump. 2. A mark on a fruit, vegetable, or plant caused by a blow or bump. *Noun.*
○ To cause a bruise on the skin of. *Verb.*
bruise (brüz) *noun, plural* **bruises**; *verb*, **bruised, bruising.**

brunette 1. Dark brown: *brunette hair.* 2. Having dark brown hair and dark-colored eyes: *Your parents are both brunette.* *Adjective.*
○ A person with dark-brown hair and dark-colored eyes. *Noun.*
bru•nette (brü net′) *adjective; noun, plural* **brunettes.**

brush¹ 1. A tool used for scrubbing, smoothing, sweeping, or painting. A brush is made of bristles or hairs attached to a stiff back or to a handle. 2. The act of using a brush: *Give your hair a good brush.* 3. A light touch in passing: *I felt a brush on my arm as the bee flew by.* *Noun.*
○ 1. To scrub, smooth, sweep, or paint with a brush: *Brush your teeth.* 2. To remove with a brush or with quick movements of the hand: *I brushed the crumbs from my lap.* 3. To touch lightly in passing: *Leaves brushed our faces as we walked through the woods.* *Verb.*
　• **to brush up.** To go over something again so as to refresh one's memory: *We started the class by brushing up on our fractions.*

brush (brush) *noun, plural* **brushes**; *verb,* **brushed, brushing.**

brush² 1. Shrubs, small trees, and bushes growing together: *The rabbit disappeared into the brush.* 2. Twigs or branches cut or broken off from trees: *We cleared the brush from the yard.* **brush** (brush) *noun.*

Brussels sprouts
A leafy plant with a thick stem that has small buds that look like cabbages growing from it. The buds are eaten as a vegetable. These buds are also called Brussels sprouts. **Brus•sels sprouts** (brus′əlz).

It is difficult to walk through thick brush.

brutal Causing or allowing pain without caring; cruel: *It's brutal to make children work in coal mines.* **bru•tal** (brü′təl) *adjective.* —**brutally** *adverb.*

brute 1. An animal. A brute cannot reason or feel the way a human being does. 2. A cruel person: *I saw that brute kicking an old dog.* **brute** (brüt) *noun, plural* **brutes.**

bu. An abbreviation for bushel.

bubble A small round body of air or other gas, usually in or on the surface of a liquid. *Noun.*
○ To form bubbles: *Water bubbles when it is boiling.* *Verb.*
bub•ble (bub′əl) *noun, plural* **bubbles**; *verb,* **bubbled, bubbling.**

buck A male deer, antelope, rabbit, or goat. *Noun.*
○ 1. To jump into the air with the back arched and the head down: *The horse bucked and threw off the rider.* 2. To work or push against: *We had to buck heavy traffic on the highway.* *Verb.*
buck (buk) *noun, plural* **bucks**; *verb,* **bucked, bucking.**

bucket A sturdy container with a round, open top and a flat bottom; pail. Buckets are used for carrying water, sand, or other things. **buck•et** (buk′it) *noun, plural* **buckets.**

buckle 1. A fastener used to hold together the two ends of a belt or strap. 2. A bend or bulge in a

PRONUNCIATION KEY:

| at | āpe | fär | câre | end | mē | it | īce | pîerce | hot | ōld | sông | fôrk |
| oil | out | up | ūse | rüle | pull | tûrn | chin | sing | shop | thin | this | |

hw in white; zh in treasure. The symbol ə stands for the unstressed vowel sound in about, taken, pencil, lemon, and circus.

99

flat surface: *The heat caused a **buckle** in the surface of the road. Noun.*

○ **1.** To fasten with a buckle: ***Buckle** your seat belts.* **2.** To bend or bulge: *The shelf **buckled** because I put too many books on it. Verb.*

• **to buckle down.** To devote oneself with energy and determination: *I **buckled down** and finished all my tasks.*

buck·le (buk′əl) *noun, plural* **buckles**; *verb,* **buckled, buckling.**

buckskin A yellowish tan leather made from the skins of deer or sheep. Buckskin is strong and soft. **buck·skin** (buk′skin′) *noun, plural* **buckskins.**

bucktooth An upper front tooth that sticks out. Braces are sometimes used to straighten buckteeth. **buck·tooth** (buk′tüth′) *noun, plural* **buckteeth** (buk′tēth′).

buckwheat A plant whose seeds are used as feed for animals or are ground into flour. **buck·wheat** (buk′hwēt′ *or* buk′wēt′) *noun, plural* **buckwheats.**

bud A small swelling on the stem or branch of a plant. A bud will later grow into a flower, leaf, or branch. *Noun.*

○ To form buds. *Verb.*

bud (bud) *noun, plural* **buds**; *verb,* **budded, budding.**

Buddha An Indian religious leader who was born about 563 B.C. and died about 483 B.C. **Bud·dha** (bŭd′ə *or* bü′də) *noun.*

Buddhism A religion based on the teachings of Buddha. **Bud·dhism** (bŭd′iz əm *or* bü′diz əm) *noun.*

buddy A close friend; pal. **bud·dy** (bud′ē) *noun, plural* **buddies.**

budge To move just a little: *We couldn't **budge** the heavy box.* **budge** (buj) *verb,* **budged, budging.**

budget A plan for using money. A budget shows how much money a person will have and the ways it will be spent: *Mother and Father made a **budget** for household expenses for the month. Noun.*

○ To make such a plan. *Verb.*

budg·et (buj′it) *noun, plural* **budgets**; *verb,* **budgeted, budgeting.**

WORD HISTORY

Budget comes from a word meaning the leather bag or leather pouch in which people put their money for safekeeping. Their coins represented all of the money they owned or could spend. Today a budget still shows how much money is available for spending.

buff **1.** A soft, strong yellowish brown leather. Buff was formerly made from the skin of buffalo and is now made from the skin of oxen. **2.** A yellowish brown color. **3.** A wheel or stick with a soft covering, used for polishing things. *Noun.*

○ Having the color of buff; yellowish brown. *Adjective.*

○ To polish; shine: *The soldier **buffed** the shoes to make them shiny. Verb.*

buff (buf) *noun, plural* **buffs**; *adjective; verb,* **buffed, buffing.**

buffalo **1.** A large North American animal that has a big shaggy head with short horns and a hump on its back; bison. **2.** Any of various oxen of Europe, Asia, and Africa. **buf·fa·lo** (buf′ə lō) *noun, plural* **buffaloes** *or* **buffalos** *or* **buffalo.**

buffalo wing A fried chicken wing served with hot, spicy sauce and blue cheese dressing.

WORD HISTORY

Buffalo wings were invented and first served in Buffalo, New York, and are not made from imaginary "wings" of a buffalo.

buffet **1.** A piece of furniture having a flat top to serve food from and drawers or shelves for storing dishes, silver, and table linen. **2.** A meal laid out on a buffet or a table so that guests may serve themselves. **buf·fet** (bə fā′ *or* bù fā′) *noun, plural* **buffets.**

bug **1.** Any of a group of insects with front wings that fold across the back. **2.** Any insect or crawling animal. Ants, spiders, and cockroaches are bugs. **3.** A germ that causes a disease: *A lot of pupils missed school because of the flu **bug.*** **4.** A fault in the working of a machine or the like:

Bugs have mouth parts that are used for sucking.

*There is a **bug** in the computer program.* **5.** A hidden microphone used to overhear conversations. *Noun.*

○ To hide a small microphone in: *The spy **bugged** the room to overhear the conversation. Verb.*

bug (bug) *noun, plural* **bugs**; *verb,* **bugged, bugging.**

buggy A light carriage with four wheels and pulled by one horse. **bug·gy** (bug′ē) *noun, plural* **buggies.**

bugle A brass musical instrument shaped like a trumpet, used in the army and navy to sound signals. **bu·gle** (bū′gəl) *noun, plural* **bugles.**

bugler A person who plays a bugle. **bugler** (būglər) *noun, plural* **buglers.**

build 1. To make by putting parts or materials together. 2. To form little by little; develop: *You can build your muscles by exercising. Verb.*
○ The way in which someone is put together: *That football player has a strong build. Noun.*
build (bild) *verb,* **built, building;** *noun, plural* **builds.**

building 1. Something built, especially a permanent structure for people to live or do things in. Houses, hotels, schools, stores, and garages are buildings. 2. The act of making houses, stores,

bridges, and similar things. **build·ing** (bil′ding) *noun, plural* **buildings.**

built Past tense and past participle of **build. built** (bilt) *verb.*

built-in Built as a permanent part of something: *built-in book shelves.* **built-in** (bilt′in′) *adjective.*

bulb 1. A round, underground part of some plants from which the plants grow. These plants live in the form of a bulb until the growing season comes and they put forth leaves and flowers. Onions, lilies, and tulips grow from bulbs. 2. Any object with a rounded part: *an electric light bulb.* **bulb** (bulb) *noun, plural* **bulbs.**

Bulgaria A country in southeastern Europe. **Bul·gar·i·a** (bul gâr′ē ə *or* bul gâr′ē ə) *noun.*

bulge A rounded part that swells out: *The big rag made a bulge in the mechanic's back pocket. Noun.*
○ To swell out. *Verb.*
bulge (bulj) *noun, plural* **bulges;** *verb,* **bulged, bulging.**

bulk 1. Large size: *The elephant's bulk made it hard for it to move around in its cage.* 2. The largest or main part: *The farming family grew corn on the bulk of their land.* **bulk** (bulk) *noun.*

bull 1. The fully grown male of cattle. 2. The fully grown male of some other animals, such as the elephant, moose, or seal. **bull** (bul) *noun, plural* **bulls.**

This bull is a Brahma, one of many different species of bulls in the world.

bulldog A small, muscular dog with a large head, square jaws, short legs, and a smooth coat. The bulldog is known for the strong, stubborn grip of its jaws. **bull·dog** (bul′dôg′) *noun, plural* **bulldogs.**

bulldozer A tractor with a powerful motor and a heavy metal blade in front, used for clearing land

---

BUILDINGS

Humans have been building structures for all of recorded history. Some of the great structures of the ancient world, known as the Seven Wonders of the World, can be found at the entry **wonder.** Great modern structures include:

Tallest freestanding structure:

CN Tower (Canada)	1,821 feet

Tallest buildings:

Oriental Pearl Television Tower (China)	1,535 feet
Petronas Towers (Malaysia)	1,483 feet
Sears Tower (US)	1,454 feet

Longest bridges:

Humber (England)	4,626 feet
Verrazano-Narrows (US)	4,260 feet
Golden Gate (US)	4,200 feet

Longest land tunnel for vehicles:

St. Gotthard (Switzerland)	10.1 miles

Longest underwater tunnel for vehicles:

Brooklyn-Battery (US)	1.7 miles

Longest railroad tunnels:

Seikan (Japan)	33.5 miles
Chunnel (UK-France)	31 miles

Longest tunnel for transporting water:

Delaware Aqueduct (US)	85 miles

PRONUNCIATION KEY:

at	āpe	fär	câre	end	mē	it	īce	pierce	hot	ōld	sông	fôrk
oil	out	up	ūse	rüle	pull	tûrn	chin	sing	shop	thin	this	

hw in white; zh in treasure. The symbol ə stands for the unstressed vowel sound in about, taken, pencil, lemon, and circus.

101

by moving earth and rocks. **bull·doz·er** (bùl′dō′zər) *noun, plural* **bulldozers.**

bullet A small piece of rounded or pointed metal, made to be shot from a small firearm, such as a gun or rifle. **bul·let** (bùl′it) *noun, plural* **bullets.**

bulletin 1. A short announcement of the latest news: *a bulletin on the radio about the hurricane.* 2. A small newspaper or magazine published regularly: *Our club bulletin lists the dates of our monthly meetings.* **bul·le·tin** (bùl′i tin) *noun, plural* **bulletins.**

bullfight A public show in which performers face and try to kill bulls in an arena. The performers do this in ways that display their skill and courage. Bullfights are popular in Spain, Mexico, and South America. **bull·fight** (bùl′fīt′) *noun, plural* **bullfights.**

bullfrog A large green or reddish brown frog. The male bullfrog has a loud, bellowing croak. The bullfrog is the largest frog in the United States. **bull·frog** (bùl′frôg′ *or* bùl′frog′) *noun, plural* **bullfrogs.**

bull's-eye 1. The center circle of a target. 2. A shot that hits this circle. **bull's-eye** (bùlz′ī′) *noun, plural* **bull's-eyes.**

bully A person who likes to frighten or threaten others. Bullies usually pick on smaller or weaker people. *Noun.*
○ To frighten or threaten into doing something. *Verb.* **bul·ly** (bùl′ē) *noun, plural* **bullies;** *verb,* **bullied, bullying.**

bumblebee A large bee with a thick, hairy body. Most bumblebees have yellow and black stripes. **bum·ble·bee** (bum′bəl bē′) *noun, plural* **bumblebees.**

bump 1. To strike or knock suddenly: *I bumped my knee on the chair.* 2. To move with jerks and jolts: *The car bumped along the dirt road. Verb.*
○ 1. A heavy knock or blow: *The bump on my head made me dizzy.* 2. A swelling or lump: *The wasp's sting left a little bump. Noun.* **bump** (bump) *verb,* **bumped, bumping;** *noun, plural* **bumps.**

bumper A heavy bar across the front or back of a car or truck that protects the vehicle from damage when it hits something. *Noun.*
○ Large: *a bumper crop of tomatoes. Adjective.* **bump·er** (bum′pər) *noun, plural* **bumpers;** *adjective.*

bun A baked piece of bread dough or cake batter; roll. **bun** (bun) *noun, plural* **buns.**

bunch 1. A number of things fastened or growing together: *a bunch of grapes.* 2. A group of people: *A bunch of us went to the movies. Noun.*
○ To gather together: *The kittens bunched together to keep warm. Verb.* **bunch** (bunch) *noun, plural* **bunches;** *verb,* **bunched, bunching.**

bundle A number of things tied or wrapped together: *Put that bundle of newspapers in the trash can. Noun.*
○ To tie or wrap together. *Verb.* **bun·dle** (bun′dəl) *noun, plural* **bundles;** *verb,* **bundled, bundling.**

bungalow A small house, usually having only one story: *a beach bungalow.* **bun·ga·low** (bung′gə lō′) *noun, plural* **bungalows.**

WORD HISTORY

The word **bungalow** comes from the country of India, where it meant "a house built in the style of Burma." Burma is a country near India that's now called Myanmar.

---

bunk A narrow bed, especially one built against a wall like a shelf. *Noun.* **bunk** (bungk) *noun, plural* **bunks.**

bunny A small animal with long ears, a short tail, and soft fur; rabbit. **bun·ny** (bun′ē) *noun, plural* **bunnies.**

Bunsen burner An instrument that uses a mixture of air and gas to make a very hot, blue flame. Bunsen burners are often used in science laboratories. **Bun·sen burner** (bun′sən).

bunt To tap a baseball pitch so that the ball goes only a short distance. *Verb.*
○ 1. The act of bunting. 2. A bunted baseball. *Noun.* **bunt** (bunt) *verb,* **bunted, bunting;** *noun, plural* **bunts.**

buoy 1. A floating object that is anchored, used to warn ships of dangerous rocks or to show the safe way through a channel. 2. A device used by a person to keep afloat in water; life preserver. **bu·oy** (bü′ē *or* boi) *noun, plural* **buoys.**

bur Another spelling for burr. **bur** (bûr) *noun, plural* **burs.**

burden 1. Something carried; load: *The mule*

carried a **burden** of logs. **2.** Something hard to bear: *Having an unusual name can be a **burden** to a child. Noun.*

○ To put too heavy a load on. *Verb.*
bur·den (bûr′dən) *noun, plural* **burdens**; *verb,* **burdened, burdening.**

bureau **1.** A chest of drawers: *I keep my sweaters in my **bureau**.* **2.** A department of a government: *the weather **bureau**.* **3.** An office or agency: *a travel **bureau**.* **bu·reau** (byūr′ō) *noun, plural* **bureaus.**

burglar A person who breaks into a house, store, or other place to steal something. **bur·glar** (bûr′glər) *noun, plural* **burglars.**

burial The act of putting a dead body in the earth, a tomb, or the sea. **bur·i·al** (ber′ē əl) *noun, plural* **burials.**

burlap A coarse cloth used for making bags, curtains, and wall coverings. **bur·lap** (bûr′lap) *noun, plural* **burlaps.**

burly Big, strong, and sturdy: *A **burly** police officer broke through the locked door.* **bur·ly** (bûr′lē) *adjective,* **burlier, burliest.**

Grain and other kinds of seeds are often stored in burlap **bags.**

Burma A country in southeastern Asia now called *Myanmar.* **Bur·ma** (bûr′mə) *noun.*

burn **1.** To set on fire; be on fire. **2.** To injure by fire, heat, or certain rays, like those of the sun. **3.** To make by fire or heat: *A spark from the campfire **burned** a hole in the scout's jacket.* **4.** To feel or cause to feel very hot: *The pepper **burned** my tongue.* **5.** To use as fuel to make light or heat: *Our furnace **burns** oil. Verb.*

○ An injury caused by fire or heat. *Noun.*

• **to burn down** or **to burn up.** To destroy or be destroyed by fire: *Three buildings **burned down** before the fire could be put out. The windmill completely **burned up** in one hour.*

burn (bûrn) *verb,* **burned** or **burnt, burning**; *noun, plural* **burns.**

burner The part of a stove or furnace from which the flame comes. **burn·er** (bûr′nər) *noun, plural* **burners.**

burnt A past tense and a past participle of **burn**. **burnt** (bûrnt) *verb.*

burp **1.** To let out gas from the stomach through the mouth; belch. **2.** To cause to burp: *He **burped** the baby by patting her lightly on the back.* **burp** (bûrp) *verb,* **burped, burping.**

burr or **bur** **1.** A prickly covering of the fruit of some plants. Burrs stick to cloth and fur. **2.** Any plant that has burrs. **burr** (bûr) *noun, plural* **burrs.**

burrito A Mexican food made of a tortilla wrapped around a filling, such as beans, meat, cheese, lettuce, tomato, salsa and spices. **bur·ri·to** (bə rē′tō) *noun, plural* **burritos.**

burro A small donkey used for riding and for carrying loads.

Other sound-alike words are **borough** and **burrow**. **bur·ro** (bûr′ō) *noun, plural* **burros.**

burrow A hole dug in the ground by an animal. Rabbits, gophers, woodchucks, and other animals use burrows. *Noun.*

○ **1.** To dig a hole in the ground. **2.** To search: *I **burrowed** in my pocket for my keys. Verb.*

Other sound-alike words are **borough** and **burro**. **bur·row** (bûr′ō) *noun, plural* **burrows**; *verb,* **burrowed, burrowing.**

burst **1.** To break open suddenly: *The buds on the roses **burst** into bloom.* **2.** To be very full: *My closet is **bursting** with clothes.* **3.** To come or go suddenly: *Please don't **burst** into my room.* **4.** To show strong emotion suddenly: *We all **burst** out laughing. Verb.*

○ **1.** The act of bursting; outbreak: *a **burst** of laughter.* **2.** A sudden effort: *a **burst** of speed. Noun.*

burst (bûrst) *verb,* **burst, bursting**; *noun, plural* **bursts.**

PRONUNCIATION KEY:
at   āpe   fär   câre   end   mē   it   īce   pîerce   hot   ōld   sông   fôrk
oil   out   up   ūse   rüle   pûll   tûrn   chin   sing   shop   thin   this
hw in white; zh in treasure. The symbol ə stands for the unstressed vowel sound in about, taken, pencil, lemon, and circus.   **103**

bury **1.** To put in the earth, a tomb, or the sea. **2.** To cover up; hide: *The letter was* **buried** *in a pile of papers.*
Another word that sounds like this is **berry.**
bur•y (ber′ē) *verb,* **buried, burying.**

bus A large motor vehicle with rows of seats for carrying many passengers. Buses usually go along a regular route. Many children go to school by bus. *Noun.*
○ To carry or go in a bus. *Verb.*
bus (bus) *noun, plural* **buses** *or* **busses;** *verb,* **bused** *or* **bussed, busing** *or* **bussing.**

In London, England, buses carry passengers on two levels.

bush A low shrub, smaller than a tree and with many branches near the ground. Berries and roses grow on bushes.
  • **to beat around the bush.** To speak in an indirect way and avoid getting to the point: *Tell me what's worrying you and stop* **beating around the bush.**
bush (bush) *noun, plural* **bushes.**

bushel A measure for grain, fruit, vegetables, and other dry things. A bushel is equal to 4 pecks, or 32 quarts: *a* **bushel** *of corn.* **bush•el** (bush′əl) *noun, plural* **bushels.**

bushy Thick and spreading like a bush. **bush•y** (bush′ē) *adjective,* **bushier, bushiest.**

business **1.** The work a person does to earn a living. **2.** An activity carried on to make money, along with the place and equipment used. Stores and factories are businesses. **3.** The buying and selling of things; trade: *The kite shop does a big* **business** *in summer.* **4.** Matters or affairs: *Don't meddle in other people's* **business.** **busi•ness** (biz′nis) *noun, plural* **businesses.**

businessman A man who owns or works in a business. **busi•ness•man** (biz′nis man′) *noun, plural* **businessmen** (biz′nis men′).

businesswoman A woman who owns or works in a business. **busi•ness•wom•an** (biz′nis wum′ən) *noun, plural* **businesswomen** (biz′nis wim′ən).

bust A statue of a person's head and shoulders: *There is a* **bust** *of that poet on a stand in our library.* **bust** (bust) *noun, plural* **busts.**

bustle To move or hurry in an excited or noisy way: *We* **bustled** *around getting everything ready for the birthday party. Verb.*
○ Noisy, excited activity. *Noun.*
bus•tle (bus′əl) *verb,* **bustled, bustling;** *noun.*

busy **1.** Doing something; active. *I am* **busy** *tonight, so I can't baby-sit.* **2.** Full of activity: *The airport is a* **busy** *place.* **3.** In use: *When I telephoned, your line was* **busy.** *Adjective.*
○ To make busy; keep busy: *While they waited, they* **busied** *themselves with cleaning the room. Verb.*
bus•y (biz′ē) *adjective,* **busier, busiest;** *verb,* **busied, busying.**

busybody A person who pries into or meddles in the affairs of other people. **bus•y•bod•y** (biz′ē bod′ē) *noun, plural* **busybodies.**

but **1.** On the other hand; in contrast: *I am tall,* **but** *my best friend is short.* **2.** In spite of this; nevertheless: *My bruised knee hurt,* **but** *I did not cry.* **3.** Other than; except: *There is no direct route* **but** *through the center of town. Conjunction.*
○ Other than; except: *Everyone has signed the card* **but** *you. Preposition.*
○ Only; just: *I saw them* **but** *a few minutes ago. Adverb.*
Another word that sounds like this is **butt.**
but (but) *conjunction; preposition; adverb.*

butcher A person who cuts up or sells meat. **butch•er** (buch′ər) *noun, plural* **butchers.**

WORD HISTORY

The related words butcher and buck both come from words having to do with male goats. At one time, the word *buck* meant only "a male goat." *Butcher* comes from a French word meaning "a person who sells goat meat."

butler A male servant. A butler is the head servant in a household. **but·ler** (but'lər) *noun, plural* **butlers.**

butt¹ **1.** The thicker or larger end of something: *The hunter held the **butt** of the rifle against his shoulder.* **2.** An end left over: *a cigarette **butt**.* Another word that sounds like this is **but.** **butt** (but) *noun, plural* **butts.**

butt² A person or thing that people make fun of: *The mascot of the rival team was the **butt** of the children's teasing.* Another word that sounds like this is **but.** **butt** (but) *noun, plural* **butts.**

butt³ To strike hard with the head or the horns: *The goat **butted** the gate. Verb.*
○ A push or blow with the head or the horns. *Noun.*
Another word that sounds like this is **but.** **butt** (but) *verb,* **butted, butting;** *noun, plural* **butts.**

butte A mountain or hill that stands alone. **butte** (būt) *noun, plural* **buttes.**

A butte has steep sides and usually a flat top.

butter **1.** A solid, yellowish fat. Butter is separated from cream or milk by churning. Butter is used as a spread for bread and in cooking. **2.** A spread like butter. Butter can be made from apples or from peanuts. *Noun.*
○ To spread with butter. *Verb.*
but·ter (but'ər) *noun, plural* **butters;** *verb,* **buttered, buttering.**

buttercup A plant that grows close to the ground and has yellow flowers shaped like cups. **but·ter·cup** (but'ər kup') *noun, plural* **buttercups.**

butterfat The yellow fat in milk. Butter is made from butterfat. **but·ter·fat** (but'ər fat') *noun.*

butterfly An insect with a thin body and four large, often brightly colored wings. Butterflies fly in the daytime. **but·ter·fly** (but'ər flī') *noun, plural* **butterflies.**

These butterflies are among the almost 15,000 different species in the world.

buttermilk The sour liquid left after milk or cream has been churned to make butter. **but·ter·milk** (but'ər milk') *noun.*

butternut The oily nut of the butternut tree. The butternut tree has large, drooping leaves and is related to the walnut tree. **but·ter·nut** (but'ər nut') *noun, plural* **butternuts.**

butterscotch A candy made from brown sugar and butter. **but·ter·scotch** (but'ər skoch') *noun.*

button **1.** A small, round, flat thing used to fasten clothing or to ornament it. **2.** A knob or disk turned or pushed to make something work: *an elevator **button**. Noun.*
○ To fasten with buttons. *Verb.*
but·ton (but'ən) *noun, plural* **buttons;** *verb,* **buttoned, buttoning.**

buttonhole A hole or slit that a button is put through in order to fasten a piece of clothing. *Noun.*
○ To stop someone and make that person listen to you: *My parents **buttonholed** the neighbor next door and talked a long time about problems on our street. Verb.*

PRONUNCIATION KEY:
at   āpe   fär   câre   end   mē   it   īce   pîerce   hot   ōld   sông   fôrk
oil   out   up   ūse   rüle   pull   tûrn   chin   sing   shop   thin   this
hw in white; zh in treasure. The symbol ə stands for the unstressed vowel sound in about, taken, pencil, lemon, and circus.

105

but·ton·hole (but′ən hōl′) *noun, plural* **button-holes;** *verb,* **buttonholed, buttonholing.**

buttress A strong, heavy structure built against a wall to hold it up or make it stronger. *Noun.*
○ To make stronger with a buttress. *Verb.*
but·tress (but′ris) *noun, plural* **buttresses;** *verb,* **buttressed, buttressing.**

buy To get something by paying money for it; purchase. *Verb.*
○ Something offered for sale at a low price; bargain: *That used car is a good* **buy.** *Noun.*
Another word that sounds like this is **by.**
buy (bī) *verb,* **bought, buying;** *noun, plural* **buys.**
—**buyer** *noun*

buzz A low humming sound. A bee makes a buzz. *Noun.*
○ **1.** To make the low, humming sound a bee makes. **2.** To fly an airplane low over something: *The pilot* **buzzed** *the bridge. Verb.*
buzz (buz) *noun, plural* **buzzes;** *verb,* **buzzed, buzzing.**

buzzard A very large bird with a sharp, hooked beak and long, sharp claws. **buz·zard** (buz′ərd) *noun, plural* **buzzards.**

buzzer An electrical device that makes a buzzing sound as a signal. **buzz·er** (buz′ər) *noun, plural* **buzzers.**

by **1.** Close to; beside: *a small table* **by** *the bed.*
2. Up to and beyond; past: *The express train went* **by** *our train.* **3.** Through the means of: *I went* **by** *bus.* **4.** Through the action of: *a book written* **by** *a famous author.* **5.** In units of: *We buy milk* **by** *the gallon.* **6.** According to: *Let's play* **by** *the rules.* **7.** Not later than: *Please be here* **by** *eight.*

8. To the extent of: *I am older than my cousin* **by** *five years.* **9.** During; at: *Some animals sleep* **by** *day.* **10.** And in the other dimension: *The room measures three yards* **by** *four. Preposition.*
○ **1.** Near: *I just stood* **by** *and watched.* **2.** Past: *Years went* **by.** *Adverb.*
Another word that sounds like this is **buy.**
• **by and by.** In a little while; shortly; soon: *I phoned to say we'd get to their place* **by and by.**
by (bī) *preposition; adverb.*

bygone Gone by; past; former: *The old couple thought of their* **bygone** *school years. Adjective.*
○ **bygones.** Something gone by or past: *Let's end our quarrel and let* **bygones** *be* **bygones.** *Noun.*
by·gone (bī′gôn′ *or* bī′gon′) *adjective; plural noun.*

bypass A road that allows someone to avoid a town or other place by passing it or going around it: *We took the* **bypass** *to avoid the center of town. Noun.*
○ To go around by a bypass: *The highway* **bypasses** *the town. Verb.*
by·pass (bī′pas′) *noun, plural* **bypasses;** *verb,* **bypassed, bypassing.**

by-product Something useful that comes from the making of something else: *Buttermilk is a* **by-product** *of the making of butter.* **by-prod·uct** (bī′prod′əkt) *noun, plural* **by-products.**

bystander A person who is at a place while something is happening but does not take part in it: *Bystanders watched as the workers poured the concrete.* **by·stand·er** (bī′stan′dər) *noun, plural* **bystanders.**

C usually sounds like the letter K when it appears before a, o, or u, as in words such as cat, coat, and cut.

C also sounds like the letter S when it appears before e, i, or y, as in cent, cider, and cyclone.

The letter C is often paired with the letter h to give the ch sound, as in chance and chosen. But this is usually spelled tch when it comes at the end of a word or syllable, as in batch, butcher, or watch. In the middle of many words, the ch sound can be spelled with other letters including: t in such words as nature and future; ti in mention and question.

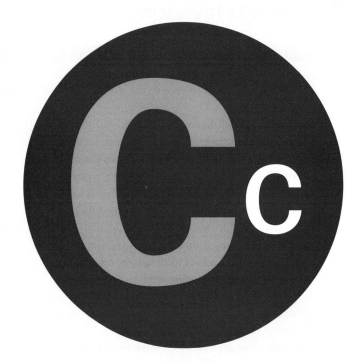

c, C 1. The third letter of the alphabet. 2. The Roman numeral for 100. **c, C** (sē) *noun, plural* **c's, C's.**

C *or* **C.** An abbreviation for **Celsius** or **centigrade.**

CA Postal abbreviation for **California.**

cab 1. A car that carries people for a charge; taxicab. 2. A small horse-drawn carriage that carries people for a charge. 3. The enclosed part of a truck, steam shovel, or other big machine: *The operator of the steam shovel sits in the cab.* **cab** (kab) *noun, plural* **cabs.**

cabbage A plant with thick leaves forming a round head eaten as a vegetable. **cab·bage** (kab′ij) *noun, plural* **cabbages.**

cabin 1. A small, simple house often built of rough boards or logs: *We stayed in a cabin on a lake last summer.* 2. A private room on a ship: *The passengers stayed in their cabins during the storm.* 3. A place in an aircraft for passengers, crew members, or cargo. **cab·in** (kab′in) *noun, plural* **cabins.**

cabinet 1. A piece of furniture with shelves or drawers. Many cabinets have doors. 2. A group of officials who give advice to the leader of a nation. A cabinet is made up of the heads of the different departments of the government. **cab·i·net** (kab′ə nit) *noun, plural* **cabinets.**

cable 1. A strong, thick rope usually made of twisted wires: *That suspension bridge hangs from huge steel cables.* 2. A bundle of wires with a protective covering, used to carry an electric current: *Telegraph messages are sent across the ocean by underwater cable.* 3. A message sent under the ocean by cable. *Noun.*

○ To send a message by cable: *I cabled that I had arrived safely at my grandparents' house. Verb.* **ca·ble** (kā′bəl) *noun, plural* **cables;** *verb,* **cabled, cabling.**

The men are attaching a long, steel cable.

cable car 1. A small car that hangs from a cable: *A cable car takes skiers up the steep mountain.* 2. A vehicle like a trolley that is pulled by a cable: *We rode a cable car in San Francisco.*

107

cable television A system that sends television programs by wire instead of through the air. People who want to receive the programs must pay a fee.

caboose A railroad car at the end of a freight train, where the train crew live, rest, or work. **ca•boose** (kə büs′) *noun, plural* **cabooses.**

cacao An evergreen tree found in warm tropical climates. Its seeds are used in making cocoa and chocolate. **cacao** (kə ka′ō *or* kə kä′ō) *noun, plural* **cacaos.**

cackle To make a shrill, broken cry, like a hen: *The children cackled with delight when the jack-in-the-box sprang open. Verb.*
○ The shrill, broken sound a hen makes. *Noun.*
cack•le (kak′əl) *verb,* **cackled, cackling;** *noun, plural* **cackles.**

cactus A plant that has a thick stem covered with spines instead of leaves, found in desert areas of North and South America. Most cacti produce bright flowers and edible fruit. **cac•tus** (kak′təs) *noun, plural* **cacti** (kaktī), **cactuses,** *or* **cactus.**

Their ability to store water enables cactus plants to thrive in dry areas.

cadet A young male or female student in a military or police academy. **ca•det** (kə det′) *noun, plural* **cadets.**

cafe A small restaurant: *They sat in the cafe drinking soda.* **ca•fe** (ka fā′) *noun, plural* **cafes.**

cafeteria A restaurant where customers buy food at a counter and carry it to tables themselves. **caf•e•te•ri•a** (kaf′i tîr′ē ə) *noun, plural* **cafeterias.**

caffeine A bitter substance found in coffee and tea and added to many soft drinks. Caffeine stimulates the body and can keep a person from feeling sleepy. This word is also spelled **caffein.** **caf•feine** (ka fēn′) *noun.*

cage **1.** A box with sides of bars or wires with open spaces between them, used to house animals or birds. **2.** A small room with one or more walls made of bars, wires, or glass: *The cashier at the amusement park sat in a cage. Noun.*
○ To put or keep in a cage. *Verb.*
cage (kāj) *noun, plural* **cages;** *verb,* **caged, caging.**

Cajun A descendant of French colonists from Canada who settled in Louisiana in the 1700's. *Noun.*
○ Having to do with the Cajuns, their language, or their culture, especially their cooking. *Adjective.*
Ca•jun (kā′jən) *noun, plural* **Cajuns;** *adjective.*

cake **1.** A baked mixture of flour, eggs, sugar, and flavoring. **2.** A flat, thin mass of baked or fried food, such as a pancake. **3.** A flattened or shaped mass of something: *a cake of soap. Noun.*
○ To become a hard, solid mass: *The mud on my boots caked as it dried. Verb.*
cake (kāk) *noun, plural* **cakes;** *verb,* **caked, caking.**

Cal. An abbreviation for California.

calamity A disaster causing great pain and sorrow; catastrophe. **cal•am•i•ty** (kə lam′ ə tē) *noun, plural* **calamities.**

calcium A soft, silver-white metal and a chemical element. Bones, teeth, and blood need calcium. **cal•ci•um** (kal′sē əm) *noun.*

---

calculate **1.** To find out by using addition, subtraction, multiplication, or division: *Let's calculate how much each person owes for the trip.* **2.** To estimate by examining numbers or quantities: *The campers calculated that they had packed* *enough food for five days.* **3.** To plan; intend: *The route was* **calculated** *to get us home quickly.* **cal·cu·late** (kal'kyə lāt') *verb,* **calculated, calculating.** —**calculation** *noun.*

Many calculators can be held in one hand.

calculator A small hand-held computer that can solve mathematical problems. **cal·cu·la·tor** (kal'kyə lā'tər) *noun, plural* **calculators.**

calendar **1.** A chart showing the days, weeks, and months of a year. **2.** A schedule of events that will take place: *In a court of law, cases to be tried are* listed on a **calendar.** **cal·en·dar** (kal'ən dər) *noun, plural* **calendars.**

WORD HISTORY

The word **calendar** comes from a Latin word meaning "the first day of the month." In ancient Rome, that was the day when people paid their bills, so it was important to have a calendar to know when the first day of the month would come.

---

calf[1] **1.** The young of cattle and related animals. **2.** A young seal, elephant, or whale. **3.** Leather made from the skin or hide of a calf. **calf** (kaf) *noun, plural* **calves.**

calf[2] The fleshy part of the back of the leg, between the knee and the ankle. **calf** (kaf) *noun, plural* **calves.**

The cowboy is roping a calf so that it can be separated from the herd.

CALENDARS

Calendars use the natural cycles of the sun, moon, and stars to divide time into days, weeks, months, and years. A day (24 hours) is the average time it takes the Earth to rotate one time. A solar year (365 days) is the average time it takes for the earth to complete one revolution around the sun.

Ancient Calendars – All cultures have calendars. Some, such as the Hebrew calendar that is still in use, are based on the cycle of the moon. They are known as lunar calendars. Lunar calendars usually have months of thirty days each. However, this totals only 360 days for the year, leaving it 5 days short when measured against the solar year. The ancient Egyptians solved this problem by holding a festival each year that lasted five days. Everyone celebrated this festival because it was supposed to be bad luck to work on those days.

The Julian Calendar – The Romans considered even numbers unlucky, so their months were either 29 or 31 days long. But the problem of the difference between the lunar and the solar years persisted. In 45 B.C. Julius Caesar solved this by setting the calendar at 365 days and adding an extra day every four years. This calendar also set the months of the year and the days of the week that we use today. It is known as the Julian calendar and it was used for over 1500 years.

The Gregorian Calendar – But the Julian calendar was slightly wrong, too. Its estimate of the length of the year was about 6 hours too high. This doesn't seem like much, but after 1500 years, this error caused the date of the beginning of spring (known as the vernal equinox) to slip 14 days, from March 25 to March 11. In 1582 Pope Gregory XIII established a new calendar, which is now called the Gregorian calendar. He dropped 10 days from the calendar, setting the vernal equinox on March 21. He also corrected the error made in the Julian calendar by decreeing that there would be no leap year in any century year except those divisible by 400. Therefore there was no leap year in 1900, but there will be one in 2000. The Gregorian calendar is the one we use today.

calico A cotton material that has small, brightly colored designs printed on it. *Noun.*
○ 1. Made of calico: *A calico dress is on sale.*
2. Having large spots or blotches of different colors: *a calico cat. Adjective.*
cal·i·co (kal′i kō) *noun, plural* **calicoes** *or* **calicos;** *adjective.*

Calif. An abbreviation for **California.**

California A state in the western United States, on the Pacific Ocean. Its capital is Sacramento.
Cal·i·for·nia (kal′ə forn′yə *or* kal′ə for′nē ə) *noun.*

Sacramento

California
U. S. Postal Abbreviation: **CA**
Capital: **Sacramento**
Population: **27,663,000**
Area: **158,706 sq. mi./411,013 sq. km**
State Nickname: **Golden State**
State Bird: **California Valley Quail**
State Flower: **Golden Poppy**

WORD HISTORY

California was the name of a make-believe island in an old Spanish story. When the Spanish explorers landed on the southern end of California, they thought they were on an island. So they named it after the island in the story. Other Spanish explorers went farther north and also call that area California. The name was finally used for all the land that became the state of California.

---

call 1. To speak or say in a loud voice: *Please raise your hand when I call your name.* 2. To ask or order to come: *The cat will come if you call.* 3. To make a request; ask: *One of the workers called for a break.* 4. To give a name to; name: *We called our puppy "Daisy."* 5. To telephone: *They called us from the airport.* 6. To make a short visit or stop: *We will call at your house tomorrow afternoon. Verb.*
○ 1. The act of speaking in a loud voice; shout; cry: *a call for help from someone in the burning building.* 2. A particular cry made by a bird or animal: *She can recognize many different bird calls.* 3. The act of telephoning someone: *I will expect your call at four.* 4. A short visit or stop: *Some old friends made a call to visit. Noun.*
• **on call.** Able to be telephoned or summoned when needed; available: *There is always someone on call for emergencies.*
• **to call for.** 1. To require because it is necessary or appropriate: *This job calls for patience.* 2. To come and get in order to accompany: *I'll call for you at 6 o'clock.*
• **to call up.** 1. To telephone: *I'll call you up after the game.* 2. To summon for military duty: *My cousins were called up just after they finished college.* 3. To cause to remember: *The music called up old memories.*
call (kôl) *verb,* **called, calling;** *noun, plural* **calls.**

call number A group of numbers or numbers and letters assigned to a book and used to help locate the book in a library.

callous 1. Having calluses. 2. Not having kindness; hardhearted.
Another word that sounds like this is **callus.**
cal·lous (kal′əs) *adjective.*

callus A hardened and thickened area of skin, caused by repeated pressing or rubbing.
Another word that sounds like this is **callous.**
cal·lus (kal′əs) *noun, plural* **calluses.**

calm 1. Not moving; still: *a calm sea.* 2. Not excited or nervous; quiet: *We all stayed calm during the fire and got out safely. Adjective.*
○ A time of quiet or stillness. *Noun.*
○ To make or become quiet and still. *Verb.*
calm (käm) *adjective,* **calmer, calmest;** *noun, plural* **calms;** *verb,* **calmed, calming.**

calorie 1. A unit used to measure the amount of heat in something. 2. A unit used to measure the amount of energy produced by food: *Some foods have more calories than others.* **cal·o·rie** (kal′ə rē) *noun, plural* **calories.**

calves Plural of **calf.** Look up calf for more information. **calves** (kavz) *plural noun.*

Cambodia A country in southeastern Asia.

Cam·bo·di·a (kam bō′dē ə) *noun.*

camcorder A portable device that includes a television camera and a videocassette recorder in one unit: *The reporter used a camcorder to record the parade.* **cam·cord·er** (kam′kôr′dər) *noun, plural* **camcorders.**

Camels are very strong and can live for many days without water.

came Past tense of **come. came** (kām) *verb.*

camel A large animal that has a hump on its back, long legs, a long neck, and lives in deserts. The camel of northern Africa and the Middle East has one hump, and the camel of central Asia has two humps. **cam·el** (kam′əl) *noun, plural* **camels.**

camera A device for taking photographs or motion pictures. A camera consists of a box with a small hole. When the hole is uncovered, light enters the camera and makes an image on the film inside. Most cameras have a lens to focus the image on the film. **cam·e·ra** (kam′ə rə *or* kam′rə) *noun, plural* **cameras.**

Cameroon A country in west-central Africa. **Cam·er·oon** (kam′ə rün′) *noun.*

camouflage A disguise used to hide something by making it look like its surroundings. The tan coat of a lion is a natural camouflage because it matches the color of the dry grasses where the lion lives. *Noun.*

○ To change the appearance of something in order to hide or trick. *Verb.*

cam·ou·flage (kam′ə fläzh′) *noun, plural* **camou-**

Its camouflage makes this lizard difficult to see.

flages; *verb,* **camouflaged, camouflaging.**

camp 1. An outdoor place with tents or cabins where people live or sleep for a time. 2. The people staying at a camp: *The whole camp woke up at dawn. Noun.*

○ To establish, equip, and live in a camp: *Last summer we went camping in western Canada. Verb.*

camp (kamp) *noun, plural* **camps;** *verb,* **camped, camping.**

campaign A series of actions planned and carried out to bring about a particular result: *the candidate's campaign for election as mayor. Noun.*

○ To carry on or take part in a campaign: *Are you going to campaign for class president? Verb.* **cam·paign** (kam pān′) *noun, plural* **campaigns;** *verb,* **campaigned, campaigning.**

camper 1. A person who stays at a camp. 2. A car or trailer designed for camping. **cam·per** (kam′pər) *noun, plural* **campers.**

campfire An outdoor fire for cooking or keeping warm in a camp. **camp·fire** (kamp′fīr′) *noun, plural* **campfires.**

campground A place for camping, such as a park. **camp·ground** (kamp′ground′) *noun, plural* **campgrounds.**

camphor A white substance with a strong odor, used in making medicines and plastics. **cam·phor** (kam′fər) *noun.*

campus The grounds and buildings of a school, college, or university. **cam·pus** (kam′pəs) *noun,*

PRONUNCIATION KEY:

at   āpe   fär   câre   end   mē   it   īce   pierce   hot   ōld   sông   fôrk
oil   out   up   ūse   rüle   pull tûrn chin   sing   shop   thin   this

hw in white; zh in treasure. The symbol ə stands for the unstressed vowel sound in about, taken, pencil, lemon, and circus.

111

plural **campuses.**

can¹ An auxiliary verb used to express the following meanings: **1.** To have the ability, skill, or knowledge to; be able to: *My neighbor can speak French. Elephants can move with surprising speed.* **2.** To have the right to; be entitled to: *You can vote when you are eighteen.* **3.** To have permission to; may: *My parents said I can stay up late tonight.* **can** (kan) *verb, past tense* **could.**

can² A cylindrical container made of metal, usually with an airtight top or cover. *Noun.*
○ To put into or preserve in a can: *We are going to can peaches this year. Verb.*
can (kan) *noun, plural* **cans;** *verb,* **canned, canning.**

Can. An abbreviation for Canada.

Canada A country in North America north of the United States. **Can•a•da** (kan′ə də) *noun.*

Canada Day A holiday in Canada that falls on July 1. It celebrates the day when the first four provinces of Canada joined together. In the past, this holiday was called *Dominion Day.*

Canadian A person who was born in or is a citizen of Canada. *Noun.*
○ Of Canada: *Ice hockey is a Canadian sport. Adjective.*
Can•a•di•an (kə nā′dē ən) *noun, plural* **Canadians;** *adjective.*

canal A waterway dug across land for boats and ships to travel through, and for carrying water from to places that need it. **can•al** (kə nal′) *noun, plural* **canals.**

canary **1.** A small yellow songbird often kept as a pet. **2.** A light, bright yellow color. *Noun.*
○ Having the color canary; light, bright yellow. *Adjective.*
ca•nar•y (kə nâr′ē) *noun, plural* **canaries;** *adjective.*

cancel **1.** To decide not to do, have, or go; call off: *The game was canceled because of rain.* **2.** To cross out or mark to show that it cannot be used again: *The post office cancels stamps on letters.* **can•cel** (kan′səl) *verb,* **canceled, canceling.**

cancer A disease in which cells in or on the body begin to divide and grow more rapidly than is normal. **can•cer** (kan′sər) *noun.*

candidate A person who seeks or is put forward by others for an office or honor: *The senator will be a candidate for president.* **can•di•date** (kan′di dāt′) *noun, plural* **candidates.**

candle A stick of wax with a string called a wick inside it. **can•dle** (kan′dəl) *noun, plural* **candles.**

candlestick A holder for a candle. **can•dle•stick** (kan′dəl stik′) *noun, plural* **candlesticks.**

candy A sweet food made of sugar or syrup with flavorings, nuts, or fruit. *Noun.*

A candle burns and gives off light when its wick is lit.

○ To cover or cook with sugar: *At home, we candy apples for holidays. Verb.*
can•dy (kan′dē) *noun, plural* **candies;** *verb,* **candied, candying.**

cane **1.** A stick used to help someone walk: *I used a cane after I sprained my ankle.* **2.** The long, woody, jointed stem of bamboo and other tall grass plants. **3.** A plant that has a long, woody, flexible stem. Bamboo is a cane. **cane** (kān) *noun, plural* **canes.**

canine **1.** Any member of the dog family, including dogs, foxes, wolves, and coyotes. **2.** One of the pointed teeth that people, dogs, and other animals use to tear off pieces of food. There is a canine on each side of the top and bottom front teeth. *Noun.*
○ Having to do with a dog or any member of the dog family. *Adjective.*
ca•nine (kā′nīn) *noun, plural* **canines;** *adjective.*

cannibal A person who eats human flesh.

can·ni·bal (kan′ə bəl) *noun, plural* **cannibals.**

cannon A large, heavy gun that is mounted on wheels or some other base. **can·non** (kan′ən) *noun, plural* **cannons** or **cannon.**

cannot Can not; be unable to. **can·not** (kan′ot *or* ka not′) *verb.*

canoe A light, narrow boat, usually pointed at both ends and moved and steered with a paddle. *Noun.*
  ○ To paddle or ride in a canoe. *Verb.*
  ca·noe (kə nü′) *noun, plural* **canoes;** *verb,* **canoed, canoeing.**

canopy A covering made of cloth or other material and hung over a bed, throne, or entrance to a building. **can·o·py** (kan′ə pē) *noun, plural*

**A canopy makes a
bed look elegant.**

canopies.

can't Shortened form of "can not." **can't** (kant) *contraction.*

cantaloupe A melon with a rough skin and sweet, yellowish orange flesh. **can·ta·loupe** (kan′tə lōp′) *noun, plural* **cantaloupes.**

canteen **1.** A small metal container for carrying water to drink. **2.** A store in a school or factory that sells food and drinks. **can·teen** (kan tēn′) *noun, plural* **canteens.**

canter The gait of a horse that is faster than a trot and slower than a gallop.
Another word that sounds like this is **cantor.**
canter (kan′tər) *noun, plural* **canters;** *verb,* **cantered, cantering.**

cantor The chief or solo singer in a synagogue.
Another word that sounds like this is **canter.**

can·tor (kan′ tər) *noun, plural* **cantors.**

canvas A strong, heavy cloth used to make tents, sails, coats, and boat covers. **can·vas** (kan′vəs) *noun, plural* **canvases.**

canyon A deep valley with very high, steep sides. **can·yon** (kan′yən) *noun, plural* **canyons.**

cap **1.** A close-fitting covering for the head, either with a short brim or no brim. **2.** Something used or shaped like a cap; a cover or top. **3.** A paper wrapping containing a small amount of explosive. Caps are used in toy guns. *Noun.*
  ○ **1.** To put a cap on; cover with a cap: *Please cap the toothpaste when you're finished.* **2.** To follow with something equal or better; match: *The speaker capped that joke with a funnier one. Verb.*
  cap (kap) *noun, plural* **caps;** *verb,* **capped, capping.**

capability The quality of being capable; ability: *I admire your capabilities as a student.*
ca·pa·bil·i·ty (kā′pə bil′i tē) *noun, plural* **capabilities.**

capable Having skill or power; able: *A capable mechanic can fix many things.*
  • **capable of.** Having the ability needed for: *I'm capable of running two miles.*
  ca·pa·ble (kā′pə bəl) *adjective.* —**ca·pa·bly** *adverb.*

capacity **1.** The amount that can be held in a space: *A gas tank with a capacity of 20 gallons.* **2.** Ability or power: *the capacity to learn.* **3.** A job or position with duties: *In my capacity as club president, I ran the club's meetings.*
ca·pac·i·ty (kə pas′i tē) *noun, plural* **capacities.**

cape¹ A piece of clothing without sleeves and worn loosely over the shoulders. **cape** (kāp) *noun, plural* **capes.**

cape² A piece of land that sticks out from the coastline into the sea or a lake. **cape** (kāp) *noun, plural* **capes.**

caper A playful act or trick; prank. **ca·per** (kā′pər) *noun, plural* **capers.**

capillary One of the tiny blood vessels connecting the arteries and veins. **cap·il·lar·y** (kap′ə ler′ē) *noun, plural* **capillaries.**

capital¹ **1.** A city where the government of a country or state is located. **2.** A large form of a letter of the alphabet. A and B are capitals; b and

PRONUNCIATION KEY:

| at | āpe | fär | câre | end | mē | it | īce | pierce | hot | ōld | sông | fôrk |
| oil | out | up | ūse | rüle | pùll | tûrn | chin | sing | shop | thin | this | |

hw in white; zh in treasure. The symbol ə stands for the unstressed vowel sound in about, taken, pencil, lemon, and circus.

113

c are not. **3.** The total amount of money or property owned by a company or person. **4.** Money accumulated to start or invest in a business. *Noun.*

○ **1.** Being where the government is: *Madrid is Spain's capital city.* **2.** Being the large form of a letter: *T and L are capital letters.* **3.** Very good or satisfying; excellent: *This is a capital pudding!* **4.** Punishable by death: *Murder is a capital crime in some places. Adjective.*

Another word that sounds like this is **Capitol.** See the entry for **Capitol** for a Language Note about this word.

cap·i·tal (kap′i təl) *noun, plural* **capitals;** *adjective.*

capital² The top part of a column or pillar. Another word that sounds like this is **Capitol.**

cap·i·tal (kap′i təl) *noun, plural* **capitals.**

capitalism An economic system in which land and factories are owned and controlled by individual people instead of by the government: *The economic system of the United States is based on capitalism.* **cap·i·tal·ism** (kap′i tə liz′əm) *noun.*

capitalize To write or print with a capital letter or letters, or begin with a capital letter: *Always capitalize proper names.* **cap·i·tal·ize** (kap′i tə līz′) *verb,* **capitalized, capitalizing.**

Capitol **1.** The building in which the U.S. Congress meets in Washington, D.C. **2. capitol.** The building in which a state legislature meets. Another word that sounds like this is **capital.**

Cap·i·tol (kap′i təl) *noun.*

LANGUAGE NOTE

Even though the words Capitol and capital sound the same, they have different meanings. It's important to spell them correctly. A capital is a city, but the Capitol is a building: *When we visited Washington, D.C., our country's capital, we stood on the steps of the Capitol to have our picture taken.*

---

capsize To turn upside down: *The strong wind capsized the small sailboat.* **cap·size** (kap′sīz or kap sīz′) *verb,* **capsized, capsizing.**

capsule **1.** A small, thin case that encloses something tightly, especially one that contains a small amount of medicine and dissolves in the stomach after it is swallowed. **2.** A compartment of a spacecraft that carries astronauts or instruments.

cap·sule (kap′səl) *noun, plural* **capsules.**

captain **1.** A person who is the leader of a group. **2.** A person who is in charge of a ship. **3.** An officer in the armed forces. In the United States Army, Marine Corps, or Air Force, a captain ranks just below a major. In the United States Navy, a captain ranks just below an admiral. *Noun.*

○ To be the captain of; lead: *Who will captain the basketball team next year? Verb.*

cap·tain (kap′tən) *noun, plural* **captains;** *verb,* **captained, captaining.**

caption The word or words under a picture that tell who or what appears in the picture. **cap·tion** (kap′shən) *noun, plural* **captions.**

captive A person or animal captured and held by force; prisoner: *The police kept the captive in jail. Noun.*

○ Held prisoner: *The captive lion was kept in a cage. Adjective.*

cap·tive (kap′tiv) *noun, plural* **captives;** *adjective.*

capture **1.** To catch and hold a person, animal, or thing. **2.** To attract and hold: *The film's strange title captured my interest.* **3.** To succeed in expressing something: *The story captures what it is like to be an only child. Verb.*

○ The act of catching and holding a person, animal, or thing: *The capture of the bank robber*

This space capsule was used by astronauts to travel to the moon.

took place the day after the robbery. Noun.
cap·ture (kap′chər) *verb*, **captured, capturing;**
noun, plural **captures.**

car 1. An automobile. 2. Any vehicle that moves
on wheels and is used to carry people or things.
A railroad train is made up of different cars
joined together. 3. The compartment of an elevator in which people and things are carried. **car**
(kär) *noun, plural* **cars.**

caramel 1. Sugar that is melted and browned by
being heated slowly. Caramel is used in cooking
for coloring and flavoring. 2. A light-brown, soft
candy flavored with caramel. **car·a·mel** (kar′ə məl
or kär′məl) *noun, plural* **caramels.**

carat A unit of weight for diamonds and other
precious stones. A carat is the same weight as ⅕
of a gram.
Another word that sounds like this is **carrot.**
car·at (kar′ət) *noun, plural* **carats.**

caravan A group of people or vehicles traveling
together: *A **caravan** of army trucks moved slowly
along the highway.* **car·a·van** (kar′ə van′) *noun,
plural* **caravans.**

carbohydrate A compound made up of carbon,
hydrogen, and oxygen. Carbohydrates are made
by green plants. Starches and sugars are carbohydrates. **car·bo·hy·drate** (kär′bō hī′drāt) *noun,
plural* **carbohydrates.**

carbon A chemical element found in all living

things and in coal. Diamonds are carbon in the
form of crystals. **car·bon** (kär′bən) *noun.*

carbon dioxide A colorless and odorless gas
made up of carbon and oxygen. It is part of the
air we breathe and is used in soft drinks and fire
extinguishers. **carbon di·ox·ide** (dī ok′sīd).

carbon monoxide A poisonous gas that has no
color or odor, formed when carbon burns with
too little air, and found among the exhaust gases
of automobiles. **carbon mon·ox·ide** (mə nok′sīd).

carburetor The part of an engine in which gasoline is mixed with air to make a mixture that
the engine burns when it runs. **car·bu·re·tor**
(kär′bə rā′tər) *noun, plural* **carburetors.**

carcass The body of a dead animal. **car·cass**
(kär′kəs) *noun, plural* **carcasses.**

card A flat piece of stiff paper with words or numbers or some kind of design on it. People have
membership cards for libraries and for clubs they
belong to: *We play many games with decks of
playing cards.* **card** (kärd) *noun, plural* **cards.**

cardboard A heavy, stiff paper used to make
boxes and posters. **card·board** (kärd′bôrd′) *noun.*

cardinal 1. One of the group of important officials who rank just below the pope in the Roman
Catholic Church. Cardinals wear bright red robes
and hats. 2. A songbird that has a crest of feathers on its head. The male cardinal has bright red
feathers. *Noun.*

car

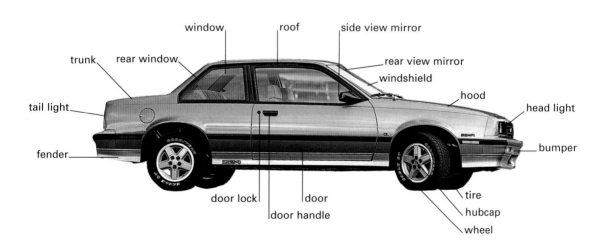

window, roof, side view mirror, rear view mirror, windshield, hood, head light, bumper, tire, hubcap, wheel, door, door handle, door lock, fender, tail light, trunk, rear window

○ Of the greatest importance; chief: *One of the cardinal issues in the town election was the vote on the new park.* Adjective.
car·di·nal (kär′də nəl) *noun, plural* **cardinals;** *adjective.*

cardinal number A number that tells how many. Numbers such as one, two, three, and four are cardinal numbers.

care 1. Close and serious attention: *Dry the dishes with* **care.** 2. A feeling of worry: *I have so many cares that it is hard to fall asleep.* 3. Keeping or custody; protection: *I left my cat in the* **care** *of a neighbor. Noun.*
○ 1. To have an interest, liking, or concern about a person or thing: *I don't* **care** *for sweets.* 2. To have a feeling against; mind: *Do you* **care** *if I borrow your bicycle?* 3. To want or wish: *Would you* **care** *to go to the movies with me?* 4. To protect or provide care: *When our neighbors go away, I* **care** *for their plants. Verb.*

  • **in care of.** At the address of: *The letter was sent to us* **in care of** *the Essex Hotel.*

  • **to take care of.** 1. To provide the care necessary for the protection, well-being, or upkeep of: *A nurse* **took care of** *me when I was sick with pneumonia.* 2. To devote one's attention and effort to: *Please* **take care of** *the most important tasks first.*

care (kâr) *noun, plural* **cares;** *verb,* **cared, caring.**

career The work that a person does through life: *My cousin chose a* **career** *as a doctor.* **ca·reer** (kə rîr′) *noun, plural* **careers.**

carefree Happy with nothing to worry about. **care·free** (kâr′frē′) *adjective.*

careful 1. Paying close attention; watchful: *Be* **careful** *and look both ways before you cross the street.* 2. Done with care: *A* **careful** *check of the paragraph showed two mistakes.* **care·ful** (kâr′fəl) *adjective.* —**carefully** *adverb.*

careless 1. Not paying close enough attention: *I was* **careless** *when I ran down the stairs, and I tripped and fell.* 2. Done without close attention or care: *You will not get a good grade on your report if you make* **careless** *spelling mistakes.* **care·less** (kâr′lis) *adjective.* —**care·less·ly** *adverb.*

caress To touch or stroke gently and with love; pet: *The child* **caressed** *the kitten fondly.* **ca·ress** (kə res′) *verb,* **caressed, caressing.** —**caress** *noun.*

caretaker 1. A person who takes care of a build-

ing or property; custodian: *The park's* **caretaker** *mows the grass every week in summer.*
2. Someone who takes care of other people.
care·tak·er (kâr′tā′kər) *noun, plural* **caretakers.**

carfare The money a person must pay for a ride, as in a bus, subway, or taxi. **car·fare** (kär′fâr′) *noun.*

This ship can carry tons of cargo from one port to another.

cargo The goods carried by a ship, airplane, or truck. **car·go** (kär′gō) *noun, plural* **cargoes** *or* **cargos.**

Caribbean A sea between North America and South America, next to the Atlantic Ocean. **Car·ib·be·an** (kar′ə bē′ən *or* kə rib′ē ən) *noun.*

caribou A large animal in the deer family that lives in northern regions. In Europe and Asia caribou are called reindeer. The female caribou is the only female deer that has antlers. **car·i·bou** (kar′ə bü′) *noun, plural* **caribou** *or* **caribous.**

caries Decay of the teeth or bone: *Brushing the teeth after every meal helps prevent dental* **caries.** The word **caries** is used with a singular verb. **car·ies** (kâr′ēz) *noun.*

carnation A flower that has a spicy, fragrant smell and comes in many colors. **car·na·tion** (kär nā′shən) *noun, plural* **carnations.**

carnival A fair or festival that has games, rides, and other amusements. **car·ni·val** (kär′nə vəl) *noun, plural* **carnivals.**

These people are attempting to win a prize at a carnival.

carnivore An animal that eats the flesh of other animals. Lions and dogs are carnivores. **car·ni·vore** (kär′nə vôr′) *noun, plural* **carnivores.**

carnivorous Eating the flesh of animals: *Wolves are carnivorous animals.* **car·niv·o·rous** (kär niv′ə rəs) *adjective.*

carob A food that tastes like chocolate, made from the beans of an evergreen tree. The tree is also called a carob. **car·ob** (kar′əb) *noun, plural* **carobs.**

carol A joyful song or hymn: *The choir practiced singing carols. Noun.*
○ To sing joyous songs. *Verb.*
car·ol (kar′əl) *noun, plural* **carols;** *verb,* **caroled, caroling.**

carp A fish that lives in fresh water and is used as food. **carp** (kärp) *noun, plural* **carp** *or* **carps.**

carpenter A person who builds and repairs houses and other things made of wood. **car·pen·ter** (kär′pən tər) *noun, plural* **carpenters.**

carpet 1. A covering for a floor, usually of heavy woven fabric. 2. Anything like a carpet: *The lawn was covered with a carpet of snow. Noun.*
○ To cover with a carpet: *We are going to carpet the stairs in our house. Verb.*
car·pet (kär′pit) *noun, plural* **carpets;** *verb,* **carpeted, carpeting.**

car pool An arrangement made by a group of people who ride to work together or whose children ride to school together in a car. Each person in the group takes a turn at driving.

carriage 1. A vehicle that moves on wheels. Some carriages are pulled by horses and carry people. Others, such as baby carriages, are small and light and are pushed by people. 2. A movable part of a machine that carries or holds up some other part. **car·riage** (kar′ij) *noun, plural* **carriages.**

carrier A person, machine, or organization that carries something. **car·ri·er** (kar′ē ər) *noun, plural* **carriers.**

carrot 1. The long, orange-colored root of a plant, eaten as a vegetable. 2. The plant that produces this root.
Another word that sounds like this is **carat.**
car·rot (kar′ət) *noun, plural* **carrots.**

carry 1. To hold something while moving it or while it is being moved: *Will you carry my suitcase if it is too heavy for me?* 2. To have some-thing. If a store carries rubber boots, it has them there for you to buy. 3. To keep doing something; continue: *If you carry your teasing too far, the puppy will bite.* 4. To move a number from one column or place and add it to another: *When I added 23 and 39, I got 52 instead of 62 because I forgot to carry the 1 from the right-hand column.*
 • **to carry on.** 1. To go on; continue: *The visitors to the classroom told the students to carry on with their work.* 2. To behave in a wild, foolish, or silly way: *The student who carried on was punished.*
 • **to carry out.** 1. To obey; follow: *The soldier carried out the order promptly.* 2. To do; accomplish; complete: *We don't have the money to carry out our plans for the party.*
car·ry (kar′ē) *verb,* **carried, carrying.**

carsick Having nausea or feeling dizzy when riding in a car, train, or bus. **car·sick** (kär′sik′) *adjective.* —**carsickness** *noun.*

cart 1. A strong wagon with two wheels, used to carry a load, and usually pulled by an animal. 2. A light vehicle pushed by a person, as in supermarkets for holding groceries. *Noun.*
○ To move something in a cart: *farmers carting vegetables into town to sell them. Verb.*
cart (kärt) *noun, plural* **carts;** *verb,* **carted, carting.**

cartilage A strong, flexible material that forms parts of the body of humans and other animals. Cartilage is not as stiff or as hard as bone. Much of a person's nose is formed of cartilage. **car·ti·lage** (kär′tə lij) *noun.*

carton A container that is made of cardboard, paper, or other material, such as plastic. **car·ton** (kär′tən) *noun, plural* **cartons.**

cartoon A drawing, often with words or a caption, that shows people or things in a way that makes you laugh. Some cartoons are made as motion pictures. Comic strips are groups of cartoons that appear in newspapers. **car·toon** (kär tün′) *noun, plural* **cartoons.**

cartridge 1. A small case that holds gunpowder and a bullet. 2. Any small case that holds something. Some cameras have special cartridges that hold the film. **car·tridge** (kär′trij) *noun, plural* **cartridges.**

PRONUNCIATION KEY:

| at | ape | fär | câre | end | mē | it | īce | pierce | hot | ōld | sông | fôrk |
| oil | out | up | ūse | rüle | pull | tûrn | chin | sing | shop | thin | this | |

hw in white; zh in treasure. The symbol ə stands for the unstressed vowel sound in about, taken, pencil, lemon, and circus.

117

cartwheel 1. The wheel of a cart. 2. A kind of jump from one's feet to one's hands and back again. If you keep your arms and legs straight when doing a cartwheel, they look like the spokes of a wheel as it turns. **cart·wheel** (kärt′hwēl′ or kärt′wēl′) *noun, plural* **cartwheels**.

carve 1. To cut something into a shape, such as statues out of wood and stone. 2. To cut meat into slices or pieces: *You will need a sharp knife to carve the turkey.* **carve** (kärv) *verb*, **carved**, **carving**.

cascade Water falling over a steep slope. *Noun.*

○ To flow down like a waterfall: *Water from the overflowing sink cascaded onto the floor. Verb.*

cas·cade (kas kād′) *noun, plural* **cascades**; *verb*, **cascaded**, **cascading**.

The water is cascading down from above.

case¹ 1. An example of something: *The forest fire was a case of carelessness.* 2. The facts; state of affairs: *They say the key is lost, and if that is the case, we are all locked out.* 3. An instance of sickness or injury: *Local doctors reported ten cases of measles to the health department.* 4. A matter to be investigated or decided by law: *The police had no suspects in the case.*

• **in case.** If: *In case anything happens, call me right away.*

• **in case of.** If there is: *In case of rain, we will go to the movies.*

case (kās) *noun, plural* **cases**.

case² A container to hold or protect something: *The new camera came in a leather case.* **case** (kās) *noun, plural* **cases**.

cash Money in the form of coins and paper bills. *Noun.*

○ To get or give cash for: *We cashed a check. Verb.*

cash (kash) *noun; verb*, **cashed**, **cashing**.

cashew An edible nut shaped like a bean. It grows on an evergreen tree found in tropical countries. **cash·ew** (kash′ü) *noun, plural* **cashews**.

cashier A person whose job it is to receive or pay out money, as in a store, bank, or restaurant. **cash·ier** (ka shîr′) *noun, plural* **cashiers**.

cash machine A machine that works by means of a computer and allows bank customers to take out and put in money.

cashmere A very soft woolen fabric woven from the hair of Asian goats: *Sweaters made of cashmere are very comfortable.* **cash·mere** (kazh′mîr or kash′mîr) *noun, plural* **cashmeres**.

cask A wooden barrel used to hold wine or other liquids. **cask** (kask) *noun, plural* **casks**.

casket A coffin. **cas·ket** (kas′kit) *noun, plural* **caskets**.

casserole 1. A deep dish in which food can be cooked and served. 2. Food prepared in such a dish. **cas·se·role** (kas′ə rōl′) *noun, plural* **casseroles**.

cassette A small case holding recording tape to place in a tape recorder or player. **cas·sette** (kə set′) *noun, plural* **cassettes**.

cast 1. To throw through the air: *We cast our fishing lines into the stream.* 2. To send or put: *The tree cast a long shadow on the ground.* 3. To pick the actors who will take the roles in a play: *They cast me as the magician in the class play.* 4. To shape by pouring a soft material into a mold to harden: *The artist cast a statue of a horse. Verb.*

It takes skill to cast a fishing line a long distance.

○ 1. The act of throwing something: *Try to make a long cast with your fishing rod.* 2. Something shaped in a mold: *a plaster cast of a deer.* 3. The actors in a show: *The whole cast came on stage to bow together.* 4. A bandage, made of plaster and cloth, that is shaped around a broken bone and protects the bone and keeps it from moving. *Noun.*

• **to cast off.** 1. Discard or shed: *Birds cast off old feathers when they molt.* 2. To release: *We cast off the boat from the dock.*

cast (kast) *verb*, **cast**, **casting**; *noun, plural* **casts**.

castanet Either of a pair of small, wooden pieces that look like the two shells of a clam. They are clicked together in a person's hand in time to the rhythm of a dance. **cas•ta•net** (kas′tə net′) *noun, plural* **castanets.**

cast iron A mixture of iron and other materials that are heated together until they melt into a liquid and are then poured into a mold. Cast iron is usually hard and brittle.

castle 1. A large building or group of buildings having high, thick walls with towers. Many castles had moats around them for defense against attack. 2. One of the pieces in a chess game; rook. **cas•tle** (kas′əl) *noun, plural* **castles.**

casual 1. Done or happening without serious thought or planning: *a casual visit.* 2. Informal: *You may wear casual clothes to dinner.* **cas•u•al** (kazh′ü əl) *adjective.* —**casually** *adverb* —**casualness** *noun.*

casualty A person injured or killed in an accident or a war. Soldiers who are captured by the enemy are also called casualties. **cas•u•al•ty** (kazh′ü əl tē) *noun, plural* **casualties.**

cat 1. A small furry animal with short ears and a long tail. Cats are kept as pets and for catching mice and rats. 2. Any animal of the family that includes lions, tigers, leopards, and the cats that are kept as pets.
• **to let the cat out of the bag.** To reveal a secret. **cat** (kat) *noun, plural* **cats.**

catalog *or* **catalogue** A list. Libraries have catalogs of the titles and authors of all their books. Stores publish catalogs with pictures and prices of the things they have for sale. *Noun.*
○ To make a list of; put in a list: *I cataloged the stamps in my collection. Verb.*
cat•a•log (kat′ə lôg′ *or* kat′ə log′) *noun, plural* **catalogs;** *verb,* **cataloged, cataloging.**

catamaran A boat with two hulls side by side and joined together. **catamaran** (kat′ ə mə ran′) *noun, plural* **catamarans.**

catapult 1. An ancient weapon that worked like a huge slingshot and threw large rocks at the enemy or over walls. 2. A modern machine that launches planes from the deck of an aircraft carrier. **catapult** (kat′ə púlt′) *noun, plural* **catapults.** —**catapult** *verb.*

cataract 1. A large, steep waterfall. 2. A cloudiness in the lens of a person's or animal's eye, causing blindness. Cataracts can usually be corrected by surgery. **cat•a•ract** (kat′ə rakt′) *noun, plural* **cataracts.**

catastrophe A great, often sudden disaster: *The plane crash was the worst catastrophe of the year.* **ca•tas•tro•phe** (kə tas′trə fē′) *noun, plural* **catastrophes.**

catbird A gray songbird with a long, slender beak and a call that sounds like a cat meowing. **cat•bird** (kat′bûrd′) *noun, plural* **catbirds.**

catch 1. To take or get hold of something or someone that is moving: *Use a pail to catch the water leaking from the roof.* 2. To be in time for: *We will have to hurry to catch the bus.* 3. To become hooked or fastened: *My sweater caught on a branch.* 4. To come upon suddenly; surprise: *The police hoped to catch the thieves before they got on the airplane.* 5. To get; receive: *Dress warmly or you will catch a cold. Verb.*
○ 1. The act of catching something or someone: *The shortstop made a great catch.* 2. Something that holds or fastens: *The catch on the door was broken.* 3. Something caught: *Our catch for the day was three fish.* 4. A game in which a ball is thrown back and forth between the players. 5. A hidden reason or condition; trick: *This problem seems so easy that there must be a catch to it. Noun.*
• **to catch on.** 1. To understand: *She had to explain the joke to me before I caught on.* 2. To become fashionable or popular: *That style of dressing caught on very quickly.*
• **to catch up.** To move fast enough to come from behind into an even position: *I caught up with the leading runner near the end of the race.*
catch (kach) *verb,* **caught, catching;** *noun, plural* **catches.**

catcher A person or thing that catches. In a baseball game the catcher is the player who crouches behind home plate to catch balls that are thrown by the pitcher. **catch•er** (kach′ər) *noun, plural* **catchers.**

catching 1. Spread from one person to another by infection; contagious: *Measles is very catching.* 2. Easily passed on to another: *The excitement of*

PRONUNCIATION KEY:

| at | āpe | fär | câre | end | mē | it | īce | pierce | hot | ōld | sông | fôrk |
| oil | out | up | ūse | rüle | púll | tûrn | chin | sing | shop | thin | this | |

hw in white; zh in treasure. The symbol ə stands for the unstressed vowel sound in about, taken, pencil, lemon, and circus.

119

the people watching the parade was catching.
catch·ing (kach'ing) *adjective*.

category A group or class of things: *The books on that shelf are divided into two categories, history and geography.* **cat·e·go·ry** (kat'i gôr'ē) *noun, plural* **categories**.

cater To provide food, supplies, and other services: *A restaurant catered the wedding dinner.* **ca·ter** (kā'tər) *verb,* **catered, catering**.

caterpillar The larva of a butterfly or moth. A caterpillar looks like a short worm and is sometimes hairy. Look up the word **larva** for more information. **cat·er·pil·lar** (kat'ər pil'ər) *noun, plural* **caterpillars**.

Most caterpillars have glands that allow them to sense odors.

catfish A type of fish with long feelers around its mouth that look like whiskers. Catfish are often used as food. **cat·fish** (kat'fish') *noun, plural* **catfish** *or* **catfishes**.

cathedral 1. The official church of a bishop. 2. A large and important church. **ca·the·dral** (kə thē'drəl) *noun, plural* **cathedrals**.

WORD HISTORY

The word **cathedral** comes from the Greek word for "chair." A bishop's official seat, which indicates his or her position of authority, is in a cathedral.

Catholic Having to do with the Christian church that is headed by the pope; Roman Catholic. *Adjective.*
○ A person who is a member of the Catholic Church; Roman Catholic. *Noun.*
Cath·o·lic (kath'ə lik) *adjective; noun, plural* **Catholics**.

CAT scan 1. A method of taking an x-ray in which a series of cross-sectional images is assembled into a three-dimensional image by a computer. 2. The three-dimensional image made by this method. **CAT scan** (kat) *noun, plural* **CAT scans**.

catsup A spicy red tomato sauce. This word is usually spelled **ketchup**. Look up **ketchup** for more information. **cat·sup** (kat'səp *or* kech'əp) *noun, plural* **catsups**.

cattail A tall plant with long flat leaves that grows in marshes. Cattails have long, furry brown flower spikes. **cat·tail** (kat'tāl') *noun, plural* **cattails**.

cattle Cows, bulls, and steers raised for meat, milk, and their hides. **cat·tle** (kat'əl) *plural noun*.

cattleman A person who owns or helps take care of cattle on a ranch. **cat·tle·man** (kat'əl mən) *noun, plural* **cattlemen** (kat'əl mən).

caught Past tense and past participle of **catch**. **caught** (kôt) *verb*.

cauliflower A plant with a round white head with green leaves around it. The head of a cauliflower is eaten as a vegetable. **cau·li·flow·er** (kô'lə flou'ər) *noun*.

caulk To fill with tar or another substance to prevent leaking; make watertight or airtight. **caulk** (kôk) *verb,* **caulked, caulking**.

cause 1. A person or thing that makes something happen. 2. Something a person or group believes in: *Stopping pollution is a cause many people work for. Noun.*
○ To make something happen; result in: *A fire caused the barn to collapse. Verb.*
cause (kôz) *noun, plural* **causes**; *verb,* **caused, causing**.

causeway A raised road or path often built across swamps, shallow water, or low ground. **cause·way** (kôz'wā') *noun, plural* **causeways**.

This causeway runs a long distance across the bay.

caution 1. Close care; watchfulness: *Use caution when you ride a bike at night.* 2. A warning about something: *There was a sign giving drivers a caution about falling rocks. Noun.* To tell to do something with great care; warn: *The cook cautioned us not to touch the hot pot. Verb.*
cau·tion (kô'shən) *noun, plural* **cautions**; *verb,* **cautioned, cautioning**; **cau·tious** *adjective;*

cau·tious·ly *adverb*.

cavalry A group of soldiers fighting on horseback or from tanks. **cav·al·ry** (kav′əl rē) *noun, plural* **cavalries**.

cave A natural hollow or hole in the ground or in the side of a mountain. *Noun.*
  • **to cave in**. To fall in or down: *The walls of the old mine are about* **to cave in**. *Verb.*
  cave (kāv) *noun, plural* **caves**; *verb*, **caved**, **caving**.

cave dweller A human being of the Stone Age who lived in a cave. **cave dwell·er** (dwel′ər).

cave-in A collapse, as of a mine or tunnel. **cave-in** (kā′vin′) *noun, plural* **cave-ins**.

cave man A man who was a cave dweller.

cavern A large cave. **cav·ern** (kav′ərn) *noun, plural* **caverns**.

Water moving underground sometimes creates a cavern.

cavity 1. A hollow place; hole. 2. A softened place on a tooth caused by decay. **cav·i·ty** (kav′i tē) *noun, plural* **cavities**.

CD An abbreviation for **compact disc**.

cease To come or bring to an end; stop: *The soldiers ceased firing.* **cease** (sēs) *verb*, **ceased**, **ceasing**.

cedar An evergreen tree that has needle-shaped leaves. The reddish wood of the cedar is very fragrant and strong and is used for making chests and cabinets. **ce·dar** (sē′dər) *noun, plural* **cedars**.

ceiling 1. The inside overhead surface of a room. 2. The distance from the earth to the bottom of the lowest clouds: *The airport canceled all flights because there was a low ceiling.* 3. An upper limit: *The class treasurer put a* **ceiling** *of ten dollars on how much we could spend on the party.* **ceil·ing** (sē′ling) *noun, plural* **ceilings**.

celebrate 1. To observe or honor a special day or event with ceremonies and other activities. 2. To perform with the proper ceremonies: *Members of the clergy* **celebrate** *religious rituals.* **cel·e·brate** (sel′ə brāt′) *verb*, **celebrated**, **celebrating**.

celebration 1. The ceremonies carried on to observe or honor a special day or event. 2. The act of celebrating: *We were there for the* **celebration** *of my cousin's graduation.* **cel·e·bra·tion** (sel′ə brā′shən) *noun, plural* **celebrations**.

celebrity A person who is well-known or often in the news. **ce·leb·ri·ty** (sə leb′ri tē) *noun, plural* **celebrities**.

celery The crisp, green or cream-colored stalks of the celery plant. The stalks are eaten raw or cooked. **cel·er·y** (sel′ə rē) *noun*.

cell 1. A small, plain room in a prison, convent, or monastery. 2. The very small, basic unit of living matter. All living things are made of cells. Cells consist of a mass of cytoplasm surrounded by a membrane. 3. A small hole or space: *Honeycombs contain many* **cells**. 4. A device that changes chemical or solar energy into electrical energy. A battery is made up of one or more cells. Another word that sounds like this is **sell**. **cell** (sel) *noun, plural* **cells**.

cellar A room or group of rooms built underground. **cel·lar** (sel′ər) *noun, plural* **cellars**.

cello A musical instrument like a violin but larger and lower in tone. A cello is held between the knees when it is played. **cel·lo** (chel′ō) *noun, plural* **cellos**.

cellophane A thin, clear material made from cellulose, used to wrap food and to make clear tape. **cel·lo·phane** (sel′ə fān′) *noun*.

celluloid A strong, clear plastic that burns easily. **cel·lu·loid** (sel′yə loid′) *noun*.

cellulose The tough material that forms the walls of plant cells. Cellulose makes up the woody part of trees and plants. **cel·lu·lose** (sel′yə lōs′) *noun*.

Celsius On or of a temperature scale on which the freezing point of water is at 0 degrees and the boiling point of water is at 100 degrees. The Celsius scale is also called the **centigrade** scale.

PRONUNCIATION KEY:

at āpe fär câre end mē it īce pierce hot ōld sông fôrk
oil out up ūse rüle pull tûrn chin sing shop thin this
hw in white; zh in treasure. The symbol ə stands for the unstressed vowel sound in about, taken, pencil, lemon, and circus.

121

Cel·si·us (sel′sē əs *or* sel′shəs) *adjective.*

cement 1. A powder made by burning a mixture of limestone and clay. Cement is mixed with water, sand, and rock to form concrete. 2. A soft, sticky substance or glue that hardens to make things hold together. *Noun.*
∘ 1. To cover with cement or concrete. 2. To fasten with cement: *Cement the wing to the model airplane. Verb.*
ce·ment (sə ment′) *noun, plural* **cements**; *verb,* **cemented, cementing.**

cemetery A place where the dead are buried.
cem·e·ter·y (sem′ə ter′ē) *noun, plural* **cemeteries.**

census An official count of the people living in a country or district. A census is taken to find out how many people there are, and their age, sex, and kind of work. **cen·sus** (sen′səs) *noun, plural* **censuses.**

cent A coin of the United States and Canada. One hundred cents is equal to one dollar. Other words sounding like this are scent and sent. **cent** (sent) *noun, plural* **cents.**

centennial The hundredth-year anniversary of an event or the celebration of that anniversary: *A fair is planned for the* **centennial** *of the founding of our city. Noun.* **cen·ten·ni·al** (sen ten′ē əl) *noun, plural* **centennials.**

center 1. The middle point of a circle or sphere. It is the same distance from any point on the circumference of the circle or any point on the surface of the sphere. 2. The middle point, part, or place of something: *We put the flowers in the* **center** *of the table.* 3. A main person, place, or thing: *The new baby was the* **center** *of attention.* 4. A player on a team who has a position in the middle of the playing line or area: *I am the* **center** *on our soccer team. Noun.*
∘ 1. To put in or at the center. 2. To come together or gather around a point or points; concentrate. *Verb.*
cen·ter (sen′tər) *noun, plural* **centers**; *verb,* **centered, centering.**

centi- A prefix that means: 1. One hundred. *Centigrade* means divided into one hundred grades, or degrees. 2. One-hundredth (1/100) of. *Centimeter* means 1/100 of a meter.

centigrade On or of the Celsius temperature scale. **cen·ti·grade** (sen′ti grād′) *adjective.*

centimeter A unit of length in the metric system.

A centimeter is equal to 1/100 of a meter. One inch equals about two and a half centimeters. **cen·ti·me·ter** (sen′tə mē′tər) *noun, plural* **centimeters.**

centipede A small animal with a long body divided into many segments. Each segment has two legs. **cen·ti·pede** (sen′tə pēd′) *noun, plural* **centipedes.**

central 1. In, at, or near the center or middle: *the* **central** *part of town.* 2. Very important; main; chief: *the* **central** *office of the bank.* **cen·tral** (sen′trəl) *adjective.* —**centrally** *adverb.*

Central African Republic A country in central Africa.

Central America The long, narrow strip of land that connects North America and South America.

century A period of one hundred years: *From 1651 to 1750 is one* **century.** **cen·tu·ry** (sen′chə rē) *noun, plural* **centuries.**

ceramic Made of baked clay: *ceramic tiles from Mexico.* **ce·ram·ic** (sə ram′ik) *adjective.*

ceramics The art of making bowls, dishes, vases, and other things out of baked clay. **ce·ram·ics** (sə ram′iks) *noun.*

Ceramics **are created in many shapes for different uses.**

cereal 1. Any grass whose grains are used for food, such as wheat, oats, rye, barley, and rice. 2. A food, such as oatmeal, made from this grain. Another word that sounds like this is serial. **ce·re·al** (sîr′ē əl) *noun, plural* **cereals.**

WORD HISTORY

The word cereal goes back to a Latin word meaning "having to do with growing crops of grain." The Latin word comes from the name Ceres, goddess of farming and crops in Roman mythology.

ceremony 1. A formal act done on a special occasion: *a graduation ceremony.* 2. Very polite or formal behavior: *The usher showed us to our seats with great ceremony.* **cer·e·mo·ny** (ser′ə mō′nē) *noun, plural* **ceremonies.**

certain 1. Sure; positive: *I am certain that my answer is correct.* 2. Known but not named; some; particular: *Certain people already know who won the contest.* **cer·tain** (sûr′tən) *adjective.*

certainly Without a doubt; surely: *Those clouds certainly mean rain.* **cer·tain·ly** (sûr′tən lē) *adverb.*

certainty The state or quality of being certain: *I watched them leave, so I can say with certainty that they are not here.* **cer·tain·ty** (sûr′tən tē) *noun, plural* **certainties.**

certificate A written statement accepted as proof of certain facts: *Your birth certificate tells where and when you were born.* **cer·tif·i·cate** (sər tif′i kit) *noun, plural* **certificates.**

Chad A country in central Africa. **Chad** (chad) *noun.*

chain 1. A row of rings or links connected to each other, usually made of metal and used to fasten, hold, or pull something. 2. A series of things connected or related to each other: *That family owns a chain of grocery stores.* 3. **chains.** Rows of rings or other objects used to fasten together the wrists or ankles of a prisoner. *Noun.*
  ○ To fasten or hold with a chain: *She chained her bike to a post. Verb.*
  chain (chān) *noun, plural* **chains;** *verb,* **chained, chaining.**

chair 1. A piece of furniture for a person to sit on. A chair has a seat, legs, and a back. Some chairs have arms. 2. A chairperson. **chair** (châr) *noun, plural* **chairs.**

chairlift A line of bench-like chairs hanging from a moving cable, used for carrying skiers to the top of a slope. **chair·lft** (châr′lift′) *noun, plural* **chairlifts.**

chairman A person, especially a man, in charge of

Chairs have been made by artisans for centuries.

a meeting or committee. **chair·man** (châr′mən) *noun, plural* **chairmen** (châr′mən).

chairperson A person in charge of a meeting or committee. **chair·per·son** (châr′pûr′sən) *noun, plural* **chairpersons.**

chairwoman A woman in charge of a meeting or committee. **chair·wom·an** (châr′wŭm′ən) *noun, plural* **chairwomen** (châr′wim′ən).

chalk 1. A type of soft white or gray limestone made up mostly of the tiny fossils of seashells and used to make lime and cement and as a fertilizer. 2. A piece of this substance, used for writing on a blackboard. *Noun.*
  ○ To write, mark, or draw with chalk. *Verb.*
    • **to chalk up.** 1. To score or record: *The hockey team chalked up three more goals.* 2. To think or say that something is caused by something else: *You can chalk up my mistake to ignorance.*
  chalk (chôk) *noun, plural* **chalks;** *verb,* **chalked, chalking.**

chalkboard A hard, smooth board made to be written on with chalk; blackboard. Look up **blackboard** for more information. **chalk·board** (chôk′bôrd′) *noun, plural* **chalkboards.**

challenge 1. To ask to take part in a contest or fight. 2. To stop someone for identification: *The guard challenged us at the door of the building.* 3. To question the truth or correctness of: *They challenged my claim that bats are mammals.* 4. To make someone think, work, or try hard: *The puzzle challenged us all. Verb.*
  ○ 1. A call to take part in a contest or fight. 2. A call to stop and give an explanation. 3. A questioning of the truth or correctness of something; objection: *There was a legal challenge to the election, because some votes were not counted.* 4. Something calling for work, effort, and the use of one's talents: *Chemistry is a real challenge. Noun.*
  chal·lenge (chal′ənj) *verb,* **challenged, challenging;** *noun, plural* **challenges.**

chamber 1. A room in a building: *While exploring the castle, we discovered a secret chamber in the tower.* 2. The office of a judge, usually in a courthouse. 3. A hall where a lawmaking body meets: *In Philadelphia, you can see the chamber where the Declaration of Independence was signed.*

PRONUNCIATION KEY:

| at | āpe | fär | câre | end | mē | it | īce | pîerce | hot | ōld | sông | fôrk |
| oil | out | up | ūse | rüle | pull | tûrn | chin | sing | shop | thin | this | |

hw in white; zh in treasure. The symbol ə stands for the unstressed vowel sound in about, taken, pencil, lemon, and circus.

123

4. A legislature: *The Senate and the House of Representatives are the two **chambers** of Congress.* **5.** An enclosed space in the body of an animal or plant: *The human heart has four **chambers**.* **6.** The part of the barrel of a gun into which the shell is put. **cham·ber** (chām′bər) *noun, plural* **chambers.**

chameleon A small lizard that can change its color to look like its surroundings. **cha·me·le·on** (kə mēl′yən) *noun, plural* **chameleons.**

champagne A fine white wine with bubbles like ginger ale. **champagne** (sham pān′) *noun, plural* **champagnes.**

champion **1.** A person or thing that is the winner in a contest or game. **2.** A person who fights or speaks for another person or a cause: *That senator is a **champion** of the rights of the poor.* **cham·pi·on** (cham′pē ən) *noun, plural* **champions.**

championship **1.** A contest held to decide who is the champion. **2.** The title or position held by a champion. **cham·pi·on·ship** (cham′pē ən ship′) *noun, plural* **championships.**

chance **1.** A good or favorable opportunity: *I'm so glad we had this **chance** to meet.* **2.** The possibility of something happening: *a **chance** of rain.* **3.** A risk: *Never take **chances** by swimming alone. Noun.*
○ **1.** To risk: *The prisoners decided to **chance** an escape.* **2.** To happen accidentally: *I **chanced** to meet them in the park. Verb.*
○ Not expected or planned; accidental: *We learned about the party through a **chance** remark. Adjective.*
  • **by chance.** Accidentally: *It was only by chance that I noticed the mistake.*
chance (chans) *noun, plural* **chances;** *verb,* **chanced, chancing;** *adjective.*

chancellor A very high official: *In certain European countries the head of the government is called the **chancellor**.* **chan·cel·lor** (chan′sə lər) *noun, plural* **chancellors.**

chandelier A kind of light that hangs from the ceiling, usually having several lights arranged on branches. **chan·de·lier** (shan′də lîr′) *noun, plural* **chandeliers.**

WORD HISTORY

The word **chandelier** comes from a French word meaning "candlestick." This French word goes back to a Latin word meaning "candle."

change **1.** To make or become different; alter: *I **changed** the way I signed my name.* **2.** To replace with another or others; exchange: *Let's **change** our seats.* **3.** To put on other clothes: *I **changed** and went for a swim. Verb.*
○ **1.** The act or result of making something different: *We made a **change** in our plans.* **2.** Something that can be put in place of another: *Bring a **change** of clothing on the camping trip.* **3.** The money given back when the amount paid is more than the amount owed. **4.** Coins: *a pocket full of **change**. Noun.*
change (chānj) *verb,* **changed, changing;** *noun, plural* **changes.**

channel **1.** The deepest part of a river, harbor, or other waterway. **2.** A body of water that connects two larger bodies of water: *The Strait of Gibraltar is a narrow **channel** between the Atlantic Ocean and the Mediterranean Sea.* **3.** A band of frequencies that a radio or television station uses to send out electronic signals: *This old television set can pick up only one **channel**. Noun.*
○ To form a channel in. *Verb.*
chan·nel (chan′əl) *noun, plural* **channels;** *verb,* **channeled, channeling.**

Ships must navigate carefully through this narrow channel.

chant A singing or shouting of words over and over. Chants usually have a strong rhythm. *Noun.*
○ To sing or shout in a chant. *Verb.*
chant (chant) *noun, plural* **chants;** *verb,* **chanted, chanting.**

Chanukah Another spelling for Hanukkah. **Cha·nu·kah** (hä′nə kə) *noun, plural* **Chanukahs.**

chaos Complete confusion; great disorder. **cha·os** (kā′os) *noun.*

chap¹ To make or become dry, cracked, and rough: *In the winter, the cold, dry air chaps my face and hands.* **chap** (chap) *verb,* **chapped, chapping.**

chap² A man or boy; fellow. **chap** (chap) *noun,* *plural* **chaps.**

chapel A room, small building, or other place for worship. **chap·el** (chap′əl) *noun,* *plural* **chapels.**

chaplain A member of the clergy who leads services and does counseling for a military unit, school, prison, or other group. **chap·lain** (chap′lin) *noun,* *plural* **chaplains.**

The chaps being worn by this rider have a fringe at their bottom.

chaps Strong leather coverings worn over trousers, usually by cowhands to protect their legs while riding horses. **chaps** (chaps *or* shaps) *plural noun.*

chapter 1. A main part of a book. 2. A local branch or division of a club or other organization: *The fan club has a chapter in every large city.* **chap·ter** (chap′tər) *noun,* *plural* **chapters.**

character 1. All the qualities that make a person or thing different from others: *That writer's stories all have a frightening character.* 2. What a person really is; inner nature: *You can judge a person's character by the way that person speaks and acts.* 3. Strength of mind, courage, and honesty taken together: *Political leaders should have great character.* 4. A person in a book, play, story, or motion picture. 5. A person who is different, funny, or strange: *Everyone thought the storekeeper was a character.* 6. A mark or sign used in writing or printing, such as the letters of the alphabet. **char·ac·ter** (kar′ik tər) *noun,* *plural* **characters.**

characteristic A quality that belongs to and helps to identify a person or thing: *Kindness and honesty are two good characteristics of my neighbor.* Noun.
○ Belonging to and helping to identify a person or thing; typical: *The characteristic taste of a lemon is sour.* Adjective.
char·ac·ter·is·tic (kar′ik tə ris′tik) *noun,* *plural* **characteristics**; *adjective.* —**characteristically** *adverb.*

characterize 1. To be a characteristic of; distinguish: *The ability to hop great distances characterizes the kangaroo.* 2. To describe the character of: *The author of the book characterizes the town as a quiet place by the ocean.*
char·ac·ter·ize (kar′ik tə rīz′) *verb,* **characterized, characterizing.**

charcoal A soft, black form of carbon, made by partially burning wood, and used as a fuel and in pencils for drawing. **char·coal** (chär′kōl′) *noun.*

charge 1. To ask as a price: *The shop charged ten dollars to repair the radio.* 2. To ask to pay for something: *The neighbor charged the children for the window they broke.* 3. To put off paying for something until later: *We charged the clothes at the store and paid for them at the end of the month.* 4. To blame; accuse: *The police charged them with robbery.* 5. To rush at; attack: *The angry bull charged the farmer.* 6. To fill or load with electricity: *The mechanic charged the car's battery.* 7. To give a task or responsibility to: *The lifeguard was charged with the care of the swimmers.* Verb.
○ 1. The price asked for something: *The charge for the repair was sixty dollars.* 2. Care or responsibility: *I had charge of my brother and sister while*

PRONUNCIATION KEY:

at   āpe   fär   câre   end   mē   it   īce   pierce   hot   ōld   sông   fôrk
oil   out   up   ūse   rüle   pull   tûrn   chin   sing   shop   thin   this
hw in white; zh in treasure. The symbol ə stands for the unstressed vowel sound in about, taken, pencil, lemon, and circus.

125

our parents were away. **3.** A statement that some-one has committed a crime; accusation: *arrested on a charge of robbery.* **4.** A rushing at an opponent; attack: *The enemy's charge was turned back by the King's soldiers. Noun.*

• **in charge.** Having the power or right to act, order, or make decisions: *One worker in the crew was in charge.*

• **in charge of.** Assigned the duty of; responsi-ble for: *You cook dinner, and I'll be in charge of washing the dishes.*
charge (chärj) *verb,* **charged, charging;** *noun, plural* **charges.**

chariot A two-wheeled vehicle drawn by horses, used in ancient times in warfare, races, and proces-sions. **char·i·ot** (char′ē ət) *noun, plural* **chariots.**

charity **1.** The giving of money or help to those who need it. **2.** A fund or organization for giving help to those who need it: *We give money to a charity for orphans.* **3.** Kindness or forgiveness toward other people: *I try to show charity even to people who are unkind to me.* **char·i·ty** (char′i tē) *noun, plural* **charities.**

charm **1.** The power to attract or delight greatly: *That fairy tale holds much charm for people of all ages.* **2.** A small ornament worn on a bracelet or necklace. **3.** An act, saying, or thing that is supposed to have magic power: *Do you carry a rabbit's foot as a charm for good luck? Noun.*
○ To attract or delight greatly. *Verb.*
charm (chärm) *noun, plural* **charms;** *verb,* **charmed, charming.**

charming Full of charm: *a charming smile.*
charm·ing (chär′ming) *adjective.*

chart **1.** A sheet that shows information in the form of a list, diagram, table, or graph. **2.** A map such as sailors use, showing where rocks, har-bors, and channels are. *Noun.*
○ To make a map or chart of. *Verb.*
chart (chärt) *noun, plural* **charts;** *verb,* **charted, charting.**

charter **1.** A document giving and explaining cer-tain rights and obligations. A charter is given by a government or ruler to a person, group of peo-ple, or company. **2.** A renting or hiring of a bus, aircraft, or automobile. *Noun.*
○ **1.** To rent or hire by charter: *The school band chartered a bus for the trip.* **2.** To give a charter to: *The state chartered a new bank. Verb.*

char·ter (chär′tər) *noun, plural* **charters;** *verb,* **chartered, chartering.**

chase **1.** To run after and try to catch. **2.** To cause to go away quickly; drive away: *We chased the birds out of our vegetable garden. Verb.*
○ The act of running and trying to catch. *Noun.*
chase (chās) *verb,* **chased, chasing;** *noun, plural* **chases.**

chasm A deep crack or opening in the earth's sur-face. **chasm** (kaz′əm) *noun, plural* **chasms.**

chassis The main framework that supports the body of an automobile or airplane, or the parts of a radio or television set. **chas·sis** (chas′ē or shas′ē) *noun, plural* **chassis** (chas′ēz or shas′ēz).

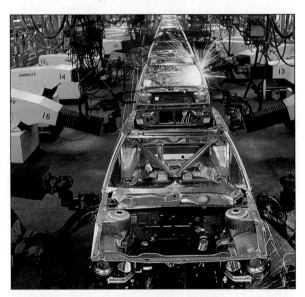
These automobile chassis are being assembled by robots.

chat To talk in a light, friendly, or relaxed way. *Verb.*
○ A light, friendly, informal talk. *Noun.*
chat (chat) *verb,* **chatted, chatting;** *noun, plural* **chats.**

chatter **1.** To talk quickly and without serious thought or purpose. **2.** To knock or click together quickly: *My teeth chattered from the cold. Verb.*
○ **1.** Quick talk without serious thought or pur-pose. **2.** Quick, short sounds: *the chatter of mon-keys. Noun.*
chat·ter (chat′ər) *verb,* **chattered, chattering;** *noun, plural* **chatters.**

chauffeur A person whose work is driving someone else's automobile. **chauf·feur** (shō′fər or shō fûr′) *noun, plural* **chauffeurs.**

cheap **1.** Low in price: *Milk is **cheap** in that store.* **2.** Charging low prices: *a **cheap** restaurant.* **3.** Having little value; not of good quality: *Clothing made of **cheap** material does not last long.* **cheap** (chēp) *adjective,* **cheaper, cheapest.** —**cheaply** *adverb* —**cheapness** *noun.*

cheat **1.** To act dishonestly: *Do not **cheat** when playing games.* **2.** To take something away from dishonestly; swindle: *The crook **cheated** them out of their money. Verb.*
 ○ A person who cheats; dishonest person. *Noun.*
cheat (chēt) *verb,* **cheated, cheating**; *noun, plural* **cheats.**

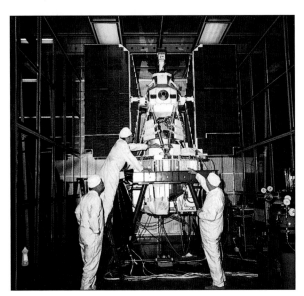

These technicians are checking **a space satellite.**

check **1.** A test to find out if something is correct or as it should be: *The teacher made a **check** of the classroom to see if everyone was present.* **2.** A mark (✓) used to show that something has been approved or is correct. **3.** A written order directing a bank to pay a certain amount of money. The money comes from the account of the person who signs the check and goes to the person named on the check. **4.** A slip of paper showing what is owed for food or drink in a restaurant. **5.** A ticket, tag, or token given to a person who has left or stored something so that the article can be claimed later. **6.** A pattern of squares: *a skirt with black and white **checks**.* **7.** A sudden stop: *A lack of time put a **check** on our plans to*

clean the yard. **8.** A person or thing that stops, controls, or limits: *The leash was a **check** on the dog. Noun.*
 ○ **1.** To test to find out if something is correct or as it should be: *The mechanic **checked** the car's engine.* **2.** To mark with a check. **3.** To leave something for a time: *We **checked** our coats at the door.* **4.** To bring to a sudden stop: *The army **checked** the attack of the enemy soldiers.* **5.** To hold in control; curb: *I had to **check** the urge to laugh. Verb.*
 • **to check in.** To register as a guest in a hotel or motel: *We **checked in** at a hotel on the beach.*
 • **to check out.** **1.** To pay one's bill and depart from a hotel or motel: *We didn't like the hotel so we **checked out** a day early.* **2.** To add up prices and accept payment for: *I have a job on weekends **checking out** groceries.*
check (chek) *noun, plural* **checks**; *verb,* **checked, checking.**

checkerboard A square board marked off into sixty-four squares of two alternating colors, used in playing checkers and chess. **check•er•board** (chek′ər bôrd′) *noun, plural* **checkerboards.**

checkers A game for two people played on a checkerboard with twelve pieces for each player. **check•ers** (chek′ərz) *plural noun.*

checkup **1.** A complete examination of the body to find out if a person is healthy. **2.** Any complete inspection: *Give your car a **checkup** before you take your trip.* **check•up** (chek′up′) *noun, plural* **checkups.**

cheek **1.** Either side of the face below the eye. **2.** Boldness or rudeness; disrespect: *I was shocked that the new student had the **cheek** to talk back to the teacher.* **cheek** (chēk) *noun, plural* **cheeks.**

cheer **1.** A shout of happiness, encouragement, or praise. **2.** Good spirits; happiness: *Summer vacation brings **cheer** to students. Noun.*
 ○ **1.** To give a shout of happiness, encouragement, or praise. **2.** To make or become happy: *My friend's joke **cheered** me up. Verb.*
cheer (chîr) *noun, plural* **cheers**; *verb,* **cheered, cheering.**

cheerful **1.** Showing or feeling cheer: *The **cheerful** carpenter whistled while building the shed.*

PRONUNCIATION KEY:

| at | āpe | fär | câre | end | mē | it | īce | pîerce | hot | ōld | sông | fôrk |
| oil | out | up | ūse | rüle | pull | tûrn | chin | sing | shop | thin | this | |

hw in white; zh in treasure. The symbol ə stands for the unstressed vowel sound in about, taken, pencil, lemon, and circus.

127

2. Bringing a feeling of cheer: *a bright, cheerful kitchen*. **cheer·ful** (chîr′fəl) *adjective.* —**cheerfully** *adverb* —**cheer·ful·ness** *noun.*

cheese A food made by pressing the less watery parts of curdled milk into a solid piece. Most cheeses are seasoned and aged. **cheese** (chēz) *noun, plural* **cheeses.**

cheetah A wild cat that has solid black spots on its coat. Cheetahs live in Africa and southern Asia and can run very fast. **chee·tah** (chēt′ə) *noun, plural* **cheetahs.**

chef The head cook of a restaurant or hotel. **chef** (shef) *noun, plural* **chefs.**

chemical Having to do with or made by chemistry: *Rusting is a chemical process in which metal combines with oxygen. Adjective.*
◦ A substance made by or used in chemistry: *Ammonia is a chemical used in household cleansers. Noun.*
chem·i·cal (kem′i kəl) *adjective; noun, plural* **chemicals.** —**chemically** *adverb.*

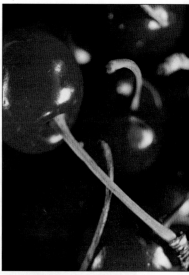

This **chef** is arranging the food attractively.

chemist A person who works or specializes in chemistry. **chem·ist** (kem′ist) *noun, plural* **chemists.**

chemistry The science that deals with substances, what they are made of, what characteristics they have, and what kinds of changes happen when they combine with other substances. **chem·is·try** (kem′ə strē) *noun.*

chemotherapy The use of chemical substances to treat diseases. **chem·o·ther·a·py** (kē′mō ther′ə pē *or* kem′ō ther′ə pē) *noun, plural* **chemotherapies.**

cherish To love and treat tenderly; hold dear: *They cherish their family pets.* **cher·ish** (cher′ish) *verb,* **cherished, cherishing.**

Cherokee A member of a Native American tribe of the southeastern United States. The Cherokee now live mostly in Oklahoma. **Cher·o·kee** (cher′ə kē) *noun, plural* **Cherokee** *or* **Cherokees.**

cherry 1. A small, round red fruit with a smooth skin and a pit in the center. 2. A bright red color. **cher·ry** (cher′ē) *noun, plural* **cherries.**

chess A game played by two people on a board, with sixteen pieces for each player. **chess** (ches) *noun.*

chest 1. The upper, front part of the body of a person, enclosed by the ribs. The lungs and the heart are in the chest. 2. A large, strong box used for holding things. **chest** (chest) *noun, plural* **chests.**

Cherries are eaten raw or used in cooking.

chestnut 1. A sweet-tasting nut that grows inside a large, prickly burr. It grows on a tree that is also called a chestnut. 2. A reddish brown color. **chest·nut** (ches′nut′) *noun, plural* **chestnuts.**

chew 1. To crush and grind something with the teeth. 2. To make by chewing: *The puppy chewed a hole in the slipper.* **chew** (chü) *verb,* **chewed, chewing.**

chewing gum A sweet gum for chewing.

Cheyenne A member of a Native American tribe that used to live on the plains of North America. The Cheyenne now live mostly in Montana and Oklahoma. **Chey·enne** (shī en′ *or* shī an′) *noun, plural* **Cheyenne** *or* **Cheyennes.**

Chicana An American woman or girl of Mexican birth or descent. **Chi·ca·na** (chi kä′nə) *noun, plural* **Chicanas.**

Chicano An American man or boy of Mexican birth or descent. **Chi·ca·no** (chi kä′nō) *noun, plural* **Chicanos.**

chick A young chicken or other young bird. **chick** (chik) *noun, plural* **chicks.**

These **chicks** have just broken through their shells.

chickadee A small bird with a gray back and wings and a black head and throat. Chickadees live in North America and have a call that sounds like their name. **chick·a·dee** (chik′ə dē′) *noun, plural* **chickadees**.

chicken **1.** A bird raised on farms for its meat and eggs. **2.** The meat of a chicken used for food. **chick·en** (chik′ən) *noun, plural* **chickens**.

chicken pox A disease caused by a virus passed from one person to another, causing a fever and rash. **chicken pox** (poks).

chief A person highest in rank or power; leader of a group: *The chief of the Indian tribe was the oldest and wisest member. Noun.*
○ **1.** Highest in rank; in charge of a group: *My cousin is chief counselor at that camp.* **2.** Most important; main: *Corn is the chief farm crop of Iowa. Adjective.*
chief (chēf) *noun, plural* **chiefs**; *adjective.*

Native American chiefs **have become a symbol of wise leadership.**

chiefly **1.** Mainly; mostly: *The house was made chiefly of wood.* **2.** More than anything; especially: *I am chiefly interested in physics.* **chief·ly** (chēf′lē) *adverb.*

chieftain A leader of a tribe or clan. **chief·tain** (chēf′tən) *noun, plural* **chieftains**.

chigger A mite that gets under the skin and causes a rash and itching. **chig·ger** (chig′ər) *noun, plural* **chiggers**.

chihuahua A tiny dog with big, pointed ears and usually a short tan coat. It is the smallest breed of dog. **chi·hua·hua** (chi wä′wə) *noun, plural* **chihuahuas**.

child **1.** A son or daughter: *The parents are proud of their child.* **2.** A young boy or girl: *That is a good book for a child.* **3.** A baby; infant. **child** (chīld) *noun, plural* **children**.

childbirth The act of giving birth to a child or children. **child·birth** (chīld′bûrth′) *noun, plural* **childbirths**.

childhood The period of a person's life when he or she is a child. **child·hood** (chīld′hùd′) *noun, plural* **childhoods**.

childish Of, like, or suitable only for a child: *Refusing to try new kinds of food is childish.* **child·ish** (chīl′dish) *adjective.* —**child·ish·ly** *adverb.* —**child·ish·ness** *noun.*

childlike Of or like a child: *My grandfather had a childlike delight in roller coasters and fireworks displays.* **childlike** (chīld′līk′) *adjective.*

children Plural of **child**. **chil·dren** (chil′drən) *plural noun.*

Chile A country in southern South America. Other words that sound like this are **chili** and **chilly**. **Chil·e** (chil′ē) *noun.*

chili **1.** The dried pod of a kind of pepper plant, used to make a hot spice. Most chilies are either red or green. **2.** A spicy food made of chilies, chopped meat, and usually beans and tomatoes. Other words sounding like this are **Chile** and **chilly**. **chil·i** (chi′lē) *noun, plural* **chilies**.

Delicious chili **is sometimes very spicy.**

chill **1.** A mild but unpleasant coldness: *a chill in the air.* **2.** A feeling of coldness in the body that makes a person shiver: *As she listened to the ghost story she felt a chill go through her. Noun.*
○ To make or become cold: *Chill the sodas before you drink them. Verb.*
○ Unpleasantly cold; chilly: *a chill wind. Adjective.*
chill (chil) *noun, plural* **chills**; *verb,* **chilled, chilling**; *adjective.*

PRONUNCIATION KEY:

| at | āpe | fär | câre | end | mē | it | īce | pîerce | hot | ōld | sông | fôrk |
| oil | out | up | ūse | rüle | pùll | tûrn | chin | sing | shop | thin | this | |

hw in white; zh in treasure. The symbol ə stands for the unstressed vowel sound in about, taken, pencil, lemon, and circus.

129

chilly 1. Causing or feeling a chill: *a chilly morning*. 2. Not warm and friendly: *a chilly welcome*. Other words sounding like this are **Chile** and **chili**. **chill•y** (chil′ē) *adjective*, **chillier, chilliest**.

chime 1. One of a set of bells or pipes tuned to make musical sounds at different pitches. 2. The sound made by these bells or pipes or a similar sound: *the chime of the doorbell. Noun.*
○ To make such a sound or sounds. *Verb.*
chime (chīm) *noun, plural* **chimes**; *verb,* **chimed, chiming**.

chimney An upright, hollow structure that is connected to a fireplace or furnace and carries away the smoke from the fire. **chim•ney** (chim′nē) *noun, plural* **chimneys**.

Most chimneys are made of stone or brick.

chimp A chimpanzee. **chimp** (chimp) *noun, plural* **chimps**.

chimpanzee A small, very intelligent ape with a dark coat that lives in groups in the forests of central and eastern Africa. **chim•pan•zee** (chim pan zē′ or chim pan′zē) *noun, plural* **chimpanzees**.

chin The part of the face below the mouth and above the neck, forming the front of the lower jaw. *Noun.*
○ To lift oneself up to an overhead bar by pulling with the arms until the chin is level with or above the bar: *How many times can you chin yourself? Verb.*
chin (chin) *noun, plural* **chins**; *verb,* **chinned, chinning**.

Chimpanzees live mainly in rain forests.

china 1. A fine, hard pottery. It is usually white and can have colored designs baked on it. 2. Dishes and other things made of china: *Set the table with our best china.* **chi•na** chī′nə) *noun.*

China A large country in eastern Asia. More people live in China than in any other country in the world. **Chi•na** (chī′nə) *noun.*

chinchilla A small South American rodent that looks like a squirrel and has a thick, soft, silver-gray fur. **chin•chil•la** (chin chil′ə) *noun, plural* **chinchillas**.

Chinese 1. A person who was born in or is a citizen of China. 2. The language spoken in China. *Noun.*
○ Having to do with China. *Adjective.*
Chi•nese (chī nēz′ or chī nēs′) *noun, plural* **Chinese**; *adjective.*

chink A small, narrow opening; crack: *Light came through chinks in the walls of the log cabin.* **chink** (chingk) *noun, plural* **chinks**.

chip 1. A very small piece that has been broken off or cut off something: *a chip of wood*. 2. A place on an object where a small piece has been broken or cut off: *The glass had a chip on the rim*. 3. A short form of the word **microchip**. Look up **microchip** for more information. *Noun.*
○ To break off in a small piece or pieces: *We had to chip the old paint. Verb.*
  • **to chip in.** To join with others in giving money or help; contribute: *We all chipped in to buy flowers for our teacher.*
chip (chip) *noun, plural* **chips**; *verb,* **chipped, chipping**.

chipmunk A small rodent with brown fur and dark stripes on its back and tail. **chip•munk** (chip′mungk) *noun, plural* **chipmunks**.

chirp A short sound with a high pitch made by birds, insects, and other small animals. *Noun.*
○ To make such a sound. *Verb.*
chirp (chûrp) *noun, plural* **chirps**; *verb,* **chirped, chirping**.

chisel A metal tool with a sharp edge at the end of a blade, used to cut or shape wood, stone, or metal. *Noun.*
○ To cut or shape with a chisel. *Verb.*
chis•el (chiz′əl) *noun, plural* **chisels**; *verb,* **chiseled, chiseling**.

chivalry The qualities that a good knight was supposed to have. Chivalry included politeness, bravery, honor, and the protecting of people who needed help. **chiv·al·ry** (shiv′əl rē) *noun*.

chlorine A greenish yellow poisonous gas that has a strong, unpleasant odor. Chlorine is a chemical element and is used to kill germs and to bleach things. **chlo·rine** (klôr′ēn) *noun*.

chlorophyll The green substance in plants that absorbs energy from sunlight. Plants use chlorophyll to change carbon dioxide and water into food and oxygen. **chlo·ro·phyll** (klôr′ə fil′) *noun*.

chocolate 1. A food made from roasted and ground cacao beans. Chocolate is used to make drinks and candy. 2. A drink made by dissolving chocolate in milk or water. 3. A candy made of or coated with chocolate. 4. A dark brown color. *Noun*.
○ 1. Made with chocolate: *chocolate cake*.
2. Having a dark brown color. *Adjective*.
choc·o·late (chôk′lit or chô′kə lit) *noun, plural* **chocolates**; *adjective*.

choice 1. The act or result of choosing: *I think my choice was the right one.* 2. The chance to choose: *a choice between going to the movies and visiting the zoo.* 3. A person or thing chosen: *Fresh fruit salad was my choice for dessert.* 4. A variety or number of things from which to choose: *The school offers a very large choice of courses. Noun.*
○ Of very good quality; excellent: *a choice spot to have a picnic. Adjective.*
choice (chois) *noun, plural* **choices**; *adjective*, **choicer**, **choicest**.

choir A group of singers who sing together, especially in a church. **choir** (kwīr) *noun, plural* **choirs**.

choke 1. To stop or

Singing in a choir requires many rehearsals.

hold back the breathing of by squeezing or blocking the windpipe: *That tight collar could choke the dog.* 2. To make or become unable to breathe easily. *I choked on a bone.* 3. To block or clog; fill up: *Grease choked the kitchen drain.* 4. To keep from growing or progressing normally: *Weeds choked the flowers in the garden. Verb.*
• **to choke back.** To keep from showing; hold in; restrain: *I choked back my anger.*
choke (chōk) *verb*, **choked**, **choking**.

choose 1. To decide to take from what is available; pick: *If you could have either a bicycle or a pair of ice skates, which would you choose?* 2. To decide or prefer to do something: *You can come with us if you choose.* **choose** (chüz) *verb*, **chose**, **chosen**, **choosing**.

chop 1. To cut by a quick blow or blows with something sharp. 2. To cut into small pieces: *They chopped onions for the stew. Verb.*
○ 1. A quick blow with something sharp.
2. A small piece of meat that has a rib in it: *lamb chops. Noun.*
chop (chop) *verb*, **chopped**, **chopping**; *noun, plural* **chops**.

chopsticks A pair of long, thin sticks used to eat with. Chopsticks are held between the thumb and fingers of one hand. **chop·sticks** (chop′stiks′) *plural noun*.

chord¹ A combination of three or more notes of music sounded at the same time to produce a harmony.
Another word that sounds like this is **cord**.
chord (kôrd) *noun, plural* **chords**.

chord² A straight line that connects any two points on the circumference of a circle.
chord (kôrd) *noun, plural* **chords**.

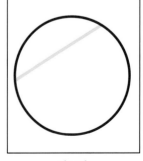

chord

chore 1. A small job or task: *Feeding the chickens was one of my chores on the farm.* 2. A hard or unpleasant task: *At first, shoveling snow was fun, but it became a chore.* **chore** (chôr) *noun, plural* **chores**.

PRONUNCIATION KEY:
at   āpe   fär   câre   end   mē   it   īce   pîerce   hot   ōld   sông   fôrk
oil   out   up   ūse   rüle   pull   tûrn   chin   sing   shop   thin   this
hw in white; zh in treasure. The symbol ə stands for the unstressed vowel sound in about, taken, pencil, lemon, and circus.

131

chorus 1. A group of people who sing or dance together: *The chorus danced in a line behind the soloist.* 2. A part of a song that is sung after each stanza: *It was hard to remember all the words of the song, but everyone knew the chorus. Noun.*
○ To sing or say at the same time: *All the children chorused "good morning." Verb.*
cho·rus (kôr′əs) *noun, plural* **choruses;** *verb,* **chorused, chorusing.**

chose Past tense of **choose. chose** (chōz) *verb.*

chosen Past participle of **choose. cho·sen** (chō′zən) *verb.*

chowder A thick soup made with fish or clams and vegetables. **chow·der** (chou′dər) *noun, plural* **chowders.**

Christ Jesus, the founder of the Christian religion. **Christ** (krīst) *noun.*

christen 1. To give a name to a person during baptism. 2. To receive into a Christian church by means of baptism. **chris·ten** (kris′ən) *verb,* **christened, christening.**

Christian A person who believes in Jesus and follows his teachings. *Noun.*
○ 1. Having to do with Jesus or the religion based on his teachings: *The cross is a Christian symbol.* 2. Believing in Jesus and following his teachings: *Easter is a holiday that is celebrated by Christian people. Adjective.*
Chris·tian (kris′chən) *noun, plural* **Christians;** *adjective.*

Christianity The religion based on the teachings of Jesus. **Chris·ti·an·i·ty** (kris′chē an′i tē) *noun.*

Christmas A Christian holiday on December 25 celebrating the anniversary of the day Jesus was born. **Christ·mas** (kris′məs) *noun, plural* **Christmases.**

Christmas tree A tree decorated with lights and ornaments at Christmas.

Christmas tree **ornaments are sometimes kept in families for generations.**

chromium A hard silver-white metal that does not easily rust or become dull. Chromium is a chemical element and is used to coat the bumpers and metal trim on automobiles so that they will stay shiny. **chro·mi·um** (krō′mē əm) *noun.*

chromosome A part of a cell in a plant or animal that carries the genes that control such things as color of the hair and eyes. **chro·mo·some** (krō′mə sōm′) *noun, plural* **chromosomes.**

chronic 1. Lasting a long time or happening again and again: *Arthritis is a chronic illness.* 2. Done by habit; habitual; constant: *Their chronic complaining irritated us.* **chron·ic** (kron′ik) *adjective.*
—**chronically** *adverb.*

chronological Arranged in the order of time in which things happened: *My history book has a chronological chart of the Civil War.* **chronological** (kron′ə loj′i kəl) *adjective.*

chrysanthemum A round flower with many small petals. Chrysanthemums may be yellow, white, or some other color. **chry·san·the·mum** (krə san′thə məm) *noun, plural* **chrysanthemums.**

chubby Round and plump. **chub·by** (chub′ē) *adjective,* **chubbier, chubbiest.** —**chubbiness** *noun.*

chuckle To laugh in a quiet way. *Verb.*
○ A quiet laugh. *Noun.*
chuck·le (chuk′əl) *verb,* **chuckled, chuckling;** *noun, plural* **chuckles.**

chug A short, steady, puffing sound such as a steam engine makes: *We could hear the chug of the fishing boat across the bay. Noun.*
○ To move slowly with such a sound: *The huge truck chugged very slowly up the steep hill. Verb.*
chug (chug) *noun, plural* **chugs;** *verb,* **chugged, chugging.**

chum A close friend; pal. **chum** (chum) *noun, plural* **chums.**

chunk A thick piece or lump. **chunk** (chungk) *noun, plural* **chunks.**

chunky 1. Full of chunks. 2. Short and solid in build or form; stocky: *a chunky build.* **chunk·y** (chung′kē) *adjective,* **chunkier, chunkiest.** —**chunkiness** *noun.*

church 1. A building where people gather together for Christian worship. 2. A group of Christians having the same beliefs; denomination: *The Roman Catholic and Episcopalian churches share many beliefs.* **church** (chûrch) *noun, plural* **churches.**

churn A container in which cream is shaken or beaten to make butter. *Noun.*
○ **1.** To shake or beat cream in a special container to make butter. **2.** To stir or move with a forceful motion: *A plow churns up the soil. Verb.*
churn (chûrn) *noun, plural* **churns;** *verb,* **churned, churning.**

chute A steep passage or slide through which things can pass: *a laundry chute.*
Another word that sounds like this is **shoot.**
chute (shüt) *noun, plural* **chutes.**

cider The juice pressed from apples, used as a drink and in making vinegar. **ci·der** (sī′dər) *noun, plural* **ciders.**

cigar A finger-shaped roll of tobacco leaves used for smoking. **ci·gar** (si gär′) *noun, plural* **cigars.**

cigarette A small roll of finely cut tobacco leaves wrapped in thin white paper and used for smoking. **cig·a·rette** (sig′ə ret′ *or* sig′ə ret′) *noun, plural* **cigarettes.**

cinder A piece of coal, wood, or other material that has been burned up or that is still burning but no longer flaming. **cin·der** (sin′dər) *noun, plural* **cinders.**

cinema **1.** A movie theater. **2.** Motion pictures as an art or industry; movies. **cinema** (sin′ə mə) *noun, plural* **cinemas.**

cinnamon **1.** A reddish brown spice made from the dried bark of a tropical tree. **2.** A light, reddish brown color. *Noun.*
○ Having a light, reddish brown color. *Adjective.*
cin·na·mon (sin′ə mən) *noun; adjective.*

circle 1. A closed, curved line made up of points that are all the same distance from a point inside called the center.
2. Anything that has a shape like a circle: *We sat in a circle around the campfire.*

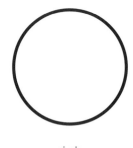
circle

3. A group of people who have interests that they share and enjoy together: *Most of my circle of friends are interested in history. Noun.*
○ **1.** To make a circle around. **2.** To move around in a circle. *Verb.*

cir·cle (sûr′kəl) *noun, plural* **circles;** *verb,* **circled, circling.**

circuit **1.** A movement around: *The earth takes one year to make its circuit around the sun.* **2.** A course or route that someone travels regularly; round: *The mail carriers start their circuits early each morning.* **3.** The path of an electric current. Electricity in a house moves in a circuit that takes it from wires outside the house to the different wall sockets in the house. **cir·cuit** (sûr′kit) *noun, plural* **circuits.**

circuit breaker A safety switch that automatically prevents current from flowing through an electric circuit. When the current becomes dangerous because it is too strong for the circuit, the circuit breaker interrupts the circuit and stops the flow.

circular Having or making the shape of a circle; round. *Adjective.*
○ A letter or an advertisement sent to many people: *a circular announcing a sale. Noun.* **cir·cu·lar** (sûr′kyə lər) *adjective; noun, plural* **circulars.**

circulate **1.** To move around widely among different places: *The fan in the window circulates air around the room.* **2.** To pass from person to person: *Bills and coins circulate.* **cir·cu·late** (sûr′kyə lāt′) *verb,* **circulated, circulating.**

circulation **1.** Movement around many different places or from person to person: *The government is putting some new coins into circulation.* **2.** The average number of copies of each issue sold of a newspaper or magazine: *The circulation of that newspaper is over 100,000.* **cir·cu·la·tion** (sûr′kyə lā′shən) *noun.*

circulatory system The system in the body made up of the heart, the blood vessels, the blood, and the lymph system. **cir·cu·la·to·ry system** (sûr′kyə lə tôr′ē).

heart
lungs
aorta
artery
vein

circulatory system

circumference **1.** A curved line that forms the outside edge of a circle. Look up circle for a picture of this. **2.** The distance around something: *That tree trunk is 15 feet in circumference.*

PRONUNCIATION KEY:
at   āpe   fär   câre   end   mē   it   īce   pierce   hot   ōld   sông   fôrk
oil   out   up   ūse   rüle   pull   tûrn   chin   sing   shop   thin   this
hw in white; zh in treasure. The symbol ə stands for the unstressed vowel sound in about, taken, pencil, lemon, and circus.

133

cir·cum·fer·ence (sər kum′fər əns) *noun, plural* **circumferences.**

circumstance A condition, act, or event that exists with other things and that may have an effect on them: *Weather is a circumstance beyond our control.* **cir·cum·stance** (sûr′kəm stans′) *noun, plural* **circumstances.**

circus A traveling show with trained animals and acrobats, clowns, and other people who entertain. **cir·cus** (sûr′kəs) *noun, plural* **circuses.**

circumference

WORD HISTORY

The word circus comes from a Latin word meaning "ring" or "circle." The ancient Romans held chariot races and other public events in a large oval theater which they called "the Circus."

cite 1. To repeat the words of another person exactly; quote: *I cited a paragraph in the encyclopedia that supported my theory.* 2. To mention as proof or support: *The firefighters cited the fire in the garage as an example of the danger of collecting oily rags.* 3. To single out for praise or honor: *The mayor cited our school for our community activities.*
Other words sounding like this are **sight** and **site.** **cite** (sīt) *verb,* **cited, citing.**

citizen 1. A person who was born in a country or who chooses to live in and become a member of a country. 2. Any person who lives in a town or city: *the citizens of our city.* **cit·i·zen** (sit′ə zən) *noun, plural* **citizens.**

citizenship The position of being a citizen of a country with all the rights, duties, and privileges that come with it. **cit·i·zen·ship** (sit′ə zən ship′) *noun.*

citrus Of or having to do with a group of

Oranges, lemons, limes, and grapefruits are citrus fruits.

trees whose fruits are juicy and often have a thick rind. **cit·rus** (sit′rəs) *adjective.*

city An area, larger than a town, where many people live and work. **cit·y** (sit′ē) *noun, plural* **cities.**

Many people are attracted to a city because of its stores and shops.

civic 1. Having to do with a city: *Keeping our streets and parks clean is a matter of civic pride.* 2. Having to do with the responsibilities or privileges of a citizen or citizenship: *It is a person's civic duty to vote.* **civ·ic** (siv′ik) *adjective.*

civics The study of the duties, rights, and privileges of citizens in relation to their government. The word "civics" is used with a singular verb. **civ·ics** (siv′iks) *noun.*

civil 1. Having to do with a citizen or citizens: *I am studying the civil life of ancient Rome.* 2. Not connected with military or church affairs: *The couple was married in a civil ceremony.* 3. Polite but not friendly; courteous. *I was very angry but managed to give a civil answer.* **civ·il** (siv′əl) *adjective.*

civilian A person not in the armed forces: *Soldiers were sent to aid civilians during the disaster.* Noun.
○ Relating to civilians: *civilian clothes.* Adjective. **ci·vil·ian** (si vil′yən) *noun, plural* **civilians;** *adjective.*

civilization A condition of human society in which agriculture, trade, government, art, and science are highly developed. Civilization is often characterized by the use of writing and the growth of cities: *In school we study the civilization of ancient Egypt.* **civ·i·li·za·tion** (siv′ə lə zā′shən) *noun, plural* **civilizations.**

civilize To bring out of a primitive or ignorant condition; educate in the arts, science, government, and agriculture. **civ·i·lize** (siv′ə līz′) *verb*, **civilized, civilizing.**

civil rights The rights of every citizen of a country, including the right to vote and the right to equal protection under the law.

civil service The branch of government service that is not part of the armed forces, the court system, or the legislature: *Postal employees belong to the civil service.*

civil war 1. A war between groups of citizens of the same country. 2. **Civil War.** The war between the northern and southern states of the United States between 1861 and 1865.

clad A past tense and past participle of **clothe. clad** (klad) *verb.*

claim 1. To declare as one's own: *The settlers claimed the land along the river.* 2. To say that something is true: *The witnesses claimed that the robber wore glasses.* 3. To take up; require; occupy: *My hobbies claim most of my free time. Verb.*
○ 1. A demand for something as one's right: *After the fire, we filed a claim with the insurance company.* 2. A statement that something is true: *Their claim was that their team was the best.* 3. Something claimed: *The miner's claim is a piece of land in the hills. Noun.*
claim (klām) *verb*, **claimed, claiming**; *noun, plural* **claims.**

clam An animal with a soft body and a hinged shell in two parts. Clams are found in the ocean and in fresh water and are used for food. *Noun.*
○ To dig in the sand or mud for clams. *Verb.*
clam (klam) *noun, plural* **clams**; *verb*, **clammed, clamming.**

clambake An outdoor party at which clams and other foods are served. The food at a clambake is usually steamed or baked over heated stones placed in a hole in the ground or sand at a beach. **clam·bake** (klam′bāk′) *noun, plural* **clambakes.**

clamber To climb by using both the hands and the feet: *We clambered slowly up the dunes.* **clam·ber** (klam′bər) *verb*, **clambered, clambering.**

clamor 1. A loud continuous noise; uproar: *the clamor of automobile horns.* 2. A loud protest or demand: *The people made a clamor against pollution. Noun.*
○ To make such a noise. *Verb.*
clam·or (klam′ər) *noun, plural* **clamors**; *verb*, **clamored, clamoring.**

clamp A device to hold things together tightly: *Use a clamp to hold the pieces of wood together until the glue dries. Noun.*
○ To fasten with a clamp. *Verb.*
clamp (klamp) *noun, plural* **clamps**; *verb*, **clamped, clamping.**

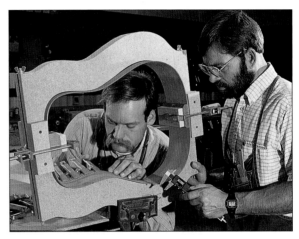

These pieces of wood are held together with clamps while being shaped to become a guitar.

clan A group of families descended from the same ancestor. **clan** (klan) *noun, plural* **clans.**

clap 1. A sharp, sudden sound like two flat pieces of wood striking each other: *a clap of thunder.* 2. A friendly slap: *My brother gave me a clap on the shoulder. Noun.*
○ 1. To strike together: *I clapped my hands twice.* 2. To strike one's hands together again and again, especially so as to show approval or enjoyment: *The children all clapped when the magician's show was over.* 3. To strike in a friendly way: *They all clapped me on the back and congratulated me for winning the prize. Verb.*
clap (klap) *noun, plural* **claps**; *verb*, **clapped, clapping.**

clarify To make something easier to understand; explain clearly. **clar·i·fy** (klar′ə fī′) *verb*, **clarified, clarifying.**

clarinet A musical instrument shaped like a tube. A clarinet is played by blowing into the mouthpiece and pressing keys or covering holes with the

PRONUNCIATION KEY:

| at | āpe | fär | câre | end | mē | it | īce | pierce | hot | ōld | sông | fôrk |
| oil | out | up | ūse | rüle | pull | tûrn | chin | sing | shop | thin | this | |

hw in white; zh in treasure. The symbol ə stands for the unstressed vowel sound in about, taken, pencil, lemon, and circus.

135

fingers to change the pitch. **clar·i·net** (klar′ə net′) *noun, plural* **clarinets.**

clarity Clearness: *The TV picture had wonderful clarity and brightness.* **clar·i·ty** (klar′i tē) *noun.*

clash 1. A loud, harsh sound like pieces of metal striking against each other: *a clash of cymbals.* 2. A strong disagreement: *There was a clash about where we should go for our vacation. Noun.*
  ○ 1. To come together with a clash: *The pots and pans clashed on the kitchen floor.* 2. To disagree strongly: *They clashed over what to do with the vacant lot.* 3. To be in sharp conflict; not match: *That suit jacket clashes with your sneakers. Verb.*
  clash (klash) *noun, plural* **clashes;** *verb,* **clashed, clashing.**

clasp 1. A device to hold two parts or objects together, such as a hook or a buckle. 2. A close or tight grasp: *They said good-bye with a clasp of hands. Noun.*
  ○ 1. To fasten with a clasp. 2. To hold or grasp tightly. *Verb.*
  clasp (klasp) *noun, plural* **clasps;** *verb,* **clasped, clasping.**

Some students in this class are ready to answer a question.

class 1. A group of persons or things alike in some way: *Pencils, pens, and crayons all belong to the class of writing tools.* 2. A group of people who share a similar way of life and have the same rank or status in society: *Members of the upper class looked to the king and queen as models.* 3. A group of students studying or meeting together. 4. A period of time during which a group of students meets. 5. A grade or quality: *That farmer grows a very high class of vegetables. Noun.*
  ○ To group in a class; classify. *I have classed the stamps in my collection by the country from which they come. Verb.*

class (klas) *noun, plural* **classes;** *verb,* **classed, classing.**

classic Excellent in the opinion of many people, past and present: *Robinson Crusoe is a classic adventure story. Adjective.*
  ○ 1. A very fine book or other work of art: *That play by William Shakespeare is a classic.* 2. the classics. The writings of ancient Greece and Rome. *Noun.*
  clas·sic (klas′ik) *adjective; noun, plural* **classics.**

classical 1. Relating to the civilization of ancient Greece or Rome. 2. Traditional; not experimental or new: *a classical sort of play, in three acts.* 3. Of or having to do with music with forms and styles developed over a long period by educated musicians and different from popular or folk music: *Symphonies, quartets, and operas are classical music.* **clas·si·cal** (klas′i kəl) *adjective.*

classify 1. To arrange in groups: *The librarian classified the books according to the authors who wrote them.* 2. To assign to a class: *Would you classify this stone as a pebble, a rock, or a boulder?* **clas·si·fy** (klas′ə fī′) *verb,* **classified, classifying.** —**classification** *noun*

classmate A member of the same class in school. **class·mate** (klas′māt′) *noun, plural* **classmates.**

classroom A room in which classes are held. **class·room** (klas′rüm′ *or* klas′rùm′) *noun, plural* **classrooms.**

clatter A loud, rattling noise: *a clatter of dishes from the kitchen. Noun.*
  ○ To make such a noise. *Verb.*
  clat·ter (klat′ər) *noun, plural* **clatters;** *verb,* **clattered, clattering.**

clause 1. A group of words that contains a subject and a predicate. In the sentence "I watched television before I went to bed," "I watched television" is the main clause because it can stand alone as a sentence. "Before I went to bed" is another clause. Its meaning depends on the main clause of the sentence. 2. A separate part of a law, treaty, or other formal agreement: *There is a clause in our lease that says we can't keep pets in our apartment.* **clause** (klôz) *noun, plural* **clauses.**

claw 1. A sharp, curved nail on the foot of a bird or animal. 2. One of the grasping parts of a lobster or crab. 3. Anything like a claw, such as the forked end of the head of a hammer used to pull out nails. *Noun.*

○ To scratch or tear with claws or hands. *Verb.*
claw (klô) *noun, plural* **claws**; *verb*, **clawed**, **clawing**.

clay A kind of fine earth. Clay can be easily shaped when wet, but it becomes hard when it is dried or baked. Clay is used to make pottery and bricks. **clay** (klā) *noun, plural* **clays**.

Clay is used to make pottery and bricks.

clean 1. Free from dirt. 2. Honorable or fair: *a clean fight.* 3. Complete; thorough: *The prisoner made a clean escape. Adjective.*
○ Completely: *The arrow went clean through the target. Adverb.*
○ To make clean. *Verb.*
clean (klēn) *adjective*, **cleaner**, **cleanest**; *adverb*; *verb*, **cleaned**, **cleaning**. —**cleanly** *adverb*

cleaner 1. A person whose work or business is cleaning: *The window cleaner washed the windows of the apartment house.* 2. Something that removes dirt: *I used a liquid cleaner on the coffee stain.* **cleaner** (klēnər) *noun, plural* **cleaners**.

cleanliness The condition of being clean; the habit of always keeping clean. **clean·li·ness** (klen'lē nis) *noun.*

cleanse To make clean. **cleanse** (klenz) *verb*, **cleansed**, **cleansing**.

cleanser Something used for cleaning. **cleans·er** (klen'zər) *noun, plural* **cleansers**.

clear 1. Free from anything that darkens; bright. 2. Easily seen through: *The water of the pond was so clear that you could see the bottom.* 3. Easily seen, heard, or understood; plain; distinct: *The directions we got were very clear.* 4. Without guilt or some other burden: *I have a clear conscience. Adjective.*
○ Completely; without obstruction: *From the cliff we could see clear across the valley. Adverb.*
○ 1. To make or become free from anything that darkens or clouds: *After the rain stopped, the sky cleared.* 2. To remove or remove things from: *Please finish clearing the table.* 3. To go by, under,

or over without touching: *The runner cleared the fence with a leap.* 4. To approve or get approved: *The council cleared the proposal.* 5. To remove suspicion or guilt from; declare innocent: *The suspect was cleared of all charges. Verb.*
• **to clear up.** 1. To explain; clarify: *The detective cleared up the mystery of who stole the jewels.* 2. To become clear: *The sky cleared up after the storm.*
clear (klîr) *adjective*, **clearer**, **clearest**; *adverb*; *verb*, **cleared**, **clearing**. —**clearly** *adverb.*

clearance 1. The act of clearing: *City officials ordered the clearance of three streets for the parade.* 2. The space in between two things that allows one or both things to move without touching each other: *There was enough clearance for the truck to go under the bridge.* **clear·ance** (klîr'əns) *noun, plural* **clearances**.

clearing A piece of land free of trees or brush. **clear·ing** (klîr'ing) *noun, plural* **clearings**.

Clearings are often used as pasture land.

cleaver A tool with a short handle and a broad blade, used by butchers for cutting up meat. **cleav·er** (klē'vər) *noun, plural* **cleavers**.

clef A sign placed on a staff in music. A clef shows the pitch of the notes on the various lines and spaces. **clef** (klef) *noun, plural* **clefs**.

cleft A space or opening made by splitting; crack: *You can climb the cliff by holding on to the clefts in the rocks. Noun.*
○ Divided by a crack or split: *Two of my cousins have cleft chins. Adjective.*
cleft (kleft) *noun, plural* **clefts**; *adjective.*

PRONUNCIATION KEY:
at   āpe   fär   câre   end   mē   it   īce   pierce   hot   ōld   sông   fôrk
oil   out   up   ūse   rüle   pull   tûrn   chin   sing   shop   thin   this
hw in white; zh in treasure. The symbol ə stands for the unstressed vowel sound in about, taken, pencil, lemon, and circus.

137

clench To grasp or close tightly: *I clench my fists when I am angry.* **clench** (klench) *verb*, **clenched**, **clenching**.

clergy Ministers, priests, rabbis, and all people appointed to carry on religious work. **cler·gy** (klûr′jē) *noun*, *plural* **clergies**.

clergyman A member of the clergy; minister, priest, or rabbi. **cler·gy·man** (klûr′jē mən) *noun*, *plural* **clergymen** (klûr′jē mən).

clerk 1. A person who keeps records and files in an office. 2. A person who sells goods to customers in a store. **clerk** (klûrk) *noun*, *plural* **clerks**; *verb*, **clerked**, **clerking**.

WORD HISTORY

The word clerk comes from a Latin word used by the church meaning "clergyman." In the Middle Ages, priests and monks were nearly the only people who could read and write. So clerk came to mean "someone who writes and keeps records."

---

clever 1. Having a quick mind; bright and alert: *The clever child soon learned to use the new toy.* 2. Showing skill or intelligence: *The cook had a clever way of cracking two eggs with one hand.* **clev·er** (klev′ər) *adjective*, **cleverer**, **cleverest**.

click A light, sharp sound. *Noun.*
○ To make such a sound. *Verb.*
click (klik) *noun*, *plural* **clicks**; *verb*, **clicked**, **clicking**.

client A person or organization that uses the services of another person or organization: *Our family's lawyer advises many clients besides us.* **cli·ent** (klī′ənt) *noun*, *plural* **clients**.

cliff A high, steep face of rock or earth. **cliff** (klif) *noun*, *plural* **cliffs**.

climate The average weather conditions of a place or region throughout the year.

A cave opening can be seen at the top of this cliff.

Climate includes average temperature, rainfall, humidity, and wind conditions. **cli·mate** (klī′mit) *noun*, *plural* **climates**.

climax The highest or most exciting moment or event: *The climax of our trip came when we canoed down the river.* **cli·max** (klī′maks) *noun*, *plural* **climaxes**.

climb 1. To move upward or over, across, or through something, using the hands and feet. 2. To grow upward or upward on: *The ivy climbed up the house.* 3. To go steadily upward; rise: *Prices could climb higher next month.* Verb.
○ 1. The act of climbing. 2. A place to be climbed: *That mountain is a tough climb.* Noun.
climb (klīm) *verb*, **climbed**, **climbing**; *noun*, *plural* **climbs**.

clinch 1. To make definite; settle: *The deal was clinched when they agreed to our terms.* 2. To make certain of winning: *By winning today's game, we clinched the race for first place.* **clinch** (klinch) *verb*, **clinched**, **clinching**.

cling To stick closely. **cling** (kling) *verb*, **clung**, **clinging**.

clinic A place where medical care is given to people who do not need to stay in a hospital: *I went to the dental clinic for a checkup.* **clin·ic** (klin′ik) *noun*, *plural* **clinics**.

clip¹ To cut; cut short: *I tried to clip the hedge evenly.* Verb.
○ A rate of speed or pace: *The bus moved along at a fast clip.* Noun.
clip (klip) *verb*, **clipped**, **clipping**; *noun*, *plural* **clips**.

clip² A device used to hold things together. *Noun.*
○ To fasten with a clip. *Verb.*
clip (klip) *noun*, *plural* **clips**; *verb*, **clipped**, **clipping**.

clip art Electronic art that can be inserted into a computer document.

clipper 1. A tool used for cutting. 2. A fast sailing ship: *American clippers sailed all over the world.* **clip·per** (klip′ər) *noun*, *plural* **clippers**.

clipping A piece that is cut out or off, especially out of a magazine or newspaper. **clip·ping** (klip′ing) *noun*, *plural* **clippings**.

cloak 1. A loose outer piece of clothing, with or without sleeves. 2. Something that covers or hides something else: *A cloak of haze concealed the valley.* Noun.

○ To cover or hide with or like a cloak. *Verb.*
cloak (klōk) *noun, plural* **cloaks**; *verb,* **cloaked,
cloaking.**

clobber To hit hard or often. **clobber** (klob′ər)
verb, **clobbered, clobbering.**

clock A device for measuring and showing the
time. *Noun.*
○ To find out the speed of something by using a
device like a clock: *We clocked the runners with a
stopwatch. Verb.*
clock (klok) *noun, plural* **clocks**; *verb,* **clocked,
clocking.**

clockwise In the direction in which the hands of a
clock move: *Move the dial clockwise to turn on
the radio.* **clock•wise** (klok′wīz′) *adverb; adjective.*

clog To block; fill up:
*Heavy traffic clogged
the roads. Verb.*
○ A shoe with a thick
wooden sole. *Noun.*
clog (klog) *verb,*
clogged, clogging;
noun, plural **clogs.**

cloister 1. A covered
walk along the wall
of a building, often
around the courtyard
of a monastery,
church, or college
building. 2. A con-
vent or a monastery.
clois•ter (klois′tər)
noun, plural **cloisters.**

**In the Netherlands, clogs
are an important part of
traditional dress.**

close 1. To shut. 2. To bring or come together:
The dog's teeth closed on the bone. 3. To bring or
come to an end: *I closed the letter with a promise
to write again soon. Verb.*
○ 1. With little space or time between; near: *Our
house is close to the school.* 2. Having affection
for each other; intimate: *close friends.* 3. Without
fresh air; stuffy: *It is close in this room.* 4. Nearly
even; almost equal: *a close race.* 5. Careful; thorough: *Pay close attention. Adjective.*
○ In a close position or way: *Your car is not
parked close enough to the curb. Adverb.*
○ End; finish: *At the close of the day, we all went
home. Noun.*

close (klōz *for verb and noun;* klōs *for adjective
and adverb*) *verb,* **closed, closing;** *adjective,*
closer, closest; *adverb; noun.*

closed-circuit television A television system
that sends images by cable to linked television sets.

closet A small room for storing things. **clos•et**
(kloz′it) *noun, plural* **closets.**

close-up A photograph or a camera shot taken
at close range. **close-up** (klōs′up′) *noun, plural*
close-ups.

clot A soft lump formed when substances in a
liquid thicken or stick together: *a clot of blood.
Noun.*
○ To form a clot or clots. *Verb.*
clot (klot) *noun, plural* **clots**; *verb,* **clotted,
clotting.**

cloth 1. Material made by weaving or knitting
fibers. Cloth is made from cotton, wool, silk,
linen, or other fibers. 2. A piece of cloth used for
a purpose: *Use this cloth to dust the living room.*
cloth (klôth) *noun, plural* **cloths.**

clothe To put clothes on someone; dress. **clothe**
(klōth) *verb,* **clothed** or **clad, clothing.**

clothes Things worn to cover the body. **clothes**
(klōz *or* klōthz) *plural noun.*

clothespin A clamp or forked piece of wood or
plastic to fasten clothes to a line. **clothes•pin**
(klōz′pin′ *or* klōthz′pin′) *noun, plural* **clothes-
pins.**

clothing Things worn to cover the body; clothes.
cloth•ing (klō′thing) *noun.*

cloud 1. A gray or white mass of tiny drops of
water or bits of ice floating high in the sky.
2. Something like a cloud: *a cloud of dust. Noun.*

cirrus

cumulus

stratus

nimbus
**Clouds are classified into
four basic types.**

1. To cover with clouds: *Smoke from the burning house* **clouded** *the whole street.* **2.** To become cloudy: *The sky suddenly* **clouded** *and it started to rain.* Verb.
cloud (kloud) *noun, plural* **clouds**; *verb,* **clouded**, **clouding**.

cloudburst A sudden, heavy rainfall. **cloud·burst** (kloud′bûrst′) *noun, plural* **cloudbursts**.

cloudy **1.** Covered with clouds. **2.** Not clear: *The stream was so* **cloudy** *that you couldn't see below the surface.* **cloud·y** (klou′dē) *adjective,* **cloudier**, **cloudiest**.

clove[1] The dried flower bud of a tropical tree. Cloves are used as a spice. **clove** (klōv) *noun, plural* **cloves**.

clove[2] A section of a garlic bulb. **clove** (klōv) *noun, plural* **cloves**.

clover A small plant with leaves of three leaflets and rounded, fragrant flower heads of white, red, or purple flowers. **clo·ver** (klō′vər) *noun, plural* **clovers**.

clown A person who makes people laugh by playing tricks or doing stunts. *Noun.*
○ To act like a clown: *Stop* **clowning** *around and do your homework.* Verb.
clown (kloun) *noun, plural* **clowns**; *verb,* **clowned**, **clowning**.

A clown in a circus often wears funny clothing and makep.

club **1.** A heavy stick often thicker at one end, used as a weapon. **2.** A stick or bat used to hit a ball in various games, as in golf. **3.** A group of people who meet together for fun or some special purpose: a chess club. **4.** The place where a club meets: *I'll see you at the swimming* **club**. **5.** A playing card marked with one or more figures shaped like this ♣. **6.** clubs. The suit of cards marked with this figure. *Noun.*
○ To beat or strike with a club. *Verb.*
club (klub) *noun, plural* **clubs**; *verb,* **clubbed**, **clubbing**.

clue A hint that helps solve a problem or mystery: *If you can't solve the riddle, I'll give you a* **clue**. **clue** (klü) *noun, plural* **clues**.

clump **1.** A group or cluster: *a* **clump** *of bushes.*

2. A thick mass or lump: *a* **clump** *of dirt.* **3.** A heavy, thumping sound: *The dead branch landed with a* **clump**. *Noun.*
○ To walk with heavy and noisy steps: *The tired hikers* **clumped** *home across the wooden bridge.* Verb.
clump (klump) *noun, plural* **clumps**; *verb,* **clumped**, **clumping**.

clumsy **1.** Awkward; not graceful. **2.** Poorly made or done: *The* **clumsy** *gate kept scraping the ground.* **clum·sy** (klum′zē) *adjective,* **clumsier**, **clumsiest**. —**clumsiness** *noun.*

clung Past tense and past participle of cling. **clung** (klung) *verb.*

cluster A number of things of the same kind that grow or are grouped together: *Grapes grow in* **clusters**. *Noun.*
○ To grow or group in a cluster: *We all* **clustered** *around the campfire.* Verb.
clus·ter (klus′tər) *noun, plural* **clusters**; *verb,* **clustered**, **clustering**.

clutch **1.** To grasp tightly. **2.** To try to grasp or seize: *I* **clutched** *at the railing when I slipped on the stairs.* Verb.
○ **1.** A tight grasp: *The girl kept a* **clutch** *on her little brother's hand.* **2.** A device in a machine that connects or disconnects the motor. *Noun.*
clutch (kluch) *verb,* **clutched**, **clutching**; *noun, plural* **clutches**.

clutter A messy collection of things; litter: *We all helped pick up the* **clutter** *after the picnic.* Noun.
○ To litter or fill with a messy collection of things. *Verb.*
clut·ter (klut′ər) *noun, plural* **clutters**; *verb,* **cluttered**, **cluttering**.

cm An abbreviation for **centimeter**.

co- A prefix that means: **1.** With: *Coworker means a person who works with others.* **2.** Together: *Cosign means to sign together.*

co. An abbreviation for **company** or **county**.

CO Postal abbreviation for **Colorado**.

coach **1.** A large, closed carriage pulled by horses. A coach has seats inside for passengers and a raised seat outside for the driver. **2.** A railroad car for passengers. **3.** A section of low-priced seats on a bus, airplane, or train. **4.** A teacher or trainer of athletes or performers. *Noun.*
○ To teach or train. *Verb.*
coach (kōch) *noun, plural* **coaches**; *verb,*

coached, coaching.

coal 1. A black mineral burned as a fuel to heat buildings or make electricity. Coal is mostly carbon and is formed from decaying plants buried deep in the earth under great pressure. 2. A piece of glowing or burned wood: *We roasted hot dogs over the hot coals.* **coal** (kōl) *noun, plural* **coals**.

coarse 1. Made up of rather large parts; not fine: *Some of the grains of coarse sand were almost as big as small pebbles.* 2. Thick and rough: *The coarse wool of the sweater made my skin itch.* 3. Crude; vulgar: *The parents scolded the child for coarse table manners.*

Another word that sounds like this is course.

coarse (kôrs) *adjective,* **coarser, coarsest;**

coast The land next to the sea; seashore. *Noun.*
○ To ride or slide along without effort or power: *We coasted down the hill on our sleds. Verb.*
coast (kōst) *noun, plural* **coasts**; *verb,* **coasted, coasting.**

coastal Near or along or at a coast: *a coastal highway.* **coast·al** (kōs′təl) *adjective.*

Coast Guard A branch of the United States armed forces that patrols and defends the nation's coasts. In wartime, it becomes part of the United States Navy.

coastline The outline or shape of a coast: *Maine has an irregular coastline.* **coast·line** (kōst′līn′) *noun, plural* **coastlines**.

The coastline is shaped by the ocean's waves.

coat 1. A piece of outer clothing with sleeves. 2. The outer covering of an animal. 3. A layer: *a new coat of paint. Noun.*
○ To cover with a layer: *Sand the floor and coat it with wax. Verb.*
coat (kōt) *noun, plural* **coats**; *verb,* **coated, coating.**

coating A layer covering a surface: *A thin coating of ice on the roads made driving dangerous.* **coat·ing** (kō′ting) *noun, plural* **coatings.**

coat of arms A design on and around a shield or on a drawing of a shield. A coat of arms can serve as the emblem of a person, family, country, or organization.

coax To persuade or influence by mild urging: *I coaxed my parents into letting me go to camp next summer.* **coax** (kōks) *verb,* **coaxed, coaxing.**

cob The hard center part of an ear of corn. The kernels grow on the cob in rows. **cob** (kob) *noun, plural* **cobs.**

cobalt A silver-white metal used in making alloys and paints. Cobalt is a chemical element. **co·balt** (kō′bôlt) *noun.*

cobbler 1. A person whose work is mending or making shoes. 2. A fruit pie baked in a deep dish: *an apple cobbler.* **cob·bler** (kob′lər) *noun, plural* **cobblers.**

cobblestone A round stone, formerly used to pave streets. **cob·ble·stone** (kob′əl stōn′) *noun, plural* **cobblestones.**

cobra A large, poisonous snake of Africa and Asia. When a cobra becomes excited it spreads the skin about its neck so that the skin looks like a hood. **co·bra** (kō′brə) *noun, plural* **cobras.**

cobweb A spider web. **cob·web** (kob′web′) *noun, plural* **cobwebs.**

cocaine A drug used in medicine to lessen pain. Cocaine is a powerful, habit-forming, dangerous drug often used illegally. **co·caine** (kō kān′) *noun.*

cock¹ 1. A male chicken; rooster. 2. The male of the turkey and other birds. 3. A faucet used to turn the flow of a gas or a liquid on and off. *Noun.*
○ To pull back the hammer of a gun so that it is ready for firing. *Verb.*
cock (kok) *noun, plural* **cocks**; *verb,* **cocked, cocking.**

cock² To turn up; tip upward: *The dog cocked its ears when it heard a meow. Verb.*
○ An upward turn: *a cock of the ears. Noun.*

PRONUNCIATION KEY:
at āpe fär câre end mē it īce pierce hot ōld sông fôrk
oil out up ūse rüle pu̇ll tûrn chin sing shop thin this
hw in white; zh in treasure. The symbol ə stands for the unstressed vowel sound in about, taken, pencil, lemon, and circus.

141

cock (kok) *verb*, **cocked**, **cocking**; *noun*, *plural* **cocks**.

cockatoo A white parrot with a large crest, found in Australia and Asia. **cock·a·too** (kok′ə tü′) *noun*, *plural* **cockatoos**.

cocker spaniel A dog with long, silky hair and short legs. **cock·er spaniel** (kok′ər).

cockle A sea clam with a shell that looks like a heart, used for food. **cock·le** (kok′əl) *noun*, *plural* **cockles**.

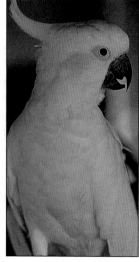

Like other parrots, cockatoos can be taught to talk.

cockpit The space in an airplane or a small boat where the pilot sits. **cock·pit** (kok′pit′) *noun*, *plural* **cockpits**.

The instruments used to fly a plane are located in the cockpit.

cockroach A brown or black insect that has a long, flat body and long feelers and is a common household pest. **cock·roach** (kok′rōch′) *noun*, *plural* **cockroaches**.

cocktail 1. A drink, usually alcoholic, made of several different beverages: *My parents had cocktails before dinner.* 2. Fruit or seafood served before a meal: *shrimp cocktail for Thanksgiving.* **cocktail** (kok′tāl′) *noun*, *plural* **cocktails**.

cocky Too sure of oneself: *a rude, cocky bully.* **cock·y** (kok′ē) *adjective*, **cockier**, **cockiest**; **cock·i·ness** *noun*.

cocoa 1. A brown powder that tastes like chocolate, made by grinding the dried seeds of the cacao tree and removing the fat. 2. A drink made by mixing cocoa powder, sugar, and milk or water. **co·coa** (kō′kō) *noun*.

coconut The large, round, brown fruit of a palm tree, having a hard shell lined with a sweet, white meat. It is filled with a white liquid called coconut milk. **co·co·nut** (kō′kə nut′) *noun*, *plural* **coconuts**.

cocoon The silky case that a caterpillar or other insect larva spins around itself. The larvae live in their cocoons while they are becoming moths or butterflies or other adult insects. **co·coon** (kə kün′) *noun*, *plural* **cocoons**.

cod A large fish that lives in cold, northern ocean waters, used for food. **cod** (kod) *noun*, *plural* **cod** *or* **cods**.

C.O.D. An abbreviation for **cash on delivery** or **collect on delivery**.

code 1. Any set of signals, words, or symbols used to send messages. 2. Any set of laws or rules that people live by: *The building code in our town requires all buildings to have smoke alarms. Noun.* ○ To put in a code. *Verb.* **code** (kōd) *noun*, *plural* **codes**; *verb*, **coded**, **coding**.

coeducation The education of both boys and girls in the same school. **co·ed·u·ca·tion** (kō ej′ə kā′shən) *noun*.

coffee 1. A dark brown drink made from the roasted and ground seeds of a small tropical tree. Coffee seeds look like beans and are often called beans. 2. The whole or ground seeds of the coffee tree. **cof·fee** (kô′fē) *noun*, *plural* **coffees**.

coffin A box in which the body of a dead person is buried. **cof·fin** (kô′fin) *noun*, *plural* **coffins**.

cog One of the teeth on the outer edge of a wheel. Cogs are made to fit between the cogs of another wheel so that one wheel can cause the other to turn. Wheels with cogs are used to run machinery. **cog** (kog) *noun*, *plural* **cogs**.

coil 1. Anything wound into rings: *Wind the hose into a coil when you finish watering the flowers.* 2. A wire wound into a spiral for carrying electricity. *Noun.* ○ To wind round and round. *Verb.* **coil** (koil) *noun, plural* **coils;** *verb,* **coiled, coiling.**

This man is working with coils of barbed wire.

coin A piece of metal used as money. A coin is stamped with official government markings to show how much it is worth. *Noun.* ○ 1. To make money by stamping metal: *The government coins money at a mint.* 2. To invent: *If you coined a new word, do you think other people would begin to use it? Verb.* **coin** (koin) *noun, plural* **coins;** *verb,* **coined, coining.**

coincide 1. To happen at the same time: *My piano lesson coincides with my appointment with the dentist.* 2. To be exactly alike; to be identical: *That photograph of you coincides with the way you look.* **co·in·cide** (kō′in sīd′) *verb,* **coincided, coinciding.**

coincidence The happening of two events at the same time or place. A coincidence seems remarkable because although it looks planned, it really is not: *It was just a coincidence that the two couples went to the same movie.* **co·in·ci·dence** (kō in′si dəns) *noun, plural* **coincidences.**

coke A grayish black substance used as fuel for making metals in special furnaces, made when coal is heated in an oven with very little air. **coke** (kōk) *noun.*

Col. An abbreviation for Colorado.

cold 1. Having a low temperature; not warm: *cold weather.* 2. Feeling a lack of warmth; chilly: *The children were cold after playing in the snow.* 3. Not friendly or kind: *a cold smile. Adjective.* ○ 1. A lack of warmth or heat. 2. A common sickness that causes sneezing, coughing, and a running or stuffy nose. *Noun.*
• **to catch cold.** To become ill with a cold. **cold** (kōld) *adjective,* **colder, coldest;** *noun, plural* **colds.**

cold-blooded 1. Having a body temperature that changes with the temperature of the surrounding air or water. Snakes, fish, and turtles are cold-blooded animals. Cats and dogs are warm-blooded. 2. Without any feeling or emotion; cruel: *cold-blooded murder.* **cold-blood·ed** (kōld′blud′id) *adjective.*

coleslaw A salad made from shredded cabbage and a dressing. **cole·slaw** (kōl′slâ′) *noun.*

coliseum A large building or stadium used for sports or other events: *We went to an ice skating show at the coliseum.* **col·i·se·um** (kol′ə sē′əm) *noun, plural* **coliseums.**

collaborate To work together on something: *The entire class collaborated on the food drive.* **col·lab·o·rate** (ka lab′ə rāt″) *verb,* **collaborated, collaborating. —collaboration** *noun.*

collage A picture made by pasting paper, cloth, metal, and other things in an arrangement on a surface. **col·lage** (kə läzh′) *noun, plural* **collages.**

collapse 1. To fall in; break down or fail: *The walls of the house collapsed.* 2. To fold together: *This cot collapses for easy storage.* 3. To lose strength or health: *The heat caused some of the marchers in the parade to collapse. Verb.* ○ The act of falling in, breaking down, or failing. *Noun.* **col·lapse** (kə laps′) *verb,* **collapsed, collapsing;** *noun, plural* **collapses.**

collar A band or strap worn around the neck. *Noun.* ○ 1. To put a collar on. 2. To seize; capture: *The police collared the thief just outside the store. Verb.* **col·lar** (kol′ər) *noun, plural* **collars;** *verb,* **collared, collaring.**

collarbone The bone connecting the breastbone and the shoulder blade. **col·lar·bone** (kol′ər bōn′) *noun, plural* **collarbones.**

collard 1. A green, leafy vegetable related to cabbage. 2. **collards.** The green leaves of a collard, used as food. **col·lard** (kol′ərd) *noun, plural* **collards.**

PRONUNCIATION KEY:
at āpe fär câre end mē it īce pierce hot ōld sông fôrk
oil out up ūse rüle pull tûrn chin sing shop thin this
hw in white; zh in treasure. The symbol ə stands for the unstressed vowel sound in about, taken, pencil, lemon, and circus.

143

colleague A fellow worker: *Our principal asked a colleague to speak at the assembly.* **col·league** (kol′ēg) *noun, plural* **colleagues.**

collect 1. To gather together. 2. To get payment for: *The state collects tolls on highways.* **col·lect** (kə lekt′) *verb,* **collected, collecting.** —**collector** *noun.*

collection 1. A gathering together: *The collection of garbage is the job of the city sanitation department.* 2. A group of things gathered together: *The museum has a large collection of dinosaur bones.* 3. Money collected: *We took up a collection to buy our teacher a present.* **col·lec·tion** (kə lek′shən) *noun, plural* **collections.**

college A school that offers more advanced education than high school. **col·lege** (kol′ij) *noun, plural* **colleges.**

collide 1. To crash against each other. 2. To disagree very strongly; clash: *The mayor collided with the governor over plans for a new highway.* **col·lide** (kə līd′) *verb,* **collided, colliding.**

The collie is one of the most popular breeds of dogs.

collie A large dog with a long, narrow head, originally raised to herd sheep. **col·lie** (kol′ē) *noun, plural* **collies.**

collision The act of colliding; a crash. **col·li·sion** (kə lizh′ən) *noun, plural* **collisions.**

Colo. An abbreviation for **Colorado.**

Colombia A country in northwestern South America. **Co·lom·bi·a** (kə lum′bē ə) *noun.*

colon¹ A punctuation mark (:) used mainly after a word to direct attention to something that fol-lows, such as a list, a quotation, or an explanation. **co·lon** (kō′lən) *noun, plural* **colons.**

colon² The main part of the large intestine. **co·lon** (kō′lən) *noun, plural* **colons.**

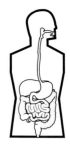

colon

colonel An officer in the United States Army, Marine Corps, or Air Force ranking below a general but above a major. Another word that sounds like this is **kernel.** **colo·nel** (kûr′nəl) *noun, plural* **colonels.**

colonial 1. Relating to a colony: *Great Britain was once a colonial power, ruling Canada, India, and South Africa.* 2. Relating to the thirteen British colonies that became the United States of America: *People marching in the parade were dressed in colonial costumes.* **co·lo·ni·al** (kə lō′nē əl) *adjective.*

colonist A person who helps found or lives in a colony; a settler. **col·o·nist** (kol′ə nist) *noun, plural* **colonists.**

colonize To found a colony or colonies in. **col·o·nize** (kol′ə nīz′) *verb,* **colonized, colonizing.**

colonnade A row of columns, often used to support the roof of a building. **col·on·nade** (kol′ə nād′) *noun, plural* **colonnades.**

colony 1. A group of people who leave their own country and settle in another land. 2. A territory ruled by another country. 3. **the Colonies.** The thirteen British colonies that became the first states of the United States. 4. A group of animals or plants of the same kind that live together: *Ants live in colonies.* **col·o·ny** (kol′ə nē) *noun, plural* **colonies.**

color 1. A quality of light as we see it with our eyes. Red, blue, yellow, and green are colors. The color of something depends on how it reflects light. 2. The coloring of the skin: *I see you have healthy color now that you are well again. Noun.* ○ To give color to: *Young children usually enjoy coloring pictures with crayons. Verb.*
  • **of color.** Having a skin coloring other than white: *people of color.*
col·or (kul′ər) *noun, plural* **colors;** *verb,* **colored, coloring.**

Colorado 1. A state in the western part of the

United States. Its capital is Denver. **2.** A river in the western United States. It flows southwest from Colorado into Mexico. **Col·o·rad·o** (kol′ə rad′ō *or* kol′ə rä′dō) *noun.*

WORD HISTORY

The name Colorado comes from a Spanish word meaning "reddish colored." Spanish explorers gave this name to a small river. Later the name was given to the Colorado River. The state of Colorado takes its name from the river.

★
Denver

Colorado
U. S. Postal Abbreviation: **CO**
Capital: **Denver**
Population: **3,296,000**
Area: **104,247 sq. mi./269,998 sq. km**
State Nickname: **Centennial State**
State Bird: **Lark Bunting**
State Flower: **Rocky Mountain Columbine**

color-blind Not able to see the difference between certain colors. Most people who are color-blind confuse red and green. **col·or-blind** (kul′ər blīnd′) *adjective.* —**colorblindness** *noun.*

colorful 1. Full of color: *colorful birds.* **2.** Interesting or vivid: *colorful stories.* **col·or·ful** (kul′ər fəl) *adjective.* —**colorfully** *adverb.*

coloring 1. The way

The mother and daughter are wearing colorful bunny outfits.

in which anything is colored: *the brilliant coloring of the autumn leaves.*
2. Something used to give color: *food coloring.* **col·or·ing** (kul′ər ing) *noun, plural* **colorings.**

colt A young horse or similar animal, such as a donkey or zebra, usually a male. **colt** (kōlt) *noun, plural* **colts.**

columbine A graceful plant related to the buttercup. The flowers of the columbine have five long petals. **col·um·bine** (kol′əm bīn′) *noun, plural* **columbines.**

column 1. An upright structure shaped like a post; pillar, used as a support or ornament for part of a building. **2.** Anything shaped like a column: *a column of black smoke.* **3.** A narrow, vertical section of printed words on a page: *This page has two columns.* **4.** A part of a newspaper written regularly by one person: *the sports column.* **5.** A long row or line: *The band marched in three columns.* **col·umn** (kol′əm) *noun, plural* **columns.**

The use of columns in buildings goes as far back as 1500 B.C.

comb 1. A piece of plastic, metal, or other material that has a row of teeth, used to smooth, arrange, or fasten the hair. **2.** A thick, fleshy red crest on the head of chickens and other birds. *Noun.*
○ **1.** To smooth or arrange with a comb. **2.** To look everywhere in; search thoroughly: *The police combed the woods for the lost child. Verb.*
comb (kōm) *noun, plural* **combs;** *verb,* **combed, combing.**

combat Fighting; battle: *The soldier was wounded*

PRONUNCIATION KEY:
| at | āpe | fär | câre | end | mē | it | īce | pierce | hot | ōld | sông | fôrk |
| oil | out | up | ūse | rūle | pull | tûrn | chin | sing | shop | thin | this | |

hw in white; zh in treasure. The symbol ə stands for the unstressed vowel sound in about, taken, pencil, lemon, and circus.

145

in combat. Noun.

○ To fight against: *Scientists have developed vaccines to combat certain diseases.* Verb.
com·bat (kom′bat *for noun;* kəm bat′ *or* kom′bat *for verb*) noun, plural **combats**; verb, **combated**, **combating.**

combination 1. Something combined: *The sandwich was a combination of ham and cheese.* 2. A series of numbers or letters used to open certain locks. **com·bi·na·tion** (kom′bə nā′shən) *noun, plural* **combinations.**

combine To join together; unite: *We combined eggs, flour, and milk to make the batter for the pancakes.* Verb.
○ A farm machine that harvests and threshes grain. *Noun.*
com·bine (kəm bīn′ *for verb;* kom′bīn *for noun*) *verb,* **combined, combining;** *noun,* plural **combines.**

combustible Capable of catching fire and burning: *Paper and dry leaves are combustible.*
com·bus·ti·ble (kəm bus′tə bəl) *adjective.*

combustion The act or process of burning. *A car's engine runs by the combustion of gasoline.*
com·bus·tion (kəm bus′chən) *noun.*

come 1. To move toward. 2. To reach a place; arrive: *Snow came early in October last year.* 3. To originate or take life from: *Apples come from trees.* 4. To turn out to be; become: *Our fear that it might rain came true.*

• **to come across.** To find or meet by chance: *I came across these old clothes in the attic.*

• **to come down.** To become sick: *I came down with the flu.*

• **to come out.** 1. To become known or be revealed: *The truth finally came out.* 2. To speak out in public: *The candidate came out for lower taxes.* 3. To be presented to the public: *That movie came out last year.* 4. To end; result; turn out: *Everything will come out all right.*

• **to come to.** 1. To become conscious again: *When did he come to?* 2. To be equal to; add up to: *The bill comes to eight dollars.* 3. To concern; have to do with: *I'm pretty good when it comes to spelling.*

come (kum) *verb,* **came, come, coming.**

comedian A person who makes people laugh by telling jokes or acting out funny stories.
co·me·di·an (kə mē′dē ən) *noun, plural* **comedians.**

comedy A play, motion picture, or television show that is funny or that has a happy ending.
com·e·dy (kom′i dē) *noun, plural* **comedies.**

comet A bright object in space that looks like a star with a long tail of light. A comet is made up of ice, frozen gases, and dust particles. A comet travels along an oval path around the sun.
com·et (kom′it) *noun, plural* **comets.**

A **comet's** tail often extends for millions of miles.

WORD HISTORY

The word **comet** comes from a Greek word that means "having long hair." The Greeks called a comet a "long-haired star" because the comet's tail looked like long hair flying behind it.

---

comfort 1. A pleasant condition with freedom from worry, pain, or want. 2. A person or thing that gives relief: *When I was in the hospital, the card that you sent was a comfort.* Noun.
○ To ease the sorrow or pain of someone. *Verb.*
com·fort (kum′fərt) *noun, plural* **comforts;** *verb,* **comforted, comforting.**

comfortable 1. Giving ease or comfort: *a comfortable bed.* 2. At ease: *After a few weeks, we felt comfortable in our new home.*
com·fort·a·ble (kum′fər tə bəl *or* kumf′tə bəl) *adjective.* —**comfortably** *adverb.*

comic Funny; amusing. *Adjective.*
○ 1. A person who makes people laugh; comedian. 2. **comics.** A group of comic strips, as in a Sunday newspaper. *Noun.*
com·ic (kom′ik) *adjective; noun,* plural **comics.**

comical Funny; amusing. **com·i·cal** (kom′i kəl) *adjective.* —**comically** *adverb.*

comic book A magazine or booklet of comic strips.

comic strip A group of drawings that tell a story that is funny or full of adventure.

comma A punctuation mark (,) that is used to separate words, phrases, or clauses in a sentence.
com·ma (kom′ə) *noun, plural* **commas.**

command **1.** To give an order to; direct. **2.** To have power over; rule: *The general commands the army.* **3.** To deserve and get: *The teacher commanded our respect.* Verb.
○ **1.** An order; direction. **2.** The power to command. **3.** The ability to use or control: *My friends from France had a good command of English.* Noun.
com·mand (kə mand′) *verb,* **commanded, commanding;** *noun, plural* **commands.**

commander **1.** A person who is in command; leader. **2.** A naval officer. In the United States Navy or Coast Guard, a commander is below a captain but above a lieutenant. **com·mand·er** kə man′dər) *noun, plural* **commanders.**

commandment A law or command.
com·mand·ment (kə mand′mənt) *noun, plural* **commandments.**

commemorate To honor or maintain the memory of: *American postage stamps commemorate many of our country's presidents.*
com·mem·o·rate (kə mem′ə rāt′) *verb,* **commemorated, commemorating.** —**commemoration** *noun.*

commence To begin; start: *Ceremonies commenced with the national anthem.* **com·mence** (kə mens′) *verb,* **commenced, commencing.**

commencement **1.** A beginning; a start: *January 1 marks the commencement of a new year.* **2.** The day or ceremony of graduation. At commencement, a school or college gives diplomas or degrees to students who have completed a course of study. **com·mence·ment** (kə mens′mənt) *noun, plural* **commencements.**

commend To speak of with approval; praise: *The teacher commended me for a fine book report.*
com·mend (kə mend′) *verb,* **commended, commending.**

comment A remark or note. A comment explains something or gives an opinion: *The coach made a few comments on the team's playing. Noun.*
○ To make a comment; remark: *Let me comment on your report. Verb.*
com·ment (kom′ent) *noun, plural* **comments;** *verb,* **commented, commenting.**

commentator A person who comments on something. Radio and television stations, newspapers,

and magazines hire commentators to explain or give opinions about the news: *The commentator said the new highway would increase business downtown.* **com·men·ta·tor** (kom′ən tā′tər) *noun, plural* **commentators.**

In recent years, stores have become part of American commerce.

commerce The buying and selling of goods; trade; business. **com·merce** (kom′ərs) *noun.*

commercial **1.** Relating to business or trade: *I plan to take accounting and other commercial subjects in high school.* **2.** Having to do with making a profit: *So many people paid to see the exhibit that it became a commercial success.* Adjective.
○ An advertising message on radio or television: *The TV show was interrupted every few minutes by a commercial. Noun.*
com·mer·cial (kə mûr′shəl) *adjective; noun, plural* **commercials.**

commission **1.** A group of persons chosen to do certain work: *The mayor named a commission to find out the causes of pollution in the city.* **2.** Money for work done: *I receive a commission for every new customer I sign up on my paper route.* **3.** The act of committing: *a rise in the commission of crimes.* **4.** A position of military rank: *The soldiers received their commissions as lieutenants after completing a training course.* **5.** A thing that a person or persons is asked and trusted to do: *The ambassador was given a commission to arrange a new treaty.* **6.** Working order: *Our car is out of commission. Noun.*
○ **1.** To give a person the right or power to do

PRONUNCIATION KEY:
at āpe fär cāre end mē it ice pierce hot old song fork
oil out up ūse rüle pull tûrn chin sing shop thin this
hw in white; zh in treasure. The symbol ə stands for the unstressed vowel sound in about, taken, pencil, lemon, and circus.

147

something: *The school commissioned the architect to design a new gym.* **2.** To put something into active service: *The ship will be commissioned today. Verb.*
com·mis·sion (kə mish'ən) *noun, plural* **commissions**; *verb,* **commissioned, commissioning.**

commissioner **1.** A person on a commission: *The commissioners decided that automobiles were the main cause of pollution in the city.* **2.** A person in charge of a department of a government: *the commissioner of public parks.*
com·mis·sion·er (kə mish'ə nər) *noun, plural* **commissioners.**

commit **1.** To do or perform: *The catcher committed two errors in the first inning.* **2.** To put into the care or under the charge of a person or institution, such as a prison. **3.** To devote; pledge: *The town committed itself to raising money for the new hospital.* **com·mit** (kə mit') *verb,* **committed, committing.**

committee A group of persons chosen to do certain work: *the decorations committee for the school dance.* **com·mit·tee** (kə mit'ē) *noun, plural* **committees.**

commodity Something that can be bought and sold: *Wheat, corn, and rice are agricultural commodities.* **com·mod·i·ty** (kə mod'i tē) *noun, plural* **commodities.**

common **1.** Happening often; familiar; usual: *Snow is common here in the winter.* **2.** Belonging equally to all; shared by all alike: *It is common knowledge that the earth is round.* **3.** Ordinary; average: *The dandelion is a common weed.*
• **in common.** Enjoyed, owned, or used together; shared: *many interests in common.*
com·mon (kom'ən) *adjective,* **commoner, commonest.** —**commonly** *adverb.*

common cold A sickness that can cause sneezing, coughing, or a sore throat. The common cold is caused by a virus.

common denominator A denominator that is the same in two or more fractions. The fractions 3/8 and 7/8 have the common denominator 8.

In the fractions

$\frac{5}{16}$	$\frac{7}{16}$	$\frac{1}{16}$	and	$\frac{15}{16}$

16 is the **common denominator.**

common noun A noun that names any one of a group of persons, places, or things. A common noun is not capitalized. In the sentence "My cousin took me to the movie," "cousin" and "movie" are common nouns.

commonplace Ordinary; not interesting, new, or remarkable: *Snow is commonplace in Alaska but not in Florida.* **com·mon·place** (kom'ən plās') *adjective.*

common sense Ordinary good judgment. A person learns common sense from experience and logical thinking, not from school or study: *It is common sense to take an umbrella with you if there is a chance of rain.*

commonwealth A nation or state governed by the people. The United States is a commonwealth. Certain states call themselves commonwealths. **com·mon·wealth** (kom'ən welth') *noun, plural* **commonwealths.**

commotion A noisy confusion; disorder: *There was a commotion at the stadium as the crowd booed the referee's decision.* **com·mo·tion** (kə mōsh'ən) *noun, plural* **commotions.**

communicable Able to be carried or passed from one person to another: *The common cold is a communicable disease.*
com·mu·ni·ca·ble (kə mū'ni kə bəl) *adjective.*

communicate To exchange or pass along feelings, thoughts, or information. People communicate by speaking or writing: *I communicated with my family by letter.*
com·mu·ni·cate (kə mū'ni kāt') *verb,* **communicated, communicating.**

The telephone is one of the most common means of communicating.

communication **1.** An exchanging or sharing of feelings, thoughts, or information: *Some Native American tribes used smoke signals as a means of communication.* **2.** A message or news exchanged or shared: *The communication from Dad said Mom's flight was late.* **3. communications.** A system for sending messages by telephone, telegraph, computers, radio, or television: *Communications in the flooded town are still not working.* **com·mu·ni·ca·tion** (kə mū′ni kā′shən) *noun, plural* **communications.**

communion 1. A sharing of feelings or thoughts: *a close communion between the parents and children.* 2. Communion. A Christian religious service commemorating the last meal of Jesus and his apostles. **com·mun·ion** (kə mūn′yən) *noun, plural* **communions.**

communism A social and economic system in which property and goods are owned by the government and are to be shared equally by all the people. The governments of China and some other countries are based on this system. **com·mu·nism** (kom′yə niz′əm) *noun.*

communist A person who believes in communism as a way of life or who belongs to a communist party. **com·mu·nist** (kom′yə nist) *noun, plural* **communists.**

communist party A political party that favors communism.

community 1. A group of people who live together in the same place: *Our community voted to build a new library.* 2. A group of people who share a common interest: *the scientific community* 3. A group of different plants and animals that live together in the same area and depend on each other for their survival. **com·mu·ni·ty** (kə mū′ni tē) *noun, plural* **communities.**

commutative property A characteristic of addition and multiplication that allows you to add or multiply two numbers in any order and still get the same answer. For example, 4 + 6 gives you

Commutative property in addition:

7 + 3 is the same as 3 + 7

OR

$$\begin{array}{r} 7 \\ +3 \end{array} \text{ is the same as } \begin{array}{r} 3 \\ +7 \end{array}.$$

They all equal 10.

Commutative property in multiplication:

7 x 3 is the same as 3 x 7

OR

$$\begin{array}{r} 7 \\ \times 3 \end{array} \text{ is the same as } \begin{array}{r} 3 \\ \times 7 \end{array}.$$

They all equal 21.

the same answer as 6 + 4, and 7 x 5 gives you the same answer as 5 x 7. **com·mu·ta·tive property** (kom′yə tā′tiv *or* kə mū′tə tiv).

commute Travel regularly to and from work or school over a long distance. *Noun.*
○ To take part in such travel. *Verb.*
com·mute (kə mūt) *noun, plural* **commutes;** *verb,* **commuted, commuting.** —**commute**r *noun.*

compact¹ 1. Tightly packed together; dense: *We pressed the snow into compact snowballs.* 2. Taking up a small amount of space: *compact cooking equipment for camping. Adjective.*
○ 1. A small case that holds face powder. 2. An automobile smaller than a standard model. *Noun.*
○ To pack tightly together: *The school has a machine that compacts trash. Verb.*
com·pact (kəm pakt′ *or* kom′pakt *for adjective;* kom′pakt *for noun;* kəm pakt′ *for verb*) *adjective; noun, plural* **compacts;** *verb,* **compacted, compacting.**

compact² An agreement: *The Mayflower Compact was an agreement among the Pilgrims concerning how their new colony would be governed.* **com·pact** (kom′pakt) *noun, plural* **compacts.**

compact disc A disc that holds stored music or information that is reproduced by putting the compact disc in a special machine that uses a laser to read it. **com·pact disc** (kom′pakt).

companion 1. A person who often goes along with another; friend; comrade: *We were constant companions last summer.* 2. Something that matches something else; one of a pair: *I lost the companion to this glove.* **com·pan·ion** (kəm pan′yən) *noun, plural* **companions.**

companionship The relation between good companions; friendship. **com·pan·ion·ship** (kəm pan′yən ship′) *noun.*

company 1. A guest or guests: *company for dinner.* 2. A business firm or organization. 3. Companionship: *I like my dog's company.* 4. A friend or friends; companions: *You can often judge people by the company they keep.* 5. A group of people gathered together: *a company of tourists in the museum.* 6. A group of performers: *a company of musicians.* 7. A group of soldiers. A captain commands a company. **com·pa·ny** (kum′pə nē) *noun, plural* **companies.**

PRONUNCIATION KEY:
at āpe fär câre end mē it īce pierce hot old sông fôrk
oil out up ūse rüle pull tûrn chin sing shop thin this
hw in white; zh in treasure. The symbol ə stands for the unstressed vowel sound in about, taken, pencil, lemon, and circus.

149

comparative 1. Having to do with or showing a comparison of one thing with another: *We made a comparative study of a frog and a worm in science class.* 2. Measured or judged by comparing with something else: *I've met your uncle many times, but your aunt is a comparative stranger to me, because we've only met once. Adjective.*
○ The form of an adjective or adverb that shows a greater degree or more of whatever is expressed by the basic form. For example, *taller* is the comparative of *tall. Noun.*
com·par·a·tive (kəm par′ə tiv) *adjective; noun, plural* **comparatives.**

compare 1. To study in order to find out how persons or things are alike or different: *We compared our watches and saw that your watch was five minutes ahead of mine.* 2. To say or think that something is like something else: *The writer compared the boom of big guns to the sound of thunder.* 3. To be thought alike; be worthy of being compared: *Seeing photographs of the Grand Canyon cannot compare with visiting it.*
com·pare (kəm pâr′) *verb,* **compared, comparing.**

comparison 1. The finding out of the likenesses and the differences between persons or things: *A comparison of the two teams shows that Saturday's game will be close.* 2. A likeness; similarity: *There is no comparison between those two cars when it comes to speed.* 3. A change in the form of an adjective or adverb that shows a difference in degree of what is expressed. **com·par·i·son** (kəm par′ə sən) *noun, plural* **comparisons.**

compartment A separate division or section: *My desk drawer has compartments for pencils, erasers, and paper clips.* **com·part·ment** (kəm pärt′mənt) *noun, plural* **compartments.**

compass 1. An instrument for showing directions; it has a magnetic needle that points to the north. Pilots, sailors, and many other people use compasses. 2. An instrument for

Since early days explorers and surveyors have depended upon the compass **to help them find their way.**

drawing circles or measuring distances, made up of two arms joined together at the top. One arm ends in a point and the other holds a pencil. **com·pass** (kum′pəs) *noun, plural* **compasses.**

compassion Sympathy for someone else's suffering or misfortune, with the desire to help: *They had compassion for the poor and delivered food to them.* **com·pas·sion** (kəm pash′ən) *noun;* **com·pas·sion·ate** *adjective.* —**compassionately** *adverb.*

compel To force: *The police compelled the owner to leave the burning building.* **com·pel** (kəm pel′) *verb,* **compelled, compelling.**

compensate 1. To make up for something: *The new player's speed compensated for lack of experience.* 2. To pay: *The government compensated the farmers for the land it took to build the highway.* **com·pen·sate** (kom′pən sāt′) *verb,* **compensated, compensating;**

compensation 1. Something that makes up for something else: *Going to the zoo was our compensation for missing the parade last week.* 2. Wages; pay. **compensation** (kom′ pən sā′ shən) *noun, plural* **compensations.**

The cowboy is competing **in a bronco-riding contest.**

compete To try to win or gain something from another or others: *They competed in the spelling contest.* **com·pete** (kəm pēt′) *verb,* **competed, competing.**

competent Able to perform basic skills; capable: *Only competent swimmers should use the deep end of the pool.* **com·pe·tent** (kom′pi tənt) *adjective.*

competition 1. The act of trying to win or gain something from another or others: *We're in competition with three others for the championship.*

2. A contest: *a swimming competition.* **com·pe·ti·tion** (kom′pi tish′ən) *noun, plural* **competitions.**

competitive **1.** Involving or decided by competition: *I won top honors in a competitive examination.* **2.** Enjoying or successful in competition: *The competitive spirit of our team captain helps us all to do our best.* **com·pet·i·tive** (kəm pet′i tiv) *adjective.* —**competitively** *adverb* —**competitiveness** *noun.*

competitor A person or thing that competes: *That store has two competitors nearby.* **com·pet·i·tor** (kəm pet′i tər) *noun, plural* **competitors.**

compile To collect or put together in a list or report: *The newspaper reporter compiled all the facts and then wrote the story.* **com·pile** (kəm pīl′) *verb,* **compiled, compiling.**

complacent Satisfied with oneself: *We should not become complacent about our success.* **com·pla·cent** (kəm plā′sənt) *adjective.* —**complacently** *adverb.*

complain **1.** To say something is wrong; find fault: *They complained that the train was late.* **2.** To make an accusation or charge: *We complained to the police about our noisy neighbors.* **com·plain** (kəm plān′) *verb,* **complained, complaining.**

complaint **1.** A statement that something is wrong: *We took our complaint about the rude clerk to the store manager.* **2.** A cause for complaining: *I have no complaints about this restaurant.* **3.** An accusation or charge: *The storekeeper made a complaint against the person who had robbed the store.* **com·plaint** (kəm plānt′) *noun, plural* **complaints.**

complement Something that completes or makes a thing whole or perfect: *Going to a movie would be the perfect complement to this weekend. Noun.*
○ To make complete: *The background music complements the acting in the movie. Verb.*
Another word sounding like this is **compliment.** **com·ple·ment** (kom′plə mənt *for noun;* kom′plə ment′ *for verb) noun, plural* **complements;** *verb,* **complemented, complementing.**

complete **1.** Having all its parts; whole; entire: *the complete writings of William Shakespeare.* **2.** Ended; finished: *I cannot go out until my homework is complete.* **3.** Thorough; perfect: *a complete success. Adjective.*
○ **1.** To make whole or perfect: *Have you completed your collection of baseball cards?* **2.** To bring to an end; finish: *After you complete the test, you may leave. Verb.*
com·plete (kəm plēt′) *adjective; verb,* **completed, completing; com·plete·ly** *adverb.*

completion **1.** The act of completing or finishing: *With the completion of the flight, the pilot relaxed.* **2.** The condition of being completed: *Bring this science project to completion before spring vacation.* **com·ple·tion** (kəm plē′shən) *noun.*

complex **1.** Hard to understand or do: *a complex arithmetic problem.* **2.** Made up of many connected parts: *a complex pattern of shapes and colors.* **com·plex** (kəm pleks′ or kom′pleks) *adjective.*

complexion **1.** The color and look of a person's skin, especially of the face: *a clear and smooth complexion.* **2.** The general look or character of anything: *The substitution of two new players changed the whole complexion of the game, and we won.* **com·plex·ion** (kəm plek′shən) *noun, plural* **complexions.**

complexity The quality of being complex: *The complexity of the arithmetic problem puzzled the class.* **com·plex·i·ty** (kəm plek′si tē) *noun, plural* **complexities.**

complicate To make hard to understand or do. **com·pli·cate** (kom′pli kāt′) *verb,* **complicated, complicating.**

complicated Hard to understand or do: *The directions for putting together the bicycle were too complicated for me to follow.* **com·pli·ca·ted** (kom′pli kā′tid) *adjective.*

complication A confused or difficult condition: *The snowstorm that closed down the airport caused a complication in our travel plans.* **com·pli·ca·tion** (kom′pli kā′shən) *noun, plural* **complications.**

compliment **1.** Something good said out of praise or admiration: *She got a compliment on her piano playing.* **2. compliments.** Friendly greetings: *Your friends asked me to send you their compliments. Noun.*
○ To express praise or admiration: *The teacher complimented him on his well-written composition. Verb.*

PRONUNCIATION KEY:

| at | āpe | fär | câre | end | mē | it | īce | pierce | hot | ōld | sông | fôrk |
| oil | out | up | ūse | rüle | půll | tûrn | chin | sing | shop | thin | <u>th</u>is | |

hw in white; zh in treasure. The symbol ə stands for the unstressed vowel sound in about, taken, pencil, lemon, and circus.

151

Another word sounding like this is **complement**.

com·pli·ment (kom′plə mənt *for noun;* kom′plə ment′ *for verb) noun, plural* **compliments;** *verb,* **complimented, complimenting.**

complimentary 1. Containing or expressing praise or admiration: *a complimentary remark.* 2. Without charge; free: *complimentary concert tickets.* **com·pli·men·ta·ry** (kom′plə men′tə rē or kom′plə men′trē) *adjective.*

comply To act in agreement with a request or rule: *I complied with the doctor's orders and stayed home until I felt better.* **com·ply** (kəm plī′) *verb,* **complied, complying.**

component A part of a machine or system: *We bought new stereo components.* **com·po·nent** (kəm pō′nənt) *noun, plural* **components.**

compose 1. To form the basis of; make up: *This material is composed of cotton and rayon.* 2. To put together; create: *compose an opera.* 3. To make quiet or calm: *I cried when I heard the sad news, but then I composed myself.* **com·pose** (kəm pōz′) *verb,* **composed, composing.**

composer A person who writes something, especially a musical work. **com·pos·er** (kəm pō′zər) *noun, plural* **composers.**

composite Made up of various parts: *a composite drawing made from several different drawings.* **com·pos·ite** (kəm poz′it) *adjective.*

composition 1. The act of putting together to form a whole: *Composition of the opera took two years.* 2. The parts that together form something: *Scientists studied the moon rock to find out its composition.* 3. Something put together or created, especially something written or a piece of music: *A symphony is a musical composition.* **com·po·si·tion** (kom′pə zish′ən) *noun, plural* **compositions.**

compost A mixture of decaying leaves, vegetables, manure, or other organic matter, used to make the soil better for gardening. **com·post** (kom′pōst) *noun.*

composure Self-control; calmness. **com·po·sure** (kəm pō′zhər) *noun.*

compound Made up of two or more parts. *Adjective.*
○ To mix or combine: *The chemist compounded a new formula out of simple ingredients. Verb.*
○ 1. A mixture or combination. 2. A substance formed by the chemical combination of two or more elements: *Water is a compound of hydrogen and oxygen.* 3. A word made up of two or more words: "Comic strip," "merry-go-round," and "nighttime" are compounds. Noun.*

com·pound (kom′pound *for adjective and noun;* kəm pound′ *for verb) adjective; verb,* **compounded, compounding;** *noun, plural* **compounds.**

compound sentence A sentence that contains two or more simple sentences joined by the conjunction *and, or,* or *but.* "I like movies, but my friend prefers books" is a compound sentence.

comprehend To understand. **com·pre·hend** (kom′pri hend′) *verb,* **comprehended, comprehending.**

comprehension Understanding or the ability to understand. **com·pre·hen·sion** (kom′pri hen′shən) *noun, plural* **comprehensions.**

comprehensive Covering or including everything or almost everything. **com·pre·hen·sive** (kom′pri hen′siv) *adjective.* —**comprehensively** *adverb;*

compress To press or squeeze together into less space: *The city trucks compress garbage. Verb.*
○ A pad or cloth used to put pressure, heat, or cold on some part of the body. *Noun.*
com·press (kəm pres′ *for verb;* kom′pres′ *for noun) verb,* **compressed, compressing;** *noun, plural* **compresses.**

comprise To include or consist of; be composed of: *The state of Hawaii comprises eight main islands and many smaller ones.* **com·prise** (kəm prīz′) *verb,* **comprised, comprising.**

compromise The settlement of an argument or dispute by agreeing that each side will give up part of its demands: *The fight over washing the dishes ended with a compromise in which they decided to share the chore. Noun.*
○ To reach a settlement by agreeing that each side will give up some part of its demands. *Verb.*
com·pro·mise (kom′prə mīz′) *noun, plural* **compromises;** *verb,* **compromised, compromising.**

compulsory Required by law or rules: *Gym class is compulsory in this school.* **com·pul·so·ry** (kəm pul′sə rē) *adjective.*

compute To find out or calculate by using mathematics; reckon: *Compute the cost of a new garage.* **com·pute** (kəm pūt′) *verb,* **computed, computing.**

computer An electronic device that can store and work with large quantities of information. Computers can do hard mathematical problems fast, can retrieve information quickly, and can help a person work with words and pictures. **com·put·er** (kəm pū′tər) *noun, plural* **computers.**

computer

floppy disk drive · power supply · monitor · CD drive · monitor screen · memory board · CPU-central processing unit · **keyboard** · mouse · number keys · function keys · letter keys

computer graphics Pictures and drawings that a computer can display on its screen or print on paper. **computer graphics** (graf′iks).

computer language A set of words and symbols used to give instructions to a computer and to write programs.

computer literacy The understanding of how computers work and how they can be used to perform tasks.

computer science The study of computers and the equipment and programs used with them.

comrade A friend who shares the same work or interests with another; companion. **com·rade** (kom′rad) *noun, plural* **comrades.**

concave Curved inward: *The inside of a spoon is con-*

concave

cave. **con·cave** (kon kāv′ *or* kon′kāv) *adjective.*

conceal To put or keep out of sight; hide: *I concealed my anger by smiling.* **con·ceal** (kən sēl′) *verb,* **concealed, concealing.**

concede 1. To admit as true: *I conceded that she was the faster runner.* 2. To yield to someone else or admit defeat: *The candidate for mayor would not concede the election until all the votes were counted.* **con·cede** (kən sēd′) *verb,* **conceded, conceding.**

conceited Having too high an opinion of oneself or of one's ability to do things: *You're conceited if you think you're better than other people.* **con·ceit·ed** (kən sē′tid) *adjective.*

conceive To form an idea of or imagine; think up: *It is hard to conceive of what life was like thousands of years ago.* **con·ceive** (kən sēv′) *verb,* **conceived, conceiving.**

concentrate 1. To bring together into one place: *The population of our country is concentrated in the cities.* 2. To make stronger or thicker: *Concentrate the liquid by boiling off some water.* 3. To put one's mind on something: *Concentrate on your homework.* **con·cen·trate** (kon′sən trāt′) *verb,* **concentrated, concentrating.**

concentration 1. The act of concentrating or the state of being concentrated. 2. Close attention: *This homework needs all your concentration.* **con·cen·tra·tion** (kon′sən trā′shən) *noun, plural* **concentrations.**

concept A general idea; thought: *Our country honors the concept of individual freedom.* **con·cept** (kon′sept) *noun, plural* **concepts.**

conception An idea; concept: *Learning about travel in space gives you some conception of how enormous the universe must be.* **con·cep·tion** (kən sep′shən) *noun, plural* **conceptions.**

concern 1. To be important to: *What my parents said about saving money concerns our whole family.* 2. To have to do with; be about: *This book concerns the American Revolution.* 3. To worry; trouble: *Your bad cough concerned us all. Verb.*
○ 1. Something important to a person: *Taking care of the puppy is my concern.* 2. Serious interest or worry: *We were full of concern after the flood destroyed our home.* 3. A business: *I work*

PRONUNCIATION KEY:
at · āpe · fär · câre · end · mē · it · ice · pierce · hot · ōld · sông · fôrk
oil · out · up · ūse · rüle · pull · tûrn · chin · sing · shop · thin · this
hw in white; zh in treasure. The symbol ə stands for the unstressed vowel sound in about, taken, pencil, lemon, and circus.

153

for a clothing **concern.** *Noun.*
con·cern (kən sûrn') *verb,* **concerned, concerning;** *noun, plural* **concerns.**

concerning About; having to do with; regarding: *My friend wrote me a letter **concerning** our vacation plans.* **con·cern·ing** (kən sûr'ning) *preposition.*

concert A performance, usually a musical performance by a number of musicians: *a band **concert** in the park.* **con·cert** (kon'sərt) *noun, plural* **concerts.**

In warm weather, concerts may
be played outdoors.

concerto A piece of music for one or more musical instruments and an orchestra. **con·cer·to** (kən cher'tō) *noun, plural* **concertos.**

concession 1. The act of conceding or yielding: *My parents made a **concession** and let me watch the football game.* 2. Something conceded: *Your admission that you were wrong was a **concession.*** 3. The permission to do something granted by a government or other authority: *The town gave our neighbor the **concession** to sell hot dogs in the park.* **con·ces·sion** (kən sesh'ən) *noun, plural* **concessions.**

conch 1. A kind of shellfish with a large, coiled shell. 2. The shell of this animal. **conch** (kongk or konch) *noun, plural* **conchs** or **conches.**

concise Expressed in few words. **con·cise** (kən sīs') *adjective.* —**concisely** *adverb.*

conclude 1. Finish: *When the music **concluded,** the baseball game began.* 2. To decide after thinking: *The judge **concluded** that no crime had been committed.* **con·clude** (kən klüd') *verb,* **concluded, concluding.**

conclusion 1. The end of something: *The conclusion of the movie was very exciting.* 2. Arrange-

ment; settlement: *The **conclusion** of the treaty between the two countries took months.* 3. Something decided after thinking: *I have come to the **conclusion** that I want to be a doctor.* **con·clu·sion** (kən klü'zhən) *noun, plural* **conclusions.**

concoct 1. To prepare by combining several different things: *We **concocted** a meal from leftovers.* 2. To devise; make up: *They **concocted** a wonderful surprise party for their parents.* **con·coct** (kon kokt') *verb,* **concocted, concocting.** —**concoction** *noun.*

concrete Able to be seen and touched: *A chair is a **concrete** object. Adjective.*
○ A mixture of cement, pebbles or sand, and water. Concrete becomes very hard when it dries. It is used in buildings, bridges, and other structures, and in paving roads and sidewalks. *Noun.* **con·crete** (kon'krēt or kon krēt') *adjective; noun, plural* **concretes.**

concur To agree; have the same opinion: *The judges **concurred** in awarding first prize to that science project.* **con·cur** (kən kûr') *verb,* **concurred, concurring.**

concussion 1. A sudden, violent shaking: *The house shook from the **concussion** of the explosion.* 2. An injury to the brain or spine caused by a fall or blow: *A blow on the head caused my **concussion.*** **con·cus·sion** (kən kush'ən) *noun, plural* **concussions.**

condemn 1. To express strong opposition to; disapprove of: *Doctors **condemn** smoking.* 2. To order as a punishment: *The judge **condemned** the thief to ten years in jail.* 3. To declare no longer safe or fit for use: *The city **condemned** the old building.* **con·demn** (kən dem') *verb,* **condemned, condemning.** —**condemnation** *noun.*

condensation 1. The act of condensing something: *The **condensation** of steam changes it into water.* 2. Something condensed: *Last year I read a **condensation** of the novel.* **con·den·sa·tion** (kon'den sā'shən) *noun, plural* **condensations.**

condense 1. To make or become less in size or volume: *Milk **condenses** when the water in it is boiled away.* 2. To change from a gas to a liquid form: *Steam **condenses** to water when cooled.* **con·dense** (kən dens') *verb,* **condensed, condensing.**

condition 1. The way a person or thing is; the state something is in: *He keeps in good **condition***

by exercising. **2.** Something needed for another event or thing to occur; something required: *Being a good skater is one of the* **conditions** *for getting on the hockey team.* **3.** An illness or an unhealthy state of the body or a part of the body. **4. conditions.** State of affairs; circumstances: *Poor working* **conditions** *caused the strike. Noun.*

○ **1.** To put in a healthy state or good shape. **2.** To make used to something; accustom: *Living at the North Pole soon* **conditioned** *them to cold weather. Verb.*

con·di·tion (kən dish′ən) *noun, plural* **conditions**; *verb,* **conditioned, conditioning.**

condominium **1.** An apartment building in which each apartment is owned by the person or persons living in it. **2.** A single apartment owned by the person or persons living in it. **con·do·min·i·um** (kon′də min′ē əm) *noun, plural* **condominiums.**

condor A large bird with a hooked bill and a head and neck without feathers. A condor is a kind of vulture found in the mountains of South America. **con·dor** (kon′dər) *noun, plural* **condors.**

conduct The way someone behaves: *Good* **conduct** *is important. Noun.*

○ **1.** To behave: *You* **conducted** *yourself very well.* **2.** To direct or lead: *Our music teacher will* **conduct** *the school orchestra.* **3.** To take charge of; control; manage: *It is a challenge to* **conduct** *a successful business.* **4.** To carry or transmit: *Cast iron* **conducts** *heat evenly. Verb.*

con·duct (kon′dukt *for noun;* kən dukt′ *for verb) noun; verb,* **conducted, conducting.**

conductor **1.** A person who conducts: *Our music teacher is also the* **conductor** *of the school orchestra.* **2.** A person on a train or bus who collects fares and helps passengers: *The* **conductor** *called out the name of the next stop.* **3.** Something that transmits heat, electricity, or sound: *Iron and copper are excellent* **conductors** *of heat.* **con·duc·tor** (kən duk′tər) *noun, plural* **conductors.**

cone **1.** A solid object that has a flat, round base with straight sides that come together at a point. **2.** Something shaped like a cone. **3.** A cone-shaped object with overlapping scales that grows

on many evergreen trees. The cone bears the seeds. **cone** (kōn) *noun, plural* **cones.**

confederacy **1.** A group of countries, states, or people joined together for a common purpose. **2. the Confederacy.** The eleven southern states that declared themselves separate from the United States in 1860 and 1861. **con·fed·er·a·cy** (kən fed′ər ə sē) *noun, plural* **confederacies.**

This cone growing on a pine tree contains the tree's seeds.

confederate **1.** A person or group that joins with another for a common purpose: *The bank robbers and their* **confederates** *were arrested by the police.* **2. Confederate.** A person who fought for or supported the Confederacy. *Noun.*

○ **1.** United in an alliance: *The two presidents signed a treaty that declared their countries* **confederate** *states.* **2. Confederate.** Of the Confederacy. *Adjective.*

con·fed·er·ate (kən fed′ər it) *noun, plural* **confederates**; *adjective.*

confederation **1.** The act of joining together to form a confederacy: *The two neighboring countries began plans for* **confederation.** **2.** A group of countries or states joined together for a common purpose; a league or alliance: *From 1781 to 1789 the American states formed a* **confederation.** **con·fed·er·a·tion** (kən fed′ə rā′shən) *noun, plural* **confederations.**

confer **1.** To meet and talk together: *The three referees* **conferred** *to decide how to rule on the play.* **2.** To give or bestow upon: *The general* **conferred** *a medal on the soldier.* **con·fer** (kən fûr′) *verb,* **conferred, conferring.**

conference A meeting to talk over important matters: *A* **conference** *of doctors was held to discuss new ways to treat disease.* **con·fer·ence** (kon′fər əns) *noun, plural* **conferences.**

PRONUNCIATION KEY:

| at | āpe | fär | câre | end | mē | it | īce | pîerce | hot | ōld | sông | fôrk |
| oil | out | up | ūse | rūle | půll | tûrn | chin | sing | shop | thin | this | |

hw in white; zh in treasure. The symbol ə stands for the unstressed vowel sound in about, taken, pencil, lemon, and circus.

155

confess **1.** To admit: *I confess that I don't like that new TV show.* **2.** To tell a priest sins to be forgiven. **con·fess** (kən fes') *verb,* **confessed, confessing. —confession** *noun.*

confetti Very small pieces of colored paper. Confetti is thrown into the air to celebrate a festive occasion. **con·fet·ti** (kən fet'ē) *noun.*

confide To tell a secret to someone who is trusted. **con·fide** (kən fīd') *verb,* **confided, confiding.**

confidence **1.** Trust or faith: *I have confidence in your honesty.* **2.** Faith in oneself: *If you studied the lesson, you can give your answer with confidence.* **3.** Trust that a person will not tell a secret: *That was told to me in confidence.* **4.** Something told as a secret to be kept. **con·fi·dence** (kon'fi dəns) *noun, plural* **confidences.**

confident **1.** Having trust or faith; sure: *I am confident we will win the game.* **2.** Having faith in oneself or one's own abilities. **con·fi·dent** (kon'fi dənt) *adjective.*

confidential Secret: *a confidential letter.* **con·fi·den·tial** (kon'fi den'shəl) *adjective;* **con·fi·den·tial·ly** *adverb.*

confine To hold or keep in; limit: *My bad cold confined me to bed. Verb.*
○ **confines.** Limits; boundaries: *The dog was not allowed to go outside the confines of the yard. Noun.*
con·fine (kən fīn') *verb,* **confined, confining;** **con·fines** (kon'fīnz) *plural noun.*

confirm **1.** To show to be true or correct: *The newspaper confirmed reports of a flood.* **2.** To consent to; approve: *The Senate confirmed the trade agreement.* **3.** To make definite: *I called my friend to confirm our date.* **4.** To admit a person to full membership in a religious congregation. **con·firm** (kən fûrm') *verb,* **confirmed, confirming.**

confirmation **1.** The act of confirming something: *Please call the hotel to get confirmation of our reservation.* **2.** Something that confirms or proves. **3.** The ceremony of admitting a person to full membership in a church or synagogue. **con·fir·ma·tion** (kon'fər mā'shən) *noun, plural* **confirmations.**

confiscate To take something by authority: *The government confiscated the property when no one would pay the taxes on it.* **con·fis·cate** (kon'fis kāt') *verb,* **confiscated, confiscating.**

conflict **1.** A long fight; war: *The War of 1812 was a conflict between the United States and England.* **2.** A strong disagreement: *The two newspaper stories are in conflict. Noun.*
○ To disagree strongly: *The two accounts of the accident conflict. Verb.*
con·flict (kon'flikt *for noun;* kən flikt' *for verb*) *noun, plural* **conflicts;** *verb,* **conflicted, conflicting.**

conform **1.** To act or think in a way that agrees with a rule or a standard: *Students have to conform to the school rules.* **2.** To be or make the same; be like: *The house conformed to the architect's plans.* **con·form** (kən fôrm') *verb,* **conformed, conforming.**

confront To meet or face: *A difficult problem confronted us.* **con·front** (kən frunt') *verb,* **confronted, confronting.**

confuse **1.** To mix up; bewilder: *That street sign confuses drivers and causes them to take a wrong turn.* **2.** To mistake for another; not see the difference between: *People are always confusing the twins.* **con·fuse** (kən fūz') *verb,* **confused, confusing.**

confusion **1.** The condition of being confused; disorder: *In my confusion, I gave the wrong answer.* **2.** A mistaking of one person or thing for another. **con·fu·sion** (kən fū'zhən) *noun, plural* **confusions.**

congeal To become thick, stiff, or hard through exposure to cold or to air: *The pudding congealed.* **con·geal** (kən jēl') *verb,* **congealed, congealing.**

Highways at rush hour are often filled with congestion.

congestion 1. Too much mucus or blood in a part of the body: *I had* **congestion** *in my nose when I had a cold.* 2. A very crowded condition: *congestion on the highway after work.* **con·ges·tion** (kən jes′chən) *noun.*

Congo A country in west-central Africa. **Con·go** (kong′gō) *noun.*

congratulate To give good wishes or praise for someone's success or for something nice that has happened: *We* **congratulated** *them on doing such a good job.* **con·grat·u·late** (kən grach′ə lāt′) *verb,* **congratulated, congratulating.**

congratulation 1. The act of congratulating. 2. congratulations. Good wishes or praise given for a person's success or for something nice that has happened: *We offered* **congratulations** *to the winning team.* **con·grat·u·la·tion** (kən grach′ə lā′shən) *noun, plural* **congratulations.**

congregate To come together in a crowd. **con·gre·gate** (kong′grə gāt′) *verb,* **congregated, congregating.**

congregation 1. A gathering or crowd of people or things. 2. The people present at a religious service. **con·gre·ga·tion** (kong′grə gā′shən) *noun, plural* **congregations.**

congress 1. An assembly of people who make laws. Many nations that are republics have a congress. 2. Congress. A branch of the government of the United States that makes laws. Congress is made up of the Senate and the House of Representatives. **con·gress** (kong′gris) *noun, plural* **congresses.**

congressman A member of Congress. **con·gress·man** (kong′gris mən) *noun, plural* **congressmen** (kong′gris mən).

congresswoman A woman who is a member of Congress. **con·gress·wom·an** (kong′gris wùm′ən) *noun, plural* **congresswomen** (kong′gris wim′ən).

congruent Exactly equal in shape and size. Two triangles are congruent if the sides and angles of one are the same as the sides and angles of the other. **con·gru·ent** (kong′grü ənt *or* kən grü′ənt) *adjective.*

conifer An evergreen tree, such as a pine, spruce, or fir, that bears cones. **con·i·fer** (kon′ə fər) *noun, plural* **conifers.** —**coniferous** *adjective.*

conjunction A word that joins other words or groups of words. In the sentence "My friends and I were late because we missed the bus," the words "and" and "because" are conjunctions. **con·junc·tion** (kən jungk′shən) *noun, plural* **conjunctions.**

Conn. An abbreviation for Connecticut.

connect 1. To fasten or join together: *Connect the trailer to the car.* 2. To consider as related; associate: *We* **connect** *robins with spring.* 3. To join together in an electrical circuit. **con·nect** (kə nekt′) *verb,* **connected, connecting.**

Connecticut A state in the northeastern United States. Its capital is Hartford. **Con·nect·i·cut** (kə net′i kət) *noun.*

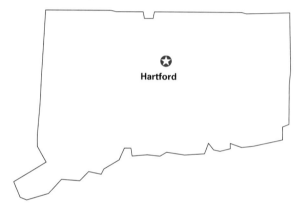

Connecticut
U. S. Postal Abbreviation: **CT**
Capital: **Hartford**
Population: **3,211,000**
Area: **5,009 sq. mi./12,973 sq. km**
State Nicknames: **Constitution State; Nutmeg State**
State Bird: **Robin**
State Flower: **Mountain Laurel**

WORD HISTORY

The name **Connecticut** comes from an Indian word that means "a place beside the long river." Settlers then gave the name to the river, too. Soon they used it for villages near the Connecticut River. Later they used it for the state in which this river is located.

connection 1. The act of fastening or joining things: *The* **connection** *of the pipes under the sink was hard work.* 2. Relationship; association: *The city council is studying the* **connection** *between heavy traffic and air pollution.* 3. Something that connects: *There's a bad* **connection** *in the radio.* **con·nec·tion** (kə nek′shən) *noun, plural* **connections.**

PRONUNCIATION KEY:
| at | āpe | fär | câre | end | mē | it | īce | pierce | hot | ōld | sông | fôrk |
| oil | out | up | ūse | rüle | pùll | tûrn | chin | sing | shop | thin | this | |

hw in white; zh in treasure. The symbol ə stands for the unstressed vowel sound in about, taken, pencil, lemon, and circus.

157

conquer To overcome; defeat: *We conquered our fears.* **con·quer** (kong′kər) *verb*, **conquered**, **conquering**.

conqueror A person who conquers. **con·quer·or** (kong′kə rər) *noun, plural* **conquerors**.

conquest 1. The act of conquering something: *Conquest of the country took months.* 2. Something conquered: *Mexico was once a conquest of Spain.* **con·quest** (kon′kwest *or* kong′kwest) *noun, plural* **conquests**.

conscience A feeling about what is right and what is wrong. Your conscience tells you to do right and warns when you are doing something wrong: *If you tell a lie, it will trouble your conscience.* **con·science** (kon′shəns) *noun, plural* **consciences**.

conscientious Showing honesty, thought, and care: *Your conscientious work at school has improved your grades.* **con·sci·en·tious** (kon′shē en′shəs) *adjective*.

conscious 1. Knowing or realizing; aware: *I was conscious of someone tapping my shoulder.* 2. Able to see and feel things; awake: *I was still conscious after being hit by the car.* 3. Done on purpose: *I made a conscious effort to stop laughing.* **con·scious** (kon′shəs) *adjective*. —**consciously** *adverb* —**consciousness** *noun*.

consecutive Following one after another without a break: *The numbers 1, 2, 3, and 4 are consecutive numbers.* **con·sec·u·tive** (kən sek′yə tiv) *adjective*. —**consecutively** *adverb*.

consent To give permission; agree: *My parents consented to my going camping. Verb.* ○ Permission. *Noun.* **con·sent** (kən sent′) *verb*, **consented**, **consenting**; *noun, plural* **consents**.

consequence 1. The result of an action: *One consequence of going to sleep late at night is waking up tired.* 2. Significance; importance: *The President is someone of consequence.* **con·se·quence** (kon′si kwəns) *noun, plural* **consequences**.

consequently As a result; therefore: *It rained, consequently I got my shoes wet.* **con·se·quent·ly** (kon′si kwent′lē) *adverb*.

conservation 1. The act of conserving. 2. The protection and wise use of the forests, rivers, minerals, and other natural resources of a country. **con·ser·va·tion** (kon′sər vā′shən) *noun*.

Conservation **involves everyone – the government, scientists, and the public.**

conservative 1. Wanting things to be as they used to be or to stay as they are; not usually favoring change or new ideas. 2. Wanting to avoid risks; using caution: *The doctor talked about the conservative use of medicines. Adjective.* ○ A person who is conservative. *Noun.* **con·serv·a·tive** (kən sûrv′ə tiv) *adjective; noun, plural* **conservatives**.

conserve To keep and protect from harm, loss, or change: *We tried to conserve our energy for the hike.* **con·serve** (kən sûrv′) *verb*, **conserved**, **conserving**.

consider 1. To think carefully about before deciding: *I'm considering whether or not to go to college.* 2. To think of as; believe to be: *I consider that movie the best I've ever seen.* 3. To show concern and care for; respect: *Always consider other people's feelings.* 4. To keep in mind: *My grandparents are very healthy if you consider their age.* **con·sid·er** (kən sid′ər) *verb*, **considered**, **considering**.

considerable Great in amount or extent: *We had considerable trouble driving up the icy hill.* **con·sid·er·able** (kən sid′ər ə bəl) *adjective*.

considerate Thoughtful of other people and their feelings. **con·sid·er·ate** (kən sid′ər it) *adjective*. —**considerately** *adverb*.

consideration 1. Thoughtfulness for other people and their feelings: *Show consideration for your neighbors.* 2. Careful thought before deciding about something: *After much consideration, my cousin decided to become a lawyer.* 3. Something thought about before deciding: *One consideration when moving to a new city is the quality of the schools.* **con·sid·er·a·tion** (kən sid′ə rā′shən) *noun, plural* **considerations**.

consist To contain; be made up: *Bricks consist mostly of clay.* **con·sist** (kən sist′) *verb,* **consisted, consisting.**

consistency **1.** Thickness or stiffness of a liquid: *This paint has the consistency of glue.* **2.** A keeping to one way of thinking or acting: *Since you change your mind so often, there is no consistency to what you say or believe.* **con·sist·en·cy** (kən sis′tən sē) *noun, plural* **consistencies.**

consistent **1.** Keeping to one way of thinking or acting: *My parents are consistent in applying rules.* **2.** In agreement: *What they said about the accident is not consistent with what really happened.* **con·sist·ent** (kən sis′tənt) *adjective.*

console¹ To comfort or cheer: *We tried to console the loser.* **con·sole** (kən sōl′) *verb,* **consoled, consoling.** **—consolation** *noun.*

console² The cabinet of a radio, television set, or phonograph that rests on the floor. **con·sole** (kon′sōl) *noun, plural* **consoles.**

consolidate To join together; combine: *The stores consolidated to form one big one.* **con·sol·i·date** (kən sol′ dāt′) *verb,* **consolidated, consolidating.**

consonant A letter of the alphabet that is not a vowel. Consonants include the letters *b, d, f, g, m, p, t,* and others. **con·so·nant** (kon′sə nənt) *noun, plural* **consonants.**

conspicuous Easily seen; attracting attention: *The ink left a conspicuous stain on the white tablecloth.* **con·spic·u·ous** (kən spik′ū əs) *adjective.*

conspiracy Secret planning together with others to do something wrong: *The gang members were arrested for conspiracy to rob a bank.* **con·spir·a·cy** (kən spir′ə sē) *noun, plural* **conspiracies.**

conspire To make a conspiracy. **con·spire** (kən spīr′) *verb,* **conspired, conspiring.**

constable **1.** A member of the police force in England; policeman or policewoman. **2.** A law officer in a town in charge of keeping order. **con·sta·ble** (kon′stə bəl *or* kun′stə bəl) *noun, plural* **constables.**

constant **1.** Not changing; continuing: *Your constant talking annoys the teacher.* **2.** Faithful; loyal: *constant friends.* **con·stant** (kon′stənt) *adjective.*

constellation A group of stars that forms a pattern in the sky that looks like a picture. The Big Dipper and the Little Dipper are parts of constellations. **con·stel·la·tion** (kon′stə lā′shən) *noun, plural* **constellations.**

WORD HISTORY

The word **constellation** comes from the old French name for a group of stars. This French word came from two Latin words meaning "together" and "stars."

---

constituent Forming a needed part: *Hydrogen and oxygen are the constituent parts of water.* *Adjective.*
○ **1.** A needed part: *Wood pulp is a constituent of paper.* **2.** A voter in a particular district: *The senators voted for the laws their constituents wanted. Noun.*
con·stit·u·ent (kən stich′ü ənt) *adjective; noun, plural* **constituents.**

constitute **1.** To make up; form; equal: *Four quarts constitute a gallon.* **2.** To set up; establish: *Congress constitutes our laws.* **3.** To appoint or elect: *The club plans to constitute you as its president.* **con·sti·tute** (kon′sti tüt′ *or* kon′sti tūt′) *verb,* **constituted, constituting.**

constitution **1.** The basic principles used to govern a state, country, or organization: *The people voted for a change in their state constitution.* **2.** Constitution: The document containing the law and plan of government of the United States. **3.** The way in which a person or thing is made: *The healthy child has a strong constitution.* **con·sti·tu·tion** (kon′sti tü′shən *or* kon′sti tū′shən) *noun, plural* **constitutions.**

constitutional Having to do with a constitution: *The United States has a constitutional form of government. Adjective.*
○ A walk taken to stay healthy. *Noun.*
con·sti·tu·tion·al (kon′sti tü′shə nəl *or* kon′sti tū′shə nəl) *adjective; noun, plural* **constitutions.**

constrict To make smaller or narrower by pressing together; to squeeze: *The dog's tight collar constricted its neck.* **con·strict** (kən strikt′) *verb,* **constricted, constricting.**

PRONUNCIATION KEY:
at   āpe   fär   câre   end   mē   it   īce   pierce   hot   ōld   sông   fôrk
oil   out   up   ūse   rüle   pull   tûrn   chin   sing   shop   thin   this
hw in white; zh in treasure. The symbol ə stands for the unstressed vowel sound in about, taken, pencil, lemon, and circus.

159

constrictor A large snake that can kill small animals by squeezing them in its coils so that they cannot breathe. The python, boa constrictor, and anaconda are constrictors. **con·stric·tor** (kən strik′tər) *noun, plural* **constrictors.**

construct To make by putting parts together; build: *We constructed a bike shed in the backyard.* **con·struct** (kən strukt′) *verb,* **constructed, constructing.**

construction The act of constructing something; building: *Construction of the new gym began last summer.* **construction** (kənstrukshən) *noun, plural* **constructions.**

Construction **is often carried out with the aid of huge vehicles.**

constructive Serving to make better; helpful: *The coach gave constructive criticism so that we played better.* **con·struc·tive** (kən struk′tiv) *adjective.*

consul A person appointed by a government to live in a foreign city: *A consul helps his or her country's citizens and business there.* **con·sul** (kon′səl) *noun, plural* **consuls.**

consult 1. To go to for advice or information: *We consulted a map to find out where we were.* 2. To talk together: *My teacher consulted with my parents.* **con·sult** (kən sult′) *verb,* **consulted, consulting. —consultation** *noun.*

consultant A person who has a lot of expert knowledge of a profession or line of work and whose job is giving advice to others in that profession or line of work. **con·sul·tant** (kən sul′tnt) *noun, plural* **consultants.**

consume 1. To use up or destroy: *The fire consumed the garage.* 2. To eat or drink: *I consumed two sandwiches at lunch.* **con·sume** (kən süm′) *verb,* **consumed, consuming.**

consumer A person who buys and uses up things. People who buy radios, books, cars, and many other things are consumers. **con·sum·er** (kən sü′mər) *noun, plural* **consumers.**

consumption The using up of something: *Consumption of gasoline is greater in a very large car than in a small car.* **con·sump·tion** (kən sump′shən) *noun, plural* **consumptions.**

contact A touching or meeting of persons or things: *The bowl began to melt when it came in contact with the stove. I lost contact with my friends when I moved.* Noun.
○ To get in touch with; communicate with; reach: *Contact your friend by telephone.* Verb. **con·tact** (kon′takt) *noun, plural* **contacts;** *verb,* **contacted, contacting.**

contact lens A thin plastic lens worn on the eyeball to improve vision.

contagious Able to be spread from person to person: *Chicken pox is contagious.* **con·ta·gious** (kən tā′jəs) *adjective.*

contain 1. To hold: *The jar contains candy.* 2. To include as a part of: *Candy contains sugar.* 3. To keep or hold back: *I tried to contain my laughter when your chair tipped over.* **con·tain** (kən tān′) *verb,* **contained, containing.**

container A box, can, or jar that holds something: *a container of milk.* **con·tain·er** (kən tā′nər) *noun, plural* **containers.**

A basket with a lid can be used as a container.

contaminate To make dirty; pollute. **con·tam·i·nate** (kən tam′ə nāt) *verb,* **contaminated, contaminating. —contamination** *noun.*

contemplate To think about or look at carefully for a long time: *We contemplated the lovely scenery.* **con·tem·plate** (kon′təm plāt′) *verb,* **contemplated, contemplating.**

contemporary 1. Belonging to the same time: *Abraham Lincoln and Robert E. Lee were contemporary figures.* 2. Modern; up-to-date: *contemporary furniture. Adjective.*

○ A person who belongs to the same time as another person. *Noun.*

con·tem·po·rar·y (kən tem′pə rer′ē) *adjective; noun, plural* **contemporaries.**

contempt **1.** A feeling that a person or act is bad, mean, or worth nothing; scorn: *I have contempt for people who are cruel to animals.* **2.** The condition of being scorned: *The noisy students were held in contempt by their classmates who were trying to study.* **con·tempt** (kən tempt′) *noun.*

contend **1.** To compete: *Only three students contended for the swimming championship.* **2.** To argue: *I contended that we ought to go to the beach instead of seeing a movie.* **3.** To struggle: *The explorers had to contend with very cold weather.* **con·tend** (kən tend′) *verb,* **contended, contending.**

content Happy and satisfied. *Adjective.*
○ To make happy; satisfy: *A pat on the head contents my dog. Verb.*
○ A feeling of being happy or satisfied: *After eating, the baby went to sleep in complete content. Noun.*
content (kən tent′) *adjective; verb,* **contented, contenting;** *noun.*

contented Content; happy. **con·ten·ted** (kən ten tid) *adjective.*

contents **1.** What something holds: *The bag's contents fell all over the floor.* **2.** What is written or spoken about: *The contents of the letter upset me.* **con·tents** (kon′tents) *plural noun.*

contest **1.** A game or race that people try to win; competition: *Our team won the swimming contest.* **2.** A struggle; fight: *The contest between the two armies lasted into the night. Noun.*
○ **1.** To struggle or fight for: *The enemy troops contested the fort.* **2.** To argue against: *The loser of the race contested the judge's decision. Verb.*
con·test (kon′test *for noun;* kən test′ *for verb*) *noun, plural* **contests;** *verb,* **contested, contesting.**

contestant A person who takes part in a contest: *a contestant in a race.* **con·test·ant** (kən tes′tənt) *noun, plural* **contestants.**

context The words before and after a word or phrase. The context influences the meaning of a word or phrase: *It was clear from the context*

that they were only joking when they said that. **con·text** (kon′tekst) *noun, plural* **contexts.**

continent One of the seven large land areas on the earth. The continents are Asia, Africa, North America, South America, Europe, Antarctica, and Australia. **con·ti·nent** (kon′tə nənt) *noun, plural* **continents.** —**continental** *adjective.*

CONTINENTS

Slightly more than one-third of the Earth's surface is covered by land. The largest pieces of land are called continents. Although they seem stable, continents do move. A discussion of continental drift can be found at the entry for Earth. The seven continents are:

Africa: With an area of 11,700,000 square miles, Africa is divided roughly into two sections. North Africa is dominated by the Sahara Desert, which covers 3,500,000 square miles. The rest of Africa consists mostly of tropical forests and great plains. Africa has a population of 720,000,000 people.

Antarctica: Covered almost entirely with ice, Antarctica has an area of 5,400,000 square miles. Except for scientists visiting work stations, Antarctica has no population.

Asia: The largest continent, Asia has an area of 17,200,000 square miles. Asia also has the largest population with 3,451,000,000 people.

Australia: The smallest continent, Australia is also the only continent made up of only one country. Australia has an area of 3,070,000 square miles. Its population is 21,500,000.

Europe: The continent of Europe covers an area of 3,800,000 miles. The population of Europe is 729,000,000.

North America: One of the two continents in the Western Hemisphere, North America has an area of 9,400,000 square miles. The population of North America, Central America, and the islands of the Caribbean is 455,000,000.

South America: The other continent in the Western Hemisphere, South America stretches southward from north of the equator almost to Antarctica. It has an area of 6,900,000 square miles. The population of South America is 319,000,000.

PRONUNCIATION KEY:

| at | āpe | fär | câre | end | mē | it | īce | pîerce | hot | ōld | sông | fôrk |
| oil | out | up | ūse | rüle | pùll | tûrn | chin | sing | shop | thin | this | |

hw in white; zh in treasure. The symbol ə stands for the unstressed vowel sound in about, taken, pencil, lemon, and circus.

161

continental shelf The edge of a continent, submerged in shallow water and gradually sloping to a point of steep descent in the ocean.

continual Happening again and again: *I had to make continual visits to the doctor until my leg healed.* **con·tin·u·al** (kən tin′ū əl) *adjective.*

continue 1. To keep happening, being, or doing; go on without stopping: *The rain continued for two days.* 2. To go on or do after stopping: *We continued the meeting after lunch.* **con·tin·ue** (kən tin′ū) *verb,* **continued, continuing.** —**continuation** *noun.*

continuous Going on without stopping; unbroken: *The river has a continuous flow of water.* **con·tin·u·ous** (kən tin′ū əs) *adjective.* —**continuously** *adverb.*

contour The outline or shape of something: *the curved contour of the earth.* **con·tour** (kon′tür) *noun, plural* **contours.**

contract 1. To make or become shorter or smaller: *The words "you had" contract to form "you'd."* 2. To get or acquire: *I contracted the flu.* 3. To make an agreement: *They contracted to paint the house.* Verb.
○ An agreement: *The star signed a movie contract.* Noun.
con·tract (kən trakt′ *for verb, definitions 1 and 2;* kən trakt′ *or* kon′trakt *for verb, definition 3;* kon′trakt′ *for noun*) *verb,* **contracted, contracting;** *noun, plural* **contracts.**

contraction 1. The act of contracting or the state of being contracted: *The contraction of the heart muscles forces blood into the arteries.* 2. A shortened form. *"Wouldn't" is the contraction of "would not."* **con·trac·tion** (kən trak′shən) *noun, plural* **contractions.**

contradict To say the opposite of; disagree with: *The newspaper contradicted what had been said on the radio about the accident.* **con·tra·dict** (kon′trə dikt′) *verb,* **contradicted, contradicting.** —**contradiction** *noun.*

contradictory 1. Contradicting; opposing; inconsistent: *There are two contradictory versions of what happened.* 2. Likely to contradict or to have a different opinion: *My contradictory cousin often disagrees with me.* **con·tra·dic·to·ry** (kon′trə dik′tə rē) *adjective.*

contrary 1. Entirely different; opposite: *My cousin's ideas about sports and music are contrary to my own.* 2. Liking to argue and oppose: *That contrary child never agrees with me.* Adjective.
○ Something completely different; the opposite: *We thought it would rain, but the contrary happened; it was sunny.* Noun.
• **on the contrary.** Just the opposite of what has been said: *You are not a clumsy dancer; on the contrary, you are very graceful.*
con·trar·y (kon′tre rē *for adjective, definition 1, and noun;* kon′tre rē *or* kən trâr′ē *for adjective, definition 2*) *adjective; noun.*

contrast To show differences that are based on comparing: *The teacher contrasted life in a big city and on a farm.* Verb.
○ 1. A difference: *There is a great contrast between summer and winter here.* 2. A person or thing that is compared to another and shows differences: *Our new car is quite a contrast to our old one.* Noun.
con·trast (kən trast′ *for verb;* kon′trast *for noun*) *verb,* **contrasted, contrasting;** *noun, plural* **contrasts.**

There is a great deal of contrast in the sizes and shapes of these buildings.

contribute 1. To give: *We contributed food and clothing to the family whose house had burned* down. **2.** To write for a newspaper or magazine: *My aunt **contributes** articles to the newspaper.*

• **to contribute to.** To help bring about: *A lack of rain **contributed to** the poor harvest.* **con·trib·ute** (kən trib′ūt) *verb*, **contributed, contributing.**

contribution **1.** The act of contributing; giving something: *Their **contribution** of money will help the hospital.* **2.** Something contributed: *We gave **contributions** to help hungry children in other countries.* **con·tri·bu·tion** (kon′trə bū′shən) *noun*, *plural* **contributions.**

contrive To plan or design cleverly: *They are **contriving** a surprise party.* **con·trive** (kən trīv′) *verb*, **contrived, contriving.**

This pilot is sitting at the controls of the glider.

control **1.** Power, authority, or regulation: *The car went out of **control**.* **2.** The power or ability to hold back or hold in: *The police lost **control** of the mob.* **3.** Something used to operate, regulate, or guide a machine or other device: *The pilot operates the **controls** of an airplane.* *Noun.*
○ **1.** To command or regulate by using power or authority: *The federal government **controls** the handling and delivery of mail.* **2.** To adjust or regulate: *This knob **controls** the loudness on my radio.* **3.** To hold back or hold in: *I always try to **control** my temper.* *Verb.*
con·trol (kən trōl′) *noun*, *plural* **controls**; *verb*, **controlled, controlling.**

control tower A tower at an airport. The movement of airplanes landing and taking off is directed from the control tower.

controversial Causing an argument: *Politics is*

often a **controversial** subject. **con·tro·ver·sial** (kon′trə vûr′shəl) *adjective*.

controversy A disagreement; dispute: *The new tax caused much **controversy**.* **con·tro·ver·sy** (kon′trə vûr′sē) *noun*, *plural* **controversies.**

convalescent **1.** Recovering from illness: *Convalescent patients often sleep a lot.* **2.** For or relating to the process of recovering from illness: *In the **convalescent** room, patients can sit in the sun.* *Adjective.*
○ A person recovering from illness. *Noun.*
con·va·les·cent (kon′və les′ənt) *adjective*; *noun*, *plural* **convalescents.**

convection The transfer of heat through a gas or a liquid by currents. *Fireplaces heat a room by convection through the air.* **con·vec·tion** (kən vek′shən) *noun*.

WORD HISTORY

Convection comes from a Latin word meaning "to carry along with." A convection oven carries its heat along with the circulating air inside.

convene To come or bring together for a meeting; assemble. **con·vene** (kən vēn′) *verb*, **convened, convening.**

convenience **1.** Ease and comfort: *I like the convenience of canned foods.* **2.** Something that gives ease or comfort: *A washing machine is a modern **convenience**.* **con·ven·ience** (kən vēn′yəns) *noun*, *plural* **conveniences.**

convenient Giving ease and comfort; useful; handy: *A dishwasher is very **convenient**.* **con·ven·ient** (kən vēn′yənt) *adjective*.

convent **1.** A group of nuns living together. **2.** A building where a group of nuns live. **con·vent** (kon′vent) *noun*, *plural* **convents.**

convention **1.** A formal meeting for some special purpose. **2.** An accepted way of acting or doing something; custom: *Shaking hands when you are introduced is a **convention**.* **con·ven·tion** (kən ven′shən) *noun*, *plural* **conventions.**

WORD HISTORY

Convention comes from two Latin words meaning "to come" and "together."

PRONUNCIATION KEY:

| at | āpe | fär | câre | end | mē | it | īce | pîerce | hot | ōld | sông | fôrk |
| oil | out | up | ūse | rüle | pùll | tûrn | chin | sing | shop | thin | this | |

hw in white; zh in treasure. The symbol ə stands for the unstressed vowel sound in about, taken, pencil, lemon, and circus.

163

conventional Following customs: *Saying "hello" is a conventional greeting.* **con•ven•tion•al** (kən ven′shə nəl) *adjective.*

conversation Talk between two or more persons: *I had a long conversation with my parents.* **con•ver•sa•tion** (kon′vər sā′shən) *noun, plural* **conversations.**

converse To talk together. **con•verse** (kən vûrs′) *verb,* **conversed, conversing.**

conversion 1. The changing of something: conversion of a garage into a den. 2. The changing of a person's belief, especially religious belief. **con•ver•sion** (kən vûr′zhən) *noun, plural* **conversions.**

convert 1. To change something into something different: *We converted the house into an inn.* 2. To cause a person to change a belief: *The political party tried to convert the voters to its beliefs.* *Verb.*
○ A person who has changed his or her beliefs. *Noun.*
con•vert (kən vûrt′ *for verb;* kon′vûrt *for noun*) *verb,* **converted, converting;** *noun, plural* **converts.**

convertible Able to be changed: *The convertible sofa can be made into a bed. Adjective.*
○ An automobile with a roof that can be folded back or removed. *Noun.*
con•vert•i•ble (kən vûrt′ə bəl) *adjective; noun, plural* **convertibles.**

convex Curving outward. The outside of a bowl is convex. **con•vex** (kon veks′ *or* kon′veks) *adjective.*

convex

convey 1. To take from one place to another; carry: *These pipes convey water from the well to the house.* 2. To make known; express: *Our parents conveyed the excitement of their trip in their letters they wrote to us.* **con•vey** (kən vā′) *verb,* **conveyed, conveying.**

conveyor belt A long, moving belt used to carry objects from one place to another. Conveyor belts are often used in factories. **con•vey•or belt** (kən vā′ər).

convict To declare or

This conveyor belt helps move ripe cranberries out of the bog.

prove a person guilty of a crime: *The jury convicted him of robbery. Verb.*
○ A person serving a prison sentence. *Noun.*
con•vict (kən vikt′ *for verb;* kon′vikt *for noun*) *verb,* **convicted, convicting;** *noun, plural* **convicts.**

conviction 1. The act of declaring or proving that a person is guilty of a crime: *New evidence led to the conviction of the thief.* 2. The state of being found guilty of a crime: *Their conviction meant they would be sent to prison.* 3. A strong belief: *I have the conviction that most people are good at heart.* **con•vic•tion** (kən vik′shən) *noun, plural* **convictions.**

convince To cause a person to believe or do something; persuade: *I convinced my parents to let me see the movie.* **con•vince** (kən vins′) *verb,* **convinced, convincing.**

WORD HISTORY

The word **convince** comes from a Latin word meaning "to conquer" or "to overcome." When you convince someone of something, you overcome the person's doubts or objections.

---

convulse To shake or disturb violently: *She was convulsed with laughter.* **con•vulse** (kən vuls′) *verb,* **convulsed, convulsing.**

convulsion 1. A violent, involuntary contraction of the muscles; spasm: *The crash victim's injuries were so severe that they caused convulsions.* 2. A fit of laughter. **con•vul•sion** (kən vul′shən) *noun, plural* **convulsions.**

cook 1. To make food ready for eating by using heat. You can cook food by broiling, roasting, baking, boiling, or frying it. 2. To be cooked: *The peas will cook quickly. Verb.*
○ A person who cooks. *Noun.*
cook (kůk) *verb,* **cooked, cooking;** *noun, plural* **cooks.**

cookbook A book of recipes and other information about food. **cook•book** (kůk′bůk′) *noun, plural* **cookbooks.**

cookie A small, flat, sweet cake. **cook•ie** (kůk′ē) *noun, plural* **cookies.**

cookout An outdoor gathering at which food is cooked and eaten. **cook•out** (kůk′out′) *noun, plural* **cookouts.**

cool 1. Somewhat cold: *a cool breeze.* 2. Protecting or giving relief from heat: *a thin, cool shirt.*

3. Not excited; calm. **4.** Not warm or friendly: *They were very **cool** after I insulted them. Adjective.*
○ Something cool: *the **cool** of the evening. Noun.*
○ To make or become cool: ***Cool** your soup by blowing on it. Verb.*
cool (kül) *adjective,* **cooler, coolest**; *noun; verb,* **cooled, cooling.**

coop A cage or pen for small animals. *Noun.*
  • **to coop up.** To put or keep in a coop or other small space: ***Coop** the dog **up** in the kitchen.*
  coop (küp) *noun, plural* **coops**; *verb,* **cooped, cooping.**

cooperate To work together: *They **cooperated** in planning a picnic.* **co·op·er·ate** (kō op′ə rāt′) *verb,* **cooperated, cooperating.**

cooperation The act of working together. **co·op·er·a·tion** (kō op′ə rā′shən) *noun.*

coordinate To work or cause to work well together; bring or put into proper working order: *In this dance, it is important to **coordinate** the movements of the feet to the beat of the music.* **co·or·di·nate** (kō ôr′də nāt′) *verb,* **coordinated, coordinating.**

coordination **1.** The act of coordinating: *Who is responsible for **coordination** of the class picnic?* **2.** The ability of parts of the body to work together well: *Athletes need good **coordination**.* **co·or·di·na·tion** (kō ôr′də nā′shən) *noun.*

cope To handle with success: *I had trouble **coping** with the extra homework.* **cope** (kōp) *verb,* **coped, coping.**

copper **1.** A reddish metal. **2.** A reddish brown color. *Noun.*
○ **1.** Made of copper. **2.** Having the color copper; reddish brown. *Adjective.*
cop·per (kop′ər) *noun; adjective.*

WORD HISTORY

The word **copper** comes from a Latin word meaning "from Cyprus." Cyprus is an island where many ancient peoples mined copper ore.

---

copperhead A poisonous snake found in the eastern United States. It has a copper-colored head and a light brown body with dark brown markings. **cop·per·head** (kop′ər hed′) *noun, plural* **copperheads.**

copy **1.** Something that looks exactly like something else. **2.** One of a number of books, magazines, or newspapers printed at the same time: *The store has only one **copy** of that new book. Noun.*
○ **1.** To make a copy of. **2.** To make or do something that is exactly like something else. *Verb.*
cop·y (kop′ē) *noun, plural* **copies**; *verb,* **copied, copying.**

coral **1.** A hard substance like stone, found in tropical seas. Coral is made up of the skeletons of tiny sea animals.
2. The tiny sea animal that makes coral. **3.** A pinkish red color. *Noun.*
○ **1.** Made of coral: *a **coral** reef.* **2.** Having the color coral; pinkish red. *Adjective.*
cor·al (kôr′əl) *noun, plural* **corals**; *adjective.*

Coral reefs are ideal places
to see fish.

coral snake A poisonous American snake with a narrow head and red, black, and yellow bands on its body.

cord **1.** A string or thin rope. **2.** A covered wire used to connect a toaster, lamp, or other appliance to an electrical outlet. **3.** A structure in the body like a cord: *The spinal **cord** extends from the brain down through the backbone.* **4.** An amount of cut wood equaling 128 cubic feet. A cord is a pile of wood 4 feet wide, 4 feet high, and 8 feet long. Another word that sounds like this is **chord.**
cord (kôrd) *noun, plural* **cords.**

PRONUNCIATION KEY:
at   āpe   fär   câre   end   mē   it   īce   pîerce   hot   ōld   sông   fôrk
oil   out   up   ūse   rüle   pull   tûrn   chin   sing   shop   thin   this
hw in white; zh in treasure. The symbol ə stands for the unstressed vowel sound in about, taken, pencil, lemon, and circus.   **165**

cordial Warm and friendly; hearty: *a cordial greeting.* cor•dial (kôr′jəl) *adjective.*

corduroy 1. A cloth with rows of ribs. It is usually made of cotton. 2. corduroys. Trousers made from corduroy. cor•du•roy (kôr′də roi′) *noun, plural* **corduroys.**

core 1. The hard part in the middle of apples, pears, and other fruits. 2. The central part of the earth. 3. The central, most important, or deepest part of anything: *The core of the teacher's talk was that the class needed to study more. Noun.*
○ To remove the core of: *We cored the apples. Verb.*
Another word that sounds like this is **corps.**
core (kôr) *noun, plural* **cores;** *verb,* **cored, coring.**

cork 1. The light, thick outer bark of a kind of oak tree. Cork is used for such things as bottle stoppers, insulation, and floats for rafts. 2. A stopper for a bottle or other container. Corks can be made of cork, rubber, plastic, or glass. *Noun.*
○ To stop with a cork: *Cork the bottle. Verb.*
cork (kôrk) *noun, plural* **corks;** *verb,* **corked, corking.**

corkscrew A device for taking corks out of bottles. Corkscrews usually have a pointed metal spiral mounted in a handle. *Noun.*
○ Shaped like a corkscrew; spiral. *Adjective.*
corkscrew (kôrk′skrü′) *noun, plural* **corkscrews;** *adjective.*

corn 1. A grain that grows in rows on the ears of a tall plant. Corn is used for food and grows on a plant that is also called corn. corn (kôrn) *noun.*

corncob The long, woody core of an ear of corn. corn•cob (kôrn′kob′) *noun, plural* **corncobs.**

cornea The clear outer covering of the front of the eyeball. The cornea covers the iris and the pupil. cor•ne•a (kôr′nē ə) *noun, plural* **corneas.**

corner 1. The place or point where two lines or surfaces come together: *the corner of the table.* 2. The place where two streets come together: *There is a mailbox on the corner.* 3. A region or place, usually a distant one: *The company has offices in many corners of the world.* 4. A place or position that is dangerous or difficult: *The sudden storm put the hikers in a corner. Noun.*
○ At or near a corner: *the corner drugstore. Adjective.*
○ To force or drive into a dangerous or difficult

place or position: *The dog cornered the cat under the bed. Verb.*
cor•ner (kôr′nər) *noun, plural* **corners;** *adjective; verb,* **cornered, cornering.**

cornet A brass musical instrument like a trumpet. cor•net (kôr net′) *noun, plural* **cornets.**

cornmeal Corn that is coarsely ground. corn•meal (kôrn′mēl′) *noun.*

coronation The ceremony of crowning a king or queen. cor•o•na•tion (kôr′ə nā′shən) *noun, plural* **coronations.**

corporal 1. A rank in the army, air force, and marines. It is below the rank of sergeant. 2. Someone who holds this rank. cor•po•ral (kôr′pər əl *or* kôr′prəl) *noun, plural* **corporals.**

corporation An organization made up of a number of people who are allowed by law to act as a single person. A corporation has the right to buy and sell property, borrow and lend money, and enter into contracts. cor•po•ra•tion (kôr′pə rā′shən) *noun, plural* **corporations.**

corps 1. A group of soldiers trained for special service: *the medical corps.* 2. A group of persons who act or work together: *That restaurant has a large corps of waiters and waitresses.*
Another word that sounds like this is **core.**
corps (kôr) *noun, plural* **corps.**

corpse A dead human body. corpse (kôrps) *noun, plural* **corpses.**

corpuscle A small cell that is part of the blood. Red and white blood cells are corpuscles. cor•pus•cle (kôr′pus′əl) *noun, plural* **corpuscles.**

corral An area with a fence around it. A corral is used to keep cattle, horses, and other animals from straying. *Noun.*
○ 1. To drive or put into a corral: *The cowhands corralled the horses.* 2. To get control or hold of by surrounding or gathering: *We corralled all the sheep in the corner of the barnyard. Verb.*
cor•ral (kə ral′) *noun, plural* **corrals;** *verb,* **corralled, corralling.**

correct 1. Not having any mistakes; accurate: *the correct answer to the arithmetic problem.* 2. In agreement with an accepted or approved way or example; proper: *It is correct to thank people for gifts. Adjective.*
○ 1. To mark the mistakes in; change to make right: *The teacher corrected our tests.* 2. To make agree with some standard: *The doctor corrected*

my poor eyesight with glasses. **3.** To punish or scold in order to improve: *The parents corrected their child for behaving badly. Verb.*
cor·rect (kə rekt′) *adjective; verb,* **corrected, correcting.**

correction **1.** The act of correcting: *Correction of the car's steering took several hours.* **2.** A change made to correct an error: *I kept a list of the corrections I made in the report.* **3.** The act of punishing in order to improve: *Criminals are sent to prison for correction.* **cor·rec·tion** (kə rek′shən) *noun, plural* **corrections.**

correspond **1.** To agree; match: *Your answer to the question does not correspond with mine.* **2.** To be similar: *The gills of a fish correspond to the lungs of a human being.* **3.** To write letters to one another: *My friends corresponded with me when I was at camp.* **cor·re·spond** (kôr′ə spond′) *verb,* **corresponded, corresponding.**

correspondence **1.** Agreement or similarity: *The police found a close correspondence between the stories of the two witnesses.* **2.** The writing of letters to one another: *We kept up a correspondence for many years.* **3.** Letters sent or received. **cor·re·spon·dence** (kor′ə spon′dəns) *noun.*

correspondent **1.** A person who writes letters to someone and receives letters in return. **2.** A person who reports news: *a newspaper correspondent.* **cor·re·spon·dent** (kôr′əs pon′dənt) *noun, plural* **correspondents.**

corridor A long hallway or passageway. **cor·ri·dor** (kôr′i dər) *noun, plural* **corridors.**

corrode To eat or wear away, little by little: *Rust corroded the iron gate.* **cor·rode** (kə rōd′) *verb,* **corroded, corroding.**

corrosion **1.** The act or condition of being eaten away or worn away: *A leaking battery caused the corrosion of my flashlight.* **2.** Something produced by corrosion. **cor·ro·sion** (kə rō′zhən) *noun.*

corrugated Shaped into parallel ridges or folds; wrinkled. **cor·ru·gat·ed** (kôr′i gā′tid) *adjective.*

corrupt **1.** Able to be bribed; crooked; dishonest. **2.** Wicked. *Adjective.*
○ **1.** To cause to be dishonest: *That judge cannot be corrupted.* **2.** To make wicked: *Bad friends may corrupt a good person. Verb.*

cor·rupt (kə rupt′) *adjective; verb,* **corrupted, corrupting.** —**corruption** *noun.*

corsage A flower or small bunch of flowers worn usually by a woman at the shoulder or waist, or on the wrist. **cor·sage** (kôr säzh′) *noun, plural* **corsages.**

cosmetic A preparation used on the face, hair, or another part of the body. Lipstick and powder are cosmetics. **cos·met·ic** (koz met′ik) *noun, plural* **cosmetics.**

cosmic Of or relating to the whole universe. **cos·mic** (koz′mik) *adjective.*

cosmonaut A Russian astronaut. **cos·mo·naut** (koz′mə nôt′) *noun, plural* **cosmonauts.**

WORD HISTORY

The word cosmonaut comes from the Russian word meaning "astronaut." The Russian word comes from two Greek words meaning "universe" and "sailor." A cosmonaut is thought of as sailing through the universe.

---

cosmos The universe considered as an ordered and harmonious system. **cos·mos** (koz′məs) *noun, plural* **cosmos** *or* **cosmoses.**

cost **1.** An amount of money paid or charged for something; price. **2.** Something lost or sacrificed: *The war was won at the cost of many lives. Noun.*
○ **1.** To be gotten or bought at the price of: *The bicycle cost too much.* **2.** To cause the loss of: *The accident cost the dog its life. Verb.*
cost (kôst) *noun, plural* **costs;** *verb,* **cost, costing.**

Costa Rica A country in Central America. **Cos·ta Ri·ca** (kos′tə rē′kə).

costly Costing a lot. **cost·ly** (kôst′lē) *adjective,* **costlier, costliest.**

costume **1.** Clothes worn to look like someone or something else: *a clown costume.* **2.** Clothes worn at a particular

This young man is dressed in Native American **costume.**

time or place or by particular people: *I collect dolls dressed in the national* **costumes** *of different countries.* **cos•tume** (kos′tüm *or* kos′tūm) *noun, plural* **costumes.**

cot A narrow bed. **cot** (kot) *noun, plural* **cots.**

cottage A small house. **cot•tage** (kot′ij) *noun, plural* **cottages.**

cottage cheese A soft, white cheese made from sour skim milk.

cotton 1. A fluffy mass of soft white or gray fibers that grow in the large seed pod of a plant. Cotton is used to make thread or cloth. 2. Thread or cloth made from fibers of cotton. *Noun.*
○ Made of cotton: *cotton shirts. Adjective.*
cot•ton (kot′ən) *noun; adjective.*

cottonmouth A poisonous snake that lives in swamps in the southeastern United States; water moccasin. **cot•ton•mouth** (kot′ən mouth′) *noun, plural* **cottonmouths.**

cottontail An American rabbit with brown or grayish fur and a short, fluffy, white tail. **cot•ton•tail** (kot′ən tāl′) *noun, plural* **cottontails.**

couch A piece of furniture that two or more people can sit on at the same time. **couch** (kouch) *noun, plural* **couches.**

cougar A member of the cat family that has a small head, long legs, and a slender, strong body. Cougars live in the mountains of North and South America. **cou•gar** (kü′gər) *noun, plural* **cougars.**

A **cougar** is also called a puma and a mountain lion.

cough 1. To force air from the lungs with a sudden, sharp sound: *I had a cold and* **coughed** *all the time.* 2. To force out of the body by coughing: *The baby* **coughed** *up a piece of cookie.* 3. To make a noise like coughing: *The car* **coughed** *when I started it. Verb.*
○ 1. The sharp sound that is made when air is suddenly forced from the lungs. 2. A sickness that causes a person to cough. *Noun.*
cough (kôf) *verb,* **coughed, coughing;** *noun, plural* **coughs.**

could An auxiliary verb used in the following ways: 1. To express the past tense of **can**[1]: *I asked if I* **could** *leave.* 2. To say that something is possible: *It* **could** *rain today.* 3. To express ability: *Many countries* **could** *do more to reduce pollution.* 4. To make polite requests: *Could you help?* 5. To ask permission: *Could I borrow a dollar?*
6. To offer a suggestion: *You* **could** *start over and do it a different way.* **could** (kùd) *verb.*

couldn't Shortened form of "could not." **could•n't** (kùd′ənt) *contraction.*

council A group of people called together to discuss a problem or other matter. A group of people elected to make laws for or help run a city or town is called a city council or a town council. Another word that sounds like this is **counsel.** **coun•cil** (koun′səl) *noun, plural* **councils.**

counsel 1. Ideas or suggestions about what to do; advice: *A wise friend gives good* **counsel.** 2. A lawyer or lawyers who give legal advice. *Noun.*
○ To advise: *My folks* **counseled** *me to work harder. Verb.*
Another word that sounds like this is **council.** **coun•sel** (koun′səl) *noun, plural* **counsels;** *verb,* **counseled, counseling.**

counselor 1. A person who helps or gives advice: *a camp* **counselor.** 2. A lawyer. **coun•se•lor** (koun′sə lər) *noun, plural* **counselors.**

count[1] 1. To find out how many of something there are; add up. 2. To say or write down numbers in order: *Count to 100.* 3. To include or be included when things are added up: *There were forty people in the bus,* **counting** *the driver.* 4. To have importance; be worth something: *Try to make every day* **count.** 5. To believe to be; think of as: *Our teachers* **count** *us their best class.* 6. To depend; rely: *Can I* **count** *on you for help? Verb.*

○ **1.** The act of counting: *We made a **count** of the cows in the barn.* **2.** The number of things there are when you add them up; total. *Noun.*
count (kount) *verb,* **counted, counting;** *noun,* *plural* **counts.**

count² A European nobleman. **count** (kount) *noun, plural* **counts.**

countdown The counting of time backward from a certain time to zero. This tells how much time is left before the start of something, such as the launch of a spacecraft. **count·down** (kount′doun′) *noun, plural* **countdowns.**

counter- A prefix that means: **1.** Against; opposing; opposite: ***Counterclockwise** means in a direction opposite the one in which the hands of a clock move.* **2.** Similar; matching: ***Counterpart** means something that matches another thing.*

counter¹ **1.** A long table: *a restaurant **counter**.* **2.** Something used for counting. Some games have round, colored disks called counters to help keep score. **count·er** (koun′tər) *noun,* *plural* **counters.**

counter² Opposite: *They acted **counter** to instructions and wrote in pencil instead of ink. Adverb.*
○ Opposite: *Your idea is **counter** to mine. Adjective.*
○ To go against; *oppose: I'll **counter** your offer with another offer. Verb.*
count·er (koun′tər) *adverb; adjective; verb,* **countered, countering.**

counterclockwise In the direction opposite the one in which the hands of a clock move: *Turn a screw **counterclockwise** to take it out.*
coun·ter·clock·wise (koun′tər klok′wīz) *adverb; adjective.*

counterfeit To make a copy or imitation of something in order to cheat or fool people: *It is a crime to **counterfeit** money. Verb.*
○ A copy or imitation made in order to cheat or fool someone: *The twenty-dollar bill was a **counterfeit**. Noun.*
○ Not genuine: *It is a crime to make **counterfeit** money. Adjective.*
coun·ter·feit (koun′tər fit′) *verb,* **counterfeited, counterfeiting;** *noun, plural* **counterfeits;** *adjective.*

counterpart A person or thing very much like or equal to another: *The United States Congress is the **counterpart** of the Canadian Parliament.*
coun·ter·part (koun′tər pärt′) *noun, plural* **counterparts.**

countess A European noblewoman, usually the wife of a count. **count·ess** (koun′tis) *noun, plural* **countesses.**

countless Too many to be counted: *There are **countless** stars in the sky.* **count·less** (kount′lis) *adjective.*

country **1.** Any area of land; region: *mountain **country**.* **2.** An area of land that has boundaries, and a government shared by all the people; nation: *The United States and Canada are **countries**.* **3.** The land a person was born in or is a citizen of: *The U.S. is my **country**.* **4.** The people of a nation: *The whole **country** feared war.* **5.** The land outside of cities and towns: *a drive in the **country**. Noun.*
○ Having to do with land outside of cities or towns; rural: *a **country** road. Adjective.*
coun·try (kun′trē) *noun, plural* **countries;** *adjective.*

countryman **1.** A person born in or a citizen of one's own country. **2.** A person who lives in the country. **coun·try·man** (kun′trē mən) *noun, plural* **countrymen** (kun′trē mən).

Many people enjoy the countryside **because of its natural beauty.**

countryside The land outside cities and towns. **coun·try·side** (kun′trē sīd′) *noun.*

PRONUNCIATION KEY:
| at | āpe | fär | câre | end | mē | it | īce | pîerce | hot | ōld | sông | fôrk |
| oil | out | up | ūse | rüle | pull | tûrn | chin | sing | shop | thin | this | |

hw in white; zh in treasure. The symbol ə stands for the unstressed vowel sound in about, taken, pencil, lemon, and circus.

169

countrywoman 1. A woman born in or a citizen of one's own country. 2. A woman who lives in the country. **coun·try·wo·man** (kun′trē wům′ən) *noun, plural* **countrywomen** (kun′trē wim′ən).

county 1. One of the sections into which a state or country is divided. 2. The people living in a county. **coun·ty** (koun′tē) *noun, plural* **counties**.

couple 1. Two things that are the same or go together in some way; pair. 2. A man and woman who are together: *a married* **couple**. *Noun*. ○ To join together: *They* **coupled** *the trailer to the car. Verb*. **cou·ple** (kup′əl) *noun, plural* **couples**; *verb*, **coupled, coupling**.

coupon A ticket or part of a ticket: *The* **coupon** *in the box of cereal was worth ten cents toward the price of the next box.* **cou·pon** (kü′pon *or* kū′pon) *noun, plural* **coupons**.

courage The strength to overcome fear and face danger; bravery. **cour·age** (kûr′ij) *noun.*

courageous Brave: *courageous firefighters*. **cou·ra·geous** (kə rā′jəs) *adjective*.

course 1. A moving onward from one point to the next; progress: *I grew four inches in the* **course** *of a year*. 2. A way; route; track: *The airplane flew off its* **course**. 3. A way of acting: *The most sensible* **course** *is to go home before it rains*. 4. An area used for certain sports or games: *a race* **course**. 5. A series of classes or lessons: *a* **course** *in cooking*. 6. A part of a meal served at one time: *Our first* **course** *was soup. Noun*. ○ To move very quickly; run; flow: *The stream* **coursed** *down the hill. Verb*. Another word that sounds like this is **coarse**.
 • **of course**. 1. Certainly; surely: *Of* **course** *I'll help you*. 2. As is or was expected; naturally: *The rain started so of* **course** *we went inside*. **course** (kôrs) *noun, plural* **courses**; *verb*, **coursed, coursing**.

court 1. An open space surrounded by walls or buildings; courtyard. 2. A short street. 3. A space or area marked off for certain games: *a basketball* **court**. 4. The place where a king or queen and his or her attendants live. 5. The family, friends, and advisers of a king or queen. 6. An official gathering headed by a judge or judges. A court hears legal cases and decides them. 7. A room or building where trials are held or where other matters are decided by law. *Noun.*
○ 1. To try to win the favor or love of a person. 2. To act in a way that invites; tempt: *Driving a car too fast* **courts** *disaster. Verb*. **court** (kôrt) *noun, plural* **courts**; *verb*, **courted, courting**.

courteous Polite: *"Thank You" is a* **courteous** *reply*. **cour·te·ous** (kûr′tē əs) *adjective*; **cour·te·ous·ly** *adverb*.

courtesy 1. A way of behaving that shows good manners and thoughtfulness toward other people; politeness. 2. A courteous act; favor. **cour·te·sy** (kûr′tə sē) *noun, plural* **courtesies**.

courthouse 1. A building in which courts of law are held. 2. A building in which the offices of a county government are located. **court·house** (kôrt′hous′) *noun, plural* **courthouses** (kôrt′hou′ziz).

courtyard An open area surrounded by walls or buildings. **court·yard** (kôrt′yärd′) *noun, plural* **courtyards**.

cousin The son or daughter of an aunt or uncle. First cousins have the same grandparents; second cousins have the same great-grandparents. **cou·sin** (kuz′in) *noun, plural* **cousins**.

cove A small, sheltered bay or inlet. **cove** (kōv) *noun, plural* **coves**.

cover 1. To put something over or on: *Cover the baby with a blanket*. 2. To hide: *Grass* **covered** *the old path*. 3. To travel over: *I* **covered** *that distance in five minutes*. 4. To deal with; include: *That magazine* **covers** *sports. Verb*. ○ 1. Something put on or over something else: *Put a* **cover** *on the pot*. 2. Something that hides or protects: *Owls hunt under the* **cover** *of darkness. Noun*. **cov·er** (kuv′ər) *verb*, **covered, covering**; *noun, plural* **covers**.

From a distance, covered wagons looked like ships and were sometimes called "prairie schooners."

covered wagon A large wagon with a canvas top spread over hoops.

covering Anything that covers: *A rug is a covering for a floor.* **cov·er·ing** (kuv′ər ing) *noun, plural* **coverings**.

covet To want something very much or with a feeling of envy: *The loser coveted the winner's prize.* **cov·et** (kuv′it) *verb*, **coveted, coveting**.

cow 1. The fully grown female of cattle. 2. The female of other large mammals. A female moose, elephant, or whale is called a cow. **cow** (kou) *noun, plural* **cows**.

coward A person lacking courage or afraid of anything dangerous or hard to do. **cow·ard** (kou′ərd) *noun, plural* **cowards**.

cowardice Complete lack of courage. **cow·ar·dice** (kou′ər dis′) *noun*.

cowardly Lacking courage. **cow·ard·ly** (kou′ərd lē) *adjective*.

cowboy A man who herds and takes care of cattle on a ranch. **cow·boy** (kou′boi′) *noun, plural* **cowboys**.

Cowboys **are skilled horsemen.**

cowgirl A woman who herds and takes care of cattle on a ranch. **cow·girl** (kou′gûrl′) *noun, plural* **cowgirls**.

cowhand A person who works on a cattle ranch; cowboy or cowgirl. **cow·hand** (kou′hand′) *noun, plural* **cowhands**.

cowhide 1. The hide of a cow. 2. Leather made from the hide of a cow. **cow·hide** (kou′hīd′) *noun, plural* **cowhides**.

coworker A person who works with others at the same place or on the same project; colleague; fellow worker. **co·work·er** (kō′wûr′kər) *noun, plural* **coworkers**.

coyote A North American animal that looks like a small, thin wolf. Coyotes are closely related to wolves, foxes, and dogs. **coy·o·te** (kī ō′tē *or* kī′ōt) *noun, plural* **coyotes** *or* **coyote**.

A coyote **can run at speeds up to 40 miles per hour.**

cozy Warm and comfortable; snug. **co·zy** (kō′zē) *adjective*, **cozier, coziest**.

CPR A method of reviving heart attack victims by mouth-to-mouth breathing and strong rhythmic pressing down on the chest. **CPR** *noun*.

crab An animal that lives in the water and is covered by a hard shell. Crabs have a wide, flat body, four pairs of legs, and a pair of claws. Many kinds of crabs are used for food. **crab** (krab) *noun, plural* **crabs**.

crab apple A small, hard, sour apple that can be used to make jelly.

crack 1. A break or narrow opening between the parts of something. A crack does not make a thing fall into parts: *The window has a crack in it.* 2. A sudden, sharp noise like that made by something breaking. 3. A sharp, hard blow: *The swinging door gave me a crack on the head.* *Noun.*

○ 1. To break without coming completely apart; split. 2. To break with a sharp, sudden noise: *The chair cracked loudly under the elephant's foot.* 3. To make a sudden, sharp noise: *The cowhand cracked the whip.* 4. To hit with a sharp, hard blow: *I cracked my head on the door.* *Verb.*

PRONUNCIATION KEY:

| at | āpe | fär | câre | end | mē | it | īce | pîerce | hot | ōld | sông | fôrk |
| oil | out | up | ūse | rüle | pull | tûrn | chin | sing | shop | thin | this | |

hw in white; zh in treasure. The symbol ə stands for the unstressed vowel sound in about, taken, pencil, lemon, and circus.

171

• to crack down. To become strict or harsh in enforcing laws or regulations.
crack (krak) *noun, plural* **cracks;** *verb,* **cracked, cracking.**

cracker A thin, crisp biscuit. **crack·er** (krak′ər) *noun, plural* **crackers.**

crackle To make slight, sharp snapping sounds: *Dry leaves crackle when you walk on them. Verb.*
○ A slight, sharp, snapping sound. *Noun.*
crack·le (krak′əl) *verb,* **crackled, crackling;** *noun, plural* **crackles.**

cradle 1. A small bed for a baby, often on rockers. 2. The place where something starts or begins to grow: *Philadelphia is the cradle of American independence.* 3. Anything like a cradle in shape or use. A box on rockers used to wash gold from earth is a cradle. The part of a phone that holds the receiver is called a cradle. *Noun.*
○ To put or hold in a cradle or as if in a cradle: *The students cradled their books in their arms. Verb.*
cra·dle (krā′dəl) *noun, plural* **cradles;** *verb,* **cradled, cradling.**

craft 1. A special skill a person has: *The chair was carved with great craft.* 2. A trade or work that needs special skill: *Woodworking is a craft that takes years to master.* 3. Skill in deceiving people; cunning: *The magician showed great craft in making things disappear.* 4. A boat or airplane: *The harbor is filled with sailing craft.* **craft** (kraft) *noun, plural* **crafts** (*for definition 2*) or **craft** (*for definition 4*).

craftsman A person with a special skill in making or doing something; artisan. **crafts·man** (krafts′mən) *noun, plural* **craftsmen** (krafts′mən).

crafty Skillful or clever in deceiving; sly; cunning: *The crafty photographer took my picture when I didn't expect it.* **craft·y** (kraf′tē) *adjective,* **craftier, craftiest.**

crag A steep, rugged rock or cliff. **crag** (krag) *noun, plural* **crags.**

cram 1. To force or crowd into a tight or crowded space: *I crammed another doughnut into my mouth.* 2. To fill completely or with more than is normally or easily held: *The elevator was crammed with people.* 3. To study hastily and intensely: *We crammed all night for the test.* **cram** (kram) *verb,* **crammed, cramming.**

cramp¹ 1. A sharp pain in a muscle that suddenly

gets tight: *I have a cramp in my leg.* 2. **cramps.** Sharp pains in the abdomen. *Noun.*
○ To cause a sharp pain in a muscle: *Holding the pencil tightly cramped my hand. Verb.*
cramp (kramp) *noun, plural* **cramps;** *verb,* **cramped, cramping.**

cramp² To limit; confine: *Space on the boat was cramped.* **cramp** (kramp) *verb,* **cramped, cramping.**

Cranberries are often an important part of a Thanksgiving meal.

cranberry A sour, red berry that grows on low bushes in bogs and swamps. **cran·ber·ry** (kran′ber′ē) *noun, plural* **cranberries.**

crane 1. A large bird with thin, very long legs and a long neck and bill. 2. A large machine with a long arm that can be moved up and down and in a circle. Cables at the end of the crane's arm are used to lift and move heavy objects. *Noun.*
○ To stretch out the neck in order to see better: *The people in back of the crowd craned to see the parade. Verb.*
crane (krān) *noun, plural* **cranes;** *verb,* **craned, craning.**

These cranes are lifting huge coils of wire.

crank 1. A part of a machine with a handle attached to a rod. When the handle is turned, the rod turns with it and makes the machine work. 2. A person with strange ideas: *An inventor with a new idea may seem to be a crank.* 3. A person who is always grouchy or cross. *Noun.*
○ To turn a crank so that something will work. *Verb.*
crank (krangk) *noun, plural* **cranks**; *verb,* **cranked, cranking.**

cranky Cross or in a bad temper; irritable; grouchy. **crank·y** (krang′kē) *adjective,* **crankier, crankiest. —crankiness** *noun.*

crash 1. A sudden, loud noise like something breaking or smashing. 2. A violent collision: *a terrible plane crash.* 3. A sudden ruin or failure in business: *A lot of money was lost in the stock market crash.* 4. A serious failure of a computer to work properly. *Noun.*
○ 1. To make a sudden, loud noise: *The lamp crashed to the floor.* 2. To collide or cause to collide violently: *The car crashed into a wall.* 3. To move or push forward with noise and strong force: *The cows crashed through the fence.* 4. To enter without being asked or having a ticket: *Strangers crashed my party.* 5. To fail to work properly or at all: *My computer crashed and I lost my work. Verb.*
crash (krash) *noun, plural* **crashes**; *verb,* **crashed, crashing.**

crate A box made of slats of wood. *Noun.*
○ To pack in a crate or crates: *The farmer crated the lettuce. Verb.*
crate (krāt) *noun, plural* **crates**; *verb,* **crated, crating.**

Most of the craters on the moon were made by meteor impacts.

crater A hollow area that looks like the inside of a bowl. **cra·ter** (krā′tər) *noun, plural* **craters.**

crave To long or yearn for; desire eagerly: *I crave a sunny day after all this rain.* **crave** (krāv) *verb,* **craved, craving.**

crawl 1. To move very slowly: *Babies crawl by moving on their hands and knees.* 2. To be covered or feel as if covered with crawling things: *a picnic table crawling with ants. Verb.*
○ 1. A very slow movement: *Traffic slowed to a crawl in the fog.* 2. A fast swimming stroke. When you do the crawl, your face is down, and you lift your arms over your head one after the other while you kick your feet. *Noun.*
crawl (krôl) *verb,* **crawled, crawling**; *noun, plural* **crawls.**

crayfish An animal that looks like a small lobster and lives in fresh water. **cray·fish** (krā′fish′) *noun, plural* **crayfish** or **crayfishes.**

crayon A colored stick made of a wax material used for drawing or writing. *Noun.*
○ To use crayons to draw or color. *Verb.*
cray·on (krā′on *or* krā′ən) *noun, plural* **crayons**; *verb,* **crayoned, crayoning.**

crazy 1. Having a mind that is sick; insane; mentally ill. 2. Foolish. 3. Very enthusiastic: *crazy about fishing.* **cra·zy** (krā′zē) *adjective,* **crazier, craziest.**

creak To make a sharp, squeaking sound: *The old stairs creak. Verb.*
○ A sharp, squeaking sound. *Noun.*
Another word that sounds like this is **creek.**
creak (krēk) *verb,* **creaked, creaking**; *noun, plural* **creaks.**

cream 1. The yellowish white part of milk. Cream has fat in it and is thicker than milk. Butter is made from cream. 2. A food like or made from cream: *cream of mushroom soup.* 3. A soft, thick lotion or foam for the skin: *hand cream.* 4. The best part of something: *The cream of society was at the party. Noun.*
○ To stir or mix until smooth like cream. *Verb.*
cream (krēm) *noun, plural* **creams**; *verb,* **creamed, creaming.**

creamy 1. Containing cream: *creamy soup.* 2. Having the texture or color of cream: *creamy gravy.* **cream·y** (krē′mē) *adjective,* **creamier, creamiest.**

PRONUNCIATION KEY:
at āpe fär câre end mē it īce pierce hot ōld sông fôrk
oil out up ūse rüle pull tûrn chin sing shop thin this
hw in white; zh in treasure. The symbol ə stands for the unstressed vowel sound in about, taken, pencil, lemon, and circus.

173

crease   A line or mark made by folding or wrinkling something: *a crease in my slacks. Noun.*
○ To make or get a line or mark in by folding or wrinkling. *Verb.*
crease (krēs) *noun, plural* **creases;** *verb,* **creased, creasing.**

create   To cause something to exist or happen: *The author created some fantastic characters in her novel.* **cre•ate** (krē āt′) *verb,* **created, creating.**

creation   1. The act of causing something to exist or happen: *Creation of the motion picture took many months.* 2. Something created: *The statue was a marvelous creation.* 3. The world and everything in it. **cre•a•tion** (krē ā′shən) *noun, plural* **creations.**

creative   Having or showing ability to make or do something in a new way: *a creative playwright.* **cre•a•tive** (krē ā′tiv) *adjective.*

creator   1. A person who makes something. 2. the Creator. God. **cre•a•tor** (krē ā′tər) *noun, plural* **creators.**

creature   A living person or animal: *Deer, bears, and wolves are creatures of the forest.* **crea•ture** (krē′chər) *noun, plural* **creatures.**

credit   1. Belief in the truth of something; faith: *Nobody gave credit to the story.* 2. Reputation: *She is a citizen of great credit in our town.* 3. Praise or honor: *The cook deserves credit for the dinner.* 4. Trust in a person to pay a debt later: *Stores give me credit.* 5. Something owed to a person: *I have a twenty-five-dollar credit at that store. Noun.*
○ 1. To believe; trust: *I credit the story of an honest person.* 2. To put an amount of money owed to someone into an account for that person: *The store credited our account with ten dollars when we returned the shirt. Verb.*
cred•it (kred′it) *noun, plural* **credits;** *verb,* **credited, crediting.**

credit card   A card from a bank or a store that gives a customer the right to buy things and pay for them later.

creditor   A person or institution to whom a debt is owed: *The business promptly paid the bills it received from creditors.* **cred•i•tor** (kred′i tər) *noun, plural* **creditors.**

creed   A statement of what a person or group of people believes in: *"Always be honest" is part of my creed.* **creed** (krēd) *noun, plural* **creeds.**

creek   A small stream.
Another word that sounds like this is **creak**.
creek (krēk *or* krik) *noun, plural* **creeks.**

A **creek** is bigger than a brook but smaller than a river.

creep   1. To move slowly and quietly; crawl: *A baby creeps on hands and knees.* 2. To grow along the ground or over a surface: *The ivy creeps over the fence.* 3. To feel as if things were crawling over one's skin: *The ghost story made my flesh creep. Verb.*
○ 1. The act or condition of moving slowly: *Traffic slowed to a creep.* 2. the creeps. A feeling as if things were crawling over the skin: *The mask gave me the creeps. Noun.*
creep (krēp) *verb,* **crept, creeping;** *noun, plural* **creeps.**

crepe   1. A cloth with a crinkled surface. 2. A thin, light pancake. **crepe** (krāp) *noun, plural* **crepes.**

crepe paper   A thin paper with a crinkled surface.

crept   Past tense and past participle of **creep**. **crept** (krept) *verb.*

crescent   1. The shape the moon has when you can only see a thin, curved part of it. 2. Something shaped like the crescent moon. *Noun.*
○ Shaped like the crescent moon. *Adjective.*
cres•cent (kres′ənt) *noun, plural* **crescents;** *adjective.*

crest   1. A tuft of longer feathers on the head of a bird: *A blue jay has a crest on its head.* 2. A plume or other decoration on the top of a helmet. 3. The highest part of something: *the crest of the hill.* 4. A decoration above a coat of arms. **crest** (krest) *noun, plural* **crests.**

crew   A group of people who work together. The people who work on and run a ship, airplane, or train are called the crew. **crew** (krü) *noun, plural* **crews.**

Racing **crews** learn to row
in unison.

crib 1. A small bed for a baby. 2. A box or trough that holds food for cattle and horses to eat from. 3. A small farm building or bin in which grain or corn is kept. **crib** (krib) *noun, plural* **cribs.**

cricket[1] A black or brown insect that hops and looks like a short grasshopper. **crick·et** (krik′it) *noun, plural* **crickets.**

cricket[2] An English game like baseball, played with a ball and bats on a grass field. **crick·et** (krik′it) *noun.*

cried Past tense and past participle of **cry.** **cried** (krīd) *verb.*

crime 1. Anything against the law. Robbery is a crime. 2. Anything that seems wrong or foolish: *It's a crime to waste food when other people are starving.* **crime** (krīm) *noun, plural* **crimes.**

criminal A person who commits a crime: *The robber was a criminal and was sent to prison. Noun.* ○ Having to do with crime or the laws about crime: *a criminal lawyer. Adjective.* **crim·i·nal** (krim′ə nəl) *noun, plural* **criminals;** *adjective.*

crimson A deep red color. *Noun.* ○ Having the color crimson. *Adjective.* **crim·son** (krim′zən) *noun, plural* **crimsons;** *adjective.*

crinkle 1. To form or cause to form wrinkles or ripples; wrinkle; crumple: *The paper crinkled in the fire and then burst into flame.* 2. To make or cause to make a rustling or crackling sound: *I crinkled the paper to catch the kitten's attention.* **crin·kle** (kring′kəl) *verb,* **crinkled, crinkling.**

cripple A person or animal that cannot move some part of the body in the usual way because of an injury or a disease. *Noun.* ○ 1. To badly injure a person or animal: *A car accident crippled him.* 2. To damage something or affect it so that it cannot work properly: *The snowstorm crippled the airport for several days. Verb.* **crip·ple** (krip′əl) *noun, plural* **cripples;** *verb,* **crippled, crippling.**

crisis 1. An important turning point that helps decide if things will get better or worse: *Having to decide whether or not to go to college was the first real crisis in my life.* 2. A difficult or dangerous situation: *The sudden death of the prime minister caused a crisis in that country.* **cri·sis** (krī′sis) *noun, plural* **crises** (krī′sēz).

crisp 1. Hard or firm but breaking easily into pieces: *Fresh celery should be crisp.* 2. Clear and cool; brisk: *a crisp autumn day.* 3. Short and to the point: *Mom gave me a crisp answer. Adjective.* **crisp** (krisp) *adjective,* **crisper, crispest.**

crisscross Marked with lines that cross one another. *Adjective.* ○ A design made by crossing lines. *Noun.* ○ 1. To mark with or make lines that cross one another: *Footprints crisscrossed in the snow.* 2. To go across back and forth: *We crisscrossed the neighborhood to find our dog. Verb.* **criss·cross** (kris′krôs′) *adjective; noun, plural* **crisscrosses;** *verb,* **crisscrossed, crisscrossing.**

The crust on top of the pie is made in a **crisscross** pattern.

critic 1. A person whose job is to say or write an opinion about what is good or bad about books, motion pictures, music, art, or plays. 2. A person who finds something wrong: *Don't be a critic; say something nice about the house.* **crit·ic** (krit′ik) *noun, plural* **critics.**

PRONUNCIATION KEY:
at   āpe   fär   câre   end   mē   it   īce   pîerce   hot   ōld   sông   fôrk
oil   out   up   ūse   rüle   pull   tûrn   chin   sing   shop   thin   this
hw in white; zh in treasure. The symbol ə stands for the unstressed vowel sound in about, taken, pencil, lemon, and circus.

175

critical 1. Finding something wrong with things: *You are **critical** of every plan we suggest.* 2. Having to do with a person whose job is to be a critic: *a **critical** review of a new book.* 3. Having to do with a crisis; dangerous; serious: *a **critical** shortage of water.* **crit·i·cal** (krit′i kəl) *adjective.*

criticism 1. The act of saying what is good or bad about something. **crit·i·cism** (krit′ə siz′əm) *noun, plural* **criticisms.**

criticize To find fault with something: *Don't always **criticize** the way I sing!* **crit·i·cize** (krit′ə sīz′) *verb,* **criticized, criticizing.**

croak A deep, hoarse sound like one made by a frog. *Noun.*
○ To make such a sound. *Verb.*
croak (krōk) *noun, plural* **croaks;** *verb,* **croaked, croaking.**

crochet To make something by looping thread or yarn into connected stitches with a needle that has a hook at one end. **cro·chet** (krō shā′) *verb,* **crocheted, crocheting.**

crocodile A long animal with short legs, thick, scaly skin, and a long, strong tail. Crocodiles are reptiles closely related to alligators. Look up **alligator** for more information. **croc·o·dile** (krok′ə dīl′) *noun, plural* **crocodiles.**

crocus A small flower that grows from an underground bulb. Crocuses can be purple, white, or yellow and have thin leaves like blades of grass. **cro·cus** (krō′kəs) *noun, plural* **crocuses.**

crook 1. A bent part; curve. 2. A shepherd's staff with a hook at the top. 3. A dishonest person. *Noun.*
○ To bend; curve; hook: *The clerk **crooked** a finger at us to tell us to come over. Verb.*
crook (krŭk) *noun, plural* **crooks;** *verb,* **crooked, crooking.**

crooked 1. Not straight; bent or curving. 2. Not honest. **crook·ed** (krŭk′id) *adjective;*

crop 1. Plants grown to be used as food or sold for profit. 2. The total amount of a plant grown as a crop that is gathered; harvest: *a huge **crop** of tomatoes.* 3. A group of persons or things that come at the same time: *a big **crop** of new students this fall.* 4. A pouch near the bottom of the throat of a bird. Food is held in the crop and is prepared for digestion. 5. A short whip. *Noun.*
○ To cut or bite off the top part of something:

*The deer **cropped** the bushes. Verb.*
• **to crop up.** To arise or appear: *Problems always **crop up** in a project like this.*
crop (krop) *noun, plural* **crops;** *verb,* **cropped, cropping.**

Cotton is a crop widely grown in the southern United States.

croquet An outdoor game played with sticks called mallets that are used to hit wooden balls along the ground and through wire hoops called wickets. **cro·quet** (krō kā′) *noun.*

cross 1. A post or stake with a bar across it. The cross is the symbol of Christianity. 2. Anything shaped like a cross. 3. Any difficulty or suffering: *He bore the **cross** of the illness without complaining.* 4. A mixing of animals or plants of different kinds: *A mule is a **cross** between a horse and a donkey. Noun.*
○ 1. To move or go from one side of something to the other: *We **crossed** the street.* 2. To go across and divide; lie across: *Main Street **crosses** Maple Street.* 3. To draw a line across or through: *You **cross** a "t" in writing.* 4. To put or lay one thing across another: *I **crossed** my legs when I sat down.* 5. To pass while going in different directions: *Our letters **crossed** in the mail.* 6. To go against; oppose: *I don't like to be **crossed**.* 7. To mix plants or animals of different kinds in order to get a new kind: *A horse **crossed** with a donkey will give birth to a mule. Verb.*
○ Grouchy. *Adjective.*
cross (krôs) *noun, plural* **crosses;** *verb,* **crossed, crossing;** *adjective,* **crosser, crossest.**

crossbow A weapon used in the Middle Ages that had a bow mounted across a wooden stock. **cross·bow** (krôs′bō′) *noun, plural* **crossbows.**

cross-eyed Having one or both eyes turned inward toward the nose. **cross-eyed** (krôs′īd′) *adjective.*

crossing 1. A place where two lines or other things cross each other: *a railroad crossing.* 2. A place where a street or river may be crossed. **cros·sing** (krô′sing) *noun, plural* **crossings.**

cross-reference A reference from one part of a book or index to another part, pointing out where more information can be found: *Under the entry crocodile there is a cross-reference to the entry for alligator.* **cross-ref·er·ence** (krôs′ref′ər əns) *noun, plural* **cross-references.**

crossroad 1. A road that crosses another one or that leads from one main road to another. 2. crossroads. The place where two or more roads cross each other. **cross·road** (krôs′rōd′) *noun, plural* **crossroads.**

cross section 1. A slice or piece made by cutting straight across something. When you cut an orange through the middle you make cross sections. 2. A sample of people or things thought to show what the whole group of people or things is like.

crosswalk A path marked off for use by pedestrians in crossing a street. **cross·walk** (krôs′wôk′) *noun, plural* **crosswalks.**

crossword puzzle A puzzle that has a pattern of squares that a person fills with words or phrases, putting one letter in each square. **cross·word puz·zle** (krôs′ wûrd′).

crotch The place where the body divides into two legs, or where a branch of a tree grows out from the trunk or from another branch. **crotch** (kroch) *noun, plural* **crotches.**

crouch To stoop or bend low with the knees bent. *Verb.*
◦ The act or position of crouching: *I got into a crouch to hide. Noun.*
crouch (krouch) *verb,* **crouched, crouching;** *noun, plural* **crouches.**

croup A children's disease of the throat and windpipe that causes difficulty in breathing and a barking cough. **croup** (krüp) *noun.*

crow¹ 1. To make the loud, sharp cry of a rooster. 2. To make a happy yell or cry: *The fans crowed with delight when we scored the first goal. Verb.*

◦ The loud, shrill cry of a rooster. *Noun.*
crow (krō) *verb,* **crowed, crowing;** *noun, plural* **crows.**

crow² A large bird with shiny black feathers and a harsh cry. **crow** (krō) *noun, plural* **crows.**

Crows are found in many parts of the United States.

crowbar A heavy steel or iron bar with one flattened end, used to lift things up or pry things apart. **crow·bar** (krō′bär′) *noun, plural* **crowbars.**

crowd A lot of people gathered together: *a crowd of people at the theater. Noun.*
◦ 1. To fill too full: *I crowded the shelf with books.* 2. To gather closely or in large numbers: *We crowded around the table.* 3. To move by pushing or shoving: *Quit crowding me. Verb.*
crowd (kroud) *noun, plural* **crowds;** *verb,* **crowded, crowding.**

crown 1. A covering for the head worn by kings and queens, often made of gold and silver set with jewels. 2. A king or queen; government headed by a king or queen: *The crown was overthrown by a revolution.* 3. A wreath or band worn on the head. 4. The highest or top part of anything: *the crown of a hat.* 5. The part of a tooth that can be seen above the gums or a substitute for this part. *Noun.*
◦ 1. To make a person a king or queen at a special ceremony during which a crown is put on his or her head. 2. To declare officially to be: *The boxer was crowned champion.* 3. To be on the

PRONUNCIATION KEY:

| at | āpe | fär | câre | end | mē | it | īce | pierce | hot | ōld | sông | fôrk |
| oil | out | up | ūse | rüle | pull | tûrn | chin | sing | shop | thin | this | |

hw in white; zh in treasure. The symbol ə stands for the unstressed vowel sound in about, taken, pencil, lemon, and circus.

177

top of: *The state flag **crowned** the office building. Verb.*

crown (kroun) *noun, plural* **crowns;** *verb,* **crowned, crowning.**

crow's-nest A small platform near the top of a ship's mast. **crow's-nest** (krōz′nest′) *noun, plural* **crow's-nests.**

crucial Very important; decisive: *a crucial test.* **cru·cial** (krü′shəl) *adjective.*

crude 1. In a natural or raw state: *Crude oil is oil as it is pumped from the ground.* 2. Done or made without skill; rough: *a crude shack.* 3. Lacking good manners or taste; not refined; rude. **crude** (krüd) *adjective,* **cruder, crudest.**

cruel 1. Willing to cause pain or suffering: *It is cruel to beat a dog.* 2. *Causing pain or suffering: a cruel, cold wind.* **cru·el** (krü′əl) *adjective,* **crueler, cruelest.**

cruelty 1. The causing of pain or suffering to others on purpose. 2. A cruel act: *The soldiers suffered many cruelties in the enemy prison camp.* **cru·el·ty** (krü′əl tē) *noun, plural* **cruelties.**

cruise 1. To sail from place to place: *The sailboat cruised along the coast.* 2. To move or ride from place to place: *A police car cruises through our neighborhood each night. Verb.*
○ A trip in a boat taken for pleasure: *a cruise to Hawaii. Noun.*
cruise (krüz) *verb,* **cruised, cruising;** *noun, plural* **cruises.**

cruiser 1. A warship faster than a battleship and carrying fewer guns. 2. A motorboat with a cabin that has space for cooking and sleeping. 3. A police car that patrols the streets. **cruis·er** (krü′zər) *noun, plural* **cruisers.**

From the crow's-nest a sailor can see a long distance.

In World War II a cruiser like this helped the United States Navy win many victories.

crumb A tiny piece of bread, cake, cracker, or cookie. **crumb** (krum) *noun, plural* **crumbs.**

crumble 1. To break into small pieces. 2. To fall apart or be destroyed: *The old house is slowly crumbling.* **crum·ble** (krum′bəl) *verb,* **crumbled, crumbling.**

crumple 1. To press or crush into wrinkles or folds. 2. To fall down or collapse: *The old shack crumpled when the bulldozer rammed it.* **crum·ple** (krum′pəl) *verb,* **crumpled, crumpling.**

crunch To chew or crush with a noisy, crackling sound: *The thin ice crunched under my shoes. Verb.*
○ A crushing, crackling sound. *Noun.*
crunch (krunch) *verb,* **crunched, crunching;** *noun, plural* **crunches.**

crusade 1. Any of the military expeditions undertaken by the Christian people of Europe between the years 1095 and 1291 to take Palestine away from the Muslims. 2. A strong fight against something evil or for something good: *a crusade to clean up the town parks. Noun.*
○ To fight in a crusade: *Our senator is crusading against pollution. Verb.*
cru·sade (krü sād′) *noun, plural* **crusades;** *verb,* **crusaded, crusading.** —**crusad·er** *noun.*

crush 1. To squeeze very hard: *The garbage can was crushed when the truck ran over it.* 2. To press into wrinkles; crumple: *The dress was crushed because it was poorly packed.* 3. To put down; subdue: *Our hopes of going to the circus were crushed when we couldn't get tickets. Verb.*
○ 1. A very strong pressure or squeezing: *The crush of the crowd pushed the student against the*

door of the gym. **2.** A sudden, strong liking for a person: *a crush on a movie star. Noun.*
crush (krush) *verb,* **crushed, crushing;** *noun, plural* **crushes.**

crust 1. The hard, crisp outside part of bread, rolls, or other food. **2.** Any hard outside part or coating: *The crust of the earth is a layer of rock 20 miles deep. Noun.*
○ To cover or become covered with a crust: *Ice crusted the pond. Verb.*
crust (krust) *noun, plural* **crusts;** *verb,* **crusted, crusting.**

crustacean An animal that has a hard shell and lives mostly in water. Lobsters, crabs, shrimp, and barnacles are crustaceans. **crus•ta•cean** (kru stā′shən) *noun, plural* **crustaceans.**

The crab is one of the most common
crustaceans.

crutch A support that helps a lame person in walking. A crutch is a pole that usually has a padded part at the top that fits under the arm so a person can lean on it. **crutch** (kruch) *noun, plural* **crutches.**

cry 1. To shed tears; weep. **2.** To call loudly; shout: *The people in the burning building cried for help.* **3.** To utter a special sound, as a bird or other animal does: *The gulls cried to each other. Verb.*
○ **1.** A loud call or shout. **2.** A fit of weeping: *I had a long cry when I learned that we had to move.* **3.** The special sound that an animal makes: *the cry of a loon. Noun.*
cry (krī) *verb,* **cried, crying;** *noun, plural* **cries.**

crystal 1. A clear kind of rock. Quartz is a kind of crystal. **2.** A body formed by certain substances when they change into a solid. Crystals have flat surfaces and a regular shape. Salt forms in crystals. Snowflakes are crystals. **3.** A very fine, clear glass. **4.** The transparent covering that protects the face of a watch. *Noun.*
○ **1.** Made of crystal: *a crystal bowl.* **2.** Like crystal; clear: *crystal water. Adjective.*
crys•tal (kris′təl) *noun, plural* **crystals;** *adjective.*

crystallize To form into crystals. **crys•tal•lize** (kris′tə līz′) *verb,* **crystallized, crystallizing.**

CT Postal abbreviation for **Connecticut.**

cu. An abbreviation for **cubic.**

cub A very young bear, wolf, lion, or tiger. **cub** (kub) *noun, plural* **cubs.**

Cuba An island country in the Caribbean Sea. **Cu•ba** (kū′bə) *noun.*

Cuban A person born in or a citizen of Cuba. *Noun.*
○ Of or having to do with Cuba or its people. *Adjective.*
Cu•ban (kū′bən) *noun, plural* **Cubans;** *adjective.*

cube 1. A solid figure with six equal, square sides. **2.** Something shaped like a cube: *ice cubes.* **3.** The product of a number multiplied by itself twice: *The cube of 2 is 8 because 2 x 2 x 2 = 8. Noun.*
○ **1.** To cut or make into cubes: *Cube some potatoes.* **2.** To multiply a number by itself twice. *Verb.*
cube (kūb) *noun, plural* **cubes;** *verb,* **cubed, cubing.**

cubic 1. Shaped like a cube: *These building blocks are cubic.* **2.** Describing or measuring length, width, and thickness. The volume of an object is given in cubic measures, such as cubic inches or cubic feet. **cu•bic** (kū′bik) *adjective.*

cub scout A boy who is a junior member of the Boy Scouts.

cuckoo A bird with a long tail and a call that sounds like its name. **cuck•oo** (kü′kü *or* kúk′ü) *noun, plural* **cuckoos.**

cucumber A long, green vegetable with white flesh and many seeds inside. The cucumber grows on a vine. **cu•cum•ber** (kū′kum bər) *noun, plural* **cucumbers.**

cud Food that comes back into the mouth from the first stomach of cows, sheep, and other animals so that they can chew it again. **cud** (kud) *noun, plural* **cuds.**

PRONUNCIATION KEY:												
at	āpe	fär	câre	end	mē	it	īce	pierce	hot	ōld	sông	fôrk
oil	out	up	ūse	rüle	pull	tûrn	chin	sing	shop	thin	this	

hw in white; zh in treasure. The symbol ə stands for the unstressed vowel sound in about, taken, pencil, lemon, and circus.

179

cuddle 1. To hold close in one's arms; hold tenderly: *cuddling a baby.* 2. To lie close and snug: *They cuddled together for warmth.* **cud•dle** (kud′əl) *verb,* **cuddled, cuddling.**

cue¹ A signal that tells someone when to do something: *The ring of the telephone was the actor's cue to walk on stage. Noun.*
○ To give a signal to someone to tell them when to do something. *Verb.*
cue (kū) *noun, plural* **cues;** *verb,* **cued, cuing.**

cue² A long, thin stick used to strike the ball in playing pool or billiards. **cue** (kū) *noun, plural* **cues.**

cuff¹ 1. A band of material at the bottom of a sleeve. 2. A fold of material turned up at the bottom of the leg of a pair of pants. **cuff** (kuf) *noun, plural* **cuffs.**

cuff² To hit with the hand: *The grocer cuffed the child on the head for stealing an apple. Verb.*
○ A hit with the hand; slap. *Noun.*
cuff (kuf) *verb,* **cuffed, cuffing;** *noun, plural* **cuffs.**

culprit A person guilty of doing something wrong. **cul•prit** (kul′prit) *noun, plural* **culprits.**

cultivate 1. To prepare and use land for growing vegetables, flowers, or other crops. To cultivate land, you dig it, fertilize it, and remove weeds from it before you plant seeds. 2. To plant and help grow: *That farmer cultivates corn.* 3. To improve or develop: *Cultivate good study habits.*
cul•ti•vate (kul′tə vāt′) *verb,* **cultivated, cultivating.**

cultivator A tool or machine used to loosen the soil and pull up weeds around growing plants. **cul•ti•va•tor** (kul′tə vā′tər) *noun, plural* **cultivators.**

cultural Having to do with culture: *This book is about the cultural history of England.* **cul•tur•al** (kul′chər əl) *adjective.*

culture 1. The arts, beliefs, and customs that make up a way of life for a group of people at a certain time: *We are studying the culture of the Inuit.* 2. An appreciation of the arts, knowledge, and good taste and manners that are the result of education: *a person of great culture.* 3. The growing and improvement of plants or animals: *Animal culture has resulted in the development of many new breeds.* 4. The growing of living cells or microorganisms, such as bacteria or viruses, for medical or scientific study. **cul•ture** (kul′chər) *noun, plural* **cultures.**

cumbersome Not easy to manage or carry; unwieldy: *I struggled up the stairs with the cumbersome box.* **cum•ber•some** (kum′bər səm) *adjective.*

cumulus A dense, white, fluffy cloud with a flat base and a sharp outline. **cu•mu•lus** (kūm′ yə ləs) *noun, plural* **cumuli** (kūm′yə lī *or* kūm′yə lē).

cunning Good at fooling or deceiving others; sly. *Adjective.*
○ Cleverness at fooling or deceiving others: *Foxes are said to show cunning in escaping from hunters. Noun.*
cun•ning (kun′ing) *adjective; noun.*

cup 1. A small bowl with a handle used to drink from. 2. The amount that a cup holds: *a cup of water.* 3. A unit of measure equal to eight ounces. There are four cups in a quart. 4. Anything that has the shape of a cup: *A silver cup was the prize for the winner. Noun.*
○ To shape like a cup: *Cup your hands when you catch the ball. Verb.*
cup (kup) *noun, plural* **cups;** *verb,* **cupped, cupping.**

cupboard A cabinet or closet with shelves to hold dishes or food. **cup•board** (kub′ərd) *noun, plural* **cupboards.**

cupcake A small cake. **cup•cake** (kup′kāk′) *noun, plural* **cupcakes.**

cupful 1. The amount that a cup holds. The size of this kind of cupful depends on the size of the cup. 2. The amount held by a standard cup in liquid or dry measurement: *A cupful of water is eight ounces of water, or half a pint.* **cup•ful** (kup′fŭl′) *noun, plural* **cupfuls.**

curb 1. A border of concrete or stone along the side of a road or sidewalk. 2. Anything that holds back or controls an action: *Keep a curb on spending by following a strict budget.* 3. A chain or strap fastened to a horse's bit, used to control the horse when the reins are pulled. *Noun.*
○ To hold back or control: *Curb your anger. Verb.*
curb (kûrb) *noun, plural* **curbs;** *verb,* **curbed, curbing.**

curd The thick part of milk that separates from the watery part when the milk sours. Curds are used in making cheese. **curd** (kûrd) *noun, plural* **curds.**

curdle To form or cause to form into a curd. **cur•dle** (kûr′dəl) *verb,* **curdled, curdling.**

cure 1. To make a person or animal healthy again. 2. To get rid of: *To cure a cold you should stay in*

bed and rest. **3.** To preserve or prepare meat and fish for use by drying, smoking, or salting. *Verb.*
○ **1.** Something that makes a person or animal healthy again: *Aspirin is the best cure for my headache.* **2.** A return to good health: *The patient's cure required a week in the hospital. Noun.* **cure** (kyŭr) *verb,* **cured, curing;** *noun, plural* **cures.**

curfew A fixed time at night when a person has to be indoors or at home. **cur•few** (kûr′fū) *noun, plural* **curfews.**

WORD HISTORY

The word curfew comes from two old French words meaning "cover" and "fire." In the Middle Ages, a bell was rung to tell people when it was time to put out or cover their fires for the night. This signal became known as the curfew.

curiosity 1. A strong wish to learn new, strange, or interesting things. **2.** Something interesting because it is strange, rare, or unusual: *A horse and buggy is a curiosity today.* **cu•ri•os•i•ty** (kyŭr′ē os′i tē) *noun, plural* **curiosities.**

curious 1. Eager to learn new, strange, or interesting things. **2.** Strange or unusual: *a curious old coin.* **cu•ri•ous** (kyŭr′ē əs) *adjective;*

curl To twist in curved rings or coils. *Verb.*
○ **1.** A curved lock of hair. **2.** Something shaped like a ring or coil: *a curl of smoke. Noun.* **curl** (kûrl) *verb,* **curled, curling;** *noun, plural* **curls.**

curly Forming or having curls: *curly hair.* **curl•y** (kûr′lē) *adjective,* **curlier, curliest.**

currant 1. A small, sour berry that grows in bunches on a bush. **2.** A small seedless raisin used in cakes, pies, and buns.
Another word that sounds like this is **current.**
cur•rant (kûr′ənt) *noun, plural* **currants.**

currency 1. The money used in a country. Dollars, quarters, and dimes are part of the currency used in the United States and Canada. Pesos are part of the currency of Mexico.
2. General use or acceptance: *As more people use a new word, they begin to give it currency.* **cur•ren•cy** (kûr′ən sē) *noun, plural* **currencies.**

current 1. Belonging to the present time: *My cur-*rent address is on the envelope. **2.** Commonly used or accepted: *At one time the belief was current that people lived on Mars. Adjective.*
○ **1.** A part of the air or of a body of water that is moving along in a path: *The rubber raft was caught in the current and carried out to sea.* **2.** A flow of electricity. **3.** The way events or thoughts seem to move along a path; trend: *The current of public opinion today seems to be that the mayor should resign. Noun.*
Another word that sounds like this is **currant.**
cur•rent (kûr′ənt) *adjective; noun, plural* **currents.**

curse 1. A wish that something evil or harmful will happen to a person or thing. A curse is often made by calling on God or gods. **2.** A word or words used when swearing. A curse is usually said in anger. **3.** Something that brings or causes evil, harm, or suffering: *War has been a curse throughout human history. Noun.*
○ **1.** To wish that something evil or harmful will happen to a person or thing. **2.** To say a word or words that show hate or anger; swear. **3.** To cause evil, harm, or suffering to: *I am cursed with a weak back. Verb.* **curse** (kûrs) *noun, plural* **curses;** *verb,* **cursed, cursing.**

cursor A special symbol on a computer monitor that shows where the next letter or number will appear. **cur•sor** (kûr′sər) *noun, plural* **cursors.**

curt Rudely brief; abrupt. **curt** (kûrt) *adjective,* **curter, curtest.**

curtain 1. A piece of cloth hung across an open space. **2.** Anything that screens or covers like a curtain: *a curtain of rain. Noun.*
○ To put a curtain over; screen: *We curtained off a part of the basement as a workshop. Verb.* **cur•tain** (kûr′tin) *noun, plural* **curtains;** *verb,* **curtained, curtaining.**

curtsy A bow showing respect made by bending the knees and lowering the body slightly: *Women and girls make a curtsy, and men and boys make a bow. Noun.*
○ To make a curtsy. *Verb.*
curt•sy (kûrt′sē) *noun, plural* **curtsies;** *verb,* **curtsied, curtsying.**

curve 1. A line that keeps bending in one direction. A curve has no straight parts or angles.
2. Something that has the shape of a curve: *the*

PRONUNCIATION KEY:

| at | āpe | fär | câre | end | mē | it | īce | pierce | hot | ōld | sông | fôrk |
| oil | out | up | ūse | rüle | pu͝ll | tûrn | chin | sing | shop | thin | this | |

hw in white; zh in treasure. The symbol ə stands for the unstressed vowel sound in about, taken, pencil, lemon, and circus.

181

curve of a river. Noun.

○ To bend or move in a curved line: *The road curves on the other side of the bridge. Verb.* **curve** (kûrv) *noun, plural* **curves;** *verb,* **curved, curving.**

Motorists should slow down when approaching a sharp curve.

cushion **1.** A pillow or soft pad used to sit, lie, or rest on. **2.** Something like a cushion in shape or use: *a cushion of grass.* **3.** Anything that softens a blow or protects against harm: *Shoes are a cushion against shock for a runner's feet. Noun.*

○ **1.** To make a pillow or soft pad for: *If you cushion the rocking chair it will be more comfortable.* **2.** To soften a blow or shock: *The pile of leaves cushioned my fall from the tree. Verb.* **cush•ion** (kūsh'ən) *noun, plural* **cushions;** *verb,* **cushioned, cushioning.**

custard A sweet dessert made of eggs, milk, and sugar. **cus•tard** (kus'tərd) *noun, plural* **custards.**

custodian A person responsible for the care of a person or thing: *The school custodian made sure the buildings were kept clean and in good repair.* **cus•to•di•an** (kə stō'dē ən) *noun, plural* **custodians.**

custody The care and keeping of a person or thing: *I was in my grandparents' custody while my parents were away.* **cus•to•dy** (kus'tə dē) *noun, plural* **custodies.**

custom **1.** A way of acting that has become accepted by many people. Customs are learned and passed down from one generation to another: *Thanksgiving Day is an American custom.* **2.** The

usual way something is done; habit: *It is my custom to walk to school every morning.* **3. customs.** Taxes a government collects on products brought in from a foreign country: *We had to pay customs on the sweaters we had bought in Scotland. Noun.*

○ Made the way the buyer wants or needs: *The custom color of the paint on our house was mixed for us at the store. Adjective.* **cus•tom** (kus'təm) *noun, plural* **customs;** *adjective.*

customary Usual: *It is customary in our family to have Thanksgiving dinner at home.* **cus•tom•ar•y** (kus'tə mer'ē) *adjective.* —**customarily** *adverb.*

customer A person who buys something at a store or uses the services of a business: *Most of the bakery's regular customers shop there at least once a week.* **cus•tom•er** (kus'tə mər) *noun, plural* **customers.**

cut **1.** To divide, pierce, open, or take away a part with something sharp: *Cut the pie into six slices.* **2.** To make by using a sharp tool: *We cut a hole in the door so the cat could come in and go out.* **3.** To do the work of a sharp tool: *This saw cuts well.* **4.** To be capable of being cut: *This steak cuts easily.* **5.** To make shorter or smaller; lessen: *I cut my speech because it was too long.* **6.** To have a tooth or teeth grow through the gum: *The baby cut a new tooth yesterday.* **7.** To put an end to or interrupt: *That lightning cut the electricity for a minute.* **8.** To cross or pass: *Let's cut through the park.* **9.** To be absent from, usually without permission: *I cut class yesterday. Verb.*

○ **1.** An opening or slit made with something sharp: *a cut on my hand from broken glass.* **2.** A piece or part that has been cut or cut off: *a nice cut of beef for dinner.* **3.** A decrease: *a cut in prices.* **4.** The way or shape in which a thing is cut; style: *The cut of that dress is old-fashioned. Noun.*

cut (kut) *verb,* **cut, cutting;** *noun, plural* **cuts.**

cute Delightful or pretty; charming: *a cute puppy.* **cute** (kūt) *adjective,* **cuter, cutest.**

cuticle A tough layer of dead skin. **cu•ti•cle** (kū'ti kəl) *noun, plural* **cuticles.**

cutlass A sword with a wide, flat, curved blade. **cut•lass** (kut'ləs) *noun, plural* **cutlasses.**

cutter **1.** A person whose job it is to cut out things: *A diamond cutter cuts away bits of the* *stone to give a diamond a special shape.* **2.** A tool or machine used to cut out things. **3.** A small, fast ship: *a Coast Guard cutter.* **cut·ter** (kut′ər) *noun, plural* **cutters.**

cutting **1.** Able to make a slit or other opening in; sharp: *the cutting edge of a knife.* **2.** Hurting a person's feelings: *a cutting remark.* *Adjective.*
○ **1.** A small part cut from a plant that is used to grow a new plant. **2.** An article or picture cut out of a newspaper or magazine; clipping. *Noun.* **cut·ting** (kut′ing) *adjective; noun, plural* **cuttings.**

cyberspace The world or environment of computer networks and electronic bulletin boards in which online computer communications takes place. **cyb·er·space** (si′bər spās′) *noun.*

cycle **1.** A series of events that happen one after another in the same order, over and over again: *the cycle of the four seasons of the year.* **2.** A bicycle, tricycle, or motorcycle. *Noun.*
To ride a bicycle, tricycle, or motorcycle. *Verb.* **cy·cle** (si′kəl) *noun, plural* **cycles;** *verb,* **cycled, cycling.**

cyclone A storm with very powerful winds. **cy·clone** (si′klōn) *noun, plural* **cyclones.**

cylinder A solid or hollow object shaped like a drum or a soup can. **cyl·in·der** (sil′ən dər) *noun, plural* **cylinders.**

cylindrical Having the shape of a cylinder. **cy·lin·dri·cal** (sə lin′dri kəl) *adjective.*

cymbal A metal musical instrument shaped like a plate.

Another word that sounds like this is **symbol.** **cym·bal** (sim′bəl) *noun, plural* **cymbals.**

cypress Any of various evergreen trees with small leaves like scales.
Another word that sounds like this is **Cyprus.** **cy·press** (si′pris) *noun, plural* **cypresses.**

Cyprus An island country in the eastern Mediterranean Sea.
Another word that sounds like this is **cypress.** **Cy·prus** (si′prəs) *noun.*

cyst An abnormal sac on the inside or the outside of the body. Cysts contain liquid and often are removed by surgery. **cyst** (sist) *noun, plural* **cysts.**

cytoplasm A substance that is like jelly and that holds all the parts inside a cell. **cy·to·plasm** (si′tə plaz′əm) *noun.*

czar One of the male rulers of Russia before the revolution of 1917. **czar** (zär) *noun, plural* **czars.**

WORD HISTORY

Czar is the Russian word for "Caesar." Julius Caesar was the first Roman emperor, and the name Caesar became the standard title for later Roman emperors, as well as for the Russian czars.

czarina The wife of a czar or a woman who ruled Russia before the revolution of 1917. **cza·ri·na** (zä rē′nə) *noun, plural* **czarinas.**

Czechoslovakia A former country in central Europe. **Czech·o·slo·va·ki·a** (chek′ə slə vä′kēə) *noun.*

Czech Republic A country in central Europe. **Czech Republic** (chek).

Cymbals make a very loud, harsh noise when they are crashed together.

PRONUNCIATION KEY:
| at | ape | far | care | end | mē | it | īce | pierce | hot | ōld | sông | fôrk |
| oil | out | up | ūse | rüle | pull | tûrn | chin | sing | shop | thin | this | |

hw in white; zh in treasure. The symbol ə stands for the unstressed vowel sound in about, taken, pencil, lemon, and circus.

183

Dd

The sound of D can be made by a single letter d as in did and dog or by dd in words such as ladder and riddle. There are also some one-syllable words, such as add and odd, that end in dd.

The D sound can also be made by ed when it indicates the past tense of a verb, such as in called and laughed.

d, D 1. The fourth letter of the alphabet. 2. The Roman numeral for 500. **d, D** (dē) *noun, plural* **d's, D's.**

dab 1. To touch lightly and gently; pat: *The school nurse dabbed my cut knee with cotton.* 2. To put on lightly and gently: *You should dab lotion on those sunburned arms. Verb.*

○ 1. A small, moist mass of something: *I took a dab of clay and molded it with my fingers.* 2. A little bit. Would you like a dab of butter on your mashed potatoes? *Noun.*

dab (dab) *verb,* **dabbed, dabbing;** *noun, plural* **dabs.**

dabble To work at or do something a little, but not in a serious way: *dabble at playing the piano;* **dab·ble** (dab′əl) *verb,* d**abbled, dabbling.** **dabbler** *noun.*

dachshund A small dog with a long body, very short legs, and drooping ears. **dachs·hund** (däks′hunt′ *or* däks′hund′) *noun, plural* **dachshunds.**

dad Father: *I call my father Dad.* **dad** (dad) *noun, plural* **dads.**

daddy Father: *Children often call their father Daddy.* **dad·dy** (dad′ē) *noun, plural* **daddies.**

daddy-longlegs A bug that looks like a spider. It has a small round body and eight very long, thin legs. **dad·dy-long·legs** (dad′ē lông′legz′) *noun, plural* **daddy-longlegs.**

daffodil A plant that has long, narrow leaves and yellow or white flowers shaped like trumpets.

daf·fo·dil (daf′ə dil) *noun, plural* **daffodils.**

dagger A small weapon that looks like a knife. A dagger has a pointed blade that is used for stabbing. **dag·ger** (dag′ər) *noun, plural* **daggers.**

daily Appearing or happening every day: *the daily newspaper. Adjective.*

The daffodil grows from a large underground bulb.

○ Every day: *That train runs daily. Adverb.*

○ A newspaper published every day or every weekday. *Noun.*

dai·ly (dā′lē) *adjective; adverb; noun, plural* **dailies.**

dainty Small and easily harmed: *a dainty design.* **dain·ty** (dān′tē) *adjective,* **daintier, daintiest.**

dairy 1. A place where milk and cream are stored or made into butter and cheese. 2. A farm where cows are raised for their milk. **dair·y** (dâr′ē) *noun, plural* **dairies.**

dais A raised platform used for making speeches or seats for guests of honor: *The mayor sat up on the dais.* **dais** (dā′is) *noun, plural* **daises.**

daisy A plant with a flower of pink, white, or yellow petals around a yellow center. **dai·sy** (dā′zē) *noun, plural* **daisies.**

WORD HISTORY

Daisy comes from the earlier phrase "the day's eye," because the flower opens during the day and closes at night.

dale A valley. **dale** (dāl) *noun, plural* **dales.**

Dalmatian A large dog that has a short white coat with small black or brown spots. **Dal·ma·tian** (dal māʹshən) *noun, plural* **Dalmatians**.

The Hoover Dam is the highest concrete dam **in the United States.**

dam A wall built across a stream or river to hold back and control the water. *Noun.*
○ To hold back with a dam: *Beavers **dam** streams with mud and sticks.* *Verb.*
dam (dam) *noun, plural* **dams**; *verb,* **dammed, damming.**

damage Harm that makes something less valuable or useful: *The flood caused great **damage** to farms. Noun.*
○ To harm or injure: *Rain **damaged** the young plants. Verb.*
dam·age (damʹij) *noun, plural* **damages**; *verb,* **damaged, damaging.**

dame 1. A woman who has a high social position or a position of honor. 2. An elderly woman.
dame (dām) *noun, plural* **dames.**

damp A little wet; moist: *a **damp** sponge; a **damp** and chilly day.* **damp** (damp) *adjective,* **damper, dampest.**

dampen 1. To make a little wet or moist: *Dampen the rag before you wipe the table.* 2. To ruin a good feeling; dull: *Losing the game **dampened** the team's spirits.* **damp·en** (dampʹən) *verb,* **dampened, dampening.**

dance 1. To move the body or feet in time to music: *We put on a record and **danced**.* 2. To move about quickly or lightly: *Sunlight **danced** on the lake. Verb.*
○ 1. A particular set of steps or movements done in time to music. The waltz, the polka, and the reel are dances. 2. A party where people dance: *I'm going to a **dance** Friday night. Noun.*
dance (dans) *verb,* **danced, dancing**; *noun, plural* **dances.**

dancer A person who dances: *The **dancers** gathered on the stage.* **danc·er** (dansʹər) *noun, plural* **dancers.**

dandelion A plant with a bright yellow flower and jagged leaves. Dandelion leaves are sometimes eaten in salads or cooked as a vegetable.
dan·de·li·on (danʹdə līʹən) *noun, plural* **dandelions.**

WORD HISTORY

The word **dandelion** comes from the old French name for this flower, which meant "lion's teeth." The plant probably got its name because its leaves are pointed like teeth.

dandruff Small white pieces of dead skin that fall from the scalp. **dan·druff** (danʹdrəf) *noun.*

dandy Very good; excellent: *a **dandy** day at the beach.* **dan·dy** (danʹdē) *adjective,* **dandier, dandiest.**

Dane A person who was born in or is a citizen of Denmark. **Dane** (dān) *noun, plural* **Danes.**

danger 1. The chance that something bad or harmful will happen: *There is great **danger** in skating on thin ice.* 2. Something that may cause harm or injury: *Busy roads are a **danger** to children on bicycles.* **dan·ger** (dānʹjər) *noun, plural* **dangers.**

dangerous Likely to cause something bad to happen: *Driving too fast is **dangerous** in the city.* **dan·ger·ous** (dānʹjər əs) *adjective.*

dangle 1. To hang or swing loosely: *An old kite **dangled** from a tree.* 2. To tease by offering something as a treat: ***dangle** a bone in front of a dog.*
• **to keep someone dangling.** To make someone wait and refuse to give him or her information: *Our teacher **kept us dangling** for days about our grades on the test.*
dan·gle (dangʹgəl) *verb,* **dangled, dangling.**

Danish The language of Denmark. *Noun.*
○ Of or having to do with Denmark, its people, or

PRONUNCIATION KEY:

| at | āpe | fär | câre | end | mē | it | īce | pîerce | hot | ōld | sông | fôrk |
| oil | out | up | ūse | rüle | pull | tûrn | chin | sing | shop | thin | this | |

hw in white; zh in treasure. The symbol ə stands for the unstressed vowel sound in about, taken, pencil, lemon, and circus.

185

its language. *Adjective.*

Dan·ish (dān′ish) *noun; adjective.*

dare **1.** To challenge someone to do something as a test of courage or ability: *I dared my friend to jump off the diving board.* **2.** To have the courage for: *No one dared to go into the dark cave. Verb.*
○ A challenge: *I accepted my friend's dare and jumped across the stream. Noun.*
dare (dâr) *verb,* **dared, daring;** *noun, plural* **dares.**

daredevil A person who does reckless or dangerous things: *My brother is a daredevil when he rides his bicycle. Noun.*
○ Bold; reckless: *Daredevil driving is foolish and unsafe. Adjective.*
dare·dev·il (dâr′dev′il) *noun, plural* **daredevils;** *adjective.*

daring Courage or boldness: *The first pilots to fly airplanes were famous for their daring. Noun.*
○ Courageous and bold; fearless: *a daring rescue of a drowning child. Adjective.*
dar·ing (dâr′ing) *noun; adjective.*

dark **1.** Having little or no light: *a dark night.* **2.** Black or brown rather than light in color: *a dark blue coat.* **3.** Bad; unlucky: *a dark day in history. Adjective.*
○ **1.** A lack of light: *Some people are afraid of the dark.* **2.** Night or nightfall; the end of daylight: *We have to be home before dark. Noun.*
• **in the dark.** Without knowledge; not aware. *The teacher kept us in the dark about the surprise party.*
dark (därk) *adjective,* **darker, darkest;** *noun.*

darken To make or become dark or darker: *rain clouds darkened the sky.* **dark·en** (där′kən) *verb,* **darkened, darkening.**

darling A person who is loved very much: *the teacher's darling. Noun.* **1.** Very much loved; dear: *our darling grandchild.* **2.** Cute and cuddly: *darling kittens. Adjective.* **dar·ling** (där′ling) *noun, plural* **darlings;** *adjective.*

darn To mend by making stitches back and forth across a hole: *You should darn that hole in your sock.* **darn** (därn) *verb,* **darned, darning.**

dart **1.** A thin, pointed object that looks like a small arrow. **2.** darts. A game in which darts are thrown at a target. *Noun.*
○ **1.** To move suddenly and quickly: *The rabbit darted into the bushes.* **2.** To do something suddenly and quickly: *Why did you dart that angry*

look at me? *Verb.*
dart (därt) *noun, plural* **darts;** *verb,* **darted, darting.**

dash **1.** To move fast; rush: *We tried to teach our dog not to dash after cars.* **2.** To hit with force; smash: *High waves dashed against the ship during the storm.* **3.** To destroy or ruin: *Rain dashed our hopes for a picnic. Verb.*
○ **1.** A small amount that is added or mixed in: *Add a dash of pepper to the beef stew.* **2.** A short race: *the 50-yard dash.* **3.** A punctuation mark (–) that is used to show a break in the thought that a sentence expresses. *Noun.*
• **dash off. 1.** To make, write, or finish quickly: *I dashed off a short letter to a friend.* **2.** To leave quickly: *dashed off to the movies.*
• **to make a dash for.** To seek quickly; flee: *The hikers made a dash for cover when the rain started.*
dash (dash) *verb,* **dashed, dashing;** *noun, plural* **dashes**

dashboard A panel under the windshield in an automobile. **dash·board** (dash′bôrd) *noun, plural* **dashboards.**

A dashboard has dials and instruments to help the driver operate the car.

data **1.** Individual facts, figures, and other items of information: *These data from the computer don't seem to be accurate.* The singular of *data* in this sense is datum. **2.** Information as a whole: *Adequate data on that subject is sometimes difficult to find.* **da·ta** (dā′tə *or* dat′ə) *plural noun.*

database A collection of information that can be examined and changed with a computer. This word is also spelled *data base.* **dat·a·base** (dā′tə bās′ *or* dat′ə bās′) *noun, plural* **databases.**

data processing The handling of information by

by the use of a computer.

date **1.** The time when something happened or happens: *The **date** of my birthday is June 3. What is today's **date**?* **2.** Writing or numerals that say when something was made or written: *The **date** on the coin was 1883.* **3.** An appointment to meet someone at a certain time and place: *We have a **date** to meet for lunch on Thursday.* **4.** A person with whom one has such an appointment: *Do you have a **date** for the dance yet? Noun.*
○ **1.** To mark with a time or date: *Be sure to **date** your test paper.* **2.** To find out or fix the time of: *The scientists are trying to **date** the dinosaur bones.* **3.** To come from a certain time: *Our old car **dates** from the 1950s.* **4.** To meet socially with a person: *I **dated** one of my classmates during the summer. Verb.*

   • **out of date.** No longer fashionable; old-fashioned: *I gave away some clothes that were **out of date**.*
   • **up-to-date.** Modern; new; recent: *Is your diary **up-to-date**?*
   date (dāt) *noun, plural* **dates**; *verb,* **dated, dating.**

date² A sweet fruit that grows on a kind of palm tree, also called a date. It grows in warm areas. **date** (dāt) *noun, plural* **dates.**

dated No longer fashionable; too old: *That kind of music is **dated**.*

datum One piece of information. Look up **data** for more information. **da•tum** (dā′təm or dat′əm) *noun, plural* **data.**

daughter A female child. A girl or woman is the daughter of her mother and father. **daugh•ter** (dô′tər) *noun, plural* **daughters.**

daughter-in-law The wife of a son. **daugh•ter-in-law** (dô′tər in lô) *noun, plural* **daughters-in-law.**

dawdle To waste time: *Don't **dawdle** over your homework.* **daw•dle** (dôd′əl) *verb,* **dawdled, dawdling.**

dawn **1.** The first light that appears in the morning; daybreak. **2.** The beginning of something: *the **dawn** of civilization. Noun.*
○ To begin to get light in the morning; become day: *The new day **dawned**. Verb.*

   • **to dawn on.** To begin to understand: *It **dawned on** us that we were being teased.*

dawn (dôn) *noun, plural* **dawns**; *verb,* **dawned, dawning.**

day **1.** The period of light between the rising and setting of the sun: *The farmer worked all **day** long.* **2.** The twenty-four hours of one day and night: *a vacation of ten **days** in the spring.* **3.** The part of a day spent working: *a **day** at school.* **4.** A certain time or period: *the horse-and-buggy **days**.* **day** (dā) *noun, plural* **days.**

DAYS

The English names for the days of the week come from several sources.

Sunday
   From the English word for the sun; Sun's day.
Monday
   From the English word for the moon; Moon's day.
Tuesday
   Named after Tiu, the ancient English god of war.
Wednesday
   From Woden, an English name for the Norse god, Odin. He was the ruler of the Norse gods.
Thursday
   From Thor, the name of the Norse god of thunder.
Friday
   Named for Frigga, the Norse goddess of love.
Saturday
   From the Roman words for Saturn's day. Saturn was the Roman god of agriculture.

---

daybreak The time each morning when light first appears; dawn. **day•break** (dā′brāk) *noun, plural* **daybreaks.**

day-care center A place where adults take care of and teach small children whose parents are not home during the day because they go to work. **day-care center** (dā′kâr).

daydream A pleasant thought about things one would like to do or have happen: *I had a **daydream** of being a famous writer someday. Noun.*
○ To think about pleasant things as if dreaming: *Sometimes I like to sit and **daydream**. Verb.*

PRONUNCIATION KEY:

| at | āpe | fär | câre | end | mē | it | īce | pierce | hot | ōld | sông | fôrk |
| oil | out | up | ūse | rüle | pùll | tûrn | chin | sing | shop | thin | this | |

hw in white; zh in treasure. The symbol ə stands for the unstressed vowel sound in about, taken, pencil, lemon, and circus.

187

day·dream (dā′drēm) *noun, plural* **daydreams**; *verb,* **daydreamed, daydreaming.**

daylight 1. The light of day; daytime. 2. The dawn; daybreak: *I get up to go to school before daylight.* **day·light** (dā′līt) *noun.*

daytime The time when it is day; daylight. **day·time** (dā′tīm) *noun.*

daze To confuse or stun; bewilder: *The fall from the tree dazed me. Verb.*
○ A confused or stunned condition: *The car accident left the driver in a daze. Noun.*
daze (dāz) *verb,* **dazed, dazing;** *noun, plural* **dazes.**

dazzle 1. To make almost blind by too much light: *The bright sun on the beach dazzled our eyes.* 2. To impress: *The acrobat's spectacular tricks dazzled the audience.* **daz·zle** (daz′əl) *verb,* **dazzled, dazzling.**

DC *or* **D.C.** 1. An abbreviation for **District of Columbia.** 2. An abbreviation for **direct current.**

de- A prefix that means: 1. To do the opposite of; undo: *Desegregate means to do the opposite of segregate.* 2. To remove: *Defrost means to remove frost.* 3. Down; lower: *Depression means a place that is lower than the area around it.*

DE Postal abbreviation for Delaware.

deacon 1. A church officer who helps a minister. 2. A member of the clergy who ranks just below a priest. **dea·con** (dē′kən) *noun, plural* **deacons.**

dead 1. No longer living: *We had to throw out the dead plant.* 2. Without power: *After the storm our telephone was dead.* 3. Lacking activity or interest: *This town is dead after the sun goes down.* 4. Complete; total: *When the curtain rose in the theater, there was dead silence.* 5. Sure or certain; exact: *Try to hit the target at dead center. Adjective.*
○ 1. Completely: *The hikers were dead tired.* 2. Directly; straight: *The exit from the highway is dead ahead. Adverb.*
○ The darkest or coldest time: *the dead of night; the dead of winter.* 2. the dead. People who are no longer living: *a prayer for the dead. Noun.*
dead (ded) *adjective,* **deader, deadest;** *adverb; noun.*

deaden To dull or weaken: *The dentist gave me an injection to deaden the pain in my sore tooth.* **dead·en** (ded′ən) *verb,* **deadened, deadening.**

dead end A street or passage that is closed at one end.

deadline A time when something must be finished; time limit: *The deadline for handing in our book*

reports is Friday. **dead·line** (ded′īn) *noun, plural* **deadlines.**

deadly 1. Causing or likely to cause death: *A knife can be a deadly weapon.* 2. Full of hatred: *The two countries became deadly enemies when they went to war.* 3. Very boring: *That new movie was deadly.* **dead·ly** (ded′lē) *adjective,* **deadlier, deadliest.**

deaf 1. Not able to hear, or not able to hear well: *The deaf children were using sign language to speak to one another.* 2. Not willing to hear or listen: *Most people were deaf to the beggar's calls for help.* **deaf** (def) *adjective,* **deafer, deafest.**

deafen To make unable to hear: *The noise of the machines deafened us for a moment.* **deafen** (defən) *verb,* **deafened, deafening.**

deal 1. To be about a subject: *I'm looking for a book that deals with dogs.* 2. To act or behave toward: *The principal dealt harshly with the fighting students.* 3. To conduct business; trade: *That store deals in newspapers and magazines.* 4. To give out: *Whose turn is it to deal the cards? Verb.*
○ A bargain or agreement: *According to our deal, I make breakfast and you wash the dishes. Noun.*
• **a great deal** *or* **a good deal.** A large amount or quantity: *I don't paint, but I draw a good deal.*
• **no big deal.** Nothing; not worth talking about: *It was no big deal; I was glad to help.*
deal (dēl) *verb,* **dealt, dealing;** *noun, plural* **deals.**

dealer 1. A person who buys or sells something for a living: *a used car dealer.* 2. A person who gives out cards in a card game. **deal·er** (dē′lər) *noun, plural* **dealers.**

dealt Past tense and past participle of deal. **dealt** (delt) *verb.*

dear 1. Much or greatly loved: *my dearest friend.* 2. Very high in price: *Strawberries are dear in the winter.* 3. Respected; esteemed: *We start a letter by writing "Dear" and following it with the name of the person we are writing to. Adjective.*
○ A much loved person: *You are a dear to come over and help. Noun.*
○ An exclamation of surprise, disappointment, or trouble: *Oh dear! I've missed the bus. Interjection.* Another word that sounds like this is **deer.**
dear (dîr) *adjective,* **dearer, dearest;** *noun, plural* **dears;** *interjection.*

dearly Very much; a great deal: *We dearly love our grandparents.* **dear·ly** (dîr′lē) *adverb.*

death 1. The end of life in people, plants, or ani-

mals: *Highway accidents cause many deaths.*
2. The end of something; destruction: *The **death**
of silent movies came in about 1930.* **death** (deth)
noun, plural **deaths.**

debate A discussion between two persons or
groups who disagree; argument. *Noun.*
○ 1. To argue about or discuss at a meeting: *The
state representatives **debated** whether or not to
change the highway speed limit.* 2. To think about;
consider: *Sometimes on a cloudy day I **debate**
whether to take an umbrella with me. Verb.*
de·bate (di bāt′) *noun, plural* **debates;** *verb,*
debated, debating.

debit An amount of money owed: *My savings
account shows several **debits**. Noun.*
○ A taking out of money: *The bank **debited** my
account. Verb.*
deb·it (deb′ət) *noun, plural* **debits;** *verb,* **debited,**
debiting.

debris The scattered remains of something; trash;
litter. **de·bris** (də brē′) *noun.*

debt 1. Something that is owed to another: *I paid
my **debts** when I got my allowance.* 2. The condition of owing: *My parents are in **debt** because
they borrowed money to buy our house.* **debt**
(det) *noun, plural* **debts.**

debtor A person who owes something to someone
else. **debt·or** (det′ər) **noun.**

debug 1. To remove errors in a computer program. 2. To remove hidden listening devices from
a place: *The police **debugged** our house.* **de·bug**
(dē bug′) *verb,* **debugged, debugging.**

debut A first appearance: *This is her acting **debut**. Noun.*
○ To perform something for the first time: ***debut**
a new play. Verb.*
de·but (dā bū′ or dā′bū) *noun, plural* **debuts;** *verb,*
debuted, debuting.

Dec. An abbreviation for December.

decade A period of
ten years. **dec·ade**
(dek′ād) *noun, plural*
decades.

decagon A figure
having ten sides and
ten angles. **dec·a·gon**
(dek′ə gon′) *noun,*
plural **decagons.**

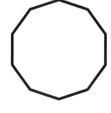

decagon

decal A design or picture on specially treated
paper. The decal can be transferred to a hard flat
surface, such as wood or glass: *We used a knife
to scrape the old **decal** off the car window.*
de·cal (dē′kal or di kal′) *noun, plural* **decals.**

decanter A glass bottle with a stopper. Decanters
are usually used to hold wine or liquor. **de·cant·er**
(di kan′tər) *noun, plural* **decanters.**

decathlon A an athletic contest in track and field
made up of ten events. **de·cath·lon** (di kath′lon)
noun, plural **decathlons.**

decay 1. A slow, natural breaking down of plant or
animal matter; rot: *The dentist told me to brush
my teeth at least twice a day to prevent tooth
decay.* 2. A slow lowering of quality or strength;
decline: *The roads show signs of **decay** because
there is no money to make repairs. Noun.*
○ 1. To rot slowly: *The oranges turned moldy and
began to **decay**.* 2. To decline slowly in quality or
strength: *Her health has steadily **decayed**. Verb.*
de·cay (di kā′) *noun, plural* **decays;** *verb,* **decayed,**
decaying.

deceased Dead: *Our school is named after
a **deceased** president. Adjective.*
○ **the deceased.** A dead person or persons. *Noun.*
de·ceased (di sēst′) *adjective; noun.*

deceit 1. The act of lying or cheating: *Using
deceit to get what you want is dangerous.* 2. The
quality that makes someone lie or cheat: *That
boy was full of **deceit** when he pretended not to
know about the missing candy.* **de·ceit** (di sēt′)
noun, plural **deceits.** —**deceitful** *adj.*

deceive To make someone believe something that
is not true; mislead: *I **deceived** my parents by
telling them I had no homework.* **de·ceive** (di sēv′)
verb, **deceived, deceiving.**

December The twelfth and last month of the
year. December has thirty-one days. **De·cember**
(di sem′bər) *noun.*

WORD HISTORY

**December comes from the Latin word for "ten." The
early Roman calendar began with March, making
December the tenth month.**

---

decent 1. Proper and respectable: *It is not **decent**
to listen to other people's private conversations.*

PRONUNCIATION KEY:

| at | āpe | fär | câre | end | mē | it | īce | pierce | hot | ōld | · | sông | fôrk |
| oil | out | up | ūse | rüle | půll | tûrn | chin | sing | shop | thin | this | | |

hw in white; zh in treasure. The symbol ə stands for the unstressed vowel sound in about, taken, pencil, lemon, and circus.

189

2. Kind or generous: *It was **decent** of them to help you with your chores.* 3. Fairly good; satisfactory: *I'll never be an A student, but I get **decent** grades.* **de·cent** (dē′sənt) *adjective*.

deception A trick or lie that fools someone: *In nature, many animals survive by **deception**.* **de·cep·tion** (di sep′shən) *noun, plural* **deceptions**.

decibel A unit used to measure the volume of sound. **dec·i·bel** (des′ə bel) *noun, plural* **decibels**.

decide 1. To make up one's mind: *I haven't **decided** whether to be a teacher or a doctor.* 2. To settle or judge a question or argument: *The judge **decided** in favor of the prisoner.* 3. To settle the outcome of: *The last touchdown **decided** the game.* **de·cide** (di sīd′) *verb*, **decided, deciding**.

deciduous Dropping leaves every year: *Maples are **deciduous** trees.* **de·cid·u·ous** (di sig′ə wəs) *adjective*.

decimal Based on the number 10. In the United States money is based on the decimal system. *Adjective.*
○ A fraction with a denominator of 10, or a multiple of 10 such as 100 or 1,000. The decimal .5 is another way of writing 5/10. This is also called a *decimal fraction.* *Noun.* **dec·i·mal** (des′ə məl) *adjective; noun, plural* **decimals**.

decimal point A period put before a decimal fraction. The periods in .5, .30, and .052 are decimal points.

decipher 1. To figure out the meaning of something difficult to read or understand: *No one could **decipher** the doctor's scribbling.* 2. To figure out a secret code: *The U.S. used Navajo for secret messages during World War II because none of our enemies could **decipher** it.* **de·ci·pher** (di sī′fər) *verb*, **deciphered, deciphering**.

decision The act or result of making up one's mind: *Think carefully about a problem before you make a **decision**.* **de·ci·sion** (di sizh′ən) *noun, plural* **decisions**.

decisive 1. Deciding something finally and completely: *Our baseball team suffered a **decisive** defeat last night.* 2. Showing firmness and determination: *The **decisive** customer quickly picked out a suit to buy.* **de·ci·sive** (di sī′siv) *adjective*.

deck 1. The floor on a ship or boat: *The ship's **deck** was slippery after the storm.* 2. A platform built onto a house: *We built a **deck** onto the back of our house.* 3. A set of playing cards. *Noun.*
○ To dress or decorate: *We all **decked** ourselves out in funny costumes for Halloween.* *Verb.* **deck** (dek) *noun, plural* **decks**; *verb*, **decked, decking**.

This ship has both an upper and lower deck.

declaration The act of making something known: *a **declaration** of war; a **declaration** of loyalty.* **dec·lar·a·tion** (dek′lə rā′shən) *noun, plural* **declarations**.

Declaration of Independence The statement made on July 4, 1776, that the thirteen American colonies were independent of Great Britain.

declarative sentence A sentence that makes a statement. An example of a declarative sentence is "The game ended in a tie." **declarative sentence** (di klar′ə tiv).

declare 1. To make something known: *The two countries **declared** war.* 2. To say strongly and firmly: *They **declared** that they were right and nothing would change their minds.* **de·clare** (di klâr′) *verb*, **declared, declaring**.

decline 1. To refuse politely: *decline an invitation to a party.* 2. To weaken or grow less: *The membership **declined** in the club.* *Verb.*
○ A lessening or weakening of something: *the **decline** and fall of an empire. My grandparents' health went into a **decline** that winter.* *Noun.* **de·cline** (di klīn′) *verb*, **declined, declining**; *noun, plural* **declines**.

decode To figure out the meaning of secret writing; decipher: *The spy **decoded** the secret message.* **de·code** (dē kōd′) *verb*, **decoded, decoding**.

decompose To rot or decay: *Dead leaves slowly decompose and become part of the soil.* **de·com·pose** (dē′kəm pōz′) *verb,* **decomposed, decomposing.**

decorate **1.** To make more beautiful: *The family decorated the living room by hanging pictures on the walls.* **2.** To give a badge or medal to: *The army decorated the soldier for bravery.* **dec·o·rate** (dek′ə rāt′) *verb,* **decorated, decorating.** —**decorator** *noun.*

decoration **1.** The act of decorating: *The decoration of the gym for the dance took all day.* **2.** Something that is used to decorate; ornament: *We took down the decorations after Christmas.* **3.** A badge or medal: *The general wore all of his decorations for the parade.* **dec·o·ra·tion** (dek′ə rā′shən) *noun, plural* **decorations.**

decoy **1.** A model of a bird that hunters use to attract real birds: *The hunter floated a wooden decoy on the lake.* **2.** A person who leads another person into danger or into a trap: *The police sometimes use decoys to arrest criminals. Noun.* ○ To attract or lead into danger or into a trap: *They decoyed the rabbit and shot it. Verb.* **de·coy** (dē′koi *or* di koi′ *for noun;* di koi′ *for verb*) *noun, plural* **decoys;** *verb,* **decoyed, decoying.**

decrease To make or become less: *decrease the speed of a car. The population of the town decreased when the coal mine closed. Verb.* ○ **1.** The act of becoming less: *a decrease in people on the beach as it got colder.* **2.** The amount by which something becomes less: *a decrease of 10 degrees in the temperature. Noun.* **de·crease** (di krēs′ *for verb;* dē′krēs *or* di krēs′ *for noun*) *verb,* **decreased, decreasing;** *noun, plural* **decreases.**

SYNONYMS

decrease, ebb, wane

The number of visitors to the museum has decreased this year. The high tide began to ebb slowly. When summer wanes, cool days arrive.

---

decree An official order or decision: *The king and queen sent out a decree that all taxes would be raised. Noun.* ○ To order or decide officially: *The dictator*

decreed *the arrest of all the rebels. Verb.* **de·cree** (di krē′) *noun, plural* **decrees;** *verb,* **decreed, decreeing.**

dedicate To set apart for a special purpose or use: *dedicated to finding a cure for cancer; dedicate a new museum* **ded·i·cate** (ded′i kāt′) *verb,* **dedicated, dedicating.**

dedication **1.** A setting apart for a special purpose or use: *the dedication of a new school.* **2.** Great focus on a purpose or goal: *The guitar player practiced the piece with dedication.* **ded·i·ca·tion** (ded′i kā′shən) *noun, plural* **dedications.**

deduct To take away or subtract from a total: *The teacher deducts five points for each wrong answer on a test.* **de·duct** (di dukt′) *verb,* **deducted, deducting.**

deduction **1.** The method or process of figuring something out from what is already known: *a master of deduction.* **2.** A conclusion based on what is known. **3.** The taking away from a total; subtraction: *a deduction of ten dollars from the price of the radio.* **de·duc·tion** (di duk′shən) *noun, plural* **deductions.**

deed **1.** Something done; act; action: *You did a good deed by helping the blind person across the street.* **2.** A written, legal agreement: *We have a deed to show that we own our house.* **deed** (dēd) *noun, plural* **deeds.**

deep **1.** Far down from the surface: *The water is over my head in the deep end of the swimming pool.* **2.** Great in degree; intense; extreme: *The weary child fell into a deep sleep.* **3.** Difficult to understand: *Organic chemistry is too deep for me.* **4.** Completely occupied with something; absorbed: *deep in thought.* **5.** Low in pitch: *a deep voice. Adjective.* ○ In, at, or to a great depth: *The explorers went deep into the jungle. Adverb.* **deep** (dēp) *adjective,* **deeper, deepest;** *adverb.*

deepen To make or become deeper: *deepen a hole.* **deep·en** (dē′pən) *verb,* **deepened, deepening.**

deer An animal with hooves that chews its cud and runs very fast. Deer are closely related to elk, moose, and caribou. Another word that sounds like this is **dear.** **deer** (dîr) *noun, plural* **deer.**

deface To damage the surface or appearance of: *The children defaced the statue by writing on it.*

PRONUNCIATION KEY:

at āpe fär câre end mē it īce pîerce hot ōld sông fôrk
oil out up ūse rüle pull tûrn chin sing shop thin this
hw in white; zh in treasure. The symbol ə stands for the unstressed vowel sound in about, taken, pencil, lemon, and circus.

191

deface (difās) *verb*, **defaced, defacing.**

defeat To win a victory over: *Our team defeated the visiting team. Verb*

○ The condition of being defeated in a contest: *The game ended in defeat. Noun.*
de·feat (di fēt′) *verb*, **defeated, defeating;** *noun, plural* **defeats.**

defect A flaw or weakness: *That glass bowl has a chip, a crack, and other defects.* **de·fect** (dē′fekt or dif ekt′) *noun, plural* **defects.**

defective Having a flaw or weakness; not perfect. **de·fec·tive** (dif ek′tiv) *adjective.*

defend 1. To protect against attack or danger: *Defend your country.* 2. To speak or act in support of: *Defend your opinion with facts.* **def·end** (di fend′) *verb*, **defended, defending.**

defense 1. The act of guarding against attack or danger. 2. A person or thing that protects: *The dam was a defense against floods.* 3. Support: *I spoke up in your defense.* 4. The defending team or players in a game: *Our hockey team has a good defense.* **de·fense** (di fens′) *noun, plural* **defenses.**

defenseless Lacking defenses; helpless: *The army's retreat left the village defenseless.* **de·fense·less** (difens′ləs) *adjective.*

defensive Guarding or protecting against attack: *Knights used to put on defensive armor before going into battle.* **de·fen·sive** (di fen′siv) *adjective.*

defer¹ To put off to a future time; delay: *The jury had to defer their judgment in the case until they had heard all the evidence.* **defer** (difûr) *verb*, **deferred, deferring.**

defer² To stop opposing the opinion or wishes of someone else; yield respectfully: *When we disagree, I usually defer to my older friend's judgment.* **de·fer** (di fûr′) *verb*, **deferred, deferring.**

defiance Bold refusal to obey or respect authority: *defiance of the law.* **de·fi·ance** (di fī′əns) *noun.*

deficiency A lack of something needed; shortage: *a vitamin deficiency.* **de·fi·cien·cy** (dif ish′ən sē) *noun, plural* **deficiencies.**

deficit 1. Something that occurs when more money has been spent than has been earned: *a trillion-dollar national deficit.* 2. Shortage: *a deficit of courage.* **def·i·cit** (def′ə sət) *noun, plural* **deficits.**

define 1. To give the meaning or meanings of: *A dictionary defines words.* 2. To describe or fix exactly: *The deed for this piece of property defines its boundaries.* **de·fine** (di fīn′) *verb*, **defined, defining.**

definite Certain; clear: *My answer was a definite no.* **def·i·nite** (def′ə nit) *adjective.*

definite article The article *the.* The definite article is used to refer to a particular person or thing. In the sentence "Give me the magazine you were reading," the definite article refers to a particular magazine.

definition An explanation of what a word or phrase means. A definition for the word "house" is "a building in which people live." **definition** (defənishən) *noun, plural* **definitions.**

deflate 1. To let the air out of something: *She deflated the balloon with a pin.* 2. To reduce in size: *Her remark deflated my ego.* **de·flate** (di flāt′) *verb*, **deflated, deflating.**

deflect To turn aside: *The awning deflected the sun's rays from entering the window.* **de·flect** (di flekt′) *verb*, **deflected, deflecting. deflector** *noun.*

deforestation The destruction of a forest. **deforestation** (dē fôr′ə stā′shən) *noun.* —**deforest** *verb.*

deform To spoil the form or shape of: *Constant winds had deformed and bent the tree.* **de·form** (di fôrm′) *verb*, **deformed, deforming.**

defrost To make free of ice or frost; thaw. *I defrosted the refrigerator this morning.* **de·frost** (dif rôst′) *verb*, **defrosted, defrosting.**

deft Skillful and clever; nimble. *The musician's deft fingers raced over the piano keys.* **deft** (deft) *adjective.*

defy 1. To refuse to obey: *Some drivers defy the law by going faster than the speed limit.* 2. To challenge someone to do something difficult: *I defy you to name all the presidents of the United States.* 3. To resist stubbornly; withstand. *The stain defied all my attempts to bleach it.* **de·fy** (di fī′) *verb*, **defied, defying.**

degrade To lower in character, quality, or rank: *The boss's cruel treatment degraded the employees.* **de·grade** (di grād′) *verb*, **degraded, degrading. degradation** *noun.*

degree 1. A stage or step in a process: *A young child learns to walk by degrees.* 2. Amount or extent: *A high degree of skill is needed to weave a rug.* 3. A title given by a school or college to a student who has finished a course of study. 4. A unit for measuring temperature: *A person's normal body temperature is 98.6 degrees Fahrenheit.* **5.** A unit for measuring angles or arcs. *Two perpendicular lines form a 90-degree angle.* **de·gree** (di grē′) *noun, plural* **degrees.**

dehydrate To make or become dry; lose or remove water: *A special process dehydrates grapes to make raisins.* **de·hy·drate** (dē hī′drāt) *verb,* **dehydrated, dehydrating.** —**dehydration** *noun.*

deity A god or goddess: *Mars was the Roman deity of war.* **de·i·ty** (dē′i tē) *noun, plural* **deities.**

dejected Sad or depressed: *The losing team felt dejected.* **de·ject·ed** (di jek′tid) *adjective.*

Del. An abbreviation for Delaware.

Delaware A state in the eastern United States. Its capital is Dover. **De·la·ware** (del′ə wâr) *noun.*

WORD HISTORY

The name **Delaware** comes from the name of the first governor of Virginia, Lord "De la Warr." An English captain named the Delaware Bay after this governor. Later, the name was given to the land west of the bay, which became the state.

Dover

Delaware
U. S. Postal Abbreviation: **DE**
Capital: **Dover**
Population: **644,000**
Area: **2,057 sq. mi./5,328 sq. km**
State Nicknames: **First State; Diamond State**
State Bird: **Blue Hen Chicken**
State Flower: **Peach Blossom**

delay **1.** To put off to a later time; postpone. We delayed the start of the hike because of rain.

2. To make late: *A flat tire delayed the start of our trip.* **3.** To slow down; linger: *I will miss my bus if I delay.* Verb.
○ The act of delaying or the condition of being delayed *There will be a delay of fifteen minutes before the train arrives.* Noun.
del·ay (di lā′) *verb,* **delayed, delaying;** *noun, plural* **delays.**

delegate A person who is chosen to act for others; representative: *Each country that belongs to the United Nations is represented by a delegate.* Noun.
○ To choose for doing a task; assign: *The club delegated me to make arrangements for a holiday party.* Verb.
del·e·gate (del′i gāt′ *or* del′i git *for noun;* del′i gāt′ *for verb) noun, plural* **delegates;** *verb,* **delegated, delegating.**

delegation A group of delegates or representatives: *A delegation from the fire department marched in the Fourth of July parade.* **del·e·ga·tion** (del′i gā′shən) *noun, plural* **delegations.**

delete To remove something from a text: *I've accidentally deleted my homework file from the computer.* **de·lete** (di lēt′) *verb,* **deleted, deleting.**

deli A short form of delicatessen. **de·li** (del′ē) *noun, plural* **delis.**

deliberate **1.** Done or said on purpose: *a deliberate trick to insult the new student.* **2.** Careful and slow; not hasty or rash: *Many people must take deliberate steps when they walk on ice.* Adjective.
○ To think over or discuss carefully: *The jury deliberated for hours before giving a decision.* Verb.
de·lib·er·ate (di lib′ər it *for adjective;* di lib′ə rāt *for verb) adjective; verb,* **deliberated, deliberating.**

delicate **1.** Fine or dainty: *The threads of a spider's web are delicate.* **2.** Pleasing in smell, taste, or color; mild: *the delicate scent of roses in the air.* **3.** Easily damaged; fragile: *Handle those delicate glasses carefully.* **4.** Very sensitive: *Delicate instruments detected an earthquake thousands of miles away.* **5.** Requiring careful skill: *a delicate operation.* **del·i·cate** (del′i kit) *adjective.*

delicatessen A store that sells food that is ready to eat. Cold meats, cheeses, and salads are sold in

PRONUNCIATION KEY:

| at | āpe | fär | câre | end | mē | it | īce | pierce | hot | ōld | sông | fôrk |
| oil | out | up | ūse | rüle | pull | tûrn | chin | sing | shop | thin | this | |

hw in white; zh in treasure. The symbol ə stands for the unstressed vowel sound in about, taken, pencil, lemon, and circus.

193

a delicatessen. **del·i·ca·tes·sen** (del′i kə tes′ən) *noun, plural* **delicatessens.**

delicious Pleasing or delightful to the taste or smell: *The stew cooking for dinner smelled* **delicious.** **de·li·cious** (di lish′əs) *adjective.*

delight Great pleasure; joy: *The children beamed with* **delight** *when they saw the baboons. Noun.*
○ To give great pleasure or joy to: *The puppet show* **delighted** *the children*
 • **delight in.** To take pleasure from: *My grandparents* **delight in** *telling us stories about their childhood. Verb.*
de·light (di līt′) *noun, plural* **delights;** *verb,* **delighted, delighting.**

delightful Very pleasing: *We had a* **delightful** *time playing games at the party.* **de·light·ful** (di līt′fəl) *adjective.*

delirious 1. Confused by a very high fever: *The patient cried out while she was* **delirious.** 2. Very excited; overcome with joy: *My brother was* **delirious** *after he won the spelling bee.* **de·lir·i·ous** (di lîr′ē əs) *adjective.*

deliver 1. To take to the proper place or person: *The department store will* **deliver** *our new television set.* 2. To say; utter: *The mayor* **delivered** *a long speech at the meeting.* 3. To strike or throw: *The pitcher* **delivered** *a curve ball to the batter.* 4. To save from danger; rescue: *The slaves were finally* **delivered** *from bondage.* **de·liv·er** (dil iv′ər) *verb,* **delivered, delivering.**

delivery 1. The act of taking something to the proper place or person: *We get a mail* **delivery** *every day except Sundays and holidays.* 2. A way of doing something: *The pitcher's* **delivery** *was low and outside.* **de·liv·er·y** (di liv′ə rē) *noun, plural* **deliveries.**

delta An area of land at the mouth of a river. A delta is formed by deposits of mud, sand, and pebbles. It is often shaped like a triangle. **del·ta** (del′tə) *noun, plural* **deltas.**

WORD HISTORY

The word delta comes from the Greek name for the fourth letter in the Greek alphabet. The letter delta was drawn as a triangle, and deltas in rivers are often in the shape of a triangle.

---

deluge A great flood or very heavy rain. *Noun.*
○ 1. To flood: *When the dam broke, nearby*

towns were **deluged.** 2. To receive a lot of something: *After our town was flooded, we were* **deluged** *with offers of help.*
del·uge (del′ūj) *verb,* **deluged, deluging.**

delusion An idea that is not real; something imagined or wished for: *Becoming an astronaut turned out to be a* **delusion** *for many people.* **de·lu·sion** (di lü′zhən) *noun, plural* **delusions.**

demand 1. To ask for forcefully; claim as a right: *The customers* **demanded** *their money back for the defective radio.* 2. To call for; need: *Portrait painting* **demands** *skill and close observation. Verb.*
○ 1. The act of demanding: *The child's* **demand** *for more spinach surprised everyone.* 2. Something that is demanded: *Higher pay and safer conditions were among the* **demands** *of the factory workers.* 3. The desire for a product or service: *The* **demand** *for turkeys is very high at Thanksgiving time. Noun.*
de·mand (di mand′) *verb,* **demanded, demanding;** *noun, plural* **demands.**

demanding Requiring great skill, attention, or effort: *Being a teacher is a* **demanding** *job.* **de·mand·ing** (di man′ding) *adjective.*

demerit A mark on a person's record that shows he or she broke a rule: *The two apprentices had received so many* **demerits** *for lateness that they were fired.* **de·me·rit** (dē me′rit) *noun, plural* **demerits.**

democracy 1. A government that is run by the people who live under it. In a democracy, the people may run the government indirectly by electing representatives who govern for them. 2. A country in which the government is a democracy. The United States is a democracy. **dem·o·cra·cy** (di mok′rə sē) *noun, plural* **democracies.**

WORD HISTORY

The word democracy comes from two Greek words meaning "the people rule." The ancient Greeks were the first to think that people might rule themselves, instead of having a king.

---

democrat 1. A person who believes that a government should be run by the people who live under it. 2. Democrat. A person who belongs to the Democratic Party. 3. A person who believes that all people are equal or should have equal rights. **dem·o·crat** (dem′ə krat) *noun, plural* **democrats.**

democratic 1. Of or supporting a democracy. The United States is a democratic country.

2. Believing that all people should be treated as equals: *a democratic approach to solving problems.* **dem•o•crat•ic** (dem'ə kra'tik) *adjective.*

Democratic Party One of the two major political parties in the United States.

demolish To tear down or destroy: *The workers demolished the old factory to make way for a new office building.* **de•mol•ish** (di mol'ish) *verb,* **demolished, demolishing, demolition** *noun.*

demon 1. An evil spirit; devil. 2. A person who does something with great enthusiasm or energy: *We worked like demons to finish the boat in time for the race.* **de•mon** (dē'mən) *noun, plural* **demons.**

demonstrate 1. To explain, prove, or show clearly: *A salesperson demonstrated the new food processor at the department store.* 2. To take part in a public meeting or parade to show feelings about a matter: *A group of citizens demonstrated against the pollution of the river by wastes from the factory.* **dem•on•strate** (dem'ən strāt') *verb,* **demonstrated, demonstrating.**

demonstration 1. Something that explains, proves, or shows clearly: *The firefighters visited our school to give us demonstration of safety procedures.* 2. A public meeting or parade to show feelings about a matter: *A group of people held a demonstration in the park to protest the war.* **dem•on•stra•tion** (dem'ən strā'shən) *noun, plural* **demonstrations.**

demonstrative Showing love openly: *Children learn how to be demonstrative from their parents.* **de•mon•stra•tive** (di mon'strə tiv) *adjective.*

den 1. A place where wild animals rest or sleep: *The bear uses a cave as a den during its long winter sleeps.* 2. A small, cozy room for reading or studying. 3. A group of about eight Cub Scouts. **den** (den) *noun, plural* **dens.**

denial The act of saying "no" or "not true" to something: *The judge listened to the prisoner's denial of the charges against him.* **de•ni•al** (di nī'əl) *noun, plural* **denials.**

denim 1. A heavy cotton cloth used for work or sports clothes. 2. denims. Pants or overalls made of this cloth. **den•im** (den'im) *noun, plural* **denims.**

Denmark A country in north-central Europe. **Den•mark** (den'märk) *noun.*

denomination 1. A religious group or sect: one of the protestant denominations. 2. One kind of unit in a system. A dime and a nickel are coins of different denominations. **de•nom•in•a•tion** (di nom'ə nā'shən) *noun, plural* **denominations.**

denominator The number below the line in a fraction. The denominator shows the number of equal parts into which the whole is divided. In the fraction, 2 is the denominator. **de•nom•in•a•tor** (di nom'ə nā'tər) *noun, plural* **denominators.**

In $\dfrac{1}{4}$; $\dfrac{2}{3}$; and $\dfrac{7}{8}$

4, 3, and 8 are **denominators.**

denote 1. To be a sign of; show: *Large dark clouds usually denote the coming of a storm.* 2. To be a name for; mean: *The word "dentist" denotes a doctor who takes care of people's teeth.* **de•note** (di nōt') *verb,* **denoted, denoting. denotation** *noun.*

denounce 1. To speak out against; object to: *The letter in the newspaper denounced bicyclists who ignore traffic lights.* 2. To give information against; accuse: *The crook denounced his partner to the police.* **de•nounce** (di nouns') *verb,* **denounced, denouncing.**

dense Packed closely together; thick: *The hikers lost the trail and got lost in the dense woods.* **dense** (dens) *adjective,* **denser, densest.**

density Closeness; thickness: *The density of population is greater in a big city than it is in the country.* **dens•i•ty** (den'si tē) *noun, plural* **densities.**

dent A small hollow made in the surface of something by a blow or pressure: *The accident put a dent in the front fender of my bike.* Noun.
○ To make a dent or hollow in: *I dented the soft clay with my thumb.* Verb.
dent (dent) *noun, plural* **dents;** *verb,* **dented, denting.**

dental 1. Having to do with the teeth: *Good dental care helps prevent tooth decay.* 2. Having to do with a dentist's work. **den•tal** (den'təl) *adjective.*

dental floss A specially treated thread used to clean between the teeth.

dentin *or* **dentine** The hard, bony material that forms the main part of the tooth. It is covered by

PRONUNCIATION KEY:
at   āpe   fär   câre   end   mē   it   īce   pierce   hot   ōld   sông   fôrk
oil   out   up   ūse   rüle   pùll   tûrn   chin   sing   shop   thin   this
hw in white; zh in treasure. The symbol ə stands for the unstressed vowel sound in about, taken, pencil, lemon, and circus.   **195**

the enamel. Dentin is very sensitive to heat, cold, and touch. **den·tin** *or* **den·tine** (den′tin *or* den tēn′) *noun.*

dentist A doctor who specializes in the care of the teeth and mouth. **den·tist** (den′tist) *noun, plural* **dentists. dentistry** *noun.*

deny 1. To say that something is not true: *The prisoners **denied** that they had robbed the bank.* 2. To refuse to give or grant: *The company **denied** the workers' request for longer vacations.* **de·ny** (di nī′) *verb,* **denied, denying.**

deodorant Something used to hide unpleasant smells: *an underarm **deodorant**.* **de·o·dor·ant** (di ōd′ə rənt) *noun, plural* **deodorants.**

depart 1. To go away; leave: *The train is due to **depart** from the station at ten o'clock.* 2. To change or differ: *We **departed** from our usual routine and held the class outdoors.* **de·part** (di pärt′) *verb,* **departed, departing.**

department A separate part of a large organization, such as a university, hospital, or government; division: *The English **department** at school has three new teachers this fall.* **de·part·ment** (di pärt′mənt) *noun, plural* **departments.**

department store A large store that sells many different kinds of goods in different departments.

departure The act of departing: *The plane's **departure** was delayed two hours.* **de·par·ture** (di pär′chər) *noun, plural* **departures.**

depend 1. To rely on or trust: *You can always **depend** on my friend to be on time.* 2. To get help or support: *Children **depend** on their parents.* 3. To be determined by how something else turns out: *Whether we go on the hike **depends** on the weather.* **de·pend** (di pend′) *verb,* **depended, depending.**

dependable Reliable or trustworthy: *A person who is **dependable** can be trusted to do a job without being watched.* **de·pen·da·ble** (di pen′də bəl) *adjective.*

dependence The state of being dependent: *A baby animal's **dependence** on its mother diminishes as it gets older.* **de·pen·dence** (di pen′dəns) *noun.*

dependent 1. Relying on someone else for what is needed or wanted: *Baby birds are **dependent** on their parents to feed them.* 2. Determined by how something else turns out: *Our plans for the picnic are **dependent** on the weather. Adjective.*

○ A person whose home, food, and other basic needs are provided by someone else: *My parents supported five **dependents**. Noun.* **de·pen·dent** (di pend′ənt) *adjective; noun, plural* **dependents.**

depict To show in pictures or words; describe: *The artist tried to **depict** the movement of the ocean's waves. The story **depicts** a typical Chinese family.* **de·pict** (di pikt′) *verb,* **depicted, depicting.**

deport To make a person return to his or her own country: *The government **deported** the criminals.* **deport** (di pôrt′) *verb,* **deported, deporting. deportation** *noun.*

deposit 1. To put money or valuable things in a bank or other safe place: *I **deposited** twenty dollars in my savings account.* 2. To put or set down; place: *The river **deposits** silt at its mouth. Verb.*

○ 1. Something put in a bank or other safe place: *a **deposit** of fifty dollars.* 2. Something given as a partial payment, with the rest to be paid later: *a **deposit** of twenty dollars on a new bicycle.* 3. Something that has settled and is left as a layer: *A **deposit** of dust covered the window sill.* 4. A large amount of mineral in rock or in the ground: *Texas has large **deposits** of oil underground. Noun.* **de·pos·it** (di poz′it) *verb,* **deposited, depositing;** *noun, plural* **deposits.**

depot A railroad or bus terminal. **de·pot** (dē′pō) *noun, plural* **depots.**

Before the automobile and the airplane, railroad depots could be found throughout the nation.

depress To make sad or gloomy: *The death of their dog **depressed** the whole family.* **depress** (dipres) *verb,* **depressed, depressing.**

depression 1. Sadness; gloom: *Troubles at home and at school contributed to my depression.* 2. A low place or hollow: *The car bumped over a depression in the road.* 3. A time when business is slow and people are out of work: *Many people lost their jobs during the depression of the 1930s.* **de•pres•sion** (di presh′ən) *noun, plural* **depressions.**

deprive To keep from having or doing: *Lack of money deprived many children of an education. The dictator deprived the people of freedom of speech.* **de•prive** (di prīv′) *verb,* **deprived, depriving.**

depth 1. The distance from top to bottom or from front to back: *The depth of the pool was 5 feet.* 2. The quality of being deep; deepness: *depth of understanding.*

  • **out of one's depth.** Unable to understand a subject or event: *Some people are out of their depth when it comes to economic problems.* **depth** (depth) *noun, plural* **depths.**

deputy A person appointed to act in the place of someone else: *The sheriff's deputy helps to keep order in the town.* **dep•u•ty** (dep′yə tē) *noun, plural* **deputies.**

derby 1. A stiff hat with a narrow brim. 2. A horse race: *the Kentucky Derby.* **der•by** (dûr′bē) *noun, plural* **derbies.**

derive 1. To come from a source; originate: *The word "dandelion" is derived from a French word.* 2. To obtain from a source: *I derive pleasure from reading.* **de•rive** (di rīv′) *verb,* **derived, deriving.**

derrick 1. A machine for lifting and moving heavy objects. It has a long arm attached to the base of an upright post. 2. The framework over an oil well or other drill hole that supports the drilling machinery. **der•rick** (der′ik) *noun, plural* **derricks.**

descend 1. To move or come from a higher place to a lower one: *They descended the mountain on skis.* 2. To come down from an earlier source or ancestor: *My family descends from French settlers in Canada.* **de•scend** (di send′) *verb,* **descended, descending.**

descendant A person who comes from a particular ancestor or group of ancestors: *Our neighbor is a descendant of the early Dutch settlers in New York.* **de•scen•dant** (di send′ənt) *noun, plural* **descendants.**

descent 1. A coming from a higher place to a lower one: *The quick descent of the elevator made my stomach feel funny.* 2. A downward slope: *The slide had a steep descent.* 3. Ancestors or birth: *We are of Polish descent.* Another word that sounds like this is **dissent.** **de•scent** (di sent′) *noun, plural* **descents.**

describe To give a picture of something in words; tell or write about: *The boy described his adventures at camp.* **de•scribe** (di skrīb′) *verb,* **described, describing.**

WORD HISTORY

The word **describe** comes from a Latin word meaning "to write down" or "to represent." This word later came to mean "to represent in words," whether the words were written down or spoken.

---

description 1. An account of something in words: *a description of a lost dog.* 2. Kind; sort; variety: *There were automobiles of every description in the show.* **des•crip•tion** (di skrip′shən) *noun, plural* **descriptions.**

descriptive Giving a picture in words: *The tourists were given descriptive pamphlets about places to visit and things to do in the city.* **de•scrip•tive** (di skrip′tiv) *adjective.*

desegregate To do away with the system of having separate schools and other facilities for people of different races: *The government ordered the town to desegregate its public schools.* **de•seg•re•gate** (dē seg′ri gāt) *verb,* **desegregated, desegregating.**

desert¹ A hot, dry, sandy area of land with few or no plants growing on it. *Noun.* **des•ert** (dez′ərt) *noun, plural* **deserts.**

desert² To go away and leave a person or thing that should not be left; abandon: *That family deserted their dog when they moved away.*

Some desert plants, like this century plant, have large flowers.

PRONUNCIATION KEY:
at ape fär câre end mē it īce pîerce hot ōld sông fôrk
oil out up ūse rüle pùll tûrn chin sing shop thin this
hw in white; zh in treasure. The symbol ə stands for the unstressed vowel sound in about, taken, pencil, lemon, and circus.

197

Another word that sounds like this is **dessert**.
de·sert (di zûrt′) *verb*, **deserted, deserting**.

deserve To have a right to; be worthy of: *The dancers **deserve** praise for their beautiful performance*. **de·serve** (di zûrv′) *verb*, **deserved, deserving**.

design 1. A drawing or outline made to serve as a guide or pattern: *Everyone liked the architect's **design** for the new school*. 2. An arrangement of shapes, parts, or colors; pattern: *The carpet in the living room has a blue and green **design***. *Noun*.
○ To make a plan, drawing, or outline of; make a pattern for: ***design** costumes for the play*. *Verb*. **de·sign** (di zīn′) *noun, plural* **designs**; *verb*, **designed, designing**.

designate 1. To mark or point out; show: *A blue line is used to **designate** rivers on many maps*. 2. To call by a particular name or title: *The time we live in could be **designated** "the Computer Age."* 3. To give a job or office to; appoint: *I was **designated** to lead the hike across the canyon*. **des·ig·nate** (dez′ig nāt) *verb*, **designated, designating**.

designated hitter In baseball, the person who bats instead of the pitcher, but without playing the pitcher's position.

desirable Worth having or wishing for; pleasing: *That corner lot is a **desirable** place for a baseball field*. **de·sir·able** (di zīr′ə bəl) *adjective*.

desire To wish for; long for: *My sister **desires** a basketball more than anything*. *Verb*.
○ A longing; wish: *a great **desire** to travel*. *Noun*. **de·sire** (di zīr′) *verb*, **desired, desiring**; *noun, plural* **desires**.

desk A piece of furniture with a flat or sloping top. A desk is used for reading or writing, and sometimes has drawers. **desk** (desk) *noun, plural* **desks**.

desktop publishing Writing, editing, and designing a book, newsletter, or flyer on a computer.

desolate 1. Without people; deserted: *In the winter, that beach is **desolate***. 2. Miserable; cheerless: *The lost child was **desolate***. **des·o·late** (des′ə lit) *adjective*.

despair A complete loss of hope: *The family was filled with **despair** when the fire destroyed their house*. *Noun*.
○ To give up or lose hope; be without hope: *I **despaired** of ever finding my lost watch in the pond*. *Verb*.

de·spair (di spâr′) *noun; verb*, **despaired, despairing**.

desperate 1. Reckless because of having no hope: *The **desperate** player hurled the basketball at the net just as the game was ending*. 2. Very bad or hopeless: *The workers trapped in the mine were in a **desperate** situation*. **des·per·ate** (des′pə rit) *adjective*.

desperation A willingness to try anything to change a hopeless situation: *They gripped the log in **desperation** as they floated toward the waterfall*. **des·per·a·tion** (des′pə rā′shən) *noun*.

despise To look down on as worthless; scorn: *My parents **despise** lying of any kind*. **de·spise** (di spīz′) *verb*, **despised, despising**.

despite In spite of; regardless of: *I went to school **despite** my bad cold*. **de·spite** (di spīt′) *preposition*.

dessert A food served at the end of a meal. Fruit, pie, cheese, and ice cream are desserts.
Another word that sounds like this is **desert**.
• **just desserts**. What a person deserves: *If you cheat on the test and are caught, you'll get your **just desserts***.
des·sert (diz ûrt′) *noun, plural* **desserts**.

destination A place to which a person is going or a thing is being sent: *My **destination** is New York*. **des·tin·a·tion** (des′tə nā′shən) *noun, plural* **destinations**.

destine To set apart for a particular purpose or use; intend. *That land is **destined** for a new hospital*. **des·tine** (des′tin) *verb*, **destined, destining**.

destiny What happens to a person or thing, especially when it seems to be determined in advance; fortune: *I felt that it was my **destiny** to be an Olympic gymnast someday*. **dest·in·y** (des′tə nē) *noun, plural* **destinies**.

destitute Without food, shelter, or money: *If you can't get a job, you'll end up **destitute***. **des·ti·tute** (des′ti tüt *or* des′ti tūt) *adjective*.

destroy To ruin completely; wreck: *The earthquake **destroyed** the city*. **de·stroy** (di stroi′) *verb*, **destroyed, destroying**.

destroyer A small, fast warship. **de·stroy·er** (di stroi′ər) *noun, plural* **destroyers**.

destruction 1. The act of destroying: *The **destruction** of an old building has become a media event*. 2. Great damage or ruin: *The earthquake caused widespread **destruction***. **de·struc·tion** (di struk′shən) *noun, plural* **destructions**.

destructive Causing destruction: *Moths can be destructive to clothes made of wool.* **de·struc·tive** (di strukʹtiv) *adjective.*

detach To unfasten and remove; take off: *The salesperson detached the price tag from the gift before wrapping it.* **de·tach** (di tachʹ) *verb,* **detached, detaching.**

detail 1. A small part of a whole; item: *Can you give me the details of our homework assignment?* 2. A dealing with matters one by one: *There's no need to go into detail about your vacation. Noun.* ○ 1. To tell or describe item by item: *The speakers detailed their experiences in Cuba.* 2. To clean a car. *Verb.* **de·tail** (di tālʹ *or* dēʹtāl) *noun, plural* **details;** *verb,* **detailed, detailing.**

There are many fine details on this doorknob and its mount.

detain 1. To keep from going; hold back: *Band practice detained me at school this afternoon, so I was late getting home.* 2. To keep in custody: *The police detained the person who was suspected of robbery.* **de·tain** (di tānʹ) *verb,* **detained, detaining.**

detect To find out or notice; discover: *I called the fire department after I detected smoke coming from the garage.* **de·tect** (di tektʹ) *verb,* **detected, detecting.**

detective A police officer or other person whose work is finding information about crimes and trying to solve them. *Noun.* ○ Having to do with detectives and their work. *Do you like to read detective stories? Adjective.* **de·tec·tive** (di tekʹtiv) *noun, plural* **detectives;** *adjective.*

detector A device that detects something such as smoke, metal, or radioactivity. **de·tec·tor** (di tekʹtər) *noun, plural* **detectors.**

detention A punishment in which a student has to come early or stay late after school. **de·ten·tion** (di tenʹchən) *noun.*

deter To discourage from doing something: *The huge waves deterred us from going swimming.* **de·ter** (di tûrʹ) *verb,* **deterred, deterring.**

detergent A chemical substance that is used for washing things. It may be a liquid or powder. **de·ter·gent** (di tûrʹjənt) *noun, plural* **detergents.**

deteriorate To make or become steadily worse: *Our car deteriorated as it got older.* **de·ter·i·or·ate** (di tîrʹē ə rātʹ) *verb,* **deteriorated, deteriorating.**

determination 1. A definite and firm purpose: *Their determination to become doctors made the students study very hard.* 2. The act of deciding or settling ahead of time: *The campers' determination of what to take on their trip took a long time.* 3. The act of finding out something by watching or checking: *The doctor hopes to make a determination about why my brother is sick.* **de·ter·min·a·tion** (di tûrʹmə nāʹshən) *noun, plural* **determinations.**

determine 1. To decide or settle definitely: *The members of the club determined the date for their next meeting.* 2. To find out by watching or checking: *We determined the name of the flower by looking for its picture in a book about plants.* 3. To be the cause of: *Sunlight, rainfall, and soil determine how well a plant grows.* **de·ter·mine** (di tûrʹmin) *verb,* **determined, determining.**

determined Firm in sticking to a purpose; showing determination: *The determined students kept phoning the senator's office until somebody answered.* **de·ter·mined** (di tûrʹmind) *adjective.*

detest To dislike very much; hate: *Drivers detest icy roads.* **de·test** (di testʹ) *verb,* **detested, detesting.**

detonate To cause something to explode: *The lit cigarette deto-*

Explosives have been detonated to topple this building.

PRONUNCIATION KEY:

| at | āpe | fär | câre | end | mē | it | īce | pierce | hot | ōld | sông | fôrk |
| oil | out | up | ūse | rüle | pull | tûrn | chin | sing | shop | thin | this | |

hw in white; zh in treasure. The symbol ə stands for the unstressed vowel sound in about, taken, pencil, lemon, and circus.

199

nated the gasoline pumps. **det·o·nate** (det′ən āt) *verb*, **detonated, detonating. detonation** *noun*.

detour A longer way to get somewhere: *We had to take a detour because the main highway was being repaired. Noun.*
  ○ To cause to make a detour: *The police detoured the traffic because of the accident. Verb.* **de·tour** (dē′tŭr) *noun, plural* **detours;** *verb,* **detoured, detouring.**

detract To take away from the value or beauty of something: *The noisy people detracted from our enjoyment of the movie.* **de·tract** (dit rakt′) *verb,* **detracted, detracting.**

detrimental Harmful: *Smoking is detrimental to your health.* **det·ri·men·tal** (de′trə ment əl) *adjective.*

devastate 1. To destroy; ruin: *The hurricane devastated the small towns along the coast.* 2. To shock; distress: *My brother was devastated when his girlfriend broke up with him.* **dev·as·tate** (dev′ə stāt′) *verb,* **devastated, devastating.**

develop 1. To bring or come gradually into being: *I developed an interest in computers while in the third grade.* 2. To grow or cause to grow: *You can develop your muscles by exercising.* 3. To put to use; make available: *That country has not developed its natural resources.* 4. To treat photographic film with a chemical so that an image appears. **de·vel·op** (di vel′əp) *verb,* **developed, developing.**

development 1. The act or process of developing: *The development of a spacecraft that could reach the moon took many years.* 2. An event or happening: *New developments in the story were broadcast every hour.* 3. A group of houses or other buildings on a large area of land. The houses often look alike and are built by one builder. **de·vel·op·ment** (di vel′əp mənt) *noun, plural* **developments.**

deviate To do something in an unusual way: *Sometimes it's fun and exciting to deviate from one's plans on a trip.* **de·vi·ate** (dē′vē āt) *verb,* **deviated, deviating. deviation** *noun.*

device 1. Something made or invented for a particular purpose. A can opener, a toothbrush, and a clock are devices. 2. A plan or scheme; trick: *Clearing the throat is sometimes just a device for getting attention.* **de·vice** (di vīs′) *noun, plural* **devices.**

devil 1. the Devil. The chief spirit of evil. 2. A wicked, mischievous, or very energetic person: *That sister of yours is a little devil.* **dev·il** (dev′əl) *noun, plural* **devils.**

devious Sneaky; untrustworthy: *a devious mind.* **devious** (dē′vē əs) *adjective.*

devise To think out; invent; plan: *We devised a secret code that no one could decipher.* **de·vise** (di vīz′) *verb,* **devised, devising.**

devote To give effort, attention, or time to some purpose; dedicate: *I want to devote all my energy to studying dancing.* **de·vote** (di vōt′) *verb,* **devoted, devoting.**

devoted Loyal; faithful: *My devoted friend would do anything for me.* **de·vot·ed** (di vō′tid) *adjective.*

devotion A strong affection; faithfulness: *They felt great devotion to their grandparents.* **de·vo·tion** (di vō′shən) *noun, plural* **devotions.**

devour 1. To eat; consume: *The hungry child devoured the sandwich.* 2. To destroy: *The flames devoured the house.* **de·vour** (di vour′) *verb,* **devoured, devouring.**

devout 1. Very religious: *devout church members.* 2. Sincere; earnest: *You have my devout wishes for your success in the school play.* **de·vout** (di vout′) *adjective.*

dew Moisture from the air that forms drops on cool surfaces. Dew gathers on grass, plants, and trees during the night. Other words that sound like this are **do** and **due**. **dew** (dü or dū) *noun, plural* **dews.**

dewlap The skin that hangs loose under the throat of cattle and certain other animals. **dew·lap** (dü′lap or dū′lap) *noun, plural* **dewlaps.**

dexterity Skill in using the hands: *Both magicians and pianists need great dexterity.* **dex·ter·i·ty** (dek ster′i tē) *noun.*

WORD HISTORY

The word dexterity goes back to a Latin word meaning "right" or "right hand." Since most people are right-handed, the right side used to be associated with strength, skill, and ability.

diabetes A disease in which there is too much sugar in the blood. A person with diabetes either cannot make or cannot use enough insulin, the substance the body needs to use sugar properly. The word *diabetes* is used with a singular verb. **di·a·be·tes** (dī′ə bē′tis *or* dī′ə bē′tēz) *noun.*

diabetic Having or having to do with diabetes. *Adjective.*
○ A person who has diabetes. *Noun.* **di·a·bet·ic** (dī′ə bet′ik) *adjective; noun, plural* **diabetics.**

diabolic Very wicked or evil: *a diabolic scheme to conquer the world.* **di·a·bol·ic** (di ə bol′ik) *adjective.* **diabolical** *adjective.*

diagnosis An opinion about what is wrong with a person or animal formed after looking at the patient and studying the symptoms: *a diagnosis of chicken pox.* **di·ag·no·sis** (dī′əg nō′sis) *noun, plural* **diagnoses** (dī′əg nō′sēz).

diagonal Having a slant: *The dress had a pattern of* **diagonal** *stripes. Adjective.*
○ A straight line that connects the opposite corners of a square or rectangle. *Noun.* **di·ag·o·nal** (dī ag′ə nəl) *adjective; noun, plural* **diagonals.**

diagram A plan or sketch that shows the parts of a thing or how the parts are put together: *We'll use this* **diagram** *of the model airplane when we build it. Noun.*
○ To show by a diagram; make a diagram of: *It's easier to* **diagram** *my house than to explain where all the rooms are. Verb.* **di·a·gram** (dī′ə gram) *noun, plural* **diagrams;** *verb,* **diagramed, diagraming.**

dial 1. The face of an instrument. A dial is marked with numbers, letters, or other signs that show time, quantity, or some other value. A clock, a compass, and a meter usually have dials. 2. The disk on a radio or television set that is turned to tune in a station or channel. 3. The disk on some telephones that is turned by the finger when the caller is selecting the number being called. *Noun.*
○ 1. To tune in by using a radio or television dial: *Dial another channel and find a better program.* 2. To select numbers when making a telephone call: *The caller* **dialed** *a wrong number. Verb.* **di·al** (dī′əl *or* dīl) *noun, plural* **dials;** *verb,* **dialed, dialing.**

dialect A form of a language that is spoken in a particular area or by a particular group of people. **di·a·ect** (dī′ə lekt) *noun, plural* **dialects.**

dialogue Conversation, especially in a play, movie, or story: *That play is full of funny dialogue.* **di·a·logue** (dī′əlôg′) *noun, plural* **dialogues.**

dial tone The sound you hear when you first pick up a telephone.

diameter 1. A straight line passing through the center of a circle or sphere, from one side to the other. 2. The length of such a line; the width or thickness of something round: *The* **diameter** *of the earth is about 8,000 miles.* **di·a·me·ter** (dī am′i tər) *noun, plural* **diameters.**

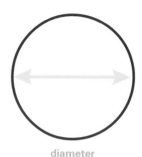

diameter

diamond 1. A mineral that consists of pure carbon in the form of a clear or pale crystal. It is the hardest natural material known. 2. A figure having four sides and four angles that is shaped like this. 3. A playing card marked with one or more red diamonds. 4. **diamonds.** The suit of cards marked with this figure ♦. 5. The space on a baseball field that is inside the lines that connect the bases. **di·a·mond** (dī′mənd *or* dī′ə mənd) *noun, plural* **diamonds.**

A baseball field is called a diamond because of its shape.

diaper A baby's underwear made of soft, folded cloth or other material. **dia·per** (dī′pər *or* dī′ə pər) *noun, plural* **diapers.**

PRONUNCIATION KEY:

| at | āpe | fär | câre | end | mē | it | īce | pierce | hot | ōld | sông | fôrk |
| oil | out | up | ūse | rüle | pull | tûrn | chin | sing | shop | thin | this | |

hw in white; zh in treasure. The symbol ə stands for the unstressed vowel sound in about, taken, pencil, lemon, and circus.

201

diaphragm 1. A thin layer of muscles that divides the chest from the abdomen. The diaphragm helps control breathing. 2. A flexible disk used to change sound into electrical signals, or to change electrical signals into sound. It is used inside telephones and microphones. 3. A kind of birth control device used by women. **di·a·phragm** (dī′ə fram) *noun, plural* **diaphragms.**

diarrhea A condition in which a person or animal has frequent and watery bowel movements. **di·ar·rhea** (dī′ə rē′ə) *noun.*

diary A written record of the things that one has done or thought each day: *I keep my diary hidden.* **di·a·ry** (dī′ə rē) *noun, plural* **diaries.**

dice Small cubes of wood, plastic, or other material marked on each side with from one to six dots. Dice are used in some games. *Noun.*
○ To cut into small cubes: *Please dice the potatoes for the stew. Verb.*
dice (dīs) *plural noun, singular* **die**; *verb,* **diced, dicing.**

dictate 1. To say or read something aloud to be written down by someone else: *The banker dictated a letter to her secretary.* 2. To order by authority: *dictate the terms of a peace treaty. Verb.*
○ A rule or command that tells what to do: *They believe in following the dictates of the law. Noun.*
dic·tate (dik′tāt *or* dik tāt′ *for verb;* dik′tāt *for noun*) *verb,* **dictated, dictating;** *noun, plural* **dictates.**

dictator A person who rules a country without sharing power or consulting anyone else: *The dictator took away the people's right to vote.* **dic·ta·tor** (dik′tā tər *or* dik tā′tər) *noun, plural* **dictators.**

dictionary A book that has words of a language arranged in alphabetical order, together with information about them: *This dictionary tells what words mean, how they are spelled, how they are used, how they are pronounced, and where they come from.* **dic·tion·ar·y** (dik′shən er′ē) *noun, plural* **dictionaries.**

did Past tense of **do. did** (did) *verb.*

didn't Shortened form of "did not": *I didn't do my homework.* **didn't** (didənt) *contraction.*

die¹ 1. To stop living: *The flowers died during the cold spell.* 2. To lose force or strength; come to an end: *The wind suddenly died as the sailboat neared the shore.* 3. To want or need: *The hikers were dying for a cold drink of water.*
Another word that sounds like this is **dye.**
die (dī) *verb,* **died, dying.**

die² A small cube used in games. Look up **dice** for more information.
Another word that sounds like this is **dye.**
die (dī) *noun, plural* **dice** (for definition 1) *or* **dies** (for definition 2).

This train is powered by a diesel engine.

diesel engine An engine that burns a heavy fuel oil. The oil is set on fire by heat produced by the compression of air in the engine. **die·sel engine** (dēz′əl).

diet 1. The food and drink usually eaten by a person or animal: *A giraffe's diet is mostly leaves.* 2. A special selection of food and drink: *a low fat diet. Noun.*
○ To eat a special selection of foods: *Wrestlers and gymnasts often diet before they compete. Verb.* **di·et** (dī′it) *noun, plural* **diets;** *verb,* **dieted, dieting.**

dietitian A person who is trained to plan balanced meals for both healthy and sick people. A dietitian usually works at a hospital or school. **di·e·ti·tian** (dī′i tish′ən) *noun, plural* **dietitians.**

differ 1. To be unlike; not be the same: *Her taste in food differs greatly from mine.* 2. To have a different opinion; disagree: *My parents and I differ about where to go on our vacation.* **dif·fer** (dif′ər) *verb,* **differed, differing.**

difference 1. The state or quality of being unlike: *Do you notice a difference in how people talk?* 2. A way of being unlike: *One of the differences* between alligators and crocodiles is that croco-diles have longer heads. **3.** The amount left after one quantity is subtracted from another; remain-der: *The **difference** between 16 and 12 is 4.* **4.** A disagreement about something: *They were able to settle their **differences** without a fight.*

• **to make a difference.** To have an effect on or change something; matter: *Getting enough sleep **makes a difference** in how I feel.*
dif·fer·ence (dif′ər əns or dif′rəns) *noun, plural* **differences.**

different **1.** Not alike or similar: *The two oppos-ing teams wore **different** uniforms.* **2.** Not the same; separate: *It rained two **different** times this afternoon.* **dif·fer·ent** (dif′ər ənt or dif′rənt) *adjective.*

difficult **1.** Needing much effort; not easy: *This is a **difficult** arithmetic problem.* **2.** Hard to get along with or please: *Some people become diffi-cult when they can't have their way.* **dif·fi·cult** (dif i kult) *adjective.*

difficulty **1.** The fact of being difficult: *The diffi-culty of learning how to ride a bicycle discour-aged me at first.* **2.** Something that is hard to do, understand, or deal with: *We had **difficulty** fit-ting everything into one suitcase.* **dif·fi·cul·ty** (dif′i kul′tē) *noun, plural* **difficulties.**

Archaeologists dig in the earth to find remains.

dig **1.** To break up or turn over the earth with a shovel, the hands, or claws: *Our dog likes to **dig** in the yard for bones.* **2.** To make or get by dig-ging: *The settlers had to **dig** a well for water.*

3. To try to find or discover by searching or by study: *The reporter had to **dig** to find the facts about the robbery.* **4.** To push or thrust: *The cat loved to **dig** its claws into the tree.* Verb.
○ **1.** A slight push or poke; nudge: *a **dig** in the ribs.* **2.** A place where scientists are looking for old cities or the bones of animals: *Some museums will let people work at **digs** during the summer.*
dig (dig) *verb,* **dug, digging;** *noun, plural* **digs.**

digest To break down food in the mouth, stom-ach, and intestines. When we digest food, we change it into a form that can be absorbed and used by the body. *Verb.*
○ A summary of a longer book or document: *I read a **digest** of a long novel. Noun.*
di·gest (di jest′ or dī′jest for *verb;* dī′jest for *noun*) *verb,* **digested, digesting;** *noun, plural* **digests.**

digestion The process of breaking down food into a form that can be absorbed and used by the body. Digestion starts in the mouth and is com-pleted in the intestines. **di·ges·tion** (di jes′chən or dī jes′chən) *noun, plural* **digestions.**

digestive Relating to or helping digestion: *Saliva is the first of the **digestive** juices that break down food.* **di·ges·tive** (di jes′tiv or dī jes′tiv) *adjective.*

digestive system

The system that breaks food down so that it can be used by the body. In humans, the digestive system includes the mouth, the esophagus, the stomach, and the in-testines. It also includes certain chemicals that help to break down the food.

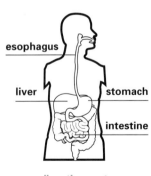

digestive system

digit **1.** One of the numerals 0, 1, 2, 3, 4, 5, 6, 7, 8, or 9. Sometimes 0 is not considered to be a digit. **2.** A finger, toe, or claw: *We have five **digits** on each hand.* **dig·it** (dij′it) *noun, plural* **digits.**

digital Using or showing information in the form of numerical digits: *My **digital** watch displays the time and the date.* **di·gi·tal** (dij′i təl) *adjective.*

digitize To change data or images into a form

PRONUNCIATION KEY:

at	āpe	fär	câre	end	mē	it	īce	pierce	hot	ōld	sông	fôrk
oil	out	up	ūse	rüle	pull	tûrn	chin	sing	shop	thin	this	

hw in white; zh in treasure. The symbol ə stands for the unstressed vowel sound in about, taken, pencil, lemon, and circus.

203

that can be used by a computer. **di•gi•tize**
(dij′i tiz′) *verb*, **digitized, digitizing.**

dignified Having or showing self-respect and self-control; confident and calm: *Our principal has a dignified manner.* **dignified** (dignəfīd) *adjective.*

dignity The condition of showing one's pride and worthiness in a confident manner: *Despite great hardship and poverty, my grandparents kept their dignity.* **dig•ni•ty** (dig′ni tē) *noun, plural* **dignities.**

dike A dam or high wall of earth built to hold back the waters of a sea or river. **dike** (dīk) *noun, plural* **dikes.**

dilapidated Fallen into ruin or decay; broken down: *I am going to rebuild my dilapidated old car.* **di•lap•i•da•ted** (di lap′i dā′tid) *adjective.*

dilemma A hard choice to make between two or more things: *My dilemma is that I can't decide where to go to college.* **di•lem•ma** (də lem′ə) *noun, plural* **dilemmas.**

diligent Working hard and steadily: *The more diligent students checked all their answers.* **dil•i•gent** (dil′i jənt) *adjective.*

dilute To make thin or weaker by adding a liquid: *If the paste is too thick, dilute it by adding water.* **di•lute** (di lüt′ *or* dī lüt′) *verb*, **diluted, diluting.**

dim 1. Having or giving little light; not bright: *There was only a dim light in the hallway.* 2. Not clear; not distinct: *I could see a dim outline of the building through the fog.* 3. Not seeing, hearing, or understanding clearly: *The old dog's eyes were growing dim. Adjective.*
○ To make or become dim: *Passing clouds dimmed the moon's light. Verb.*
dim (dim) *adjective*, **dimmer, dimmest**; *verb*, **dimmed, dimming.**

dime A coin in the United States and Canada that is worth ten cents. **dime** (dīm) *noun, plural* **dimes.**

dimension 1. The measurement of length, width, or height: *The dimensions of the room are 15 feet long, 12 feet wide, and 8 feet high.* 2. Size or importance: *Few people seem to realize the true dimensions of racism in this country.* **di•men•sion** (di men′shən) *noun, plural* **dimensions.**

diminish To make or become smaller: *The campers' supply of food diminished as the days wore on.* **di•min•ish** (di min′ish) *verb*, **diminished, diminishing.**

diminutive Very small; tiny: *A baby has diminu-*

tive hands and feet. **diminutive** (diminyətiv) *adjective.*

dimmer A device that regulates the brightness of an electric light or automobile headlight: *We have a dimmer for the ceiling light in the living room.* **dim•mer** (dim′ər) *noun, plural* **dimmers.**

dimple A small hollow on or in something: *There are many people who have dimples in their cheeks whenever they smile. Noun.*
○ To mark with or form dimples: *The hail dimpled the surface of our new car. Verb.*
dim•ple (dim′pəl) *noun, plural* **dimples**; *verb*, **dimpled, dimpling.**

din A loud noise that goes on for some time: *The din of the car horns kept us awake. Noun.*
○ To say over and over: *The coach dinned into our ears that we must run faster and faster. Verb.*
din (din) *noun, plural* **dins**; *verb*, **dinned, dinning.**

dine To eat dinner: *My parents dined at a restaurant on their anniversary.* **dine** (dīn) *verb*, **dined, dining.**

There were once thousands of diners in the United States.

diner 1. A person who is eating dinner. 2. A small restaurant that is usually inexpensive: *That diner is a favorite stop for truck drivers on their way through town.* **din•er** (dī′nər) *noun, plural* **diners.**

dinette A small dining room. **di•nette** (dī net′) *noun, plural* **dinettes.**

dinghy A small rowboat: *The sailors rowed a dinghy from the ship to shore.* **din•ghy** (ding′ē) *noun, plural* **dinghies.**

dingy Having a dirty and dull appearance; not bright. *The dingy curtains needed to be washed.* **din•gy** (din′jē) *adjective*, **dingier, dingiest.**

dining room A room where meals are served and eaten: *We eat breakfast in the kitchen and dinner* *in the dining room.*

dinner 1. The main meal of the day: *On Sunday we eat **dinner** at four o'clock in the afternoon.* 2. A formal meal in honor of some person or event: *The school gave the members of the soccer team a **dinner** to celebrate their winning season.* **din•ner** (din′ər) *noun, plural* **dinners.**

dinosaur Any of a large group of extinct animals that lived millions of years ago. There were dinosaurs that lived on land, in the oceans, and some flew through the air. Some dinosaurs were the largest animals that have ever lived, and others were as small as cats. **din•o•saur** (dīn′ə sôr) *noun, plural* **dinosaurs.**

WORD HISTORY

The word dinosaur comes from two Greek words meaning "terrible lizard." Scientists named these animals this because of their great size.

---

diocese A church district that is under the authority of a bishop. **di•o•cese** (dī′ə sis *or* dī′ə sēz) *noun, plural* **dioceses** (dīə sēz *or* dīə sisiz).

dip 1. To put into a liquid for a moment: *Carefully **dip** the brush into the paint can.* 2. To go in water and come out quickly: *We **dipped** in the swimming pool to cool off.* 3. To lift out by using a scoop or ladle: *I **dipped** some oats from the bag.* 4. To lower and raise again: *The soldier **dipped** the flag in salute as the president of the United States rode by.* 5. To slope downward: *Be careful; the road **dips** suddenly up ahead. Verb.*
○ 1. The act of dipping: *Let's take one last **dip** in the ocean before we go home.* 2. A liquid into which something is dipped for cleaning or coloring: *We put the eggs in a **dip** to color them for Easter.* 3. An amount taken out in a scoop or ladle: *a **dip** of ice cream?* 4. A sinking or drop: *a **dip** in the road.* 5. A thick sauce that is scooped up on crackers or vegetables. 6. A stupid or foolish person: *What a **dip** you are sometimes. Noun.* **dip** (dip) *verb,* **dipped, dipping;** *noun, plural* **dips.**

diploma A printed piece of paper given by a school or college to a graduating student that says he or she has finished a course of study. **di•plo•ma** (di plō′mə) *noun, plural* **diplomas.**

DINOSAURS

Dinosaur fossils have been found throughout the world. From them, scientists have been able to learn what dinosaurs looked like, how they lived, and what they ate.

The Age of the Dinosaurs: The various kinds of dinosaurs lived for about 160 million years, ending about 65 million years ago. Scientists call this time the Mesozoic era. They divide this period into three shorter periods:

The **Triassic Period** lasted from 225 to 195 million years ago. The first dinosaurs are called theropods. They are small meat-eating dinosaurs such as the *Eoraptor*, which was only about three feet long. Plant-eaters that appeared during this period are called *Prosauropds*.

The **Jurassic Period** lasted from 195 to 135 million years ago. This was the period of gigantic dinosaurs, including the largest land animals ever, *Apatosaurus* and *Brachiosaurus*. The *Stegosaurus*, with bony plates along its back, lived during this period, as did the giant meat-eaters, *Allosaurus* and *Megalosaurus*.

The **Cretaceous Period** lasted from 135 to 65 million years ago. Horned dinosaurs such as *Triceratops* appeared during this period, along with duck-billed dinosaurs and heavily armored dinosaurs such as *Ankylosaurus*. The best-known dinosaur, *Tyrannosaurus Rex*, also lived during this period. This meat-eater stood over 20 feet tall and had teeth seven inches long.

The Extinction of the Dinosaurs: The Cretaceous Period ended abruptly 65 million years ago with the extinction of the dinosaurs. Some scientists have suggested that an asteroid collided with Earth causing a blanket of dust to cloud the atmosphere and cool the planet. This killed most of the plant life, leaving the dinosaurs to die out. Other scientist have suggested that some dinosaurs are still with us today, having evolved into birds. These questions remain open, waiting for new evidence to help solve them.

diplomat **1.** A person whose job is to handle relations between his or her own country and other countries. **2.** A person who is good at dealing with people without making enemies or hurting anyone's feelings: *Our coach is a diplomat who can handle referees.* **dip•lo•mat** (dip′lə mat) *noun, plural* **diplomats.**

diplomatic **1.** Of or having to do with diplomats: *I hope some day to join the diplomatic service.* **2.** Good at dealing with people without hurting feelings: *It's diplomatic to thank someone for a gift even if you don't like it.* **dip•lo•mat•ic** (dip′lə mat′ik) *adjective.*

dipper A cup with a long handle that is used to lift water or other liquids. **dip•per** (dip′ər) *noun, plural* **dippers.**

dire Very urgent: *a dire need for fresh water.* **dire** (dir) *adjective.*

direct **1.** To manage or control; guide: *A police officer directs traffic at the busy intersection.* **2.** To supervise and guide the performers in the making of a play, movie, or other performance. **3.** To order; command: *The general directed the troops to attack.* **4.** To tell or show someone the way: *Can you direct me to the nearest bus stop?* **5.** To aim in a particular direction or to a particular place: *I directed the hose at the flowers. Verb.*
◦ **1.** Going in a straight line without stopping or turning: *Main Street is a direct route between my house and yours.* **2.** Plain and straightforward. "Yes" and "no" are direct answers to a question: "If you say so" and "maybe" are not direct answers. *Adjective.*
◦ In a straight line without stopping or turning: *This plane goes direct to New York from Los Angeles. Adverb.*
di•rect (di rekt′ *or* dī rekt′) *verb,* **directed, directing;** *adjective; adverb.*

direct current An electric current that flows only in one direction. Batteries generate direct current.

direction **1.** Management or control; guidance:. *The young doctor performed the operation under the direction of an older, more experienced doctor.* **2.** The line or course along which something moves, faces, or lies: *We decided to walk in the direction of the lake.* **3.** An order or instruction on how to do something or how to act: *Follow the directions on the package to cook the vegetables.* **di•rec•tion** (di rek′shən *or* dī rek′shən) *noun, plural* **directions.**

directly **1.** In a direct line or manner; straight: *The fielder threw the ball directly to a teammate covering first base.* **2.** At once; without delay: *Please come home directly after the concert.* **di•rect•ly** (di rekt′lē *or* dī rekt′lē) *adverb.*

direct object A word or group of words in a sentence that tells who or what directly receives the action expressed by the verb. In the sentence "I like oatmeal," the noun "oatmeal" is the direct object because it directly receives the action of the verb "like."

director A person who supervises and guides the performers in a play, movie, or other performance. **di•rect•or** (di rek′tər *or* dī rek′tər) *noun, plural* **directors.**

directory A list of names and addresses: *A telephone directory lists the telephone numbers of people living in a particular area.* **di•rec•tor•y** (di rek′tə rē *or* dī rek′tə rē) *noun, plural* **directories.**

dirigible A large aircraft that has areas filled with gas to make it float. A dirigible is driven by a motor and can be steered. **dir•i•gi•ble** (dir′i jə bəl *or* də rij′ə bəl) *noun, plural* **dirigibles.**

dirt **1.** Mud, dust, or other material that makes something unclean: *The children washed the dirt off their hands before coming to dinner.* **2.** Loose earth or soil: *The gardener filled the pots with dirt before planting the bulbs in them.* **dirt** (dûrt) *noun.*

dirty **1.** Soiled; not clean: *Cleaning out the garage was a hard and dirty job.* **2.** Not honest or decent; unfair or low: *That's a dirty lie.* **3.** Full of anger; resentful: *The bully gave us a dirty look.* **4.** Not decent; obscene: *Dirty words.* **dirt•y** (dûr′tē) *adjective,* **dirtier, dirtiest.**

dis- A prefix that means: **1.** Not or opposite: *Disapprove means not to approve. Disinfect means to do the opposite of infect.* **2.** Lack of: *Disrespect means lack of respect.*

disable To take away ability; cripple: *A broken leg can disable a person for months.* **dis•a•ble** (dis ā′bəl) *verb,* **disabled, disabling.**

disabled Unable to do some things because of a condition present from birth or an illness or accident: *My father is disabled because of a car accident.* **dis•a•bled** (dis ā′bəld) *adjective.* **—disability** *noun.*

disadvantage **1.** Something that makes it harder to succeed: *Not being able to read is a disadvantage in life.* **2.** A loss or injury; harm: *It will be to your dis-*

advantage if you are late to school. **dis•ad•van• tage** (dis′ad van′tij) *noun, plural* **disadvantages.**

disagree 1. To differ in opinion: *I think life has a purpose, but my cousin disagrees.* 2. To quarrel; argue: *They disagreed about which movie to see.* 3. To be different or unlike: *The stories of the two witnesses disagreed so much that the police didn't know which one to believe.* 4. To cause indigestion or discomfort: *Hot, spicy foods disagree with me.* **dis•a•gree** (dis′ə grē′) *verb,* **disagreed, disagreeing.**

disagreeable 1. Not pleasant or likable; unpleasant: *The sour milk had a disagreeable taste.* 2. Likely to go against other people's wishes or opinions: *Sometimes my best friend can be downright disagreeable.* **dis•a•gree•a•ble** (dis′ə grē′ə bəl) *adjective.*

disagreement 1. A difference of opinion: *There is no disagreement about whether we have to solve the problems of pollution.* 2. A quarrel; argument: *They settled their disagreement and shook hands.* **dis•a•gree•ment** (dis′ə grē′mənt) *noun, plural* **disagreements.**

disappear 1. To go out of sight: *We watched the sun disappear behind a cloud.* 2. To stop existing; become extinct: *Dinosaurs disappeared from the earth about 65 million years ago.* **dis•ap•pear** (dis′ə pˆir′) *verb,* **disappeared, disappearing.**

disappearance The act or fact of disappearing: *The disappearance of the two mountain climbers worried us all.* **dis•ap•pear•ance** (dis′ə pˆir′əns) *noun, plural* **disappearances.**

disappoint To fail to live up to the hopes of: *You will disappoint the children if you do not keep your promise to them.* **dis•ap•point** (dis′ə point′) *verb,* **disappointed, disappointing.**

disappointment 1. A feeling of being disappointed: *The class couldn't hide its disappointment when the field trip was called off.* 2. A person or thing that disappoints: *My new boots were supposed to be very warm, but they are a disappointment.* **dis•ap•point•ment** (dis′ə point′mənt) *noun, plural* **disappointments.**

disapprove To have a strong feeling against: *My parents disapprove of smoking.* **dis•ap•prove** (dis′ə prüv′) *verb,* **disapproved, disapproving.**

disarm 1. To take weapons away from someone: *The police quickly disarmed the robber.* **dis•arm**

(dis ärm′) *verb,* **disarmed, disarming.**

disaster 1. An event that causes much suffering or loss: *The flood was a disaster.* 2. Something that does not go right or fails: *My birthday party was a disaster because it rained.* **dis•as•ter** (di zas′tər) *noun, plural* **disasters.**

disbelief Lack of belief; refusal to believe: *Thanks to my disbelief in ghosts, I wasn't afraid of the empty old house.* **dis•be•lief** (dis′bi lēf′) *noun, plural* **disbeliefs.**

disc 1. A phonograph record. 2. Another spelling for *disk.* Look up **disk** for more information. **disc** (disk) *noun, plural* **discs.**

discard To throw away: *I discarded all my worn-out clothes.* **dis•card** (dis′kärd) *verb,* **discarded, discarding.**

discharge 1. To let go or release; dismiss: *When the company went out of business it had to discharge all its workers.* 2. To fire or shoot: *It is illegal to discharge a firearm within the city limits.* 3. To send or let out: *The factory should not be allowed to discharge its wastes into the river. Verb.*
○ 1. Dismissal from service or a job: *Many soldiers received their discharges from the army in 1946.* 2. A firing of a weapon: *The discharge of the cannon made the ship shudder. Noun.* **dis•charge** (dis chärj′ *for verb;* dis′chärj *for noun*) *verb,* **discharged, discharging;** *noun, plural* **discharges.**

disciple 1. A person who believes in a leader or a leader's teachings: *The young doctor was a devoted disciple of the famous surgeon.* 2. One of the twelve original followers of Jesus; Apostle. **dis•ci•ple** (di sī′pəl) *noun, plural* **disciples.**

discipline 1. Training that develops skill, good character, or orderly behavior: *Those wild children have had no discipline from their parents.* 2. Punishment given to train or correct someone: *If you break a rule here, you will receive severe discipline.* 3. A field of study: *Mathematics and science are related disciplines. Noun.*
○ 1. To train to be obedient: *An officer in the army must be able to discipline troops.* 2. To punish: *We disciplined our dog for barking too much. Verb.*
dis•ci•pline (di′sə plin) *noun,* **plural** *disciplines;*

PRONUNCIATION KEY:
| at | āpe | fär | câre | end | mē | it | īce | pierce | hot | ōld | sông | fôrk |
| oil | out | up | ūse | rüle | pull | tûrn | chin | sing | shop | thin | this | |
hw in white; zh in treasure. The symbol ə stands for the unstressed vowel sound in about, taken, pencil, lemon, and circus.

207

verb, **disciplined, disciplining.**

disc jockey 1. An announcer on a radio program that broadcasts recorded music. 2. A person who selects, announces, and plays recordings of music at clubs or parties. **disc jockey** (disk)

disclose To make known: *I promise not to disclose this secret to anyone.* **dis•close** (dis klōz′) *verb*, **disclosed, disclosing.**

disco 1. A kind of music that is good for dancing. 2. A club where this kind of dance music is featured. **dis•co** (dis′kō) *noun, plural* **discos.**

discomfort The condition or fact of being uncomfortable or uneasy: *The cold wind caused us some discomfort.* **dis•com•fort** (dis kum′fərt) *noun, plural* **discomforts.**

disconnect To separate from another part or from a source of electricity; break the connection of: *You must disconnect the television set before fixing it.* **dis•con•nect** (dis′kə nekt′) *verb*, **disconnected, disconnecting.**

discontented Unhappy and restless: *The worker was discontented with the dull job.* **dis•con•tent•ed** (dis′kən ten′tid) *adjective.*

discontinue To put an end to; stop: *We asked the telephone company to discontinue our service when we moved.* **dis•con•tin•ue** (dis′kən tin′ū) *verb*, **discontinued, discontinuing.**

discord A lack of agreement or harmony; disagreement: *There was much discord among the members of the committee.* **dis•cord** (dis kôrd′) *noun.*

discount An amount subtracted from the regular price: *I bought a suit on sale at a 25 percent discount.* **dis•count** (dis kount′) *noun, plural* **discounts.**

discourage 1. To cause to lose courage, hope, or confidence: *Failing to have your first story published should not discourage you from be-coming a writer.* 2. To try to keep a personfrom doing something: *They discouraged us from starting our trip because of the heavy snowstorm.* **dis•cour•age** (dis kûr′ij) *verb*, **discouraged, discouraging.**

discourteous Impolite; rude: *It is discourteous to interrupt people.* **dis•cour•te•ous** (dis kûr′tē əs) *adjective.*

discover 1. To see or find out for the first time: *Marie and Pierre Curie discovered radium.* 2. To notice; come upon: *I discovered a spelling error in my essay.* **dis•cov•er** (dis kuv′ər) *verb*, **discovered, discovering.**

discovery 1. The act of seeing or finding out

something for the first time: *The discovery of yet another planet in our solar system may be only a matter of time.* 2. Something that is seen or found out for the first time: *Electricity was an important discovery.* **dis•cov•er•y** (dis kuv′ər ē) *noun, plural* **discoveries.**

discriminate 1. To treat some people unjustly because they are different in a way that people with power believe is bad: *It is against the law for an employer to discriminate against people because of their race, religion, sex, or age.* 2. To tell the difference between things: *Can you discriminate between a dolphin and a porpoise?* **dis•crim•i•nate** (di skrim′ə nāt′) *verb*, **discriminated, discriminating.**

discrimination 1. An unfair difference in treatment: *That company hires people without discrimination as to race or sex.* 2. The act or ability of seeing differences: *Discrimination between right and wrong is the basis for good decisions.* **dis•crim•i•na•tion** (di skrim′ə nā′shən) *noun.*

discus A track-and-field event in which athletes compete to see who can throw a large, heavy disk the farthest. **dis•cus** (dis′kəs) *noun, plural* **discuses.**

A **discus** thrower needs to have good balance, strength, and timing.

discuss To talk over; speak about: *After dinner my friends and I **discussed** our plans for tomorrow.* **dis•cuss** (dis kus′) *verb*, **discussed, discussing**.

discussion The act of talking something over; a serious exchange of opinions: *My question about when a person becomes a grown-up started an interesting **discussion**.* **dis•cus•sion** (di skush′ən) *noun, plural* **discussions**.

disease 1. Something inside a living organism that makes it sick; illness: *Five children in my school have died of a **disease**.* 2. A specific sickness: *Chicken pox is a common **disease** among children.* **dis•ease** (di zēz′) *noun, plural* **diseases**.

disfavor Lack of favor or approval; dislike: *The students looked with **disfavor** on the plan to shorten spring vacation.* **dis•fa•vor** (dis fā′vər) *noun*.

disfigure To ruin the shape or appearance of: *The wax statue was **disfigured** by the heat of the fire.* **dis•fig•ure** (dis fig′yər) *verb*, **disfigured, disfiguring**.

disgrace 1. The loss of honor or respect; shame: *The president of the company resigned in **disgrace** when the police learned about the stolen money.* 2. A person or thing that causes a loss of honor or respect: *It is a **disgrace** that so many people in this society are hungry. Noun.* ○ To bring shame to: *Football players who do drugs **disgrace** their teams. Verb.* **dis•grace** (dis grās′) *noun, plural* **disgraces**; *verb*, **disgraced, disgracing**.

disgruntled Unhappy: *The **disgruntled** secretaries decided to take a two-hour lunch.* **dis•grun•tled** (dis grun′təld) *adjective*.

disguise 1. To change the way one looks in order to hide one's real identity or look like someone else: *The children **disguised** themselves as ghosts, pirates, and monsters on Halloween.* 2. To hide: *We **disguised** our hiding place with branches and leaves. Verb.* ○ Something that changes or hides the way one looks: *A mustache was part of the thief's **disguise**. Noun.* **dis•guise** (dis gīz′) *verb*, **disguised, disguising**; *noun, plural* **disguises**.

disgust A sick feeling caused by strong dislike: *I felt **disgust** when I smelled the rotting garbage.* *Noun.* To cause a sick feeling of strong dislike in. *Verb.* **dis•gust** (dis gus′t) *noun; verb*, **disgusted, disgusting**.

disgusting Very unpleasant; nasty: *His behavior in the lunchroom today was **disgusting**.* **dis•gust•ing** (dis gus′ting) *adjective*.

dish 1. A plate or shallow bowl used for holding food: *We set the table with our good china dishes.* 2. Food made in a particular way: *Spaghetti with tomato sauce is my favorite **dish**.* 3. In basketball, a short, quick pass. *Noun.* ○ To put or serve in a dish. *We **dished** up dinner as soon as everyone sat down. Verb.* **dish** (dish) *noun, plural* **dishes**; *verb*, **dished, dishing**.

disheveled Very messy; mussed: *I was **disheveled** when I got home from playing football.* **di•shev•eled** (di shev′əld) *adjective*.

dishonest Not fair or honest: *A student who cheats on a test is **dishonest**.* **dis•hon•est** (dis on′ist) *adjective*.

dishonor Loss of honor; disgrace; shame: *It is no **dishonor** to admit that you have made a mistake.* *Noun.* ○ To cause disgrace or shame. *Verb.* **dis•hon•or** (dis on′ər) *noun, plural* **dishonors**; *verb*, **dishonored, dishonoring**.

dishwasher A machine that washes dishes, glasses, and pots. **dish•wash•er** (dish′wô′shər *or* dish′wosh′ər) *noun, plural* **dishwashers**.

disillusion To cause a person to let go of a belief or ideal: *I was **disillusioned** when I found out my coach had been fixing games.* **dis•il•lu•sion** (dis′ə lü′zhən) *verb*, **disillusioned, disillusioning**.

disinfect To destroy germs that cause disease: *The nurse **disinfected** the thermometer before I used it.* **dis•in•fect** (dis′in fekt′) *verb*, **disinfected, disinfecting**.

disinfectant A chemical used to destroy germs that can cause diseases or infections. **dis•in•fect•ant** (dis′in fekt′ənt) *noun, plural* **disinfectants**.

disintegrate To break into many small pieces: *A blow with the heavy hammer caused the stone to **disintegrate**.* **dis•in•te•grate** (dis in′ti grāt) *verb*, **disintegrated, disintegrating**.

disinterested Free from selfish interest; fair: *A*

PRONUNCIATION KEY:
| at | āpe | fär | câre | end | mē | it | īce | pierce | hot | old | sông | fôrk |
| oil | out | up | ūse | rüle | pull | tûrn | chin | sing | shop | thin | this | |

hw in white; zh in treasure. The symbol ə stands for the unstressed vowel sound in about, taken, pencil, lemon, and circus.

209

referee should remain **disinterested**. **dis·in·ter·est·ed** (dis in′trə stid *or* dis in′tə res′tid) *adjective*.

disk 1. A flat, thin, round object. 2. A device that stores information in a computer. This word is also spelled *disc*. **disk** (disk) *noun, plural* **disks**.

disk drive The device inside or attached to a computer that allows the computer to store and retrieve information on a disk.

diskette A small piece of plastic in a square cover that is used to store information for a computer. Some diskettes are floppy disks. **disk·ette** (dis ket′) *noun, plural* **diskettes**.

disk operating system The main program that instructs a computer how to work.

dislike A feeling of not liking something: *I have a dislike of baseball so I did not try out for the team. Noun.*
○ To have a feeling of not liking: or of being against. *Our messy neighbor dislikes doing housework. Verb.*
dis·like (dis līk′) *noun, plural* **dislikes**; *verb*, **disliked, disliking**.

dislocate To put out of a proper or normal position: *I dislocated my hip when I slipped and fell on the ice.* **dis·lo·cate** (dis′lō kāt′ *or* dis lō′kāt) *verb*, **dislocated, dislocating**.

dislodge To move or force out of a place or position: *The flood dislodged two of the supports that held up the bridge.* **dis·lodge** (di sloj′) *verb*, **dislodged, dislodging**.

dismal Causing sadness; dreary; miserable: *The weather has been rainy and dismal lately.* **dis·mal** (diz′məl) *adjective*.

dismantle To take something apart piece by piece: *The workers dismantled the grandstand very quickly.* **dis·man·tle** (dis man′təl) *verb*, **dismantled, dismantling**.

dismay To shock or surprise in an unpleasant way: *The rising flood dismayed the people of the town. Verb.*
○ A feeling of shock or surprise: *The family was filled with dismay when they learned that the fire was approaching their house. Noun.*
dis·may (dis mā′) *verb*, **dismayed, dismaying**; *noun*.

dismayed Shocked; upset: *She was dismayed when I told her how much the coat cost.* **dis·mayed** (dis mād′) *adjective*.

dismiss 1. To send away or allow to leave: *The teacher decided to dismiss the class early.* 2. To take away the job of; fire: *The supervisor dismissed the employee for being late too often.* **dis·miss** (dis mis′) *verb*, **dismissed, dismissing**.

dismount To get off or down from: *The clowns at the rodeo help the cowboys to dismount from the broncos.* **dis·mount** (dis mount′) *verb*, **dismounted, dismounting**.

disobedient Refusing or failing to obey: *The disobedient child crossed the road without the babysitter's permission.* **dis·o·be·di·ent** (dis′ə bē′dē ənt) *adjective*.

disobey To refuse or fail to obey: *The driver disobeyed the traffic laws by not stopping at a red light.* **dis·o·bey** (dis′ə bā′) *verb*, **disobeyed, disobeying**.

disorder 1. A lack of order; confusion: *The room was in complete disorder after the birthday party.* 2. A sickness; ailment: *Doctors are investigating ways to treat lung disorders. Noun.*
○ To disturb the order of; throw into confusion: *The sudden downpour of rain disordered the parade. Verb.*
dis·or·der (dis ôr′dər) *noun, plural* **disorders**; *verb*, **disordered, disordering**.

disorderly 1. Messy; untidy: *The old newspapers lay in a disorderly pile.* 2. Behaving without proper self-control in public; unruly: *The disorderly crowd had to be held back by the police.* **dis·or·der·ly** (dis ôr′dər lē) *adjective*.

disown To state that a person is no longer part of a family: *My grandfather disowned one of my uncles.* **dis·own** (dis ōn′) *verb*, **disowned, disowning**.

dispatch To send off quickly: *The travelers dispatched a telegram to announce their time of arrival. Verb.*
○ A written message or report: *The newspaper received a dispatch from its reporter in England. Noun.*
dis·patch (dis pach′) *verb*, **dispatched, dispatching**; *noun, plural* **dispatches**.

dispel To drive away or cause to disappear: *The babysitter's kind words helped to dispel the child's fear of the dark.* **dis·pel** (di spel′) *verb*, **dispelled, dispelling**.

dispense To give out: *The town dispensed food and clothing to the homeless people.* **dispense** (di spens′) *verb*, **dispensed, dispensing**.

disperse To break up and scatter in different directions: *The police **dispersed** the angry crowd before anyone got hurt.* **dis•perse** (di spûrs′) *verb*, **dispersed, dispersing.**

displace 1. To take the place of: *The airplane **displaced** the train as the fastest way to travel.* 2. To move from the usual or proper place: *You can use my desk, but please don't **displace** the things on it.* **dis•place** (dis plās′) *verb*, **displaced, displacing.**

display To show or exhibit: *The art museum is now **displaying** some of Monet's paintings. Verb.*
○ A show or exhibit: *A hug is a **display** of affection. Noun.*
dis•play (dis plā′) *verb*, **displayed, displaying;** *noun, plural* **displays.**

The boy is proudly *displaying* his catch.

displease To annoy; disappoint: *You **displeased** the teacher when you didn't do your homework.* **dis•please** (dis plēz′) *verb*, **displeased, displeasing.**

disposable Made to be thrown away after being used: *We used **disposable** paper plates at the picnic.* **dis•pos•able** (di spōz′ə bəl) *adjective.*

disposal 1. The act of getting rid of something: *The city is responsible for the **disposal** of garbage.* 2. A machine under a sink that grinds up food. **dis•pos•al** (di spōz′əl) *noun, plural* **disposals.**

dispose 1. To get rid of: *I **disposed** of the wrappers by putting them in a garbage can.* 2. To finish up with; settle: *We quickly **disposed** of our morning chores so we could go to the zoo in the afternoon.* **dis•pose** (di spōz′) *verb*, **disposed, disposing.**

disposition 1. A person's usual way of acting, thinking, or feeling; mood: *You always have a cheerful **disposition**, even when you're tired.* 2. A natural tendency: *I have a **disposition** to agree with others too readily.* **dis•po•si•tion** (dis′pə zish′ən) *noun, plural* **dispositions.**

disprove To show that something is not true: *Can you **disprove** her claim to have seen ghosts?* **dis•prove** (dis prüv′) *verb*, **disproved, disproving.**

dispute 1. To argue against; disagree with: *They **disputed** your statement that you were a faster swimmer.* 2. To argue or fight over: *The two countries are **disputing** the boundary between them. Verb.*
○ An argument or quarrel: *A judge had to settle the **dispute** between the farmers. Noun.*
dis•pute (dis pūt′) *verb*, **disputed, disputing;** *noun, plural* **disputes.**

disqualify To make or declare not fit or able to do something: *The judges **disqualified** the runner from the race for starting too soon.* **dis•qual•i•fy** (dis kwol′ə fī) *verb*, **disqualified, disqualifying.**

disregard To pay no attention to; ignore: *I tried to **disregard** the noise on the bus and read my book. Verb.*
○ Lack of attention or consideration; neglect: *Playing the radio loudly shows a **disregard** for your neighbors. Noun.*
dis•re•gard (dis′ri gärd′) *verb*, **disregarded, disregarding;** *noun.*

disreputable Having a bad reputation: *a **disreputable** part of the city.* **dis•rep•u•ta•ble** (dis rep′yət ə bəl) *adjective.*

disrespect Lack of respect: *Some spectators showed their **disrespect** for the judge by talking loudly during the trial.* **dis•re•spect** (dis′ri spekt′) *noun.*

disrupt To break up or apart: *By talking together, the two pupils were **disrupting** the whole class.* **dis•rupt** (dis rupt′) *verb*, **disrupted, disrupting.**

dissatisfaction A feeling of being displeased or disappointed; discontent: *My dissatisfaction with my study habits grew until I finally changed them.* **dis·sat·is·fac·tion** (dis sat is fak'shən) *noun.*

dissatisfied Not content; displeased: *The salesperson said that if we were dissatisfied with the encyclopedia, we could return it.* **dissatisfied** (dis'sat'is fīd) *adjective.*

dissect 1. To cut up an animal to study it. 2. To analyze something in great detail: *dissect a person's approach to life.* **dis·sect** (di sekt' or dī sekt') *verb,* **dissected, dissecting.**

dissent To differ in opinion; disagree: *Six judges of the Supreme Court agreed on the decision, but three judges dissented. Verb.*
○ A difference of opinion; disagreement: *The dictator did not allow dissent against the actions of the government. Noun.*
Another word that sounds like this is descent. **dis·sent** (di sent') *verb,* **dissented, dissenting;** *noun.*

dissident A person who disagrees with the way things are done: *The dissidents had a rally to protect the new curfew. Noun.*
○ Not agreeing: *One judge wrote a dissident opinion. Adjective.*
dis·si·dent (dis'i dənt) *noun,* **dissidents;** *adjective.*

dissolve 1. To mix thoroughly with a liquid: *Dissolve the powder in milk to make the instant pudding.* 2. To bring to an end: *The club members voted to dissolve the dance committee after the dance.* **dis·solve** (di zolv') *verb,* **dissolved, dissolving.**

distance 1. The amount of space between two things or points: *The distance from my house to the school is two blocks.* 2. A point or place that is far away: *The driver saw a large truck in the distance.*
• **to keep one's distance.** To stay away from someone or something: *She prefers to keep her distance from the rowdy crowd.*

dis·tance (dis'təns) *noun, plural* **distances.**

distant 1. Far away in space or time; not near: *Dinosaurs lived in the distant past.* 2. Away: *The farm was 10 miles distant from the nearest town.* 3. Not friendly: *The two roommates have been distant since their quarrel.* **dis·tant** (dis'tənt) *adjective.*

distasteful Unpleasant; offensive: *I find gory movies distasteful.* **dis·taste·ful** (dis tāst'fəl) *adjective.*

distemper A very contagious disease that dogs and other animals can catch. Distemper is caused by a virus. **dis·temper** (dis temp'ər) *noun.*

distinct 1. Not the same; separate; different: *The envelopes were sorted into three distinct piles.* 2. Easy to see, hear, or understand; clear: *The coach noticed a distinct improvement in the team's playing.* **dis·tinct** (di stingkt') *adjective.*

distinction 1. The act of making or noticing a difference between things: *It is not always easy to make a distinction between poison ivy and some other plants.* 2. Something that makes a thing different or exceptional: *The cheetah has the distinction of being the fastest animal on land.* 3. Excellence; worth: *The senator was a person of distinction.* **dis·tinc·tion** (di stingk'shən) *noun, plural* **distinctions.**

distinctive Making something or someone easy to recognize; characteristic: *I spotted you from a distance, because you have a distinctive walk.* **dis·tinc·tive** (di stingk'tiv) *adjective.*

distinguish 1. To know or show that there is a difference between certain things: *The jeweler distinguished the real diamond from the fake one.* 2. To make something special or different; set apart: *The male cardinal's bright red feathers distinguish it from other birds.* 3. To see or hear clearly: *We could not distinguish your faces in the dark.* 4. To make famous or deserving of special honor or attention; make well known: *The doctors distinguished themselves by their work in cancer research.* **dis·tin·guish** (di sting'gwish) *verb,* **distinguished, distinguishing.**

This woman is using binoculars to see into the distance.

distinguished Recognized for the good things one has done: *a distinguished surgeon.* **dis·tin·guished** (dis ting′gwisht) *adjective.*

distort **1.** To twist or bend out of shape: *The curved mirror distorted my image.* **2.** To change so as to be misleading: *Don't distort the facts when you tell what happened.* **dis·tort** (di stôrt′) *verb,* **distorted, distorting.**

distract To draw one's attention away from what one is doing or thinking: *The noise distracted me from my homework.* **dis·tract** (di strakt′) *verb,* **distracted, distracting.**

distress **1.** Great pain or sorrow; misery: *My grandfather's illness was a great distress to me.* **2.** Danger, trouble, or great need: *The ship sent a message that it was in distress. Noun.*
○ To cause pain, sorrow, or misery: *The bad news distressed us. Verb.*
dis·tress (di stres′) *noun; verb,* **distressed, distressing.**

distribute **1.** To give out in shares: *The teacher distributed new books to the class.* **2.** To spread something out over a large area; scatter: *The farm machines distributed seed over the plowed field.* **3.** To arrange or sort into groups: *The post office distributes mail.* **dis·tri·bute** (di strib′ūt) *verb,* **distributed, distributing.**

distribution The act of distributing:. *The fire department supervised the distribution of food and clothing to the flood victims.* **dis·tr·ibu·tion** (dis′trə bū′shən) *noun, plural* **distributions**

distributive property A law of mathematics that allows you to multiply a group of numbers and get the same answer that you would by multiplying each member of the group separately. For example, 5 x (2 + 3 + 4) = (5 x 2) + (5 x 3) + (5 x 4) = 45. **distributive property**(di strib′yə tiv).

Distributive property in multiplication:
2 x (3 + 6 + 8)
is the same as
(2 x 3) + (2 x 6) + (2 x 8)
They both equal 34.

district An area that is part of a larger area: *That store is in the business district of the city.* **dis·trict** (dis′trikt) *noun, plural* **districts.**

District of Columbia An area in the eastern United States between Maryland and Virginia. It is completely occupied by the city of Washington, the national capital. **District of Columbia** (kəlumbēə).

> ### WORD HISTORY
> The **District of Columbia** was named after Christopher Columbus, the Italian explorer who landed in America in 1492.

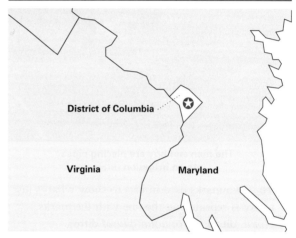

District of Columbia
The site of the Federal capital consists of the city of Washington, Georgetown, and Washington County.
U.S. Postal Abbreviation: DC
Population: 554,256
Area: 68 sq. mi./262.5 sq. km
District Bird: Wood Thrush
District Flower: American Beauty Rose

distrust To not trust someone or something about the person: *I distrust her motives for wanting to help me.* **dis·trust** (dis trust′) *verb,* **distrusted, distrusting.**

disturb **1.** To make uneasy or nervous; upset: *Loud music disturbs my grandmother.* **2.** To break in on; interrupt: *The telephone call disturbed everyone's sleep.* **3.** To upset or change the order or arrangement of things: *The children disturbed the books on the shelf.* **dis·turb** (di stûrb′) *verb,* **disturbed, disturbing.**

disturbance **1.** An interruption: *After the phone call, I went back to work without further disturbance.* **2.** Something that disturbs: *When people complained of a barking dog, the police went to investigate the disturbance.* **dis·turb·ance**

PRONUNCIATION KEY:
at   āpe   fär   câre   end   mē   it   īce   pierce   hot   ōld   sông   fôrk
oil   out   up   ūse   rüle   pull   tûrn   chin   sing   shop   thin   this
hw in white; zh in treasure. The symbol ə stands for the unstressed vowel sound in about, taken, pencil, lemon, and circus.

213

(di stûrb′əns) *noun, plural* **disturbances**

ditch A long, narrow hole dug in the ground. Ditches are used to drain off water. *Noun.*
○ To make an emergency landing in water: *No pilot wants to have to **ditch** an airplane. Verb.*
ditch (dich) *noun, plural* **ditches**; *verb,* **ditched, ditching.**

The man and boy are placing pipes into an irrigation ditch.

ditto Two marks used in lists to show what is just above is repeated on the line with the marks. *Noun.* **dit•to** (dit′ō) *noun, plural* **dittos.**

dive 1. To plunge headfirst into water: *At first, I was afraid to **dive** from the high board into the pool.* 2. To plunge downward quickly and at a steep angle: *We watched the eagle **dive** from the sky.* 3. To go, move, or drop suddenly and quickly: *At the sound of thunder the frightened puppy **dived** under the bed. Verb.*
○ 1. A headfirst plunge into water: *It's not safe to do a **dive** from the rocks into the lake.* 2. A quick, steep plunge: *The plane went into a **dive** when it was hit by enemy fire. Noun.*
dive (dīv) *verb,* **dived** or **dove, dived, diving**; *noun, plural* **dives.**

diver 1. A person who dives. 2. A person who works or explores underwater. Divers usually carry tanks of air on their backs so that they can breathe underwater. **div•er** (dī′vər) *noun, plural* **divers.**

diverse Not all the same; varied: *The students in the class come from **diverse** backgrounds.* **di•verse** (di vûrs′ *or* dī vûrs′) *adjective.*

diversion 1. A changing of the direction in which something is going: *A storm forced the **diversion** of the plane to a different city.* 2. Something that turns the attention in a different direction: *You*

create a **diversion**, *and we'll sneak up from behind to surprise them.* 3. Entertainment; amusement; pastime: *My favorite **diversions** are drawing and listening to music.* **di•ver•sion** (di vûr′zhən *or* dī vûr′zhən) *noun, plural* **diversions.**

diversity Great difference; variety: *The exhibition of paintings included a **diversity** of styles.* **di•ver•si•ty** (di vûr′si tē *or* dī vûr′si tē) *noun, plural* **diversities.**

divert 1. To change the direction in which something is going: *The police **diverted** traffic from the street where the accident happened.* 2. To turn the attention in a different direction: *I tried to **divert** the crying baby by singing a song.* 3. To entertain; amuse: *The television show **diverted** me while I waited for dinner.* **di•vert** (di vûrt′ *or* dī vûrt′) *verb,* **diverted, diverting.**

divide 1. To separate into parts, pieces, or groups: *The class **divided** into two teams for the spelling contest.* 2. To separate into parts or pieces and give some to each; share: *The three children who found the lost dog **divided** the reward money.* 3. To show how many times one number contains another number: *When you **divide** 6 by 2 you get 3, because the number 6 contains the number 2 three times.* 4. To split into opposing sides because of different feelings or opinions: *The class **divided** on the choice of a site for the picnic. Verb.*
○ A ridge of land that separates two areas that are drained by different rivers. *Noun.*
di•vide (di vīd′) *verb,* **divided, dividing**; *noun, plural* **divides.**

dividend 1. A number that is to be divided by another number: *When you **divide** 6 by 3, the dividend is 6.* 2. Money that is earned by a business; profit. **div•i•dend** (di′vi dend) *noun, plural* **dividends.**

In **12 ÷ 6 = 2** or $6\overline{)12}^{\,2}$
12 is the **dividend.**

In **9 ÷ 3 = 3** or $3\overline{)9}^{\,3}$
9 is the **dividend.**

divine 1. Of or from God or a god: *The workers trapped in the mine prayed for **divine** mercy.* 2. Religious; sacred: *The church bell called the people to **divine** worship.* **di•vine** (di vīn′) *adjective.*

diving board A board that swimmers use for jumping or diving into water. One end of the board is attached to the ground or a support, and the other end sticks out over the water.

divisible Capable of being divided: *The number 8 is evenly divisible by the numbers 8, 4, 2, and 1.* **di·vis·ible** (di viz′ə bəl) *adjective.*

division 1. The act of dividing or the condition of being divided: *The division of the house into apartments provided homes for five families.* 2. One of the parts into which something is divided: *Asian history is one of the divisions of our social studies course.* 3. Something that divides or separates: *The wooden fence formed a division between the farms.* 4. A large unit of an army that is made up of different regiments. **di·vi·sion** (di vizh′ən) *noun, plural* **divisions.**

divisor A number by which another number is to be divided: *When you divide 6 by 3, the divisor is 3.* **di·vi·sor** (di vī′zər) *noun, plural* **divisors.**

$$\text{In } 12 \div 6 = 2 \text{ or } 6\overline{)12}^{\,2}$$
6 is the **divisor.**
$$\text{In } 9 \div 3 = 3 \text{ or } 3\overline{)9}^{\,3}$$
3 is the **divisor.**

divorce The legal ending of a marriage. *Noun.* ◦ To legally end a marriage. *Verb.* **di·vorce** (di vôrs′) *noun, plural* **divorces;** *verb,* **divorced, divorcing.**

dizzy 1. Having the feeling of spinning and being about to fall: *The children ran in circles until they were dizzy.* 2. Overwhelmed; confused: *Having to learn so many dates for the history test made me dizzy.* 3. Silly; foolish: *Sometimes you have the dizziest ideas.* **diz·zy** (diz′ē) *adjective,* **dizzier, dizziest.**

DJ Short for disc jockey. (dē′jā′)

DNA The biological molecule that gives living things their special features. The letters stand for DeoxyriboNucleic Acid. (dē′en a′)

do 1. To carry out an action; perform: *Let's do something this afternoon.* 2. To produce or create; make: *First the artist did a sketch.* 3. To bring to an end; finish: *I've already done my homework.* 4. To take care of: *Let's do the dishes.*

5. To work out; solve: *I can't do this mathematics problem.* 6. To cause; result in: *It does little good to complain.* 7. To act in a certain way; behave: *The naughty children never did as they were told.* 8. To get along; manage: *How are you doing with that homework assignment?* 9. To be suitable: *That light jacket won't do for cold weather.* 10. Used in place of a verb or a verb phrase that has just been used: *You can ice-skate as well as I do.* 11. An auxiliary verb that is used in asking questions, in making negative statements, and in making another verb seem stronger: *Do horses run faster than dogs? Now I do understand.* Other words that sound like this are **dew** and **due.**

• **to do away with.** 1. To put an end to; get rid of: *The Thirteenth Amendment to the Constitution did away with slavery in the United States.* 2. To kill: *The poison did away with the rats in our basement.*

• **to make do.** To manage; get along: *They can make do without new clothes for spring.* **do** (dü) *verb,* **did, done, doing.**

Doberman pinscher A dog that has a long head, slender legs, and a shiny black or brown coat. Doberman pinschers are often kept as watchdogs. **Do·ber·man pin·scher** (dō′bər mən pin′shər).

docile Easy to teach, train, or handle: *A child can pet and ride that docile pony.* **do·cile** (dos′əl) *adjective.*

dock 1. A platform where boats or ships are tied up. A dock is built along the shore or out into the water. Docks are used for loading and unloading a ship's cargo and passengers. 2. An area of water between two piers where boats and ships tie up: *The tugboat towed the ocean liner into the dock. Noun.* ◦ 1. To bring or come to a dock: *The tanker docked and unloaded its cargo.* 2. To bring two spacecraft together in space. *Verb.* **dock** (dok) *noun, plural* **docks;** *verb,* **docked, docking.**

doctor 1. A person who has been trained and licensed to treat the sick and injured: *A physician, a dentist, and a veterinarian are all doctors.* 2. A person who has the highest degree from a university. **doc·tor** (dok′tər) *noun, plural* **doctors.**

doctrine Something that is believed by a group of

PRONUNCIATION KEY:

| at | āpe | fär | câre | end | mē | it | īce | pierce | hot | ōld | sông | fôrk |
| oil | out | up | ūse | rüle | pull | tûrn | chin | sing | shop | thin | this | |

hw in white; zh in treasure. The symbol ə stands for the unstressed vowel sound in about, taken, pencil, lemon, and circus.

215

people: *The beliefs of a religion and the ideals of a political party are* **doctrines**. **doc·trine** (dok′trin) *noun, plural* **doctrines**.

document A written or printed statement that gives official proof and information about something: *A birth certificate, a deed to a house, and a diploma are* **documents**. *Noun.*

○ To record something as evidence: *The teacher documented the number of times I missed class. Verb.* **doc·u·ment** (dok′yə mənt) *noun, plural* **documents**; *verb,* **documented, documenting.**

documentary A movie or television program about real events and real people: *a* **documentary** *about tigers in India.* **doc·u·men·ta·ry** (dok′yə men′trē *or* dok′ū ment′ə rē) *noun, plural* **documentaries.**

dodge **1.** To keep away from something by moving aside quickly: *I* **dodged** *the snowball that someone threw at me.* **2.** To get away from something in a tricky way: *The witness* **dodged** *the lawyer's question by pretending not to remember. Verb.*

○ **1.** A quick move to the side: *The boxer avoided being hit by making a* **dodge** *to the left.* **2.** A trick that is used to fool or cheat someone: *I tried every* **dodge** *I could think of to avoid taking the history test. Noun.*

dodge (doj) *verb,* **dodged, dodging**; *noun, plural* **dodges.**

dodo A large bird that no longer exists. Its body was so large and its wings were so small that it was not able to fly. **do·do** (d;ab′odō) *noun, plural* **dodos** *or* **dodoes.**

doe **1.** A female deer. **2.** The female of several other animals, such as the antelope or hare. Another word that sounds like this is **dough**. **doe** (dō) *noun, plural* **does.**

does A form of the present tense of do that is used with she, he, it or the name of a person, place, or thing: *The artist* **does** *beautiful paintings.* **does** (duz) *verb.*

doesn't Shortened form of "does not": *That cup* **doesn't** *hold much milk.* **does·n't** (duz′ənt) *contraction.*

dog An animal that has four legs and makes a barking noise. Dogs are related to coyotes, wolves, and foxes, and eat meat. *Noun.*

○ To follow closely in the way a hunting dog would: *I* **dogged** *the babysitter through the park so that I wouldn't get lost. Verb.*

dog (dôg) *noun, plural* **dogs**; *verb,* **dogged, dogging.**

dogwood A tree or shrub that has small flowers with a greenish yellow center and pink or white leaves that look like petals. **dog·wood** (dôg′wŭd) *noun, plural* **dogwoods.**

The dogwood grows in North America, Europe, and Asia.

doily A small piece of linen, lace, paper, or some other material. Doilies are usually placed under something, such as a vase or plate, as a decoration or to protect furniture. **doi·ly** (doi′lē) *noun, plural* **doilies.**

doings Activities, deeds, or events: *The* **doings** *of the club were reported on the news.* **do·ings** (dü′ingz) *plural noun.*

do-it-yourself Having to do with home projects that people do themselves instead of hiring someone to do them: *a* **do-it-yourself** *book.* **do-it-your·self** (dü′i chər self′ *or* dü′it yər self′) *adjective.* **do-it-yourselfer** *noun.*

doll A toy that looks like a baby, a child, or a grown-up. **doll** (dol) *noun, plural* **dolls.**

dollar A unit of money in the United States and in Canada. A dollar is worth one hundred cents. **dol·lar** (dol′ər) *noun, plural* **dollars.**

dolphin A very intelligent sea animal that has two flippers and a snout that is like a beak. Although a dolphin

A dolphin has a longer snout and a more slender body than a porpoise.

looks like a fish, it is a mammal. **dol·phin** (dol′fin) *noun, plural* **dolphins.**

domain 1. All the land that is controlled by a ruler or government: *The news spread throughout the king's domain.* 2. A field of knowledge or interest: *Volcanoes and earthquakes fall within the domain of geology.* **do·main** (dō mān′) *noun, plural* **domains.**

dome A round roof that looks like an upside down cup. Domes are built on a base that is circular or has many sides. **dome** (dōm) *noun, plural* **domes.**

Some state capitol buildings have domes.

domestic 1. Having to do with the home and family: *domestic chores.* 2. Not wild; tame: *Dogs, cows, and chickens are domestic animals.* 3. Having to do with one's own country; not foreign: *The president of the United States handles both foreign and domestic affairs.* **do·mes·tic** (də mes′tik) *adjective.*

domesticate To train or change a wild animal so that it can live with or be used by people; tame: *People first domesticated wild horses to pull loads and help in farming.* **do·mes·ti·cate** (də mes′tik āt) *verb,* **domesticated, domesticating.**

dominant 1. Most powerful or important: *Rome was the dominant power in Europe 2,000 years ago.* 2. The most common feature: *Blue is the dominant color in my wardrobe.* **dominant** (domənənt) *adjective.*

dominate To rule or control because of power, strength, or importance: *In spite of women's efforts, men continue to dominate in business and politics.* **dom·i·nate** (dom′ə nāt) *verb,* **dominated, dominating.**

Dominican Republic A country that occupies part of an island in the Caribbean Sea. **Do·min·i·can Republic** (də min′i kən).

dominion 1. A land or territory that is controlled by a ruler or government: *In 1770, Virginia was still among the dominions of Great Britain.* 2. The power to rule; authority: *An able ruler held dominion over the land for forty years.* **do·min·ion** (də min′yən) *noun, plural* **dominions.**

Dominion Day The former name of *Canada Day.* Look up **Canada Day** for more information.

domino 1. One of a set of small black tiles marked with dots. Dominoes are used in playing a game. 2. dominoes. The game that is played with these tiles. **do·min·o** (dom′ə ˙nō) *noun, plural* **dominoes.**

don To put on: *Don your hat before you go outside.* **don** (don) *verb,* **donned, donning.**

donate To give; contribute: *The family donated their old clothes to people who needed them.* **do·nate** (dō′nāt) *verb,* **donated, donating.**

donation A gift; contribution: *The hospital fund received donations of more than $1,000 from the citizens in our town.* **do·na·tion** (dō nā′shən) *noun, plural* **donations.**

done Past participle of do: *Verb.*
○ Cooked: *When the meat is done, we can start our dinner. Adjective.*
done (dun) *verb; adjective.*

donkey A tame ass. Donkeys are related to horses but have longer ears and a shorter mane than horses do. They are often used to pull or carry loads. **don·key** (dong′kē or dung′kē) *noun, plural* **donkeys.**

donor A person who gives or contributes something: *a blood donor.* **do·nor** (dōn′ər) *noun, plural* **donors.**

don't Shortened form of "do not." **don't** (dōnt) *contraction.*

donut Another way to spell *doughnut.* **do·nut** (dō′nut) *noun, plural* **donuts.**

doodle To draw designs and sketches of nothing in particular: *I often doodled while talking on the phone. Verb.*
○ A design or drawing that is the result of doodling: *The notepad by our telephone is full of doodles. Noun.*
doo·dle (dü′dəl) *verb,* **doodled, doodling;** *noun, plural* **doodles.**

doom A sad end or death; a terrible fate: *The mountain climbers met their doom when their rope snapped. Noun.*
○ To make sure that a bad end will come; des-

PRONUNCIATION KEY:

| at | ape | far | care | end | me | it | ice | pierce | hot | old | song | fork |
| oil | out | up | use | rule | pull | turn | chin | sing | shop | thin | this | |

hw in white; zh in treasure. The symbol ə stands for the unstressed vowel sound in about, taken, pencil, lemon, and circus.

217

tined to fail or die: *A sudden thunderstorm doomed our hiking trip. Verb.*
doom (düm) *noun, plural* **dooms**; *verb,* **doomed, dooming.**

doomed Sure to fail or die: *a doomed project.* **doomed** (dümd) *adjective.*

door A movable object that is used to open or close an entrance in something. Doors are usually made of wood, metal, or glass. **door** (dôr) *noun, plural* **doors.**

doorbell A bell or buzzer that is rung by someone who is outside a door and who wants to come in. **door·bell** (dôr′bel) *noun, plural* **doorbells.**

doorknob A rounded handle used to open and close a door: *We were locked in the room because the doorknob was jammed.* **door·knob** (dô′rnob) *noun, plural* **doorknobs.**

doorstep A step or flight of steps leading from the outside door of a building to the ground or sidewalk. **door·step** (dôr′step) *noun, plural* **doorsteps.**

doorway An opening in a wall that leads in and out of a room or building and can be closed by a door. **door·way** (dôr′wā) *noun, plural* **doorways.**

dope 1. A very stupid person. 2. A harmful drug that causes addiction. 3. A varnish or similar liquid. Dope is used in building models of airplanes. **dope** (dōp) *noun, plural* **dopes.**

dormant Not active. A volcano that had been dormant for years suddenly erupted. **dor·mant** (dôr′mənt) *adjective.*

dormitory A building in which there are many bedrooms. Many colleges have dormitories where students live. **dorm·i·to·ry** (dôr′mi tôr′ē) *noun, plural* **dormitories.**

dormouse An animal that looks like a small squirrel with black or gray fur. Dormice are rodents and are found in Europe and northern Africa. They hibernate in the winter. **dor·mouse** (dôr′mous) *noun, plural* **dormice** (dôrmīs).

dory A rowboat that has a flat bottom and high sides. **do·ry** (dôr′ē) *noun, plural* **dories.**

DOS An abbreviation for disk operating system. **DOS** (dos *or* dôs)

dose An amount of medicine that a person is given at one time: *The doctor prescribed a small dose of aspirin for the sick child.* **dose** (dōs) *noun, plural* **doses.**

dot A small, round mark; small spot or speck: *The*

dot *on the map showed the location of the town. Noun.*
○ 1. To mark with a dot or dots: *Don't forget to dot your i's.* 2. To be scattered here and there: Small houses dotted the seashore. *Verb.*
dot (dot) *noun, plural* **dots**; *verb,* **dotted, dotting.**

dote To give too much affection: *The grandparents doted on their two grandchildren and spoiled them.* **dote** (dōt) *verb,* **doted, doting.**

double 1. Twice as many or as much: *The worker got double pay for the extra hours of work.* 2. Having or made up of two parts: *People stood in a double line in front of the theater.* That author led a double life during the war as a German citizen and a spy for the British. *Adjective.*
○ Two instead of one; in pairs: *The ride on the merry-go-round made me feel dizzy and see everything double. Adverb.*
○ 1. Something that is twice as much: *Ten is the double of five.* 2. A person or thing that is very much or just like another: *I saw your double on the street today.* 3. A hit in baseball that lets the batter reach second base. 4. **doubles.** In tennis and similar games, a game in which there are two people on each side of the net who play as a team. *Noun.*
○ 1. To make or become twice as many or as much: *I asked my parents to double my weekly allowance.* 2. To bend, fold, or turn over or back: *The funny story made the listeners double over with laughter.* 3. To be a substitute: *Another actor doubled for the star when we saw the play.* 4. To serve a second purpose: *This sofa doubles as a bed.* 5. To hit a double in baseball. *Verb.*
dou·ble (dub′əl) *adjective; adverb; noun, plural* **doubles**; *verb,* **doubled, doubling.**

double-cross To cheat or betray someone by not doing what one has promised: *The robber double-crossed a partner by running off with the money that they were supposed to share.* **dou·ble-cross** (dub′əl krôs′) *verb,* **double-crossed, double-crossing.**

double-header Two baseball games that are played one right after the other on the same day. **dou·ble-head·er** (dub′əl hed′ər) *noun, plural* **double-headers.**

doubt 1. To be uncertain about; not believe or trust fully: *The judge doubted that the prisoner* *was telling the truth.* **2.** To think of as unlikely: *I brought my umbrella, even though I **doubt** that it will rain. Verb.*

○ **1.** A feeling of not believing or trusting: *I had **doubts** about the honesty of the salesperson who was trying to sell me the **car.*** **2.** A state of being undecided or unsure: *The result of the race was in **doubt** until the horses reached the finish line. Noun.*

doubt (dout) *verb,* **doubted, doubting;** *noun, plural* **doubts.**

doubtful Feeling, showing, or causing doubt; not sure or certain: *The outcome of the game was **doubtful** until the last minute.* **doubt·ful** (dout′fəl) *adjective.* **doubtfully** *adv.*

doubtless Without doubt; certainly: *A person who draws as well as you will **doubtless** become an artist someday.* **doubtl·ess** (dout′lis) *adverb.*

dough **1.** A thick mixture of flour, liquid, and other ingredients that is usually baked. Dough is used to make bread, cookies, pie crusts, and other food. **2. Money.** This is an informal usage. **dough** (dō) *noun, plural* **doughs.**

doughnut A small, round cake that has a hole in the middle. A doughnut is cooked in fat. **dough·nut** (dō′nut) *noun, plural* **doughnuts.**

Doughnuts may be plain, frosted, or sprinkled with sugar.

WORD HISTORY

The word **doughnut** developed from an earlier form of the word *dough-nought,* a "dough circle." Nought is an old-fashioned word for "zero."

dove¹ Any member of a group of plump birds with small heads; pigeon. A white dove is sometimes used as a symbol of peace. **dove** (duv) *noun, plural* **doves.**

A dove makes a pleasant cooing sound.

dove² A past tense of dive: *The swimmer dove from the rocks into the lake.* **dove** (dōv) *verb.*

down¹ **1.** From a higher to a lower place: *The painter climbed **down** from the ladder.* **2.** To or in a lower position, level, or condition: *The price of milk has gone **down**.* **3.** To or on the ground or floor: *I fell **down**.* **4.** To a calmer condition: *The noisy crowd quieted **down**. Adverb.*

○ From a higher to a lower place; along, through, or into: *We rolled **down** the hillside. Preposition.*

○ **1.** To bring or put down: *The rocket **downed** the aircraft.* **2.** To swallow quickly: *It's best to **down** the bitter medicine in one gulp. Verb.*

○ One of four chances that a football team gets to move the ball 10 yards. If it does not move the ball that far, the other team gets possession of the ball. *Noun.*

down (doun) *adverb; preposition; verb,* **downed, downing;** *noun, plural* **downs.**

down² Fine, soft feathers. Baby birds have down until their regular feathers grow in. **down** (doun) *noun.*

downcast Sad; gloomy: *We were all **downcast** when the game was rained out.* **down·cast** (doun′kast′) *adjective.*

download To transfer information from one computer to another: *download a file.* **down·load** (doun′lōd′) *verb,* **downloaded, downloading.**

downpour A very heavy rain. **down·pour** (doun′pôr) *noun, plural* **downpours.**

PRONUNCIATION KEY:

at ā pe fär câre end mē it īce pierce hot old sông fôrk
oil out up ūse rüle pull tûrn chin sing shop thin this
hw in white; zh in treasure. The symbol ə stands for the unstressed vowel sound in about, taken, pencil, lemon, and circus.

219

downright Thorough; complete: *The rumor about me is a downright lie. Adjective.*
○ Thoroughly; completely: *First I was annoyed by the delay, then I became downright angry. Adverb.*
down·right (doun′rīt) *adjective; adverb.*

downsize 1. To make something smaller: *Detroit downsized cars last year.* 2. To get rid of employees: *My dad lost his job when the company downsized.* **downsize** (doun′sīz′) *verb,* **downsized, downsizing.**

downstairs 1. Down the stairs: *The child tripped and fell downstairs.* 2. On or to a lower floor: *The closest bathroom is downstairs. Adverb.*
○ On a lower or main floor: *a downstairs bathroom. Adjective.*
down·stairs (doun′stârz′) *adverb; adjective.*

downstream Moving in the same direction as the current of a stream: *Downstream river traffic is faster than upstream traffic. Adjective.*
○ 1. Down a stream: *The raft drifted downstream.* 2. At a point farther down the stream: *The water becomes rough downstream. Adverb.*
down·stream (doun′strēm′) *adjective; adverb.*

downtown To or in the main part or business district of a town: *We went downtown to see a movie. Adverb.*
○ Going to or located in the main part or business district of a town: *The downtown stores are larger than the stores in our neighborhood. Adjective.*
down·town (doun′toun′) *adverb; adjective.*

downward From a higher to a lower place: *The road is level and then goes downward into the valley. Adverb.*
○ Moving from a higher place to a lower place: *The hikers followed the downward course of the stream from the mountain top. Adjective.*
down·ward (doun′wərd) *adverb; adjective.*

downwards Another spelling of the adverb downward. **down·wards** (doun′wərdz) *adverb.*

dowry In some countries, the money or property that a woman brings to her marriage. **dow·ry** (dou′rē) *noun, plural* **dowries.**

doz. An abbreviation for **dozen.**

doze To sleep lightly or for a short time; take a nap. *Verb.*
○ A short, light sleep. *Noun.*
doze (dōz) *verb,* **dozed, dozing;** *noun, plural* **dozes.**

dozen A group of twelve: a dozen doughnuts.
doz·en (duz′ən) *noun, plural* **dozens** *or* **dozen.**

Dr. An abbreviation for **doctor.**

drab Not cheerful or bright; dull: *The dark, drab room was much nicer after we put up new curtains.* **drab** (drab) *adjective,* **drabber, drabbest.**

draft 1. A current of air in an enclosed space: *a cold draft from an open window.* 2. A device that controls the flow of air in something: *Furnaces, fireplaces, and some stoves have drafts.* 3. A sketch, plan, or rough copy of something written: *The author wrote three drafts of the novel.* 4. The selecting of persons for military service or some other special duty: *During World War II, most young men in the United States were subject to the draft. Noun.*
○ 1. To make a sketch, plan, or rough copy of something: *I drafted the letter in pencil and then typed it.* 2. To select a person or persons for some special duty: *Many people were drafted to serve in that war. Verb.*
○ Used for pulling loads: *Elephants are used as draft animals in some countries. Adjective.*
draft (draft) *noun, plural* **drafts;** *verb,* **drafted, drafting;** *adjective.*

drag 1. To pull or move along slowly or heavily: *The mover dragged the heavy trunk across the room.* 2. To trail along the ground: *The dog's leash dragged behind it.* 3. To search the bottom of a body of water with a hook or net: *The sailors dragged the bottom of the lake for the sunken rowboat.* **drag** (drag) *verb,* **dragged, dragging.**

dragon An imaginary beast that is supposed to look like a giant lizard with claws and wings.
drag·on (drag′ən) *noun, plural* **dragons.**

dragonfly An insect that has a long, thin body and two pairs of wings. Dragonflies eat mosquitoes and other insects. They live near fresh water.
drag·on·fly (drag′ən flī) *noun, plural* **dragonflies.**

A dragonfly has large eyes that have some 30,000 parts.

drain 1. To empty water or other liquid from something: *The thirsty players drained a pitcher of lemonade.* 2. To tire or use up; exhaust: *The long hike drained our energy. Verb.*

○ **1.** An opening, pipe, or other device that draws off water or another liquid: *The **drain** in the sink is clogged.* **2.** Something that uses up or exhausts: *Having to buy lunch every day is a **drain** on my allowance.* Noun.

drain (drān) *verb*, **drained, draining**; *noun, plural* **drains.**

drainage A drawing off or emptying of water or other liquid: *The **drainage** of the swamp has killed a lot of animals that lived there.* **drainage** (drān´ij) *noun, plural* **drainages.**

drainpipe A pipe used for carrying water or sewage away. **drain·pipe** (drān´pīp) *noun, plural* **drainpipes.**

drake A male duck. **drake** (drāk) *noun, plural* **drakes.**

drama **1.** A story that is written for actors to perform on the stage; play. **2.** A happening that is as exciting or interesting as a play: *the **drama** of astronauts walking in space.* **3.** The quality of excitement and suspense that good plays and stories have: *We enjoyed the movie, because it was full of **drama**.* **dra·ma** (drä´mə *or* dram´ə) *noun, plural* **dramas.**

These actors are performing a drama.

dramatic **1.** Of or having to do with plays or acting: *My cousin is studying **dramatic** literature.* **2.** As exciting and interesting as a good play or story: *Our team won a **dramatic** victory by scoring the winning point in the last minutes of the game.* **dra·ma·tic** (drə mat´ik) *adjective.*

dramatist A person who writes plays. **dram·a·tist** (dram´ə tist *or* dräm´ə tist) *noun, plural* **dramatists.**

dramatize **1.** To write or perform something as a play: *The class **dramatized** several stories from the books they had read.* **2.** To make something seem very exciting: *I **dramatized** what happened so that it sounded like a great adventure.* **dram·a·tize** (dram´ə tīz *or* dräm´ə tīz) *verb,* **dramatized, dramatizing.**

drank Past tense of drink. **drank** (drangk) *verb.*

drape **1.** To cover or decorate with cloth that hangs loosely: *I **draped** a shawl over my shoulders.* **2.** To arrange or spread loosely: *You **draped** your feet over the chair. Verb.*

○ Cloth that is hung at a window; drapery: *I opened the **drapes** to let sunlight into the room. Noun.*

drape (drāp) *verb,* **draped, draping**; *noun, plural* **drapes.**

drapery Cloth that is hung in loose folds. Draperies are usually used as window curtains. **dra·per·y** (drā´pə rē) *noun, plural* **draperies.**

drastic Very strong or harsh; extreme: *Fasting is a **drastic** way to lose weight.* **dras·tic** (dras´tik) *adjective.*

draw **1.** To move by pulling; haul: *Four horses **drew** the hay wagon.* **2.** To approach; move: *The train **drew** near the station.* **3.** To take out; bring out: *The nurse carefully **drew** the splinter from my foot.* **4.** To make a mark or picture with lines, using a pencil, crayon, or other writing tool: *Would you like to learn how to **draw**?* **5.** To cause to come; attract: *That band always **draws** a large audience.* **6.** To bring forth; result in: *The mayor's mistakes **drew** a lot of criticism.* **7.** To close; shut: *Please **draw** the curtains.* **8.** To take in by inhaling: *Draw a deep breath. Verb.*

○ **1.** The act of pulling a gun: *The hero in the movie was quick on the **draw** and fired first.* **2.** A game or contest that ends with an even score or no winner; tie: *The chess game ended in a **draw**. Noun.*

• **to draw out. 1.** To make longer: *He **drew** out the story until I thought it would never end.*

2. To cause to relax and talk: *The teacher had a hard time **drawing** out the shy girl.*

• **to draw up. 1.** To come or bring to a stop:

PRONUNCIATION KEY:

at	āpe	fär	câre	end	mē	it	īce	pierce	hot	ōld	sông	fôrk
oil	out	up	ūse	rüle	pull	tûrn	chin	sing	shop	thin	this	

hw in white; zh in treasure. The symbol ə stands for the unstressed vowel sound in about, taken, pencil, lemon, and circus.

221

The taxi **drew up** in front of our house. **2.** To prepare: *I **drew up** the plans for our vacation.* **draw** (drô) *verb,* **drew, drawn, drawing;** *noun, plural* **draws.**

drawback A thing that makes something more difficult or unpleasant; disadvantage: *One **drawback** of our new house is that it is so far away from my school.* **draw·back** (drô′bak) *noun, plural* **drawbacks.**

drawbridge A kind of bridge that can be raised or moved so that ships can pass under it. **draw·bridge** (drô′brij) *noun, plural* **drawbridges.**

drawer A box that fits into a piece of furniture and can be pulled out and pushed in. Bureaus, desks, and cabinets have drawers. **draw·er** (drôr) *noun, plural* **drawers.**

Some of the world's oldest drawings are found on the walls of ancient caves.

drawing **1.** A picture or design made using a pencil, pen, chalk, or other writing tool; sketch. **2.** The choosing of a winning chance or ticket in a raffle or other contest: *The **drawing** for the winning number will be next Saturday night.* **draw·ing** (drô′ing) *noun, plural* **drawings.**

drawl To speak slowly, drawing out the vowel sounds: *The sleepy child **drawled** an answer to the question. Verb.*
○ A slow way of speaking, with the vowel sounds drawn out: *Many people from the South speak with a **drawl**. Noun.*
drawl (drôl) *verb,* **drawled, drawling;** *noun, plural* **drawls.**

drawn Past participle of draw: *The artist has **drawn** many sketches of the church.* Look up draw for more information. **drawn** (drôn) *verb.*

drawstring A string or cord that is used to close

an opening or to make something tighter: *My pajamas have a **drawstring** around the waist.* **drawstring** (drôstring) *noun, plural* **drawstrings.**

dread To look forward to with fear; be very afraid or anxious about: *I **dreaded** going to the dentist. Verb.*
○ A feeling of great fear: *I think of mountain climbing with **dread** because I am afraid of heights. Noun.*
○ Causing fear; dreadful: *Smallpox is one of the **dread** diseases that has been almost completely wiped out. Adjective.*
dread (dred) *verb,* **dreaded, dreading;** *noun; adjective.*

dreadful **1.** Very frightening; terrible: *The **dreadful** storm damaged many trees.* **2.** Very bad; awful: *a **dreadful** movie.* **dread·ful** (dred′fəl) *adjective.*

dreadlocks A way of wearing the hair in long, ropelike locks. **dread·locks** (dred′loks′) *noun.*

dream **1.** A series of thoughts, feelings, and sights that a person has while asleep: *I had a **dream** last night that I was flying through the air.* **2.** A hope or ambition to do or succeed at something: *My great **dream** is to become an actor.* **3.** A very attractive person: *Isn't the new kid a **dream**? Noun.*
○ **1.** To see, feel, or think about in a dream: *I dozed off and **dreamed** about riding a white horse.* **2.** To imagine: *I didn't take an umbrella because I never **dreamed** it would rain. Verb.*
dream (drēm) *noun, plural* **dreams;** *verb,* **dreamed** *or* **dreamt, dreaming.**

dreamt A past tense and a past participle of dream: *I **dreamt** I was living in a castle.* Look up dream for more information. **dreamt** (dremt) *verb.*

dreary Sad or dull; gloomy: *Painting the dark room bright yellow made it less **dreary**.* **drear·y** (drîr′ē) *adjective,* **drearier, dreariest.**

dredge A large machine that scoops up mud, sand, and other material from the bottom of a body of water: *The engineers used a **dredge** to make the canal deeper. Noun.*
○ To clean out or deepen with a dredge: *The machine **dredged** mud from the river. Verb.*
dredge (drej) *noun, plural* **dredges;** *verb,* **dredged, dredging.**

dregs **1.** Small pieces that settle at the bottom of a liquid: *There were **dregs** at the bottom of the cof-*

fee cup. **2.** The bottom layer of anything: *He hangs out with the **dregs** of the school.* **dregs** (dregz) *plural noun.*

drench To make something completely wet; soak: *The big wave **drenched** the children on the raft.* **drench** (drench) *verb,* **drenched, drenching.**

dress **1.** An outer garment usually worn by women or girls. A dress is usually one piece and extends from the neck to just above or below the knees. **2.** Clothing or a particular style of clothing: *The guests at the ball were all wearing formal **dress**.* *Noun.*

○ **1.** To put clothes on: *I **dressed** quickly because I was late for school.* **2.** To select and wear clothes: *Salespersons often **dress** in the latest styles.* **3.** To decorate; trim: *Thank you for helping us **dress** the store windows for the holidays.* **4.** To comb and arrange the hair: *I went to the barber to have my hair **dressed**.* **5.** To clean and prepare for use or sale: *The butcher **dressed** the turkey for us.* **6.** To clean and treat with medicine: *The nurse **dressed** my wound and bandaged it.* *Verb.*

• **to dress up.** To put on clothing more elaborate or fancy than what is usually worn: *It's fun to **dress up** for parties.*

dress (dres) *noun, plural* **dresses**; *verb,* **dressed, dressing.**

dresser A piece of furniture that has drawers for storing clothes and other things. A dresser often has a large mirror attached to it. **dress•er** (dresər) *noun, plural* **dressers.**

dressing **1.** A sauce that is put on salads and some other foods. **2.** A mixture of bread crumbs and seasonings that is used to stuff turkey, chicken, or other fowl. **3.** A medicine or bandage that is put on a wound or sore. **dress•ing** (dres'ing) *noun, plural* **dressings.**

dress rehearsal The last rehearsal before a play, in full costume.

drew Past tense of draw: **drew** (drü) *verb.*

dribble **1.** To flow or let flow in small drops; trickle: *Rain **dribbled** through the cracks in the roof.* **2.** To move a ball along by bouncing or kicking it: *Players **dribble** the ball in basketball and soccer.* *Verb.*

○ A dripping; trickle: *A **dribble** of juice from the*

plum ran down the child's chin. *Noun.* **drib•ble** (drib'əl) *verb,* **dribbled, dribbling**; *noun, plural* **dribbles.**

dried Past tense and past participle of dry: *I washed my hair and then **dried** it.* Look up dry for more information. **dried** (drīd) *verb.*

drier Comparative of dry: *Adjective.*

○ Another spelling for the word dryer. *Noun.* **dri•er** (drī'ər) *adjective; noun, plural* **driers.**

drift **1.** To move because of a current of air or water: *We stopped rowing and let our boat **drift** downstream.* **2.** To pile up in masses from the action of the wind: *The snow **drifted** to 6 feet outside our cabin.* **3.** To move from place to place without a goal or purpose: *The tramp **drifted** from town to town.* *Verb.*

○ **1.** Movement caused by a current of air or water: *Scientists measured the **drift** of the glacier over the past one hundred years.* **2.** Something that has been moved along or piled up by air or water currents: *The storm caused **drifts** of snow more than 10 feet deep.* *Noun.*

• **to get the drift.** To understand what someone means: *She didn't say a lot, but we **got the drift**.*

drift (drift) *verb,* **drifted, drifting**; *noun, plural* **drifts.**

driftwood Wood that floats on water or is brought to the shore by water. **driftwood** (driftwüd) *noun.*

drill **1.** A tool that is used to cut holes in wood, plastic, and other hard material. A drill usually has a long, pointed end that is turned with a crank or by an electric motor. **2.** Training or teaching by making someone do something again and again; practice: *For our social studies **drill**, the teacher asked us to name the capital of each state.* *Noun.*

○ **1.** To make a hole in something with a drill; use a drill: *The carpenter **drilled** a hole in the wood.* **2.** To train or teach by having someone do something again and again: *The school band **drilled** by marching back and forth.* *Verb.*

drill (dril) *noun, plural* **drills**; *verb,* **drilled, drilling.**

drink **1.** To swallow a liquid: *I **drink** a glass of milk with every meal.* **2.** To soak up: *The plants **drank** in the rain.* **3.** To drink alcoholic beverages. *Verb.*

PRONUNCIATION KEY:

| at | āpe | fär | câre | end | mē | it | tûrn | īce | pierce | hot | ōld | sông | fôrk |
| oil | out | up | ūse | rüle | pull | | | chin | sing | shop | thin | this | |

hw in white; zh in treasure. The symbol ə stands for the unstressed vowel sound in about, taken, pencil, lemon, and circus.

223

○ **1.** A liquid for drinking: *Lemonade is my favorite* **drink** *in the summer.* **2.** A portion of liquid to be swallowed: *The tennis players stopped to have a* **drink** *of orange juice.* **3.** An alcoholic beverage. *Noun.*

• **to drink up. 1.** To drink completely: *I just couldn't leave the table until I* **drank up** *my milk.* **2.** To use up completely: *Her long illness* **drank up** *our savings.*
drink (dringk) *verb,* **drank, drunk, drinking;** *noun,* plural **drinks.**

SYNONYMS

drink, sip, swallow, gulp
The animals gathered to **drink** *from the stream. The cocoa is hot so* **sip** *it slowly. That vitamin pill is hard to* **swallow.** *They* **gulped** *their orange juice and ran for the bus.*

drip To fall or let fall in drops: *Please don't* **drip** *paint from the brush onto the floor. Verb.*
○ A falling of liquid in drops: *There was a* **drip** *of water from the faucet. Noun.*
drip (drip) *verb,* **dripped, dripping;** *noun, plural* **drips.**

drive 1. To operate and steer a car or other vehicle: *I didn't learn to* **drive** *until I was eighteen years old.* **2.** To go or carry in a car or other vehicle: *We plan to* **drive** *to the city on Saturday.* **3.** To move with a strong force: *The waves* **drove** *the ship toward the rocks.* **4.** To strike or send with a powerful blow: *The baseball player tried to* **drive** *the ball over the fence.* **5.** To force into some act or condition: *The noises were* **driving** *us crazy.* **6.** To supply the power for; set and keep going: *Electricity* **drives** *this motor. Verb.*
○ **1.** A trip in a car or other vehicle: *The* **drive** *here was unpleasant because there was so much traffic.* **2.** A road or driveway: *The visitor parked the car in the* **drive** *and walked to the front door.* **3.** A strong hit: *In the golf tournament, the winner hit a* **drive** *more than 250 yards.* **4.** In football, a long period of time when the offense has the ball and keeps moving it toward the goal line: *That last* **drive** *used up a lot of time.* **5.** A great desire to do something; ambition: *My sister has more* **drive** *than I do.* **6.** A special group effort to do something; campaign: *The town started a* **drive** *to raise money for a new hospital. Noun.*

• **to drive crazy or mad.** To irritate; annoy: *Turn that music down; it's* **driving me crazy.**
• **To drive up the wall.** To frustrate: *This arithmetic problem is* **driving me up the wall.**
drive (drīv) *verb,* **drove, driven, driving;** *noun, plural* **drives.**

drive-in A restaurant, movie theater, or bank that can take care of customers in their cars. **drive-in** (drī′vin) *noun, plural* **drive-ins.**

drive-in window. A window in a fastfood restaurant, bank, or other place of business where customers can drive up to buy something, make a deposit, etc.

driver 1. A person who drives an automobile, truck, or other vehicle. **2.** A kind of golf club. **driv·er** (drī′vər) *noun, plural* **drivers.**

driveway A private road that leads from a street to a house, garage, or other building. **drive·way** (drīv′wā) *noun, plural* **driveways.**

Some driveways are
extremely long.

drizzle To rain steadily in fine, misty drops. *Verb.*
○ A fine, misty rain. *Noun.*
driz·zle (driz′əl) *verb,* **drizzled, drizzling;** *noun, plural* **drizzles.**

dromedary A kind of camel that has one hump. Dromedaries live in Arabia and northern Africa.

drom·e·dar·y (drom′ə der ē)*noun, plural* **dromedaries.**

drone¹ A male bee. **drone** (drōn) *noun, plural* **drones.**

drone² **1.** To make a low, steady, humming sound: *The small airplane droned as it climbed higher.* **2.** To talk in a dull, boring way: *The speaker droned on and on. Verb.*
○ A low, steady humming sound: *The drone of the car's engine made me sleepy. Noun.*
drone (drōn) *verb,* **droned, droning**; *noun, plural* **drones.**

drool To let saliva drip from the mouth: *Babies often drool when they are teething.* **drool** (drül) *verb,* **drooled, drooling.**

droop To hang or sink down; sag: *After a few days the flowers in the vase began to droop.* **droop** (drüp) *verb,* **drooped, drooping.**

drop **1.** To fall or cause to fall to a lower position; move or fall down: *The wet dish dropped from my hand. The temperature dropped to below freezing last night.* **2.** To go into a less active condition: *After a while I must have dropped off to sleep.* **3.** To stop talking about or pursuing: *No one seemed interested, so I decided to drop the subject.* **4.** To pay a casual, unplanned visit: *Our neighbor dropped by to say hello.* **5.** To let out of a vehicle: *The bus drops the children in front of the school.* **6.** To leave out; omit: *I accidentally dropped a stitch as I knitted. Verb.*
○ **1.** A very small amount of liquid: *There was a drop of blood on my hand where the cat had scratched me.* **2.** The act of dropping or falling: *The weather reporter said there would be a drop in temperature tonight.* **3.** The distance between one thing and another thing that is below it: *From the top of the cliff to the beach was a drop of 100 feet. Noun.*
• **to drop in.** To pay a visit that is informal or not planned: *We were passing your house and decided to drop in.*
• **to drop off.** To deliver: *Please drop off this order at the grocery on your way to school.*
• **drop out.** To leave a place or stop an activity: *I never see her anymore since she dropped out of school.*
drop (drop) *verb,* **dropped** *or* **dropt, dropping**; *noun, plural* **drops.**

drought A long period of time when there is very little rain or no rain at all. **drought** (drout) *noun, plural* **droughts.**

drove¹ Past tense of drive: **drove** (drōv) *verb.*

drove² **1.** A group of animals that move or are driven along together: *The cowhands brought a drove of cattle to the ranch.* **2.** A large number of people; crowd: *People went to the beach in droves on the hot summer day.* **drove** (drōv) *noun, plural* **droves.**

drown **1.** To die by suffocating in water or another liquid: *The swimmer went out too far and almost drowned.* **2.** To kill by keeping under water or another liquid and not getting air to breathe: *Two people were drowned in the flood.* **3.** To cover up the sound of something by a louder sound: *We tried to say good-bye, but our words were drowned by the roar of the airplane engines.*
• **to drown out.** To cover up the sound of: *I couldn't hear you because the baby's screams drowned you out.*
drown (droun) *verb,* **drowned, drowning.**

drowsy Half asleep; sleepy: *I felt drowsy after dinner and decided to take a nap.* **drow·sy** (drou′zē) *adjective,* **drowsier, drowsiest.**

drudgery Hard, unpleasant, and uninteresting labor: *Compared to the drudgery of scrubbing the floor, dusting the shelves was enjoyable.* **drudg·er·y** (druj′ər ē) *noun.*

drug **1.** A chemical substance taken to treat a disease or make a person feel better. **2.** A harmful substance that can make a person who takes it become addicted. *Noun.*
○ To give a drug to: *The nurse drugged the patient so that falling asleep would be easier. Verb.*
drug (drug) *noun, plural* **drugs**; *verb,* **drugged, drugging.**

druggist **1.** A person who has a license to make and sell medicine; pharmacist. **2.** A person who owns or runs a drugstore. **drug·gist** (drug′ist) *noun, plural* **druggists.**

drugstore A store where medicines and drugs are sold. Drugstores often also sell cosmetics, candy, magazines, and other things. **drug·store** (drug′stôr) *noun, plural* **drugstores.**

PRONUNCIATION KEY:
at   āpe   fär   câre   end   mē   it   īce   pierce   hot   ōld   sông   fôrk
oil   out   up   ūse   rüle   půll   tûrn   chin   sing   shop   thin   this
hw in white; zh in treasure. The symbol ə stands for the unstressed vowel sound in about, taken, pencil, lemon, and circus.

225

drum 1. A musical instrument that is hollow and covered at the top and at the bottom with material that is stretched tight. A drum is beaten to make sounds. 2. A container that is shaped like a drum: *The oil was stored in large metal drums. Noun.*
○ 1. To beat or play on a drum. 2. To make a sound like a drum: *The woodpecker drummed on the tree trunk with its bill.* 3. To force into a person's head by repeating: *I finally drummed the idea into your head that I don't like to be called by my nickname. Verb.*
drum (drum) *noun, plural* **drums**; *verb,* **drummed, drumming.**

This drum was used in the Civil War.

drum major A person who leads a marching band.

drum majorette A girl who twirls a baton while marching with a band in a parade. **drum major•ette** (mā′jə ret′).

drummer A person who plays drums. **drum•mer** (drum′ər) *noun, plural* **drummers.**

drumstick 1. A stick used to beat a drum. 2. The lower part of the leg of a cooked chicken, turkey, or other fowl. **drum•stick** (drum′stik) *noun, plural* **drumsticks.**

drunk Past participle of **drink.** *Verb.*
○ Having had too much to drink of an alcoholic beverage: *A person who is drunk should not drive a car. Adjective.*
○ A person who has had or often has too much to drink of an alcoholic beverage. *Noun.*
drunk (drungk) *verb; adjective,* **drunker, drunkest;** *noun, plural* **drunks.**

dry 1. Not wet or damp; with very little or no water or other liquid: *Cactuses grow well in a dry climate.* 2. Not in or under water: *After the long voyage, the sailors were happy to be back on dry land again.* 3. Thirsty: *I was so dry after playing tennis that I drank three glasses of water.* 4. Not interesting; dull: *The long, dry speech put some of the listeners to sleep. Adjective.*
○ To make or become dry: *If you wash the dishes, I'll dry them. Verb.*
dry (drī) *adjective,* **drier, driest;** *verb,* **dried, drying.**

dry cell An electric cell or battery in which the substance that conducts the electrical current is made of a paste so that it will not spill.

dry-clean To clean clothes by using chemicals instead of water. **dry-clean** (drī′klēn) *verb,* **dry-cleaned, dry-cleaning.**

dryer A machine or device for drying something: *I put the wet laundry in the clothes dryer.* This word is also spelled **drier. dry•er** (drī′ər) *noun, plural* **dryers.**

dual Made up of or having two parts: *The driving instructor and the student used a car that had dual controls.*
Another word that sounds like this is **duel.**
dual (dü′əl *or* dū′əl) *adjective.*

duchess The wife or widow of a duke. **duch•ess** (duch′is) *noun, plural* **duchesses.**

duck¹ 1. A water bird that has a broad, flat bill and webbed feet that help it to swim. There are both wild and tame ducks. Tame ducks are often raised for food. 2. A female duck. The male is often called a **drake. duck** (duk) *noun, plural* **ducks.**

duck² 1. To push someone under water suddenly: *I swam behind my friends and playfully ducked them.* 2. To lower the head or bend down quickly: *The batter ducked to keep from being hit by the ball.* 3. To avoid; evade: *I ducked the embarrassing question by bringing up another subject.* **duck** (duk) *verb,* **ducked, ducking.**

duckling A young duck: *The ducklings followed their parents into the pond.* **duck•ling** (duk′ling) *noun, plural* **ducklings.**

duct A tube, pipe, or channel that carries a liquid or air. Tears are formed in glands behind the eyes and are carried to the eyes by tiny ducts. Ducts are used in some buildings to carry hot or cold air to control the temperature in rooms. **duct** (dukt) *noun, plural* **ducts.**

dud Something that does not do what it is supposed to do: *Our last car was a dud.* **dud** (dud) *noun, plural* **duds.**

due 1. Owed or owing: *The rent for the apartment is due on the first day of each month.* 2. Expected or supposed to arrive or be ready: *The train is due at noon.* 3. Appropriate; proper: *I addressed the principal with due respect. Adjective.*
○ 1. Something that is owed: *You should give the others their due and congratulate them for beat-*

ing you in the contest. **2. dues.** A fee that a person pays to a club for being a member. *Noun.*
○ Straight; directly: *The explorers walked* **due** *west toward the setting sun. Adverb.*
Other words that sound like this are **dew** and **do.**

• **due to. 1.** Caused by: *Our delay was* **due to** *heavy traffic.* **2.** Because of: *The project was abandoned* **due to** *lack of support.*
due (dü *or* dū) *adjective; noun, plural* **dues;** *adverb.*

duel A formal fight between two people with swords or pistols. Duels were held to settle an argument or to decide a question of honor. *Noun.*
○ To fight a duel. *Verb.*
Another word that sounds like this is **dual.**
duel (düəl *or* dūəl) *noun, plural* **duels;** *verb,* **dueled, dueling.**

duet A piece of music written for two singers or two musical instruments. **duet** (düet *or* dūet) *noun, plural* **duets.**

dug Past tense and past participle of **dig. dug** (dug) *verb.*

Baseball dugouts are located between home plate and first base and third base.

dugout 1. A rough shelter that is made by digging a hole in the ground or in the side of a hill. 2. A long, low shelter in which baseball players sit during a game when they are not playing. Dugouts are built at the side of the field. 3. A canoe or boat that is made by hollowing out a large log. **dug·out** (dug′out) *noun, plural* **dugouts.**

duke A nobleman who has the highest rank below a prince. **duke** (dük *or* dūk) *noun, plural* **dukes.**

dull 1. Not sharp or pointed; blunt: *The knife was so* **dull** *that I could not cut the steak.* 2. Not interesting; plain or boring: *The movie was so* **dull** *that we left before it was over.* 3. Slow to learn or understand; not intelligent: *A person would have to be very* **dull** *not to understand that joke.* 4. Not bright, clear, or distinct: *I felt a* **dull** *ache in my legs the day after the long hike. Adjective.*
○ To make or become dull: *Using the kitchen scissors for cutting wire* **dulled** *them. Verb.*
dull (dul) *adjective,* **duller, dullest;** *verb,* **dulled, dulling.**

dumb 1. Not able to speak: *Although they were born deaf and* **dumb,** *those children learned to communicate through sign language.* We were struck dumb by the surprising news. 2. Stupid: *You have to be really* **dumb** *to believe such a silly lie.* **dumb** (dum) *adjective,* **dumber, dumbest.**

dumbbell A short bar with a heavy weight at each end. Dumbbells are lifted to develop the muscles of the arms and back. **dumb·bell** (dum′ bel) *noun, plural* **dumbbells.**

dumbfounded At a loss for words; shocked: *We were* **dumbfounded** *by the way you talked to the teacher.* **dumb·founded** (dum′foun′dəd *or* dum foun′dəd) *adjective.*

dummy 1. A figure that is made to look like a person: *The* **dummy** *in the department store window was dressed in a wedding gown.* 2. Something that is made to look like something else that is real: *The bullets used in the movie were* **dummies.** 3. A foolish person. **dum·my** (dum′ē) *noun, plural* **dummies.**

dump To drop, unload, or empty: *The truck* **dumped** *the gravel on the sidewalk. Verb.*
○ A place where garbage and trash are dumped: *At the end of the day, the garbage trucks unloaded at the city* **dump.** *Noun.*
dump (dump) *verb,* **dumped, dumping;** *noun, plural* **dumps.**

PRONUNCIATION KEY:
at āpe fär cåre end mē it īce pierce hot old sông fôrk
oil out up ūse rüle pull tûrn chin sing shop thin this
hw in white; zh in treasure. The symbol ə stands for the unstressed vowel sound in about, taken, pencil, lemon, and circus.

227

dune A mound or ridge of sand that has been piled up by the wind. **dune** (dün or dūn) *noun, plural* **dunes.**

As winds blow on it, a dune gradually shifts its position.

dungaree 1. A heavy cotton cloth that is used to make clothing and sails. 2. **dungarees.** Pants or work clothes that are made from this cloth. **dun·ga·ree** (dung′gə rē′) *noun, plural* **dungarees.**

WORD HISTORY

The word dungaree comes from the country of India, where this kind of cloth was first produced.

dungeon A dark prison or cell that is built underground: *The royal guards captured the traitors and put them in the dungeon of the castle.* **dun·geon** (dun′jən) *noun, plural* **dungeons.**

dunk 1. To dip something, such as a doughnut, in a liquid: 2. To shove a basketball into the basket forcefully: *dunk* (dungk) *verb,* **dunked, dunking.**

duplicate Just like something else: *My parents gave me a duplicate key to our front door. Adjective.* Something that is just like something else; exact copy: *My parents liked the snapshot so much that I had a duplicate made for them. Noun.* ○ 1. To make an exact copy of something: *The secretary duplicated the letter.* 2. To do again; repeat: *Our tennis team tried to duplicate last year's victory. Verb.* **du·pli·cate** (dü′pli kit *or* dū′pli kit *for adjective and noun;* dü′pli kāt′ *or* dū′pli kāt′ *for verb) adjective; noun, plural* **duplicates;** *verb,* **duplicated, duplicating.**

durable Able to last a long time in spite of much use or wear: *I'm still wearing those durable shoes with heavy soles.* **du·ra·ble** (dùr′ə bəl *or* dyùr′ə bəl) *adjective.*

duration The length of time during which something continues: *I stayed in bed for the duration of my illness.* **du·ra·tion** (dù rā′shən *or* dyù rā′shən) *noun, plural* **durations.**

during 1. Throughout the time of: *The trees and grass are green during the summer.* 2. At some time in the course of: *We were awakened by a telephone call during the night.* **dur·ing** (dùr′ing *or* dyùr′ing) *preposition.*

dusk The time of day just before the sun goes down; twilight: *The farmer worked in the fields from dawn to dusk.* **dusk** (dusk) *noun.*

dust Tiny pieces of earth, dirt, or other matter: *The horse kicked up a cloud of dust. Noun.* ○ 1. To remove the dust from something by brushing or wiping: *I dusted the table and then polished it with wax.* 2. To cover or sprinkle: *The baker dusted the doughnuts with powdered sugar. Verb.* **dust** (dust) *noun; verb,* **dusted, dusting.**

dusty 1. Covered with dust: *The attic was filled with dusty old chairs and pictures.* 2. Like dust: *Those flowers give off a dusty pollen.* **dust·y** (dust′ē) *adjective,* **dustier, dustiest.**

Dutch Of or relating to the Netherlands, its people, or their language. *Adjective.* ○ 1. **the Dutch.** The people of the Netherlands. 2. The language of the Netherlands. *Noun.* **Dutch** (duch) *adjective; noun.*

dutiful Doing what one ought to do; obedient: *Dutiful children help their parents with chores.* **du·ti·ful** (dü′ti fəl *or* dū′ti fəl) *adjective.*

duty 1. Something that a person is supposed to do: *Locking up the store at night was one of the manager's duties.* 2. A tax paid on goods that are brought into or taken out of a country. **du·ty** (dü′tē *or* dū′tē) *noun, plural* **duties.**

dwarf 1. A person, animal, or plant that is much smaller than the normal size when fully grown. 2. A little man in fairy tales who has magical powers. *Noun.* ○ To make seem small: *The skyscraper dwarfed all the buildings around it. Verb.* **dwarf** (dwôrf) *noun, plural* **dwarfs** *or* **dwarves** (dwôrvz); *verb,* **dwarfed, dwarfing.**

dwell To make one's home; live in a place: *After living in the country for many years, they decided to **dwell** in the city.*

> • **to dwell on** or **to dwell upon.** To think, write, or speak about for a long time: *Don't **dwell on** unpleasant memories.*
>
> **dwell** (dwel) *verb,* **dwelt** or **dwelled, dwelling.**

dwelling A place where a person lives: *We live in a two-family **dwelling**.* **dwel·ling** (dwel′ing) *noun,* *plural* **dwellings.**

dwindle To become less or smaller; shrink slowly: *The crowd began to **dwindle** after the parade passed by.* **dwin·dle** (dwin′dəl) *verb,* **dwindled, dwindling.**

dye A substance that is used to give a particular color to cloth, hair, food, or other materials. *Noun.*

> ○ To color or stain something with a dye: *When the blue curtains faded, we **dyed** them red. Verb.* Another word that sounds like this is **die.**
>
> **dye** (dī) *noun,* *plural* **dyes**; *verb,* **dyed, dyeing.**

dying Present participle of die: **dy·ing** (dī′ing) *verb.*

dynamic Having or showing a lot of energy; active; forceful: *That **dynamic** young person is sure to become a leader.* **dy·nam·ic** (dī nam′ik) *adjective.*

dynamite A substance that explodes with great force. Dynamite is used to blow up old buildings and blast openings in rocks. *Noun.*

> ○ To blow something up with dynamite: *The builders **dynamited** the mountain so that they could put a road through. Verb.*
>
> **dy·na·mite** (dī′nə mīt) *noun; verb,* **dynamited, dynamiting.**

dynamo An electric motor or generator. Dynamos usually produce a direct current. **dy·na·mo** (dī′nə mō) *noun,* *plural* **dynamos.**

dynasty A series of rulers who belong to the same family: *I read about a **dynasty** of emperors in a book on ancient China.* **dy·nas·ty** (dī′nə stē) *noun,* *plural* **dynasties.**

dz. An abbreviation for **dozen.**

PRONUNCIATION KEY:
at   āpe   fär   câre   end   mē   it   īce   pîerce   hot   ōld   sông   fôrk
oil   out   up   ūse   rüle   pùll   tûrn   chin   sing   shop   thin   this
hw in white; zh in treasure. The symbol ə stands for the unstressed vowel sound in about, taken, pencil, lemon, and circus.

229

E e

The sound of E in b**e** and m**e** can also be made by:

ea in words such as b**ea**t and **ea**sy; ee in b**ee** and **ee**l; ey in k**ey**, ie in f**ie**ld; and y, especially at the end of words with more than one syllable, such as luck**y**.

Less often, the sound of E in b**e** is made by:

ei in rec**ei**ve; and i in mach**i**ne.

In words such as tak**e**n and ag**e**nt the sound of the letter E is represented in the pronunciations in this dictionary by a schwa (ə).

Silent E

The letter E is silent in some words, but it often makes the vowel in front of the E say its name. For example, adding silent E will change car to car**e**, rip to rip**e**, not to not**e**, and cub to cub**e**.

Also:

Adding silent E to a word ending in the letter G makes it sound like J, as in changing wag to wag**e**; and a silent E that follows the letter C often makes it sound like S, as in lac**e** and nic**e**.

Spelling Hints

The letter E has two sounds in English, but these sounds can also be made by other combinations of letters.

The sound of E in b**e**d, p**e**t, and t**e**n can also be made by:

a in **a**ny and m**a**ny; ai in s**ai**d; ay in s**ay**s; ei in words such as th**ei**r; eo in l**eo**pard; ie in fri**e**nd; and u in b**u**ry.

e, E The fifth letter of the alphabet. **e, E** (ē) *noun, plural* **e's, E's.**

E *or* **E.** An abbreviation for **east** or **eastern.**

each Every one of two or more things or persons thought of as individuals or one at a time: *Each player gets a turn. Adjective.*
○ Every individual person or thing in a group: *The farmer gave each of us a ride on the horse. Pronoun.*
○ For each one: *These apples are a quarter each. Adverb.*

• **each other.** Each of two or more people or things involved in an action or relationship that is shared by the other or others: *The twins love each other.*

each (ēch) *adjective; pronoun; adverb.*

eager Wanting very much to do something: *The children were eager to go to the circus.* **ea·ger** (ē′gər) *adjective.*

eagle A large, powerful bird that hunts and feeds on small animals and fish. Eagles have sharp eyesight, a hooked bill, and strong claws. One kind of eagle, the bald eagle, is the national symbol of the United States. **ea·gle** (ē′gəl) *noun, plural* **eagles.**

ear¹ 1. The organ of the body by which people and animals hear. 2. In people and mammals, the outer, visible part of this organ: *The rabbit turned its long ears toward the sound.* 3. The sense of hearing: *Our singing teacher's voice is pleasing to the ear.*

• **to play by ear.** To play a piece of music without following written music: *I **played** a song I had heard on the radio **by ear.*** **ear** (îr) *noun, plural* **ears**.

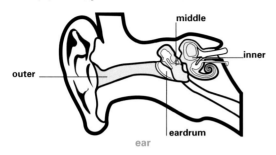

ear

ear² The part of certain plants on which the grains or seeds grow: *The grains of corn and wheat grow on **ears.*** **ear** (îr) *noun, plural* **ears**.

earache A pain inside the ear. **ear·ache** (îr′āk) *noun, plural* **earaches**.

eardrum The thin tissue that is stretched like the top of a drum inside the ear. When sound waves strike the eardrum, it vibrates and passes the sound waves on to the hearing nerves. **ear·drum** (îr′drum) *noun, plural* **eardrums**.

earl A nobleman in Great Britain. **earl** (ûrl) *noun, plural* **earls**.

early **1.** In or near the beginning: *My birthday is **early** in March.* **2.** Before the usual time: *We had an **early** dinner so we could go to the carnival in the evening.*

ear·ly (ûr′lē) *adjective,* **earlier, earliest;** *adverb.*

earmuffs A pair of fluffy coverings worn on the ears to protect them from the wind and cold. **ear·muffs** (îr′mufs) *plural noun.*

earn **1.** To get as pay for work done: *I **earned** fifty dollars mowing lawns.* **2.** To deserve or win because of hard work or good behavior: *The student **earned** high marks by studying hard.* Another word that sounds like this is **urn.** **earn** (ûrn) *verb,* **earned, earning.**

earnest Not joking or fooling about something; serious: *The children were being **earnest** when they said they wanted to help.* **ear·nest** (ûr′nist) *adjective.*

earnings Money that has been received as pay, profit, or interest: *I put all my **earnings** in the bank to save up for a bicycle.* **earn·ings** (ûr′ningz) *plural noun.*

earphone A part of an electrical device that turns electric signals into sound. Earphones are placed over or held next to the ear so that a person can listen to a radio, phonograph, or other device. **ear·phone** (îr′fōn) *noun, plural* **earphones**.

earring A piece of jewelry worn on or through the ear. **ear·ring** (îr′ring) *noun, plural* **earrings**.

earth **1.** The planet on which we live. It is the fifth largest planet in our solar system and the third planet in order of distance from the sun. The

---

EARTH

The Origin of the Earth: The planets of the Solar System, including Earth, are thought to have been formed 4.5 billion years ago from dust left over from the creation of the sun. As gravity pulled the dust together, pressure and radioactivity heated it. This heat melted the dust, allowing the heavier elements, such as iron, to sink toward the center. Lighter elements, such as silicon, were forced upward. This heaving and sinking must have been a time of turmoil, with volcanoes erupting, lava flowing, and steam spouting out of the Earth. Eventually, the Earth cooled and great rains fell. The water collected in depressions on the Earth's surface and formed oceans.

Inside the Earth: The iron core of Earth is still very hot, with a temperature of about 11,000° F. The core is about 2,100 miles in diameter. It is surrounded by the mantle, which extends about 1,800 miles, nearly to the surface. The mantle is like a very thick liquid. It flows, but usually very slowly. Above the mantle is the crust that we stand on. It ranges in thickness from 5 to 25 miles.

The Continents: Recent evidence suggests that the land we stand on is actually moving. This confirms a theory known as *continental drift*. If you look at a map of the continents, some of them, such as Africa and South America, look as though they could fit together like parts of a jigsaw puzzle.

Continents are part of a system of pieces of crust, known as plates, that float on the mantle. Over long periods of time, these plates slowly shift position. Where plates move together, earthquakes occur frequently and mountain chains are formed.

word "earth" in this sense is sometimes capitalized. **2.** Dry land; the ground: *After weeks at sea, the sailors were glad to feel the earth under their feet.* **3.** Soil; dirt: *We planted the seeds in the earth.* **earth** (ûrth) *noun.*

earthen 1. Made out of earth: *The log cabin had an earthen floor.* **2.** Made of clay that has been baked and made hard: *In the museum we saw earthen bowls made by American Indians.* **earth·en** (ûr′thən) *adjective.*

earthly 1. Having to do with the earth or this world, rather than with heaven: *The couple left all their earthly goods to their children.* **2.** Possible; that can be imagined: *These old shoes are of no earthly use.* **earth·ly** (ûrth′lē) *adjective.*

earthquake A shaking or trembling of the ground. Earthquakes are caused by rock, lava, or hot gases moving deep inside the earth. Some earthquakes are so powerful that they cause the ground to split and buildings to fall down. **earth·quake** (ûrth′kwāk) *noun, plural* **earthquakes.**

earthworm A common worm made up of many round segments. Earthworms loosen the soil by making tunnels. **earth·worm** (ûrth′wûrm) *noun, plural* **earthworms.**

ease Freedom from trouble, pain, or hard work: *After working for many years, our neighbors sold their business and lived a life of ease. Noun.*
○ **1.** To make free from trouble, pain, or worry: *The news that the flood would not reach our house eased our minds.* **2.** To make less; lighten: *This medicine will ease the ache in your back.* **3.** To move slowly or carefully: *The driver eased the car into the small parking space. Verb.*
 • **ease into.** To begin to do gradually: *I'm trying to ease into my new job, learning slowly.*
 • **ease up.** To use, go, or stop slowly: *ease up on the meatloaf; ease up on the gas pedal; ease up to a stoplight.*
ease (ēz) *noun; verb,* **eased, easing.**

easel A tall stand or rack. Easels are used to hold blackboards, signs, and paintings. **ea·sel** (ē′zel) *noun, plural* **easels.**

easily 1. Without trouble, pain, or hard work: *I can touch my toes easily.* **2.** Without any doubt; certainly: *That student is easily the best player on the team.* **3.** Very likely; possibly: *If the books are too heavy, you could easily drop them.* **eas·ily** (ē′zə lē) *adverb.*

east 1. The direction a person faces to watch the sun rise in the morning. East is one of the four main points of the compass. It is directly opposite west. **2. East.** Any area or place that is in the east. **3. the East.** The eastern part of the United States, along the Atlantic coast. **4. the East.** Asia and the islands close to it. *Noun.*
○ **1.** Toward or in the east: *Our school is on the east side of town.* **2.** Coming from the east: *An east wind was blowing. Adjective.*
○ Toward the east: *You bicycle east to get to the park. Adverb.*
east (ēst) *noun; adjective; adverb.*

Easter A Christian holiday that celebrates Jesus's rising from the grave. Easter falls on the Sunday after the first full moon between March 21 and April 25. **Eas·ter** (ēs′tər) *noun, plural* **Easters.**

WORD HISTORY

The word **Easter** comes from the name of a pagan goddess, Eastre. Before Christianity came to England, the pagan people there celebrated Eastre's festival in the spring. Later the new Christian festival of Easter was also held in the spring, so the old name was kept.

eastern 1. In or toward the east: *There is a large river in the eastern part of that state.* **2.** Coming from the east: *An eastern breeze was blowing.* **3. Eastern.** Of or in the part of the United States that is in the East. **4. Eastern.** Of or in Asia and the islands close to it. **east·ern** (ēs′tərn) *adjective.*

easterner 1. A person living in the east. **2. Easterner.** A person living in the eastern part of the United States. **east·ern·er** (ēs′tər nər) *noun, plural* **easterners.**

Eastern Hemisphere The half of the earth that includes Europe, Asia, Africa, and Australia.

East Germany After World War II and until 1990, when it was reunited with West Germany, a country in north-central Europe.

eastward Toward the east: *The river flows eastward through the state. Adverb.*
○ Toward or in the east: *The eastward flight of those ducks will bring them to the lake. Adjective.*
east·ward (ēst′wərd) *adverb; adjective.*

eastwards Another spelling of the adverb eastward: *The ship sailed eastwards.* **east·wards** (ēst′wərdz) *adverb.*

easy **1.** Needing only a little work; not hard to do: *The arithmetic problems were easy.* **2.** Without pain, trouble, or worry: *Many people wish for an easy life, but only a few get their wish.* **3.** Not strict or difficult to please: *We have an easy science teacher.*

• **easy does it.** An expression used to caution someone to be careful: *When you put your foot on the gas pedal of the car, easy does it.*

• **to go easy on. 1.** To use just a little at a time: *Go easy on the peanut butter; we don't have any more.* **2.** To punish less harshly: *Go easy on her. She didn't know matches were dangerous.* **eas·y** (ē′zē) *adjective,* **easier, easiest.**

eat **1.** To chew on and swallow: *I like to eat popcorn when I'm at the movies.* **2.** To have a meal: *Our family usually eats at six o'clock.* **3.** To wear away or destroy: *Rust has eaten away the iron railing on the porch.* **eat** (ēt) *verb,* **ate, eaten, eating.**

The family is eating in the outdoor section of a restaurant.

eaves The under part of a roof that hangs over the side of a building. **eaves** (ēvz) *plural noun.*

eavesdrop To listen to other people talking without letting them know you are listening: *I learned about my own surprise party by eavesdropping as my friends planned it.* **eaves·drop** (ēvz′drop) *verb,* **eavesdropped, eavesdropping.**

WORD HISTORY

The word eavesdrop once meant the area at the side of a house, where rainwater on the roof would drop from the eaves to the ground. A person who stood in this place to listen in secret to people talking inside the house was said to be *eavesdropping.*

---

ebb The flowing of the ocean away from the shore: *The beach was covered with seaweed and shells at the tide's ebb.* Noun.
○ **1.** To flow out: *We sat on the beach and watched the tide ebb.* **2.** To become less or weaker: *Hope of finding the lost plane began to ebb.* Verb.
ebb (eb) *noun, plural* **ebbs;** *verb,* **ebbed, ebbing.**

ebony A hard, black wood. It comes from trees that grow in Africa and Asia. The black piano keys are made of ebony. **eb·o·ny** (eb′ə nē) *noun, plural* **ebonies.**

eccentric Not ordinary or normal in behavior or appearance; different and odd: *Some people think that my cousin who goes swimming in winter is eccentric.* Adjective.
○ A person who does things that some people find strange: *My sister will be an eccentric when she grows up.*
ec·cen·tric (ek sen′trik) *adjective.* **eccentricity** *noun.*

echo The repeating of a sound. Echoes are caused when sound waves bounce off a surface: *We shouted "hello" toward the hill and soon heard the echo of our voices.* Noun.
○ **1.** To send back the sound of something: *The halls of the school echoed with voices and footsteps.* **2.** To be heard again: *His warning echoed in her ears.* **3.** To repeat or imitate closely: *The students echoed the words of their teachers.* Verb.
ech·o (ek′ō) *noun, plural* **echoes;** *verb,* **echoed, echoing.**

eclipse A darkening or hiding of the sun, a planet, or a moon by another heavenly body. In an eclipse of the moon, the earth moves between the sun and the moon. *Noun.*
○ **1.** To cause an eclipse of: *The moon eclipsed the sun.* **2.** To be better or more important than: *Our team eclipsed its*

In an eclipse of the sun the moon passes between the sun and the earth.

PRONUNCIATION KEY:

| at | ape | far | care | end | mē | it | ice | pierce | hot | old | song | fork |
| oil | out | up | use | rule | pull | turn | chin | sing | shop | thin | this | |

hw in white; zh in treasure. The symbol ə stands for the unstressed vowel sound in about, taken, pencil, lemon, and circus.

233

rivals to win the championship. *Verb.*
e·clipse (i klips') *noun, plural* **eclipses**; *verb,*
eclipsed, eclipsing.

ecology The science that deals with how plants, animals, and other living things live in relation to each other and to their environment. **e·col·o·gy** (ē kol'ə jē) *noun.* —**ecological** *adjective.*

Ecology shows us how animals relate
to their surroundings.

economic Having to do with the money system: *The president spoke on television about the need for a new economic program.* **ec·o·nom·ic** (ek ə nom'ik *or* ē'kə nom'ik) *adjective.*

economical Using only a small amount of something; not wasting anything. **ec·o·nom·i·cal** (ek ə nom'i kəl *or* ē'kə nom'i kəl) *adjective.*

economics The science that studies how money, goods, and services are produced, how they are distributed among people, and how they are used. The word *economics* is used with a singular verb. **ec·o·nom·ics** (ek ə nom'iks *or* ē'kə nom'iks) *noun.*

economize 1. To spend less money; reduce expenses: *It is hard to economize when prices are so high.* 2. To be careful to use only a small amount of something; not waste: *To economize on water they closed the country club.* **e·con·o·mize** (ikon'ə mīz) *verb,* **economized, economizing.**

economy 1. The way a country produces, distributes, and uses its money, goods, natural resources, and services: *The economy of the United States is different from that of China.* 2. The careful use of money and other things to reduce waste: *My cousins try to practice economy in buying groceries.* **e·con·o·my** (i kon'ə mē) *noun, plural* **economies.**

ecosystem All the living and nonliving things in a certain area. Soil, water, algae, insects, fish, and frogs are some of the things that make up the ecosystem of a pond. **ec·o·sys·tem** (ek'ō sis'təm *or* ē'kō sis'təm) *noun, plural* **ecosystems.**

ecstasy A feeling of being very happy, thrilled, or delighted: *The children were in ecstasy when their parents brought the puppy home.* **ec·sta·sy** (ek'stə sē) *noun, plural* **ecstasies.**

Ecuador A country in northwestern South America. **Ec·ua·dor** (ek'wə dôr) *noun.*

-ed A suffix that: **1.** Shows that an action or state is in the past. The word "walked" in the sentence "We walked to work yesterday" is the past tense of "walk." The word "walked" in the sentence "I have walked to work every day this week" is the past participle of "walk." **2.** Means having or having the quality of. The word "horned" means "having horns."

eddy A spinning current in water or air. *Noun.*
○ To swirl in circles: *The water eddied as it flowed down the drain.* *Verb.*
ed·dy (ed'ē) *noun, plural* **eddies**; *verb,* **eddied, eddying.**

edge **1.** A line or place where something ends; side: *The pencil rolled off the edge of the desk. The house is near the edge of the woods.* **2.** The side of a tool that cuts: *That knife has a sharp edge.* **3.** An advantage: *A taller player has an edge in basketball. Noun.*
○ **1.** To move slowly or carefully, little by little: *The cat edged toward the toy.* **2.** To put an edge on; form an edge on: *Please edge this handkerchief with lace. Verb.*
• **on edge.** Nervous; irritated: *Waiting for the storm has everyone on edge.*
edge (ej) *noun, plural* **edges**; *verb,* **edged, edging.**

edgewise In a slanted manner; sideways: *We had to move the refrigerator through the door edgewise to get it into the house.*
• **to get a word in edgewise.** To be able to say something: *He talked so fast none of us could get a word in edgewise.*
edge·wise (ej'wīz) *adverb.*

edgy On edge; nervous: *Knowing I have a big test coming up makes me edgy.* **edg·y** (ej'ē) *adjective,* **edgier, edgiest.**

edible Fit or safe to eat: *Not all kinds of berries are edible.* **ed·i·ble** (ed'ə bəl) *adjective.*

edit To correct and check something written so that it is ready to be printed: *Our neighbor edits the town newspaper.* **ed·it** (ed'it) *verb,* **edited, editing.**

edition 1. The form in which a book is printed: *That dictionary is now for sale in a paperback edition.* 2. The total number of copies of a book, newspaper, or magazine printed at one time: *The first edition of that novel sold quickly.* 3. One of the copies of a book, newspaper, or magazine printed at one time: *I buy the morning edition of the newspaper.* **e·di·tion** (i dish′ən) *noun, plural* **editions.**

editor 1. A person who edits: *The editor made changes in the book after talking with its author.* 2. A person who writes editorials: *The newspaper editor wrote an article in favor of raising city taxes.* **ed·i·tor** (ed′i tər) *noun, plural* **editors.**

editorial 1. An article in a newspaper or magazine written by the editor. An editorial gives an opinion on some subject: *The editorial praised Congress for passing the new law.* 2. A statement on a television or radio program that gives the opinion of the management of the station. *Noun.*
○ Of or having to do with editors or their work: *My cousin does editorial work at a publishing company. Adjective.*
ed·i·to·ri·al (ed′i tôr′ē əl) *noun, plural* **editorials;** *adjective.*

educate 1. To teach or train: *Teachers educate children.* 2. To send to school: *The cost of educating students at college is very high.* **ed·u·cate** (ej′ə kāt) *verb,* **educated, educating. educator** *noun.*

education 1. The act or process of gaining knowledge: *A person's education at college usually takes four years.* 2. The knowledge or skill a person gains by being taught or trained: *I wish I had received more education in science.* **ed·u·ca·tion** (ej′ə kā′shən) *noun, plural* **educations.**

educational 1. Of or having to do with education: *This state's educational system is one of the largest in the country.* 2. Giving knowledge or skill: *Our class saw an educational film about how steel is made.* **ed·u·ca·tion·al** (ej′ə kā′shən əl) *adjective.*

eel A long, thin fish that looks like a snake. **eel** (ēl) *noun, plural* **eels** or **eel.**

eerie Strange in a scary way; making people frightened or nervous: *Walking through that abandoned house was an eerie experience.* **ee·rie** (îr′ē) *adjective,* **eerier, eeriest.**

effect 1. Something that happens as a result of something else: *One effect of prices going up was that people began to buy less.* 2. The power to change something or to make something happen; influence: *Punishment has no effect on that naughty child.* 3. The condition of being in force or in operation: *The new traffic law will be in effect next month.* 4. effects. Belongings; possessions: *We lost only a few personal effects when the canoe sank. Noun.*
○ To make happen; bring about; cause: *The medicine effected a cure of my sore throat. Verb.*
Another word that sounds close to this is **affect.**
• **to go into effect.** To become active: *The new curfew goes into effect tonight.*
ef·fect (i fekt′) *noun, plural* **effects;** *verb,* **effected, effecting.**

effective 1. Able to change something or to make something happen: *The two students used effective arguments and got the others to agree with them.* 2. In operation: *The new rules on riding bicycles in the park become effective next week.* **ef·fec·tive** (i fek′tiv) *adjective.*

efficient Able to get the results wanted with a minimum of time or effort: *With our efficient new washing machine, the laundry gets done much faster.* **ef·fi·cient** (i fish′ənt) *adjective.* —**efficiently** *adverb.*

effluent Something that flows out, especially sewage and waste matter: *Out town's water supply was poisoned by effluent.* **ef·flu·ent** (ef′lü ənt or e flü′ənt) *noun, plural* **effluents.**

It is taking real effort for these people to climb this wall.

effort 1. Hard work: *Climbing the steep hill took much effort.* 2. A hard try: *Make an effort to get there on time.* **ef·fort** (ef′ərt) *noun, plural* **efforts.**

PRONUNCIATION KEY:

| at | ape | fär | câre | end | mē | it | īce | pierce | hot | ōld | sông | fôrk |
| oil | out | up | ūse | rüle | pull | tûrn | chin | sing | shop | thin | this | |

hw in white; zh in treasure. The symbol ə stands for the unstressed vowel sound in about, taken, pencil, lemon, and circus.

235

egg¹ 1. A round or oval body with a shell or other covering produced by certain female animals. Young birds, reptiles, fish, and snakes hatch from eggs. 2. The inside of an egg, especially a chicken egg, that is used for food. 3. A cell produced in the bodies of female animals that can develop into a new individual after joining with a special cell from a male animal. Human beings, cats, dogs, and many other animals grow from these cells. **egg** (eg) *noun, plural* **eggs.**

Decorating eggs at Easter is a tradition that began in the Ukraine.

egg² Egg on. To urge: *The two children began to fight after they were egged on by the others in the playground.* **egg** (eg) *verb,* **egged, egging.**

eggplant An oval-shaped vegetable that usually has a shiny, dark purple skin. **egg·plant** (eg′plant) *noun, plural* **eggplants.**

egocentric Being completely concerned with oneself; self-absorbed: *He was too egocentric to care about other people's feelings.* **ego·cen·tric** (ē′gō sen′trik) *adjective.*

The eggplant was first grown in tropical Asia.

egret A large bird with white feathers and long legs. It is related to the heron. **e·gret** (ē′grət) *noun, plural* **egrets.**

Egypt A country in the Middle East. Ancient Egypt was the center of one of the world's earliest civilizations. **E·gypt** (ē′jipt) *noun.*

Egyptian 1. A person who was born in or is a citizen of Egypt. 2. A person who lived in ancient Egypt. 3. The language of the people of Egypt in ancient times. *Noun.*
○ Of or having to do with Egypt or its people. *Adjective.*
E·gyp·tian (i jip′shən) *noun, plural* **Egyptians;** *adjective.*

eight One more than seven; 8.
Another word that sounds like this is **ate.**
eight (āt) *noun, plural* **eights;** *adjective.*

eighteen Eight more than ten; 18. **eight·een** (ā′tēn′) *noun, plural* **eighteens;** *adjective.*

eighteenth Next after the seventeenth. *Adjective, noun.*
○ One of eighteen equal parts; $1/18$. *Noun.*
eight·eenth (ā′tēnth′) *adjective; noun, plural* **eighteenths.**

eighth Next after the seventh. *Adjective, noun.*
○ One of eight equal parts; $1/8$. *Noun.*
eighth (āth) *adjective; noun, plural* **eighths.**

eightieth Next after the seventy-ninth. *Adjective, noun.*
One of eighty equal parts; $1/80$. *Noun.*
eight·i·eth (ā′tē ith) *adjective; noun, plural* **eightieths.**

eighty Eight times ten; 80. **eight·y** (ā′tē) *noun, plural* **eighties;** *adjective.*

either 1. One or the other: *I would be happy to see either movie.* 2. One and the other; each of two: *There were tall trees on either side of the street. Adjective.*
○ One or the other: *Can either of you two children help me? Pronoun.*
○ One or the other. The word either is used before the first of two or more choices or possibilities that are connected by the word or: *They will come either tonight, tomorrow, or the day after. Conjunction.*
○ Also; likewise: *You can't go to the game, and I can't go either. Adverb.*
ei·ther (ē′thər *or* ī′thər) *adjective; pronoun; conjunction; adverb.*

eject 1. To throw out; force to leave: *The manager ejected the noisy couple from the theater.* 2. To use a special seat to propel oneself out of a plane that is about to crash: *The pilot ejected as soon as she saw the flames coming from the engine.* **ej·ect** (ij ekt′) *verb,* **ejected, ejecting. —ejection** *noun.*

elaborate Worked out or made with great care and in great detail: *Elaborate plans were made for the wedding. Adjective.*
○ To work out with great care; add details to: *The reporters asked the astronauts to elaborate on their answer. Verb.*
e·lab·o·rate (i lab′ər it *for adjective;* i lab′ə rāt *for verb*) *adjective; verb,* **elaborated, elaborating.**

elapse To go by; pass: *Three years elapsed before we saw each other again.* **e·lapse** (i laps′) *verb,* **elapsed, elapsing.**

elastic Able to go back to its own shape soon after being stretched, squeezed, or pressed together. Rubber bands, balloons, and metal springs are elastic. *Adjective.*

○ A tape or fabric that can stretch: *This skirt has elastic around the waist. Noun.*

e·las·tic (i las′tik) *adjective; noun, plural* **elastics.**

elbow 1. The joint between the upper arm and the lower arm. The elbow allows the arm to bend. 2. Something having the same shape as a bent elbow. In plumbing, a pipe that curves at a sharp angle is called an elbow. *Noun.*

○ To push with the elbows; shove: *The bully tried to elbow me off the line. Verb.*

• **elbow room.** Room to move around in easily: *This small kitchen doesn't provide much elbow room for working.*

el·bow (el′bō) *noun, plural* **elbows;** *verb,* **elbowed, elbowing.**

elder Born earlier; older: *My elder cousins are in high school. Adjective.*

○ A person who is older: *I have great respect for my elders. Noun.*

el·der (el′dər) *adjective; noun, plural* **elders.**

elderly Rather old: *Our elderly neighbor has no plans to retire.* **eld·er·ly** (el′dər lē) *adjective.*

eldest Born first; oldest: *I am the eldest of three children.* **eld·est** (el′dist) *adjective.*

elect 1. To choose by voting: *The people of the town elected a new mayor.* 2. To make a choice; choose; decide: *Will you elect to study history in college?* **e·lect** (i lekt′) *verb,* **elected, electing.**

election The act of electing: *There is an election for the president every four years in the United States.* **e·lec·tion** (i lek′shən) *noun, plural* **elections.**

electric 1. Having to do with electricity; run or produced by electricity: *My electric clock keeps good time.* 2. Exciting: *The actor's electric performance thrilled the audience.* **e·lec·tric** (i lek′trik) *adjective.*

electrical Having to do with electricity; electric: *Irons and other electrical appliances are sold at that store.* **e·lec·tri·cal** (i lek′tri kəl) *adjective.*

electric eel A long fish that looks like an eel. It is able to give off electric shocks to protect itself and to catch small fish for food.

electrician A person who works with electricity or installs or repairs things that are electric, such as wires, motors, and appliances. **e·lec·tri·cian** (i lek trish′ən) *noun, plural* **electricians.**

This train runs on electricity.

electricity 1. One of the basic forms of energy. Electricity can run motors and produce light and heat. It makes radios, televisions, and telephones work. Electricity can be produced by burning coal, water power, or wind generators. 2. Electric current: *Electricity is running through those wires.* 3. A lot of tension or excitement; strong feeling: *You could feel the electricity when the mayor entered the room.* **e·lec·tri·ci·ty** (i lek tris′i tē) *noun.*

electrocute To kill by means of a very strong electric shock. **e·lec·tro·cute** (i lek′trə kūt) *verb,* **electrocuted, electrocuting.**

electrode A place where an electric current flows into or out of a device. **e·lec·trode** (ə lek′trōd) *noun, plural* **electrodes.**

electromagnet A piece of iron with wire wound around it. It becomes a magnet when an electric current is passed through the wire. **e·lec·tro·mag·net** (i lek′trō mag′nit) *noun, plural* **electromagnets.**

electron A very tiny particle that moves around the nucleus of an atom and has a negative electrical charge. **e·lec·tron** (i lek′tron) *noun, plural* **electrons.**

PRONUNCIATION KEY:

| at | āpe | fär | câre | end | mē | it | īce | pierce | hot | ōld | sông | fôrk |
| oil | out | up | ūse | rüle | pull | tûrn | chin | sing | shop | thin | this | |

hw in white; zh in treasure. The symbol ə stands for the unstressed vowel sound in about, taken, pencil, lemon, and circus.

237

electronic Of or relating to electrons or electronics. **e·lec·tron·ic** (i lek tron′ik) *adjective*.

electronic mail The longer name for e-mail.

electronics The science that deals with electrons and how they act and move. The discoveries of electronics have led to the development of radio, television, and computers. The word *electronics* is used with a singular verb. **e·lec·tron·ics** (i lek tron′iks) *noun*.

elegant Rich and fine in quality: *The museum has a display of elegant costumes.* **el·e·gant** (el′i gənt) *adjective.* —**elegance** *noun* —**elegantly** *adverb*.

element 1. One of the materials from which all other materials are made. Each element has its own kind of atom. There are more than one hundred known elements. Iron, oxygen, gold, and carbon are elements. 2. One of the parts that something is made of. 3. The natural or most comfortable place to be: *The ocean is the whale's element.* 4. **the elements.** Rain, wind, snow, and other forces of nature: *The mountain climbers struggled against the elements.* **el·e·ment** (el′ə mənt) *noun, plural* **elements**.

elementary Dealing with the simple parts or beginnings of something: *We learned about addition and subtraction when we studied elementary arithmetic.* **el·e·ment·ar·y** (el′ə men′tə rē *or* el′ə men′trē) *adjective*.

elementary school A school for children from the ages of about six to twelve or fourteen. Elementary schools usually cover the first six or eight grades. An elementary school is also called a *grade school* or a *grammar school*.

elephant A huge gray animal with a long trunk, large, floppy ears, and two ivory tusks. Elephants come from parts of Asia and Africa. **el·e·phant** (el′ə fənt) *noun, plural* **elephants** *or* **elephant**.

Elephants are the largest and strongest land animals.

elevate To raise to a higher level; lift up: *The workers in the garage elevated the car so that they could repair the muffler.* **el·e·vate** (el′ə vāt) *verb,* **elevated, elevating**.

elevation 1. The act of raising or lifting up: *The cranes beside those docks are used for the elevation of boats from the water.* 2. A raised thing or place: *The cabin is on a slight elevation that looks over the lake.* 3. The height above the earth's surface or above sea level: *The plane flew at an elevation of 30,000 feet.* **el·e·va·tion** (el′ə vā′shən) *noun, plural* **elevations**.

Grain elevators are a common sight in the Midwest and Canada.

elevator 1. A small room or cage that can be raised or lowered.

ELEMENTS

An element is a substance composed of only one kind of atom. Elements can combine to form compounds. Alone or in compounds, elements make up everything we see and use: wood, plastic, cloth, metal, even the air we breathe. The elements include hydrogen and oxygen, which are gases that combine to make water; sodium and chlorine, which combine to form the compound we know as table salt; and heavier elements such as iron, lead, and uranium.

Identifying Elements: Each element has a particular atomic form. An element is identified by its atomic number. The atomic number is equal to the number of positively charged protons inside its nucleus, and to the number of negatively charged electrons outside the nucleus. For example, hydrogen has one proton and one electron, so its atomic number is 1. Oxygen has 8 of each, so its atomic number is 8. Lead has an atomic number of 82. So far, scientists have identified 112 elements, but only 92 of those are regularly found in nature.

It is used for carrying people and things from one floor to another in a building or from one level to another in mines and other places. **2.** A building for storing grain. **el·e·va·tor** (el′ə vā′tər) *noun, plural* **elevators.**

eleven One more than ten; 11. **e·lev·en** (i lev′ən) *noun, plural* **elevens;** *adjective.*

eleventh Next after the tenth. *Adjective, noun.* ○ One of eleven equal parts; $\frac{1}{11}$. *Noun.* **e·lev·enth** (i lev′ənth) *adjective; noun, plural* **elevenths.**

elf A kind of fairy who has magical powers. In legends and folk tales, elves are small and are often full of mischief. **elf** (elf) *noun, plural* **elves.**

eligible Having the qualities needed for something; fit to be chosen: *A person must be thirty-five years old to be **eligible** to run for president of the United States.* **el·i·gi·ble** (el′i jə bəl) *adjective.*

eliminate To get rid of; remove: *The city is trying to **eliminate** pollution.* **e·lim·i·nate** (i lim′ə nāt) *verb,* **eliminated, eliminating. —elimination** *noun.*

elk 1. A large deer of North America. The male elk has very large antlers. **2.** A moose. **elk** (elk) *noun, plural* **elk** *or* **elks.**

ellipse A figure that looks like a narrow or flattened circle. **el·lipse** (i lips′) *noun, plural* **ellipses.**

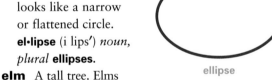
ellipse

elm A tall tree. Elms were once planted to shade streets and lawns. Many of the elms in the United States were killed by a disease. **elm** (elm) *noun, plural* **elms.**

elope To run away in order to get married. **e·lope** (i lōp′) *verb,* **eloped, eloping.**

eloquent Having or showing an ability to use words well: *The lawyer made an **eloquent** plea to the jury to find the accused person innocent of the crime.* **el·o·quent** (el′ə kwənt) *adjective.* **—eloquence** *noun.*

El Salvador A country in Central America. **El Sal·va·dor** (el sal′və dôr).

else 1. Other; different: *I mistook that student for someone **else**. Would you like something **else** instead?* **2.** More; further; additional: *If anyone **else** comes, we won't have enough chairs. Adjective.*

○ **1.** At a different time or in a different place or manner; instead: *What **else** could you have done?* **2.** If not; otherwise: *We'd better hurry, or **else** we'll miss the train. Adverb.* **else** (els) *adjective; adverb.*

elsewhere In, at, or to another place; somewhere else: *We wanted to go to the park, but we'll have to go **elsewhere** because it's raining.* **else·where** (els′hwâr *or* els′wâr) *adverb.*

elude To avoid or escape by being clever or quick: *The bandit **eluded** the police by hiding in an abandoned building. The comet has so far **eluded** astronomers' attempts to take a clear photograph of it.* **e·lude** (i lüd′) *verb,* **eluded, eluding.**

elusive Hard to find or catch; tricky: *Because of their good camouflage, many insects are **elusive**.* **e·lu·sive** (ē lü′siv) *adjective.*

elves Plural of **elf**. **elves** (elvz) *plural noun.*

e-mail Messages that are sent between computers connected through telephone lines by means of a modem. E-mail is a very fast means of communication. The longer name for it is *electronic mail.* **e-mail** (ē′māl) *noun; verb,* **e-mailed, e-mailing.**

emancipate To set free from slavery or control: *President Abraham Lincoln's proclamation **emancipated** the slaves in some states in 1863.* **e·man·ci·pate** (i man′sə pāt) *verb,* **emancipated, emancipating. emancipation** *noun.*

embankment A mound of earth, stones, or bricks used to hold up a road or to hold back water. **em·bank·ment** (em bangk′mənt) *noun, plural* **embankments.**

embargo 1. An order by a government that forbids certain ships from entering or leaving its ports. **2.** A restriction that a government puts on the buying and selling of certain goods, especially importing or exporting those goods. **em·bar·go** (em bär′gō) *noun, plural* **embargoes.**

embark 1. To go on board a ship or airplane for a trip: *The passengers **embarked** at New York.* **2.** To start out or set out: *The explorers **embarked** on a dangerous journey.* **em·bark** (em bärk′) *verb,* **embarked, embarking.**

embarrass To make someone feel shy, uncomfortable, or ashamed: *My foolish mistake **embarrassed** me.* **em·bar·rass** (em bar′əs) *verb,* **embarrassed, embarrassing.**

PRONUNCIATION KEY:

| at | āpe | fär | câre | end | mē | it | īce | pierce | hot | ōld | sông | fôrk |
| oil | out | up | ūse | rüle | pùll | tûrn | chin | sing | shop | thin | <u>th</u>is | |

hw in white; zh in treasure. The symbol ə stands for the unstressed vowel sound in about, taken, pencil, lemon, and circus.

239

embarrassment 1. A feeling of shyness or being ashamed: *I turned red with embarrassment when the teacher called my name.* 2. Something that embarrasses: *My falling asleep during the recital was an embarrassment.* **em·bar·rass·ment** (em bar′əs mənt) *noun, plural* **embarrassments.**

embassy The official home and office in a foreign country of an ambassador and his or her staff. **em·bas·sy** (em′bə sē) *noun, plural* **embassies.**

embed To place or set firmly in something: *The flagpole was embedded in concrete.* **em·bed** (em bed′) *verb,* **embedded, embedding.**

ember A piece of wood or coal that is still glowing in the ashes of a fire: *The campers put water on the embers of their fire before they left.* **em·ber** (em′bər) *noun, plural* **embers.**

embezzle To steal money or goods that one was supposed to take care of: *The teller embezzled thousands of dollars from the bank.* **em·bez·zle** (em bez′əl) *verb,* **embezzled, embezzling. embezzler** *noun.*

The emblems on this astronaut's suit tell us what country and what organization he is from.

emblem A sign or figure that stands for something: *The shamrock is the emblem of Ireland.* **em·blem** (em′bləm) *noun, plural* **emblems.**

embody To be a definite form that can be seen; be real: *The U.S. Constitution embodies our democratic ideals.* **em·bod·y** (em bod′ē) *verb,* **embodied, embodying. —embodiment** *noun.*

emboss To decorate or cover a surface with a design that is raised: *I have stationery embossed with my initials.* **em·boss** (em bôs′) *verb,* **embossed, embossing.**

embrace 1. To take or hold in the arms as a sign of love or friendship; hug: *The children embraced their parents as soon as they got off the plane.* 2. To take up willingly: *We embraced the opportunity to visit our cousins in France.* 3. To include; contain: *Biology embraces the study of all things that have life. Verb.*
  ○ A holding in the arms; hug: *The puppy wiggled out of the child's embrace. Noun.*
  em·brace (em brās′) *verb,* **embraced, embracing;** *noun, plural* **embraces.**

embroider 1. To decorate with designs sewn on with thread: *I embroidered the napkins with flowers.* 2. To make a story more interesting by adding parts that have been made up: *They embroidered their stories about their first day at camp to make us laugh.* **em·broid·er** (em broi′dər) *verb,* **embroidered, embroidering.**

embroidery Designs that have been sewn on cloth with thread: *I did the embroidery on my jeans.* **em·broid·er·y** (em broi′də rē) *noun, plural* **embroideries.**

embryo An animal or plant that is just starting to grow, before its birth, hatching, or sprouting. A baby inside its mother, a chick inside an egg, and a plant inside a seed are embryos. **em·bry·o** (em′brē ō) *noun, plural* **embryos.**

The embroidery on this girl's blouse is in a floral design.

emerald 1. A bright green, clear stone that is very valuable. Emeralds are often used in rings, pins, and other jewelry. 2. A bright green color. *Noun.*
  ○ Having a bright green color. *Adjective.*
  em·er·ald (em′ər əld) *noun, plural* **emeralds;** *adjective.*

emerge 1. To come into view: *The sun emerged*

from behind a cloud. **2.** To come out; become known: *New facts about the case* **emerged** *during the trial.* **e·merge** (i mûr′j) *verb,* **emerged, emerging.**

emergency Something serious that comes without any warning and calls for fast action: *In case of an* **emergency,** *the doctor can be reached at home. Noun.*

○ Having to do with an emergency; used during an emergency: *There is an* **emergency** *exit at the back of the theater. Adjective.*
e·mer·gen·cy (i mûr′jən sē) *noun, plural* **emergencies;** *adjective.*

emery A hard black or brown mineral in the form of a powder. Emery is used for grinding and polishing metals or stones. **em·er·y** (em′ə rē) *noun.*

emigrant A person who leaves his or her own country to live in another: *My parents were emigrants from China.* **em·i·grant** (em′i grənt) *noun, plural* **emigrants.**

emigrate To leave one's own place or country to live in another: *Our neighbors plan to* **emigrate** *from the United States to Australia.* **emigrate** (em′i grāt) *verb,* **emigrated, emigrating.** —**emigration** *noun.*

LANGUAGE NOTE

The verbs *emigrate* and *immigrate* have nearly opposite meanings. *Emigrate* means to leave a country. My grandparents *emigrated* from Italy in 1930. *Immigrate* means to enter a new country to live. Many Irish *immigrated* to the United States in the 1800s.

---

eminent Above others in rank, power, or achievement; outstanding: *Our neighbor is an* **eminent** *lawyer in the town.* **em·i·nent** (em′ə nənt) *adjective.*

emit To send out; give off: *The sun* **emits** *heat and light. You* **emitted** *a shriek when I surprised you.* **e·mit** (i mit′) *verb,* **emitted, emitting.**

emotion A strong feeling. Love, hate, happiness, sorrow, and fear are emotions. **e·mo·tion** (i mō′shən) *noun, plural* **emotions.**

emotional **1.** Having to do with emotion or the feelings a person has: *I get* **emotional** *satisfaction from knowing I've done a job well.* **2.** Easily moved by emotion: *An* **emotional** *person has*

strong feelings. **3.** Arousing or attempting to arouse emotion: *The general made an* **emotional** *speech at the ceremony honoring the soldiers who had died in battle.* **e·mo·tion·al** (i mō′shə nəl) *adjective.*

emperor The ruler of an empire. **em·per·or** (em′pə rər) *noun, plural* **emperors.**

emphasis **1.** Special attention or importance given to something: *I've been taught to place much* **emphasis** *on telling the truth.* **2.** Special force used when saying a particular word or syllable; stress: *The* **emphasis** *is on the first syllable in the word "empty" and on the second syllable in the word "employ."* **em·pha·sis** (em′fə sis) *noun, plural* **emphases** (em′fə sēz).

emphasize To give emphasis to; stress: *The mayor's speech* **emphasized** *the need for a new hospital.* **em·pha·size** (em′fə sīz) *verb,* **emphasized, emphasizing.**

empire **1.** A group of countries, lands, or peoples under one government or ruler: *The* **empire** *of ancient Rome was powerful.* **2.** A country ruled by an emperor or empress. **em·pire** (em′pīr) *noun, plural* **empires.**

employ **1.** To pay someone to do work; hire: *The store* **employed** *extra workers during its big sale.* **2.** To use: *I* **employ** *a hoe when weeding the garden. Verb.*

○ Service for pay; employment: *That engineer is in the* **employ** *of a large railroad. Noun.*
em·ploy (em ploi′) *verb,* **employed, employing;** *noun.*

employee A person who works for some person or business for pay: *The store gives its* **employees** *a raise once a year.* **em·ploy·ee** (em ploi′ē or em′ploi ē′) *noun, plural* **employees.**

employer A person or business that pays a person or group of people to work: *My cousin's* **employer** *has an office in Japan.* **em·ploy·er** (em ploi′ər) *noun, plural* **employers.**

employment **1.** The work that a person does; job: *After the factory closed, it was hard for many of the workers to find new* **employment.** **2.** The act of employing or the condition of being employed: *Employment of more workers made it possible for the automobile company to manufacture cars faster.* **em·ploy·ment** (em ploi′mənt) *noun, plural* **employments.**

PRONUNCIATION KEY:
at   āpe   fär   câre   end   mē   it   īce   pîerce   hot   ōld   sông   fôrk
oil   out   up   ūse   rüle   pull   tûrn   chin   sing   shop   thin   this
hw in white; zh in treasure. The symbol ə stands for the unstressed vowel sound in about, taken, pencil, lemon, and circus.

241

empress 1. A woman who is the ruler of an empire. 2. The wife or widow of an emperor. **em·press** (em′pris) *noun, plural* **empresses.**

empty 1. Having nothing in it; without what is usually inside: *The bottom drawer of the dresser is* ***empty****, and you can use it for your shirts.* 2. Lacking value, force, or meanings: *The people didn't want to vote for a candidate who made* ***empty*** *promises. Adjective.*

These stalls are empty of horses.

○ 1. To remove all that is in something: *I* ***emptied*** *my pockets.* 2. To become empty: *The theater* ***emptied*** *when the movie was over.* 3. To pour or flow out: *That river* ***empties*** *into the sea. Verb.* **emp·ty** (emp′tē) *adjective,* **emptier, emptiest;** *verb,* **emptied, emptying.**

empty set A mathematical set that has no members. The set of all even numbers between 8 and 10 is an example of an empty set.

emu A bird of Australia that looks like an ostrich. An emu can be as large as a grown person. **e·mu** (ē′mū) *noun, plural* **emus.**

Although they cannot fly, emus can run very fast.

enable To make able: *The school raised enough money to* ***enable*** *the library to buy many new books.* **en·a·ble** (e nā′bəl) *verb,* **enabled, enabling.**

enact 1. To make into law: *Congress* ***enacted*** *a new bill on education this year.* 2. To act out on stage; play: *I am going to* ***enact*** *the part of Amelia Earhart in this year's class play.* **en·act** (e nakt′) *verb,* **enacted, enacting.**

enamel 1. A smooth, hard coating like glass. Enamel is put on metal, pottery, or other material to protect or decorate it. 2. A paint that dries to form a hard, glossy surface: *They painted the kitchen with white* ***enamel****.* 3. The hard, white outer layer of the teeth: *Decay can eat through a tooth's* ***enamel****. Noun.*
○ To cover with enamel: *The jeweler* ***enameled*** *the bracelet with a pattern of tulips. Verb.* **e·nam·el** (i nam′əl) *noun, plural* **enamels;** *verb,* **enameled, enameling.**

-ence A suffix that means: 1. The state or quality of being: *Independence means the state or quality of being independent.* 2. The act of: *Occurrence means the act of occurring.*

enchant 1. To put a magical spell on: *The magician had* ***enchanted*** *the kingdom and turned its people into statues.* 2. To delight; charm: *The children were* ***enchanted*** *by the beautiful costumes the dancers wore.* **en·chant** (en chant′) *verb,* **enchanted, enchanting.**

enchanted 1. Having been put under a magic spell: *The old castle was said to be* ***enchanted****.* 2. Impressed by; awed: *I was* ***enchanted*** *by the baby's tiny fingers.* **en·chant·ed** (en chan′təd) *adjective.*

enchanting Very likable or enjoyable; charming: *My sister thought the music at the dance was* ***enchanting****.* **en·chant·ing** (en chan′ting) *adjective.*

enchantment The act of enchanting or the condition of being enchanted: *The* ***enchantment*** *of the kingdom by the magical spell was to last one hundred years.* **en·chant·ment** (en chant′mənt) *noun, plural* **enchantments.**

encircle 1. To form a circle around; surround: *The soldiers* ***encircled*** *the enemy's camp.* 2. To move in a circle around: *Many satellites* ***encircle*** *the earth.* **en·cir·cle** (en sûr′kəl) *verb,* **encircled, encircling.**

enclose 1. To surround on all sides: *Our back yard is* ***enclosed*** *by a picket fence.* 2. To include with a letter or parcel: *They* ***enclosed*** *pictures of the children with their letter.* **en·close** (en klōz′) *verb,* **enclosed, enclosing.**

enclosure 1. The act of enclosing or the condition of being enclosed: *The family finished the* ***enclosure*** *of the pool by building a fence.*

2. Something that is enclosed: *The check was sent as an enclosure with the letter.* **en·clos·ure** (en klō′zhər) *noun, plural* **enclosures.**

encompass 1. To form a circle around; surround: *A stone wall encompasses the castle.* 2. To contain or include: *This article encompasses the early years of the senator's life.* **en·com·pass** (en kum′pəs) *verb,* **encompassed, encompassing.**

encore A word meaning "again" that is said by members of an audience to request that a performer continue performing: *"Encore! Encore!" cried the audience when the musicians had finished their delightful performance.* Interjection.
○ 1. A demand made by an audience to a performer to go on performing. People usually clap or cheer for a long time to call for an encore: *The band received four encores at the end of their performance.* 2. Something that is performed in answer to such a demand: *As an encore, the chorus sang a well-known song.* Noun. **en·core** (äng′kôr) *interjection; noun, plural* **encores.**

encounter 1. To meet, usually unexpectedly: *I encountered an old friend on my way to the library.* 2. To face; confront: *We encountered much opposition to our plan.* 3. To meet in battle: *The soldiers encountered the enemy and defeated them.* Verb.
○ A usually unexpected meeting: *Your encounter with the movie star is the talk of the neighborhood.* Noun. **en·coun·ter** (en koun′tər) *verb,* **encountered, encountering;** *noun, plural* **encounters.**

encourage 1. To give courage, hope, or confidence to; urge on: *The coach encouraged the students to try out for the swimming team.* 2. To give help to or help bring about; help or foster: *The low price of homes encouraged many people to settle in that town.* **en·cour·age** (en kûr′ij) *verb,* **encouraged, encouraging.**

encouragement 1. The act of encouraging or the condition of being encouraged: *Your encouragement of our project helped us to complete it.* 2. Something that encourages: *My father's praise of my marks at school has been an encouragement to me.* **en·cour·age·ment** (en kûr′ij mənt) *noun, plural* **encouragements.**

encyclopedia A book or set of books giving a great deal of information about many things. Encyclopedias often contain a large number of articles about various subjects. **en·cy·clo·pe·di·a** (en sī′klə pē′dē ə) *noun, plural* **encyclopedias.**

WORD HISTORY

The word encyclopedia **goes back to a Greek phrase meaning "general education." The ancient idea of a total or complete education included training in a variety of fields. The modern encyclopedia also tries to include all areas of knowledge in its coverage.**

---

end 1. The last part: *The end of the movie was happy.* 2. The part where something starts or stops: *They each held an end of the rope. My vacation is at an end.* 3. Purpose; goal; outcome: *Are you putting all your knowledge to a good end?* Noun.
○ To bring or come to an end: *The heavy rain ended their picnic.* Verb. **end** (end) *noun, plural* **ends;** *verb,* **ended, ending.**

endanger 1. To put in a situation that is dangerous: *The flood endangered the lives of hundreds of people.* 2. To threaten with becoming extinct: *Pollution is endangering many different species of animals.* **en·dan·ger** (en dān′jər) *verb,* **endangered, endangering.**

endangered species A species of wild animals or plants that is close to becoming extinct. **en·dan·gered** (en dān′jərd).

endeavor To make an effort; try: *The judge always endeavored to be fair and just.* Verb.
○ A serious attempt to do or achieve something: *My endeavors to do well on the test were rewarded with a high mark.* Noun. **en·deav·or** (en dev′ər) *verb,* **endeavored, endeavoring;** *noun, plural* **endeavors.**

ending The last or final part: *I like stories that have happy endings.* **end·ing** (en′ding) *noun, plural* **endings.**

endless 1. Having no limit or end; going on forever: *The drive across the desert seemed endless.* 2. Without ends: *A circle is endless.* **end·less** (end′lis) *adjective.*

endorse 1. To sign one's name on the back of a check or similar paper: *You have to endorse the*

PRONUNCIATION KEY:

at	āpe	fär	câre	end	mē	it	īce	pîerce	hot	ōld	sông	fôrk
oil	out	up	ūse	rüle	pull	tûrn	chin	sing	shop	thin	this	

hw in white; zh in treasure. The symbol ə stands for the unstressed vowel sound in about, taken, pencil, lemon, and circus.

243

check or the bank won't cash it. **2.** To give support or approval to: *The senator endorsed the president's statement.* **en·dorse** (en dôrs′) *verb,* **endorsed, endorsing.**

endow **1.** To give money or property to: *Many wealthy people have endowed that museum with valuable paintings.* **2.** To provide with an ability, a talent, or some other good quality at birth: *The singer was endowed with a beautiful voice.* **en·dow** (en dou′) *verb,* **endowed, endowing.** —**endowment** *noun.*

endurance The power to put up with hardships or difficulties: *The pioneers who crossed the wilderness in covered wagons had much endurance.* **en·dur·ance** (en dùr′əns *or* en dyùr′əns) *noun.*

endure **1.** To undergo and survive; put up with: *The first explorers of the North Pole had to endure many hardships.* **2.** To continue; last: *That great artist's name will endure forever.* **en·dure** (en dùr′ *or* en dyùr′) *verb,* **endured, enduring.**

enemy **1.** A person or group of people who hates or wishes to harm another: *Many people were enemies of the cruel dictator.* **2.** A country that is at war with another country: *France and Germany were enemies in World War II.* **3.** Something that is dangerous or harmful: *A lack of rain can be a farmer's enemy.* **en·e·my** (en′ə mē) *noun, plural* **enemies.**

energetic Full of energy. An energetic person is eager and ready to work or do things: *After eating lunch the hikers felt energetic again.* **en·er·get·ic** (en′ər jet′ik) *adjective.*

energy **1.** The strength or eagerness to work or do things: *My parents have so much energy that they get up early to do exercises.* **2.** The capacity for doing work. Some forms of energy are light, heat, and electricity: *A windmill uses the energy of the wind.* **en·er·gy** (en′ərj ē) *noun, plural* **energies.**

enforce To make certain that people obey; put or keep in force: *The police in that town enforce the parking laws strictly.* **en·force** (en fôrs′) *verb,* **enforced, enforcing.**

Eng. An abbreviation for **England** or **English.**

engage **1.** To hire: *The automobile factory engaged more workers.* **2.** To take the time or attention of: *A stranger engaged them in a conversation at the bus stop.* **3.** To involve oneself; take part: *The committee engaged in a serious discussion of the problem.* **4.** To promise; pledge: *In 1978 my parents were engaged to be married.*

5. To meet and fight in a battle; fight: *After marching all night, the soldiers engaged the enemy outside the town.* **en·gage** (en gāj′) *verb,* **engaged, engaging.**

engaged Planning to get married: *an engaged couple.* **en·gaged** (in gājd′) *adjective.*

engagement **1.** The act or process of engaging or the condition of being engaged: *The engagement of workers at the printing plant was the job of the recruiter.* **2.** A promise to marry: *That young couple's engagement was announced last week by their parents.* **3.** A meeting with someone at a certain time; appointment: *My parents have a dinner engagement this evening.* **en·gage·ment** (en gāj′mənt) *noun, plural* **engagements.**

engine **1.** A machine that uses energy to run other machines. Engines can get their energy from the burning of oil or gasoline or from steam. The engine of a car provides the power that moves the car. **2.** A machine that pulls a railroad train; locomotive. **en·gine** (en′jin) *noun, plural* **engines.**

engineer **1.** A person who is trained in engineering. An engineer may plan and design bridges, roads, or airplanes. **2.** A person who drives a locomotive: *The engineer blew the train's whistle as it neared the station.* **en·gi·neer** (en′jə nîr′) *noun, plural* **engineers.**

A railroad **engineer** has to be continually alert.

engineering The work that uses scientific knowledge for practical things, such as building bridges and dams, drilling for oil, producing plastics, or designing machines. **en·gi·neer·ing** (en′jə nîr′ing) *noun.*

England A section of the United Kingdom. It is on the southern part of the island of Great Britain. **Eng·land** (ing′glənd) *noun.*

WORD HISTORY

The name **England** comes from Old English and means "Land of the Angles." The Angles were the main tribe of invaders from Germany who conquered Britain around A.D. 450. Their name and their language have been with us for the last 1,500 years.

English 1. A language spoken in England, the United States, Canada, India, Australia, and many other places. 2. **the English.** The people of England. *Noun.*
○ 1. Of England or its people: *This report tells about various English customs.* 2. Of or in the English language: *The book was written in French, but you can buy an English translation of it. Adjective.*
Eng·lish (ing'glish) *noun; adjective.*

English horn A long, thin musical instrument that resembles the oboe but has a deeper tone.

Englishman A person who was born in or is a citizen of England. **Eng·lish·man** (ing'glish mən) *noun, plural* **Englishmen** (ingglish mən).

Englishwoman A woman who was born in or is a citizen of England. **Eng·lish·wo·man** (ing'glish wu'mən) *noun, plural* **Englishwomen** (ing'glish wim'ən).

engrave 1. To cut or carve letters, figures, or designs into a surface: *The jeweler engraved my name on the back of my watch.* 2. To print something from a metal plate or other surface that has been cut with letters, figures, or designs: *The printer engraved the wedding invitations.*
en·grave (en grāv)' *verb,* **engraved, engraving.**

engraving 1. The art of cutting or carving letters, figures, or designs into a surface. 2. A picture or design that is printed by using a surface that has been engraved: *This engraving shows a famous ancient battle.* **en·grav·ing** (en grā'ving) *noun, plural* **engravings.**

engross To take all the attention of someone; absorb: *I was so engrossed in the novel I didn't notice the time passing.* **en·gross** (en grōs') *verb,* **engrossed, engrossing.**

engulf To swallow up or cover completely, as if by a flood; overwhelm: *The waves engulfed the small boat.* **en·gulf** (en gulf') *verb,* **engulfed, engulfing.**

enhance To make greater; add to: *The rose bushes by the front door enhance the beauty of the house.* **en·hance** (en hans') *verb,* **enhanced, enhancing.**

enjoy 1. To get joy or pleasure from; be happy with: *Our whole family enjoys skiing in the winter.* 2. To have as an advantage: *That city enjoys warm weather throughout the year.*
• **to enjoy oneself.** To have a good time: *We all enjoyed ourselves at the movies.*
en·joy (en joi') *verb,* **enjoyed, enjoying.**

enjoyable Giving joy or happiness; pleasant: *The class had an enjoyable time at the museum.* **en·joy·a·ble** (en joi'ə bəl) *adjective.*

enjoyment Pleasure; joy: *Many people get enjoyment out of collecting stamps.* **en·joy·ment** (en joi'mənt) *noun, plural* **enjoyments.**

enlarge To make or become larger: *We are enlarging our house by adding an extra bedroom.* **en·large** (en lärj') *verb,* **enlarged, enlarging.**

enlargement 1. The act of enlarging or the condition of being enlarged: *The enlargement of the building was achieved by adding another room.* 2. Something, such as a photograph, that has been made larger than the original: *Many details could be seen in the enlargement of the photograph.* **en·large·ment** (en lärj'mənt) *noun, plural* **enlargements.**

enlighten To give knowledge or wisdom to: *The news reports enlightened us about the effect of the drought on this year's harvest.* **en·light·en** (en līt'ən) *verb,* **enlightened, enlightening.**

enlist 1. To join or persuade to join the Army, Navy, or some other part of the armed forces: *Many enlisted in the Navy as soon as the war broke out.* 2. To get the help or support of: *The mayor enlisted the entire town in the drive to clean up the city.* **en·list** (en list) *verb,* **enlisted, enlisting.**

Some construction vehicles have enormous tires.

enormous Much greater than the usual size or amount; very

PRONUNCIATION KEY:
at	āpe	fär	câre	end	mē	it	īce	pîerce	hot	ōld	sông	fôrk
oil	out	up	ūse	rüle	pull	tûrn	chin	sing	shop	thin	this	

hw in white; zh in treasure. The symbol ə stands for the unstressed vowel sound in about, taken, pencil, lemon, and circus.

245

large: *Many dinosaurs were **enormous**. The flood caused an **enormous** amount of damage.* **e·nor·mous** (i nôr′məs) *adjective.*

enough As much or as many as needed: *There were **enough** players for a game of baseball. Adjective.*

○ An amount that is as much or as many as needed: *There is **enough** here to feed the whole family. Noun.*

○ To an amount or degree that is wanted or needed: *Are you feeling well **enough** to go out? Adverb.* **e·nough** (i nuf′) *adjective; noun;* **adverb.**

enrage To make very angry; put into a rage: *The dictator's cruel actions **enraged** the people.* **en·rage** (en rāj′) *verb,* **enraged, enraging.**

enrich 1. To make rich or richer: *The discovery of the shipwreck and its treasure **enriched** the divers.* 2. To improve or make better by adding something: *They **enrich** bread at this bakery by adding vitamins to it.* **en·rich** (en rich′) *verb,* **enriched, enriching.**

enroll To make or become a member: *The teacher **enrolled** seven new students in the class.* **en·roll** (en rōl′) *verb,* **enrolled, enrolling.**

enrollment 1. The act of enrolling or the condition of being enrolled: *My **enrollment** in this club entitles me to two free books.* 2. The number of persons enrolled: *The class has an **enrollment** of twenty-five.* **en·roll·ment** (en rōl′mənt) *noun, plural* **enrollments.**

en route On the way: *They stopped for lunch **en route** to the movie.* **en route** (än rüt′).

ensign 1. A flag or banner: *The **ensign** of the United States was flying on the ship.* 2. A naval officer of the lowest rank: *In the United States Navy, an **ensign** is next below a lieutenant.* **ensign** (en′sən *or* en′sīn *for definition 1;* en′sən *for definition 2) noun, plural* **ensigns.**

ensure 1. To make sure or certain; guarantee: *Careful planning helped to **ensure** the success of the project.* 2. To make safe; protect: *A vaccination will **ensure** you against getting that disease.* **en·sure** (en shùr′) *verb,* **ensured, ensuring.**

entangle 1. To catch in a tangle or net: *The kitten **entangled** its claws in the yarn.* 2. To get into a difficult situation: *I don't know how you got **entangled** in such a mess!* **en·tan·gle** (en tang′gəl) *verb,* **entangled, entangling.**

enter 1. To go or come into or in: *Doubts **entered***

my mind. 2. To pass through something; pierce: *The nail **entered** the sole of my shoe.* 3. To enroll; register: *I **entered** my dog in the contest.* 5. To put down in writing; make a record of: *The bank **entered** the amount of the deposit in my account.* 4. To type information into a computer. **en·ter** (en′tər) *verb,* **entered, entering.**

enterprise Something that a person plans or tries to do. An enterprise is often something difficult or important: *The search for the treasure was an exciting **enterprise**.* **en·ter·prise** (en′tər prīz) *noun, plural* **enterprises.**

enterprising Willing to take a risk; ambitious: *That **enterprising** student has started a new business.* **en·ter·pris·ing** (en′tər prī′zing) *adjective.*

entertain 1. To keep interested and amused: *The clown **entertained** the children.* 2. To have as a guest: *They often **entertain** people in their house in the country.* 3. To keep in mind; consider: *Our neighbor is **entertaining** an offer for a new job.* **en·ter·tain** (en′tər tān′) *verb,* **entertained, entertaining.**

entertainer Someone who entertains people for a living. Singers, dancers, and comedians are entertainers. **en·ter·tain·er** (en′tər tān′ər) *noun, plural* **entertainers.**

entertainment 1. The act of entertaining: *The **entertainment** of guests is the job of a host.* 2. Something that interests and amuses: *The **entertainment** at the party was a puppet show.* **en·ter·tain·ment** (en′tər tān′mənt) *noun, plural* **entertainments.**

enthrall To hold the attention and interest of someone completely: *The audience was **enthralled** as they watched the acrobats.* **en·thrall** (en thrôl′) *verb,* **enthralled, enthralling.**

enthusiasm 1. A strong feeling of excitement and interest about something: *The children looked forward to the puppet show with **enthusiasm**.* 2. Something a person likes to do: *In-line skating is her new **enthusiasm**.* **en·thu·si·asm** (en thü′zē az′əm) *noun.*

enthusiastic Full of enthusiasm. A person who is enthusiastic is very excited, interested, and eager about something: *We were all **enthusiastic** about going to the picnic.* **en·thu·si·as·tic** (en thü′zē as′tik) *adjective.*

entire Having all the parts; with nothing left out; whole: *Did you eat the **entire** bowl of salad?* **en·tire** (en tīr′) *adjective.*

entirely In every way or detail; completely: *It will be entirely your fault if you don't get there on time.* **en·tire·ly** (en tīr′lē) *adverb.*

entitle **1.** To give a right to: *Buying a ticket to the amusement park entitles you to one free ride.* **2.** To give the title of; call: *I entitled my story "How Our Cat Got Up the Tree."* **en·ti·tle** (en tī′təl) *verb,* **entitled, entitling.**

entrance¹ **1.** A place through which one enters: *The entrance to the building is in the middle of the block.* **2.** The act of entering: *Everyone stood up at the judge's entrance.* **3.** The power, right, or permission to enter: *Students were given free entrance to the game.* **en·trance** (en′trəns) *noun, plural* **entrances.**

entrance² **1.** To put into a trance. When a person is hypnotized, he or she is entranced. **2.** To fill with delight or wonder: *The children were entranced by the tricks that the clown and the dog performed.* **en·trance** (en trans′) *verb,* **entranced, entrancing.**

entrant Someone who takes part in a contest or game: *There were over 50 entrants in the marathon.* **en·trant** (en′trənt) *noun, plural,* **entrants.**

entreat To ask earnestly; beg: *The prisoners entreated the judge to let them go.* **en·treat** (en trēt′) *verb,* **entreated, entreating.**

entrust **1.** To trust a person with something: *We entrusted our neighbors with the care of our dog over the weekend.* **2.** To put someone or something in the care of a person: *I entrusted my money to my cousin when I left for vacation.* **en·trust** (en trust′) *verb,* **entrusted, entrusting.**

entry **1.** The act of entering: *At the president's entry into the hall, the band began to play.* **2.** A place through which one enters; entrance: *The ladder blocked the entry to the building.* **3.** Something written in a book, list, diary, or other record: *I made an entry in my diary. Each word explained in a dictionary is an entry.* **4.** A person or thing that is entered in a contest or race: *The judges must have all entries for the art show by next Friday.* **en·try** (en′trē) *noun, plural* **entries.**

enunciate To speak or pronounce words: *It is difficult to understand someone who does not enunciate words clearly.* **e·nun·ci·ate** (i nun′sē āt′) *verb,* **enunciated, enunciating.**

envelop To wrap or cover completely: *Fog enveloped the city.* **en·vel·op** (en vel′əp) *verb,* **enveloped, enveloping.**

envelope A flat covering or container made of paper. Envelopes are used for mailing letters and other papers. **en·ve·lope** (en′və lōp′ *or* än′və lōp′) *noun, plural* **envelopes.**

enviable Worth being wanted: *After college, he was in the enviable position of being able to choose his job.* **en·vi·a·ble** (en′vē ə bəl) *adjective.*

envious Feeling or showing envy; jealous. When people are envious, they often feel dislike for a person who has something they would like to have: *I was envious of your school's new gymnasium.* **en·vi·ous** (en′vē əs) *adjective.*

environment **1.** The air, the water, the soil, and all the other things that surround a person, animal, or plant. The environment can affect the growth and health of living things: *The zoo tries to make each animal's cage like its natural environment.* **2.** Surroundings; atmosphere: *I loved summer camp because of the friendly environment.* **en·vi·ron·ment** (en vī′rən mənt *or* en vī′ərn mənt) *noun, plural* **environments.**

This woman is taking notes about the environment.

envy **1.** A feeling of not being happy about another person's good luck or belongings. A person who feels envy wishes that he or she could have what the other person has: *I felt envy when your grandparents were at our graduation and mine couldn't be.* **2.** A person or thing that makes one

PRONUNCIATION KEY:

| at | āpe | fär | câre | end | mē | it | īce | pîerce | hot | ōld | sông | fôrk |
| oil | out | up | ūse | rüle | pŭll | tûrn | chin | sing | shop | thin | this | |

hw in white; zh in treasure. The symbol ə stands for the unstressed vowel sound in about, taken, pencil, lemon, and circus.

247

feel envy: *The child's new bicycle was the envy of his classmates. Noun.*

○ To feel envy toward or because of: *Everyone in our class envies you because of your good grades. Verb.*
en·vy (en′vē) *noun, plural* **envies**; *verb,* **envied, envying.**

enzyme A protein in living animals that makes chemical reactions occur. **en·zyme** (en′zim) *noun,* **enzymes.**

eon A very long period of time: *That deposit of coal was formed eons ago.* **e·on** (ē′ən *or* ē′on) *noun, plural* **eons.**

epic A long poem that tells of the adventures of heroes in legend or history. *Noun.*

○ **1.** Being or having to do with an epic: *The class read an epic poem about how Rome was founded.* **2.** Like something in an epic; great: *We admire the epic courage of the American pioneers. Adjective.*
ep·ic (e′pik) *noun, plural* **epics**; *adjective.*

epicenter The place directly above an earthquake: *The epicenter of the earthquake was near the San Andreas fault, in California.* **ep·i·cen·ter** (ep′i sen′tər) *noun,* **epicenters.**

epidemic An outbreak of a disease that makes many people in an area ill at the same time. In an epidemic the disease may spread very fast. **ep·i·dem·ic** (ep′i dem′ik) *noun, plural* **epidemics.**

WORD HISTORY

The word **epidemic** goes back to a Greek word that means "among the people." An epidemic happens when a disease spreads quickly among many people.

---

epilepsy A disorder of the brain that can make a person sometimes be unconscious and have convulsions. Sometimes drugs can prevent a person who has epilepsy from becoming unconscious or having convulsions. **ep·i·lep·sy** (ep′ə lep′sē) *noun.* —**epileptic** *adjective, noun.*

episode One part of a series of events in a story or real life: *I watched the third episode of that series on television.* **ep·i·sode** (ep′ə sōd′) *noun, plural* **episodes.**

epoch A period of time during which something important developed or happened: *The first airplane flight marked a new epoch in travel.* **ep·och** (ep′ək) *noun, plural* **epochs.**

equal **1.** Being the same, as in amount, size, value, or quality: *Four quarts are equal to one gallon. Both teams have an equal chance to win the game because they both have good players.* **2.** Having the same rights and duties: *All people are equal under the law. Adjective.*

○ A person or thing that is equal: *You are my equal in softball because you play as well as I do. Noun.*

○ To be equal to: *Two plus two equals four. Verb.*
e·qual (ē′kwəl) *adjective; noun, plural* **equals**; *verb,* **equaled, equaling.**

equality The quality or condition of being equal: *The Constitution of the United States provides for the equality of all Americans under the law.* **e·qual·i·ty** (i kwol′i tē) *noun.*

equation A statement in mathematics that two quantities are equal. $5 + 4 = 9$ is an equation. **e·qua·tion** (i kwā′zhən) *noun, plural* **equations.**

equator An imaginary line around the earth. It is halfway between the North and South Poles. The United States and Canada are north of the equator. Most of South America is south of the equator. **e·qua·tor** (i kwā′tər) *noun, plural* **equators.**

equatorial **1.** At or near the equator: *Some of the countries in South America and Africa are equatorial countries.* **2.** Showing the qualities of the area at or near the equator: *The equatorial heat was unusual for our area.* **e·qua·tor·i·al** (ē′kwə tôr′ē əl *or* ek′wə tôr′ē əl) *adjective.*

equestrian Having to do with riding horses: *equestrian events in the Olympics. Adjective.*
○ A person who is skilled at riding horses. *Noun.*
e·ques·tri·an (i kwes′trē ən) *adjective; noun, plural* **equestrians.**

equilateral triangle A triangle in which all three sides are equal in length. **e·qui·lat·er·al triangle** (ē′kwə lat′ər əl).

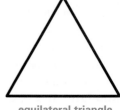
equilateral triangle

equilibrium Balance: *Many tightrope walkers carry poles to help them keep their equilibrium.* **e·qui·lib·ri·um** (ē′kwə lib′rē əm) *noun.*

WORD HISTORY

The word **equilibrium** goes back to a Latin phrase meaning "equal in weight" or "equal on a scale." Roman scales had two pans. You put an object to be weighed in one pan and little weights in the second pan on the other side. When the two pans were equal in weight, the scale would be balanced, or *in equilibrium.*

equinox One of the two days of the year when daytime and nighttime are equal in length all over the earth. During these two days the sun is directly above the equator. The equinoxes take place about March 21 and September 23. **e•qui•nox** (ē′kwə noks) *noun, plural* **equinoxes.**

equip To provide with whatever is needed: *The ship was equipped with hoses to be used in case of fire.* **e•quip** (i kwip′) *verb,* **equipped, equipping.**

equipment **1.** Anything that is provided for a particular purpose or use; supplies: *The students bought a tent, sleeping bags, and other camping equipment.* **2.** The act of equipping: *The equipment of the entire football team with new uniforms cost a lot of money.* **e•quip•ment** (i kwip′mənt) *noun.*

It takes special equipment to build bridges and roads.

equivalent Equal: *A quarter is equivalent to five nickels. Shaking your head from side to side is equivalent to saying "no." Adjective.*
○ Something that is equal: *Ten dimes are the equivalent of one dollar. Noun.*
e•quiv•a•lent (i kwiv′ə lənt) *adjective; noun, plural* **equivalents.** —**equivalence** *noun.*

-er¹ A suffix that means: **1.** A person or thing that does something: *Teacher means a person who teaches. Opener means a tool that opens.* The suffix **-or** has the same meaning. **2.** A person who studies or works at something: *Astronomer means a person who studies astronomy.* The suffix **-ist** has the same meaning. **3.** A person living in: *Northerner means a person living in the north.*

-er² A suffix that means more: *Colder means more cold than.* The suffix -er shows that an adjective or adverb is in its comparative form: *Colder is the comparative form of* **cold.** *Faster is the comparative form of* **fast.** The comparative of some words is formed with more rather than by adding -er. Look up **more** for more information.

era A period of time or of history. An era often begins or ends with an important event: *The colonial era in American history began when the first permanent settlements of Europeans were established.* **e•ra** (îr′ə or er′ə) *noun, plural* **eras.**

eradicate To get rid of something, especially something that is harmful; wipe out: *eradicate a disease.* **e•rad•i•cate** (i rad′ə kāt) *verb,* **eradicated, eradicating.** —**eradication** *noun.*

erase **1.** To remove by rubbing, scratching, or wiping off: *Erase the word that is spelled wrong and write in the correct spelling.* **2.** To remove recording from: *I accidentally erased a part of the tape.* **e•rase** (i rās′) *verb,* **erased, erasing.**

eraser Something used to rub out or remove marks: *This pencil has a rubber eraser on one end.* **e•ras•er** (i rā′sər) *noun, plural* **erasers.**

ere Before. This word is used mainly in poetry, and in writing from long ago.
Other words that sound like this are **air** and **heir.**
ere (âr) *preposition; conjunction.*

erect Upright; raised: *The dog's ears became erect when its owner whistled. Adjective.*
○ **1.** To build: *A new apartment house will be erected on that lot.* **2.** To put or raise into an upright position: *They hurried to erect the tent so they could get inside before the rain began. Verb.* **e•rect** (i rekt′) *adjective; verb,* **erected, erecting.**

ermine A small animal with short legs that is a member of the weasel family. It has brown fur that changes to white in the winter. **er•mine** (ûr′min) *noun, plural* **ermines** or **ermine.**

PRONUNCIATION KEY:
| at | āpe | fär | câre | end | mē | it | īce | pierce | hot | ōld | sông | fôrk |
| oil | out | up | ūse | rüle | pull | tûrn | chin | sing | shop | thin | this | |

hw in white; zh in treasure. The symbol ə stands for the unstressed vowel sound in about, taken, pencil, lemon, and circus.

249

erode To wear or wash away slowly; eat away: *Ocean waves eroded the shore. Rust had eroded the tin roof of the shed.* **e•rode** (i rōd′) *verb,* **eroded, eroding.**

erosion A wearing, washing, or eating away. Erosion usually happens gradually over a long time: *The trees and grass helped prevent the erosion of soil on the hill by protecting it from the wind and rain.* **e•ro•sion** (i rō′zhən) *noun.*

The ridges on this mountain were created by erosion.

errand 1. A short trip to do something: *I have to go to the grocery store, stop at the post office, and do several other errands this morning.* 2. Something a person is sent to do; the purpose of such a trip: *Our errand was to buy the newspaper.* **er•rand** (er′ənd) *noun, plural* **errands.**

erratic 1. Acting or moving in an irregular or confused way: *We knew something was wrong because of the bird's erratic flight.* 2. Straying from an accepted or usual standard; eccentric: *The captain's erratic behavior made the crew of the ship nervous.* **er•rat•ic** (i rat′ik) *adjective.*

error 1. Something that is wrong; mistake: *There were five spelling errors on that test paper.* 2. A poor play made by a fielder in baseball: *An error lets a runner get to a base safely or lets a batter remain at bat when either one would have been out if the play had been made correctly.* **er•ror** (er′ər) *noun, plural* **errors.**

erupt 1. To break out suddenly and with force: *A fight erupted between the two hockey teams.* 2. To release lava through a volcano with great force: *The volcano erupted and covered the surrounding land with lava.* 3. To lose one's temper: *Our teacher erupted and scolded us for being so noisy.* **e•rupt** (i rupt′) *verb,* **erupted, erupting.**

escalator A moving stairway. It is made of a series of steps pulled by a continuous chain. **es•ca•la•tor** (es′kə lā′tər) *noun, plural* **escalators.**

An escalator is used to carry people from one floor to another.

escape 1. To get free: *The bird escaped from the cage and flew into the woods.* 2. To remain free from: *The workers escaped harm when the building collapsed. Verb.*
○ 1. The act of escaping: *The rabbit made its escape when its owner forgot to lock the cage door.* 2. A way of escaping: *A rope ladder served as an escape from the burning house. Noun.* **es•cape** (e skāp′) *verb,* **escaped, escaping;** *noun, plural* **escapes.**

escort 1. A person or persons who go along with others. An escort does this to show respect or to honor or protect someone: *The president's car had a police escort.* 2. One or more ships or airplanes that travel with or protect another ship or airplane: *The escort for the battleship included three destroyers. Noun.*
○ To act as an escort: *The police escorted the mayor in the parade. Verb.* **es•cort** (es′kôrt *for noun;* e skôrt′ *for verb*) *noun, plural* **escorts;** *verb,* **escorted, escorting.**

Eskimo A member of a people living in Alaska, northern Canada, and other arctic regions. **Es•ki•mo** (es′kə mō′) *noun, plural* **Eskimo** *or* **Eskimos.**

esophagus The muscular tube through which food moves from the throat to the stomach. **e•soph•a•gus** (i sof′ə gəs) *noun.*

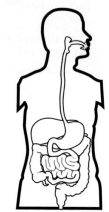

esophagus

especially 1. More than usually; to an unusual degree: *Be especially careful not to slip on the icy sidewalk.* 2. Mainly; chiefly: *We came over especially to see* *your new computer.* **es·pe·cial·ly** (e spesh′ə lē) *adverb.*

espionage The use of spies to gather secret information: *The government discovered its enemy's plans by using espionage.* **es·pi·o·nage** (es′pē ə näzh′ *or* es′pē ə nij) *noun.*

essay A short written composition on a subject: *I wrote an essay about the need for world peace.* **es·say** (es′ā) *noun, plural* **essays.**

WORD HISTORY

The word **essay** comes from a French word meaning "to try." The first essays modestly claimed to be only attempts to set down the writer's thoughts.

---

essence 1. Something that makes a thing what it is; necessary and basic part: *Respect for each other is the essence of a good friendship.* 2. A concentrated substance or solution: *We used essence of peppermint to add flavoring to the cake we made.* **es·sence** (es′ əns) *noun, plural* **essences.**

essential Very important or necessary: *It is essential that we leave now or we'll miss the last train.* *Adjective.*
○ A necessary or basic part: *We brought food, sleeping bags, a tent, and other essentials for our camping trip. Noun.*
es·sen·tial (i sen′shəl) *adjective; noun, plural* **essentials. —essentially** *adverb.*

-est A suffix that means most: *Coldest means the most cold. The suffix -est shows that an adjective or adverb is in its superlative form: Coldest is the superlative form of cold. Soonest is the superlative form of soon. The superlative of some words is formed with most rather than by adding -est.*
Look up **most** for more information.

establish 1. To begin or create; set up: *The college established a new course for students interested in computers.* 2. To show or prove to be true: *The lawyer established the fact that the accused people were out of town on the day of the crime.* **es·tab·lish** (e stab′lish) *verb,* **established, establishing.**

establishment 1. The act of establishing: *The establishment of a new hospital for the town took longer than was planned.* 2. Something established: *A department store, a school, a busi-*

ness, and a household are establishments. 3. the Establishment. The group of people who have the most power in a society. **es·tab·lish·ment** (e stab′lish mənt) *noun, plural* **establishments.**

estate 1. A large piece of land, usually with a large house on it: *Our neighbors have an estate in the country.* 2. Everything that a person owns: *The old couple left their entire estate to their children.* **es·tate** (e stāt′) *noun, plural* **estates.**

esteem To think highly of; respect: *The captain esteemed the soldiers for their bravery. Verb.*
○ High respect and admiration: *Many people have great esteem for that judge's opinions. Noun.*
es·teem (e stēm′) *verb,* **esteemed, esteeming;** *noun, plural* **esteems.**

estimate An opinion of the value, quality, size, or cost of something: *The worker gave an estimate of what it would cost to patch the roof. Noun.*
○ To form an opinion by reasoning: *We estimated that the trip would take an hour, but it took longer because of heavy traffic. Verb.*
es·ti·mate (es′tə mit *for noun;* es′tə māt′ *for verb*) *noun, plural* **estimates;** *verb,* **estimated, estimating.**

estimation An opinion or judgment: *In my estimation, the project will be finished in two weeks.* **es·ti·ma·tion** (es′tə mā′shən) *noun, plural* **estimations.**

estuary The mouth of a river where its current meets the sea and is affected by the tides. **es·tu·a·ry** (es′chü erē) *noun, plural* **estuaries.**

etc. An abbreviation for the Latin words *et cetera,* which mean *and so forth* or *and others: We went to the store and bought milk, fish, vegetables, etc.*

etch To engrave a picture or design on metal or glass by letting acid eat away parts of the metal or glass: *The artist etched a portrait of a couple.* **etch** (ech) *verb,* **etched, etching.**

etching A picture or design that is printed from a surface that has been etched. **etch·ing** (ech′ing) *noun, plural* **etchings.**

eternal 1. Lasting forever: *The laws of nature are eternal.* 2. Seeming to last or go on forever: *We complained about the eternal noise that our neighbors made.* **e·ter·nal** (i tûr′nəl) *adjective.*

eternity 1. Time without beginning or end; all time. 2. A period of time that seems endless:

PRONUNCIATION KEY:
| at | āpe | fär | câre | end | mē | it | ice | pierce | hot | ōld | sông | fôrk |
| oil | out | up | ūse | rüle | pull | tûrn | chin | sing | shop | thin | this | |
hw in white; zh in treasure. The symbol ə stands for the unstressed vowel sound in about, taken, pencil, lemon, and circus.

251

*An **eternity** passed before the bus arrived.*
e·ter·ni·ty (i tûr′ni tē) *noun, plural* **eternities.**

ether A liquid that burns easily and has a strong smell and no color. It was once used in medicine to make people unconscious during surgery. **e·ther** (ē′thər) *noun.*

Ethiopia A country in east-central Africa. **E·thi·o·pi·a** (ē′thē ō′pē ə) *noun.*

ethnic Having to do with a group of people who have the same language and culture: *Many different **ethnic** groups live in our city.* **eth·nic** (eth′nik) *adjective.* —**ethnically** *adverb* —**ethnicity** *noun.*

etiquette Rules of correct behavior: *It is not proper **etiquette** to interrupt someone who is talking.* **et·i·quette** (et′i kit′ *or* et′i ket) *noun, plural* **etiquettes.**

etymology The history of a word from its beginning to its present form. An etymology tells what other language a word has come from and any changes that have occurred in the word's spelling or meaning. In this dictionary, etymologies are printed in red boxes with the heading "Word History." **et·y·mol·o·gy** (et′ə mol′ə jē) *noun, plural* **etymologies.**

WORD HISTORY

The word **etymology** comes from a Greek term meaning "true word." The ancient Greeks and Romans looked for what they thought was the original meaning of a word. They called this meaning the "true word," or *etymology.*

---

eucalyptus A tall evergreen tree or shrub that grows in warm climates. Oil made from its leaves is used in medicine. **eu·ca·lyp·tus** (ū′kə lip′təs) *noun, plural* **eucalyptuses.**

Europe The continent that is between Asia and the Atlantic Ocean. **Eu·rope** (yûr′əp) *noun.*

European Of Europe or the people who were born or live there. *Adjective.*
○ A person who was born or is living in Europe. *Noun.*
Eu·ro·pe·an (yûr′ə pē′ən) *adjective; noun, plural* **Europeans.**

evacuate To leave or cause to leave; empty or remove: *Firefighters **evacuated** the people from the burning building.* **e·vac·u·ate** (i vak′ū āt′) *verb,* **evacuated, evacuating.** —**evacuation** *noun.*

evade To escape from or avoid: *The escaped pris-*

oner **evaded** the police by hiding on the roof of an old building. Some people try to **evade** paying their income taxes.* **e·vade** (i vād′) *verb,* **evaded, evading.**

evaluate To judge or discover the value of: *That test is used to **evaluate** how well students are doing in the reading program.* **e·val·u·ate** (i val′ū āt′) *verb,* **evaluated, evaluating.** —**evaluation** *noun.*

evaporate 1. To change from a liquid or solid into a gas: *Water **evaporates** when it is boiled and becomes steam.* 2. To fade away or disappear; vanish: *Our big lead in the game **evaporated** when the other team scored five runs in the ninth inning.* **e·vap·o·rate** (i vap′ə rāt) *verb,* **evaporated, evaporating.** —**evaporation** *noun.*

eve The evening or day before a holiday or other important day: *On the **eve** of the school elections, no one was sure who would be elected class president.* **eve** (ēv) *noun, plural* **eves.**

even 1. Free from changes; regular: *My cousin has an **even** temper.* 2. At the same height: *The drifts of snow were **even** with the tops of the parked cars.* 3. Completely flat: *Our house is built on a piece of **even** ground.* 4. The same or equal: *At the end of the fifth inning the score in the game was **even**.* 5. Able to be divided by 2 without leaving a remainder: *The numbers 4, 28, and 72 are **even** numbers.* *Adjective.*
○ 1. As a matter of fact; actually: *They were willing, **even** eager, to help us.* 2. Though it may seem unlikely: *Our dog is always friendly, **even** to strangers.* 3. Still; yet: *Your grade on the test was **even** better than mine.* 4. At the same moment: *Your parents called **even** as you knocked on our door.* *Adverb.*
○ To make or become even: *The workers **evened** the bumpy road by filling in the holes with gravel.* *Verb.*
e·ven (ē′vən) *adjective; adverb; verb,* **evened, evening.** —**evenly** *adverb.*

evening The late afternoon and early nighttime. *Noun.*
○ Relating to or occurring in the evening: *We eat our **evening** meal at seven o'clock.* *Adjective.*
eve·ning (ēv′ning) *noun, plural* **evenings;** *adjective.*

event 1. Anything that happens, especially anything that is important: *We studied the **events***

leading up to the American Revolution. **2.** A contest in a program of sports: *The mile run was the main event at the track meet.*

- **in any event.** No matter what happens; in any case: *The train may be late, but in any event we'll be there in time for dinner.*

e·vent (i vent′) *noun, plural* **events**.

eventual Happening at the end; final: *The eventual decision on whether to build a public swimming pool depends on how much money the town can raise.* **e·ven·tu·al** (i ven′chü əl) *adjective.*

eventually At the end; finally: *We waited and waited for our friends, but eventually we went to the movies without them.* **e·ven·tu·al·ly** (i ven′chü ə lē) *adverb.*

ever **1.** At any time: *Have you ever visited the White House?* **2.** At all times; always: *Our parents are ever willing to listen to what we have to say.* **3.** In any way: *How can I ever thank you enough for all your help?* **ev·er** (ev′ər) *adverb.*

everglade An area of low, swampy ground with dense grasses and many slow-moving streams or small rivers. Everglades are found in warm climates. **ev·er·glade** (ev′ər glād′) *noun, plural* **everglades**.

These evergreens may become Christmas trees.

evergreen Having green leaves or needles all year long. *Adjective.*

○ An evergreen shrub, tree, or other plant. Pine trees, spruce trees, and holly trees are evergreens. *Noun.*

ev·er·green (ev′ər grēn′) *adjective; noun, plural* **evergreens**.

everlasting Lasting forever; eternal: *The war made the people wish for everlasting peace.* **ev·er·last·ing** (ev′ər las′ting) *adjective.*

every Each person or thing of all the people or things that are part of a group: *Every student in the class is here today. Answer every question on the test.*

- **every now and then** or **every now and again.** Once in a while; occasionally: *We get to visit my grandparents every now and then.*
- **every other.** Each second; each alternate: *The garbage collector comes to our house every other day.*
- **every so often.** Now and then; occasionally: *Every so often I wonder what it's like to walk on the moon.*

eve·ry (ev′rē) *adjective.*

everybody Every person: *Everybody in the family went next door to meet the new neighbors.* **eve·ry·bod·y** (ev′rē bod′ē) *pronoun.*

everyday **1.** Having to do with every day; daily: *Walking the dog is an everyday chore for me.* **2.** Fit for normal days; not special: *Most people get dressed up to go to a party instead of wearing their everyday clothes.* **eve·ry·day** (ev′rē dā′) *adjective.*

everyone Every person; everybody: *There was enough food for everyone at the party.* **eve·ry·one** (ev′rē wun′) *pronoun.*

Everyone in this band is wearing a uniform.

everything **1.** All things or all the things: *It is impossible for a person to know everything. We showed our parents everything we had bought.* **2.** A very important thing: *Getting a good education means everything to me.* **eve·ry·thing** (ev′rē thing′) *pronoun.*

PRONUNCIATION KEY:
at   āpe   fär   câre   end   mē   it   īce   pîerce   hot   ōld   sông   fôrk
oil   out   up   ūse   rüle   pull   tûrn   chin   sing   shop   thin   this
hw in white; zh in treasure. The symbol ə stands for the unstressed vowel sound in about, taken, pencil, lemon, and circus.

253

everywhere In every place; in all places: *Have you looked **everywhere** for the book you lost?* **eve·ry·where** (ev′rē hwâr′ *or* ev′rē wâr′) *adverb.*

evict To force someone to leave the place in which they live. **e·vict** (i vikt′) **evicted, evicting.** —**eviction** *noun.*

evidence Proof of something: *The footprints were **evidence** that the suspect had been in the area.* **ev·i·dence** (ev′i dəns) *noun.*

evident Easily seen or understood; clear: *It was **evident** that they didn't like the movie since they left before the end.* **ev·i·dent** (ev′i dənt) *adjective.*

evil Bad, wicked, or harmful. *Adjective.*
○ 1. The condition of being wicked: *The minister's sermon was about good and **evil**.* 2. Something that causes trouble or harm: *War is an **evil** that has ruined many people's lives. Noun.* **e·vil** (ē′vəl) *adjective; noun, plural* **evils.**

evolution 1. A development, growth, or change that happens slowly and in steps: *The exhibit at the museum showed the **evolution** of the automobile with pictures and models of old and new cars.* 2. Changes in the members of a group of plants, animals, or other living things. These changes result from tiny changes in the genes that are passed from one generation to the next over many years. 3. The theory that all living animals and plants slowly developed over millions of years from much earlier and simpler forms of life. **ev·o·lu·tion** (ev′ə lü′shən) *noun, plural* **evolutions.**

evolve To develop or grow gradually: *The buds of roses **evolve** into beautiful flowers. The plan for the new park **evolved** in discussions between the mayor and the council.* **e·volve** (i volv′) *verb,* **evolved, evolving.**

ewe A female sheep.
Other words that sound like this are **yew** and **you.** **ewe** (ū) *noun, plural* **ewes.**

ex- A prefix that means *former*: *Ex-president means former president.* This prefix is followed by a hyphen.

exact Without anything wrong; very accurate: *This clock always gives the **exact** time. Adjective.*
○ To demand and get: *The criminals **exacted** a ransom from the family of the child that they had kidnapped. Verb.* **ex·act** (eg zakt′) *adjective; verb,* **exacted, exacting.**

exacting Requiring a lot of attention to detail; precise: *Our teacher is **exacting** about our homework.* **ex·act·ing** (eg zak′ting) *adjective.*

exactly 1. Without any mistake; in an accurate way: *Measure the boards for the bookcase **exactly**.* 2. In the exact way; quite: *The accident happened **exactly** as I told him.* **ex·act·ly** (eg zakt′lē) *adjective.*

exaggerate To make something seem larger, greater, or more important than it is: *The camper **exaggerated** the size of the fish that had gotten away.* **ex·ag·ger·ate** (eg zaj′ə rāt′) *verb,* **exaggerated, exaggerating.** —**exaggeration** *noun.*

examination 1. The act or process of examining: *The dentist's **examination** of my teeth showed that I had no cavities.* 2. A test: *The students prepared for their **examinations** at the end of the year.* **ex·am·i·na·tion** (eg zam′ə nā′shən) *noun, plural* **examinations.**

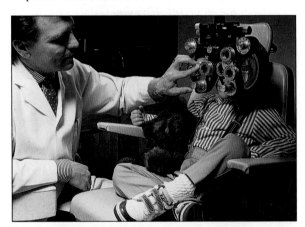
Regular eye examinations are important for healthy vision.

examine 1. To look at closely and carefully; check: *We **examined** the baseball bat to be sure it wasn't cracked.* 2. To question in a careful way or test, usually to discover what a person knows: *The lawyer **examined** the witness during the trial.* **ex·am·ine** (eg zam′in) *verb,* **examined, examining.**

example 1. A thing that is used to show what other similar things are like: *Three pictures were hung up as **examples** of the work the class was doing in art.* 2. A problem given to show how similar problems are solved: *The arithmetic **example** on the blackboard was hard to understand.* 3. A person or thing that ought to be copied: *Your good care of your dog is an* *example* for all of us. **4.** Something used to serve as a warning to others: *The judge made* **examples** *of the criminals by giving them harsh sentences.*

> • **for example.** As an example or examples: *I would like to visit many foreign countries,* **for example,** *China and Japan.*

> • **to set an example.** To serve as a model for others: *The student's hard work in class* **set an example** *for the others.*

ex·am·ple (eg zam′pəl) *noun, plural* **examples.**

exasperate To annoy greatly; make angry: *The constant barking of our neighbor's dog has* **exasperated** *our family.* **ex·as·per·ate** (eg zas′pə rāt′) *verb,* **exasperated, exasperating.**

excavate **1.** To remove by digging: *The workers* **excavated** *the dirt and rocks with a steam shovel.* **2.** To uncover by digging: *The museum sent a group of people to* **excavate** *the ruins of the ancient city.* **3.** To make by digging: *The mining company* **excavated** *a tunnel in the side of the mountain.* **ex·ca·vate** (ek′skə vāt′) *verb,* **excavated, excavating. —excavation** *noun.*

exceed To go beyond or be greater than: *The driver* **exceeded** *the speed limit and was stopped by the police. The money given to the charity* **exceeded** *$10,000.* **ex·ceed** (ek sēd′) *verb,* **exceeded, exceeding.**

exceedingly To an unusual or extreme degree: *Last night it was* **exceedingly** *hot.* **ex·ceed·ing·ly** (ek sēd′ing lē) *adverb.*

excel To be better or greater than others: *I would like to* **excel** *as a football player.* **ex·cel** (ek sel′) *verb,* **excelled, excelling.**

excellence The condition of being very good or outstanding: *Your* **excellence** *as a pitcher is known to everyone in school.* **ex·cel·lence** (ek′sə ləns) *noun.*

excellent Very good; outstanding: *The teacher told my parents that my work in arithmetic was* **excellent.** **ex·cel·lent** (ek′sə lənt) *adjective.*

except With the exception of; not including: *The store is open every day* **except** *Sunday. Preposition.*

> ○ If it were not for the fact that; only: *I would go,* **except** *that I have work to do. Conjunction.*

ex·cept (ek sept′) *preposition; conjunction.*

exception **1.** The act of leaving out or the condition of being left out: *Everyone went on the picnic with the* **exception** *of two students, who were sick.* **2.** A person or thing that is left out or that is different from others: *Most birds can fly, but the penguin is an* **exception.** **ex·cep·tion** (ek sep′shən) *noun, plural* **exceptions.**

exceptional Not ordinary; unusual; extraordinary: *We had an* **exceptional** *amount of rain this August. This young child is an* **exceptional** *piano player.* **ex·cep·tion·al** (ek sep′shə nəl) *adjective.*

excerpt A short part taken from a longer piece of writing: *We read an* **excerpt** *from* A Tale of Two Cities *in class today. Noun.*

> ○ To take a small part from a longer piece of writing: **excerpting** *one of Shakespeare's plays. Verb.*

ex·cerpt (ek′sûrpt *for noun;* ik sûrpt′ *or* ek sûrpt′ *for verb*) *noun, plural* **excerpts;** *verb,* **excerpted, excerpting.**

excess An amount greater than what is needed or usual: *An* **excess** *of water in the fish tank caused it to overflow. Noun.*

> ○ Greater than what is needed or usual; extra: *When you travel on an airplane you have to pay for* **excess** *luggage. Adjective.*

ex·cess (ek′ses *or* ek ses′) *noun, plural* **excesses;** *adjective.*

excessive More than is necessary or usual: *Don't spend an* **excessive** *amount of money during your trip.* **ex·ces·sive** (ek ses′iv) *adjective.* **—excessively** *adverb.*

exchange **1.** To give or give up for something else: *You can* **exchange** *the shirt I gave you as a present and get a belt instead.* **2.** To give and receive things of the same kind back: *My friend and I* **exchange** *recipes for desserts. Verb.*

> ○ **1.** The act of giving one thing for another: *The two friends* **enjoyed** *their exchange of letters.* **2.** A place where things are bought, sold, or traded: *a currency* **exchange;** *the stock* **exchange.** **3.** A central office where telephone lines are connected for a town or in part of a large city. *Noun.*

ex·change (eks chānj′) *verb,* **exchanged, exchanging;** *noun, plural* **exchanges.**

PRONUNCIATION KEY:

at	āpe	fär	câre	end	mē	it	īce	pierce	hot	ōld	sông	fôrk
oil	out	up	ūse	rüle	pull	tûrn	chin	sing	shop	thin	<u>th</u>is	

hw in white; zh in treasure. The symbol ə stands for the unstressed vowel sound in about, taken, pencil, lemon, and circus.

255

excite To stir up; arouse: *The team's great play excited the fans.* **ex·cite** (ek sīt′) *verb,* **excited,** **exciting** (eg zak′ting).

excitement 1. The condition of being excited: *We could hardly sleep because of our excitement about starting the trip tomorrow.* 2. Something that stirs up or excites: *Winning the contest was an excitement I shall never forget.* **ex·cite·ment** (ek sīt′mənt) *noun.*

exciting Causing excitement: *For me, the acrobats who walk on the tightrope are the most exciting part of the circus.* **ex·cit·ing** (ek sīt′ing) *adjective.*

exclaim To speak or shout suddenly, or with force; to express surprise or other strong feeling: *"My bicycle's missing!" I exclaimed.* **ex·claim** (ek sklām′) *verb,* **exclaimed,** **exclaiming.**

exclamation 1. The act of exclaiming: *There was no excuse for your constant exclamations during the meeting.* 2. Something that is spoken or shouted suddenly or with force: *Hurrah! and Ouch! are exclamations.* **ex·clam·a·tion** (eks′klə mā′shən) *noun,* *plural* **exclamations.**

exclamation point or **exclamation mark** A punctuation mark (!) that is used after a word or group of words that is an exclamation.

exclamatory sentence A sentence that expresses excitement or strong feelings. An example of an exclamatory sentence is: What a scary movie that was! **ex·clam·a·tory sentence** (ek sklam′ə tôr′ē).

exclude To keep from entering; shut out: *All those who aren't eighteen years old or older are excluded from voting.* **ex·clude** (ek sklüd′) *verb,* **excluded,** **excluding.**

exclusive 1. Belonging to a single person or group: *Because my parents own our family's house together, neither one is the exclusive owner.* 2. Open to a certain kind of person or group only: *That is an exclusive club for lawyers only.* 3. Complete; entire: *The students gave the visitor their exclusive attention.* **ex·clu·sive** (ek sklü′siv) *adjective.*

excrete To give off waste from the body. **ex·crete** (ek skrēt′) *verb,* **excreted, excreting. excretion** *noun.* —**excretory** *adjective.*

excruciating Causing great discomfort or pain: *The noise of the sirens was excruciating.* **ex·cru·ci·a·ting** (ek skrü′shē ā ting) *adjective.*

excursion 1. A short trip made for a special reason or for pleasure: *Tomorrow the class will take an excursion to the zoo.* 2. A trip, as on an airplane or train, at a reduced fare. **ex·cur·sion** (ek skûr′zhən) *noun,* *plural* **excursions.**

excuse 1. To forgive; pardon; overlook: *We excused your rude remark because we knew you were tired.* 2. To let off from duty: *I was excused from football practice because I had hurt my knee.* 3. To serve as a reason or explanation for: *Your illness excused your absence from the meeting.* Verb. ○ A reason given to explain something: *Waking up late is not a good excuse for being late to school.* Noun.

• **to excuse oneself.** 1. To apologize for oneself; ask to be pardoned: *I excused myself for being late.* 2. To ask permission to leave: *You should excuse yourself if you want to leave the table during dinner.*

ex·cuse (ek skūz′ *for verb;* ek skūs′ *for noun*) *verb,* **excused, excusing;** *noun,* *plural* **excuses.**

execute 1. To carry out or enforce: *The captain executed the colonel's orders.* 2. To kill according to a legal order. 3. To make or do by following a plan or design: *The two dancers executed the unusual steps perfectly.* **ex·e·cute** (ek′si kūt′) *verb,* **executed, executing.**

execution 1. The act of executing: *The execution of the plan to clean up the neighborhood will call for everyone's help.* 2. The act of killing according to a legal order. 3. The performance of an action: *The diver's execution on the high board was outstanding.* **ex·e·cu·tion** (ek′si kū′shən) *noun,* *plural* **executions.**

executive Having to do with directing or managing matters in business or government: *The president heads the executive branch of the United States government.* Adjective. ○ 1. A person who directs or manages: *All the executives of the company met to discuss ways of selling their new product.* 2. The branch of government that manages the affairs of a nation and sees that the laws are carried out. Noun. **ex·ec·u·tive** (eg zek′yə tiv) *adjective;* *noun,* *plural* **executives.**

exempt To free from a duty or requirements excuse: *One student was exempted from taking the final test because of excellent marks during the year.* Verb.

○ Freed from doing or giving something; excused: *Land belonging to a church is usually **exempt** from taxes. Adjective.*
ex·empt (eg zempt′) *verb,* **exempted, exempting;** *adjective.*

exercise 1. Activity that trains or improves the body or the mind: *Walking is good **exercise**. That book has arithmetic **exercises** at the end of each chapter.* 2. Use or practice: *The **exercise** of power by the dictator led to many cruel acts.* 3. A ceremony or program: *Graduation **exercises** included speeches by teachers and students. Noun.*
○ 1. To put or go through exercises: *I **exercise** my dog in the park. That athlete **exercises** by running five miles every day.* 2. To make use of: *You should **exercise** your rights as a citizen by voting. Verb.*
ex·er·cise (ek′sər sīz′) *noun, plural* **exercises;** *verb,* **exercised, exercising.**

exert To make use of; use: *The firefighters had to **exert** all their strength to break down the door.*
ex·ert (eg zûrt′) *verb,* **exerted, exerting.**

exhale To breathe out: *The doctor listened to my lungs as I inhaled and **exhaled**.* **ex·hale** (eks′hāl) *verb,* **exhaled, exhaling.**

exhaust 1. To make very weak or tired: *The long, hot hike **exhausted** us.* 2. To use up completely: *The campers **exhausted** their supply of water, so they drank from a fresh spring. Verb.*
○ 1. The steam or gases that escape from an engine: *An automobile has a pipe at the rear to let out the **exhaust**.* 2. A pipe or other device that allows used steam or gases to escape. *Noun.*
ex·haust (eg zôst′) *verb,* **exhausted, exhausting;** *noun, plural* **exhausts.**

exhaustion The act of exhausting or condition of being exhausted: *The runner's **exhaustion** was caused by a seven-mile run.* **ex·haus·tion** (eg zôs′chən) *noun.*

exhibit To show: *The school **exhibited** the students' best art-*

Space vehicles are often placed on exhibit.

*work. Your cousin **exhibits** great talent in playing the piano. Verb.*
○ Something shown: *We went to see the **exhibit** of African art at the museum. Noun.*
ex·hib·it (eg zib′it) *verb,* **exhibited, exhibiting;** *noun, plural* **exhibits.**

exhibition 1. The act of exhibiting: *Being rude is an **exhibition** of bad manners.* 2. A public show: *The class went to an **exhibition** of rare books shown at the town library.* **ex·hi·bi·tion** (ek sə bish′ən) *noun, plural* **exhibitions.**

exhilarate To make cheerful, lively, or excited: *The brisk air of the mountains **exhilarated** the hikers.* **ex·hil·a·rate** (eg zil′ə rāt′) *verb,* **exhilarated, exhilarating** (eg zil′ə rā ting). —**exhilaration** *noun.*

exile To send a person away from his or her country or home as a punishment: *The country **exiled** the scientist for being a spy for another country. Verb.*
○ 1. The state of being exiled: *The government decided that **exile** would be the punishment for the traitors.* 2. A person who is sent away from his or her country or home. *Noun.*
ex·ile (eg′zīl or ek′sīl) *verb,* **exiled, exiling;** *noun, plural* **exiles.**

exist 1. To be real: *I do not believe that ghosts **exist**.* 2. To have life; live: *A person cannot **exist** for long without water.* 3. To be found: *Outside of zoos, polar bears **exist** only in arctic regions.* **ex·ist** (eg zist′) *verb,* **existed, existing.**

existence 1. The fact of being alive or real: *The **existence** of some wild animals is in danger because of pollution.* 2. A way of living; life: *The early colonists in America led a dangerous **existence**.* **ex·ist·ence** (eg zis′təns) *noun, plural* **existences.**

exit 1. The way out or off: *We left the movies by the **exit** on the left.* 2. The act of leaving: *My **exit** from the room was not noticed. Noun.*
○ To go out; leave; depart: ***Exit** by the side door during the fire drill. Verb.*
ex·it (eg′zit or ek′sit) *noun, plural* **exits;** *verb,* **exited, exiting.**

exodus The leaving of many people at the same time: *the **exodus** from the cities.* **ex·o·dus** (ek′səd əs) *noun.*

PRONUNCIATION KEY:
at āpe fär câre end mē it īce pierce hot ōld sông fôrk
oil out up ūse rüle pull tûrn chin sing shop thin this
hw in white; zh in treasure. The symbol ə stands for the unstressed vowel sound in about, taken, pencil, lemon, and circus.
257

exotic Foreign; strange; unusual: *These **exotic** flowers come from Africa.* **ex•ot•ic** (eg zot′ik) *adjective.*

Exotic **plants like these can be found in many countries of the world.**

expand To make larger or become larger: *Metal **expands** when it is heated.* **ex•pand** (ek spand′) *verb,* **expanded, expanding.**

SYNONYMS

expand, balloon, inflate, swell
*The warm air **expanded** to fill the room. A boat's sails will **balloon** in the wind. You can **inflate** the tire with a pump. The sea **swelled** with huge waves.*

---

expanse A wide, open area: *the great **expanse** of the prairies.* **ex•panse** (ek spans′) *noun, plural* **expanses.**

expansion 1. The act of expanding or the condition of being expanded: *After its **expansion**, the school had thirty new classrooms.* 2. The expanded form of something: *This novel is an **expansion** of a story in a magazine.* **ex•pan•sion** (ek span′shən) *noun, plural* **expansions.**

expect 1. To look forward to: *I **expect** to see my grandparents at Thanksgiving.* 2. To want something because it is right or necessary: *The teacher **expected** an apology from the rude child.* 3. To think; suppose: *I **expect** I won't be going to school if I still have the flu tomorrow.* **ex•pect** (ek spekt′) *verb,* **expected, expecting.**

expectation 1. The act of expecting: *The sailors anchored the boat securely in **expectation** of the coming storm.* 2. A reason for expecting: *The student had studied hard and had **expectations** of a good mark on the text.* **ex•pec•ta•tion** (ek′spek tā′shən) *noun, plural* **expectations.**

expedition 1. A journey made for a particular reason: *The scientists made an **expedition** to Alaska to study the animals in the area.* 2. The people making such a journey: *The **expedition** camped beside the river for the night.* **ex•pe•di•tion** (ek′spi dish′ən) *noun, plural* **expeditions.**

expel To drive or force out: *They **expelled** the child from school for disobeying everyone.* **ex•pel** (ek spel′) *verb,* **expelled, expelling.**

expenditure 1. The spending of time, money, or energy: *Building a new house requires the **expenditure** of a great deal of money.* 2. Something that is spent: *The **expenditure** for the flowers was $25.00.* **ex•pend•i•ture** (ek spen′di chər) *noun, plural* **expenditures.**

expense 1. Money spent to buy or do something; cost: *My family cannot afford the **expense** of a new car.* 2. A cause or reason for spending money: *Building the swimming pool was a big **expense**.* **ex•pense** (ek spens′) *noun, plural* **expenses.**

expensive Having a high price; very costly: *The town bought an **expensive** new fire engine.* **ex•pen•sive** (ek spen′siv) *adjective.*

experience 1. Something that a person has done, seen, or taken part in: *Our **experience** camping in the national park is something we won't forget. The soldiers told our class about their **experiences** in the army.* 2. The knowledge or skill a person gains from doing something: *The youngest firefighter already has three years of **experience**. Noun.*
○ To have something happen to one; feel; undergo: *I didn't **experience** much pain when the dentist drilled my tooth. Verb.*
ex•pe•ri•ence (ek spîr′ē ̣ əs) *noun, plural* **experiences;** *verb,* **experienced, experiencing.**

experiment A test that is used to discover or prove something by watching results very carefully: *The class did an **experiment** to show that a fire needs oxygen to burn. Noun.*
○ To make an experiment or experiments: *Scientists tested the new drug by **experimenting** with rats. Verb.*
ex•per•i•ment (ek sper′ə mənt *for noun;* ek sper′ə ment′ *for verb*) *noun, plural* **experiments;** *verb,* **experimented, experimenting.**

experimental From or relating to experiments: *The scientists were working on an experimental project in the chemistry laboratory.* **ex·per·i·ment·al** (ek sper′ə ment′əl) *adjective.*

expert A person who knows a great deal about some special thing: *One of our teachers is an expert on American history.* Noun.
○ Having or showing a great deal of knowledge: *The swimming coach gave the team expert advice on how to dive.* Adjective.
ex·pert (eks′pûrt *for noun*; eks′pûrt *or* ek spûrt′ *for adjective*) *noun, plural* **experts**; *adjective.*

expiration 1. The act of coming to an end or close: *I must get a new library card before the expiration of my old one.* 2. The act of breathing out air: *The sick child's expirations were weak.* **ex·pi·ra·tion** (eks′pə rā′shən) *noun, plural* **expirations.**

expire 1. To come to an end: *Your membership at the pool expires at the end of the month.* 2. To breathe out; exhale: *When we expire, our bodies let air out of our lungs.* 3. To die. **ex·pire** (ek spīr′) *verb,* **expired, expiring.**

The art teacher is explaining paintings to the class.

explain 1. To make something plain or clear; tell the meaning of: *Explain how to get the answer to this mathematics problem.* 2. To give or have a reason for: *Can you explain why you were late for school?* **ex·plain** (ek splān′) *verb,* **explained, explaining.**

explanation 1. The act or process of making something plain or clear: *My friend's explanation of how to make a kite helped me understand how to do it.* 2. A reason or meaning: *My parents wanted an explanation for why the vase was broken.* **ex·pla·na·tion** (eks′plə nā′shən) *noun, plural* **explanations.**

explicit Stated clearly or shown clearly: *Our teacher gave explicit instructions on how we should do the work.* **ex·pli·cit** (ek splis′it) *adjective.*

explode 1. To burst or cause to burst suddenly and with a loud noise; blow up: *I pumped too much air into the tire, and it exploded.* 2. To show an emotion noisily or forcefully: *The audience exploded with laughter at the funny joke.* **ex·plode** (ek splōd′) *verb,* **exploded, exploding.**

exploit A brave deed or act: *The story is about the daring exploits of a knight.* Noun.
○ 1. To use in an unfair or unjust way for selfish reasons: *The American colonists felt that the British government exploited them by taxing the tea they drank.* 2. To make the fullest possible use of: *This new drill will enable us to exploit oil buried far under the ground.* Verb.
ex·ploit (ek′ sploit *for noun*; ek sploit′ *for verb*) *noun, plural* **exploits**; *verb,* **exploited, exploiting.**

exploration The act of exploring: *Sometimes people really mean conquest when they talk about exploration.* **ex·plo·ra·tion** (ek′splə rā′shən) *noun, plural* **explorations.**

explore 1. To go to a place that one knows nothing about: *Astronauts explored the moon and brought back rocks.* 2. To try to figure out: *Doctors explore the causes of diseases.* **ex·plore** (ek splôr′) *verb,* **explored, exploring.**

explorer A person who explores. **ex·plor·er** (ek splôr′ər) *noun, plural* **explorers.**

explosion 1. The act of bursting or expanding suddenly and noisily: *The explosion of the bomb broke windows in the buildings nearby.* 2. A sudden outburst: *The funny joke caused an explosion of laughter.* **ex·plo·sion** (ek splō′zhən) *noun, plural* **explosions.**

explosive 1. Likely to explode or cause an explosion: *A bomb is an explosive device.* 2. Likely to cause a lot of trouble: *an explosive political situation.* Adjective.
○ Something that can explode or cause an explosion: *Dynamite is an explosive.* Noun.
ex·plo·sive (ek splō′siv) *adjective; noun, plural* **explosives.**

PRONUNCIATION KEY:
at   āpe   fär   câre   end   mē   it   īce   pierce   hot   ōld   sông   fôrk
oil   out   up   ūse   rüle   pull   tûrn   chin   sing   shop   thin   this
hw in white; zh in treasure. The symbol ə stands for the unstressed vowel sound in about, taken, pencil, lemon, and circus.

259

exponent 1. A smaller number that is placed beside and above another number to show many times that number is to be multiplied by itself.

In 4^2 the **2** is an **exponent**.
In 10^{23} the **23** is an **exponent**.

2. A person who explains or argues for something: *My professor is an* **exponent** *of abstract art.* **ex•po•nent** (eks pō′nent) *noun, plural* **exponents.** —**exponential** *adjective* —**exponentially** *adverb.*

export To send goods to other countries to be sold or traded: *Brazil* **exports** *coffee to the United States. Verb.*

○ 1. Something that is sold or traded to another country: *Wheat is an* **export** *of the United States and Canada.* 2. The act or process of selling or trading to another country: *Many farmers depend on the money that comes from the* **export** *of corn. Noun.*
ex•port (ek spôrt′ or ek′spôrt′ for verb; ek′spôrt′ for noun) *verb,* **exported, exporting;** *noun, plural* **exports.**

expose 1. To leave open or without protection: *We were* **exposed** *to the mumps when a friend had them.* 2. To make something known; reveal: *The magazine article* **exposed** *the real age of the movie star.* 3. To allow light to reach a photographic film or plate: *You will* **expose** *the film if you load your camera under the lamp.* **ex•pose** (ek spōz′) *verb,* **exposed, exposing.**

exposition A large public display: *There was an* **exposition** *of camping equipment at the convention center.* **ex•po•si•tion** (ek′spə zish′ən) *noun, plural* **expositions.**

exposure 1. The act of exposing: *The government's* **exposure** *of the plot to kill the president shocked the public.* 2. The condition of being exposed: *The mountain climbers were suffering from* **exposure** *after the climb in the terrible cold and wind.* 3. A position in relation to the sun or wind: *This room has a southern* **exposure**, *so it gets a lot of sunlight.* 4. The act of exposing a photographic film to light. **ex•po•sure** (ek spō′zhər) *noun, plural* **exposures.**

express To say or show: *The Declaration of Independence* **expresses** *the idea that people are created equal. Verb.*

○ 1. Special or particular: *We came here for the* **express** *purpose of seeing the monument.* 2. Having to do with fast transportation or delivery: *The* **express** *bus to the city travels on the superhighway. Adjective.*

○ 1. A system of fast transportation or delivery: *I sent my trunk to camp by* **express.** 2. A train, bus, or elevator that is fast and makes few stops. *Noun.*

• **to express oneself.** To put what one thinks or feels into words: *I want to learn how* **to express** *myself clearly when speaking to a large group.*
ex•press (ek spres′) *verb,* **expressed, expressing;** *adjective; noun, plural* **expresses.**

expression 1. The act of putting thoughts or feelings into words or actions: *These flowers are an* **expression** *of our thanks to you.* 2. An outward show; look: *The students all had* **expressions** *of surprise on their faces after the magician performed the trick.* 3. A way of speaking that shows a feeling: *The child told the exciting story with* **expression.** 4. A common word or group of words. "Look before you leap" and "A penny saved is a penny earned" are well-known expressions. **ex•pres•sion** (ek spresh′ən) *noun, plural* **expressions.**

expressive Full of meaning or feeling: *The poet read the poem to the audience in a very* **expressive** *voice.* **ex•pres•sive** (ek spres′iv) *adjective.*

expressway A wide highway with several lanes so that cars, trucks, and buses can go long distances without stopping for lights or signs. **ex•press•way** (ek spres′wā) *noun, plural* **expressways.**

These expressways lead in and out of the city.

exquisite 1. Of great beauty or perfection: *The view of the sunrise over the lake was* **exquisite.** 2. Of high quality: *The detailed sculpture showed* **exquisite** *workmanship.* **ex•qui•site** (ek skwiz′it or ek′skwiz′it) *adjective.*

extend 1. To make or be longer; stretch out: *The bird* **extended** *its wings and flew away.* 2. To reach; stretch: *This electrical cord doesn't* **extend** *far enough.* 3. To offer or give: *We* **extended** *our welcome to the new neighbors.* **ex•tend** (ek stend′) *verb,* **extended, extending.**

extension 1. The act of extending or the condition of being extended: *The town that was damaged by*

the tornado accepted the state's **extension** of help.
2. Something that extends; addition: *They built an*
extension *to the house so they would have a room*
for the new baby. **3.** An extra telephone added to
the same line as the main telephone. **ex·ten·sion** (ek
sten′shən) *noun, plural* **extensions.**

extensive Large; great; broad: *The flood caused*
extensive damage to the farms in the area.
ex·ten·sive (ek sten′siv) *adjective.*

extent The space, size, amount, degree, or limit to
which something extends: *I would go to any* **extent**
to help a friend. **ex·tent** (ek stent′) *noun, plural*
extents.

exterior The outer part; outward look or manner:
The **exterior** *of the building is made of brick.*
Although you have a calm **exterior**, *I think you*
must feel nervous about running in the race. Noun.
○ On or having to do with the outside; outer:
The **exterior** *walls of the house were painted white.*
Adjective.
ex·te·ri·or (ek stîr′ē ər) *noun, plural* **exteriors**;
adjective.

exterminate To wipe out; destroy: *We used a spray*
to **exterminate** *the bugs.* **ex·ter·mi·nate**
(ek stûr′mə nāt) *verb*, **exterminated, exterminating.**
—**exterminator** *noun.*

external On or having to do with the outside; outer:
The peel of a banana is its **external** *covering.*
ex·ter·nal (ek stûr′nəl) *adjective.*

extinct **1.** No longer existing: *The dodo became*
extinct *because people hunted it for food.*
2. No longer active or burning: *The village is built*
on an **extinct** *volcano.* **ex·tinct** (ek stingkt′) *adjec-*
tive. **extinction** *noun.*

extinguish **1.** To cause to stop burning; put out:
The firefighters **extinguished** *the fire in about twen-*
ty minutes. **2.** To end; destroy: *The heavy rain*
extinguished *any hope for a picnic that day.*
ex·tin·guish (ek sting′gwish) *verb*, **extinguished,**
extinguishing.

extra More than what is usual, expected, or needed;
additional: *I spent* **extra** *time studying so I would*
get a better grade on that test. Adjective.
○ **1.** Something added to what is usual, expected, or
needed: *That car has many* **extras***, such as a clock,*
a radio, and air conditioning. **2.** A special edition of
a newspaper that is printed to report something

important: *The paper printed an* **extra** *to announce*
that the war was over. Noun.
○ To a degree that is greater than what is usual,
expected, or needed: *My parents bought an* **extra**
large cake for my birthday party. Adverb.
ex·tra (ek′strə) *adjective; noun, plural* **extras**; *adverb.*

extract To take, get, or pull out: *The dentist* **extract-**
ed *the tooth. Scientists have found a way to* **extract**
salt from sea water. Verb.
○ Something that is extracted: *The cake was fla-*
vored with vanilla **extract***. Noun.*
ex·tract (ek strakt′ *for verb*; ek′strakt *for noun*)
verb, **extracted, extracting**; *noun, plural* **extracts.**
—**extraction** *noun.*

extraordinary Very unusual; remarkable: *The*
art teacher said that my friend had **extraordinary**
talent. **ex·tra·or·di·nar·y** (ek strôr′də ner′ē *or*
ek′strə ôr′də ner′ē) *adjective.*

extraterrestrial Coming from, existing, or operating outside the earth or its atmosphere: *Scientists*
can determine if a rock is **extraterrestrial** *from its*
chemical composition. Adjective.
○ A being from another planet: *In the movie,*
extraterrestrials *came to earth in a spaceship.*
Noun.
ex·tra·ter·res·tri·al (ek′strə tə res′trē əl) *adjective;*
noun, plural **extraterrestrials.**

extravagance The spending of too much money:
When our parents go shopping, they avoid **extrava-**
gance *and only buy what they need.*
ex·trav·a·gance (ek strav′ə gəns) *noun, plural*
extravagances.

extravagant Spending too much money; spending
in a free or careless way: *The extravagant movie*
star bought only very **expensive** *clothes.*
ex·trav·a·gant (ek strav′ə gənt) *adjective.*

WORD HISTORY

The word **extravagant** goes back to a Latin word meaning "wandering outside of the limits." A person who is
extravagant in some way has gone beyond the usual
limits of behavior.

---

extreme **1.** Going beyond what is usual; very great
or severe: *The campers were in* **extreme** *danger*
when they were caught in the avalanche. **2.** Very
far; farthest: *My best friend lives at the* **extreme** *end*

PRONUNCIATION KEY:

| at | āpe | fär | câre | end | mē | it | īce | pîerce | hot | ōld | sông | fôrk |
| oil | out | up | ūse | rüle | pull | tûrn | chin | sing | shop | thin | this | |

hw in white; zh in treasure. The symbol ə stands for the unstressed vowel sound in about, taken, pencil, lemon, and circus.

261

of the block. *Adjective.*

○ **1.** Farthest points; end: *The lighthouse is at one* **extreme** *of the island.* **2. extremes.** Complete opposites: *Hot and cold are* **extremes** *of each other. Noun.*

ex•treme (ek strēm′) *adjective; noun, plural* **extremes.**

extremely Very: *The friends were* **extremely** *happy when they won the contest. These mountains are* **extremely** *old.* **ex•treme•ly** (ek strēm′lē) *adverb.*

extremity 1. The farthest point or end of something: *go to the* **extremities** *of the earth.* **2.** A person's hands and feet. **3.** A very desperate situation or feeling: *In his* **extremity,** *the climber clung to the side of the cliff.* **4.** A very extreme thing to do: *She will go to any* **extremity** *to feed the hungry.* **ex•trem•i•ty** (ek strem′ə tē) *noun, plural* **extremities.**

extrovert A person is very outgoing and enjoys being with other people: *Everyone in my family but me is an* **extrovert.** **ex•tro•vert** (ek′strə vərt) *noun,* **extroverts.**

extroverted Very outgoing; lively: *My cousin is* **extroverted,** *but I prefer to be alone.* **ex•tro•verted** (ek′stra vər təd) *adjective.*

eye 1. One of the organs of the body by which humans and other animals see or sense light. **2.** The colored part of the eye; iris: *I have brown* **eyes.** **3.** The part of the face around the eye. *Many children rub their* **eyes** *when they are tired.* **4. eyes.** The ability to see; vision. *My* **eyes** *are not as good as they used to be.* **5.** A look. *We cast an* **eye** *at the bicycle in the store window.* **6.** Something like an eye in shape, position, or use. The bud of a potato and the hole in a needle are called eyes. A hook attaches to an eye. **7.** The center of a hurricane: *The* **eye** *has no clouds and light winds. Noun.*

○ To watch carefully or closely: *The detective* **eyed** *every move the suspect made. Verb.*

Other words that sound like this are **aye** and **I.**

• **to catch one's eye.** To attract one's attention: *A poster in the shop window* **caught my eye** *and I stopped to look at it.*

• **to have an eye for.** To be able to spot some-

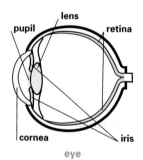

eye

thing: *He has an* **eye** *for bargains.*

• **to keep an eye on.** To watch or tend carefully: *I* **kept an eye on** *the twins when their parents were out for the evening.*

• **to see eye to eye.** To agree completely: *The team didn't* **see eye to eye** *on the strategy for the game.*

eye (ī) *noun, plural* **eyes;** *verb,* **eyed, eying** *or* **eyeing.**

eyeball The round part of the eye that is shaped like a ball, without the eyelids or other surrounding parts. **eye•ball** (ī′bôl) *noun, plural* **eyeballs.**

eyebrow 1. The hair that grows on the bony part of the face above the eye. **2.** The bony ridge above each eye. The eyebrows help to shade and protect the eyes. **eye•brow** (ī′brou) *noun, plural* **eyebrows.**

eyedropper A small glass or plastic tube with a rubber bulb at one end and a hole at the other. It is used to measure and apply drops of medicine to the eye. **eye•drop•per** (ī′drop′ər) *noun, plural* **eyedroppers.**

eyeglasses A pair of lenses in a frame that helps a person to see better. **eye•glass•es** (ī′glas′iz) *noun plural.*

eyelash One of the small, stiff hairs growing on the edge of the eyelid. The eyelashes help keep dust out of the eyes. **eye•lash** (ī′lash) *noun, plural* **eyelashes.**

eyelet A small hole in a material for a cord or lace to go through. Shoelaces are put through eyelets. Another word that sounds like this is **islet.** **eye•let** (ī′lit) *noun, plural* **eyelets.**

eyelid The covering of skin that can open and close over the eye. The eyelids protect the eyes and help keep them moist. **eye•lid** (ī′lid) *noun, plural* **eyelids.**

eyesight 1. The ability to see; vision: *They tested our* **eyesight** *in school by asking us to read a chart.* **2.** The range or distance the eye can see; view: *The whistling train soon came within* **eyesight.** **eye•sight** (ī′sīt) *noun.*

eyetooth Either of the two pointed teeth in the upper jaw between the front teeth and the molars, used for biting or tearing. **eye•tooth** (ī′tüth) *noun, plural* **eyeteeth** (ī tēth).

eyewitness A person who has seen something happen, and therefore is able to report or give testimony about it: *Reporters interviewed the* **eyewitnesses** *to the accident.* **eye•wit•ness** (ī′wit nis) *noun, plural* **eyewitnesses.**

The letter F has only one sound, but it can be made in several ways:

f as in fall and fifty; ff in the middle of words like different and at the end of words such as off and staff.

Less often, the sound of F is made by:

gh as in enough and laugh; ph as in phone; lf at the end of some words such as calf.

f, F The sixth letter of the alphabet.
f, F (ef) *noun, plural* **f's, F's.**

F *or* **F.** An abbreviation for **Fahrenheit.**

fable 1. A story meant to teach a lesson. The characters in fables are often animals that talk and act like people. 2. A made-up or untrue story: *Have you heard the old fable about alligators living in the city sewers?* **fa·ble** (fā′bəl) *noun, plural* **fables.**

fabric A material that is woven or knitted; cloth. Fabric is made from natural or synthetic fibers such as cotton, silk, or nylon. **fab·ric** (fab′rik) *noun, plural* **fabrics.**

fabulous Unbelievable; seeming impossible; amazing: *fabulous creatures like dragons. They spent fabulous amounts of money on books.* **fab·u·lous** (fab′yə ləs) *adjective.* —**fabulously** *adverb.*

face 1. The front of the head. The eyes, nose, and mouth are parts of the face. 2. A look on the face; expression: *a sad face.* 3. The front, main, or outward part of something: *the face of a clock.* 4. Importance in the opinion of other people; prestige: *If we don't keep our streets clean, our town will lose face. Noun.*
○ 1. To have or turn the face toward: *Face the camera.* 2. To deal with firmly or courageously: *You must face the problem immediately. Verb.*
face (fās) *noun, plural* **faces;** *verb,* **faced, facing.**

facet One of the small, polished, flat surfaces of a cut gem. **fac·et** (fa′shəl) *noun, plural* **facets.**

facial Of or for the face: *A smile is a happy facial expression.* **fa·cial** (fā′shəl) *adjective.*

facilitate To make easier; help in the doing of: *Zip codes facilitate the sorting and delivery of mail.* **fa·cil·i·tate** (fə sil′i tāt′) *verb,* **facilitated, facilitating.**

facility 1. Ease or skill in doing something: *You ride your new bicycle with great facility.* 2. Something that makes a job easier to do or serves a particular purpose: *The kitchen facilities include a stove, refrigerator, and sink.* **fa·cil·i·ty** (fə sil′i tē′) *noun, plural* **facilities.**

fact Something known to be true or real: *It is a fact that the world is round.* **fact** (fakt) *noun, plural* **facts.**

factor 1. Something that matters or that counts: *Sunny weather and good food were important factors in the success of the picnic.* 2. Any of the numbers that form a product when they are multiplied together. The factors of 12 are 12 and 1, 6 and 2, and 3 and 4. *Noun.*
○ To find the factors of a product: *What answer do you get when you factor 6? Verb.*
fac·tor (fak′tər) *noun, plural* **factors;** *verb,* **factored, factoring.**

factory A building or group of buildings where things are manufactured; plant. **fac·to·ry** (fak′tə rē) *noun, plural* **factories.**

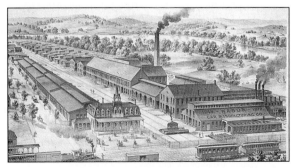

In the 1800s, factories **like this helped make the United States an industrial giant.**

factual True; accurate: *This book contains a factual account of the battle.* **fac·tu·al** (fak′chü əl) *adjective;* **fac·tu·al·ly** *adverb.*

faculty 1. All the teachers of a school, college, or university. 2. A natural power of the mind or body: *Hearing and speaking are two human faculties.* 3. A special talent or skill for doing something: *a faculty for making friends.* **fac·ul·ty** (fak′əl tē) *noun, plural* **faculties.**

fad Something that is very popular for a short period of time: *The hula hoop was a fad.* **fad** (fad) *noun, plural* **fads.**

fade 1. To lose or cause to lose color or brightness: *Clothes may fade when they are washed.* 2. To lose freshness; wither: *The flowers faded.* 3. To become gradually weaker, fainter, or dimmer: *The sound faded away.* **fade** (fād) *verb,* **faded, fading.**

Fahrenheit The name of a temperature scale on which the freezing point of water is at 32 degrees and the boiling point of water is at 212 degrees: *It was 30 degrees Fahrenheit and the ice on the pond was frozen.* **Fahr·en·heit** (far′ən hīt) *adjective.*

WORD HISTORY

The word Fahrenheit comes from the name of Gabriel Daniel Fahrenheit. He was the German scientist who devised this scale for measuring temperature.

fail 1. To not succeed in doing or getting something: *We failed to get there on time.* 2. To get too low a grade in a test or course of study; not pass: *I didn't study for the test, so I failed.* 3. To be of no use or help to; disappoint: *Their friends failed them when they refused to keep their promise.* 4. To not be enough; run out: *The water supply failed during the emergency.* 5. To become weaker in strength or health: *His eyesight is beginning to fail.* 6. To be unable to pay what one owes; go bankrupt: *The small store failed because it had so few customers.* 7. To not do; neglect: *If you fail to answer when your name is called, you will be marked absent.* **fail** (fāl) *verb,* **failed, failing.**

failure 1. The act of not succeeding in doing or getting something: *I was disappointed at the failure of the plant to grow.* 2. A person or thing that does not succeed: *Our play was a failure.* 3. The condition of not being large or good enough: *Bad weather caused a crop failure.* **fail·ure** (fāl′yər) *noun, plural* **failures.**

faint 1. Not clear or strong; weak: *the faint cry of a kitten. There was a faint light ahead.* 2. Weak and dizzy: *I'm faint with hunger. Adjective.*
○ A condition in which a person becomes suddenly unconscious for a short time. *Noun.*
○ To become suddenly unconscious for a short time. *Verb.*
Another word that sounds like this is **feint.**
faint (fānt) *adjective,* **fainter, faintest;** *noun, plural* **faints;** *verb,* **fainted, fainting.**

fair¹ 1. Not in favor of any one more than another or others; just: *The judges were fair in awarding prizes.* 2. According to the rules: *a fair tackle.* 3. Neither too good nor too bad; average: *a fair chance of winning.* 4. Light in coloring; not dark: *fair hair.* 5. Not cloudy; clear; sunny: *fair weather.* 6. Attractive; beautiful: *a fair young princess. Adjective.*
○ In a fair manner; according to the rules: *Play fair! Adverb.*
Another word that sounds like this is **fare.**
fair (fâr) *adjective,* **fairer, fairest;** *adverb.*

fair² 1. A public showing of farm products. Fairs are held to show and judge crops and cows, pigs, and other livestock. Fairs often have shows, contests, and entertainment. 2. Any large showing of products or objects: *a photography fair.* 3. The showing and selling of things for a particular cause or reason: *Our school book fair is going to raise money for a new playground.*
Another word that sounds like this is **fare.**
fair (fâr) *noun, plural* **fairs.**

At fairs prizes are awarded for the best animals and produce.

fairground An outdoor place where fairs are held. **fair•ground** (fâr′ground′) *noun, plural* **fairgrounds.**

fairly 1. In a fair manner; honestly; justly: *Distribute the toys fairly, one to each child.* 2. Somewhat; rather: *a fairly large amount.* **fair•ly** (fâr′lē) *adverb.*

fairy A tiny being in stories who is supposed to have magic powers. **fair•y** (fâr′ē) *noun, plural* **fairies.**

faith 1. Belief or trust without proof: *I have faith in your honesty.* 2. A religion: *There are people of many faiths in our city.* **faith** (fāth) *noun, plural* **faiths.**

faithful 1. Loyal and devoted: *faithful friends.* 2. Accurate; true: *a faithful copy of a drawing.* **faith•ful** (fāth′fəl) *adjective;* **faith•ful•ly** *adverb.* —**faithfulness** *noun.*

fake A person or thing that is not what it seems or claims to be: *That is not a real fireplace; it's a fake. Noun.* ∘ 1. To take on the appearance of; pretend: *I faked illness to stay home from school.* 2. To make something seem true or real in order to fool: *The banker stole the money and faked the records so that no one would know. Verb.* ∘ Not real or genuine; false: *a fake mustache. Adjective.* **fake** (fāk) *noun, plural* **fakes;** *verb,* **faked, faking;** *adjective.*

Sometimes falcons are trained to hunt birds and small animals.

falcon A bird with pointed wings and a long tail. Falcons are powerful flyers and can catch other birds in the air with their feet. **fal•con** (fôl′kən *or* fal′kən) *noun, plural* **falcons.**

fall 1. To come down from a higher place; drop: *The leaves have fallen.* 2. To become lower or less: *Their voices fell to a whisper.* 3. To take place; happen: *Night fell quickly.* 4. To pass into a particular condition; become: *They fell in love.* 5. To be defeated, captured, or overthrown: *The city fell to the invaders.* 6. To hang down: *The dress fell from the shoulders in soft folds. Verb.* ∘ 1. A coming down from a higher place: *a fall from a ladder.* 2. The amount of something that comes down: *a 6-inch fall of rain.* 3. A loss of power; capture or defeat: *The country was in confusion after the fall of the government.* 4. A lowering or lessening: *a fall in prices.* 5. The season between summer and winter; autumn. 6. **falls.** A fall of water from a higher place; waterfall. *Noun.*
- **to fall back.** To retreat; withdraw: *The army fell back to a safer position.*
- **to fall back on.** To rely on for help; resort to: *It's good to have friends to fall back on in an emergency.*
- **to fall behind.** To not keep up: *I fell behind in my math.*
- **to fall through.** To fail: *Their plans fell through.*

fall (fôl) *verb,* **fell, fallen, falling;** *noun, plural* **falls.**

fallen Past participle of **fall.** *Verb.* ∘ 1. Having come down from a higher place; dropped: *fallen snow.* 2. Having died in battle: *fallen soldiers. Adjective.* **fall•en** (fôl′ən) *verb; adjective.*

fallout Radioactive particles that fall to the earth as dust after a nuclear bomb explodes. **fall•out** (fôl′out′) *noun.*

false 1. Not true or correct; wrong: *a false answer.* 2. Not real; artificial: *a false beard.* 3. Not faithful: *Our false friends let us down.* 4. Used or intended to deceive: *The magician's trunk has a false bottom.* **false** (fôls) *adjective,* **falser, falsest;** **false•ly** *adverb.*

falsehood An untrue statement; a lie. **false•hood** (fôls′hùd′) *noun, plural* **falsehoods.**

falter 1. To act or move in an unsteady or hesitating way: *The baby faltered while trying to take a step.* 2. To pause while speaking because of being unsure or confused; hesitate. **fal•ter** (fôl′tər) *verb,* **faltered, faltering.**

PRONUNCIATION KEY:

| at | āpe | fär | câre | end | mē | it | īce | pierce | hot | ōld | sông | fôrk |
| oil | out | up | ūse | rüle | pùll | tûrn | chin | sing | shop | thin | this | |

hw in white; zh in treasure. The symbol ə stands for the unstressed vowel sound in about, taken, pencil, lemon, and circus.

265

fame The quality of being famous or well-known: *The tennis player's fame spread across the country.* **fame** (fām) *noun*.

familiar 1. Often heard or seen: *Cows are a familiar sight on a farm.* 2. Known because of having been heard or seen before: *The announcer's voice was familiar.* 3. Knowing something well: *A good mechanic is familiar with all sorts of tools.* 4. Friendly or informal; close: *I'm on familiar terms with our new neighbors.* **fa·mil·iar** (fə mil′yər) *adjective.* —**familiarly** *adverb.*

WORD HISTORY

The word **familiar** goes back to a Latin word meaning "household." People in a household are people with whom you are familiar.

---

family 1. A group of people who are related and who live together, including parents, children, and sometimes other relatives. 2. The children of a father and mother: *My parents raised a large family.* 3. A group of people related to each other; relatives: *The whole family will get together for the holidays.* 4. A group of related animals or plants: *Zebras and donkeys belong to the horse family.* 5. Any group of things that are similar or connected to each other in some way: *English and German belong to the same language family.* **fam·i·ly** (fam′ə lē *or* fam′lē) *noun*, *plural* **families**.

For many people activities with their family are the most fun.

family room A room in a house used for activities by the whole family.

famine A great lack of food in an area or country: *Many people died of starvation during the famine*

in Ireland in the 1840s. **fam·ine** (fam′in) *noun*, *plural* **famines**.

famous Very well-known; having great fame: *A crowd of fans gathered around the famous baseball player to ask for his autograph.* **famous** (fā′məs) *adjective*.

fan¹ 1. A device held in the hand and waved back and forth to make air move. 2. A mechanical device having several blades turned by an electric motor. Fans are used to make air move for cooling or heating. 3. Anything that looks like a fan. The open tail of the peacock is called a fan. *Noun*.
○ To move air toward or on: *Fan yourself with a newspaper to keep cool.* *Verb*.
fan (fan) *noun*, *plural* **fans**; *verb*, **fanned**, **fanning**.

These fans are an important part of the dance that is being performed.

fan² A person who is very interested in or enthusiastic about something: *Some football fans watch games on television all weekend.* **fan** (fan) *noun*, *plural* **fans**.

fanatic A person much too devoted to a cause or too enthusiastic about something. *Noun*.
○ Much too devoted or enthusiastic: *Fanatic chess players.* *Adjective*.
fa·nat·ic (fə natik) *noun*, *plural* **fanatics**; *adjective*. —**fanatically** *adverb*.

fancy 1. The picturing of things in the mind; imagination: *A unicorn is a creature of fancy.* 2. Something imagined in a playful or wishful way: *Being a movie star was his fancy.* 3. A liking or fondness: *You have a fancy for big words.* *Noun*.
○ Very decorated: *a fancy dress.* *Adjective*.
○ 1. To imagine in a playful or wishful way: *I like to fancy myself as a famous pianist.*

2. To be fond of; like: *Which of these books do you fancy? Verb.*
fan·cy (fan′sē) *noun, plural* **fancies;** *adjective,* **fancier, fanciest;** *verb,* **fancied, fancying.**

fang A long, pointed tooth. **fang** (fang) *noun, plural* **fangs.**

fantastic **1.** Very strange; odd: *driftwood with fantastic shapes.* **2.** Very good; excellent: *a fantastic view from the hilltop.* **fan·tas·tic** (fan tas′tik) *adjective.* —**fantastically** *adverb.*

fantasy **1.** Playful or wishful imagination: *Your claim that you can fly is pure fantasy.* **2.** A story with characters, places, or events that are very strange: *I wrote fantasies about life on other planets.* **fan·ta·sy** (fan′tə sē) *noun, plural* **fantasies.**

far **1.** At a long way: *We're far from home.*
2. To or at a certain place, time, or distance: *The meeting lasted far into the afternoon.*
3. Very much: *It would be far better if you stayed until the rain stops. Adverb.*
○ **1.** Distant: *Polar bears live in the far north.*
2. More distant; farther away: *the far side of the moon. Adjective.*
• **as far as.** To the distance, degree, or extent that: *As far as I know, no one has run a mile in less than 3 minutes.*
• **so far. 1.** Until now: *So far it's been a nice day.* **2.** To a certain point: *The road only goes so far into the park; then it becomes a trail.*
far (fär) *adverb,* **farther** or **further, farthest** or **furthest;** *adjective.*

faraway **1.** A long way away; remote: *faraway places.* **2.** Showing deep thought; dreamy: *There is a faraway look in the eyes of that quiet child.* **far·a·way** (fär′ə wā′) *adjective.*

fare **1.** The cost of a ride on a bus, train, airplane, ship, or taxi. **2.** A passenger who pays a fare: *The cab driver had five fares during the morning. Noun.*
○ To get along: *Are you faring well at your new school? Verb.*
Another word that sounds like this is **fair.**
fare (fâr) *noun, plural* **fares;** *verb,* **fared, faring.**

farewell Good-bye and good luck: *"Farewell!" said the passengers as the ship pulled away. The guests said their farewells and left.* **fare·well** (fâr′wel′) *interjection; noun, plural* **farewells.**

farm **1.** A piece of land used to raise crops or animals. **2.** An enclosed area of water in which fish or shellfish are raised. *Noun.*
○ **1.** To raise crops or animals on a farm: *We farm for a living.* **2.** To cultivate: *The settlers had to remove trees and rocks before they could farm the land. Verb.*
farm (färm) *noun, plural* **farms;** *verb,* **farmed, farming.**

The main crop raised on this farm is flowers.

farmer A person who owns or works on a farm. **farmer** (färmər) *noun, plural* **farmers.**

farming The business of raising crops or animals on a farm; agriculture. **farm·ing** (fär′ming) *noun.*

farsighted **1.** Able to see things that are far away better than things that are close. Many farsighted people wear glasses for reading but not for driving. **2.** Able to guess the future and plan for it: *They were farsighted to save their money for the future.* **far·sight·ed** (fär′sī′tid) *adjective.* —**farsightedness** *noun.*

farther A comparative of **far:** *The little boat drifted farther from the dock. The farther mountain seems smaller than the nearer one.* **far·ther** (fä′rthər) *adverb; adjective.*

LANGUAGE NOTE

Farther **and** further **can sometimes be confused. Use farther when you are speaking about distances. We live farther from town than you do. Use further when you mean "additional" or "additionally." There are two further points that I want to make.**

PRONUNCIATION KEY:

| at | āpe | fär | câre | end | mē | it | īce | pierce | hot | ōld | sông | fôrk |
| oil | out | up | ūse | rüle | pull | tûrn | chin | sing | shop | thin | this | |

hw in white; zh in treasure. The symbol ə stands for the unstressed vowel sound in about, taken, pencil, lemon, and circus.

267

farthest A superlative of far: *I sat farthest from the front of the room. He lives farthest from school.* **far•thest** (fär′thist) *adverb; adjective.*

fascinate To attract and hold the interest of; charm: *The magician's tricks fascinated the children in the audience.* **fas•ci•nate** (fasənāt) *verb,* **fascinated, fascinating.** —**fascination** *noun.*

The small animals have fascinated these children.

fashion 1. The current custom or style in dress or behavior: *It's the fashion to carry books in backpacks.* 2. Manner or way: *During the fire, residents left the building in an orderly fashion. Noun.*
○ To give form to; make; shape: *I fashioned a boat out of a block of wood. Verb.*
fash•ion (fash′ən) *noun, plural* **fashions;** *verb,* **fashioned, fashioning.**

fast¹ 1. Acting, moving, or done in a short time; quick; rapid: *a fast train.* 2. Ahead of the correct time: *My watch is fast.* 3. Faithful; loyal: *fast friends.* 4. Firmly attached; secure: *Get a fast grip on the ladder.* 5. Not easily faded: *Are the colors in this material fast? Adjective.*
○ 1. In a firm way; tightly; securely: *The tent was held fast by stakes.* 2. Soundly; deeply: *fast asleep.* 3. With speed; quickly: *The horse ran fast. Adverb.*
fast (fast) *adjective; adverb,* **faster, fastest.**

fast² To eat little or no food, or only certain kinds of food: *In many religions, people fast on certain days. Verb.*
○ A day or time of fasting. *Noun.*
fast (fast) *verb,* **fasted, fasting;** *noun, plural* **fasts.**

fasten 1. To attach firmly: *Mother fastened the gold pin to her dress.* 2. To close so that it will not come loose or open; secure: *Please fasten the door.* 3. To direct steadily; fix: *He fastened his attention on the book.* **fas•ten** (fas′ən) *verb,* **fastened, fastening.**

fastener A device used to hold things together. A snap, buckle, zipper, and paper clip are all fasteners. **fastener** (fasənər) *noun, plural* **fasteners.**

fast food A food that can be cooked easily and quickly, without much preparation, and then sold to customers.

fat A yellowish or whitish oily substance. Fat is found in certain body tissues of animals and in some plants. *Noun.*
○ 1. Having a lot of fat or flesh on the body. 2. Having a lot in it; full: *a fat book. Adjective.*
fat (fat) *noun, plural* **fats;** *adjective,* **fatter, fattest.**

fatal 1. Causing death: *a fatal accident.* 2. Causing great harm; very bad: *Risking your money in investments could be a fatal mistake.* **fa•tal** (fā′təl) *adjective.* —**fatally** *adverb.*

fate 1. The power believed to control what is going to happen or how things will turn out: *Some gamblers think fate is on their side and will make them win.* 2. What finally happens to someone or something; final outcome: *It was my fate to be last in line.* **fate** (fāt) *noun, plural* **fates.**

father 1. A male parent. 2. A man important in beginning or inventing something: *George Washington is called the father of his country.* 3. A priest. **fa•ther** (fä′thər) *noun, plural* **fathers.**

father-in-law The father of one's husband or wife. **fa•ther-in-law** (fä′thər in lô′) *noun, plural* **fathers-in-law.**

fathom A measure of length equal to 6 feet, used mainly in measuring the depth of the ocean. *Noun.*
○ To get to the bottom of and understand: *I could never fathom algebra.*
fath•om (fath′əm) *noun, plural* **fathoms** or **fathom;** *verb,* **fathomed, fathoming.**

fatigue The condition of being tired: *After nine hours on the road, the truck driver was suffering from fatigue. Noun.*
○ To cause to be tired: *The long hours of studying fatigued me. Verb.*

fa·tigue (fə tēg′) *noun; verb,* **fatigued, fatiguing.**

fatten To make or become fat: *The farmer fattened the turkeys for Thanksgiving. Our pigs fattened on grain and scraps.* **fat·ten** (fat′ən) *verb,* **fattened, fattening.**

faucet A device for turning on or off the flow of water or another liquid from a pipe, sink, or container. **fau·cet** (fô′sit) *noun, plural* **faucets.**

fault **1.** Something that is wrong with and spoils something else: *The roof fell in because of a fault in the beams. A bad temper is a serious fault in a person.* **2.** The responsibility for a mistake: *It was my fault that I was late to class.* **3.** A mistake; error: *The teacher corrected the spelling faults on the student's paper.*
• **to find fault with.** To criticize: *Why did you find fault with my ideas for the party?*
fault (fôlt) *noun, plural* **faults.**

favor **1.** An act of kindness: *I did them a favor by giving them a ride to school.* **2.** Friendliness or approval; liking: *The candidate won the favor of the voters.* **3.** A small gift: *party favors. Noun.*
○ **1.** To show kindness or favor to; oblige: *Please favor us with an answer to our letter.* **2.** To approve of; believe in; support: *The candidate favored the law.* **3.** To show special treatment or kindness: *The mother cat favored the sick kitten over the others.* **4.** To look like; resemble: *The baby favors his father. Verb.*
• **in favor of.** **1.** Approving of; supporting: *Everyone was in favor of the trip.* **2.** To the advantage of: *The score is three to one in favor of the home team.*
fa·vor (fā′vər) *noun, plural* **favors;** *verb,* **favored, favoring.**

favorable **1.** Showing approval or liking; approving: *I hope you will give me a favorable answer and come to the party.* **2.** In one's favor; benefiting: *favorable weather for a picnic.* **fa·vor·a·ble** (fā′vər ə bəl) *adjective.* —**favorably** *adverb.*

favorite Liked best: *Summer is my favorite time of year. Adjective.*
○ A person or thing liked best: *Mystery stories are my favorites. Noun.*
fa·vor·ite (fā′vər it) *adjective; noun, plural* **favorites.**

The resourceful young woman is feeding three fawns at the same time.

fawn A young deer. **fawn** (fôn) *noun, plural* **fawns.**

fax A copy of a letter, picture, or document sent electronically by machine over telephone lines. *Noun.*
○ To send such a copy. *Verb.*
fax (faks) *noun, plural* **faxes;** *verb,* **faxed, faxing.**

fear A strong feeling caused by knowing that danger, pain, or evil is near: *a fear of falling. Noun.*
○ **1.** To be afraid of: *The baby fears the dark.* **2.** To be worried or anxious: *I fear it's too late to see a movie. Verb.*
fear (fîr) *noun, plural* **fears;** *verb,* **feared, fearing.**

fearful **1.** Feeling or showing fear; afraid: *The cat was fearful of the dog.* **2.** Causing fear; frightening: *The lightning was fearful.* **fear·ful** (fîr′fəl) *adjective.* —**fearfully** *adverb.*

fearless Feeling or showing no fear; brave. **fear·less** (fîr′lis) *adjective.* —**fearlessly** *adverb* —**fearlessness** *noun.*

feast A large, rich meal on a special occasion. *Noun.*
○ To have a feast; eat richly. *We feasted on turkey and stuffing on Thanksgiving. Verb.*
feast (fēst) *noun, plural* **feasts;** *verb,* **feasted, feasting.**

PRONUNCIATION KEY:
at   ā pe   fär   câre   end   mē   it   īce   pierce   hot   ōld   sông   fôrk
oil   out   up   ūse   rüle   pùll   tûrn   chin   sing   shop   thin   this
hw in white; zh in treasure. The symbol ə stands for the unstressed vowel sound in about, taken, pencil, lemon, and circus.

269

feat An act or deed that shows great courage, strength, or skill: *Climbing that mountain was quite a feat.*
Another word that sounds like this is **feet**.
feat (fēt) *noun, plural* **feats**.

feather One of the light, soft body parts that cover a bird's skin. Feathers protect the bird's skin from injury, help keep the bird warm, and help it to fly. *Noun.*
○ To supply, line, or cover with feathers: *The birds feathered the inside of their nest. Verb.*
feath·er (feth′ər) *noun, plural* **feathers**; *verb,* **feathered**, **feathering**.

This costume contains **feathers** from many different kinds of birds.

feature 1. A part or quality of something: *An important feature of the camel is its ability to go for days without water.* 2. A part of the face: *The eyes, nose, mouth, and chin are features.* 3. A motion picture of standard length. 4. A story of special interest in a newspaper or magazine. *Noun.*
○ To have as a main attraction: *The concert features a pianist. Verb.*
fea·ture (fē′chər) *noun, plural* **features**; *verb,* **featured, featuring.**

Feb. An abbreviation for **February**.

February The second month of the year. February has twenty-eight days except in a leap year, when it has twenty-nine. **February** (feb′rü er′ē or feb′ū er′ē) *noun, plural* **Februaries**.

> ### WORD HISTORY
>
> **The word February comes from the Latin name of a religious holiday that the ancient Romans used to hold in the middle of this month.**

fed Past tense and past participle of **feed**.
• **fed up.** Annoyed, bored, or disgusted: *After waiting an hour, we got fed up and left.*
fed (fed) *verb.*

federal 1. Formed by an agreement between states or provinces to join together as one nation:

The United States has a federal government.
2. Having to do with the central government of the United States, thought of as separate from the government of each state: *The power to provide for defense is a federal power.* **fed·er·al** (fed′ər əl) *adjective.*—**federally** *adverb.*

federation A union formed by agreement between states, nations, or other groups. **fed·er·a·tion** (fed′ə rā′shən) *noun, plural* **federations.**

fee Money requested or paid for some service or right: *a fee of ten dollars for a dog license.* **fee** (fē) *noun, plural* **fees.**

feeble Not strong; weak. **fee·ble** (fē′bəl) *adjective,* **feebler, feeblest.** —**feebleness** *noun* —**feebly** *adverb.*

feed 1. To give food to: *May I feed the baby?* 2. To give as food: *We fed oats to the horse.* 3. To supply with something: *Melting snow from the mountains feeds the rivers.* 4. To take in food; eat: *Frogs feed on flies. Verb.*
○ Food for farm animals. *Noun.*
feed (fēd) *verb,* **fed, feeding;** *noun, plural* **feeds.**

feel 1. To find out about by touching or handling; touch: *The doctor felt my pulse.* 2. To be aware of by touch: *Can you feel the rain on your face?* 3. To seem to be: *The water feels warm.* 4. To be: *I felt happy.* 5. To think: *I feel I haven't done my share.* 6. To find by touching: *We felt our way in the dark. Verb.*
○ The way that something seems to the touch: *the feel of silk. Noun.*
• **to feel like.** To have an interest in or desire for: *Do you feel like going to a museum today?*
feel (fēl) *verb,* **felt, feeling;** *noun, plural* **feels.**

feeler A part of an animal's body used for touching things. Many insects have feelers on their heads. **feel·er** (fē′lər) *noun, plural* **feelers.**

feeling 1. The ability to feel by touching; sense of touch: *Rub your cold hands to bring back the feeling.* 2. The condition of being aware; awareness; sensation: *I had a feeling of hunger long before noon.* 3. An emotion. Joy, fear, and anger are feelings. 4. **feelings.** The tender or sensitive part of a person's nature: *Some people's feelings are hurt when you don't say hello to them.*
5. An opinion; belief: *It is my feeling that you are right.* **feel·ing** (fē′ling) *noun, plural* **feelings.**

feet More than one foot.

Another word that sounds like this is **feat**. **feet** (fēt) *plural noun*.

feign To put on a false show of; pretend: *Opossums feign death to escape their enemies.* **feign** (fān) *verb*, **feigned**, **feigning**.

feint A blow or movement meant to trick or take away attention from the real or main point of attack. *Noun.*
○ To make a feint: *The boxer feinted with the left hand and then punched with the right. Verb.* Another word that sounds like this is **faint**. **feint** (fānt) *noun, plural* **feints**; *verb*, **feinted**, **feinting**.

fell¹ Past tense of **fall**: *I fell on the ice.* **fell** (fel) *verb*.

fell² 1. To hit and knock down: *One of the boxers felled the other.* 2. To cut down: *The lumberjack felled the tree.* **fell** (fel) *verb*, **felled**, **felling**.

fellow 1. A man or boy; guy: *a good fellow.* 2. A person who is like another; companion; associate: *Scientists like to talk with their fellows at professional meetings. Noun.*
○ Belonging to the same group or kind: *my fellow workers. Adjective.*
fel·low (fel′ō) *noun, plural* **fellows**; *adjective.*

fellowship 1. A warm, friendly feeling among people. 2. A group of people with common interests or goals. **fel·low·ship** (fel′ō ship′) *noun, plural* **fellowships**.

felt¹ Past tense and past participle of **feel**. **felt** (felt) *verb*.

felt² A material made of wool, hair, or fur pressed together in layers instead of being woven or knitted. **felt** (felt) *noun, plural* **felts**.

female 1. Of or having to do with the sex that gives birth to young or produces eggs: *A mare is a female horse.* 2. Having to do with women or girls; feminine. *Adjective.*
○ A female person or animal: *Our dog is a female. Noun.*
fe·male (fē′māl) *adjective; noun, plural* **females**.

feminine Of or having to do with women or girls: *"Mary" is a feminine name.* **fem·i·nine** (fem′ənin) *adjective.*

fence 1. A structure used to surround, protect, or mark off an area. 2. A person who buys and sells stolen goods. *Noun.*
○ 1. To put a fence around: *We fenced our*

vegetable garden to keep rabbits out. 2. To fight with a sword or a foil; take part in the sport of fencing. 3. To buy and sell stolen goods. *Verb.*
fence (fens) *noun, plural* **fences**; *verb*, **fenced**, **fencing**.

This type of structure is called a split-rail fence.

fencing The art or sport of fighting with a sword or a foil. **fenc·ing** (fen′sing) *noun.*

fender 1. A metal piece over the wheel of an automobile or bicycle for protection against splashed water or mud. 2. A metal screen in front of a fireplace to protect against sparks. **fen·der** (fen′dər) *noun, plural* **fenders**.

ferment To undergo or cause a chemical change that makes gas bubbles: *When grape juice ferments, it turns into wine. Verb.*
○ 1. Something that causes a substance to ferment: *Yeast is used as a ferment in making wine.*
2. A state of excitement and activity: *The school was in a ferment over who would be the new principal. Noun.*
fer·ment (fər ment′ *for verb;* fûr′ment *for noun*) *verb*, **fermented**, **fermenting**; *noun, plural* **ferments**.

fern A plant with big leaves called fronds and no flowers. **fern** (fûrn) *noun, plural* **ferns**.

A fern **reproduces by means of spores instead of seeds.**

PRONUNCIATION KEY:
at āpe fär câre end mē it īce pierce hot ōld sông fôrk
oil out up ūse rüle pull tûrn chin sing shop thin this
hw in white; zh in treasure. The symbol ə stands for the unstressed vowel sound in about, taken, pencil, lemon, and circus.

271

ferocious Savage; fierce: *A lion can be ferocious.* **fe·ro·cious** (fə rō′shəs) *adjective.* —**ferociously** *adverb.*

ferret A long, thin animal related to the weasel and sometimes trained to hunt rats, mice, and rabbits. *Noun.*
○ **1.** To hunt with ferrets. **2.** To look for; search: *I ferreted through my drawers looking for the missing sock. Verb.*
fer·ret (fer′it) *noun, plural* **ferrets**; *verb,* **ferreted, ferreting.**

Ferris wheel A big upright revolving wheel with seats hung from the rim. **Fer·ris wheel** (fer′is).

A **Ferris wheel** is usually found at amusement parks and fairs.

ferry A boat used to carry people, cars, and goods across a narrow body of water. *Noun.*
○ To go or carry in a ferry: *We ferried to the island. Verb.*
fer·ry (fer′ē) *noun, plural* **ferries**; *verb,* **ferried, ferrying.**

fertile **1.** Able to produce crops and plants easily and plentifully: *fertile soil.* **2.** Able to produce eggs, seeds, pollen, or young: *An animal is fertile when it can give birth to young.* **3.** Able to develop into or become a new person or animal: *An egg must be fertile for a chick to hatch from it.* **4.** Thinking up a lot of good ideas; creative: *a fertile imagination.* **fer·tile** (fûr′təl) *adjective.*

fertilize **1.** To make fertile. **2.** To put fertilizer on: *We fertilized the field with manure.* **fer·ti·lize** (fûr′tə līz′) *verb,* **fertilized, fertilizing.**

fertilizer A substance added to soil to make it better for the growing of crops. Manure and certain chemicals are used as fertilizers. **fer·ti·liz·er** (fûr′tə lī′zər) *noun, plural* **fertilizers.**

festival **1.** A celebration or holiday: *a religious festival.* **2.** A program of special activities or shows: *a film festival.* **fes·ti·val** (fes′tə vəl) *noun, plural* **festivals.**

festivity **1.** Rejoicing and fun: *The party was full of festivity.* **2.** festivities. Activities that are part of a celebration: *Parades were among the festivities for the town's hundredth anniversary.* **fes·tiv·i·ty** (fes tiv′i tē) *noun, plural* **festivities.**

Dancing is a common feature of a festival.

fetch To go after and bring back; get: *Please fetch two more chairs from the other room.* **fetch** (fech) *verb,* **fetched, fetching.**

feud A bitter quarrel that lasts for a long time. *Noun.*
○ To take part in such a quarrel. *Verb.*
feud (fūd) *noun, plural* **feuds**; *verb* **feuded, feuding.**

feudalism A political and economic system in western Europe during the Middle Ages. Under feudalism, a lord provided land and protection for people under his rule, who were known as vassals. In return they gave services and a share of their crops to the lord. **feu·dal·ism** (fū′də liz′əm) *noun.*

fever A body temperature higher than normal. Most people have a fever if their temperature is more than 98.6 degrees Fahrenheit. A fever usually means that a person is fighting an infection. **fe·ver** (fē′vər) *noun, plural* **fevers.**

few Not many: *Few people live to be 100. Adjective.*
○ A small number of persons or things: *Only a few of the papers had been sold. Noun.*
few (fū) *adjective,* **fewer, fewest**; *noun.*

fiancé A man to whom a woman is engaged to be married. **fi·an·cé** (fē′än sā′) *noun, plural* **fiancés.**

fiancée A woman to whom a man is engaged to be married. **fi·an·cée** (fē′än sā′) *noun, plural* **fiancées.**

fib A lie about something unimportant: *I told a fib about the size of the fish that I had caught. Noun.*
○ To tell such a lie: *Why did you fib about your age? Verb.*
fib (fib) *noun, plural* **fibs**; *verb,* **fibbed, fibbing.**

fiber **1.** A long, thin piece of flexible material: *a rope made of hemp fibers.* **2.** Material in a plant that cannot be digested by the body; roughage. Fiber helps move food through the intestines. Bran, fruit, vegetables, and whole-wheat bread have a lot of fiber. **fi·ber** (fī′bər) *noun, plural* **fibers.**

fiberglass A strong material made of fine threads of glass. Fiberglass does not burn easily. It is used for insulation, in textiles, and in the making of boats and automobiles. **fi·ber·glass** (fī′bər glas′) *noun.*

fiction **1.** Written works that tell a story or stories about characters and events that are not real. Novels and short stories are fiction. **2.** Something imaginary or not true: *The monster turned out to be a fiction.* **fic·tion** (fik′shən) *noun, plural* **fictions; fic·tion·al** *adjective.*

fiddle A violin. *Noun.*
○ **1.** To play a violin. **2.** To make aimless movements with the hands: *I fiddled nervously with my pencil. Verb.*
fid·dle (fid′əl) *noun, plural* **fiddles;** *verb,* **fiddled, fiddling.**

Sometimes fiddling on a fiddle is pure fun.

field **1.** A piece of open or cleared land: *a wheat field.* **2.** Land that contains or gives a natural resource: *an oil field.* **3.** An area of land on which a game is played: *a football field.* **4.** An area of interest or activity: *the field of medicine. Noun.*
○ To catch, stop, or pick up a ball that has been hit in baseball: *The shortstop fielded the ball and threw to first. Verb.*
field (fēld) *noun, plural* **fields;** *verb,* **fielded, fielding.**

fielder A baseball player who has a position in the outfield while the other team is at bat. **field·er** (fēl′dər) *noun, plural* **fielders.**

field glasses A pair of binoculars.

field trip A trip away from the classroom to see things and learn: *Classes take field trips to museums, parks, and other places.*

fierce **1.** Likely to make violent attacks; dangerous; savage: *Bears are shy animals, but they can be fierce.* **2.** Very strong or violent; raging: *a fierce storm.* **fierce** (fîrs) *adjective,* **fiercer, fiercest. —fiercely** *adverb* **—fierceness** *noun.*

fiery **1.** Having to do with fire or like fire: *a fiery furnace.* **2.** Very excitable; emotional: *a fiery temper.* **fier·y** (fir′ē *or* fī′ə rē) *adjective.*

fiesta A festival or celebration. **fi·es·ta** (fē es′tə) *noun, plural* **fiestas.**

fife A musical instrument like a flute. The fife makes a high, clear sound and is often used with drums in a marching band. **fife** (fīf) *noun, plural* **fifes.**

fifteen Five more than ten; 15. **fif·teen** (fif′tēn′) *noun, plural* **fifteens;** *adjective.*

fifteenth Next after the fourteenth. *Adjective, noun.*
○ One of fifteen equal parts; 1/15. *Noun.*
fif·teenth (fif′tēnth′) *adjective; noun, plural* **fifteenths.**

fifth Next after the fourth. *Adjective, noun.*
○ One of five equal parts; 1/5. *Noun.*
fifth (fifth) *adjective; noun, plural* **fifths.**

fiftieth Next after the forty-ninth. *Adjective, noun.*
○ One of fifty equal parts; 1/50. *Noun.*
fif·ti·eth (fif′tē ith) *adjective; noun, plural* **fiftieths.**

fifty Five times ten; 50. **fif·ty** (fif′tē) *noun, plural* **fifties;** *adjective.*

fig The sweet fruit of a shrub or small tree that grows in warm regions. Figs have many tiny seeds, and are often preserved by drying. **fig** (fig) *noun, plural* **figs.**

fight **1.** A struggle between animals, persons, or groups who use weapons or their bodies against each other. In a fight, each side tries to hurt the other or to protect itself against the other: *The two dogs had a fight over the bone.* **2.** A quarrel: *Let's not have a fight over which program to watch.* **3.** A hard effort to gain a goal; struggle: *the fight against cancer. Noun.*

PRONUNCIATION KEY:

| at | āpe | fär | câre | end | mē | it | īce | pierce | hot | ōld | sông | fôrk |
| oil | out | up | ūse | rüle | pull | tûrn | chin | sing | shop | thin | this | |

hw in white; zh in treasure. The symbol ə stands for the unstressed vowel sound in about, taken, pencil, lemon, and circus.

273

○ **1.** To use weapons or the body to try to hurt or overcome: *Soldiers **fight** in wars.* **2.** To struggle against; try to gain power over: ***fought** the blaze for hours.* **3.** To carry on a battle, contest, or struggle: *I had to **fight** the urge to laugh. Verb.* **fight** (fīt) *noun, plural* **fights**; *verb,* **fought**, **fighting.**

fighter **1.** A person who fights. **2.** A person who boxes; boxer. **fight•er** (fī′tər) *noun, plural* **fighters.**

figure **1.** A symbol that stands for a number. 0, 1, 2, 3, 4, and 5 are figures. **2.** An amount given in figures: *The population **figures** of the cities and towns are on the back of the map.* **3. figures.** Arithmetic: *You're good at **figures.*** **4.** A form or outline; shape: *a slim **figure.*** **5.** A person; character: *The mayor is a public **figure.*** **6.** A design; pattern: *a cloth with red **figures** on it. Noun.*
○ **1.** To find out by using numbers; calculate: *We **figured** the cost of the trip.* **2.** To stand out; have importance; appear: *Well-known people **figured** in the news today. Verb.*

• **to figure out.** To learn, understand, or solve: *I couldn't **figure out** how the magician did those tricks.*

fig•ure (fig′yər) *noun, plural* **figures**; *verb,* **figured, figuring.**

figurehead **1.** A carved wooden figure placed on the bow of a ship for decoration: *The **figurehead** was carved in the shape of a bird.* **2.** A person with a title that sounds important but with no real power or responsibility: *The queen is only a **figurehead.*** **fig•ure•head** (fig′yər hed′) *noun, plural* **figureheads.**

figure of speech An expression in which words are used differently from their true or main meanings. Figures of speech are used to make writing or speaking fresher and more expressive. "When I saw I was late, I flew out of the house" is a figure of speech.

filament A very fine thread or wire. In an electric light bulb, the filament is a fine wire that gives off light when an electric current passes through it. **fil•a•ment** (fil′ə mənt) *noun, plural* **filaments.**

file¹ **1.** A folder, drawer, or cabinet in which papers, cards, or records are arranged in order. **2.** A set of papers, cards, or records arranged in order: *a **file** of addresses.* **3.** A collection of information, program instructions, or words stored on a computer disk: *Each **file** has a name that identi-*

fies it. **4.** A line of persons, animals, or things placed one behind the other: *We marched in a single **file.** Noun.*
○ **1.** To put away in a set of papers, cards, or records arranged in order: *The secretary **filed** the letters.* **2.** To hand in or put on a record: *The police officer **filed** a report of the accident.* **3.** To march or move in a file: *The passengers **filed** off the airplane. Verb.*

• **on file.** Kept in a file: *The medical records are **on file** in the nurse's office.*

file (fīl) *noun, plural* **files**; *verb,* **filed, filing.**

file² A metal tool having tiny ridges on one or two sides. A file is used to cut, smooth, or grind down hard surfaces. *Noun.*
○ To cut, smooth, or grind with a file: *I **filed** my fingernails. Verb.*
file (fīl) *noun, plural* **files**; *verb,* **filed, filing.**

filename The name given to a computer file when it is saved so that it can be easily found again. **file•name** (fīl′nām′) *noun, plural* **filenames.**

filet A spelling sometimes used for the word fillet. **fi•let** (fi lā′ *or* fil′ā) *noun, plural* **filets**; *verb,* **fileted, fileting.**

filings Small bits of a material that have been removed by a file. A magnet attracts iron filings. **fil•ings** (fī′lingz) *plural noun.*

fill **1.** To make or become full: ***Fill** the bucket with water.* **2.** To take up the whole space of: *The students **filled** the auditorium.* **3.** To give or have whatever is asked for or needed: *The grocery store **filled** our order.* **4.** To stop up or close up by putting something in: *The dentist **filled** a cavity in my tooth.* **5.** To do the duties or job of: *Who will **fill** the office of treasurer? Verb.*
○ Something used to fill: *Gravel was used as **fill** for the hole in the road. Noun.*

• **to fill in.** **1.** To complete by writing something: ***Fill in** all the blanks on the test.*
2. To write something missing or needed: ***Fill in** your name in the space on the form.*
3. To act as a substitute: *An assistant **filled in** for our teacher.*

• **to fill up.** To make or become completely full: *The bathtub **filled up** in a few minutes.*

fill (fil) *verb,* **filled, filling**; *noun, plural* **fills.**

fillet *or* **filet** A slice of meat or fish without bones or fat. *Noun.*
○ To cut meat or fish into fillets. *Verb.*

fil·let (fi lā′ or fil′ā) *noun, plural* **fillets;** *verb,* **filleted, filleting.**

filling A substance used to fill something: *We used cherries as a **filling** for the pie. I broke the **filling** in one of my teeth when I bit into the hard candy.* **fill·ing** (fil′ing) *noun, plural* **fillings.**

filly A young female horse. **fil·ly** (filē) *noun, plural* **fillies.**

film 1. A very thin layer or covering: *a **film** of grease.* 2. A thin roll or strip of material coated with a substance that changes when it is exposed to light. It is placed inside a camera and used to take photographs or to make motion pictures. 3. A motion picture. *Noun.*
○ 1. To cover or become covered with a thin layer of something: *The windows were **filmed** with dust.* 2. To take pictures of with a motion-picture camera. *We **filmed** the spacecraft as it took off. Verb.* **film** (film) *noun, plural* **films;** *verb,* **filmed, filming.**

Motion picture film is stored in tight metal containers.

filter A device or material with tiny spaces in it. A liquid or gas is passed through a filter in order to clean out any dirt or other matter: *The **filter** in an air conditioner collects dust. Noun.*
○ 1. To pass a liquid or air through a filter; strain: *The water was **filtered** through sand.* 2. To take out or separate by a filter: *The dirt was **filtered** from the water.* 3. To go through very slowly: *The sunlight **filtered** through the trees. Verb.* **fil·ter** (fil′tər) *noun, plural* **filters;** *verb,* **filtered, filtering.**

filth Disgusting dirt or other material. **filth** (filth) *noun.*

filthy Extremely dirty; foul. *No one wanted to swim in the **filthy** river.* **filthy** (filthē) *adjective,* **filthier, filthiest.**

fin 1. One of the thin, flat parts that stick out from the body of a fish. A fish uses its fins to swim and balance itself in the water. Certain other water animals, such as whales and porpoises, also have fins. 2. Something with the same shape or use as a fin. A rocket may have fins to keep it steady during flight. **fin** (fin) *noun, plural* **fins.**

final 1. Coming at the end; last. 2. Not to be changed: *The decision of the judges is **final**. Adjective.*
○ 1. The last examination of a school or college course of study: *history **finals**.* 2. The last or deciding game or match in a series: *basketball **finals**. Noun.* **fi·nal** (fī′nəl) *adjective; noun, plural* **finals.**

finale The last part of something; conclusion: *The band played a lively march as the **finale** of its concert.* **fi·na·le** (fi nä′lē) *noun, plural* **finales.**

finalist A person who takes part in the final game or other contest in a series of games or contests: *Each of the **finalists** had run 100 meters in less than 15 seconds.* **fi·nal·ist** (fī′inə list) *noun, plural* **finalists.**

finally At the end; at last: *We **finally** got home at midnight.* **fi·nal·ly** (fī′nə lē) *adverb.*

finance 1. The management of money matters for people, businesses, or governments: *A bank president should be an expert in **finance**.* 2. **finances.** The amount of money that a person, business, or government has; funds: *We checked our **finances** to see if we could afford a vacation. Noun.*
○ To provide money for: *Profits from the bake sale **financed** our field trip. Verb.* **fi·nance** (fi′nans or fī nans′) *noun, plural* **finances;** *verb,* **financed, financing.**

financial Having to do with money matters: *Banks, stock exchanges, and insurance companies handle **financial** affairs.* **fi·nan·cial** (fi nan′shəl or fī nan′shəl) *adjective.*

finch A small songbird with a strong bill shaped like a cone. There are a lot of different kinds of finches. **finch** (finch) *noun, plural* **finches.**

find 1. To discover or come upon by accident; happen on: *I **found** a wallet on the sidewalk.*

PRONUNCIATION KEY:

| at | āpe | fär | câre | end | mē | it | īce | pierce | hot | ōld | sông | fôrk |
| oil | out | up | ūse | rüle | pull | tûrn | chin | sing | shop | thin | this | |

hw in white; zh in treasure. The symbol ə stands for the unstressed vowel sound in about, taken, pencil, lemon, and circus.

275

fine ▸ fire

2. To get or learn by thinking or calculating: *Please find the sum of these numbers.* **3.** To learn or discover: *I found that I liked school.* **4.** To look for and get something lost or left: *I finally found my old compass.* **5.** To come to a decision about and declare: *The jury found the defendant guilty. Verb.*

○ Something found: *I came up with some great finds at the sale of old furniture. Noun.*

• **to find out.** To learn: *Find out what time the meeting is.*

find (fīnd) *verb,* **found, finding;** *noun, plural* **finds.**

fine¹ **1.** Very good; excellent: *a fine musician.* **2.** Very small or thin: *a fine thread.* **3.** Without clouds or rain; clear: *fine weather. Adjective.*

○ Very well: *The children are doing fine in school. Adverb.*

fine (fīn) *adjective,* **finer, finest;** *adverb.*

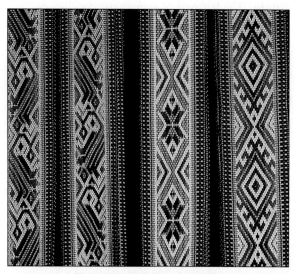

There are many fine details in this woven textile.

fine² An amount of money paid as a punishment for breaking a rule or law. *Noun.*

○ To punish by making pay a fine: *The judge fined the driver for going through a red light. Verb.*

fine (fīn) *noun, plural* **fines;** *verb,* **fined, fining.**

finger **1.** One of the five separate parts at the end of the hand. Usually, a person is said to have four fingers and a thumb. **2.** A part of a glove that covers a finger. *Noun.*

○ To touch, handle, or play with the fingers: *The woman fingered her necklace. Verb.*

fin·ger (fing′gər) *noun, plural* **fingers;** *verb,* **fingered, fingering.**

fingernail A thin, hard layer of material that grows at the end of each finger. **fin·ger·nail** (fing′gər nāl′) *noun, plural* **fingernails.**

fingerprint An impression of the markings on the tip of a finger. Fingerprints help to identify people because no two people have the same fingerprints. *Noun.*

○ To take the fingerprints of: *The police fingerprinted the suspect. Verb.*

fin·ger·print (fing′gər print′) *noun, plural* **fingerprints;** *verb,* **fingerprinted, fingerprinting.**

finish **1.** To bring to an end; come to the end of; complete: *Finish your homework* **2.** To use up completely: *We finished the candy.* **3.** To treat the surface of in some way: *I used varnish to finish the cabinet. Verb.*

○ **1.** The last part of something; end: *the finish of a race.* **2.** The surface of something: *The table has a shiny finish. Noun.*

fin·ish (fin′ish) *verb,* **finished, finishing;** *noun, plural* **finishes.**

Finland A country in northern Europe. **Fin·land** (fin′lənd) *noun.*

Finn A person born in or a citizen of Finland. Another word that sounds like this is **fin.** **Finn** (fin) *noun, plural* **Finns.**

Finnish The language of Finland. *Noun.*

○ Of or having to do with Finland, its people, or its language. *Adjective.* Another word that sounds like this is **finish.** **Fin·nish** (fin′ish) *noun; adjective.*

fiord A spelling sometimes used for *fjord.* Look up fjord for more information. **fiord** (fyôrd) *noun, plural* **fiords.**

fir An evergreen tree related to the pine. Another word that sounds like this is **fur.** **fir** (fûr) *noun, plural* **firs.**

fire **1.** The flame, heat, and light given off when wood, paper, or another material burns. **2.** Something burning: *Add another log to the fire.* **3.** Burning that destroys or causes damage: *The bad wiring in the house started a fire.* **4.** A very strong emotion or spirit; passion: *Her eyes were full of fire.* **5.** The shooting of guns: *the sound of rifle fire. Noun.*

○ **1.** To set on fire; cause to burn: *We fired the heap of leaves.* **2.** To dismiss from a job: *The company fired me.* **3.** To cause to be excited or stirred up: *Stories about pirates fired the* *child's imagination.* **4.** To shoot: *The ship* **fired** *a flare. Verb.*

- **on fire.** Burning.
- **to catch fire.** To begin to burn.
- **under fire. 1.** Being shot at by an enemy: *The soldiers were* **under fire. 2.** Being criticized or blamed: *The politician was* **under fire** *from the press.*

fire (fīr) *noun, plural* **fires**; *verb,* **fired, firing.**

firearm A gun. Rifles and pistols are firearms. **fire·arm** (fīr′ärm′) *noun, plural* **firearms.**

firecracker A paper tube containing gunpowder and a fuse. Firecrackers make a loud noise when they explode. **fire·crack·er** (fīr′krak·ər) *noun, plural* **firecrackers.**

fire department A group set up by a government to prevent and put out fires.

fire engine A truck that carries equipment for fighting and putting out fires.

fire escape A metal stairway on the outside of a building, used for escape in case of fire.

fire extinguisher A device containing water, chemicals, or some other substance that can be sprayed on a fire to put it out. **fire ex·tin·guish·er** (ek sting′gwishər)

firefighter A person whose work is to put out and prevent fires. **fire·fight·er** (fīr′fī′tər) *noun, plural* **firefighters.**

firefly A small beetle that flies at night and gives off short flashes of light from its body; lightning bug. **fire·fly** (fīr′flī′) *noun, plural* **fireflies.**

firehouse A building for firefighters and their trucks and equipment. **fire·house** (fīr′hous′) *noun, plural* **firehouses** (fīr′hou′ziz).

fireman 1. A firefighter. **2.** A person who takes care of the fire in a furnace or steam engine. **fire·man** (fīr′mən) *noun, plural* **firemen** (fīr′mən).

fireplace 1. An opening in a room, with a chimney leading up from it, used for building fires. **2.** An outdoor structure of brick or stone in which fires are built. **fire·place** (fīr′plās′) *noun, plural* **fireplaces.**

fireproof Not able to burn or to burn easily: *Iron is fireproof.* **fire·proof** (fīr′prüf′) *adjective.*

fireside 1. The area around a fireplace; hearth. **2.** Home; family life: *The travelers were happy to be back at their own* **fireside. fire·side** (fīr′sīd′) *noun, plural* **firesides.**

firewood Wood used for a fire. **fire·wood** (fīr′wùd′) **noun.**

---

fire engine

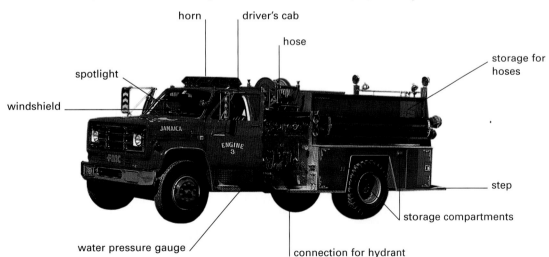

This fire engine is sometimes called a pumper. Its powerful pumps pull water from a fire hydrant or other source and spray it on the fire.

horn · driver's cab · hose · storage for hoses · spotlight · windshield · step · storage compartments · water pressure gauge · connection for hydrant

PRONUNCIATION KEY:
at   āpe   fär   câre   end   mē   it   īce   pîerce   hot   ōld   sông   fôrk
oil   out   up   ūse   rüle   pùll   tûrn   chin   sing   shop   thin   this
hw in white; zh in treasure. The symbol ə stands for the unstressed vowel sound in about, taken, pencil, lemon, and circus.

277

fireworks Firecrackers and other things burned or exploded to make loud noises or brilliant shows of light. **fire·works** (fīr′wûrks′) *plural noun.*

Many Fourth of July celebrations include displays of fireworks.

firm¹ **1.** Not giving in much when pressed; solid: *a firm mattress.* **2.** Not easily moved; secure: *fence posts firm in the ground.* **3.** Not changing; staying the same: *a firm belief that they did the right thing.* **4.** Steady or strong: *a firm voice. Adjective.*
○ So as not to move or change: *The soldiers stood firm. Adverb.*
firm (fûrm) *adjective; adverb,* **firmer, firmest.**

SYNONYMS

firm, hard, solid, sound
Give your friend a good, firm handshake. This mattress is as hard as a rock. The bank's vault is made of solid steel. The house is very old but it's still sound.

---

firm² A company in which two or more people go into business together: *There are five partners in my cousin's law firm.* **firm** (fûrm) *noun, plural* **firms.**

first Before all others: *George Washington was the first president of the United States. Adjective.*
○ **1.** Before all others: *She was called on first in English today.* **2.** For the first time: *He first heard the news yesterday. Adverb.*
○ **1.** A person or thing that is first: *This invention is the first of its kind.* **2.** The beginning: *I liked the new car from the first. Noun.*
first (fûrst) *adjective; adverb; noun, plural* **firsts.**

first aid Help given to a sick or hurt person before a doctor gets there.

first-class **1.** Of the best kind: *a first-class performance.* **2.** Having to do with a class of mail that includes mainly personal letters, packages, and postcards. **3.** Having to do with the best and most expensive seats or rooms on a ship, train, or airplane: *first-class tickets. Adjective.*
○ By first-class mail or transportation: *I sent the package first-class. Adverb.*
first-class (fûrs′tklas′) *adjective; adverb.*

firsthand Direct from the first or original source: *That forest ranger has firsthand knowledge of these woods. I learned about horses firsthand when I worked at a stable.* **first·hand** (fûrst′hand′) *adjective; adverb.*

first-rate Of the highest quality or importance; excellent. **first-rate** (fûrst′rāt′) *adjective.*

fish **1.** A cold-blooded animal that lives in water. Fish have backbones, gills for breathing, and,

---

fish

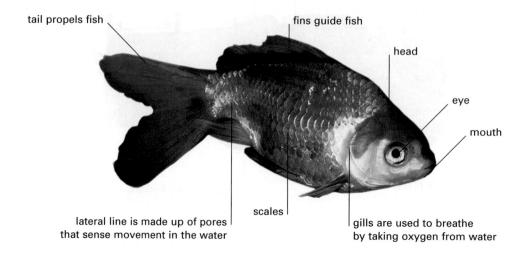

tail propels fish

fins guide fish

head

eye

mouth

lateral line is made up of pores that sense movement in the water

scales

gills are used to breathe by taking oxygen from water

usually, fins and scales. **2.** The flesh of fish used as food. *Noun.*
▫ **1.** To catch or try to catch fish: *We fished for trout.* **2.** To search by groping: *I fished in my pocket for the key. Verb.*
fish (fish) *noun, plural* **fish** *or* **fishes**; *verb,* **fished, fishing.**

fisherman A person who fishes for a living or for sport. **fish·er·man** (fish′ər mən) *noun, plural* **fishermen** (fish′ər mən).

fishery **1.** A place for catching fish. **2.** A place where fish are bred. **fish·er·y** (fish′ə rē) *noun, plural* **fisheries.**

fishhook A hook used for catching fish. **fish·hook** (fish′hük′) *noun, plural* **fishhooks.**

fishing rod A long pole made of wood, metal, or fiberglass. It has a hook, line, and usually a reel attached to it and is used for catching fish.

fishy **1.** Like a fish in odor or taste: *My hands smelled fishy after cleaning the fish.* **2.** Not likely to be true: *a fishy excuse for being late.* **fish·y** (fish′ē) *adjective,* **fishier, fishiest.**

fission The splitting or breaking apart of an atomic nucleus. A lot of energy is released during fission. **fis·sion** (fish′ən) *noun.*

fist A hand that is tightly closed with the fingers folded into the palm. **fist** (fist) *noun, plural* **fists.**

fit¹ **1.** Suitable, right, or proper: *This dirty water is not fit to drink.* **2.** In good health; healthy: *You should exercise to keep fit. Adjective.*
▫ **1.** To be suitable, right, or proper for: *The part of the witch in the play does not fit me.* **2.** To be the right size or shape for: *That coat fits you well.* **3.** To make right, proper, or suitable: *Fit your speech to the audience.* **4.** To supply with what is needed: *The store fitted the campers with supplies for the trip.* **5.** To join, adjust, or put in snugly: *We fitted the pieces of the jigsaw puzzle together. Verb.*
▫ The way in which something fits: *The jacket has a tight fit. Noun.*
fit (fit) *adjective,* **fitter, fittest**; *verb,* **fitted, fitting**; *noun, plural* **fits.**

fit² **1.** A sudden, sharp attack of something: *a fit of coughing.* **2.** A sudden burst: *a fit of anger.* **fit** (fit) *noun, plural* **fits.**

five One more than four; 5. **five** (fīv) *noun, plural* **fives**; *adjective.*

fix **1.** To repair; mend: *I fixed the broken chair.* **2.** To get ready or arrange; prepare: *I'll fix dinner.* **3.** To make firm or secure; fasten tightly: *We fixed the tent pegs in the ground.* **4.** To arrange definitely; settle: *Fix a wedding date.* **5.** To direct or hold steadily: *I fixed my eyes straight ahead.* **6.** To place; put: *The police fixed the responsibility for the accident on the pedestrian.* **7.** To try to get something to come out the way one wants: *They fixed the race. Verb.*
▫ Trouble; difficulty: *I got into quite a fix by promising to go to two parties on the same day. Noun.*
• **to fix up.** **1.** To mend; repair. **2.** To provide with something needed or wanted: *We fixed them up with a place to spend the night.*
fix (fiks) *verb,* **fixed, fixing**; *noun, plural* **fixes.**

fixture Something firmly and permanently fastened into place. A bathtub, a toilet, and a sink are bathroom fixtures. **fix·ture** (fiks′chər) *noun, plural* **fixtures.**

fjord A long, narrow inlet of the sea between high cliffs. This word is sometimes spelled *fiord.* **fjord** (fyôrd) *noun, plural* **fjords.**

FL Postal abbreviation for Florida.

Fla. An abbreviation for Florida.

This flag was used by colonists during the American Revolution.

flag A piece of cloth with different colors and designs on it, used as a symbol of a country or an organization. Flags are also sometimes used for giving signals. *Noun.*
▫ To stop or signal: *I flagged a taxicab. Verb.*
flag (flag) *noun, plural* **flags**; *verb,* **flagged, flagging.**

flagpole A pole used for raising and flying a flag. **flag·pole** (flag′pōl′) *noun, plural* **flagpoles.**

PRONUNCIATION KEY:
at   āpe   fär   câre   end   mē   it   īce   pierce   hot   ōld   sông   fôrk
oil   out   up   ūse   rüle   pùll   tûrn   chin   sing   shop   thin   this
hw in white; zh in treasure. The symbol ə stands for the unstressed vowel sound in about, taken, pencil, lemon, and circus.

279

flail A long wooden staff or handle with a shorter stick swinging on the end, used for threshing grain. *Noun.*
○ **1.** To use such a tool. **2.** To hit with a flail.
flail (flāl) *noun, plural* **flails;** *verb,* **flailed, flailing.**

flair A natural talent: *a flair for acting.*
Another word that sounds like this is **flare.**
flair (flâr) *noun, plural* **flairs.**

flake A small, thin, flat piece: flakes of snow. *Noun.*
○ To chip or peel off in flakes: *Old paint can crack and flake. Verb.*
flake (flāk) *noun, plural* **flakes;** *verb,* **flaked, flaking.**

flame **1.** One of the streams of light given off by a fire. **2.** Gas or vapor burning to give off light or heat. **3.** The condition of burning: *The house burst into flame. Noun.*
○ **1.** To burn with flames; blaze: *The fire flamed for hours.* **2.** To light up or glow: *Their eyes flamed with anger.* **3.** To send a rude or nasty message to someone by e-mail. *Verb.*
flame (flām) *noun, plural* **flames;** *verb,* **flamed, flaming.**

flamingo A pink or red bird with a long, thin neck and legs, and webbed feet. **fla·min·go** (flə ming′gō) *noun, plural* **flamingos** or **flamingoes.**

Flamingos **get their pink color from eating shellfish.**

flammable Able to be set on fire easily: *Gasoline is flammable.* **flam·ma·ble** (flam′ə bəl) *adjective.*

flank **1.** The area between the lower ribs and the hip on either side of the body. **2.** The left or right side of something, especially a military group: *The army protected its flanks. Noun.*
○ **1.** To be at the side of: *Two statues of lions flanked the entrance to the library.* **2.** To attack or move around the side of: *Our troops flanked the enemy. Verb.*
flank (flangk) *noun, plural* **flanks;** *verb,* **flanked, flanking.**

flannel A soft cotton or woolen material. Flannel is used for such things as nightgowns, babies' clothes, and shirts. **flan·nel** (flan′əl) *noun, plural* **flannels.**

flap **1.** To move up and down: *The bird flapped its wings.* **2.** To swing or wave loosely and with noise: *The curtain flapped in the breeze. Verb.*
○ **1.** The motion or the noise made by something when it flaps: *We could hear the flap of the shutters against the house.* **2.** Something attached at only one edge so that its other edge can move freely: *The part of an envelope that is folded down to close the envelope is a flap. Noun.*
flap (flap) *verb,* **flapped, flapping;** *noun, plural* **flaps.**

flapjack A word sometimes used for *pancake.* Look up **pancake** for more information. **flap·jack** (flap′jak′) *noun, plural* **flapjacks.**

flare **1.** To start to burn with a sudden, very bright light: *The match flared and went out.* **2.** To break out with sudden or violent feeling: *The insult caused my temper to flare.* **3.** To open or spread outward: *This skirt flares from the waist. Verb.*
○ **1.** A sudden bright light. A flare usually lasts only a short time. **2.** A fire or burst of light used as a signal or to give light. *Noun.*
Another word that sounds like this is **flair.**
• **to flare up.** To break out or grow more intense: *The infection flared up just as I seemed to be getting better.*
flare (flâr) *verb,* **flared, flaring;** *noun, plural* **flares.**

flash **1.** A sudden, short burst of light or flame: *a flash of lightning.* **2.** A very short period of time; instant: *The fire engines were at the fire in a flash. Noun.*
○ **1.** To burst out in sudden light or fire: *Lightning flashed.* **2.** To be suddenly bright; shine briefly: *Her eyes flashed with anger.* **3.** To come or move suddenly or quickly: *The ambulance flashed by. The answer to the riddle flashed into my mind. Verb.*
flash (flash) *noun, plural* **flashes;** *verb,* **flashed, flashing.**

flashlight An electric light powered by batteries

and small enough to be carried. **flash·light** (flash′līt′) *noun, plural* **flashlights**.

flask A small bottle used to hold a liquid. **flask** (flask) *noun, plural* **flasks**.

American prairie land is extremely flat, making it excellent for farming.

flat 1. Smooth and even; level: *a flat road.* 2. Lying, placed, or stretched at full length; spread out: *The dog lay flat on its back.* 3. Not very deep or thick; shallow: *a flat tray.* 4. Not changing in amount; fixed: *a flat charge for lunch.* 5. Without much interest, energy, or flavor: *a flat performance.* 6. Containing little or no air: *a flat tire.* 7. Lower than the true or intended musical pitch: *I hit a flat note on my trombone. Adjective.*
○ 1. A flat part or surface: *the flat of the hand.* 2. A tire that has little or no air. 3. A musical tone or note that is one half step below its natural pitch. 4. A symbol (♭) that shows this tone or note. *Noun.*
○ 1. In a flat manner: *The fallen tree lay flat on the ground.* 2. Exactly; precisely: *The winner ran the race in four minutes flat.* 3. Below the true pitch in music: *Both cello players were fine, but the violinist played flat. Adverb.*
flat (flat) *adjective,* **flatter, flattest;** *noun, plural* **flats;** *adverb.*

flatcar A railroad car with a floor but no roof or sides, used for carrying freight. **flat·car** (flat′kär′) *noun, plural* **flatcars**.

flatfish A fish with a flattened body and both eyes on the upper side of the body. Flounder, sole, and halibut are flatfish. **flat·fish** (flat′fish′) *noun, plural* **flatfish** *or* **flatfishes**.

flatten To make or become flat or flatter. **flat·ten** (flat′ən) *verb,* **flattened, flattening**.

flatter 1. To praise too much or insincerely: *If you think you'll change my mind by flattering me, you're wrong.* 2. To show as more attractive than is actually true: *I think that picture flatters me.* **flat·ter** (flat′ər) *verb,* **flattered, flattering**.

flattery Praise that is not sincere or not deserved: *It is often easy to tell the difference between genuine praise and mere flattery.* **flat·ter·y** (flat′ə rē) *noun.*

flavor 1. A particular taste: *Pepper gives food a spicy flavor.* 2. A special or main quality: *Her experiences as a police officer gave flavor to the lecture. Noun.*
○ To give flavor or taste to: *The cook flavored the fish with lemon juice. Verb.*
fla·vor (flā′vər) *noun, plural* **flavors;** *verb,* **flavored, flavoring**.

flavoring Something added to food or drink to give flavor. **fla·vor·ing** (flā′vər ing) *noun, plural* **flavorings**.

flaw A scratch, crack, or other defect: *Selfishness is a character flaw.* **flaw** (flô) *noun, plural* **flaws**.

flawless Perfect: *a flawless performance.* **flaw·less** (flô′lis) *adjective.* —**flawlessly** *adverb.*

flax 1. A fiber that comes from the stem of a certain plant. This fiber is spun into thread which is used to make linen. Flax can also be used to make rope and rugs. 2. The plant that produces this fiber. A kind of oil comes from the seeds of flax plants. **flax** (flaks) *noun.*

flea An insect without wings. Fleas feed on the blood of human beings, dogs, cats, and other animals. A flea can sometimes carry a disease and give it to the person or animal it is living on. Another word that sounds like this is **flee**. **flea** (flē) *noun, plural* **fleas**.

fled Past tense and past participle of **flee**. **fled** (fled) *verb.*

flee 1. To run away: *The family fled the burning house.* 2. To move or pass away quickly: *The vacation fled by.* Another word that sounds like this is **flea**. **flee** (flē) *verb,* **fled, fleeing**.

fleece The coat of wool covering a sheep. *Noun.*
○ To cut the fleece from: *The farmer used a pair*

PRONUNCIATION KEY:

| at | āpe | fär | câre | end | mē | it | īce | pîerce | hot | ōld | sông | fôrk |
| oil | out | up | ūse | rûle | pull | tûrn | chin | sing | shop | thin | this | |

hw in white; zh in treasure. The symbol ə stands for the unstressed vowel sound in about, taken, pencil, lemon, and circus.

281

of electric clippers to *fleece* the sheep. *Verb.*
fleece (flēs) *noun, plural* **fleeces;** *verb,* **fleeced,**
fleecing.

fleet¹ 1. A group of warships under one command:
The admiral ordered the *fleet* *to sail.* 2. A group
of ships, airplanes, or cars: *a* *fleet* *of taxicabs.*
fleet (flēt) *noun, plural* **fleets.**

**This fishing fleet hunts for tuna
in the ocean.**

fleet² Capable of moving very quickly; swift:
The deer is a *fleet* *animal.* **fleet** (flēt) *adjective,*
fleeter, fleetest.

fleeting Passing very quickly; very brief: *I had
only a* *fleeting* *look at the car because it drove
by so fast.* **fleet·ing** (flē'ting) *adjective.*
—**fleetingly** *adverb.*

flesh 1. The soft layers of muscle and fat between
the bones and the skin. 2. The soft part of fruit
or vegetables that can be eaten: *A cantaloupe has
greenish skin and orange* *flesh.* 3. The meat of an
animal. **flesh** (flesh) *noun.*

fleshy Plump; fat: *The base of the thumb is the
fleshy part of the hand.* **flesh·y** (flesh'ē) *adjective,*
fleshier, fleshiest.

flew Past tense of **fly.**
Other words that sound like this are **flu** and **flue.**
flew (flü) *verb.*

flex To bend: *If your arm is tired,* *flex* *it to keep it
loose.* **flex** (fleks) *verb,* **flexed, flexing.**

flexible 1 . Able to bend without breaking; not
stiff: *Rubber is* *flexible.* 2. Able to change or
adjust when necessary: *a* *flexible* *schedule.*
flex·i·ble (flek'səbəl) *adjective.*

flick A light, quick snap: *a* *flick* *of the wrist. Noun.*
○ To hit or move with a quick, light snap: *The
waiter* *flicked* *the crumbs off the table. Verb.*
flick (flik) *noun, plural* **flicks;** *verb,* **flicked, flicking.**

flicker¹ 1. To burn with an unsteady or wavering
light: *The candles* *flickered.* 2. To move back and
forth with a quick, unsteady movement: *Shadows
flickered on the door. Verb.*
○ 1. An unsteady or wavering light: *a* *flicker* *of
light from the fireplace.* 2. A quick, unsteady
movement: *the* *flicker* *of a snake's tongue. Noun.*
flick·er (flik'ər) *verb,* **flickered, flickering;** *noun,*
plural **flickers.**

flicker² A large woodpecker of North America. It
is mostly brown and white, with a curved black
mark across its breast. **flick·er** (flik'ər) *noun, plural* **flickers.**

flied Past tense of **fly:** *The batter* *flied* *to left field.*
flied (flīd) *verb.*

flier A person or thing that flies. This word is also
spelled *flyer.* **fli·er** (flī'ər) *noun, plural* **fliers.**

flight¹ 1. Movement through the air with the use of
wings; flying. 2. The distance or course traveled by
a bird or aircraft: *a* *flight* *from the United States
to China.* 3. A group of things flying through the
air together: *a* *flight* *of birds.* 4. A trip in an airplane. 5. A set of stairs or steps between floors
or landings of a building. **flight** (flīt) *noun,*
plural **flights.**

flight² The act of running away; escape: *People
were hurt during their* *flight* *from the burning
building.* **flight** (flīt) *noun, plural* **flights.**

flight attendant A person who serves passengers
on an airplane; a steward or stewardess.

flimsy Without strength; light and thin; frail:
a *flimsy* *summer shirt. That's a pretty* *flimsy
excuse.* **flim·sy** (flim'zē) *adjective,* **flimsier,
flimsiest.**

flinch To draw back from something painful,
dangerous, or unpleasant: *I* *flinched* *when the
doctor gave me the shot.* **flinch** (flinch) *verb,*
flinched, flinching.

fling To throw hard or carelessly: *Just* *fling* *your
coat on the bed. Verb.*
○ 1. A throw: *I gave the pebble a* *fling.* 2. A time
of carefree enjoyment: *Our day at the beach was
our last* *fling* *before vacation ended. Noun.*
fling (fling) *verb,* **flung, flinging;** *noun, plural*
flings.

flint A very hard, gray stone that makes sparks
when steel is struck against it. Before the invention of matches, flint was used to light fires.
flint (flint) *noun, plural* **flints.**

flintlock   An old-fashioned gun. In a flintlock, steel is struck against flint to make sparks that set the gunpowder on fire. **flint·lock** (flint′lok′) *noun*, *plural* **flintlocks**.

flip   To toss or turn over with a quick, jerking motion: We *flipped a coin to see who would go first. Verb.*
○ **1.** A toss: *a flip of a coin.* **2.** A somersault done in the air. *Noun.*
flip (flip) *verb*, **flipped**, **flipping**; *noun*, *plural* **flips**.

flipper   **1.** A broad, flat limb on a seal, turtle, penguin, or other animal, used for swimming and moving along on land. **2.** One of a pair of rubber shoes shaped like a duck's feet, worn to make swimming or skin diving easier. **flip·per** (flip′ər) *noun*, *plural* **flippers**.

flirt   To act romantic in a playful way: *They flirted at the party. Verb.*
○ A person who flirts. *Noun.*
flirt (flûrt) *verb*, **flirted**, **flirting**; *noun*, *plural* **flirts**.

flit   To move quickly and lightly: *Butterflies flit among flowers.* **flit** (flit) *verb*, **flitted**, **flitting**.

A float in a parade is usually highly decorated and carries several people.

float   **1.** To rest on top of a liquid like water and not sink: *In swimming class we learned how to float on our backs.* **2.** To move along slowly in the air or on water: *Far above us, a balloon floated by. Verb.*
○ **1.** Anything that rests on top of water. A raft anchored in the lake is a float. **2.** A low, flat platform on wheels that carries an exhibit in a parade. *Noun.*
float (flōt) *verb*, **floated**, **floating**; *noun*, *plural* **floats**.

flock   **1.** A group of animals of one kind herded or gathered together: *a flock of sheep.* **2.** A large number or group: *a flock of reporters crowded around. Noun.*
○ To move or gather in crowds: *People flock to the beaches during the summer. Verb.*
flock (flok) *noun*, *plural* **flocks**; *verb*, **flocked**, **flocking**.

floe   A mass or sheet of floating ice. Another word that sounds like this is **flow**.
floe (flō) *noun*, *plural* **floes**.

flood   **1.** A great flow of water over normally dry land. **2.** A great flow of anything: *a flood of words. Noun.*
○ **1.** To cover with water: *The town was flooded.* **2.** To fill, cover, or overwhelm: *The baseball field was flooded with light for the night game. Verb.*
flood (flud) *noun*, *plural* **floods**; *verb*, **flooded**, **flooding**.

floodlight   A lamp that shines brightly over a wide area. **flood·light** (flud′līt′) *noun*, *plural* **floodlights**.

floor   **1.** The surface of a room that people walk or stand on. **2.** A surface like the floor of a room: *the ocean floor.* **3.** A number of rooms that are the same height from the ground and that make up one level of a building; story: *My office is on the second floor. Noun.*
○ **1.** To cover with a floor. **2.** To knock down. **3.** To bewilder or surprise completely: *We were floored by the news. Verb.*
floor (flôr) *noun*, *plural* **floors**; *verb*, **floored**, **flooring**.

flop   **1.** To drop or fall heavily: *I flopped into bed.* **2.** To move around or flap loosely: *My dog's ears flop when she runs.* **3.** To fail completely: *The new play flopped after a week. Verb.*
○ **1.** The act or sound of dropping or falling heavily. **2.** A complete failure: *The TV show was a flop that lasted only two episodes. Noun.*
flop (flop) *verb*, **flopped**, **flopping**; *noun*, *plural* **flops**.

PRONUNCIATION KEY:
at   āpe   fär   cāre   end   mē   it   ice   pierce   hot   ōld   sông   fôrk
oil   out   up   ūse   rule   pull   turn   chin   sing   shop   thin   this
hw in white; zh in treasure. The symbol ə stands for the unstressed vowel sound in about, taken, pencil, lemon, and circus.

283

floppy Able to or tending to flop: *a large, floppy hat brim. Adjective.*
○ A floppy disk. *Noun.*
flop·py (flop′ē) *adjective,* **floppier, floppiest;** *noun, plural* **floppies.**

floppy disk A flexible piece of plastic that can store information for a computer. Look up **diskette** for more information.

This decorated tray has a floral design.

floral Of, relating to, or showing flowers: *The wallpaper in their room has a floral design.* **flo·ral** (flôr′əl) *adjective.*

Florida A state in the southeastern United States. Its capital is Tallahassee. **Flor·i·da** (flôr′i də *or* flor′i də) *noun.*

Tallahassee

Florida
U. S. Postal Abbreviation: **FL**
Capital: **Tallahassee**
Population: **12,023,000**
Area: **58,560 sq. mi./151,670 sq. km**
State Nickname: **Sunshine State**
State Bird: **Mockingbird**
State Flower: **Orange Blossom**

WORD HISTORY

Florida is a Spanish word that means "flowery." Ponce de Leon landed in Florida during the Easter season, which in Spanish is pasqua florida, "festival of flowers." He named the place from the name of the holiday.

---

florist A person who sells flowers and indoor plants. **flo·rist** (flôr′ist) *noun, plural* **florists.**

floss **1.** A soft, shiny thread of cotton or silk used for embroidering. **2.** A term sometimes used for *dental floss.* Look up **dental floss** for more information. *Noun.*
○ To clean between the teeth with dental floss. *Verb.*
floss (flôs) *noun, plural* **flosses;** *verb,* **flossed, flossing.**

flounder¹ To struggle or stumble about: *The colt floundered as it tried to walk.* **floun·der** (floun′dər) *verb,* **floundered, floundering.**

flounder² A flatfish that lives in salt water. **floun·der** (floun′dər) *noun, plural* **flounder** *or* **flounders.**

flour A fine powder made by grinding and sifting wheat, rye, or other grains, and used to make bread and cake. **flour** (flour) *noun, plural* **flours.**

flourish **1.** To grow or develop strongly and with vigor: *Those plants will flourish in a sunny garden.* **2.** To wave in the air boldly: *The guard flourished a gun at the escaping prisoners. Verb.*
○ **1.** A showy gesture or sound: *The actor walked on stage with a flourish.* **2.** An extra stroke for decoration: *I signed my name with a flourish below it. Noun.*
flour·ish (flûr′ish) *verb,* **flourished, flourishing;** *noun, plural* **flourishes.**

flow **1.** To move along steadily in a stream: *Water flows through these pipes.* **2.** To hang or fall loosely: *When I was young, my hair flowed to my waist. Verb.*
○ **1.** The act of flowing: *the flow of a river.* **2.** A long series of things coming steadily one after another; stream: *an endless flow of cars. Noun.*
Another word that sounds like this is **floe.**
flow (flō) *verb,* **flowed, flowing;** *noun, plural* **flows.**

flowchart A chart or diagram showing the development or growth of something step by step. **flow·chart** (flō′chärt′) *noun, plural* **flowcharts**.

flower **1.** The part of a plant that makes seeds; blossom. **2.** A plant grown for its showy, sometimes brightly colored petals: *The garden was full of purple, yellow, and red flowers. Noun.*
○ To produce flowers; blossom: *Cherry trees flower in the early spring. Verb.*
flow·er (flou′ər) *noun, plural* **flowers**; *verb,* **flowered, flowering.**

**These straw flowers
are annuals.**

flown Past participle of **fly:** *The bird had flown out of the cage.* **flown** (flōn) *verb.*

flu A disease that is like a very bad cold. It is caused by a virus and can easily spread from one person to another through coughing and sneezing. This word is a short form of the word *influenza.*
Other words that sound like this are **flew** and **flue.**
flu (flü) *noun, plural* **flus.**

flue The hollow inside part of a chimney that draws the smoke from a fireplace out of the room and into the outside air.
Other words that sound like this are **flew** and **flu.**
flue (flü) *noun, plural* **flues.**

fluff A soft, light material: *Some tree seeds are held inside floating bits of fluff. Noun.*
○ To pat or puff into a soft, light mass: *Fluff up the cushions on the couch. Verb.*
fluff (fluf) *noun; verb,* **fluffed, fluffing.**

fluffy Covered with or like fluff. **fluff·y** (fluf′ē) *adjective,* **fluffier, fluffiest.**

fluid A gas or liquid. Fluids can flow easily and take the shape of any container they are in. Air and water are fluids. *Noun.*
○ Flowing; not solid: *Water is fluid unless it is frozen. Adjective.*
flu·id (flü′id) *noun, plural* **fluids**; *adjective*

WORD HISTORY

Fluid comes from a Latin word meaning "to flow."

---

fluke¹ **1.** The triangular blade at the end of an anchor, designed to dig into the ground. **2.** One of the two flat horizontal tail pieces of a whale, dolphin, or porpoise. **fluke** (flük) *noun, plural* **flukes.**

fluke² An accidental stroke of good luck: *We won the game by the most amazing fluke of luck.* **fluke** (flük) *noun, plural* **flukes.**
—**fluky** *adjective.*

flung Past tense and past participle of *fling.* **flung** (flung) *verb.*

fluorescent **1.** Able to give off light when exposed to electricity or X rays. Fluorescent lamps often are made of glass tubes and are filled with gas. **2.** Very bright and colorful: *Fluorescent colors can attract your attention, so they are sometimes used for warning signs.* **fluo·res·cent** (flù res′ənt *or* flô res′ənt) *adjective.*

fluoridate To add fluoride to something: *The town fluoridated its drinking water to reduce tooth decay among the townspeople.* **fluor·i·date** (flùr′i dāt′ *or* flôr′i dāt′) *verb,* **fluoridated, fluoridating.**

fluoride A compound that contains fluorine. **fluo·ride** (flùr′īd *or* flôr′īd) *noun.*

fluorine A yellow-green gas. Fluorine is a chemical element. It combines very easily with other elements. Compounds of fluorine are added to drinking water to prevent tooth decay. **fluo·rine** (flùr′ēn *or* flôr′ēn) *noun.*

flurry **1.** A brief, light fall of snow. **2.** A sudden outburst: *a flurry of excitement.* **flur·ry** (flûr′ē) *noun, plural* **flurries.**

flush¹ **1.** To turn red or cause to turn red; blush. **2.** To flow or rush suddenly: *Water flushed through the pipes.* **3.** To empty or wash with a

PRONUNCIATION KEY:

at   āpe   fär   câre   end   mē   it   īce   pierce   hot   ōld   sông   fôrk
oil   out   up   ūse   rüle   pùll   tûrn   chin   sing   shop   thin   this
hw in white; zh in treasure. The symbol ə stands for the unstressed vowel sound in about, taken, pencil, lemon, and circus.

285

sudden rush of water: *A plumber **flushed** the clogged drain.* Verb.

○ **1.** A reddish color or glow: *a healthy **flush** on his cheeks.* **2.** A sudden rush or flow: *A **flush** of water burst from the broken pipe.* **3.** An exciting sensation; thrill: *the **flush** of success.* Noun.
flush (flush) *verb,* **flushed, flushing;** *noun, plural* **flushes.**

flush² Even or level: *The orange juice was **flush** with the rim of the glass. We tried to fit the shelf **flush** with the wall.* **flush** (flush) *adjective; adverb.*

fluster To make embarrassed or nervous; confuse. Verb.
○ Nervous confusion: *I was in a **fluster** the morning of the wedding.* Noun.
flus•ter (flus′tər) *verb,* **flustered, flustering;** *noun.*

flute A long, thin musical instrument you play by blowing. A person plays a flute by blowing across a hole at one end. The player makes different notes by covering the holes with the fingers or by pushing down keys that cover the holes. **flute** (flüt) *noun, plural* **flutes.**

Some music is written especially for the flute.

flutter To move or fly with quick, light, flapping movements: *Butterflies **fluttered** past us.* Verb.
○ **1.** A quick, light, flapping movement: *the **flutter** of pigeon wings.* **2.** A state of excitement or confusion: *The appearance of the movie star caused a **flutter** among the crowd.* Noun.
flut•ter (flut′ər) *verb,* **fluttered, fluttering;** *noun, plural* **flutters.**

fly¹ One of a large group of insects that have two wings. Houseflies, mosquitoes, and gnats are flies. **fly** (flī) *noun, plural* **flies.**

fly² **1.** To move through the air with wings: *Some birds **fly** south for the winter.* **2.** To pilot or travel in an aircraft: *My cousin **flies** jets for a large airline. The children **flew** to Puerto Rico to visit their grandparents.* **3.** To move, float, or wave in the air: *I **flew** my kite. A flag **flies** from the ship's mast.* **4.** To go swiftly: *They **flew** up the stairs when they heard the baby crying.* **5.** To hit a baseball high into the air: *The batter **flied** to left field.* Verb.
○ **1.** A flap of material that covers buttons or a zipper on a piece of clothing. **2.** A baseball hit high into the air. Noun.
fly (flī) *verb,* **flew, flown, flying** *(for definitions 1-4)* or **flied, flying** *(for definition 5); noun, plural* **flies.**

One must be constantly alert to fly this light aircraft.

flycatcher A songbird that catches flying insects for food. There are many kinds of flycatchers. **fly•catch•er** (flī′kach′ər) *noun, plural* **flycatchers.**

flyer Another spelling for the word *flier.* **fly•er** (flī′ər).

flying fish A saltwater fish with fins that look like wings. The flying fish can leap into the air and use its fins to glide above the surface of the water.

flying saucer A flying object that someone thinks he or she sees but that cannot be identified. Some people think that flying saucers are real and are sent by beings from outer space.

A foal stays close to its mother until it learns to care for itself.

foal A young horse, donkey, zebra, or similar animal. Noun.
○ To give birth to a foal: *The mare **foaled** this morning.* Verb.
foal (fōl) *noun, plural* **foals;** *verb,* **foaled, foaling.**

foam A mass of tiny bubbles. *Noun.*
  ○ To form or flow in a mass of tiny bubbles: *The rushing stream **foamed** over the rocks. Verb.* **foam** (fōm) *noun; verb,* **foamed, foaming.**

foam rubber A firm kind of rubber that is like sponge and is used for seats, mattresses, and pillows.

focus 1. The point at which light rays meet after being bent by a lens. 2. The distance from the lens to the point where the rays meet: *The eye of a farsighted person has a longer **focus** than the eye of a person with normal eyesight.* 3. An adjustment that gives a clear image: *The binoculars were out of **focus**.* 4. A center of activity or interest: *The speaker was the **focus** of attention. Noun.*
  ○ 1. To bring to a meeting point or focus: *A magnifying glass **focuses** light.* 2. To bring into focus to make a clear image: *The photographer **focused** the camera.* 3. To fix or direct: *The wedding guests **focused** all their attention on the bride and groom. Verb.*
  fo·cus (fō′kəs) *noun, plural* **focuses;** *verb,* **focused, focusing.**

WORD HISTORY

The word **focus** comes from Latin; in Latin it meant "fireplace" or "hearth." The fireplace which gave warmth to the room and where cooking was done would be the natural place for a family or others to gather for many activities.

---

fodder Food for horses, cows, and other farm animals. Hay and corn are kinds of fodder. **fodder** (fod′ər) *noun, plural* **fodders.**

foe An enemy: *The knight said to the stranger, "Are you friend or **foe**?"* **foe** (fō) *noun, plural* **foes.**

fog 1. A cloud of small drops of water close to the earth's surface: *The **fog** made driving dangerous.* 2. A state of confusion; daze: *I was in a **fog** all morning. Noun.*
  ○ To cover or become covered with fog: *The heavy mist **fogged** the road. Verb.*
  fog (fôg *or* fog) *noun, plural* **fogs;** *verb,* **fogged, fogging.**

foggy 1. Full of or hidden by fog; misty. 2. Confused or unclear: *a **foggy** idea.* **fog·gy** (fôg′ē *or* fog′ē) *adjective,* **foggier, foggiest.**

foghorn A horn with a deep sound that gives warning to boats when fog makes it hard to see. **fog·horn** (fôg′hôrn′ *or* fog′hôrn′) *noun, plural* **foghorns.**

foil¹ To stop from being successful: *The hero of the story **foiled** the pirates' plan to take over the ship.* **foil** (foil) *verb,* **foiled, foiling.**

foil² Metal in very thin, flexible sheets: *aluminum foil.* **foil** (foil) *noun, plural* **foils.**

foil³ A long sword used in fencing. The tip of a foil is covered to prevent injury. **foil** (foil) *noun, plural* **foils.**

fold¹ 1. To bend or double over on itself: *I **folded** the letter and put it in the envelope.* 2. To bring together close to the body: *The bird **folded** its wings. Verb.*
  ○ 1. A part bent or doubled over on itself: *The dress hung in graceful **folds**.* 2. A mark or crease made by folding: *Cut the paper along the **fold**. Noun.*
  fold (fōld) *verb,* **folded, folding;** *noun, plural* **folds.**

fold² A pen or other closed-in area for sheep. **fold** (fōld) *noun, plural* **folds.**

folder 1. A holder for loose papers. A folder is often a folded sheet of thin cardboard. 2. A booklet made up of folded sheets of paper. **fold·er** (fōl′dər) *noun, plural* **folders.**

In the fall many people go to the mountains to view the foliage.

foliage The leaves on a tree or other plant. **fo·li·age** (fō′lē ij) *noun.*

PRONUNCIATION KEY:
at   āpe   fär   câre   end   mē   it   īce   pierce   hot   ōld   sông   fôrk
oil   out   up   ūse   rüle   pùll   tûrn   chin   sing   shop   thin   this
hw in white; zh in treasure. The symbol ə stands for the unstressed vowel sound in about, taken, pencil, lemon, and circus.

287

folk 1. People: *city folk on vacation in the country.* 2. Family or relatives: *My folks live in a small town. Noun.*
○ Coming from or belonging to the common people: *folk music. Adjective.*
folk (fōk) *noun, plural* **folks** or **folk**; *adjective.*

folk dance 1. A traditional dance originally invented by the common people of a region or country. 2. The music for this kind of dance.

folklore The tales, beliefs, customs, or other traditions handed down from one generation to the next among a group of people. **folk·lore** (fōk′lôr′) *noun.*

folk music The traditional music of the common people of a region or country.

folk singer A singer who sings folk songs.

folk song 1. A traditional song of a region or country that has been handed down among the common people. 2. A song imitating or in the style of a real folk song.

folktale A traditional story been handed down among the common people. **folk·tale** (fōk′tāl′) *noun, plural* **folktales.**

follow 1. To go or come after, behind, or in back of: *The dog followed us down the street.* 2. To go along: *Follow this road for a mile.* 3. To act according to; obey: *Follow the instructions.* 4. To pay attention to and understand: *We followed the story with interest.* 5. To make a living from: *Most people here follow the fishing trade.*
• **to follow up.** To follow an action with something that strengthens its effect: *I wrote a letter of complaint to the company, and I followed up with a phone call a few days later.*
fol·low (fol′ō) *verb,* **followed, following.**

follower Someone who supports or admires a person or a set of beliefs: *The followers of the religious leader gathered to listen to the sermon.* **fol·low·er** (fol′ō ər) *noun, plural* **followers.**

following Coming after in order or time: *We packed Thursday night and left the following morning. Adjective.*
○ A group of supporters: *That author has a large following. Noun.*
fol·low·ing (fol′ō ing) *adjective; noun, plural* **followings.**

folly A lack of good sense; foolishness: *It is folly to think that you can drive in this blizzard.*

fol·ly (fol′ē) *noun, plural* **follies.**

fond Liking or loving: *I'm fond of my classmates.* **fond** (fond) *adjective,* **fonder, fondest.**

font A basin used to hold water for baptism. **font** (font) *noun, plural* **fonts.**

food Something eaten or taken in by people, animals, or plants that keeps them alive and helps them grow; nourishment. **food** (füd) *noun, plural* **foods.**

food chain A group of living things that form a chain in which the first living thing is eaten by the second, the second is eaten by the third, and so on. An example of a food chain is a peach which is eaten by a fly, which is eaten by a spider, which is eaten by a snake, which is eaten by a hawk.

food processor An appliance for slicing, chopping, grating, and blending foods. **food proc·es·sor** (pros′e sər *or* prō′se sər).

food web The complex system of different food chains in an ecological community.

fool 1. A person without good sense: *You're a fool to think that you can fool her.* 2. A person whose job was to entertain people in the household of a king, queen, or noble. *Noun.*
○ 1. To trick: *His story didn't fool me.* 2. To be silly; joke; tease: *I said I could swim a mile, but I was only fooling. Verb.*
fool (fül) *noun, plural* **fools;** *verb,* **fooled, fooling.**

foolish Without good sense; unwise: *It's foolish to dive into a lake without knowing how deep it is.* **fool·ish** (fü′lish) *adjective.* —**foolishly** *adverb* —**foolishness** *noun.*

foot 1. The end part of the leg that humans and other animals walk on or stand on. 2. The lowest or supporting part: *the foot of a mountain.* 3. The part opposite the head: *the foot of a bed.* 4. A measure of length equal to 12 inches. One foot is the same as 0.3048 meters.
• **on foot.** By walking: *We went to the park on foot.*
• **to put one's foot down.** To act firmly according to one's rights or authority: *My friend had kept the borrowed sweater much too long, so I had to put my foot down and demand that it be returned the next day.*
• **under foot.** In the way: *The kittens were always under foot.*
foot (fut) *noun, plural* **feet.**

football 1. A game played by two teams of eleven players each on a big field with goals at each end. Each team tries to make points by carrying, passing, or kicking the ball over the other team's goal. 2. The oval ball used in this game. **foot·ball** (fut′bôl′) *noun, plural* **footballs.**

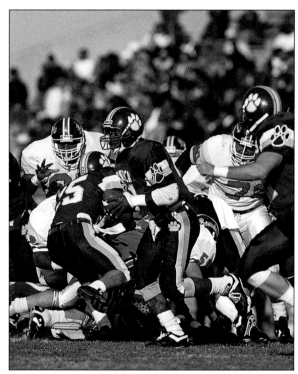

The game of football is one of the oldest sports in the United States.

foothill A low hill near the lower part of a mountain or mountain range. **foot·hill** (fut′hil′) *noun, plural* **foothills.**

footing 1. The safe or firm placing of the feet: *You can lose your footing on those slippery rocks.* 2. A safe place or support for the feet: *The icy ledge provided no footing for the mountain climbers.* 3. A position or relationship: *We started off on a bad footing with our neighbors.* **foot·ing** (fut′ing) *noun, plural* **footings.**

footlights The row of lights along the front edge of a stage in a theater. **foot·lights** (fut′līts′) *plural noun.*

footnote A note or explanation at the bottom of a page. **foot·note** (fut′nōt′) *noun, plural* **footnotes.**

footprint A mark made by a foot or shoe. **foot·print** (fut′print′) *noun, plural* **footprints.**

footstep 1. The sound made by a step. 2. A step of the foot.

  • **to follow in someone's footsteps.** To imitate or follow the same course as someone: *I'm going to follow in my cousin's footsteps and become a musician.*
foot·step (fut′step′) *noun, plural* **footsteps.**

footstool A low stool on which a person can rest the feet while sitting down. **foot·stool** (fut′stül′) *noun, plural* **footstools.**

for 1. Throughout a time or distance of: *We worked for two hours.* 2. Intended or reserved to accommodate: *This room is for guests.* 3. As a result of; because of: *We were praised for our success in the debate.* 4. In support or defense of: *They fought for their beliefs.* 5. In the amount of: *a bill for fifty dollars.* 6. At the cost of: *I bought a ticket for fifteen dollars.* 7. Directed to, sent to, given to, or belonging to: *This letter is for you.* 8. In place of; instead of: *They used a cardboard carton for a table. Preposition.*
  ○ Because: *We should go, for it is late. Conjunction.*
Other words that sound like this are **fore** and **four.**
for (fôr; *unstressed* fər) *preposition; conjunction.*

forage Hay, grain, and other food for cows, horses, and similar animals. *Noun.*
  ○ To hunt or search, especially for food or supplies: *The birds foraged in the snow. Verb.*
for·age (fôr′ij *or* for′ij) *noun; verb,* **foraged, foraging.**

forbade Past tense of forbid. **for·bade** (fər bad′ *or* fər bād′) *verb.*

forbid To order not to do something; prohibit: *I forbid you to go swimming.* **for·bid** (fər bid′) *verb,* **forbade, forbidden, forbidding.**

force 1. Power or strength: *The batter hit the ball with great force.* 2. Power or strength used against a person or thing: *The sheriff used force to arrest the suspect.* 3. A group of people who work together: *a police force.* 4. Something that moves a body or stops or changes its motion: *The force of gravity causes things to fall.* 5. The power to convince or influence: *the force of an argument. Noun.*
  ○ 1. To cause someone to do something against his or her wishes; make: *The rain forced us to*

PRONUNCIATION KEY:
at   āpe   fär   câre   end   mē   it   īce   pierce   hot   old   sông   fôrk
oil   out   up   ūse   rüle   pull   tûrn   chin   sing   shop   thin   this
hw in white; zh in treasure. The symbol ə stands for the unstressed vowel sound in about, taken, pencil, lemon, and circus.

289

cancel the picnic. **2.** To cause to open by using force: *I had to **force** the lock on my suitcase.* **3.** To get or make by using power or strength: *They **forced** their way through the crowd.* Verb.
 • **in force.** Being observed or enforced; in effect: *Despite yesterday's rain, rules for saving water are still **in force.***
force (fôrs) *noun, plural* **forces;** *verb,* **forced, forcing.**

forceful Having much strength or power; vigorous: *a **forceful** speech.* **force•ful** (fôrs'fəl) *adjective.* —**forcefully** *adverb* —**forcefulness** *noun.*

forceps A small tool for gripping and holding things, used by doctors and dentists in operations. **for•ceps** (fôr'seps) *noun, plural* **forceps.**

ford A shallow place where a river or other body of water can be crossed. *Noun.*
 ○ To cross at a shallow place. *Verb.*
ford (fôrd) *noun, plural* **fords;** *verb,* **forded, fording.**

fore At or toward the front: *The pilot stood at the **fore** part of the ship.*
Other words that sound like this are **for** and **four.**
fore (fôr) *adjective.*

fore- A prefix that means: **1.** At or near the front: *Foreleg means a front leg.* **2.** Ahead of time; before: *Foresee means to see ahead of time.*

forearm The part of the arm between the elbow and the wrist. **fore•arm** (fôr'ärm') *noun, plural* **forearms.**

forecast To tell what will or may happen; predict: *Political experts tried to **forecast** the results of the election.* Verb.
 ○ A statement that tells what will or may happen; prediction: *a weather **forecast.** Noun.*
fore•cast (fô'rkast') *verb,* **forecast** or **forecasted, forecasting;** *noun, plural* **forecasts.**

forefather An ancestor. **fore•fa•ther** (fôr'fä'thər) *noun, plural* **forefathers.**

forefinger The finger next to the thumb; index finger. **fore•fin•ger** (fôr'fing'gər) *noun, plural* **forefingers.**

forefoot One of the front feet of an animal that has four feet. **fore•foot** (fôr'fŭt') *noun, plural* **forefeet.**

foregone Known or decided ahead of time: *His election as captain of the hockey team was a **foregone** conclusion.* **fore•gone** (fôr'gôn' or fôr'gon') *adjective.*

foreground The part of a picture or view that is or seems to be nearest to the person looking at it. **fore•ground** (fôr'ground') *noun, plural* **foregrounds.**

The tree appears in the foreground of this photograph.

forehead The part of the face above the eyebrows. **fore•head** (fôr'id *or* fôr'hed') *noun, plural* **foreheads.**

foreign **1.** Of or from another country: *My French friend speaks English with a **foreign** accent.* **2.** Outside a person's own country: *foreign countries.* **3.** Having to do with other nations or governments: *The president makes many decisions on **foreign** policy.* **for•eign** (fôr'ən) *adjective.*

foreigner A person from another country. **for•eign•er** (fôr'ə nər) *noun, plural* **foreigners.**

foreleg One of the front legs of an animal that has four or more legs. **fore•leg** (fôr'leg') *noun, plural* **forelegs.**

foreman **1.** A worker in charge of a group of workers. **2.** The chairperson of a jury. **fore•man** (fôr'mən) *noun, plural* **foremen** (fôr'mən).

foremost First in position or importance: *She was considered the **foremost** citizen of the town.* **fore•most** (fôr'mōst') *adjective.*

forerunner **1.** A person or thing that comes before another: *The bicycle was the **forerunner** of the motorcycle.* **2.** A sign of something coming: *A brisk wind and a dark sky are often **forerunners** of a storm.* **fore•run•ner** (fôr'run'ər) *noun, plural* **forerunners.**

foresaw Past tense of foresee. **fore•saw** (fôr sô') *verb.*

foresee To know or see ahead of time: *No one can really foresee the future.* **fore·see** (fôr sē′) *verb,* **foresaw, foreseen, foreseeing.**

foreseen Past participle of foresee. **fore·seen** (fôr sēn′) *verb.*

foresight Care or thought for the future: *You showed foresight in bringing along an umbrella.* **fore·sight** (fôr′sīt′) *noun.*

forest A lot of trees and plants covering a large area of land; woods. **for·est** (fôr′ist) *noun, plural* **forests.**

forest ranger A person whose job is to protect forests.

foretell To tell ahead of time; predict. **fore·tell** (fôr tel′) *verb,* **foretold, foretelling.**

foretold Past tense and past participle of foretell. **fore·told** (fôr tōld′) *verb.*

forever 1. Throughout all time; without ever coming to an end: *No one can expect things to remain the same forever.* 2. Without letting up; always; constantly: *He is forever complaining about things.* **for·ev·er** (fə rev′ər) *adverb.*

forfeit To lose or have to give up because of some fault, accident, or mistake: *I had to forfeit my place in line because I forgot my wallet. Verb.*
○ Something lost because of some fault, accident, or mistake: *The game ended with forfeit. Noun.* **for·feit** (fôr′fit) *verb,* **forfeited, forfeiting;** *noun, plural* **forfeits.**

forgave Past tense of forgive. **for·gave** (fôr gāv′) *verb.*

forge¹ A furnace or hearth in which metal is heated. The fire softens the metal so that it can be hammered into shape. A blacksmith uses a forge to make horseshoes. *Noun.*
○ 1. To heat in a forge until very hot and then hammer into shape: *Blacksmiths forged iron into horseshoes.* 2. To make or form: *Diplomats forged a peace agreement.* 3. To copy in order to trick or cheat: *It is a crime to forge someone else's signature on the check. Verb.*
forge (fôrj) *noun, plural* **forges;** *verb,* **forged, forging.**

forge² To move forward slowly but steadily: *The tugboat forged through the rough waters of the bay.* **forge** (fôrj) *verb,* **forged, forging.**

forget 1. To not be able to remember: *I forgot my homework.* 2. To fail to think of or do: *I forgot to tell my parents that I would be late for dinner.* **for·get** (fər get′) *verb,* **forgot, forgotten** or **forgot, forgetting.**

forgetful Likely to forget; having a poor memory: *My forgetful cousin can never remember my telephone number.* **for·get·ful** (fər get′fəl) *adjective.*
—**forgetfulness** *noun.*

forget-me-not A low plant with small blue, pink, or white flowers shaped like trumpets and growing in clusters. **for·get-me-not** (fər get′mē not′) *noun, plural* **forget-me-nots.**

forgive To stop blaming or feeling anger toward; pardon or excuse: *I was sorry for breaking the window, and my parents forgave me.* **for·give** (fər giv′) *verb,* **forgave, forgiven, forgiving.**

forgiven Past participle of forgive. **forgiven** (fərgivən) *verb.*

forgiveness 1. The act of forgiving; pardon: *I beg your forgiveness for my being late.* 2. A willingness to *forgive.* **for·give·ness** (fər giv′nis) *noun.*

forgot Past tense of forget. **for·got** (fər got′) *verb.*

forgotten Past participle of forget. **for·got·ten** (fər got′ən) *verb.*

fork 1. A tool with a handle at one end and two or more thin pointed parts at the other. One kind of fork is used for eating food. A larger kind of fork is used for pitching hay. 2. The place where something divides: *a fork in a road. Noun.*
○ 1. To lift or pitch with a fork. 2. To divide into branches: *The river forks two miles upstream. Verb.*
fork (fôrk) *noun, plural* **forks;** *verb,* **forked, forking.**

form 1. The outline of something; shape: *We saw the dim form of the bridge through the fog.* 2. Kind or type: *Electricity is a form of energy.* 3. A way of behaving or of doing something: *I have been working to improve my form in diving.* 4. A sheet of paper with blanks that are to be filled in. 5. One of the different ways that a word may appear. "Was" is a form of the verb "be." *Noun.*
○ 1. To make or shape: *The artist formed a head out of clay.* 2. To take shape: *The water dripping from the roof formed into icicles.* 3. To make up:

PRONUNCIATION KEY:

at	āpe	fär	câre	end	mē	it	īce	pierce	hot	ōld	sông	fôrk
oil	out	up	ūse	rüle	püll	tûrn	chin	sing	shop	thin	this	

hw in white; zh in treasure. The symbol ə stands for the unstressed vowel sound in about, taken, pencil, lemon, and circus.

291

Students **formed** *the biggest part of the crowd. Verb.*
form (fôrm) *noun, plural* **forms**; *verb,* **formed, forming.**

formal 1. Very stiff and proper: *The teacher's manner was so* **formal** *that the students were a little afraid.* 2. Following strict custom, ceremony, or rules: *At a* **formal** *dinner, the guest of honor sits to the right of the host.* 3. Done or made with authority; official: *A* **formal** *agreement has to be written, signed, and witnessed. Adjective.*
○ 1. A formal dress. 2. A formal dance. *Noun.*
for·mal (fôr′məl) *adjective; noun, plural* **formals.**
—formally *adverb.*

formation 1. The process of forming or making: *The* **formation** *of ice from water requires a temperature below 32 degrees Fahrenheit.*
2. Something formed or made. 3. The way in which the members or units of a group are arranged: *The band lined up in parade* **formation.**
for·ma·tion (fôr mā′shən) *noun, plural* **formations.**

This rock formation was cut by wind and water.

former 1. The first of two: *Greenland and Madagascar are both islands; the* **former** *is in the North Atlantic Ocean and the latter is in the Indian Ocean.* 2. Belonging to or happening in the past; earlier: *In* **former** *times, people used fireplaces to heat their houses.* **for·mer** (fôr′mər) *adjective.*

formerly In time past; once: *Trains were* **formerly** *pulled by steam locomotives.* **for·mer·ly** (fôr′mər lē) *adverb.*

formula 1. An explanation of how to prepare a medicine, food, or other mixture. A formula says how much of each ingredient to use: *The* **formula** *for mixing this drink is to add one part powder to three parts of cold water.* 2. A rule expressed in symbols or numbers: *The* **formula** *for changing miles into kilometers is: 1 mile equals 1.61 kilometers.* 3. A way of naming a chemical compound that uses a symbol for each element in a molecule of the compound: *The chemical* **formula** *for water is H_2O.* 4. A set method for doing or getting something: *There is no real* **formula** *for making friends.* **for·mu·la** (fôr′myə lə) *noun, plural* **formulas.**

forsake To give up or leave: *I decided to* **forsake** *the city and live on a farm.* **for·sake** (fôr sāk′) *verb,* **forsook, forsaken, forsaking.**

forsaken Past participle of forsake. **for·sak·en** (fôr sā′kən) *verb.*

forsook Past tense of forsake. **for·sook** (fôr sük′) *verb.*

forsythia A shrub that has yellow flowers shaped like little bells. The flowers grow in clusters along the stem and bloom in the early spring before the leaves appear. **for·syth·i·a** (fôr sith′ē ə) *noun, plural* **forsythias.**

fort A strong building or area that can be defended against attacks by an enemy. **fort** (fôrt) *noun, plural* **forts.**

forth 1. Forward: *From that day* **forth,** *I was never lonely.* 2. Out into view: *The flowers burst* **forth** *on the first warm day of spring.* Another word that sounds like this is **fourth.** **forth** (fôrth) *adverb.*

fortieth Next after the thirty-ninth. *Adjective, noun.*
○ One of forty equal parts; 1/40. *Noun.*
for·ti·eth (fôr′tē ith) *adjective; noun, plural* **fortieths.**

fortification 1. The act of strengthening something: *a wall built as part of the fortification of the town.* 2. Something that strengthens, such as a wall or embankment. **for·ti·fi·ca·tion** (fôr′tə fi kā′shən) *noun, plural* **fortifications.**

fortify 1. To make stronger or more secure: *They fortified the town by building high walls around it* 2. To add strengthening ingredients to; enrich: *This breakfast cereal is fortified with vitamins and iron.* **for·ti·fy** (fôr′tə fī) *verb,* **fortified, fortifying.**

fortress A strong place that can be defended against attack; fort. **for·tress** (fôr′tris) *noun, plural* **fortresses.**

fortunate Having or resulting from good luck; lucky: *One fortunate person has won the contest twice.* **for·tu·nate** (fôr′chə nit) *adjective.* —**fortunately** *adverb.*

fortune 1. Something either good or bad that will happen to a person: *The gypsy in the circus told my fortune.* 2. Luck: *It was my good fortune to find the job I wanted.* 3. Great wealth; riches: *a fortune in jewels.* **for·tune** (fôr′chən) *noun, plural* **fortunes.**

fortuneteller A person who claims to be able to tell people's fortunes. **for·tune·tell·er** (fôr′chən tel′ər) *noun, plural* **fortunetellers.**

forty Four times ten; 40. **for·ty** (fôr′tē) *noun, plural* **forties;** *adjective.*

forum 1. The public square of an ancient Roman city. Business and other important activities took place in the forum. 2. A meeting to discuss issues or questions of public interest: *A forum was held at the school to discuss littering in the neighborhood.* **fo·rum** (fôr′əm) *noun, plural* **forums.**

forward Toward what is in front or ahead: *We are looking forward to our vacation. Adverb.*
○ 1. At or toward the front: *I took a forward seat on the plane.* 2. Bold or rude: *Some forward children made fun of the old couple. Adjective.*
○ To send ahead to a new address: *My parents forwarded the mail I got during the summer to my address at camp. Verb.*
○ A player whose position is near the front of the team in certain games. *Noun.*
for·ward (fôr′wərd) *adverb; adjective; verb,* **forwarded, forwarding;** *noun, plural* **forwards.**

forwards Another spelling for the adverb forward. **for·wards** (fôr′wərdz) *adverb.*

fossil The hardened remains or traces of an animal or plant that lived long ago: *The fossils we found were imprints of ancient seashells in rock.* **fos·sil** (fos′əl) *noun, plural* **fossils.**

fossil fuel A fuel formed from the remains of prehistoric plants and animals. Coal and petroleum are fossil fuels.

foster To help the growth or development of: *My parents fostered my interest in music. Verb.*
○ Giving or receiving care in a family without being related by birth or adoption: *The state has a special department that tries to find foster parents for homeless children. Adjective.*
fos·ter (fôs′tər) *verb,* **fostered, fostering;** *adjective.*

fought Past tense of fight. **fought** (fôt) *verb.*

foul 1. Very unpleasant or dirty: *a foul odor. Foul water.* 2. Cloudy, rainy, or stormy: *foul weather.* 3. Very bad; evil: *foul deeds.* 4. Breaking the rules; unfair: *foul play.* 5. Outside the foul line in a baseball game: *a foul ball. Adjective.*
○ 1. A breaking of rules: *The basketball player committed a foul.* 2. A baseball hit outside the foul line. *Noun.*
○ 1. To make dirty: *The factory fouled the lake by pumping waste into it.* 2. To tangle or become tangled: *I fouled the fishing line in the bushes.* 3. To hit a foul ball in baseball. *Verb.*
Another word that sounds like this is fowl.
foul (foul) *adjective,* **fouler, foulest;** *noun, plural* **fouls;** *verb,* **fouled, fouling.**

foul line Either of the two lines in baseball that go from home plate through first or third base to the limits of the playing field.

found¹ Past tense and past participle of find. **found** (found) *verb.*

found² To start or bring into being; establish: *The students founded a science club.* **found** (found) *verb,* **founded, founding.**

foundation 1. The act of founding: *We studied the American Revolution and the foundation of the United States.* 2. The base on which a structure is built: *the foundation of a house.* 3. Something that supports or justifies; basis: *a story without foundation.* **foun·da·tion** (foun dā′shən) *noun, plural* **foundations.**

PRONUNCIATION KEY:
at   āpe   fär   câre   end   mē   it   īce   pîerce   hot   ōld   sông   fôrk
oil   out   up   ūse   rüle   pull   tûrn   chin   sing   shop   thin   this
hw in white; zh in treasure. The symbol ə stands for the unstressed vowel sound in about, taken, pencil, lemon, and circus.

293

foundry A place where metal is melted and formed into different shapes. **found·ry** (foun'drē) *noun, plural* **foundries.**

fountain 1. A stream of water made to shoot from the ground or from a structure designed for it. 2. An abundant source of something: *That teacher is a fountain of knowledge about history.* **foun·tain** (foun'tən) *noun, plural* **fountains.**

Some fountains are used to drink from; others are for decoration.

fountain pen A pen that has a little tube inside to hold and feed liquid ink to the writing point.

four One more than three; 4.

Another word that sounds like this is **for.**
four (fôr) *noun, plural* **fours;** *adjective.*

Four-H club One of a group of organizations for young people that teach and promote skills in farming and maintaining a home. The Four-H clubs are named for their purpose of improving the heads, hearts, hands, and health of their members. **Four-H club** (fôr'āch').

fourteen Four more than ten; 14. **four·teen** (fôr'tēn') *noun, plural* **fourteens;** *adjective.*

fourteenth Next after the thirteenth. *Adjective, noun.*
○ One of fourteen equal parts; 1/14. *Noun.*
four·teenth (fôr'tēnth') *adjective; noun, plural* **fourteenths.**

fourth Next after the third. *Adjective, noun.*
○ One of four equal parts. *Noun.*

Another word that sounds like this is **forth.**
fourth (fôrth) *adjective; noun, plural* **fourths.**

Fourth of July A holiday celebrated in the United States. Look up **Independence Day** for more information.

fowl One of a number of birds used for food. The chicken, turkey, and duck are kinds of fowl. Another word that sounds like this is **foul.**
fowl (foul) *noun, plural* **fowl** or **fowls.**

fox 1. A wild animal closely related to the dog. A fox has a pointed nose and ears, a bushy tail, and thick fur. 2. The fur of a fox. 3. A sly or cunning person. **fox** (foks) *noun, plural* **foxes.**

foxhound A hound with a very good sense of smell. It is trained to hunt foxes. A foxhound has a tan, black, and white coat. **fox·hound** (foks'hound') *noun, plural* **foxhounds.**

fraction 1. A part of a whole: *Only a small fraction of the people watching the football game left before it was over.* 2. A number that stands for one or more of the equal parts of a whole. A fraction shows the division of one number by a second number. 2/3, 3/4, and 1/16 are fractions. **frac·tion** (frak'shən) *noun, plural* **fractions.**

WORD HISTORY

Fraction comes from a Latin word meaning "to break." A fraction is a broken-off part of a large whole.

fracture To crack or break: *I fell and fractured an ankle.* Verb.
○ A crack or break: *Your bone fracture will heal.* Noun.
frac·ture (frak'chər) *verb,* **fractured, fracturing;** *noun, plural* **fractures.**

fragile Easily broken; delicate: *a fragile china cup.* **frag·ile** (fraj'əl) *adjective.*

fragment A part broken off; small piece: *The students found some fragments of pottery in the woods.* **frag·ment** (frag'mənt) *noun, plural* **fragments.**

fragrance A sweet or pleasing smell: *Roses have a beautiful fragrance.* **fra·grance** (frā'grəns) *noun, plural* **fragrances.**

fragrant Having a sweet or pleasing smell: *The flowers made the whole room fragrant.* **fra·grant** (frā'grənt) *adjective*

frail 1. Lacking in strength; weak: *The child was too frail to play sports.* 2. Easily broken or torn;

delicate: *That lace is very old and frail.* **frail** (frāl) *adjective*, **frailer**, **frailest**.

frame 1. A structure that borders or supports something: *a window frame.* 2. The structure of a person's body; build: *That football player has a large frame. Noun.*
○ 1. To set in a bordering or supporting structure: *The painter framed the drawing.* 2. To enclose as a picture frame does: *The hat frames your face nicely.* 3. To express or construct carefully: *The teacher framed each question so that everyone would understand. Verb.*
frame (frām) *noun, plural* **frames**; *verb*, **framed**, **framing**.

framework A structure that gives shape or support to something: *The framework of the building is steel.* **frame•work** (frām′wûrk′) *noun, plural* **frameworks**.

The wooden framework of this house is being constructed.

franc A unit of money and a coin of France, Belgium, Switzerland, and other countries. Another word that sounds like this is **frank**. **franc** (frangk) *noun, plural* **francs**.

France A country in western Europe. **France** (frans) *noun*.

frank Honest and open in expressing one's real thoughts and feelings: *Let me be frank and tell you that your voice is not good enough for the choir.* Another word that sounds like this is **franc**. **frank** (frangk) *adjective*, **franker**, **frankest**. —**frankly** *adverb*.

frankfurter A sausage made of beef or beef and pork, often served on a long roll. **frank•furt•er** (frangk′fər tər) *noun, plural* **frankfurters**.

WORD HISTORY

The word frankfurter comes from a German word that means "from Frankfurt." This kind of sausage may have been first made in the city of Frankfurt in Germany.

frantic Wildly excited by worry or fear: *The children became frantic when they realized they were lost.* **fran•tic** (fran′tik) *adjective.* —**frantically** *adverb.*

fraud 1. A tricking of someone in order to cheat: *To sell fake diamonds that are supposed to be real is fraud.* 2. A person or thing that tricks or cheats; fake: *Someone who claims to be a doctor but really isn't is a fraud.* **fraud** (frôd) *noun, plural* **frauds**.

fray To separate into loose threads: *Many years of wear had frayed the cuffs of the coat.* **fray** (frā) *verb*, **frayed**, **fraying**.

freak 1. A person, animal, or plant that has not developed normally. A mouse with two tails would be a freak. 2. Anything odd or unusual. **freak** (frēk) *noun, plural* **freaks**.

freckle A small brownish spot on the skin. **freck•le** (frek′əl) *noun, plural* **freckles**.

free 1. Having one's liberty; not under control of another: *I set my white mice free.* 2. Not held back or confined: *You are free to come and go as you like.* 3. Not troubled or affected by something: *free from disease.* 4. Not obstructed; clear: *The stairway should be kept free of toys.* 5. Without cost: *free tickets to the show. Adjective.*
○ Without cost: *Children are admitted free. Adverb.*
○ To make or set free: *We freed the trapped animal. Verb.*
free (frē) *adjective*, **freer**, **freest**; *adverb*; *verb*, **freed**, **freeing**. —**freely** *adverb*.

freedom 1. The condition of being free; liberty: *The slaves struggled for their freedom.* 2. The condition of being able to move or act without being held back: *Our dog has freedom of the house.* **free·dom** (frē′dəm) *noun, plural* **freedoms**.

A woman who had been a slave made this quilt to celebrate her freedom.

free fall During a jump from a plane, the time when the person jumping drops straight down, before the parachute opens and slows the person down.

freeware Software that may be copied without charge. The person who wrote the software remains its legal owner.

freeway A highway with more than two lanes and no intersections or stoplights. A freeway is used for fast and direct driving. **free·way** (frē′wā′) *noun, plural* **freeways**.

freeze 1. To harden because of the cold: *When water freezes, it becomes ice.* 2. To cover or block with ice: *The cold weather froze the pipes.* 3. To make or become very cold: *We stood there freezing as we waited for the bus.* 4. To become fixed or motionless: *The campers froze when they saw the snake.* 5. To damage or be damaged by cold or frost: *The orange crop in Florida froze this winter.* **freeze** (frēz) *verb,* **froze, frozen, freezing**.

freezer A refrigerator or part of a refrigerator used to freeze food quickly or to store food already frozen. **freez·er** (frēz′ər) *noun, plural* **freezers**.

freight 1. The carrying of goods by land, air, or water: *Most of this airline's business is freight.* 2. The goods carried in this way; cargo. **freight** (frāt) *noun.*

freighter A ship used for carrying cargo. **freight·er** (frā′tər) *noun, plural* **freighters**.

French 1. The people of France. 2. The language of France. *Noun.*
  ○ Having to do with France, its people, their language, or their culture. *Adjective.*
  French (french) *noun; adjective.*

French fries Thin strips of potatoes fried in fat until brown and crisp. **French fries** (frīz).

French Guiana A territory of France that is on the northeastern coast of South America. **French Gui·a·na** (gē ä′nə *or* gē an′ə).

French horn A brass musical instrument.

A French horn has a long tube that widens into the shape of a bell.

Frenchman A person born in or a citizen of France. **French·man** (french′mən) *noun, plural* **Frenchmen** (french′mən).

Frenchwoman A woman born in or a citizen of France. **French·wom·an** (french′wùm′ən) *noun, plural* **Frenchwomen** (french′wim′ən).

frenzy Wild excitement: *We were in a frenzy to escape from the bees.* **frenzy** (frenzē) *noun, plural* **frenzies**.

frequency 1. A happening again and again: *The frequency of storms this spring caused the pond* to *overflow.* **2.** The number of times something happens or takes place during a period of time: *The frequency of a person's heartbeat is usually between sixty and ninety beats a minute.* **3.** The number of cycles per second of a radio wave or other kind of wave or radiation. **fre·quen·cy** (frē′kwən sē) *noun, plural* **frequencies.**

frequent Happening often: *There are frequent thunderstorms in this area in the summer.* **fre·quent** (frē′kwənt) *adjective.* —**frequently** *adverb.*

fresh **1.** Newly done, made, or gathered: *fresh vegetables.* **2.** New; another: *a fresh piece of paper.* **3.** Clean or refreshing: *a breath of fresh air.* **4.** Not salty: *fresh water.* **5.** Rude; impudent: *I was kept after school for being fresh to the teacher.* **fresh** (fresh) *adjective,* **fresher, freshest.**

freshen To make or become fresh: *The rain freshened the air.* **fresh·en** (fresh′ən) *verb,* **freshened, freshening.**

freshman A student in the first year of high school or college. **fresh·man** (fresh′mən) *noun, plural* **freshmen** (fresh′mən).

freshwater Of or living in fresh water rather than in salt water: *The perch is a freshwater fish.* **fresh·wa·ter** (fresh′wô′tər) *adjective.*

Fri. An abbreviation for **Friday.**

friar A man who belongs to one of several religious orders of the Roman Catholic Church. **fri·ar** (frī′ər) *noun, plural* **friars.**

friction **1.** The rubbing of one thing against another: *The friction of the rope on the climber's hands was painful.* **2.** A force that resists movement between two surfaces that touch one another: *The friction between two parts of a machine can be reduced by oiling them.* **3.** Conflict or disagreement: *friction between the neighbors.* **fric·tion** (frik′shən) *noun.*

Friday The sixth day of the week. **Friday** (frī′dē or frī′dā) *noun, plural* **Fridays.**

WORD HISTORY

Friday comes from the Old English word meaning "Frigga's day." Frigga was the queen of the pagan English gods.

---

fried Past tense and past participle of **fry.** **fried** (frīd) *verb.*

friend **1.** A person you like who likes you. **2.** A person who supports or favors something: *The governor is a friend of public education.* **friend** (frend) *noun, plural* **friends.**

True friends enjoy each other's company.

friendly **1.** Like or wanting to be a friend; warm and pleasant: *a friendly smile.* **2.** Not angry or fighting; not hostile: *Canada and the United States are on friendly terms.* **friend·ly** (frend′lē) *adjective,* **friendlier, friendliest.** —**friendliness** *noun.*

friendship The warm feeling between friends. **friend·ship** (frend′ship′) *noun, plural* **friendships.**

fright **1.** A sudden fear or alarm. **2.** A person or thing that is ugly or shocking: *You looked a fright in that witch costume.* **fright** (frīt) *noun, plural* **frights.**

frighten **1.** To make or become suddenly afraid or alarmed: *The explosion frightened everyone.* **2.** To drive away by scaring: *The dog frightened away the squirrels.* **fright·en** (frī′tən) *verb,* **frightened, frightening.**

frightful **1.** Causing sudden fear; alarming. **2.** Disgusting or shocking: *a frightful amount of litter.* **fright·ful** (frīt′fəl) *adjective.*

frigid **1.** Very cold: *a frigid climate.* **2.** Cold in feeling; unfriendly: *a frigid greeting.* **frig·id** (frij′id) *adjective.* —**frigidly** *adverb.*

fringe **1.** A border of hanging threads or cords: *The bedspread has a fringe around the edge.*

PRONUNCIATION KEY:

at   āpe   fär   câre   end   mē   it   īce   pierce   hot   ōld   sông   fôrk
oil   out   up   ūse   rüle   pull   tûrn   chin   sing   shop   thin   this

hw in white; zh in treasure. The symbol ə stands for the unstressed vowel sound in about, taken, pencil, lemon, and circus.

297

2. Anything like a fringe: *A **fringe** of bushes lined the driveway.* **fringe** (frinj) *noun, plural* **fringes**.

Frisbee A trademark for a plastic disk that players throw back and forth in a game. **Fris·bee** (friz′bē) *noun, plural* **Frisbees**.

frivolous Lacking seriousness or sense; silly: *Frivolous people can't keep their minds on anything for very long.* **friv·o·lous** (friv′ə ləs) *adjective.*

frog A small animal with moist skin, webbed feet, and no tail. Frogs are amphibians and are closely related to toads. They live in or near water. **frog** (frôg *or* frog) *noun, plural* **frogs**.

A **frog** uses its strong back legs
for hopping.

frogman A swimmer specially trained and equipped to work underwater. **frog·man** (frôg′man′ *or* frog′man′) *noun, plural* **frogmen** (frôg′men′ *or* frog′men′).

frolic To play about happily and gaily. **frol·ic** (frol′ik) *verb,* **frolicked, frolicking.**

from 1. Starting at; beginning with: *We flew **from** New York to Chicago.* 2. With a particular person, place, or thing as the source: *I got a letter **from** my friends in Canada.* 3. Off or out of: *Two **from** five leaves three.* 4. Out of the material of: *a house made **from** bricks.* 5. At a distance relative to: *ten miles **from** our house.* 6. Because of: *shivering **from** the cold.* 7. As being different from: *It's easy to tell lions **from** tigers.* **from** (from *or* frum *or unstressed* frəm) *preposition.*

frond The leaf of a fern or palm. **frond** (frond) *noun, plural* **fronds**.

front 1. The part that faces forward or comes first: *The introduction comes at the **front** of the book.* 2. A place or position at the forward part: *He entered the store while I waited in **front**.* 3. The land that lies along a street or body of water: *a cabin on the lake **front**.* 4. A place where fighting is going on between enemy forces: *The general visited the **front** to encourage the soldiers.* 5. The boundary line between two air masses of different temperatures: *Temperature dropped as the cold **front** moved into the area.* Noun.
◦ On or near the front: the front door. *Adjective.*
◦ To face: *Our house **fronts** on a busy street. Verb.*
  • **in front of.** In a place or position directly before; ahead of: *A tall person sat **in front of** me.*
front (frunt) *noun, plural* **fronts**; *adjective; verb,* **fronted, fronting.**

frontier 1. The far edge of a country, where people are just beginning to settle: *The development of the railroad helped to move the American **frontier** farther west.* 2. The border between two countries: *We crossed the **frontier** between Canada and the United States.* 3. The part of a subject or field of study where new discoveries are being made: *exploring the **frontiers** of medicine.* **fron·tier** (frun tîr′) *noun, plural* **frontiers**.

frost 1. Tiny ice crystals that form on a surface when water vapor in the air freezes. 2. Very cold weather during which the temperature is below freezing. *Noun.*
◦ 1. To cover with frost: *The first cold night **frosted** my windows.* 2. To cover with frosting or something like frosting: *We **frosted** the cake. Verb.*
frost (frôst) *noun, plural* **frosts**; *verb,* **frosted, frosting.**

frostbite Injury to some part of the body caused by exposure to extreme cold. *Noun.*
◦ To injure by exposure to extreme cold: *toes were **frostbitten** by the cold. Verb.*
frost·bite (frôst′bīt′) *noun; verb,* **frostbit, frostbitten, frostbiting.**

frosting A mixture of sugar, butter, and flavoring used to cover a cake or cookies; icing. **frost·ing** (frôs′ting) *noun, plural* **frostings**.

frosty Cold enough for frost; freezing. **frost·y** (frôs′tē) *adjective,* **frostier, frostiest.**

froth A mass of bubbles formed in or on a liquid; foam: *A froth appeared on the milk as it boiled.* Noun.

○ To give out or form froth: *The mixture frothed as it boiled.* Verb.

froth (frôth) *noun, plural* **froths**; *verb,* **frothed, frothing.** —**frothy** *adjective.*

frown A wrinkling of the forehead. A person who is thinking hard or is angry or worried may make a frown. *Noun.*

○ 1. To wrinkle the forehead in thought, anger, or worry. 2. To regard with anger or disapproval: *My parents frown on my staying out late at night.* Verb.

frown (froun) *noun, plural* **frowns**; *verb,* **frowned, frowning.**

froze Past tense of **freeze. froze** (frōz) *verb.*

frozen Past participle of **freeze. fro·zen** (frō′zən) *verb.*

frugal 1. Careful in spending money and using resources; not wasteful: *a frugal shopper.* 2. Costing little: *a frugal meal of beans and bread.* **fru·gal** (frü′gəl) *adjective.* —**frugally** *adverb.*

fruit 1. The part of a plant that contains the seeds. Nuts, berries, and pods are fruits. 2. A plant part that contains seeds and is fleshy or juicy and good to eat. **fruit** (früt) *noun, plural* **fruit** *or* **fruits.**

Oranges, apples, melons, bananas, and grapes are fruit.

frustrate 1. To keep from doing something; prevent: *I was frustrated in trying to learn the address.* 2. To prevent from being fulfilled: *The rain frustrated our plans for a hike.* 3. To make someone feel helpless or incapable; discourage: *Not being able to find a job frustrated me.*

frus·trate (frus′trāt) *verb,* **frustrated, frustrating; frus·tra·tion** *noun.*

fry To cook in hot fat: *We fried bacon and eggs for our breakfast.* **fry** (frī) *verb,* **fried, frying.**

ft. An abbreviation for **feet, foot,** or **fort.**

fudge A soft candy made of sugar, milk, butter, and often chocolate flavoring. **fudge** (fuj) *noun, plural* **fudges.**

fuel Something burned to provide heat or power. Coal, wood, and oil are fuels. **fu·el** (fū′əl) *noun, plural* **fuels.**

fugitive A person who runs away or tries to escape: *The police caught the fugitive.* **fu·gi·tive** (fū′ji tiv) *noun, plural* **fugitives.**

-ful A suffix that means: 1. Having the qualities of; full of: *Fearful means full of fear.* 2. Able to; likely to: *Forgetful means likely to forget.* 3. The amount that will fill something: *Cupful means the amount that will fill a cup.*

fulcrum The support on which a lever rests or turns when it is moving or lifting something: *The farmer used a rock as a fulcrum to move the heavy boulder.* **ful·crum** (fůl′krəm) *noun, plural* **fulcrums.**

fulfill 1. To carry out or finish: *I fulfilled my obligations and left for home.* 2. To meet or satisfy: *If you are a citizen and if you are at least eighteen years old, you fulfill two requirements for voting.* **ful·fill** (fůl fil′) *verb,* **fulfilled, fulfilling.**

full 1. Holding as much or as many as possible: *a full glass of milk.* 2. Having or containing a large number or quantity: *a house full of guests.* 3. Complete; entire: *a full two weeks of vacation.* 4. Having a rounded outline; plump: *a full, round face.* Adjective.

○ Completely; entirely: *I filled the pitcher full with lemonade.* Adverb.

full (fůl) *adjective,* **fuller, fullest;** *adverb.*

full moon 1. The moon when all of the side that faces the earth is shining. 2. The time when this happens: *Tonight is the full moon.*

fully 1. Completely; entirely: *I don't fully understand that arithmetic problem.* 2. At least; not less than: *The train was fully an hour late.* **ful·ly** (fůl′ē) *adverb.*

PRONUNCIATION KEY:

| at | āpe | fär | câre | end | mē | it | īce | pierce | hot | ōld | sông | fôrk |
| oil | out | up | ūse | rüle | půll | tûrn | chin | sing | shop | thin | this | |

hw in white; zh in treasure. The symbol ə stands for the unstressed vowel sound in about, taken, pencil, lemon, and circus.

299

fumble 1. To grope: *I fumbled around in my pocket for my keys.* 2. To handle clumsily or drop: *The runner fumbled the ball. Verb.*
○ The act of fumbling: *The fumble cost us the game. Noun.*
fum·ble (fum′bəl) *verb,* **fumbled, fumbling;** *noun,* *plural* **fumbles.**

fume A smoke or gas that is harmful or has a bad smell. *Noun.*
○ To be very angry or irritated: *The driver fumed while stuck in traffic. Verb.*
fume (fūm) *noun, plural* **fumes;** *verb,* **fumed, fuming.**

fun 1. Enjoyment or amusement: *We had fun riding our sleds.* 2. Playfulness: *full of fun.*
• **to make fun of** *or* **to poke fun at.** To laugh at; ridicule: *They made fun of my haircut.*
fun (fun) *noun.*

function 1. Use or purpose: *An usher's function is to help people find their seats.* 2. A formal gathering: *All the supporters of the art museum went to a function to celebrate the museum's fiftieth anniversary. Noun.*
○ To work or serve: *A motor functions best when it is kept well oiled. Verb.*
func·tion (fungk′shən) *noun, plural* **functions;** *verb,* **functioned, functioning.**

fund 1. A sum of money set aside for a purpose: *the fund for my college education.* 2. A supply: *This book has a fund of information on American Indians.* 3. **funds.** Money ready for use: *The state does not have the funds to repair the highway.* **fund** (fund) *noun, plural* **funds.**

fundamental Serving as a basis; essential; basic: *Learning the rules is a fundamental part of any game. Adjective.*
○ An essential part: *Addition and subtraction are two of the fundamentals of arithmetic. Noun.*
fun·da·men·tal (fun′də men′təl) *adjective; noun, plural* **fundamentals.**

WORD HISTORY

The word fundamental comes from a Latin word meaning "foundation" or "base." Something which is fundamental is basic.

funeral The ceremony and services held before the burial of a dead person. **fu·ner·al** (fū′nər əl) *noun, plural* **funerals.**

fungi More than one fungus. **fun·gi** (fun′jī) *plural noun.*

Mushrooms, mildews, and molds are fungi.

fungus One of a large group of living things that have cell walls similar to those of plants but that have no flowers, leaves, or green coloring. Fungi live on plant or animal matter. **fun·gus** (fung′gəs) *noun, plural* **fungi** (fun′jī) *or* **funguses.**

funnel 1. A utensil with a wide cone at one end and a thin tube at the other, used to pour something into a container with a small opening without spilling. 2. A round chimney or smokestack on a steamship or steam engine. **fun·nel** (fun′əl) *noun, plural* **funnels.**

funny 1. Causing laughter or amusement: *a funny joke.* 2. Strange; odd: *It's funny you never told us your real name.* **fun·ny** (fun′ē) *adjective,* **funnier, funniest.**

fur 1. The soft, thick, hairy coat of certain animals: *The raccoon has striped fur.* 2. The skin of an animal that has fur. Fur is used in making clothing, rugs, and other things. 3. A piece of clothing made of fur.
Another word that sounds like this is **fir.**
fur (fûr) *noun, plural* **furs.**

furious 1. Very angry. 2. Violent; fierce: *a furious thunderstorm.* **fu·ri·ous** (fyùr′ē əs) *adjective.*

furlough An absence from duty for which permission has been given; vacation: *The soldiers spent their furlough seeing the sights in the city.*

fur·lough (fûr′lō) *noun, plural* **furloughs.**

furnace A large, enclosed, metal box where heat is produced. A furnace is used to heat a building or to melt metal. **fur·nace** (fûr′nis) *noun, plural* **furnaces.**

furnish 1. To supply with furniture: *We furnished our den with some old chairs table.* 2. To supply or provide: *The book furnished us with useful facts about the American Revolution.* **fur·nish** (fûr′nish) *verb,* **furnished, furnishing.**

furniture Tables, chairs, beds, and other movable articles used in a home or office. **fur·ni·ture** (fûr′ni chər) *noun.*

furrow A long, narrow groove: *The wheels of the car made furrows in the mud.* **fur·row** (fûr′ō) *noun, plural* **furrows.**

furry Like fur or covered with fur: *The new rug in the living room is soft and furry.* **fur·ry** (fûr′ē) *adjective,* **furrier, furriest.**

further A comparative of far: *We left without further delay. I swam to the further side of the pond. We'll talk further about this later. Let's walk a little further.* Look up **far** for more information. *Adjective; adverb.*
○ To help forward; support: *The United Nations was formed to further the cause of peace.* Verb. **fur·ther** (fûr′thər) *adjective; adverb; verb,* **furthered, furthering.**

furthermore In addition; moreover; besides: *I don't want to go to bed yet, and furthermore I still have homework to do.* **fur·ther·more** (fûr′thər môr′) *adverb.*

furthest A superlative of far: *Going swimming is the furthest thing from my mind today. Of all the family, you have gone furthest in your education.* Look up **far** for more information. **fur·thest** (fûr′thist) *adjective; adverb.*

fury 1. Violent anger; rage. 2. Violent or fierce action: *the fury of a storm.* **fu·ry** (fyùr′ē) *noun, plural* **furies.**

fuse¹ 1. A strip of metal in an electric circuit. The fuse melts and breaks the circuit if the current becomes too strong. Fuses are used to prevent fires caused by wires that carry too much electricity. 2. A piece of cord that can burn. A fuse is used to explode a bomb or other explosive device. **fuse** (fūz) *noun, plural* **fuses.**

fuse² 1. To melt by heating: *I fused the metal with a torch.* 2. To blend or unite: *Because gold is such a soft metal, it is fused with silver or copper to harden it.* **fuse** (fūz) *verb,* **fused, fusing.**

fuselage The main body of an airplane, carrying the passengers, cargo, and crew. **fu·se·lage** (fū′sə läzh′ *or* fū′sə lij) *noun, plural* **fuselages.**

fusion 1. The act or process of melting or blending: *The fusion of copper and tin makes bronze.* 2. The combining of the nuclei of two atoms to form the nucleus of a heavier atom. Large amounts of energy are released during fusion. **fu·sion** (fū′zhən) *noun, plural* **fusions.**

fuss An unnecessary stir or bother over small or unimportant things: *a big fuss over who would go first.* Noun.
○ To make an unnecessary stir or bother. *Verb.* **fuss** (fus) *noun, plural* **fusses;** *verb,* **fussed, fussing.**

future Happening in the time after the present; coming: *I hope that your future work will be better.* Adjective.
○ 1. The time to come: *In the future, please call if you are going to be late.* 2. Another word for *future tense.* Noun. **fu·ture** (fū′chər) *adjective; noun.*

future tense A form of a verb that shows that an action will happen or a condition will exist in the future. In the sentence "We will go to the beach tomorrow," "will go" is a verb in the future tense. In the sentence "I will be on time," "will be" is a verb in the future tense. The future tense is also called the *future.*

fuzz Fine, loose fibers or hair: *peach fuzz.* **fuzz** (fuz) *noun.*

fuzzy 1. Covered with or like fuzz: *Some caterpillars are fuzzy.* 2. Not clear; blurred: *That would be a good photograph except that it's too fuzzy.* **fuzz·y** (fuz′ē) *adjective,* **fuzzier, fuzziest.** **—fuzziness** *noun.*

The letter G has two sounds in English. Both of these sounds can be made in several ways:

The sound of G in words such as get, give, and go is often made by:
> gg in the middle or at the end of words such as egg and wriggle.

The sound of G in get is made less often by:
> gu as in guard.

The letter G also sounds like the letter J in words such as gem and page.

The letter G also appears silently in combinations with other letters such as:
> gh in laugh and though; ght as in light, sight, and thought.

g, G The seventh letter of the alphabet. **g, G** (jē) *noun, plural* **g's, G's.**

g An abbreviation for **gram.**

GA Postal abbreviation for **Georgia.**

Ga. An abbreviation for **Georgia.**

gable The part of an outside wall between the sides of a sloping roof. The gable is shaped like a triangle. **ga·ble** (gā′bəl) *noun, plural* **gables.**

Gabon A country in west-central Africa. **Ga·bon** (ga bōn′) *noun.*

gadget A small, useful tool or device. **gad·get** (gaj′it) *noun, plural* **gadgets.**

gag 1. Something put in the mouth to keep a person from talking or shouting. 2. A joke. *Noun.*
○ 1. To keep someone from talking or shouting by using a gag. 2. To feel as if one were about to vomit; choke: *The dog gagged on a bone. Verb.*
gag (gag) *noun, plural* **gags;** *verb,* **gagged, gagging.**

gaiety Joy and fun; being merry: *the gaiety of a circus.* **gai·e·ty** (gā′i tē) *noun, plural* **gaieties.**

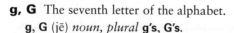

SYNONYMS

gaiety, glee, festivity, fun
The gaiety of the children at the party delighted all the grown ups. We laughed with glee at the monkey's tricks. The festivity of the carnival made up for the long trip we took to get there. The children couldn't stop talking about the fun they had in the amusement park on the boardwalk.

gaily In a gay manner; happily. **gai·ly** (gā′lē) *adverb.*

gain 1. To get or win: *You will gain experience by working at the store.* 2. To benefit in some way: *We all gained from the building of the new bridge.* 3. To get to; reach: *The ship gained the port before the storm. Verb.*
○ Something gained: *a gain of ten yards. Noun.*
gain (gān) *verb,* **gained, gaining;** *noun, plural* **gains.**

gait A way of walking or running: *The horse's gait changed from a trot to a gallop.*
Another word that sounds like this is **gate.**
gait (gāt) *noun, plural* **gaits.**

A zebra's gait allows it to move at a rapid pace.

gal. An abbreviation for **gallon.**

gala Festive; suitable for a celebration: *a gala banquet. Adjective.*
○ A festive occasion; celebration. *Noun.*
ga·la (gā′lə *or* gal′ə) *adjective; noun, plural* **galas.**

galaxy A very large group of stars. There are billions of galaxies in the universe. The Milky Way is the galaxy that contains our sun and the planets. **gal·ax·y** (gal′ək sē) *noun, plural* **galaxies**.

WORD HISTORY

The first galaxy we ever knew about was the Milky Way, our own galaxy. The word galaxy comes from a Greek word meaning ``milky,'' because the Milky Way looks like a milky white path in the sky.

---

gale 1. A strong wind. 2. A loud outburst: *gales of laughter.* **gale** (gāl) *noun, plural* **gales**.

gallant Good and brave. **gal·lant** (gal′ənt) *adjective.* **—gallantly** *adverb* **—gallantry** *noun.*

Many art galleries contain paintings, drawings, sculpture, and other fine objects.

gallery 1. A balcony in a theater or large hall. 2. A room or building where works of art are shown or sold. **gal·ler·y** (gal′ə rē) *noun, plural* **galleries**.

galley 1. A long, low ship with sails and oars, used in early times. 2. The kitchen of a ship or aircraft. **gal·ley** (gal′ē) *noun, plural* **galleys**.

gallon A unit of measure for liquids. A gallon equals four quarts or about 3.8 liters. **gal·lon** (gal′ən) *noun, plural* **gallons**.

gallop The fastest gait of a horse. *Noun.*
○ To move or ride at a gallop. *Verb.*
gal·lop (gal′əp) *noun, plural* **gallops;** *verb,* **galloped, galloping**.

gallows A framework from which criminals are hanged. **gal·lows** (gal′ōz) *noun, plural* **gallows** *or* **gallowses**.

galoshes Waterproof overshoes made of rubber or plastic, worn in snowy or rainy weather.

ga·losh·es (gə losh′iz) *plural noun.*

gamble 1. To play a game for money; bet: *I gambled a dollar at the bingo game.* 2. To take a chance: *The coach decided to gamble and use the new player. Verb.*
○ An act that involves a risk. *Noun.*
gam·ble (gam′bəl) *verb,* **gambled, gambling;** *noun, plural* **gambles.** **—gambler** *noun.*

game 1. Something done for fun or pleasure. 2. A sport or contest with rules: *In the third inning the game was tied.* 3. Materials or equipment needed in playing a game. *My grandparents gave me a croquet game for my birthday.* 4. Wild animals, birds, or fish hunted or caught for sport or food: *They went hunting for deer and other game. Noun.*
○ Full of spirit and courage. *Are you game for a swim? Adjective.*
game (gām) *noun, plural* **games;** *adjective,* **gamer, gamest**.

These children are playing a hand-clapping game.

gander A grown male goose. **gan·der** (gan′dər) *noun, plural* **ganders**.

gang 1. A group of people who do things or work together. 2. A group of people involved in crime. **gang** (gang) *noun, plural* **gangs**.

gangplank A movable bridge for getting on and off a boat or ship; gangway. **gang·plank** (gang′plangk′) *noun, plural* **gangplanks**.

gangster A member of a criminal gang. **gang·ster** (gang′stər) *noun, plural* **gangsters**.

gangway 1. A passageway on either side of a ship's deck. 2. A gangplank. **gang·way** (gang′wā′) *noun, plural* **gangways**.

gap 1. A break, crack, or opening: *a gap in the fence.* 2. A narrow passage through a mountain range; mountain pass. 3. A part or space where something is missing: *There are several gaps in the recording where you can't hear the music.* **gap** (gap) *noun, plural* **gaps**.

PRONUNCIATION KEY:

| at | āpe | fär | câre | end | mē | it | īce | pîerce | hot | ōld | sông | fôrk |
| oil | out | up | ūse | rûle | pull | tûrn | chin | sing | shop | thin | this | |

hw in white; zh in treasure. The symbol ə stands for the unstressed vowel sound in about, taken, pencil, lemon, and circus.

303

garage A building where cars and trucks are parked or repaired. **ga·rage** (gə räzh′ *or* gə räj′) *noun, plural* **garages.**

garbage Food and other things that are thrown out. **gar·bage** (gär′bij) *noun.*

garden A piece of ground for growing flowers or vegetables. *Noun.*
○ To work in a garden. *Verb.*
gar·den (gär′dən) *noun, plural* **gardens;** *verb,* **gardened, gardening. —gardener** *noun.*

gardenia A yellow or white flower with a sweet smell and petals that feel like wax. **gar·de·nia** (gär dēn′yə) *noun, plural* **gardenias.**

WORD HISTORY

The **gardenia** was named after Alexander Garden, a botanist who lived in the eighteenth century.

---

gargle To rinse the mouth with a liquid. The liquid is moved around by breathing out through the mouth, which makes a bubbling sound. *Verb.*
○ A liquid used for gargling. *Noun.*
gar·gle (gär′gəl) *verb,* **gargled, gargling;** *noun, plural* **gargles.**

gargoyle A pipe or spout in the form of an odd or ugly person or animal. **gar·goyle** (gär′goil) *noun, plural* **gargoyles.**

A **gargoyle** sticks out from the roof of a building.

garland A wreath of flowers, leaves, or vines. **gar·land** (gär′lənd) *noun, plural* **garlands.**

garlic An herb related to the onion, with a strong smell and flavor. **gar·lic** (gär′lik) *noun, plural* **garlics.**

garment A piece of clothing. **gar·ment** (gär′mənt)

The bulb of the **garlic** is used in cooking.

noun, plural **garments.**

garnet A deep red gem used in jewelry. **gar·net** (gär′nit) *noun, plural* **garnets.**

garnish To decorate: *The cook garnished the fish with slices of lemon. Verb.*
○ Something placed on or around food to improve the way it looks or tastes: *A garnish of parsley decorated the bowl of carrots. Noun.*
gar·nish (gär′nish) *verb,* **garnished, garnishing;** *noun, plural* **garnishes.**

garrison A place where soldiers are stationed; military base. *Noun.*
○ **1.** To station soldiers in: *The general garrisoned the town to protect it.* **2.** To station at a military base: *I was garrisoned at that base. Verb.*
gar·ri·son (gar′ə sen) *noun, plural* **garrisons;** *verb,* **garrisoned, garrisoning.**

garter A strap or band that holds up a stocking or sock. **gar·ter** (gär′tər) *noun, plural* **garters.**

garter snake A snake that is green or brown with long yellow stripes on its back. It is harmless to people.

gas **1.** A form of matter that is not solid or liquid. Gas can move about freely and does not have a definite shape. The air we breathe is made of gases. **2.** A gaseous substance burned as a fuel for heating or cooking. **3.** gasoline. Look up gasoline for more information. **gas** (gas) *noun, plural* **gases.**

gaseous In the form of gas; like gas. **gas·e·ous** (gas′ē əs *or* gash′əs) *adjective.*

gas mask A mask worn over the nose and mouth. It has a filter that keeps a person from breathing poisonous gases.

gasoline A clear liquid that burns easily. It is made mostly from petroleum and is used as a fuel for cars, airplanes, and other vehicles. **gas·o·line** (gas′ə lēn′ *or* gas′ə lēn′) *noun, plural* **gasolines.**

gasp **1.** To draw in air suddenly or with effort: *The runner gasped for breath.* **2.** To utter while breathing in suddenly or with effort: *"Lifeguard! Help!" gasped the struggling swimmer. Verb.*
○ The act or sound of gasping. *Noun.*
gasp (gasp) *verb,* **gasped, gasping;** *noun, plural* **gasps.**

gas station A place that sells gasoline, oil, and other things vehicles and travelers need. Many gas stations also have mechanics who repair cars and trucks.

gate A movable object like a door, used to close an opening in a fence or wall.
Another word that sounds like this is **gait**.
gate (gāt) *noun, plural* **gates**.

gateway 1. An open place in a fence or wall for a gate. 2. The way to get somewhere or do something: *Education is a gateway to success.*
gate·way (gāt′wā′) *noun, plural* **gateways**.

gather 1. To come or bring together; collect. 2. To increase bit by bit: *The sled gathered speed as it slid down the hill.* 3. To reach an opinion; conclude: *We gathered from the dark clouds that a storm was coming.* **gath·er** (gath′ər) *verb,* **gathered, gathering.**

SYNONYMS

gather, accumulate, assemble, collect
*The principal **gathered** all the teachers for a meeting. The snow kept **accumulating** on all the roads and sidewalks. The entire school **assembled** for the play. Our class **collects** over 3,000 cans in the drive every year.*

gathering A meeting, assembly, or crowd.
gath·er·ing (gath′ər ing) *noun, plural* **gatherings**.

The people at this gathering come from various backgrounds.

gaudy Too bright and showy. **gaud·y** (gô′dē) *adjective,* **gaudier, gaudiest.** —**gaudily** *adverb* — —**gaudiness** *noun.*

gauge 1. A standard of measurement. There are gauges for measuring the barrel of a gun and for measuring the distance between two rails on a railroad track. 2. An instrument for measuring: *An air pressure gauge. Noun.*
○ 1. To measure: *Scientists can gauge the exact amount of rain that falls.* 2. To estimate: *It is hard to gauge ability. Verb.*
gauge (gāj) *noun, plural* **gauges**; *verb,* **gauged, gauging.**

gaunt So thin that bones show through the skin.
gaunt (gônt) *adjective,* **gaunter, gauntest.**
—**gauntly** *adverb* —**gauntness** *noun.*

gauze A very thin cloth that you can see through, used in making bandages. **gauze** (gôz) *noun.*

gave Past tense of give. Look up **give** for more information. **gave** (gāv) *verb.*

gavel A small wooden hammer used by the person in charge of a meeting or trial to call for order or attention. **gav·el** (gav′əl) *noun, plural* **gavels**.

gay 1. Full of joy and fun; merry; bright. 2. Brightly colored or showy. **gay** (gā) *adjective,* **gayer, gayest.**

gaze To look at something a long time: *We all gazed at the beautiful sunset. Verb.*
○ A long, steady look. *Noun.*
gaze (gāz) *verb,* **gazed, gazing**; *noun, plural* **gazes**.

gazelle A graceful antelope that can run very fast, found in Africa and Asia. **ga·zelle** (gə zel′) *noun, plural* **gazelles** *or* **gazelle**.

The teeth of a gear cause other gears to turn.

gear 1. A wheel with teeth on the edge. The teeth are made to fit in between the teeth of another gear, so that one gear can cause the other to turn. 2. Equipment for a purpose. *My hiking gear included a knapsack. Noun.*
○ To make suitable or right: *The school was*

PRONUNCIATION KEY:

| at | āpe | fär | câre | end | mē | it | īce | pierce | hot | ōld | sông | fôrk |
| oil | out | up | ūse | rüle | pull | tûrn | chin | sing | shop | thin | this | |

hw in white; zh in treasure. The symbol ə stands for the unstressed vowel sound in about, taken, pencil, lemon, and circus.

305

geared to meet the needs of all. *Verb.*
gear (gîr) *noun, plural* **gears;** *verb,* **geared, gearing.**

gearshift A device that connects a set of gears to a motor. An automobile has a gearshift. **gear·shift** (gîr′shift′) *noun, plural* **gearshifts.**

geese Plural of **goose.** Look up **goose** for more information. **geese** (gēs) *plural noun.*

Geiger counter A device used to discover and measure the strength of rays from a radioactive substance. **Gei·ger counter** (gī′gər)

WORD HISTORY

The **Geiger counter** was named after Hans Geiger, a German scientist who helped invent this device.

---

gelatin A substance like jelly, made from the skin and bones of animals, and used in jellies and desserts and in making glue. **gel·a·tin** (jel′ə tən) *noun.*

gem 1. A precious stone that has been cut and polished; jewel. 2. A person or thing thought of as perfect or valuable: *Your garden is a gem.* **gem** (jem) *noun, plural* **gems.**

Diamonds, emeralds, rubies, and sapphires are regarded as gems.

gene One of the tiny units of a cell of an animal or plant that determines the characteristics that an offspring inherits from its parent or parents. **gene** (jēn) *noun, plural* **genes.**

genera Plural of **genus.** Look up **genus** for more information. **gen·er·a** (jen′ə rə) *plural noun.*

general 1. For all; for the whole: *an exhibit open to the general public.* 2. By all or many; among all or many: *There was general panic during the landslide.* 3. Having no limit or restriction: *The store had a general sale.* 4. Not concerned with details: *The president spoke in a general way about increasing taxes. Adjective.*
○ An armed forces officer of the highest rank. The five ranks of general in the United States Army are brigadier general, major general, lieutenant general, general, and general of the army. *Noun.*

• **in general.** Usually; generally: *In general, the weather here is very good.*
gen·er·al (jen′ər əl) *adjective; noun, plural* **generals.**

generalize 1. To form a general rule from particular facts: *After studying the temperature and rainfall in the city during June, July, and August, we were able to generalize about the summer weather there.* 2. To treat a subject in a general way, without discussing details: *I had to generalize in my report because I did not have enough time to be more specific.* **gen·er·al·ize** (jen′ər ə līz′) *verb,* **generalized, generalized.** —**generalization** *noun*

generally 1. Almost always; usually: *I generally walk to school.* 2. To a large extent or great degree: *It is generally believed that the Vikings visited America before Columbus.* 3. Without discussing the details: *Generally speaking, the book was good.* **gen·er·al·ly** (jen′ər ə lē) *adverb.*

generate To bring about or produce: *That machine generates electricity.* **gen·er·ate** (jen′ə rāt′) *verb,* **generated, generating.**

generation 1. A group of persons born around the same time: *My parents call us the younger generation.* 2. One step in the line of descent from a common ancestor: *A grandparent, parent, and child make up three generations.* 3. The period of time, about thirty years, between the births of the parents and the births of their children. 4. The act or process of generating; production. **gen·er·a·tion** (jen′ə rāsh′ən) *noun, plural* **generations.**

generator A machine that produces electricity, steam, or other energy. **gen·er·a·tor** (jen′ə rā′tər) *noun, plural* **generators.**

generic 1. Applied to a whole group; general: *"Fruit" is a generic term; "apple" is a specific term.* 2. Not having a trademark: *Generic products often cost less than brand-name products.* **ge·ner·ic** (jə ner′ik) *adjective.*

generosity The quality of being generous: *Although those people were poor, they were well-known for their generosity.* **gen·er·os·i·ty** (jen′ər os′i tē) *noun.*

generous 1. Willing and happy to share; not selfish: *Be generous with your new bicycle and let your friends ride it.* 2. Large; abundant: *a generous helping of French fries.* **gen·er·ous** (jen′ər əs) *adjective.*

genetics The science that deals with how characteristics are passed from a parent or parents to the offspring. The word "genetics" is used with a singular verb. **ge·net·ics** (jə net′iks) *noun*.

genial Friendly and cheerful; welcoming: *a genial host*. **gen·ial** (jē′yəl) *adjective*. —**genially** *adverb*.

genie A spirit with magic powers in Middle Eastern fairy tales. **ge·nie** (jē′nē) *noun, plural* **genies**.

genius 1. Great ability to think or to invent or create things: *an artist of genius*. 2. A person who has this ability: *That musician is a genius*. 3. Ability or talent for a particular thing: *a genius for drawing*. **gen·ius** (jēn′yəs) *noun, plural* **geniuses**.

gentile or **Gentile** A person who is not a Jew. *Noun*.
  ◦ Not Jewish. *Adjective*.
  gen·tile or **Gen·tile** (jen′tīl) *noun, plural* **gentiles** or **Gentiles**; *adjective*.

gentle 1. Mild and kindly. 2. Soft or low: *the gentle tapping of the rain on the window*. 3. Easy to handle; tame: *a gentle horse*. 4. Not steep: *a gentle slope*. **gen·tle** (jen′təl) *adjective*, **gentler**, **gentlest**. —**gently** *adverb* —**gentleness** *noun*.

WORD HISTORY

The word **gentle** comes from an old French word meaning "noble" or "born of a good family." Because being kind was thought to be a quality of people of noble birth, gentle came to be used to mean "mild and kindly."

gentleman 1. A man who is polite, kind, and honorable. 2. A man of high social position. 3. Any man: *"A gentleman is here to see you," my cousin said*. **gen·tle·man** (jen′təl mən) *noun, plural* **gentlemen** (jen′təl mən).

gentlewoman 1. A woman who is polite, kind, and honorable. 2. A woman of high social position. **gen·tle·wom·an** (jen′təl wùm′ən) *noun, plural* **gentlewomen** (jen′təl wim′ən).

genuine 1. Being what it seems or is claimed to be; real: *a belt of genuine leather*. 2. Sincere; honest: *We made a genuine effort to get here on time*. **gen·u·ine** (jen′ū in) *adjective*. —**genuinely** *adverb*.

genus A large group of closely related plants or animals. A genus consists of many separate species: *Wolves, coyotes, and dogs are three species of the same genus*. **ge·nus** (jē′nəs) *noun, plural* **genera** (jen′ə rə).

geodesic dome A dome made of light, straight bars that lock together in a geometric pattern. A geodesic dome is very strong and needs no poles for support. **ge·o·des·ic** (jē ə dēs′ik) *adjective*.

geographical or **geographic** Having to do with geography. **ge·o·graph·i·cal** (jē′ə graf′i kəl) or **ge·o·graph·ic** (jē′ə graf′ik) *adjective*.

geography 1. The science dealing with the surface of the earth and the plant, animal, and human life on it. When you study geography, you learn about the earth's countries and people, and about its climate, oceans and rivers, mountains, and natural resources. 2. The surface or natural features of a place or region: *The Grand Canyon is part of the geography of Arizona*. **ge·og·ra·phy** (jē og′rə fē) *noun, plural* **geographies**.

geology The science that deals with the structure of the earth. Geologists study rocks, mountains, and cliffs to find out what the earth is made of and what changes have taken place over the years. **ge·ol·o·gy** (jē ol′ə jē) *noun, plural* **geologies**. —**geological** or **geologic** *adjective* —**geologist**, *noun*.

geometric 1. Having to do with geometry: *A triangle is a geometric shape*. 2. Consisting of or decorated with lines, angles, circles, triangles, or similar shapes: *The rug in my room has a geometric design of circles and squares*. **ge·o·met·ric** (jē′ə met′rik) *adjective*.

This quilt has a geometric pattern.

PRONUNCIATION KEY:

at	āpe	fär	câre	end	mē	it	īce	pierce	hot	ōld	sông	fôrk
oil	out	up	ūse	rüle	pùll	tûrn	chin	sing	shop	thin	<u>th</u>is	

hw in white; zh in treasure. The symbol ə stands for the unstressed vowel sound in about, taken, pencil, lemon, and circus.

307

geometry The branch of mathematics that deals with the measurement and relation of points, lines, angles, plane figures, and solids. **ge·om·e·try** (jē om′i trē) *noun.*

Georgia A state in the southeastern United States. Its capital is Atlanta. **Geor·gia** (jôr′jə) *noun.*

WORD HISTORY

Georgia was named after King George II of England. He gave some people the right to start a colony in part of what is now this state.

Georgia
U. S. Postal Abbreviation: **GA**
Capital: **Atlanta**
Population: **6,222,000**
Area: **58,876 sq. mi./152,488 sq. km**
State Nicknames: **Empire State of the South;**
Peach State; Goober State
State Bird: **Brown Thrasher**
State Flower: **Cherokee Rose**

geothermal Relating to intense heat produced deep within the earth: *The geothermal geysers of hot water are located in Yellowstone National Park.* **ge·o·ther·mal** (jē′ə thûrm′əl) *adjective.*

geranium A plant with bright red, pink, white, or lavender flowers. **ge·ra·ni·um** (jə rā′nē əm) *noun, plural* **geraniums.**

gerbil A small rodent of the deserts of Africa and Asia. It lives in a burrow and

The leaves of some geraniums have a scent.

is kept as a pet. **ge·rbil** (jûr′bəl) *noun, plural* **ger·bils.**

germ A tiny particle that can cause disease. Viruses and bacteria are germs and are so small that they can be seen only through a microscope. **germ** (jûrm) *noun, plural* **germs.**

German 1. A person born in or a citizen of Germany. 2. The language of Germany. *Noun.*
○ Having to do with Germany, its people, or their language. *Adjective.*
Ger·man (jûr′mən) *noun, plural* **Germans;** *adjective*

germanic 1. Having to do with Germany, the German people, or the German language. 2. Having to do with a family of languages that includes English, Dutch, German, Danish, Norwegian, and Swedish. **ger·man·ic** (jər man′ik) *adjective.*

German shepherd A dog originally from Germany and used to herd sheep. It has a thick coat of black, brown, or gray fur.

Germany A country in north central Europe. **Ger·ma·ny** (jûr′mə nē) *noun.*

germinate To begin growing from a seed; to sprout: *The seeds need water to germinate.* **ger·mi·nate** (jûr′mə nāt′) *verb,* **germinated, germinating.**

gesture 1. A movement of the hands or head, showing what a person is thinking or feeling: *Holding out your hand with the palm up is a gesture that you want something.* 2. Something said or done to express a feeling or for effect: *Going to visit your sick classmate was a kind gesture. Noun.*
○ To make or use gestures: *The police officer gestured for the driver to stop. Verb.*
ges·ture (jes′chər) *noun, plural* **gestures;** *verb,* **gestured, gesturing.**

get 1. To come to have; receive; gain; earn: *I got a radio for my birthday.* 2. To come to or reach: *When will we get home?* 3. To come or go; move: *Get down from the ladder.* 4. To seek and bring back; catch or fetch: *Please get me a glass of milk.* 5. To become ill with: *Several of my classmates got the flu.* 6. To cause to be, be done, or become: *Get a haircut.* 7. To be or become: *The children got lost in the park.* 9. To have permission or be able: *We hoped we would get to fish in the lake.* 10. To persuade; convince: *Get them* to wear warmer clothes. **11.** To understand: *I don't **get** the joke.*

- **to get along. 1.** To be friendly: *Try **to get along** with everyone.* **2.** To manage to survive: *A camel **gets along** on very little water.*

- **to get away with.** To do something without being noticed, caught, or punished: *No one should **get away with** lying.*

- **to get back. 1.** To come back; return: *When did you **get back** from your trip?* **2.** To get again something one used to have; regain: *It took me a month **to get back** my strength after the flu.*

- **to get in. 1.** To go in; enter: *I couldn't **get into** the house.* **2.** To arrive: *The train **got in** at noon.*

- **to get out. 1.** To leave; depart: *Someone locked the door to my room, and I couldn't **get out**.* **2.** To become known; leak out: *How did the secret **get out**?*

- **to get over.** To recover from: *I just **got over** a cold.*

- **to get together.** To meet or gather: *Let's **get together** for lunch.*

- **to get up. 1.** To rise from bed: *I usually **get up** at seven.* **2.** To sit up or stand up: *When I fell off my bicycle, I couldn't **get up** right away.* **get** (get) *verb,* **got, got** *or* **gotten, getting.**

getaway A quick escape, especially from the scene of a crime or from the police. **get·a·way** (get′ə wā′) *noun, plural* **getaways.**

geyser A hot, underground spring from which steam and hot water shoot into the air. **gey·ser** (gī′zər) *noun, plural* **geysers.**

Ghana A country in western Africa. **Gha·na** (gä′nə) *noun.*

ghastly 1. Terrible; horrible: *a **ghastly** murder.* **2.** Very pale; like a ghost: *The sick person had a **ghastly** look.* **ghast·ly** (gast′lē) *adjective,* **ghastlier, ghastliest.** —**ghastliness** *noun*

ghetto A part of a city where members of a certain race or religion live because they are poor or because they are discriminated against. **ghet·to** (get′ō) *noun, plural* **ghettos** *or* **ghettoes.**

ghost The spirit of a dead person, especially when it haunts people or houses. **ghost** (gōst) *noun, plural* **ghosts.** —**ghostly** *adjective.*

ghost town A deserted town, especially one in the western United States after local gold or silver mines closed.

giant 1. An imaginary creature that looks like a huge person and has great strength. **2.** A person or thing that is very large, powerful, or important: *a **giant** in automobile manufacturing. Noun.* ◦ Very large: *a **giant** telescope. Adjective.* **gi·ant** (jī′ənt) *noun, plural* **giants;** *adjective.*

gibbon A small ape that has long arms and no tail and lives in trees in Asia. **gib·bon** (gib′ən) *noun, plural* **gibbons.**

giddy 1. Having a spinning feeling in the head; dizzy: *I felt **giddy** after swinging high on the swing.* **2.** Playful; silly: *We became so **giddy** that we laughed at anything.* **gid·dy** (gid′ē) *adjective,* **giddier, giddiest.** —**giddily** *adverb* —**giddiness** *noun.*

gift 1. Something given; present. **2.** Talent; ability. **gift** (gift) *noun, plural* **gifts.**

gifted Having natural ability or talent; talented: *a **gifted** musician.* **gift·ed** (gift′id) *adjective.*

gigantic Like a giant; huge and powerful. **gi·gan·tic** (jī gan′tik) *adjective.*

giggle To laugh in a high, silly, or nervous way. *Verb.* ◦ A high, silly, or nervous laugh. *Noun.* **gig·gle** (gig′əl) *verb,* **giggled, giggling;** *noun, plural* **giggles.**

gild To cover with a thin layer of gold: *The artist **gilded** the picture frame.* Another word that sounds like this is **guild.** **gild** (gild) *verb,* **gilded** *or* **gilt, gilding.**

gill The part of a fish that is used for breathing. *A **gill** takes in oxygen from the water.* **gill** (gil) *noun, plural* **gills.**

gilt A past tense and a past participle of **gild.** Look up **gild** for more information. ◦ A thin layer of gold or gold paint, used for decoration. *Noun.* ◦ Covered with gilt: *a **gilt** mirror frame. Adjective.* (gilt) Another word that sounds like this is **guilt.** **gilt** (gilt) *noun; adjective.*

gimmick A clever device, idea, or trick to catch a person's attention. **gim·mick** (gim′ik) *noun, plural* **gimmicks.**

PRONUNCIATION KEY:
at āpe fär câre end mē it īce pierce hot ōld sông fôrk
oil out up ūse rüle pull tûrn chin sing shop thin this
hw in white; zh in treasure. The symbol ə stands for the unstressed vowel sound in about, taken, pencil, lemon, and circus.
309

gin¹ A colorless alcoholic drink flavored with juniper berries. **gin** (jin) *noun, plural* **gins.**

gin² A machine for separating cotton from the seeds. **gin** (jin) *noun, plural* **gins.**

ginger A hot spice from the root of a tropical plant, used in food. **gin·ger** (jin′jər) *noun, plural* **gingers.**

gingerbread A dark, sweet cake or cookie flavored with ginger and molasses. **gin·ger·bread** (jin′jər bred′) *noun, plural* **gingerbreads.**

gingham A strong cotton fabric, usually having a pattern of checks, stripes, or plaid. **ging·ham** (ging′əm) *noun, plural* **ginghams.**

giraffe A large African animal with a very long neck, long, thin legs, and a coat with brown patches. **gi·raffe** (jə raf′) *noun, plural* **giraffes.**

Giraffes are the tallest animals.

girder A large, heavy beam used to support floors and the frameworks of buildings and bridges. **gir·der** (gûr′dər) *noun, plural* **girders.**

girl A female child from birth to the time she is a young woman. **girl** (gûrl) *noun, plural* **girls.**

WORD HISTORY

The word **girl** used to mean "a child or young person." The word was used for both boys and girls, and boys were sometimes called "knave girls." Later people began to use **girl** for female children only.

---

girlfriend 1. The sweetheart of a boy or a man. 2. A friend who is a girl or a woman. **girl·friend** (gûrl′frend′) *noun, plural* **girlfriends.**

girlhood 1. The time of being a girl. 2. The state of being a girl. **girl·hood** (gûrl′hùd′) *noun, plural* **girlhoods.**

girl scout A member of the Girl Scouts.

Girl Scouts An organization for girls. It helps girls to develop character and physical fitness.

girth The measurement around an object: *the girth of a tree.* **girth** (gûrth) *noun, plural* **girths.**

give 1. To hand, pass, present, or grant. 2. To make or do; bring about; cause: *The noise gives me a headache.* 3. To produce: *The sun gives off light.* 4. To break down; yield: *If the dam gives, the town will be flooded. Verb.*

○ The quality of being able to bend without breaking or yielding: *A hard mattress has very little give. Noun.*

• **to give away.** 1. To give as a gift: *They gave away prizes at the party.* 2. To cause to become known; reveal: *My friends gave away their hiding place when they laughed.*

• **to give back.** To return: *I gave back the money I had borrowed.*

• **to give in.** To stop being or acting against something; yield: *Our parents gave in and let us stay up late.*

• **to give out.** 1. To distribute: *The store is giving out free samples.* 2. To become tired, broken down, or used up: *The swimmer gave out before the end of the race.*

• **to give up.** 1. To surrender; yield: *We lost because our team gave up too many points.* 2. To stop or abandon: *Our neighbor gave up playing golf.* 3. To stop trying: *I know the problem is hard, but don't give up so soon.*

give (giv) *verb,* **gave, given, giving;** *noun.*

given Past participle of **give.** Look up **give** for more information. **giv·en** (giv′ən) *verb.*

glacier A large mass of ice in very cold regions or on the tops of high mountains. A glacier is formed by snow that does not melt. **gla·cier** (glā′shər) *noun, plural* **glaciers.**

glad 1. Happy; pleased: *I am glad to meet you.* 2. Causing joy or pleasure: *We heard the glad news.* 3. Very willing: *I was glad to help you clean the garage.* **glad** (glad) *adjective,* **gladder, gladdest.** —**gladly** *adverb.*

gladiator In ancient Rome, a man who fought another man in an arena to entertain the spectators. **glad·i·a·tor** (glad′ē ā′tər) *noun, plural* **gladiators.**

gladiolus A plant with brightly colored spikes of flowers and leaves shaped like swords. **glad·i·o·lus** (glad′ē ō′ləs) *noun, plural* **gladioli** (glad′ē ō′lī) *or* **gladioluses.**

glamour The quality of being fascinating, exciting, and charming: *The glamour of the big city made us eager to visit it again.* This word is also spelled *glamor.* **glam·our** *or* **glam·or** (glam′ər) noun. —**glamorous** *adjective* —**glamorously** *adverb*.

glance A quick look: *One glance and I knew it was you. Noun.*
  ○ **1.** To take a quick look. **2.** To hit something and move off at a slant: *The ax glanced off the tree. Verb.*
  glance (glans) *noun, plural* **glances**; *verb*, **glanced, glancing.**

gland A part inside the body that takes certain substances from the blood and changes them into chemicals that the body uses or gives off. Glands near the eyes make tears. **gland** (gland) *noun, plural* **glands.**

glare **1.** A strong, unpleasant light: *the glare of the headlights.* **2.** An angry look or stare: *I gave the cat a glare when it refused to come in. Noun.*
  ○ **1.** To shine with a strong, unpleasant light: *The sunlight glared at the beach.* **2.** To give an angry look. *Verb.*
  glare (glâr) *noun, plural* **glares**; *verb*, **glared, glaring.**

glaring **1.** Shining with a glare. **2.** Very easily noticed: *a glaring error in my addition.* **3.** Staring in an angry way: *The glaring driver told us never to run out into the street without looking.* **glar·ing** (glâr′ing) *adjective.*

glass **1.** A hard, clear material that breaks easily and is made by heating together sand and certain chemicals. Windows and camera lenses are made of glass. **2.** A container made of glass that is used for drinking. **3. glasses.** A pair of eyeglasses. **glass** (glas) *noun, plural* **glasses.**

glaze **1.** To put a hard, shiny finish on something: *My mother glazed a ham.* **2.** To fit a pane of glass into a window. *Verb.*
  ○ **1.** A thin coat of liquid put on pottery to make it glossy.
  glaze (glāz) *verb* **glazed, glazing**; *noun, plural* **glazes.**

gleam **1.** A flash or beam of bright light. **2.** A faint or short appearance or sign: *a gleam of hope. Noun.*
  ○ To shine; glow: *The new car gleamed in the sunlight. Verb.*
  gleam (glēm) *noun, plural* **gleams**; *verb*, **gleamed, gleaming.**

glee Joy or delight: *The little child laughed with glee.* **glee** (glē) *noun*; **gleeful**, *adjective* **gleefully**, *adverb*

glen A small, narrow valley. **glen** (glen) *noun, plural* **glens.**

glide **1.** To move smoothly along without any effort: *The skater glided across the ice.* **2.** To fly or descend slowly without using a motor for power: *The hawk glided over the field. Verb.*
  ○ *The act of gliding. Noun*
  glide (glīd) *verb*, **glided, gliding**; *noun, plural* **glides.**

glider An aircraft that flies without a motor. Rising air currents keep a glider in the air. **glid·er** (glī′dər) *noun, plural* **gliders.**

glimmer **1.** A dim, unsteady light: *the glimmer of a distant star.* **2.** A weak sign; hint: *a glimmer of hope. Noun.*
  ○ To shine with a dim, unsteady light: *The lights*

glider

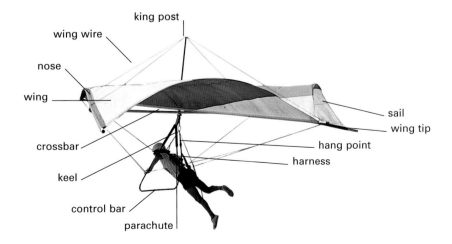

This hang glider is one of the newest types of gliders.

king post
wing wire
nose
wing
crossbar
keel
control bar
parachute
sail
wing tip
hang point
harness

on the airplane **glimmered** in the night sky. Verb. **glim·mer** (glim′ər) noun, plural **glimmers**; verb, **glimmered, glimmering.**

glimpse A quick look; glance: I caught a **glimpse** of my friend in the mall. Noun.
○ To see for a moment; glance. Verb.
glimpse (glimps) noun, plural **glimpses**; verb, **glimpsed, glimpsing.**

glint To sparkle or flash: Her eyes **glinted** with merriment. **glint** (glint) verb **glinted, glinting**; noun, plural **glints.**

glisten To shine with reflected light: The snow **glistened** in the sun. **glis·ten** (glis′ən) verb, **glistened, glistening.**

glitch A problem that prevents a computer or program from operating properly. **glitch** (glich) noun, plural **glitches.**

glitter To shine with bright flashes; sparkle: Stars **glittered** in the sky. Verb.
○ 1. Sparkling brightness or light: the **glitter** of a diamond. 2. Small bits of sparkling material used in decoration: We glued the **glitter** onto our costumes. Noun.
glit·ter (glit′ər) verb, **glittered, glittering**; noun.

gloat To look at or think about something with great satisfaction: The team **gloated** over their victory. **gloat** (glōt) verb, **gloated, gloating.**

global 1. Having the shape of a globe. 2. Having to do with the world: **global** weather conditions. **glob·al** (glō′bəl) adjective.

global warming An increase in the average temperature of the atmosphere of the earth. Global warming may result from the greenhouse effect.

globe 1. The world: The group traveled around the **globe**. 2. A round ball with a map of the world on it. 3. Anything shaped like a ball: We bought a new glass **globe** to cover the light bulb in the hall. **globe** (glōb) noun, plural **globes.**

gloom 1. Dim light or darkness: the **gloom** of the forest at night. 2. Low spirits; sorrow; sadness: I was filled with **gloom** when my best friend moved away. **gloom** (glüm) noun. —**gloominess** noun —**gloomy** adjective.

glorify 1. To praise or worship: The people **glorified** the hero. 2. To cause to appear more glorious than it is: The television show **glorified** the life of sailors at sea. **glo·ri·fy** (glôr′ə fī′) verb, **glorified, glorifying.**

glory 1. Great praise; honor; fame: They both did the work, but only one got the **glory**. 2. A person or thing that brings praise or honor: This forest is one of the **glories** of our state. 3. Great beauty; splendor: The sun shone in all its **glory**. Noun.
○ To rejoice proudly: The team **gloried** in their unexpected victory. Verb.
glor·y (glôr′ē) noun, plural **glories**; verb, **gloried, glorying.** —**glorious** adjective.

gloss A smooth, bright look; shine: I waxed the floor to give it a nice **gloss**. **gloss** (glôs) noun, plural **glosses**. —**glossy** adjective.

glossary A list of difficult words and their meanings. The words in a glossary are in alphabetical order. Some books have a glossary at the end. **glos·sa·ry** (glos′ə rē) noun, plural **glossaries.**

WORD HISTORY

Glossary comes from a Greek word meaning "tongue" or "speech." The Romans later borrowed this word and in Latin used it to mean "a difficult word" or "a word needing to be explained." It is from this Latin usage that our word glossary comes.

---

glove A covering for the hand. Most gloves have separate parts for each of the four fingers and for the thumb. However, boxing gloves and some baseball gloves hold the four fingers together in one part. **glove** (gluv) noun, plural **gloves.**

A baseball player uses a glove designed for the position he or she plays.

glow 1. A light or shine: At sunrise, the sky has an orange **glow**. 2. An appearance that suggests warmth or warm feeling: the **glow** of good health. Noun.
○ 1. To shine or burn without catching on fire: The light bulb **glows** brightly. 2. To have an appearance that suggests warmth or warm

feeling: *The parents' faces **glowed** as a friend admired their baby. Verb.*

glow (glō) *noun, plural* **glows**; *verb,* **glowed, glowing.**

glowworm A firefly. **glow·worm** (glō′wûrm′) *noun, plural* **fireflies.**

glue A substance used for sticking things together. *Noun.*
○ 1. To stick things together with glue. 2. To fasten or hold tightly. *Verb.* **glue** (glü) *noun, plural* **glues**; *verb,* **glued, gluing.**

glum Very unhappy or disappointed: *Every member of the losing team looked **glum** after the game.* **glum** (glum) *adjective.*

gm An abbreviation for **gram.**

gnarled Having a rough, twisted, or rugged look: *a **gnarled** old oak tree.* **gnarled** (närld) *adjective.*

gnat A small fly. Some gnats bite and suck blood from people and animals. Others feed on plants. **gnat** (nat) *noun, plural* **gnats.**

gnaw To bite again and again in order to wear away little by little: *The dog **gnawed** the bone.* **gnaw** (nô) *verb,* **gnawed, gnawing.**

gnome A kind of dwarf in fairy tales. **gnome** (nōm) *noun, plural* **gnomes.**

gnu A large African animal. A gnu is a kind of antelope but has a large head and a stocky build like an ox.
Other words that sound like this are **knew** and **new.** **gnu** (nü or nū) *noun, plural* **gnus** or **gnu.**

go 1. To move from one place to another; move along, ahead, or away. 2. To pass, be spent, or be lost: *Where did all the money **go**?* 3. To reach; lead: *The road **goes** east from here.* 5. To work; run: *Our car won't **go.*** 6. To have as a result; turn out: *The game **went** well for us.* 7. To be given: *First prize **went** to two students.* 8. To have a place or be suitable; belong or match: *The curtains **go** well with the new rug.* 9. To sound or make the sound of: *A cow **goes** "moo."* 10. To be capable of being divided: *How many times does eight **go** into forty?*
• **to go on.** 1. To continue or proceed: *The meeting **went on** until midnight.* 2. To take place; happen; occur: *What's **going on** here?*
• **to go out.** 1. To stop burning: *The candles **went out** from the wind.* 2. To go to a social

event or have a date: *My parents **go out** on Saturday nights.*
• **to let go.** 1. To release or free: *The dog wouldn't **let go** of the bone.* 2. To cause to be without a job; fire; discharge: *Because business was bad, the company had **to let** a lot of workers **go.***
go (gō) *verb,* **went, gone, going.**

goal 1. Something that a person wants and tries to get or become; aim; purpose. 2. A place in certain games where players must get the ball or puck in order to score. 3. The point or points made by getting the ball or puck into such a place. **goal** (gōl) *noun, plural* **goals.**

goalie The player who defends the goal in soccer, hockey, and some other games. **goal·ie** (gō′lē) *noun, plural* **goalies.**

goalkeeper A goalie. **goal·keep·er** (gōl′kē′pər) *noun, plural,* **goalkeepers.**

A goat is one of the most sure-footed of all animals.

goat An animal related to the sheep, having short horns and a tuft of hair like a beard under the chin. Goats are raised for their milk, hair, meat, and skin. **goat** (gōt) *noun, plural* **goats** or **goat.**

goatee A small pointed beard looking like a goat's beard. It is only large enough to cover the chin and ends in a point just below the chin. **goat·ee** (gō tē′) *noun, plural* **goatees.**

gobble¹ To eat something quickly and in large chunks. **gob·ble** (gob′əl) *verb,* **gobbled, gobbling.**

gobble² The sound that a turkey makes. *Noun.*
○ To make such a sound. *Verb.*

PRONUNCIATION KEY:
| at | ape | fär | câre | end | mē | it | īce | pïerce | hot | ōld | sông | fôrk |
| oil | out | up | ūse | rüle | pull | tûrn | chin | sing | shop | thin | this | |

hw in white; zh in treasure. The symbol ə stands for the unstressed vowel sound in about, taken, pencil, lemon, and circus.

313

gob·ble (gob′əl) *noun, plural* **gobbles;** *verb,* **gobbled, gobbling.**

goblet A kind of tall drinking glass set on a long stem. **gob·let** (gob′lit) *noun, plural* **goblets.**

goblin An ugly, mischievous spirit or elf. **gob·lin** (gob′lin) *noun, plural* **goblins.**

god 1. A being having power over the lives and doings of people: *The ancient Romans believed in many gods.* 2. A person or thing considered very important: *Their god is money.* **god** (god) *noun, plural* **gods.**

God The all-good, all-powerful being worshiped by Jews, Christians, and Muslims as the maker and ruler of the universe. **God** (god) *noun.*

goddess A female god. Gods and goddesses ruled the world in Greek myths. **god·dess** (god′is) *noun, plural* **goddesses.**

godfather A man who acts as a sponsor, usually at a baptism. **god·fa·ther** (god′fä′<u>th</u>ər) *noun, plural* **godfathers.**

godmother A woman who acts as a sponsor, usually at a baptism. **god·moth·er** (god′mu<u>th</u>′ər) *noun, plural* **godmothers.**

godparent A godfather or godmother. **god·par·ent** (god′pâr′ənt) *noun, plural* **godparents.**

goes A form of the present tense of **go** that is used with *he, she, it,* or the name of a person, place, or thing. Look up **go** for more information. **goes** (gōz) *verb.*

The safety **goggles** this woman is wearing are made of heavily coated plastic.

goggles Special eyeglasses that are worn to protect the eyes from water, glare, wind, dust, or sparks. **gog·gles** (gog′əlz) *plural noun.*

gold 1. A soft, heavy yellow metal, used to make jewelry and coins. Gold is a chemical element. 2. The yellow color of this metal. *Noun.*
○ 1. Made of or containing the metal gold. 2. Having the color gold. *Adjective.* **gold** (gōld) *noun, plural* **golds;** *adjective.*

golden 1. Made of or containing gold: *a golden crown.* 2. Having the color or shine of gold; bright or shining: *The baby's hair is soft and golden.* 3. Very good or valuable; excellent: *a golden opportunity.* 4. Very happy, with much success, wealth, or good fortune: *That was the golden age of Roman history when the empire was at peace.* **gold·en** (gōl′dən) *adjective.*

goldenrod A tall plant with long stalks of yellow flowers. Goldenrods bloom in late summer and autumn. **gold·en·rod** (gōl′dən rod′) *noun, plural* **goldenrods.**

goldfinch Any of a large group of small birds with thick bills and brightly colored feathers. The male American goldfinch is yellow with black markings. **gold·finch** (gōld′finch′) *noun, plural* **goldfinches.**

goldfish A fish that is usually orange-gold in color, often raised in home aquariums. **gold·fish** (gōld′fish′) *noun, plural* **goldfish** or **goldfishes.**

A **goldfish** can see an extraordinary range of colors.

golf A game played outdoors on a special course. It is played with a small, hard ball and a set of long, thin clubs with steel or wooden heads. The object of the game is to hit the ball into each of a series of holes with as few strokes at the ball as possible. *Noun.*
○ To play the game of golf. *Verb.* **golf** (golf) *noun; verb,* **golfed, golfing; golfer,** *noun.*

gondola 1. A long, narrow boat with a high peak at each end, rowed at one end by a man with an oar or pole. Gondolas are used to carry passengers on the canals of Venice, Italy. 2. A compartment under a blimp or large balloon, used to carry passengers and equipment. **gon·do·la** (gon′də lə) *noun, plural* **gondolas.**

gone Past participle of **go**. Look up **go** for more information. *Verb.*
  ○ Used up or spent: *The oranges are all* **gone**. *Adjective.*
  gone (gôn) *verb; adjective.*

gong A piece of metal shaped like a plate and used as a musical instrument. It is played with a padded hammer or drumstick and makes a deep sound when it is struck. **gong** (gông *or* gong) *noun, plural* **gongs**.

good 1. Of high quality; not bad or poor: *My health is* **good**. 2. Nice or pleasant: **good** *news*. 3. Giving help or an advantage: *The new trade agreement is* **good** *for the economy.* 4. Behaving properly: *The children were* **good** *while you were gone.* 5. Safe or correct; reliable: **good** *advice*. 6. Real; true; genuine: *I have a* **good** *excuse for being late. Adjective.*
  ○ 1. Benefit; advantage: *I'm doing this for your own* **good**. 2. Kindness or honesty: *There is some* **good** *in everybody. Noun.*
    • **as good as**. Almost; practically: *With our team leading by ten runs, the game was* **as good as** *over.*
    • **for good**. Forever; permanently: *The school might be closing* **for good**.
    • **no good**. Worthless or useless: *It's* **no good** *trying to please them.*
  good (gůd) *adjective,* **better**, **best**; *noun.*

good-bye Farewell: *After saying our* **good-byes**, *we left the party.* This word is also spelled *good-by*. **good-bye** (gůd'bī') *interjection; noun, plural* **good-byes**.

WORD HISTORY

Good-bye is a shortened modern form of God be with you! meaning "May God be with you!" This phrase was used as a form of farewell.

Good Friday A Christian holiday on the Friday before Easter marking the anniversary of the day Jesus died.

goodhearted Kind and generous. **good·heart·ed** (gůd'här'tid) *adjective.*

good-natured Pleasant, kindly, and cheerful toward others. **good-na·tured** (gůd'nā'chərd) *adjective.*

goodness The condition of being good: *They helped us out of the* **goodness** *of their hearts. Noun.*
  ○ A word used to express surprise: *My* **goodness**, *you've grown so tall! Interjection.*
  good·ness (gůd'nis) *noun; interjection.*

goods 1. Things that are sold; merchandise: *All of the store's* **goods** *are on sale.* 2. Things that belong to someone; belongings: *We moved all our household* **goods** *into our new apartment.* **goods** (gůdz) *plural noun.*

Many goods are being sold at this outdoor market.

good will or **goodwill** 1. Kindness or friendliness: *Show* **good will** *to your neighbors.* 2. Cheerful agreement to something: *Both sides accepted the decision with* **good will**. 3. The advantage a business has because of good relations with its customers: *Over the years, the supermarket on our block developed* **good will** *by charging fairer prices than its competitors.*

goose 1. A bird like a duck but larger and with a longer neck. 2. A female bird of this kind. A male goose is called a gander.
  • **to cook one's goose**. To spoil or destroy one's hopes, plans, or chances: *Their* **goose** *was cooked when they ran out of money for the project.*
  goose (gůs) *noun, plural* **geese**.

Many kinds of geese are wild but some are tame.

PRONUNCIATION KEY:
at   āpe   fär   câre   end   mē   it   īce   pîerce   hot   ōld   sông   fôrk
oil   out   up   ūse   rüle   pull   tûrn   chin   sing   shop   thin   this
hw in white; zh in treasure. The symbol ə stands for the unstressed vowel sound in about, taken, pencil, lemon, and circus.

315

goose bumps A rough condition of the skin caused by cold or fear. Goose bumps last only a short time.

gopher A North American animal that looks like a large chipmunk. Gophers have large pouches in their cheeks and burrow under the ground to build long tunnels to live in. **go•pher** (gō′fər) *noun, plural* **gophers.**

gorge A deep, narrow valley with steep, rocky walls. *Noun.*
○ 1. To eat food in a greedy way: *The children quickly gorged their dinner.* 2. To stuff with food: *I gorged myself with four helpings of spaghetti.* *Verb.*
gorge (gôrj) *noun, plural* **gorges;** *verb,* **gorged, gorging.**

gorgeous Very pleasing to look at; beautiful: *the gorgeous colors of the autumn leaves.* **gor•geous** (gôr′jəs) *adjective.*

A gorilla is a highly intelligent animal.

gorilla A large, very strong African ape. Gorillas have big, heavy bodies, short legs, and long arms. Another word that sounds like this is **guerrilla**. **go•ril•la** (gə ril′ə) *noun, plural* **gorillas.**

WORD HISTORY

The word gorilla comes from a Greek word that means "wild, hairy person." Some early explorers in Africa thought that the gorillas were wild people instead of animals.

gospel 1. The teachings of Jesus and the Apostles. 2. Gospel. In the Bible, any of the first four books of the New Testament about the life and teachings of Jesus. 3. Anything believed as absolutely true: *The patients took their doctor's advice as gospel.* **gos•pel** (gos′pəl) *noun, plural* **gospels.**

gossip 1. Talk or rumors about other people, often untrue and unkind: *There's a lot of gossip about why the mayor is resigning.* 2. A person who enjoys talking about other people or who repeats rumors to others: *Those two are nothing but gossips.* *Noun.*
○ To use gossip in one's speech. *Verb.*
gos•sip (gos′ip) *noun, plural* **gossips;** *verb,* **gossiped, gossiping.**

got Past tense and a past participle of **get**. Look up **get** for more information. **got** (got) *verb.*

gotten A past participle of **get**. Look up **get** for more information. **got•ten** (got′ən) *verb.*

gouge 1. A chisel with a curved, hollow blade, used for making holes or grooves in wood. 2. A hole, groove, or cut: *We made a gouge in the floor when we dragged the table.* Noun.
○ To cut or scoop out: *The carpenter gouged the wood for the shelves. Verb.*
gouge (gouj) *noun, plural* **gouges;** *verb,* **gouged, gouging.**

gourd A rounded fruit related to the pumpkin or squash. Gourds grow on vines and have a hard outer rind. They are dried and used to make bowls, jugs, and dippers and are also used for decoration. **gourd** (gôrd) *noun, plural* **gourds.**

gourmet A person who loves fine food and knows a great deal about it. **gour•met** (gùr mā′ or gùr′mā) *noun, plural* **gourmets.**

gov. *or* **Gov.** An abbreviation for **governor** or **government.**

govern To rule, control, or manage: *Their actions were governed by a desire for money.* **gov•ern** (guv′ərn) *verb,* **governed, governing.**

government 1. The group of people in charge of ruling or managing a country, state, city, or other place. 2. A way of ruling or governing: *Canadians have a democratic government.* **gov•ern•ment** (guv′ərn mənt *or* guv′ər mənt) *noun, plural* **governments.**

governor 1. The person elected to be the head of government of a state of the United States. 2. A person appointed to govern a province, colony, or territory. **gov•er•nor** (guv′ər nər) *noun, plural* **governors.**

govt. An abbreviation for **government.**

gown 1. A woman's dress usually worn on special occasions. 2. A long, loose robe such as a student at graduation ceremonies and a judge in court wears. **gown** (goun) *noun, plural* **gowns.**

grab To take hold of suddenly; seize; snatch: *Grab your jacket and run to get the bus. Verb.*
○ A sudden, snatching movement. *Noun.*
grab (grab) *verb,* **grabbed, grabbing;** *noun, plural* **grabs.**

grace 1. Beautiful or pleasing design, movement, or style: *The ballerina danced with grace.* 2. A short prayer said before or after a meal. 3. Kindness and courtesy to others; manners: *They had the grace to apologize for being so rude. Noun.*
○ To add honor or beauty to: *A bouquet of roses graced the table. Verb.*
• **in someone's good graces.** Liked or approved by someone: *I'm not in their good graces because I behaved badly at their party.*
grace (grās) *noun, plural* **graces;** *verb,* **graced, gracing.**

graceful Beautiful or pleasing in design, movement, or style: *The dancer made a graceful bow to the audience.* **grace·ful** (grās′fəl) *adjective;* **gracefully,** *adverb.*

gracious Full of grace and charm: *The gracious host made each guest feel welcome.* **gra·cious** (grā′shəs) *adjective.*—**graciously** *adverb.*

grackle A kind of blackbird with a long tail and shiny black feathers. **grack·le** (grak′əl) *noun, plural* **grackles.**

grade 1. A year or level of work in school. 2. A number or letter showing how well a student has done in work at school; mark. 3. A degree or step in value, quality, or rank: *This beef is of the highest grade.* 4. The slope of a road or a railroad track: *There was a steep grade on the road. Noun.*
○ 1. To place or arrange in grades; sort: *The farmer graded the eggs by size and color.* 2. To give a grade to; mark. 3. To make more level; make less steep. *The bulldozer graded the new road. Verb.*
grade (grād) *noun, plural* **grades;** *verb,* **graded, grading.**

grade school A school for children from the ages of about six to twelve or fourteen. This school is also called an elementary school or a grammar school.

gradual Happening little by little: *We watched the gradual growth of the seeds into plants in our vegetable garden.* **grad·u·al** (graj′ü əl) *adjective.*—**gradually** *adverb.*

graduate 1. To finish studying at a school or college and be given a diploma. 2. To mark with evenly spaced lines for measuring: *This thermometer is graduated in degrees. Verb.*
○ A person who has finished studying at a school or college and has been given a diploma. *Noun.*
grad·u·ate (graj′ü ā′t *for verb;* graj′ü it *for noun*) *verb,* **graduated, graduating;** *noun, plural* **graduates.**

graduation 1. The act or process of graduating: *You must pass English for graduation.* 2. The ceremony of graduating from a school or college: *My whole family went to my graduation.* **grad·u·a·tion** (graj′ü ā′shən) *noun, plural* **graduations.**

graffiti Words or pictures scratched or painted on subway cars, buses, or the walls of buildings. **graf·fi·ti** (grə fē′tē) *noun plural,* **graffito** (grə fē′tō).

graft 1. To put a shoot, bud, or branch from one plant into a slit in another plant so that the two pieces will grow together and form one plant. 2. To transfer a piece of skin or bone onto an injured part of the body: *The doctors grafted skin from the patient's leg onto the burned arm. Verb.*
○ 1. A shoot, bud, or branch that has been grafted. 2. A piece of living or synthetic tissue that is to be grafted. *Noun.*
graft (graft) *verb,* **grafted, grafting;** *noun, plural* **grafts.**

grain 1. The seed of wheat, corn, rice, oats, and other cereal plants. 2. A tiny, hard piece of something: *grains of sand.* 3. The lines and other marks that run through wood, stone, and other things. **grain** (grān) *noun, plural* **grains.**

gram A unit of mass or weight in the metric system. One ounce is equal to about 28 grams. One pound is equal to about 450 grams. **gram** (gram) *noun, plural* **grams.**

grammar 1. A system of arranging words in sentences so that the meaning of what is said is clearly communicated. Grammar is based on a series of rules. Most of these rules come naturally

PRONUNCIATION KEY:

| at | āpe | fär | câre | end | mē | it | īce | pierce | hot | ōld | sông | fôrk |
| oil | out | up | ūse | rüle | pull | tûrn | chin | sing | shop | thin | this | |

hw in white; zh in treasure. The symbol ə stands for the unstressed vowel sound in about, taken, pencil, lemon, and circus.

317

to us as we use our language or hear it used by other people. **2.** A book containing the rules of grammar: *I have my father's old Latin grammar.* **3.** The use of words in a way thought of as standard: *Many people think that the word "ain't" is bad grammar.* **gram·mar** (gram'ər) *noun, plural* **grammars**.

grammar school A school for children from the ages of about six to twelve or fourteen. This school is also called an *elementary school* or a *grade school.*

grammatical **1.** Following the rules of grammar. The sentence "Bought I shirt a white" is not grammatical, while "I bought a white shirt" is. **2.** Having to do with grammar: *This book report has several grammatical errors.* **gram·mat·i·cal** (grə mat'i kəl) *adjective.*

grand **1.** Large and splendid: *a grand palace.* **2.** Including everything; complete: *a grand total of one thousand dollars.* **3.** Most important; main: *The grand prize in this contest is a trip.* **4.** Very good or excellent: *We had a grand time at the party.* **grand** (grand) *adjective,* **grander,** **grandest**.

grandchild A child of one's son or daughter. A grandchild is either a granddaughter or grandson. **grand·child** (grand'chīld') *noun, plural* **grandchildren** (grand'chil'drən).

granddaughter A daughter of one's son or daughter. **grand·daugh·ter** (gran'dô'tər) *noun, plural* **granddaughters**.

grandfather The father of one's mother or father. **grand·fath·er** (grand'fä'thər) *noun, plural* **grandfathers**.

A clock in a tall, narrow cabinet that stands on the floor.

A **grandfather clock** keeps time with the help of a pendulum beneath its face.

grandmother The mother of one's mother or father. **grand·moth·er** (grand'muth'ər) *noun, plural* **grandmothers**.

grandparent A parent of one's mother or father. A grandparent is either a grandmother or a grandfather. **grand·par·ent** (grand'pâr'ənt) *noun, plural* **grandparents**.

grandson A son of one's son or daughter. **grand·son** (grand'sun') *noun, plural* **grandsons**.

grandstand The main place where people sit when watching a parade or sports event. It has raised rows of seats that are sometimes covered by a roof. **grand·stand** (grand'stand') *noun, plural* **grandstands**.

Granite usually contains quartz.

granite A hard kind of rock used to build monuments and buildings. **gran·ite** (gran'it) *noun.*

granola A food made of oats and other ingredients, such as dried fruit, nuts, and honey, and eaten as a breakfast cereal and as a snack. **gra·no·la** (grə nō'lə) *noun.*

grant **1.** To give or allow: *My teacher granted me permission to go home early.* **2.** To admit to be true: *I'll grant that it will be faster if we ride bikes rather than walk. Verb.*
○ Something is granted; a gift: *The settlers got a grant of land from the government. Noun.*
• **to take for granted.** To suppose something to be true or probable: *I took it for granted that you wanted to sleep late; so I turned off the alarm clock.*
grant (grant) *verb,* **granted,** **granting;** *noun, plural* **grants**.

grape A small, juicy, round fruit that grows in bunches on vines. Grapes have a smooth, thin skin that is usually green, red, or purple in color. **grape** (grāp) *noun, plural* **grapes.**

grapefruit A round fruit with a yellow rind and juicy yellow or pink pulp inside. It is like an orange, but larger and more sour. **grape•fruit** (grāp′früt′) *noun, plural* **grape-fruits** *or* **grapefruit.**

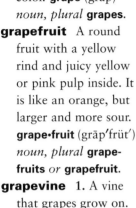

Juice, jelly, jam, raisins, and wine are made from grapes.

grapevine 1. A vine that grapes grow on. 2. A secret or informal way of spreading news or rumors from person to person: *We heard it through the grapevine that your birthday is today.* **grape•vine** (grāp′vīn′) *noun, plural* **grapevines.**

graph A drawing that shows the relationship between changing things: *The class drew a graph to show how the population of the United States has grown over the past one hundred years.* **graph** (graf) *noun, plural* **graphs.**

-graph A suffix that means: 1. An instrument that writes or records: *Seismograph means an instrument that records earthquakes.* 2. Something written or recorded: *Photograph means a picture recorded on film.*

graphic 1. Having to do with handwriting. 2. Having to do with pictures or designs. 3. Described or told in detail: *Alice gave us a graphic account of the hurricane.* **graph•ic** (graf′ik) *adjective.* **—graphically** *adverb.*

graphics 1. The charts, designs, pictures, and artwork that a person can make on a computer and show on the screen. 2. The drawings, photographs, maps, and other images in a printed work: *This dictionary has beautiful graphics.* **graphi•cs** (graf′iks) *plural noun.*

graphite A soft, black form of the element carbon, used as the writing lead in pencils. **graph•ite** (graf′īt) *noun.*

WORD HISTORY

The mineral **graphite** takes its name from the Greek word meaning "to write."

---

grasp 1. To take hold of firmly with or as if with the hand. 2. To see the meaning of; understand: *I had a hard time grasping the meaning of that poem. Verb.*
○ 1. The act of grasping. 2. The power or ability to grasp. 3. Knowledge; understanding. *Noun.*
grasp (grasp) *verb,* **grasped, grasping;** *noun, plural* **grasps.**

grass Any of a large number of plants with narrow leaves called blades. Grasses grow in lawns, fields, and pastures. Horses, cows, and sheep eat grass. Wheat, rye, oats, corn, sugarcane, rice, and bamboo are kinds of grasses. **grass** (gras) *noun, plural* **grasses.** **—grassy** *adjective.*

grasshopper A flying insect with long, powerful legs for jumping. Many grasshoppers eat grasses and crops and can become great pests to farmers. **grass•hop•per** (gras′hop′ər) *noun, plural* **grasshoppers.**

When a grasshopper rubs its hind legs together it produces a chirping sound.

grassland Land covered mainly with grass, used as pasture for animals. **grass•land** (gras′land′) *noun, plural* **grasslands.**

grate¹ 1. A frame of iron bars set over a window or other opening. It is used as a cover, guard, or screen. 2. A frame of iron bars for holding burning fuel in a fireplace or furnace. Another word that sounds like this is **great.** **grate** (grāt) *noun, plural* **grates.**

PRONUNCIATION KEY:

| at | āpe | fär | câre | end | mē | it | īce | pierce | hot | old | sông | fôrk |
| oil | out | up | ūse | rüle | pull | tûrn | chin | sing | shop | thin | this | |

hw in white; zh in treasure. The symbol ə stands for the unstressed vowel sound in about, taken, pencil, lemon, and circus.

319

grate² **1.** To make into small pieces by rubbing against a rough surface: *The cook grated some cheese to sprinkle on the spaghetti.* **2.** To scrape with a harsh, grinding noise: *The chalk grated on the blackboard.* **3.** To be annoying, irritating, or unpleasant: *A shrill laugh really grates on me.* Another word that sounds like this is **great.** **grate** (grāt) *verb,* **grated, grating.**

grateful Full of thanks for a favor or for something that makes one happy: *We were grateful to be inside on such a cold, stormy night.* **grate·ful** (grāt′fəl) *adjective.* —**gratefully** *adverb.*

gratify To give pleasure to; please: *I was gratified by the good news.* **grat·i·fy** (grat′ə fī′) *verb,* **gratified, gratifying.**

grating¹ A grate. **grat·ing** (grāt′ing) *noun, plural* **gratings.**

grating² **1.** Making a harsh, grinding sound: *There was a loud grating noise as we pulled the rusty lid open.* **2.** Not pleasant; annoying: *I find your habit of chewing your fingernails very grating.* **grat·ing** (grāt′ing) *adjective.*

gratitude A feeling of gratefulness: *We are full of gratitude for your help.* **grat·i·tude** (grat′i tüd′ *or* grat′i tūd′) *noun.*

grave¹ A hole dug in the ground for burying a dead person. **grave** (grāv) *noun, plural* **graves.**

grave² **1.** Thoughtful and solemn; serious: *The doctors became grave as they described the operation.* **2.** Very important: *The general had to make grave decisions when the war broke out.* **grave** (grāv) *adjective,* **graver, gravest.**

gravel Pebbles and small pieces of rock, used for making driveways and roads. **grav·el** (grav′əl) *noun.*

graveyard A place where dead people are buried; cemetery. **grave·yard** (grāv′yärd′) *noun, plural* **graveyards.**

gravitation The force or pull that draws all the bodies in the universe toward one another. Gravitation is the force that keeps the planets in their orbit around the sun. It also keeps people and objects on the surface of the earth. **grav·i·ta·tion** (grav′i tā′shən) *noun.*

gravity **1.** The force that pulls things toward the center of the earth. Gravity is the force that causes objects to fall when they are dropped. It also pulls them back to earth when they are thrown upward and causes objects to have weight.

2. Serious nature: *Because of the gravity of the situation, troops were sent in.* **grav·i·ty** (grav′i tē) *noun, plural* **gravities.**

gravy A sauce made from the juices that come from meat during cooking. **gra·vy** (grā′vē) *noun, plural* **gravies.**

gray A color made by mixing black and white. *Noun.* **1.** Having the color gray: *gray eyes.* **2.** Dark, gloomy, or dreary: *It was gray and rainy all week. Adjective.* This word is also spelled *grey.* **gray** (grā) *noun, plural* **grays;** *adjective,* **grayer, grayest.**

graze¹ **1.** To feed on growing grass: *The sheep grazed on the hillside.* **2.** To put out to feed on growing grass: *The farmer grazed the cattle in the pasture.* **graze** (grāz) *verb,* **grazed, grazing.**

graze² To scrape or touch lightly in passing: *The tree grazed the house when the wind knocked it over.* **graze** (grāz) *verb,* **grazed, grazing.**

grease **1.** Melted animal fat: *Please clean the grease from the pan you used to cook the bacon.* **2.** A very thick, oily material put on the parts of an automobile engine that move against one another. *Noun.*
○ To rub or put grease on or in *Verb.* Another word that sounds like this is **Greece.** **grease** (grēs *for noun;* grēs *or* grēz *for verb*) *noun, plural* **greases;** *verb,* **greased, greasing.**

greasy **1.** Soiled with grease: *The mechanics' uniforms were greasy after they repaired the car.* **2.** Containing much grease or fat; oily: *This fried chicken is greasy.* **3.** Like grease; oily; slick: *This lotion feels greasy.* **greas·y** (grē′sē *or* grē′zē) *adjective,* **greasier, greasiest.** —**greasiness** *noun.*

great **1.** Very large in size, number, or amount: *A great crowd gathered.* **2.** Very important, excellent, or remarkable: *a great discovery.* **3.** More than is usual; much: *We'll never forget your great kindness to us.* Another word that sounds like this is **grate.** **great** (grāt) *adjective,* **greater, greatest.**

Great Britain **1.** An island off the western coast of Europe. Great Britain includes England, Scotland, and Wales. **2.** A term sometimes used for *United Kingdom.* Look up **United Kingdom** for more information.

Great Dane A large, powerful dog with a smooth, short coat. **Great Dane** (dān).

great-grandchild The child of one's grandchild.

great-grand·child (grāt′gran′chīld) *noun, plural* **great-grandchildren** (grāt′grand′chil′drən).

great-grandfather The father of one's grandparent. **great-grand·fa·ther** (grāt′grand′fä′<u>th</u>ər) *noun, plural* **great-grandfathers.**

great-grandmother The mother of one's grandparent. **great-grand·moth·er** (grāt′grand′mu<u>th</u>′ər) *noun, plural* **great-grandmothers.**

great-grandparent The mother or father of one's grandparent. **great-grand·par·ent** (grā′t grand′pâr′ənt) *noun, plural* **great-grandparents.**

greatly Very much; highly: *We greatly appreciated your gift.* **great·ly** (grāt′lē) *adverb.*

Greece A country in southeastern Europe, on the Mediterranean Sea. In ancient times, Greece was a center of learning and the arts. Another word that sounds like this is **grease.** **Greece** (grēs) *noun.*

greed A very great and selfish desire for more than one's share: *Because of their greed, the owners of that store try to cheat their customers.* **greed** (grēd) *noun, plural* **greeds.** —**greedy** *adjective.*

Greek Having to do with Greece, its people, or their language or culture. *Adjective.*
○ **1.** A person who was born in or is a citizen of Greece. **2.** A person who lived in ancient Greece. **3.** The language of Greece. *Noun.*
Greek (grēk) *adjective; noun, plural* **Greeks.**

green 1. The color of growing grass and leaves, made by mixing blue and yellow. **2.** Ground covered with grass: *the village green.* **3.** On a golf course, the area around the hole that has very thick, closely cut grass. **4.** greens. Green leaves and stems of plants that are used for food or decoration: *We are having beet greens with dinner. Noun.*
○ **1.** Having the color green: *a green coat.* **2.** Covered with growing plants, grass, or leaves: *green pastures.* **3.** Not finished growing or not ripe: *green tomatoes.* **4.** Having little or no training or experience: *The pitcher and catcher are green compared to the other players on their team. Adjective.*
green (grēn) *noun, plural* **greens;** *adjective,* **greener, greenest.**

greenhouse A room or building with walls and sides made of glass, where plants can be grown all year long. **green·house** (grēn′hous′) *noun, plural* **greenhouses** (grēn′hou′ziz).

greenhouse effect The trapping of heat from the sun within the earth's atmosphere. This can happen from an increase of carbon dioxide created by the burning of fossil fuels on earth. The gases keep the heat from escaping into space, just as the glass windows keep heat inside a greenhouse.

Greenland An island northeast of North America, in the Atlantic Ocean. It belongs to Denmark and is the largest island in the world. **Green·land** (grēn′ land′ *or* grēn′ lənd) *noun.*

green thumb A special talent for growing plants.

greet 1. To speak to or welcome in a friendly way. **2.** To respond to; meet; receive: *The announcement that school would end early was greeted with cheers.* **3.** To present itself to; appear to: *A snowy scene greeted us in the morning.* **greet** (grēt) *verb,* **greeted, greeting.**

greeting 1. The act or words of a person who greets others: *Our host gave us a friendly greeting.* **2.** greetings. A friendly message sent by someone: *My friends send greetings to me on my birthday.* **greet·ing** (grēt′ing) *noun, plural* **greetings.**

grenade A small bomb that can be thrown by hand or fired by a rifle. **gre·nade** (gri nād′) *noun, plural* **grenades.**

grew Past tense of **grow.** Look up **grow** for more information. **grew** (grü) *verb.*

grey Another spelling for **gray.** Look up **gray** for more information. **grey** (grā).

greyhound A slender dog that has a smooth coat and a long nose and can run very fast. **grey·hound** (grā′hound′) *noun, plural* **greyhounds.**

grid 1. An arrangement of parallel or crossing bars or wires, with openings between them; grating. **2.** A pattern of intersecting parallel lines used to divide a map or chart into squares. **grid** (grid) *noun, plural* **grids.**

griddle A heavy, flat metal pan with a handle, used for cooking pancakes and other food. **grid·dle** (grid′əl) *noun, plural* **griddles.**

gridiron 1. A grill used for broiling food. **2.** A football field. **grid·i·ron** (grid′ī′ərn) *noun, plural* **gridirons.**

PRONUNCIATION KEY:

| at | āpe | fär | câre | end | mē | it | īce | pierce | hot | ōld | sông | fôrk |
| oil | out | up | ūse | rüle | pull | tûrn | chin | sing | shop | thin | <u>th</u>is | |

hw in white; zh in treasure. The symbol ə stands for the unstressed vowel sound in about, taken, pencil, lemon, and circus.

321

A football field is called a gridiron because its yard line markers are in the form of a grid.

WORD HISTORY

The Middle English word which gave us gridiron meant "a grating or lattice." A football field is called a gridiron because it is crisscrossed with yard markings that look like a lattice.

gridlock A traffic jam so large that no vehicles can move in any direction. **grid·lock** (grid'lok') *noun, plural* **gridlocks.**

grief A very great feeling of being sad: *My grief at the death of my dog was something I'll never forget.* **grief** (grēf) *noun.*

grieve 1. To feel grief; mourn: *The nation grieved at the death of the president.* 2. To make someone feel grief or sorrow: *Your unkind words grieved your friends.* **grieve** (grēv) *verb,* **grieved, grieving.**

grill 1. A framework of metal bars for cooking food over an open fire. 2. A restaurant that mainly serves food cooked on a grill. *Noun.*
○ 1. To cook on a grill. 2. To question closely, harshly, and for a long time: *The*

A grill can be fueled by gas, electricity, or treated coals.

sergeant **grilled** the soldiers until they confessed their crime. *Verb.*
grill (gril) *noun, plural* **grills;** *verb,* **grilled, grilling.**

grim 1. Stern, frightening, and harsh: *a grim expression on his face.* 2. Refusing to give up; very stubborn: *grim determination.* **grim** (grim) *adjective,* **grimmer, grimmest.**

grimace A twisting of the face. People often make a grimace when they are not comfortable, pleased, or happy about something. *Noun.*
○ To make a grimace. *Verb.*
gri·mace (grim'əs *or* gri mās') *noun, plural* **grimaces;** *verb,* **grimaced, grimacing.**

grime Dirt that is covering or rubbed into a surface. **grime** (grīm) *noun.* —**grimy** *adjective.*

grin To smile very broadly and happily. *Verb.*
○ A very broad, happy smile. *Noun.*
grin (grin) *verb,* **grinned, grinning;** *noun, plural* **grins.**

grind 1. To crush into small pieces or into a fine powder: *We watched the butcher grind the meat.* 2. To make something smooth or sharp by rubbing it against something rough: *The farmer ground the ax on the grindstone.* 3. To rub or press down in a harsh or noisy way: *I grind my teeth when I'm angry.* **grind** (grīnd) *verb,* **ground, grinding.**

grindstone A round, flat stone, set in a frame. By spinning it around a person can use it to sharpen knives, axes, and other tools. **grind·stone** (grīnd'stōn') *noun, plural* **grindstones.**

grip 1. A firm hold; tight grasp: *I kept a good grip on the dog.* 2. Firm control or power: *The city was in the grip of a heavy snowstorm. Noun.*
○ 1. To take hold of firmly and tightly. 2. To attract and keep the interest of: *That novel really gripped us. Verb.*
grip (grip) *noun, plural* **grips;** *verb,* **gripped, gripping.**

grit 1. Very small bits of sand or stone. 2. Bravery; courage: *It takes grit to climb a cliff without any equipment. Noun.*
○ To press together hard: *I gritted my teeth. Verb.*
grit (grit) *noun; verb,* **gritted, gritting.**

grits Ground grain, usually white corn, boiled and eaten as a cereal. **grits** (grits) *plural noun.*

grizzled Gray or mixed with gray. **griz·zled** (griz'əld) *adjective.*

grizzly bear A very large, powerful bear with

long claws and brown or gray fur. Grizzly bears live in western North America. **griz·zly bear** (griz′lē).

groan A deep, sad sound that people make when they are unhappy, annoyed, or in pain. *Noun.*
○ To make this sound *Verb.*
Another word that sounds like this is **grown.**
groan (grōn) *noun, plural* **groans**; *verb,* **groaned, groaning.**

grocer A person who sells food and household supplies. **gro·cer** (grō′sər) *noun, plural* **grocers.**

grocery 1. A store that sells food and household supplies. 2. groceries. Food and other things sold by a grocer. **gro·cer·y** (grō′sə rē) *noun, plural* **groceries.**

groggy Not fully alert or awake: *I'm pretty groggy when I wake up in the morning.* **grog·gy** (grog′ē) *adjective,* **groggier, groggiest.** —**groggily** *adverb* —**grogginess** *noun.*

groom 1. A man who has just been married. 2. A person whose work is taking care of horses. *Noun.*
○ 1. To wash, brush, and take care of horses. 2. To make neat and pleasant in appearance: *A barber grooms people's hair for a living. Verb.* **groom** (grüm) *noun, plural* **grooms**; *verb,* **groomed, grooming.**

groove A long, narrow cut or dent: *The wheels of the car made grooves in the dirt road. Noun.*
○ 1 To make a groove or grooves in. *Verb* **groove** (grüv) *noun, plural* **grooves**; *verb,* **grooved, grooving.**

grope 1. To feel about with the hands: *The child groped for the light switch in the dark.* 2. To search for something in a blind or uncertain way: *The student groped for the right answer.* **grope** (grōp) *verb,* **groped, groping.**

gross 1. With nothing taken out; total; entire: *A person's gross income is all the money he or she earns before taxes are taken out of it.* 2. Very easily seen or understood: *It is a gross injustice that this innocent person was sent to prison.* 3. Coarse; vulgar: *gross jokes. Adjective.*
○ 1. The total amount received before anything is taken out. 2. Twelve dozen; 144: *a gross of tennis balls. Noun.* **gross** (grōs) *adjective,* **grosser, grossest**; *noun, plural* **grosses** (for definition 1) or **gross**

(for definition 2).

grotesque Strange or ugly in shape or appearance: *There were grotesque monsters in the movie.* **gro·tesque** (grō tesk′) *adjective.* —**grotesquely** *adverb.*

WORD HISTORY

The word **grotesque** comes from an Italian word meaning "of or from a cave." The Italian word was first used to describe strange paintings found on the walls of caves in Italy. The word **grotesque** is now used for anything that is strange and ugly.

---

grouch A person who is often cross, has a bad temper, and usually complains a great deal. **grouch** (grouch) *noun, plural* **grouches.**

grouchy Easily annoyed or angered; in a bad mood. **grouch·y** (grou′chē) *adjective,* **grouchier, grouchiest.**

ground¹ 1. The part of the earth that is solid; soil; land. 2. grounds. The land around a building: *The school grounds were planted with flowers.* 3. An area of land used for a special purpose: *picnic grounds.* 4. The reason why something is said, done, or thought: *What grounds do you have for thinking they are lying?* 5. grounds. The bits that settle at the bottom of a liquid: *coffee grounds. Noun.*
○ 1. To force to stay on the ground or to come down to the ground: *The airport grounded the plane because of bad weather.* 2. To cause to hit the bottom of a body of water: *The captain grounded the ship on the sand bar.* 3. To hit a baseball so that it rolls or bounces along the ground. 4. To fix or base firmly: *Ground your argument on facts.* 5. To connect with the ground so that electricity passes into it. Electrical wires or devices are grounded to prevent a person from receiving a shock from any electricity that might collect in them. *Verb.*
ground (ground) *noun, plural* **grounds**; *verb,* **grounded, grounding.**

ground² Past tense and past participle of **grind.** Look up **grind** for more information. **ground** (ground) *verb.*

groundhog A woodchuck. Look up **woodchuck** for more information. **ground·hog** (ground′hôg′

PRONUNCIATION KEY:
| at | āpe | fär | câre | end | mē | it | īce | pierce | hot | ōld | sông | fôrk |
| oil | out | up | ūse | rüle | pull | tûrn | chin | sing | shop | thin | this | |

hw in white; zh in treasure. The symbol ə stands for the unstressed vowel sound in about, taken, pencil, lemon, and circus.

323

or ground'hog') *noun, plural* **groundhogs.**

group **1.** A number of persons or things together: *A* **group** *of people gathered on the corner to watch the fire.* **2.** A number of persons or things belonging together or put together: *The teacher divided the class into* **groups.** *Noun.*
○ To form or put into a group or groups: *The counselor at summer camp* **grouped** *us by age. Verb.*
group (grüp) *noun, plural* **groups;** *verb,* **grouped, grouping.**

GROUPS

Many kinds of animals are often seen in groups and over the years names have been developed for these gatherings. Most of us know about a herd of cattle or a pack of wolves, but many other animals have special group names. Often the members of these groups are related to each other. Some of the most common names are:

Ants gather in a **colony.**
Bees gather in a **swarm.**
Eggs are laid in a **clutch.**
Ducks gather in a **brace.**
Elks gather in a **gang.**
Geese gather in a **flock** *or* **gaggle.**
Gorillas gather in a **band.**
Hens gather in a **brood.**
Kangaroos gather in a **troop.**
Lions gather in a **pride.**
Monkeys gather in a **troop.**
Oxen gather in a **yoke.**
Sheep gather in a **flock.**
Whales gather in a **pod.**

---

grouse A plump bird with brown, black, or gray feathers. Grouse live in forests and on open land and are often hunted as game. **grouse** (grous) *noun, plural* **grouse** *or* **grouses.**

grove A group of trees standing together: *Orange trees are grown in orange* **groves.** **grove** (grōv) *noun, plural* **groves.**

grow **1.** To become bigger; increase. **2.** To come into being and live; exist: *Cactuses don't* **grow** *here.* **3.** To cause to grow: *Farmers* **grow** *corn.* **4.** To become: *It* **grew** *cold as the sun went down.*
• **to grow up.** To become an adult: *I want to be a musician when I* **grow up.**
grow (grō) *verb,* **grew, grown, growing.**

growl To make a deep, harsh, rumbling sound in the throat. Dogs and other animals often growl when they are angry. *Verb.*
○ A deep, harsh, rumbling sound made in the throat. *Noun.*
growl (groul) *verb,* **growled, growling;** *noun, plural* **growls.**

grown Past participle of **grow.** Look up **grow** for more information.
Another word that sounds like this is **groan.**
grown (grōn) *verb.*

grown-up **1.** Fully grown; adult. *Your cousin is a* **grown-up** *person now.* **2.** Of or like an adult: *Those children have* **grown-up** *manners. Adjective.*
○ An adult: *The* **grown-ups** *watched as the children swam in the pool. Noun.*
grown-up (grōn'up' *for adjective;* grōn'up' *for noun) adjective; noun, plural* **grown-ups.**

growth **1.** The process of growing: *The* **growth** *of my parents' business has been very rapid.* **2.** Something that has grown: *a thick* **growth** *of weeds.* **growth** (grōth) *noun, plural* **growths.**

grub **1.** An insect in an early stage of growth, when it looks like a worm. **2.** Food. *Noun.*
○ To dig in the ground; dig up from the ground: *Pigs* **grub** *for food with their hooves and snouts. Verb.*
grub (grub) *noun, plural* **grubs;** *verb,* **grubbed, grubbing.**

grubby Dirty and messy: *The baby's face and hands were* **grubby** *with food.* **grub•by** (grub'ē) *adjective,* **grubbier, grubbiest.**

grudge Dislike or anger that has been felt for a long time: *Those two have held a* **grudge** *against each other ever since kindergarten. Noun.*
○ To be unwilling to give or allow: *Although they don't like you, they won't* **grudge** *you first prize if you deserve it. Verb.*
grudge (gruj) *noun, plural* **grudges;** *verb,* **grudged, grudging.**

grueling Very difficult or exhausting: *a* **grueling** *race.* **gru•el•ing**

A marathon presents a grueling **challenge to runners.**

(grü′ə ling) *adjective.*

gruesome Causing disgust or fear; horrible: *gruesome* ghost stories. **grue·some** (grü′səm) *adjective;* **gruesomely,** *adverb.*

gruff 1. Deep and rough-sounding: *a gruff* voice. 2. Not friendly, warm, or polite. Some people have a gruff manner but are really very kind. **gruff** (gruf) *adjective,* **gruffer, gruffest. —gruffly** *adverb* **—gruffness** *noun.*

grumble 1. To complain in a low voice. 2. To make a low, rumbling sound: *My stomach grumbles when I am hungry. Verb.*
○ 1. Unhappy complaining or muttering. 2. A low, rumbling sound. *Noun.*
grum·ble (grum′bəl) *verb,* **grumbled, grumbling;** *noun, plural* **grumbles.**

grumpy In a bad mood; cross or grouchy. **grum·py** (grum′pē) *adjective,* **grumpier, grumpiest.**

grunt A short, deep sound. *Noun.*
○ 1. To make a short, deep sound: *The lifeguards grunted as they pulled the boat out of the water.* 2. To say with a grunt: *The exhausted runner grunted, "I did it," at the finish of the race. Verb.*
grunt (grunt) *noun, plural* **grunts;** *verb,* **grunted, grunting.**

guarantee 1. A promise to repair or replace something or to give back the money for it, if anything goes wrong with it before a certain time has passed. 2. Anything that makes an outcome or condition certain: *Wealth is no guarantee of happiness. Noun.*
○ 1. To give a guarantee for. 2. To make sure or certain: *Having that band play will guarantee that the dance will be a success.* 3. To promise something: *The plumber guaranteed the work would be finished on time. Verb.*
guar·an·tee (gar′ən tē′) *noun, plural* **guarantees;** *verb,* **guaranteed, guaranteeing.**

guard 1. To keep safe from harm or danger; protect. 2. To watch carefully or control the actions of: *Two soldiers guarded the prisoner.* 3. To try to prevent a player on another team from scoring. 4. To do something to prevent a bad thing from happening; take precautions: *I always guard against catching a cold by dressing warmly. Verb.*
○ 1. A person or group of persons that guards: a museum guard. 2. A careful watch: *A sentry kept*

guard at the camp. 3. Something that protects: *a chin guard.* 4. In football, a player at either side of the center. 5. In basketball, either of two players whose position is near their team's basket. *Noun.*
• **on guard** *or* **on one's guard.** Prepared or watchful, as for danger, difficulties, or attack; alert: *The watchdog was on guard for burglars.*
guard (gärd) *verb,* **guarded, guarding;** *noun, plural* **guards.**

guardian 1. A person or thing that guards or watches over: *It was the judge's duty to be a guardian of justice.* 2. A person chosen by law to take care of someone who is young or not able to care for himself or herself: *After the children's parents died, their grandparents became their guardians.* **guard·i·an** (gär′dē ən) *noun, plural* **guardians.**

Guatemala A country in Central America. **Gua·te·ma·la** (gwä′tə mä′lə) *noun.*

guava A pear-shaped, yellow tropical fruit, used in jams. **gua·va** (gwov′ə) *noun, plural* **guavas.**

guerrilla A member of a small band of soldiers. Guerrillas are not part of the regular army of a country and often fight the enemy by making quick, surprise attacks. This word is also spelled guerilla.
Another word that sounds like this is **gorilla.**
guer·ril·la (gə ril′ə) *noun, plural* **guerrillas.**

guess 1. To form an opinion without having enough knowledge to be sure: *I could only guess what time it was.* 2. To get the correct answer by guessing: *I guessed the end of the mystery.* 3. To think; believe; suppose: *I guess they didn't come because they forgot we were having a party. Verb.*
○ An opinion formed without having enough knowledge to be sure: *My guess is that it will rain tomorrow. Noun.*
guess (ges) *verb,* **guessed, guessing;** *noun, plural* **guesses.**

guest 1. Someone who is at another person's house for a meal or a visit. 2. A customer in a restaurant, hotel, or similar place. **guest** (gest) *noun, plural* **guests.**

guidance 1. The act or process of guiding; direction: *I learned how to swim under the guidance of an instructor.* 2. Advice about one's plans for

PRONUNCIATION KEY:
at āpe fär câre end mē it īce pierce hot ōld sông fôrk
oil out up ūse rüle pull tûrn chin sing shop thin this
hw in white; zh in treasure. The symbol ə stands for the unstressed vowel sound in about, taken, pencil, lemon, and circus.

325

attending school or getting a job: *The school gives guidance to students who want to work after graduation.* **guid·ance** (gī′dəns) *noun.*

guide To show the way; direct. *Verb.*

○ A person or thing that shows the way or directs: *A guide took us through the museum. Noun.*

guide (gīd) *verb,* **guided, guiding;** *noun,* *plural* **guides.**

SYNONYMS

guide, conduct, escort, lead

The scout guided the settlers across the mountains. Our teachers conducted our class through the museum. Police cars often escort the governor on her way through our town. The older students will lead the younger ones on a nature trail.

A guide needs to be able to
give clear directions.

guided missile A missile that automatically moves along a certain course throughout its flight toward a target. It is guided by an automatic control inside it or by radio signals that it receives from the ground.

guide word A word that appears at the top of a page in dictionaries and some other books. A guide word shows the first or last dictionary entry that appears on a page. The guide words on this page of your dictionary are *guide* and *gull.*

guild 1. In the Middle Ages, a group of people in the same trade or craft who joined together. Guilds were set up to see that the quality of work done was good and to look out for the interests of their members. 2. An organization of people with the same interests or aims: *The amateur actors' guild is holding an auction to raise money.*

Another word that sounds like this is **gild.** **guild** (gild) *noun, plural* **guilds.**

guillotine A machine for executing a person by cutting off the head. A heavy blade is dropped between two posts. **guil·lo·tine** (gil′ə tēn′) *noun, plural* **guillotines.**

guilt 1. The condition or fact of having done something wrong or having broken the law: *The evidence proved the robber's guilt.* 2. A feeling of having done something wrong; shame: *I felt guilt because I got angry at a good friend.* Another word that sounds like this is **gilt.** **guilt** (gilt) *noun, plural* **guilts.** —**guilty** *adjective.*

Guinea A country in western Africa. **Guin·ea** (gin′ē) *noun.*

guinea pig A small, plump rodent with short ears, short legs, and no tail, often used in scientific experiments. Guinea pigs are very gentle and are often kept as pets.

Some kinds of guitars use electricity
to make their sound louder.

guitar A musical instrument with a long neck and six or more strings, played by plucking or strumming the strings. **gui·tar** (gi tär′) *noun, plural* **guitars.** —**guitarist** *noun.*

gulch A narrow valley with steep sides; ravine. **gulch** (gulch) *noun, plural* **gulches.**

gulf 1. A part of an ocean or sea partly enclosed by land and usually larger and deeper than a bay. 2. A deep opening in the earth; chasm. 3. A large difference or wide separation: *There is a big gulf between my age and my teacher's age.* **gulf** (gulf) *noun, plural* **gulfs.**

gull A bird with gray and white feathers. It lives on or near bodies of water and has long wings and a thick, slightly hooked beak. It is also called a *sea gull*. **gull** (gul) *noun, plural* **gulls.**

gullible Believing or trusting in almost anything; easily fooled, tricked, or cheated: *That gullible person would believe that bears fly.* **gul·li·ble** (gul′ə bəl) *adjective.*

gully A narrow ditch made by flowing water: *After it rained, there were deep gullies along the sides of the road.* **gul·ly** (gul′ē) *noun, plural* **gullies.**

gulp 1. To swallow quickly, greedily, or in large amounts: *I gulped a glass of milk.* 2. To draw in or swallow air; gasp: *I gulped when I heard about the spelling test. Verb.*
○ 1. The act of gulping: *You finished that lemonade in two gulps!* 2. The amount swallowed at one time: *The child took a big gulp from the glass. Noun.*
gulp (gulp) *verb,* **gulped, gulping;** *noun, plural* **gulps.**

gum¹ 1. A thick, sticky juice that comes from various trees and plants. Gum hardens when it is dry. It is used for sticking paper and other things together and in candy and medicine. 2. Gum that is made sweet and thick for chewing; chewing gum. *Noun.*
○ 1. To glue or become glued with gum or another sticky substance. 2. To make or become sticky or clogged. *Verb.* **gum** (gum) *noun, plural* **gums;** *verb,* **gummed, gumming.**

gum² The pink flesh around the teeth. **gum** (gum) *noun, plural* **gums.**

gumdrop A small piece of candy that is like jelly coated with sugar. **gum·drop** (gum′drop′) *noun, plural* **gumdrops.**

gun 1. A weapon made up of a metal tube through which a bullet is shot. Pistols, rifles, and cannons are guns. 2. Something like a gun in shape or use: *a staple gun. Noun.*
○ To increase the speed of something quickly: *The police officer gunned his cruiser. Verb.*
• **to gun down.** To shoot someone with a gun. **gun** (gun) *noun, plural* **guns;** *verb,* **gunned, gunning.**

gunfire The firing of guns. **gun·fire** (gun′fīr′) *noun.*

gunner A soldier who handles and fires cannons. **gun·ner** (gun′ər) *noun, plural* **gunners.**

gunpowder A powder that burns and explodes when touched with fire. It is used in guns, fireworks, and blasting. **gun·pow·der** (gun′pou′dər) *noun, plural* **gunpowders.**

gunwale The upper edge of the side of a ship or boat. **gun·wale** (gun′əl) *noun, plural* **gunwales.**

guppy A very small fish. There are many different kinds of guppies. Some are very colorful and are kept as pets. **gup·py** (gup′ē) *noun, plural* **guppies.**

WORD HISTORY

The **guppy** was named after R. J. L. Guppy, a naturalist who knew a great deal about these fish and who gave some of them to a museum.

gurgle 1. To flow or run with a bubbling sound: *The water gurgled as it went down the drain.* 2. To make a sound like this: *The baby gurgled with delight. Verb.*
○ A sound of or like a bubbling liquid. *Noun.* **gur·gle** (gûr′gəl) *verb,* **gurgled, gurgling;** *noun, plural* **gurgles.**

gush 1. To pour out suddenly and in large amounts. 2. To talk with so much feeling and eagerness that it seems silly: *Our neighbors are always gushing about their grandchildren. Verb.*
○ A sudden, heavy flow. *Noun.* **gush** (gush) *verb,* **gushed, gushing;** *noun, plural* **gushes.**

gust 1. A sudden, strong rush of wind or air. 2. A short or sudden bursting out of feeling: *a gusts of laughter.* **gust** (gust) *noun, plural* **gusts.**

gut 1. The stomach and intestines of the body. 2. Tough, strong string made from the intestines of some animals, used as strings in musical instruments and in surgery. 3. **guts.** The inside of something, such as a machine: *We examined the guts of the old washing machine.* 4. **guts.** The stomach and intestines; gut. 5. **guts.** Courage. *Noun.*
○ To empty out or destroy the inside of: *The fire gutted the building. Verb.* **gut** (gut) *noun, plural* **guts;** *verb,* **gutted, gutting.**

gutter 1. A channel or ditch along the side of a street or road to carry off water. 2. A pipe or trough along the lower edge of a roof. It carries off rain water. **gut·ter** (gut′ər) *noun, plural* **gutters.**

guy¹ A rope, chain, or wire used to steady or fas-

PRONUNCIATION KEY:
at āpe fär câre end mē it īce pierce hot ōld sông fôrk
oil out up ūse rūle pull tûrn chin sing shop thin this
hw in white; zh in treasure. The symbol ə stands for the unstressed vowel sound in about, taken, pencil, lemon, and circus. **327**

ten something, such as a tent, a tall antenna, or the masts of a ship. **guy** (gī) *noun, plural* **guys.**

guy² 1. A boy or man; fellow. 2. guys. Persons of either sex; people: *Call those guys and tell them we're having a party.* This word is used only in everyday conversation. **guy** (gī) *noun, plural* **guys.**

Guyana A country in northern South America. **Guy·an·a** (gī an′ə) *noun.*

gym 1. A gymnasium. 2. A course in physical education given in a school or college: *We played volleyball in gym today.* **gym** (jim) *noun, plural* **gyms.**

gymnasium A room or building with equipment for physical exercise or training and for indoor sports. **gym·na·si·um** (jim nā′zē əm) *noun, plural* **gymnasiums.**

gymnast A person skilled in gymnastics. **gym·nast** (jim′nast *or* jim′nəst) *noun, plural* **gymnasts.**

Gymnasts perform in the Olympics.

gymnastics 1. Exercises done to develop strength, balance, and agility. 2. The art, practice, or sport of these exercises. In this sense, the word "gymnastics" is used with a singular verb. **gym·nas·tics** (jim nas′tiks) *plural noun.*

Gypsy A person belonging to a group of people who came to Europe from India long ago. Gypsies are a wanderers and live scattered throughout the world. **Gyp·sy** (jip′sē) *noun, plural* **Gypsies.**

WORD HISTORY

The word Gypsy is short for Egyptian. People used to think that Gypsies came from Egypt.

---

gyroscope An instrument with a wheel that is mounted so that its axis can point in any direction. A gyroscope is used as a compass and to keep aircraft and ships steady. **gy·ro·scope** (jī′rə skōp′) *noun, plural* **gyroscopes.**

The sound of the letter H can be made in two ways:

> h as in happy and her;

And also by:

> wh as in who.

The letter H also appears silently in combinations with other letters such as:

> gh as in laugh; ght as in light and sight.

H forms new sounds as in these combinations:

> ch in change and much; sh in shadow and mush; th in then and thought.

h, H The eighth letter of the alphabet.
h, **H** (āch) *noun, plural* **h's, H's.**

ha **1.** A word used to show surprise, joy, or victory. **2.** A word used to express laughter. **ha** (hä) *interjection.*

habit **1.** An action that you do so often or for so long that you do it without thinking. A habit is hard to stop or control. **2.** A certain kind of clothing: *The nun wore a long habit of black and white.* **hab·it** (hab′it) *noun, plural* **habits.**

SYNONYMS

habit, characteristic, pattern, trait
I used to have the bad habit of biting my nails. Our teacher's sense of humor is his best-known characteristic. The rats in the experiment always showed the same patterns of behavior. Musical talent has always been a trait in my family.

---

habitat The place where an animal or plant naturally lives and grows: *The natural habitat of fish is water.* **hab·i·tat** (hab′i tat′) *noun, plural* **habitats.**

habitual **1.** Done by habit. **2.** Commonly occurring or used; usual: *The teacher took his habitual seat in front of the class.* **ha·bit·u·al** (hə bich′ü əl) *adjective.* —**habitually** *adverb.*

hacienda A large country estate for farming or for raising cattle. There are haciendas in the southwest United States and Mexico. **ha·ci·en·da** (hä′sē en′də) *noun, plural* **haciendas.**

hack **1.** To cut or chop unevenly with heavy blows, with a hatchet or cleaver: *They hacked their way*

through the forest. **2.** To cough with short, harsh sounds. **hack** (hak) *verb,* **hacked, hacking.**

hacker A person who is an expert at getting into a computer system, sometimes illegally: *The hacker logged in to the system to change the records.* **hacker** (hak′ər) *noun, plural* **hackers.**

had Past tense of **have.** Look up **have** for more information. **had** (had; *unstressed* həd *or* əd) *verb.*

hadn't Shortened form of "had not." **had·n't** (had′ənt) *contraction.*

haggard Having a worn, tired, and worried look. **haggard** (hag′ərd) *adjective.* —**haggardly** *adverb.*

haiku A form of Japanese poetry. A haiku has three lines with five, seven, and five syllables. Many haiku are about nature. **hai·ku** (hī′kü) *noun, plural* **haiku.**

hail¹ To greet or attract the attention of by calling or shouting: *We hailed a taxi by waving our arms. Verb.*
○ A motion or call used as a greeting or to attract attention. *Noun.*
hail (hāl) *verb,* **hailed, hailing;** *noun, plural* **hails.**

hail² **1.** Small round pieces of ice that fall like rain. **2.** A heavy shower of anything: *The married couple ran off in a hail of rice thrown by the guests. Noun.*
○ **1.** To pour down hail. **2.** To send in large amounts; shower: *The burning building hailed sparks on the firefighters. Verb.*
hail (hāl) *noun; verb,* **hailed, hailing.**

hair 1. A very thin, threadlike growth on the skin of people and animals. 2. A mass of such growths. 3. A very thin, threadlike growth on the outer layer of plants.
Another word that sounds like this is **hare**.
hair (hâr) *noun, plural* **hairs**.

haircut The act or style of cutting the hair. **hair·cut** (hâr′kut′) *noun, plural* **haircuts**.

hairdo A way of arranging the hair. **hair·do** (hâr′dü′) *noun, plural* **hairdos**.

hairpin A piece of wire bent into a U, used to hold the hair in place. *Noun.*
○ Shaped like a hairpin: *a hairpin curve*. *Adjective.*
hair·pin (hâr′pin′) *noun, plural* **hairpins**; *adjective.*

hairy Covered with hair; having a lot of hair. **hair·y** (hâr′ē) *adjective,* **hairier, hairiest.** —**hairiness** *noun.*

Haiti A country that occupies part of an island in the Caribbean Sea. **Hai·ti** (hā′tē) *noun.*

half 1. One of two equal parts of something: *A pint is half of a quart.* 2. Either of two time periods in certain sports: *A basketball game is divided into two halves.* *Noun.*
○ Being one of two equal parts: *a half gallon of ice cream.* *Adjective.*
○ 1. To the extent of one half: *The glass was half full.* 2. Partly; somewhat: *I was half asleep.* *Adverb.*
half (haf) *noun, plural* **halves**; *adjective; adverb.*

half brother A brother who shares only one parent with someone else: *My half brother and I have the same mother, but we have different fathers.*

halfhearted Without much hope or spirit: *a halfhearted attempt at doing homework.* **half·heart·ed** (haf′här′tid) *adjective;* **halfheartedly,** *adverb.*

half-mast The position of a flag halfway down from the top of a pole. It is used as a sign of mourning for someone who has died or as a signal of distress. **half-mast** (haf′mast′) *noun.*

half sister A sister who shares only one parent with someone else: *My half sister and I have the same father, but we have different mothers.*

halftime A rest period in the middle of some games, such as football and basketball. **half·time** (haf′tīm′) *noun, plural* **halftimes**.

halfway To or at half the distance; midway: *The movie is halfway over.* *Adverb.*
○ 1. Half the way between two points: *My horse was leading in the race at the halfway mark.*
2. Not thorough or adequate; partial: *halfway measures at solving the pollution problem.* *Adjective.*
half·way (haf′wā′) *adverb; adjective.*

halibut A large flatfish with both eyes on the top of the body and eaten as food. It may weigh several hundred pounds and is found in the northern Atlantic and Pacific oceans. **hal·i·but** (hal′ə bət) *noun, plural* **halibut** *or* **halibuts**.

WORD HISTORY

The word **halibut** comes from two earlier English words that meant "holy" and "flatfish." This fish was called "holy" because it was eaten on holy days when Christians were not allowed to eat meat.

---

hall 1. A passageway in a building. A hall has doors or openings that lead into rooms. 2. A room at the entrance to a building; lobby: *We left our coats in the hall.* 3. A building or large room used for a purpose: *a concert hall.*
Another word that sounds like this is **haul**.
hall (hôl) *noun, plural* **halls**.

hallelujah A word used to express joy, thanks, and praise to God. *Interjection.*
○ The interjection or exclamation "Hallelujah." *Noun.*
hal·le·lu·jah (hal ə lü′yə) *interjection; noun, plural* **hallelujahs**.

Halloween A holiday on October 31 celebrated by dressing up in costumes, collecting treats, and playing tricks. **Hal·low·een** (hal′ə wēn′) *noun, plural* **Halloweens**.

Halloween costumes can be simple or fancy.

Halloween is short for All-hallow-even, meaning "the evening before All Saints' (day)." In the ancient pagan religion of Britain, October 31 was considered to be the last day of the old year and a time when witches roamed about. When Christianity came to Britain, the Church made November 1 a holiday honoring all the saints (called "hallows"). But the tradition of imagining witches on the day before All Saints' Day is still part of Halloween.

hallway A hall or passageway. **hall·way** (hôl′wā′) *noun, plural* **hallways**.

halo 1. A ring of light around the head of a saint or angel in a work of art. 2. A circle of light that seems to surround the sun or the moon. **ha·lo** (hā′lō) *noun, plural* **halos** *or* **haloes**.

halt A stop for a short time. *Noun.*
○ To stop: *The troops **halted** when the sergeant gave the order. Verb.*
halt (hôlt) *noun, plural* **halts**; *verb*, **halted, halting**.

halter 1. A rope or strap used for leading or tying an animal. It fits over the animal's nose and over or behind its ears. 2. A kind of blouse that fastens behind the neck and leaves the arms and back bare. **hal·ter** (hôl′tər) *noun, plural* **halters**.

**This large melon has been
halved for eating.**

halve 1. To divide into two equal parts: *I **halved** an apple so that I could share it with my friend.* 2. To make less by half: *We **halved** the pancake recipe.* Another word that sounds like this is **have**.
halve (hav) *verb*, **halved, halving**.

halves Plural of **half**. Look up **half** for more information. **halves** (havz) *plural noun*.

ham 1. The meat from the back leg or shoulder of a hog, usually salted or smoked. 2. The back part of the thigh of a human being. 3. An amateur radio operator. **ham** (ham) *noun, plural* **hams**.

hamburger 1. Ground beef. 2. A rounded, flat portion of ground beef, fried and usually served on a bun or roll. **ham·burg·er** (ham′bûr′gər) *noun, plural* **hamburgers**.

What we now call **hamburger** used to be called Hamburger steak or Hamburg steak. This form of meat was named after the city of Hamburg in Germany.

hamlet A very small village. **ham·let** (ham′lət) *noun, plural* **hamlets**.

hammer 1. A tool with a heavy metal head on a handle, used for driving nails and for beating or shaping metals. 2. Anything like a hammer in shape or use: *The padded **hammers** inside a piano strike the strings and produce the sound. Noun.*
○ 1. To strike again and again; pound: *The carpenter **hammered** nails into the wood.* 2. To pound into shape with a hammer: *In camp, we learned to **hammer** a bowl out of copper. Verb.*
ham·mer (ham′ər) *noun, plural* **hammers**; *verb*, **hammered, hammering**.

hammock A swinging bed hung between two trees or poles, made from a long piece of canvas or netting. **ham·mock** (ham′ək) *noun, plural* **hammocks**.

**A hammock is a great
place to relax.**

hamper¹ To get in the way of action or progress: *Stalled cars **hampered** efforts at snow removal.* **ham·per** (ham′pər) *verb*, **hampered, hampering**.

hamper² A large basket or container with a cover: *There are food **hampers** for picnics and clothes **hampers** for dirty laundry.* **ham·per** (ham′pər) *noun, plural* **hampers**.

PRONUNCIATION KEY:
at āpe fär câre end mē it īce pierce hot ōld sông fôrk
oil out up ūse rüle pull tûrn chin sing shop thin this
hw in white; zh in treasure. The symbol ə stands for the unstressed vowel sound in about, taken, pencil, lemon, and circus.

331

hamster A small furry rodent with a plump body, a short tail, and large cheek pouches, often kept as a pet. **ham·ster** (ham′stər) *noun, plural* **hamsters.**

hand 1. The end part of the arm from the wrist down in humans and some other animals. It is made up of the palm, four fingers, and a thumb. 2. A pointer on a clock, meter, or dial. 3. **hands.** Control or possession: *The decision is in your hands.* 4. A member of a group or crew; laborer: *The hands on the farm get up early.* 5. A way of using the hands: *The magician needs a quick hand to do magic tricks.* 6. A part in something; share; role: *Each student had a hand in the class play.* 7. Help; aid: *Please give me a hand with this table.* 8. A round of applause; clapping. 9. One round of a card game. 10. The cards a player holds in one round of a card game. 11. Handwriting style: *a note written in a large, clear hand.* 12. Either the left or the right side or direction: *A nurse was at the doctor's right hand.* 13. A promise of marriage. 14. A measurement equal to four inches, used to tell the height of a horse. *Noun.*

○ To give or pass with the hand: *I handed the book to the librarian. Verb.*

• **by hand.** With the hands: *Delicate clothing should be washed by hand.*

• **on hand.** Ready or available for use: *We always keep canned foods on hand.*

• **to hand down.** To transmit, as from a parent to a child or from one generation to another: *This ring was handed down from my great-grandmother.*

• **to hand out.** To distribute; give out; pass out: *I handed out advertisements for a department store.*

hand (hand) *noun, plural* **hands;** *verb,* **handed, handing.**

handbag A bag or case for carrying personal articles such as a wallet. **hand·bag** (hand′bag′) *noun, plural* **handbags.**

handball 1. A game in which players take turns hitting a small rubber ball against a wall with the hand. 2. The ball used in this game. **hand·ball** (hand′bôl′) *noun, plural* **handballs.**

handbook A book with information about a subject. **hand·book** (hand′buk′) *noun, plural* **handbooks.**

handcuff One of two metal rings joined by a chain and locked around the wrists of a prisoner. *Noun.*

○ To put handcuffs on. *Verb.*
hand·cuff (hand′kuf′) *noun, plural* **handcuffs;** *verb,* **handcuffed, handcuffing.**

handful 1. The amount the hand can hold at one time. 2. A small number: *Only a handful of people showed up for the club meeting.* **hand·ful** (hand′fül′) *noun, plural* **handfuls.**

handicap 1. Anything that makes it harder for a person to do well or get ahead: *Despite its handicap, the injured dog was able to get around the house.* 2. An advantage given to a weaker player or team or a disadvantage given to a stronger player or team at the start of a game. *Noun.*

○ To put at a disadvantage; hinder: *Poor eyesight handicaps me in my work. Verb.*
hand·i·cap (han′dē kap′) *noun, plural* **handicaps;** *verb,* **handicapped, handicapping.**

handicapped 1. Having some handicap: *We were handicapped in the race because we started late.* 2. Having some disability: *Handicapped people often find it harder to get around the city than others do.* **hand·i·capped** (han′dē kapt′) *adjective.*

handicraft A trade, work, or art in which skill with the hands is needed, such as making pottery or weaving. **hand·i·craft** (han′dē kraft′) *noun, plural* **handicrafts.**

handkerchief A square, soft piece of cloth used to wipe the nose or face. **hand·ker·chief** (hang′kər chif′) *noun, plural* **handkerchiefs.**

Various handicrafts are sold at this fair.

handle The part of an object grasped by the hand. A frying pan has a handle. *Noun.*

○ 1. To touch or hold with the hand: *Please handle the glass carefully.* 2. To manage, control, or deal with: *I know how to handle dogs. Verb.*
han·dle (han′dəl) *noun, plural* **handles;** *verb,* **handled, handling.**

handlebars The curved bar on the front of a bicycle or motorcycle. The rider grips the ends of the bars and uses them to steer. **han·dle·bars** (han′dəl bärz′) *plural noun.*

handmade Made by hand rather than by machine: *handmade lace.* **hand·made** (hand′mād′) *adjective.*

handout Money or something else given to a poor person. **hand·out** (hand′out′) *noun, plural* **handouts.**

handrail A railing that can be gripped by the hand, used on stairways and balconies to support and protect people. **hand·rail** (hand′rāl′) *noun, plural* **handrails.**

handshake An act in which two people grip and shake each other's hands. A handshake can be a way of greeting someone, a way of saying good-bye, or a way of marking an agreement. **hand·shake** (hand′shāk′) *noun, plural* **handshakes.**

handsome 1. Having a pleasing appearance: *a handsome old desk.* 2. Large or generous: *a handsome reward.* **hand·some** (han′səm) *adjective,* **handsomer, handsomest.**

handspring A kind of somersault in which a person springs forward or backward onto both hands, flips the feet over the head, and then lands back on the feet again. **hand·spring** (hand′spring′) *noun, plural* **handsprings.**

handwriting Writing done by hand with a pen or pencil, not with a machine. **hand·writ·ing** (hand′rī′ting) *noun, plural* **handwritings.**

handy 1. Within reach; nearby: *When I have a cold, I keep a handkerchief handy.* 2. Working well with one's hands; skillful: *handy with tools.* 3. Easy to use or handle: *a handy carrying case for pencils and drawings.* **hand·y** (han′dē) *adjective,* **handier, handiest.**

hang 1. To fasten or be attached from above only, without support from below: *pictures hung on the wall.* 2. To fasten or be attached so as to move freely back and forth: *We hung the gate on hinges.* 3. To put a person to death by hanging by a rope tied around the neck. 4. To float; hover: *Fog hung over the city. Verb.*
○ 1. The way something hangs or falls: *I didn't like the hang of my new coat.* 2. The way of doing something; knack: *It takes a while to get the hang of riding a bicycle. Noun.*
　　• **to hang up.** 1. To put on a hanger or peg: *Please hang up your clothes!* 2. To end a telephone conversation by putting the receiver back on its cradle.

hang (hang) *verb,* **hung** (*for definitions 1, 2, and 4*) *or* **hanged** (*for definition 3*), **hanging;** *noun.*

hangar A building to keep aircraft in.
Another word that sounds like this is **hanger.**
han·gar (hang′ər *or* hang′gər) *noun, plural* **hangars.**

Aircraft are repaired in a hangar.

hanger A frame with three corners made of wire, wood, or plastic with a hook at the top, used to hang up clothes.
Another word that sounds like this is **hangar.**
hang·er (hang′ər) *noun, plural* **hangers.**

hang glider A glider like a large kite. The person operating it holds on to a frame underneath the wing and launches the hang glider from a cliff or hilltop.

hangnail A piece of skin that hangs loosely at the side or bottom of a fingernail. **hang·nail** (hang′nāl′) *noun, plural* **hangnails.**

hanker To wish for something strongly; desire. **han·ker** (hang′kər) *verb,* **hankered, hankering.** —**hankering** *noun, plural* **hankerings.**

Hanukkah *or* **Chanukah** A Jewish holiday that lasts for eight days in December. It celebrates the anniversary of the dedication of the temple in Jerusalem. **Ha·nuk·kah** (hä′nə kə) *noun.*

haphazard Put together or chosen without any order: *You'll never find your socks in that haphazard pile of clothing in your closet.* **hap·haz·ard** (hap haz′ərd) *adjective.* —**haphazardly** *adverb.*

happen 1. To take place; occur: *The accident happened last week.* 2. To take place without

PRONUNCIATION KEY:
| at | āpe | fär | câre | end | mē | it | īce | pierce | hot | ōld | sông | fôrk |
| oil | out | up | ūse | rüle | pùll | tûrn | chin | sing | shop | thin | this | |

hw in white; zh in treasure. The symbol ə stands for the unstressed vowel sound in about, taken, pencil, lemon, and circus.

333

plan or reason: *My cousin's birthday just **happens** to be the same day as mine.* **3.** To come or go by chance: *A police officer **happened** along just after the robbery.* **4.** To be done: *Something must have **happened** to the telephone, because it isn't working.* **hap·pen** (hap′ən) *verb,* **happened, happening.**

happening Something that happens; event. **hap·pen·ing** (hap′ə ning) *noun, plural* **happenings.**

happily **1.** With pleasure or gladness: *The children played **happily** together. The dog jumped up happily when I reached for the leash.* **2.** Luckily. *Happily, no one was hurt in the fire.* **hap·pi·ly** (hap′ə lē) *adverb.*

happiness The condition of being glad or content: *Their vacation on the farm was full of happiness.* **hap·pi·ness** (hap′ē nis) *noun.*

happy **1.** Feeling or showing pleasure or gladness: *The children were **happy** with their new dog.* **2.** Satisfied and pleased with one's condition; contented: *All I need is one good friend to be **happy**.* **3.** Lucky; fortunate: *By a **happy** chance, one tennis court was empty.* **hap·py** (hap′ē) *adjective,* **happier, happiest.**

happy-go-lucky Without any worries or serious thoughts; carefree: *My **happy-go-lucky** friend does not worry about the future.* **hap·py-go-luck·y** (hap′ē gō luk′ē) *adjective.*

harass To bother or annoy again and again: *The bully **harassed** the younger children.* **har·ass** (ha′rəs *or* hə ras′) *verb,* **harassed, harassing.** —**harassment** *noun.*

harbor A sheltered place along a coast. Ships and boats often anchor in a harbor. *Noun.*
○ **1.** To give protection or shelter to: *It is against the law to **harbor** a criminal in your home.* **2.** To keep in one's mind: *I **harbored** a grudge against the rude student. Verb.*
har·bor (här′bər) *noun, plural* **harbors;** *verb,* **harbored, harboring.**

hard **1.** Solid and firm to the touch; not soft. **2.** Needing or using much effort: *a **hard** worker.* **3.** Full of sorrow, pain, or worry: *Life was **hard** for them after both parents lost their jobs.* **4.** Having great force or strength: *The boxer knocked out his opponent with one **hard** blow.* **5.** Not gentle or yielding; stern: *The judge had a **hard** face. Adjective.*
○ **1.** With effort or energy: *They worked **hard**.* **2.** With force or strength: *It rained so **hard** yesterday that the roads flooded.* **3.** With difficulty: *The runner was breathing **hard** after the race.* **4.** With great sadness or pain: *They took the news **hard**. Adverb.*
• **hard of hearing.** Partially deaf: *My grandfather wears a hearing aid because he is **hard** of hearing.*
hard (härd) *adjective,* **harder, hardest;** *adverb.*

hard-boiled **1.** Boiled until hard: *A **hard-boiled** egg is boiled until its yolk and white are solid.* **2.** Tough and not sympathetic: *a **hard-boiled** police detective.* **hard-boiled** (härd′boild′) *adjective.*

hard copy Numbers, letters, or pictures from a computer that have been printed on paper.

harden **1.** To make or become hard: *I put the clay bowl in the sun to **harden**.* **2.** To make or become tougher or less sensitive: *Seeing crime every day can **harden** the feelings of police officers.* **hard·en** (här′dən) *verb,* **hardened, hardening.**

hardly **1.** Just about; barely: *We could **hardly** see in the dim light.* **2.** Not likely; surely not: *Since you are sick, you will **hardly** be able to go to the party tonight.* **hard·ly** (härd′lē) *adverb.*

hardship Something that causes difficulty, pain, or suffering: *The flood was a great **hardship**.* **hard·ship** (härd′ship′) *noun, plural* **hardships.**

hardware **1.** Metal articles for making and fixing things. Tools, nails, and screws are hardware. **2.** The electronic and mechanical parts of a computer system, such as the keyboard, the monitor, the printer, and the computer itself. **hard·ware** (härd′wâr′) *noun.*

hardwood The strong, heavy wood of trees that have leaves rather than needles. Oaks, beeches, and maples are hardwood trees. Hardwood is used for furniture, floors, and sports equipment. **hard·wood** (härd′wūd′) *noun, plural* **hardwoods.**

hardy Capable of standing hardship or harsh conditions: *Ivy is a **hardy** plant.* **har·dy** (här′dē) *adjective,* **hardier, hardiest.** —**hardiness** *noun.*

Hardwood trees are harvested throughout the world.

SYNONYMS

hardy, robust, rugged, tough
Hardy pioneers crossed deserts and mountains in covered wagons. Everyone in my family has always had robust good health. The long camping trip in the mountains required rugged endurance. The tough old sailor survived the open sea in a lifeboat for over a month.

hare An animal of the rabbit family with very long ears, strong back legs and feet, and a short tail. Another word that sounds like this is **hair**.
hare (hâr) *noun, plural* **hares** *or* **hare**.

The hare, unlike the rabbit, does not burrow.

harm 1. Injury or hurt: *To make sure no harm would come to the children, their parents made them wear life jackets when they went sailing.* 2. An evil; wrong: *The bad child saw no harm in stealing. Noun.*
○ To do damage to; hurt: *The dog won't harm you. Verb.*
harm (härm) *noun, plural* **harms**; *verb,* **harmed, harming. —harmful** *adjective* **—harmless** *adjective.*

harmonica A musical instrument. It is a small case with slots that contain a series of metal reeds. It is played by blowing in and out through the slots. **har·mon·i·ca** (här mon′i kə) *noun, plural* **harmonicas.**

harmonize 1. To arrange, sing, or play in harmony: *The voices of the choir harmonized beautiful-*ly. 2. To go together in a pleasing way: *The colors of the curtains and the rug harmonize well.* 3. To add notes to a melody to form chords in music. **har·mo·nize** (här′mə nīz′) *verb,* **harmonized, harmonizing.**

harmony 1. A combination of musical notes or voices that sound pleasing together: *You take the bass part, I'll take the soprano part, and we'll sing in harmony.* 2. A pleasing combination of parts: *The colors in the plaid dress have a nice harmony.* 3. Friendly agreement or cooperation; smooth relation: *Often the Native Amercians lived in harmony with the first colonists from England.* **har·mo·ny** (här′mə nē) *noun, plural* **harmonies.**

harness The straps, bands, and other gear used to attach a work animal to a cart, plow, or wagon. *Noun.*
○ 1. To put a harness on. 2. To control and make use of: *At that dam, engineers harness water power to generate electricity. Verb.*
har·ness (här′nis) *noun, plural* **harnesses**; *verb,* **harnessed, harnessing.**

harp A musical instrument with strings. The strings are set in an upright frame shaped like a triangle with a curved top.
harp (härp) *noun, plural* **harps.**

A harp is played by plucking the strings with the fingers.

harpoon A weapon similar to a spear with a rope attached, used to kill whales. It is shot from a gun or thrown by hand. *Noun.*
○ To strike, catch, or kill with a harpoon. *Verb.*
har·poon (här pün′) *noun, plural* **harpoons**; *verb,* **harpooned, harpooning.**

harpsichord A musical instrument that is like a small piano. The harpsichord was widely used in the sixteenth through eighteenth centuries.
harp·si·chord (härp′si kôrd′) *noun, plural* **harpsichords.**

PRONUNCIATION KEY:
| at | āpe | fär | câre | end | mē | it | īce | pierce | hot | ōld | sông | fôrk |
| oil | out | up | ūse | rüle | pull | tûrn | chin | sing | shop | thin | this | |

hw in white; zh in treasure. The symbol ə stands for the unstressed vowel sound in about, taken, pencil, lemon, and circus.

335

harrow A farm tool that is a heavy frame with upright disks or teeth. It is usually pulled behind a tractor to break up and level plowed land. *Noun.*
  ∘ **1.** To drag a harrow over. **2.** To make someone suffer or worry very much: *The people at the funeral looked harrowed by grief. Verb.*
har·row (har′ō) *noun, plural* **harrows;** *verb,* **harrowed, harrowing.**

harsh **1.** Rough or unpleasant to the ear, eye, taste, or touch: *The towel felt harsh against my sunburned skin.* **2.** Very cruel or severe: *The prisoners got harsh treatment.* **harsh** (härsh) *adjective,* **harsher, harshest.** —**harshly** *adverb* —**harshness** *noun.*

harvest **1.** The gathering in of a crop when it is ripe: *The farmers began the corn harvest.* **2.** The crop gathered: *We stored our harvest of potatoes in sacks. Noun.*
  ∘ To gather in a crop. *Verb.*
har·vest (här′vist) *noun, plural* **harvests;** *verb,* **harvested, harvesting.**

Tractors and other farm machinery
are used in the harvest.

harvester A machine for harvesting crops in fields. **har·vest·er** (här′və stər) *noun, plural* **harvesters.**

has A form of the present tense of **have** that is used with *he, she, it,* and the name of a person, place, or thing. **has** (haz) *verb.*

hash **1.** A cooked mixture of chopped meat, potatoes, and other vegetables. **2.** A mess; jumble: *I made such a real hash of the test.* **hash** (hash) *noun, plural* **hashes.**

hasn't Shortened form of "has not." **has·n't** (haz′ənt) *contraction.*

hassle To keep annoying someone about something: *Quit hassling me about polishing my shoes! Verb.*
  ∘ An annoying or troublesome problem. *Noun.*
has·sle (has′əl) *verb,* **hassled, hassling; hassle,** *noun, plural* **hassles.**

haste Quickness in moving or in acting; speed; hurry: *We left in great haste for the bus.* **haste** (hāst) *noun.*

hasten **1.** To move quickly; hurry: *It was getting dark, so I hastened home.* **2.** To make something happen faster; speed up: *The medicine hastened the child's recovery.* **has·ten** (hās′ən) *verb,* **hastened, hastening.**

hasty **1.** Quick; hurried: *We barely had time for a hasty breakfast.* **2.** Too quick; careless or reckless: *Don't make a hasty decision that you'll be sorry for later.* **hast·y** (hās′tē) *adjective,* **hastier, hastiest.** —**hastily** *adverb* —**hastiness** *noun.*

hat A covering for the head, often with a brim and crown. **hat** (hat) *noun, plural* **hats.**

These hats are worn as
part of a uniform.

hatch¹ **1.** To cause young to come from an egg: *The mother robin hatched her eggs.* **2.** To come from an egg: *The chicks hatched by pecking through their shells.* **3.** To plan or invent, usually in secret: *We hatched a plan to catch them in the act.* **hatch** (hach) *verb,* **hatched, hatching.**

hatch² **1.** An opening in the deck of a ship. It leads to lower decks or to the cargo hold. **2.** A cover or trap door for such an opening. **hatch** (hach) *noun, plural* **hatches.**

hatchback A car with a panel or door in the back that opens up. **hatch·back** (hach′bak′) *noun, plural* **hatchbacks.**

hatchery A place where the eggs of fish or birds are hatched. **hatch·er·y** (hach′ə rē) *noun, plural* **hatcheries.**

hatchet A small ax with a short handle, made to be used with one hand. **hatch·et** (hach′it) *noun, plural* **hatchets.**

hate To have very strong feelings against; dislike very much. **hate** (hāt) *verb,* **hated, hating.**

hateful 1. Marked by hatred: *The bully was hateful to the new student.* 2. Causing or arousing hatred: *a hateful crime.* **hate·ful** (hāt′fəl) *adjective.* —**hatefully** *adverb.*

hatred A strong feeling against a person or thing: *The people felt hatred toward the dictator.* **ha·tred** (hā′trid) *noun, plural* **hatreds.**

haughty Thinking of oneself as much better than other people; arrogant: *The haughty king refused to speak to common people.* **haugh·ty** (hô′tē) *adjective,* **haughtier, haughtiest.** —**haughtily** *adverb* —**haughtiness** *noun.*

haul 1. To pull or move with force; drag: *We hauled the trunk up the stairs.* 2. To carry; transport: *Railroads haul freight. Verb.*
○ 1. The act of hauling: *Give the rope a haul.*
2. Something caught or won: *a big haul of fish.*
3. The distance something is hauled: *It's a long haul from here to the dump. Noun.*
Another word that sounds like this is **hall.**
haul (hôl) *verb,* **hauled, hauling;** *noun, plural* **hauls.**

Fishermen depend on a large haul for their livelihood.

haunch A part of the body including the hip and upper thigh: *The lion sat on its haunches.* **haunch** (hônch) *noun, plural* **haunches.**

haunt 1. To visit or live in: *Ghosts haunt the old house.* 2. To come often to the mind of: *Memories of the shipwreck he had been in haunted the old sailor.* **haunt** (hônt) *verb,* **haunted, haunting.**

have 1. To own; possess: *Everyone in my family has black hair.* 2. To consist of; contain: *A year has twelve months.* 3. To hold in the mind: *I have a good idea.* 4. To carry on; engage in: *We had a discussion in class.* 5. To experience: *Have a good time!* 6. To give birth to: *My cat will have kittens in a week.* 7. To be forced or obligated: *I have to be home by five.* 8. To receive or obtain; get: *You had a phone call while you were out.* 9. To permit; allow: *I wanted to keep snakes as pets, but my parents wouldn't have it.* 10. To cause something to be done; arrange for: *We had wallpaper put up.* 11. Also used as an auxiliary verb to show that the action of the main verb is finished: *We have done all of our homework.*
Another word that sounds like this is **halve.**
• **to have to do with.** To be about, be concerned with, or be related to: *That book has to do with the history of our state.*
have (hav) *verb,* **had, having.**

haven A place of safety or shelter: *The cool woods were a haven for the hot and tired hikers.* **ha·ven** (hā′vən) *noun, plural* **havens.**

haven't Shortened form of "have not." **have·n't** (hav′ənt) *contraction.*

Hawaii An island state of the United States in the Pacific Ocean. Its capital is Honolulu. **Ha·wai·i** (hə wī′ē) *noun.*

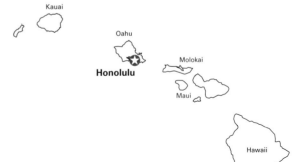

Hawaii
U. S. Postal Abbreviation: **HI**
Capital: **Honolulu**
Population: **1,083,000**
Area: **6,450 sq. mi./16,705 sq. km**
State Nickname: **Aloha State**
State Bird: **Nene (Hawaiian Goose)**
State Flower: **Hibiscus**

WORD HISTORY

Hawaii was originally the name for the biggest island of the state. An ancient island song says that Hawaii was the traditional home of the first people who lived there. This name was given to the island by later settlers.

PRONUNCIATION KEY:
| at | āpe | fär | câre | end | mē | it | īce | pierce | hot | old | sông | fôrk |
| oil | out | up | ūse | rüle | pull | tûrn | chin | sing | shop | thin | this | |
hw in white; zh in treasure. The symbol ə stands for the unstressed vowel sound in about, taken, pencil, lemon, and circus.

337

hawk¹ A bird with a sharp, hooked beak, strong claws, and sharp eyesight. **hawk** (hôk) *noun, plural* **hawks.**

A **hawk** hunts small animals
and is related to the eagle.

hawk² To offer goods for sale by calling out: *The peddler hawked fruit in the street.* **hawk** (hôk) *verb,* **hawked, hawking.**

hawthorn A thorny shrub or tree with white or pink flowers and small red, orange, purple, or black berries. **haw·thorn** (hô′thôrn′) *noun, plural* **hawthorns.**

hay Grass, alfalfa, or clover cut and dried for use as feed for livestock.
Another word that sounds like this is **hey.**
hay (hā) *noun, plural* **hays.**

Hay is often left to dry in the field
in huge rolls.

hay fever A condition that causes a stuffy nose, itching eyes, and sneezing. Hay fever is an allergy caused by breathing pollen in the air.

hayloft An upper floor in a barn or stable, used for storing hay. **hay·loft** (hā′lôft′) *noun, plural* **haylofts.**

haystack A pile of hay stacked outdoors. **hay·stack** (hā′stak) *noun, plural* **haystacks.**

hazard Something that can cause harm or injury; danger: *Icy roads are a hazard to drivers.* **haz·ard** (haz′ərd) *noun, plural* **hazards.**

hazardous Likely to cause harm or injury; dangerous: *Smoking is hazardous to your health because it can cause cancer and heart disease.* **haz·ard·ous** (haz′ər dəs) *adjective.*

hazardous waste A chemical or nuclear substance dangerous to people, animals, or the earth. Hazardous wastes often come from factories and nuclear power plants.

haze Mist, smoke, or dust in the air: *The bridge was hidden in the haze.* **haze** (hāz) *noun, plural* **hazes.**

hazel 1. A tree or shrub with light brown nuts that can be eaten. 2. A light brown color like the color of this nut. *Noun.*
○ Having the color hazel; light brown: *My cousin has beautiful hazel eyes. Adjective.*
ha·zel (hā′zəl) *noun, plural* **hazels;** *adjective.*

hazy Not clear; blurred or confused: *On a hazy day, we can see only a dim outline of the mountains.* **ha·zy** (hā′zē) *adjective,* **hazier, haziest; haziness,** *noun.*

H-bomb A powerful bomb usually called a **hydrogen bomb.** Look up **hydrogen bomb** for more information. **H-bomb** (āch′bom′) *noun, plural* **H-bombs.**

he 1. A male person or animal that is being talked about: *Bob promised that he would be on time.* 2. A person; anyone: *He who hesitates is lost. Pronoun.*
○ A male person or animal: *Is the kitten a he or a she? Noun.*
he (hē) *pronoun; noun, plural* **hes.**

head 1. The top part of the human body, where the eyes, ears, nose, and mouth are. 2. The top or front part of any other animal that is like a human head. 3. The top or front part of something: *Hit the nail on the head.* 4. A firm, rounded cluster of leaves or flowers: *a head of lettuce.* 5. A person above others in rank; chief: *The president is the head of our country's government.* 6. A single animal of a group: *The cowhands rounded up forty head of cattle.* 7. Mental ability: *a good head for figures.*

8. heads. The side of a coin that shows the main design, usually a picture of a person's head. *Noun.*
○ Top, chief, or front: *the head lifeguard at the pool. Adjective.*
○ **1.** To be or go to the top or front of; lead: *The scout leader headed our troop in the parade.* **2.** To be in charge of: *Our best writer heads the school newspaper.* **3.** To direct or move in a direction: *We head for the beach on hot days. Verb.*
  • **over one's head.** Beyond one's ability to understand or manage: *Physics is over my head.*
  • **to head off.** To get ahead of and cause to stop or turn back: *The posse headed off the bank robbers.*
head (hed) *noun, plural* **heads** (*for definitions 1-5*) *or* **head** (*for definitions 6 and 7*); *adjective; verb,* **headed, heading.**

headache **1.** A pain felt inside the head. **2.** Something that causes trouble or worry: *The flat tire was another headache on the trip.* **head·ache** (hed′āk′) *noun, plural* **headaches.**

headband A band worn around the head, used to hold the hair in place or for an ornament. **head·band** (hed′band′) *noun, plural* **headbands.**

headdress A covering or decoration for the head: *an Indian headdress.* **head·dress** (hed′dres′) *noun, plural* **headdresses.**

headfirst With the head going in front: *We dived headfirst into the water.* **head·first** (hed′fûrst′) *adverb.*

heading A title for a page or chapter. **head·ing** (hed′ing) *noun, plural* **headings.**

headland A point of high land that sticks out into the water; cape. **head·land** (hed′lənd) *noun, plural* **headlands.**

headlight A bright light on the front of an automobile or other vehicle. **head·light** (hed′līt′) *noun, plural* **headlights.**

headline A line printed at the top of a newspaper or magazine article. A headline tells what the article is about. It is printed in large or heavy type. *Noun.*
○ To be the main attraction of a show: *A magic act headlined the show. Verb.*
head·line (hed′līn′) *noun, plural* **headlines**; *verb,* **headlined, headlining.**

headlong **1.** With the head first: *The runner slid headlong into second base.* **2.** In a reckless way; rashly: *I rushed headlong into buying the bicycle. Adverb.*
○ Made with the head first: *I made a headlong dive into the lake. Adjective.*
head·long (hed′lông′) *adverb; adjective.*

head-on With the head or front end first: *The car hit the pole head-on. Adverb.*
○ Occuring head-on: *The two cars were in a head-on crash. Adjective.*
head-on (hed′ôn′ *or* hed′on′) *adverb; adjective.*

headphone A radio or telephone receiver held against the ear by a band that fits over the head. **head·phone** (hed′fōn′) *noun, plural* **headphones.**

headquarters A center of operations where leaders work and give orders; main office: *That company's headquarters are in New York.* The word *headquarters* may be used with a singular or plural verb. **head·quar·ters** (hed′kwôr′tərz) *noun.*

headrest A support for the head. Headrests in automobiles are designed to prevent injuries to the neck in a collision. **head·rest** (hed′rest′) *noun, plural* **headrests.**

head start An early start or other advantage given to someone starting out in a race or other competition.

headstone A stone set at the head of a grave; tombstone. **head·stone** (hed′stōn′) *noun, plural* **headstones.**

headstrong Insisting on one's own way; stubborn: *The headstrong child would not listen to advice.* **head·strong** (hed′strông′) *adjective.*

headwaters The small streams that come together to form the beginning of a river. **head·wa·ters** (hed′wô′tərz) *plural noun.*

headway Forward movement or progress: *I can't make much headway with this arithmetic problem.* **head·way** (hed′wā′) *noun.*

heal To make or become healthy or sound again: *The cut healed without leaving a scar.* Other words that sound like this are **heel** and **he'll**. **heal** (hēl) *verb,* **healed, healing.**

health **1.** The condition of being well and without disease or injury: *You'll lose your health if you don't eat the proper foods.* **2.** The condition of the body or mind: *The doctor examined me and decided that I was in good health.* **health** (helth) *noun.*

PRONUNCIATION KEY:

at	āpe	fär	câre	end	mē	it	īce	pïerce	hot	ōld	sông	fôrk
oil	out	up	ūse	rüle	pull	tûrn	chin	sing	shop	thin	this	

hw in white; zh in treasure. The symbol ə stands for the unstressed vowel sound in about, taken, pencil, lemon, and circus.

339

health food Any food held to be or promoted as being good for the health.

healthful Good for people's health; wholesome: *Exercise is healthful.* **health·ful** (helth'fəl) *adjective.* —**healthfully** *adverb* —**healthfulness** *noun.*

healthy Having, showing, or giving good health: *I love the healthy country air.* **health·y** (hel'thē) *adjective,* **healthier, healthiest.**

heap A collection of things piled together: *a heap of books. Noun.*
○ **1.** To make into a pile: *We heaped the fallen leaves.* **2.** To give or fill in large amounts: *I heaped my plate with mashed potatoes. Verb.* **heap** (hēp) *noun, plural* **heaps;** *verb,* **heaped, heaping.**

hear **1.** To receive sound through the ears: *I hear someone calling my name.* **2.** To listen to: *Please hear my side of the story, too.* **3.** To get information about: *I heard about the fire on the radio.* **4.** To get a letter or other communication: *Have you heard from your friend lately?* Another word that sounds like this is **here.** **hear** (hîr) *verb,* **heard, hearing.**

heard Past tense and past participle of hear. Another word that sounds like this is **herd.** **heard** (hûrd) *verb.*

hearing **1.** The ability to hear: *You have very good hearing.* **2.** The act of listening or getting information: *Hearing that my friend won the contest made me happy.* **3.** The chance to be heard: *The judge gave both sides a fair hearing.* **hear·ing** (hîr'ing) *noun, plural* **hearings.**

hearing aid A small electronic device that makes sounds louder. It is worn in or near the ear to make poor hearing better.

hearsay Information heard from someone else: *Is that a fact or just hearsay?* **hear·say** (hîr'sā') *noun.*

heart **1.** The organ in the body that pumps blood through the arteries and veins. The heart is located in the chest. It is divided into four chambers. **2.** The center of a person's feelings: *The happy child spoke from the heart when thanking us for finding the puppy.*

aorta
artery
atrium
ventricle
heart

3. Spirit; courage: *The team lost heart after their defeat.* **4.** The center or middle of anything: *We got lost in the heart of the forest.* **5.** A playing card marked with one or more red figures like this: ♥. **6.** Anything shaped like a heart: *We cut out paper hearts to make Valentine's Day cards.*
• **by heart.** From or by memory: *I'm learning my lines for the play by heart.* **heart** (härt) *noun, plural* **hearts.**

heartbeat One complete pumping motion of the heart. **heart·beat** (härt'bēt') *noun, plural* **heartbeats.**

heartbroken Filled with sorrow or grief: *We were heartbroken when our dog died.* **heart·bro·ken** (härt'brō'kən) *adjective.*

hearth **1.** The floor of a fireplace or the space in front of it. **2.** Home. **hearth** (härth) *noun, plural* **hearths.**

heartless Unkind and cruel. **heartless** (härt'ləs) *adjective.*

hearty **1.** Full of warmth, friendliness, or enthusiasm: *a hearty welcome.* **2.** Big and satisfying: *a hearty meal.* **heart·y** (här'tē) *adjective,* **heartier, heartiest.** —**heartily** *adverb* —**heartiness** *noun.*

heat **1.** High temperature; warmth. Heat is a form of energy: *The sun gives off heat.* **2.** Strong feeling, excitement: *in the heat of anger. Noun.*
○ To make or become hot or warm: *We heated the milk before giving it to the baby. Verb.* **heat** (hēt) *noun, plural* **heats;** *verb,* **heated, heating.**

heater A device, such as a radiator or furnace, that gives heat. **heat·er** (hē'tər) *noun, plural* **heaters.**

heath A flat, open piece of land covered with heather or low bushes. **heath** (hēth) *noun, plural* **heaths.**

heathen A person who does not believe in the God of the Christians, Jews, or Muslims. *Noun.*
○ Having to do with heathens: *Ancient heathen tribes worshiped many gods. Adjective.* **hea·then** (hē'thən) *noun, plural* **heathens** *or* **heathen;** *adjective.*

WORD HISTORY

The word **heathen** comes from an Old English word which originally meant "someone who lives on the heath." *On the heath* meant "in the country." The cities were the first places to be converted to Christianity. People in the country held on to the old beliefs longer.

heather A low evergreen shrub that has pink, purple, or white flowers and grows wild in Scotland and England. **heath•er** (he<u>th</u>′ər) *noun, plural* **heathers.**

heave 1. To lift, raise, pull, or throw using force or effort: *I heaved a rock across the stream.* 2. To give out in a loud or heavy way: *I heaved a sigh of relief.* 3. To rise and fall: *The runner's chest heaved after the race.* **heave** (hēv) *verb,* **heaved, heaving.**

heaven 1. In Christianity and other religions, the place where God and the angels live. 2. **heavens.** The space above and around the earth; sky: *You can see many stars in the heavens on a clear, dark night.* **heav•en** (hev′ən) *noun, plural* **heavens.**

heavenly 1. Having to do with heaven; divine: *Angels are heavenly beings.* 2. Of or in the sky or outer space. 3. Happy, pleasing, or beautiful: *a heavenly spot for a picnic.* **heav•en•ly** (hev′ən lē) *adjective.*

The sun in the sky is considered
a heavenly body.

heavy 1. Having great weight; hard to lift or move: *The desk was too heavy for me to move.* 2. Having more than the usual weight: *It's so cold that I need a heavy blanket.* 3. Large in size or amount: *heavy traffic.* 4. Hard to do, carry out, or bear: *heavy responsibilities.* **heav•y** (hev′ē) *adjective,* **heavier, heaviest.** —**heavily** *adverb* —**heaviness** *noun.*

Hebrew 1. A member of one of the Jewish tribes of ancient times. 2. The language spoken by the ancient Jews. The people of Israel speak a form of this language. *Noun.* ○ Of the Hebrews or their language. *Adjective.* **He•brew** (hē′brü) *noun, plural* **Hebrews;** *adjective.*

The message on this
early poster is written
in Hebrew.

heckle To keep annoying and interrupting a speaker by shouting and making noise. **heck•le** (hek′əl) **heckled, heckling.** —**heckler** *noun.*

hectare A unit of area in the metric system. It is equal to 10,000 square meters, or about 2½ acres. **hec•tare** (hek′târ) *noun, plural* **hectares.**

hectic Very rushed, confused, and excited: *a hectic day at work.* **hec•tic** (hek′tik) *adjective.*

he'd 1. Shortened form of "he had." 2. Shortened form of "he would." Another word that sounds like this is **heed.** **he'd** (hēd) *contraction.*

hedge A row of shrubs or small trees planted close together, used as a fence. *Noun.* ○ 1. To surround, close in, or separate with a hedge. 2. To avoid answering a question directly: *When they asked me for help, I hedged and said I would think about it.* *Verb.* **hedge** (hej) *noun, plural* **hedges;** *verb,* **hedged, hedging.**

hedgehog 1. An animal with a pointed snout and sharp, hard spines on its back and sides. When it is frightened or attacked, it rolls up into a ball with only its spines showing. Hedgehogs eat insects and are found in western Europe. 2. A porcupine. **hedge•hog** (hej′hôg′ *or* hej′hog′) *noun, plural* **hedgehogs.**

heed To pay attention to; listen or mind: *I heeded my parents' advice.* Another word that sounds like this is **he'd.** **heed** (hēd) *verb,* **heeded, heeding.**

PRONUNCIATION KEY:

| at | āpe | fär | câre | end | mē | it | īce | pierce | hot | ōld | sông | fôrk |
| oil | out | up | ūse | rüle | pull | tûrn | chin | sing | shop | thin | <u>th</u>is | |

hw in white; zh in treasure. The symbol ə stands for the unstressed vowel sound in about, taken, pencil, lemon, and circus.

341

heel¹ 1. The rounded back part of the human foot below the ankle. The heel has many bones in it that carry the weight of the body. 2. Anything like a heel in shape, use, or position. The heel of the hand is the part of the palm near the wrist. *Noun.*
○ To follow closely: *The dog **heeled** at its master's side. Verb.*
Other words that sound like this are **heal** and **he'll**. **heel** (hēl) *noun, plural* **heels**; *verb,* **heeled**, **heeling**.

heel² To lean to one side: *The wind forced the sailboat to **heel** to the left.*
Other words that sound like this are **heal** and **he'll**. **heel** (hēl) *verb,* **heeled**, **heeling**.

heifer A young cow that has not had a calf. **heif·er** (hef′ər) *noun, plural* **heifers**.

height 1. The distance from bottom to top: *The **height** of the statue is 11 feet.* 2. A high place: *The little child was afraid of **heights**.* 3. The highest point: *at the **height** of a brilliant career.* **height** (hīt) *noun, plural* **heights**.

heighten To make or become high or higher: *The excitement **heightened** as the story went on.* **height·en** (hī′tən) *verb,* **heightened**, **heightening**.

Heimlich maneuver An emergency treatment used to help a person who is choking on something. You stand behind the person who is choking, put your arms around the person, and press hard into the upper abdomen. This should force the object out. **Heim·lich maneuver** (hīm′lik).

WORD HISTORY

The **Heimlich maneuver** is named after Henry J. Heimlich, the American physician who developed it.

heir A person who is to receive the money or property of a person after that person has died. Other words that sound like this are **air** and **ere**. **heir** (âr) *noun, plural* **heirs**.

heiress A woman who is to receive or has received the money or property of a person after that person has died. **heir·ess** (âr′is) *noun, plural* **heiresses**.

heirloom An object handed down from generation to generation in a family. **heir·loom** (âr′lüm′) *noun, plural* **heirlooms**.

held Past tense and past participle of **hold**. Look up **hold** for more information. **held** (held) *verb.*

helicopter An aircraft kept in the air by blades that rotate above the craft. **hel·i·cop·ter** (hel′i kop′tər) *noun, plural* **helicopters**.

helium A very light gas that has no color or odor. Helium is used in balloons and blimps. Helium is a chemical element. **he·li·um** (hēl′ē əm) *noun.*

WORD HISTORY

The word **helium** comes from the Greek word for "sun." Helium was first discovered by people who were studying the rays of light that come from the sun.

hell 1. In Christianity and other religions, the place where Satan lives and where wicked people will

helicopter

rotor
rotor hub
rotor blade
canopy
boom
tail rotor (keeps helicopter from spinning)

be punished after death. **2.** A place or condition of great suffering: *The prison was a **hell** on earth.* **hell** (hel) *noun, plural* **hells.**

he'll **1.** Shortened form of "he will." **2.** Shortened form of "he shall."
Other words that sound like this are **heal** and **heel**.
he'll (hēl) *contraction.*

hello A word used as a greeting: *a warm **hello**.* **hel·lo** (he lō′ *or* hə lō′) *interjection; noun, plural* **hellos.**

helm The part of a ship used for steering. It is usually a wheel or large lever: *The captain stood at the **helm** of the ship.* **helm** (helm) *noun, plural* **helms.**

Soldiers, firefighters, football players, and astronauts wear helmets.

helmet A covering for the head, worn for protection. **hel·met** (hel′mit) *noun, plural* **helmets.**

help **1.** To give or do something useful, wanted, or needed; assist: *I **helped** my parents paint the living room.* **2.** To make better; ease; relieve: *Cough drops will **help** your sore throat.* **3.** To stop or avoid: *I couldn't **help** laughing. Verb.*
○ **1.** The act of helping: *Do you need **help**?*

2. A person or thing that helps: *The new vacuum cleaner is a big **help** around the house. Noun.*
• **to help oneself to.** To take, especially without being urged: *The food is on the table, so **help** yourself.*
• **to help out.** To provide help, support, or service: *I always **help out** when we have company for dinner.*
help (help) *verb,* **helped, helping;** *noun, plural* **helps.**

helpful Giving help; useful. **help·ful** (help′fəl) *adjective.* —**helpfully** *adverb* —**helpfulness** *noun.*

helping A serving of food for one person: *Would you like a second **helping** of cake?* **help·ing** (hel′ping) *noun, plural* **helpings.**

helping verb A term sometimes used for **auxiliary verb.** Look up **auxiliary verb** for more information.

helpless Not able to take care of oneself: *A newborn kitten is **helpless**.* **help·less** (help′lis) *adjective.* —**helplessly** *adverb* —**helplessness** *noun.*

hem The border of a garment or piece of cloth. It is made by folding under the edge and sewing it down. Dresses, pillowcases, and curtains have hems. *Noun.*
○ To fold under the edge of a piece of cloth and sew it down. *I **hemmed** the curtains. Verb.*
• **to hem in.** To close in; surround: *I felt **hemmed in** by the crowd.*
hem (hem) *noun, plural* **hems;** *verb,* **hemmed, hemming.**

hemisphere One half of the earth or another sphere. The equator divides the earth into the Northern Hemisphere and the Southern Hemisphere. The earth is also divided into the Eastern Hemisphere and the Western Hemisphere. Europe, Africa, Asia, and Australia are in the Eastern Hemisphere. North and South America are in the Western Hemisphere. **hem·i·sphere** (hem′ə sfir′) *noun, plural* **hemispheres.**

hemlock **1.** A tall evergreen tree with reddish bark, flat needles, and small cones. Its wood is used for pulp and as lumber. **2.** A poisonous plant with spotted, hollow stems and clusters of white flowers. **hem·lock** (hem′lok′) *noun, plural* **hemlocks.**

PRONUNCIATION KEY:

| at | āpe | fär | câre | end | mē | it | īce | pierce | hot | ōld | sông | fôrk |
| oil | out | up | ūse | rüle | pull | tûrn | chin | sing | shop | thin | this | |

hw in white; zh in treasure. The symbol ə stands for the unstressed vowel sound in about, taken, pencil, lemon, and circus.

343

hemp A strong, tough fiber made from the stem of a tall plant, used to make rope. **hemp** (hemp) *noun, plural* **hemps.**

hen 1. An adult female chicken. 2. The female of various other birds. **hen** (hen) *noun, plural* **hens.**

hence 1. As a result; therefore: *I've seen the movie before, and* ***hence*** *I know the story.* 2. From this time or place: *The friends agreed to meet two weeks* ***hence*** *at the same place.* **hence** (hens) *adverb.*

her A female person or animal that is being talked about: *I invited* ***her*** *to the dance. Pronoun.*
  ○ Of, belonging to, or having to do with her: ***Her*** *cousin is my best friend. Adjective.*
  her (hûr) *pronoun; adjective.*

herb 1. A plant whose leaves, stems, seeds, or roots are used in cooking for flavoring, in medicines, or because they are fragrant. Mint and parsley are herbs. 2. Any flowering plant that dies at the end of one growing season and does not form a woody stem. **herb** (ûrb *or* hûrb) *noun, plural* **herbs.**

Herbs **like this are used in cooking.**

herbivore An animal that eats only plants. Cows are herbivores. **her·bi·vore** (hûr′bə vôr′) *noun, plural* **herbivores.**

herbivorous Feeding on plants. **her·biv·o·rous** (hûr biv′ər əs) *adjective.*

These riders are herding **this flock of sheep.**

herd A group of animals that live or travel together. *Noun.*
  ○ To group or lead in or like a herd: *Our tour guide* ***herded*** *us into the bus. Verb.*
  Another word that sounds like this is **heard.**
  herd (hûrd) *noun, plural* **herds;** *verb,* **herded, herding.**

here 1. At, in, or to this place: *Bring the book* ***here,*** *and I'll read it to you.* 2. At this time: *Let's stop reading* ***here.*** *Adverb.*
  ○ This place: *How do I get home from* ***here***? *Noun.*
  ○ A word used in answering a roll call, calling an animal, or attracting attention. *Interjection.*
  Another word that sounds like this is **hear.**
  here (hîr) *adverb; noun; interjection.*

hereafter From now on; after this: *The guard told me that* ***hereafter,*** *I should not run in school halls.* **here·af·ter** (hîr af′tər) *adverb.*

hereby By means of this: *The certificate said, "You are* ***hereby*** *entitled to one free admission to the zoo."* **here·by** (hîr′bī′) *adverb.*

hereditary 1. Passed on or able to be passed on by heredity: *Blue eyes are* ***hereditary.*** 2. Passed on from an ancestor to an heir: *The noble inherited the* ***hereditary*** *title from ancestors.* **he·red·i·tar·y** (hə red′i ter′ē) *adjective.*

heredity 1. The passing on of characteristics from an animal or plant to its offspring. 2. The characteristics passed on: *Brown hair is part of my* ***heredity.*** **he·red·i·ty** (hə red′i tē) *noun, plural* **heredities.**

here's Shortened form of "here is." **here's** (hîrz) *contraction.*

heritage Something handed down from earlier generations or from the past; tradition: *The right* *to free speech is part of the American **heritage**.* **her·i·tage** (her′i tij) *noun, plural* **heritages**.

hermit A person who lives alone and away from other people, often for religious reasons. **her·mit** (hûr′mit) *noun, plural* **hermits**.

hero 1. A person looked up to by others because of great achievements or fine qualities: *The swimmer who saved the child from drowning was a **hero**.* 2. The main male character in a play, story, or poem. 3. A big sandwich on a long roll with a thick crust: *a meatball **hero**.* **he·ro** (hîr′ō) *noun, plural* **heroes**.

heroic 1. Very brave; courageous: *a **heroic** rescue.* 2. Describing the deeds of heroes: *a **heroic** poem about a great warrior.* **he·ro·ic** (hi rō′ik) *adjective.* —**heroically** *adverb.*

heroin A very addictive, illegal drug. Another word that sounds like this is **heroine**. **her·o·in** (her′ō in) *noun.*

heroine 1. A woman or girl looked up to by others for great achievements or fine qualities: *Our school doctor is my **heroine**, because I want to be a doctor too some day.* 2. The main female character in a play, story, or poem. Another word that sounds like this is **heroin**. **her·o·ine** (her′ō in) *noun, plural* **heroines**.

heron A bird with a long slender neck, a long pointed bill, and long thin legs. **her·on** (her′ən) *noun, plural* **herons**.

herring A small saltwater fish that is a member of the sardine family. Herring are found in the northern Atlantic Ocean and can be eaten smoked, fresh, or canned. **her·ring** (her′ing) *noun, plural* **herring** *or* **herrings**.

hers The one or ones that belong or have to do with her:

Herons feed on fish and frogs.

*Whose book is it, his or **hers**?* **hers** (hûrz) *pronoun.*

herself 1. Her own self: *The principal **herself** is opposed to the plan.* 2. Her usual, normal, or true self: *Mother has not been **herself** since she caught a cold.* **her·self** (hûr self′) *pronoun.*

he's 1. Shortened form of "he is." 2. Shortened form of "he has." **he's** (hēz) *contraction.*

hesitant Showing hesitation; not quite willing: *I was **hesitant** about jumping into the lake.* **hes·i·tant** (hez′i tənt) *adjective;* **hesitantly**, *adverb.*

hesitate 1. To wait or stop a moment, especially because of feeling unsure: *The speaker **hesitated** and looked down at some notes.* 2. To be unwilling: *I **hesitated** to telephone you because it was late.* 3. To wait to act because of doubt or fear: *If you **hesitate** too long, you will lose your chance to get the job.* **hes·i·tate** (hez′i tāt′) *verb,* **hesitated, hesitating**.

hesitation A delay or pause because of fear, uncertainty, or forgetting: *The brave child picked up the garden snake without **hesitation**.* **hes·i·ta·tion** (hez′i tā′shən) *noun, plural* **hesitations**.

hexagon A shape or figure with six sides. **hex·a·gon** (heks′ə gon) *noun, plural* **hexagons**.

hexagon

hey A word used to attract attention or to show surprise or pleasure: *"**Hey**! Watch where you're going!"* Another word that sounds like this is **hay**. **hey** (hā) *interjection.*

hi A word used to say "hello." Another word that sounds like this is **high**. **hi** (hī) *interjection.*

HI Postal abbreviation for **Hawaii**.

H.I. An abbreviation for **Hawaiian Islands**.

hibernate To spend the winter sleeping. Some bears, woodchucks, frogs, and snakes hibernate. **hi·ber·nate** (hī′bər nāt′) *verb,* **hibernated, hibernating**. —**hibernation** *noun.*

PRONUNCIATION KEY:
at   āpe   fär   câre   end   mē   it   īce   pîerce   hot   ōld   sông   fôrk
oil   out   up   ūse   rüle   půll   tûrn   chin   sing   shop   thin   this
hw in white; zh in treasure. The symbol ə stands for the unstressed vowel sound in about, taken, pencil, lemon, and circus.

345

hiccup ▸ highly

WORD HISTORY

Hibernate comes from a Latin word meaning "winter quarters." The Roman legions usually did not fight during the winter season; instead they would stay near camp until spring. Hibernate now refers to how animals become inactive during the winter.

hiccup 1. A quick catching of the breath that one cannot control. A hiccup is caused by a short spasm of the breathing muscles. 2. **hiccups.** The condition of having one hiccup after another. *Noun.*
○ To have hiccups. *Verb.*
hic·cup (hik′up) *noun, plural* **hiccups;** *verb,* **hiccupped, hiccupping.**

hickory A tall tree of North America. The hickory has nuts that are used as food and strong, hard wood. **hick·o·ry** (hik′ə rē) *noun, plural* **hickories.**

hid Past tense and a past participle of **hide.** Look up **hide** for more information. **hid** (hid) *verb.*

The man is almost hidden by the high grass.

hidden A past participle of **hide.** Look up **hide** for more information. **hid·den** (hid′ən) *verb.*

hide¹ 1. To put or keep out of sight: *The heavy snow hid the deer's tracks.* 2. To keep secret: *The lost children tried to hide their fears from each other.* **hide** (hīd) *verb,* **hid, hidden** *or* **hid, hiding.**

hide² The skin of an animal. Leather shoes are made from hides. **hide** (hīd) *noun, plural* **hides.**

hide-and-seek A children's game in which one player has to find all of the other players who are hiding. **hide-and-seek** (hīd′ən sēk′) *noun.*

hideous Very ugly; horrible: *a hideous monster.* **hid·e·ous** (hid′ē əs) *adjective.* —**hideously** *adverb* —**hideousness** *noun.*

hideout A place where someone can hide, especially from the police. **hide·out** (hīd′out′) *noun, plural* **hideouts.**

hieroglyphic A picture or symbol that stands for a word, sound, or idea. **hi·er·o·glyph·ic** (hī′ər ə glif′ik) *noun, plural* **hieroglyphics.**

The ancient Egyptians used hieroglyphics in their writing.

high 1. Tall: *That mountain is very high.* 2. At a great distance from the ground: *The bird was high in the sky.* 3. Above or more important than others: *a high rank in the army.* 4. Greater than others: *high winds.* 5. Above other sounds in pitch: *a high note.* 6. Noble or lofty: *high ideals. Adjective.*
○ At or to a high place: *The hikers climbed high up the hill. Adverb.*
○ 1. A high place or point: *The temperature today reached a new high.* 2. The arrangement of gears in an automobile, bicycle, or other vehicle that gives the greatest speed. *Noun.*
Another word that sounds like this is **hi.**
• **high and dry.** 1. Completely up out of water: *The ship was stranded high and dry on the rocks.* 2. Without aid or assistance; alone; abandoned: *The outlaws drove off in the stagecoach, leaving the passengers high and dry.* **high** (hī) *adjective,* **higher, highest;** *adverb; noun, plural* **highs.**

high jump A contest in which a person jumps as high as possible over a bar set between two upright poles.

highland A high or hilly part of a country. **high·land** (hī′lənd) *noun, plural* **highlands.**

highly 1. Very much; very: *a highly entertaining movie.* 2. With much praise or admiration: *The* *students think **highly** of their teacher.* **3.** At a high price: *I was not **highly** paid for mowing the lawn.* **high•ly** (hī′lē) *adverb.*

Highness A title of respect used when speaking to or about a member of a royal family: *A king is spoken of as "His **Highness**," and a queen is spoken of as "Her **Highness**."* **High•ness** (hī′nis) *noun, plural* **Highnesses.**

high-rise A very tall building. **high-rise** (hī′rīz′) *noun, plural* **high-rises.**

high school A school attended after elementary school or junior high school. High school goes up to the twelfth grade.

high seas The open waters of an ocean. They are not under the control of any country.

high-strung Very tense or nervous by nature: *a **high-strung** horse.* **high-strung** (hī′strung′) *adjective.*

high tide The tide when the level of the ocean is at its highest.

highway A main road: *Main Street becomes a **highway** just outside of town.* **high•way** (hī′wā′) *noun, plural* **highways.**

highwayman A robber who holds up travelers on a road. **high•way•man** (hī′wā′mən) *noun, plural* **highwaymen** (hī′wā′mən).

hijack To take over a truck, airplane, or other vehicle by force. **hi•jack** (hī′jak′) *verb,* **hijacked, hijacking.**

hike To take a long walk. *Verb.*
○ A long walk: *We took a long **hike** in the woods. Noun.* **hike** (hīk) *verb,* **hiked, hiking;** *noun, plural* **hikes.**

Going on a long outdoor hike is a good way to learn about nature.

hilarious Very funny: *a **hilarious** joke.* **hi•lar•i•ous** (hi lâr′ē əs) *adjective.* —**hilariously** *adverb.*

hill **1.** A raised, rounded part of the earth's surface. A hill is not as high as a mountain. **2.** A small heap or mound: *Ants have made **hills** in our backyard.* **hill** (hil) *noun, plural* **hills.** —**hilly** *adjective.*

hillside The side or slope of a hill. **hill•side** (hil′sīd′) *noun, plural* **hillsides.**

hilltop The top of a hill. **hill•top** (hil′top′) *noun, plural* **hilltops.**

hilt The handle of a sword or dagger. **hilt** (hilt) *noun, plural* **hilts.**

him A male person or animal that is being talked about: *I lent a book to **him**.*

The **hilt** of this sword is cushioned so it can be easily gripped.

Another word that sounds like this is **hymn.** **him** (him *or* im) *pronoun.*

himself **1.** His own self: *Jim hit **himself** by accident with the hammer.* **2.** His usual, normal, or true self: *Mike just wasn't **himself** during the game today.* **him•self** (him self′) *pronoun.*

hind At the back; rear: ***hind** legs.* **hind** (hīnd) *adjective.*

hinder To hold back the progress of: *The snowstorm **hindered** the search for the missing plane.* **hin•der** (hin′dər) *verb,* **hindered, hindering.**

hindrance Something that hinders; obstacle: *The noisy traffic outside was a **hindrance** to our conversation.* **hin•drance** (hin′drəns) *noun, plural* **hindrances.**

Hinduism A religion, philosophy, and social system that originated in India. The supreme being of Hinduism takes many different forms. **Hin•du•ism** (hin′dü iz′əm) *noun.*

hinge A joint on which a door, gate, or lid moves back and forth or up and down: *The **hinges** on the gate squeak when you open or close it. Noun.*
○ **1.** To put hinges on; attach by hinges. **2.** To depend: *The team's chances **hinge** on next week's game. Verb.* **hinge** (hinj) *noun, plural* **hinges;** *verb,* **hinged, hinging.**

hint A slight sign or suggestion: *There is a **hint** of spring in the air this morning. Noun.*
○ To give a slight sign or suggestion. *Verb.* **hint** (hint) *noun, plural* **hints;** *verb,* **hinted, hinting.**

PRONUNCIATION KEY:

at	āpe	fär	câre	end	mē	it	ice	pîerce	hot	ōld	sông	fôrk
oil	out	up	ūse	rüle	pull	tûrn	chin	sing	shop	thin	this	

hw in white; zh in treasure. The symbol ə stands for the unstressed vowel sound in about, taken, pencil, lemon, and circus.

347

hip The part on either side of the body just below the waist; the joint where either leg meets the body. **hip** (hip) *noun, plural* **hips**.

hipbone Either of two large bones that form the sides of the pelvis in a person's skeleton. **hip·bone** (hip′bōn′) *noun, plural* **hipbones**.

hippo A hippopotamus. **hip·po** (hip′ō) *noun, plural* **hippos**.

hippopotamus A very large, heavy animal that eats plants. It lives in and near rivers and lakes in Africa. **hip·po·pot·a·mus** (hip′ə pot′ə məs) *noun, plural* **hippopotamuses**.

The **hippopotamus** lives in Africa and has short legs and thick, hairless skin.

hire 1. To give a job to; employ: *The school **hired** three new teachers.* 2. To get the temporary use of something in return for payments; rent: *We **hired** a car to drive to Florida. Verb.*
○ The act of hiring: *I couldn't afford the **hire** of a rowboat. Noun.*
hire (hīr) *verb,* **hired, hiring;** *noun, plural* **hires**.

his The one or ones that belong or have to do with him: *This book is mine and that book is **his**. Pronoun.*
○ Of, belonging to, or having to do with him: *His best friend lives next door. Adjective.*
his (hiz) *pronoun; adjective.*

Hispanic Of or having to do with Spain or Latin America, or with the people of Spain or Latin America. *Adjective.*
○ A person who lives in the United States and has Spanish or Latin American parents or ancestors. *Noun.*
His·pan·ic (hi span′ik) *adjective; noun, plural* **Hispanics**.

hiss A sound like the letter "s" that is held for a long time and is used to show dislike. *Noun.*
○ To make this sound. *Verb.*
hiss (his) *noun, plural* **hisses;** *verb,* **hissed, hissing**.

historian A person who knows a great deal about history. Historians write history books. **his·to·ri·an** (hi stôr′ē ən) *noun, plural* **historians**.

General Lee's surrender to General Grant in the Civil War was a historic event.

historic Important in history: *a **historic** old house.* **his·tor·ic** (hi stôr′ik) *adjective.*

historical Having to do with history: *This book has **historical** information, such as how our town began, how it changed, and who its leaders have been.* **his·tor·i·cal** (hi stôr′i kəl) *adjective.*

history The story or record of what has happened in the past: *That old house has an interesting **history**.* **his·to·ry** (his′tə rē) *noun, plural* **histories**.

hit 1. To give a blow to; strike: *The bully **hit** my friend.* 2. To send by striking with a bat or racket: *The batter **hit** the ball over the fence.* 3. To come against with force: *The arrow **hit** the target.* 4. To come to; reach: *We finally **hit** upon the answer.* 5. To have a strong effect on; impress: *The unhappy news **hit** us hard. Verb.*
○ 1. A blow or strike. 2. A person or thing that is successful or popular: *The band was the **hit** of the party.* 3. The hitting of a baseball so that the batter gets on base. *Noun.*
• **to hit it off.** To like or get along with one another: *When I first met the twins, we didn't **hit it off**.*
hit (hit) *verb,* **hit, hitting;** *noun, plural* **hits**.

hitch 1. To fasten with a rope, strap, or hook: *The farmer **hitched** the horse to the wagon.* 2. To move or lift with a jerk: *I **hitched** up my suspenders. Verb.*
○ 1. A fastening: *The **hitch** between the car and the trailer broke.* 2. An unexpected delay or problem: *The storm put a **hitch** in their plans to leave that day.* 3. A quick, upward pull: *I gave my trousers a **hitch**.* 4. A kind of knot used to attach things together temporarily. *Noun.*
hitch (hich) *verb,* **hitched, hitching;** *noun, plural* **hitches**.

hitchhike To travel by getting free rides from cars or trucks that are passing by. **hitch·hike** (hich′hīk′) *verb*, **hitchhiked**, **hitchhiking**.

hive 1. A box or house for bees to live in. 2. All the bees that live together in the same hive. **hive** (hīv) *noun*, *plural* **hives**.

hives A rash of raised red or white bumps that itch. Hives are often caused by an allergy. **hives** (hīvz) *plural noun*.

hoard To save and store or hide away: *I hoarded my allowance. Verb.*
○ Something stored or hidden away. *Noun.*
Another word that sounds like this is **horde**.
hoard (hôrd) *verb*, **hoarded**, **hoarding**; *noun*, *plural* **hoards**.

hoarse 1. Having a rough or harsh, deep sound: *My voice was hoarse from a bad cold.* 2. Having a harsh voice: *I was hoarse after all the shouting I did at the game.*
Another word that sounds like this is **horse**.
hoarse (hôrs) *adjective*, **hoarser**, **hoarsest**.

hoax A trick or made-up story meant to fool people. **hoax** (hōks) *noun*, *plural* **hoaxes**.

hobble 1. To move or walk awkwardly with a limp. 2. To keep from moving easily or freely: *You hobble a horse by tying its front legs or its back legs together. Verb.*
○ A rope, strap, or other thing used to hobble a horse or other animal. *Noun.*
hob·ble (hob′əl) *verb*, **hobbled**, **hobbling**; *noun*, *plural* **hobbles**.

hobby Something done regularly in one's spare time for pleasure. **hob·by** (hob′ē) *noun*, *plural* **hobbies**.

hockey 1. A game played on ice by two teams of six players each. The players wear ice skates and hit a rubber disk, called a puck, with curved sticks. Each team tries to get the puck into the other team's goal. 2. A game played on a field by

Hockey has long been the national sport of Canada.

two teams of eleven players each. Curved sticks are used to hit a ball along the ground into the other team's goal. **hock·ey** (hok′ē) *noun*.

hoe A tool with a wide, thin blade set across the end of a long handle. Hoes are used to loosen the soil around plants and dig up weeds. *Noun.*
○ To dig with a hoe. *Verb.*
hoe (hō) *noun*, *plural* **hoes**; *verb*, **hoed**, **hoeing**.

hog 1. A fully grown pig, raised for its meat. 2. Any of several wild animals in the pig family. 3. A greedy or dirty person. *Noun.*
○ To take more than one's share: *The truck hogged the narrow road so that no cars could pass. Verb.*
hog (hôg *or* hog) *noun*, *plural* **hogs**; *verb*, **hogged**, **hogging**.

Hogs are more intelligent than dogs but will eat almost anything.

hogan A house made of stones or logs with a roof of branches covered with earth. Some Navajo Indians live in hogans. **ho·gan** (hō′gän) *noun*, *plural* **hogans**.

hoist To lift or pull up: *We hoisted the flag up the pole. Verb.*
○ A device used to lift or pull up something heavy: *The mechanic at the garage put the car on a hoist to raise it. Noun.*
hoist (hoist) *verb*, **hoisted**, **hoisting**; *noun*, *plural* **hoists**.

hold¹ 1. To take and keep in the hands or arms; grasp: *If you hold the packages, I'll unlock the door.* 2. To keep from falling; support: *Will this chair hold my weight?* 3. To keep in a certain place or position: *A good book holds your attention.* 4. To remain attached or fastened: *The ship's anchor held in rough seas.* 5. To contain: *This bottle holds two quarts.* 6. To take part in; carry on: *We were holding a conversation.* 7. To have in the mind: *I hold strong opinions about religion.* 8. To believe to be; think: *The judge held them responsible for the accident. Verb.*
○ 1. A grasp; grip: *I didn't have a good hold on the heavy lamp.* 2. Something that can be gripped: *The hikers couldn't find enough holds to*

PRONUNCIATION KEY:
at   āpe   fär   câre   end   mē   it   īce   pierce   hot   ōld   sông   fôrk
oil   out   up   ūse   rüle   pull   tûrn   chin   sing   shop   thin   this
hw in white; zh in treasure. The symbol ə stands for the unstressed vowel sound in about, taken, pencil, lemon, and circus.

349

climb the side of the cliff. **3.** A mark or symbol in music that shows a pause. *Noun.*

• **to hold back.** To restrain; control: *I tried to hold back the tears.*

• **to hold out. 1.** To last; continue: *Our food will hold out another week.* **2.** To keep fighting or resisting: *The troops in the fort held out for weeks.*

• **to hold up. 1.** To support; keep from falling: *These columns hold up the roof.* **2.** To raise in order to show or display: *Hold up your hand if you want to ask a question.* **3.** To last or continue: *These shoes have held up for years.* **4.** To stop or delay: *Traffic held us up.* **5.** To rob while threatening with a weapon: *A gang held up three stores.*

hold (hōld) *verb,* **held, holding;** *noun, plural* **holds.**

hold² A space in a ship or airplane where cargo is stored. **hold** (hōld) *noun, plural* **holds.**

holder 1. A person who holds something; owner: *You must be the holder of a driver's license.* **2.** A thing used to hold something else with: *That jar will make a good holder for pencils.* **hold·er** (hōl′dər) *noun, plural* **holders.**

holdup 1. An armed robbery. **2.** A stopping or delay: *a holdup of traffic.* **hold·up** (hōld′up′) *noun, plural* **holdups.**

hole 1. A hollow place in something solid: *The dog dug a hole in the ground.* **2.** An opening through something: *I wore a hole in the elbow of my old sweater.* **3.** A small hollow place on the green of a golf course. The ball is hit into the hole. **4.** The burrow of an animal. Another word that sounds like this is **whole.** **hole** (hōl) *noun, plural* **holes.**

holiday 1. A day on which most people do not work. Many holidays celebrate the anniversaries of great events. Thanksgiving Day is an American

---

HOLIDAYS

Although the Federal Government decides what holidays its employees will get, each state is free to choose the holidays it will celebrate. The most common public holidays are:

New Year's Day: Celebrated on January 1. Chinese New Year is celebrated between January 10 and February 19.

Martin Luther King, Jr. Day: Celebrated in the third Monday in January, it honors the birthday of the African-American civil rights leader.

President's Day or **Washington's Birthday:** This holiday celebrates the birthdays of both George Washington (February 22) and Abraham Lincoln (February 12). It is celebrated on the third Monday in February.

Memorial Day: On the last Monday of May, this holiday honors all those who died serving the United States during war.

Fourth of July or **Independence Day:** This holiday celebrates the signing of the Declaration of Independence in 1776 when the American colonies announced their independence from Great Britain.

Labor Day: On the first Monday of September, this holiday honors the workers in the United States.

Columbus Day: Celebrated on the second Monday in October, this holiday celebrates the day when Christopher Columbus first saw the New World, October 12, 1492.

Election Day: Falling on the first Tuesday after the first Monday in November, Election Day is a holiday in some states.

Veteran's Day: Honoring the veterans of United States wars, this day marks the signing of the agreement that ended World War I. That agreement was signed on the eleventh hour of the eleventh day of the eleventh month in 1918.

Thanksgiving: First celebrated by the Pilgrims in 1621, Thanksgiving is a day of thanks celebrated on the fourth Thursday of November. The following Friday is usually also a holiday.

Christmas: Both a religious and a public holiday, Christmas is celebrated on December 25th.

Other special holidays include **Valentine's Day** on February 14, **Mother's Day** in May, **Father's Day** in June, **Halloween** on October 31, and **Kwanzaa**, a week-long celebration that begins on December 26.

holiday. **2.** A vacation: *My neighbor is home from college for the spring holidays.* **hol·i·day** (hol′i dā′) *noun, plural* **holidays.**

WORD HISTORY

The word **holiday** comes from an Old English word that meant "holy day." In England long ago, the only days when people did not work were days set aside as special religious feast days.

Holland A country in northwestern Europe. This country is also called **the Netherlands. Hol·land** (hol′ənd) *noun.*

hollow **1.** Having a hole or an empty space inside; not solid: *A water pipe is hollow.* **2.** Curved in like a cup or bowl; sunken: *The thin child had hollow cheeks.* **3.** Deep and echoing: *Our footsteps made a hollow sound in the empty tunnel. Adjective.*
○ **1.** A hole or empty space: *The car bounced over a hollow in the dirt road.* **2.** A valley: *The farm nestled in the hollow between the hills. Noun.*
○ **1.** To make hollow: *Woodpeckers had hollowed out the dead tree trunk.* **2.** To make by digging out: *The rabbits hollowed out a burrow in the ground. Verb.*
hol·low (hol′ō) *adjective,* **hollower, hollowest;** *noun, plural* **hollows;** *verb,* **hollowed, hollowing.**

This hollow **tube serves as a special kind of water slide.**

holly An evergreen tree or shrub usually having very shiny leaves with sharp, pointed edges and bright red berries. Its leaves and berries are often used as Christmas decorations. **hol·ly** (hol′ē) *noun, plural* **hollies.**

hollyhock A tall plant with round wrinkled leaves and spikes of large, brightly colored flowers. **hol·ly·hock** (hol′ē hok′) *noun, plural* **hollyhocks.**

holocaust **1.** A great or complete destruction, as by fire: *The holocaust leveled the city.* **2.** the **Holocaust.** The murder of millions of European Jews and others by the Nazis during World War II. **hol·o·caust** (hol′ə kôst′ *or* hō′lə kôst′) *noun, plural* **holocausts.**

WORD HISTORY

The word **holocaust** comes from a Greek word meaning "burnt up whole." This was the term applied to an ancient form of sacrifice to a particular god. In this ritual an animal was killed, and then all or part of it was burned on an altar.

holster A leather case for carrying a gun. Holsters for pistols are often worn on a belt around a person's waist. **hol·ster** (hōl′stər) *noun, plural* **holsters.**

holy **1.** Belonging to or set apart for the worship of God; sacred. **2.** Close to God; very religious and pure: *The nun led a holy life.* Another word that sounds like this is **wholly. ho·ly** (hō′lē) *adjective,* **holier, holiest.**

home **1.** The place where a person lives: *Our home is in an apartment house.* **2.** A person's family; household: *I grew up in a happy home.* **3.** The place that a person comes from: *Colorado is my home.* **4.** The goal or place of safety in some sports and games. **5.** A place for the shelter and care of certain people: *That big house is a home for elderly people. Noun.*
○ **1.** At or to the place where a person lives: *The whole family will come home for Christmas.* **2.** To the place or mark aimed at: *The arrow hit home. Adverb.*
• **at home.** As if one were in one's own home; comfortable; relaxed: *Whenever I visit your family, they always make me feel at home.*
home (hōm) *noun, plural* **homes;** *adverb.*

homeland A country where a person was born or has a home: *Their homeland is Sweden, although they now live in New York.* **home·land** (hōm′land′) *noun, plural* **homelands.**

PRONUNCIATION KEY:
at āpe fär câre end mē it īce pîerce hot ōld sông fôrk
oil out up ūse rüle pu̇ll tûrn chin sing shop thin this
hw in white; zh in treasure. The symbol ə stands for the unstressed vowel sound in about, taken, pencil, lemon, and circus.

351

homeless Having no home: *Homeless people sleep in the streets and parks of this city.* **home·less** (hōm′lis) *adjective.*

homely 1. Having a plain appearance; not handsome or pretty: *Our old dog is homely, but we love him.* 2. Simple and modest; not fancy or special: *The hotel manager's homely manners put us at ease.* **home·ly** (hōm′lē) *adjective,* **homelier, homeliest.**

homemade Made at home or by hand. **home·made** (hōm′mād′) *adjective.*

In baseball, both a catcher and an umpire are positioned behind home plate.

home plate The place where a baseball player stands to hit a pitched ball. A runner must touch home plate after rounding the bases in order to score a run.

homer A short form of the phrase "home run." Look up **home run** for more information. **hom·er** (hōm′ər) *noun, plural* **homers.**

homeroom A classroom to which all the pupils in a class go in the mornings. Attendance is checked and special announcements are made there. **home·room** (hōm′rüm′ *or* hōm′rùm′) *noun, plural* **homerooms.**

home run A hit in baseball that lets the batter go around all the bases to home plate and score a run.

homesick Sad because of being away from one's home or family. **home·sick** (hōm′sik′) *adjective.* —**homesickness** *noun.*

homespun A cloth woven by hand at home, instead of in a factory by machines. **home·spun** (hōm′spun′) *noun.*

homestead 1. A farm with its house and other buildings. 2. A piece of land that was given by the United States government to a settler for

farming. **home·stead** (hōm′sted′) *noun, plural* **homesteads.**

homeward Toward home: *The hikers turned homeward for the walk back. Adverb.*
○ Toward home: *This train ticket is good for our homeward trip. Adjective.* **home·ward** (hōm′wərd) *adverb; adjective.*

homework A school assignment to be done at home, not in the classroom. **home·work** (hōm′wûrk′) *noun.*

hominy Kernels of white corn that are hulled and ground up. Hominy is mixed with water and boiled before it is eaten. **hom·i·ny** (hom′ə nē) *noun.*

homogenize To mix milk so that the cream is spread evenly throughout and will not separate and rise to the top. **ho·mog·e·nize** (hə moj′ə nīz′) *verb,* **homogenized, homogenizing.**

homograph A word with the same spelling as another, but with a different origin and meaning and, sometimes, a different pronunciation. *Bow* meaning "to bend forward" and *bow* meaning "a weapon for shooting arrows" are homographs. **hom·o·graph** (hom′ə graf′) *noun, plural* **homographs.**

homonym A word with the same pronunciation as another, but with a different meaning and, often, a different spelling. *Lean* meaning "to bend" and *lean* meaning "thin" are homonyms. **hom·o·nym** (hom′ə nim′) *noun, plural* **homonyms.**

homophone A word with the same pronunciation as another, but with a different meaning and spelling. *Know* and *no* are homophones. **hom·o·phone** (hom′ə fōn′) *noun, plural* **homophones.**

Honduras A country in Central America. **Hon·du·ras** (hon dùr′əs *or* hon dyùr′əs) *noun.*

honest 1. Truthful, fair, or trustworthy. An honest person does not cheat, lie, or steal. 2. Earned or gotten fairly: *an honest living.* **hon·est** (on′ist) *adjective.*

honesty The quality of being honest; truthfulness: *Answer the questions with honesty.* **hon·est·y** (on′ə stē) *noun.*

honey 1. A thick, sweet liquid made by bees. Bees collect nectar from flowers and make honey, which they store in honeycombs. 2. A very dear person or thing. **hon·ey** (hun′ē) *noun, plural* **honeys.**

honeybee A bee that makes and stores honey. **hon·ey·bee** (hun′ē bē′) *noun, plural* **honeybees**.

honeycomb 1. A wax structure made by bees to store their eggs and honey in. A honeycomb is made up of layers of cells that have six sides. 2. Something that looks like a bee's honeycomb: *There was a honeycomb of subway tunnels under the city. Noun.*
○ To make full of tunnels or cells like a bee's honeycomb: *Secret passages honeycombed the castle. Verb.* **hon·ey·comb** (hun′ē kōm′) *noun, plural* **honeycombs;** *verb,* **honeycombed, honeycombing.**

honeydew melon A kind of melon with light green pulp and a smooth green or yellow rind. **hon·ey·dew melon** (hun′ē dü′).

honeymoon A vacation taken by a couple who have just been married. *Noun.*
○ To be or go on a honeymoon. *Verb.* **hon·ey·moon** (hun′ē mün′) *noun, plural* **honeymoons;** *verb,* **honeymooned, honeymooning.**

honeysuckle A shrub or vine with many small, sweet-smelling flowers. **hon·ey·suck·le** (hun′ē suk′əl) *noun, plural* **honeysuckles.**

Hong Kong A colony of Great Britain on the southern coast of China. It became part of China in 1997. **Hong Kong** (hong′kong′).

honk 1. The cry of a goose or a sound like it. 2. A sound made by an automobile horn. *Noun.*
○ To make the cry of a goose or the sound of an automobile horn. *Verb.* **honk** (hongk) *noun, plural* **honks;** *verb,* **honked, honking.**

honor 1. A sense of what is right or honest; high moral standards. 2. A good name or reputation: *My honor was at stake.* 3. Something given or done to show great respect or appreciation: *The hero received a medal and other honors.* 4. Honor. A title of respect used in speaking to or of a judge, mayor, or other official: *Everyone at the trial called the judge "Your Honor." Noun.*
○ To show or feel great respect for a person or thing: *The city honored the astronauts with a parade. Verb.* **hon·or** (on′ər) *noun, plural* **honors;** *verb,* **honored, honoring.**

honorable Deserving honor; worthy of respect. **hon·or·a·ble** (on′ər ə bəl) *adjective.* —**honorably** *adverb.*

honorary Given as an honor or award, without the usual requirements or duties: *an honorary degree.* **hon·or·ar·y** (on′ə râr ē) *adjective.*

hood 1. A covering for the head and neck, often attached to the collar of a coat. 2. The metal cover over the engine of an automobile. 3. Something that looks like a hood or is used as a cover: *A cobra has a fold of loose skin called a hood that it can stretch open around its head.* **hood** (hủd) *noun, plural* **hoods.**

hoodlum A rough and nasty person who causes trouble for other people. **hood·lum** (hüd′ləm or hủd′ləm) *noun, plural* **hoodlums.**

hoof 1. The hard covering on the feet of horses, cattle, deer, and some other animals. 2. A foot with this covering: *The horse's hoof pawed the ground.* **hoof** (hủf or hüf) *noun, plural* **hooves** or **hoofs.**

A horseshoe is used to protect a horse's hoof from injury.

hook 1. A bent piece of metal, wood, or other strong material used to hold or fasten something: *a coat hook.* 2. Anything bent or shaped like a hook. A curved piece of wire with a barb at one end used for catching fish is a hook. *Noun.*
○ 1. To hang, fasten, or attach with a hook. 2. To catch with or on a hook: *We hooked three fish.* 3. To have or make into the shape of a hook: *She hooked a leg over the arm of the chair. Verb.* **hook** (hủk) *noun, plural* **hooks;** *verb,* **hooked, hooking.**

hooked 1. Having a hook or curved like a hook: *a hooked nose.* 2. Having a strong liking for: *hooked on playing the piano.* **hooked** (hủkt) *adjective.*

hoop A ring made of wood, metal, or other material: *Lions leap through flaming hoops in the circus.* Another word that sounds like this is **whoop.** **hoop** (hüp or hủp) *noun, plural* **hoops.**

PRONUNCIATION KEY:

| at | āpe | fär | câre | end | mē | it | īce | pierce | hot | ōld | sông | fôrk |
| oil | out | up | ūse | rüle | pùll | tûrn | chin | sing | shop | thin | <u>th</u>is | |

hw in white; zh in treasure. The symbol ə stands for the unstressed vowel sound in about, taken, pencil, lemon, and circus.

353

hooray Another form of the word **hurrah**. Look up **hurrah** for more information. **hoo·ray** (hu̇ rā′) *noun, plural* **hoorays**; *interjection.*

hoot 1. The sound an owl makes. 2. A shout that expresses dislike, scorn, or disbelief: *Our friends gave a hoot when we said we saw a ghost. Noun.* ○ To make the sound of an owl or a shout of scorn or disbelief. *Verb.*
hoot (hüt) *noun, plural* **hoots**; *verb,* **hooted**, **hooting.**

hooves Plural of **hoof**. Look up **hoof** for more information. **hooves** (hu̇vz *or* hüvz) *plural noun.*

hop 1. To make a short jump on one foot: *When you play hopscotch, you have to hop from one square to another.* 2. To move by jumping on both feet or all feet at once: *Rabbits hop.* 3. To jump over: *We hopped the fence. Verb.* ○ 1. A short jump or leap: *The bunny took three hops and was gone.* 2. A bounce: *The ball took a high hop over the shortstop's head. Noun.*
hop (hop) *verb,* **hopped**, **hopping**; *noun, plural* **hops.**

hope To wish for something very much, usually with some belief that it could happen: *I hope that you will feel better soon. Verb.* ○ 1. A strong wish and belief that a thing will happen: *We hope you enjoy your vacation.* 2. Something wished for: *My hope is that we will catch enough fish for dinner. Noun.*
hope (hōp) *verb,* **hoped**, **hoping**; *noun, plural* **hopes.**

hopeful 1. Having or showing hope: *The many branches on the tree made me hopeful that I could climb it.* 2. Giving promise that what is wished for will happen: *A clear moon is a hopeful sign of good weather to come.* **hope·ful** (hōp′fəl) *adjective.*

hopeless Having or giving no hope: *The student had studied hard and felt hopeless after failing the test.* **hope·less** (hōp′lis) *adjective.* —**hopelessly** *adverb* —**hopelessness** *noun.*

hopper 1. A person or an animal that hops. Grasshoppers, rabbits, and kangaroos are hoppers. 2. A container wide open at the top with a small opening at the bottom, used to store grain, coal, or other material and then to empty it into another container. **hop·per** (hop′ər) *noun, plural* **hoppers.**

hopscotch A children's game on numbered squares drawn on the ground. The players hop into the squares in a certain order and try to pick up a stone or other object that has been tossed into one of the squares. **hop·scotch** (hop′skoch′) *noun.*

horde A very large group that is close together; a crowd or swarm: *a horde of ants.* Another word that sounds like this is **hoard**. **horde** (hôrd) *noun, plural* **hordes.**

This fishing boat is heading out to sea just as the sun rises above the horizon.

horizon 1. The line where the sky and the ground or the sea seem to meet. 2. The limit of a person's knowledge, interests, or experience: *You can widen your horizons by reading books.* **hor·i·zon** (hə rī′zən) *noun, plural* **horizons.**

horizontal Flat and straight across; parallel to the horizon. **hor·i·zon·tal** (hôr′ə zon′təl) *adjective.* —**horizontally** *adverb.*

The road is horizontal while the cliffs are vertical.

hormone A chemical made by certain glands in the body. Hormones travel through the bloodstream and help control growth, digestion, and other body processes. **hor·mone** (hôr′mōn) *noun, plural* **hormones.**

The large **horns** of these animals are used for protection.

horn 1. A hard, pointed growth on the head of some animals that have hooves. Deer, sheep, and rhinoceroses have horns. 2. Something that looks like the horn of an animal. Some owls have tufts of feathers on their heads called horns. 3. A brass musical instrument. Horns have a narrow end that you blow into to play them. 4. A device used to make a loud warning sound. **horn** (hôrn) *noun, plural* **horns**.

horned toad A lizard with spikes that look like horns on its head and scales on its body. Horned toads live in the southwestern United States. **horned toad** (hôrnd).

hornet A large wasp that can give a very painful sting. **hor·net** (hôr′nit) *noun, plural* **hornets**.

horny 1. Made of horn. 2. Being hard like a horn: *A deer's antlers are* **horny** *growths.* **horn·y** (hôr′nē) *adjective,* **hornier, horniest**.

horrible 1. Causing great fear or shock: *Murder is a* **horrible** *crime.* 2. Very bad, ugly, or unpleasant: *There was a* **horrible** *smell from the garbage.* **hor·ri·ble** (hôr′ə bəl) *adjective*.

horrid 1. Causing great fear or shock; horrible: *a* **horrid** *monster movie.* 2. Very bad, ugly, or unpleasant: *Spinach tastes* **horrid**. **hor·rid** (hôr′id) *adjective*.

horrify To cause horror: *Seeing the two cars crash* **horrified** *them.* **hor·ri·fy** (hôr′ə fī′) *verb,* **horrified, horrifying**.

horror 1. A feeling of great fear and dread: *I have a* **horror** *of being alone in the dark.* 2. A strong feeling of dislike or shock: *We looked around the dirty old house with* **horror**. 3. A person or thing that causes great fear, shock, or dislike: *The war was a* **horror**. **hor·ror** (hôr′ər) *noun, plural* **horrors**.

horse 1. A large animal with four legs, hooves, and a long, flowing mane and tail, used for riding and pulling heavy loads. 2. Any mammal belonging to the horse family that includes horses, zebras, and asses. 3. A frame with legs, used to hold things like wood being sawed. 4. A heavy leather pad on supporting legs, used in gymnastics for doing exercises. Another word that sounds like this is **hoarse**. **horse** (hôrs) *noun, plural* **horses**.

horse

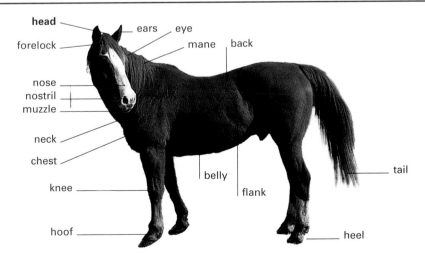

head
ears   eye
forelock   mane   back
nose
nostril
muzzle
neck
chest
belly
flank
knee
tail
hoof
heel

PRONUNCIATION KEY:
at   āpe   fär   câre   end   mē   it   īce   pierce   hot   ōld   sông   fôrk
oil   out   up   ūse   rūle   pull   tûrn   chin   sing   shop   thin   this
hw in white; zh in treasure. The symbol ə stands for the unstressed vowel sound in about, taken, pencil, lemon, and circus.

355

horseback The back of a horse: *The mail was delivered by riders on horseback. Noun.*
○ On the back of a horse: *Some of us are going to ride horseback to the camp. Adverb.*
horse•back (hôrs′bak′) *noun; adverb.*

horsefly A large fly with two black wings. The female gives a painful bite to horses and other animals and to humans. **horse•fly** (hôrs′flī′) *noun, plural* **horseflies.**

horseman 1. A person who rides on a horse. 2. A person skilled in riding or handling horses. **horse•man** (hôrs′mən) *noun, plural* **horsemen** (hôrs′mən).

horseplay Rough, lively play: *We started wrestling for fun, but the horseplay ended with both of us getting hurt.* **horse•play** (hôrs′plā′) *noun.*

horsepower A unit for measuring the power of an engine. One horsepower is equal to the energy needed to raise 550 pounds one foot in one second. **horse•pow•er** (hôrs′pou′ər) *noun.*

horseshoe 1. A metal U-shaped plate curved to fit the shape of a horse's hoof and nailed onto the hoof to protect it. 2. **horseshoes.** A game played by throwing U-shaped plates toward a post so that they will land around the post. **horse•shoe** (hôrs′shü′) *noun, plural* **horseshoes.**

horsewoman 1. A woman who rides on a horse. 2. A woman skilled in riding or handling horses. **horse•wom•an** (hôrs′wùm′ən) *noun, plural* **horse•women** (hôrs′wim′ən).

Riding, grooming and caring for horses are skills that a horsewoman develops.

hose 1. A tube of rubber or other material that will bend easily, used to carry fluids from one place to another. 2. Stockings or socks. *Noun.*
○ To wash or water with a hose: *Will you hose off the front porch? Verb.*
hose (hōz) *noun, plural* **hoses** (for definition 1) or **hose** (for definition 2); *verb,* **hosed, hosing.**

A strong hose is an important piece of equipment for fighting a fire.

hosiery Stockings and socks. **ho•sier•y** (hō′zhə rē) *noun.*

hospitable Making a guest or visitor feel welcome and comfortable; friendly: *a hospitable host.* **hos•pi•ta•ble** (hos′pi tə bəl *or* ho spit′ə bəl) *adjective.* —**hospitably** *adverb.*

hospital A place where people who are sick or hurt are taken care of. **hos•pi•tal** (hos′pi təl) *noun, plural* **hospitals.**

WORD HISTORY

The word hospital comes from a Latin word meaning "a place where travelers can find rest and food." These places often also took care of the needs of poor people who could not pay to stay at other places. Hospital then was used to mean "a place for the care of poor sick people." Today, a hospital is "a place for the care of sick people."

hospitality A friendly welcome and treatment of guests or visitors. **hos•pi•tal•i•ty** (hos′pi tal′i tē) *noun, plural* **hospitalities.**

hospitalize To put a person in a hospital. **hos•pi•tal•ize** (hos′pi tə līz′) *verb,* **hospitalized, hospitalizing.**

host¹ A person who invites people to visit as guests: *We thanked our host for a wonderful party.* **host** (hōst) *noun, plural* **hosts.**

host² A large number: *a host of stars in the sky.* **host** (hōst) *noun, plural* **hosts.**

hostage A person held as a prisoner until money is paid or promises are kept. **hos•tage** (hos′tij) *noun, plural* **hostages.**

hostel A place that gives simple, cheap lodging to

travelers, especially young people on bicycle tours or hikes.

Another word that sounds like this is **hostile**.
hos·tel (hos′təl) *noun, plural* **hostels**.

hostess 1. A woman who invites people to come to her home as her guests: *My aunt was the hostess at a large dinner party.* 2. A woman who serves food and greets people in a restaurant or on an airplane. **host·ess** (hōs′tis) *noun, plural* **hostesses**.

hostile Feeling or showing hostility, hatred, or dislike: *hostile looks.*
Another word that sounds like this is **hostel**.
hos·tile (hos′təl) *adjective.*

hostility 1. A readiness to fight; unfriendliness; antagonism: *There was still hostility between the two old enemies.* 2. hostilities. Acts of war; warfare: *Hostilities between the two countries lasted for years.* **hos·til·i·ty** (ho stil′i tē) *noun, plural* **hostilities**.

hot 1. Having a high temperature. 2. Having a burning, sharp taste: *hot mustard.* 3. Showing anger or passion; violent: *a hot temper.* 4. Following very closely: *in hot pursuit of the robbers.* 5. Just made or heard; fresh: *hot news.* **hot** (hot) *adjective,* **hotter, hottest.** —**hotly** *adverb.*

hot dog A long, thin sausage; frankfurter.

hotel A building with many rooms that people pay to sleep in. Most hotels serve meals. **ho·tel** (hō tel′) *noun, plural* **hotels**.

hothouse A heated building made mainly of glass where plants are grown; greenhouse. **hot·house** (hot′hous′) *noun, plural* **hothouses** (hot′houz′iz).

hot spring A spring whose water is heated naturally in the earth.

hound A dog raised and trained to hunt by scent or sight. A beagle is a hound. *Noun.*
○ To keep urging; pester: *My parents hounded me to clean my room.* *Verb.*
hound (hound) *noun, plural* **hounds**; *verb,* **hounded, hounding.**

hour 1. A unit of time equal to sixty minutes. There are twenty-four hours in a day. 2. The time for anything: *an hour of need.*
Another word that sounds like this is **our**.
hour (our) *noun, plural* **hours**.

hourglass A device used in former times for measuring time. It is a glass tube with a narrow middle. A quantity of sand runs from the top part of the tube to the bottom part in one hour. **hour·glass** (our′glas′) *noun, plural* **hourglasses**.

hourly Done or happening every hour: *hourly flights to California.* *Adjective.*
○ Every hour: *The weather is reported hourly on the radio.* *Adverb.*
hour·ly (our′lē) *adjective; adverb.*

house 1. A building in which people live; home. 2. The people who live in a house: *Our whole house was awakened by the noise.* 3. Any building used for a special purpose: *The town has a new movie house.* 4. A group of people who make laws: *The United States Congress is made up of two houses, the House of Representatives and the Senate.* 5. An audience: *There was a full house for the show.* 6. A royal or noble family. *Noun.*
○ To give a place to live or stay: *We housed our friends until their new home was ready.* *Verb.*
house (hous *for noun;* houz *for verb) noun, plural* **houses** (hou′ziz); *verb,* **housed, housing.**

Not all houses are for people; these are for birds to live in.

houseboat A boat that people can live on. **house·boat** (hous′bōt′) *noun, plural* **houseboats**.

housefly A grayish black fly with transparent wings that lives in and near people's houses. It eats food and garbage. **house·fly** (hous′flī′) *noun, plural* **houseflies**.

household 1. A place where people live; home: *Our household was very busy the week before Christmas.* 2. All the people who live in a home: *The household took a vote on what to have for dinner. Noun.*

PRONUNCIATION KEY:

| at | āpe | fär | câre | end | mē | it | īce | pîerce | hot | ōld | sông | fôrk |
| oil | out | up | ūse | rüle | pùll | tûrn | chin | sing | shop | thin | this | |

hw in white; zh in treasure. The symbol ə stands for the unstressed vowel sound in about, taken, pencil, lemon, and circus.

357

○ Having to do with a household: *household chores. Adjective.*

house·hold (hous′hōld′) *noun, plural* **households;** *adjective.*

housekeeper A person whose job is to take care of a home. A housekeeper is responsible for housework and sometimes child care.
house·keep·er (hous′kē′pər) *noun, plural* **house-keepers.**

House of Commons One of the houses of the British or Canadian Parliament. The members of the House of Commons are elected.

House of Lords One of the houses of the British Parliament. The members of the House of Lords are nobles or members of the clergy.

House of Representatives One of the two houses of the United States Congress.

houseplant A plant grown indoors. **house·plant** (hous′plant′) *noun, plural* **houseplants.**

housewife A woman who takes care of a home and the needs of a family. **house·wife** (hous′wīf′) *noun, plural* **housewives** (hous′wīvz′).

housework Washing, ironing, cleaning, cooking, and other work that has to be done in taking care of a home. **house·work** (hous′wûrk′) *noun.*

housing 1. A number of houses: *There is a lot of new housing in our town.* 2. A covering for the moving parts of a machine: *The housing on the drill gets very hot when the drill is used for a long time.* **hous·ing** (hou′zing) *noun, plural* **housings.**

hovel A small, dirty, broken-down house or shack. **hov·el** (huv′əl *or* hov′əl) *noun, plural* **hovels.**

hover 1. To stay in the air, flying right above one place: *The bees hovered over the flowers.* 2. To stay close by: *The reporters hovered around the candidate.* **hov·er** (huv′ər *or* hov′ər) *verb,* **hovered, hovering.**

Some birds hover over a spot where food is to be found.

how 1. In what way; by what means: *How will you go home?* 2. To what degree, amount, or extent: *How did you like the circus?* 3. In what condition: *How are you today?* 4. For what reason; why: *How did you happen to be so late?*
 • **how about.** What do you think of: *How about a game of cards?*
 • **how come.** Why does it happen that: *How come I didn't think of that?*
how (hou) *adverb.*

however In spite of that; yet: *It is the middle of winter; however, it is very warm outside. Conjunction.*
○ 1. In whatever way: *You may each draw the house however you like.* 2. To whatever degree: *However far our dogs wander, they always come home. Adverb.*
how·ev·er (hou ev′ər) *conjunction; adverb.*

howl To make a loud, wailing cry: *Dogs and wolves howl. Verb.*
○ A loud, wailing cry: *the howl of the wind. Noun.*
howl (houl) *verb,* **howled, howling;** *noun, plural* **howls.**

hr. An abbreviation for **hour.**

ht. An abbreviation for **height.**

HTML A language used to create pages for the World Wide Web. The letters stand for *Hypertext Markup Language.*

hub 1. The middle part of a wheel: *A round cap covers the hub of a car wheel.* 2. A center of interest or movement: *The refreshment table was the hub of activity during the party.* **hub** (hub) *noun, plural* **hubs.**

hubcap A round metal or plastic covering on the outer side of the tire of a car or truck. A hubcap must be removed before changing the tire. **hub·cap** (hub′cap′) *noun, plural* **hubcaps.**

huckleberry A small, shiny, dark blue berry. They are like blueberries but are smaller, darker, and have harder seeds. These berries grow on a small, low shrub that is also called a huckleberry. **huck·le·ber·ry** (huk′əl ber′ē) *noun, plural* **huckleberries.**

huddle To gather close together in a bunch: *The scouts huddled around the campfire to keep warm. Verb.*
○ A group of people or animals gathered close together: *The football players formed a huddle to plan their next play. Noun.*

hud·dle (hud′əl) *verb*, **huddled**, **huddling**; *noun*, *plural* **huddles**.

hue A color or a shade of a color: *The sunset had an orange hue.* **hue** (hū) *noun*, *plural* **hues**.

huff A sudden feeling of anger, resentment, or hurt pride: *Don't leave the party in a huff just because you didn't win the prize for best costume. Noun.*
○ To take in or give out a quick, noisy breath; puff: *We were huffing and puffing from the long climb. Verb.*
huff (huf) *noun*, *plural* **huffs**; *verb*, **huffed**, **huffing**.

hug 1. To put the arms around a person or thing and hold close and tightly: *I hugged my grandparents because I was so glad to see them.* 2. To keep close to: *Try to hug the curb when you're bicycling on a busy street. Verb.*
○ A close, tight clasp with the arms. *Noun.*
hug (hug) *verb*, **hugged**, **hugging**; *noun*, *plural* **hugs**.

huge Great in size or amount; very big; enormous: *An elephant is a huge animal.* **huge** (hūj) *adjective*, **huger**, **hugest**. —**hugely** *adverb* —**hugeness** *noun*.

hulk 1. The remains of a wrecked ship. 2. Something hard to handle. 3. Someone large and clumsy. **hulk** (hulk) *noun*, *plural* **hulks**.

hull 1. The outer covering of a nut, grain, or other seed. 2. The small leaves around the stem of a strawberry and other fruits. 3. The sides and bottom of a boat or ship. *Noun.*
○ To remove the hull from a seed or fruit: *I hulled the strawberries and then sliced them. Verb.*
hull (hul) *noun*, *plural* **hulls**; *verb*, **hulled**, **hulling**.

The sleek hull of this boat enables the vessel to move swiftly through the water.

hum 1. To make a soft, murmuring sound for a long time, like a bee. If you keep saying "m" with your mouth closed, you are humming. 2. To sing with the lips closed and without saying words: *I didn't know the words to the song so I just hummed the tune. Verb.*
○ A soft, murmuring sound that keeps going: *the hum of an air conditioner. Noun.*
hum (hum) *verb*, **hummed**, **humming**; *noun*, *plural* **hums**.

human Being or having to do with a person or persons: *Men, women, and children are human beings. Adjective.*
○ A person: *Every man, woman, and child is a human. Noun.*
hu·man (hū′mən) *adjective*; *noun*, *plural* **humans**.

human being A man, woman, or child; person; human.

humane Having sympathy for others; wanting to prevent pain: *The humane doctor helped many poor people.* **hu·mane** (hū mān′) *adjective*. —**humanely** *adverb*.

humanity 1. People; all human beings: *Keeping our air and water clean will help all humanity.* 2. Deep concern for the suffering of others; human sympathy: *The volunteers showed great humanity in caring for the flood victims.* **hu·man·i·ty** (hū man′i tē) *noun*.

humble 1. Not proud; modest. A humble person does not think he or she is better than other people. 2. Not big or important; lowly: *a humble cottage. Adjective.*
○ To make humble: *We were humbled when we saw what good work the others had done without our help. Verb.*
hum·ble (hum′bəl) *adjective*, **humbler**, **humblest**; *verb*, **humbled**, **humbling**.

humid Having humidity; damp; moist: *a hot, humid summer day.* **hu·mid** (hū′mid) *adjective*.

humidity Water vapor in the air; dampness: *The high humidity that day made us feel uncomfortable.* **hu·mid·i·ty** (hū mid′i tē) *noun*.

humiliate To make a person feel ashamed or foolish: *I was humiliated when I failed the test after I thought I would do well.* **hu·mil·i·ate** (hū mil′ē āt′) *verb*, **humiliated**, **humiliating**. —**humiliation** *noun*.

hummingbird A tiny bird with brightly colored feathers and a long, narrow bill. The hummingbird beats its wings so fast that they make a humming sound. It can fly backward or sideways, and can hover above flowers while it drinks their nectar. **hum·ming·bird** (hum′ing bûrd′) *noun*, *plural* **hummingbirds**.

PRONUNCIATION KEY:
| at | āpe | fär | câre | end | mē | it | īce | pîerce | hot | ōld | sông | fôrk |
| oil | out | up | ūse | rüle | pull | tûrn | chin | sing | shop | thin | this | |

hw in white; zh in treasure. The symbol ə stands for the unstressed vowel sound in about, taken, pencil, lemon, and circus.

359

humor 1. The funny part of something. Humor is what makes a person laugh. 2. The ability to make people laugh or to enjoy funny things: *Our guests had no sense of **humor**, because they never even smiled at any of our jokes.* 3. The state of mind that a person is in; mood: *We were in a good **humor** after our vacation. Noun.*
○ To give in to what a person wants: *When I was sick, my mother **humored** me by reading my favorite story several times. Verb.*
hu•mor (hū′mər) *noun, plural* **humors**; *verb,* **humored, humoring.**

humorous Making people laugh; funny; comical: *They saw a **humorous** movie about a fish that thought it could fly.* **hu•mor•ous** (hū′mər əs) *adjective.* —**humorously** *adverb.*

hump A rounded lump or bump: *Some camels have two **humps** on their backs.* **hump** (hump) *noun, plural* **humps.**

humus A dark part of the soil. Humus comes from dead plants. **hu•mus** (hū′məs) *noun.*

hunch To draw up or bend: *The cold wind made me **hunch** my shoulders. Verb.*
○ A guess or feeling about what will happen: *We had a **hunch** our friends might visit. Noun.*
hunch (hunch) *verb,* **hunched, hunching**; *noun, plural* **hunches.**

hundred Ten times ten; 100. **hun•dred** (hun′drid) *noun, plural* **hundreds**; *adjective.*

hundredth Next after the ninety-ninth. *Adjective, noun.*
○ One of a hundred equal parts; ¹⁄₁₀₀. *Noun.*
hun•dredth (hun′dridth) *adjective; noun, plural* **hundredths.**

hung A past tense and a past participle of **hang.** Look up **hang** for more information. **hung** (hung) *verb.*

These T-shirts have been **hung** so that customers can see them easily.

Hungary A country in east-central Europe. **Hun•ga•ry** (hung′gə rē) *noun.*

hunger 1. Pain or weakness caused by not eating enough food: *Many wild animals die of **hunger.*** 2. The feeling of wanting or needing food: *My **hunger** made me gobble my lunch.* 3. A strong wish or need for something: *a **hunger** for power. Noun.*
○ To have a strong wish or need for something: *I **hungered** for pizza after camping for two weeks. Verb.*
hun•ger (hung′gər) *noun, plural* **hungers**; *verb,* **hungered, hungering.**

hungry 1. Wanting or needing food: *We were **hungry** all morning because we didn't have time to eat breakfast.* 2. Having a strong wish or need for anything: *The orphans were **hungry** for love.*
hun•gry (hung′grē) *adjective,* **hungrier, hungriest.**

hunk A large lump or piece; chunk: *Take a **hunk** of bread with your cheese.* **hunk** (hungk) *noun, plural* **hunks.**

hunt 1. To chase wild animals in order to catch or kill. 2. To look hard to try to find something or someone: *We **hunted** all over for the keys. Verb.*
○ 1. A chase made to catch or kill wild animals: *a buffalo **hunt.*** 2. A search to try to find something or someone. *Noun.*
hunt (hunt) *verb,* **hunted, hunting**; *noun, plural* **hunts.**

hunter 1. A person who chases wild animals in order to kill or catch them. 2. An animal that chases other animals for its own food or to help human beings: *My dog is a good **hunter.*** 3. A person who searches for something: *A fossil **hunter** looks for the remains of animals and plants that lived long ago.* **hunt•er** (hun′tər) *noun, plural* **hunters.**

hurdle 1. A barrier to be jumped over in a race: *The horse cleared the **hurdle.*** 2. **hurdles.** A race in which the runners must jump over barriers while they run. 3. A difficulty or problem: *Final exams were the last **hurdle** before graduation. Noun.*
○ To jump over while running: *The farmer had to **hurdle** a fence to get away from the angry bull. Verb.*
hur•dle (hûr′dəl) *noun, plural* **hurdles**; *verb,* **hurdled, hurdling.**

hurl To throw hard and fast; fling: *We **hurled** the pebbles far out into the water.* **hurl** (hûrl) *verb,* **hurled, hurling.**

hurrah A shout of joy or encouragement: *We gave a big **hurrah** for our team. Noun.*
○ A word used to express joy. *"**Hurrah!**" I yelled when my sister crossed the finish line. Interjection.* **hur·rah** (hə rä′) *noun, plural* **hurrahs**; *interjection.*

hurricane A storm with very strong winds and heavy rain. **hur·ri·cane** (hûr′i kān′) *noun, plural* **hurricanes**.

HURRICANES

The word *hurricane* comes from the name of the wind god of the Carib people, Huracán. To be called a hurricane, a storm must have winds blowing faster than 74 miles per hour. The word *hurricane* usually refers to violent storms that occur in the Atlantic. A similar storm is called a typhoon in the Pacific or a cyclone in the Indian Ocean.

Naming Hurricanes: In 1953, the US Weather Service began using women's names to identify hurricanes. Men's names began to be used as well in 1978. Recently, representatives from countries that have hurricanes agreed upon a new naming system. There are now six sets of names for hurricanes in the Atlantic and another six for Pacific hurricanes. The names that are used in 1998 will be used again in 2004.

---

hurried Done or made quickly or too quickly: *I wrote a **hurried** note to tell my family where I was going.* **hur·ried** (hûr′ēd) *adjective.*

hurry To move faster than usual; rush; speed: *If we don't **hurry** we'll miss the train. Verb.*
○ **1.** The act of moving very quickly: *In your **hurry** to pack, you forgot your toothbrush.* **2.** The wish or need to act or move very quickly: *The children were in a **hurry** to go outside and play. Noun.* **hur·ry** (hûr′ē) *verb,* **hurried, hurrying**; *noun, plural* **hurries.**

SYNONYMS

hurry, hasten, rush
I had to hurry to school this morning. A lot of rest and mild exercise hastened my brother's recovery from his accident. The senator rushed the bill through Congress.

---

hurt **1.** To cause pain or injury: *I **hurt** my arm.* **2.** To be painful: *My knee **hurts** because I twisted it.* **3.** To be bad for; harm: *Being sick so often **hurt** my chances of making the team. Verb.*
○ A pain or injury. *Noun.* **hurt** (hûrt) *verb,* **hurt, hurting**; *noun, plural* **hurts.**

hurtle To move or throw with great force and speed: *The comet **hurtled** toward the sun.* **hur·tle** (hûr′təl) *verb,* **hurtled, hurtling.**

husband A man who is married. **hus·band** (huz′bənd) *noun, plural* **husbands.**

WORD HISTORY

The word husband comes from an old Scandinavian word meaning "master of a household." In Old English times, any man who was head of his own household could be a "husband." Only later did husband mean that the man was married, even if he did not own his own land.

---

hush A silence or stillness when noise suddenly stops. *Noun.*
○ **1.** To make quiet or silent: *The dimming of the lights **hushed** the audience.* **2.** To keep secret: *They all agreed to **hush** up about the party. Verb.*
○ Be quiet: *"**Hush**," the babysitter said, "or you will wake the baby." Interjection.* **hush** (hush) *noun, plural* **hushes**; *verb,* **hushed, hushing**; *interjection.*

husk The dry outside covering of some vegetables and fruits: *We took the green **husks** off the corn. Noun.*
○ To take off the husk from: *We cracked and **husked** the coconut. Verb.* **husk** (husk) *noun, plural* **husks**; *verb,* **husked, husking.**

husky¹ **1.** Big and strong: ***husky** football players.* **2.** Rough and deep in sound: *a **husky** voice.* **husk·y** (hus′kē) *adjective,* **huskier, huskiest.**

husky² A strong dog with a thick coat of hair and a bushy tail, used to pull sleds in the Arctic. **husk·y** (hus′kē) *noun, plural* **huskies.**

hustle To move or do something very quickly and with energy: *We had to **hustle** to finish all our work.* **hus·tle** (hus′əl) *verb,* **hustled, hustling.**

hut A small, roughly built house or shelter. **hut** (hut) *noun, plural* **huts.**

PRONUNCIATION KEY:
| at | āpe | fär | câre | end | mē | it | īce | pierce | hot | ōld | sông | fôrk |
| oil | out | up | ūse | rüle | pull | tûrn | chin | sing | shop | thin | this | |

hw in white; zh in treasure. The symbol ə stands for the unstressed vowel sound in about, taken, pencil, lemon, and circus.

361

hutch A house for rabbits or other small animals. **hutch** (huch) *noun, plural* **hutches**.

A **hyacinth** has long leaves that grow up from the ground.

hyacinth A plant that has a thick stem with small flowers growing on it. Hyacinths grow from bulbs. **hy•a•cinth** (hī′ə sinth′) *noun, plural* **hyacinths**.

hybrid The offspring of two different kinds of plants or animals. *Noun.*
○ Having to do with or being a hybrid: *hybrid roses. Adjective.*
hy•brid (hī′brid) *noun, plural* **hybrids**; *adjective.*

A mule is a **hybrid** because its father is a donkey and its mother is a horse.

hydrant A wide, covered pipe that sticks out of the ground and is attached underground to a water supply. Firefighters attach hoses to hydrants to get water to put out fires. **hy•drant** (hī′drənt) *noun, plural* **hydrants**.

hydroelectric Relating to electricity created by generators run by rapidly flowing water: *There is a hydroelectric power station at the waterfall.* **hy•dro•e•lec•tric** (hī′drō i lek′trik) *adjective.*

hydrogen A gas that has no color, taste, or odor and that burns very easily. Hydrogen is a chemical element. It is the lightest and most abundant element in the universe. **hy•dro•gen** (hī′drə jən) *noun.*

WORD HISTORY

The word **hydrogen** is formed from two Greek words, one meaning "water" and the other meaning "forming." Hydrogen combines with oxygen to form water.

hydrogen bomb A very powerful bomb that explodes with great force. The fusion of atoms of hydrogen to form atoms of helium causes the explosion. The hydrogen bomb is more powerful than the atomic bomb. It is also called an **H-bomb**.

hyena An animal that has a large head and front legs that are longer than the back legs. Hyenas are meat eaters and live in Africa and Asia. **hy•e•na** (hī ē′nə) *noun, plural* **hyenas**.

hygiene Things that must be done to keep people and places healthy and clean: *Washing yourself and brushing your teeth are part of your personal hygiene.* **hy•giene** (hī′jēn) *noun.*

hygienist A person trained to know what must be done to keep people and places healthy and clean: *A dental hygienist cleans teeth and instructs people in how to care for them.* **hy•gien•ist** (hī jē′nist or hī′jē en′ist) *noun, plural* **hygienists**.

hymn A song of praise, especially to God. Another word that sounds like this is **him**. **hymn** (him) *noun, plural* **hymns**.

hymnal A book of hymns. **hym•nal** (him′nəl) *noun, plural* **hymnals**.

hype Publicity of an exaggerated kind: *The newest version of the Internet browser was announced with a lot of hype.* **hype** (hīp) *noun.*

WORD HISTORY

The word **hype** may be based on the Greek word **hyperbole**, which is used in English to mean "extreme exaggeration," as in "The shoulders on that suit are a mile wide."

hyperactive Being very restless and unable to concentrate well: *A hyperactive person may find it difficult to sit quietly and listen in class.* **hy·per·ac·tive** (hī′pər ak′tiv) *adjective.* —**hyperactivity** *noun.*

hypertext A method of presenting information on a computer. A document with hypertext will have links to other things, such as pictures, sound, or other documents. **hy·per·text** (hī′pər tekst′) *noun.*

hyphen A punctuation mark (-) that is used to connect two or more words or parts of words to form a compound word, as in the word *merry-go-round.* A hyphen is also used to connect the syllables of a word that has been divided at the end of a line. **hy·phen** (hī′fən) *noun, plural* **hyphens.**

hyphenate To put a hyphen or hyphens in a word: *We must hyphenate a word when it has to be divided between two lines.* **hy·phen·ate** (hī′fə nāt′) *verb,* **hyphenated, hyphenating.**

hypnosis A special kind of sleep in which one can still hear and see. People who are under hypnosis sometimes remember things that they had forgotten, and they respond to what the hypnotist says to them. **hyp·no·sis** (hip nō′sis) *noun.* —**hypnotist** *noun.*

hypnotize To put someone into hypnosis. **hyp·no·tize** (hip′nə tīz′) *verb,* **hypnotized, hypnotizing.** —**hypnotism** *noun.*

hypocrite Someone who pretends to be one sort of person but acts or behaves differently. A hypocrite is often a person who pretends to be honest, thoughtful, loyal, or religious, and is not. **hyp·o·crite** (hip′ə krit) *noun, plural* **hypocrites.**

hypotenuse The side of a right triangle that is opposite the 90 degree angle. The hypotenuse is always the longest side of a right triangle. **hy·pot·e·nuse** (hī pot′ə nüs′ *or* hī pot′ə nūs′) *noun.*

hypothermia A condition of having the body's temperature dangerously below normal: *Someone who has been in freezing water may suffer from hypothermia.* **hy·po·ther·mi·a** (hī′pə ther′mē ə) *noun.*

hypothesis Something that is suggested as being true for the purposes of argument or of further investigation: *Their hypothesis was that the light in the refrigerator stayed on after the door was closed, but they didn't know if they could prove it.* **hy·poth·e·sis** (hī pôth′ə sis) *noun, plural* **hypotheses** (hī pôth′ə sēz).

hysterical 1. Emotionally violent and uncontrollable: *The frightened child burst into hysterical crying.* 2. Crying or laughing uncontrollably, usually because of an emotional upset: *If you ever get lost in the woods, keep calm and don't become hysterical.* **hys·ter·i·cal** (hi ster′i kəl) *adjective.* —**hysterically** *adverb.*

PRONUNCIATION KEY:

| at | āpe | fär | câre | end | mē | it | īce | pierce | hot | ōld | sông | fôrk |
| oil | out | up | ūse | rüle | pull | tûrn | chin | sing | shop | thin | this | |

hw in white; zh in treasure. The symbol ə stands for the unstressed vowel sound in about, taken, pencil, lemon, and circus.

363

SPELLING HINTS

The letter I has two sounds in English, but these sounds can be made in many different ways.

The sound of i as in big, fit, and tip can be made by:

e as in English; ee as in been; o as in women;
u as in busy; ui as in build; y as in hymn.

The sound of i in fine, ice, and kite can be made by:

ai as in aisle; ei as in height; ey as in eye;
ie as in lie and tie; igh as in right and sigh;
uy as in buy; y as in fly and my;
ye as in rye.

The sound you would hear if the letter I combined with the letter R is made by several other combinations in English. These are:

ear in hear; eer in deer and eerie;
eir in weird; ere in here and mere;
ier in pier and pierce.

In words such as pencil the sound of the letter I is represented in the pronunciations in this dictionary by a schwa (ə).

---

i, I The ninth letter of the alphabet. **i, I** (ī) *noun, plural* **i's, I's.**

I The person who is speaking or writing: *I have a dog and a cat.*
Other words that sound like this are **aye** and **eye.**
I (ī) *pronoun.*

Ia. An abbreviation for **Iowa.**

IA Postal abbreviation for **Iowa.**

-ic or **-ical** Suffixes that mean: 1. Having to do with: *Symbolic means having to do with symbols. Mythical means having to do with myths.* 2. Like: *Poetic means like a poem.* 3. Made of; containing: *Alcoholic means containing alcohol.*

ice 1. Water that is solid because it is below 32 degrees Fahrenheit; frozen water: *We cut a hole through the ice on the lake.* 2. A frozen dessert made with sweetened water and fruit flavors. *Noun.*
○ 1. To chill with ice: *Ice your ankle before it swells.* 2. To decorate with icing: *The baker iced the cake after it had cooled. Verb.*
• **ice over.** To become covered with ice: *The lake ices over in the winter.*
• **put on ice.** To hold back from doing some-

thing: *The weather was so bad we had to put the field trip on ice.*
ice (īs) *noun, plural* **ices;** *verb,* **iced, icing.**

ice age A period on earth or another planet when temperatures are so cold over a long period of time, usually for millions of years, that glaciers form over vast areas. The most recent ice age on earth ended about 10,000 years ago.

iceberg A very large piece of floating ice that has broken off from a glacier. **ice·berg** (īs'bûrg') *noun, plural* **icebergs.**

icebox 1. A box or chest cooled with ice that is used for storing food and drinks. 2. A refrigerator. This is an old usage of this word. **ice·box** (īs'boks') *noun, plural* **iceboxes.**

icebreaker 1. A specially designed ship that is used to break a passage through ice. 2. Something done that makes people feel more comfortable: *What this dull party needs is a good icebreaker!* **ice·break·er** (īs'brāk'ər) *noun, plural* **icebreakers.**

icecap A sheet of ice that covers an area of land and moves out from the center in all directions as it becomes larger. **ice·cap** (īs'kap') *noun, plural* **icecaps.**

Ice cream **is one of the most popular
of all treats.**

ice cream A frozen dessert made from milk products, sweeteners, and flavoring.

ice hockey Hockey as it is played on ice.

Iceland An island country northwest of Europe in the Atlantic Ocean. **Ice·land** (īs′lənd) *noun.*

ice-skate To skate on ice. **ice-skate** (īs′skāt′) *verb,* **ice-skated, ice-skating.**

ice skate A shoe with a metal blade on the bottom, used for ice-skating.

Ice-skating **requires both
strength and balance.**

icicle A pointed, hanging piece of ice formed by water that freezes as it drips. **i·ci·cle** (ī′si kəl) *noun,* *plural* **icicles.**

icing A mixture of sugar, butter, flavoring, and sometimes eggs. Icing is used to cover or decorate cakes or other baked goods. **ic·ing** (ī′sing) *noun,* *plural* **icings.**

icon 1. A small picture on a computer screen that represents a program or a function. 2. A small religious picture. **i·con** (ī′kon) *noun,* *plural* **icons.**

icy 1. Made of or covered with ice: *I slipped on the icy sidewalk.* 2. Very cold: *When the icy winds blew, it grew cold in the house.* 3. Cold and unfriendly: *My friend gave me an icy stare the next time we met after our big argument.* **i·cy** (ī′sē) *adjective,* **icier, iciest.**

ID Postal abbreviation for **Idaho.**

I.D. A short form of **identification.** (ī dē′)

I'd 1. Shortened form of "I had": *They asked me if I'd seen their dog.* 2. Shortened form of "I would": *I'd go if you would.* **I'd** (īd) *contraction.*

Ida. An abbreviation for **Idaho.**

Idaho A state in the western United States. Its capital is Boise. **I·da·ho** (ī′də hō′) *noun.*

Idaho
U. S. Postal Abbreviation: **ID**
Capital: **Boise**
Population: **998,000**
Area: **83,557 sq. mi./216,412 sq. km**
State Nickname: **Gem State**
State Bird: **Mountain Bluebird**
State Flower: **Mock Orange**

WORD HISTORY

The Apache and the Comanche are two Native American tribes who live in the West. The word Idaho probably comes from the Apache word used to mean "Comanche." The name was first used in the area that is now Colorado, but the United States Senate officially gave the name Idaho to a nearby territory. This other territory kept the name when it became the state of Idaho.

idea 1. A picture or thought formed in the mind: *The author had an idea for a new novel.* 2. A belief; opinion: *My parents have some firm ideas about religion.* 3. The purpose: *The idea of the game of baseball is to score runs for your team.* 4. The main meaning; point: *Do you understand the idea of the poem?* **i·de·a** (ī dē′ə) *noun,* *plural* **ideas.**

PRONUNCIATION KEY:

| at | āpe | fär | câre | end | mē | it | īce | pierce | hot | ōld | sông | fôrk |
| oil | out | up | ūse | rüle | pull | tûrn | chin | sing | shop | thin | this | |

hw in white; zh in treasure. The symbol ə stands for the unstressed vowel sound in about, taken, pencil, lemon, and circus.

365

ideal 1. A person or thing thought of as perfect: *That star quarterback was my **ideal** when I played football.* 2. The best or most perfect goal or result: *Justice is the **ideal** that a judge tries to achieve. Noun.*
○ Being exactly what one would hope for; perfect: *The breeze makes it an **ideal** day for going sailing. Adjective.*
i·de·al (ī dē′əl) *noun, plural* **ideals**; *adjective.*

identical 1. The very same: *This is the **identical** hotel we stayed at two years ago.* 2. Exactly alike: *The twins always wore **identical** clothes.* i·den·ti·cal (ī den′ti kəl) *adjective.*

identification 1. The act of saying who a person is or what a thing is: *I had to make an **identification** of my lost wallet before the principal could return it to me.*

These Irish dancers are wearing identical outfits.

2. Something used to show who a person is: *Many people use their driver's license as **identification**.*
i·den·ti·fi·ca·tion (ī den′tə fi kā′shən) *noun, plural* **identifications.**

identify To find out or tell exactly who a person is or what a thing is; recognize: *Can you **identify** this strange object?*
• **identify with.** 1. To feel that a person or group is worthy of being imitated: *When I was growing up I **identified with** nurses.* 2. To connect a person or group in one's mind: *Nurses are **identified with** the field of medicine.*
i·den·ti·fy (ī den′tə fī′) *verb,* **identified, identifying.**

identity 1. Who a person is or what a thing is: *Famous people sometimes hide their **identity** so that they can have some privacy.* 2. The condition of being exactly the same: *The **identity** of the twins made it hard for their friends to tell them apart.*
i·den·ti·ty (ī den′ti tē) *noun, plural* **identities.**

idiom A phrase or expression whose meaning cannot be understood from the ordinary meanings of the separate words in it. "To put off" is an idiom that means "to delay or postpone." "To pull a

person's leg" is an idiom that means "to trick or tease." id·i·om (id′ē əm) *noun, plural* **idioms.**

LANGUAGE NOTE

Idioms are a part of everyday language. People who have grown up speaking English use them without thinking about the fact that they have a special meaning. For someone learning English as a foreign language, though, idioms do not make sense and can be very confusing. Imagine, for example, what a student of English thinks when he or she first hears someone say, "I don't believe you; you're pulling my leg."

idiot A very silly or foolish person: *Only an **idiot** would believe that such a fantastic story was true.* id·i·ot (id′ē ət) *noun, plural* **idiots.**

idle 1. Not wanting to be active; lazy: *The **idle** children seldom helped with the chores.* 2. Having little worth or usefulness: *I exchanged some **idle** chatter with the person waiting in front of me in line.* 3. Not working or being used; not busy: *The piano in our house is **idle** because two keys are broken. Adjective.*
○ 1. To spend time doing nothing: *Instead of doing my homework, I **idled** around the house all evening.* 2. To run slowly and out of gear: *We left the car **idling** in the driveway while we delivered the package. Verb.*
Another word that sounds like this is **idol**.
i·dle (ī′dəl) *adjective,* **idler, idlest;** *verb,* **idled, idling.**

idol 1. A statue or other object that is worshiped as a god. 2. A person who is greatly loved or admired: *That movie star is an **idol** to people around the world.*
Another word that sounds like this is **idle**.
i·dol (ī′dəl) *noun, plural* **idols.**

if 1. In case; in the event that; supposing that: *If I hurt your feelings, I'm sorry.* 2. With the requirement or agreement that; on condition that; provided: *I can go to the movies if I finish my chores first.* 3. Whether: *I don't know if they'll be there.* if (if) *conjunction.*

igloo A hut shaped like a dome used by the Inuit to live in. It is usually built of blocks of hardened snow. ig·loo (ig′lü) *noun, plural* **igloos.**

igneous Produced with great heat or by a volcano: *An **igneous** rock is formed when lava from a volcano hardens.* ig·ne·ous (ig′nē əs) *adjective.*

A small fire is used to ignite a campfire.

ignite 1. To set on fire: *We **ignited** the sticks for the campfire with a match.* 2. To begin to burn; catch on fire: *You must be careful with how you store oily rags because they **ignite** easily.* **ig·nite** (ig nīt′) *verb*, **ignited**, **igniting**.

ignition 1. The act of igniting: *The **ignition** of the rockets sent the spacecraft on its way to the moon.* 2. The electrical system of a vehicle, used to start the engine: *The **ignition** starts the fuel and air burning in the engine.* 3. The firing of a rocket: *We have **ignition**!* **ig·ni·tion** (ig nish′ən) *noun, plural* **ignitions**.

ignorance A lack of knowledge; being ignorant: *My **ignorance** of current affairs meant that I couldn't join the debate team this year.* **ig·no·rance** (ig′nər əns) *noun*.

ignorant 1. Showing a lack of knowledge: *The young cowhands were **ignorant** at first of how to brand cattle, but they learned quickly.* 2. Not informed or aware: *I wasn't wearing my watch, so I was **ignorant** of the time.* **ig·no·rant** (ig′nər ənt) *adjective*.

ignore To pay no attention to: *I tried to **ignore** the noise of the subway as I read my book.* **ig·nore** (ig nôr′) *verb*, **ignored**, **ignoring**.

iguana A large greenish brown lizard that has a ridge of scales down its back. It is found in the very warm parts of Central and South America. **i·gua·na** (i gwä′nə) *noun, plural* **iguanas**.

IL Postal abbreviation for Illinois.

ill 1. Not healthy or well; sick: *Many children in our class were **ill** with colds last week.* 2. Bad or evil: *the **ill** effects of a drug. Adjective.*

○ Unkindly; badly: *Don't speak **ill** of anyone. Adverb.*

○ Trouble, evil, or misfortune: *War is one of the **ills** of humanity. Noun.*

ill (il) *adjective*, **worse**, **worst**; *adverb; noun, plural* **ills**.

Ill. An abbreviation for Illinois.

I'll Shortened form of "I will" or "I shall": *I'll win the contest no matter what it takes.* Other words that sound like this are **aisle** and **isle**. **I'll** (īl) *contraction*.

illegal Not legal; against laws or rules: *It is **illegal** to shoot off fireworks in that town.* **il·le·gal** (i lē′gəl) *adjective*.

illegible Very hard or impossible to read: *The handwriting on the envelope was **illegible**.* **il·leg·i·ble** (i lej′ə bəl) *adjective*.

Illinois A state in the north-central United States. Its capital is Springfield. **Il·li·nois** (il′ə noi′ *or* il′ə noiz′) *noun*.

WORD HISTORY

Illinois is the way French explorers wrote the Indian name for a tribe that used to live in the place that is now the state of Illinois. The Indian word means "men" or "tribe of great men."

Illinois
U. S. Postal Abbreviation: **IL**
Capital: **Springfield**
Population: **11,582,000**
Area: **56,400 sq. mi./146,075 sq. km**
State Nicknames: **Prairie State; Land of Lincoln**
State Bird: **Cardinal**
State Flower: **Violet**

PRONUNCIATION KEY:

| at | āpe | fär | câre | end | mē | it | īce | pierce | hot | ōld | sông | fôrk |
| oil | out | up | ūse | rüle | pùll | tûrn | chin | sing | shop | thin | this | |

hw in white; zh in treasure. The symbol ə stands for the unstressed vowel sound in about, taken, pencil, lemon, and circus.

367

illiterate Not able to read or write: *The illiterate person needed help in filling out the form.* **il·lit·er·ate** (i lit′ər it) *adjective*.

illness A sickness or disease: *Many illnesses can be cured by taking the right medicine.* **ill·ness** (il′nis) *noun, plural* **illnesses.**

illogical Not logical or reasonable: *I try not to be illogical when I write an essay.* **il·log·i·cal** (i loj′i kəl) *adjective*.

Hundreds of lights illuminate these buildings and trees.

illuminate 1. To light up; give light to: *A lamp illuminated one corner of the dark room.* 2. To make clear or easier to understand: *The teacher's explanation in class illuminated the chapter for me.* **il·lu·mi·nate** (i lü′mə nāt′) *verb,* **illuminated, illuminating.**

illusion A false impression or belief; misleading idea: *We were under the illusion that the party was on Friday and not Saturday.* **il·lu·sion** (i lü′zhən) *noun, plural* **illusions.**

illustrate 1. To make clear or explain: *The teacher illustrated how the human eye works by comparing it to a camera.* 2. To draw a picture or diagram to explain or decorate something written: *The famous artist illustrated a book about birds.* **il·lus·trate** (il′ə strāt′ *or* i lus′trāt) *verb,* **illustrated, illustrating.**

WORD HISTORY

The word **illustrate** comes from a Latin word meaning "to throw light upon" or "to illuminate." This word came to be used to mean "to make clear to the mind," and later "to make clear or explain by pictures."

---

illustration 1. An example or comparison that explains, teaches, or shows something: *The teacher gave us an illustration of how to solve other arithmetic problems of the same kind.* 2. A picture or diagram used to explain or decorate something written: *The illustrations in this dictionary help to explain words that have been defined.* **il·lus·tra·tion** (il′ə strā′shən) *noun, plural* **illustrations.**

illustrator An artist who makes illustrations for books, magazines, or other works. **il·lus·tra·tor** (il′ə strā′tər) *noun, plural* **illustrators.**

ill will Unfriendly feeling: *After their argument, the two classmates felt ill will toward each other.*

im- A prefix that means: 1. Not, or a lack of: *Imperfect* means not perfect. *Impatience* means a lack of patience. 2. In or into: *Imperil* means to put in peril or danger. *Im-* has the same meaning as *in-*. It is used instead of *in-* before words or roots that begin with the letters *b, m,* or *p.*

I'm Shortened form of "I am": *I'm going to the zoo today.* **I'm** (īm) *contraction*.

image 1. A picture or other likeness of a person or thing: *A penny has an image of Abraham Lincoln on one side of it.* 2. A picture of an object formed by a mirror or lens. 3. A person who looks very similar to someone else: *That girl is the image of her mother.* **im·age** (im′ij) *noun, plural* **images.**

imagery Language used in poetry, novels, and other kinds of literature that creates vivid images in the mind: *Metaphors are a kind of imagery.* **im·ag·er·y** (im′ij rē) *noun*.

imaginary Existing only in the mind; unreal: *Most people believe that ghosts are imaginary.* **i·mag·i·nar·y** (i maj′ə ner′ē) *adjective*.

imagination 1. The forming in a person's mind of pictures or ideas of things that are elsewhere or not real: *Your imagination led you to believe that you and I might be cousins, but we aren't.* 2. The ability or power to create or form new images or ideas: *It took great imagination to write such a clever story.* **i·mag·i·na·tion** (i maj′ə nā′shən) *noun, plural* **imaginations.**

SYNONYMS

imagination, fancy, fantasy

Our class wrote and produced a play that showed a great deal of imagination and humor. It is just the little girl's fancy that she has an invisible bunny for a friend. His fantasy is to learn to fly planes.

imaginative **1.** Having a good imagination: *The imaginative child made up stories to tell the younger children.* **2.** Showing imagination: *an imaginative solution to our problem.* **i•mag•i•na•tive** (i maj′ə nə tiv) *adjective.*

imagine **1.** To picture a person or thing in the mind: *Try to imagine a dragon breathing fire.* **2.** To suppose; guess: *I don't imagine we will go on a picnic if it rains.* **i•mag•ine** (i maj′in) *verb,* **imagined, imagining.**

imitate **1.** To try to act just as another person does; copy: *People often imitate those whom they admire.* **2.** To look like; resemble: *Some plastics imitate leather.* **im•i•tate** (im′i tāt′) *verb,* **imitated, imitating.**

imitation **1.** The act of copying: *That student does a great imitation of the president's voice.* **2.** Something that is a copy of something else: *We bought an imitation of a famous painting. Noun.*
○ Made to look like something real; not real: *imitation flowers. Adjective.*
im•i•ta•tion (im′i tā′shən) *noun, plural* **imitations;** *adjective.*

immaculate Extremely clean or neat: *The shirt was immaculate after we washed it.* **im•mac•u•late** (i mak′yə lit) *adjective.*

WORD HISTORY

Immaculate comes from a Latin word meaning "without spots" or "without stains."

---

immature **1.** Not having reached full growth; not mature: *Immature corn is not ready to pick and eat.* **2.** Foolish or childish: *The immature visitor fussed about not liking the food at the party.* **im•ma•ture** (im′ə chu′r *or* im′ə tùr′ *or* im′ə tyùr′) *adjective.*

immeasurable Unable to be measured; very great: *The help you gave us was immeasurable.* **im•meas•ur•a•ble** (i mezh′ər ə bəl) *adjective.*

immediate **1.** Done or happening right away; without delay: *When you do an arithmetic problem on a calculator, you get an immediate answer.* **2.** Close in time or space; near: *I can remember the immediate past better than what happened five years ago.* **im•me•di•ate** (i mē′dē it) *adjective.*

immediately Right away; now: *If we leave*

immediately, we can get to the movie in time.
im•me•di•ate•ly (i mē′dē it lē) *adverb.*

immense Of great size; very large; huge: *The whale is an immense animal that can grow as long as 100 feet.* **im•mense** (i mens′) *adjective.*

immerse **1.** To cover completely by dipping into water or another liquid: *We immersed our feet in the pool.* **2.** To involve or occupy completely: *I did not hear the doorbell because I was immersed in a good book.* **im•merse** (i mûrs′) *verb,* **immersed, immersing.**

At the turn of the century, millions of immigrants settled in American cities.

immigrant A person who comes to live in a country in which he or she was not born: *My grandparents were immigrants to the United States from Italy.* **im•mi•grant** (im′i grənt) *noun, plural* **immigrants.**

immigrate To come to live in a country where one was not born: *My grandparents immigrated to Canada from Poland.* **im•mi•grate** (im′i grāt′) *verb,* **immigrated, immigrating.**

immigration The act of coming to a new country to make one's home. **im•mi•gra•tion** (im′i grā′shən) *noun.*

imminent Expected to happen; likely to occur or take place very soon: *The dark clouds may mean that a storm is imminent.* **im•mi•nent** (im′ə nənt) *adjective.* —**imminently** *adverb.*

immoral Wicked; evil; not moral: *Lying about a friend is an immoral thing to do.* **im•mor•al** (i môr′əl) *adjective.* —**immorality** *noun* —**immorally** *adverb.*

PRONUNCIATION KEY:

| at | āpe | fär | câre | end | mē | it | īce | pierce | hot | ōld | sông | fôrk |
| oil | out | up | ūse | rüle | pull | tûrn | chin | sing | shop | thin | *this* | |

hw in white; zh in treasure. The symbol ə stands for the unstressed vowel sound in about, taken, pencil, lemon, and circus.

369

immortal Living, lasting, or remembered forever: *Some literature is immortal.* **im·mor·tal** (i môr′təl) *adjective.*

immune 1. Protected from a disease: *The doctor gave me a vaccination that made me immune to measles.* 2. Safe from undergoing something; free from: *No one is immune from criticism.* **im·mune** (i mūn′) *adjective.*

immune system The system that protects the body from disease. In humans, the immune system includes white blood cells and antibodies.

immunity The ability of the body to resist a disease. A person can gain immunity to a disease by being inoculated or vaccinated. **im·mu·ni·ty** (i mū′ni tē) *noun, plural* **immunities.**

immunize To make immune to a disease: *Many children are immunized against certain diseases before they can go to school.* **im·mu·nize** (im′yə nīz) *verb,* **immunized, immunizing.** —**immunization** *noun.*

impact 1. The force of one object striking against another: *The impact of the car crashing into the pole smashed the front fender.* 2. A strong, immediate effect: *That book has an emotional impact on its readers.* **im·pact** (im′pakt) *noun, plural* **impacts.**

impair To lessen the quality or strength of; weaken: *The heavy fog impaired the driver's vision.* **im·pair** (im pâr′) *verb,* **impaired, impairing.**

Impalas **spring high in the air when they are frightened.**

impala A small, slender antelope that lives in Africa. It has a reddish or golden brown coat and a black line down the hind part of each thigh. **im·pal·a** (im pal′ə) *noun, plural* **impalas.**

impartial Not favoring one more than others; fair: *The judges of a contest should be impartial.*

im·par·tial (im pär′shəl) *adjective.* —**impartiality** *noun* —**impartially** *adverb.*

impatience An inability to put up with delay or opposition calmly and without anger: *The teacher could sense the children's impatience for summer vacation to begin.* **im·pa·tience** (im pā′shəns) *noun.*

impatient Not able to put up with delay or opposition calmly and without anger: *Toward the end of the movie, the children became impatient to leave.* **im·pa·tient** (im pā′shənt) *adjective.*

impeach To bring formal charges of wrong conduct against a public official. An official can be removed from office if he or she is found guilty of the charges. **im·peach** (im pēch′) *verb,* **impeached, impeaching.**

imperative Absolutely necessary; urgent: *If we are to arrive on time, it is imperative that we leave right away.* **im·per·a·tive** (im per′ə tiv) *adjective.*

imperative sentence A sentence that tells or asks someone to do something. An example of an imperative sentence is "Go to the store and buy some bread."

imperfect Having a mistake or fault: *The fit was imperfect but I liked the shoes so much that I bought them anyway.* **im·per·fect** (im pûr′fikt) *adjective.*

SYNONYMS

imperfect, defective, faulty

My mother said her French was imperfect, but she had no trouble communicating when we were in France. The modem in our new computer was defective; so we exchanged it for another one. The lights in our dining room flicker because the wiring is faulty.

---

imperial 1. Having to do with an empire or an emperor or empress: *The emperor and empress live in the imperial palace.* 2. Having to do with one country's control over another or others: *The United States was formed from a group of colonies under the imperial rule of England.* **im·pe·ri·al** (im pîr′ē əl) *adjective.*

impersonal 1. Not having or showing warm feelings: *a cold, impersonal greeting.* 2. Not relating to a particular person; general: *Try to keep this discussion impersonal and don't identify any of the people involved.* **im·per·son·al** (im pûr′sə nəl) *adjective.* —**impersonally** *adverb.*

impersonate To copy the appearance and actions

of in order to amuse or deceive: *My friend can **impersonate** famous actors.* **im·per·son·ate** (im pûr′sə nāt′) *verb*, **imperso-nated, impersonating.**

impertinent Very rude or bold; impudent: *It would be **impertinent** to interrupt someone who is speaking.* **im·per·ti·nent** (im pûr′tə nənt) *adjective.* —**impertinence** *noun* —**impertinently** *adverb.*

impetuous Acting or done too quickly, without planning or thought: *I later regretted my **impetuous** decision.* **im·pet·u·ous** (im pech′ü əs) *adjective.*

implant To put an organ or a device into the body. *Verb.*
○ An organ or a device placed in the body by surgery. *Noun.*
im·plant (im plant′ *for verb*; im′plant′ *for noun*) *verb*, **implanted, implanting;** *noun, plural* **implants.**

implement An object used to do a particular job; tool: *Hoes, rakes, and spades are gardening **implements**. Noun.*
○ To put a plan into action: *Will the government **implement** a relief plan soon? Verb.*
im·ple·ment (im′plə mənt) *noun, plural* **implements;** *verb*, **implemented, implementing.**

implication A hidden meaning: *When she says she's too warm, the **implication** is she would like you to open a window.* **im·pli·ca·tion** (im plə kā′shən) *noun, plural* **implications.**

imply To suggest without saying directly: *Did you **imply** that I'm old-fashioned when you said my clothes were out of style?* **im·ply** (im plī′) *verb*, **implied, implying.**

LANGUAGE NOTE

People often confuse the verbs imply and infer because the words describe two sides of the same idea. Someone who hints at something is *implying*. The frown on your face *implied* that something was wrong. Someone who reaches a conclusion by examining things is *inferring*. I *inferred* from your smile that you won the game.

---

impolite Having or showing bad manners; not polite; rude: *It is **impolite** to arrive late for dinner.* **im·po·lite** (im′pə līt′) *adjective.*

import To bring in goods from another country for sale or use: *The United States **imports** tea from India. Verb.*
○ Something that is imported. *Noun.*
im·port (im pôrt′ *for verb*; im′pôrt′ *for noun*) *verb*, **imported, importing;** *noun, plural* **imports.**

Many imports arrive in America by ship.

importance The state of being important: *Rain is of great **importance** to farmers since crops can't grow without water.* **im·por·tance** (im pôr′təns) *noun.*

important 1. Having great value or meaning: *A proper diet is **important** to good health.* 2. Having a high position or much power: *Members of the city council are **important** civic figures.* **im·por·tant** (im pôr′tənt) *adjective.*

impose 1. To put or set on a person: *The judge **imposed** a sentence of three years.* 2. To make unfair or impolite demands: *I won't **impose** on you by taking your time.* **im·pose** (im pōz′) *verb*, **imposed, imposing.**

impossible 1. Not able to happen or be done: *It is **impossible** for a person to fly by flapping the arms.* 2. Hard to deal with: *an **impossible** child.* **im·pos·si·ble** (im pos′ə bəl) *adjective.*

impostor A person who tries to trick others by pretending to be someone else. **im·pos·tor** (im pos′tər) *noun, plural* **impostors.**

impractical 1. Not useful or practical: *Doing nothing is an **impractical** answer to your problem.* 2. Not wise with money: *It's **impractical** not to save a few dollars from your allowance.* **im·prac·ti·cal** (im prak′ti kəl) *adjective.* —**impracticality** *noun* —**impractically** *adverb.*

PRONUNCIATION KEY:

| at | āpe | fär | câre | end | mē | it | īce | pierce | hot | ōld | sông | fôrk |
| oil | out | up | ūse | rüle | pull | tûrn | chin | sing | shop | thin | this | |

hw in white; zh in treasure. The symbol ə stands for the unstressed vowel sound in about, taken, pencil, lemon, and circus.

371

impress **1.** To have a strong effect on the mind or feelings: *The height of the skyscraper **impressed** me.* **2.** To fix in the mind: *Our parents tried to **impress** a sense of right and wrong on each of us.* **im•press** (im pres′) *verb*, **impressed, impressing.**

impression **1.** An effect on the mind or feelings: *What was your **impression** of the new student in our class?* **2.** An uncertain belief, notion, or memory; feeling: *I had the **impression** that they were related, but I was wrong.* **3.** A mark or design produced by pressing or stamping: *We made **impressions** of our hands in the wet concrete.* **4.** Imitation: *The clown did a very funny **impression** of a monkey.* **im•pres•sion** (im presh′ən) *noun, plural* **impressions.**

impressive Making a strong impression: *Their science project was so **impressive** that the judges awarded them first prize.* **im•pres•sive** (im pres′iv) *adjective.*

imprint **1.** A mark made by pressing or stamping: *Your boots have made **imprints** in the snow.* **2.** A mark or effect: *Age has left its **imprint** on the crumbling building. Noun.*
○ **1.** To mark by pressing or stamping: *The store **imprinted** envelopes with my name and address.* **2.** To fix firmly in the mind: *That beautiful scene became **imprinted** in my memory. Verb.* **im•print** (im′print′ *for noun;* im print′ *for verb*) *noun, plural* **imprints;** *verb*, **imprinted, imprinting.**

imprison To put or keep in prison; lock up. **im•pris•on** (im priz′ən) *verb*, **imprisoned, imprisoning.**

improper **1.** Not correct: *A screwdriver is an **improper** tool for driving nails.* **2.** Showing bad manners or bad taste: *It is **improper** to talk with food in your mouth.* **im•prop•er** (im prop′ər) *adjective.*

improper fraction A fraction that is equal to or greater than 1. $\frac{8}{5}$ and $\frac{6}{6}$ are both improper fractions because $\frac{8}{5}$ is equal to $1\frac{3}{5}$ and $\frac{6}{6}$ is equal to 1.

improve To make or become better: *I am taking lessons to **improve** my singing.* **im•prove** (im prüv′) *verb*, **improved, improving.**

improvement **1.** The act of improving or the state of being improved: *I've noticed an **improvement** in your health.* **2.** A change or a thing added that improves something: *The new yellow curtains are an **improvement** to the room.* **3.** A person or thing that is better than another: *This new wagon is an **improvement** over our old rusty one.* **im•prove•ment** (im prüv′mənt) *noun, plural* **improvements.**

improvise **1.** To make up and perform without planning beforehand: *The class **improvised** a program of skits and songs for the unexpected visitors.* **2.** To make out of whatever materials are around: *The children **improvised** bookcases out of some old wooden crates.* **im•pro•vise** (im′prə vīz′) *verb*, **improvised, improvising.**

impudent Bold and rude: *The **impudent** student talked back to the teacher.* **im•pu•dent** (im′pyə dənt) *adjective.* —**impudence** *noun* —**impudently** *adverb.*

impulse **1.** A sudden feeling that makes a person act without thinking: *An **impulse** made me give the new baseball mitt to my best friend.* **2.** A sudden force that causes motion; push: *The **impulse** of the falling water turned the water wheel.* **im•pulse** (im′puls) *noun, plural* **impulses.**

impulsive **1.** Acting without thinking or planning: *It's hard to guess what an **impulsive** person will do next.* **2.** Done because of a sudden feeling or urge; not planned or thought out: *When I had to pay the bills, I regretted my **impulsive** shopping trip.* **im•pul•sive** (im pul′siv) *adjective.* —**impulsively** *adverb.*

impure **1.** Not clean; dirty: ***Impure** water may be harmful to drink.* **2.** Containing another substance that is not as good: *This **impure** gold has traces of other metals in it.* **im•pure** (im pyůr′) *adjective.*

in **1.** Surrounded by; inside or within: *The suitcase is **in** the closet.* **2.** To or toward the inside of; into: *We all got **in** the car.* **3.** While, during, or after: *The weather here is cold **in** the winter.* **4.** Affected by or having: *The new worker is **in** trouble because of lateness. Preposition.*
○ **1.** To or toward a place inside: *Come **in** out of the cold.* **2.** At a certain place; at one's home or an office: *I stayed **in** because I had a cold. Adverb.*

The woman is putting oranges in a bag.

Another word that sounds like this is **inn.**

• **ins and outs.** All of the details of some activity or process: *I'm learning the **ins and outs** of my family's business.*
in (in) *preposition; adverb.*

in- A prefix that means: **1.** Not: *Inappropriate means not appropriate.* **2.** In or into: *Inborn means born in a person.* **Intake means the amount of something taken in.* *In-* has the same meaning as *im-.* *Im-* is used instead of *in-* before words or roots that begin with *b, m,* or *p.*

in. An abbreviation for **inch.**

IN Postal abbreviation for **Indiana.**

inability Lack of power or ability to do something: *My **inability** to sing well kept me from joining the school chorus.* **in•a•bil•i•ty** (in′ə bil′i tē) *noun.*

inaccurate Not correct or accurate; wrong: *I got lost because the directions were **inaccurate.*** **in•ac•cu•rate** (in ak′yər it) *adjective.*

inadequate Not enough; not good enough: *That amount of money is **inadequate** to our need.* **in•ad•e•quate** (in ad′i kwit) *adjective.* —**inadequately** *adverb.*

inappropriate Not suitable or correct; not appropriate: *A formal suit is **inappropriate** for a beach party.* **in•ap•pro•pri•ate** (in′ə prō′prē it) *adjective.*

inaudible Impossible to hear: *The sound of distant thunder was almost **inaudible.*** **in•au•di•ble** (in ôd′ə bəl) *adjective.*

inaugurate **1.** To put a person in office with a formal ceremony: *The president of the United States is **inaugurated** in January after the election.* **2.** To open or begin to use formally: *The governor **inaugurated** the new bridge by riding in the first car to drive across it.* **in•au•gu•rate** (in ô′gyə rāt′) *verb,* **inaugurated, inaugurating.**

WORD HISTORY

The word **inaugurate** comes from a Latin word meaning "to look for omens." The Romans believed that such things as the flight of birds were signs, or omens, that could be used to help predict the future. They watched for these signs when they inaugurated someone into public office.

inauguration **1.** The ceremony of putting a person in office: *At the **inauguration**, the new president took the oath of office.* **2.** A formal beginning or opening: *We went to the **inauguration** of the city's new swimming pool.* **in•au•gu•ra•tion** (in ô′gyə rā′shən) *noun, plural* **inaugurations.**

A presidential inauguration takes place every four years.

inborn Born in a person; natural: *That youngster seems to have an **inborn** talent for playing musical instruments.* **in•born** (in′bôrn′) *adjective.*

Inca A member of an Indian people of the Andes Mountains of South America. The Inca developed an advanced civilization and controlled an empire in the fifteenth and sixteenth centuries. **In•ca** (ing′kə) *noun, plural* **Inca** or **Incas.**

incandescent **1.** Glowing with a hot bright light: *an **incandescent** bulb.* **2.** Glowing with happiness: *an **incandescent** smile.* **in•can•des•cent** (in′kən des′ənt) *adjective.*

incapable Lacking the necessary power or skill to do something; not capable: *An infant is **incapable** of walking.* **in•ca•pa•ble** (in kā′pə bəl) *adjective.*

incense¹ A substance that has a fragrant smell when it is burned: *After the **incense** was lighted, it created a spicy smell in the room.* **in•cense** (in′sens′) *noun, plural* **incenses.**

incense² To make very angry: *I was **incensed** when I discovered my bike was missing.* **in•cense** (in sens′) *verb,* **incensed, incensing.**

incentive Something that urges a person on: *The possibility of a higher allowance was a powerful **incentive** for me to do extra chores.* **in•cen•tive** (in sen′tiv) *noun, plural* **incentives.**

incessant Going on without stopping; continuous: *The campers were bothered by the*

PRONUNCIATION KEY:
| at | āpe | fär | câre | end | mē | it | īce | pierce | hot | ōld | sông | fôrk |
| oil | out | up | ūse | rüle | pu̇ll | tûrn | chin | sing | shop | thin | this | |

hw in white; zh in treasure. The symbol ə stands for the unstressed vowel sound in about, taken, pencil, lemon, and circus.

373

incessant buzz of mosquitoes. **in•ces•sant** (in ses′ənt) *adjective.*

inch A measure of length that equals ¹⁄₁₂ of a foot. Twelve inches equal 1 foot. One inch is the same as 2.54 centimeters. *Noun.*
○ To move very slowly: *We **inched** our way along the narrow ledge. Verb.*
inch (inch) *noun, plural* **inches**; *verb,* **inched, inching.**

inchworm A kind of moth caterpillar that has legs in the front and the back but not in the middle. It moves by pulling the rear of its body up toward the front and then stretching the front end forward. **inch•worm** (inch′wûrm′) *noun, plural* **inchworms.**

incident Something that happens; event: *My neighbors told us some of the funny **incidents** of their trip to Florida.* **in•ci•dent** (in′si dənt) *noun, plural* **incidents.**

incidentally By the way: *Let's play catch; incidentally, do you still have my baseball?* **in•ci•den•tal•ly** (in′si den′tə lē *or* in′si dent′lē) *adverb.*

incinerator A furnace that burns garbage or trash. **in•cin•er•a•tor** (in sin′ə rā′tər) *noun, plural* **incinerators.**

incision An opening made with a sharp knife: *The surgeon closed the **incision** neatly with five stitches.* **in•ci•sion** (in sizh′ən) *noun, plural* **incisions.**

incite To urge someone to do something: *a troublesome child who **incited** others to misbehave.* **in•cite** (in sit′) *verb,* **incited, inciting.**

inclination 1. A natural tendency: *My **inclination** to check small details often helps me in planning projects.* 2. A liking: *I have an **inclination** to go to the movies rather than stay home.* 3. A slope; slant: *The steep **inclination** of the hill makes it great for sledding.* **in•cli•na•tion** (in′klə nā′shən) *noun, plural* **inclinations.**

incline To slope or slant: *The road is hard to climb because it **inclines** upward. Verb.*

Steep inclines can make hiking difficult.

○ A surface that slopes: *The ball rolled down the **incline** to the bottom of the hill. Noun.* **in•cline** (in klīn′ *for verb;* in′klīn′ *or* in klīn′ *for noun*) *verb,* **inclined, inclining;** *noun, plural* **inclines.**

include 1. To have as part of the whole; contain: *The batteries for that toy are **included** in the box.* 2. To put in a group or total: *We **included** all of our close friends in the list of people invited to the party.* **in•clude** (in klüd′) *verb,* **included, including.**

incoherent Not clear; not logical: *The speaker was almost **incoherent** with nervousness.* **in•co•her•ent** (in′kō hîr′ənt) *adjective.* —**incoherence** *noun.*

income Money received for work or from property or other things that are owned. **in•come** (in′kum′) *noun, plural* **incomes.**

income tax A tax on a person's income.

incompatible 1. Not able to be brought or kept together in harmony: *The couple had become **incompatible** and so they separated.* 2. Not matching: *Your story is **incompatible** with the facts.* **in•com•pat•i•ble** (in′kəm pat′ə bəl) *adjective.*

incompetent Not able to do something well; not competent: *Only an **incompetent** typist could make so many mistakes on just one page.* **in•com•pe•tent** (in kom′pi tənt) *adjective.*

incomplete Not complete; not finished: *The report was **incomplete** because certain information was still missing.* **in•com•plete** (in′kəm plēt′) *adjective.*

incomprehensible Not capable of being understood; not clear: *Your bad behavior to your good friends is **incomprehensible**.* **in•com•pre•hen•si•ble** (in′kom prē hen′sə bəl) *adjective.*

inconceivable Not believable or thinkable: *Getting a high grade on the test was **inconceivable** to me, since I hadn't studied.* **in•con•ceiv•a•ble** (in′kən sē′və bəl) *adjective.*

inconclusive Not leading to a clear or certain conclusion: *The tests the doctor did were **inconclusive**.* **in•con•clu•sive** (in′kən klü′siv) *adjective.*

inconsiderate Not thoughtful of others; rude: *It is **inconsiderate** not to thank someone for a gift.* **in•con•sid•er•ate** (in′kən sid′ə rət) *adjective.*

inconspicuous Not easily seen or noticed; not attracting attention: *The plaid of my shirt helped to make the mend **inconspicuous**.*

in·con·spic·u·ous (in′kən spik′ū əs) *adjective.*

inconvenience 1. Lack of comfort or ease; trouble or bother: *I don't like the inconvenience of living far away from school.* 2. Something that causes trouble or bother: *Not having a telephone is an inconvenience. Noun.*
○ To cause bother to; trouble: *We hope the bus delay won't inconvenience you. Verb.* **in·con·ven·ience** (in′kən vēn′yəns) *noun,* plural **inconveniences**; *verb,* **inconvenienced, inconveniencing.**

inconvenient Troublesome: *The movie starts at an inconvenient time, so we won't go.* **in·con·ven·ient** (in′kən vēn′yənt) *adjective.*

incorporate 1. To include something as part of a larger thing: *I incorporated the photographs into our big picture album.* 2. To make or become a corporation. **in·cor·po·rate** (in kôr′pə rāt′) *verb,* **incorporated, incorporating.**

incorrect Not right or correct: *You must do this problem over because your answer is incorrect.* **in·cor·rect** (in′kə rekt′) *adjective.*

increase To make or become larger in number or size: *The number of students trying out for the band has increased this year. Verb.*
○ An amount by which something is made larger: *I got an increase of fifty cents in my allowance. Noun.*
in·crease (in krēs′ *for verb;* in′krēs′ *for noun*) *verb,* **increased, increasing;** *noun,* plural **increases.**

incredible 1. Hard or impossible to believe: *Your excuse that the dog ate your homework is incredible.* 2. Amazing; astonishing: *The amount of money they spend on clothes is incredible.* **in·cred·i·ble** (in kred′ə bəl) *adjective.*

incredulous Not able to believe something: *Many people were incredulous when the workers from the mine said they had found gold.* **in·cred·u·lous** (in krej′ə ləs) *adjective.*

incriminate To claim or show that someone is guilty of or involved in a crime: *The bits of chocolate incriminated me in the theft of the cookies.* **in·crim·i·nate** (in krim′ə nāt′) *verb,* **incriminated, incriminating.**

incubate To sit on eggs and keep them warm for hatching: *A hen incubates her eggs.* **in·cu·bate** (ing′kyə bāt′) *verb,* **incubated, incubating.**

incubator 1. A heated container that is used to hatch eggs. 2. A similar container that supplies heat, moisture, and oxygen to babies who are born too early. **in·cu·ba·tor** (ing′kyə bā′tər) *noun,* plural **incubators.**

incurable Not capable of being cured: *Some diseases are incurable.* **in·cur·a·ble** (in kyùr′ə bəl) *adjective.*

indebted 1. Owing money; in debt: *Until I pay back this loan, I am indebted to the bank.* 2. Owing gratitude to another for a favor: *I am indebted to you for all your help.* **in·debt·ed** (in det′id) *adjective.*

Ind. An abbreviation for **Indiana.**

indecent Rude or shocking; not decent: *That store charges indecent prices for clothes.* **in·de·cent** (in dē′sənt) *adjective.*

indeed Really; truly: *They do indeed have a talking parrot, just as they said they did.* **in·deed** (in dēd′) *adverb.*

indefinite 1. Not clear, set, or exact; vague: *Our plans for the summer are still indefinite.* 2. Having no limits; not fixed: *I will be in the hospital for an indefinite number of days.* **in·def·i·nite** (in def′ə nit) *adjective.*

indefinite article Either of the articles *a* or *an.* An indefinite article is used to refer to an indefinite person or thing. In the sentence "I'd like a piece of fruit," the indefinite article "a" refers to an indefinite "piece."

indent To start a written line farther in than the other lines: *We indent the first sentence of a paragraph.* **in·dent** (in dent′) *verb,* **indented, indenting.**

independence Freedom from the control of another or others: *The American colonies fought to win independence from England.* **in·de·pend·ence** (in′di pen′dəns) *noun.*

Independence Day A holiday in the United States that falls on the fourth of July. It celebrates the anniversary of the signing of the Declaration of Independence in 1776. This holiday is also called the Fourth of July.

independent Free from the control or rule of another or others; separate: *Mexicans fought against the Spanish to make Mexico an independent country.* **in·de·pend·ent** (in′di pen′dənt) *adjective.*

PRONUNCIATION KEY:
at   āpe   fär   câre   end   mē   it   īce   pîerce   hot   ōld   sông   fôrk
oil   out   up   ūse   rüle   pùll   tûrn   chin   sing   shop   thin   this
hw in white; zh in treasure. The symbol ə stands for the unstressed vowel sound in about, taken, pencil, lemon, and circus.

375

index An alphabetical list at the end of a book. An index tells on what page or pages a particular subject or name can be found: *To find information about robins, look up the word "robin" in the indexes of some books on birds.* Noun.
○ To make an index for: *The editor indexed the book about Indians so the reader could look up information easily.* Verb.
in·dex (in′deks) *noun, plural* **indexes**; *verb,* **indexed, indexing.**

WORD HISTORY

The word index comes from a Latin word that means "to show or point out." In Latin, the word index was first used to mean "forefinger," which is the finger we use for pointing.

India A country in southern Asia. **In·di·a** (in′dē ə) *noun.*

Indian 1. A member of one of the peoples who have been living in North and South America since before the Europeans discovered the continents; Native American. 2. A person who was born in or is a citizen of India. *Noun.*
○ 1. Having to do with American Indians; Native American. 2. Having to do with India or its people. *Adjective.*
In·di·an (in′dē ən) *noun, plural* **Indians**; *adjective.*

Indiana A state in the north-central United States. Its capital is Indianapolis. **In·di·an·a** (in′dē an′ə) *noun.*

Indian tribes were once found throughout the United States and Canada.

WORD HISTORY

The name Indiana comes from a modern Latin word meaning "Indian." There were many American Indians living in this region when other Americans began to settle there. This name was used for the territory and then the state.

Indiana
U. S. Postal Abbreviation: **IN**
Capital: **Indianapolis**
Population: **5,531,000**
Area: **36,291 sq. mi./93,993 sq. km**
State Nickname: **Hoosier State**
State Bird: **Cardinal**
State Flower: **Peony**

Indian corn A plant whose grain grows on large ears. Look up corn for more information.

Indian Ocean An ocean south of Asia, between Africa and Australia.

indicate 1. To be a sign of; show: *A high fever indicates that a person is sick.* 2. To point out: *The guide indicated the best path for us to take.* 3. To say or express briefly: *By nodding, I indicated that I agreed.* **in·di·cate** (in′di kāt′) *verb,* **indicated, indicating.**

indication Something that indicates; a sign: *Good grades are often an indication of hard work.* **in·di·ca·tion** (in′di kā′shən) *noun, plural* **indications.**

indict To accuse and charge a person with committing a crime. *A person is indicted by a special jury and then is given a trial.* **in·dict** (in dīt′) *verb,* **indicted, indicting.**

indifferent Having or showing a lack of interest, concern, or care: *The football game was so exciting that the fans were indifferent to the rain.* **in·dif·fer·ent** (in dif′ər ənt *or* in dif′rənt) *adjective.*

indigestion Difficulty or discomfort in digesting foods: *Food that is very spicy may cause indigestion.* **in·di·ges·tion** (in′di jes′chən *or* in′dī jes′chən) *noun.*

indignant Filled with anger about something unfair, wrong, or bad: *People in the town became indignant when they learned of plans to turn the park into a garbage dump.* **in·dig·nant** (in dig′nənt) *adjective.*

indigo 1. A very dark blue dye. It can be obtained from various plants but is now usually made artificially. 2. A plant that usually has purple or red flowers from which this dye is obtained. 3. A deep violet-blue color. *Noun.*
○ Having the color indigo; deep violet-blue. *Adjective.*
in·di·go (in′di gō′) *noun, plural* **indigos** *or* **indigoes**; *adjective.*

indirect 1. Not in a straight line; roundabout: *We took the indirect route through small towns because it is prettier than the main highway.* 2. Not straight to the point: *Yawning is an indirect way of saying that you are bored.* 3. Not directly connected. **in·di·rect** (in′də rekt′ *or* in′dī rekt′) *adjective.*

indirect object A word or group of words in a sentence to whom, to what, for whom, or for what the action of a *verb* is done. In the sentence "I showed them how to solve the problem," the *pronoun* "them" is the indirect object of the *verb* "showed."

indispensable Absolutely necessary: *Studying is indispensable to doing well in school.* **in·dis·pens·a·ble** (in′di spen′sə bəl) *adjective.*

individual 1. Of or for one person or thing: *You can announce your party to the whole class, or you can send out individual invitations.* 2. Single; separate: *The coffee was served with individual packets of sugar.* 3. Characteristic of a particular person or thing: *My cousin has an individual way of laughing. Adjective.*
○ A single person or thing: *In this group picture, the tallest individual stands out. Noun.*
in·di·vid·u·al (in′də vij′ü əl) *adjective; noun, plural* **individuals.**

individuality A quality that makes one person or thing different from others: *Some people try to express their individuality in the way they dress.* **in·di·vid·u·al·i·ty** (in′dəvij′ü al′i tē) *noun, plural* **individualities.**

individually One at a time: *The teacher explained the assignment to the class as a whole and then answered our questions individually.* **in·di·vid·u·al·ly** (in′də vij′ü ə lē) *adverb.*

indivisible Not able to be divided or separated: *The United States is an indivisible nation.*

in·di·vis·i·ble (in′də viz′ə bəl) *adjective.*

Indonesia A country made up of a group of islands in southeastern Asia. **In·do·ne·sia** (in′də nē′zhə) *noun.*

indoor Used, done, or built within a house or building: *The school had an indoor swimming pool.* **in·door** (in′dôr′) *adjective.*

indoors In or into a house or building: *We went indoors when it began to rain.* **in·doors** (in′dôrz′) *adverb.*

indulge 1. To allow oneself to have, do, or enjoy something: *I indulged in an hour of relaxation after I finished all my chores.* 2. To give in to the wishes of: *Grandparents sometimes indulge children by giving them everything they ask for.* **in·dulge** (in dulj′) *verb,* **indulged, indulging.**

industrial 1. Having to do with or produced by industry: *Iron smelting, coal mining, and the production of plastics are industrial processes.* 2. Having highly developed industries: *Canada is an industrial country.* **in·dus·tri·al** (in dus′trē əl) *adjective.*

industrialize To set up or develop industry in an area or country: *The governor wanted to industrialize the state in order to provide more jobs.* **in·dus·tri·al·ize** (in dus′trē ə līz′) *verb,* **industrialized, industrializing. industrialization** *noun.*

industrious Working hard: *The industrious student finished the report a week before it was due.* **in·dus·tri·ous** (in dus′trē əs) *adjective.*

The industrious girl is making valentines.

industry 1. Making of things on a large scale, especially by people and machines working together: *Industry came to the town when a tire factory and an electric power plant were opened.* 2. A branch of business, trade, or manufacturing: *The tourist industry employs many people in Hawaii.* 3. Hard work; steady effort: *The students showed much industry in preparing their homework.* **in·dus·try** (in′dəs trē) *noun, plural* **industries**.

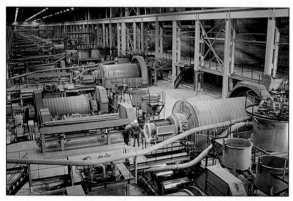

Many industries operate with huge machinery.

inedible Not fit as food; not suitable for eating: *The burned meat was inedible.* **in·ed·i·ble** (in ed′ə bəl) *adjective.*

inefficient Not offering a good use of time, effort, or money: *Computers can end the inefficient method of writing with pen and pencil.* **in·ef·fi·cient** (in′ə fish′ənt) *adjective.* **inefficiency** *noun.* —**inefficiently** *adverb.*

inequality The condition of not being equal: *Often there is an inequality between what we hope for and what we get.* **in·e·qual·i·ty** (in′i kwol′i tē) *noun, plural* **inequalities**.

inert Not able to move or act: *The huge effort left the workers inert.* **in·ert** (i nûrt′) *adjective.*

inertia 1. The tendency of a body to stay in motion if it is in motion, and to stay at rest if it is at rest, unless acted upon by some external force. 2. Unwillingness to move or to exert oneself: *The heavy Thanksgiving dinner had left them all with a feeling of inertia.* **in·er·tia** (i nûr′shə *or* in ûr′shə) *noun.*

inevitable Not able to be avoided; bound to happen: *An inevitable result of closing your eyes is not being able to see.* **in·ev·i·ta·ble** (i nev′i tə bəl) *adjective.* —**inevitably** *adverb.*

inexpensive Not expensive; reasonable in price:

I bought inexpensive shorts for the summer. **in·ex·pen·sive** (in′ek spen′siv) *adjective.*

inexperienced Lacking the knowledge or skill gained from doing something: *The driver was inexperienced in maneuvering the car through snow.* **in·ex·pe·ri·enced** (in′ek spîr′ē ənst) *adjective.*

infant A child during the earliest period of life; baby. *Noun.*
  ○ 1. Having to do with a baby. 2. In an early stage of growth; young: *The United States was an infant republic when its constitution was written. Adjective.*
  in·fant (in′fənt) *noun, plural* **infants**; *adjective.*

infantry Soldiers trained and equipped to fight on foot: *The infantry used to be very important in winning wars.* **in·fan·try** (in′fən trē) *noun, plural* **infantries**.

infatuated Filled with an excessive love or admiration: *They become infatuated with a new rock group every year.* **in·fat·u·at·ed** (in fach′ə wā təd) *adjective.*

infect 1. To spread a disease that is caused by a germ: *Mosquitoes infected many of the workers in the jungle with malaria.* 2. To enter a living thing and cause disease: *The doctor said that bacteria had infected the cut on my hand.* **in·fect** (in fekt′) *verb,* **infected, infecting**.

infection 1. The process of infecting: *The infection of the wound was caused by bacteria.* 2. A disease that is caused by germs entering the body: *I got a very bad infection in my foot after stepping on some pieces of broken glass.* **in·fec·tion** (in fek′shən) *noun, plural* **infections**.

infectious 1. Spread by infection: *Mumps is an infectious disease.* 2. Spreading quickly: *Happiness is an infectious emotion.* **in·fec·tious** (in fek′shəs) *adjective.*

infer To find out by reasoning; conclude: *From your high grades, I inferred that you were a good student.* Look up imply for a Language Note about this word. **in·fer** (in fûr′) *verb,* **inferred, inferring**.

inferior 1. Of poor quality; below average: *The food at that restaurant is inferior.* 2. Low or lower in quality, importance, or value: *The rank of private is inferior to the rank of sergeant.* **in·fe·ri·or** (in fîr′ē ər) *adjective.*

infertile 1. Not useful for farming: *This infertile land won't produce crops.* 2. Not able to have children. **in·fer·tile** (in fûr′təl) *adjective.* **infertility** *noun.*

infield 1. The area of a baseball field that is inside and around the bases. 2. In baseball, the people who play the positions at first base, second base, third base, and shortstop. **in·field** (in′fēld′) *noun, plural* **infields.**

infiltrate To enter into something in secret: *The soldiers discovered an enemy agent had infiltrated their headquarters.* **in·fil·trate** (in′fil trāt) *verb,* **infiltrated, infiltrating.**

infinite 1. Without limits or an end: *Outer space seems to be infinite.* 2. Very great: *The artist painted the tiny figures with infinite care.* **in·fi·nite** (in′fə nit) *adjective.* —**infinitely** *adverb* —**infinity** *noun.*

infinitive A simple *verb* form. An infinitive is often preceded by the word "to." In the sentence "I like to swim," "to swim" is an infinitive. **in·fin·i·tive** (in fin′i tiv) *noun, plural* **infinitives.**

infirm Not strong; sick: *The infection left him infirm for the rest of his life.* **in·firm** (in fûrm′) *adjective.*

inflame 1. To excite greatly; stir up: *The plan to turn the park into a parking lot inflamed the whole town.* 2. To make hot, red, or swollen: *The infection in the cut inflamed my finger.* **in·flame** (in flām′) *verb,* **inflamed, inflaming.**

inflammable Easily set on fire; flammable: *Gasoline is an inflammable liquid.* **in·flam·ma·ble** (in flam′ə bəl) *adjective.*

inflammation A condition of a part of the body in which there is heat, redness, swelling, and pain. It is usually caused by an infection or injury. **in·flam·ma·tion** (in′flə mā′shən) *noun, plural* **inflammations.**

inflatable Designed to be filled with air: *This rubber raft boat is inflatable.* **inflatable** (in flā′tə bəl) *adjective.*

A special kind of heater is used to inflate a hot air balloon.

inflate To cause to swell by filling with air or gas: *Use a pump to inflate the bicycle tire.* **in·flate** (in flāt′) *verb,* **inflated, inflating.**

inflation 1. The act or process of inflating: *The inflation of the balloons for the party took all morning.* 2. A rise in the usual prices of goods and services. **in·fla·tion** (in flā′shən) *noun, plural* **inflations.**

inflexible 1. Not able to bend; rigid: *Steel is an inflexible metal.* 2. Firm; determined: *Mother is an inflexible judge of our manners.* 3. Not capable of being changed or ignored: *The city has an inflexible rule against parking near a fire hydrant.* **in·flex·i·ble** (in flek′sə bəl) *adjective.*

inflict To cause harm or damage: *The storm inflicted great damage on the town.* **in·flict** (in flikt′) *verb,* **inflicted, inflicting.**

influence 1. The power of a person or thing to produce an effect on others without using force or a command: *Use your influence to persuade your friend to study harder.* 2. A person or thing that has the power to produce an effect on others: *Working with that classmate has had a good influence on my study habits.* Noun.
○ To have an effect on; especially by giving suggestions or by serving as an example: *The older members of my family influence me in many ways.* Verb. **in·flu·ence** (in′flü əns) *noun, plural* **influences;** *verb,* **influenced, influencing.**

influential Having or using influence: *Some influential teachers persuaded the principal to change the rule.* **in·flu·en·tial** (in′flü en′shəl) *adjective.*

influenza A disease that causes fever, coughing, and muscle pains. Influenza is caused by a virus. It is also called flu. **in·flu·en·za** (in′flü en′zə) *noun.*

PRONUNCIATION KEY:

| at | āpe | fär | câre | end | mē | it | īce | pierce | hot | ōld | sŏng | fôrk |
| oil | out | up | ūse | rüle | pŏll | tûrn | chin | sing | shop | thin | this | |

hw in white; zh in treasure. The symbol ə stands for the unstressed vowel sound in about, taken, pencil, lemon, and circus.

379

info A shortened way of spelling **information**. **in·fo** (in′fō) *noun*.

infomercial A television commercial that tells about a product or service in great detail and at great length. Infomercials are usually designed to look more like a regular program than like a commercial. **in·fo·mer·cial** (in′fə mûr′shəl) *noun*, **infomercials**.

inform 1. To give information to; tell: *Please inform us of the date you will arrive.* 2. To tell secret or damaging information. **in·form** (in fôrm′) *verb*, **informed, informing**.

informal Without ceremony; not formal; casual: *We gave a very informal party where everyone wore old clothes.* **in·for·mal** (in fôr′məl) *adjective*.

information 1. Knowledge or facts about something: *Where can I ask for information about the bus schedule?* 2. A person or service that answers questions and gives facts: *You can call information for the telephone number of the school.* **in·for·ma·tion** (in′fər mā′shən) *noun*.

information superhighway A worldwide network of computers and other telecommunications links planned for the future.

infrequent Not happening often; not frequent: *Serious accidents are infrequent on our quiet street.* **in·fre·quent** (in frē′kwənt) *adjective*. —**infrequently** *adverb*.

infuriate To make very angry; make furious: *Their constant teasing infuriates me.* **in·fu·ri·ate** (in fyùr′ē āt′) *verb*, **infuriated, infuriating**.

-ing A suffix that: 1. Forms the present participle of verbs. The word talking is the present participle of talk: *We are **talking** about something important.* 2. Forms nouns from verbs. The *noun* that is formed names the action that the *verb* describes: ***Talking** is not allowed in the halls.*

ingenious Clever, imaginative: *My friend is ingenious at thinking of new ideas for class projects.* **in·gen·ious** (in jēn′yəs) *adjective*.

ingenuity The quality of being clever and imaginative: *You showed ingenuity in making bookcases out of orange crates.* **in·ge·nu·i·ty** (in′jə nü′i tē) *noun*.

ingot A mass of metal that is often shaped like a bar or block. **in·got** (ing′gət) *noun*, *plural* **ingots**.

Blueberries are the main ingredients in this pie.

ingredient Any one of the parts that go into a mixture: *Flour, eggs, sugar, and butter are the main ingredients of this cake.* **in·gre·di·ent** (in grē′dē ənt) *noun*, *plural* **ingredients**.

inhabit To live in or on: *Many birds inhabit the woods.* **in·hab·it** (in hab′it) *verb*, **inhabited, inhabiting**.

inhabitant A person or animal that lives in a place. **in·hab·it·ant** (in hab′i tənt) *noun*, *plural* **inhabitants**.

inhale To take into the lungs; breathe in: *I inhaled the fresh, clean mountain air.* **in·hale** (in hāl′) *verb*, **inhaled, inhaling**.

inherit 1. To receive the property or money of a person who has died: *We inherited this house from our grandparents.* 2. To get from one's parent or parents: *The little boy inherited his mother's black hair.* **in·her·it** (in her′it) *verb*, **inherited, inheriting**.

inheritance Something that is inherited: *We set aside my inheritance from my grandparents for my college education.* **in·her·it·ance** (in her′i təns) *noun*, *plural* **inheritances**.

inhuman Without kindness, pity, or mercy; cruel; brutal: *Making the tired old horse work in the heat was inhuman.* **in·hu·man** (in hū′mən) *adjective*.

initial Coming at the beginning; first: *The initial letter of the word "ring" is "r."* Adjective.
○ The first letter of a word or a name: *"B.R." are the initials of Betsy Ross.* Noun.
○ To mark or sign with one's initial or initials: *The teacher initialed the report after reading it.* Verb. **i·ni·tial** (i nish′əl) *adjective*; *noun*, *plural* **initials**; *verb*, **initialed, initialing**.

initiate 1. To be the first to do; begin; start: *The new librarian **initiated** the practice of lending books for a month.* 2. To make a person a member of an organization or club: *The new members were **initiated** into the club at a special ceremony.* **i·ni·ti·ate** (i nish′ē āt′) *verb*, **initiated**, **initiating**.

initiative 1. The first step in doing or beginning something: *I took the **initiative** at the party by introducing myself to the people I didn't know.* 2. The ability or willingness to take a first step in doing or learning something: *The new campers showed **initiative** by setting up the tent without being asked.* **i·ni·tia·tive** (i nish′ə tiv) *noun*.

inject 1. To force a liquid through the skin into a muscle, vein, or other part of the body: *The doctor **injected** the vaccine into my arm.* 2. To put in: *The principal tried to **inject** some humor into the speech by telling several jokes.* **in·ject** (in jek′t) *verb* **injected**, **injecting**.

injection The forcing of a liquid through the skin into the body for a medical purpose: *The veterinarian gave the dog an **injection** with a needle.* **in·jec·tion** (in jek′shən) *noun*, *plural* **injections**.

injure To cause harm to; damage or hurt: *I **injured** myself when I fell off my bicycle.* **in·jure** (in′jər) *verb*, **injured**, **injuring**.

injury Harm or damage done to a person or thing: *The accident caused an **injury** to my leg.* **in·ju·ry** (in′jə rē) *noun*, *plural* **injuries**.

injustice 1. The lack of justice; unfairness: *The class protested against the **injustice** of punishing everyone because one student was noisy.* 2. Something unjust: *You do your friends an **injustice** when you lie to them.* **in·jus·tice** (in jus′tis) *noun*, *plural* **injustices**.

ink A colored liquid used for writing, drawing, or printing. **ink** (ingk) *noun*, *plural* **inks**.

inkling A vague idea; hint: *I had an inkling she might be at the party, so I wasn't surprised to see her there.* **ink·ling** (ingk′ling) *noun*, *plural* **inklings**.

inland Away from the coast or border: *Kansas is an **inland** state. Adjective.*
○ In or toward the inner part of a country or region: *We drove **inland** from the coast for many miles. Adverb.*
in·land (in′lənd) *adjective*; *adverb*.

inlet A narrow body of water leading inland from a larger body of water. **in·let** (in′let′) *noun*, *plural* **inlets**.

This **inlet** allows ships to enter the port from the sea.

inn A small hotel. An inn is usually in the country. Another word that sounds like this is **in.** **inn** (in) *noun*, *plural* **inns**.

inner 1. Farther in: *The principal's office is in the **inner** room.* 2. More private; personal: *I hid my **inner** feelings of disappointment at having lost the contest.* **in·ner** (in′ər) *adjective*.

inning One of the parts into which a baseball or softball game is divided. Both teams bat during an inning until three players on each team are put out. **in·ning** (in′ing) *noun*, *plural* **innings**.

This model reveals some **inner** parts of an airplane.

innkeeper A person who owns or manages an inn. **inn·keep·er** (in′kē′pər) *noun*, *plural* **innkeepers**.

innocence The state or quality of being innocent: *The **innocence** of the prisoner was proven during the trial.* **in·no·cence** (in′ə səns) *noun*.

innocent 1. Free from guilt or wrong: *An **innocent** person was accused of the crime, but a jury found the person not guilty.* 2. Not doing harm; harmless: *The children hid from their parents as an **innocent** joke.* **in·no·cent** (in′ə sənt) *adjective*.

PRONUNCIATION KEY:
at āpe fär câre end mē it īce pierce hot ōld sông fôrk
oil out up ūse rūle pull tûrn chin sing shop thin this
hw in white; zh in treasure. The symbol ə stands for the unstressed vowel sound in about, taken, pencil, lemon, and circus.

381

innovation Something new that is introduced: *The development of the first antibiotic was a great innovation in medicine.* **in·no·va·tion** (in′ə vā′shən) *noun, plural* **innovations.**

inoculate To give a healthy person or animal a small amount of a substance that contains weakened disease germs. This helps the body protect itself against the disease. A person can be inoculated against diseases such as smallpox and typhoid fever. **in·oc·u·late** (in ok′yə lāt′) *verb,* **inoculated, inoculating.**

input 1. Information that is put into a computer. 2. Advice: *We need your input before we make a decision.* **in·put** (in′pùt′) *noun.*

inquire To ask for information: *We stopped at a gas station to inquire the way to the park.* **in·quire** (in kwīr′) *verb,* **inquired, inquiring.**

inquiry 1. A looking for information or knowledge; investigation: *The fire department is making an inquiry into the cause of the fire.* 2. A request for information: *There were many inquiries about the summer job that was advertised in the paper.* **in·qui·ry** (in kwīr′ē or in′kwə rē) *noun, plural* **inquiries.**

inquisitive Eager to know; curious: *An inquisitive student asks a lot of questions.* **in·quis·i·tive** (in kwiz′i tiv) *adjective.*

insane 1. Not having a healthy mind; not sane; crazy. 2. Of or for insane people: *The state runs that insane asylum.* 3. Very foolish: *It is insane to think that you can fly.* **in·sane** (in sān′) *adjective.*

insanity A state in which the mind is seriously sick. **in·san·i·ty** (in san′i tē) *noun, plural* **insanities.**

inscribe To write, carve, engrave, or mark words or letters on something: *an inscribed locket.* **in·scribe** (in skrīb′) *verb,* **inscribed, inscribing.**

insect 1. Any of a large group of small animals without a backbone. Insects have a body divided into three parts, three pairs of legs, and usually two pairs of wings. Flies, ants, grasshoppers, and beetles are insects. 2. An animal that is similar to an insect: *Ticks and spiders are sometimes called insects but they are another kind of animal.* **in·sect** (in′sekt) *noun, plural* **insects.**

WORD HISTORY

The word **insect** comes from a Latin word that means "cut into." An insect was called "an animal that has been cut into" because its body is divided into three sections.

---

insecticide A chemical for killing insects. **in·sec·ti·cide** (in sek′tə sīd′) *noun, plural* **insecticides.**

insecure 1. Likely to fail; not firm or stable: *The latch was so insecure that the wind could blow the door open.* 2. Not safe from danger, harm, or loss: *The fort was insecure because there were not enough troops to defend it.* 3. Not confident; fearful: *The student felt nervous and insecure before the start of the spelling contest.* **in·se·cure** (in′si kyùr′) *adjective.*

insensitive Not caring about the feelings of other people; not sensitive: *It was insensitive of you to ask such personal questions of your new neighbors.* **in·sen·si·tive** (in sen′si tiv) *adjective.*

---

insect

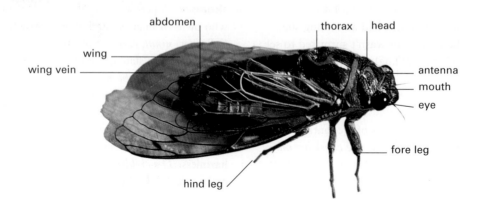

abdomen · wing · wing vein · thorax · head · antenna · mouth · eye · fore leg · hind leg

insert To put, set, or place in: *I inserted a coin in the vending machine. Verb.*
○ Something inserted: *The Sunday edition of the newspaper has an eight-page color insert on vacations. Noun.*
in•sert (in sûrt′ *for verb;* in′sûrt′ *for noun*) *verb,* **inserted, inserting;** *noun, plural* **inserts.**

inside 1. The inner side or part; interior: *The inside of the house was dark.* 2. **insides:** *The internal organs of the body. Noun.*
○ 1. On or in the inside: *I took an inside seat on the train.* 2. Known or done by only a few: *The reporter got the inside story on the mayor's meeting with the governor. Adjective.*
○ 1. On, in, or into the inner side or part of within: *I opened the door of the house and stepped inside.* 2. Indoors: *The children played inside because of the rain. Adverb.*
○ In, into, or on the inner side or part of: *I looked inside the closet for my coat. Preposition.*
• **inside out.** 1. So that the inside is facing out: *Your sweater is turned inside out.* 2. Completely; thoroughly: *They had worked at the office so many years that they knew their job inside out.*
in•side (in′sīd′ *or* in sīd′ *or* in′sīd′) *noun, plural* **insides;** *adjective; adverb; preposition.*

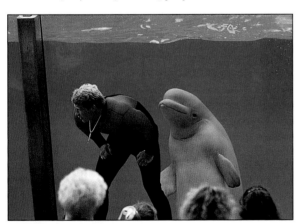

The beluga whale is on display inside a huge tank.

insight A special understanding about something: *She had a sudden insight that the bright lights were what made her head ache.* **in•sight** (in′sit) *noun, plural* **insights. —insightful** *adjective.*

insignia A badge, medal, or other mark showing a person's rank, position, or membership: *The police officer wore the insignia of a captain.*
in•sig•ni•a (in sig′nē ə) *noun, plural* **insignias.**

insignificant Having little or no importance or meaning: *My problems seem insignificant compared to the difficulties of others.* **in•sig•ni•fi•cant** (in′sig nif′i kənt) *adjective.*

insincere Not sincere; dishonest: *It is insincere to say that you like a person when you really don't.* **in•sin•cere** (in′sin sîr′) *adjective.* **—insincerity** *noun.*

insist To demand or say in a strong, firm manner: *The doctor insisted that the sick patient stay in bed.* **in•sist** (in sist′) *verb,* **insisted, insisting.**

insolent Very rude or sdisrespectful: insulting: *They have to stay after school for being insolent to the teacher.* **in•so•lent** (in′sə lənt) *adjective.*
—insolently *adverb.*

insomnia A condition in which a person finds it hard to fall asleep and to stay asleep. **in•som•ni•a** (in som′nē ə) *noun.*

inspect To look at closely and carefully: *The official inspected our car and declared that it was safe to drive.* **in•spect** (in spekt′) *verb,* **inspected, inspecting.**

The farmer is inspecting the peppers he has grown.

inspection The act of inspecting: *The mechanic's inspection of the elevator took an hour.* **in•spec•tion** (in spek′shən) *noun, plural* **inspections.**

inspector A person who makes inspections. **in•spec•tor** (in spek′tər) *noun, plural* **inspectors.**

inspiration 1. The stirring of the mind, feelings, or imagination, especially so that some good idea comes: *Hoping for inspiration, I looked at a list of possible topics for my essay.* 2. A person or thing that stirs the mind, feelings, or imagination: *The author's family was the inspiration for many of the characters in the novel.* 3. A sudden, bright idea: *Your plan to put your bed on a platform was an inspiration.* **in•spi•ra•tion** (in′spə rā′shən) *noun, plural* **inspirations.**

PRONUNCIATION KEY:
at   āpe   fär   câre   end   mē   it   īce   pierce   hot   ōld   sông   fôrk
oil   out   up   ūse   rüle   pull   tûrn   chin   sing   shop   thin   <u>th</u>is
hw in white; zh in treasure. The symbol ə stands for the unstressed vowel sound in about, taken, pencil, lemon, and circus.

383

inspire 1. To stir the mind, feelings, or imagination of: *The senator's* **speech** *inspired the audience.* 2. To fill with a strong, encouraging feeling: *Success in school* **inspired** *me with hope for the future.* 3. To move to action: *What inspired you to take up knitting?* **in·spire** (in spīr′) *verb,* **inspired, inspiring.**

install 1. To put in place for use or service: *We had a new air conditioner installed today.* 2. To place a person in an office with a ceremony: *The new club president will be installed at the next meeting.* **in·stall** (in stôl′) *verb,* **installed, installing.**

installment 1. One of the parts of a sum of money that is owed and is to be paid at particular times: *My parents paid for our new car in thirty-six monthly installments.* 2. A part of a story that is issued or shown separately: *The book was first published in a magazine in weekly installments.* **in·stall·ment** (in stôl′mənt) *noun, plural* **installments.**

instance An example; case: *There are many* **instances** *of immigrants becoming famous Americans.*

• **for instance.** As an example or illustration: *I enjoy many team sports,* **for instance,** *baseball, football, basketball, and hockey.* **in·stance** (in′stəns) *noun, plural* **instances.**

instant 1. A very short period of time; moment: *For an* **instant,** *lightning lit up the sky.* 2. A particular moment: *I want you to leave this* **instant!** *Noun.*
○ 1. Without delay; immediate: *The computer gave us an* **instant** *reply to our question.* 2. Very important or necessary; urgent: *The town had an* **instant** *need for help during the flood.* 3. Needing only additional liquid to prepare: *I added hot water to make the* **instant** *mashed potatoes. Adjective.* **in·stant** (in′stənt) *noun, plural* **instants;** *adjective.*

instantly At once; without delay: *I picked up a very hot frying pan and* **instantly** *dropped it.* **in·stant·ly** (in′stənt lē) *adverb.*

instead In place of another person or thing: *The recipe called for butter, but we used margarine* **instead.**
• **instead of.** As a substitute for; in place of: *We watched television* **instead of** *going to the movies.* **in·stead** (in sted′) *adverb.*

instep The arched upper part of the human foot

between the toes and the ankle. **in·step** (in′step′) *noun, plural* **insteps.**

instill To put in or introduce little by little: *The English teachers instilled a love of books into their pupils.* **in·still** (in stil′) *verb,* **instilled, instilling.**

instinct A way of acting or behaving that a person or animal is born with and does not have to learn: *Birds build nests by* **instinct.** **in·stinct** (in′stingkt′) *noun, plural* **instincts.**

instinctive Having to do with a way of acting or behaving that a person or animal is born with and does not have to learn: *Building a nest is* **instinctive** *behavior in a bird.* **in·stinc·tive** (in stingk′tiv) *adjective.*

institute A school or other organization that is set up for a special purpose: *Both of my parents are doctors at the medical* **institute** *for cancer research. Noun.*
○ To set up; establish: *The neighbors instituted a weekly clean-up campaign. Verb.* **in·sti·tute** (in′sti tüt′ *or* in′sti tūt′) *noun, plural* **institutes;** *verb,* **instituted, instituting.**

institution 1. An organization that is set up for a special purpose: *A school is an* **institution** *of learning.* 2. A custom or practice that has been followed for a long time: *Having Thanksgiving dinner at my grandparents' house is an* **institution** *in our family.* **in·sti·tu·tion** (in′sti tü′shən *or* in′sti tū′shən) *noun, plural* **institutions.**

instruct 1. To show how to do or use something; teach: *Has someone instructed you in the correct use of the saw?* 2. To give directions or orders to: *Our folks instructed us to lock the door when we left.* **in·struct** (in strukt′) *verb,* **instructed, instructing.**

instruction 1. The act of teaching: *We learned how to swim from the coach's* **instruction.** 2. An explanation or direction: *If you follow the* **instructions,** *you can put the model airplane together easily.* **in·struc·tion** (in struk′shən) *noun, plural* **instructions.**

instructor A person who instructs; teacher: *My friend is*

The instructor is explaining the workings of a computer to his students.

a swimming **instructor** at the town pool.
in·struc·tor (in struk′tər) *noun, plural* **instructors**.

instrument **1.** A device used for doing a certain kind of work; tool: *The dental hygienist used a sharp instrument to scrape my teeth.* **2.** A device for producing musical sounds: *Our music teacher plays the guitar, flute, and several other instruments.* **in·stru·ment** (in′strə mənt) *noun, plural* **instruments**.

These musicians are accompanying each other on their musical instruments.

insufficient Not enough; inadequate: *I had insufficient time to change my clothes before the party.* **in·suf·fi·cient** (in′sə fish′ənt) *adjective*.

insulate To cover or surround with a material that slows or stops the flow of electricity, heat, or sound: *The electrician insulated the electric wire with rubber.* **in·su·late** (in′sə lāt′) *verb*, **insulated, insulating**.

insulation **1.** The act of insulating or the condition of being insulated: Insulation of the water pipes keeps them from freezing in winter. **2.** Material that is used to slow or stop the flow of electricity, heat, or sound: *The builders put fiberglass insulation under the roof of our new house.* **in·su·la·tion** (in′sə lā′shən) *noun*.

insulin A hormone that controls the amount of sugar in a person's body. It is produced in the pancreas. **in·su·lin** (in′sə lin) *noun*.

insult To hurt the feelings or pride of: *You insulted your friends when you refused to attend their party. Verb.*

○ A remark or action that hurts someone's feelings or pride: *My old friend wouldn't say hello to me, and this was a painful insult. Noun.* **in·sult** (in sult′ *for verb;* in′sult′ *for noun*) *verb*, **insulted, insulting**; *noun, plural* **insults**.

insurance Protection against loss or damage. A person who wants insurance agrees to pay a small amount of money at regular times to a company. In exchange, the company promises to pay a certain amount in case of death, accident, fire, or theft: *My parents' medical insurance paid for the doctors' bills when I broke my arm.* **in·sur·ance** (in shùr′əns) *noun*.

insure To protect by insurance: *The car is insured against accident or theft.* **in·sure** (in shùr′) *verb*, **insured, insuring**.

intact With nothing missing, broken, or injured; complete: *We all survived the accident intact.* **in·tact** (in takt′) *adjective*.

intake **1.** The amount of something taken in: *I was advised to increase my intake of liquids while I had a cold.* **2.** A place in a channel or pipe where a liquid or gas is taken in. **in·take** (in′tāk′) *noun, plural* **intakes**.

integer A number that is not a fraction; a whole number: *The numbers 0, 15, -2, and 365 are integers.* **in·te·er** () *noun, plural* **integers**.

integrate **1.** To make open to people of all races: *The town integrated all its schools long ago.* **2.** To bring parts together into a whole: *The reporter tried to integrate all the different accounts of the accident into one clear story.* **in·te·grate** (in′ti grāt′) *verb*, **integrated, integrating**.

integration The act of making something open to people of all races: *In 1954 the Supreme Court ruled that there should be integration of the public schools of the United States.* **in·te·gra·tion** (in′ti grā′shən) *noun*.

integrity Complete honesty: *A person who lies has no integrity.* **in·teg·ri·ty** (in teg′ri tē) *noun*.

intellect The power of the mind to think, learn, and understand, especially when this power is developed and trained; intelligence: *That chemistry professor is a scientist of great intellect.* **in·tel·lect** (in′tə lekt′) *noun*.

intellectual **1.** Having to do with the power to think, learn, and understand: *It takes intellectual ability to solve difficult problems.* **2.** Having or showing highly developed intelligence: *Intellectual people often like to think and to express ideas. Adjective.*

○ A person who has a highly developed and

PRONUNCIATION KEY:

| at | āpe | fär | câre | end | mē | it | īce | pierce | hot | ōld | sông | fôrk |
| oil | out | up | ūse | rüle | pùll | tùrn | chin | sing | shop | thin | this | |

hw in white; zh in treasure. The symbol ə stands for the unstressed vowel sound in about, taken, pencil, lemon, and circus.

385

trained intelligence: *The person who wrote that book was one of the great* **intellectuals** *of the time. Noun.*

in·tel·lec·tu·al (in′tə lek′chü əl) *adjective; noun, plural* **intellectuals**.

intelligence 1. The ability to think, learn, and understand. 2. Information, especially about foreign countries or enemy forces: *The army's* **intelligence** *showed that the enemy was going to attack at dawn.* **in·tel·li·gence** (in tel′i jəns) *noun*.

intelligent Having or showing the ability to think, learn, and understand: *Intelligent people learn from their mistakes.* **in·tel·li·gent** (in tel′i jənt) *adjective*.

intelligible Able to be understood; clear: *Your question wasn't* **intelligible** *to some of the class.* **in·tel·li·gi·ble** (in tel′i jə bəl) *adjective*.

intend 1. To have in mind as a purpose; plan: *What do you* **intend** *to do with this money?* 2. To mean for a particular person or purpose: *That present is* **intended** *for you.* **in·tend** (in tend′) *verb*, **intended, intending**.

intense 1. Very great or strong; extreme: *The heat from the iron was so* **intense** *that it burned a hole in the cloth.* 2. Having or showing strong feeling, purpose, or effort; concentrated: *The worried parent had an* **intense** *look.* **in·tense** (in tens′) *adjective*.

intensify To make or become stronger: *Before we could find shelter, the storm had* **intensified**. **in·ten·si·fy** (in ten′sə fī) *verb*, **intensified, intensifying**.

intensity 1. The state or quality of being intense: *The light from the searchlight shone with great* **intensity**. 2. Amount or degree of something that varies: *The* **intensity** *of my toothache lessened after I took aspirin.* **in·ten·si·ty** (in ten′si tē) *noun, plural* **intensities**.

intent 1. Something that is intended; purpose;

These people are intent **on watching a television program.**

aim: *My* **intent** *has always been to go to college.* 2. Meaning; significance: *What was the precise* **intent** *of what you said? Noun.*

○ Having the mind firmly fixed on something: *I asked them to stay, but they were* **intent** *on leaving. Adjective.*

in·tent (in tent′) *noun, plural* **intents**; *adjective*.

intention Something that is intended; purpose; plan. *Our* **intention** *is to wash all the windows before dinner.* **in·ten·tion** (in ten′shən) *noun, plural* **intentions**.

intentional Done on purpose; planned; meant: *I know that your bumping into me was not* **intentional**. **in·ten·tion·al** (in tens′hə nəl) *adjective*. —**intentionally** *adverb*.

interactive Allowing two-way communication: *an* **interactive** *story on CD-ROM that lets the player make choices about the story's outcome.* **in·ter·ac·tive** (in′tər ak′tiv) *adjective*.

intercept To stop or take something on its way from one person or place to another: *I tried to pass the ball to a teammate, but an opposing player* **intercepted** *it.* **in·ter·cept** (I′ntər sept′) *verb*, **intercepted, intercepting**. —**interception** *noun*.

interchangeable Capable of being put or used in place of each other: *These typewriter ribbons are* **interchangeable**, *although they were made by different companies.* **in·ter·change·a·ble** (in′tər chān′jə bəl) *adjective*.

intercom A radio or telephone system between different parts of a building, airplane, or ship: *The pilot welcomed the passengers over the* **intercom**. **in·ter·com** (in′tər kom′) *noun, plural* **intercoms**.

interest 1. A desire or eagerness to know about or take part in something: *Do you have any* **interest** *in football?* 2. Something that causes such a desire: *Collecting records is my main* **interest** *now.* 3. The power to cause such a desire: *That book about horses had little* **interest** *for us.* 4. Advantage; benefit: *A selfish person cares only about his or her own* **interests**. 5. Money that is paid for the use of borrowed or deposited money. When a person keeps money in a bank, the bank pays the person a certain amount of interest. 6. A right or share: *The four partners each have a one-quarter* **interest** *in the business they own. Noun.*

○ 1. To cause to want to know about or take part in something: *The teacher* **interested** *me in gardening by giving me several books on the subject.*

2. To persuade to do or take something: *Could I interest you in a walk? Verb.*
in•ter•est (in′trist *or* in′tər ist) *noun, plural* **interests**; *verb,* **interested, interesting.**

interesting Causing or holding interest or attention: *The pictures in this book on underwater photography are interesting.* **in•ter•est•ing** (in′tris ting *or* in′tə res′ting) *adjective.*

interface Something that connects and allows communication between separate things or individuals: *The graphic part of a computer program that you see on the monitor is the interface that helps a person use the program.* **in•ter•face** (in′tər fās′) *noun, plural* **interfaces.**

interfere **1.** To take part in the affairs of others without having been asked; meddle: *Our neighbor is always interfering by giving us advice that we don't want.* **2.** To disturb or interrupt; prevent or hinder: *That loud music interferes with my studying.* **in•ter•fere** (in′tər fîr′) *verb,* **interfered, interfering.**

interference **1.** An unwelcome involvement in the affairs of other people: *She didn't appreciate your interference in our argument.* **2.** An interruption of a radio or television signal: *I missed my favorite program because of the interference.* **3.** In sports, illegally keeping an opponent from making a play. **in•ter•fer•ence** (in′tər fîr′əns) *noun.*

intergalactic Existing between or among galaxies: *intergalactic molecules of hydrogen.* **in•ter•ga•lac•tic** (in′tər gə lak′tik) *adjective.*

interior **1.** The inner side, surface, or part: *The interior of the cave was dark.* **2.** The part of a country or region that is away from the coast or border: *The interior of Australia is mostly desert. Noun.*
○ Having to do with or on the inner side; inside: *The interior walls of the building are painted gray. Adjective.*
in•te•ri•or (in tîr′ē ər) *noun, plural* **interiors**; *adjective.*

interjection A word or phrase that shows strong feeling. An interjection can be used alone. "Oh!" and "Hey!" are interjections. **in•te•rjec•tion** (in′tər jek′shən) *noun, plural* **interjections.**

intermediate In the middle; being between: *The school offers beginning, intermediate, and advanced classes in gymnastics.* **in•ter•me•di•ate** (in′tər mē′dē it) *adjective.*

intermission A time of rest or stopping between periods of activity: *There was an intermission of ten minutes between the first and second acts of the play.* **in•ter•mis•sion** (in′tər mish′ən) *noun, plural* **intermissions.**

intern A doctor who has just graduated from medical school and is working in a hospital under more experienced doctors. **in•tern** (in′tûrn′) *noun, plural* **interns.**

internal **1.** Having to do with or on the inside; interior: *The stomach and kidneys are internal organs of the body.* **2.** Having to do with matters within a country; domestic: *A national government deals with internal affairs as well as foreign policy.* **in•ter•nal** (in tûr′nəl) *adjective.* —**internally** *adverb.*

international Having to do with or made up of two or more countries: *The United Nations is an international organization.* **in•ter•na•tion•al** (in′tə rnash′ə nəl) *adjective.* —**internationally** *adverb.*

Internet A network of computers that connects people around the world. A user can get onto the Internet by means of a modem and by using a browser. **In•ter•net** (in′tər net) *noun.*

Internet service provider A business that provides subscribers to the Internet for a fee. It also offers services like e-mail, newsgroups, and all kinds of information.

interplanetary Having to do with or operating in the space between the planets in the solar system: *The movie was about an interplanetary flight from Earth to Mars and beyond.* **in•ter•plan•e•tar•y** (in′tər plan′i ter′ē) *adjective.*

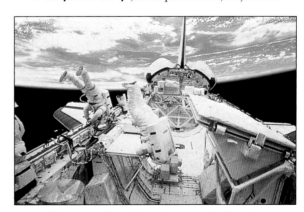

The space shuttle has been used to launch interplanetary probes.

PRONUNCIATION KEY:
| at | āpe | fär | câre | end | mē | it | īce | pierce | hot | ōld | sông | fôrk |
| oil | out | up | ūse | rüle | pull | tûrn | chin | sing | shop | thin | this | |

hw in white; zh in treasure. The symbol ə stands for the unstressed vowel sound in about, taken, pencil, lemon, and circus.

387

interpret 1. To explain the meaning of: *The teacher interpreted what the author meant in the poem.* 2. To change from one language to another; translate: *Since my friends couldn't speak Spanish, I interpreted what my cousin from Mexico was saying.* 3. To take as meaning; understand: *You can usually interpret a nod as meaning "yes."* 4. To perform so as to bring out the meaning: *The pianist interpreted the musical piece with great feeling.* **in·ter·pret** (in tûr′prit) *verb,* **interpreted, interpreting.**

interpretation 1. An explanation of the meaning of something: *The two students disagreed in their interpretation of the poem.* 2. A performance of a work of art that shows the performer's idea of its meaning. **in·ter·pre·ta·tion** (in tûr′pri tā′shən) *noun, plural* **interpretations.**

interrogate To question harshly and in great detail: *The detectives interrogated the suspect.* **in·ter·ro·gate** (in ter′ə gāt) *verb,* **interrogated, interrogating.** —**interrogation** *noun.*

interrogative Having the form of a question. *Adjective.*
○ A word or form used in asking a question. In the sentence "Who is it?" the word "who" is an interrogative. *Noun.*
in·ter·rog·a·tive (in′tə rog′ə tiv) *adjective; noun, plural* **interrogatives.**

interrogative sentence A sentence that asks a question. An example of an interrogative sentence is "Where are you going tonight?"

interrupt 1. To break in upon or stop a person who is acting or speaking: *Please do not interrupt me when I'm talking.* 2. To stop for a time; break off: *I interrupted my work to answer the telephone.* **in·ter·rupt** (in′tə rupt′) *verb,* **interrupted, interrupting.**

interruption 1. The state of being interrupted: *There was an interruption in the radio program for a special report.* 2. Something that interrupts: *Please make no interruption while the principal is addressing the class.* **in·ter·rup·tion** (in′tə rup′shən) *noun, plural* **interruptions.**

intersect 1. To divide by passing through or cutting across: *The river intersects the valley.* 2. To meet and cross each other: *The two roads intersect near our house.* **in·ter·sect** (in′tər sekt′) *verb,* **intersected, intersecting.**

intersection The place where two or more things meet and cross each other: *There was a traffic signal at the intersection of the two roads.* **in·ter·sec·tion** (in′tər sek′shən *or* in′tər sek′shən) *noun, plural* **intersections.**

interstate Between or among two or more states of the United States: *We traveled on an interstate highway.* **in·ter·state** (in′tər stāt′) *adjective.*

interval A time or space between two things: *There is an interval of 20 yards between each streetlight on our block.* **at intervals.** 1. With spaces between: *Signs were placed at intervals along the road.* 2. Now and then; occasionally: *We visited them at intervals during the summer.* **in·ter·val** (in′tər vəl) *noun, plural* **intervals.**

interview 1. A meeting in which people talk face to face: *I had an interview with the store manager for a summer job.* 2. A meeting in which someone, such as a reporter or television commentator, obtains information: *The magazine writer arranged for an interview with the scientist.* 3. A written or broadcast reproduction of the information obtained at such a meeting. *Noun.*
○ To have an interview with: *The mayor was interviewed about the growing traffic problem. Verb.*
in·te·rview (in′tər vū′) *noun, plural* **interviews;** *verb,* **interviewed, interviewing.**

By interviewing older people, we can learn much about our history.

intestine A long tube that extends down from the stomach. The intestine is part of the digestive system. It carries and digests food and stores waste products. The intestine is divided into the small intestine and the large intestine. **in·tes·tine** (in tes′tin) *noun, plural* **intestines.**

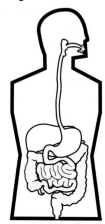

intestine

intimate **1.** Close and familiar; well-acquainted: *The two neighbors have been* **intimate** *friends for years.* **2.** Very personal; private: *Do you keep a diary of your* **intimate** *thoughts?* **in·ti·mate** (in′tə mit) *adjective.*

into **1.** To or toward the inside of: *We walked* **into** *the house.* **2.** So as to make contact with; against: *The child bumped* **into** *the door.* **3.** To the form or condition of: *The water turned* **into** *ice. You'll get* **into** *trouble if you do that.* **4.** Dividing: *8* **into** *16 is 2.* **in·to** (in′tü or in′tə) *preposition.*

intolerable Being very hard to put up with; unbearable: *That dog's barking has become* **intolerable.** **in·tol·er·a·ble** (in tol′ə rə bəl) *adjective.*

intolerant Not willing to accept or respect different opinions, practices, or people: *I used to be* **intolerant** *of people who disagreed with my religious beliefs.* **in·tol·er·ant** (in tol′ər ənt) *adjective.*

intoxicate **1.** To make drunk: *Drinking too much liquor will* **intoxicate** *a person.* **2.** To excite greatly: *The sights and sounds of the circus* **intoxicated** *the children.* **in·tox·i·cate** (in tok′si kā′t) *verb,* **intoxicated, intoxicating.**

intransitive verb A verb that cannot have a direct object. In the sentence "The clock stopped," "stopped" is an intransitive verb. **in·tran·si·tive verb** (in tran′si tiv).

intravenous Within or put into a vein: *The nurse gave the patient* **intravenous** *fluids.* **in·tra·ve·nous** (in′trə vē′nəs) *adjective.*

intricate Very involved or complicated; complex: *This* **intricate** *dance takes weeks of practice to learn.* **in·tri·cate** (in′tri kit) *adjective.*

intrigue To make curious or interested; fascinate: *The story of the sailor's adventures* **intrigued** *us all.* **in·trigue** (in trēg′) *verb,* **intrigued, intriguing.**

introduce **1.** To make known or acquainted: *My parents* **introduced** *me to the dinner guests.* **2.** To

The stone carvings around this door are very intricate.

bring into use, knowledge, or notice: *The potato was* **introduced** *to Europe from the New World.* **3.** To begin; start: *The lecturer* **introduced** *the poem with a short explanation.* **in·tro·duce** (in′trə düs′ or in′trə düs′) *verb,* **introduced, introducing.**

SYNONYMS

introduce, inaugurate, initiate, launch, originate
The senator introduced a new bill to the Senate. The end of the war inaugurated a period of prosperity. The mayor initiated a campaign to clean up graffiti. Our club will launch a drive to collect cans and bottles. The plan to feed the homeless of our city originated among the clergy.

introduction **1.** The act of introducing or the state of being introduced: *We shook hands after our* **introduction.** **2.** A beginning part that explains what is going to follow: *Many books have* **introductions.** **in·tro·duc·tion** (in′trə duk′shən) *noun, plural* **introductions.**

introductory Giving an introduction; preliminary: *The speaker's* **introductory** *remarks told us what the lecture would be about.* **in·tro·duc·to·ry** (in′trə duk′tə rē) *adjective.*

intrude To go into a place without being invited: *He doesn't like people who* **intrude** *when he's concentrating on work.* **in·trude** (in trüd′) *verb,* **intruded, intruding. intruder** *noun*

intuition The ability to guess about something correctly: *They relied on their* **intuition** *to help them find their way out of the cave.* **in·tu·i·tion** (in′tə wish′ən) *noun, plural* **intuitions.**

Inuit An Eskimo of North America. **I·nu·it** (in′ü it or in′ū it) *noun, plural* **Inuit** *or* **Inuits.**

invade **1.** To go or and attack in order to conquer: *Enemy troops* **invaded** *the country.* **2.** To go or break into something without being asked or wanted: *You* **invade** *my privacy when you read my mail without asking.* **in·vade** (in vād′) *verb,* **invaded, invading.**

invalid[1] A person who is not able to take care of himself or herself because of a sickness or injury: *A broken hip made our neighbor an* **invalid** *for several months.* **in·va·lid** (in′və lid) *noun, plural* **invalids.**

PRONUNCIATION KEY:

| at | āpe | fär | câre | end | mē | it | īce | pîerce | hot | ōld | sông | fôrk |
| oil | out | up | ūse | rüle | pull | tûrn | chin | sing | shop | thin | this | |

hw in white; zh in treasure. The symbol ə stands for the unstressed vowel sound in about, taken, pencil, lemon, and circus.

389

invalid² Not valid; no longer in force: *My bus pass is invalid on weekends.* **in·val·id** (in val′id) *adjective.*

invaluable Having a value or worth that is too great to be measured; extremely valuable: *My neighbor's invaluable advice helped me solve my problem.* **in·val·u·a·ble** (in val′ū ə bəl) *adjective.*

invasion 1. The entrance of an army into a region in order to conquer it: *That country has survived the several invasions.* 2. A breaking into something without being asked or wanted: *an invasion of privacy.* **in·va·sion** (in vā′zhən) *noun, plural* **invasions.**

invent 1. To make or think of for the first time; create: *Do you know who invented the phonograph?* 2. To make up: *I'm ashamed to say I invented an excuse for being late.* **in·vent** (in vent′) *verb,* **invented, inventing.**

WORD HISTORY

The word **invent** comes from a Latin word meaning "to come upon" or "find." At first the word *invent* was used to describe the finding of an answer, the solution to a problem, or the means to do something. This use led to our modern meaning "to make or think of for the first time."

invention 1. The act of inventing: *The invention of the airplane had a great effect on travel.* 2. Something that is invented: *Such inventions as the telephone and the computer have changed our way of life.* 3. A false or untrue story: *Their story about seeing a monster is nothing but an invention.* **in·ven·tion** (in ven′chən) *noun, plural* **inventions.**

inventive Good at thinking up new things; creative: *The inventive campers kept their food cool*

An **inventive** person created this water vehicle.

by putting it in a closed jar in the river. **in·ven·tive** (in ven′tiv) *adjective.*

inventor A person who invents: *Alexander Graham Bell was the inventor of the telephone.* **in·ven·tor** (in ven′tər) *noun, plural* **inventors.**

inventory 1. A detailed list of articles on hand: *The inventory showed all the goods the clothing store had on its shelves.* 2. The articles that are on such a list: *The store has a large inventory of sports equipment.* **in·ven·to·ry** (in′vən tôr′ē) *noun, plural* **inventories.**

invert 1. To turn upside down: *Invert the bank and try to shake some coins out.* 2. To reverse the order or position of: *If you invert the letters of the word "star," you have the word "rats."* **in·vert** (in vûrt′) *verb,* **inverted, inverting.**

invertebrate Having to do with an animal that does not have a backbone. *Adjective.*
○ An animal that does not have a backbone. Sponges, worms, lobsters, and insects are invertebrates. *Noun.*
in·ver·te·brate (in vûr′tə brit *or* in vûr′tə brāt′) *adjective; noun, plural* **invertebrates.**

invest 1. To use money to buy something that will make more money: *Some people invest their savings in stocks and bonds.* 2. To give or spend time or effort: *We invested many hours in planning the annual class trip.* **in·vest** (in vest′) *verb,* **invested, investing.**

investigate To look into carefully in order to find facts and get information: *The police are responsible for investigating crimes.* **in·ves·ti·gate** (in ves′ti gāt′) *verb,* **investigated, investigating.**

investigation The act of investigating: *The investigation of the moon has been accomplished by astronauts.* **in·ves·ti·ga·tion** (in ves′ti gā′shən) *noun, plural* **investigations.**

investment 1. The act of investing money, time, or effort: *They made a lot of money on that investment in real estate.* 2. The amount of money that is invested: *How large is your investment in your friend's business?* 3. Something in which money is invested: *That savings certificate was a good investment.* **in·vest·ment** (in vest′mənt) *noun, plural* **investments.**

investor A person or company that invests money. **in·ves·tor** (in ves′tər) *noun, plural* **investors.**

invisible Not able to be seen; not visible: *Oxygen is an invisible gas.* **in·vis·i·ble** (in viz′ə bəl) *adjective.*

invitation A written or spoken request to do something: *Have you received an **invitation** to the party?* **in•vi•ta•tion** (in′vi tā′shən) *noun, plural* **invitations.**

invite 1. To ask someone to go somewhere or to do something: *Please **invite** your friends to come with us to the concert.* 2. To ask for; request: *The teacher **invited** questions from the students on the arithmetic lesson.* 3. To risk causing: *To fail to do your homework is to **invite** trouble.* **in•vite** (in vīt′) *verb*, **invited, inviting.**

involuntary 1. Not done willingly or by choice; not voluntary: *I let out an **involuntary** cry when I accidentally stuck myself with the pin.* 2. Happening without a person's control: *Breathing is an **involuntary** action.* **in•vol•un•tar•y** (in vol′ən ter′ē) *adjective.*

involve 1. To have as a necessary part; include: *This job as a salesperson **involves** a great deal of traveling.* 2. To bring into difficulty: *I tried not to become **involved** in the argument.* 3. To take up completely; absorb: *We were **involved** all day in household chores.* **in•volve** (in volv′) *verb*, **involved, involving.**

inward Toward the inside or center: *The front gate opens **inward**. Adverb.*
○ Of or toward the inside: *I opened the heavy door with an **inward** push. Adjective.* **in•ward** (in′wərd) *adverb; adjective.*

inwardly 1. Toward the inside; inward. 2. In the mind; privately: *Although the tightrope walkers seemed calm, they were **inwardly** terrified.* **in•ward•ly** (in′wərd lē) *adverb.*

inwards Another spelling of the *adverb* inward: *Both the front door and the back door open **inwards.*** Look up inward for more information. **in•wards** (in′wərdz) *adverb.*

iodine 1. A chemical element that occurs as shiny gray crystals. It is found in seaweed and saltwater. Iodine is used in medicine and in photography. 2. A brown medicine that contains iodine. It is put on cuts to kill germs. **i•o•dine** (ī′ə dīn′ *or* ī′ə dēn′) *noun.*

ion An atom or group of atoms that has an electrical charge. **i•on** (ī′ən *or* ī′on) *noun, plural* **ions.**

-ion A suffix that means: 1. The act of: *Discussion means the act of discussing.* 2. The condition of being: *Confusion means the state of being confused.* The suffix *-tion* has the same meanings.

Iowa A state in the north-central United States. Its capital is Des Moines. **I•o•wa** (ī′ə wə) *noun.*

WORD HISTORY

The name **Iowa** comes from a name of a tribe of Native Americans who lived in what is now Iowa. Pioneers gave this name to the area's largest river. Later it was chosen as the name of the state.

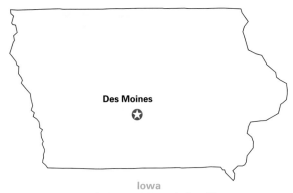

Iowa

U. S. Postal Abbreviation: **IA**
Capital: **Des Moines**
Population: **2,834,000**
Area: **56,290 sq. mi./145,790 sq. km**
State Nickname: **Hawkeye State**
State Bird: **Eastern Goldfinch**
State Flower: **Wild Rose**

Iran A country in southwestern Asia. This country was formerly known as Persia. **I•ran** (i ran′) *noun.*

Iraq A country in southwestern Asia. **I•raq** (i rak′) *noun.*

irate Very angry: *My mother was **irate** because I got home late.* **i•rate** (ī rāt′) *adjective.*

Ireland 1. An island west of Great Britain that is divided into two countries, Ireland and Northern Ireland. 2. The country called the Republic of Ireland that is in the southern part of this island. **Ire•land** (īr′lənd) *noun.*

iris 1. The round, colored part of the eye. The iris is between the cornea and the lens. It controls the amount of light that enters the eye. 2. A plant that has long leaves shaped like swords and large, showy flowers. **i•ris** (ī′ris) *noun, plural* **irises.**

Irish 1. The people of Ireland or their descendants in other countries. 2. A language spoken in Ireland. **I•rish** (ī′rish) *noun.*

PRONUNCIATION KEY:

| at | āpe | fär | cãre | end | mē | it | īce | pierce | hot | ōld | sông | fôrk |
| oil | out | up | ūse | rūle | pull | tûrn | chin | sing | shop | thin | this | |

hw in white; zh in treasure. The symbol ə stands for the unstressed vowel sound in about, taken, pencil, lemon, and circus.

391

Irish setter A hunting dog that originally came from Ireland. It has a coat of silky, reddish hair.

iron 1. A gray-white metal that is a chemical element. It is the most important metal and is used to make steel. It is magnetic and is a good conductor of heat and electricity. All plants and animals need iron. 2. Any of various tools made of iron or a similar metal: *The cowhand branded the cattle with a hot iron.* 3. An appliance with a flat surface that is heated and used to press or smooth cloth: *The laundry used a large iron to press shirts.* 4. irons. Heavy chains that are used to keep a prisoner from moving. *Noun.*
○ 1. Made of iron: *The lion's cage has iron bars.* 2. Strong and hard: *I have an iron will once I make up my mind to do something. Adjective.*
○ To press or smooth with a heated iron: *Can you iron your own shirt? Verb.*

• **to iron out.** To settle, adjust, or eliminate: *We talked for an hour and ironed out our differences. Verb.*

i•ron (ī′ərn) *noun, plural* **irons;** *adjective; verb,* **ironed, ironing.**

This iron pot holds heat for slow cooking.

irony A way of speaking or writing in which what a person says is the opposite of what he or she really means or feels. *To say "Oh, wonderful!" when you hear bad news is irony.* i•ro•ny (ī′rə nē) *noun.*

Iroquois A member of a confederation of American Indian tribes of New York. **Ir•o•quois** (ir′ə kwoi′) *noun, plural* **Iroquois.**

irrational Not logical or sensible: an irrational fear of snakes. ir•ra•tion•al (i rash′ə nəl) *adjective.* —**irrationality** *noun* —**irrationally** *adverb.*

irregular 1. Not following a pattern; unequal or uneven in length, shape, or spacing: *The irregular row of trees had gaps and clusters in it.* 2. Not smooth; bumpy or rugged: *The surface of the moon is irregular.* 3. Not going by a rule, custom, or habit; unusual: *It's irregular to call a teacher by his or her first name.* ir•reg•u•lar (i reg′yə lər) *adjective.*

irregularity 1. The quality of being irregular: *The irregularity of rainfall in this area makes it hard for farmers to know when to plant.* 2. Something that goes against a pattern, rule, or custom: *That lone hill is the only irregularity in the flat landscape.* ir•reg•u•lar•i•ty (i reg′yə lar′i tē) *noun, plural* **irregularities.**

irrelevant Having no connection to something of immediate concern; unimportant: *Your answer was irrelevant to the question I asked.* ir•rel•e•vant (i rel′ə vənt) *adjective.*

irresistible Not capable of being resisted or posed: *The delicious watermelon was irresistible to the children.* ir•re•sist•i•ble (ir′i zis′tə bəl) *adjective.*

irresponsible Not trustworthy or reliable; not responsible: *It would be irresponsible to borrow a book and not return it.* ir•re•spon•si•ble (ir′i spon′sə bəl) *adjective.*

irreversible Not able to be changed or reversed: *Our teacher's decision to have a test was irreversible.* ir•re•vers•i•ble (ir′i vûr′sə bəl) *adjective.*

irrigate To supply land with water through streams, channels, or pipes: *The farmer irrigated the dry land so that crops could be grown.* ir•ri•gate (ir′i gāt′) *verb,* **irrigated, irrigating.**

irrigation The act of supplying land with water: *Irrigation made it possible for crops to grow in the desert.* ir•ri•ga•tion (ir′i gā′shən) *noun.*

Through irrigation, crops can be grown in even the driest places.

irritable Easily irritated; grumpy: *Hot weather makes some people uncomfortable and irritable.* ir•ri•ta•ble (ir′ə tə bəl) *adjective.*

irritate 1. To make angry or impatient, especially over a small thing: *Your constant teasing irritates me.* 2. To make sore or sensitive: *The smoke irritated my eyes.* **ir·ri·tate** (ir′i tāt′) *verb,* **irritated, irritating.** —**irritation** *noun.*

is A form of the present tense of *be* that is used with *he, she, it,* or the name of a person, place, or thing: *He is four years old. Who is at the door?* **is** (iz) *verb.*

-ish A suffix that means: 1. Of or having to do with: *Polish means of or having to do with Poland.* 2. Like: *Childish means like a child.* 3. Somewhat: *Yellowish means somewhat yellow.*

Islam A religion that is based on the teachings of Muhammad. Its sacred book is the Koran, and its followers are known as Muslims. **Is·lam** (is läm′ *or* is′läm) *noun.* **Islamic** *adjective.*

island 1. A body of land that is completely surrounded by water. An island is smaller than a continent. Ireland is an island. 2. Something that looks like an island: *There was an island of floating ice in the middle of the lake.* **is·land** (ī′lənd) *noun, plural* **islands.**

ISLANDS

Islands are found in almost every large body of water, and in many small ones, too. Some of the largest are:

Greenland: The largest island, Greenland is located in the North Atlantic. It covers an area of 840,000 square miles and has a population of around 50,000.

New Guinea: Located in the Pacific Ocean north of Australia, it has an area of 306,000 square miles.

Borneo: Also located in the Pacific, it covers an area of 290,012 square miles.

Madagascar: Located in the Indian Ocean off the east coast of Africa, Madagascar has an area of 226,657 square miles.

There are also a number of nations that consist entirely of islands, including Japan and New Zealand. Indonesia consists of over 17,000 islands. The nations of Iceland, Cyprus, and Jamaica are basically single islands.

---

islander A person who was born or is living on an island. **i·sland·er** (ī′lən dər) *noun, plural* **islanders.**

isle An island. Isles are usually small islands. Other words that sound like this are **aisle** and **I'll.** **isle** (īl) *noun, plural* **isles.**

islet A little island. Another word that sounds like this is **eyelet.** **is·let** (ī′lit) *noun, plural* **islets.**

isn't Shortened form of "is not": *Our dog isn't a puppy anymore.* **is·n't** (iz′ənt) *contraction.*

isolate To place or set apart; separate from others: *I was isolated from my sister and brother when I had the mumps so that they wouldn't get it.* **i·so·late** (ī′sə lāt′) *verb,* **isolated, isolating.**

isosceles triangle A triangle with two sides of equal length. **i·sos·ce·les triangle** (ī sos′ə lēz).

ISP Abbreviation for Internet service provider.

Israel A country in the Middle East. **Is·ra·el** (iz′rē əl *or* iz′rā əl) *noun.*

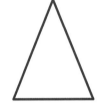
isosceles triangle

Israeli A person born in or a citizen of Israel. *Noun.* ○ Having to do with Israel or the people of Israel. *Adjective.* **Isr·ae·li** (iz rā′lē) *noun, plural* **Israelis;** *adjective.*

issue 1. The act of sending or giving out: *I was in charge of the issue of tents to all the campers.* 2. Something that is sent or given out: *Do you have the latest issue of this magazine?* 3. A subject that is being discussed or considered: *The student council debated the issue of safety in the hallways. Noun.* ○ To send or give out: *The Department of the Treasury issues paper money and coins. Verb.* **is·sue** (ish′ü) *noun, plural* **issues;** *verb,* **issued, issuing.**

-ist A suffix that means: 1. A person who does or makes something: *Tourist means a person who tours. Novelist means a person who writes novels.* 2. A person who is skilled in or works at something: *Biologist means a person who is skilled in biology. Machinist means a person who is skilled in using machinery.* 3. A person who

PRONUNCIATION KEY:
at   āpe   fär   câre   end   mē   it   īce   pîerce   hot   ōld   sông   fôrk
oil   out   up   ūse   rüle   pull   tûrn   chin   sing   shop   thin   this
hw in white; zh in treasure. The symbol ə stands for the unstressed vowel sound in about, taken, pencil, lemon, and circus.   393

supports or is in favor of: *Socialist means a person who is in favor of socialism.*

isthmus A narrow strip of land that connects two larger land areas. An isthmus has water on two sides. North America and South America are connected by an isthmus. **isth·mus** (is′məs) *noun, plural* **isthmuses.**

it 1. A thing, person, or situation that is being talked about: *My cousin threw the ball to me and I caught it.* 2. It is used with some verbs that show an action or condition: *It isn't very cold this morning. Pronoun.*
○ In certain children's games, the person who has to do something special: I*n playing tag, the person who is it has to chase the other players. Noun.*
it (it) *pronoun; noun.*

Italian 1. A person born in or a citizen of Italy. 2. The language spoken in Italy. *Noun.*
○ Of or having to do with Italy, its people, or their language. *Adjective.*
I·tal·ian (i tal′yən) *noun, plural* **Italians;** *adjective.*

italic Of or having to do with a style of type whose letters slant to the right: *This sentence is printed in italic type. Adjective.*
○ italics. Italic type: *Print the sentence in italics. Noun.*
i·tal·ic (i tal′ik) *adjective; noun, plural* **italics.**

italicize To print in italics. **i·tal·i·cize** (i tal′ə sīz′) *verb,* **italicized, italicizing.**

Italy A country in southern Europe. **It·a·ly** (it′ə lē) *noun.*

itch 1. A tickling or stinging feeling in the skin. An itch is relieved by scratching or rubbing. 2. A restless, uneasy feeling or longing: *Some people have an itch to travel around the world. Noun.*
○ 1. To have or cause a tickling or stinging feeling in the skin: *The rash on my hand itches.* 2. To have a restless, uneasy feeling or desire: *The bully was itching for a fight. Verb.*
itch (ich) *noun, plural* itches; *verb,* **itched, itching.**

item 1. A single thing in a group or list: *The shopping list has ten items on it.* 2. A bit of news: *There was an item in the newspaper about the football team's victory.* **i·tem** (ī′təm) *noun, plural* **items.**

itemize To make a list of each item in a group: *If you itemize all your expenses, you can make up a budget.* **i·tem·ize** (ī′tə mīz′) *verb,* **itemized, itemizing.**

it'll Shortened form of "it will": *It'll soon be spring. It'll take me an hour to get home.* **it'll** (it′əl) *contraction.*

its Of, belonging to, or having to do with it: *The last volume of the encyclopedia is not in its proper place.*
Another word that sounds like this is **it's.**
its (its) *adjective.*

it's 1. Shortened form of "it is": *It's cold out today.* 2. Shortened form of "it has": *It's been nice to see you.*
Another word that sounds like this is **its.**
it's (its) *contraction.*

itself Its own self: *The cat washed itself. The yard is full of weeds, but the house itself is in good condition.* **it·self** (it self′) *pronoun.*

-ity A suffix that means the state or quality of being: *The word* **finality** *means the state or quality of being final.*

IV *or* **I.V.** An abbreviation of the word **intravenous.** **IV** (i′vē′)

-ive A suffix that means doing or tending to do something: *The word* **destructive** *means tending to destroy.*

I've Shortened form of "I have": *I've been home all day.* **I've** (īv) *contraction.*

ivory 1. A smooth, hard, white substance. It forms the tusks of elephants, walruses, and certain other animals. 2. A creamy white color. *Noun.*
○ 1. Made of or like ivory: *The piano has ivory keys.* 2. Having the color ivory: *The room was ivory with red trim. Adjective.*
i·vo·ry (ī′və rē) *noun, plural* **ivories;** *adjective.*

Piano keys used to be made of real ivory.

Ivory Coast A country in western Africa.

ivy 1. A vine with shiny, evergreen leaves. Some kinds of ivy climb up walls or grow along the ground. 2. Any plant that climbs up walls or grows along the ground. **i·vy** (ī′vē) *noun, plural* **ivies.**

SPELLING HINTS

The letter J has only one sound, as in job and jump, but that sound is also commonly made by:

dge as in badge, judge, and ridge; g, especially when it appears before *e*, *i*, or *y*, as in gem, gist, and stingy;

and less often by:

d as in graduate;
di as in soldier;
dj, especially in words with *ad* as in adjective and adjourn;

and rarely by:

gg as in exaggerate.

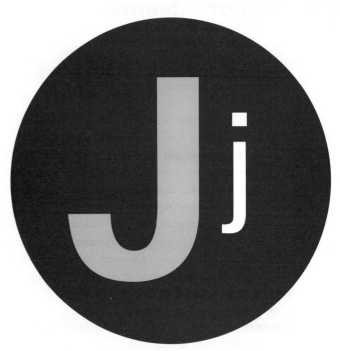

j, J The tenth letter of the alphabet. **j, J** (jā) *noun, plural* **j's, J's.**

jab To poke with something pointed: *I accidentally jabbed my finger with a pin while I was sewing. Verb.*

○ A poke with something pointed: *Please give me a jab if I start to fall asleep during the movie. Noun.* **jab** (jab) *verb,* **jabbed, jabbing;** *noun, plural* **jabs.**

jack 1. A tool that is used for lifting heavy objects a short distance above the ground: *The mechanic used a jack to raise the front end of the car in order to change the flat tire.* 2. A playing card with a picture of a young man on it. 3. **jacks.** A game that is played with a small rubber ball and little pieces of metal that are also called jacks. A player has to pick up a number of the metal jacks while bouncing and catching the ball with the same hand. *Noun.*

○ To lift with a jack: *The mechanic jacked the car up so he could work on it. Verb.* **jack** (jak) *noun, plural* **jacks;** *verb,* **jacked, jacking.**

WORD HISTORY

The word jack comes from the man's name Jack. Tools and other objects are often named after personal names. This same word *jack* is also found in the words *jack-in-the-box, jackknife, jack-o'-lantern, jackpot,* and *jackrabbit.*

jackal An animal that looks like a small dog. A jackal has a pointed face, a bushy tail, and ears that point straight up. Jackals live on plains in Africa and Asia. They eat plants, small animals, and the remains of other animals' prey. **jack·al** (jak'əl) *noun, plural* **jackals.**

jacket 1. A short coat: *Our team wears jackets with the name of the team across the back.* 2. An outer covering for a record or book: *On the back of this book jacket there is a picture of the author.* **jack·et** (jak'it) *noun, plural* **jackets.**

jack-in-the-box A toy that is made up of a box with a doll that pops out when the lid is opened. **jack-in-the-box** (jak' in <u>th</u>ə boks') *noun, plural* **jack-in-the-boxes.**

jackknife 1. A large pocketknife. 2. A kind of dive in which a diver bends double while in the air and then straightens out before entering the water. *Noun.*

○ To bend double: *The truck jackknifed on the tight curve because it was going too fast. Verb.* **jack·knife** (jak'nīf') *noun, plural* **jackknives** (jak'nīvz'); *verb,* **jackknifed, jackknifing.**

jack-o'-lantern A pumpkin that has been hollowed out and carved to look

Jack-o'-lanterns **are commonly used at Halloween.**

395

like a face. Jack-o'-lanterns are used at Halloween as lanterns or decorations. **jack-o'-lan·tern** (jak'ə lan'tərn) *noun, plural* **jack-o'-lanterns.**

jackpot The largest prize in a game or contest: *That game show has a jackpot of $100,000.*

• **to hit the jackpot. 1.** To win a jackpot: *Someone from our town hit the jackpot on a television game show.* **2.** To have a great success or unexpected good fortune: *My parents' friends hit the jackpot with their new business.* **jack·pot** (jak'pot') *noun, plural* **jackpots.**

jackrabbit A large hare of western North America that has very long ears and strong back legs for leaping. **jack·rab·bit** (jak'rab'it) *noun, plural* **jackrabbits.**

Jacuzzi A trademark for a large bathtub that has underwater jets. **Ja·cuz·zi** (jə kü'zē) *noun, plural* **Jacuzzis.**

jade A hard, green stone that is used for jewelry and carved ornaments. **jade** (jād) *noun, plural* **jades.**

jagged Having sharp points that stick out: *Some eagles build nests on jagged cliffs.* **jag·ged** (jag'id) *adjective.*

jaguar A large animal that belongs to the cat family. The short fur of a jaguar is golden and is marked with black rings with spots in their centers. **jag·uar** (jag'wär) *noun.*

The **jaguar** is found in Mexico, Central America, and South America.

jail A building where people who are waiting for a trial or who have been found guilty of breaking the law are kept; prison. *Noun.*

○ To put or keep in a jail: *The police jailed the people they caught robbing the bank.* Verb. **jail** (jāl) *noun, plural* **jails;** *verb,* **jailed, jailing.**

jailbird A prisoner in a jail. This is an informal expression. **jail·bird** (jāl'bûrd') *noun, plural* **jailbirds.**

jam¹ 1. To press or squeeze into a tight space: *The traveler tried to jam too many clothes into one small suitcase. People jammed onto the bus to get to work.* **2.** To fill or block completely: *Cars jammed the road to the beach. The store was jammed with customers.* **3.** To become or cause to become stuck so as not to work: *The rifle jammed when the soldier tried to fire it. Rust and dirt jammed the lock on the gate.* **4.** To push hard: *The driver jammed on the brakes to stop the car.* **5.** To bruise by crushing: *I jammed my hand when I closed the drawer on it.* **6.** To play music in a group: *The band jammed into the wee hours of the morning. Verb.*

○ **1.** A mass of people or things so crowded together that it is difficult to move: *We were three hours late because we got stuck in a traffic jam in the city.* **2.** A difficult situation: *The tourists were in a real jam when the police found drugs and the stolen money in their car.* **3.** A meeting in which musicians play together without planning; jam session. *Noun.*

• **jam session.** A meeting during which musicians play together without having planned to. **jam** (jam) *verb,* **jammed, jamming;** *noun, plural* **jams.**

jam² A sweet food made by boiling fruit and sugar together until it is thick. Jam is used as a spread on bread or other foods. **jam** (jam) *noun, plural* **jams.**

Jamaica An island country in the Caribbean Sea. **Ja·mai·ca** (jə mā'kə) *noun.*

Jan. An abbreviation for **January.**

jangle 1. To make or cause to make a harsh or unpleasant sound: *The metal blinds jangled in the wind. The janitor jangled a bunch of keys.* **2.** To irritate or upset: *The noise from the party at my neighbor's apartment jangled my nerves and made it hard for me to concentrate. Verb.*

○ A harsh or unpleasant sound: *Everything fell from the shelf with a loud jangle. Noun.* **jan·gle** (jang'gəl) *verb,* **jangled, jangling;** *noun, plural* **jangles.**

janitor A person whose job is to take care of and clean a building. **jan·i·tor** (jan'i tər) *noun, plural* **janitors.**

January The first month of the year. January has thirty-one days. **Jan•u•ar•y** (jan′ū er′ē) *noun.*

WORD HISTORY

The Romans named January after Janus, their god of doors and gates. A holiday in his honor was held during this month. Janus was shown with two faces that looked in opposite directions. His holiday was probably held in January because this month looks in two directions, back on the year that has passed and ahead to the year to come.

Japan An island country in the Pacific Ocean. It is off the eastern coast of Asia. **Ja•pan** (jə pan′) *noun.*

Japanese 1. A person who was born in or is a citizen of Japan. 2. The language of Japan. *Noun.*
○ Having to do with Japan, its people, or their language. *Adjective.*
Jap•a•nese (jap′ə nēz′ *or* jap′ə nēs′) *noun, plural* **Japanese;** *adjective.*

Japanese beetle A beetle that came to the United States from Asia. Its head parts are blue-green and its wings are copper colored. The larvae feed on roots, and the adults eat leaves and flowers and can be serious pests.

Peanut butter, pickles, and jelly often come in jars.

jar¹ 1. A container that has a wide mouth. A jar is usually made out of glass, plastic, or pottery. 2. The amount that a jar will hold: *This recipe calls for a small jar of olives.* **jar** (jär) *noun, plural* **jars.**

jar² 1. To shake or vibrate: *The explosion jarred the building.* 2. To have a harsh, unpleasant effect on: *The sudden clatter of dishes jarred my nerves. Verb.*

○ A shake or sudden movement; shock: *We wrapped the glass bowl well so all the jars and bumps it would get in the mail would not break it. Noun.*
jar (jär) *verb,* **jarred, jarring;** *noun, plural* **jars.**

jargon Words used by members of a group that share a specific interest: *Computer jargon is sometimes hard to understand if you don't use computers.* **jar•gon** (jär′gən) *noun.*

jaundice A disease of the liver that makes the skin turn yellow. **jaun•dice** (jôn′dis) *noun.*

jaundiced Having an unhealthy, yellowish color of the skin caused by jaundice. **jaun•diced** (jôn′dist) *adjective.*

jaunt A short trip: *Let's go for a jaunt in the country.* **jaunt** (jônt) *noun, plural* **jaunts.**

jaunty Carefree and confident: *That athlete has a jaunty walk.* **jaun•ty** (jôn′tē) *adjective,* **jauntier, jauntiest.**

javelin 1. A light spear that was once used as a weapon. 2. A long, thin spear of metal that is thrown in athletic contests. The athlete who throws it the farthest wins. **jave•lin** (jav′lin) *noun, plural* **javelins.**

jaw 1. The lower or upper bony part of the mouth. The jaws give shape to the mouth and hold the teeth in place. 2. A similar mouth part or parts in insects and other animals without backbones. 3. One of two parts of a tool that can be closed to grasp or hold something: *The jaws of this vise hold the piece of wood tight while I sand it.* **jaw** (jô) *noun, plural* **jaws.**

jawbone A bone of the jaw, especially the lower jaw: *He wiggled his jawbone back and forth.* **jaw•bone** (jô′bōn′) *noun, plural* **jawbones.**

jay Any of various noisy, brightly colored birds that belong to the crow family. **jay** (jā) *noun, plural* **jays.**

Some jays have crests on their heads.

PRONUNCIATION KEY:
at   āpe   fär   câre   end   mē   it   īce   pîerce   hot   ōld   sông   fôrk
oil   out   up   ūse   rüle   pull   tûrn   chin   sing   shop   thin   this
hw in white; zh in treasure. The symbol ə stands for the unstressed vowel sound in about, taken, pencil, lemon, and circus.

397

jaywalk To cross the street without paying attention to the traffic lights or laws. **jay·walk** (jā'wôk') verb, **jaywalked, jaywalking.**

jazz Music that has strong rhythm and accented notes that fall in unexpected places. Jazz was originated by American blacks in the late nineteenth century. Musicians frequently add notes of their own as they play a jazz piece. **jazz** (jaz) noun.

jealous 1. Fearful of losing someone's love to another person: *A young child will often be jealous of a new baby in the family.* 2. Having envy of a person, or what a person has or can do: *I used to be jealous of my friend's ability to play football well.* **jeal·ous** (jel'əs) adjective.

jealousy A jealous feeling: *My jealousy over my friend's new bicycle was silly.* **jeal·ous·y** (jel'ə sē) noun, plural **jealousies.**

jeans Pants made from denim or similar strong cloth and worn for work or informal dress: *I wore old jeans while cleaning the house.* **jeans** (jēnz) plural noun.

jeep A small, powerful automobile that moves easily over poor, rough roads. The jeep was originally used by soldiers. **jeep** (jēp) noun, plural **jeeps.**

jelly A soft, firm food. The most common kind of jelly is made from fruit juice boiled with sugar and is eaten with bread, toast, muffins, and other foods: *Peanut butter and jelly sandwiches are my favorite. Noun.*
○ To make into or become jelly: *My neighbor jellies plums every fall. Verb.*
jel·ly (jel'ē) noun, plural **jellies;** verb, **jellied, jellying.**

jellyfish A sea animal with a body that is soft and firm like jelly and has the shape of an umbrella. There are many long, slender tentacles hanging down from this body. The jellyfish uses its tentacles to sting its prey and move the prey to its mouth. **jel·ly·fish** (jel'ē fish') noun, plural **jellyfish** or **jellyfishes.**

jeopardy The danger of loss, injury, or death: *Firefighters are in jeopardy when they enter burning buildings.* **jeop·ar·dy** (jep'ər dē) noun.

jerk 1. A sudden, sharp pull or twist; start: *The worker gave the rope a jerk. The train moved forward with a violent jerk.* 2. An annoying person. *Noun.*
○ To move with a sudden, sharp motion: *I jerked my head around when I heard the loud noise. The fishing rod jerked when the fish bit the bait. Verb.* **jerk** (jûrk) noun, plural **jerks;** verb, **jerked, jerking.** —**jerky** adjective.

SYNONYMS

jerk, snap, tug, wrench, yank
I jerked my hand away from the hot stove. The fish snapped at the bait. The baby tugged the dog's tail. The door was stuck and I had to wrench it open. No one dared to yank the lion's tail that hung outside his cage.

---

jerkin A short, tight jacket that does not have sleeves. Jerkins were worn by men and boys in the 1500s and 1600s. **jer·kin** (jûr'kin) noun, plural **jerkins.**

jerky Meat that has been dried so it can be eaten at a later time. **jer·ky** (jûr'kē) noun.

jersey 1. A cloth that is knitted by machine out of wool, cotton, or other materials. Jersey is very soft and is used to make clothing. 2. A sweater or shirt made out of this cloth. It is pulled on over the head. **jer·sey** (jûr'zē) noun, plural **jerseys.**

jest A playful joke; prank: *I meant my remark as a jest, and I'm sorry it hurt your feelings. Noun.*
○ To speak or act in a playful way: *You must be jesting; I can't believe what you're saying is true. Verb.*
jest (jest) noun, plural **jests;** verb, **jested, jesting.**

jester An entertainer at court in the Middle Ages; court jester. **jest·er** (jes'tər) noun, plural **jesters.**

Jesus The founder of the Christian religion. He was born in about 4 B.C. and died in about 29 A.D. He is also called Christ or Jesus Christ. **Je·sus** (jē'zəs).

jet 1. A stream of liquid, gas, or vapor that comes with force from a small opening: *This fountain is a jet of water that rises fifty feet into the air.* 2. An aircraft that is driven by a stream of hot gas: *When we went to Puerto Rico, we flew on a jet. Noun.*
○ To shoot forth in a stream; spurt: *Water jetted onto the street from the break in the water pipe. Verb.*
jet (jet) noun, plural **jets;** verb, **jetted, jetting.**

jet airplane An airplane driven by jet engines. It is also called a *jet plane.*

jet engine An engine that is driven by a stream of gases.

jet lag The feeling of extreme tiredness people feel after traveling a long distance through different time zones in an airplane: *It took us two days to recover from jet lag.*

jet-propelled Driven by a stream or jet of hot gas: *The jet-propelled rocket was launched into an orbit around the earth.* **jet-pro·pelled** (jet′prə peld′) *adjective.*

jet propulsion A method of moving an airplane, rocket, or other vehicle in one direction by using a stream or jet of hot gas forced out in the opposite direction.

jet stream A very strong wind current that usually moves from west to east.

jettison To throw away something that is no longer useful: *The air balloon jettisoned some of its sand bags so that it could rise higher.* **jet·ti·son** (jet′ə sən) *verb*, **jettisoned, jettisoning.**

jetty 1. A wall that is built out into a body of water. Jetties are used to control the flow of a river or to protect the coast from breaking waves. 2. A platform where boats and ships can dock; wharf. **jet·ty** (jet′ē) *noun, plural* **jetties.**

Jetties can be built of rocks, wood, concrete, or steel.

Jew 1. A person who is descended from the ancient Hebrews. 2. A person whose religion is Judaism. **Jew** (jü) *noun, plural* **Jews.**

jewel 1. A precious stone; gem. Jewels are used in rings and bracelets because of their beauty. They are also used in watches or machines because they are very hard and last a long time. 2. A valuable necklace, pin, bracelet, or other ornament that is decorated with precious stones. 3. A person or thing that has great value or excellence: *That battleship is the jewel of the navy.* **jew·el** (jü′əl) *noun, plural* **jewels.**

jeweler A person who makes, repairs, or sells jewelry or watches. **jew·el·er** (jü′ə lər) *noun, plural* **jewelers.**

jewelry Necklaces, pins, bracelets, or other ornaments. **jew·el·ry** (jü′əl rē) *noun.*

Jewish Having to do with Jews, their religion, or their culture. **Jew·ish** (jü′ish) *adjective.*

jib A sail in the shape of a triangle that is set in front of the mast and is attached to the bow. **jib** (jib) *noun, plural* **jibs.**

Jewelry is often decorated with precious stones.

jet engine

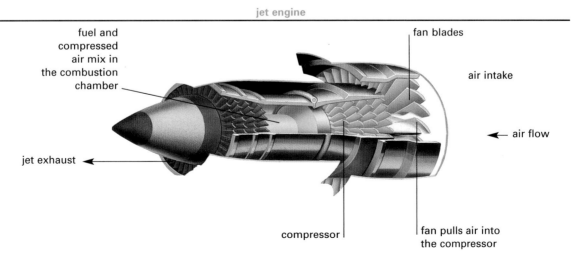

fuel and compressed air mix in the combustion chamber

fan blades

air intake

air flow

jet exhaust

compressor

fan pulls air into the compressor

PRONUNCIATION KEY:

| at | āpe | fär | câre | end | mē | it | īce | pîerce | hot | ōld | sông | fôrk |
| oil | out | up | ūse | rüle | pull | tûrn | chin | sing | shop | thin | this | |

hw in white; zh in treasure. The symbol ə stands for the unstressed vowel sound in about, taken, pencil, lemon, and circus.

399

jiffy A very short time; moment: *Wait for me; I'll be there in a jiffy.* **jif·fy** (jif′ē) *noun.*

jig 1. A fast, lively dance. 2. The music for this dance: *The bagpipes played a jig, and everyone danced. Noun.*

○ 1. To dance a jig. 2. To move with a rapid jerking or bobbing motion: *As I watched, the float on my fishing line jigged up and down. Verb.*

• **the jig is up.** Someone has caught on to a secret that someone else has been keeping and is going to reveal it: *OK, the jig is up. I know you've been hiding presents around the house.*

jig (jig) *noun, plural* **jigs**; *verb,* **jigged, jigging.**

jigsaw A saw that has a narrow blade set vertically in a frame. A jigsaw is used to cut along wavy or curved lines. **jig·saw** (jig′sô′) *noun, plural* **jigsaws.**

jigsaw puzzle A puzzle made up of small pieces that have irregular shapes and can be fitted together to make a picture.

jingle To make or cause to make a tinkling or ringing sound: *Whenever the kitten moved, the bell on its collar jingled. The child shook the bank to jingle the coins inside. Verb.*

○ 1. A tinkling or ringing sound: *Whenever the cowhands walked you could hear the jingle of their spurs.* 2. A light, short tune that is easy to remember, usually used in commercials: *I can't stop humming a new jingle I've heard on the radio. Noun.*

jin·gle (jing′gəl) *verb,* **jingled, jingling**; *noun, plural* **jingles.**

jinx 1. A person or thing that is believed to bring bad luck. 2. A spell of bad luck: *There seems to be a jinx on this garden, because nothing will grow. Noun.*

○ To bring or try to bring bad luck to: *Some people think a black cat will jinx you if it walks in front of you. Verb.*

jinx (jingks) *noun, plural* **jinxes**; *verb,* **jinxed, jinxing.**

job 1. A position of work; employment: *Did you get a job in the grocery store for the summer?* 2. Something that has to be done; piece of work: *It's my job to feed and walk the dog. The repair job on the television set will cost fifty dollars.* **job** (job) *noun, plural* **jobs.**

jockey A person who rides horses in races. **jock·ey** (jok′ē) *noun, plural* **jockeys.**

A **jockey** is usually small so that his horse will not have to carry too much weight.

jog To run or move at a slow, steady pace, often as exercise: *My parents jog in the park every morning before work. Verb.*

○ A slow, steady pace: *The runner moved at a jog. Noun.*

jog (jog) *verb,* **jogged, jogging**; *noun, plural* **jogs.**

join 1. To put or fasten together so as to become one: *Tie a knot to join the two ends of the rope. We all joined hands and formed a circle.* 2. To come together or come together with: *Where do the two rivers join? This road joins the main highway just ahead.* 3. To become a member of: *Two students who are graduating from high school plan to join the army.* 4. To come into the company of; get together with: *Our friends at the other table joined us after they had finished eating.* 5. To take part with others: *Many people joined in singing the old songs.*

• **to join up.** To enlist in a military group: *They're joining up after high school because the Navy will help pay for their college education.*

join (join) *verb,* **joined, joining.**

joint 1. The place or part where two or more bones meet or come together. The knee and the elbow are joints. Most joints act like hinges, allowing the bones to move in one or more directions. 2. The part or space between two joints: *The ring was stuck on the middle joint of my finger.* 3. The place or part where any two or more things meet or come together: *The old chair was very unsteady because the joint in one of its legs was coming loose.* 4. A cheap place to eat or spend the night: *Let's have a snack at the joint on the corner. Noun.*

○ Belonging to or done by two or more people: *You and I have a **joint** responsibility to feed and walk the dog after school. My parents are **joint** owners of a travel agency. Adjective.*
joint (joint) *noun, plural* **joints;** *adjective.*

joke Something that is said or done to make people laugh: *The child started to tell a **joke** but forgot the funny line at the end. My parents pretended to forget my birthday as a **joke**. Noun.*
○ To tell or make jokes: *At the party everyone laughed and **joked**. Verb.*
joke (jōk) *noun, plural* **jokes;** *verb,* **joked, joking.**

jolly Full of fun; merry and cheerful: *The person who was dressed as a clown was very **jolly**. We sat around the campfire singing songs and having a **jolly** time.* **jol·ly** (jol′ē) *adjective,* **jollier, jolliest.**

The young people are having a jolly time trying to knock each other off the log.

jolt To move or cause to move with a sudden, rough jerk or jerks: *The jeep **jolted** along the dirt road. When the car behind us hit our car, we were **jolted** out of our seats. Verb.*
○ **1.** A jerk or jar: *The bus stopped with a **jolt**.* **2.** An unpleasant surprise; shock: *The bad news gave us quite a **jolt**. Noun.*
jolt (jōlt) *verb,* **jolted, jolting;** *noun, plural* **jolts.**

jonquil A fragrant yellow flower that is a kind of daffodil. A jonquil has a short center petal shaped like a cup. Jonquils grow from bulbs: *The flower garden in the park is full of **jonquils** and tulips in the spring.* **jon·quil** (jong′kwəl) *noun, plural* **jonquils.**

Jordan A country in the Middle East. **Jor·dan** (jôr′dən) *noun.*

jostle To bump or push roughly: *A group of people at the stage door **jostled** one another to get a chance to meet the actors after the show. Verb.*
○ A bump or push: *I accidentally gave the person next to me a **jostle** as I tried to get off the bus. Noun.*
jos·tle (jos′əl) *verb,* **jostled, jostling;** *noun, plural* **jostles.**

jot To write quickly or briefly: *I always keep a pad by the telephone so I can **jot** down messages.* **jot** (jot) *verb,* **jotted, jotting.**

journal **1.** A regular record or account. A diary is one kind of journal: *Each student was told to keep a **journal** during the summer. The scientist entered the results of the experiments in a **journal**.* **2.** A magazine or newspaper: *The medical **journal** published a report on the doctor's most recent discoveries.* **jour·nal** (jûr′nəl) *noun, plural* **journals.**

journalism The writing and publishing of articles on news and opinions in newspapers, magazines, and similar publications. **jour·nal·ism** (jûr′nə liz′əm) *noun.*

journalist A writer who works for a newspaper or magazine. **jour·nal·ist** (jûr′nə list) *noun, plural* **journalists.**

journey A long trip: *The Pilgrims crossed the Atlantic on their **journey** to the New World. Noun.*
○ To make a trip; travel: *My cousin wants to **journey** through Africa after graduating from college. Verb.*
jour·ney (jûr′nē) *noun, plural* **journeys;** *verb,* **journeyed, journeying.**

joust A formal contest or combat in the Middle Ages between two knights on horseback. Each knight was armed with a lance and wore armor. *Noun.*
○ To fight or take part in a joust: *The two knights **jousted** to win the favor of the royal couple. Verb.*
joust (joust) *noun, plural* **jousts;** *verb,* **jousted, jousting.**

jovial Full of fun; merry; jolly: *I'm always in a **jovial** mood on my birthday.* **jo·vi·al** (jō′vē əl) *adjective.*

jowl Heavy, loose flesh hanging from or under the lower jaw. **jowl** (joul) *noun, plural* **jowls.**

PRONUNCIATION KEY:
at āpe fär câre end mē it īce pierce hot ōld sông fôrk
oil out up ūse rūle pull tûrn chin sing shop thin this
hw in white; zh in treasure. The symbol ə stands for the unstressed vowel sound in about, taken, pencil, lemon, and circus.

401

joy 1. A strong feeling of happiness or delight: *The young children jumped with joy when their grandparents arrived for a visit.* 2. A person or thing that causes a strong feeling of happiness: *The friendly, helpful children were a joy to their neighbors.* **joy** (joi) *noun, plural* **joys.**

joyful Feeling, showing, or causing great happiness; glad: *The parents had joyful looks on their faces when they saw that their child was not hurt in the accident. The couple's wedding anniversary was a joyful occasion.* **joy·ful** (joi′fəl) *adjective.*

joyous Joyful or happy: *The wedding was a joyous occasion for the families of the bride and groom.* **joy·ous** (joi′əs) *adjective.* —**joyously** *adverb.*

joystick or **joy stick** A control shaped like a rod that is attached to some computers. The joystick controls figures on the monitor. **joy·stick** (joi′stik′) *noun, plural* **joysticks.**

jr. or **Jr.** An abbreviation for **junior.**

jubilant Feeling or showing great joy: *The players were jubilant over their victory.* **ju·bi·lant** (jü′bə lənt) *adjective.*

Judaism The religion of the Jews. It is based chiefly on a belief in one God and the teachings of the Hebrew Bible. **Ju·da·ism** (jü′dē iz′əm) *noun.*

judge 1. To agree on a verdict or make a decision about a case in a court of law: *The court could not judge the case properly because of a lack of evidence.* 2. To settle or decide: *Three men and three women have been chosen to judge the dog show.* 3. To form an opinion of: *Judge the movie by seeing it yourself; don't listen to what other people say about it.* 4. To find something wrong with: *Don't be quick to judge other people. Verb.* ○ 1. A person who decides on questions and disagreements in a court of law. A judge can be chosen by a government official or elected by the voters. 2. A person who decides the winner in a contest or dispute. 3. A person who knows enough about a subject to give an opinion about it: *My cousin is a good judge of horses. Noun.* **judge** (juj) *verb,* **judged, judging;** *noun, plural* **judges.**

judgment 1. The ability to decide or judge: *They showed good judgment in deciding to buy this car.* 2. An opinion: *In my judgment, that student is very good at drawing.* 3. A verdict agreed on or a decision made by a court of law: *It was the judgment of the court that the accused person was guilty.* **judg·ment** (juj′mənt) *noun, plural* **judgments.**

judicial Having to do with courts of law or judges: *It is the responsibility of the judicial branch of government to make the meaning of the law clear.* **ju·di·cial** (jü dish′əl) *adjective.*

judo A way of fighting and defending oneself without weapons. **ju·do** (jü′dō) *noun.*

WORD HISTORY

The word **judo** comes from a Japanese word that means "gentle way." This method of fighting is not so rough as other ways of fighting.

jug A rounded container that has a handle and a narrow neck. A jug is used for holding liquids and is usually made out of pottery, glass, or plastic. **jug** (jug) *noun, plural* **jugs.**

juggernaut Something so powerful that it can overcome or destroy everything in its path: *That school's football team is a juggernaut—no one can beat them.* **jug·ger·naut** (jug′ər nôt′) *noun, plural* **juggernauts.**

Sometimes jugs are designed to look like people or other figures.

juggle 1. To keep balls or other objects in continuous motion from the hands into the air by skillful tossing and catching: *That clown can juggle five plates at once without dropping them.* 2. To change in order to cheat or deceive: *The criminals juggled the records to hide the theft from the company.* **jug·gle** (jug′əl) *verb,* **juggled, juggling.**

juice 1. The liquid from vegetables, fruits, or meats: *I love fresh orange juice.* 2. A fluid produced inside the body: *The stomach releases digestive juices when we eat.* **juice** (jüs) *noun, plural* **juices.**

juicy Having much juice: *The juicy peach squirted my shirt when I bit into it.* **juic·y** (jü′sē) *adjective,* **juicier, juiciest.**

jukebox A machine that plays music when money is put into it. **juke·box** (jük′boks′) *noun, plural* **jukeboxes.**

July The seventh month of the year. July has thirty-one days. **Ju·ly** (jù lī′) *noun.*

WORD HISTORY

The Romans named the month of July in honor of Julius Caesar because he was born in this month.

---

jumble To mix or throw into confusion: *All the toys were jumbled together in the box. Verb.*
○ *A confused mixture or condition; mess: A jumble of clothes, toys, and books lay on the floor of the children's room. The child threw everything in the closet into a jumble in trying to find a missing shoe. Noun.*
jum·ble (jum′bəl) *verb,* **jumbled, jumbling;** *noun, plural* **jumbles.**

jumbo Extremely large. **jum·bo** (jum′bō) *adjective.*

WORD HISTORY

The word jumbo comes from Jumbo, the name of a large elephant that appeared about one hundred years ago in a famous circus.

---

jump 1. To use a push from one's feet to move through or into the air: *The shortstop had to jump to catch the ball. I can jump off the high diving board.* 2. To move or get up suddenly: *The students jumped to their feet when they heard the fire alarm ring.* 3. To pass over through the air: *The horse jumped the fence.* 4. To increase or rise in a quick or unexpected way: *The price of gasoline jumped. Verb.*
○ 1. The act of jumping: *The fox made a jump across the stream.* 2. The distance covered by jumping: *The athlete made a jump of 20 feet.* 3. A sudden move or start. 4. A sudden increase or rise: *My parents complained about the jump in the price of milk. Noun.*
• **to jump at.** To accept quickly and eagerly: *I jumped at the chance to work at the library during the summer.*
jump (jump) *verb,* **jumped, jumping;** *noun, plural* **jumps.**

jumper A dress that is in one piece and does not

have sleeves. A jumper is usually worn over a blouse or sweater. **jump·er** (jum′pər) *noun, plural* **jumpers.**

jump rope 1. A game or exercise in which a person jumps over a rope that is swung over the head and under the feet. This may be done by one person, or two people may swing the rope while one or more others jump. 2. The rope used for this.

jumpsuit A one-piece garment that covers the body, arms, and legs and opens down the front. **jumpsuit** (jump′süt′) *noun, plural* **jumpsuits.**

junction 1. A place where things meet or cross. A place where railroad tracks meet is called a junction. 2. The act of joining or the condition of being joined. **junc·tion** (jungk′shən) *noun, plural* **junctions.**

June The sixth month of the year. June has thirty days. **June** (jün) *noun.*

WORD HISTORY

The Romans named the month of June in honor of Juno, queen of the gods in Roman mythology.

---

jungle Land in tropical areas that is covered with a thick mass of trees, vines, and bushes. **jun·gle** (jung′gəl) *noun, plural* **jungles.**

junior 1. The younger of two. The word "junior" is used after the name of a son who has the same name as his father: *Robert Edwards, Junior, is the son of Robert Edwards, Senior.* 2. Of or for younger people: *The twins are playing in the junior tennis tournament.* 3. Having to do with the year before the last year in high school or college. 4. Having a lower position or rank: *A junior executive does not have as important a job as a senior executive. Adjective.*
○ 1. A person who is younger than another: *My cousin is my junior by three years.* 2. A student who is in the year before the last year of high school or college. *Noun.*
jun·ior (jün′yər) *adjective; noun, plural* **juniors.**

junior high school A school between elementary school and high school. It usually includes grades seven and eight and sometimes grades six or nine.

juniper An evergreen shrub or tree. Junipers have purple cones that look like berries. **ju·ni·per** (jü′nə pər) *noun, plural* **junipers.**

PRONUNCIATION KEY:

at āpe fär câre end mē it ice pierce hot ōld sóng fork
oil out up ūse rüle pull tûrn chin sing shop thin this
hw in white; zh in treasure. The symbol ə stands for the unstressed vowel sound in about, taken, pencil, lemon, and circus.

403

junk¹ 1. Old pieces of metal, wood, rags, or other things that are thrown away; trash. 2. Old things that are no longer useful: *My bedroom closet is full of junk. Noun.*

○ To throw something away because it is no longer useful: *My father had to junk our old car. Verb.*

junk (jungk) *noun; verb,* **junked, junking.**

This artist has created sculptures out of junk.

junk² A sailing ship usually found in China and southeastern Asia. **junk** (jungk) *noun, plural* **junks.**

junk food Food that has a large amount of sugar or fat and small amounts of other nutrients.

junk mail Mail, usually advertisements, that arrives without being asked for.

junkyard A place where junk is collected and stored, especially a place for cars that are old or wrecked. **junk·yard** (jungk′yärd′) *noun, plural* **junkyards.**

Jupiter The largest planet in our solar system.

Jupiter
This planet is so large that more than 1,000 Earths could fit inside it. The Great Red Spot is a huge storm in Jupiter's atmosphere that has been observed for more than 300 years.

Average distance from sun: **483,900,000 miles**
Diameter: **88,865 miles**
Length of Day: **9 hours, 55 minutes**
Length of Year: **11.9 years**
Average Temperature: **-243°F**
Mass compared to Earth: **318**
Weight of 100 pounds: **254**
Atmosphere: **Hydrogen, Helium**
Number of rings: **3**
Number of satellites: **16**

It is the fifth closest planet to the sun. **Ju·pi·ter** (jü′pi tər) *noun.*

juror A member of a jury: *The jurors left the court to decide on their verdict.* **ju·ror** (jùr′ər) *noun, plural* **jurors.**

jury 1. A group of people chosen to hear the facts in a matter that has been brought before a court of law. The jury makes a decision on the matter based on the facts they hear and on the law. 2. A group of people who choose the winners and award the prizes in a contest. **ju·ry** (jùr′ē) *noun, plural* **juries.**

just Fair and right; honest: *The principal is a stern but just person. Adjective.*

○ 1. Not more or less than; exactly: *You said just what I was going to say.* 2. A little while ago: *If you're looking for your parents, I just saw them in the garage.* 3. By very little; barely: *Because of all the traffic, they just made their plane on time.* 4. No more than; only: *I'm not really hurt; it's just a scratch. Adverb.*

just (just) *adjective; adverb.*

justice 1. Fair or right treatment or action: *The lawyer demanded justice for the innocent person.* 2. The quality or condition of being fair and right: *Justice demands that all people be treated as equals in a court of law.* 3. A judge of the Supreme Court of the United States. **jus·tice** (jus′tis) *noun, plural* **justices.**

justify 1. To show to be fair or reasonable: *You justified our teacher's faith in you when you won the scholarship.* 2. To prove to be without blame or guilt: *The lawyer tried to justify the suspect's action.* **jus·ti·fy** (jus′tə fī′) *verb,* **justified, justifying. —justification** *noun.*

jut To stick out: *The lighthouse is on a piece of land that juts into the sea.* **jut** (jut) *verb,* **jutted, jutting.**

jute A strong fiber that is used to make heavy cord or a coarse material called burlap. Jute comes from a plant that is grown mostly in tropical areas of Asia. **jute** (jüt) *noun.*

juvenile 1. Of or for children or young people: *Our town library keeps its collection of juvenile books on the second floor.* 2. Childish: *The teenagers were criticized for their juvenile behavior. Adjective.*

○ A young person: *Our youth center offers many activities for juveniles. Noun.*

ju·ve·nile (jü′və nəl *or* jü′və nīl′) *adjective; noun, plural* **juveniles.**

The letter K has one sound in English, as in kayak and kite, but that sound is commonly made by:

c, especially when it appears before *a*, *o*, and *u*, as in can, cost, and cut, or with other consonants, as in clutch and crease;

ck as in luck;

and rarely by:

ch as in ache and anchor;

cqu as in lacquer;

cu as in biscuit;

kh as in khaki;

lk as in talk and walk;

qu as in liquid;

que as in unique.

k, K The eleventh letter of the alphabet. **k, K** (kā) *noun, plural* **k's, K's.**

kaleidoscope A tube that contains mirrors and often small pieces of colored glass or other colored objects at one end. When the other end of the tube is held up to the eye and turned, the mirrors reflect a series of changing patterns. **ka·lei·do·scope** (kə lī′də skōp′) *noun, plural* **kaleidoscopes.**

kangaroo An animal that has small front legs, very strong back legs for leaping, and a long, powerful tail for balance. The female carries her young in a pouch for about six months after birth. Kangaroos are marsupials and live in Australia and New Guinea. **kan·ga·roo** (kang′gə rü′) *noun, plural* **kangaroos** *or* **kangaroo.**

karaoke A popular kind of entertainment in which a person sings along to music being played by a

Some kangaroos are over 5 feet tall.

special device. Karaoke originated in Japan. **ka·ra·o·ke** (kar′ē ō′kē) *noun.*

karate A Japanese style of self-defense in which people fight each other using only kicks and punches. **ka·ra·te** (kə rä′tē) *noun.*

Kans. An abbreviation for Kansas.

Kansas A state in the west-central United States. Its capital is Topeka. **Kan·sas** (kan′zəs) *noun.*

WORD HISTORY

Kansas was named for a river in the northeastern part of the state. The word was an Indian name for a tribe that used to live near this river.

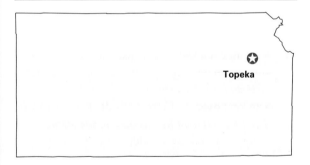

Topeka

Kansas
U. S. Postal Abbreviation: **KS**
Capital: **Topeka**
Population: 2,476,000
Area: **82,264 sq. mi./213,063 sq. km**
State Nickname: **Sunflower State**
State Bird: **Western Meadowlark**
State Flower: **Sunflower**

katydid A large, green insect that resembles a grasshopper. A katydid has two long antennae and wings that look like leaves. By rubbing its two wings together, the male katydid can make a shrill noise that sounds like its name. **ka•ty•did** (kā′tē did′) *noun, plural* **katydids**.

A kayak has an opening in the center where a person can sit.

kayak 1. A type of canoe first used by the Inuit. It is made by stretching animal skins over a frame. 2. A light canoe that looks like this, usually made of fiberglass. **kay•ak** (kī′ak) *noun, plural* **kayaks**.

WORD HISTORY

Kayak is the Inuit word for this special kind of canoe.

keel A wooden or metal piece that runs along the center of the bottom of many ships and boats. The keel supports the whole structure of a boat and helps keep it balanced. *Noun.*

• **on an even keel.** On a steady course: *Try to stay* **on an even keel** *for the rest of the school year and don't waste any more time.*

• **to keel over.** 1. To turn upside down; capsize: *The little sailboat* **keeled over** *in the strong wind.* 2. To fall over suddenly; collapse: *The heat in the crowded subway caused two people to* **keel over.**

keel (kēl) *noun, plural* **keels**; *verb,* **keeled, keeling**.

keen 1. Sharp or quick in seeing, hearing, or thinking: *That hound has a* **keen** *sense of smell.* 2. Full of enthusiasm; eager: *I am* **keen** *about sports of all kinds.* 3. Having a sharp cutting edge or point: *A* **keen** *knife is an important tool in any kitchen.* *Adjective.*

○ Used to express approval or agreement: *We're going to the video arcade for my birthday.* **Keen!** *Interjection.*

keen (kēn) *adjective,* **keener, keenest**; *interjection.*

keep 1. To continue to have, hold, or do: *Keep mixing the batter until it is smooth.* 2. To continue or cause to continue in a certain place or condition; stay or cause to stay: *The doctor* **kept** *the sick patient in the hospital for a week.* 3. To store or put: *Do you* **keep** *your shoes in the closet?* 4. To hold back or stop: *The cold weather may* **keep** *the plants from budding.* 5. To be faithful to; fulfill: *I* **kept** *my promise and mowed the lawn.* 6. To take care of: *That farmer* **keeps** *a big herd of cows.* 7. To write or make entries in: *Do you* **keep** *a diary? Verb.*

○ 1. Food and a place to live: *When the children grew up, they had to start earning their own* **keep.** 2. The strongest part in a castle or fort. *Noun.*

• **to keep up.** 1. To match the rate of speed of someone or something else: *The rest of the team is trying* **to keep up** *with the lead runner.* 2. To continue: *The noise of the machines* **kept up** *all through the night.* 3. To maintain something in good condition: *The house hasn't been* **kept up** *for years so no one wants to buy it.*

keep (kēp) *verb,* **kept, keeping**; *noun, plural* **keeps**.

SYNONYMS

keep, reserve, retain
We **keep** *most of what we grow in our garden and eat it ourselves. I* **reserve** *my evenings for reading instead of watching television. I forgot to* **retain** *the sales receipt they gave me when I bought my stereo.*

keeping 1. The condition of being in charge of or having control over something: *We left our house in our neighbor's* **keeping** *while we were on vacation.* 2. Agreement or harmony: *Your jokes were not in* **keeping** *with the serious nature of the occasion.* **keep•ing** (kē′ping) *noun.*

keg A small metal or wooden barrel. Beer is often put in kegs. **keg** (keg) *noun, plural* **kegs**.

kelp A large, brown seaweed that grows in cold waters along ocean coasts. Kelp provides food for people and animals and is used to make many products. **kelp** (kelp) *noun.*

kennel 1. A building where dogs are kept. 2. A place where dogs are raised and trained or cared for while an owner is away. **ken•nel** (ken′əl) *noun, plural* **kennels.**

Kentucky A state in the east-central United States. Its capital is Frankfort. **Ken•tuck•y** (kən tuk′ē) *noun.*

WORD HISTORY

Kentucky comes from an Indian name for this area that probably meant "meadowland" or "flat land." Later the name was used for the river running through this flat land south of the Ohio River. When Virginia established a county in this area in 1776, it used the name *Kentucky*. When the county was made a state, it kept the same name.

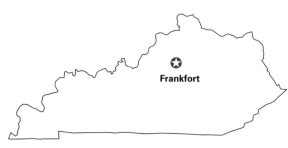

Kentucky
U. S. Postal Abbreviation: **KY**
Capital: **Frankfort**
Population: **3,727,000**
Area: **40,409 sq. mi./104,623 sq. km**
State Nickname: **Bluegrass State**
State Bird: **Cardinal**
State Flower: **Goldenrod**

Kenya A country in east-central Africa. **Ken•ya** (ken′yə *or* kēn′yə) *noun.*

kept Past tense and past participle of **keep:** *I kept the ball I found in the playground when no one claimed it.* **kept** (kept) *verb.*

kerchief A piece of cloth that is worn over the head or around the neck. **ker•chief** (kûr′chif) *noun, plural* **kerchiefs.**

kernel 1. The whole grain or seed of wheat, corn, and some other plants. 2. The soft part inside the shell of a seed, fruit, or nut. 3. The central or most necessary part: *There is a **kernel** of truth in what our opponent says.*

Another word that sounds like this is **colonel.** **ker•nel** (kûr′nəl) *noun, plural* **kernels.**

**When we eat corn on the cob,
we are eating the kernels.**

kerosene A thin, colorless oil that is made from petroleum. Kerosene was once used as a fuel for lamps before the electric light bulb was invented. Today it is used in fuel for jet engines, portable heaters, and farm equipment. **ker•o•sene** (ker′ə sēn′) *noun.*

ketchup or **catsup** A thick red sauce that is made of tomatoes, onions, vinegar, salt, sugar, and spices. Ketchup is used to give flavor to hamburgers, French fries, and many other foods. **ketch•up** (kech′əp) *noun.*

kettle A metal pot used for boiling liquids or for cooking foods. **ket•tle** (ket′əl) *noun, plural* **kettles.**

kettledrum A drum, shaped like a bowl, that is made of copper or brass with a thin material called parchment stretched over the top. **ket•tle•drum** (ket′əl drum′) *noun, plural* **kettledrums.**

key¹ 1. A shaped piece of metal that can open a lock on a door, drawer, or other thing: *We lost the key, so we can't unlock the front door.* 2. Anything that is used or shaped like such a piece of metal: *I used a roller skate key to tighten the skates on my shoes.* 3. Something that solves or explains: *The detective found the key to the mystery when she located the missing documents. There is a key to the pronunciations in this dictionary at the bottom of this page.* 4. Something that leads to or is a way of getting something: *Hard work can sometimes be the key to success.* 5. The part on a machine or musical instrument that is pressed down to make it work. The keys of

PRONUNCIATION KEY:

at	āpe	fär	câre	end	mē	it	īce	pîerce	hot	ōld	sông	fôrk
oil	out	up	ūse	rüle	pull	tûrn	chin	sing	shop	thin	this	

hw in white; zh in treasure. The symbol ə stands for the unstressed vowel sound in about, taken, pencil, lemon, and circus.

407

a typewriter or computer are marked with different numbers, symbols, and letters of the alphabet. A piano has black and white keys. **6.** A group of notes in which all the notes are related to each other and are based on the lowest note in the group. *Noun.*

○ Very important; chief: *The quarterback holds a key position on a football team. Adjective.*

○ To regulate or adjust the musical pitch of: *The musicians in the orchestra have to key their instruments before a performance. Verb.* Another word that sounds like this is **quay.**

• **keyed up.** Very excited: *Don't get all keyed up right before bedtime.*

• **to key in.** To enter information in a computer. **key** (kē) *noun, plural* **keys;** *adjective; verb,* **keyed, keying.**

key² A low island or reef. There are keys along the southern tip of Florida. **key** (kē) *noun, plural* **keys.**

keyboard A set or row of keys. A piano, a typewriter, or a computer has a keyboard. **key·board** (kē′bôrd′) *noun, plural* **keyboards.**

Information is entered into a computer through the use of a keyboard.

keyhole The hole in a lock where a key is put. **key·hole** (kē′hōl′) *noun, plural* **keyholes.**

keypad A small panel of buttons, as on a computer keyboard or an ATM machine, for doing arithmetic or keying in commands. **key·pad** (kē′pad′) *noun, plural* **keypads.**

key ring A metal or plastic ring for holding keys.

keystone **1.** The top stone in the middle of an arch. The keystone holds the other stones of the arch together. **2.** Something important in a system or plan that holds the other elements

together: *Studying hard is the keystone of his success at school.*

• **keystone sack.** In baseball, second base. **key·stone** (kē′stōn′) *noun, plural* **keystones.**

kg An abbreviation for **kilogram.**

khaki **1.** A dull, yellowish brown color. **2.** A heavy cotton cloth of this color. Khaki is most often used to make military uniforms. **3. khakis.** A military uniform or other clothing made from khaki. **khak·i** (kak′ē or kä′kē) *noun, plural* **khakis.**

kick **1.** To hit or strike out with the foot: *The mule kicked the fence. Knowing how to kick correctly is important when you are learning to swim.* **2.** To move by hitting with the foot: *The child kicked a stone along on the way home from school.* **3.** To spring back when fired: *The rifle kicked so hard that it hurt the hunter's shoulder. Verb.*

○ **1.** A hit or blow with the foot: *The police opened the door with a kick.* **2.** The sudden springing back of a gun when it is fired: *The kick of the gun bruised my shoulder.* **3.** A feeling of excitement; thrill: *Did you get a kick out of going for your first ride on an airplane? Noun.*

• **to kick in.** **1.** To contribute to something: *Can you kick in a dime so I can buy a candy bar?* **2.** To begin: *The rain had barely kicked in before the storm had passed.*

• **to kick off.** **1.** In football or soccer, to start play at the beginning of a game or resume play after a score. **2.** To start: *Our school band will kick off the big parade tomorrow.*

• **to kick up.** To start or create: *I used to kick up a fuss when I had to go to bed.* **kick** (kik) *verb,* **kicked, kicking;** *noun, plural* **kicks.**

kickoff A kick of the ball in football or soccer that begins the action: *The crowd in the stands stood up to watch the opening kickoff of the football game.* **kick·off** (kik′ôf′) *noun, plural* **kickoffs.**

kid **1.** A young goat. **2.** A child. This meaning is used mostly in informal conversation. **3.** A kind of leather that is made from the skin of a young goat: *These gloves are made of tan kid. Noun.*

○ **1.** To make fun of or tease: *My friends kidded me about my new short haircut.* **2.** To say something that is not true as a joke: *I was only kidding when I told my parents there wouldn't be any school today. Verb.*

kid (kid) *noun, plural* **kids;** *verb,* **kidded, kidding.**

kidnap To seize or hold a person by force: *Three people kidnaped the rich couple and demanded one million dollars for their release.* **kid·nap** (kid′nap′) *verb,* **kidnaped** or **kidnapped**, **kidnaping** or **kidnapping**.

kidney 1. Either of two organs in the body that are shaped like a very large bean. The kidneys are located underneath the lowest ribs in the back. They filter out waste from the bloodstream and pass it to the bladder in the form of urine. 2. The kidneys of certain animals when used as food. **kid·ney** (kid′nē) *noun, plural* **kidneys**.

kill 1. To end the life of: *Automobile accidents kill thousands of Americans every year. Many deer are killed during the hunting season.* 2. To end; destroy: *Failing the test killed the student's chances of getting an A in the course.* 3. To use up: *While we were waiting for the bus, we killed fifteen minutes by looking in store windows.* 4. To cause much pain to; hurt very much: *I hurt my back and it's killing me. Verb.*
○ 1. The act of killing: *Once the dogs had chased the animal up a tree, the hunters moved in for the kill.* 2. An animal that is killed: *The wolf dragged its kill back to the den to feed its family. Noun.*
kill (kil) *verb,* **killed**, **killing**; *noun, plural* **kills**.

killdeer A noisy bird whose song sounds like its name. The killdeer is a plover of North America, Central America, and western South America, with brownish feathers and two black stripes along the breast. **kill·deer** (kil′dîr′) *noun, plural* **killdeers** or **killdeer**.

killer whale A medium-size, carnivorous whale; orca. For more information see the entry for orca. **kill·er whale** (kil′ər).

kiln A furnace or oven for burning, baking, or drying. A kiln is used in making bricks, pottery, and charcoal. **kiln** (kiln or kil) *noun, plural* **kilns**.

kilo A short form of kilogram. **ki·lo** (kē′lō) *noun, plural* **kilos**.

kilo- A prefix that means 1,000: *Kilowatt means 1,000 watts.*

kilogram A unit of weight and mass in the metric system. A kilogram is equal to 1,000 grams, or about two pounds and three ounces. **kil·o·gram** (kil′ə gram′) *noun, plural* **kilograms**.

kilohertz A unit that measures the frequency of radio waves. One kilohertz is equal to 1,000 vibrations per second. **kil·o·hertz** (kil′ə hûrts′) *noun, plural* **kilohertz**.

kilometer A unit of length in the metric system. A kilometer is equal to 1,000 meters, or about 0.62 of a mile. **ki·lom·e·ter** (ki lom′i tər or kil′ə mē′tər) *noun, plural* **kilometers**.

kilowatt A unit of electrical power. A kilowatt is equal to 1,000 watts. **kil·o·watt** (kil′ə wot′) *noun, plural* **kilowatts**.

Scottish men sometimes wear kilts.

kilt A pleated, plaid skirt that reaches to the knees. **kilt** (kilt) *noun, plural* **kilts**.

kimono A loose robe that is tied with a sash. **ki·mo·no** (ki mō′nə) *noun, plural* **kimonos**.

Kimonos are a traditional way of dress in Japan.

kin A person's whole family; relatives: *All of my neighbor's kin live in Alabama.* **kin** (kin) *noun.*

kind¹ Gentle, generous, and friendly: *A kind person is thoughtful of others. It was kind of you to help me.* **kind** (kīnd) *adjective,* **kinder**, **kindest**.

kind² 1. A group of things that are the same in some way: *The whales are one kind of mammal. That store sells many different kinds of sports equipment.* 2. One of a group of people or things

PRONUNCIATION KEY:

| at | āpe | fär | câre | end | mē | it | īce | pierce | hot | ōld | sông | fôrk |
| oil | out | up | ūse | rüle | pull | tûrn | chin | sing | shop | thin | this | |

hw in white; zh in treasure. The symbol ə stands for the unstressed vowel sound in about, taken, pencil, lemon, and circus.

409

that are different or special in some way: *That's not the **kind** of saw that can cut a metal pipe.* **kind** (kīnd) *noun, plural* **kinds**.

kindergarten A class in school for children between the ages of four and six. It comes before first grade. **kin·der·gar·ten** (kin′dər gär′tən) *noun, plural* **kindergartens**.

WORD HISTORY

The word **kindergarten** comes from a German word that means ``children's garden.''

---

kindle **1.** To begin burning or cause to burn: *The campers **kindled** the logs of the campfire. The trash **kindled** when a spark landed on it.* **2.** To stir or excite: *The factory's pollution of the river **kindled** the anger of the people who lived nearby.* **kin·dle** (kin′dəl) *verb,* **kindled, kindling**.

kindling Small pieces of dry material, such as twigs and leaves, used to start a fire: *The campers searched the woods for **kindling** to light the campfire.* **kind·ling** (kind′ling) *noun*.

kindly Having or showing kindness: *I looked for the **kindly** faces of my friends in the audience before I gave my speech. Adjective.*
○ **1.** In a kind or gentle manner: *The police officer spoke **kindly** to the lost child.* **2.** As a favor; please: ***Kindly** mail this letter for me on your way to school.* **3.** Very much; sincerely: *Thank you **kindly** for your help. Adverb.*
kind·ly (kīnd′lē) *adjective,* **kindlier, kindliest**; *adverb*.

kindness **1.** The quality or condition of being kind: *The **kindness** of my friends when I was sick made me very grateful.* **2.** A thoughtful, friendly act; favor: *The guests thanked their hosts for their many **kindnesses**.* **kind·ness** (kīnd′nis) *noun, plural* **kindnesses**.

king **1.** A man who rules a country. A man usually becomes king because he is related to the ruler before him and usually rules until he dies. **2.** A person or thing that is the best, most important, or most powerful of its group: *The lion is often called the **king** of the jungle.* **3.** A playing card with a picture of a king on it. **4.** An important piece in a game of chess or checkers. **king** (king) *noun, plural* **kings**.

kingdom **1.** A country that is ruled by a king or a queen. **2.** One of the main divisions of living

things, such as the animal kingdom, the plant kingdom, or the fungus kingdom. **king·dom** (king′dəm) *noun, plural* **kingdoms**.

kingfisher Any of various birds that have a short tail and a long beak. A kingfisher can dive from a tree branch into the water to catch small fish. **king·fish·er** (king′fish′ər) *noun, plural* **kingfishers**.

king-size Larger or longer than is ordinary: *After I bought a **king-size** bed, I had to move my other furniture to make room for it.* **king-size** (king′sīz′) *adjective*.

kink **1.** A tight curl of hair, wire, rope, or something similar: *He sat combing out the **kinks** in the dog's fur. The water wouldn't flow because the hose had a **kink**.* **2.** A pain in a muscle; cramp: *You got a **kink** in your back because you tried to move the heavy piano alone.* **3.** An unexpected problem: *At the last minute, we found out there was a **kink** in our plans. Noun.*
○ To form a kink or kinks: *The thread **kinked** as I was sewing the button onto the coat. Verb.*
kink (kingk) *noun, plural* **kinks**; *verb,* **kinked, kinking**. —**kinky** *adjective*.

kiss To touch with the lips as a sign of greeting or affection: *I **kissed** my aunt and uncle before they left. Verb.*
○ **1.** A touch with the lips as a sign of greeting or affection: *The children gave each parent a **kiss** before going to bed.* **2.** A small piece of candy that is sometimes wrapped in foil: *The store had chocolate **kisses** on sale.* **3.** In basketball, a gentle bounce of the ball as it strikes the backboard. *Noun.*
kiss (kis) *verb,* **kissed, kissing**; *noun, plural* **kisses**.

A **kiss** is one of the most common signs of affection.

kit **1.** A set of parts or materials to be put together: *Have you ever built a model of a rocket from a **kit**?* **2.** A collection of tools or equipment for a particular purpose: *My sewing **kit** has a thimble, needles, pins, and thread.* **kit** (kit) *noun, plural* **kits**.

kitchen A room or place where food is cooked. **kitch·en** (kich′ən) *noun, plural* **kitchens**.

kitchenette A very small kitchen. **kitch·en·ette** (kich′ə net′) *noun, plural* **kitchenettes.**

kite 1. A light, wooden frame that is covered with paper, plastic, or cloth. A kite can be flown in the air at the end of a long string. **2.** A hawk that has a hooked bill and long, narrow wings. Some kites have a forked tail. **kite** (kīt) *noun, plural* **kites.**

kite

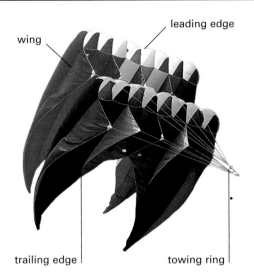

wing

leading edge

trailing edge

towing ring

kitten A young cat; *The cat gave birth to four kit-tens.* **kit·ten** (kit′ən) *noun, plural* **kittens.**

kitty 1. A young cat; a kitten: *I called my pet by saying, "Here, kitty!"* **2.** An amount of money collected from everyone in a group and then used to buy something: *Come on, kick something in to the kitty for our class party.* **kit·ty** (kit′ē) *noun, plural* **kitties.**

kiwi¹ A bird that lives in New Zealand. The kiwi has a round body covered with brown feathers that look like fur. It cannot fly. **ki·wi** (kē′wē) *noun, plural* **kiwis.**

kiwi² A small, round fruit often grown in New Zealand. It has brown, fuzzy skin and green flesh. The kiwi was first grown in China, and is some-times called the *Chinese gooseberry.* **ki·wi** (kē′wē) *noun, plural* **kiwis.**

klutz A very clumsy person: *Only a klutz would spill his drink twice at the same meal.* This is a slang word. **klutz** (kluts) *noun, plural* **klutzes.**

km. An abbreviation for **kilometer.**

knack A special ability or skill for doing some-thing easily: *My classmate has a knack for repair-ing things.* **knack** (nak) *noun.*

knapsack A bag made of canvas, leather, nylon, or other material that is used for carrying clothes, books, equipment, or other supplies. A knapsack is strapped over the shoulders and carried on the back. **knap·sack** (nap′sak′) *noun, plural* **knapsacks.**

knead To mix and press together with the hands: *The baker had to knead the dough before baking it.* Another word that sounds like this is **need.** **knead** (nēd) *verb,* **kneaded, kneading.**

knee 1. The joint between the thigh and the lower leg. **2.** Something that works or looks like a knee. **knee** (nē) *noun, plural* **knees.**

kneecap A flat, movable bone in front of the knee. The kneecap protects the knee joint from getting injured. **knee·cap** (nē′kap′) *noun, plural* **kneecaps.**

kneel To go down on a bent knee or knees: *The knights were seen kneeling before the king and queen.* **kneel** (nēl) *verb,* **knelt** or **kneeled, kneeling.**

knelt A past tense and a past participle of **kneel.** **knelt** (nelt) *verb.*

knew Past tense of **know.** Other words that sound like this are **gnu** and **new.** **knew** (nü *or* nū) *verb.*

knickknack A small object used as an ornament: *The man-tel was crowded with small figures of ani-mals and other knick-knacks.* **knick·knack** (nik′nak′) *noun, plural* **knickknacks.**

knife 1. A tool that is used for cutting. A knife has a sharp blade attached to a handle. **2.** The part of a tool or machine that cuts; blade. *Noun.*

This chef needs to be careful while using such a large knife.

PRONUNCIATION KEY:

at   āpe   fär   câre   end   mē   it   īce   pierce   hot   ōld   sông   fôrk
oil   out   up   ūse   rüle   pull   tûrn   chin   sing   shop   thin   this

hw in white; zh in treasure. The symbol ə stands for the unstressed vowel sound in about, taken, pencil, lemon, and circus.

411

○ To cut or stab with a knife. *Verb.*
knife (nīf) *noun, plural* **knives**; *verb*, **knifed**, **knifing.**

knight 1. A soldier in the Middle Ages. A knight gave his loyalty to a king or lord and in return was given the right to hold land. A man had to serve as a page before he could become a knight. 2. A man who holds this title today as an honor for service to his country. In Great Britain, a knight uses the word "Sir" before his name. 3. One of the pieces in a game of chess. A knight is usually in the shape of a horse's head. *Noun.*
○ To raise to the rank of knight: *Queen Elizabeth II has knighted many writers, actors, and musicians. Verb.*
Another word that sounds like this is **night.**
knight (nīt) *noun, plural* **knights**; *verb*, **knighted**, **knighting.**

knighthood The rank of a knight: *After many years of service to the country, the page was awarded knighthood at a grand ceremony.* **knight·hood** (nīt'húd') *noun.*

knit 1. To make cloth or clothing by looping yarn together, either by hand with long needles or by machine: *I knitted a sweater for my grandchild.* 2. To join or come together closely and securely: *The doctor said that broken bone would take six months to knit.*
• **to knit one's brows.** To frown so that the forehead wrinkles: *My sister knits her brows when she concentrates on doing arithmetic.*
knit (nit) *verb*, **knitted** or **knit**, **knitting.**

knives Plural of knife: *These knives are not very sharp.* **knives** (nīvz) *plural noun.*

knob 1. A rounded handle for opening a door or drawer, or for working a radio, television, or other machine: *The knob on the drawer came off in my hand.* 2. A rounded lump: *There were knobs all over the trunk of the huge old tree.* **knob** (nob) *noun, plural* **knobs.**

knock 1. To strike with a sharp, hard blow or blows; hit: *The branch knocked the hunter on the head. I knocked on the door but no one answered.* 2. To push and cause to fall: *The cat jumped on the table and knocked the lamp over.* 3. To make a pounding or rattling noise: *The engine of the old car knocked.* 4. To find something wrong with: *It's a good idea; don't knock it. Verb.*
○ 1. A sharp, hard blow; hit: *The player got a knock on the head in the soccer game. I heard a knock on the door.* 2. A pounding or rattling noise: *Our old car had a knock in the engine. Noun.*
• **to knock out.** To hit so hard as to make unconscious: *The blow on the head knocked out the football player.*
• **to knock for a loop.** 1. To knock out: *That last punch knocked his opponent for a loop.* 2. To amaze; astonish: *The news that he was fired knocked us all for a loop.*
knock (nok) *verb*, **knocked**, **knocking**; *noun, plural* **knocks.**

knocker A metal knob or ring that is attached to a door with a hinge. A knocker is used to knock on a door. **knock·er** (nok'ər) *noun, plural* **knockers.**

knoll A small, rounded hill. **knoll** (nōl) *noun, plural* **knolls.**

knot 1. The place where pieces of thread, string, or cord are tied around each other: *Tie the rope around the tree with a tight knot.* 2. A tangle or lump: *There were knots in the dog's coat because it hadn't been brushed for a long time.* 3. A small group of people or things: *A knot of people waited on the platform for the train.* 4. A dark, hard, round spot in a board. A knot is the spot where a branch grew out of the trunk of a tree. 5. A measurement of speed used on ships, boats, and aircraft. A knot is the same as one nautical mile per hour, which equals 6,076 feet per hour. *Noun.*
○ To tie or tangle in or with a knot or knots: *I knotted the string around the package. Your hair is all knotted from the wind. Verb.*
Another word that sounds like this is **not.**
knot (not) *noun, plural* **knots**; *verb*, **knotted**, **knotting.**

knotty 1. Having, covered with, or full of knots: *We used knotty wood to make this table.* 2. Difficult to understand or solve: *No one got the correct answer to the knottiest problem on the test.* **knot·ty** (not'ē) *adjective*, **knottier**, **knottiest.**

know 1. To understand clearly; be certain of the facts or truth of: *The police know how the accident happened.* 2. To be acquainted or familiar with: *I am a friend of theirs, but I don't know their parents.* 3. To have skill or experience with: *That student knows how to type very well.*
Another word that sounds like this is **no.**

• **to know about.** To be aware of: *Do you know about the dance tomorrow night?*

• **to know of.** To be aware of: *I know of a good place to eat.*
know (nō) *verb,* **knew, known, knowing.**

know-how The knowledge of how to do something; practical skill: *To fix this lawn mower, you'll need some know-how with small engines.* **know-how** (nō′hou′) *noun.*

knowledge 1. An understanding that is gained through experience or study: *I have enough knowledge of football to be able to follow a game. I have no knowledge of Dutch.* 2. The fact of knowing: *The knowledge that the car could slide on the icy road made the driver more careful.* **knowl·edge** (nol′ij) *noun.*

knowledgeable Having a lot of information about something: *She's very knowledgeable about field hockey.* **knowl·edge·a·ble** (nol′i jə bəl) *adjective.* —**knowledgeably** *adverb.*

known Past participle of **know**: *A great deal is known about the harmful effects of pollution.* **known** (nōn) *verb.*

knuckle A joint of a finger.

• **to knuckle under.** To give in; yield: *The general refused to knuckle under to the enemy's demands.*

knuck·le (nuk′əl) *noun, plural* **knuckles;** *verb,* **knuckled, knuckling.**

koala A furry, chubby animal that lives in Australia. It has large bushy ears, a black nose, and hands that help it grasp the limbs of trees. Koalas are marsupials. **ko·a·la** (kō ä′lə) *noun, plural* **koalas.**

A female koala carries her young in a pouch.

kook Someone who behaves strangely or

has strange ideas: *People will think you're a kook if you dye your hair a funny color.* This is a slang word. **kook** (kük) *noun, plural* **kooks.**

kookaburra A bird found in Australia with a call that sounds like wild laughter. **kook·a·bur·ra** (kŭk′ə bûr′ə) *noun, plural* **kookaburras.**

Koran The sacred book of Muslims, containing the religious and moral code of Islam. **Ko·ran** (kô ran′ *or* kô rän′) *noun.*

Korea A former country in east-central Asia. It is now divided into North Korea and South Korea. **Ko·re·a** (kə rē′ə) *noun.*

Korean 1. A person who was born in or is a citizen of North Korea or South Korea. 2. The language spoken in North Korea and South Korea. *Noun.*
○ Of or having to do with North Korea or South Korea, its people, or its language. *Adjective.* **Ko·re·an** (kə rē′ən) *noun, plural* **Koreans;** *adjective.*

kosher 1. Prepared according to Jewish ceremonial law: *Milk and meat are not served together at a kosher meal.* 2. Selling or preparing kosher food: *There is a kosher butcher's shop on the main street in our neighborhood.* **ko·sher** (kō′shər) *adjective.*

KS Postal abbreviation for **Kansas.**

Kuwait A country in southwest Asia. **Ku·wait** (kü wāt′) *noun.*

Kwanza *or* **Kwanzaa** A week-long African-American holiday based on traditional African harvest festivals and celebrated from December 26 to January 1. Each day of the holiday is centered around a theme, such as faith, unity, or purpose.

WORD HISTORY

Kwanza comes from the Swahili word *kwanzaa,* which means "first fruit of the harvest." Swahili is a language spoken in east and central Africa.

Ky. An abbreviation for **Kentucky.**
KY Postal abbreviation for **Kentucky.**

PRONUNCIATION KEY:
| at | āpe | fär | câre | end | mē | it | īce | pierce | hot | ōld | sông | fôrk |
| oil | out | up | ūse | rüle | pùll | tûrn | chin | sing | shop | thin | this | |

hw in white; zh in treasure. The symbol ə stands for the unstressed vowel sound in about, taken, pencil, lemon, and circus.

413

SPELLING HINTS

In English, the letter L has only one sound,
    as in lag and lily,

but that sound can be made by:
    ll as in call and doll;

Or very rarely by:
    sl as in island.

Labor Day A holiday in the United States that honors working people, celebrated on the first Monday in September.

labor union An association of workers formed to protect and advance their interests. Labor unions help workers obtain better wages and working conditions.

lace 1. A string or cord used to pull or hold parts together: *The lace on this shoe broke.* 2. An open fabric of fine threads that form elaborate designs: *a dress trimmed with lace. Noun.*
    ○ To pull or tighten together with a string or cord: *Lace up your skates. Verb.*
lace (lās) *noun, plural* **laces**; *verb,* **laced, lacing.**

Europe has long been a center for making lace.

WORD HISTORY

The word lace comes from a Latin word meaning "snare" or "noose." *Lace* later came to be used for any cord or string used for tying things together.

I, L The twelfth letter of the alphabet. **I, L** (el) *noun, plural* **I's, L's.**

l An abbreviation for **liter.**

La. or **LA** An abbreviation for **Louisiana.**

lab A short form of the word "laboratory." Look up **laboratory** for more information. **lab** (lab) *noun, plural* **labs.**

label A piece of cloth, paper, or other material that is fastened to something and gives information about it: *The label inside the shirt tells the brand name. Noun.*
    ○ 1. To put a label on: *Label the package you want to mail.* 2. To describe as, using a word or phrase: *The teacher labeled the picnic a success. Verb.*
la·bel (lā′bəl) *noun, plural* **labels**; *verb,* **labeled, labeling.**

labor 1. Hard work; toil: *The farmers were tired after their labor.* 2. People who work at jobs that require physical strength or skills, or are members of a union of workers: *Labor supported the senator for another term. Noun.*
    ○ 1. To do hard work. 2. To move slowly and with difficulty: *The tired runners labored up the steep hill. Verb.*
la·bor (lā′bər) *noun, plural* **labors**; *verb,* **labored, laboring.**

laboratory A room used for doing scientific experiments or for teaching science. **lab·o·ra·to·ry** (lab′ər ə tôr′ē *or* lab′rə tôr′ē) *noun, plural* **laboratories.**

lack To be without or have too little of; need: *That movie lacked excitement. Verb.*
    ○ 1. The condition of needing something: *The lack of rain caused the crops to fail.* 2. Something that is needed or is missing: *The most serious lack in that person's character is honesty. Noun.*
lack (lak) *verb,* **lacked, lacking**; *noun, plural* **lacks.**

lacquer A liquid that is put on wood or metal and dries quickly to form a shiny coat. *Noun.*

○ To coat with lacquer: *The worker lacquered the wooden chairs. Verb.*
lac·quer (lak'ər) *noun, plural* **lacquers**; *verb,* **lacquered, lacquering.**

lacrosse A game played by two teams of ten players each. The players use sticks with a net on one end to throw, catch, and carry a ball. Points are scored by getting the ball into a goal. **la·crosse** (lə krôs') *noun.*

WORD HISTORY

The name **lacrosse** comes from the French word for the staff that a bishop carries. French explorers first saw lacrosse played by Indians in Canada and thought that a lacrosse stick looked like a bishop's staff.

lad A boy or young man: *Our proud neighbors always said that their grandson was a fine lad.* **lad** (lad) *noun, plural* **lads.**

ladder A device used for climbing. A ladder is made of two long side pieces joined together by short pieces, called rungs, which are used as steps: *I stood on a ladder to paint the ceiling.* **lad·der** (lad'ər) *noun, plural* **ladders.**

Ladders **can be either wooden or metal.**

laden Filled; loaded: *a pirate chest laden with jewels.* **lad·en** (lā'dən) *adjective.*

ladle A spoon with a long handle and a bowl shaped like a cup. It is used to scoop up liquids. **la·dle** (lā'dəl) *noun, plural* **ladles.**

lady 1. Any woman: *There is a lady at the door to see you.* 2. A girl or woman who is polite or has good manners. 3. A woman of high social position. 4. Lady. In Great Britain, a title for a woman of noble rank. **la·dy** (lā'dē) *noun, plural* **ladies.**

ladybug A small, round, bright red or orange beetle with black spots. Ladybugs eat insects harmful to plants. **la·dy·bug** (lā'dē bug') *noun, plural* **ladybugs.**

lag To move less quickly and follow: *The little child always lags behind the older children. Verb.*
○ An act, amount, or example of moving less quickly and following: *After we saw the lightning, there was a lag of a few seconds before we heard the thunder. Noun.*
lag (lag) *verb,* **lagged, lagging**; *noun, plural* **lags.**

lagoon A shallow body of water usually connected to a larger body of water. **la·goon** (lə gün') *noun, plural* **lagoons.**

laid Past tense and past participle of lay: *I laid the book on the table.* **laid** (lād) *verb.*

lain Past participle of lie: *The toys have lain on the floor all day.*
Another word that sounds like this is **lane.**
lain (lān) *verb.*

lair A place where a wild animal lives or rests; den: *The fox's lair was in a hole in the ground.* **lair** (lâr) *noun, plural* **lairs.**

lake A body of water surrounded by land. A lake is larger than a pond. **lake** (lāk) *noun, plural* **lakes.**

A lake **is larger than a pond.**

lamb 1. A young sheep. 2. The meat from a lamb. **lamb** (lam) *noun, plural* **lambs.**

lame 1. Not able to walk well: *The lame horse won't be able to run in this race.* 2. Stiff and painful: *My back is lame from moving the heavy chest.* 3. Poor or weak: *The student*

A lamb **is an affectionate animal.**

PRONUNCIATION KEY:

at   āpe   fär   câre   end   mē   it   īce   pierce   hot   ōld   sông   fôrk
oil   out   up   ūse   rüle   pull   tûrn   chin   sing   shop   thin   this
hw in white; zh in treasure. The symbol ə stands for the unstressed vowel sound in about, taken, pencil, lemon, and circus.

415

had a **lame** excuse for not doing the homework. Adjective.
○ To make lame: *The accident had **lamed** the runner. Verb.*
lame (lām) *adjective,* **lamer, lamest;** *verb,* **lamed, laming.**

lamp A device that produces light. Some lamps hold light bulbs and work by electricity. Other lamps burn oil, kerosene, or gas to provide light. **lamp** (lamp) *noun, plural* **lamps.**

LAN A shortened form of "local area network." **LAN** (lan) *noun, plural* **LANs.**

lance A long spear made of a wooden pole with a sharp metal point at one end. *Noun.*
○ To cut open with a sharp instrument: *The doctor **lanced** the boil in order to drain it. Verb.*
lance (lans) *noun, plural* **lances;** *verb,* **lanced, lancing.**

land 1. All or any part of the earth's surface that is not water; ground. 2. A country or region: *The tourists went to Europe to visit foreign **lands**. Noun.*
○ 1. To come or bring to the ground: *The airplane **landed** safely at the airport. The pilot **landed** the helicopter in the field.* 2. To come or bring ashore: *The marines have **landed**. The ship **landed** its cargo at the dock.* 3. To bring to land or into a boat; catch: *After fishing for an hour, we **landed** only one fish.* 4. To end up or cause to end up: *Stealing could **land** you in jail. Verb.*
land (land) *noun, plural* **lands;** *verb,* **landed, landing.**

landing 1. The act or process of coming to the ground or to land, or coming ashore: *The airplane had a smooth **landing**. The capture of the island began with the **landing** of the Marines.* 2. The place on a dock or pier where people and goods are brought ashore or put on a boat. 3. A level area at the end of a flight of stairs. **land·ing** (lan′ding) *noun, plural* **landings.**

landlady A woman who owns houses, apartments, or rooms that she rents to other people. **land·la·dy** (land′lā′dē) *noun, plural* **landladies.**

landlord A person or organization that owns houses, apartments, or rooms to be rented to other people. **land·lord** (land′lôrd′) *noun, plural* **landlords.**

landmark 1. An object that is familiar and serves as a guide: *The church steeple is a well-known* **landmark** in our town. 2. An important building, structure, or place: *This Civil War battlefield is a national **landmark**.* 3. An important event: *The first landing of astronauts on the moon was a **landmark** in history.* **land·mark** (land′märk′) *noun, plural* **landmarks.**

landscape 1. The stretch of land that can be seen from a place; view: *The train passengers watched the passing **landscape**.* 2. A picture of such a view: *The artist painted a **landscape**. Noun.*
○ To make an area of land more beautiful by planting trees, shrubs, and other plants and by designing gardens: *A gardener **landscaped** the grounds around these offices. Verb.*
land·scape (land′skāp′) *noun, plural* **landscapes;** *verb,* **landscaped, landscaping.**

landslide 1. The sliding down a slope of rocks and soil: *The rumble of the **landslide** echoed in the valley.* 2. Rocks and soil that slide down a slope: *The road was buried under a **landslide**.* 3. A great victory in an election: *The mayor won the election by a **landslide**.* **land·slide** (land′slīd′) *noun, plural* **landslides.**

lane 1. A narrow way or road: *The child walked down the country **lane**.* 2. A route for traffic going in one direction: *The cars kept in the right-hand **lane** on the highway.* 3. A long, narrow path down which bowling balls are rolled; alley. Another word that sounds like this is **lain**.
lane (lān) *noun, plural* **lanes.**

LANGUAGES

There are thousands of languages spoken in different parts of the world, some by millions of people, and some by small groups of a few dozen. The native languages of the largest number of people are listed here:

Mandarin (Chinese)	**853 million**
Hindi	**348 million**
Spanish	**346 million**
English	**330 million**
Bengali	**197 million**
Arabic	**195 million**
Portuguese	**173 million**
Russian	**168 million**
Japanese	**125 million**

language 1. Spoken or written words; human speech: *We are able to express our thoughts and* feelings by means of **language**. **2.** The speech of a country or group: *In Mexico, people speak the Spanish language.* **3.** A way of expressing thoughts and feelings without words: *Many deaf people use sign language.* **4.** A set of words and symbols used to give instructions to a computer and to write programs; computer language. **lan·guage** (lang'gwij) *noun, plural* **languages**.

WORD HISTORY

The word language comes from a Latin word that means "tongue." In Latin and the languages closely related to it, such as English, the word for "tongue" can also be used to mean "speech" and "language."

---

lanky Tall and thin: *a lanky basketball player.* **lank·y** (lang'kē) *adjective,* **lankier, lankiest**.

lantern A covering or container for a light. Some lanterns are made of metal with sides of glass. Most lanterns can be carried: *The camper used a lantern to light the path.* **lan·tern** (lan'tərn) *noun, plural* **lanterns**.

Most lanterns can be carried.

Laos A country in southeastern Asia. **La·os** (lä'ōs *or* lā'os) *noun*.

lap¹ The front part of the body between the waist and the knees of a person who is seated: *The cat lay curled up asleep on its owner's lap.* **lap** (lap) *noun, plural* **laps**.

lap² To lie partly over another; extend over; overlap: *The shingles on a roof lap over each other. Verb.*
○ One time around or over the entire length of something: *Run three laps around the track. Noun.*
lap (lap) *verb,* **lapped, lapping;** *noun, plural* **laps**.

lap³ **1.** To drink a liquid by lifting it up with the tongue: *The kitten lapped its milk.* **2.** To wash or move gently against: *The waves lapped against the shore. Verb.*

○ The act of lapping: *The dog drank all its water in a few laps. Noun.*
lap (lap) *verb,* **lapped, lapping;** *noun, plural* **laps**.

lapel The front part of a coat or jacket that is folded back: *Will you pin this carnation to the lapel of my jacket?* **la·pel** (lə pel') *noun, plural* **lapels**.

lapse **1.** A slight mistake or failure: *The report was perfect except for a few lapses in grammar.* **2.** An amount of time between events; interval: *We met again after a lapse of a year. Noun.*
○ **1.** To slip or fall gradually: *The old building lapsed into ruin.* **2.** To end or be discontinued: *My insurance policy lapsed when I failed to make the monthly payment. Verb.*
lapse (laps) *noun, plural* **lapses;** *verb,* **lapsed, lapsing**.

larch A tall tree with small cones and needles that turn yellow and drop off in the fall. The hard wood of the larch is often used for telephone poles. **larch** (lärch) *noun, plural* **larches**.

lard A soft, white grease obtained by melting the fat of pigs and hogs. It is used in cooking. *Noun.*
○ To add lard to or cover with lard: *This recipe says to lard the pan before using it. Verb.*
lard (lärd) *noun, plural* **lards;** *verb,* **larded, larding**.

larder A pantry or small room for storing food. **lar·der** (lärd'ər) *noun, plural* **larders**.

This large machine is used for making carpets.

large Big in size or amount: *That large house has twenty rooms. The museum has a large stamp collection.*
• **at large. 1.** Free: *The police are searching for the thieves who are still at large.* **2.** Of or repre-

PRONUNCIATION KEY:

| at | āpe | fär | câre | end | mē | it | īce | pierce | hot | ōld | sông | fôrk |
| oil | out | up | ūse | rüle | pull | tûrn | chin | sing | shop | thin | this | |

hw in white; zh in treasure. The symbol ə stands for the unstressed vowel sound in about, taken, pencil, lemon, and circus.

417

senting an entire area: *The United States senators from each state are elected by the people at large.* **large** (lärj) *adjective,* **larger, largest.**

SYNONYMS

large, big, great, huge
The museum has a large stamp collection. A Saint Bernard is a very big dog. Countries both great and small belong to the United Nations. We sat down to a huge Thanksgiving dinner.

---

large intestine The lower section of the intestines including the appendix, colon, and rectum. The large intestine is the part of the digestive system that removes water from digested food.

largely To a great extent; mostly: *The houses on that street are largely made of wood.* **large·ly** (lärj′lē) *adverb.*

lariat A long rope with a loop at one end, used to catch animals; lasso: *The rancher used a lariat to rope the calf.* **lar·i·at** (lar′ē ət) *noun, plural* **lariats.**

lark¹ A small songbird with gray-brown feathers, known for its beautiful song. Larks live in most parts of the world. **lark** (lärk) *noun, plural* **larks.**

lark² Something done for fun: *The children went running and sliding through the snow for a lark.* **lark** (lärk) *noun, plural* **larks.**

larkspur A plant with tall stalks of blue, purple, or white flowers. **lark·spur** (lärk′spûr′) *noun, plural* **larkspurs.**

larva The newly hatched form of some insects and other animals without backbones. A larva has a soft body that looks like a worm and has no wings. A caterpillar is the larva of a moth or butterfly, and a grub is the larva of a beetle. **lar·va** (lär′və) *noun, plural* **larvae** (lär′vē).

WORD HISTORY

The word **larva** comes from a Latin word that means "mask." People used to think that this stage in an insect's growth hid or "masked" the way the insect would finally look.

---

laryngitis Inflammation of the larynx. A person with laryngitis sounds hoarse. **lar·yn·gi·tis** (lar′in jī′tis) *noun.*

larynx The top part of the windpipe. The larynx holds the vocal cords. **lar·ynx** (lar′ingks) *noun, plural* **larynxes.**

laser A device that makes a very narrow but strong beam of light. A laser may be used to perform surgery, cut metal, or send electronic messages. **la·ser** (lā′zər) *noun, plural* **lasers.**

lash¹ 1. A blow with a whip. 2. A movement such as a whip makes: *The lash of the dog's tail knocked the lamp over.* 3. A small, stiff hair that grows on the edge of the eyelid; eyelash. *Noun.*
○ 1. To beat with a whip: *The farmer lashed the stubborn mule.* 2. To strike against with force: *Violent winds lashed the trees.* 3. To move back and forth quickly: *The tiger lashed its tail furiously. Verb.*
lash (lash) *noun, plural* **lashes;** *verb,* **lashed, lashing.**

lash² To tie with a rope: *The shipwrecked sailors lashed boards together to make a raft.* **lash** (lash) *verb,* **lashed, lashing.**

lass A girl or young woman. **lass** (las) *noun, plural* **lasses.**

lasso A long rope with a loop. It is used to catch animals. *Noun.*
○ To catch with a lasso: *The cowhands will lasso the steer. Verb.*
las·so (las′ō *or* la sü′) *noun, plural* **lassos** or **lassoes;** *verb,* **lassoed, lassoing.**

A **lasso** is used to catch animals.

last¹ 1. Coming at the end; final: *December is the last month of the year.* 2. Being the only one that is left: *I spent my last dollar on a gift for my friend.* 3. Coming just before this; most recent; latest: *How old were you on your last birthday? We watched television last night.* 4. Most unlikely: *A giraffe is the last thing you would expect to see in the middle of Main Street. Adjective.*
○ 1. At the end: *Wash the dishes first and the pots and pans last.* 2. Most recently: *When did your cousin last write to you? I last saw the mayor two weeks ago. Adverb.*
○ A person or thing that is last: *I was the last in line in the cafeteria. Noun.*
• **at last.** After a long time or much effort; finally: *At last it's stopped raining.*
last (last) *adjective; adverb; noun.*

last² 1. To go on; continue: *The show will last an hour.* 2. To stay in good condition: *That coat will last if you take care of it.* **last** (last) *verb*, **lasted, lasting.**

lasting Going on or continuing for a long time: *The speech made a lasting impression on the listeners.* **last•ing** (las′ting) *adjective.*

latch A small piece of metal or wood for holding a door, window, or gate closed: *Please lift the latch and open the gate. Noun.*
○ To fasten or close the latch of something: *We were forgot to latch the back door. Verb.* **latch** (lach) *noun, plural* **latches**; *verb*, **latched, latching.**

late 1. Coming after the usual time: *I was late to school today. The campers had a late lunch.* 2. Coming near the end: *It was late afternoon when we started our trip.* 3. Done, made, or happening not long ago: *My parents bought a late model car.* 4. Recently dead: *The late senator had served for thirty years. Adjective.*
○ 1. After the usual time: *We arrived late at the party. They came home late last night.* 2. Near or toward the end: *The football team scored its first touchdown late in the second quarter. Adverb.* **late** (lāt) *adjective; adverb,* **later, latest.**

lately Not long ago; recently: *Have you seen the principal lately?* **late•ly** (lāt′lē) *adverb.*

lateral On, from, or to the side: *A lateral pass in football is made to a side of the field rather than forward or backward.* **lat•er•al** (lat′ər əl) *adjective.*

lathe A machine that spins around a piece of wood or metal while a cutting tool is pressed against the spinning piece to shape it: *The table leg was shaped on a lathe.* **lathe** (lāth) *noun, plural* **lathes.**

lather 1. Foam made by mixing soap and water: *This shampoo makes a thick lather.* 2. Foam caused by sweating: *The horse was covered with lather*

A lathe is used to make round pieces for furniture.

from running. Noun.
○ 1. To cover with lather: *The barber lathered the customer's face before shaving it.* 2. To form a lather: *This soap does not lather well in cold water. Verb.* **lath•er** (lath′ər) *noun, plural* **lathers**; *verb,* **lathered, lathering.**

Latin 1. The language of the ancient Romans. 2. A person who speaks a language that developed from Latin. The Italians, Spanish, French, and Portuguese are Latins. *Noun.*
○ 1. Having to do with Latin: *The class is studying Latin grammar.* 2. Having to do with the people or countries that use languages coming from Latin: *Spain and Mexico are Latin countries. Adjective.* **Lat•in** (lat′in) *noun, plural* **Latins**; *adjective.*

Latina 1. A girl or woman born in or living in Latin America. 2. A girl or woman born in Latin America but living in the United States. *Noun.*
○ Relating to Latinas or their culture. *Adjective.* **La•ti•na** (lə tē′nə) *noun, plural* **Latinas**; *adjective.*

Latin America The countries of North America and South America that are south of the United States, where languages based on Latin are spoken.

Latin American A person who was born in or is a citizen of a country in Latin America. *Noun.*
○ Of or having to do with Latin America or its people. *Adjective.*

Latino 1. A boy or man born or living in Latin America. 2. A boy or man born in Latin America but living in the United States. *Noun.*
○ Relating to Latinos or their culture. *Adjective.* **La•ti•no** (lə tē′nō) *noun, plural* **Latinos**; *adjective.*

latitude Distance measured on the earth's surface north and south of the equator. On a map or globe, lines of latitude are drawn running east and west. Latitude is expressed in degrees. Each degree is equal to around sixty-nine miles. **lat•i•tude** (lat′i tüd′ *or* lat′i tūd′) *noun, plural* **latitudes.**

latter 1. The second of two things mentioned: *Of baseball and football, our friends like the latter sport better.* 2. Near the end; later: *I spend the latter part of each day doing my homework.* **lat•ter** (lat′ər) *adjective.*

lattice A framework of thin strips of wood or metal placed across each other with open spaces

PRONUNCIATION KEY:

at	āpe	fär	câre	end	mē	it	īce	pierce	hot	ōld	sông	fôrk
oil	out	up	ūse	rüle	pull	tûrn	chin	sing	shop	thin	this	

hw in white; zh in treasure. The symbol ə stands for the unstressed vowel sound in about, taken, pencil, lemon, and circus.

419

between them: *The roses grew over a white wood-en lattice.* **lat·tice** (lat′is) *noun, plural* **lattices.**

laugh To make sounds that show amusement, happiness, or ridicule: *The children laughed at the silly monkeys in the zoo. We laughed at the idea of losing. Verb.*

○ The act or sound of laughing: *His joke got a big laugh. Noun.*

laugh (laf) *verb,* **laughed, laughing;** *noun, plural* **laughs.**

Synonyms

laugh, chuckle, giggle

My funny costume made everyone laugh out loud.
The teacher smiled and chuckled quietly at the joke.
My little sister giggles when we tickle her.

---

laughable Causing or likely to cause a person to laugh: *It was laughable to think that all those clowns could fit in one tiny car.* **laugh·a·ble** (laf′ə bəl) *adjective.*

laughter The act or sound of laughing: *We could hear laughter coming from the playground.* **laugh·ter** (laf′tər) *noun.*

launch¹ 1. To start in motion; send off: *The scientists at the space center will launch a rocket.* 2. To put into the water: *The sailors launched the sailboat.* 3. To start something: *The company launched its store with a big sale. Verb.*

○ The act or process of launching: *a rocket launch. Noun.*

launch (lônch) *verb,* **launched, launching;** *noun, plural* **launches.**

launch² An open motorboat. **launch** (lônch) *noun, plural* **launches.**

launch pad A platform from which a rocket is launched.

launder To wash or wash and iron clothing and linens: *Some delicate clothing must be laundered by hand.* **laun·der** (lôn′dər) *verb,* **laundered, laundering.**

Laundromat A trademark for a laundry where people can wash their own clothes. It has washing machines and clothes dryers that work when coins are put in them. **Laun·dro·mat** (lôn′drə mat) *noun, plural* **Laundromats.**

laundry 1. Clothes and linens that are to be or have been washed: *I folded the laundry.* 2. A place where clothes, sheets, and other things are washed: *We sent the shirts to the laundry.* **laun·dry** (lôn′drē) *noun, plural* **laundries.**

laurel 1. An evergreen tree with stiff, pointed leaves. 2. A flowering shrub that is also called the *mountain laurel.* **lau·rel** (lôr′əl) *noun, plural* **laurels.**

Various species of laurel are found worldwide.

lava 1. Very hot, melted rock that comes out of an erupting volcano. 2. Rock formed by lava that has cooled and hardened. **la·va** (lä′və *or* lav′ə) *noun.*

lavatory 1. A room with toilets and sinks; bathroom. 2. A sink for washing. **lav·a·to·ry** (lav′ə tôr′ē) *noun, plural* **lavatories.**

lavender 1. A plant with fragrant purple flowers. The dried leaves and flowers of lavender are used in chests or closets to give a pleasant odor to clothes and sheets. Oil from the flowers is used in perfumes. 2. A light purple color. *Noun.*

○ Having the color lavender; light purple: *At sunset the sky was lavender and orange. Adjective.* **lav·en·der** (lav′ən dər) *noun, plural* **lavenders;** *adjective.*

lavish 1. Giving or spending in great amounts; extravagant: *I was so lavish with the shampoo that I used the whole bottle in a week.* 2. Being or costing a great amount or an amount that is greater than usual: *The wedding was followed by a lavish dinner. Adjective.*

○ To give or spend in great amounts: *Our grandparents always lavished presents on us. Verb.* **lav·ish** (lav′ish) *adjective; verb,* **lavished, lavishing.**

law 1. A rule made by a government for all the people in a town, state, or country: *The state and city police enforce the **laws** against driving too fast.* 2. A set or system of such rules: *The **law** of the United States is based on the system used in England.* 3. The profession of a lawyer: *a career in **law**.* 4. Any rule or custom: *This book covers the **laws** of English grammar.* 5. A statement that says a group of scientific events will always happen the same way when all the conditions are the same: *This science book tells us about the **law** of gravity.* **law** (lô) *noun, plural* **laws**.

lawful Allowed by the law: *It is not **lawful** to park near a fire hydrant.* **law·ful** (lô′fəl) *adjective.* —**lawfully** *adverb.*

lawn An area with grass that is kept mowed: *The **lawn** around the old house was full of weeds.* **lawn** (lôn) *noun, plural* **lawns**.

lawn mower A machine with blades for cutting grass. Some lawn mowers are run by motors powered by gasoline or electricity.

lawsuit A legal case begun in a court by one person who claims something from another; suit. **law·suit** (lô′süt′) *noun, plural* **lawsuits**.

lawyer A person who has studied the law and can give legal advice and represent people in court. **law·yer** (lô′yər) *noun, plural* **lawyers**.

lay¹ 1. To put or place: *May I **lay** my coat over this chair? **Lay** the plates on the table.* 2. To place or spread upon a surface: *They **laid** new sod on our front yard. The workers will **lay** the new carpet.* 3. To produce an egg or eggs: *These chickens **lay** almost every day.*
Another word that sounds like this is **lei**.

• **to lay aside** or **to lay away** or **to lay by**. To save or reserve: *I try **to lay aside** a little of my allowance every week.*
lay (lā) *verb,* **laid**, **laying**.

lay² Past tense of lie: *The tired dog **lay** down to rest.*
Another word that sounds like this is **lei**.
lay (lā) *verb.*

layer 1. One thickness of something: *A **layer** of dust covered the table. The wall has several **layers** of paint.* 2. A chicken that lays eggs. **lay·er** (lā′ər) *noun, plural* **layers**.

layoff The act of putting a person or group of people out of work, usually temporarily: *A slow-down in the economy caused **layoffs** at the factory.* **lay·off** (lā′ôf′) *noun, plural* **layoffs**.

lazy Not willing to work: *He's too **lazy** to help us clean the garage.* **la·zy** (lā′zē) *adjective,* **lazier**, **laziest**.

lb. An abbreviation for **pound**¹.

lead¹ 1. To show the way: *The guide **led** us through the cave.* 2. To go or be first; be ahead of others: *The general will **lead** the parade. Our team **leads** by a score of three to nothing. You now **lead** the class in arithmetic.* 3. To be a way; go: *This hall **leads** to the cafeteria.* 4. To be the head of; direct: *That teacher **leads** the school orchestra.* 5. To live: *Our doctor **leads** a busy life. Verb.*
○ 1. The first position; being ahead: *The fastest runner took the **lead** in the race.* 2. The amount or extent by which one is ahead: *Our team has a **lead** of seven points.* 3. Clue: *The detectives don't know who stole the money yet, but they have a few **leads**.* 4. The main actor or role in a play, motion picture, or the like: *They want a well-known actor for the **lead** in that movie. Noun.*
lead (lēd) *verb,* **led**, **leading**; *noun, plural* **leads**.

lead² 1. A heavy, soft, gray metal that is easy to bend and melt and is used to make pipes and solder. Lead is a chemical element. 2. The soft black substance in a pencil.
Another word that sounds like this is **led**.
lead (led) *noun, plural* **leads**.

leader A person who leads: *My friend is the **leader** of the school band. The youngest swimmer was the **leader** in the race.* **lead·er** (lē′dər) *noun, plural* **leaders**.

leaf 1. One of the flat, green parts growing from a stem of a plant. Some leaves are made up of smaller parts called leaflets. 2. A sheet of paper: *The student tore a **leaf** out of the notebook.* 3. A movable flat part of the top of a table: *We added a **leaf** to make the table bigger. Noun.*
○ 1. To grow leaves: *Many trees **leaf** in the spring.* 2. To turn pages and glance at them quickly: *I **leafed** through a magazine in the dentist's office. Verb.*

leaflet 1. A single printed sheet of paper or pamphlet: *The candidate for mayor handed out **leaflets** to people on the street. This game comes with a **leaflet** that gives the rules.* 2. A small or young

PRONUNCIATION KEY:
| at | āpe | fär | câre | end | mē | it | īce | pierce | hot | old | sông | fôrk |
| oil | out | up | ūse | rüle | pull | tûrn | chin | sing | shop | thin | this | |
hw in white; zh in treasure. The symbol ə stands for the unstressed vowel sound in about, taken, pencil, lemon, and circus.

421

leaf: *In the spring this tree has fuzzy leaflets.* **3.** One part of a larger leaf: *This leaf is made up of six leaflets.* **leaf·let** (lēf′lĭt) *noun, plural* **leaflets.**

league¹ A number of people, groups, or countries joined together for a common purpose: *Those two baseball teams belong to the same league.* **league** (lēg) *noun, plural* **leagues.**

league² A measure of distance that was used in the past. A league is equal to about three miles. **league** (lēg) *noun, plural* **leagues.**

leak A hole or tear that lets something pass through by accident: *The leak in the milk carton let the milk drip on the table. The tire went flat because of a leak. Noun.*
○ **1.** To have a leak: *The roof of that old house leaks.* **2.** To pass or cause to pass through a hole or tear: *All the air leaked out of the tire.* **3.** To allow or be allowed to become no longer secret: *The official leaked the government secret to the newspapers. Verb.*
Another word that sounds like this is **leek.**
leak (lēk) *noun, plural* **leaks;** *verb,* **leaked, leaking.**

lean¹ **1.** To be at a slant; bend: *The walls of the shed lean out.* **2.** To rest or rely on a person or thing for support or help: *The monkey leaned against the branch. Whom do you lean on when you have a problem?* **3.** To put something at a slant: *Lean the rake against the wall.* **lean** (lēn) *verb,* **leaned, leaning.**

lean² **1.** Having little or no fat; not fat: *That student is tall and lean. Did you see that lean meat at the supermarket?* **2.** Not producing much; poor: *That was a lean year for farmers.* **lean** (lēn) *adjective,* **leaner, leanest.**

leap To jump: *The soldiers leaped to their feet. The horse leaped the fence. Verb.*
○ A jump: *The cat made a leap from the chair. Noun.*
leap (lēp) *verb,* **leaped** or **leapt, leaping;** *noun, plural* **leaps.**

leapfrog A game in which players take turns leaping over the backs of other players. **leap·frog** (lēp′frôg′ or lēp′frŏg′) *noun.*

leapt A past tense and a past participle of **leap:** *The squirrel leapt from the branch to the garage.* **leapt** (lĕpt) *verb.*

leap year A year that has an extra day, February 29. The years 2000, 2004, and 2008 will be leap years.

learn **1.** To get to know through study or practice; gain knowledge or skill: *I want to learn to speak French. The children learned how to swim this summer.* **2.** To memorize: *The students had to learn their lines for the school play.* **3.** To get information about: *The police never learned who had taken the bicycle.* **learn** (lûrn) *verb,* **learned** or **learnt, learning.**

learned Having or showing knowledge: *Our teacher is a learned person.* **learn·ed** (lûr′nĭd) *adjective.*

learning Knowledge gained by careful study: *This book about the ancient Greeks was written by a person of learning.* **learn·ing** (lûr′nĭng) *noun.*

learnt A past tense and a past participle of **learn.** *The child had learnt how to spell all the words on the list.* **learnt** (lûrnt) *verb.*

lease A written agreement for renting a house, apartment, or land: *My parents have a lease for this apartment for three years. Noun.*
○ To rent: *The family leased a cabin for the summer. Verb.*
lease (lēs) *noun, plural* **leases;** *verb,* **leased, leasing.**

leash A strap, cord, or chain for holding or tying an animal: *Fasten the leash to the dog's collar. Noun.*
○ To fasten to a leash: *The child leashed the puppy before taking her for a walk. Verb.*
leash (lēsh) *noun, plural* **leashes;** *verb,* **leashed, leashing.**

least Smallest; littlest: *A second is the least amount of time that is shown on most watches. Of all my houseplants, the cactus requires the least care. Adjective.*
○ The smallest thing or amount: *Saying you are sorry for breaking the vase is the least you can do. Noun.*
○ In the smallest degree: *This year's crop is the least abundant in years. Adverb.*
● **at least. 1.** Not less or fewer than: *At least twenty people will come to the party.* **2.** No matter what happens; at any rate: *We may not succeed with our project, but at least we'll try.*
least (lēst) *adjective; noun; adverb.*

leather A material made from an animal skin that has been cleaned and tanned. Leather is used for making shoes, gloves, jackets, and many other things. **leath·er** (lĕth′ər) *noun, plural* **leathers.**

leave¹ **1.** To go from a place; go away: *We have to leave and go home. The plane leaves at six o'clock. You may leave the table if you have finished eating.* **2.** To withdraw from; quit: *I must leave the softball team. At the end of the summer, I will leave my job.* **3.** To let something stay behind: *Leave the note on the desk. The spilled grape juice left a stain on my shirt. Did you leave your notebook at school?* **4.** To let stay in a certain way: *Why did you leave your work unfinished? Leave the dog alone. The good news left us feeling happy.* **5.** To let another do something: *Why don't you leave the cooking to me tonight?* **6.** To give in a will: *The painting was left to the museum.* **7.** To have remaining: *10 minus 3 leaves 7.*

• **to leave off.** To stop: *Where did we leave off in our discussion?*

• **to leave out.** To omit: *We didn't have enough onions for the stew, so I left them out.*

leave (lēv) *verb*, **left**, **leaving**.

leave² **1.** Permission; consent: *Our parents gave us leave to go camping.* **2.** Permission to be absent: *The soldier asked for a leave to visit a sick friend.*

• **to leave behind.** To forget to bring: *Don't leave anything behind when you get off the bus.*

• **on leave.** Away from one's duty with permission: *The sailors decided to see a play while they were on leave.*

leave (lēv) *noun, plural* **leaves**.

leaves Plural of leaf: *We raked the leaves into a pile.* **leaves** (lēvz) *plural noun*.

The leaves of different trees change color at different times.

Lebanon A country in the Middle East. **Leb·a·non** (leb'ə non') *noun*.

lecture **1.** A talk given to an audience: *The writer gave a lecture on Japanese poets.* **2.** A scolding: *I got a lecture from my parents for breaking the window. Noun.*

○ **1.** To give a lecture: *The scientist lectures on the history of aviation at the college.* **2.** To scold: *The teacher lectured us for not doing our homework. Verb.* **lec·ture** (lek'chər) *noun, plural* **lectures**; *verb*, **lectured**, **lecturing**.

led Past tense and past participle of **lead¹**. *The guide led the hunters through the forest.* Another word that sounds like this is **lead**. **led** (led) *verb*.

ledge A narrow shelf or surface like a shelf: *A window ledge juts out from the wall of a building. The climbers rested on a ledge of the mountain.* **ledge** (lej) *noun, plural* **ledges**.

This rock formation has a long ledge.

lee The side of a ship sheltered from the wind. *Noun.*

○ Sheltered from the wind: *The sailors stayed on the lee side of the ship. Adjective.* **lee** (lē) *noun, plural* **lees**; *adjective*.

leech A kind of worm that sucks the blood of animals. Leeches are found in ponds, rivers, and damp soil. **leech** (lēch) *noun, plural* **leeches**.

leek A plant with long, thick leaves. It tastes like a mild onion. The leaves and bulb of the leek are eaten as vegetables. Another word that sounds like this is **leak**. **leek** (lēk) *noun, plural* **leeks**.

left¹ On the west side of your body when you face north: *I write with my left hand. Adjective.*

○ The left side: *Who's that standing on your left in the photograph? Noun.*

○ Toward the left: *Turn left at the corner. Adverb.* **left** (left) *adjective; noun; adverb*.

left² Past tense and past participle of **leave**: *I left my books at home.* Look up **leave** for more information. **left** (left) *verb*.

PRONUNCIATION KEY:

| at | āpe | fär | câre | end | mē | it | īce | pierce | hot | ōld | sông | fôrk |
| oil | out | up | ūse | rüle | pull | tûrn | chin | sing | shop | thin | this | |

hw in white; zh in treasure. The symbol ə stands for the unstressed vowel sound in about, taken, pencil, lemon, and circus.

423

left-hand 1. On or toward the left:. *Look in the left-hand drawer.* 2. For the left hand: *I lost my left-hand glove.* **left-hand** (left′hand′) *adjective.*

left-handed 1. Using the left hand more easily than the right hand: *My parents are both left-handed.* 2. Done with the left hand: *The quarterback made a left-handed pass.* 3. Made to be held in or used by the left hand: *These are left-handed scissors.* **left-hand·ed** (left′han′did) *adjective.*

leftover Something that remains unused or not eaten: *We had the leftovers from last night's dinner for our lunch. Noun.*
○ Unused or uneaten; remaining: *We ate the leftover pizza for lunch. Adjective.*
left·o·ver (left′ō′vər) *noun, plural* **leftovers;** *adjective.*

leg 1. One of the parts of the body that a person or animal stands and walks on. 2. Something like a leg: *The leg of the chair is broken.* 3. One part of a trip or journey: *On the first leg of our trip, we'll travel 300 miles.*
• **to pull one's leg.** To trick or tease: *I was pulling your leg when I told you we would get six feet of snow.*
leg (leg) *noun, plural* **legs.**

legacy 1. Money or property left to someone in a will. 2. Something handed down by custom or tradition: *a legacy of public service.* **leg·a·cy** (leg′ə sē) *noun, plural* **legacies.**

legal 1. Relating to law: *Go to a lawyer for legal advice.* 2. Allowed by or according to the law or the rules; lawful: *They're the legal owners of the farm. That's not a legal move in checkers.* **le·gal** (lē′gəl) *adjective.* —**legally** *adverb.*

legend 1. A story passed down through the years that many people believe, but that is not entirely true: *There are many legends about the knights of the Middle Ages.* **leg·end** (lej′ənd) *noun, plural* **legends.**

legendary Relating to a legend or legends: *a legendary king and queen.* **leg·end·ar·y** (lej′ən der′ē) *adjective.*

leggings Outer coverings for the legs, made of cloth or leather: *When I was younger, I wore leggings when I played in the snow.* **leg·gings** (leg′ingz) *plural noun.*

legible Easily read: *This sloppy writing is not legible.* **leg·i·ble** (lej′ə bəl) *adjective.* —**legibly** *adverb.*

legion 1. A unit of the army of ancient Rome, having five or six thousand soldiers and several hundred more on horseback. 2. An army: *The enemy sent its legions to conquer the small country.* 3. A great number of persons or things: *Legions attended the county fair.* **le·gion** (lē′jən) *noun, plural* **legions.**

legislation 1. The making or passing of laws: *The work of the Senate and House of Representatives is legislation.* 2. The laws made or passed: *Congress passed new legislation dealing with housing.* **leg·is·la·tion** (lej′is lā′shən) *noun, plural* **legislations.**

legislative 1. Of or having to do with making or passing laws: *Senators and Representatives have legislative duties.* 2. Having the power to make or pass laws: *Congress is the legislative branch of the United States government.* **leg·is·la·tive** (lej′is lā′tiv) *adjective.*

legislature A body of persons that has the power to make or pass laws: *The state legislature voted on a new tax bill.* **leg·is·la·ture** (lej′is lā′chər) *noun, plural* **legislatures.**

Every state in the United States has its own legislature.

legitimate According to what is right or lawful: *The judge ruled that the state was the legitimate owner of the land. The student could not give a legitimate excuse for being late.* **le·git·i·mate** (li jit′ə mit) *adjective.* —**legitimately** *adverb.*

legume A plant whose seeds grow in pods. Peas, beans, lentils, and peanuts are legumes. **leg·ume** (leg′ūm *or* li gūm′) *noun, plural* **legumes.**

lei A wreath of flowers, leaves, or other material, often worn around the neck in Hawaii. Another word that sounds like this is **lay.** **lei** (lā) *noun, plural* **leis.**

leisure The time to do what one likes; free time: *The busy farmer did not have much leisure. Noun.*
○ Not taken up by work, school, or duty. *I spend my leisure time reading. Adjective.*
lei·sure (lē′zhər *or* lezh′ər) *noun; adjective.*

lemon A yellow citrus fruit with a sour taste. Lemons have an oval or round shape, a rind, and juicy pulp. Lemons grow on small, thorny trees in warm regions. *Noun.*

○ Made from or flavored with lemon: *The bakery sells **lemon** pies. Adjective.*

lem·on (lem′ən) *noun, plural* **lemons**; *adjective.*

lemonade A drink made from lemon juice, water, and sugar. **lem·on·ade** (lem′ə nād′) *noun, plural* **lemonades.**

lend 1. To let a person have or use something for a while: *Please **lend** me your pen.* 2. To give a person money to use for a certain period of time. When the money is repaid, the person also pays interest. *The bank will **lend** my parents money to buy a car.* 3. To provide; give: *Bright lights **lend** excitement to the city.* **lend** (lend) *verb,* **lent, lending.**

length 1. The distance from one end to the other end: *the **length** of a football field.* 2. The amount or extent from beginning to end: *My vacation was three months in **length**.* 3. A piece of something: *a **length** of rope.* **length** (lengkth *or* length) *noun, plural* **lengths.**

lengthen To make or become longer: *Can you **lengthen** this dress? The days **lengthened** as summer grew near.* **length·en** (lengk′thən *or* leng′thən) *verb,* **lengthened, lengthening.**

lengthwise In the same direction as the length: *Split these logs **lengthwise**. These towels should be folded **lengthwise**.* **length·wise** (lengkth′wīz′ *or* length′wīz′) *adverb; adjective.*

lenient Tolerant or merciful; not strict: *My parents are **lenient** about my staying up late.* **len·i·ent** (lē′nē ənt *or* lēn′yənt) *adjective.* —**leniently** *adverb.*

lens 1. A piece of glass or other clear material curved to make light rays move apart or come together. A lens can make an object look larger or closer. Lenses for sunglasses are tinted. 2. The curved, clear part of the eye that focuses light on the retina. The lens is located behind the pupil. **lens** (lenz) *noun, plural* **lenses.**

Lenses are used in eyeglasses, telescopes, and cameras.

lent Past tense and past participle of **lend**: *I **lent** my classmate a pencil for the test.* **lent** (lent) *verb.*

Lent The forty days before Easter, not including Sundays. In many Christian churches, Lent is observed as a time to pray, fast, and repent for sins. **Lent** (lent) *noun.*

lentil A flat, round seed that grows on a certain kind of legume. Lentils are eaten cooked, especially in soups. **len·til** (len′təl) *noun, plural* **lentils.**

leopard A large animal of the cat family. Leopards have short fur that is usually yellow or gray with black spots grouped in circles. They live in Africa and southern Asia. **leop·ard** (lep′ərd) *noun, plural* **leopards.**

Leopards live in Africa and southern Asia.

leotard A single garment that fits tightly from the neck to the top of the legs or to the feet, worn especially by acrobats and dancers. **le·o·tard** (lē′ə tärd) *noun, plural* **leotards.**

leprechaun In Irish folklore, a kind of elf who reveals hidden treasure to the one who can catch him. **leprechaun** (lep′rə kon′) *noun, plural* **leprechauns.**

leprosy A disease that attacks the nerves, skin, and muscles. People with leprosy lose sensation in parts of their bodies and can easily injure themselves without knowing it. Leprosy is caused by an infection. **lep·ro·sy** (lep′rə sē) *noun.*

less Not as much: *I have **less** work to do today than I had yesterday. Adjective.*

○ To a smaller extent or degree: *This watch is **less** expensive than that one. Adverb.*

○ A smaller number or quantity: *I finished **less** of*

PRONUNCIATION KEY:

| at | āpe | fär | câre | end | mē | it | īce | pierce | hot | ōld | sông | fôrk |
| oil | out | up | ūse | rüle | púll | tûrn | chin | sing | shop | thin | this | |

hw in white; zh in treasure. The symbol ə stands for the unstressed vowel sound in about, taken, pencil, lemon, and circus.

425

the work than I had planned. Noun.

○ With the subtraction of; minus: *10 less 7 is 3.* Preposition.

less (les) *adjective; adverb; noun; preposition.*

LANGUAGE NOTE

It isn't difficult to remember when to use less and when to use fewer. Use "less" when you are speaking about something that cannot be counted: There is *less* sugar in the bowl. Use "fewer" when you are speaking about something that can be counted: *Fewer* students attended the game.

-less A suffix that means: **1.** Having no; without: *Hopeless means having no hope.* **2.** That cannot be: *Countless means that cannot be counted.*

lessen To make or become less: *The teacher lessened the amount of homework. The pain of my sprained ankle began to lessen.* Another word that sounds like this is **lesson.** **less•en** (les′ən) *verb,* **lessened, lessening.**

lesser Smaller or less in number, size, degree, or importance: *From the high peak, we could see the lesser mountains around us.* **less•er** (les′ər) *adjective.*

lesson **1.** Something to be learned, taught, or studied: *Today's arithmetic lesson was on fractions. We have five more lessons to study in our social studies book.* **2.** A period of time given to instruction; class or course of study: *Do you have a piano lesson today? My cousin is taking skating lessons.* Another word that sounds like this is **lessen.** **les•son** (les′ən) *noun, plural* **lessons.**

let **1.** To allow; permit: *Mom and Dad let me go to the party. Do you let your friends ride your bicycle?* **2.** To allow to pass or go: *The hole in the roof lets in the rain. Open the cage and let the bird out.* **3.** To cause or make: *I will let my parents know what I would like for my birthday.* **4.** To rent: *My family lets a cabin for the summer every year.*

• **to let down.** To disappoint: *I let down my friends when I didn't help them.*

• **to let off.** To set free with little or no punishment: *The police officer let the driver off with just a warning.*

• **to let on.** To show that one knows something; admit: *I didn't let on that I had heard about my surprise party.*

• **to let out.** **1.** To utter: *At one point in the movie, the person sitting next to me let out a scream.* **2.** To make larger: *These jeans will have to be let out.*

• **to let up.** To lessen or stop: *It seemed the rain would never let up.*

let (let) *verb,* **let, letting.**

let's Shortened form of "let us": *Let's go for a walk.* **let's** (lets) *contraction.*

letter **1.** A mark that stands for a spoken sound: *The word "run" has three letters.* **2.** A written message: *I wrote a letter to my friend.* **3.** The initial of a school or college that is given to a student as an award: *The pitcher for our high school team has received a letter every year for playing so well.* **let•ter** (let′ər) *noun, plural* **letters.**

letter carrier A person who carries and delivers mail.

lettering Letters that have been drawn, painted, or formed by some other means: *The lettering on this statue is carefully carved.* **let•ter•ing** (let′ə ring) *noun.*

lettuce A plant with large green or reddish leaves. Lettuce is eaten in salads. Lettuce can be either green or red in color. **let•tuce** (let′is) *noun, plural* **lettuces.**

There are many different kinds of lettuce.

leukemia A cancer in which the body makes too many white blood cells. **leu•ke•mi•a** (lü kē′mē ə) *noun, plural* **leukemias.**

levee **1.** An embankment built along a river to keep the river from overflowing. **2.** A landing place for boats and ships to dock along a river. Another word that sounds like this is **levy.** **lev•ee** (lev′ē) *noun, plural* **levees.**

level 1. Having a flat, horizontal surface; even: *The airport was built on* **level** *ground.* 2. At the same height or position: *The top of the tree is* **level** *with the roof of the house. Adjective.*
○ 1. Height: *The flood in the basement rose to a* **level** *of two feet.* 2. A position or rank in a process, series, or order: *Our neighbor has risen to the* **level** *of manager of the store. The students in this class read at a high* **level**. 3. A floor or story of a structure: *The car is parked on the lower* **level**. 4. A tool used to show whether a surface is flat. A level is a long, narrow box with a liquid inside that shows when the surface that it is on is flat: *The carpenter put a* **level** *on the shelf to make sure it was straight. Noun.*
○ 1. To make flat: *The workers* **leveled** *the hilly land with a bulldozer.* 2. To bring to the level of the ground; destroy: *The fire* **leveled** *the house. Verb.*
lev•el (lev′əl) *adjective; noun, plural* **levels**; *verb,* **leveled, leveling.**

lever 1. A rod or bar used to lift things or pry things open: *A crowbar is a kind of* **lever**. 2. A rod or bar attached to a machine, used to work or control it: *The operator moved a* **lever** *to lower the arm of the crane.* **lev•er** (lev′ər *or* lē′vər) *noun, plural* **levers.**

levy To impose or collect by lawful actions or force: *The county plans to* **levy** *new taxes. Verb.*
○ 1. A tax: *The legislature has passed a new levy on gasoline.* 2. The act of levying: *The* **levy** *of new taxes angered many citizens. Noun.*
Another word that sounds like this is **levee.**
lev•y (lev′ē) *verb,* **levied, levying**; *noun, plural* **levies.**

liable 1. Likely; apt: *You are* **liable** *to be cold if you don't wear a jacket.* 2. Responsible by law: *The driver who caused the accident is* **liable** *for the damage done to the other car.* **li•a•ble** (lī′ə bəl) *adjective.*

liar A person who tells lies. **li•ar** (lī′ər) *noun, plural* **liars.**

liberal 1. Generous: *The family gave a* **liberal** *donation to the library.* 2. More than enough; plentiful: *The school has a* **liberal** *supply of chalk.* 3. Favoring change as a way of improving things in political and social matters; favoring progress and

reform: *The two candidates in the election were a* **liberal** *politician and a conservative one.* 4. Not limited or narrow; broad: *Science and literature are two parts of a* **liberal** *education.* 5. Not narrow in one's thinking; tolerant. *Adjective.*
○ A person who is liberal. *Noun.*
lib•er•al (lib′ər əl) *adjective; noun, plural* **liberals.**

liberate To set free: *The soldiers* **liberated** *the prisoners.* **lib•er•ate** (lib′ə rāt′) *verb,* **liberated, liberating.** —**liberation** *noun* —**liberator.**

Liberia A country in western Africa. **Li•be•ri•a** (lī bîr′ē ə) *noun.*

liberty 1. The ability to act, speak, or think the way one pleases: *The people lost their* **liberty** *under the dictator's rule.* 2. Freedom from control of another: *England was forced to give the American colonies their* **liberty**. 3. Time granted to a sailor in the navy to go ashore: *During their* **liberty***, the sailors watched a bullfight.*
• **at liberty.** 1. Not confined; free: *The escaped prisoners are still* **at liberty**. 2. Permitted; allowed: *I am not* **at liberty** *to tell you.*
lib•er•ty (lib′ər tē) *noun, plural* **liberties.**

librarian A person who is in charge of or works in a library. **li•brar•i•an** (lī brâr′ē ən) *noun, plural* **librarians.**

library 1. A collection of books, magazines, and newspapers. Many libraries also have computers, recorded music, films, and videotapes: *My parents gave me some books for my* **library**. 2. A room or building for such a collection: *You can study in the school* **library**. **li•brar•y** (lī′brer′ē) *noun, plural* **libraries.**

Libya A country in northern Africa. **Lib•y•a** (lib′ē ə) *noun.*

lice Plural of louse: *The dog was scratching because it had* **lice**. **lice** (līs) *plural noun.*

license A card or paper showing that a person has legal permission to do or have something: *The police asked the drivers in the accident for their* **licenses**. *Noun.*
○ To give a license to or for: *Doctors are* **licensed** *to practice medicine. Verb.*
li•cense (lī′səns) *noun, plural* **licenses**; *verb,* **licensed, licensing.**

lichen An organism made up of a kind of algae and a fungus. Lichens grow on tree trunks, rocks,

PRONUNCIATION KEY:

at	āpe	fär	câre	end	mē	it	īce	pierce	hot	old	song	fôrk
oil	out	up	ūse	rüle	pull	tûrn	chin	sing	shop	thin	this	

hw in white; zh in treasure. The symbol ə stands for the unstressed vowel sound in about, taken, pencil, lemon, and circus.

427

or the ground. **li·chen** (lī′kən) *noun, plural* **lichens.**

lick **1.** To move the tongue over something: *I licked the envelope to seal it.*
2. To eat or drink something by taking it up with the tongue: *I licked my ice cream cone.* **3.** To defeat: *Our team can lick theirs.* **4.** To move over or touch lightly or quickly: *The flames began to lick the tree above the burning shed. Verb.*
○ **1.** A movement of the tongue over something: *The cat gave the milk a lick.*
2. Salt that animals

Licking an ice cream
cone can be messy.

can lick: *The farmer put a block of salt in the pasture as a lick for the cows.* **3.** A small amount; bit: *didn't do a lick of work. Noun.*
lick (lik) *verb,* **licked, licking;** *noun, plural* **licks.**

licorice **1.** A plant whose sweet-tasting root is used in medicine and candy. **2.** A candy flavored with licorice. **lic·o·rice** (lik′ər is *or* lik′ər ish) *noun.*

lid **1.** A movable cover: *a garbage can lid.* **2.** Either of the upper or lower protective coverings of the eye; eyelid. **lid** (lid) *noun, plural* **lids.**

lie¹ Something a person says that he or she knows is not true: *You told a lie when you said you were at school today. Noun.*
○ To say something that is not true; tell a lie: *Those two students lie so often that you never know when to believe them. Verb.*
Another word that sounds like this is **lye.**
lie (lī) *noun, plural* **lies;** *verb,* **lied, lying.**

lie² **1.** To put oneself in a flat position on a surface: *I like to lie on the grass and watch the clouds.*
2. To be or rest on something: *The book lies on the table.* **3.** To stay in a certain place or condition: *The treasure lies at the bottom of the ocean.*
4. To be located or placed: *Mexico lies south of the United States.* **5.** To be found; exist: *The problem with the car lies in the ignition.*
Another word that sounds like this is **lye.**
lie (lī) *verb,* **lay, lain, lying.**

LANGUAGE NOTE		

The verbs **lie** and **lay,** and their inflected forms, are easy to confuse. Remember that *lay* is followed by a noun or pronoun that is used as a direct object. *Lie* does not take a direct object. Here are the various inflected forms of *lie* and *lay:*

Present	Past	Past Participle
lie	lay	lain
lay	laid	laid

lieutenant An officer in the armed forces. In the United States Army, Marine Corps, and Air Force, a lieutenant is next below a captain in rank. The two ranks of lieutenant in the Army, Air Force, and Marines are second lieutenant and first lieutenant. In the United States Navy and Coast Guard, a lieutenant is next below a commander. The two ranks of lieutenant in the Navy and Coast Guard are lieutenant junior grade and lieutenant. **lieu·ten·ant** (lü ten′ənt) *noun, plural* **lieutenants.**

life **1.** The quality that makes it possible for things to grow and reproduce. Plants and animals have life, rocks do not. **2.** The fact of having this quality: *Don't risk your life in a dangerous stunt.* **3.** A living being; person: *Firefighters save many lives every year.* **4.** Living beings: *There was no plant life in the cave.* **5.** The period from birth to death: *My grandparents had long lives.* **6.** The period during which something lasts or works: *Poor driving can shorten the life of a car.* **7.** A way of living: *Life in the city can be exciting.* **8.** A story of a person's life: *I am reading the life of a great scientist.* **9.** Energy; spirit: *You are always full of life.* **life** (līf) *noun, plural* **lives.**

lifeboat A boat used for saving lives at sea or along the shore. Lifeboats are often carried on larger ships. **life·boat** (līf′bōt′) *noun, plural* **lifeboats.**

life cycle The sequence of changes each living thing passes through during its life. The life cycle of animals includes birth, development, reproduction, growing old, and death.

lifeguard A person hired to protect and help swimmers at a beach or pool: *The lifeguard blew a whistle to warn the swimmers that they were too far from shore.* **life·guard** (līf′gärd′) *noun, plural* **lifeguards.**

life jacket A life preserver that looks like a vest or sleeveless jacket.

lifeless Not having life: *the cold and **lifeless** moon*. **life·less** (līf′lis) *adjective*. —**lifelessly** *adverb*.

lifelike Like something alive or real: *The doll was so **lifelike** that for a moment we thought it was a real baby*. **life·like** (līf′līk′) *adjective*.

lifelong Lasting or continuing through a person's life: *The children became **lifelong** friends*. **life·long** (līf′lông′) *adjective*.

life preserver A device used to keep a person floating in water. A life preserver can be a belt, a vest, or a ring: *I wear a **life preserver** whenever I go sailing*. **life pre·ser·ver** (pri zûr′və) *noun*, *plural* **life preservers**.

A life preserver is filled with air or made with material that floats.

lifesaving The skill or method of saving a person's life. Lifeguards and firefighters are trained in lifesaving. *Noun*.

○ Used or made for saving a person's life: *The fire engine carried **lifesaving** equipment*. *Adjective*. **life·sa·ving** (līf′sā′ving) *noun; adjective*.

life span The period of time that a person, animal, or plant is expected to live.

lifetime The period of time that the life of a person or thing lasts: *My grandfather has seen many changes in his **lifetime***. **life·time** (līf′tīm′) *noun*, *plural* **lifetimes**.

lift 1. To raise or be raised; pick up: *I can't **lift** this heavy suitcase. The team's spirits **lifted** after their victory over the league champions*. 2. To rise into the air: *The jet **lifted** from the runway*. 3. To rise or seem to rise and go; disappear: *The fog **lifted**, and we had a clear day*. *Verb*.

○ 1. The act of lifting: *Give me a **lift** into the tree.*

2. A free ride given to a person: *Our neighbor gave us a **lift** into town*. 3. A happy feeling: *Your compliment gave me a **lift***. *Noun*.

lift (lift) *verb*, **lifted**, **lifting**; *noun*, *plural* **lifts**.

lift-off The movement of a rocket or spacecraft as it rises from its launch pad: *After the **lift-off**, the rocket went into orbit*. **lift-off** (lift′ôf′) *noun*, *plural* **lift-offs**.

ligament A band of strong tissue that connects bones or holds an organ of the body in place. **lig·a·ment** (lig′ə mənt) *noun*, *plural* **ligaments**.

light¹ 1. The form of energy that makes it possible for us to see. The sun gives off light. 2. Something that gives off light or brightness. Candles and lamps are lights. *We could see the dim **lights** of the distant town*. 3. Something used to set fire to something else. A flame and a spark are lights. *Give me a **light** so I can start the logs burning*. 4. The time of day when the sun first shines; daybreak: *Because I deliver newspapers, I have to wake up before **light***. 5. Knowledge or information; understanding: *The scientific study shed new **light** on preventing pollution*. 6. Public knowledge: *Some new clues to the mystery have come to **light***. 7. The way that someone thinks about something: *We saw the problem in a new **light***. *Noun*.

○ 1. To burn or cause to burn: *Wet wood will not **light** easily. We will **light** candles if the electricity goes off*. 2. To cause to give off light: *When you **light** that lamp, it makes the whole room bright*. 3. To give brightness to: *One large bulb **lights** the hallway*. 4. To make or become bright or lively: *Your face **lighted** up when you heard you had passed the test*. 5. To show the way by means of a light or lights: *Please **light** our way up these dark steps with your flashlight*. *Verb*.

○ 1. Bright; not dark: *a **light** and airy room*. 2. Pale in color: *a **light** complexion*. *Adjective*. **light** (līt) *noun*, *plural* **lights**; *verb*, **lighted** or **lit**, **lighting**; *adjective*, **lighter**, **lightest**.

light² 1. Having little weight; not heavy: *The empty box was **light***. 2. Not great in amount or force: *a **light** rain. The leaves hardly moved in the **light** breeze*. 3. Easy to do or bear; not hard: *We did some **light** cleaning*. 4. Moving easily; graceful; nimble: *Good dancers are **light** on their feet*.

PRONUNCIATION KEY:

| at | āpe | fär | câre | end | mē | it | īce | pîerce | hot | ōld | sông | fôrk |
| oil | out | up | ūse | rüle | püll | tûrn | chin | sing | shop | thin | this | |

hw in white; zh in treasure. The symbol ə stands for the unstressed vowel sound in about, taken, pencil, lemon, and circus.

429

5. Happy; cheerful: *We whistled a* **light** *tune.*
6. Entertaining; amusing; not serious: *I read a good,* **light** *novel last week.* **7.** Few or slight; not serious: *The army suffered* **light** *losses in the battle.* **light** (līt) *adjective,* **lighter, lightest.**

lighten¹ To make or become brighter or lighter: *The sky* **lightened** *after the thunderstorm.* **light‧en** (lī′tən) *verb,* **lightened, lightening.**

lighten² **1.** To make or become less heavy or harsh: *You'll have to* **lighten** *that suitcase because no one can lift it. The teacher* **lightened** *the homework assignment.* **2.** To make or become more cheerful; ease: *My spirits* **lightened** *after the test.* **light‧en** (lī′tən) *verb,* **lightened, lightening.**

lighthearted Not bothered by worries; cheerful; gay: *The* **lighthearted** *child was always laughing.* **light‧heart‧ed** (līt′här′tid) *adjective.* —**lightheartedly** *adverb.*

lighthouse A tower with a strong light on top, built near a dangerous place in the water to warn or guide ships. **light‧house** (līt′hous′) *noun, plural* **lighthouses** (līt′hou′ziz).

Lighthouses **have saved the lives of millions of sailors.**

lighting The system or arrangement of lights in a room, building, or area: *This room is too dark; we need better* **lighting.** **light‧ing** (lī′ting) *noun.*

lightning A flash of light in the sky caused by electricity moving between clouds or between a cloud and the ground: *Lightning struck our house during the storm.* **light‧ning** (līt′ning) *noun.*

lightning bug A small beetle that gives off flashes of light as a signal to a mate; firefly.

light pen An instrument shaped like a pen and used to draw or change images on a computer screen or to give commands to the computer.

light-year The distance that light travels through space in one year. Since light moves at a speed of about 186,000 miles per second, it travels

about 5,880,000 miles in one year. If a star is 30 light-years away, it takes 30 years for its light to reach the earth. **light-year** (līt′yîr′) *noun, plural* **light-years.**

likable or **likeable** Easy to like; agreeable; pleasant: *It's hard to argue with someone who is so* **likable.** **lik‧a‧ble** or **like‧a‧ble** (lī′kə bəl) *adjective.*

-like A suffix that means similar to; like: *Lifelike* means like life.

like¹ **1.** Almost the same as; similar to: *Your bicycle is* **like** *mine.* **2.** In the same or a similar way as: *I tried to crow* **like** *a rooster.* **3.** Such as: *I do well in subjects* **like** *math and science.* **4.** Having the desire to; inclined to: *Do you feel* **like** *watching television or playing a game?* **5.** Giving a promise or indication of; likely to: *It looks* **like** *rain.* Preposition.
◦ Similar or equal: *The twins wore* **like** *outfits to the party. The boss gave me a fifty-dollar bonus and a* **like** *amount to all the other workers.* Adjective.
◦ **1.** In the way that; as: *This soup doesn't taste* **like** *it has enough salt.* **2.** As if; as though: *It looks* **like** *it will snow today.* Conjunction.
like (līk) *preposition; adjective; conjunction.*

like² To be fond of; enjoy: *Do you* **like** *sports? Out of the litter, I* **like** *the brown puppy the most. I* **like** *swimming in the ocean.* Verb.
◦ **likes.** The things a person enjoys or prefers: *I have strong* **likes** *and dislikes in clothes.* Noun.
like (līk) *verb,* **liked, liking;** *plural noun.*

likelihood The condition or quality of being expected: *Is there any* **likelihood** *that it will rain tonight? In all* **likelihood,** *I will leave tomorrow.* **like‧li‧hood** (līk′lē hůd′) *noun.*

likely **1.** Seeming to be true; probable: *The damp weather is the* **likely** *cause of this year's poor strawberry crop.* **2.** To be expected: *It is* **likely** *to rain tomorrow. We are* **likely** *to finish painting the fence by sundown.* **3.** Right for the time or purpose; suitable: *That student has many good ideas and is a* **likely** *candidate for school president.* Adjective.
◦ Almost certainly, probably: *Judging from the porch they built, they're most* **likely** *good carpenters.* Adverb.
like‧ly (līk′lē) *adjective,* **likelier, likeliest;** *adverb.*

likeness **1.** The condition of looking alike; resemblance: *The girl's* **likeness** *to her mother was very* *strong.* **2.** A portrait: *The one-dollar bill has a likeness of George Washington on it.* **like·ness** (līk′nis) *noun, plural* **likenesses.**

likewise **1.** In a like way; similarly: *Watch what the swimming teacher does and then do likewise.* **2.** Also: *The class president is a fine athlete and a good student likewise.* **like·wise** (līk′wīz′) *adverb.*

liking A feeling of being fond or preferring: *a liking for folk music.* **lik·ing** (lī′king) *noun, plural* **likings.**

lilac **1.** A shrub that has clusters of purple, pink, or white flowers. Some lilacs have flowers that smell very sweet. **2.** A pale, pinkish purple color. *Noun.*
○ Having a pale, pinkish purple color. *Adjective.* **li·lac** (lī′lək) *noun, plural* **lilacs;** *adjective.*

lily **1.** A large, showy flower shaped like a trumpet. The lily grows from a bulb. **2.** Any plant like a lily: *A water lily grows in the water.* **lil·y** (lil′ē) *noun, plural* **lilies.**

lily of the valley A plant that grows from a bulb and has tiny flowers growing down one side of its stem. The flowers smell very sweet and are shaped like bells.

lima bean A flat, pale green bean that is eaten cooked. **li·ma bean** (lī′mə).

limb **1.** A part of a body used in moving or grasping. Arms, legs, wings, and flippers are limbs. **2.** One of the large branches of a tree: *We hung a swing from a limb of the old tree.* **limb** (lim) *noun, plural* **limbs.**

This limb has fallen across the stream.

lime¹ A white substance like powder made up of calcium and oxygen. Lime is found in seashells or is made by burning limestone. Lime is used in making plaster and cement and as a fertilizer. **lime** (līm) *noun.*

lime² A small, yellowish green citrus fruit. The lime has an oval or round shape, a thin rind, and a juicy pulp. It grows on a thorny evergreen tree. **lime** (līm) *noun, plural* **limes.**

limerick A funny poem five lines long. An example of a limerick is: There once was a man named Paul/ Who went to a masquerade ball./ He decided to risk it/ And go as a biscuit/ But a dog ate him up in the hall. **lim·er·ick** (lim′ə rik) *noun, plural* **limericks.**

WORD HISTORY

The word **limerick** comes from the name of a place in Ireland. It was the custom at parties to take turns making up funny poems. At the end of a poem, everyone would sing, "Will you come up to Limerick?" This may be how these funny poems got their name.

limestone A hard rock used for building and for making lime. Most limestone is light gray. **lime·stone** (līm′stōn′) *noun.*

limit The point at which something ends or must end: *Stay inside the limits of the park. That car was going faster than the speed limit. Noun.*
○ To keep within a bound or bounds; restrict: *I have to limit my spending because I'm trying to save money. Verb.*
lim·it (lim′it) *noun, plural* **limits;** *verb,* **limited, limiting.**

limp¹ To walk unevenly or with difficulty: *My dog is limping because he hurt his leg. Verb.*
○ A lame or uneven walk. *His fall on the court caused the basketball player to limp. Noun.*
limp (limp) *verb,* **limped, limping;** *noun, plural* **limps.**

limp² Not stiff or firm: *After three days of heat, the flowers became limp and died.* **limp** (limp) *adjective,* **limper, limpest.**

Lincoln's Birthday A holiday on February 12 observed in some states to celebrate Abraham Lincoln's birthday. This holiday is observed by many states on Presidents' Day. Look up **Presidents' Day** for more information. **Lin·coln's Birthday** (ling′kənz).

PRONUNCIATION KEY:
| at | āpe | fär | câre | end | mē | it | īce | pierce | hot | ōld | sông | fôrk |
| oil | out | up | ūse | rüle | pull | tûrn | chin | sing | shop | thin | this | |

hw in white; zh in treasure. The symbol ə stands for the unstressed vowel sound in about, taken, pencil, lemon, and circus.

431

line¹ 1. A long, thin mark or stroke: *White lines divide the lanes of the highway.* 2. Anything like a line: *Your forehead is full of lines from frowning.* 3. A limit or boundary; edge: *That row of trees marks the line of our property.* 4. A number of persons or things arranged one after the other; row: *We waited in a long line outside the movie theater.* 5. A row of words or letters on a page: *The journalist wrote a column of thirty lines for the newspaper.* 6. A short letter, note, or verse: *While you're at camp, don't forget to drop us a line once in a while.* 7. **lines.** The words spoken by a person in a play: *the actor was so nervous that he forgot his lines.* 8. A kind of goods: *That store is selling a new line of bicycles.* 9. A system of transportation in which vehicles travel over a route on a regular schedule: *The bus line runs buses on most of the main streets of the city.* 10. A cord, rope, wire, or cable used for a special purpose: *We hung the wash on the line to dry. I telephoned you, but your line was busy.* 11. A pipe that carries a fluid from one place to another. *The water line broke, and our neighborhood was without water for three days. Noun.*
○ 1. To mark or cover with lines: *I always line blank paper before I write on it.* 2. To form a line along: *Trees lined the road. Verb.*

  • **in line.** 1. In a line or row: *We waited in line for tickets.* 2. In agreement: *Most of your ideas are in line with mine.*

  • **out of line.** Lacking proper respect: *His behavior was rude and out of line.*

  • **to line up.** 1. To form or cause to form a line: *The workers lined up to get their pay. The teacher lined the students up according to their height.* 2. To obtain or gather: *The mayor is trying to line up supporters for the new tax law.*
line (līn) *noun, plural* **lines;** *verb,* **lined, lining.**

line² 1. To cover the inside of: *The tailor lined the wool suit with silk.* 2. To be used as a lining or covering for: *Paintings lined the walls of the museum.* **line** (līn) *verb,* **lined, lining.**

linear Having to do with length: *Feet, miles, centimeters, and inches are linear measurements.* **lin·e·ar** (lin'ē ər) *adjective.*

linen 1. A cloth woven from fibers of flax. 2. **linens:** Household things made of linen or a similar cloth. Sheets, tablecloths, towels, and napkins are linens. *Noun.*
○ Made of linen. *Adjective.*
lin·en (lin'ən) *noun, plural* **linens;** *adjective.*

liner A ship or airplane that belongs to a transportation line. **lin·er** (lī'nər) *noun, plural* **liners.**

linger To stay on as if not wanting to leave; move slowly: *The fans lingered outside the stadium to see the team.* **lin·ger** (ling'gər) *verb,* **lingered, lingering.**

lining The layer or coating that covers the inside of something: *The fur lining of the jacket made it very warm.* **lin·ing** (lī'ning) *noun, plural* **linings.**

link 1. One of the rings or loops of a chain. 2. Anything that joins or connects: *That museum provides a link to our country's history.* 3. Something that looks like a link in a chain, such as a link of sausage. 4. A place on a Web page that you click on to be taken to another Web page. *Noun.*
○ To join or be joined; connect: *We linked arms to form a circle. Verb.*
link (lingk) *noun, plural* **links;** *verb,* **linked, linking.**

linking verb A verb that links a subject with a predicate noun or a predicate adjective. A linking verb does not express action. In the sentence "The movie was a thrilling mystery," "was" is a linking verb.

linoleum A floor covering made with a hardened mixture of linseed oil and finely ground cork or wood put on a canvas back. It is nailed or glued in place. **li·no·le·um** (li nō'lē əm) *noun, plural* **linoleums.**

linseed oil An oil from the seed of certain flax plants, used to make paints, varnish, ink, patent leather, and linoleum. **lin·seed oil** (lin'sēd').

**The male lion usually lets the
female lions do the hunting.**

lion A large, strong animal of the cat family. The lion lives mainly in Africa and southern Asia. It has a yellowish brown coat of short, coarse hair. The male has long, shaggy hair around its neck, head, and shoulders. **li·on** (lī′ən) *noun, plural* **lions.**

lioness A female lion. **li·on·ess** (lī′ə nis) *noun, plural* **lionesses.**

lip 1. Either of the two soft flaps of flesh that form the opening to the mouth. 2. The edge or rim of an opening: *I chipped the lip of the pitcher.* **lip** (lip) *noun, plural* **lips.**

lip-read To understand what a person says only by watching the speaker's mouth and not by hearing. **lip-read** (lip′rēd′) *verb,* **lip-read, lip-reading.** —**lip-reading** *noun.*

lipstick A stick of oily material used as a cosmetic for coloring the lips. **lip·stick** (lip′stik′) *noun, plural* **lipsticks.**

liquid A form of matter that is not a solid or a gas. A liquid can flow easily and take on the shape of any container into which it is poured. Water, milk, and ink are liquids. *Noun.*
○ In the form of a liquid; not solid or gaseous: *The nurse gave me the liquid medicine with a spoon. Adjective.*
liq·uid (lik′wid) *noun, plural* **liquids;** *adjective.*

liquor A kind of alcoholic drink: *Whiskey and gin are liquors.* **liq·uor** (lik′ər) *noun, plural* **liquors.**

lira A unit of money in Italy. **li·ra** (lîr′ə) *noun, plural* **lire** (lîr′ā).

lisp A way of speaking in which a person says the sound of *s* as the sound of *th* in *thing* and the sound of *z* as the sound of *th* in *them. Noun.*
○ To speak with a lisp. *Verb.*
lisp (lisp) *noun, plural* **lisps;** *verb,* **lisped, lisping.**

list¹ A series of names, numbers, or other things: *Make a list of the groceries we need to buy. Noun.*
○ To make a list of or enter in a list: *The teacher listed the students in the class. Is your name listed in the telephone book? Verb.*
list (list) *noun, plural* **lists;** *verb,* **listed, listing.**

list² A leaning to one side: *The list of the sailboat was caused by the strong wind. Noun.*
○ To lean to one side; tilt: *The ship listed sharply. Verb.*
list (list) *noun, plural* **lists;** *verb,* **listed, listing.**

listen To try to hear; pay attention in order to hear: *Listen for the school bus.* **lis·ten** (lis′ən) *verb,* **listened, listening.**

lit A past tense and a past participle of **light.** Look up **light¹** for more information. **lit** (lit) *verb.*

liter A unit of measurement in the metric system, a little larger than a quart of liquid. **li·ter** (lē′tər) *noun, plural* **liters.**

literacy The ability to read and write: *Literacy is essential in the modern world.* **lit·er·a·cy** (lit′ər ə sē) *noun.*

literally 1. Considering each word; word for word: *I translated the story from Spanish into English literally.* 2. Really; actually: *The village was literally destroyed by the earthquake.* **lit·er·al·ly** (lit′ər ə lē) *adverb.*

literate 1. Able to read and write. 2. Very educated; learned. **lit·er·ate** (lit′ər it) *adjective.*

literature 1. Writing of lasting value, including plays, poems, and novels: *My cousin studies American literature in college.* 2. Printed matter of any kind: *Some literature came with the new dryer.* **lit·er·a·ture** (lit′ər ə chər *or* lit′ər ə chŭr′) *noun.*

litmus paper A paper soaked in a dye and used in chemistry experiments. Red litmus paper turns blue in a base solution, and blue litmus paper turns red in an acid solution. **lit·mus paper** (lit′məs).

litter 1. Bits or scraps of paper or other rubbish; mess: *Broken bottles and other litter filled the empty lot.* 2. A group of young animals born at one time to the same mother: *Our cat gave birth to a litter of five kittens.* 3. A stretcher for carrying a sick or injured person. *Noun.*
○ To scatter or leave bits of rubbish around; make dirty with litter. *Verb.*
lit·ter (lit′ər) *noun, plural* **litters;** *verb,* **littered, littering.**

little 1. Small in size or amount: *A pebble is a little stone. Give the plant a little water.* 2. Short in time or distance: *We will be home in a little while. Adjective.*
○ Not much; slightly: *Snow is little seen in warm places. Adverb.*
○ 1. A small amount: *I ate only a little because I wasn't hungry.* 2. A short time or distance. *Step back a little. Noun.*

PRONUNCIATION KEY:
| at | āpe | fär | câre | end | mē | it | īce | pierce | hot | ōld | sông | fôrk |
| oil | out | up | ūse | rüle | pull | tûrn | chin | sing | shop | thin | this | |
hw in white; zh in treasure. The symbol ə stands for the unstressed vowel sound in about, taken, pencil, lemon, and circus.

433

• **little by little.** In small amounts or steps; gradually: *After a long illness, she built up her strength little by little.*

lit·tle (lit′əl) *adjective*, **less** *or* **lesser** *or* **littler**, **least** *or* **littlest**; *adverb*, **less**, **least**; *noun*.

SYNONYMS

little, small, tiny, miniature

I ate so much I had room for only a little piece of cake. As the girl grew her shoes became too small for her. The baby has such tiny fingers! The doll's house was filled with miniature furniture.

Little Dipper A group of seven stars in the northern sky. They form the outline of a dipper. The star at the end of the Little Dipper's handle is called the North Star.

live¹ 1. To be alive; have life: *That ruler lived during the Middle Ages.* 2. To stay alive: *Most fish cannot live out of water.* 3. To support oneself: *I live on a small income.* 4. To feed: *Some birds live on bugs and worms.* 5. To make one's home: *We live on the east side of town. This kind of spider lives in the desert.* **live** (liv) *verb*, **lived**, **living**.

live² 1. Having life; living: *The hunter brought back a live elephant to the zoo.* 2. Burning: *Be careful because there are still live coals in the fireplace.* 3. Carrying an electric current: *After the thunderstorm, we had to be careful of live wires that were blown down.* 4. Seen while actually happening; not taped: *a live television show.* 5. Containing an explosive; capable of exploding: *The police discovered a live bomb in the suitcase.* **live** (līv) *adjective*.

livelihood The means of staying alive or supporting life: *That journalist earns her livelihood by writing for newspapers.* **live·li·hood** (līv′lē hùd′) *noun*, *plural* **livelihoods**.

lively 1. Full of life or energy; gay or cheerful: *The lively kitten played with the ball of string. The band played a lively tune.* 2. Bright and strong. *The colors of the clown's costume were very lively. Adjective.*

○ In a lively manner; with vigor: *The horses stepped lively. Adverb.*

live·ly (līv′lē) *adjective*, **livelier**, **liveliest**; *adverb*.

liver 1. A large, reddish brown organ in the body. The liver cleans the blood, stores fats and sugars, and makes bile. 2. The liver of certain animals when used as food. **liv·er** (liv′ər) *noun*, *plural* **livers**.

livery 1. A uniform worn by servants or the members of a profession: *The livery of the cook included a white hat and apron.* 2. A stable where horses are cared for and rented out. **liv·er·y** (liv′ə rē) *noun*, *plural* **liveries**.

lives Plural of **life**: *The firefighters saved many lives during the fire.* **lives** (līvz) *plural noun*.

livestock Animals raised on a farm or ranch for profit. Cows, horses, sheep, and pigs are livestock: *We enjoy seeing the livestock when we go to the county fair.* **live·stock** (līv′stok′) *noun*.

livid 1. Having a pale, usually bluish, color: *Your face was livid with anger.* 2. Changed in color because of a bruise: *I had a livid mark on my arm where the ball had hit me.* **liv·id** (liv′id) *adjective*.

living 1. Having life; alive: *All animals are living creatures. We read a book on famous living artists.* 2. Of or for life: *Living conditions were bad after the flood.* 3. Still active or in use: *Russian is a living language. Adjective.*

○ 1. The condition or fact of being alive: *I enjoy living by the sea.* 2. A means of maintaining the condition of being alive; livelihood: *My cousin earns a living as a firefighter.* 3. A way of life: *The athlete believed in healthy living. Noun.*

liv·ing (liv′ing) *adjective*; *noun*, *plural* **livings**.

living room A room in a home for the general use of the family or for entertaining guests.

lizard An animal with a scaly body, four legs, and a long tail. Lizards are reptiles, related to snakes and alligators. **liz·ard** (liz′ərd) *noun*, *plural* **lizards**.

llama A shaggy animal of the camel family. Llamas live in the mountains of South America. They are used for carrying heavy loads. **lla·ma** (lä′mə) *noun*, *plural* **llamas**.

Lizards love to bask in the sun for warmth.

load 1. Something carried: *The wagon has a load of hay.* 2. The amount or number that can be carried: *One load of bricks will be enough to build the patio.* **3.** Something that burdens the mind or heart: *Finishing my book report took a load off my mind. Noun.*

○ **1.** To put a load in or on something: *I loaded the box with old clothes. The workers loaded the rocks onto the truck.* **2.** To put something needed into a device: *The photographer loaded the camera with film. Our teacher will show us how to load the program into the computer.* **3.** To put a charge of gunpowder or ammunition into a gun: *The hunter loaded the rifle. Verb.*
Another word that sounds like this is **lode.**
load (lōd) *noun, plural* **loads;** *verb,* **loaded, loading.**

Machines are used to lift a heavy load.

loaf¹ **1.** Bread baked in one piece. **2.** Any mass of food in the shape of a loaf of bread: *meat loaf.* **loaf** (lōf) *noun, plural* **loaves.**

loaf² To spend time doing little or nothing: *I like to loaf when I'm on vacation.* **loaf** (lōf) *verb,* **loafed, loafing.**

loan **1.** The act of lending something: *Thank you for the loan of your pencil.* **2.** Something lent: *We received a loan of five thousand dollars from the bank. Noun.*
○ To lend: *Please loan me your bicycle. Verb.*
Another word that sounds like this is **lone.**
loan (lōn) *noun, plural* **loans;** *verb,* **loaned, loaning.**

loathe To dislike strongly; to feel disgust toward: *I loathe small bugs that crawl, but my cousin finds them interesting.* **loathe** (lōth) *verb,* **loathed, loathing.**

loathsome Extremely disgusting or hateful: *a loathsome monster.* **loath·some** (lōth'səm) *adjective.*

loaves Plural of loaf: *The loaves of bread were delivered by the bakery.* **loaves** (lōvz) *plural noun.*

lobby **1.** A hall or room at the entrance to a building: *The movie theater had a large lobby.* **2.** A person or group that tries to convince legislators to vote in a certain way. *Noun.*
○ To try to convince legislators to vote in a certain way: *A group of citizens lobbied against the bill to build a new highway. Verb.*
lob·by (lob'ē) *noun, plural* **lobbies;** *verb,* **lobbied, lobbying.** —**lobbyist** *noun.*

lobster A saltwater animal that has a hard shell and five pairs of legs. The front pair of legs ends in large claws. Lobsters are crustaceans eaten as food. **lob·ster** (lob'stər) *noun, plural* **lobsters.**

local **1.** Having to do with a particular place: *We went to the local library. My neighbor writes for the local newspaper.* **2.** Stopping at all or most of the stops along a route; not an express: *We rode the local train.* **3.** Having to do with or affecting only a part of the body: *The dentist gave the patient a local anesthetic. Adjective.*
○ A train, bus, or subway that stops at all or most of the stops along its route. *Noun.*
lo·cal (lō'kəl) *adjective; noun, plural* **locals.**

local area network A network of computers linked together in a small area, such as an office.

locality A place and the area around it: *You'll like the camp's locality because it is on the lake.* **lo·cal·i·ty** (lō kal'i tē) *noun, plural* **localities.**

locate **1.** To find the place or position of: *He could not locate his lost book. She located Kansas on the map.* **2.** To put or settle in a particular place: *The bakery is located on Main Street. The family left the large city to locate in a small town.* **lo·cate** (lō'kāt) *verb,* **located, locating.**

location **1.** The place where something is located; site: *Where is the location of your school? Their new house is in a beautiful location on top of a hill.* **2.** The act of locating: *Your location of the North Pole on the map was correct.* **lo·ca·tion** (lō kā'shən) *noun, plural* **locations.**

lock¹ **1.** A fastener for a door, window, chest, or other thing. Many locks can be opened with a

PRONUNCIATION KEY:

| at | āpe | fär | câre | end | mē | it | īce | pierce | hot | ōld | sông | fôrk |
| oil | out | up | ūse | rüle | pull | tûrn | chin | sing | shop | thin | this | |

hw in white; zh in treasure. The symbol ə stands for the unstressed vowel sound in about, taken, pencil, lemon, and circus.

435

key or combination. **2.** A part of a canal or other waterway through which water can be pumped in or out to raise or lower ships. Ships use a lock to pass from one body of water to another that is at a different level. *Noun.*
○ **1.** To fasten with a lock: *Lock the front door.* **2.** To shut in or out of a place: *Lock the money in a metal box. We were locked out of the house.* **3.** To join or hold firmly: *The two cars locked bumpers in the accident. Verb.*
lock (lok) *noun, plural* **locks;** *verb,* **locked, locking.**

lock² **1.** A piece of hair, cotton, or wool. **2. locks:** The hair on a person's head: *The child's locks were soft and curly.* **lock** (lok) *noun, plural* **locks.**

locker A small closet, cabinet, or chest that can be locked: *At school, we have metal lockers to keep our coats, books, and other belongings in.* **lock·er** (lok′ər) *noun, plural* **lockers.**

locket A small case for holding a picture of someone, often worn on a chain around the neck. **lock·et** (lok′it) *noun, plural* **lockets.**

lockjaw A disease caused by germs that enter the body through a wound. One of the first signs of this disease is tight muscles in the jaw. This disease is also called **tetanus.** Look up **tetanus** for more information. **lock·jaw** (lok′jô′) *noun.*

locksmith A person who makes or fixes locks and keys: *We had to call a locksmith when we locked ourselves out of the house.* **lock·smith** (lok′smith′) *noun, plural* **locksmiths.**

locomotion The act or capability of moving from place to place: *A steam engine provided the locomotion of the freight train.* **lo·co·mo·tion** (lō′kə mō′shən) *noun.*

While early locomotives were powered by steam, today they are diesel or electric.

locomotive An engine that moves on its own power, used to pull railroad cars. **lo·co·mo·tive** (lō′kə mō′tiv) *noun, plural* **locomotives.**

WORD HISTORY

The word **locomotive** comes from two Latin words that mean "place" and "moving." Locomotive first meant "moving from place to place."

locust **1.** A type of large grasshopper that travels in huge swarms and destroys crops. **2.** A tree that has small leaves and fragrant white, pink, or purple flowers. **lo·cust** (lō′kəst) *noun, plural* **locusts.**

lode A deposit of a metal in the earth: *The prospectors discovered and mined a lode of silver.* Another word that sounds like this is **load.** **lode** (lōd) *noun, plural* **lodes.**

lodestone A stone containing iron that acts as a magnet. **lode·stone** (lōd′stōn′) *noun, plural* **lodestones.**

lodge **1.** A small house, cottage, or cabin: *The hunters stayed at a lodge in the mountains.* **2.** A branch of a club or other organization. *Noun.*
○ **1.** To live in a place for a while: *People lodged in the school during the flood.* **2.** To provide with a place to live for a while; rent rooms to: *That couple lodges tourists in their home.* **3.** To become stuck or fixed in a place: *A pebble lodged in my shoe and made walking very uncomfortable.* **4.** To bring to someone in authority: *We lodged a complaint with the owner of the building about our noisy neighbors. Verb.*
lodge (loj) *noun, plural* **lodges;** *verb,* **lodged, lodging.**

lodger A person who rents a room or rooms in someone else's home. **lodg·er** (loj′ər) *noun, plural* **lodgers.**

lodging **1.** A place to live in for a while: *The family wanted lodging for the weekend.* **2. lodgings.** A rented room or rooms in someone else's home. **lodg·ing** (loj′ing) *noun, plural* **lodgings.**

loft **1.** The upper floor, room, or space in a building. Lofts in office buildings are used as work or storage areas. Lofts in stables and barns are used for storing hay. **2.** An upper floor or balcony in a large hall or church: *The choir sang in the choir loft.* **3.** A large, open room in a building: *The owner of the building divided the loft into three apartments.* **loft** (lôft) *noun, plural* **lofts.**

lofty 1. Very high; towering: *We saw many lofty skyscrapers in the city. The hikers climbed to the lofty mountain peak.* 2. High and noble: *Many knights of olden times believed in lofty ideals.* 3. Too proud; haughty: *A lofty manner can offend people.* **loft·y** (lôf′tē) *adjective,* **loftier, loftiest.**

log 1. A piece of a tree cut with the bark still on: *The pioneers used logs to build cabins.* 2. The record of the voyage of a ship or the flight of an airplane: *The captain of the ship kept a log. Noun.*
○ 1. To cut down trees in a forest and shape them into logs. 2. To make a record of a ship's voyage in a log. *Verb.*
○ Made of logs: *a log cabin. Adjective.*
• **to log off.** To exit from a computer system.
• **to log on.** To enter into a computer system, especially with a password.
log (lôg *or* log) *noun, plural* **logs;** *verb,* **logged, logging;** *adjective.*

Several early United States presidents were born in log cabins.

loganberry The reddish purple fruit of a thorny shrub. It has a sharp taste. **lo·gan·ber·ry** (lō′gən ber′ē) *noun, plural* **loganberries.**

logger A person who logs trees; lumberjack. **log·ger** (lô′gər *or* log′ər) *noun, plural* **loggers.**

logic 1. Sound reasoning: *There is much logic in your argument.* 2. Any method of reasoning: *I don't understand the logic behind planting flowers in winter.* 3. The study of the rules for reasoning and for proving things by reasoning. **log·ic** (loj′ik) *noun.*

logical 1. Having to do with or done by sound reasoning: *The dealer gave a logical explanation for how the gears on my bicycle work.* 2. Capable of reasoning correctly: *You have a logical mind.* 3. Naturally to be expected: *It is logical that if you make fun of them, you will hurt their feelings.* **log·i·cal** (loj′i kəl) *adjective.*

logo A symbol, design, or trademark that represents a company or organization. **lo·go** (lō′gō) *noun, plural* **logos.**

LOGO A computer language that is very easy to learn. LOGO can be used to draw pictures. **LOGO** (lō′gō) *noun.*

loin 1. The part of a person or animal between the ribs and hip on each side of the body. 2. A cut of meat from this part of an animal. **loin** (loin) *noun, plural* **loins.**

loiter 1. To stand around; be idle: *Students loitered in the hall.* 2. To move slowly: *I loitered on my way to the dentist.* **loi·ter** (loi′tər) *verb,* **loitered, loitering.**

loll To stand or sit in a very relaxed, casual manner. **loll** (lol) *verb,* **lolled, lolling.**

lollipop A piece of hard candy on the end of a stick. **lol·li·pop** (lol′ē pop) *noun, plural* **lollipops.**

lone 1. Away from others; alone; solitary: *A lone star twinkled in the early evening sky.* 2. Only; sole: *the lone survivor of the crash.* Another word that sounds like this is **loan.** **lone** (lōn) *adjective.*

lonely 1. Unhappy from being alone: *The student felt lonely at the new school.* 2. Away from others; alone: *A lonely house stood by itself on the hill.* 3. Not often visited or used by people; deserted: *We were the only people on the lonely beach.* **lone·ly** (lōn′lē) *adjective,* **lonelier, loneliest.**

lonesome 1. Unhappy from being alone: *Were you lonesome when your best friend was away at camp?* 2. Not often visited or used by people; deserted: *a dark, lonesome road.* **lone·some** (lōn′səm) *adjective.*

long¹ 1. Of or having great length; not short: *It's a long way from our school to the lake. There was a long wait before the movie started.* 2. Having or lasting for a certain length: *The room is ten feet long. The program was an hour long.* 3. Taking more time to pronounce: The "e" in the word "be" is a *long vowel. Adjective.*
○ 1. For a long time: *Our guests did not stay long.* 2. Throughout the length of: *It snowed all*

PRONUNCIATION KEY:

| at | āpe | fär | câre | end | mē | it | īce | pierce | hot | ōld | sông | fork |
| oil | out | up | ūse | rüle | pull | tûrn | chin | sing | shop | thin | this | |

hw in white; zh in treasure. The symbol ə stands for the unstressed vowel sound in about, taken, pencil, lemon, and circus.

437

morning **long**. **3.** At a time in the far past: *That castle was built* **long** *ago. Adverb.*

○ A long time: *They should return before* **long**. *Noun.*

long (lông) *adjective,* **longer, longest;** *adverb; noun.*

long² To want very much; yearn: *I* **longed** *to see my old friends again.* **long** (lông) *verb,* **longed, longing.**

long-distance **1.** Covering or capable of covering a long distance: *These trucks are* **long-distance** *carriers.* **2.** Connecting distant locations: *We made a* **long-distance** *call to our grandparents on their anniversary. Adjective.*

○ By means of a long-distance connection: *I called my friend* **long-distance**. *Adverb.*

long-dis·tance (lông′dis′təns) *adjective; adverb.*

longhand Writing that is done by hand. When you write in longhand, you write the words out in full. **long·hand** (lông′hand′) *noun.*

A **longhorn** can travel great distances without needing much water.

longhorn A breed of cattle with very long horns. Longhorns were once common in the southwestern United States. **long·horn** (lông′hôrn′) *noun, plural* **longhorns.**

longing A feeling of strong desire; yearning: *The children have a* **longing** *to visit the zoo. Noun.*

○ Feeling or showing a strong desire: *The hungry child cast* **longing** *glances at the food. Adjective.*

long·ing (lông′ing) *noun, plural* **longings;** *adjective.*

longitude Distance that is measured on the earth's surface east and west of an imaginary line

passing through the town of Greenwich, England. On a map or globe, lines of longitude are drawn from the North Pole to the South Pole. Longitude is expressed in degrees. **lon·gi·tude** (lôn′ji tüd′ or lôn′ji tūd′) *noun, plural* **longitudes.**

look **1.** To use one's eyes; see: *I* **looked** *at my friend's stamp collection.* **Look** *carefully before you cross the street.* **2.** To turn one's eyes or attention: **Look** *at the camera and smile!* **3.** To make a search or examination: *I* **looked** *through the magazine for the article on fishing.* **4.** To appear; seem: *You* **look** *tired.* **5.** To face in a certain direction or have a certain view: *The windows* **look** *north. Verb.*

○ **1.** The act of looking; a glance or inspection: *Take a* **look** *at this bicycle. Don't buy the car if you haven't had a good* **look** *at it.* **2.** Appearance: *The guest had a cheerful* **look**. *The new car has a shiny* **look**. **3. looks.** The outward appearance: *I don't like the* **looks** *of those clouds. Noun.*

• **to look after.** To take care of: *I* **looked after** *her dog for a week.*

• **to look down on.** To have a feeling of dislike for and of being better than: *Don't* **look down on** *people who are different from you.*

• **to look forward to.** To wait for eagerly: *We* **look forward to** *our vacation.*

• **to look into.** To ask questions about, examine, or search for: *The police* **looked into** *the reason for the accident.*

• **to look up.** **1.** To search for in a dictionary or other reference: *I* **looked up** *the date of the battle in an encyclopedia.* **2.** To locate and visit: *When I got to the city, I* **looked up** *an old friend.* **3.** To get better; improve: *Business is* **looking up**.

• **to look up to.** To respect: *People in the United States* **look up to** *the Supreme Court.*

look (lŭk) *verb,* **looked, looking;** *noun, plural* **looks.**

looking glass A surface made with glass that reflects light; mirror.

lookout **1.** A careful watch for someone or something: *When crossing the street, be on the* **lookout** *for cars.* **2.** A person who keeps a careful watch: *The* **lookout** *in the tower watched for forest fires.* **3.** A place from which to keep a careful watch: *The high tower served as a* **lookout**. **look·out** (lŭk′out′) *noun, plural* **lookouts.**

Looms were in use as far back
as 5000 B.C.

loom¹ A machine or frame for weaving thread into cloth. **loom** (lüm) *noun, plural* **looms**.

loom² To appear as large and dangerous or full of trouble: *A ship* **loomed** *in the fog. The most important test for the new airplane still* **loomed** *ahead.* **loom** (lüm) *verb,* **loomed, looming**.

loon A water bird with short legs and webbed feet that dives and swims in the water for fish. The loon has a loud, laughing call. **loon** (lün) *noun, plural* **loons**.

Some amusement park rides are
in the shape of a loop.

loop 1. The rounded shape formed by the part of a string, wire, or rope that crosses itself. 2. Anything like a loop: *The curly ribbon on the*

package had many **loops**. *The belt goes through the* **loops** *of the pants.* 3. A series of commands for a computer that is repeated until the computer is instructed to stop. *Noun.*
○ To make a loop or loops in something; form a loop or loops: *You* **loop** *the laces when you tie your shoes. As the dog ran, the chain* **looped** *around the tree. Verb.* **loop** (lüp) *noun, plural* **loops**; *verb,* **looped, looping**.

loose 1. Not fastened or attached firmly: *A page was* **loose** *in the book. A* **loose** *wire caused the radio to stop playing.* 2. Free: *The canary is* **loose** *in the house.* 3. Not tight: *a* **loose** *jacket.* 4. Not tied or joined together: *I carry* **loose** *keys in my pocket.* 5. Not in a package or container: *We bought some* **loose** *carrots at the store.* 6. Not packed or pressed tightly together: *The workers put* **loose** *gravel on the driveway. The tablecloth has a* **loose** *weave. Adjective.*
○ 1. To set free; let go: *We* **loosed** *the dog in the field.* 2. To make or become less tight; loosen or unfasten: *You* **loosed** *the knot. Verb.*
loose (lüs) *adjective,* **looser, loosest;** *verb,* **loosed, loosing**.

loose-leaf 1. Holding or made to hold pages that have holes and are easily removed: *I keep my book reports in a* **loose-leaf** *notebook.* 2. Made to be put in and removed from a special notebook that has rings that open: **Loose-leaf** *paper is available with two or three holes.* **loose-leaf** (lüs′lēf′) *adjective.*

loosen 1. To make or become loose or looser: **Loosen** *your necktie.* 2. To set free or release: *The dog had been* **loosened** *from its leash.* **loos•en** (lü′sən) *verb,* **loosened, loosening**.

loot Things that have been stolen: *The thieves hid their* **loot** *in a barn. Noun.*
○ To steal valuable things from; plunder: *The enemy soldiers* **looted** *the town. Verb.*
Another word that sounds like this is **lute**.
loot (lüt) *noun; verb,* **looted, looting**.

lopsided Larger or heavier on one side than on the other; leaning more to one side than to the other: *The dog's uneven ears gave it a* **lopsided** *appearance.* **lop•sid•ed** (lop′sī′did) *adjective.*

lord 1. A man who has power over others or is of noble rank. In the Middle Ages, a lord was a

PRONUNCIATION KEY:

| at | āpe | fär | cāre | end | mē | it | ice | pierce | hot | ōld | sông | fôrk |
| oil | out | up | ūse | rüle | pùll | tûrn | chin | sing | shop | thin | this | |

hw in white; zh in treasure. The symbol ə stands for the unstressed vowel sound in about, taken, pencil, lemon, and circus.

439

powerful man who lived in a castle and had many people under his rule. **2. Lord.** In Great Britain, a title for a man of noble rank. **3. Lord. a.** God. **b.** Jesus. **lord** (lôrd) *noun, plural* **lords.**

WORD HISTORY

The word **lord** comes from an Old English word that meant "keeper of the loaf." The lady of the house made the bread, and the lord kept the bread and distributed it to the other members of the household.

---

lose **1.** To have no longer; be without: *I lost my pencil. We don't want to lose your friendship. The roof lost some of its shingles in the storm.* **2.** To fail to keep: *Do you lose your temper easily? Those acrobats never lose their balance.* **3.** To fail to win: *We lost the game.* **4.** To fail to use; waste: *The travelers will lose time if the bus breaks down.* **lose** (lüz) *verb,* **lost, losing.**

loss **1.** The act of losing something or the condition of being lost: *The loss of the game was a disappointment to the team. I'm worried about the loss of my wallet.* **2.** Something that has been lost: *The store owner suffered great losses in the fire.* **3.** The suffering or damage caused by losing something: *We felt a loss when our neighbors moved.*

• **at a loss.** Puzzled; confused: *Their sudden departure left me at a loss.*

loss (lôs) *noun, plural* **losses.**

lost Past tense and past participle of **lose**: *I lost my gloves. The team has lost the game. Verb.*
○ **1.** That cannot be found; missing: *a lost toy.* **2.** No longer possessed: *They thought sadly about their lost fortune.* **3.** Not knowing where one is or the way to go: *The lost driver asked the police officer for directions. That dog looks lost to me.* **4.** Not won or able to be won: *We are playing well, but the game is lost.* **5.** Not used; wasted: *They drove all night to make up for lost time.* **6.** Ruined; destroyed: *Many lives were lost in the fire. Adjective.*

• **lost in.** So busy with or interested in something that one is not aware of other things: *I was lost in thought and didn't hear your question.*

lost (lôst) *verb; adjective.*

lot **1.** A great amount: *There are a lot of cars on this road. This horse eats lots of hay.* **2.** A number or group of persons or things: *This is a poor lot of vegetables.* **3.** A piece of land: *We play*

baseball on an empty *lot.* **4.** A bit of paper, wood, straw, or other material used to decide something by chance: *The children drew lots to decide who would be first at bat in the game.* **5.** Fate or fortune in life: *It was the hermit's lot to live alone.*

• **a lot.** By a great amount or to a great degree; much: *I don't want to be a lot taller than I am now.*

lot (lot) *noun, plural* **lots.**

lotion A special liquid for the skin. A lotion heals, soothes, softens, or cleans the skin. **lo•tion** (lō'shən) *noun, plural* **lotions.**

lottery A kind of contest or gambling in which people buy numbered tickets. Money or prizes are given to those whose tickets have been chosen by chance. **lot•ter•y** (lot'ə rē) *noun, plural* **lotteries.**

lotus A plant with large pink, white, or yellow flowers. The roots of the lotus grow under water, and the leaves and flowers grow above water. **lo•tus** (lō'təs) *noun, plural* **lotuses.**

Lotus plants appear frequently in Egyptian art.

loud **1.** Having a strong sound; not quiet: *The jet plane made a loud noise.* **2.** Too bright; gaudy: *a loud tie. Adjective.*
○ In a loud way: *We hear you loud and clear. Adverb.*
loud (loud) *adjective,* **louder, loudest;** *adverb.*
—**loud•ly** *adverb.*

loudspeaker A device that can change electrical signals into sounds and make the sounds louder. Loudspeakers are used in radios and phonographs. **loud•speak•er** (loud'spē'kər) *noun, plural* **loudspeakers.**

Louisiana A state in the southern United States. Its capital is Baton Rouge. **Lou·i·si·an·a** (lü ē′zē an′ə *or* lü′ə zē an′ə) *noun.*

WORD HISTORY

A French explorer named the Mississippi Valley Louisiana after King Louis XIV of France. When the land was divided into states, Louisiana became the name of one of the states.

Louisiana
U. S. Postal Abbreviation: **LA**
Capital: **Baton Rouge**
Population: **4,461,000**
Area: **48,523 sq. mi./125,674 sq. km**
State Nickname: **Pelican State**
State Bird: **Brown Pelican**
State Flower: **Magnolia**

lounge To stand, sit, or lie down in a comfortable or lazy way: *Don't lounge on the sofa all day. Verb.*
   ○ **1.** A place where a person may lounge: *The hotel has a lounge where guests may relax.* **2.** A long seat for more than one person that has a back and arms; sofa; couch. *Noun.*
   lounge (lounj) *verb,* **lounged, lounging;** *noun,* *plural* **lounges.**

louse A tiny insect without wings. It lives on people and animals by biting them and sucking their blood. Lice can spread disease. **louse** (lous) *noun,* *plural* **lice.**

lovable *or* **loveable** Having qualities that make one easy to love or worthy of being loved: *a lovable child.* **lov·a·ble** (luv′ə bəl) *adjective.*

love **1.** A strong, warm feeling for another; deep affection: *The love of a friend is special.* **2.** A strong liking for something: *They go to concerts because of their love of music.* **3.** Someone that is loved or something that is liked very much: *Playing chess is a love of mine. They share a love of gardening. Noun.*
   ○ **1.** To have a strong, warm feeling for another: *Parents love their children.* **2.** To have a strong liking for something: *I love to read. My cousin loves fresh, raw carrots. Verb.*
   love (luv) *noun, plural* **loves;** *verb,* **loved, loving.**

lovely **1.** Having a beautiful appearance or a warm character: *The lovely flowers were a gift. Our neighbor is a kind, lovely person.* **2.** Enjoyable: *We had a lovely time at your party.*
   love·ly (luv′lē) *adjective,* **lovelier, loveliest.**

An array of flowers makes a lovely **garden.**

loving Feeling or showing love: *The parents were very loving toward their children.* **lov·ing** (luv′ing) *adjective.*

low **1.** Not high or tall: *A low wall surrounds the yard. The branches of the tree are low enough for me to reach.* **2.** Below the usual level: *The river was low. The car was going at a low speed.* **3.** Below what is regarded as average; below others: *I got a low grade on the test. That meat is low in quality.* **4.** Not favorable; bad: *I have a low opinion of people who are cruel to animals.* **5.** Not having enough: *Our car is low on gas.*

PRONUNCIATION KEY:
| at | āpe | fär | câre | end | mē | it | īce | pierce | hot | ōld | sông | fôrk |
| oil | out | up | ūse | rüle | pu̇ll | tûrn | chin | sing | shop | thin | this | |
hw in white; zh in treasure. The symbol ə stands for the unstressed vowel sound in about, taken, pencil, lemon, and circus.

441

6. Not loud; soft: *Speak in a **low** voice.* 7. Deep in pitch: *You can sing very **low** notes.* 8. Not lively or happy; sad; gloomy: *Everyone felt **low** after losing the game.* Adjective.

○ At or to a low place or level: *The airplane flew **low** over the town. The campers' supplies ran **low** after they had been in the woods for two weeks.* Adverb.

○ 1. A low place or point: *The temperature reached a new **low**.* 2. The position of gears in an automobile that gives the lowest speed and greatest power: *The driver shifted into **low** to go up the steep hill.* Noun.

low (lō) *adjective,* **lower, lowest;** *adverb; noun, plural* **lows.**

lower Comparative of low: *They live on a **lower** floor of the apartment house. Our supply of heating oil is **lower** than it should be.* Look up low for more information. *Adjective.*

○ 1. To move or cause to move from one position to another that is not as high: *The soldiers will **lower** the flag at dusk. I **lowered** my arm when the teacher called my name.* 2. To make or become less; lessen: *The store **lowered** its prices during the sale.* 3. To make soft or less loud: ***Lower** your voice.* Verb.

low·er (lō′ər) *adjective; verb,* **lowered, lowering.**

lower case Letters that are not capitals. The letters a, b, c, and d are printed in lower case.

low tide The tide when the level of the ocean or a lake along the shore is at its lowest.

loyal Having or showing strong and lasting affection and support for someone or something. *The old friends were **loyal** to each other. The **loyal** soldiers refused to betray their country.* **loy·al** (loi′əl) *adjective.*

loyalty Strong and lasting affection and support; allegiance: *You showed your **loyalty** to your friends by helping them when they were in need.* **loy·al·ty** (loi′əl tē) *noun, plural* **loyalties.**

lubricate 1. To put oil or grease on the parts of a machine that move against each other so that the parts will move easily: *The mechanic **lubricated** the car's wheels and axles.* 2. To help the parts of a machine move easily: *That oil **lubricated** the fan well.* **lu·bri·cate** (lü′bri kāt′) *verb,* **lubricated, lubricating. —lubrication** *noun.*

luck 1. What seems to happen to a person by chance: *It was good playing and not **luck** that*

caused the team to win. Some of their problems were the result of bad **luck**. 2. Good fortune: *Wish me **luck**! They had no **luck** in looking for the lost ring.* **luck** (luk) *noun.*

luckily By or with good fortune: ***Luckily**, they found my missing wallet.* **luck·i·ly** (luk′ə lē) *adverb.*

lucky 1. Having or bringing good luck: *You were very **lucky** to win the prize. The child believed the rabbit's foot was **lucky**.* 2. Happening by good fortune; caused by good luck: *That home run was just a **lucky** hit.* **luck·y** (luk′ē) *adjective,* **luckier, luckiest.**

lug To carry or drag with much effort: *I didn't want to **lug** that heavy suitcase upstairs.* **lug** (lug) *verb,* **lugged, lugging.**

luggage The suitcases, trunks, and bags a traveler takes along on a trip; baggage. **lug·gage** (lug′ij) *noun.*

lukewarm 1. Slightly warm; neither hot nor cold. 2. Having or showing little enthusiasm; indifferent: *The audience's response to the new play was only **lukewarm**.* **luke·warm** (lük′wôrm′) *adjective.*

lull To make or become calm: *The sound of rain on the roof **lulled** the baby to sleep.* Verb.

○ A short period of calm or quiet: *a **lull** in the wind.* Noun.

lull (lul) *verb,* **lulled, lulling;** *noun, plural* **lulls.**

lullaby A song to lull a baby to sleep. **lul·la·by** (lul′ə bī′) *noun, plural* **lullabies.**

lumber¹ Boards cut from logs: *The carpenter bought **lumber** to build a shed.* **lum·ber** (lum′bər) *noun.*

At a sawmill, special saws are used to turn logs into lumber.

lumber² To move about in a clumsy, noisy way: *The wagon **lumbered** down the dirt road. The elephant **lumbered** along the trail.* **lum·ber** (lum′bər) *verb,* **lumbered, lumbering.**

lumberjack A person who cuts down trees and gets logs ready for the sawmill. **lum·ber·jack** (lum′bər jak′) *noun, plural* **lumberjacks.**

luminous Bright; shining: *We could see the luminous glow of a campfire through the trees.* **lu·mi·nous** (lü′mə nəs) *adjective.*

lump **1.** A shapeless piece of something; chunk: *The sculptor took the **lump** of clay and made a figure of a dog with it.* **2.** A swollen place; bump: *You have a **lump** on your head where the ball hit you. Noun.*
   ○ **1.** To put or bring together: *The teenagers **lumped** their allowances to buy a camera.* **2.** To form lumps: *Oatmeal sometimes **lumps** when it cools. Verb.*
   lump (lump) *noun, plural* **lumps;** *verb,* **lumped, lumping.**

lunar Of or having to do with the moon: *The astronauts brought back **lunar** rocks for study. A **lunar** eclipse is the darkening of the moon when the earth moves between the sun and the moon.* **lu·nar** (lü′nər) *adjective.*

lunch A meal eaten between breakfast and dinner. *Noun.*
   ○ To eat lunch: *We **lunched** at noon. Verb.*
   lunch (lunch) *noun, plural* **lunches;** *verb,* **lunched, lunching.**

luncheon A lunch: *We went to a formal **luncheon** given by the school.* **lunch·eon** (lunchən) *noun, plural* **luncheons.**

lung One of two organs for breathing in the chest of human beings and other animals with backbones. The lungs supply the blood with oxygen and rid the blood of carbon dioxide. **lung** (lung) *noun, plural* **lungs.**

lunge A sudden movement forward: *The catcher made a **lunge** for the ball. Noun.*
   ○ To move forward suddenly: *I **lunged** to catch the plate as it fell. Verb.*
   lunge (lunj) *noun, plural* **lunges;** *verb,* **lunged, lunging.**

lurch¹ To move suddenly in an unsteady manner: *The car **lurched** forward. Verb.*

   ○ A lurching movement: *The train started up with a **lurch**. Noun.*
   lurch (lûrch) *verb,* **lurched, lurching;** *noun, plural* **lurches.**

lurch² A decisive defeat in a game called cribbage.
   • **to leave in the lurch.** To leave someone in a difficult position and needing help.
   lurch (lûrch) *noun.*

lure **1.** A strong attraction: *the **lure** of adventure in unknown lands.* **2.** Artificial bait used in fishing: *I used a plastic worm as a **lure**. Noun.*
   ○ To attract strongly: *We were **lured** to the park by the sound of music. Verb.*
   lure (lur) *noun, plural* **lures;** *verb,* **lured, luring.**

lurk **1.** To lie hidden, especially to attack. **2.** To move about quietly; sneak: *The thief **lurked** in the shadows.* **3.** To read messages posted to an electronic bulletin board or discussion group, as on the Internet, without posting any messages of one's own. **lurk** (lûrk) *verb,* **lurked, lurking.**

A colorful lure will attract the eye of feeding fish.

luscious Smelling or tasting delicious: *We're having a **luscious** apple crisp for dessert.* **lus·cious** (lush′əs) *adjective.*

lush Thick, rich, and abundant: *That land is covered with **lush** forests.* **lush** (lush) *adjective,* **lusher, lushest.**

lust A strong desire: *a **lust** for glory. Noun.*
   ○ To want or desire very strongly: *The young actor **lusted** after fame. Verb.*
   lust (lust) *noun, plural* **lusts;** *verb,* **lusted, lusting.**

luster A bright shine; glow: *You can give the table a nice **luster** by waxing it.* **lus·ter** (lus′tər) *noun, plural* **lusters.**

PRONUNCIATION KEY:

| at | āpe | fär | câre | end | mē | it | īce | pierce | hot | ōld | sông | fôrk |
| oil | out | up | ūse | rüle | pull | tûrn | chin | sing | shop | thin | this | |

hw in white; zh in treasure. The symbol ə stands for the unstressed vowel sound in about, taken, pencil, lemon, and circus.

443

lute A musical instrument like a guitar but with a body shaped like a pear. It is played by plucking the strings.

Another word that sounds like this is **loot.**
lute (lüt) *noun, plural* **lutes.**

Luxembourg A country in northwestern Europe. **Lux·em·bourg** (luk'səm bûrg') *noun.*

luxuriant 1. Having thick or abundant growth of plants. *The jungle was **luxuriant** and green after the rainy season.* 2. Rich in decoration; very fancy: *The drapes behind the queen's throne were **luxuriant**.* **lux·u·ri·ant** (luk shûr'ē ənt *or* lug zhûr'ē ənt) *adjective.*

The lute dates back to the 14th century.

luxurious 1. Giving much comfort and pleasure: *a **luxurious** hotel.* 2. Fond of luxuries or luxury: *Don't get a **luxurious** taste for jewels and furs.* **lux·u·ri·ous** (luk shûr'ē əs *or* lug zhûr'ē əs) *adjective.*

luxury 1. Something that gives much comfort and pleasure but is not necessary: *Eating dinner at the fancy restaurant was a **luxury** for our family.* 2. A way of life that gives comfort and pleasure: *The opera star is used to **luxury**.* **lux·u·ry** (luk'shə rē *or* lug'zhə rē) *noun, plural* **luxuries.**

-ly¹ A suffix that means: 1. In a certain way or manner: ***Perfectly** means in a perfect way.* 2. To a certain degree or extent: ***Highly** means to a high degree.*

-ly² A suffix that means: 1. Like: ***Friendly** means like a friend.* 2. Happening at a certain period of time: ***Weekly** means happening every week.*

lye A strong substance used in making soap and detergents. Lye is obtained by soaking wood ashes in water.

Another word that sounds like this is **lie.**
lye (lī) *noun.*

lying¹ Present participle of **lie¹**: *They are **lying** if they say they don't know what happened. Verb.* ○ The act of telling lies: *The witness will be punished for **lying**. Noun.* **ly·ing** (lī'ing) *verb; noun.*

lying² Present participle of **lie²**: *The dog is **lying** on the rug.* **ly·ing** (lī'ing) *verb.*

lymph A clear, yellowish liquid in the tissues of the body, containing water, proteins, and white blood cells. **lymph** (limf) *noun.*

lynx A wild animal in the cat family, about the size of a large domestic cat. It has yellowish brown fur with black spots and has black tufts on the ears. Lynx are found in eastern Europe and Asia. **lynx** (lingks) *noun, plural* **lynx** *or* **lynxes.**

lyre A musical instrument with strings that is like a harp. The lyre was played by ancient Egyptians, Hebrews, and Greeks. **lyre** (līr) *noun, plural* **lyres.**

lyric Expressing a strong, personal emotion: *The poet wrote **lyric** poems about nature. Adjective.* ○ 1. A poem that expresses a strong personal emotion. 2. **lyrics.** The words of a song: *I wrote both the **lyrics** and the melody of this song. Noun.* **lyr·ic** (lir'ik) *adjective; noun, plural* **lyrics.**

WORD HISTORY

The word lyric comes from a Greek word meaning "of a lyre." Lyric poetry was originally sung accompanied by a lyre.

lyrical Expressing a strong, personal emotion; lyric: *The **lyrical** poem was about love.* **lyr·i·cal** (lir'ik əl) *adjective.* —**lyrically** *adverb.*

The letter M has one sound in English, but that sound can be made in several different ways. It is commonly made by:

m as in words such as di**m**, dru**m**, and **m**ur**m**ur;

mm as in ha**mm**er;

and rarely by:

mb as in cli**mb**;

mn as in hy**mn** and autu**mn**;

lm as in ca**lm** and pa**lm**;

gm as in diaphra**gm**.

m, M The thirteenth letter of the alphabet. **m, M** (em) *noun, plural* **m's, M's.**

m. An abbreviation for **meter.**

MA Postal abbreviation for **Massachusetts.**

ma'am Madam: *Excuse me, ma'am; do you know what time it is?* This word is used mostly in everyday conversation. **ma'am** (mam) *noun, plural* **ma'ams.**

macaroni A food that is made from dough and then dried. It is usually shaped like short, hollow tubes. The way to cook macaroni is by boiling it in water. **mac·a·ro·ni** (mak′ə rō′nē) *noun.*

Macedonia 1. A country in southern Europe. 2. An ancient kingdom in southeastern Europe. **Mac·e·do·ni·a** (mas′i dō′nē ə) *noun.*

machine 1. A device that does some particular job. It is made up of a number of parts that work together. A lawn mower, a hair dryer, and a printing press are machines. 2. A simple device that lessens the force needed to move an object. A lever and a pulley are simple machines. **ma·chine** (mə shēn′) *noun, plural* **machines.**

This large machine is used for picking cotton.

machine gun A rifle that keeps firing bullets as long as the trigger is pressed.

machinery 1. Machines or parts of machines: *The mechanics fixed the machinery of the elevator.* 2. A group of things or people that make something work: *The president and Congress are part of the machinery of the federal government.* **ma·chin·er·y** (mə shē′nə rē) *noun.*

machinist A skilled worker who operates machinery that makes tools and parts. **ma·chin·ist** (mə shē′nist) *noun, plural* **machinists.**

mackerel A saltwater fish used for food. It has a silver-colored body with wavy dark markings on its back. **mack·er·el** (mak′ər əl) *noun, plural* **mackerels** *or* **mackerel.**

macron A short line (ˉ) placed over a vowel to show that it has a long sound. **ma·cron** (mā′kron) *noun, plural* **macrons.**

mad 1. Feeling or showing anger; angry: *I was mad when I found that my new bicycle was scratched.* 2. Crazy; insane. 3. Very foolish or reckless; not wise or sensible: *Walking across the canyon on a tightrope is a mad idea.* 4. Very enthusiastic: *My family is mad about camping.* 5. Wild and excited: *We made a mad dash to the airport.* 6. Sick with rabies: *a mad dog.* **mad** (mad) *adjective,* **madder, maddest. —madly** *adverb.*

Madagascar An island country in the Indian Ocean, off the coast of southeastern Africa. **Mad·a·gas·car** (mad′ə gas′kər) *noun.*

madam A title for a woman: *May I help you, madam?* **mad·am** (mad′əm) *noun, plural*

mesdames (mā däm′) *or* **madams.**

madame The French title for a married woman or a widow. **mad•ame** (mə dam′) *noun, plural* **mesdames.**

made Past tense and past participle of **make.** Another word that sounds like this is **maid.** **made** (mād) *verb.*

mademoiselle The French title for a girl or an unmarried woman. **mad•e•moi•selle** (mad′ə mə zel′) *noun, plural* **mademoiselles** *or* **mesdemoiselles** (mād mwä zel′).

made-up 1. Not real or true: *The author used made-up names for the characters in the book.* 2. Wearing make-up: *He had the made-up face of a clown.* **made-up** (mād′up′) *adjective.*

magazine 1. A printed collection of stories, articles, and pictures that is usually bound in a paper cover. Most magazines are issued every week or every month. 2. A room or building for storing ammunition. 3. The part of a gun or rifle that holds the bullets. **mag•a•zine** (mag′ə zēn′ *or* mag′ə zēn′) *noun, plural* **magazines.**

maggot A fly that has just come out of its egg; fly larva. It has a thick body with no legs. **mag•got** (mag′ət) *noun, plural* **maggots.**

magic 1. The power to control forces of nature and events by using special charms or spells: *The fairy tale told of wizards who used magic.* 2. The art or skill of doing tricks to entertain people. *Noun.*
○ Using magic; done by or seeming to be done by magic: *The magic trick was done with mirrors. Adjective.*
mag•ic (maj′ik) *noun; adjective.*

magical Using or done by magic: *The wizard used magical powers to disappear.* **mag•i•cal** (maj′i kəl) *adjective.* —**magically** *adverb.*

magician 1. A person who entertains people by doing magic tricks. 2. A person thought to have magical powers; wizard. **ma•gi•cian** (mə jish′ən) *noun, plural* **magicians.**

magma Melted rock below the surface of the earth. Magma

It takes much practice to become a magician.

rises to the surface of the earth and hardens into rock or flows as lava out of volcanoes. **mag•ma** (mag′mə) *noun.*

magnesium A silver-white metal. Magnesium is very light in weight and is used in alloys. It burns with a brilliant, white light, and is often used in making fireworks. Magnesium is a chemical element. **mag•ne•si•um** (mag nē′zē əm *or* mag nē′zhəm) *noun.*

magnet A piece of stone or metal that can attract iron or steel. Magnets are often made in the shape of a bar or horseshoe. **mag•net** (mag′nit) *noun, plural* **magnets.**

WORD HISTORY

The word **magnet** comes from the the Greek name of the city of Magnesia, in western Asia. The first magnets were discovered there.

magnetic 1. Acting like a magnet; having to do with magnets or magnetism: *The magnetic needle of a compass points to the earth's magnetic poles.* 2. Able to attract or fascinate people: *a magnetic personality.* **mag•net•ic** (mag net′ik) *adjective.* —**magnetically** (mag net′ik lē) *adverb.*

magnetic field The space around a magnet in which the magnet has the power to attract other metals.

magnetic pole 1. Either of the two points of a magnet where its magnetic force is strongest. 2. Either of the two points on the earth's surface toward which the needle of a compass points. One of these points is near the North Pole and the other is near the South Pole. They are the points where the earth's magnetic pull is strongest.

magnetic tape Tape that has a special magnetic coating and is used for recording and playing sound and for recording and displaying images. A videocassette contains magnetic tape.

magnetism 1. The power to attract iron, steel, and certain other materials. Certain stones and metals and all electric currents have magnetism. 2. The ability to attract or fascinate people: *Many political leaders have strong personal magnetism.* **mag•net•ism** (mag′ni tiz′əm) *noun.*

magnetize To cause an object to act like a magnet; give the power of magnetism to a metal: *We magnetized the iron bar by setting it against a strong magnet for a few days.* **mag•ne•tize**

(mag′ni tīz′) *verb*, **magnetized**, **magnetizing**.

magnificence The quality of being magnificent: *the magnificence of the royal palace.* **mag·nif·i·cence** (mag- nif′ə səns) *noun*.

magnificent Very beautiful and grand; splendid: *a magnificent view of the valley.* **mag·nif·i·cent** (mag nif′ə sənt) *adjective*. —**magnificently** *adverb*.

magnify 1. To make something look bigger than it really is: *The microscope magnified the cells one hundred times.* 2. To make something seem more important than it really is; exaggerate: *Some people always magnify their health problems.* **mag·ni·fy** (mag′nə fī′) *verb*, **magnified**, **magnifying**.

This building has a magnificent design.

magnifying glass A lens or combination of lenses that make things look bigger than they really are.

magnitude 1. Greatness of size: *We could only guess at the magnitude of the mountain.* 2. Importance: *The discovery of America was an event of great magnitude.* **mag·ni·tude** (mag′ni tüd′ *or* mag′ni tūd′) *noun*.

magnolia A tree or shrub with large white, pink, purple, or yellow flowers. **mag·no·lia** (mag nōl′yə) *noun*, *plural* **magnolias**.

magpie A bird with a long tail, a thick bill, and a noisy, chattering call. They are related to crows. **mag·pie** (mag′pī) *noun*, *plural* **magpies**.

mahogany 1. An evergreen tree that grows in warm parts of North and South America. The reddish brown wood of this tree is strong and hard and is often used in making furniture. 2. A dark reddish brown color. *Noun.* ○ Having the color mahogany; dark reddish brown. *Adjective.* **ma·hog·a·ny** (mə hog′ə nē) *noun*, *plural* **mahoganies**; *adjective*.

maid 1. A woman paid to do housework. 2. A girl or a young unmarried woman. Another word that sounds like this is **made**. **maid** (mād) *noun*, *plural* **maids**.

maiden A girl or young unmarried woman. *Noun.* ○ First or earliest: *The ship's maiden voyage was from England to New York. Adjective.* **maid·en** (mā′dən) *noun*, *plural* **maidens**; *adjective*.

maiden name The original last name of a woman who has married and changed her last name.

maid of honor An unmarried woman who is the main female attendant of the bride at a wedding.

mail¹ 1. Letters, cards, and packages sent or received through a post office. 2. The system by which mail is sent, moved, or delivered. It is usually run by the government of a country: *We received the invitation by mail. Noun.* ○ To send by mail: *I mailed your letter this morning. Verb.* Another word that sounds like this is **male**. **mail** (māl) *noun*, *plural* **mails**; *verb*, **mailed**, **mailing**.

mail² Armor made of linked rings. **mail** (māl) *noun*.

mailbox 1. A box in which letters are put so that they can be picked up by a mail carrier. 2. A box into which a person's mail is put when it is delivered. **mail·box** (māl′boks) *noun*, *plural* **mailboxes**.

mail carrier A person who carries and delivers mail.

mailing A batch of mail sent at one time. **mail·ing** (mā′ling) *noun*, *plural* **mailing**.

mailman A person whose job is carrying and delivering mail; mail carrier; postman. **mail·man** (māl′man′) *noun*, *plural* **mailmen** (māl′men′).

maim To hurt someone so much that the injured part is useless; cripple: *Many soldiers had been maimed in the fighting.* **maim** (mām) *verb*, **maimed**, **maiming**.

main Greatest in size or importance: *This is the main branch of the library. Adjective.* ○ A large pipe or cable that is usually underground. Mains are used to carry water, gas, and electricity to homes or other buildings. *Noun.* Other sound alike words are **Maine** and **mane**. **main** (mān) *adjective*; *noun*, *plural* **mains**.

PRONUNCIATION KEY:

| at | āpe | fär | câre | end | mē | it | īce | pierce | hot | ōld | sông | fôrk |
| oil | out | up | ūse | rüle | pull | tûrn | chin | sing | shop | thin | this | |

hw in white; zh in treasure. The symbol ə stands for the unstressed vowel sound in about, taken, pencil, lemon, and circus.

447

Maine A state in the northeastern United States, on the Atlantic Ocean. Its capital is Augusta. Other sound alike words are are **main** and **mane**. **Maine** (mān) *noun*.

Maine
U. S. Postal Abbreviation: **ME**
Capital: **Augusta**
Population: **1,187,000**
Area: **33,215 sq. mi./86,026 sq. km**
State Nickname: **Pine Tree State**
State Bird: **Chickadee**
State Flower: **White Pine Cone and Tassel**

WORD HISTORY

The name **Maine** comes from the earlier English words "the maine," which meant "mainland." People who explored this region used these words to show the difference between the North American continent and the islands along the coast in this area.

mainframe A powerful computer that is much larger than a microcomputer. Mainframes are usually used by big companies and organizations to process large amounts of information. **main·frame** (mān′frām′) *noun*, *plural* **mainframes**.

mainland The chief land mass of a country or continent, as distinguished from an island: *Hong Kong is an island located off the mainland of China*. **main·land** (mān′land′ or mān′lənd′) *noun*.

mainly For the most part; chiefly: *Although they are interested mainly in popular music, they sometimes listen to classical music too*. **main·ly** (mān′lē) *adverb*.

mainstay 1. A heavy rope or cable that supports or steadies the mast of a sailing ship. 2. A person or thing that is the main support of something:

Agriculture is the mainstay of our state. **main·stay** (mān′stā′) *noun*, *plural* **mainstays**.

maintain 1. To continue to have or do; go on with; keep: *It was hard for the skiers to maintain their balance on the icy hill*. 2. To take care of: *Gardeners maintain the park*. 3. To say in a firm and sure way: *No matter what you say, I still maintain that I am right*. **main·tain** (mān tān′) *verb*, **maintained**, **maintaining**.

maintenance 1. A maintaining or being maintained: *The city government is responsible for the maintenance of streets and sidewalks*. 2. Money, food, and shelter needed for living; means of support: *My job provides a comfortable maintenance*. **main·te·nance** (mān′tə nəns) *noun*.

maize A grain that grows in rows on the ears of a tall plant. This grain is usually called corn. Another word that sounds like this is **maze**. **maize** (māz) *noun*.

majestic Having majesty: *The majestic mountains rose high above the valley*. **ma·jes·tic** (mə jes′tik) *adjective*. —**majestically** (mə jes′ tik lē) *adverb*.

majesty 1. Great dignity; grandness: *The crowds were thrilled by the majesty of the royal procession*. 2. Majesty. A title used in speaking to or about a king, queen, or other royal ruler. **ma·jes·ty** (maj′əs tē) *noun*, *plural* **majesties**.

major Bigger or more important: *The major expense of my vacation was the cost of the airplane ticket*. *Adjective*.
○ An officer in the armed forces. In the United States Army, Marine Corps, or Air Force, a major ranks below a colonel but above a captain. *Noun*.
maj·or (mā′jər) *adjective*; *noun*, *plural* **majors**.

majorette A woman or girl who leads a marching band and twirls a baton. **ma·jor·ette** (mā jə ret′) *noun*, *plural* **majorettes**.

majority 1. The larger number or part of something; more than half: *The majority of the students voted for you for class president*. 2. The amount by which a larger number is greater than a smaller number: *I won the election by twenty-five votes to ten votes, so I had a majority of fifteen votes*. 3. The age at which a person is legally permitted to manage his or her own affairs. In the United States this age is different in different states. **ma·jor·i·ty** (mə jôr′i tē) *noun*, *plural* **majorities**.

make **1.** To cause to be, become, or happen: *A robin has begun to* **make** *a nest in the tree outside my window. The smell of food* **makes** *me hungry.* **2.** To cause or force to do: *A funny movie always* **makes** *me laugh.* **3.** To add up to; amount to: *Thirty-six inches* **make** *a yard.* **4.** To earn: *The author* **makes** *a living by writing novels.* **5.** To go or get to: *I rushed to* **make** *the bus on time.* **6.** To win a place or position on: *My friend* **made** *the school basketball team this year.* Verb.
○ The style or type of something made and sold; brand: *Our new car is the same* **make** *as our old car.* Noun.
   • **to make believe.** To pretend: *The two playmates like* **to make believe** *that they are firefighters.*
   • **to make it.** To succeed: *That movie actor has also* **made it** *in television.*
   • **to make up.** **1.** To become friends again: *The two friends argue a lot, but they always* **make up.** **2.** To put cosmetics on: *The actor* **made up** *before going on stage.* **3.** To invent in the mind: *The baby-sitter* **made up** *a funny story to amuse us.* **4.** To be the parts of; form: *Nine players* **make up** *a baseball team.*
make (māk) *verb,* **made, making;** *noun, plural* **makes.**

make-believe Imagination: *The book contained stories of ghosts and witches and other tales of* **make-believe.** *Noun.*
○ Not real; imaginary: *The attic became the children's* **make-believe** *castle. Adjective.*
make·be·lieve (māk′bi lēv′) *noun; adjective.*

makeshift Something used for a time in place of the correct or usual thing: *When the Venetian blind broke, we used a sheet as a* **makeshift.** *Noun.*
○ Used for a time in place of the correct or usual thing: *We sometimes use our sofa as a* **makeshift** *bed. Adjective.* **make·shift** (māk′shift′) *noun, plural* **makeshifts;** *adjective.*

makeup **1.** Lipstick, powder, and other cosmetics that are put on the face. **2.** The way in which something is put together: *The* **makeup** *of the kennel is half dogs and half cats.* **3.** A person's nature; personality: *You are such a polite person that it is not in your* **makeup** *to be rude to anyone.*

make·up (māk′up) *noun, plural* **makeups.**

malaria A disease that causes chills, a high fever, and sweating. Malaria is spread by the bite of a certain type of mosquito that carries the disease from infected persons. **mal·ar·i·a** (mə lâr′ē ə) *noun.*

Malawi A country in southeastern Africa. **Ma·la·wi** (mə lä′wē) *noun.*

Malaysia A country in southeastern Asia. **Ma·lay·sia** (mə lā′zhə) *noun.*

male **1.** Of or having to do with men or boys: *The school play will have four* **male** *parts and four female parts.* **2.** Having to do with or belonging to the sex that can fertilize female eggs: *A* **male** *deer is called a buck. Adjective.*
○ A male person or animal. *Noun.*
Another word that sounds like this is **mail.**
male (māl) *adjective; noun, plural* **males.**

Mali A country in northwestern Africa. **Ma·li** (mä′lē) *noun.*

malice The desire to cause harm or pain to someone; ill will: *It was* **malice** *that made the child spread the nasty rumor.* **mal·ice** (mal′is) *noun.*

malicious Feeling, showing, or caused by malice: *Malicious lies can hurt others.* **ma·li·cious** (mə lish′əs) *adjective.* —**maliciously** (mə lish′əs lē) *adverb.*

malign To tell damaging lies about; slander: *During the election campaign, many people* **maligned** *the mayor. Verb.* **ma·lign** (mə līn′) *verb,* **maligned, maligning.**

malignant **1.** Tending to spread disease through the body: *The surgeon removed the* **malignant** *growth.* **2.** Showing ill will; harmful: *The soldiers spread* **malignant** *lies about their new commander.* **ma·lig·nant** (mə lig′nənt) *adjective.*

mall **1.** A large, enclosed, air-conditioned shopping center. **2.** A street lined with stores and closed off to motor vehicles. **3.** A large open space, often like a park, for people to walk and relax in.
Another word that sounds like this is **maul.**
mall (môl) *noun, plural* **malls.**

mallard A common wild duck of North America, Europe and Asia. The male mallard has a green head, a white band around the neck, a reddish brown chest, and a grayish back.
mal·lard (mal′ərd) *noun, plural* **mallards** *or* **mallard.**

PRONUNCIATION KEY:

| at | āpe | fär | câre | end | mē | it | īce | pîerce | hot | ōld | sông | fôrk |
| oil | out | up | ūse | rüle | pull | tûrn | chin | sing | shop | thin | this | |

hw in white; zh in treasure. The symbol ə stands for the unstressed vowel sound in about, taken, pencil, lemon, and circus.

449

mallet A type of hammer with a head made of wood or other soft material. In some sports, such as croquet or polo, mallets with long handles are used to hit the ball. **mal·let** (mal′it) *noun, plural* **mallets.**

Mallets with short handles are used as tools.

malnutrition An unhealthy condition of the body, caused by not eating enough food or not eating the right kinds of food. **mal·nu·tri·tion** (mal′nü trish′ən *or* mal′nū trish′ən) *noun.*

malt Barley or other grain that is soaked in warm water until it sprouts and then is dried. Malt is used in making beer and ale. **malt** (môlt) *noun.*

malted milk A drink made by mixing milk and ice cream with a powder made of malt. **malt·ed milk** (môl′tid).

mama An informal word for mother. **ma·ma** (mä′mə) *noun, plural* **mamas.**

Most mammals like this lesser panda are covered with fur or have some hair.

mammal A kind of animal that is warm-blooded and has a backbone. Female mammals have glands that produce milk to feed their young. Human beings, cattle, dogs, cats, and whales are mammals. **mam·mal** (mam′əl) *noun, plural* **mammals.**

mammoth A kind of ancient elephant with long, curving tusks and shaggy, brown hair. The last mammoths on earth died about 10,000 years ago. *Noun.*

○ Very large; gigantic; huge: *Building that cabin was a mammoth job.* Adjective. **mam·moth** (mam′əth) *noun, plural* **mammoths;** *adjective.*

Mammoths were larger than elephants.

man 1. An adult male person: *Until 1920, only men were allowed to vote in the U.S.* 2. A human being or the human race; a person or all people: *Man is the only animal that can use language.* 3. One of the pieces used in playing chess, checkers, and other games. *Noun.*

○ To supply with people who do a certain job: *Ten soldiers manned the fort. Verb.* **man** (man) *noun, plural* **men;** *verb,* **manned, manning.**

manage 1. To direct or control: *The president of the company managed its business affairs. Only a very good rider could manage such a wild horse.* 2. To succeed at doing something; be able to: *Our team managed to win, even though our best player was sick.* **man·age** (man′ij) *verb,* **managed, managing.**

management 1. The act or process of managing: *The business failed because of bad management.* 2. The person or persons who manage something, such as a business: *The company's management planned to hire more workers.* **man·age·ment** (man′ij mənt) *noun.*

manager A person who manages something: *The manager of the baseball team decided which player would pitch.* **man·a·ger** (man′i jər) *noun, plural* **managers.**

manatee A large animal that looks somewhat like a seal and lives in the tropical waters of the Atlantic coast. **man·a·tee** (man′ə tē′) *noun, plural* **manatees.**

mandarin 1. A high public official in imperial China. 2. Mandarin. A dialect of the Chinese language. It is the official language of the Chinese government. 3. A small citrus fruit with a loose rind that is easy to peel. It is also called a mandarin orange. **man·da·rin** (man′də rin) *noun, plural* **mandarins.**

mandate 1. Instruction or support given by voters

to their representatives in government through the votes cast in an election: *The president got a mandate to work for tax reform.* **2.** An official command or order. *Noun.*

○ To demand or require: *Trouble with the lights mandated moving the slide show to another room. Verb.*

man·date (man′dāt) *noun, plural* **mandates**; *verb,* **mandated, mandating.**

mandolin A musical instrument like a guitar, with a pear-shaped body and metal strings. **man·do·lin** (man′də lin′ *or* man′də lin′) *noun, plural* **mandolins.**

mane The long, thick hair on the neck of certain animals, such as horses and male lions.

Other sound alike words are **main** and **Maine.**

mane (mān) *noun, plural* **manes.**

maneuver **1.** A planned movement of soldiers or ships: *The generals discussed a maneuver to capture the enemy's supplies.* **2.** A skillful or clever move or plan: *The candidate used many maneuvers to win. Noun.*

○ **1.** To cause soldiers or ships to move in a certain way: *The captain maneuvered the soldiers into a position for attacking the enemy.* **2.** To move or manage skillfully or cleverly: *We maneuvered our way to the front of the crowd so we could see the parade. Verb.*

ma·neu·ver (mə nü′vər) *noun, plural* **maneuvers**; *verb,* **maneuvered, maneuvering.**

manganese A brittle, silver gray metal used in making steel. Manganese is a chemical element. **man·ga·nese** (mang′gə nēz′ *or* mang′gə nēs′) *noun.*

manger A large box that holds food for horses or cattle. **man·ger** (mān′jər) *noun, plural* **mangers.**

mangle To destroy by tearing, cutting, or crushing. **man·gle** (mang′gəl) *verb,* **mangled, mangling.**

mango A yellowish red fruit with a sweet, spicy taste and a hard seed in the center. It grows on a tropical evergreen tree. **man·go** (mang′gō) *noun, plural* **mangoes** *or* **mangos.**

manhole An opening or hole, usually in a street, through which a worker can go to build or repair a sewer, wires, pipes, or the like. Manholes have lids that can be removed. **man·hole** (man′hōl′) *noun, plural* **manholes.**

manhood **1.** The condition or the time of being an adult male person: *The adolescent boy will soon enter manhood.* **2.** Men as a group: *The manhood and womanhood of our country always respond well in a national crisis.* **man·hood** (man′hùd) *noun.*

maniac **1.** An insane or violent person. **2.** A person who is very enthusiastic about something: *a football maniac.* **ma·ni·ac** (mā′nē ak) *noun, plural* **maniacs.**

manicure A cleaning, shaping, and sometimes polishing of the fingernails. *Noun.*

○ To give a manicure to. *Verb.*

man·i·cure (man′i kyùr) *noun, plural* **manicures**; *verb,* **manicured, manicuring.**

Manitoba A province in central Canada. Its capital is Winnipeg. **Man·i·to·ba** (man′i tō′bə) *noun.*

mankind The human race; human beings as a group: *The exploration of outer space is one of the greatest achievements of mankind.* **man·kind** (man′kīnd′) *noun.*

man-made Made by people rather than by nature: *Glass, steel, and plastic are man-made; water, coal, and wood are not.* **man-made** (man′mād′) *adjective.*

manner **1.** The way in which something is done: *The children dropped their jackets on the floor in a careless manner.* **2.** A way of acting or behaving: *Our librarian has a warm and friendly manner.* **3. manners.** Polite ways of behaving or acting: *Those children are too young to have good table manners.*

Another word that sounds like this is **manor.**

man·ner (man′ər) *noun, plural* **manners.**

man-of-war A warship, usually a sailing ship. **man-of-war** (man′əv wôr′) *noun, plural* **men-of-war** (men′əv wôr′).

manor **1.** A large estate belonging to a lord in the Middle Ages. The lord lived on part of the land and the rest was divided among peasants, who paid rent to the lord in the form of goods or work. **2.** A mansion.

Another word that sounds like this is **manner.**

man·or (man′ər) *noun, plural* **manors.**

mansion A very large and grand home: *a beautiful old mansion by the ocean.* **man·sion** (man′shən) *noun, plural* **mansions.**

PRONUNCIATION KEY:

| at | āpe | fär | câre | end | mē | it | īce | pierce | hot | ōld | sông | fôrk |
| oil | out | up | ūse | rüle | pùll | tûrn | chin | sing | shop | thin | <u>th</u>is | |

hw in white; zh in treasure. The symbol ə stands for the unstressed vowel sound in about, taken, pencil, lemon, and circus.

451

manslaughter The crime of killing someone without having intended to do so. A driver who accidentally kills someone may be guilty of manslaughter.
man·slaugh·ter (man′slô′tər) *noun.*

mantel 1. The structure that surrounds a fireplace opening. 2. The shelf above a fireplace. This is also called a *mantelpiece.*
Another word that sounds like this is **mantle.**
man·tel (man′təl) *noun, plural* **mantels.**

mantle A loose, sleeveless cape.
Another word that sounds like this is **mantel.**
man·tle (man′təl) *noun, plural* **mantles.**

manual Done with or using the hands: *Carpenters use many **manual** skills in their work. Adjective.*
○ A book that gives instructions or information about something; handbook: *Study the driver's **manual** before you take the test for your driver's license. Noun.*
man·u·al (man′ū əl) *adjective; noun, plural* **manuals.**

manufacture 1. To make or process something, especially in quantity and with the use of machinery: *That company **manufactures** bicycles.* 2. To make up; invent: *I **manufactured** an excuse for forgetting my friend's birthday. Verb.*
○ The act or process of manufacturing: *The city is famous for the **manufacture** of automobiles. Noun.*
man·u·fac·ture (man′yə fak′chər) *verb,* **manufactured, manufacturing;** *noun.*

manure Waste matter from animals used to fertilize soil. **ma·nure** (mə nùr′ *or* mə nyùr′) *noun.*

manuscript A book or article written or typed by hand. Manuscripts are sent to a publisher or printer to be made into printed books or magazines. **man·u·script** (man′yə skript′) *noun, plural* **manuscripts.**

many Made up of a large number: *We have **many** books on American history here. Adjective.*
○ A large number: *The meeting was canceled because **many** of the members could not be there. Noun.*
○ A large number of people or things: *Many were late for school because of the bad weather. Pronoun.*
man·y (men′ē) *adjective,* **more, most;** *noun; pronoun.*

map A drawing that shows the surface features of an area, as of a state or country. Maps of large areas usually show cities, rivers, oceans, and other features. *Noun.*
○ 1. To make a map of; show on a map: *The explorers **mapped** the wilderness as they explored it.* 2. To plan in detail; arrange: *The committee **mapped** out a campaign to raise money for a new hospital. Verb.*
map (map) *noun, plural* **maps;** *verb,* **mapped, mapping.**

This woman is studying a topographical **map.**

maple A tree that has leaves with deep notches. Its seeds are contained in a small fruit that looks like two wings. **ma·ple** (mā′pəl) *noun, plural* **maples.**

maple syrup A sweet syrup made by boiling the sap of a certain kind of maple tree.

Mar. An abbreviation for March.

marathon 1. A race for runners over a course of 26 miles and 385 yards. 2. A long race or competition testing endurance: *The baseball game turned into a **marathon** of six hours, because neither team could score.* **ma·ra·thon** (mar′ə thon′) *noun, plural* **marathons.**

The wood from a **maple** is hard and is used in making furniture.

marble 1. A type of hard, smooth stone. Marble is white, or streaked with different colors. It is often used in building and sculpture. 2. A small, hard ball of glass used in games: *At recess we played with **marbles.***
mar·ble (mär′bəl) *noun, plural* **marbles.**

march 1. To walk with regular, measured steps as soldiers do. People who march walk in step with others in an orderly group: *The firefighters and police* **marched** *in the parade.* **2.** To move forward steadily: *Time* **marches** *on. Verb.*

○ **1.** The act of marching: *The parade started its* **march** *at noon.* **2.** A musical piece that has a strong rhythm and is suitable for marching: *The band played a military* **march.** *Noun.*

march (märch) *verb,* **marched, marching;** *noun, plural* **marches.**

March The third month of the year. March has thirty-one days. **March** (märch) *noun.*

WORD HISTORY

The Romans named the month of March in honor of Mars, the god of war in Roman mythology.

mare The female of the horse, donkey, zebra, or certain other animals. **mare** (mâr) *noun, plural* **mares.**

margarine A food used as a spread or in cooking and baking. It may contain animal or vegetable oil, milk, water, and salt. Margarine was originally made as a substitute for butter. Another word for this is oleomargarine. **mar·ga·rine** (mär′jər in) *noun, plural* **margarines.**

margin **1.** The blank space around the written or printed part of a page: *I wrote in the* **margin** *of my notebook.* **2.** An edge or border: *There was a fence around the* **margin** *of the property.* **3.** An extra amount; amount in addition to what is necessary: *Allow a* **margin** *of ten minutes for your trip just in case.* **mar·gin** (mär′jin) *noun, plural* **margins.**

There are many different types of marigolds.

marigold A garden plant that bears yellow, orange, or red flowers in summer. **mar·i·gold** (mar′i gōld′) *noun, plural* **marigolds.**

marina A small harbor where boats and yachts can be docked and serviced. **ma·ri·na** (mə rē′nə) *noun, plural* **marinas.**

marine **1.** Having to do with or living in the sea: *Whales are* **marine** *animals.* **2.** Having to do with ships or navigation: *Several stores here sell* **marine** *supplies.* **3.** Having to do with the Marine Corps. *Adjective.*

○ **Marine.** A member of the Marine Corps. *Noun.* **ma·rine** (mə rēn′) *adjective; noun, plural* **Marines.**

Marine Corps A branch of the United States armed forces, trained to fight both on land and at sea.

marionette A doll or puppet, usually made of wood, moved by strings or wires held from above. **mar·i·o·nette** (mar′ē ə net′) *noun, plural* **marionettes.**

The use of marionettes dates back to the 16th century.

maritime **1.** Of or having to do with the sea, ships, or sea travel: *The Coast Guard enforces* **maritime** *laws.* **2.** Close to or living near the sea: *That* **maritime** *nation has a large fishing fleet.* **mar·i·time** (mar′i tīm) *adjective.*

mark¹ **1.** A spot or trace made on one thing by another. A line, scratch, stain, or scar is a mark. **2.** A sign or symbol: *Does this sentence end with a question* **mark?** **3.** A letter or number that shows how good a person's work is: *I get good* **marks** *in history.* **4.** A line or object that shows position: *The white pole was the halfway* **mark** *on the track.* **5.** Something aimed at; target or goal: *The arrow missed the* **mark.** *Noun.*

○ **1.** To make or put a mark or marks on: *My boots* **marked** *the kitchen floor.* **2.** To show clearly: *A stone wall* **marks** *the end of the farmer's land.* **3.** To be a sign or feature of: *Happiness* **marked** *the occasion of their wedding.* **4.** To give a mark to; grade: *The teacher* **marked** *the spelling tests. Verb.*

• **to make one's mark.** To become famous or

PRONUNCIATION KEY:

| at | āpe | fär | câre | end | mē | it | īce | pierce | hot | ōld | sông | fôrk |
| oil | out | up | ūse | rüle | pu̇ll | tûrn | chin | sing | shop | thin | this | |

hw in white; zh in treasure. The symbol ə stands for the unstressed vowel sound in about, taken, pencil, lemon, and circus.

453

successful: *Our state senators have **made their mark** in this session of Congress.*
• **to mark down.** To reduce the price of: *Our grocery store **marked down** apples this week.*
• **to mark up.** To increase the price of: *The store has **marked up** these jackets since last week.*
mark (märk) *noun, plural* **marks;** *verb,* **marked, marking.**

mark² A unit of money in Germany. **mark** (märk) *noun, plural* **marks.**

market 1. A place or store where food or goods are for sale: *I bought shrimp at the fish **market**.* 2. A demand for something that is for sale: *There is a very large **market** for television sets now in this country. Noun.*
○ To buy or sell goods at a market: *I go **marketing** for groceries every weekend. The rancher **marketed** the cattle in town. Verb.*
mar·ket (mär′kit) *noun, plural* **markets;** *verb,* **marketed, marketing.**

marketplace A place where food and other products are bought and sold: *In old towns the **marketplace** was often in a square.* **mar·ket·place** (mär′kit plās′) *noun, plural* **marketplaces.**

marking A mark or marks; patch or patches of color: *The bird had brown and white **markings** on its wings.* **mark·ing** (mär′king) *noun, plural* **markings.**

marmalade A type of jam made with fruit and sugar and usually with citrus fruits and their peel: *orange **marmalade**.* **mar·ma·lade** (mär′mə lād′) *noun, plural* **marmalades.**

maroon¹ A dark brownish red color. *Noun.*
○ Having the color maroon. *Adjective.*
ma·roon (mə rün′) *noun, plural* **maroon;** *adjective.*

maroon² To leave a person alone on a deserted island or coast: *The pirates **marooned** their prisoner on a tiny, lonely island.* **ma·roon** (mə rün′) *verb,* **marooned, marooning.**

marquee A large awning or a rooflike structure over the entrance of a theater, store, or hotel. **mar·quee** (mär kē′) *noun, plural* **marquees.**

marquis A nobleman ranking next below a duke and above an earl or count. **mar·quis** (mär′kwis *or* mär kē′) *noun, plural* **marquises** *or* **marquis.**

marquise 1. The wife or widow of a marquis. 2. A noblewoman whose rank equals that of a marquis. **mar·quise** (mär kēz′) *noun, plural* **marquises.**

marriage 1. The state of being married: *My grandparents' **marriage** was happy.* 2. The act of marrying: *The couple's **marriage** was in June.* **mar·riage** (mar′ij) *noun, plural* **marriages.**

marrow The soft substance that fills the hollow parts of bones. The marrow makes cells for the bloodstream. **mar·row** (mar′ō) *noun.*

marry 1. To take as a husband or wife; wed: *They plan to **marry** after college.* 2. To join as husband and wife: *The minister **married** them in a church.* **mar·ry** (mar′ē) *verb,* **married, marrying.**

Mars The seventh largest planet in our solar system. It is the fourth planet in order of distance from the sun. **Mars** (märz) *noun.*

Mars
The red planet Mars has long been a source of fantasies about alien civilizations. Although no life has been discovered there so far, it is thought that microorganisms may be found there eventually.
Average distance from sun: **141,700,000 miles**
Diameter: **4,223 miles**
Length of Day: **24 hours, 37 minutes**
Length of Year: **1.8 years**
Average Temperature: **-81°F**
Mass compared to Earth: **.11**
Weight of 100 pounds: **38**
Atmosphere: **Carbon Dioxide**
Number of rings: **0**
Number of satellites: **2**

marsh Low, wet land. Grasses and reeds grow in marshes. **marsh** (märsh) *noun, plural* **marshes.**

marshal 1. An officer of a federal court who has the duties of a sheriff. 2. A person who arranges certain ceremonies. *Noun.*
○ To arrange in proper order: *The general **marshaled** all the troops for battle. Verb.*
Another word that sounds like this is **martial.**
mar·shal (mär′shəl) *noun, plural* **marshals;** *verb,* **marshaled, marshaling.**

marshmallow A soft, white candy with a texture like a sponge. Marshmallows are sometimes toasted before being eaten. **marsh·mal·low** (märsh′mel′ō *or* märsh′mal′ō) *noun, plural* **marshmallows.**

marsupial A kind of animal. The female has a pouch in which young are carried. Kangaroos and opossums are marsupials. **mar·su·pi·al** (mär sü′pē əl) *noun, plural* **marsupials.**

martial Of, having to do with, or suitable for war or military life: *My sister and I take lessons in martial arts.*
Another word that sounds like this is **marshal.**
mar·tial (mär′shəl) *adjective.*

martin One of several kinds of swallows. Martins live throughout the world and eat insects that they catch while in flight. **mar·tin** (mär′tən) *noun, plural* **martins.**

Martin Luther King Day A holiday observed on the third Monday in January to celebrate the birthday of Martin Luther King, Jr., the black civil-rights leader.

martyr A person who chooses to suffer or die rather than give up his or her beliefs. **mar·tyr** (mär′tər) *noun, plural* **martyrs.**

marvel A wonderful or astonishing thing: *Space travel is one of the marvels of modern science. Noun.*
○ To feel wonder and astonishment: *We marveled at the acrobat's skill. Verb.*
mar·vel (mär′vəl) *noun, plural* **marvels;** *verb,* **marveled, marveling.**

marvelous 1. Causing wonder or amazement: *The story tells of marvelous events.* 2. Outstanding; excellent: *I went to a marvelous birthday party.* **marvelous** (mär′ və ləs) *adjective.*
—marvelously *adverb.*

Maryland A state in the eastern United States. Its capital is Annapolis. **Mar·y·land** (mer′ə lənd) *noun.*

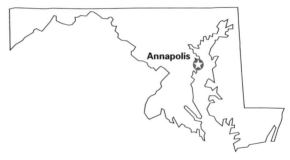

Maryland
U. S. Postal Abbreviation: **MD**
Capital: **Annapolis**
Population: **4,535,000**
Area: **10,577 sq. mi./27,394 sq. km**
State Nicknames: **Old Line State; Free State**
State Bird: **Baltimore Oriole**
State Flower: **Black-Eyed Susan**

mascara A cosmetic paste put on the eyelashes to make them look longer, darker, and thicker. **mas·car·a** (mas kâr′ə) *noun, plural* **mascaras.**

mascot An animal, person, or thing supposed to bring good luck. Sports teams sometimes have a pet animal as a mascot. **mas·cot** (ma′skot) *noun, plural* **mascots.**

masculine Having to do with a man; like that of a man: *My cousin has a deep, masculine voice.* **mas·cu·line** (mas′kyə lin) *adjective.*

mash 1. A soft mass or mixture. 2. A mixture of grains that is fed to livestock or poultry. *Noun.*
○ To make into a soft mass: *After I boiled the potatoes, I mashed them. Verb.*
mash (mash) *noun, plural* **mashes;** *verb,* **mashed, mashing.**

mask 1. A covering worn to hide or protect the face: *The children wore masks to the Halloween party. The baseball bounced off of the catcher's mask.* 2. Anything that hides or covers up something: *Their boasting is just a mask to hide their lack of self-confidence. Noun.*
○ 1. To cover with a mask: *The surgeons masked*

Some masks are hung on a wall for decoration.

their faces before the operation. **2.** To hide or cover up: *A high stone wall* **masked** *the house from the road. I tried to* **mask** *my disappointment with a smile. Verb.* **mask** (mask) *noun, plural* **masks;** *verb,* **masked, masking.**

mason A person whose work is building with stone, bricks, or cement. **ma•son** (mā′sən) *noun, plural* **masons.**

masonry Something built of stone, brick, or concrete by a mason. **ma•son•ry** (mā′sən rē) *noun.*

masquerade **1.** A party at which masks and costumes are worn: *The children dressed as famous people from history for the* **masquerade.** **2.** A false appearance; disguise: *The spy's* **masquerade** *of friendship fooled the soldier into revealing secret information. Noun.*
○ To disguise oneself; put on a false appearance: *We* **masqueraded** *as pirates for the dance. Verb.* **mas•quer•ade** (mas′kə rād′) *noun, plural* **masquerades;** *verb,* **masqueraded, masquerading.**

mass **1.** A body of matter with no particular shape: *A* **mass** *of snow piled up along the fence.* **2.** A large quantity or number: *A* **mass** *of people showed up for the game.* **3.** Size or bulk: *An elephant has great* **mass.** **4.** The main or larger part; majority: *The* **mass** *of voters turned out for the election.* **5.** The quantity of matter that a body contains. *Noun.*
○ Involving many people or things: *There was a* **mass** *meeting in front of the library. Adjective.*
○ To gather or form into a mass: *The people* **massed** *together in front of the theater. Verb.* **mass** (mas) *noun, plural* **masses;** *adjective; verb,* **massed, massing.**

Mass The main religious ceremony in the Roman Catholic Church and certain other churches. **Mass** (mas) *noun, plural* **Masses.**

Mass. An abbreviation for Massachusetts.

Massachusetts A state in the northeastern United States. Its capital is Boston. **Mas•sa•chu•setts** (mas′ə chü′sits) *noun.*

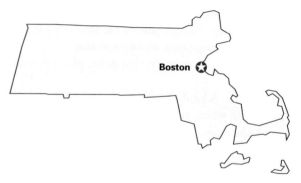

Boston ✪

Massachusetts
U. S. Postal Abbreviation: **MA**
Capital: **Boston**
Population: **5,855,000**
Area: **8,257 sq. mi./21,386 sq. km**
State Nicknames: **Bay State; Old Colony State**
State Bird: **Chickadee**
State Flower: **Mayflower**

massacre A brutal, bloody killing of many people or animals. *Noun.*
○ To kill many people or animals in a brutal, bloody way: *The cruel ruler ordered the army to* **massacre** *the enemy. Verb.* **mas•sa•cre** (mas′ə kər) *noun, plural* **massacres;** *verb,* **massacred, massacring.**

massage The rubbing or kneading of the muscles and joints of the body: *A* **massage** *relaxes the muscles and helps the circulation of the blood. Noun.*
○ To give a massage to: *The trainer* **massaged** *the athlete's sore back after a long practice session. Verb.* **mas•sage** (mə säzh′ *or* mə säj′) *noun, plural* **massages;** *verb,* **massaged, massaging.**

massive Of great size or extent; very big; large and solid: *The safe in the bank has* **massive** *steel doors.* **mas•sive** (mas′iv) *adjective.*

mass media All the different forms of communication used to reach large numbers of people, including television, radio, newspapers, and advertising.

mass production The process of making things in large quantities, especially by machinery.

mass transit A system of buses and trains used to carry many people from place to place within a city: *The city plans to extend its* **mass transit** *to our neighborhood.*

mast **1.** A tall pole on a sailing ship or boat that supports the sails and rigging. **2.** Any long pole or post. **mast** (mast) *noun, plural* **masts.**

master 1. A person who has power or control over something. 2. A person who has great skill or knowledge about something: *That author is a master of the mystery novel.* 3. A male teacher. 4. **Master.** A title for a young boy: *"Will Master Charles be dining with his parents tonight?" the cook asked. Noun.*

Wooden masts are made from very tall trees.

○1. Very skillful in an art or trade: *a master carpenter.* 2. Most important; main: *All the lights in the building were controlled by a master switch. Adjective.*

○ 1. To gain control over: *I finally mastered my fear of heights.* 2. To become expert in: *That student mastered French easily. Verb.*

mas•ter (mas′tər) *noun, plural* **masters;** *adjective;* *verb,* **mastered, mastering.**

masterful 1. Tending to control; showing power: *I use a masterful voice when I give my dog a command.* 2. Having great skill or knowledge: *The singer gave a masterful performance.*

mas•ter•ful (mas′tər fəl) *adjective.* —**masterfully** *adverb.*

masterly Having great skill or knowledge: *The singer gave a masterly performance.* **mas•ter•ly** (mas′tər lē) *adjective.*

masterpiece 1. Something done with great skill: *Several masterpieces were sold at the art auction.* 2. A person's greatest achievement or finest work: *This novel is her masterpiece.* **mas•ter•piece** (mas′tər pēs′) *noun, plural* **masterpieces.**

mat 1. A small, flat piece of material, often made of rubber or woven material, used as a floor covering or placed in front of a door. 2. A small, flat piece of material put under a dish, vase, or other object and used for decoration or to protect a surface. 3. A large, thick pad or covering put on the floor to protect wrestlers or gymnasts. 4. A

thick, tangled mass: *A mat of seaweed clung to the boat's anchors. Noun.*

○ To become tangled in a thick mass: *The dog's coat was matted with rain and mud. Verb.*

mat (mat) *noun, plural* **mats;** *verb,* **matted, matting.**

match¹ 1. A person or thing suitable for or very much like another: *I bought a pocketbook that was a perfect match for my shoes.* 2. A game or contest: *a bowling match. Noun.*

○ 1. To be suitable with, equal to, or like something: *These gloves don't match.*

2. To find or bring together things that are exactly equal to or like one another: *I matched the socks in pairs.* 3. To compete with as an equal: *No one on their team could match our pitcher. Verb.*

match (mach) *noun, plural* **matches;** *verb,* **matched, matching.**

match² A short, thin piece of wood or cardboard used to start a fire. Matches are coated on one end with a chemical substance that makes a flame when it is struck against something. **match** (mach) *noun, plural* **matches.**

People should never play with matches.

mate 1. One of a pair: *I've lost the mate to this sock.* 2. A husband or wife. 3. The male or female of a pair of animals: *The robin helped his mate build their nest.* 4. An officer on a ship lower in rank than the captain: *The mate gave orders to mop the deck.* 5. A friend or companion. *Noun.*

○To join in a pair for breeding: *Birds mate in the spring. Verb.*

mate (māt) *noun, plural* **mates;** *verb,* **mated, mating.**

material What something is made of or used for: *I used my experiences in camp as material for my story. Noun.*

○ 1. Made from or having to do with matter; physical: *Scientists study things that exist in the material world.* 2. Having to do with the body or

PRONUNCIATION KEY:

at	āpe	fär	câre	end	mē	it	īce	pierce	hot	ōld	sông	fôrk
oil	out	up	ūse	rüle	pull	tûrn	chin	sing	shop	thin	this	

hw in white; zh in treasure. The symbol ə stands for the unstressed vowel sound in about, taken, pencil, lemon, and circus.

457

physical well-being: *Food, clothing, and shelter are material needs. Adjective.*
ma·te·ri·al (mə tîr′ē əl) *noun, plural* **materials;** *adjective.*

maternal 1. Of or like a mother; motherly: *maternal instincts.* 2. Related through one's mother: *Your maternal grandparents are your mother's parents.* **ma·ter·nal** (mə tûr′nəl) *adjective.*

math An abbreviation for **mathematics. math** (math) *noun.*

mathematical Having to do with or using mathematics: *a mathematical problem.* **math·e·mat·i·cal** (math′ə mat′i kəl) *adjective.*

mathematician A person who works or specializes in mathematics. **math·e·ma·ti·cian** (math′ə mə tish′ən) *noun, plural* **mathematicians.**

mathematics The study of numbers, quantities, measurements, and shapes, and how they relate to each other. Arithmetic, algebra, and geometry are parts of mathematics: *Mathematics is my favorite subject.* The word "mathematics" is used with a singular verb. **math·e·mat·ics** (math′ə mat′iks) *noun.*

matinee A play or other performance given in the afternoon. **mat·i·nee** (mat′ə nā′) *noun, plural* **matinees.**

matter 1. Anything that has weight and takes up space. All things are made of matter. Matter can be a solid, liquid, or gas. 2. A subject of discussion, interest, or action: *The secretary talked on the telephone about a business matter.* 3. Problem; trouble: *I went to the dentist to find out what was the matter with my tooth.* 4. Written or printed material: *The store sells all sorts of reading matter.* 5. An amount or quantity: *It's only a matter of minutes before the train arrives. Noun.*
○ To be of importance: *It doesn't matter to me where we go. Verb.*

• **as a matter of fact.** Truly; actually: *I know them very well; as a matter of fact, they're my good friends.*

• **no matter.** Regardless of; it makes no difference: *No matter how hard we try, we cannot always succeed.*
mat·ter (mat′ər) *noun, plural* **matters;** *verb,* **mattered, mattering.**

mattress A thick pad that is used as a bed or part of a bed. It is usually covered with cloth and stuffed with cotton, foam rubber, or hair.

mat·tress (mat′ris) *noun, plural* **mattresses.**

mature 1. Having reached full growth or development; ripe: *When a puppy becomes mature it is called a dog.* 2. Like or having the qualities of a mature person; adult: *My classmate did the mature thing by not hitting back. Adjective.*
○ To become fully grown or developed: *The tomatoes are maturing fast. Verb.*
ma·ture (mə chùr′ *or* mə tùr′ *or* mə tyùr′) *adjective; verb,* **matured, maturing.**

SYNONYMS

mature, adult, grown-up
A mature male deer develops antlers. It was very adult of you to offer to pay your own way to the movie. Sometimes that boy seems too grown-up for his age.

---

maul To hurt someone or damage something by rough treatment: *The stuffed toy had been mauled by the two large dogs.*
Another word that sounds like this is **mall.**
maul (môl) **mauled, mauling.**

Mauritania A country in western Africa. **Mau·ri·tan·i·a** (môr′i tān′ē ə) *noun.*

maximum 1. The greatest possible number or amount: *Six dollars was the maximum that we could spend.* 2. The highest point or degree reached or recorded: *The temperature rose to a maximum of 98 degrees today. Noun.*
○ The greatest possible: *The maximum number of people allowed on the merry-go-round at any one time is forty. Adjective.*
max·i·mum (mak′sə məm) *noun, plural* **maximums** *or* **maxima** (mak′sə mə); *adjective.*

may An auxiliary verb used in the following ways: 1. To ask or give permission: *May I leave the table?* 2. To say that something is possible or likely: *It may snow today.* 3. To express hope or a wish: *May you have a happy life.* Look up **can** for a Language Note about this word. **may** (mā) *verb.*

May The fifth month of the year. May has thirty-one days. **May** (mā) *noun.*

WORD HISTORY

The Romans named the month of May in honor of Maia, the earth goddess in Roman mythology.

Maya A member of an American Indian people of southern Mexico and Central America. The Maya had an advanced civilization that flourished until about A.D. 1000. **Ma•ya** (mä′yə) *noun, plural* **Maya** or **Mayas**.

maybe Possibly; perhaps: *I don't agree with you, but maybe you are right.* **may•be** (mā′bē) *adverb*.

mayonnaise A thick, creamy sauce or dressing made of egg yolks, oil, and vinegar or lemon juice and used on sandwiches and in salads. **may•on•naise** (mā′ə nāz′ *or* mā′ə nāz′) *noun*.

mayor The person who is the official head of a city or town government. **may•or** (mā′ər) *noun, plural* **mayors**.

maze A confusing series of paths or passageways through which people may have a hard time finding their way: *I got lost in the maze of hallways in my new school.*
Another word that sounds like this is **maize**.
maze (māz) *noun, plural* **mazes**.

MB Postal abbreviation for **Manitoba**.

Md. An abbreviation for **Maryland**.

MD Postal abbreviation for **Maryland**.

M.D. An abbreviation for **doctor of medicine**.

me The person who is speaking or writing: *The bus takes me to school.* **me** (mē) *pronoun*.

Me. An abbreviation for **Maine**.

ME Postal abbreviation for **Maine**.

meadow A field of grassy land often used for growing hay or as a pasture for animals. **mead•ow** (med′ō) *noun, plural* **meadows**.

meadowlark A songbird with a pointed bill, a short tail, and a yellow breast with a black bar across it. Meadowlarks live in North America, Central America, and South America. **mead•ow•lark** (med′ō lärk′) *noun, plural* **mead-owlarks**.

meager Very little; hardly enough: *The sick child ate a meager meal of tea and toast.* **mea•ger** (mē′gər) *adjective*.

meal¹ The food served or eaten at one time: *Breakfast is the first meal of the day.* **meal** (mēl) *noun, plural* **meals**.

meal² Grain or other food that has been ground: *I ground the almonds into meal and added it to the batter for the cake.* **meal** (mēl) *noun, plural* **meals**.

Doctors tell us we should eat three healthy meals a day.

mean¹ 1. To have in mind; want to do or say: *I do not know what you mean by that remark.* 2. To have as a purpose; intend: *I didn't mean to hurt your feelings.* 3. To be defined as; have a particular sense: *"To start" means "to begin."* **mean** (mēn) *verb*, **meant**, **meaning**.

mean² 1. Cruel; not kind; not nice: *It is mean to tease animals.* 2. Low in quality or rank: *Abraham Lincoln grew up in mean conditions, but still achieved fame and success.* 3. Hard to deal with; difficult: *Drive slowly because there's a mean curve in the road just ahead.* **mean** (mēn) *adjective*, **meaner**, **meanest**.

mean³ 1. Something halfway between two extremes: *Warmth is a happy mean between freezing cold and great heat.* 2. **means.** The way that something is or may be done: *We used the back door as a means of escape.* 3. **means.** Money or property; wealth: *The money was donated by a family of means.* *Noun.*
○Halfway between two extremes; average: *The mean temperature for last Saturday was 60 degrees.* *Adjective.*
• **by means of.** By the use of; with the help of: *They climbed out of the window by means of a ladder.*
mean (mēn) *noun, plural* **means**; *adjective*.

meander To go along while in a winding way: *The river meandered along the plain.* **me•an•der** (mē an′dər) *verb*, **meandered**, **meandering**.

meaning An idea or sense that is meant or intended: *The word "run" has many meanings.* **mea•ning** (mē′ning) *noun, plural* **meanings**.

PRONUNCIATION KEY:
at   āpe   fär   câre   end   mē   it   īce   pierce   hot   ōld   sông   fôrk
oil   out   up   ūse   rüle   pu̇ll   tûrn   chin   sing   shop   thin   this
hw in white; zh in treasure. The symbol ə stands for the unstressed vowel sound in about, taken, pencil, lemon, and circus.

459

meant Past tense and past participle of **mean**.
meant (ment) *verb.*

meantime The time between: *I'll be gone for an hour; in the* **meantime**, *please answer the telephone if it rings.* **mean·time** (mēn'tīm') *noun.*

meanwhile 1. In or during the time between: *The train doesn't leave for an hour;* **meanwhile**, *I'm going to read a book.* 2. At the same time: *My cousin washed the car;* **meanwhile**, *I mowed the lawn.* **mean·while** (mēn'hwīl' *or* mēn'wīl') *adverb.*

measles A disease that causes a rash of small red spots, a fever, and the symptoms of a bad cold. It is caused by a virus. The word "measles" is used with a singular or plural verb. **mea·sles** (mē'zəlz) *noun.*

The geologist is measuring the size of one of the rocks in the wall.

measure 1. To find or show the size, weight, or amount of something: *The doctor* **measured** *me and found that I had grown two inches in a year.* 2. To have as a measurement: *The painting* **measured** *three feet by two feet.* 3. To mark off or set apart by measuring: *I* **measured** *out two cups of flour. Verb.*
○1. The size, weight, or amount of something: *Without a ruler, I could only guess at the* **measure** *of the piece of wood.* 2. A unit, standard, or system of measurement: *Inches and meters are* **measures** *of length.* 3. An instrument, container, or other device used for measuring: *The cook used a cup* **measure** *to add milk to the batter.* 4. An amount, degree, or portion that can be measured: *Our success was due in large* **measure** *to your help.* 5. Something done to make something else happen: *The police took harsh* **measures** *to stop*

crime. 6. A bill or law: *The Senate has passed the* **measure**. 7. A bar of music. *Noun.*
meas·ure (mezh'ər) *verb,* **measured, measuring;** *noun, plural* **measures.**

measurement 1. The act of measuring: *Rulers are used for* **measurement**. 2. Something found or shown by measuring; the size, height, or amount of something: *The carpenter used a ruler to get the* **measurements** *of the shelf.* 3. A system of measuring: *Metric* **measurement** *is used in most countries of the world.* **meas·ure·ment** (mezh'ər mənt) *noun, plural* **measurements.**

meat 1. The flesh of an animal used as food. The flesh of a cow, pig, or lamb is meat. 2. The part of a fruit or nut that can be eaten: *The solid, white part of a coconut is called the* **meat**. 3. The most important part of something: *The story of the author's childhood was the* **meat** *of the book.* Another word that sounds like this is **meet**.
meat (mēt) *noun, plural* **meats.**

meatball A small ball made from ground meat and other ingredients and then cooked. **meat·ball** (mēt'bôl) *noun, plural* **meatballs.**

mechanic A person who is skilled in repairing and operating machines: *A* **mechanic** *fixed our car.* **me·chan·ic** (mi kan'ik) *noun, plural* **mechanics.**

mechanical 1. Using or having to do with machines or machinery: *The* **mechanical** *toy was run by a small motor.* 2. Like or suitable for a machine; lacking feeling: *A* **mechanical** *task like folding clothes can be more pleasant if you do it with someone else.* **me·chan·i·cal** (mi kan'i kəl) *adjective.* —**mechanically** *adverb.*

mechanism The working parts of a machine; a mechanical device: *The jeweler said that the only thing wrong with the* **mechanism** *of my watch was a broken spring.* **mech·a·nism** (mek'ə niz əm) *noun, plural* **mechanisms.**

medal A flat piece of metal that is often similar in shape to a coin and attached to a ribbon. Medals are usually given as a reward for bravery or achievement.
Another word that sounds like this is **meddle**.
med·al (med'əl) *noun, plural* **medals.**

meddle To take part in another person's business without being asked or wanted; interfere: *It is often wise not to* **meddle** *in other people's affairs.* Another word that sounds like this is **medal**.
med·dle (med'əl) *verb,* **meddled, meddling.**

media 1. Plural of **medium**. 2. **the media.** Sources of news and information, such as newspapers, television, and magazines: *The president's trip abroad was reported on television and in other news media.* **me·di·a** (mē′dē ə) *plural noun.*

median The middle number in a series of numbers arranged from smallest to largest. If the series has an even number of elements, the median equals the average of the two middle numbers. **me·di·an** (mē′dē ən) *noun, plural* **medians.**

medic 1. An informal word for a medical doctor. 2. A medical intern. 3. Someone trained to give first aid or medical assistance in an emergency or on a battlefield: *As soon as the ambulance arrived, the medics began to help the accident victim.* **med·ic** (med′ik) *noun, plural* **medics.**

medical Having to do with doctors and medicine: *a medical school.* **med·i·cal** (med′i kəl) *adjective.* —**medically** *adverb.*

medicine 1. A drug or other substance used to prevent or cure disease or to relieve pain: *cough medicine.* 2. The science or practice of detecting, treating, or preventing disease or injury: *a career in medicine.* **med·i·cine** (med′ə sin) *noun, plural* **medicines.**

medicine man A person in certain North American Indian tribes who was called upon to cure sickness and was believed to have magic powers.

medieval Having to do with or belonging in the Middle Ages. **me·di·e·val** (mē′dē ē′vəl *or* mid ē′vəl) *adjective.*

Medicine men **were highly respected by the tribes they served.**

meditate To think seriously, carefully, and quietly; reflect: *a peaceful spot to meditate.* **med·i·tate** (med′i tāt′) *verb,* **meditated, meditating.** —**meditation** *noun.*

Mediterranean A large sea between southern Europe, western Asia, and northern Africa. **Med·i·ter·ra·ne·an** (med′i tər ā′nē ən) *noun.*

medium 1. Something in the middle: *I try to find a happy medium between working too hard and* not doing anything. 2. A substance or means through which something acts or is done: *The newspaper is a medium of communication.* 3. The substance or conditions in which something lives: *The ideal medium for growing potatoes is moist, sandy, soil. Noun.*
○ Having a middle position in size, amount, quality, or degree: *Although my parents are both short, I am of medium height. Adjective.* **me·di·um** (mē′dē əm) *noun, plural* **media** *or* **mediums;** *adjective.*

medley 1. A mixture of things that usually don't belong together; jumble: *The dinner was a medley of Chinese, Italian, and Mexican dishes that tasted awful when they were combined on one plate.* 2. A series of musical compositions or parts of musical compositions combined into a single piece of music: *The orchestra played a medley of songs from popular movies.* **med·ley** (med′lē) *noun, plural* **medleys.**

meek Humble, quiet, and mild-mannered: *The traveler was too meek to ask for directions and so got lost.* **meek** (mēk) *adjective,* **meeker, meekest.** —**meekly** *adverb* —**meekness** *noun.*

meet 1. To come upon or find by chance: *While walking downtown, they met a friend they hadn't seen in months.* 2. To be introduced to: *I hope to meet your parents some day soon.* 3. To keep an appointment with: *We'll meet you outside of school.* 4. To be equal to; satisfy: *This book should meet your needs.* 5. To come into contact with; join: *The Mississippi River meets the Gulf of Mexico in southern Louisiana.* 6. To come together; assemble: *The school board will meet on Thursday. Verb.*
○ A meeting or contest: *a swimming meet. Noun.*
Another word that sounds like this is **meat.**
• **to meet with.** 1. To receive: *My suggestion met with everyone's approval.* 2. To experience; undergo: *The explorers met with danger in the jungle.*
meet (mēt) *verb,* **met, meeting;** *noun, plural* **meets.**

meeting 1. A gathering of people: *All the members of the club came to the meeting.* 2. The act of coming together: *a chance meeting with some*

PRONUNCIATION KEY:

| at | āpe | fär | câre | end | mē | it | īce | pierce | hot | ōld | sông | fôrk |
| oil | out | up | ūse | rüle | pull | tûrn | chin | sing | shop | thin | this | |

hw in white; zh in treasure. The symbol ə stands for the unstressed vowel sound in about, taken, pencil, lemon, and circus.

461

old friends. **3.** The place where things meet: *The town was located at the **meeting** of two rivers. Noun.* **meet·ing** (mē′ting) *noun, plural* **meetings.**

megaphone A device used to make the voice sound louder so that it can be heard far away. It is usually shaped like a cone. **meg·a·phone** (meg′ə fōn′) *noun, plural* **megaphones.**

melancholy **1.** Low in spirits; sad; gloomy: *I was in a **melancholy** mood because I didn't want the vacation to end.* **2.** Causing low spirits or sadness: *I don't like **melancholy** music. Adjective.* ○ Low spirits; a mood of sadness: *Melancholy filled the town when the mayor died. Noun.* **mel·an·cho·ly** (me′lən kol′ē) *adjective; noun.*

mellow **1.** Soft, sweet, and juicy from being ripe: *Those peaches are **mellow** and ready to eat.* **2.** Full, soft, and rich; not harsh: *The room echoed with the **mellow** sound of the violin.* **3.** Made wise and understanding by age: *You used to get angry easily, but now you are more **mellow**.* **mel·low** (mel′ō) *adjective,* **mellower, mellowest.**

melodious Making agreeable sounds; pleasant to hear: *a **melodious** voice.* **mel·o·di·ous** (mə lō′dē əs) *adjective.* —**melodiously** *adverb.*

melody A series of musical notes that make up a tune: *a pleasing **melody**.* **mel·o·dy** (mel′ə dē) *noun, plural* **melodies.**

melon A large, juicy fruit that grows on a vine. Melons have a sweet, soft pulp that can be eaten. Cantaloupes and watermelons are types of melons. **mel·on** (mel′ən) *noun, plural* **melons.**

melt **1.** To change from a solid to a liquid by heating: *The warm sun **melted** the ice on the pond.* **2.** To slowly dissolve: *The lump of sugar **melted** in the hot tea.* **3.** To disappear or fade away gradually: *The clouds **melted** away.* **4.** To become gentle or understanding; soften: *My heart **melted** when the child began to cry.* **melt** (melt) *verb,* **melted, melting.**

SYNONYMS

melt, dissolve, thaw
The ice sculptures are melting in the sun. Sugar will dissolve in water. With the coming of spring, the glacier began to thaw.

---

member **1.** A person, animal, or thing that belongs to a group: *The lion is a **member** of the cat family.* **2.** A limb of a person or an animal.

A leg or arm is a **member**. **mem·ber** (mem′bər) *noun, plural* **members.**

membership **1.** The condition of being a member: *We have a **membership** in the tennis club.* **2.** All of the members of a group: *The union **membership** voted to strike.* **3.** The number of members in a group: *Membership in the club has been growing each year.* **mem·ber·ship** (mem′bər ship) *noun, plural* **memberships.**

membrane A thin, flexible layer of skin or tissue. Membranes line parts of the body. **mem·brane** (mem′brān) *noun, plural* **membranes.**

memento Something kept or given as a reminder of someone or some place or event: *This rock collection is a **memento** of my trip to the West.* **me·men·to** (mə men′tō) *noun, plural* **mementos** or **mementoes.**

memo An abbreviation for **memorandum**; short note: *The principal sent a **memo** to the teachers.* **mem·o** (mem′ō) *noun, plural* **memos.**

memorable Worth remembering; notable: *Our trip to Europe was **memorable**.* **mem·o·ra·ble** (mem′ər ə bəl) *adjective.* —**memorably** *adverb.*

memorandum A short note written as a reminder or to give information to people at work. **mem·o·ran·dum** (mem′ə ran′dəm) *noun, plural* **memorandums** or **memoranda.** (mem′ə ran′də).

memorial A reminder of a person or event: *The town built a **memorial** to honor soldiers who had died in the war. Noun.* ○ Serving as a reminder: *The **memorial** parade was held every year on the anniversary of the founding of the city. Adjective.* **me·mo·ri·al** (mə môr′ē əl) *noun, plural* **memorials;** *adjective.*

Monuments and statues often serve as memorials.

Memorial Day A holiday in the United States honoring Americans who have died while fighting in wars. Memorial Day is observed on the last Monday in May.

memorize To learn by heart; fix in the memory: *I*

memorized the words of the poem by repeating them over and over. **mem·o·rize** (mem′ə rīz) *verb,* **memorized, memorizing.**

memory **1.** The ability to remember things: *In studying history it is necessary to have a good memory for facts and dates.* **2.** A person or thing remembered: *The trip to Canada was one of their happiest memories.* **3.** All that a person can remember: *The student recited the poem from memory.* **4.** The length of time in the past that is remembered: *It was the worst snowstorm in our memory.* **5.** The part of a computer that very quickly stores information that can be retrieved very quickly. RAM and ROM are different kinds of memory. **mem·o·ry** (mem′ə rē) *noun, plural* **memories.**

men Plural of **man. men** (men) *plural noun.*

menace A person or thing that is a danger or a threat: *Careless drivers are a menace to everyone else on the road.* Noun.

○ To threaten something; put in danger: *The sudden storm menaced the small ship.* Verb.
men·ace (men′is) *noun, plural* **menaces;** *verb,* **menaced, menacing.**

mend **1.** To put in good condition again; fix or repair: *I used glue to mend the broken cup.* **2.** To heal; improve: *My sprained ankle is mending nicely.* Verb.

○ A mended place: *You could see the mend where the hole in the shirt had been sewed up.* Noun.

• **on the mend.** Getting better; improving: *I was sick for a week, but now I'm on the mend.*
mend (mend) *verb,* **mended, mending;** *noun, plural* **mends.**

menorah A candle-

Fishermen continually need to mend their nets.

stick for seven or nine candles used in Jewish ceremonies. Menorahs with nine candles are used during Hanukkah. **me·no·rah** (mə nôr′ə) *noun, plural* **menorahs.**

-ment A suffix that means: **1.** The act of: *Development means the act of developing.* **2.** The state of being: *Amazement means the state of being amazed.* **3.** The result or product of: *Improvement means the result of improving.*

mental **1.** Done by or having to do with the mind: *Learning to speak is one stage of a child's mental development.* **2.** Having to do with or affected by a disease of the mind: *a mental patient.*
men·tal (men′təl) *adjective.* —**mentally** *adverb.*

mention To speak about or refer to: *I mentioned your party to my friend.* Verb.

○ A short remark or statement: *There was no mention of the parade in the newspaper.* Noun.
men·tion (men′shən) *verb,* **mentioned, mentioning;** *noun.*

menu **1.** A list of the food available in a restaurant: *See if you find anything you like on the menu.* **2.** A list of operations to choose from on a computer screen. **men·u** (men′ū) *noun, plural* **menus.**

meow The sound that a cat or kitten makes. *Noun.*

○ To make this sound: *The cat meowed because it was hungry.* Verb.
me·ow (mē ou′) *noun, plural* **meows;** *verb,* **meowed, meowing.**

merchandise Things for sale; goods: *The hardware store sells tools, paint, and other merchandise.* **mer·chan·dise** (mûr′chən dīz′ or mûr′chən dīs′) *noun.*

merchant **1.** A person whose business is buying goods and selling them for profit: *My grandparents were clothing merchants.* **2.** A person who owns or runs a store: *All the merchants in town decorated their store windows for the holiday season.* **mer·chant** (mûr′chənt) *noun, plural* **merchants.**

merchant marine **1.** The ships of a nation used to carry cargo and passengers. **2.** The officers and crews of these ships.

mercury A heavy, silver-colored metal that is a liquid at normal temperatures. It is used in thermometers and barometers. Mercury is a chemical element. **mer·cu·ry** (mûr′kyə rē) *noun.*

PRONUNCIATION KEY:

| at | āpe | fär | câre | end | mē | it | īce | pîerce | hot | ōld | sông | fôrk |
| oil | out | up | ūse | rüle | pûll | tûrn | chin | sing | shop | thin | this | |

hw in white; zh in treasure. The symbol ə stands for the unstressed vowel sound in about, taken, pencil, lemon, and circus.

463

Mercury The second smallest planet in our solar system and the closest planet to the sun. **Mer·cur·y** (mûr′kyə rē) *noun.*

Mercury
Closest planet to the sun, the temperatures on Mercury range from roasting during the day to freezing at night. At over 100,000 miles per hour, Mercury moves faster in its orbit than any other planet.
Average distance from sun: **36,000,000 miles**
Diameter: **3,028 miles**
Length of Day: **58 days, 16 hours**
Length of Year: **88 days**
Average Temperature: **800˚F (day); -300˚F (night)**
Mass compared to Earth: **.06**
Weight of 100 pounds: **18**
Atmosphere: **None**
Number of rings: **0**
Number of satellites: **0**

mercy 1. Kindness or forgiveness greater than what is expected or deserved: *The ruler showed no* **mercy** *to the rebels.* 2. Something to be thankful for; blessing: *Your help in our time of need was a real* **mercy.**

 • **at the mercy of.** Under the control of; subject to: *The troops were* **at the mercy of** *the enemy.* **mer·cy** (mûr′sē) *noun, plural* **mercies.** —**merciful** *adjective* —**merciless** *adjective.*

mere Nothing more than; only: *The* **mere** *thought of all that work made me feel tired.* **mere** (mîr) *adjective.* —**merely** *adverb.*

merge To join and become one; come together: *The two paths* **merged** *at the foot of the hill.* **merge** (mûrj) *verb,* **merged, merging.**

merger The combination of two or more things, especially businesses, into one: *A* **merger** *produced one huge media corporation from two smaller companies.* **merg·er** (mûr′jər) *noun, plural* **mergers.**

meridian 1. An imaginary line on the earth's surface. It passes through the North and South poles. Meridians are shown on maps and globes and are used in navigation. 2. The highest point that the sun or a star reaches in the sky. *The sun's* **meridian** *is reached at about noon.* **me·rid·i·an** (mə rid′ē ən) *noun, plural* **meridians.**

WORD HISTORY

The word meridian comes from two Latin words meaning "middle" and "day." At the middle of the day, the sun is highest in the sky and directly south. From this come both the meanings "highest point in the sky" and "the imaginary line from north to south."

merit 1. Goodness, worth, or value: *Your idea has great* **merit.** 2. **merits.** The actual facts of a matter: *The judge will decide the case on its* **merits.** *Noun.*
 ○ To deserve; be worthy of: *The book report you wrote* **merits** *a very good grade. Verb.* **mer·it** (mer′it) *noun, plural* **merits;** *verb,* **merited, meriting.**

mermaid An imaginary creature believed to live in the sea. A mermaid is thought of as having the head and body of a woman and the tail of a fish. **mer·maid** (mûr′mād) *noun, plural* **mermaids.**

merry Cheerful and jolly; full of fun: *a* **merry** *group of clowns. During the holidays we sang* **merry** *songs.* **mer·ry** (mer′ē) *adjective,* **merrier, merriest.** —**merrily** *adverb.*

merry-go-round A round platform that has wooden animals and seats on which people ride while the platform turns.

Many merry-go-round figures are beautifully crafted.

mer·ry-go-round (mer′ē gō round′) *noun, plural* **merry-go-rounds.**

merrymaking The act of being merry and having fun; gaiety. **mer·ry·mak·ing** (mer′ē mā′king) *noun.*

Mesas are found in the desert areas of the United States and in Mexico.

mesa A hill or mountain with a flat top and steep sides; a high plateau. **me·sa** (mā′sə) *noun, plural* **mesas.**

WORD HISTORY

Mesa comes from a Spanish word which means "table." The Spanish called a raised area of land a mesa because it resembled a large rock table.

---

mesh A net made of threads or wires woven together with openings between them. *The screen on a window is a mesh. Noun.*
○ To fit together: *The teeth on a zipper mesh very closely. Verb.*
mesh (mesh) *noun, plural* **meshes;** *verb,* **meshed, meshing.**

mess 1. A dirty or disorderly condition; untidy group of things: *Clean up the mess in your room!* 2. An unpleasant, difficult, or confusing state: *Problems with our car made a mess of our vacation.* 3. A group of people, such as campers, who eat their meals together. 4. A meal eaten by a group, such as campers. *Noun.*
○ 1. To make dirty or disorderly: *Our muddy boots messed the floor.* 2. To spoil or confuse: *The rain messed up our plans for a picnic. Verb.*
mess (mes) *noun, plural* **messes;** *verb,* **messed, messing.**

message 1. Words or information sent from one person or group to another. *Please leave a message for me if I am not home when you call.* 2. An official speech or other communication: *The president's message to the nation was broadcast on television.* **mes·sage** (mes′ij) *noun, plural* **messages.**

messenger A person who delivers messages or runs errands. **mes·sen·ger** (mes′ən jər) *noun, plural* **messengers.**

messy 1. In a sloppy or dirty condition; not tidy: *Our attic is messy.* 2. Unpleasant or difficult: *Cleaning the oven is a messy job.* **mes·sy** (mes′ē) *adjective,* **messier, messiest.**

met Past tense and past participle of **meet. met** (met) *verb.*

metabolism All of the chemical and biological changes that take place in a living thing. Metabolism is the means by which our bodies make use of the food we eat. **me·tab·o·lism** (mə tab′ə liz′əm) *noun, plural* **metabolisms.**

metal A substance that usually has a shiny surface, can be melted, and can conduct heat and electricity. Iron, silver, copper, lead, brass, and bronze are metals. **met·al** (met′əl) *noun, plural* **metals.**

metallic Of or containing a metal: *The box was made of a metallic substance. There are gold metallic threads in the material.* **me·tal·lic** (mə tal′ik) *adjective.*

metamorphic 1. Of or having to do with metamorphosis: *A caterpillar goes through metamorphic changes to become a butterfly.* 2. Produced beneath the surface of the earth by processes that change the texture, structure, and mineral makeup of rocks: *Marble is a metamorphic rock that began as limestone.* **met·a·mor·phic** (met′ə môr′fik) *adjective.*

metamorphosis 1. The series of changes in shape and function that certain animals go through as they develop from an egg to an adult: *Caterpillars become butterflies and tadpoles become frogs through the process of metamorphosis.* 2. A complete change in form or appearance.
met·a·mor·pho·sis (met′ə môr′fə sis) *noun, plural* **metamorphoses** (met′ə môr′fə sēz).

metaphor A statement in which one thing is compared to another to suggest a similarity.

PRONUNCIATION KEY:
| at | āpe | fär | câre | end | mē | it | īce | pierce | hot | ōld | sông | fôrk |
| oil | out | up | ūse | rüle | pùll | tûrn | chin | sing | shop | thin | this | |
hw in white; zh in treasure. The symbol ə stands for the unstressed vowel sound in about, taken, pencil, lemon, and circus.

465

Metaphors are often used in writing, especially poetry: *"You are the sunshine of my life"* is an example of a *metaphor.* **met·a·phor** (met′ə fôr′) *noun, plural* **metaphors.** —**metaphoric** *adjective* —**metaphorically** *adverb.*

meteor A mass of metal or stone that comes into the earth's atmosphere from space. As it passes through the atmosphere at high speed, it becomes very hot and burns with a bright light as it falls to the earth. This is also called a shooting star. **me·te·or** (mē′tē ər) *noun, plural* **meteors.**

meteorite A meteor that has fallen to earth. **me·te·or·ite** (mē′tē ə rīt′) *noun, plural* **meteorites.**

meteorologist A person who studies meteorology or who knows a great deal about meteorology: *The weather forecaster on that TV station is a trained meteorologist.* **me·te·or·ol·o·gist** (mē′tē ə rol′ə jist) *noun, plural* **meteorologists.**

meteorology The science that studies the earth's atmosphere and the changes that take place within it. One important branch of meteorology is the study of the weather. **me·te·or·ol·o·gy** (mē′tē ə rol′ə jē) *noun.*

meter¹ The basic unit of length in the metric system. A meter is equal to 39.37 inches, or slightly more than 3¼ feet. **me·ter** (mē′tər) *noun, plural* **meters.**

meter² 1. The regular pattern of rhythm that accented and unaccented syllables give to a line of poetry. 2. The basic pattern of rhythm that accented notes or beats give to a piece of music. **me·ter** (mē′tər) *noun, plural* **meters.**

meter³ A device that measures or records. Meters are used to show how much electricity, water, or gas is used in a building or how fast a car is moving. **me·ter** (mē′tər) *noun, plural* **meters.**

methane A gas with no color or odor. Methane burns easily. The gas that we use for heating or cooking is mostly methane. **meth·ane** (meth′ān) *noun.*

method 1. A way of doing something: *Speaking on the telephone is a method of communicating.*

2. Order or system: *I could not find the book I wanted because the books had been put on the shelves without method.* **meth·od** (meth′əd) *noun, plural* **methods.**

metric Of or having to do with the metric system: *The gram is a metric measurement.* **met·ric** (met′rik) *adjective.*

metric system A system of measurement based on counting by tens. In the metric system, the meter is the basic unit of length, the gram is the basic unit of weight, and the liter is the basic unit of capacity.

metronome A device with a pendulum that can be adjusted to swing back and forth at different speeds. Musicians use a metronome to help them keep correct time when they practice playing music. **met·ro·nome** (met′rə nōm′) *noun, plural* **metronomes.**

metropolis A large and important city. **me·trop·o·lis** (mə trop′ə lis) *noun, plural* **metropolises.**

New York is one of the world's greatest metropolises.

metropolitan Belonging to or having to do with a metropolis: *There were more than 5,000 officers on the metropolitan police force.* **met·ro·pol·i·tan** (met′rə pol′i tən) *adjective.*

Mexican A person who was born in Mexico or is a citizen of Mexico. *Noun.*
○ Of or having to do with Mexico or its people. *Adjective.*
Mex·i·can (meks′i kən) *noun, plural* **Mexicans;** *adjective.*

Mexico A country in North America, south of the United States. **Mex·i·co** (meks′i kō′) *noun.*

mg An abbreviation for **milligram.**

mi. An abbreviation for **mile.**

MI Postal abbreviation for **Michigan.**

mice Plural of **mouse. mice** (mīs) *plural noun.*

Mich. An abbreviation for **Michigan.**

Michigan A state in the north-central United States. Its capital is Lansing. **Mich·i·gan** (mish′i gən) *noun.*

WORD HISTORY

Michigan is the way French explorers wrote an Indian name for Lake Michigan that meant "big water." The state was named for Lake Michigan.

Michigan
U. S. Postal Abbreviation: **MI**
Capital: **Lansing**
Population: **9,200,000**
Area: **58,216 sq. mi./150,779 sq. km**
State Nickname: **Wolverine State**
State Bird: **Robin**
State Flower: **Apple Blossom**

microbe A very tiny living thing; a microorganism. Some microbes cause disease. **mi·crobe** (mī′krōb) *noun, plural* **microbes.**

microchip A small, thin slice of special material that usually contains a large number of tiny electronic parts. **mi·cro·chip** (mī′krə chip) *noun, plural* **microchips.**

microcomputer A small computer usually designed to be used by one person at a time. Although they are small, microcomputers are powerful enough to perform many tasks. A microcomputer is also called a **personal computer** or a **PC. mi·cro·com·pu·ter** (mī′krō kəm pū′tər) *noun, plural* **microcomputers.**

microorganism A living thing too small to be seen with the naked eye. Bacteria are microorganisms. **mi·cro·or·gan·ism** (mī′krō ôr′gə niz′əm) *noun, plural* **microorganisms.**

microphone A device used to transmit sound or to make it louder. A microphone changes sound waves into electrical signals: *Speak into the microphone and your voice will be recorded on the tape.* **mi·cro·phone** (mī′krə fōn′) *noun, plural* **microphones.**

microscope A device for looking at things that are too small to be seen with the naked eye. It has one or more lenses that produce an enlarged image of anything seen through it: *The biologist studied the leaf under a microscope.* **mi·cro·scope** (mī′krə skōp′) *noun, plural* **microscopes.**

microscope

eyepiece magnifies the image for your eye

arm

objective lenses magnify specimen

body tube

rotating lens mount holds different power lenses

slide clips hold the slide in place

specimen is mounted on a glass slide

stage

focus knob adjusts image

base

lamp shines light through specimen

microscopic 1. So small it can be seen only through a microscope: *a microscopic piece of material.* 2. Using a microscope to examine something: *a microscopic examination of a bacterium.* **mi·cro·scop·ic** (mī′ krə skop′ik) *adjective.* —**microscopically** *adverb.*

microwave 1. A type of radio wave that can pass through solid objects and other materials, such as

---

PRONUNCIATION KEY:

at	āpe	fär	câre	end	mē	it	īce	pïerce	hot	ōld	sông	fôrk
oil	out	up	ūse	rüle	pull	tûrn	chin	sing	shop	thin	this	

hw in white; zh in treasure. The symbol ə stands for the unstressed vowel sound in about, taken, pencil, lemon, and circus.

467

fog, that would block light waves. Microwaves are used to transmit messages over long distances and to cook food in microwave ovens. **2.** A short form of the term "microwave oven." **mi·cro·wave** (mī′krə wāv′) *noun, plural* **microwaves.**

microwave oven An oven that cooks or heats food very quickly by means of microwaves instead of the heat from electricity or burning gas. This is also called a **microwave.**

mid Being at or near the middle: *My cousin was born in the mid 1960s.* **mid** (mid) *adjective.*

midday The middle of the day; noon: *We ate our lunch at midday.* **mid·day** (mid′dā′) *noun.*

middle Halfway between two things, sides, times, or the like: *We sat in the middle row of the class. Adjective.*
○ Something halfway between two things, sides, times, or the like: *There is a white line down the middle of the road. Noun.*
mid·dle (mid′əl) *adjective; noun, plural* **middles.**

middle-aged In the time of life between youth and old age, between about forty and sixty-five years old. **mid·dle-aged** (mid′əl ājd′) *adjective.*

Middle Ages The period of European history from about A.D. 400 to 1450.

middle class The class of people between those who are rich and those who are poor.

Middle East A region made up of Israel, Egypt, Syria, Turkey, Iran, and other countries. The Middle East consists of parts of northeastern Africa and southwestern Asia.

Middle English The English language as it was spoken and written in the period between about 1100 and 1500.

Middle West A region of the north-central United States. This area is also called the **Midwest.**

midget A very small person or thing. A person who is a midget is much smaller than, but has the same proportions as, a normal adult. **midg·et** (mij′it) *noun, plural* **midgets.**

midland The middle or interior part of a country or region: *Kansas is in the midland of the United States. Noun.*
○ Of or located in the midland: *Iowa is a midland state. Adjective.*
mid·land (mid′lənd) *noun, plural* **midlands**; *adjective.*

midnight Twelve o'clock at night; the middle of the night. **mid·night** (mid′nīt) *noun.*

midst **1.** The middle; center: *The child got lost in the midst of the crowd.* **2.** A position in the middle of a group of people or things: *They were afraid that there was a spy in their midst.* **midst** (midst) *noun.*

midway In the middle; halfway: *I'll meet you at a midway point. Their house is midway between my house and yours. Adjective, Adverb.*
○ A place for games, rides, and other amusements at a circus, carnival, or fair. *Noun.*
mid·way (mid′wā′) *adjective; adverb; noun, plural* **midways.**

Midwest A region of the north-central United States. This area is also called the **Middle West.** **Mid·west** (mid′west′) *noun.*

might¹ An auxiliary verb used in the following ways: **1.** To express the past tense of **may**: *I asked the teacher if I might leave.* **2.** To say that something is possible: *The story we heard might be true, but I'm not sure.* **3.** To ask permission: *Might I borrow your dictionary?* **4.** To offer a suggestion: *You might try using a pencil so that you can erase your mistakes.*
Another word that sounds like this is **mite.**
might (mīt) *verb.*

might² Power or strength: *I slammed the door with all my might.*
Another word that sounds like this is **mite.**
might (mīt) *noun.*

mighty Great in power, size, or amount: *The Pacific is a mighty ocean.* **might·y** (mī′tē) *adjective,* **mightier, mightiest.**

migrant A person or animal that migrates: *These birds are migrants from South America. Noun.*
○ Migrating: *Migrant workers go from farm to farm looking for work. Adjective.*
mi·grant (mī′grənt) *noun, plural* **migrants**; *adjective.*

migrate To move from one place to another: *Many birds migrate to the south in the fall.* **migrate** (mī′grāt′) *verb,* **migrated, migrating.** **—migration** *noun.*

mild Gentle or calm; not harsh or sharp: *A mild winter is not very cold and snowy.* **mild** (mīld) *adjective,* **milder, mildest. —mildly** *adverb* **—mildness** *noun.*

mildew A kind of fungus that looks like white powder or fuzz. It grows on plants and materials such as cloth, leather, and paper when they are left damp. **mil•dew** (mil′dü) *noun, plural* **mildews**.

mile A measure of distance equal to 5,280 feet. **mile** (mīl) *noun, plural* **miles**.

mileage 1. Distance traveled in miles: *The mileage on our car is about 150,000 miles.* 2. The distance in miles that a vehicle can travel on a given amount of fuel: *Small cars get better mileage than large ones.* **mile•age** (mīl′ij) *noun.*

milestone 1. A marker made of stone placed at the side of a road. It gives the distance in miles to some place or places. 2. An important event or development: *The invention of the telephone was a milestone in the history of communications.* **mile•stone** (mīl′stōn) *noun, plural* **milestones**.

military 1. Having to do with the armed forces, soldiers, or war: *a military career in the Marine Corps.* 2. the military. The armed forces as a whole: *The army, navy, and air force are branches of the military.* **mil•i•tar•y** (mil′i ter′ē) *adjective.*

militia A group of citizens trained to fight and help in emergencies. Each state in the United States has a militia called the National Guard. **mi•li•tia** (mi lish′ə) *noun, plural* **militias**.

milk 1. A white liquid food produced by glands in female mammals, used to feed their babies. The milk of cows is used as food by people. 2. A white liquid like this that is made in plants. *Coconuts are filled with milk that people use as food. Noun.*
○ To take milk from a cow or other animal. *Verb.* **milk** (milk) *noun; verb,* **milked, milking**.

On clear nights, the Milky Way appears as a cloudy white patch across the sky.

Milky Way A galaxy that includes billions of stars. Our sun, the earth, and the rest of the solar sys-

tem are part of the Milky Way. **Mil•ky Way** (mil′kē).

mill 1. A building where machines grind grain into flour or meal. 2. A machine that grinds grain or other seeds. 3. A building where machines make raw materials into finished products: *Steel mills make steel. Noun.*
○ 1. To grind: *The machines milled the wheat into flour.* 2. To move around in a confused way: *The frightened sheep milled around in the pen. Verb.* **mill** (mil) *noun, plural* **mills;** *verb,* **milled, milling**.

milli- A prefix that means one thousandth (1/ 1000) of: *A milliliter is 1/1000 of a liter.*

milligram A unit of weight in the metric system. A milligram is equal to one thousandth of a gram. **mil•li•gram** (mil′ə gram′) *noun, plural* **milligrams**.

millimeter A unit of length in the metric system. A millimeter is equal to one thousandth of a meter, or about .039 of an inch. **mil•li•me•ter** (mil′ə mē′tər) *noun, plural* **millimeters**.

million 1. One thousand times one thousand; 1,000,000. 2. A very large or very exaggerated number: *There must be a million people waiting in line for this movie.* **mil•lion** (mil′yən) *noun, plural* **millions;** *adjective.*

millionaire A person who has money or property worth a million or more dollars. **mil•lion•aire** (mil′yə nâr′) *noun, plural* **millionaires**.

mimeograph A machine that makes copies of written pages using an ink process. **mim•e•o•graph** (mim′ē ə graf′) *noun, plural* **mimeographs**.

mimic To imitate, especially in order to make fun of: *The comedian could mimic the voices and gestures of famous people. Verb.*
○ A person or thing that imitates. *Noun.* **mim•ic** (mim′ik) *verb,* **mimicked, mimicking;** *noun, plural* **mimics**.

min. An abbreviation for **minute**.

minaret A tall, slender tower on top of a mosque. A person calls people to prayer from a balcony near the top of a minaret. **min•a•ret** (min′ə ret′) *noun, plural* **minarets**.

mince To chop into very small pieces: *I minced onions and garlic for the spaghetti sauce.* **mince** (mins) *verb,* **minced, mincing**.

PRONUNCIATION KEY:

| at | āpe | fär | câre | end | mē | it | īce | pîerce | hot | ōld | sông | fôrk |
| oil | out | up | ūse | rüle | pùll | tûrn | chin | sing | shop | thin | <u>th</u>is | |

hw in white; zh in treasure. The symbol ə stands for the unstressed vowel sound in about, taken, pencil, lemon, and circus.

469

mincemeat A filling for pies made of finely chopped apples, raisins, currants, sugar, spices, and sometimes meat. **mince·meat** (mins′mēt) *noun*.

mind 1. The part of a person that thinks, knows, learns, remembers, understands, and feels: *Keep your mind on what you're doing.* 2. A wish or opinion: *I changed my mind about visiting when I heard you were sick. Noun.*
○ 1. To pay attention to or worry about: *Mind your manners at the dinner table.* 2. To take care of: *A baby-sitter minded the children when their parents went out.* 3. To dislike something; object to: *Do you mind going to the movies alone? Verb.*

• **never mind.** To not worry or pay attention: *Never mind about the dirty dishes.*

• **to make up one's mind.** To decide: *I made up my mind to leave.*
mind (mīnd) *noun, plural* **minds;** *verb,* **minded, minding.**

mine¹ The one or ones that belong to me: *This bicycle is mine.* **mine** (mīn) *pronoun.*

mine² 1. A large area dug out in or under the ground. Coal, gold, diamonds, and other minerals are dug out of mines. 2. Any rich source or supply: *The book was a mine of information about life under the sea.* 3. A bomb put underground or underwater. *Noun.*
○ 1. To take a mineral from the ground by digging: *Workers mine coal in Pennsylvania.* 2. To put bombs in: *The navy divers mined the harbor during the war. Verb.*
mine (mīn) *noun, plural* **mines;** *verb,* **mined, mining.**

mineral A substance found in nature that is not an animal or a plant. Salt, coal, and gold are minerals. *Noun.*
○ Containing minerals: *Mineral water is water that has minerals in it naturally. Adjective.*
min·er·al (min′ər əl) *noun, plural* **minerals;** *adjective.*

mingle 1. To put or come together; mix; join: *This stream mingles with others to form a river.* 2. To move about freely; join; associate: *We mingled with the guests at the party.* **min·gle** (ming′gəl) *verb,* **mingled, mingling.**

miniature Much smaller than the usual size: *My parents made miniature furniture for my doll house. Adjective.*
○ A model or copy of something in a much small-

er size: *We bought a miniature of the Statue of Liberty as a souvenir of our trip to New York. Noun.*
min·ia·ture (min′ē ə chər *or* min′ə chər) *adjective; noun, plural* **miniatures.**

Many animals come in miniature **form.**

minimize 1. To make something as small as possible: *Well-lighted stairways minimize the risk of falling.* 2. To make something seem unimportant: *The public official minimized the size of the debt.* **min·i·mize** (min′ə mīz) *verb,* **minimized, minimizing.**

minimum 1. The smallest or least possible amount: *I need a minimum of two weeks to finish my report.* 2. The lowest point or number reached: *The temperature dropped to a minimum of 20 degrees. Noun.*
○ Lowest; smallest: *The minimum pay for the job was five dollars an hour. Adjective.*
min·i·mum (min′ə məm′) *noun, plural* **minimums;** *adjective.*

mining The act, process, or industry of digging for minerals in the ground, such as gold, coal, and diamonds. **min·ing** (mī′ning) *noun.*

minister 1. A person authorized to conduct religious services, especially in a Protestant church; member of the clergy; pastor. 2. A person in charge of a department of the government. 3. A person who represents his or her government in a foreign country. *Noun.*
○ To take care of: *Nurses minister to sick people. Verb.*
min·is·ter (min′əs tər) *noun, plural* **ministers;** *verb,* **ministered, ministering.**

mink 1. A slender animal of the weasel family with short legs and soft, thick fur. Minks live in woods near water. 2. The fur of this animal. **mink** (mingk) *noun, plural* **mink** *or* **minks.**

Minn. An abbreviation for Minnesota.

Minnesota A state in the north-central United States. Its capital is St. Paul. **Min·ne·so·ta** (min′ə sō′tə) *noun.*

Minnesota
U. S. Postal Abbreviation: **MN**
Capital: **St. Paul**
Population: **4,246,000**
Area: **84,068 sq. mi./217,735 sq. km**
State Nicknames: **North Star State; Gopher State**
State Bird: **Common Loon**
State Flower: **Pink and White Lady's Slipper**

WORD HISTORY

Minnesota was an Indian name for the Minnesota River. It means "water the color of the sky" or "cloudy water." Congress gave this name to the area that became the state of Minnesota.

minnow A very small, freshwater fish. **min·now** (min′ō) *noun, plural* **minnows.**

minor Small in importance or size: *The teacher found a few* ***minor*** *errors in my report. Adjective.*
○ A person who is not old enough to vote or be legally responsible for his or her own affairs. *Noun.*
mi·nor (mī′nər) *adjective; noun, plural* **minors.**

minority **1.** The smaller part of a group or whole; less than half: *Out of twenty students, a* ***minority*** *of only six voted for the new plan.* **2.** A group of people different from the larger group of which it is a part because of race, religion, politics, or nationality. **mi·nor·i·ty** (mə nôr′i tē *or* mī nôr′i tē) *noun, plural* **minorities.**

minstrel A wandering poet and singer in the Middle Ages. **min·strel** (min′strəl) *noun, plural* **minstrels.**

mint¹ **1.** A plant with fragrant leaves used as flavoring and in medicine. Peppermint and spearmint are kinds of mint. **2.** A candy flavored with mint. **mint** (mint) *noun, plural* **mints.**

mint² **1.** A place where metal is made into coins, usually under government authority. **2.** A large amount of money: *A car like this must cost a* ***mint.*** *Noun.*
○ To make coins. *The government* ***minted*** *new half dollars this year. Verb.*
mint (mint) *noun, plural* **mints;** *verb,* **minted, minting.**

minuend The number from which another number is subtracted. **min·u·end** (min′ū end′) *noun, plural* **minuends.**

$$\text{In} \quad 6 - 2 = 4 \quad \text{or} \quad \begin{matrix} 6 \\ \underline{-2} \\ 4 \end{matrix}$$

6 is the **minuend.**

minus **1.** Decreased by; less: *Ten* ***minus*** *seven is three.* **2.** Lacking; without: *The chair was* ***minus*** *a leg. Preposition.*
○ **1.** Less than zero: *It was* ***minus*** *four degrees this morning.* **2.** Lower than or less than: *I got an A* ***minus*** *on my paper.* **3.** Showing that something is to be or has been taken away: *A* ***minus*** *sign means that the number following it is to be subtracted. Adjective.*
○ A sign (−) that shows something is to be or has been subtracted. In the equation 9 − 6 = 3, the sign between 9 and 6 is a minus. *Noun.*
mi·nus (mī′nəs) *preposition; adjective; noun, plural* **minuses.**

minute¹ **1.** A unit of time equal to sixty seconds. There are sixty minutes in an hour. **2.** A moment in time; instant: *I knew who you were the* ***minute*** *you walked into the room.* **3. minutes.** A written report of what was said and done at a meeting. **min·ute** (min′it) *noun, plural* **minutes.**

minute² **1.** Very small; tiny: *a* ***minute*** *piece of dust.* **2.** Paying close attention to details; very careful and thorough: *The detective made a* ***minute*** *examination of the desk for fingerprints.* **mi·nute** (mī nüt′ *or* mī nūt′) *adjective.*

minuteman A volunteer soldier who was not part of the regular army during the American Revolution, but was ready to fight at a minute's

PRONUNCIATION KEY:

| at | āpe | fär | câre | end | mē | it | īce | pierce | hot | ōld | sông | fôrk |
| oil | out | up | ūse | rüle | pùll | tûrn | chin | sing | shop | thin | this | |

hw in white; zh in treasure. The symbol ə stands for the unstressed vowel sound in about, taken, pencil, lemon, and circus.

471

notice. **min·ute·man** (mi'nit man') *noun, plural* **minutemen** (min'it men').

miracle 1. Something amazing or wonderful that cannot be explained by the laws of nature. 2. An amazing or wonderful thing: *It was a miracle that our team won the championship.* **mir·a·cle** (mir'ə kəl) *noun, plural* **miracles.**

miraculous 1. Impossible to explain by the laws of nature: *The child's recovery from the loss of hearing seemed miraculous.* 2. Amazing; marvelous: *The magician made a miraculous escape from a locked trunk.* **mi·rac·u·lous** (mi rak'yə ləs) *adjective.*

mirage An illusion in which an object that is seen at a distance is not really there. A common mirage is the appearance of a sheet of water that you see ahead of you on a highway on a hot day. A mirage is caused by light rays that are bent by layers of air at different temperatures. **mi·rage** (mi räzh') *noun, plural* **mirages.**

mirror 1. A smooth, polished surface that shows the image of the person or thing in front of it by reflecting light. Most mirrors are made of glass with an aluminum or silver coating on the back. 2. Something that gives a true picture: *This story is a mirror of life in colonial America.*
○ *Noun.* To reflect a picture or image: *I can see myself mirrored in your sunglasses. Verb.* **mir·ror** (mir'ər) *noun, plural* **mirrors;** *verb,* **mirrored, mirroring.**

**Most mirrors are
made of glass.**

mis- A prefix that means: 1. Bad; wrong: *Misfortune means bad fortune.* 2. In a bad or wrong way: *Mispronounce means to pronounce in the wrong way.*

misbehave To do something wrong; behave badly: *The child misbehaved by writing on the wall.* **mis·be·have** (mis'bi hāv') *verb,* **misbehaved, misbehaving.**

miscellaneous Made up of different kinds of things: *There was a miscellaneous collection of papers, toys, and clothes in the drawer.* **mis·cel·la·ne·ous** (mis'ə lā'nē əs) *adjective.*

mischief Conduct that may seem playful but that causes harm or trouble: *Our parents told us not to get into any mischief while they were away.* **mis·chief** (mis'chif) *noun.*

mischievous 1. Full of mischief; playful but naughty: *That mischievous child hid my slippers again.* 2. Causing trouble; harmful: *The candidate was hurt by mischievous rumors spread by opponents.* **mis·chie·vous** (mis'chə vəs) *adjective.* —**mischievously** *adverb.*

misconduct Bad behavior or immoral actions. **mis·con·duct** (mis kon'dukt) *noun.*

miscount To count incorrectly: *The votes were miscounted. Verb.*
○ An incorrect count: *Because of a miscount of the tickets sold, extra seats had to be brought into the auditorium. Noun.* **mis·count** (mis kount' *for verb;* mis'kount' *for noun) verb,* **miscounted, miscounting;** *noun, plural* **miscounts.**

miser A person who prefers to live poorly and save money rather than spend it; a stingy person. **mi·ser** (mī'zər) *noun, plural* **misers.**

miserable 1. Very unhappy; wretched: *We all felt miserable about losing our dog.* 2. Causing discomfort or unhappiness: *I had a miserable cold.* 3. Of little or no value; poor: *They did such a miserable job of fixing the chair that it broke again.* **mis·er·a·ble** (miz'ər ə bəl) *adjective.* —**miserably** *adverb.*

misery Great unhappiness or suffering: *The flood caused misery for many people.* **mis·e·ry** (miz'ə rē) *noun, plural* **miseries.**

misfortune 1. Bad luck: *It was my misfortune to lose my new watch.* 2. An unlucky event or happening: *The pitcher's injury was a great misfortune for our baseball team.* **mis·for·tune** (mis fôr'chən) *noun, plural* **misfortunes.**

misgiving A feeling of doubt, suspicion, or worry: *We had misgivings about making the long trip with so little money.* **mis·giv·ing** (mis giv'ing) *noun, plural* **misgivings.**

misguided Having mistaken ideas; misled. **mis·guid·ed** (mis gīd′əd) *adjective.*

mishap An accident; misfortune. **mis·hap** (mis′hap) *noun, plural* **mishaps.**

mislay To put in a place that is later forgotten: *I mislaid my skates and couldn't find them for a week.* **mis·lay** (mis lā′) *verb,* **mislaid, mislaying.**

mislead 1. To lead or guide in the wrong direction: *Our map misled us and so we never found our way to the beach.* 2. To lead into a mistaken or wrong thought or action: *The advertisement for this product misled us.* **mis·lead** (mis lēd′) *verb,* **misled** (mis led′), **misleading.**

misleading Causing a mistake or wrong idea: *The witnesses told the detective a misleading story.* **mis·lead·ing** (mis lē′ding) *adjective.*

misplace 1. To put something in a place and forget where it is; lose: *I misplaced my key and had to get a new one.* 2. To put in the wrong place: *In the sentence "If you go please, tell me first," the comma after "please" is misplaced. It should be after "go."* **mis·place** (mis plās′) *verb,* **misplaced, misplacing.**

misprint A mistake in printing: *The word "try" appeared as the misprint "rty."* **mis·print** (mis′print′) *noun, plural* **misprints.**

mispronounce To pronounce a word or sound in the wrong way: *If you pronounce the "k" in the word "knife," you are mispronouncing it.* **mis·pro·nounce** (mis′prə nouns′) *verb,* **mispronounced, mispronouncing.** —**mispronunciation** *noun.*

misread To read or understand incorrectly: *We misread the sign on the highway and missed the exit.* **mis·read** (mis rēd′) *verb,* **misread** (mis red′), **misreading.**

miss¹ 1. To fail to do something attempted or planned; fail to get, reach, hit, meet, find, or catch: *The player swung the bat but missed the ball. We missed the bus.* 2. To notice or feel the absence or loss of a person or thing: *I missed my parents when they went on vacation.* 3. To get away from; escape: *We just missed being hit by the falling rock.* 4. To be without; lack: *This coat is missing a button. Verb.*

○ A failure to hit or reach something: *I shot five*

arrows at the target without a miss. Noun.
miss (mis) *verb,* **missed, missing;** *noun, plural* **misses.**

miss² A title for a girl or for an unmarried woman. When "miss" is used with a person's name, it is written with a capital "M": *Our friend, Miss Lane, will be visiting this weekend.* **miss** (mis) *noun, plural* **misses.**

Miss. An abbreviation for Mississippi.

misshapen badly shaped; deformed. **mis·shap·en.** (mis shā′pen) *adjective.*

missile 1. Anything thrown or shot through the air. An arrow, a bullet, and a rock can be missiles. 2. A rocket that is used to launch a space capsule, satellite, or weapon. **mis·sile** (mis′əl) *noun, plural* **missiles.**

missing 1. Lost; not to be found: *I finally found my missing sock.* 2. Not there; absent or lacking: *This jigsaw puzzle has a missing piece.* **miss·ing** (mis′ing) *adjective.*

mission 1. A group of people sent somewhere to do a special job: *Four rangers formed a rescue mission to search for the lost child.* 2. A special job or task: *a mission to the moon.* 3. A church or other place where a group of missionaries work. **mis·sion** (mish′ən) *noun, plural* **missions.**

This is the early Texas mission now known as the Alamo.

missionary A person sent by a religious group to spread the religion and promote good will in another country: *Their grandparents were missionaries in India.* **mis·sion·ar·y** (mish′ə ner′ē) *noun, plural* **missionaries.**

PRONUNCIATION KEY:

at	āpe	fär	câre	end	mē	it	īce	pierce	hot	ōld	sông	fôrk
oil	out	up	ūse	rüle	pu̇ll	tûrn	chin	sing	shop	thin	this	

hw in white; zh in treasure. The symbol ə stands for the unstressed vowel sound in about, taken, pencil, lemon, and circus.

473

Mississippi 1. A state in the southern United States. Its capital is Jackson. 2. The longest river in the United States. It flows from Minnesota to the Gulf of Mexico. **Mis·sis·sip·pi** (mis′ə sip′ē) *noun*.

Mississippi
U. S. Postal Abbreviation: **MS**
Capital: **Jackson** Population: **2,625,000**
Area: **47,716 sq. mi./123,584 sq. km**
State Nickname: **Magnolia State**
State Bird: **Mockingbird** State Flower: **Magnolia**

WORD HISTORY

Mississippi comes from two Indian words that mean "big river." The name was first used in the northern part of the country for what is now called the Mississippi River, but later Congress gave the name to the area at the southern end of the river that became the state of Mississippi.

Missouri
U. S. Postal Abbreviation: **MO**
Capital: **Jefferson City** Population: **5,103,000**
Area: **69,686 sq. mi./180,486 sq. km**
State Nickname: **Show Me State**
State Bird: **Bluebird** State Flower: **Hawthorn**

Missouri 1. A state in the central United States. Its capital is Jefferson City. 2. A large river in the United States. It flows from Montana to the Mississippi River. **Mis·sou·ri** (mi zŭr′ē *or* mi zŭr′ə) *noun*.

WORD HISTORY

Missouri is an Indian word that means "people with the big canoes." It was the name of a tribe that lived near the mouth of the Missouri River when French explorers first went there. Later the name was used for the river near this tribe's home, and finally it was given to the state.

misspell To spell a word incorrectly: *I misspelled "until" on the test when I spelled it with two l's at the end.* **mis·spell** (mis spel′) *verb*, **misspelled** *or* **misspelt, misspelling.**

mist A cloud of tiny drops of water or other liquid in the air; fog: *There was a heavy mist over the lake. Noun.*
○ 1. To be or become covered with a mist: *My glasses misted in the fog.* 2. To rain in fine drops; drizzle: *It misted in the morning, but by noon the sky was clear. Verb.* **mist** (mist) *noun*; *verb*, **misted, misting.**

In the early morning, mist often rises out of mountain ranges.

mistake Something that is not correctly done, said, or thought; error. I made two spelling mistakes on the test: *It was a mistake to mention the party, since it was supposed to be a surprise. Noun.*
○ To make an error about something: *It is easy to mistake one twin for the other because they look exactly alike. Verb.* **mis·take** (mi stāk′) *noun, plural* **mistakes;** *verb,* **mistook, mistaken, mistaking.**

mistaken In error; wrong: *We had a mistaken idea about when the party was to begin. Adjective.*
○ Past participle of **mistake:** *I've mistaken your coat for mine Verb.* **mis·tak·en** (mi stā′kən) *adjective; verb.*

474

mister A title for a man. When "mister" is used with a man's name, it is written with a capital "M" or more often abbreviated as "Mr": *Mr. Jackson lives next door to us.* **mis·ter** (mis′tər) *noun, plural* **misters.**

mistletoe A plant with small, yellowish green leaves and bunches of little white berries. Mistletoe is a parasite that grows on the branches of trees and is used as a Christmas decoration. **mis·tle·toe** (mis′əl tō′) *noun, plural* **mistletoes.**

mistook Past tense of mistake. **mis·took** (mis tůk′) *verb.*

mistreat To be cruel, rough, or unkind to; treat badly: *The child mistreated the cat by pulling on its tail.* **mis·treat** (mis trēt′) *verb,* **mistreated, mis-treating.** —**mistreatment** *noun.*

mistress A woman in charge or control of something. A woman who has a home is mistress of the household. **mis·tress** (mis′tris) *noun, plural* **mistresses.**

mistrust A lack of trust or confidence; suspicion; doubt: *I discussed my mistrust of the plan with the committee. Noun.*
○ To have no trust or confidence in; be suspicious of; doubt: *We mistrust a lot of television commercials. Verb.*
mis·trust (mis trust′) *noun; verb,* **mistrusted, mistrusting.**

misty 1. Covered or clouded with mist: *The harbor was misty with morning fog. The child's eyes were misty with tears.* 2. Not clear; vague: *I have only a misty memory of my first day of school.* **mist·y** (mis′tē) *adjective,* **mistier, mistiest.**

misunderstand To understand someone or something incorrectly: *I misunderstood the question and wrote my answers in pencil instead of ink.* **mis·un·der·stand** (mis′un dər stand′) *verb,* **misunderstood, misunderstanding.**

misunderstanding 1. The failure to understand correctly: *Misunderstanding can lead to mistakes.* 2. A disagreement between people: *The two friends settled their misunderstanding by discussing it.* **mis·un·der·stand·ing** (mis′un dər stan′ding) *noun, plural* **misunderstandings.**

misunderstood Past tense of misunderstand. **mis·un·der·stood** (mis′un dər stůd′) *verb.*

misuse Wrong or incorrect use: *The teacher warned us that misuse of laboratory equipment can be dangerous. Noun.*
○ 1. To use wrongly or incorrectly: *My essay was criticized because I misused pronouns in several sentences.* 2. To treat badly: *We misused our new car by driving on rocky roads. Verb.*
mis·use (mis ūs′ *for noun;* mis ūz′ *for verb*) *noun, plural* **misuses;** *verb,* **misused, misusing.**

mite 1. A tiny animal similar to a spider. Most mites are parasites and live on animals 2. A very small object or creature: *The baby was a mite compared to the adults.* 3. A small amount. Another word that sounds like this is **might.** **mite** (mīt) *noun, plural* **mites.**

mitt 1. A type of glove used in baseball. Mitts have padding to protect a person's hand when a ball is caught. 2. A glove that covers the palm of the hand but not the fingers. **mitt** (mit) *noun, plural* **mitts.**

mitten A warm covering for the hand. **mit·ten** (mit′ən) *noun, plural* **mittens.**

A mitten covers four fingers together and the thumb separately.

mix 1. To put two or more different things together: *We mixed yellow roses and white roses in the bouquet.* 2. To blend, combine, or join: *Oil and water will not mix.* 3. To get along with other people: *It was a great party because all the guests mixed well. Verb.*
○ Something made by mixing; mixture: *We bought a pancake mix. Noun.*
• **to mix up.** 1. To confuse: *I was so mixed up that I got lost.* 2. To involve: *The police suspect that the gang was mixed up in the robberies.*
mix (miks) *verb,* **mixed, mixing;** *noun, plural* **mixes.**

PRONUNCIATION KEY:

| at | āpe | fär | câre | end | mē | it | īce | pierce | hot | ōld | sông | fôrk |
| oil | out | up | ūse | rüle | půll | tûrn | chin | sing | shop | thin | this | |

hw in white; zh in treasure. The symbol ə stands for the unstressed vowel sound in about, taken, pencil, lemon, and circus.

475

mixed number A number made up of a whole number and a fraction. The number 4⅞ is a mixed number.

mixer A machine for mixing different things together: *A cement mixer mixes cement, water, and sand to make concrete.* **mix·er** (mik′sər) *noun, plural* **mixers.**

mixture **1.** Something made up of different things that are put together: *Pink paint is a mixture of red and white paints.* **2.** The act or process of mixing: *The mixture of oil, vinegar, and spices makes a salad dressing.* **mix·ture** (miks′chər) *noun, plural* **mixtures.**

mix-up An instance or condition of confusion: *We missed the bus because of a mix-up in the schedule.* **mix-up** (miks′up) *noun, plural* **mix-ups.**

ml An abbreviation for **milliliter.**

mm An abbreviation for **millimeter.**

MN Postal abbreviation for **Minnesota.**

mo. An abbreviation for **month.**

Mo. An abbreviation for **Missouri.**

MO Postal abbreviation for **Missouri.**

moan A long, low sound that usually shows that a person or animal feels pain or grief. *Noun.*
○ To make or say with a long, low sound: *I moaned when I accidentally bumped my sore arm. Verb.*
Another word that sounds like this is **mown.**
moan (mōn) *noun, plural* **moans;** *verb,* **moaned, moaning.**

moat A deep, wide ditch that surrounds a castle or town for protection against an enemy. Moats are usually filled with water. A drawbridge is lowered over the moat so that people can cross it. **moat** (mōt) *noun, plural* **moats.**

mob A large number of people; crowd. A mob is sometimes made up of people who are so angry or upset about something that they break the law and cause damage: *An angry mob gathered in front of the jail to demand that the prisoner be set free. Noun.*
○ To crowd around in excitement or anger: *Shoppers mobbed the store during the sale. Verb.*
mob (mob) *noun, plural* **mobs;** *verb,* **mobbed, mobbing.**

mobile Capable of moving or being moved: *The crew set up mobile television cameras. Adjective.*
○ A kind of sculpture with movable parts that are usually hung from rods or thin wires. These parts can be easily moved by currents of air. *Noun.*
mobile (mō′bəl *or* mō′bēl *for adjective;* mō′bēl *for noun) adjective; noun, plural* **mobiles.**

mobile home A large trailer that people can live in.

moccasin A soft leather shoe or slipper with no heel. Moccasins were first worn by Native Americans. **moc·ca·sin** (mok′ə sin) *noun, plural* **moccasins.**

WORD HISTORY
The word moccasin comes from the an Indian word for this sort of leather shoe.

mock **1.** To make fun of in a mean way: *Instead of helping, they laughed and mocked me when I fell off my bike.* **2.** To imitate or copy in a joking or rude way: *That comedian mocks several famous politicians. Verb.*
○ Not real; imitation: *In history class we had a mock battle with cardboard shields and wooden swords. Adjective.*
mock (mok) *verb,* **mocked, mocking;** *adjective.*

Most mockingbirds have dark gray feathers with white markings.

mockingbird A bird of North and Central America that can imitate the calls of other birds. **mock·ing·bird** (mok′ing bûrd′) *noun, plural* **mockingbirds.**

mode¹ A way of doing something: *Automobiles are a popular mode of transportation.* **mode** (mōd) *noun, plural* **modes.**

mode² A style of dress, fashion, or behavior popular at a particular time: *Hats with wide brims may be the mode next spring.* **mode** (mōd) *noun, plural* **modes.**

model 1. A small-sized copy of something: *making model cars from kits.* 2. A person or thing that is a good example of something and is copied: *The U.S. Constitution is used as a model by many new governments.* 3. A person who poses for an artist or photographer. 4. A person whose job is to wear new clothes so that customers can see what they look like. Models may work in stores or in fashion shows, or be photographed for magazines. 5. A style or type of thing: *That car is a very old model. Noun.*
○ 1. Worthy of being imitated: *The children showed model behavior.* 2. Serving as or being a small copy: *We built the model airplane from a kit. Adjective.*
○ 1. To make or design something: *The sculptor modeled a pony in clay.* 2. To follow or copy someone or something: *I hope to model my career after my favorite teacher's.* 3. To work as a model: *My cousin models for a clothing store. Verb.*
mod·el (mod′əl) *noun, plural* **models;** *adjective; verb,* **modeled, modeling.**

These astronauts are holding a model of the space shuttle they have just flown.

moderate Not too much or too little; not extreme: *We have had moderate temperatures this winter. Adjective.*
○ To become or make less extreme or violent: *The heavy winds moderated during the night. Verb.* **mod·er·ate** (mod′ə rit *for adjective;* mod′ə rāt′ *for verb) adjective; verb,* **moderated, moderating.** —**moderation** *noun.*

modern 1. Having to do with the present time or recent time: *Nuclear energy as a source of power is a modern development.* 2. Having to do with the period from about the year 1450 to the present: *Last year, we studied ancient history; now we are learning about modern history.* 3. Up-to-date; not old-fashioned: *The laboratory has the most modern equipment.* **mod·ern** (mod′ərn) *adjective.*

modernize To make or become modern or up-to-date: *We modernized our kitchen by installing new cabinets, a dishwasher, and a microwave oven.* **mod·ern·ize** (mod′ərn īz′) *verb,* **modernized, modernizing.**

modest 1. Not thinking too highly of oneself: *A modest person does not brag or show off.* 2. Within reason; limited or restrained; not extreme: *We spent only a modest amount of money on the trip.* **modest** (mod′ist) *adjective.* —**modestly** *adverb* —**modesty** *noun.*

modify 1. To change in some way: *We modified our plan for the new kitchen.* 2. To make less; reduce: *The union leaders modified their demands for better working conditions.* 3. To limit the meaning of a word: *In the sentence "They live in a white house," the adjective "white" modifies the noun "house."* **mod·i·fy** (mod′ə fī′) *verb,* **modified, modifying.**

module A part of a spacecraft that has a special use and can be separated from the rest of the craft. A lunar module is the small craft in which astronauts landed on the moon. **mod·ule** (moj′ūl *or* mod′ūl) *noun, plural* **modules.**

Mohawk A member of a tribe of American Indians of New York. The Mohawk are part of the Iroquois confederation. **Mo·hawk** (mō′hôk) *noun, plural* **Mohawk** *or* **Mohawks.**

moist Slightly wet; damp: *I wiped the shelves with a moist cloth.* **moist** (moist) *adjective,* **moister, moistest.**

PRONUNCIATION KEY:
at   āpe   fär   câre   end   mē   it   īce   pîerce   hot   ōld   sông   fôrk
oil   out   up   ūse   rüle   pull   tûrn   chin   sing   shop   thin   this
hw in white; zh in treasure. The symbol ə stands for the unstressed vowel sound in about, taken, pencil, lemon, and circus.

477

moisten To make or become slightly wet: *I moistened the soil around the plant.* **moist·en** (mois′ən) *verb,* **moistened, moistening.**

moisture Water or other liquid in the air or on a surface; slight wetness: *There was moisture on the window from the steam in the kitchen.* **mois·ture** (mois′chər) *noun.*

molar Any one of the large teeth at the back of the mouth. Molars have broad surfaces for grinding food. **mo·lar** (mō′lər) *noun,* plural **molars.**

WORD HISTORY

The word molar comes from a Latin word meaning "of a mill" or "millstone." Because the molars grind food, they were called grinding "millstones."

---

molasses A sweet, thick, yellowish brown syrup made from sugarcane. **mo·las·ses** (mə las′iz) *noun.*

mold¹ A hollow form made in a special shape. A liquid or soft material is poured into a mold. When it hardens, it takes the shape of the mold. *Noun.*
○ **1.** To make into a special shape; form: *We molded the clay with our hands.* **2.** To influence and give form to: *Our parents help mold our habits. Verb.*
mold (mōld) *noun,* plural **molds;** *verb,* **molded, molding.**

mold² A furry-looking covering of fungus that grows on food and damp surfaces. **mold** (mōld) *noun,* plural **molds.** —**moldy** *adjective.*

molding A strip of wood, plaster, or other material used along the edges of walls, windows, or doorways for decoration. **mold·ing** (mōld′ing) *noun,* plural **moldings.**

mole¹ A small, often raised, brown spot on the skin. **mole** (mōl) *noun,* plural **moles.**

mole² A small animal with very soft, grayish fur that burrows holes underground. Moles have long claws and very small eyes. **mole** (mōl) *noun,* plural **moles.**

molecule The smallest particle into which a substance can be divided without being changed chemically. *For example, a molecule of water has two atoms of hydrogen and one atom of oxygen.* **mol·e·cule** (mol′ə kūl) *noun,* plural **molecules.**

mollusk Any of a group of animals without backbones that usually have a soft body protected by a hard shell. Mollusks often live in or near water. Clams, snails, and oysters are mollusks. **mol·lusk** (mol′əsk) *noun,* plural **mollusks.**

molt To shed the hair, feathers, skin, or shell and grow a new covering. Birds and snakes molt. **molt** (mōlt) *verb,* **molted, molting.**

molten Melted by heat: *Lava from a volcano is molten rock.* **molten** (mōl′tən) *adjective.*

mom An informal word for **mother. mom** (mom) *noun,* plural **moms.**

moment **1.** A short period of time: *I'll answer you in a moment.* **2.** A particular point in time: *Please come home the moment I call you.* **mo·ment** (mō′mənt) *noun,* plural **moments.**

momentary Lasting only a short time: *There was a momentary lull in the storm and then it rained heavily again.* **mo·men·tar·y** (mō′mən ter′ē) *adjective.*

momentous Having great importance: *The end of the war was a momentous event.* **mo·men·tous** (mō men′təs) *adjective.*

momentum The force or speed that an object has when it is moving: *A rock gains momentum as it rolls down a hill.* **mo·men·tum** (mō men′təm) *noun,* plural **momentums.**

Mon. An abbreviation for **Monday.**

monarch **1.** A king or queen of a country. **2.** A large orange and black butterfly found in North America. **mon·arch** (mon′ərk) *noun,* plural **monarchs.**

monarchy **1.** Government by a king or queen. **2.** A nation or state ruled by a monarch. **mon·ar·chy** (mon′ər kē) *noun,* plural **monarchies.**

monastery A place where monks live and work together. **mon·as·ter·y** (mon′ə ster′ē) *noun,* plural **monasteries.**

Monday The second day of the week. **Mon·day** (mun′dē or mun′dā) *noun,* plural **Mondays.**

WORD HISTORY

The Romans dedicated the second day of the week to the moon. This name was translated as an Old English word meaning "moon's day," or Monday as it became in modern English.

---

monetary Of, in, or having to do with money or currency: *This vase has great monetary value. The dollar is the monetary unit of the United States.* **monetary** (mon′i ter′ē) *adjective.*

money The coins and paper currency of a country used to buy goods and pay people for services. Dimes, quarters, and dollar bills are money. **mon•ey** (mun′ē) *noun, plural* **moneys.**

Mongolia A country in central Asia. **Mon•go•li•a** (mong gō′lē ə) *noun.*

mongoose A slender animal with a pointed face, a long tail, and rough, shaggy fur. Mongooses live in Africa and Asia, are very quick, and eat rats and mice. **mon•goose** (mong′güs) *noun, plural* **mongooses.**

mongrel A plant or an animal, especially a dog, that is a mixture of breeds. **mon•grel** (mung′grəl *or* mong′grəl) *noun, plural* **mongrels.**

monitor **1.** A student who is given a special duty to do, such as taking attendance. **2.** A person who warns or keeps watch: *The sailor's job was to be monitor of the radar screen.* **3.** The screen that a computer uses to display numbers, letters, and pictures. It is similar to a television screen. *Noun.*
○ To watch over or observe something: *Our teacher monitored the fire drill. Verb.*
mon•i•tor (mon′i tər) *noun, plural* **monitors;** *verb,* **monitored, monitoring.**

monk A man who has joined a religious order, lives in a monastery, and is bound by religious vows. **monk** (mungk) *noun, plural* monks.

monkey **1.** Any of a group of intelligent, furry primates with long tails and hands and feet that can grasp things. Most monkeys live in trees in tropical areas of the world. **2.** A playful or naughty child. *Noun.*
○ To fool or play around in a mischievous way: *The lifeguard asked us to quit monkeying around in the water. Verb.*
mon•key (mung′kē) *noun, plural* **monkeys;** *verb,* **monkeyed, monkeying.**

Most monkeys **live in trees in tropical areas of the world.**

MONEY

Since the earliest times humans have traded items for things they couldn't make or grow themselves. Farmers traded animals and crops for salt or cloth. Weavers traded cloth and thread for food of other items. The items traded are known as a medium of exchange. A wide range of items have been used as mediums of exchange throughout the world. Knives and rice were used in China as early as 3000 BC. Cattle and clay tablets were used as early as 2500 BC by the Babylonians. In fact, in some parts of the world cattle and other animals are still used as a medium of exchange today.

Coins: As trade spread, however, a simpler, more portable medium of exchange was invented: coins. The first known coins were issued by the Greek city of Lydia around the 7th century BC. These metal coins were shaped like beans, but coins like the ones we use today appeared soon after. Coins were widely used by the Greeks and Romans, and by the Chinese.

Paper Money: But there are problems with coins. They can be heavy and precious metal such as gold or silver is easy to steal and melt down for reuse. Paper money was probably invented in China, but our use of it comes to us from Europe. Merchants in Europe in the Middle Ages developed a system of sending notes from city to city promising to pay a certain amount of gold to the person carrying the note, something like the bank checks we use today.

National Currency: This system of notes led banks to printing their own money, backed by their holdings of gold or silver. Eventually the government of France noticed that issuing money could be a source of wealth. In the 18th century France began issuing uniform bills similar to the ones we use. Other countries quickly followed and today most countries issue their own money. In the United States paper money is issued by the U. S. Treasury and coins are made by the U. S. Mint.

PRONUNCIATION KEY:
at   āpe   fär   câre   end   mē   it   īce   pierce   hot   ōld   sông   fôrk
oil   out   up   ūse   rüle   pull   tûrn   chin   sing   shop   thin   this
hw in white; zh in treasure. The symbol ə stands for the unstressed vowel sound in about, taken, pencil, lemon, and circus.

479

monkey wrench A wrench with a jaw that can be adjusted to fit different sizes of nuts and bolts.

monogram A design made by combining two or more initials of a person's name. You see monograms on such things as clothing, towels, and stationery. **mon•o•gram** (mon′ə gram′) *noun, plural* **monograms.**

monologue 1. A long dramatic or comic speech or performance given by one person: *The audience wept during the actor's* **monologue.** 2. A long speech made by one person who is part of a group. **mon•o•logue** (mon′ə lôg′ *or* mon′ə log′) *noun, plural* **monologues.**

monopolize 1. To get or have a monopoly of. 2. To get, have, or use all of: *Don't monopolize the teacher's attention.* **mo•nop•o•lize** (mə nop′ə līz)′ *verb,* **monopolized, monopolizing.**

monopoly 1. The sole control of a product or service by a person or company: *That bus company has a monopoly on public transportation in our town.* 2. A person or company that has such control. **mo•nop•o•ly** (mə nop′ə lē) *noun, plural* **monopolies.**

monorail 1. A train that runs on or is suspended from a single rail. 2. A railroad track that has only one rail. Some modern trains run on monorails. **mon•o•rail** (mon′ə rāl′) *noun, plural* **monorails.**

monotone Speech or vocal sound uttered with no change in tone: *The announcer's dull monotone made the program boring.* **mon•o•tone** (mon′ə tōn′) *noun.*

monotonous Tiring or uninteresting because it does not change in any way: *That job is monotonous because you have to do the same thing over and over.* **mo•not•o•nous** (mə not′ə nəs) *adjective.* —**monotonously** *adverb.*

monsieur The French title for a man. **mon•sieur** (mə syûr′) *noun, plural* **messieurs** (mes ərz′).

monsoon A very strong wind that blows in the Indian Ocean and southern Asia. In the summer, it blows from the ocean toward the land and brings very heavy rains. In the winter, it blows from the land toward the ocean. **mon•soon** (mon sün′) *noun, plural* **monsoons.**

monster 1. An imaginary creature that is huge and frightening. 2. A huge animal, plant, or thing. 3. A wicked, cruel person. 4. An animal or plant not normal in form or appearance. **mon•ster** (mon′stər) *noun, plural* **monsters.**

monstrous 1. Horrible or frightening: *a monstrous dragon.* 2. Very, very large; enormous: *The child thought the elephant at the zoo was a monstrous animal.* 3. Very evil: *Murder is a monstrous crime.* **monstrous** (monstrəs) *adjective.* —**monstrously** *adverb.*

Mont. An abbreviation for **Montana.**

Montana A state in the northwestern United States. Its capital is Helena. **Mon•tan•a** (mon tan′ə) *noun.*

Montana
U. S. Postal Abbreviation: **MT**
Capital: **Helena**
Population: **809,000**
Area: **147,138 sq. mi./381,086 sq. km**
State Nickname: **Treasure State**
State Bird: **Western Meadowlark**
State Flower: **Bitterroot**

month One of the twelve parts of a year. **month** (munth) *noun, plural* **months.**

monthly 1. Done or happening once a month: *monthly meetings.* 2. Of or for a month: *The monthly rainfall for April was 12 inches.* *Adjective.*

○ Once a month; every month: *The bill from the telephone company arrives* **monthly.** *Adverb.*

○ A magazine published once a month. *Noun.* **month•ly** (munth′lē) *adjective; adverb; noun, plural* **monthlies.**

monument 1. A building, statue, or other object made to honor a person or event: *The Lincoln Memorial in Washington, D.C., is a* **monument** *to Abraham Lincoln.* 2. An achievement of lasting importance: *The discovery of a polio vaccine was a **monument** in medicine.* **mon•u•ment** (mon′yə mənt) *noun, plural* **monuments.**

—**monumental** *adjective.*

moo The sound that a cow makes. *Noun.* ○ To make this sound. *Verb.* **moo** (mü) *noun, plural* **moos;** *verb,* **mooed, mooing.**

mood The way that a person feels at a certain time. Our moods change; sometimes we are happy and other times we are sad: *Learning to swim put me in a good **mood**.* **mood** (müd) *noun, plural* **moods.**

moody 1. Tending to change moods often: *You can never predict the reactions of such a **moody** person.* 2. Being in or showing a gloomy or sullen mood: *Some people are **moody** because of rainy weather.* **mood•y** (müd′ē) *adjective,* **moodier, moodiest.**

The Washington Monument is over 550 feet high.

Moon
The only extraterrestrial object visited by humans, one side of the Moon always faces Earth. The Moon's gravitation causes the tides on Earth.
Average distance from Earth: **235,000 miles**
Diameter: **2,160 miles**
Length of Day: **27 days, 7 hours, 43 minutes**
Time to orbit Earth: **27.3 days**
Average Temperature: **214˚F (day); -300˚F (night.)**
Mass compared to Earth: **.1**
Weight of 100 pounds: **17**
Atmosphere: **None**

moon 1. A heavenly body that revolves around the earth from west to east once every 29 days. The moon seems to shine because it reflects light from the sun. The moon is the earth's satellite. 2. A satellite of any planet: *Mars has two **moons**.* **moon** (mün) *noun, plural* **moons.**

moonbeam A ray of light from the moon. **moon•beam** (mün′bēm) *noun, plural* **moonbeams.**

moonlight The light that shines from the moon. **moon•light** (mün′līt) *noun.*

moor¹ To fasten or tie a boat in place: *We **moored** the sailboat at the dock with a rope.* **moor** (mùr) *verb,* **moored, mooring.**

moor² An open area of wild land with few trees. There are moors in England and Scotland that are often covered with heather and have wet, marsh-like ground. **moor** (mùr) *noun, plural* **moors.**

The boat is moored to the dock.

moose A large, heavy animal related to the deer that lives in forests in cold northern regions of North America, Europe, and Asia. The male has enormous, broad antlers. **moose** (müs) *noun, plural* **moose.**

mop 1. A cleaning device made of a bundle of yarn or cloth or a sponge attached to a long handle. 2. A thick, tangled mass, as of hair: *Please comb that **mop** of hair. Noun.* ○ To clean or dry with a mop: *I **mopped** the deck of the ship.* **mop** (mop) *noun, plural* **mops;** *verb,* **mopped, mopping.**

mope To be depressed and gloomy: *Find something useful to do and stop **moping** around.* **mope** (mōp) *verb,* **moped, moping.**

moped A heavy bicycle with a small engine. **mo•ped** (mō′ped) *noun, plural* **mopeds.**

moral 1. Good and honest in behavior and character: *A **moral** person would admit to breaking the window.* 2. Having to do with what is right and wrong: *Whether to report that your friend cheated*

PRONUNCIATION KEY:

| at | āpe | fär | câre | end | mē | it | īce | pîerce | hot | ōld | sông | fôrk |
| oil | out | up | ūse | rüle | pùll | tûrn | chin | sing | shop | thin | this | |

hw in white; zh in treasure. The symbol ə stands for the unstressed vowel sound in about, taken, pencil, lemon, and circus.

481

*is a **moral** question. Adjective.*
○ **1.** A lesson about right and wrong that is taught in a story, event, or fable: *The **moral** of the story was "Don't put off until tomorrow what you can do today."* **2. morals.** The beliefs that a person has about what is right and what is wrong. *Noun.*
mor·al (môr′əl) *adjective; noun, plural* **morals.** —**morally** *adverb.*

morale The way a person or a group of people feel in general; attitude or spirit: *The team's **morale** was low after they lost the game.* **mo·rale** (mə ral′) *noun.*

more **1.** Greater in number, amount, or degree: *A gallon is **more** than a quart.* **2.** Additional; further: *I need **more** charcoal for the fire. Adjective.*
○ **1.** To a greater amount or degree: *Be **more** careful.* **2.** In addition; again: *I will only tell you once **more**. Adverb.*
○ An extra amount: *Our dogs always want **more** to eat. Noun.*
more (môr) *adjective; adverb; noun.*

LANGUAGE NOTE

More is used to make the comparative form of some adjectives and adverbs. Most English comparatives are formed by adding -er to the end of a word. For example, *tall* + *-er* forms the comparative *taller*. But many words would sound awkward if we added -er to the end of the word. So instead we put the word "more" in front of it. We would say "more familiar," not "familiarer."

---

moreover In addition to what has been said; not only that: *It's dark and cold, and **moreover** it's raining.* **more·o·ver** (môr ō′vər) *adverb.*

Mormon **1.** A member of the Church of Jesus Christ of Latter-Day Saints. *Noun.*
○ **2.** Having to do with Mormons or their church. *Adjective.*
Mor·mon (môr′mən) *noun, plural* **Mormons;** *adjective.*

morning The early part of the day, ending at noon. Another word that sounds like this is **mourning.** **morn·ing** (môr′ning) *noun, plural* **mornings.**

morning glory A white, pink, purple, or blue flower that is shaped like a trumpet and grows on a vine. The flower opens in early morning and then closes later in the day.

Morocco A country in northwestern Africa. **Mo·roc·co** (mə rok′ō) *noun.*

morsel A small bite of food or piece of something: *The birds ate every **morsel** of bread we put out for them.* **mor·sel** (môr′səl) *noun, plural* **morsels.**

mortal **1.** Certain to die: *All things that live are **mortal**.* **2.** Causing death: *a **mortal** wound.* **3.** Very great; intense: *I have a **mortal** fear of wasps.* **4.** Very hostile: ***mortal** enemies. Adjective.*
○ A person; human being. *Noun.*
mor·tal (môr′təl) *adjective; noun, plural* **mortals.**

mortar¹ A building material made of sand, water, and lime. **mor·tar** (môr′tər) *noun.*

Mortar is used like cement to hold bricks and stones together.

mortar² A thick, heavy bowl in which things are crushed or ground by using a pestle. Look up pestle for a picture of a mortar. **mort·ar** (môr′tər) *noun, plural* **mortars.**

mosaic A picture or design made by fitting together bits of stone, glass, or tile of different colors, and cementing them in place. **mo·sa·ic** (mō zā′ik) *noun, plural* **mosaics.**

Moslem Another spelling for Muslim. **Mos·lem** (moz′ləm) *adjective; noun, plural* **Moslems.**

mosque A Muslim place of worship. **mosque** (mosk) *noun, plural* **mosques.**

mosquito A small insect with two wings. The female gives a sting or bite that itches. Some mosquitoes carry malaria and other diseases. **mos·quit·o** (məs kē′tō) *noun, plural* **mosquitoes** *or* **mosquitos.**

moss A small green plant that grows in groups to form a soft, thick mat on the ground, on rocks, or on trees. Mosses grow in shady places where it is damp. **moss** (môs) *noun, plural* **mosses.**

most **1.** Greatest in number, amount, or degree: *Who received the most votes?* **2.** The majority of: *Most children like games. Adjective.*
○ The greatest number, amount, or degree: *One dollar is the most I can give you. Noun.*
○ **1.** Very: *That musician is a most unusual person.* **2.** To the greatest degree: *That was the most interesting book I have ever read. Adverb.*
most (mōst) *adjective; noun; adverb.*

LANGUAGE NOTE

Most is used to make the superlative form of some adjectives and adverbs. Most English superlatives are formed by adding *-est* to the end of a word. For example, *fast* + *-est* forms the superlative *fastest.* But many words would sound awkward if we added *-est* to the end of the word. So instead we put the word "most" in front of it. We would say "most famous," not "famousest."

mostly For the most part; mainly; chiefly: *The dress is mostly blue, with some white trim.* **most·ly** (mōst'lē) *adverb.*

motel A kind of hotel built near a main road. Travelers can drive up to it easily and park their cars near their rooms. **mo·tel** (mō tel') *noun, plural* **motels.**

moth An insect that looks like a butterfly. Unlike butterflies, moths have thick bodies and fly mostly at night. The larvae of some moths eat holes in wool and other fabrics. **moth** (môth) *noun, plural* **moths.**

There about 100,000 species of moths.

mother **1.** A female parent. **2.** The source or origin of something: *Necessity is the mother of invention. Noun.*
○ To produce or care for something as a mother does: *We mothered the injured bird until it was well enough to fly. Verb.*
○ **1.** Being a mother: *a mother hen.* **2.** Relating to or characteristic of a mother: *mother love.*

3. Being related or attached to something as a mother is to her children: *mother country. Adjective.*
moth·er (muth'ər) *noun, plural* **mothers;** *verb,* **mothered, mothering;** *adjective.*

mother-in-law The mother of one's husband or wife. **moth·er-in-law** (muth'ər in lô') *noun, plural* **mothers-in-law.**

motherly Of, having to do with, or like a mother: *The doctor treated her patients with motherly care.* **moth·er·ly** (muth'ər lē) *adjective.*

motion **1.** The act of changing place or position; movement: *The steady motion of the boat made me feel sick.* **2.** A formal suggestion made at a meeting: *I made a motion to take a vote on the proposal. Noun.*
○ To move the hand or another part of the body as a sign: *The teacher motioned for us to sit. Verb.*
mo·tion (mō'shən) *noun, plural* **motions;** *verb,* **motioned, motioning.**

motionless Not moving; without motion: *The deer stood motionless at the edge of the meadow.* **mo·tion·less** (mō'shən lis) *adjective.* —**motionlessly** *adverb.*

motion picture A series of pictures on a film. They are projected onto a screen at such a high speed that it appears to the viewer that the people and things in the pictures are moving. This is also called a **moving picture** or **movie.**

motive The reason that a person does something: *A desire to go to college can be a strong motive for trying to get good grades. Fear of being scolded was their motive for telling the lie.* **mo·tive** (mō'tiv) *noun, plural* **motives.**

motor A machine that provides motion or power to make things run or work. Some motors use electricity and others burn fuel: *The motor of a fan makes the fan blades turn. Noun.*
○ **1.** Having to do with a motor or something run by a motor: *A car is a motor vehicle.* **2.** Having to do with the nerves of a person's body that control motion: *Pulling your hand back from a hot object is a motor reflex. Adjective.*
○ To travel by car: *We motored through New England. Verb.*
mo·tor (mō'tər) *noun, plural* **motors;** *adjective; verb,* **motored, motoring.**

PRONUNCIATION KEY:
| at | āpe | fär | câre | end | mē | it | īce | pîerce | hot | ōld | sông | fôrk |
| oil | out | up | ūse | rüle | pull | tûrn | chin | sing | shop | thin | this | |

hw in white; zh in treasure. The symbol ə stands for the unstressed vowel sound in about, taken, pencil, lemon, and circus.

483

motorboat A boat that is run by a motor. **mo·tor·boat** (mō′tər bōt′) *noun*, *plural* **motorboats.**

A motorboat **travels very quickly across the water.**

motorcycle A vehicle with two wheels that is bigger and heavier than a bicycle and is powered by an engine. **mo·tor·cy·cle** (mō′tər sī′kəl) *noun*, *plural* **motorcycles.**

motto A short sentence or phrase that says what someone believes or what something stands for: The Latin phrase, "E pluribus unum," which means "out of many, one," is the motto on the seal of the United States. **mot·to** (mot′ō) *noun*, *plural* **mottoes** or **mottos.**

mound **1.** A hill or heap of earth, stones, or other material: *There are* **mounds** *of garbage at the dump.* **2.** A slightly higher area in the center of a baseball diamond. *The pitcher stands on the* **mound** *to pitch the ball. Noun.*

○ To pile in a hill or heap: *I like to* **mound** *ice cream on top of my pie. Verb.*
mound (mound) *noun*, *plural* **mounds**; *verb*, **mounded, mounding.**

These chemicals are being piled into mounds.

mount¹ **1.** To go up; climb: *The firefighters* **mounted** *the stairs two at a time.* **2.** To get up on: *The sheriff* **mounted** *the horse and rode off.* **3.** To set in place: *I* **mounted** *the stamps in my album.* **4.** To rise or increase: *The cost of food has been* **mounting** *steadily this year. Verb.*

○ **1.** A horse or other animal for riding: *The rider stopped for a fresh* **mount** *at the midway point of the journey.* **2.** A stand, frame, or other object used to hold something: *We bought a wooden frame as a* **mount** *for the picture. Noun.*
mount (mount) *verb*, **mounted, mounting**; *noun*, *plural* **mounts.**

---

motorcycle

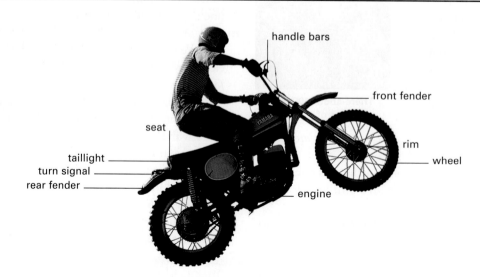

handle bars

front fender

seat

rim

wheel

taillight

turn signal

rear fender

engine

mount² A hill or mountain. **mount** (mount) *noun,* *plural* **mounts**.

mountain 1. A mass of land that rises very high above the surrounding area. 2. A very large pile or amount of something: *There was a **mountain** of trash at the dump.* **moun·tain** (moun′tən) *noun, plural* **mountains**.

mountaineer 1. A person who lives in the mountains: *The **mountaineer's** shack was stocked with food for the winter.* 2. A person who climbs mountains as a sport: *The **mountaineers** prepared their equipment for the climb.* **moun·tain·eer** (moun′tə nîr′) *noun, plural* **mountaineers**.

mountain lion A large wild cat that lives in the mountains of North and South America. This animal is also called a **cougar**. Look up **cougar** for more information.

mountainous 1. Having many mountains: *There is good skiing in that **mountainous** area.* 2. Very big; huge: *The storm piled up **mountainous** drifts of snow.* **moun·tain·ous** (moun′tə nəs) *adjective*.

mountain range A series of mountains that form a group.

mourn To feel or show sorrow or grief: *We **mourned** for all the people who died in the war.* **mourn** (môrn) *verb,* **mourned**, **mourning**.

mourning 1. The act of showing sorrow or grief: *They were in **mourning** for the victims of the fire.* 2. Black clothing or some other symbol worn to show grief over a person's death. Another word that sounds like this is **morning**. **mourn·ing** (môr′ning) *noun.*

A **mouse**, like a rat and a squirrel, is a rodent.

mouse 1. A small, furry animal with a pointed nose, small ears, and a long, thin tail. Mice that live in houses are often gray. Mice are rodents, as are rats and squirrels. 2. A small instrument that can be connected to a computer to move the cursor on a monitor. A mouse is moved by hand across the top of a desk or table to control the movement of the cursor. **mouse** (mous) *noun,* *plural* **mice**.

moustache Another spelling for **mustache**.

mouth 1. The opening through which people and animals take in food. The human mouth contains the tongue and the teeth. Many animals make sounds through their mouths. 2. Any opening that is like a mouth: *We entered the **mouth** of the cave. The **mouth** of a river is where it empties into another body of water, such as a lake or the sea.* Noun.
○ To say or repeat in a false or insincere way: *Try to recite the poem with feeling and not just **mouth** the words.* Verb.
mouth (mouth *for noun;* mou<u>th</u> *for verb*) *noun,* *plural* **mouths** (mou<u>th</u>z); *verb,* **mouthed**, **mouthing**.

mouthful The amount of food or drink that is taken into the mouth at one time: *I took a **mouthful** of the soda.* **mouth·ful** (mouth′fúl) *noun, plural* **mouthfuls**.

mouth organ Another name for **harmonica**.

mouthpiece The part of a musical instrument, telephone, or other object that is put between or near the lips. **mouth·piece** (mouth′pēs) *noun,* *plural* **mouthpieces**.

movable or **moveable** 1. Able to be moved: *The shelves in that cabinet are **movable**.* 2. That changes from one date to another in different years: *Thanksgiving is a **movable** holiday.* **mov·a·ble** (müv′ə bəl) *adjective.*

move 1. To change the place or direction of something: *We had to **move** to different seats to get a better view of the movie screen. **Move** the chair closer to the window.* 2. To change the location of a home or business: *We are **moving** to a new city.* 3. To go forward; advance: *Time **moves** quickly when you are having fun.* 4. To put in motion: *Wind **moves** a windmill.* 5. To cause someone to do something: *The teacher was **moved** by curiosity*

PRONUNCIATION KEY:
at   āpe   fär   câre   end   mē   it   ice   pierce   hot   ōld   sông   fôrk
oil   out   up   ūse   rüle   pull   tûrn   chin   sing   shop   thin   <u>th</u>is
hw in white; zh in treasure. The symbol ə stands for the unstressed vowel sound in about, taken, pencil, lemon, and circus.

485

to open the package. **6.** To stir a person's feelings: *I was **moved** to tears when I found the starving kittens.* **7.** To make a suggestion at a meeting: *The secretary **moved** that the meeting be ended. Verb.* ○ **1.** The act of moving: *The basketball player made a quick **move** toward the basket.* **2.** An action planned to bring about a result: *It was a smart **move** to shop early before the crowds arrived.* **3.** A person's turn to move a playing piece in certain games: *The player with the white chess pieces makes the first **move**. Noun.* **move** (müv) *verb*, **moved, moving**; *noun, plural* **moves.**

movement **1.** The act of moving: *A fan causes **movement** of air in a room.* **2.** A group of moving parts that make something work: *The **movement** of a watch turns the hands.* **3.** The actions of a group of people to reach some goal: *the civil rights **movement**.* **4.** A tendency or trend: *a **movement** toward reform in the school system.* **5.** A part of a long musical piece, such as a symphony: *The orchestra rehearsed the first **movement** several times.* **move·ment** (müv'mənt) *noun, plural* **movements.**

mover A person or company whose job is to move people's furniture and other things from one house or office to another. **mov·er** (mü'vər) *noun, plural* **movers.**

movie **1.** A series of pictures on a film that is projected onto a screen; *motion picture.* **2. movies.** The showing of a motion picture: *I went to the **movies** last weekend.* **3.** The industry of making movies: *They are studying acting in the hope of becoming successful in **movies**.* **mov·ie** (mü'vē) *noun, plural* **movies.**

moving **1.** That moves or is able to move: *It's hard to hit a **moving** target.* **2.** Causing or producing action or motion: *The mayor was a **moving** force behind the new law.* **3.** Affecting the emotions; touching: *The actor's **moving** performance left the audience amazed.* **mov·ing** (mü'ving) *adjective.*

mow To cut grass, grain, or hay with a sharp blade or machine. *Caretakers of the property mow the lawns regularly.* **mow** (mō) *verb*, **mowed, mowed** or **mown, mowing.**

mower A device or person that mows. Look up **lawn mower** for more information. **mow·er** (mō'ər) *noun, plural* **mowers.**

mown Past participle of **mow.**

Another word that sounds like this is **moan.**
mown (mōn) *verb.*

Mozambique A country in southeastern Africa. **Mo·zam·bique** (mō'zəm bēk') *noun.*

mpg or **m.p.g.** An abbreviation for **miles per gallon.**

mph or **m.p.h.** An abbreviation for **miles per hour.**

Mr. The abbreviation for **Mister**, used before a man's name: *"Dear **Mr.** Andrews," I wrote.* **Mr.** (mistər) *plural* **Messrs.**

Mrs. A title used before the name of a married woman or a widow: ***Mrs.** Whitney was my kindergarten teacher.* **Mrs.** (misiz) *plural* **Mmes.**

Ms. A title used before a woman's name: ***Ms.** Simpson is the school principal.* **Ms.** (miz) *plural* **Mss.** or **Mses.**

MS Postal abbreviation for **Mississippi.**

Mt. An abbreviation for **Mount** or **Mountain.**

MT Postal abbreviation for **Montana.**

much Great in amount or degree: *I don't have **much** money left after buying that expensive gift. We had too **much** rain this week. Adjective.* ○ **1.** To a great degree; very: *I was very **much** upset when I lost my keys.* **2.** Just about; nearly: *They feel **much** the same as you do. Adverb.* ○ A great amount: ***Much** has been written about the Civil War. Noun.* **much** (much) *adjective*, **more, most**; *adverb*, **more, most**; *noun.*

mucilage A sticky substance made from plants; glue. **mu·ci·lage** (mü'sə lij) *noun, plural* **mucilages.**

mucus A slimy fluid that coats and protects the inside of the mouth, nose, throat, and other parts of the body. **mu·cus** (mükəs) *noun.*

mud Soft, wet, sticky earth or dirt: *We tracked **mud** into the house after walking through the wet streets.* **mud** (mud) *noun.*

muddle A confused condition; mess: *My school papers are in a **muddle**. Noun.* ○ **1.** To cause to be in a confused condition; mix up: *The two speakers **muddled** the issues in their debate.* **2.** To make a mess of; do in a bad or clumsy way: *We **muddled** the job of straightening up the files. Verb.* **mud·dle** (mud'əl) *noun, plural* **muddles**; *verb*, **muddled, muddling.**

muddy Covered with mud. *Adjective.* ○ **1.** To cover with mud: *The children were mud-*

died with dirt from the yard. **2.** To make vague or unclear: *If you keep interrupting you will* **muddy** *my train of thought. Verb.*
mud·dy (mud′ē) *adjective,* **muddier, muddiest;** *verb,* **muddied, muddying.**

muff A roll of fur made so a person can put one hand in each end. Muffs keep the hands warm.
muff (muf) *noun, plural* **muffs.**

muffin A small, cup-shaped cake or bread.
muf·fin (muf′in) *noun, plural* **muffins.**

muffle **1.** To soften the sound that something makes: *The carpet in the hallway* **muffled** *our footsteps.* **2.** To wrap or cover so as to soften the sound or protect: *I* **muffled** *my face against the cold wind.* **muf·fle** (muf′əl) *verb,* **muffled, muffling.**

muffler **1.** A warm scarf for wrapping around the neck in cold weather. **2.** A device that reduces the noise made by an engine. Cars have mufflers.
muf·fler (muf′lər) *noun, plural* **mufflers.**

mug A large drinking cup with a handle. Mugs are often made of pottery or metal. *Noun.*
○ To attack and rob someone. *Verb.*
mug (mug) *noun, plural* **mugs;** *verb* **mugged, mugging.**

muggy Warm and damp: *It was a muggy day with no breeze.* **mug·gy** (mug′ē) *adjective,* **muggier, muggiest.**

Muhammad An Arab religious leader who founded Islam. He was born around A.D. 570 and died in 632.
Mu·ham·mad (mů ham′əd).

mulberry A tree with sweet, dark reddish purple berries that look like blackberries and can be eaten. *The leaves of some* **mulberry** *trees are fed to silkworms.*
mul·ber·ry (mul′ber′ē) *noun, plural* **mulberries.**

mule **1.** An animal that is the offspring of a female horse and

Mules are used to carry and pull things.

a male donkey. A mule is as large as a horse, but it has longer ears and a tail like a donkey. **2.** A stubborn person. **mule** (mūl) *noun, plural* **mules.**

multiple Having or involving many parts; made up of more than one: *I got* **multiple** *cuts and bruises when I fell off my bicycle. Adjective.*
○ A number that is the product of multiplying one number by another: *The numbers 8 and 12 are* **multiples** *of 4. Noun.*
mul·ti·ple (mul′tə pəl) *adjective; noun, plural* **multiples.**

multiplicand A number that is to be multiplied by another number. **mul·ti·pli·cand** (mul′tə pli kand′) *noun, plural* **multiplicands.**

$$\text{In} \quad 3 \times 6 = 18 \quad \text{or} \quad \begin{array}{r} 3 \\ \times 6 \\ \hline 18 \end{array}$$

3 is the **multiplicand.**

multiplication The mathematical operation of taking a number and adding it to itself a certain number of times. In the multiplication of 2 times 4, you are adding 2 sets of 4, which equals 8.
mul·ti·pli·ca·tion (mul′tə pli kā′shən) *noun.*

multiplier A number that tells how many times to multiply another number. **mul·ti·pli·er** (mul′tə plī′ər) *noun, plural* **multipliers.**

$$\text{In} \quad 3 \times 6 = 18 \quad \text{or} \quad \begin{array}{r} 3 \\ \times 6 \\ \hline 18 \end{array}$$

6 is the **multiplier.**

multiply **1.** To add a number to itself a certain number of times: *If we* **multiply** *2 times 4, we get 8.* **2.** To grow in number: *The longer you wait to ask for help, the more your problems* **multiply. mul·ti·ply** (mul′tə plī′) *verb,* **multiplied, multiplying.**

multitude A great number of people or things: *A* **multitude** *of people came to the outdoor music festival.* **mul·ti·tude** (mul′ti tüd′ or mul′ti tūd′) *noun, plural* **multitudes.**

multivitamin A vitamin compound made up of several different vitamins. It is usually in the form of a tablet. **mul·ti·vi·ta·min** (mul′ti vī′te min) *noun, plural* **multivitamins.**

PRONUNCIATION KEY:

| at | āpe | fär | câre | end | mē | it | īce | pîerce | hot | ōld | sông | fôrk |
| oil | out | up | ūse | rüle | půll | tûrn | chin | sing | shop | thin | this | |

hw in white; zh in treasure. The symbol ə stands for the unstressed vowel sound in about, taken, pencil, lemon, and circus.

487

SYNONYMS

mumble, murmur, mutter

I can't understand what you are saying when you mumble. The brook murmured softly as it flowed through the forest. The cook was muttering a list of ingredients to himself in the kitchen.

mumble To speak low and unclearly, as with the mouth partly closed: *The shy student mumbled the answer.* **mum·ble** (mum′bəl) *verb,* **mumbled, mumbling.** —**mumbler** *noun.*

mummy A dead body that has been wrapped in cloth and specially treated to preserve it. Some ancient Egyptian mummies are over 3,000 years old. **mum·my** (mum′ē) *noun, plural* **mummies.**

mumps A disease that causes the glands at the sides of the face to become swollen and sore. The mumps spreads from person to person. It is caused by a virus. The word "mumps" can be used with a singular or plural verb. **mumps** (mumps) *noun.*

munch To chew something in a noisy way: *The rabbits munched carrots and lettuce.* **munch** (munch) *verb,* **munched, munching.**

municipal Having to do with the government and affairs of a city or town: *a municipal election.* **mu·ni·ci·pal** (mū nis′ə pəl) *adjective.*

mural A picture painted on a wall or ceiling. A mural usually covers most of a wall. **mu·ral** (myur′əl) *noun, plural* **murals.**

murder The deliberate and unlawful killing of a person. *Noun.*
○ To kill a person deliberately and unlawfully. *Verb.* **mur·der** (mûr′dər) *noun, plural* **murders;** *verb,* **murdered, murdering.**

murky Dark and gloomy: *We couldn't see beneath the surface of the murky water in the pond.* **murk·y** (mûr′kē) *adjective,* **murkier, murkiest.**

murmur A low, soft sound: *We heard the murmur of the brook. When in the library I always speak in a murmur. Noun.*
○ To make or say with a low, soft sound: *I heard you murmur in your sleep. Verb.* **mur·mur** (mûr′mər) *noun, plural* **murmurs;** *verb,* **murmured, murmuring.**

muscle 1. A tissue in the body that is made of strong fibers. Muscles can be tightened or relaxed to make the body move. Most muscles, like those that move our arms and legs, are controlled by us. Other muscles, like those that make the heart beat, work by themselves. 2. A bundle of this tissue that moves a particular part of the body: *The biceps muscle is tightened to move the arm.* 3. Strength: *We'll need some muscle to move that piano.* Another word that sounds like this is **mussel.** **mus·cle** (mus′əl) *noun, plural* **muscles.**

WORD HISTORY

The word **muscle** comes from the Latin word meaning "little mouse." Muscles under the skin reminded the Romans of little mice.

---

mummy

Mummies have been found in many parts of the world, but best known are those from ancient Egypt.

A portrait of the person's face appeared on the outside of the mummy case.

The outside mummy case was often made of wood.

The lid and sides of the mummy cases were painted with pictures and hieroglyphic writing.

Writings often give the name and rank of the dead person.

Mummies were often buried facing east toward the rising sun.

The mummy inside is wrapped in as many as 20 layers of linen.

Mummy cases of high-ranking people were sometimes made of solid gold.

muscular **1.** Having strong or well-developed muscles: *My arms were **muscular** after a summer of working on the farm.* **2.** Having to do with muscle: *The pain in my leg is from a **muscular** strain.* **mus·cu·lar** (mus′kyə lər) *adjective*.

muse To think long and quietly: *My grandfather was **musing** about his childhood.* **muse** (mūz) *verb*, **mused**, **musing**.

Museums **are entertaining places to visit.**

museum A building where objects of art, science, or history are kept and displayed for people to see. **mu·se·um** (mū zē′əm) *noun, plural* **museums**.

mush **1.** A kind of porridge made by boiling corn-meal in water or milk. **2.** Any soft, thick mass: *An increase in temperature turned the snow into **mush**.* **mush** (mush) *noun*.

Mushrooms **are used in cooking in many different ways.**

mushroom A fast-growing fungus that is shaped like a small umbrella. Some mushrooms can be eaten, but others are poisonous. *Noun*.
○ To grow or appear suddenly and quickly: *New office buildings **mushroomed** all over the city. Verb.*
mush·room (mush′rüm′ or mush′rùm′) *noun, plural* **mushrooms**; *verb*, **mushroomed**, **mushrooming**.

music **1.** A pleasing combination of sounds. **2.** The art of creating a pleasing combination of sounds.

3. A musical composition: *Does the pianist know the **music** to that song?* **4.** The written or printed signs that tell a person what sounds are used for a musical composition: *Can you read **music**?* **mu·sic** (mū′zik) *noun*.

musical Having to do with or producing music: *The trombone is a **musical** instrument. Adjective.*
○ A play that has songs and dancing in it. *Noun.*
mu·si·cal (mū′zi kəl) *adjective; noun, plural* **musicals**. — **musically** *adverb*.

music box A box containing a device that plays music mechanically. Many music boxes have to be wound in order to play.

musician A person who is skilled in playing a musical instrument, composing music, or singing. **mu·si·cian** (mū zish′ən) *noun, plural* **musicians**.

This musician **is playing a saxophone.**

musk **1.** A substance with a strong odor, produced by a certain male deer and used to make perfume. **2.** The odor of this substance. **musk** (musk) *noun*.

musket A gun with a long barrel like a rifle, used in warfare before modern rifles were invented. **mus·ket** (mus′kit) *noun, plural* **muskets**.

musketeer A soldier armed with a musket. **mus·ket·eer** (mus′ki tîr′) *noun, plural* **musketeers**.

muskmelon A large, juicy fruit; a type of melon. Cantaloupes are muskmelons. **musk·mel·on** (musk′mel′ən) *noun, plural* **muskmelons**.

musk ox A shaggy, dark brown animal that chews its cud. Musk oxen have horns that lie flat over the forehead and sides of the head and curve upward at the tips. They live in northern Canada and Greenland. **musk ox** (musk).

muskrat A small North American animal that looks like a large rat. Muskrats live in and near the water. A muskrat has webbed back feet and a flat tail that help it to swim. **mus·krat** (muskrat) *noun, plural* **muskrat** *or* **muskrats**.

PRONUNCIATION KEY:

at	āpe	fär	câre	end	mē	it	īce	pierce	hot	ōld	sông	fôrk
oil	out	up	ūse	rüle	pùll	tûrn	chin	sing	shop	thin	this

hw in white; zh in treasure. The symbol ə stands for the unstressed vowel sound in about, taken, pencil, lemon, and circus.

489

Muslim Having to do with Islam, the religion founded by Muhammad. *Adjective.*
○ A person who follows the religion founded by Muhammad. *Noun.* **Mus•lim** (muz′lim) *adjective; noun, plural* **Muslims.**

muslin A cotton cloth used to make sheets and clothing. **mus•lin** (muz′lin) *noun.*

muss To make untidy; mess: *The wind and rain mussed their hair.* **muss** (mus) *verb,* **mussed, mussing.**

mussel An animal that looks like a clam. Saltwater mussels are mollusks that have bluish black shells and are used as food. The shells of freshwater mussels are used to make buttons and jewelry.
Another word that sounds like this is **muscle.**
mus•sel (musəl) *noun, plural* **mussels.**

must An auxiliary verb used to express the following meanings: **1.** To be obliged to; have to: *I must return this book to the library.* **2.** To be forced or required to: *People must eat to live.* **3.** To be likely to: *They must have forgotten about the meeting.* **must** (must) *verb.*

mustache or **moustache** Hair that grows above the upper lip. *My grandfather has a big mustache that curls up at each end.* **mus•tache** (mus′tash *or* mə stash′) *noun, plural* **mustaches.**

mustang A wild horse that lives on the American plains; bronco. **mus•tang** (mus′tang) *noun, plural* **mustangs.**

mustard A sharp-tasting yellow paste or powder that is made from the seeds of a plant and is used to flavor food. The mustard plant has bunches of small, yellow flowers. **mus•tard** (mustərd) *noun, plural* **mustards.**

muster **1.** To bring or call together; assemble: *The captain mustered the troops for the march.* **2.** To gather from within oneself: *The timid child mustered up the courage to read aloud in class. Verb.*
○ An assembled group, as of military units. *Noun.*
mus•ter (mus′tər) *verb,* **mustered, mustering;** *noun, plural* **musters.**

mustn't Shortened form of "must not." **must•n't** (mus′ənt) *contraction.*

musty Having a stale or moldy smell or taste, often because of dampness or decay: *After the flood, the house smelled musty.* **must•y** (mus′tē) *adjective,* **mustier, mustiest.**

mutant A plant or animal that has genetic characteristics different from its parents and can pass these characteristics along to its own offspring. **mu•tant** (mū′tənt) *noun, plural* **mutants.**

mute **1.** Not able to speak because of an illness, birth defect, or injury. **2.** Not willing to speak; silent: *The student stood mute and would not answer the principal's questions.* **3.** Not pronounced: *The "b" in "lamb" is mute. Adjective.*
○ **1.** A person who cannot speak. **2.** A device put on a musical instrument to soften the tone. Mutes are usually used with trumpets and other brass instruments. *Noun.*
mute (mūt) *adjective; noun, plural* **mutes.**

mutilate To damage severely, as by tearing or ripping: *The books had been mutilated and were now tattered and torn.* **mu•ti•late** (mū′tə lāt) *verb,* **mutilated, mutilating. —mutilation** *noun.*

mutineer A person who takes part in a mutiny: *The mutineers tied up their captain and seized control of the ship.* **mu•tin•eer** (mūt′ə nîr′) *noun, plural* **mutineers.**

mutiny An open rebellion against authority: *The sailors who took part in the mutiny were punished. Noun.*
○ To take part in an open rebellion: *The crew mutinied against their captain. Verb.*
mu•tin•y (mūt′ən ē) *noun, plural* **mutinies;** *verb,* **mutinied, mutinying.**

mutt A dog, especially one that is a mixture of breeds; a mongrel. **mutt** (mut) *noun, plural* **mutts.**

mutter To speak in a low, unclear way with the mouth almost closed: *I muttered to myself that I would be late if I didn't hurry. Verb.*
○ Word spoken in a low, unclear way: *There was a mutter of disapproval from the audience at the speaker's remarks. Noun.*
mut•ter (mut′ər) *verb,* **muttered, muttering;** *noun.*

mutton Meat from an adult sheep. **mut•ton** (mut′ən) *noun.*

mutual Given and received equally; shared: *My friend and I have a mutual interest in sports.* **mu•tu•al** (mū′chü əl) *adjective.* **—mutually** *adverb.*

muzzle **1.** The part of the head of an animal made up of the nose, mouth, and jaws: *A collie has a long muzzle.* **2.** A set of straps that fit over the muzzle of an animal to keep it from biting. **3.** The opening at the front end of a gun. The bullet comes out through the muzzle. *Noun.*

○ To put a muzzle on an animal: *The dog had to be muzzled because it bites. Verb.*
muz·zle (muz′əl) *noun, plural* **muzzles**; *verb,* **muzzled, muzzling.**

my Of, belonging to, or done by me: *my pencil; my opinion; my essay.* **my** (mī) *adjective.*

Myanmar A country in southeast Asia. It was formerly called **Burma. Myan·mar** (myän′mär′) *noun.*

myrtle 1. An evergreen tree with white or pink flowers and shiny leaves. 2. A vine that grows along the ground and has shiny leaves and blue, pink, or white flowers. **myrt·le** (mûr′təl) *noun, plural* **myrtles.**

myself 1. My own self: *I cut myself. I can cook for myself. I myself will do the job.* 2. My usual, normal, or true self: *I haven't been myself since the accident.* **my·self** (mī self′) *pronoun.*

mysterious Very hard or impossible to explain or understand; full of mystery: *We heard mysterious sounds from the deserted house.* **mys·te·ri·ous** (mi stîr′ē əs) *adjective.* —**mysteriously** *adverb.*

mystery 1. Something that is not or cannot be known, explained, or understood: *The identity of the poem's author is a mystery.* 2. A book, play, or other story about a crime that is puzzling.

mys·ter·y (mis′tə rē) *noun, plural* **mysteries.**

mystify To confuse or puzzle; bewilder: *The audience was mystified by the magician's tricks.* **mys·ti·fy** (mis′tə fī′) *verb,* **mystified, mystifying.**

myth 1. A story that tells about a belief of a group of people. Myths often tell about gods and heroes. They were made up as an explanation for something that happens in nature or for a custom: *Long ago people explained thunder by the myth that it was the noise made by the chariot of the god Thor as he rode across the skies.* 2. A person or thing that is not real or true: *The idea that a person gets warts from touching a frog is a myth.* **myth** (mith) *noun, plural* **myths.**

mythical Having to do with myths: *A unicorn is a mythical creature. Apollo was a mythical god.* **myth·i·cal** (mith′i kəl) *adjective.*

mythology A group or collection of myths and legends: *All the myths that were told and written in ancient Greece are known as Greek mythology.* **my·thol·og·y** (mi thol′ə jē) *noun, plural* **mythologies.**

PRONUNCIATION KEY:

| at | āpe | fär | câre | end | mē | it | īce | pierce | hot | ōld | sông | fôrk |
| oil | out | up | ūse | rüle | pull | tûrn | chin | sing | shop | thin | this | |

hw in white; zh in treasure. The symbol ə stands for the unstressed vowel sound in about, taken, pencil, lemon, and circus.

491

SPELLING HINTS

The letter N has one sound in English, which is made in several ways. It is commonly made by:

n as in words such as banana, nose and garden;

nn as in dinner;

and more rarely by:

kn as in kneel;

gn as in gnat, gnome, and gnu;

pn in some words of Greek origin such as pneumonia.

The letter N also combines with G to form the ng sound in words such as long and sing. This sound of N can also be made by nk in words such as pink and think or by ngue in words such as tongue.

---

n, N The fourteenth letter of the alphabet. **n, N** (en) *noun, plural* **n's, N's.**

N or N. An abbreviation for **north** or **northern.**

nag¹ To annoy with scolding and complaining: *My parents* ***nag*** *me about my clothes.* **nag** (nag) *verb,* **nagged, nagging.**

nag² A horse, especially a worn-out old horse: *A tired* ***nag*** *pulled the wagon.* **nag** (nag) *noun, plural* **nags.**

nail 1. A thin piece of metal that is pointed at one end and flat at the other. A nail is hammered into pieces of wood to hold them together. 2. The thin, hard layer of tough material at the end of a finger or toe. *Noun.*

○ To fasten with a nail or nails: *The carpenter* ***nailed*** *pieces of wood together to make a bookcase. Will you* ***nail*** *that picture to the wall? Verb.* **nail** (nāl) *noun, plural* **nails;** *verb,* **nailed, nailing.**

naked 1. Without clothing or covering of any kind: *A person is* ***naked*** *when taking a bath or shower. The tree was* ***naked*** *after the caterpillars ate every leaf on it.* 2. Without anything added: *I'm telling you the* ***naked*** *truth.* 3. Without the help of any device: *You don't need a telescope; you can see that star with the* ***naked*** *eye.* **na·ked** (nā′kid) *adjective.*

name 1. The word or words by which a person,

animal, place, or thing is known: *The new baby's* ***name*** *is Taylor. Salmon is the* ***name*** *of a kind of fish. Denver is the* ***name*** *of a city.* 2. A bad or insulting word or words used to refer to someone or something: *The bully called everyone* ***names.*** 3. Reputation or character: *Don't ruin your good* ***name*** *by telling lies. Noun.*

○ 1. To give a name or names to: *The couple* ***named*** *their first child Leslie.* 2. To speak of; mention: *The newspaper article* ***named*** *the topics of the coming debate.* ***Name*** *some of your favorite songs.* 3. To appoint or choose: *The teacher* ***named*** *three students to hand out books. Verb.*

name (nām) *noun, plural* **names;** *verb,* **named, naming.**

namely In other words: *We visited two southern states,* ***namely*** *Mississippi and Louisiana.* **name·ly** (nām′lē) *adverb.*

nanny A person who works for a family taking care of their young child or children. **nan·ny** (nan′ē) *noun, plural* **nannies.**

nap¹ A short sleep: *The baby is taking a* ***nap.*** *Noun.*

○ 1. To sleep for a short while: *Dad* ***napped*** *in his easy chair.* 2. To be not prepared or ready: *The storm caught us* ***napping.*** *Verb.*

nap (nap) *noun, plural* **naps;** *verb,* **napped, napping.**

nap² The soft, fuzzy surface of cloth: *This sweater is so old that all the nap has worn off.* **nap** (nap) *noun.*

napkin A piece of cloth or paper used at meals to protect clothing and wipe the lips and hands. **nap•kin** (nap′kin) *noun, plural* **napkins.**

narcissus A plant that has yellow or white flowers in the spring and long, thin leaves. The daffodil is a kind of narcissus. **nar•cis•sus** (när sis′əs) *noun, plural* **narcissuses.**

narcotic A drug that dulls the senses, produces sleep, and eases pain when used in small doses. People can become addicted to narcotics. **nar•cot•ic** (när kot′ik) *noun, plural* **narcotics.**

narrate To tell or relate: *The reporter narrated an interesting story of travels in Africa.* **nar•rate** (nar′āt *or* na rāt′) *verb,* **narrated, narrating.**

narrative A story or report on something that happened: *The writer gave a long narrative on her travels. Noun.*
○ Telling a story: *a narrative poem. Adjective.*
nar•ra•tive (nar′ə tiv) *noun, plural* **narratives;** *adjective.*

narrator A person who tells a story: *The narrator of the film started by explaining the historical background of the story.* **nar•ra•tor** (na′rā tər *or* na′rā tər) *noun, plural* **narrators.**

narrow **1.** Not wide or broad: *The deer jumped across the narrow stream.* **2.** Limited or small: *The small library had only a narrow choice of books. People with narrow minds don't like new ideas.* **3.** Barely successful; close: *The firefighter saved the child, but they had a narrow escape. Adjective.*
○ To make or become narrow: *The workers narrowed the sidewalk when the street was made wider. The river narrows at the bridge. Verb.*
○ **narrows.** The narrow part of a body of water,

This building's narrow shape fits the land upon which it was built.

especially one that connects two larger bodies of water: *a bridge across the narrows. Noun.*
nar•row (nar′ō) *adjective,* **narrower, narrowest;** *verb,* **narrowed, narrowing;** *plural noun.*

NASA An abbreviation for **National Aeronautics and Space Administration. NASA** (nas′ə)

nasal **1.** Having to do with the nose: *A cold usually stuffs up the nasal passages and makes it hard to breathe through the nose.* **2.** Spoken by releasing the breath through the nose rather than the mouth. The "m" sound is nasal. **na•sal** (nā′zəl) *adjective.*

nasturtium A plant that has yellow, orange, or red flowers. Nasturtiums have sharp-tasting leaves and petals that are sometimes used in salads. The seeds are used in pickles. **nas•tur•tium** (nə stûr′shəm) *noun, plural* **nasturtiums.**

nasty **1.** Resulting from hate or spite; mean: *That nasty rumor is not true.* **2.** Disagreeable or unpleasant: *The weather today is cold and nasty. The filthy canal had a nasty smell.* **3.** Harmful or severe: *I took a nasty fall while skiing.* **nas•ty** (nas′tē) *adjective,* **nastier, nastiest. —nastiness,** *noun.*

nation **1.** A group of people living in a particular area under one government, usually sharing the same history, culture, and language: *Presidents often speak to the nation on television.* **2.** A particular land where such a people lives; country: *Canada is a nation.* **na•tion** (nā′shən) *noun, plural* **nations.**

SYNONYMS

nation, country, land, state
How many new nations have been created in Africa since 1960? All the industrialized countries supported the plan to aid poorer countries. The President is the highest elected official in the land. Those citizens belong to the state of France.

---

national **1.** Having to do with a land united under one government: *The national government of the United States is headed by the president.* **2.** Characteristic of or having to do with the people of a nation: *Their national costume is very colorful.* **3.** Covering or relating to an entire land: *The national road system is very impressive.*

PRONUNCIATION KEY:

| at | āpe | fär | câre | end | mē | it | īce | pierce | hot | ōld | sông | fôrk |
| oil | out | up | ūse | rüle | pull | tûrn | chin | sing | shop | thin | this | |

hw in white; zh in treasure. The symbol ə stands for the unstressed vowel sound in about, taken, pencil, lemon, and circus.

493

Adjective.

○ A citizen of a country: *There were many American* **nationals** *living in Japan at the time. Noun.*

na·tion·al (nash′ə nəl) *adjective*; *noun, plural* **nationals.** —**nationally** *adverb.*

national anthem A special song that expresses love for one's country. People sing their national anthem at public events as a way of honoring the country and showing patriotism.

nationalism A feeling of deep loyalty to one's nation. **na·tion·al·ism** (nash′ə nə liz′əm) *noun.* —**nationalist** *noun* —**nationalistic** *adjective.*

nationality **1.** The fact or condition of belonging to a particular nation: *That painter's* **nationality** *is French.* **2.** A group of people who share the same language, culture, and history: *People of many* **nationalities** *work at the United Nations.* **na·tion·al·i·ty** (nash′ə nal′i tē) *noun, plural* **nationalities.**

native **1.** A person who was born in a particular country or place: *One of my classmates is a* **native** *of Germany. The mayor is a* **native** *of this town.* **2.** One of the original people, animals, or plants of a region or country: *The* **natives** *of Australia are called Aborigines. Noun.*

○ **1.** Belonging to a person by birth: *My grandparents'* **native** *language is Italian.* **2.** Originally living or growing in a region or country: *Raccoons are* **native** *to America. Adjective.*

na·tive (nā′tiv) *noun, plural* **natives**; *adjective.*

Native American A member of any of the peoples, except the Inuit, who have lived in North and South America since long before European settlers arrived; American Indian.

NATO An alliance of nations, among them the United States, Britain, Germany, France, and Italy. Each nation helps to defend the others in time of need. NATO stands for **North Atlantic Treaty Organization. NATO** (nā′tō) *noun.*

natural **1.** Found in nature; not made by people; not artificial: *Natural rock formations overlook the river.* **2.** Possessed or being from birth; not resulting from teaching or training: *a* **natural** *athlete. Is your musical talent* **natural**, *or did you take lessons? The new sergeant was a* **natural** *leader.* **3.** Happening in the normal course of things: *My grandparents both died of* **natural** *causes when they were very old.* **4.** Closely fol-

lowing nature; lifelike: *This painting of the garden is very* **natural.** **5.** Not pretending to feel what one does not; sincere: *a* **natural** *smile. Adjective.*

○ A person who is good at something because of a special talent or ability: *a* **natural** *at basketball. Noun.*

nat·u·ral (nach′ər əl) *adjective*; *noun, plural* **naturals.**

natural gas A gas that is found beneath the surface of the earth. Natural gas burns very easily and is used for cooking and heating.

natural history The study of objects and living things in nature, including plants, animals, and minerals.

naturalist A person who specializes in the study of things in nature, especially animals and plants. **nat·u·ral·ist** (nach′ər ə list) *noun, plural* **naturalists.**

naturalize To make a citizen of someone who was born in another country: *After living in the United States for several years, the immigrants passed a test and were* **naturalized. nat·u·ral·ize** (nach′ər ə līz′) *verb,* **naturalized, naturalizing.**

naturally **1.** As would be expected; of course: *Naturally I'll help you.* **2.** By nature: *I sleep late* **naturally.** **3.** In a normal manner: *I was too nervous to act* **naturally. nat·u·ral·ly** (nach′ər ə lē) *adverb.*

natural resources Materials found in nature that are useful or necessary for life. Water, forests, and minerals are natural resources.

There is an enormous amount of beauty to be found in nature.

nature **1.** The basic character and quality of a person or thing: *The doctor has a kindly* **nature.** *It is the* **nature** *of fire to be hot.* **2.** The physical universe; all the things that are not made by people: *The mountains, the woods, and the oceans are parts of nature.* **3.** Sort or kind; variety: *I enjoy camping, hiking, and things of that nature.* **na·ture** (nā′chər) *noun, plural* **natures.**

naught **1.** Nothing: *All our plans came to naught.* **2.** Zero: *Five plus naught equals five.* **naught** (nôt) *noun.*

naughty Behaving badly; mischievous or disobedient: *The teacher sent the naughty boy out of the classroom.* **naugh·ty** (nô′tē) *adjective,* **naughtier, naughtiest.** —**naughtily** *adverb* —**naughtiness** *noun.*

nausea A sick feeling in the stomach: *I take special pills to prevent nausea when I go on a boat.* **nau·sea** (nô′zē ə *or* nô′shə) *noun.*

nauseated Feeling or suffering from nausea: *The long car trip made me nauseated.* **nau·se·at·ed** (nô′zē ā′tid *or* nô′shē ā′tid) *adjective.*

nautical Having to do with ships, sailors, or navigation: *A shop at the harbor sells nautical equipment.* **nau·ti·cal** (nô′ti kəl) *adjective.*

nautical mile A measurement of distance used by sailors. It is equal to about 6,076 feet.

Navajo or **Navaho** A member of a tribe of Native Americans of the southwest United States. **Na·va·jo** (nav′ə hō′) *noun, plural* **Navajo, Navajos,** *or* **Navajoes.**

naval **1.** Having to do with a navy: *Naval supplies are stored near the docks.* **2.** Having a navy: *England was once the greatest naval power in the world.* Another word that sounds like this is **navel.** **na·val** (nā′vəl) *adjective.*

navel A round scar in the middle of a person's abdomen. The navel results when the cord that connected a newborn baby to its mother is cut or falls off. **na·vel** (nā′vəl) *noun, plural* **navels.**

navigate 1. To sail, steer, or direct the course of: *They navigated the ship through the storm.*

It takes skill and experience to navigate a sailboat.

2. To sail on or across: *Ships can navigate the Atlantic in under a week.* **nav·i·gate** (nav′i gāt′) *verb,* **navigated, navigating.**

navigation **1.** The act of navigating a ship or aircraft: *The pilot found navigation difficult in the high winds.* **2.** The art or science of figuring out the position and course of boats, ships, and aircraft: *Knowing the position of the stars and the sun is useful in navigation.* **nav·i·ga·tion** (nav′i gā′shən) *noun.*

navigator **1.** A person on a boat, ship, or aircraft who is in charge of determining or steering a course. **2.** A person who explores by ship: *The navigator Ferdinand Magellan organized the first voyage around the world.* **nav·i·ga·tor** (nav′i gā′tər) *noun, plural* **navigators.**

navy **1.** All the warships of a country: *The United States has one of the most powerful navies in the world.* **2.** The large, organized group of sailors who are trained to fight at sea. The word *navy* is often capitalized: *Our neighbor is a lieutenant in the Navy.* **3.** A very dark blue color; navy blue. *Noun.*
  ○ Very dark blue. *Adjective.*
na·vy (nā′vē) *noun, plural* **navies;** *adjective.*

navy blue A very dark blue color.

nay No: *"Nay," said the knight, "I do not know the way to Westwood Castle." Adverb.* This adverb was once common, but is not used often today.
  ○ A vote or voter against: *A narrow majority of nays defeated the proposal. Noun.*
Another word that sounds like this is **neigh.**
nay (nā) *adverb; noun, plural* **nays.**

Nazi A member of the political party led by Adolph Hitler that controlled Germany from 1933 to 1945, before and during World War II. **Na·zi** (nät′sē *or* nat′sē) *noun, plural* **Nazis.**

NB Postal abbreviation for **New Brunswick.**

N.B. An abbreviation for **New Brunswick.**

NC Postal abbreviation for **North Carolina.**

N.C. An abbreviation for **North Carolina.**

ND Postal abbreviation for **North Dakota.**

N. Dak. An abbreviation for **North Dakota.**

NE Postal abbreviation for **Nebraska.**

NE or **N.E.** An abbreviation for **northeast.**

near **1.** Not far or distant: *Night is drawing near.* **2.** Almost; nearly: *We were near exhausted when*

PRONUNCIATION KEY:

at	āpe	fär	câre	end	mē	it	īce	pierce	hot	ōld	sông	fôrk
oil	out	up	ūse	rüle	pull	tùrn	chin	sing	shop	thin	this	

hw in white; zh in treasure. The symbol ə stands for the unstressed vowel sound in about, taken, pencil, lemon, and circus.

495

we got home. *Adverb.*

○ **1.** Not far or distant: *Will I see you in the near future?* **2.** Done or missed by only a small amount; narrow: *The people in that building had a near escape from the fire.* **3.** Close in feeling or association: *You can rely on help from those who are near to you.* **4.** Being the closer of two: *The telephone is on the near side of the street. Adjective.*

○ Close to or by: *My grandparents live near the beach. Preposition.*

○ To come or draw near: *The airplane neared the landing field. The animals fled as the hunters neared. Verb.*

near (nîr) *adverb,* **nearer, nearest;** *adjective,* **nearer, nearest;** *preposition; verb,* **neared, nearing.**

SYNONYMS

near, close, immediate, nearby

The subway is near my house. The bookstore is close to my school. There is a post office in the immediate vicinity. The nearby convenience store carries a lot of handy things.

nearby A short distance away; not far off: *My parents work in a nearby town. My neighbor and I go to school nearby.* **near·by** (nîr′bī′) *adjective; adverb.*

nearly All but; almost: *I nearly forgot your birthday. It is nearly midnight.* **near·ly** (nîr′lē) *adverb.*

nearsighted Able to see objects that are close by more clearly than faraway ones: *A nearsighted person should not drive a car without wearing eyeglasses.* **near·sight·ed** (nîr′sī′tid) *adjective.*

neat **1.** Clean and orderly; tidy: *You have neat handwriting.* **2.** Having or showing care for keeping things in order: *Her roommate is neater than she is.* **3.** Done in a clever way: *We learned a neat trick in school today.* **4.** Wonderful or fine: *I had a neat time at the party.* **neat** (nēt) *adjective,* **neater, neatest.** —**neatly** *adverb.*

Neb. or **Nebr.** An abbreviation for Nebraska.

Nebraska A state in the central United States. Its capital is Lincoln. **Ne·bras·ka** (nə bras′kə) *noun.*

WORD HISTORY

Nebraska was an Indian name for the Platte River. It means "flat water." The river's name was changed, but the Indian name was kept for the state.

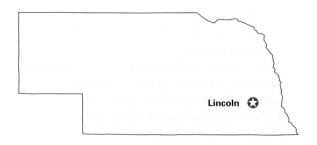

Nebraska
U. S. Postal Abbreviation: **NE**
Capital: **Lincoln**
Population: **1,594,000**
Area: **77,227 sq. mi./200,017 sq. km**
State Nickname: **Cornhusker State**
State Bird: **Western Meadowlark**
State Flower: **Goldenrod**

nebula A huge, bright cloud of gas and dust that can be found in space between the stars. **neb·u·la** (neb′yə lə) *noun, plural* **nebulas** or **nebulae** (neb′yə lē′ *or* neb′yə lī′).

necessarily As a certain result: *Tall people are not necessarily good basketball players.* **nec·es·sar·i·ly** (nes′ə ser′ə lē) *adverb.*

necessary **1.** That must be had or done; needed; required: *Proper food is necessary for good health.* **2.** That cannot be avoided; certain: *Low grades were a necessary result of the student's poor work. Adjective.*

○ Something that cannot be done without; necessity; essential: *We can't go on without necessaries like fresh water. Noun.*

nec·es·sar·y (nes′ə ser′ē) *adjective; noun, plural* **necessaries.**

necessity **1.** Something that is needed; requirement: *Food, clothing, and shelter are the necessities of life.* **2.** The fact of being necessary: *I realize the necessity of finishing school if I want to be a doctor.* **ne·ces·si·ty** (ni ses′i tē) *noun, plural* **necessities.**

Their long necks allow these tall birds to bend or reach for food.

neck **1.** The part of the body of a person or animal that connects the head and the shoulders. **2.** The part of a piece of clothing that fits around the neck: *I like to leave the neck of my shirt open in hot weather.* **3.** A narrow part that is like a neck in shape or position: *This bottle has a stopper that fits into its neck. We have a summer cottage on a little neck of land that juts out into the lake.* **neck** (nek) *noun, plural* **necks**.

neckerchief A scarf or kerchief that is worn around the neck. **neck·er·chief** (nek′ər chif′) *noun, plural* **neckerchiefs**.

necklace A string of beads or other piece of jewelry that is worn around the neck for decoration. **neck·lace** (nek′lis) *noun, plural* **necklaces**.

More than one necklace can be worn at a time.

necktie A piece of cloth that is worn around the neck by putting it under a shirt collar and knotting it in front. A man wearing a suit usually wears a necktie. **neck·tie** (nek′tī′) *noun, plural* **neckties**.

nectar The sweet liquid formed in flowers. Bees use nectar to make honey. **nec·tar** (nek′tər) *noun, plural* **nectars**.

nectarine A kind of peach that has a smooth skin. **nec·tar·ine** (nek′tə rēn′) *noun, plural* **nectarines**.

need **1.** A lack of something necessary, useful, or desired: *The team's defeat showed their need for practice.* **2.** Something that is necessary, useful, or desired: *What are the needs for our camping trip?* **3.** A necessity or obligation: *There is no need to stay.* **4.** A condition or time of trouble or want: *Thank you for helping me in my time of need after my accident.* **5.** Poverty or hardship: *They lived in need, barely having enough food.* Noun.
○ **1.** To lack or require: *I need a new coat. The town needs a library.* **2.** To have to: *Do you need to wait for them?* Verb.

Another word that sounds like this is **knead**.

need (nēd) *noun, plural* **needs**; *verb,* **needed, needing**.

needle **1.** A thin, pointed instrument with a hole in one end. It is used in sewing. The thread is passed through the hole and the needle carries the thread through the cloth. **2.** A pointer on a compass or dial: *The needle on the compass shows that north is to our right.* **3.** A sharp, thin, hollow tube that is used to put fluid into or take fluid out of the body: *The doctor stuck a needle in my arm to give me a flu shot.* **4.** A thin rod that is used in knitting: *a sweater knitted on large needles.* **5.** The thin, pointed leaves on a fir tree or pine tree: *Pine needles do not fall off when winter comes.* **6.** Anything that is thin and pointed like a needle: *We had a hard time trying to replace the needle on our old record player.* Noun.
○ To annoy or tease: *My friends needled me about my new haircut.* Verb.
nee·dle (nē′dəl) *noun, plural* **needles**; *verb,* **needled, needling**.

needless Not needed; unnecessary: *Buying a new stove would be a needless expense.* **need·less** (nēd′lis) *adjective.* —**needlessly** *adverb.*

needlework Work, such as sewing or embroidery, that is done with a needle. **nee·dle·work** (nē′dəl wûrk′) *noun.*

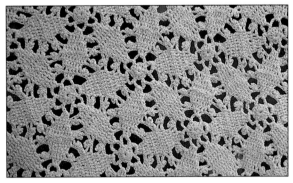

Fine needlework is often very delicate.

needn't Shortened form of "need not": *You needn't hurry because we have plenty of time.* **need·n't** (nē′dənt) *contraction.*

needy Not having enough to live on; very poor: *The church helps needy families.* **need·y** (nē′dē) *adjective,* **needier, neediest**.

negative **1.** Saying or indicating "no": *I accompa-*

PRONUNCIATION KEY:

| at | āpe | fär | câre | end | mē | it | īce | pîerce | hot | ōld | sông | fôrk |
| oil | out | up | ūse | rüle | pull | tûrn | chin | sing | shop | thin | this | |

hw in white; zh in treasure. The symbol ə stands for the unstressed vowel sound in about, taken, pencil, lemon, and circus.

497

nied my **negative** answer to the question with a **negative** shake of my head. **2.** Not helpful or constructive: *If you have a **negative** attitude toward learning French, you will never be good at it.* **3.** Less than zero: *The result of 6 minus 8 is a **negative** number.* **4.** Having one of two opposite kinds of electric charge: *Magnets have a **negative** pole at one end and a positive pole at the other.* **5.** Not showing a certain disease or condition: *The doctor knew that it was not a broken leg because the X rays were **negative**. Adjective.*
○ **1.** A photographic image that is created when film is developed. In a negative, the areas that were light in the original subject are dark and those that were dark are light. Prints can be made from a negative. **2.** A word or phrase that expresses a denial or says "no." "Not" is a negative. *Noun.*
neg·a·tive (neg′ə tiv) *adjective; noun, plural* **negatives.** —**negatively** *adverb.*

neglect **1.** To fail to give proper attention or care to: *I **neglected** my plants and they died.* **2.** To fail to do: *You **neglected** to make your bed this morning. Verb.*
○ **1.** A failure to give proper attention; lack of care: ***Neglect** of a pet may cause it to get sick.* **2.** The condition of not being cared for: *The house fell into **neglect**. Noun.*
neg·lect (ni glekt′) *verb,* **neglected, neglecting;** *noun.* —**neglectful** *adjective.*

negligent Not showing proper care or concern; careless or neglectful: *The **negligent** waiter forgot our drinks.* **neg·li·gent** (neg′li jənt) *adjective.* —**negligence** *noun.*

negotiate **1.** To talk over and arrange the terms of: *The factory owners met with the workers to **negotiate** an end to the strike.* **2.** To have a discussion in order to bring about an agreement: *The two warring countries refused to **negotiate**.* **ne·go·ti·ate** (ni gō′shē āt′) *verb,* **negotiated, negotiating.** —**negotiator** *noun.*

negotiation A discussion to try to reach an agreement: *The **negotiations** to end the war are going well.* **ne·go·ti·a·tion** (ni gō′shē ā′shən) *noun, plural* **negotiations.**

Negro A member of one of the major divisions of the human race; black. Negroes have dark skin. The native peoples of southern and central Africa are Negroes. *Noun.*
○ Of or having to do with Negroes; black. *Adjective.*
In recent times, the word *black* has replaced the word *Negro*, and in the United States, *African-American* has come to be preferred.
Ne·gro (nē′grō) *noun, plural* **Negroes;** *adjective.*

neigh The sound that a horse makes. *Noun.*
○ To make the sound of a horse. *Verb.*
Another word that sounds like this is **nay.**
neigh (nā) *noun, plural* **neighs;** *verb,* **neighed, neighing.**

neighbor **1.** A person who lives in a house or apartment next to or near one's own: *Our **neighbor** took care of our dog while we were away.* **2.** A person, place, or thing that is next to or near another: *Mexico is a **neighbor** of the United States.* **3.** A fellow human being: *Concern for our **neighbors** is important to society.* **neigh·bor** (nā′bər) *noun, plural* **neighbors.** —**neighboring** *adjective.*

WORD HISTORY

The word neighbor goes back to two Old English words that meant "near" and "a person who dwells." A person's neighbor is someone who dwells nearby.

Neighbors sometimes get together
to share in a celebration.

neighborhood **1.** A small area or district in a town or city where people live: *The **neighborhood** near the river is one of the oldest in town.* **2.** The people living in the same area or district: *The whole **neighborhood** is talking about the fire last night.* **3.** An area near something: *In the **neighborhood** of the factory it is very noisy and crowded.* **neigh·bor·hood** (nā′bər hùd′) *noun, plural* **neighborhoods.**

neighboring Located next to or nearby: *Students from several **neighboring** towns attend the high* *school.* **neigh•bor•ing** (nā′bər ing) *adjective.*

neighborly Having or showing the kindness of a good neighbor: *a neighborly offer to help.* **neigh•bor•ly** (nā′bər lē) *adjective.* —**neighborliness** *noun.*

neither 1. Not either. The word *neither* is used before the first of two or more negative choices or possibilities connected by *nor*: *When I was sick I could neither eat nor drink.* 2. Nor: *They don't want to see the movie, and neither do I. Conjunction.*

○ Not one or the other; not either: *Neither team played well. Adjective.*

○ Not the one nor the other: *I tried on two coats, but neither fit me. Pronoun.*

nei•ther (nē′thər or nī′thər) *conjunction; adjective; pronoun.*

neon A gas that has no color or odor. It makes up a very small part of the air. Neon glows when electricity passes through it. Tubes filled with neon are used in electric signs. Neon is a chemical element. **ne•on** (nē′on) *noun.*

Tubes filled with neon are used in electric signs.

WORD HISTORY

The word neon comes from the Greek word meaning "new." The gas neon was given this name late in the nineteenth century because it was at that time the newest gas was discovered.

Nepal A country in central Asia. **Ne•pal** (nə pôl′ or nə päl′) *noun.*

nephew 1. The son of one's brother or sister. 2. The son of one's brother-in-law or sister-in-law. **neph•ew** (nef′ū) *noun, plural* **nephews.**

Neptune The fourth largest planet in our solar system. It is the eighth planet in order of distance from the sun. Neptune can be seen from earth only by telescope. **Nep•tune** (nep′tün or nep′tūn) *noun.*

Neptune
Usually the second farthest planet from the Sun, because of Pluto's orbit, Neptune will be farthest until 1999. Neptune was discovered in 1846 following a calculation of where it should be found based on the movement of Uranus.
Average distance from sun: **2,795,700,000 miles**
Diameter: **30,782 miles**
Length of Day: **16 hours, 7 minutes**
Length of Year: **165 years**
Average Temperature: **-373°F**
Mass compared to Earth: **17**
Weight of 100 pounds: **119**
Atmosphere: **Hydrogen, Helium**
Number of rings: **3**
Number of satellites: **8**

nerd 1. An unattractive and socially awkward person. 2. A person who spends a lot of time with and is good at some activity: *a computer nerd.* **nerd** (nûrd) *noun, plural* **nerds.** —**nerdy** *adjective.*

nerve 1. A bundle of fibers that carries messages between the brain and spinal cord and other parts of the body. If a person touches a hot stove, the brain receives a message of pain from the nerves in the hand. The brain then sends a message through the nerves to make the hand pull away from the stove. 2. Courage or bravery: *It takes nerve to jump off a high diving board.* 3. **nerves.** The way one feels; state of mind: *It's important to have calm nerves when driving in traffic .*

• **to get on one's nerves.** To annoy or irritate one: *Their constant bragging gets on my nerves.* **nerve** (nûrv) *noun, plural* **nerves.**

nervous 1. Not able to relax; tense: *Loud noises make me nervous.* 2. Fearful or timid: *I am very nervous about taking the exam.* 3. Relating to nerves or the nervous system: *A rash may be*

PRONUNCIATION KEY:

at	āpe	fär	câre	end	mē	it	īce	pierce	hot	ōld	sông	fôrk
oil	out	up	ūse	rüle	pull	tûrn	chin	sing	shop	thin	this	

hw in white; zh in treasure. The symbol ə stands for the unstressed vowel sound in about, taken, pencil, lemon, and circus.

499

caused by a **nervous** reaction to something upsetting. **nerv·ous** (nûr′vəs) *adjective.* —**nervously** *adverb* —**nervousness** *noun.*

nervous system The system in the body that includes the brain, spinal cord, and nerves. The nervous system controls all the actions and reactions of the body.

-ness A suffix that means the "state or quality of being": *Likeness means the state of being similar; kindness means the quality of being kind.*

nest 1. A place built by a bird for laying its eggs and raising its young. A nest can be made out of grass, twigs, mud, or many other materials. 2. A place made by insects, fish, turtles, or other animals for laying their eggs or raising their young. Some fish make nests by making a hole in the mud or sand with their tails. 3. A group of birds, insects, or other animals living in a nest: *There was a **nest** of robins in the maple tree by the barn.* 4. A cozy place or shelter: *The kitten made a **nest** among the rags in the closet and fell asleep. Noun.*
○ To build or live in a nest: *Every spring sparrows **nest** under the attic roof. Verb.*
nest (nest) *noun, plural* **nests**; *verb,* **nested, nesting.**

nestle To get very close to; snuggle; cuddle: *The kittens **nestled** against their mother.* **nes·tle** (nes′əl) *verb,* **nestled, nestling.**

Large nets can be used to trap many fish.

net¹ 1. A fabric made of threads, cords, ropes or wires that are woven together so as to leave evenly spaced holes. Net is used to make stockings, veils, and other articles of clothing. 2. A device made of such fabric: *We used a **net** to catch the fish and pull them out of the water. Hit the tennis ball over the **net**. Noun.*

○ To catch with or as if with a net: *I **netted** three large fish on my first day of fishing. Verb.*
net (net) *noun, plural* **nets**; *verb,* **netted, netting.**

net² Remaining after all costs and deductions or after allowances are made for other factors. A storekeeper's net profit is the money left over from selling goods after the rent and the other costs of running the business are paid. *Adjective.*
○ To earn or get as a profit: *The sale of a new car may **net** the dealer a good sum of money. Verb.*
net (net) *adjective; verb,* **netted, netting.**

Netherlands A country in northwest Europe. This country is also called **Holland**. **Neth·er·lands** (neth′ər ləndz) *noun.*

nettle A plant with hairs on its leaves and stem that sting when they are touched. **net·tle** (net′əl) *noun, plural* **nettles.**

network 1. A system of lines or structures that cross or connect: *a **network** of electric wires. a computer **network**. A railroad yard is a **network** of tracks.* 2. A group of radio or television stations that usually broadcast many of the same programs, often at the same time. *Noun*
○ To connect so a group of computers can work together. *Verb.*
net·work (net′wûrk′) *noun, plural* **networks**; *verb,* **networked, networking.**

neurotic Having or showing unreasonable fears or worries: *a **neurotic** patient. a **neurotic** concern for neatness.* **neu·rot·ic** (nù rot′ik *or* nyù rot′ik) *adjective.*

neutral 1. Not taking or belonging to either side in a conflict: *During the war many people fled to a **neutral** country.* 2. Having no particular shade or tint: *Gray is a **neutral** color.* 3. Being neither an acid nor a base in chemistry: *The right mixture of an acid and a base will produce a **neutral** salt. Adjective.*
○ 1. A person or country that is neutral: *Switzerland and Sweden were **neutrals** in World War II.* 2. A position of gears in an automobile. When a car is in neutral, the engine cannot make the car move. *Noun.*
neu·tral (nü′trəl *or* nū′trəl) *adjective; noun, plural* **neutrals.**

neutralize To stop the effect of: *Our team's strong defense **neutralized** their offense.* **neu·tral·ize** (nü′trə līz′ *or* nū′trə līz′) *verb,* **neutralized, neutralizing**

neutron A small particle that is part of the nucleus, or center, of every atom except that of hydrogen. A neutron has no electric charge. It is a little heavier than a proton. **neu·tron** (nü′tron *or* nū′tron) *noun, plural* **neutrons**.

Nev. An abbreviation for Nevada.

Nevada A state in the western United States. Its capital is Carson City. **Ne·vad·a** (nə vad′ə *or* nə vä′də) *noun*.

WORD HISTORY

The name Nevada comes from the Spanish word meaning "snowy" or "covered with snow." Spanish explorers gave this name to the Sierra Nevada mountains. The state of Nevada takes its name from these mountains.

Carson City

Nevada
U. S. Postal Abbreviation: **NV**
Capital: **Carson City**
Population: **1,007,000**
Area: **110,540 sq. mi./286,297 sq. km**
State Nicknames: **Silver State; Sagebrush State**
State Bird: **Mountain Bluebird**
State Flower: **Sagebrush**

never 1. At no time; not ever: *I have* **never** *been to China*. 2. In no way; not at all: *We* **never** *thought he could do it!* **nev·er** (nev′ər) *adverb*.

nevertheless In spite of that; in any case; however: *It was a cloudy day;* **nevertheless**, *we went to the beach*. **nev·er·the·less** (nev′ər th̲ə les′) *adverb*.

new 1. Having existed only a short time; recently grown or made: *In spring there are* **new** *leaves on the trees. The* **new** *boat was launched yesterday.* 2. Seen, known, made, or thought of for the first time; strange; unfamiliar: *When I came back to school there were* **new** *faces in my class. They are slow to act on* **new** *ideas. On the expedition we found several* **new** *rocks for the collection. The sailors discovered a* **new** *land.* 3. Not yet familiar or experienced: *I was still* **new** *to the job.* 4. Having recently come into a certain state, relationship, position, or role: *I made lots of* **new** *friends when we moved. The* **new** *mayor acted quickly to improve the traffic situation.* 5. Not yet used or worn: *Do you like my* **new** *shoes? Our house has a* **new** *coat of paint.* 6. Coming or beginning again: *Tomorrow is a* **new** *day. The* **new** *year began with a heavy snowstorm.* 7. Changed, as for the better: *Today I feel like a* **new** *person.* Other words sounding like this are **gnu** and **knew**. **new** (nü *or* nū) *adjective*, **newer**, **newest**.

newbie A person who is new to using the World Wide Web and doesn't know much about how it works. **new·bie** (nü′bē *or* nū′bē) *noun, plural* **newbies**.

newborn 1. Born very recently: *A* **newborn** *baby sleeps most of the time.* 2. As if born again; fresh: *After resting we started to climb again with* **newborn** *determination.* **new·born** (nü′bôrn′ *or* nū′bôrn′) *adjective*.

New Brunswick A province in southeastern Canada. Its capital is Fredericton. **New Bruns·wick** (brunz′wik) *noun*.

newcomer A person who has recently arrived: *a* **newcomer** *in town.* newcomer (nü′kum′ər *or* nū′kum′ər) *noun, plural* **newcomers**.

This newborn calf will quickly learn to walk.

PRONUNCIATION KEY:
at   āpe   fär   câre   end   mē   it   īce   pierce   hot   ōld   sông   fôrk
oil   out   up   ūse   rüle   pu̇ll   tûrn   chin   sing   shop   thin   this
hw in white; zh in treasure. The symbol ə stands for the unstressed vowel sound in about, taken, pencil, lemon, and circus.

501

New England A region of the northeast United States. Maine, Vermont, New Hampshire, Massachusetts, Rhode Island, and Connecticut are the New England states.

Newf. An abbreviation for **Newfoundland.**

newfangled New and often needlessly different: *My grandparents don't like newfangled appliances.* **new•fan•gled** (nü′fang′gəld *or* nū′fang′gəld) *adjective.*

Newfoundland An island province in northeastern Canada. Its capital is St. John's. **New•found•land** (nü′fənd lənd *or* nū′fənd lənd) *noun.*

New Hampshire A state in the northeast United States. Its capital is Concord. **New Hamp•shire** (hamp′shər).

WORD HISTORY

New Hampshire was named after the county of Hampshire, in England. The English county was the home of one of the men who started the American colony of New Hampshire.

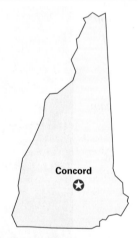

New Hampshire
U. S. Postal Abbreviation: **NH**
Capital: **Concord**
Population: **1,057,000**
Area: **9,403 sq. mi./24,097 sq. km**
State Nickname: **Granite State**
State Bird: **Purple Finch**
State Flower: **Purple Lilac**

New Jersey A state in the eastern United States. Its capital is Trenton. **New Jer•sey** (jûr′zē).

WORD HISTORY

New Jersey was named after the island of Jersey, in the English Channel. One of the first owners of the American colony was born on this island.

New Jersey
U. S. Postal Abbreviation: **NJ**
Capital: **Trenton**
Population: **7,672,000**
Area: **7,836 sq. mi./20,295 sq. km**
State Nickname: **Garden State**
State Bird: **Eastern Goldfinch**
State Flower: **Purple Violet**

newly Lately; recently: *This bread is so newly made that it is still warm.* **new•ly** (nü′lē *or* nū′lē) *adverb.*

New Mexico A state in the southwestern United States. Its capital is Santa Fe. **New Mex•i•co** (mek′si kō′).

WORD HISTORY

A Spanish explorer who had been in Mexico named this area New Mexico. The name *Mexico* comes from the name of an Indian god.

New Mexico
U. S. Postal Abbreviation: **NM**
Capital: **Santa Fe**
Population: **1,500,000**
Area: **121,666 sq. mi./315,113 sq. km**
State Nickname: **Land of Enchantment**
State Bird: **Roadrunner**
State Flower: **Yucca**

new moon The moon when it cannot be seen or when it appears as a thin crescent with the hollow part on the right side. A new moon happens every month.

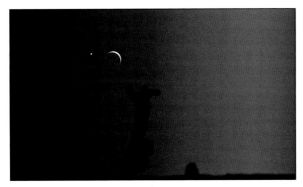

A **new moon** is the opposite of a full moon.

news A report or information of something that happened recently: *People at home heard no **news** from the traveler. Everyone was excited by the **news** that the spacecraft had landed safely on the moon.* **news** (nüz *or* nūz) *noun.*

newscast A radio or television program that presents the news: *Our family watches a **newscast** every evening.* **news•cast** (nüz′kast′ *or* nūz′kast′) *noun, plural* **newscasts.** —**newscaster** *noun.*

newsgroup A discussion group on the World Wide Web where people who are interested in the same things can exchange messages. **news•group** (nüz′ grüp′ *or* nūz′ grüp′) *noun, plural* **newsgroups.**

newspaper A publication printed on sheets of paper that contain news, opinions on local and national happenings, and advertisements. Most newspapers are published every day or every week. **news•pa•per** (nüz′pā′pər *or* nūz′pā′pər) *noun, plural* **newspapers.**

newsstand A place where newspapers and magazines are sold. **news•stand** (nüz′stand′ *or* nūz′stand′) *noun, plural* **newsstands.**

newt A small, brightly colored salamander that lives in or around water. **newt** (nüt *or* nūt) *noun, plural* **newts.**

New Testament The second part of the Christian Bible. It contains the life and teachings of Jesus, the founder of the Christian religion, and his disciples.

New World North and South America; the Western Hemisphere.

New Year's Day A holiday that celebrates the first day of the year, January 1.

New York A state in the eastern United States. Its capital is Albany. **New York** (yôrk). —**New Yorker** *noun.*

WORD HISTORY

When the English took over the Dutch colony of New Netherland, the English king gave the colony to his brother, the Duke of York. It was renamed New York in honor of its official protector, who was later crowned King James II.

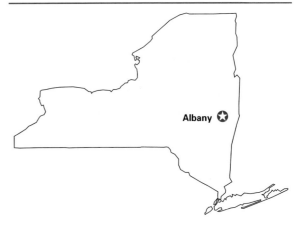

New York
U. S. Postal Abbreviation: **NY**
Capital: **Albany**
Population: **17,825,000**
Area: **49,576 sq. mi./128,401 sq. km**
State Nickname: **Empire State**
State Bird: **Bluebird**
State Flower: **Rose**

New Zealand A country made up of two islands in the Pacific Ocean. It is off the east coast of Australia. **New Zea•land** (zē′lənd). —**New Zealander** *noun.*

next 1. Following immediately in time or order: *It rained on Thursday, but the **next** morning it was sunny.* 2. Nearest: *The **next** house is my cousin's. Adjective.*
○ 1. Immediately afterward: *January is the first month, and February comes **next.*** 2. At the first time after this: *Call us when you are **next** in town. Adverb.*

PRONUNCIATION KEY:
at   āpe   fär   câre   end   mē   it   īce   pierce   hot   ōld   sông   fôrk
oil   out   up   ūse   rüle   pùll   tûrn   chin   sing   shop   thin   this
hw in white; zh in treasure. The symbol ə stands for the unstressed vowel sound in about, taken, pencil, lemon, and circus.

503

• **next door.** In or at the building, house, or apartment that is nearest: *My best friend lives **next door** to me.*

• **next to.** **1.** Almost; nearly: *Fixing the old toaster was **next to** impossible.* **2.** Beside: *I was standing **next to** you.*
next (nekst) *adjective; adverb.*

next-door In the nearest building, house, or apartment: *Our **next-door** neighbors share a driveway with us.* **next-door** (nekst′dôr′) *adjective.*

Nez Percé A member of a tribe of Native Americans of the northwest United States.
Nez Percé (nez′pûrs′) *noun, plural* **Nez Percé** *or* **Nez Percés.**

Nfld. An abbreviation for **Newfoundland.**

NH Postal abbreviation for **New Hampshire.**

N.H. An abbreviation for **New Hampshire.**

nibble **1.** To eat quickly and with small bites: *The mouse **nibbled** the cheese.* **2.** To bite gently. *Verb.*
○ A small bite: *A fish took a **nibble** at the bait. Noun.*
nib•ble (nib′əl) *verb,* **nibbled, nibbling;** *noun, plural* **nibbles.**

Nicaragua A country in Central America.
Nic•a•ra•gua (nik′ə rä′gwə) *noun.* —**Nicaraguan** *adjective; noun.*

nice **1.** Pleasant or agreeable: *The weather was **nice** yesterday. We had a **nice** time at the dance.* **2.** Kind and thoughtful: *It was **nice** of you to ask us to the party.* **3.** Showing or needing care and skill; fine: *Those wooden cabinets are a **nice** piece of work.* **4.** Having or showing good manners; polite: *It isn't **nice** to grab things at dinner.* **nice** (nīs) *adjective,* **nicer, nicest.** —**nicely** *adverb.*

niche **1.** A hollow in a wall used as a setting for statues or vases. **2.** A place, position, or situation especially suitable for someone or something: *I've found my **niche** in the science club.* **niche** (nich) *noun, plural* **niches.**

nick A place on a surface or edge that has been cut or chipped: *The mirror made a **nick** in the table when it fell. Noun.*
○ To make a small cut or chip on the surface or edge of: *I **nicked** my finger with a knife. Verb.*
• **in the nick of time.** Just before it is too late; just in time: *The lifeguard reached the drowning swimmer **in the nick of time**.*
nick (nik) *noun, plural* **nicks;** *verb,* **nicked, nicking.**

nickel **1.** A hard, silver-colored metal. Nickel is added to alloys to make them strong. Nickel is a chemical element. **2.** A coin of the United States and Canada equal to five cents. **nick•el** (nik′əl) *noun, plural* **nickels.**

nickname A name that is used instead of or in addition to a person's real name: *Walter's **nickname** is "Ace." "Sandy" is a **nickname** for Sandra or Alexandra. Noun.*
○ To give a nickname to: *I was **nicknamed** "Red" because of my red hair. Verb.*
nick•name (nik′nām′) *noun, plural* **nicknames;** *verb,* **nicknamed, nicknaming.**

nicotine A poisonous, oily substance that is found in the leaves, roots, and seeds of the tobacco plant. It is what makes people addicted to cigarettes. **nic•o•tine** (nik′ə tēn′) *noun.*

niece **1.** The daughter of one's brother or sister. **2.** The daughter of one's brother-in-law or sister-in-law. **niece** (nēs) *noun, plural* **nieces.**

Niger A country in north-central Africa. **Ni•ger** (nī′jər) *noun.*

Nigeria A country in west-central Africa.
Ni•ge•ri•a (nī jîr′ē ə) *noun.* —**Nigerian** *adjective; noun.*

night **1.** The time when it is dark; time between the setting and rising of the sun: *The baby slept all **night**.* **2.** The darkness of night: *The prisoner escaped under the cover of **night**.* **3.** The beginning of night; nightfall: ***Night** comes earlier in the autumn.*
Another word that sounds like this is **knight.**
night (nīt) *noun, plural* **nights.**

At night the lights from a city give it a different appearance than in daytime.

nightfall The beginning of night; the end of the

day: *My parents told me to be sure to be home before **nightfall**.* **night·fall** (nīt′fôl′) *noun.*

nightgown A loose gown that is worn to bed. **night·gown** (nīt′goun′) *noun, plural* **nightgowns.**

nightingale A small bird that lives in Europe and western Asia. The nightingale has brown wings and a white chest. Male nightingales are known for their beautiful song. **night·in·gale** (nī′tən gāl′ *or* nī′ting gāl′) *noun, plural* **nightingales.**

nightly Done or happening every night: *the **nightly** news on TV. Adjective.*
○ Every night: *Brush your teeth **nightly**. Adverb.* **night·ly** (nīt′lē) *adjective; adverb.*

nightmare 1. A bad or frightening dream: *My cousin had a **nightmare** about being chased by a lion.* 2. Any bad or frightening experience: *Being lost in the city was a **nightmare** for the children.* **night·mare** (nīt′mâr′) *noun, plural* **nightmares.**

WORD HISTORY

The word nightmare is made up of the word *night* and an Old English word for an imaginary monster. The word was first used for an imaginary creature that was supposed to sit on people when they were asleep so that they could not breathe.

---

nighttime The time when it is dark; night: *I don't like to go out alone at **nighttime**.* **night·time** (nīt′tīm′) *noun.*

nimble 1. Light and quick in movement: *The circus has **nimble** acrobats.* 2. Quick to understand or respond: *In a debate, a **nimble** mind helps.* **nim·ble** (nim′bəl) *adjective,* **nimbler, nimblest.** —**nimbly** *adverb.*

nine One more than eight; 9. **nine** (nīn) *noun, plural* **nines;** *adjective.*

nineteen Nine more than ten; 19. **nine·teen** (nīn′tēn′) *noun, plural* **nineteens;** *adjective.*

nineteenth Next after the eighteenth. *Adjective, noun.*
○ One of nineteen equal parts; ¹/₁₉. *Noun.* **nine·teenth** (nīn′tēnth′) *adjective; noun, plural* **nineteenths.**

ninetieth Next after the eighty-ninth. *Adjective, noun.*
○ One of ninety equal parts; ¹/₉₀. *Noun.*

nine·ti·eth (nīn′tē ith) *adjective; noun, plural* **ninetieths.**

ninety Nine times ten; 90. **nine·ty** (nīn′tē) *noun, plural* **nineties;** *adjective.*

ninja A warrior in medieval Japan who was an expert in martial arts and often acted as a spy or an assassin. **nin·ja** (nin′jə) *noun.*

ninth Next after the eighth. *Adjective, noun.*
○ One of nine equal parts; ¹/₉. *Noun.* **ninth** (nīnth) *adjective; noun, plural* **ninths.**

nip 1. To bite or pinch quickly and not hard: *The parrot **nipped** my finger.* 2. To cut by pinching: *The gardener **nipped** the dead leaves off the branch.* 3. To cause to smart or sting: *The cold night air **nipped** our faces.* 4. To stop or destroy the growth of: *Bad weather **nipped** our plans for the weekend. Verb.*
○ 1. A bite or pinch: *I felt the **nip** of a crab on my toe.* 2. A sharp, biting cold: *a **nip** in the air. Noun.* **nip** (nip) *verb,* **nipped, nipping;** *noun, plural* **nips.**

nipple 1. The small rounded tip in the center of a breast or udder. A baby or other newly born mammal sucks milk from its mother's nipple. 2. The rubber tip or mouthpiece of a baby's bottle. A baby sucks on the nipple to get milk or other liquids. **nip·ple** (nip′əl) *noun, plural* **nipples.**

nitrogen A gas that has no color or smell. Nitrogen makes up almost ⅘ of the air on earth. All living things need nitrogen. Nitrogen is a chemical element. **ni·tro·gen** (nī′trə jən) *noun.*

NJ Postal abbreviation for **New Jersey.**

N.J. An abbreviation for **New Jersey.**

NM Postal abbreviation for **New Mexico.**

N.M. *or* **N. Mex.** An abbreviation for **New Mexico.**

no¹ 1. Not so: *No, this is not the right road.* 2. Not at all; not any: *The bird was **no** larger than your hand.* In this sense, the word "no" is used with the comparative form of an adjective. *Adverb.*
○ A word used to show surprise, wonder, or disbelief: *No! I can't believe it! Interjection.*
○ 1. The saying of the word "no"; denial; refusal: *The boss answered his request with a **no**.* 2. A vote or voter against: *The **noes** were in the majority, so the proposal lost. Noun.*
Another word that sounds like this is **know.**
no (nō) *adverb; interjection; noun, plural* **noes** *or* **nos.**

PRONUNCIATION KEY:

at	āpe	fär	câre	end	mē	it	īce	pierce	hot	ōld	sông	fôrk
oil	out	up	ūse	rüle	pùll	tûrn	chin	sing	shop	thin	this	

hw in white; zh in treasure. The symbol ə stands for the unstressed vowel sound in about, taken, pencil, lemon, and circus.

505

no² **1.** Not any: *It was a clear day, with no clouds in the sky.* **2.** Not a: *It was no surprise when the old car stopped running.* **no** (nō) *adjective.*

no. An abbreviation for **number.**

nobility **1.** A class of people who have a high rank or title. Dukes, duchesses, earls, and countesses belong to the nobility. **2.** Greatness of character. Courage and honesty are two elements of nobility. **no·bil·i·ty** (nō bil′i tē) *noun, plural* **nobilities.**

noble **1.** Having a high rank or title: *The duke comes from a noble family.* **2.** Having or showing greatness of character: *The fight for freedom is a noble cause.* **3.** Impressive in appearance; magnificent: *It is a noble view from the top of the mountain. Adjective.*
○ A person of high rank or title: *the king and his nobles. Noun.*
no·ble (nō′bəl) *adjective,* **nobler, noblest;** *noun, plural* **nobles.**

nobleman A man of high rank or title. **no·ble·man** (nō′bəl mən) *noun, plural* **noblemen** (nō′bəl mən).

noblewoman A woman of high rank or title. **no·ble·wom·an** (nō′bəl wùm′ən) *noun, plural* **noblewomen** (nō′bəl wim′ən).

nobody No person; no one: *I rang the doorbell, but nobody answered. Pronoun.*
○ A person of no importance or rank: *I felt like a nobody at the party. Noun.*
no·bod·y (nō′bod′ē) *pronoun; noun, plural,* **nobodies.**

nocturnal **1.** Happening or appearing at night: *We sat quietly on our porch and listened to the nocturnal sounds.* **2.** Active at night: *The raccoon is nocturnal and spends a large part of the day sleeping.* **noc·tur·nal** (nok tûr′nəl) *adjective.*

nod **1.** To move the head up and down: *Nod if you understand, and shake your head if you don't.* **2.** To let the head fall forward with a quick motion: *The student sat nodding over the dull book and finally fell asleep.* **3.** To show by quickly moving the head up and down: *The librarian nodded approval of our request.* **4.** To bend forward with a swaying motion: *The wheat nodded in the breeze. Verb.*
○ A movement up and down of the head: *My friend greeted me with a nod. Noun.*
nod (nod) *verb,* **nodded, nodding;** *noun, plural* **nods.**

noise **1.** A sound that is loud and harsh: *The noise*

of the traffic outside the window made it hard to sleep. **2.** Any sound: *I heard a noise in the bushes.* **noise** (noiz) *noun, plural* **noises.**

noisy Making much noise: *The noisy children had to leave the theater.* **nois·y** (noi′zē) *adjective,* **noisier, noisiest.** —**noisily** *adverb.*

nomad **1.** A member of a group or tribe that does not have a permanent home. Nomads wander from place to place looking for food for themselves or for their animals. **2.** A person who wanders from place to place: *I was a nomad for years before I settled down.* **no·mad** (nō′mad) *noun, plural* **nomads.**

nomadic Relating to nomads or to wandering from place to place: *Many Inuit are nomadic.* **no·mad·ic** (nō mad′ik) *adjective.*

nominate **1.** To choose as a candidate: *The political parties nominate candidates for president.* **2.** To appoint to an office or name for an honor: *The mayor nominated a new police chief.* **nom·i·nate** (nom′ə nāt′) *verb,* **nominated, nominating.**

nomination **1.** The choice of a person to run for an office: *The nominations for president took place this summer.* **2.** The appointment of a person to an office or the naming of a person for an honor: *We'll celebrate your nomination as town manager.* **nom·i·na·tion** (nom′ə nā′shən) *noun, plural* **nominations.**

nominee A person who is nominated: *The two presidential nominees had a debate.* **nom·i·nee** (nom′ə nē′) *noun, plural* **nominees.**

non- A prefix that means "not" or "the opposite of": *Nonfiction means "not fiction." Nonsense means "the opposite of sense."*
If the root word begins with a capital letter, we use a hyphen when we add *non-*. For example, *non-Chinese* is written with a hyphen. *Non-Chinese* means "not Chinese."

none **1.** No one; not one: *All the children tried, but none could catch the rabbit.* **2.** No part; not any: *None of the stolen money was ever found. Pronoun.*
○ Not at all: *Help came none too soon. Adverb.*
Another word that sounds like this is **nun.**
none (nun) *pronoun; adverb.*

nonfiction Writing that is not fiction. Nonfiction deals with real people and events: *Biographies and history books are examples of nonfiction.* **non·fic·tion** (non fik′shən) *noun.*

nonsense 1. A way of talking or acting that is silly and makes no sense: *No **nonsense** in class, please.* 2. Language or behavior that is annoying or lacking in good sense: *I don't want to hear any more **nonsense** about not being able to sleep!* **non·sense** (nonʹsens) *noun.* —**nonsensical** *adjective.*

nonstop Not making any stops: *Your reservation is on a **nonstop** flight. Adjective.*
○ Without stops: *We flew **nonstop** from Boston to Denver. Adverb.*
non·stop (nonʹstopʹ) *adjective; adverb.*

noodle A flat strip of dried dough. Noodles are made out of flour, water, and eggs. **noo·dle** (nüʹdəl) *noun, plural* **noodles.**

noon Twelve o'clock in the daytime; the middle of the day. **noon** (nün) *noun.*

no one No person; nobody: *I thought I heard the doorbell, but **no one** was there.*

noontime Twelve o'clock in the daytime; noon: *"It's **noontime**; let's eat!"* **noon·time** (nünʹtīmʹ) *noun.*

noose A loop of rope with a special knot that lets the loop tighten when the end of the rope is pulled. **noose** (nüs) *noun, plural* **nooses.**

nor 1. And not. The word *nor* is used as a connector between a word or group of words that begins with *neither* (or some other negative) and one or more other words or groups of words: *Neither Mom **nor** Dad **nor** I saw the eclipse. We could neither watch television **nor** listen to the radio.* 2. A word that is used in place of *and* and *not* to continue a negative idea: *They didn't like the concert, **nor** did I.* **nor** (nôr) *conjunction.*

normal 1. Conforming to a standard, pattern, or model; regular; usual: *Heavy rain is **normal** at this time of year.* 2. Having or showing average mental or physical development; healthy: *We were happy to hear that the baby is **normal**. Adjective.*
○ The usual or regular condition or level: *This year's rainfall is above **normal**. Noun.*
nor·mal (nôrʹməl) *adjective; noun.* —**normality** *noun* —**normally** *adverb.*

Norse Relating to ancient Scandinavia: *Norse explorers.* **Norse** (nôrs) *adjective.*

north 1. The direction to your right as you watch the sun set in the evening. North is one of the four main points of the compass. It is located directly opposite south. 2. **North.** Any region or place that is in this direction. 3. **the North.** The region of the United States that is north of Maryland, the Ohio River, and Missouri. *Noun.*
○ 1. Toward or in the north: *The oak tree is on the **north** side of the backyard.* 2. Coming from the north: *a **north** wind. Adjective.*
○ Toward the north: *We hiked **north** for a mile. Adverb.*
north (nôrth) *noun; adjective; adverb.*

North America A continent in the Western Hemisphere. North America lies between the Atlantic and Pacific oceans. North America contains the countries of Mexico, the United States, and Canada. It is the third largest continent.

North American 1. A person who was born or is living in North America. 2. Relating to North America or its people.

North Carolina A state in the United States on the Atlantic Ocean. Its capital is Raleigh. **North Car·o·li·na** (karʹə līʹnə)

WORD HISTORY

North Carolina was created from the northern part of the English colony of Carolina. The founder of the colony had asked that it be given the Latin name Carolina, which means "from Charles" or "belonging to Charles," in honor of Charles I, who was then king of England.

North Carolina
U. S. Postal Abbreviation: **NC**
Capital: **Raleigh**
Population: **6,413,000**
Area: **52,586 sq. mi./136,197 sq. km**
State Nickname: **Tar Heel State**
State Bird: **Cardinal**
State Flower: **Dogwood**

PRONUNCIATION KEY:

| at | āpe | fär | câre | end | mē | it | īce | pierce | hot | ōld | sông | fôrk |
| oil | out | up | ūse | rüle | pull | tûrn | chin | sing | shop | thin | this | |

hw in white; zh in treasure. The symbol ə stands for the unstressed vowel sound in about, taken, pencil, lemon, and circus.

507

North Dakota A state in the north-central United States. Its capital is Bismarck. **North Da·ko·ta** (də kō′tə).

WORD HISTORY

North Dakota was made from the northern part of the Dakota Territory. The territory was named after the Dakota Indians, who lived there. Their name is a Native American word that means "allied tribes."

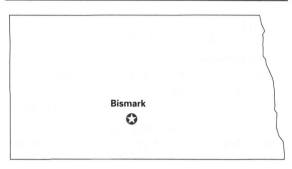

Bismark
★

North Dakota
U. S. Postal Abbreviation: **ND**
Capital: **Bismarck**
Population: **672,000**
Area: **70,665 sq. mi./183,022 sq. km**
State Nicknames: **Flickertail State; Peace Garden State; Sioux State**
State Bird: **Western Meadowlark**
State Flower: **Wild Prairie Rose**

northeast 1. The direction halfway between north and east. 2. A region or place in this direction: *The northeast of the island has few trees.* 3. the Northeast. The region in the north and east of the United States, including New England and New York. *Noun.*
○ 1. Toward or in the northeast: *the northeast section of town.* 2. Coming from the northeast: *a northeast wind. Adjective.*
○ Toward the northeast: *We drove northeast. Adverb.*
north·east (nôrth′ēst′) *noun; adjective; adverb.* —**northeasterly** *adjective.*

northeastern 1. Toward or in the northeast: *The northeastern sky grew darker in the afternoon.* 2. Characteristic of or relating to the northeast or Northeast: *Northeastern summers are cool and pleasant.* 3. Coming from the northeast: *The northeastern storm blew all the leaves off the trees.* **north·east·ern** (nôrth′ēs′tərn) *adjective.*

northerly 1. Toward the north: *We traveled in a northerly direction.* 2. From the north: *The wind blew northerly.* **north·er·ly** (nôr<u>th</u>′ər lē) *adjective; adverb.*

northern 1. In or toward the north: *There is a large lake in the northern part of our state. I spent my vacation in northern Michigan.* 2. Coming from the north: *a cold northern breeze.* 3. Northern. Of or in the part of the United States that is in the north. **north·ern** (nôr′<u>th</u>ərn) *adjective.*

northerner 1. A person born or living in the north. 2. Northerner. A person born or living in the northern part of the United States. **north·ern·er** (nôr′<u>th</u>ər nər) *noun, plural* **northerners.**

Northern Hemisphere The half of the earth that is north of the equator. Europe and North America and most of Asia and Africa are located in the Northern Hemisphere.

Northern Ireland A country in the northeastern part of Ireland. It is a part of the United Kingdom. Look up **Ireland** for more information.

Northern lights are so named because they are seen most commonly in the North.

northern lights Shining bands or streams of light sometimes seen in the northern sky at night; aurora borealis. Look up **aurora borealis** for more information.

North Korea A country in east-central Asia. **North Ko·re·a** (kə rē′ə).

North Pole The point on earth that is farthest

north. It is the northern end of the earth's axis.

North Star A bright star that is in the northern sky above the North Pole.

northward Toward the north: *The train sped* **northward.** *Adverb.*

○ Toward or in the north: *The* **northward** *slope is often covered with ice. Adjective.*
north•ward (nôrth′wərd) *adverb; adjective.*

northwards Another spelling of the adverb northward: *The storm traveled* **northwards.** Look up **northward** for more information. **north•wards** (nôrth′wərdz) *adverb.*

northwest 1. The direction halfway between north and west. 2. A region or place in this direction: *The* **northwest** *is a region of forests.* 3. **the Northwest.** The region in the north and west of the United States: *Oregon is in* **the Northwest.** *Noun.*

○ 1. Toward or in the northwest: *We drove to the* **northwest** *part of town.* 2. Coming from the northwest: *a* **northwest** *wind. Adjective.*

○ Toward the northwest: *Turn* **northwest** *at the next corner. Adverb.*
north•west (nôrth′west′) *noun; adjective; adverb.*
—northwesterly *adjective.*

northwestern 1. Toward or in the northwest: *The army's* **northwestern** *advance was slowed by the coming of winter.* 2. Characteristic of or relating to the northwest or Northwest: *Washington is a* **northwestern** *state.* 3. Coming from the northwest: *a* **northwestern** *wind.* **north•west•ern** (nôrth′wes′tərn) *adjective.*

Northwest Territories A division of Canada located in the north-central part of the country. Its capital is Yellowknife.

Norway A country in northern Europe. **Nor•way** (nôr′wā) *noun.*

Norwegian 1. A person who was born in or is a citizen of Norway. 2. The language spoken in Norway. *Noun.*

○ Of or relating to Norway, its people, or its language. *Adjective.*
Nor•we•gian (nôr wē′jən) *noun, plural* **Norwegians;** *adjective.*

nose 1. The part of the face or head that is used for breathing and smelling. Air comes into and goes out of the nose through the nostrils. 2. The sense of smell: *Dogs have good* **noses.** 3. The

point or front of something that sticks out: *The* **nose** *of the plane points slightly upward when it takes off. Noun.*

○ 1. To find or notice by smell: *The dog* **nosed** *the rabbit in the bushes.* 2. To push or move forward slowly and gently: *Our dog* **nosed** *the back door open. The big car* **nosed** *around the corner. Verb.*

• **under one's nose.** In a place that is clearly visible: *I felt silly when I found the pen I'd lost right* **under my nose.**
nose (nōz) *noun, plural* **noses;** *verb,* **nosed, nosing.**

nosebleed A bleeding from the nose. **nose•bleed** (nōz′blēd′) *noun, plural* **nosebleeds.**

nose cone The cone-shaped front part of a rocket sent into space. It separates from the rest of the rocket during flight. It often has a special shield that protects it from the enormous heat that builds up when it comes back into the earth's atmosphere.

nostalgia A longing for the past: *Grandpa feels* **nostalgia** *for his childhood when he looks at old photos.* **nos•tal•gi•a** (nos tal′jə) *noun.* **—nostalgic** *adjective* **—nostalgically** *adverb.*

nostril One of two outer openings of the nose. Air is taken in and let out through the nostrils. **nos•tril** (nos′trəl) *noun, plural* **nostrils.**

WORD HISTORY

The word **nostril** goes back to two Old English words meaning "nose" and "hole."

---

nosy Having or showing too much interest in other people's concerns: *She asked me a lot of* **nosy** *questions that were none of her business.* **nos•y** (nō′zē) *adjective,* **nosier, nosiest.** **—nosily** *adverb* **—nosiness** *noun.*

not An adverb that is used in the following ways: 1. To mean "at no time" or "in no way:" *It did* **not** *rain this week.* 2. To make a statement negative: *You may* **not** *sit there.* 3. After a statement to represent the negative or opposite: *Sometimes I'm hungry, sometimes* **not.**
Another word that sounds like this is **knot.**
not (not) *adverb.*

notable Worthy of notice; important or remarkable: *The author's first book was a* **notable**

PRONUNCIATION KEY:

| at | ape | fär | câre | end | mē | it | īce | pierce | hot | ōld | sông | fôrk |
| oil | out | up | ūse | rüle | pull | tûrn | chin | sing | shop | thin | this | |

hw in white; zh in treasure. The symbol ə stands for the unstressed vowel sound in about, taken, pencil, lemon, and circus.

509

success. A **notable** scientist spoke to us last night. *Adjective.*

○ A person who is important: *The mayor and other **notables** led the parade. Noun.*

no·ta·ble (nō′tə bəl) *adjective; noun, plural* **notables. —notably** *adverb.*

notation 1. A system of signs or symbols that are used to represent numbers, words, or other information: *musical **notation**. The sign ÷ is a **notation** in arithmetic that means "divided by."* 2. A quick note, as to assist memory or help organize information: *Many students make **notations** in the margins of their books.* **no·ta·tion** (nō tā′shən) *noun, plural* **notations.**

Notation shows a musician how a
musical score should be played.

notch 1. A nick or cut on the edge or surface of something: *I cut V-shaped **notches** in the ends of the ribbons. The scouts made **notches** in the trees as they went along so they could find their way back to camp.* 2. A narrow pass between mountains: *a stream at the bottom of the **notch**. Noun.*

○ To make a notch or notches in: *Some Native Americans counted the passing days by **notching** sticks. Verb.*

notch (noch) *noun, plural* **notches;** *verb,* **notched, notching.**

note 1. A word or words written down to help a person remember what was in a talk or book: *I took **notes** during the history class.* 2. A comment that explains a word or part of a book: *Our poetry book has **notes** at the bottom of the pages.*

3. A short message or letter: *Send your grandparents a thank-you **note**.* 4. Careful notice; regard: *Take **note** of how he catches the ball.* 5. Importance: *A judge is a person of **note**.* 6. A hint or suggestion; indication: *We thought we heard a **note** of jealousy in their voices.* 7. A single sound in music, or a sign that represents such a sound. 8. A piece of paper with a written promise to pay someone a sum of money. *Noun.*

○ 1. To put down in writing: *I will **note** your telephone number in my address book.* 2. To take careful notice of; regard: *Please **note** the enclosed newspaper article. Verb.*

note (nōt) *noun, plural* **notes;** *verb,* **noted, noting.**

notebook A book with blank pages for notes: *I have a **notebook** for each of the five subjects I take at school.* **note·book** (nōt′bŭk′) *noun, plural* **notebooks.**

noted Noticed for a particular reason; well-known; famous: *A **noted** speaker will talk at our graduation.* **not·ed** (nō′tid) *adjective.*

nothing 1. No thing; not anything: *We bought **nothing** at the store. They were so shy that they sat in a corner and said **nothing**.* 2. A person or thing that is of no importance: *One dollar is **nothing** to a rich person.* 3. Zero: *The final score was two to **nothing**. Noun.*

○ In no way; not at all: *You look **nothing** like your parents. Adverb.*

noth·ing (nŭth′ing) *noun, plural* **nothings;** *adverb.*

notice 1. The condition of being seen or observed: *The children tiptoed out of the room to escape **notice**.* 2. The act of seeing or observing: *This problem deserves your **notice**.* 3. A warning or announcement: *The ship's horn gave **notice** that it was about to sail. The enemy attacked without **notice**.* 4. A printed or written announcement: *The principal sent home a **notice** about school pictures. Noun.*

○ To become aware of; observe: *I **noticed** that the room was getting cooler. Verb.*

no·tice (nō′tis) *noun, plural* **notices;** *verb,* **noticed, noticing.**

noticeable Easily noticed: *a **noticeable** drop in the temperature.* **no·tice·a·ble** (nō′ti sə bəl) *adjective.* **—noticeably** *adverb.*

notify To tell about something; inform: *The store **notified** us of the sale.* **no·ti·fy** (nō′tə fī′) *verb,* **notified, notifying.**

notion 1. An idea or belief: *I don't have the slightest* **notion** *of what you're talking about. Where did you get the silly* **notion** *that I'm angry at you?* 2. A desire or whim: *a sudden* **notion** *to go swimming.* 3. **notions.** Ribbons, pins, needles, and other small, useful items. **no‧tion** (nō′shən) *noun, plural* **notions.**

notorious Well-known for something bad: *Who do you think was the most* **notorious** *outlaw in the old West?* **no‧to‧ri‧ous** (nō tôr′ē əs) *adjective.* —**notoriously** *adverb.*

noun A word that names a person, place, or thing. In the sentence "My parents took Tom and me to the country," "parents," " Tom," and "country" are nouns. **noun** (noun) *noun, plural* **nouns.**

nourish 1. To provide food needed for life and growth: *Milk* **nourishes** *a baby or newborn animal. Sun, rain, and good soil* **nourish** *plants and trees.* 2. To provide with other things that promote life, growth, development, or success: *Studying at the university* **nourished** *the scientist's career.* **nour‧ish** (nûr′ish) *verb,* **nourished, nourishing.** —**nourishing** *adjective.*

nourishment Something needed for life and growth: *It is important that growing children get good* **nourishment.** **nour‧ish‧ment** (nûr′ish mənt) *noun.*

Nov. An abbreviation for **November.**

Nova Scotia A province in southeastern Canada. Its capital is Halifax. **No‧va Sco‧tia** (nō′və skō′shə) *noun.*

novel[1] A long story about imaginary people and events. A novel usually tells about events that might really take place and people like those in real life. **nov‧el** (nov′əl) *noun, plural* **novels.**

novel[2] New and unusual: *A* **novel** *design for the book cover will make people notice it.* **nov‧el** (nov′əl) *adjective.*

novelist A person who writes novels: *Jane Austen and Charles Dickens were famous English* **novelists.** **nov‧el‧ist** (nov′ə list) *noun, plural* **novelists.**

novelty 1. The quality of being new: *Once the* **novelty** *of mowing the lawn wore off, I got bored.* 2. Something that is new or unusual: *Riding the subway was a* **novelty** *for the children who lived on a farm.* 3. **novelties.** Small, cheap toys and decorations. **nov‧el‧ty** (nov′əl tē) *noun, plural* **novelties.**

November The eleventh month of the year.

November has thirty days. **No‧vem‧ber** (nō vem′bər) *noun.*

novice 1. A person who is new to something; beginner: *Some of the drivers are* **novices** *taking part in their first race.* 2. A person who is taken into a religious order for a trial period of time before taking vows for that order. Monks and nuns must go through a time as novices. **nov‧ice** (nov′is) *noun, plural* **novices.**

now 1. At this time; at this moment: *He's on the phone* **now.** *My friends are at the beach* **now,** *while I'm here working.* 2. Without delay; immediately: *Eat your food* **now,** *before it gets cold.* 3. Under the present conditions or circumstances: *The tire is flat, so* **now** *we must walk.* 4. A short while ago: *I finished the book just* **now.** 5. At that time; then: *Her homework was done, and* **now** *she could go out. Adverb.*
◦ Since: *Now that the rain has stopped, the game can go on. Conjunction.*
◦ The present time: *The time to act is* **now.** *Noun.*
◦ A word used to express warning, sympathy, or disapproval: *Now, stop that! Interjection.*
• **now and again** or **now and then.** At times; once in a while; occasionally.
now (nou) *adverb; conjunction; noun; interjection.*

nowadays In the present day: *Nowadays, most people making long trips travel by plane.* **now‧a‧days** (nou′ə dāz′) *adverb.*

nowhere To, at, or in no place; not anywhere: *I've looked all over, but the cat is* **nowhere** *to be found. Noun.*
◦ 1. A place that is remote or not well known: *Our car ran out of gas in the middle of* **nowhere,** *and we couldn't find a service station.* 2. A condition of being unknown: *The new baseball star rose quickly from* **nowhere.** *Noun.*
no‧where (nō′hwâr′ or nō′wâr′) *adverb; noun.*

nozzle A spout at the end of a hose or pipe: *Turn the* **nozzle** *on the hose and the water comes out.* **noz‧zle** (noz′əl) *noun, plural* **nozzles.**

PRONUNCIATION KEY:

| at | āpe | fär | câre | end | mē | it | īce | pierce | hot | ōld | sông | fôrk |
| oil | out | up | ūse | rüle | püll | tûrn | chin | sing | shop | thin | this | |

hw in white; zh in treasure. The symbol ə stands for the unstressed vowel sound in about, taken, pencil, lemon, and circus.

511

NS Postal abbreviation for **Nova Scotia**.

N.S. An abbreviation for **Nova Scotia**.

NT Postal abbreviation for **Northwest Territories**.

nuclear 1. Of or forming a nucleus: *Protons and neutrons are* **nuclear** *particles. The* **nuclear** *membrane is a thin layer that surrounds the nucleus.* 2. Coming from or relating to energy created when the nucleus of an atom is split or combined: *Some electricity is made from* **nuclear** *energy.* **nu•cle•ar** (nü′klē ər *or* nū′klē ər) *adjective.*

nuclear energy Energy that can be released from the nucleus of an atom. The release of this energy may be uncontrolled, as in the explosion of an atomic bomb. It may also be controlled and used to produce electric power, to run ships, and to treat certain diseases. This is also called **atomic energy**.

nuclei Plural of **nucleus**. **nu•cle•i** (nü′klē ī′ *or* nū′klē ī′) *plural noun.*

nucleus 1. The center point or core around which other things gather: *The* **nucleus** *of the party was the table with the food and drinks.* 2. The small oval center of a plant or animal cell. The nucleus controls important activities in the cell, such as cell growth and cell division. It also contains the genes that control heredity. 3. The center of an atom. The nucleus of an atom is made up of protons and neutrons. The nucleus carries a positive charge of electricity.

NUMBERS LARGE AND SMALL

You may be familiar with kilobytes or even gigabits, but what about a yottabyte? The prefixes listed here are used for very large numbers:

Prefix	Units	Number of Zeros	Written Number
deca-	tens	1	10
cent-	hundreds	2	100
kilo-	thousands	3	1,000
mega-	millions	6	1,000,000
giga-	billions	9	1,000,000,000
tera-	trillions	12	1,000,000,000,000
peta-	quadrillions	15	1,000,000,000,000,000
exa-	quintillions	18	1,000,000,000,000,000,000
zetta-	sextillions	21	1,000,000,000,000,000,000,000
yotta-	septillions	24	1,000,000,000,000,000,000,000,000
multi-; poly-	many		

The largest number named so far is a **googol**. A googol has 100 zeros!

SMALL NUMBERS

Just as numbers are getting larger and larger, they are also getting smaller and smaller. Prefixes are also used to indicate very small numbers.

Prefix	Units	Number of zeros	Written Number
deci-	one tenth		.1
centi-	one hundredth	1	.01
milli-	one thousandth	2	.001
micro-	one millionth	5	.000,001
nano-	one billionth	8	.000,000,001
pico-	one trillionth	11	.000,000,000,001
femto-	quadrillionth	15	.000,000,000,000,001
atto-	one quintillionth	17	.000,000,000,000,000,001
zepto-	one sextillionth	20	.000,000,000,000,000,000,001
yocto-	one septillionth	23	.000,000,000,000,000,000,000,001

nu·cle·us (nü′klē əs *or* nū′klē əs) *noun, plural* **nuclei** *or* **nucleuses**.

WORD HISTORY

The word nucleus comes from a Latin word meaning "kernel" or "inner part of a nut."

---

nude Naked. *Adjective.*
○ A human figure without any clothes, especially a sculpture or a figure in a painting. *Noun.*
nude (nüd *or* nūd) *adjective; noun, plural* **nudes.** —**nudity** *noun.*

nudge To push or touch gently in order to attract attention: *My friend nudged me when the teacher called my name. Verb.*
○ A gentle push or touch: *My dog gave me a nudge to get my attention. Noun.*
nudge (nuj) *verb,* **nudged, nudging;** *noun, plural* **nudges.**

nugget A solid lump: *Gold as it is found in nature is often in nuggets.* **nug·get** (nug′it) *noun, plural* **nuggets.**

nuisance A person, thing, or action that annoys or offends: *Loud radios on the beach are a nuisance. I think it's a nuisance having to get up early.* **nui·sance** (nü′səns *or* nū′səns) *noun, plural* **nuisances.**

numb 1. Lacking or having lost feeling or movement: *The skier's face was numb with cold. Ten minutes after the dentist gave me the shot, my mouth was completely numb.* 2. Lacking or seeming to lack feelings: *When I spoke to them about the loss of their dog, they were still numb. Adjective.*
○ To make or become numb: *The dentist numbed my mouth. Verb.*
numb (num) *adjective,* **number, numbest;** *verb,* **numbed, numbing.** —**numbness** *noun.*

number 1. The total amount of things in a group; how many there are of something: *The number of children in our family is three.* 2. A symbol or word that tells how many or which one. 2, 77, and 396 are numbers: *Their apartment number is 2D. Do you have my telephone number?* 3. A total or sum: *The person who guesses the right number of peanuts in the jar will win a prize.* 4. A large quantity or group: *A number of people gathered outside the store before the sale started. Noun.*
○ 1. To find out the number of; count: *The police numbered the crowd at about 1,000.* 2. To give a number or numbers to: *Number the pages of your book reports, please.* 3. To amount to or include; contain: *The sixth grade numbered fifty-two students.* 4. To limit: *The days before summer vacation ends are numbered. Verb.*
num·ber (num′bər) *noun, plural* **numbers;** *verb,* **numbered, numbering.**

number line A line on which points are marked with numbers.

numeral A figure or group of figures that stand for a number: *The numerals 7 and VII both stand for seven.* **nu·mer·al** (nü′mər əl *or* nū′mər əl) *noun, plural* **numerals.**

numerator The number above or to the left of the line in a fraction. In the fraction ½, 1 is the numerator and 2 is the denominator. **nu·mer·a·tor** (nü′mə rā′tər *or* nū′mə rā′tər) *noun, plural* **numerators.**

In $\underline{\mathbf{1}}$; $\underline{\mathbf{2}}$; and $\underline{\mathbf{7}}$
 4 3 8
1, 2, and **7** are **numerators.**

numerical Relating to or expressed by a number or numbers: $2 + 3 = 5$ *is a numerical equation;* $a + b = c$ *is not.* **nu·mer·i·cal** (nü mer′i kəl *or* nū mer′i kəl) *adjective.* —**numerically** *adverb.*

Numerous cactuses are growing in the sun.

numerous 1. Forming a large number; many: *Our parents have numerous friends in this*

PRONUNCIATION KEY:

| at | āpe | fär | câre | end | mē | it | īce | pîerce | hot | ōld | sông | fôrk |
| oil | out | up | ūse | rüle | pùll | tûrn | chin | sing | shop | thin | this | |

hw in white; zh in treasure. The symbol ə stands for the unstressed vowel sound in about, taken, pencil, lemon, and circus.

513

neighborhood. **2.** Containing a large number; large: *Counting all my cousins, this is a numerous family.* **nu·mer·ous** (nü′mər əs *or* nū′mər əs) *adjective.*

nun A woman who has taken special vows and belongs to a religious order. Many nuns live in convents, while others live and work in different communities.
Another word that sounds like this is **none.**
nun (nun) *noun, plural* **nuns.**

It takes a good deal of training to become a nurse.

nurse **1.** A person who is trained to take care of sick people and to teach people how to stay healthy: *The school nurse reminded us to wash our hands before meals.* **2.** A person hired to take care of children. *Noun.*
○ **1.** To take care of: *We nursed the injured rabbit back to health.* **2.** To feed a baby or young animal from a nipple: *a mother nursing her baby.* **3.** To be fed from a nipple: *At first, the puppies did nothing but nurse and sleep.* **4.** To treat with care: *I'm nursing a sore elbow. Verb.*
nurse (nûrs) *noun, plural* **nurses;** *verb,* **nursed, nursing.**

WORD HISTORY

The word **nurse** goes back to a Latin word meaning "nourishing" or "the nourishing one." Originally, a nurse was the woman who tended and fed babies.

nursery **1.** A baby's bedroom. **2.** A place where young children are taken care of during the day. **3.** A place where plants and trees are raised and sold. **nurs·er·y** (nûr′sə rē) *noun, plural* **nurseries.**

nursery school A school for children who are too young to go to kindergarten.

nut **1.** The dry fruit of a plant. Nuts have a hard outer shell and a softer kernel inside. **2.** The edible inside kernel of a nut. **3.** A piece of metal with a hole in the center. The nut screws onto a bolt and helps keep the bolt in place. **4.** A crazy or silly person. **nut** (nut) *noun, plural* **nuts.** — **nutty** *adjective.*

The soft kernel inside a nut can usually be eaten.

nutcracker **1.** A tool used for breaking open the hard outer shell of a nut. **2.** A bird with a tough pointed beak for feeding on nuts. Nutcrackers are related to crows. **nut·crack·er** (nut′krak′ər) *noun, plural* **nutcrackers.**

nuthatch A small bird with a narrow head and sharp beak. Nuthatches look for food along tree trunks and branches. They often move down a tree trunk head first. **nut·hatch** (nut′hach′) *noun, plural* **nuthatches.**

nutmeat The kernel of a nut, especially when it can be eaten. **nut·meat** (nut′mēt′) *noun, plural* **nutmeats.**

nutmeg The hard seed of a tropical evergreen tree. Nutmeg is dried, then ground or grated, and used in flavoring foods. **nut·meg** (nut′meg′) *noun, plural* **nutmegs.**

nutshell The hard outer covering of a nut: *You will need a nutcracker to break that nutshell.* **nut·shell** (nut′shel′) *noun, plural* **nutshells.**

nutrient Something that is needed by people, animals, or plants for life and growth: *The protein in meat is a **nutrient** for people and many animals. Plants use the **nutrients** in water and soil to grow.* **nu·tri·ent** (nü′trē ənt *or* nū′trē ənt) *noun,* plural **nutrients**.

nutrition 1. Food; nourishment: *The lack of proper nutrition made the child sick.* 2. The process by which food is taken in and used by a living thing: *We are studying plant **nutrition** in science this month.* **nu·tri·tion** (nü trish′ən *or* nū trish′ən) *noun.*

nutritious Giving nourishment; useful as a food: *It is important for children to have **nutritious** food.* **nu·tri·tious** (nü trish′əs *or* nū trish′əs) *adjective.* —**nutritiously** *adverb.*

nuzzle To touch or rub with the nose: *The dog nuzzled its owner when it wanted to be fed.* **nuz·zle** (nuz′əl) *verb,* **nuzzled, nuzzling**.

NV Postal abbreviation for **Nevada**.

NW or **N.W.** An abbreviation for **northwest**.

N.W.T. An abbreviation for **Northwest Territories**.

NY Postal abbreviation for **New York**.

N.Y. An abbreviation for **New York**.

nylon A strong fabric manufactured from chemicals. Nylon is used to make thread, clothes, stockings, tires for automobiles, tents for camping, and many other things **ny·lon** (nī′lon) *noun.*

Many tents are made of nylon.

nymph 1. In old legends, a goddess that lived in forests, hills, or rivers. Nymphs usually took the form of beautiful young women. 2. A newly hatched insect that looks like a tiny adult. A newly hatched grasshopper is a nymph. **nymph** (nimf) *noun,* plural **nymphs**.

PRONUNCIATION KEY:
at   āpe   fär   câre   end   mē   it   īce   pierce   hot   ōld   sông   fôrk
oil   out   up   ūse   rüle   pull   tûrn   chin   sing   shop   thin   this
hw in white; zh in treasure. The symbol ə stands for the unstressed vowel sound in about, taken, pencil, lemon, and circus.

515

SPELLING HINTS

The letter O has several sounds in English and each of these sounds can be made in several different ways.

The sound of o in hot, odd, and spot can also be made by:

a, especially when it follows a w as in words such as wand and watch; ah as in hurrah.

The sound of o as in coffee and moth can also be made by:

a when it comes before ll as in fall and small;
a when it follows w in some words such as want; aw as in awful, law and saw;
au, especially when it occurs in the middle of a syllable, as in haunt and taut;

or less commonly by:

ou as in cough and fought;

and rarely by:

oa in words such as broad.

The sound of O in go can also be made by:

oa as in oat and soap; oe as in toe;
ow as in low, grow, and know;

and less commonly by:

ou as in soul; ough as in though;
ew as in sew;

and in some words from foreign languages by:

au as in mauve; eau as in plateau.

In words such as *atom*, *lemon*, and *mother*, the sound of the letter O is represented in the pronunciations in this dictionary by a (ə).

o, O The fifteenth letter of the alphabet. **o, O** (ō) *noun, plural* **o's, O's.**

O. An abbreviation for Ohio.

oak Any of a large group of trees or shrubs that bear acorns. Oaks have a strong, heavy wood that is used in making furniture and boats and for covering floors. **oak** (ōk) *noun, plural* **oaks.**

oar A long pole with a flat or curved blade at one end. Oars are usually made of wood. They are used to row or steer a boat.
Other words that sound like this are or and ore. **oar** (ôr) *noun, plural* **oars.**

oasis A place in a desert where trees and other plants can grow because there is water. **o•a•sis** (ō ā′sis) *noun, plural* **oases.**

oat The grain of a plant that is related to grass. Oats are used as food by humans and as feed for horses, cattle, and other animals. **oat** (ōt) *noun, plural* **oats.**

oath 1. A statement or promise in which a person swears that what he or she says is true: *The witness took an oath in court.* 2. A strong or foul word used by someone who is angry; curse. **oath** (ōth) *noun, plural* **oaths.**

oatmeal 1. Meal that is made by grinding or rolling oats. 2. A cooked cereal that is made from this meal. **oat•meal** (ōt′mēl′) *noun, plural* **oatmeals.**

obedient Tending or willing to obey: *The obedient children went right to bed.* **o•be•di•ent** (ō bē′dē ənt) *adjective.* —**obedience** *noun.*

obese Very fat: *This diet helps obese people lose weight.* **o•bese** (ō ′bēs) *adjective.* **obesity,** *noun.*

obey 1. To carry out the orders, wishes, or instructions of: *I obeyed my parents and came home before dark.* 2. To carry out or follow: *The driver obeyed the speed limit.* 3. To do what one is ordered or instructed to do: *The dog wouldn't obey when I told him to go home.* **o•bey** (ō bā′) *verb,* **obeyed, obeying.**

SYNONYMS

obey, comply, follow, mind
*The driver obeyed the traffic policeman's signal.
I complied with the teacher's request to distribute
the books. The students followed their teacher's
instructions. I always mind my parents' request to
phone if I'm going to be out late.*

---

obi A wide sash worn with a kimono. **o·bi** (ō'bē) *noun, plural* **obis**.

object **1.** Anything that can be seen and touched; thing: *What is that object in your hand?* **2.** A person or thing toward which feeling, thought, or action is directed: *the object of someone's love.* **3.** A thing that one wants to achieve; purpose; goal: *The object of his call was to invite her to a party.* **4.** A word or group of words in a sentence that tells who or what receives or is affected by the action of a verb. In the sentence "I already gave them permission," the pronoun "them" and the noun "permission" are objects of the verb "gave." **5.** A noun or pronoun that ends a phrase begun with a preposition. In the sentence "I put it on the desk," the noun "desk" is the object of the preposition "on." *Noun.*
○ To be against; have or raise an objection: *The students objected to the increase in homework. Verb.*
ob·ject (ob'jikt *for noun*; əb jekt' *for verb*) *noun, plural* **objects**; *verb,* **objected, objecting**.

objection **1.** A cause or reason for not liking or approving of something: *My teacher's objection to my answer was that it was incomplete.* **2.** A feeling of not liking or approving: *Their objection to the idea showed on their faces.* **ob·jec·tion** (əb jek'shən) *noun, plural* **objections**.

objectionable Tending to cause objection. **ob·jec·tion·able** (əb jek'shə nə bəl) *adjective.*
—objectionably

objective Not influenced by one's personal feelings or opinions: *The witnesses tried to be objective when they talked to the police. Adjective.*
○ Something that one wants to achieve; purpose; goal: *What was your objective in going to see the mayor? Noun.*
ob·jec·tive (əb jek'tiv) *adjective; noun, plural* **objectives**. **—objectively** *adverb.*

obligate To make a person do something because of a law, promise, or sense of duty: *A driver is obligated to obey traffic laws.* **ob·li·gate** (ob'li gāt') *verb,* **obligated, obligating**.

obligation Something a person is supposed to do; duty; responsibility: *It is the obligation of all citizens to vote.* **ob·li·ga·tion** (ob'li gā'shən) *noun, plural* **obligations**. **—obligatory** *adjective.*

oblige **1.** To make a person do something by a law, promise, or sense of duty: *My parents were obliged to pay for the window I broke.* **2.** To make thankful for a service or favor: *We are obliged to you for your help.* **o·blige** (ə blīj') *verb,* **obliged, obliging**.

obliging Willing to help or do favors for others: *an obliging neighbor.* **o·blig·ing** (ə blī'jing) *adjective.*

oblique angle Any angle that is not a right angle. **ob·lique angle** (ə blēk').

oblong Longer than wide: *an oblong box. Adjective.*
○ An object or shape that is oblong: *A rectangle that is not square is an oblong. Noun.*
ob·long (ob'lông') *adjective; noun, plural* **oblongs**.

obnoxious Extremely unpleasant or offensive: *He's a good ballplayer but his obnoxious manner offends his teammates.* **ob·nox·ious** (əb nok'shəs *or* ob nok'shəs) *adjective.*

oboe A musical instrument that makes a high tone. The oboe is played by blowing into a mouthpiece made from two reeds. **o·boe** (ō'bō) *noun, plural* **oboes**.

obscene Offensive and indecent: *The film is rated unsuitable for children because of the obscene language in its dialogue.* **ob·scene** (əb sēn' *or* ob sēn') *adjective.* **—obscenity** *noun.*

obscure **1.** Hard to understand; not clearly expressed: *The poem was full of symbols and very obscure.* **2.** Not clearly seen, felt, or heard: *an obscure figure in a faded photograph.* **3.** Not well-known: *an obscure writer. Adjective.*
○ To hide; conceal: *Fog obscured the moon. Verb.*
ob·scure (əb skyür') *adjective; verb,* **obscured, obscuring**. **—obscurity** *noun.*

observation **1.** The act or power of noticing: *The detective's careful observation helped solve the crime.* **2.** The condition of being seen; notice: *The thief escaped observation.* **3.** Something said; comment; remark: *I made an observation about*

PRONUNCIATION KEY:

| at | āpe | fär | câre | end | mē | it | īce | pîerce | hot | ōld | sông | fôrk |
| oil | out | up | ūse | rüle | pull | tûrn | chin | sing | shop | thin | this | |

hw in white; zh in treasure. The symbol ə stands for the unstressed vowel sound in about, taken, pencil, lemon, and circus.

517

the weather. **ob·ser·va·tion** (ob′zər vā′shən) *noun*, *plural* **observations**.

Modern observatories were made possible by the invention of the telescope.

observatory A place or building that has telescopes for observing and studying the sun, moon, planets, and stars. **ob·serv·a·to·ry** (əb zûr′və tôr′ ē) *noun*, *plural* **observatories**.

observe 1. To see or notice: *I observed a large truck parked next door.* 2. To make a careful study of: *The scientist observed how the mice acted after they had the medicine.* 3. To follow, obey, or celebrate: *The driver of the car observed the speed limit. We observe Thanksgiving with my grandparents.* 4. To comment; remark. *"We have a strong team," the coach observed.* **ob·serve** (əbzûrv′) *verb*, **observed**, **observing**. **—observant** *adjective*.

obsolete No longer in use or practice; out-of-date: *Stagecoaches are obsolete.* **ob·so·lete** (ob′sə lēt′ *or* ob′sə lēt′) *adjective*.

obstacle A person or thing that stands in the way or blocks progress: *The heavy snowstorm was an obstacle to traffic.* **ob·sta·cle** (ob′stə kəl) *noun*, *plural* **obstacles**.

obstinate Unwilling to change one's mind; stubborn: *He's being obstinate and won't even listen to our point of view.* **ob·sti·nate** (ob′stə nət) *adjective*.

obstruct 1. To fill and block: *Fallen trees obstructed the road.* 2. To stand or be in the way of: *The hat on the person in front of me obstructed my view.* **ob·struct** (əb strukt′) *verb*, **obstructed**, **obstructing**.

WORD HISTORY

The word **obstruct** comes from two Latin words meaning "in the way" and "to build." To obstruct means "to build something in the way" and thus block a path or action.

---

obstruction 1. Something that obstructs; obstacle; block: *The tree that fell in the road was an obstruction to traffic.* 2. The act of obstructing or the condition of being obstructed: *Your obstruction of this road is illegal.* **ob·struc·tion** (əb struk′shən) *noun*, *plural* **obstructions**.

obtain To get through effort; gain: *I went to the library to obtain information for my report.* **ob·tain** (əb tān′) *verb*, **obtained**, **obtaining**.

obtuse angle Any angle that is greater than a right angle. **ob·tuse angle** (əb tüs′ *or* əb tūs′).

obvious Easily seen or understood: *The dog made it obvious that it didn't want a bath.* **ob·vi·ous** (ob′vē əs) *adjective*.

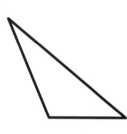

obtuse angle

occasion 1. The time when something happens: *I have met that person on several occasions.* 2. An important or special event: *The baby's first birthday was an occasion.* 3. A suitable time; good opportunity: *I haven't had an occasion to talk to them lately.* **oc·ca·sion** (ə kā′zhən) *noun*, *plural* **occasions**.

occasional Happening or appearing now and then; not frequent: *The weather report said there will be occasional showers.* **oc·ca·sion·al** (ə kāzh′ə nəl) *adjective*. **—occasionally** *adverb*.

occupant A person or thing that occupies a place or position: *I don't know the present occupant of the apartment.* **oc·cu·pant** (ok′yə pənt) *noun*, *plural* **occupants**.

occupation 1. The work that a person does in order to earn a living; profession:

Farming is one of the world's oldest occupations.

OCEAN

Water covers more than two-thirds of the surface of the Earth and the largest amount of water is held in four great oceans.

Pacific Ocean: Lying between Asia and the Americas, the Pacific is the largest ocean. It covers 64,186,300 square miles and has an average depth of 12,925 feet. The deepest point on Earth, the Mariana Trench, is located in the southern Pacific and is 35,840 feet deep. If the tallest mountain, Mount Everest, was placed in the trench, its peak would be a mile below the surface of the water.

Atlantic Ocean: Located between the Americas, Europe, and Africa, the Atlantic covers 33,420,00 square miles. Its average depth is 11,730 feet.

Indian Ocean: Bordered by Africa and India, this ocean covers 28,350,500 square miles at an average depth of 12,598 feet.

Arctic Ocean: Surrounding the North Pole, much of this ocean is covered by ice. However, submarines can cross this ocean by traveling beneath the ice. The Arctic Ocean covers 5,105,700 square miles with an average depth of 3,407 feet.

Her occupation is teaching. **2.** The act of occupying or the condition of being occupied: *the enemy soldiers' occupation of the town.* **oc·cu·pa·tion** (ok′yə pā′shən) *noun, plural* **occupations.**

occupy **1.** To take up time or space; fill: *Running errands for my parents occupied most the morning.* **2.** To take and keep control of: *Enemy soldiers occupied the fort.* **3.** To live in: *occupy a house.* **4.** To keep busy: *The children occupied themselves by working on model airplanes.* **5.** To have as one's own; possess: *Two of our neighbors occupy a position in the town's government.* **oc·cu·py** (ok′yə pī′) *verb,* **occupied, occupying.**

occur **1.** To take place; happen: *The fire occurred last week.* **2.** To be found; appear: *How many times does the word "to" occur on this page?* **3.** To come into one's thoughts; suggest itself: *It did not occur to me to take my umbrella.* **oc·cur** (ə kûr′) *verb,* **occurred, occurring.**

occurrence **1.** The act of occurring: *The occurrence of snow at this time of year is rare.* **2.** Something that takes place or happens: *Rain is an unusual occurrence in the desert.* **occurrence** (ə kûr′əns) *noun, plural* **occurrences.**

ocean **1.** The whole body of salt water that covers nearly three fourths of the earth's surface. **2.** Any one of the four main parts of this body of water: *the Atlantic, Pacific, Indian, or Arctic Ocean.* **o·cean** (ō′shən) *noun, plural* **oceans.**

ocean floor The land lying at the bottom of the ocean: *The diver found many exotic fish while exploring the ocean floor.*

oceanography The science that deals with the ocean and the animals and plants that live in it. **o·cean·og·ra·phy** (ō′shə nog′rə fē) *noun.*

ocelot A wildcat of medium size that has yellow fur with black stripes on its face and spots on its body. Ocelots live in the southwestern United States and in Central and South America. **o·ce·lot** (os′ə lot′ *or* ō′sə lot′) *noun, plural* **ocelots.**

o'clock Of or according to the clock: *They will meet us at two o'clock.* **o'clock** (ə klok′) *adverb.*

Oct. An abbreviation for October.

octagon A figure having eight sides and eight angles. **oc·ta·gon** (ok′tə gon′) *noun, plural* **octagons.**

octagon

octave **1.** The musical interval between the first and last notes of a scale. **2.** All the notes or keys of an instrument that make up this interval. Most pianos have a range of seven and one half octaves. **oc·tave** (ok′tiv) *noun, plural* **octaves.**

October The tenth month of the year. October has thirty-one days. **Oc·to·ber** (ok tō′bər) *noun.*

WORD HISTORY

October comes from the Latin word for "eight." The early Roman calendar began with March, making October the eighth month.

PRONUNCIATION KEY:

| at | āpe | fär | câre | end | mē | it | īce | pierce | hot | ōld | sông | fôrk |
| oil | out | up | ūse | rüle | pull | tûrn | chin | sing | shop | thin | this | |

hw in white; zh in treasure. The symbol ə stands for the unstressed vowel sound in about, taken, pencil, lemon, and circus.

519

octopus An animal that lives in salt water and has a soft, rounded body and eight arms. The octopus has suckers on its arms that help it move along the ocean bottom and catch food. **oc·to·pus** (ok′tə pəs) *noun, plural* **octopuses.**

odd 1. Different from the usual or normal; strange; peculiar: *The car was making an* **odd** *sound, so we took it to be fixed. It is* **odd** *that they never answered my letter.* 2. Remaining from a pair or set: *I have an* **odd** *glove and can't find its mate. This is an* **odd** *plate left from the set of old dishes.* 3. Happening or appearing now and then; occasional: *She makes a living doing* **odd** *jobs.* 4. Leaving a remainder of one when divided by two: *5, 7, and 19 are* **odd** *numbers.* **odd** (od) *adjective,* **odder, oddest.**

oddity 1. A person or thing that is odd or strange: *An animal with two heads would be quite an* **oddity.** 2. The condition or quality of being odd or strange: *The* **oddity** *of their green hair made the clowns look funnier than ever.* **odd·i·ty** (od′i tē) *noun, plural* **oddities.**

odds The difference in favor of or against something being true or happening: *The* **odds** *are ten to one against that horse's winning the race. The* **odds** *are in favor of your being elected class president.*

• **at odds.** Disagreeing or quarreling: *The twins are often* **at odds** *with each other.*
odds (odz) *plural noun.*

odds and ends Things of various kinds, usually with little value: *You'll find all sorts of* **odds and ends** *in that drawer.* (od′zə nendz′)

odor Smell; scent: *The* **odor** *of flowers filled the room. The* **odor** *of garbage bothered the people who lived near the town dump.* **o·dor** (ō′dər) *noun, plural* **odors.**

odorless Having no smell; without an odor: *Some gases are* **odorless.** **odorless** (ō′dər lis) *adjective.*

of 1. Belonging to: *The cover* **of** *the book is red. Are you a member* **of** *the club?* 2. Away from: *We live five miles north* **of** *the city.* 3. That is or that is called: *The city* **of** *Boston is very historic.* 4. Characterized by; having; with: *a girl* **of** *many talents* 5. Relating to; concerning; about: *I thought* **of** *you last night.* 6. Resulting from; caused by: *The plant died* **of** *the cold.* 7. Having or containing: *I drank a glass* **of** *milk.* 8. Made from or with: *A wall* **of** *bricks surrounded the yard.* **of** (uv *or* ov *or unstressed* əv) *preposition.*

off No longer on, attached to, or connected with; away from: *Take the books* **off** *the shelf, please. A button is* **off** *my jacket. Preposition.*
○ 1. So as to be no longer on, attached, or connected: *The bike skidded and I fell* **off.** *I broke a piece of bread* **off** *from the loaf.* 2. So as to be no longer working or functioning. *Please switch* **off** *the lights in the living room.* 3. So as to be away from work or duty: *Did you take yesterday* **off?** *Adverb.*
○ 1. No longer working, continuing, or taking place: *Is the electricity* **off?** 2. Away from work or duty: *The students are* **off** *for the day.* 3. Not accurate or correct: *Your addition was* **off** *by three cents. Adjective.*

• **off and on.** Stopping and starting with periods of time between; not continuously: *Yesterday it rained* **off and on** *all day.*
off (ôf) *preposition; adverb; adjective.*

offend To cause to be angry or unhappy: *Your rude remark* **offended** *me.* **of·fend** (ə fend′) *verb,* **offended, offending.**

offense 1. The act of breaking the law or a rule: *The thieves will be punished for their* **offense.** 2. The act of causing anger or unhappiness: *I'm sorry I hurt your feelings; I meant no* **offense.** 3. The attacking team or players in a game: *Our team has a good* **offense.** **off·ense** (ə fens′ *for definitions 1 and 2;* ô′fəns *for definition 3*) *noun, plural* **offenses.** —**offender** *noun.*

offensive 1. Causing anger or unhappiness: *They got into an argument over an* **offensive** *remark.* 2. Not pleasing; unpleasant; disagreeable: *There was an* **offensive** *smell in the garbage can.* 3. Used for attack: *A knife is an* **offensive** *weapon. Adjective.*
○ A position, course, or attitude of attack: *The enemy took the* **offensive** *and surrounded the fort. Noun.*
of·fen·sive (ə fen′siv) *adjective; noun, plural* **offensives.** —**offensively** *adverb.*

offer 1. To present to be accepted or turned down: *I offered an apology for being late. They* **offered** *me a cold drink. We* **offered** *ten dollars for the book.* 2. To show a desire to do or give something; volunteer: *My friend* **offered** *to help me.* 3. To make a show of: *The enemy* **offered** *little resistance when the soldiers attacked. Verb.*

○ **1.** The act of offering: *We accept your offer of help.* **2.** Something offered: *We made an offer of $500 for the old car.* Noun.
of·fer (ôf′ər) *verb,* **offered, offering**; *noun, plural* **offers.**

SYNONYMS

offer, extend, present
I offered my guest another drink. The principal extended an invitation to all the parents to visit the new school library. The teacher presented the new student to the class.

---

offhand Done or said without preparation or careful thought: *offhand remarks.* **off·hand** (ôf′hand′) *adjective.*

office **1.** A place where the work of a business or profession is done: *The door to the doctor's office was open. That company's office is upstairs.* **2.** All the people who work in such a place: *The office gave the secretary a birthday party.* **3.** A position of authority, trust, or responsibility: *Who is running for the office of mayor?* **of·fice** (ô′fis) *noun, plural* **offices.**

Captains, generals, and admirals are officers.

officer **1.** A person who has the power to command and lead others in the army or navy. **2.** A person who has a position of authority, trust, or responsibility: *The president and vice president of a company are two of its officers.* **3.** A member of the police; policeman or policewoman: *We asked the officer for directions.* **of·fi·cer** (ô′fə sər) *noun, plural* **officers.**

official A person who holds a certain office or position: *The president and vice president are the two highest officials in the executive branch of the United States government.* Noun.
○ **1.** Of or relating to an office or position of authority: *Taking notes at each meeting is one of the official duties of the club secretary.* **2.** Coming from or approved by an authority: *The governor made an official statement to the press.* **3.** Having the authority to do a specific job: *the official referee at the basketball game.* **4.** Formal and proper: *an official reception for a visiting prime minister.* Adjective.
of·fi·cial (ə fish′əl) *noun, plural* **officials**; *adjective.*
—**officially** *adverb.*

off-road Built or used on the rough roads: *off-road vehicles.* **off·road** (ôf′rōd′) *adjective.*

offset To act against or lessen the effect of; make up for: *The teacher's kindness offset the strict rules of the school.* **off·set** (ôf′set′) *verb,* **offset, offsetting.**

offshoot Something that develops or grows from something else. A shoot or stem that grows from the main stem of a plant is an offshoot. **off·shoot** (ôf′shüt′) *noun, plural* **offshoots.**

offshore Moving or in a direction away from the shore: *We saw some people doing offshore fishing from their boats.* Adjective.
○ Away from the shore: *The storm has moved offshore.* Adverb.
off·shore (ôf′shôr′) *adjective; adverb.*

offspring The young of a person, animal, or plant: *At the zoo we saw a mother lion and three offspring.* **off·spring** (ôf′spring′) *noun, plural* **offspring.**

often Many times; frequently: *We went swimming often this summer.* **of·ten** (ô′fən) *adverb.*

ogre **1.** A monster or giant that eats people. Ogres appear in fairy tales and legends. **2.** A person who is cruel and frightening: *That man is an ogre to children who cross his yard.* **o·gre** (ō′gər) *noun, plural* **ogres.**

oh A word used to express surprise, happiness, sadness, pain, or other feeling: *Oh! I didn't hear you come into the room!*
Another word that sounds like this is **owe.**
oh (ō) *interjection.*

OH Postal abbreviation for **Ohio.**

PRONUNCIATION KEY:
at   āpe   fär   câre   end   mē   it   īce   pîerce   hot   ōld   sông   fôrk
oil   out   up   ūse   rüle   pùll   tûrn   chin   sing   shop   thin   this
hw in white; zh in treasure. The symbol ə stands for the unstressed vowel sound in about, taken, pencil, lemon, and circus.

521

Ohio **1.** A state in the north-central United States. Its capital is Columbus. **2.** A river in the east-central United States. **O•hi•o** (ō hī′ō) *noun.*

Ohio
U. S. Postal Abbreviation: **OH**
Capital: **Columbus**
Population: **10,784,000**
Area: **41,222 sq. mi./106,764 sq. km**
State Nickname: **Buckeye State**
State Bird: **Cardinal**
State Flower: **Scarlet Carnation**

WORD HISTORY

Ohio was a Native American name for the Ohio River that means "fine, great, beautiful river." Settlers used the name for the land around the river. When this land was made a county of Virginia, it was called Ohio, too. When the county became a separate state, it kept the same name.

Oil well pumps like these are sometimes called grasshoppers because of their shape.

oil **1.** Any one of a large group of substances that are greasy and will dissolve in alcohol but not in water. Oils are usually liquid or will easily become liquid when warmed. Oil comes from animals, vegetables, and minerals. **2.** A liquid that is found beneath the earth's surface; petroleum. Look up **petroleum** for more information.
○ *Noun.* To cover, polish, or supply with oil: *I helped **oil** the furniture. The worker **oiled** the rusty hinges of the door. Verb.*
oil (oil) *noun, plural* **oils;** *verb,* **oiled, oiling.**

oil paint A paint that is made by mixing colored powders with oil.

oil well A well that is dug or drilled in the earth to get petroleum.

oily **1.** Of or like oil: *oily suntan lotion.* **2.** Containing, covered, or soaked with oil: *We threw away the oily rags.* **oil•y** (oi′lē) *adjective,* **oilier, oiliest.** **oiliness,** *noun.*

ointment A soft, oily substance that is put on the skin to heal, protect, or soften it. Ointments frequently contain medicine. **oint•ment** (oint′mənt) *noun, plural* **ointments.**

Ojibwa A member of a Native American people who live mostly in the area around Lake Superior and in the Northern Great Plains. The Ojibwa are also known as *Chippewa.* **O•jib•wa** (ō jib′wā or ō jib′wə) *noun, plural* **Ojibwa or Ojibwas.**

OK¹ All right: *Is it OK if I borrow your book? OK! I'll do it! Adjective; adverb; interjection.*
○ Agreement or approval: *We need the teacher's OK to have a party. Noun.*
○ To approve or agree to: *The teacher OK'd our project. Verb.*
This word is also spelled O.K. and okay.
O•K (ō′kā′) *adjective; adverb; interjection; noun, plural* **OK's;** *verb,* **OK'd, OK'ing.**

OK² Postal abbreviation for Oklahoma.

Okla. An abbreviation for Oklahoma.

Oklahoma A state in the south-central United States. Its capital is Oklahoma City. **O•kla•ho•ma** (ō′klə hō′mə) *noun.*

WORD HISTORY

In an Indian treaty of 1866, one tribe used the name Oklahoma for its lands. This Native American word means "red people." The name was given to a railroad station that used to be where Oklahoma City is today. Later it was chosen as the name for the state.

Oklahoma
U. S. Postal Abbreviation: **OK**
Capital: **Oklahoma City**
Population: **3,272,000**
Area: **69,919 sq. mi./181,089 sq. km**
State Nickname: **Sooner State**
State Bird: **Scissor-Tailed Flycatcher**
State Flower: **Mistletoe**

okra The green pods of a plant. Okra is soft and sticky inside. It is used in soups and eaten as a vegetable. **o•kra** (ō′krə) *noun.*

old 1. Having lived or existed for a long period of time: *That church is a very old building.* 2. Of a certain age: *Our car is three years old.* 3. From the past; not new or recent: *The comedian told an old joke.* 4. Known for a long time; familiar: *We are old friends.* 5. Former: *when I lived in my old neighborhood.* 6. Worn-out; used: *We gave away all our old clothes. Adjective.*
○ A time in the past; former times: *a story of the knights of old. Noun.*
old (ōld) *adjective,* **older** *or* **elder,** **oldest** *or* **eldest;** *noun.*

Synonyms

old, aged, elderly, senior
My father met an old friend he hadn't seen since his Army days. *He's an aged veteran of World War I.*
The elderly lady had a hard time climbing the stairs.
Our town just built a senior citizens center.

olden Very old or ancient: *Chariots were used in olden days.* **old•en** (ōl′dən) *adjective.*
Old English The oldest form of the English language, used until about the year 1100.
old-fashioned 1. Attached to or favoring old ways, ideas, or customs: *My grandparents are a little old-fashioned in the way they think.*

2. Out-of-date; no longer in fashion: *I found an old-fashioned hat in the attic.* **old-fash•ioned** (ōld′fash′ənd) *adjective.*
Old Testament A collection of writings that make up the Jewish Bible and form the first part of the Christian Bible.
Old World The part of the world that includes Europe, Asia, and Africa: *Columbus sailed from the Old World to the New World.*
oleomargarine A substitute for butter. This is also called *margarine.* Look up **margarine** for more information. **o•le•o•mar•ga•rine** (ō′lē ō mär′jə rin) *noun, plural* **oleomargarines.**
olive 1. The small, oily fruit of an evergreen tree. Olives have a single hard seed and firm flesh. They are often eaten pickled and are used to make olive oil. 2. A dull yellowish green color. *Noun.*
○ Having the color olive; dull yellowish green. *Adjective.*
ol•ive (ol′iv) *noun, plural* **olives;** *adjective.*
olive oil A yellow or green oil obtained from olives. It is used in salads and in cooking.

OLYMPIC GAMES

The tradition of athletes coming together from all parts of the world to compete dates back to the Greeks more than 2,700 years ago. The ancient Olympic Games were held every four years near the city of Olympia starting in 776 BC. At first, there was only one competition, a foot race, but soon other events were added, including wrestling, chariot racing, discus and javelin throwing, and boxing. The games continued for more than 1,000 years until it was stopped by a Roman Emperor in 393 AD.

The Modern Olympics: The idea of an international sports competition was revived in 1896 when the first modern Olympics were held in Athens, Greece. Athletes from 13 nations participated. The Olympics now draw athletes from all over the world and are divided into the summer and winter games. They are still held every four years, but the summer games will be held in 2000 and 2004, and the winter games will be held in 2002 and 2006.

Olympic games 1. An ancient Greek festival during which a series of competitions in athletics,

PRONUNCIATION KEY:

| at | āpe | fär | câre | end | mē | it | īce | pierce | hot | ōld | sông | fôrk |
| oil | out | up | ūse | rüle | pùll | tûrn | chin | sing | shop | thin | <u>th</u>is | |

hw in white; zh in treasure. The symbol ə stands for the unstressed vowel sound in about, taken, pencil, lemon, and circus.

523

poetry, and dancing were held. **2.** A modern series of athletic contests in which athletes from many countries take part. The Olympic games are held in winter and summer every four years. These games are also called the Olympics. **O·lym·pic games** (ō lim′pik *or* ə lim′pik).

WORD HISTORY

The Olympic games were named after Olympia, the city in Greece where the first games were held in 776 B.C.

---

omelet A food that is made of eggs that have been beaten, cooked in a pan, and then folded over. Omelets often have fillings. **om·e·let** (om′lit *or* om′ə lit) *noun, plural* **omelets.**

omen Something that is supposed to be a sign of good or bad luck to come: *Breaking a mirror is thought to be a bad* **omen. o·men** (ō′mən) *noun, plural* **omens.**

ominous Telling of trouble or bad luck to come; threatening: *There were* **ominous** *black storm clouds coming in from the sea.* **om·i·nous** (om′ə nəs) *adjective.*

omit To leave out; not include: *Did you* **omit** *butter from the recipe?* **o·mit** (ō mit′) *verb,* **omitted, omitting.** —**omission** *noun.*

omnivore An animal that eats both animal flesh and plants: *Bears are* **omnivores. om·ni·vore** (om′nə vôr′) *noun, plural* **omnivores.** —**omnivorous** *adjective.*

on 1. In a position above and supported by; atop: *The blankets are* **on** *the bed.* **2.** So as to be in contact with: *Please spread butter* **on** *the bread.* **3.** In a position at, near, or next to: *Their house is* **on** *the lake.* **4.** In the direction of; toward; to: *Our classroom is* **on** *the left.* **5.** In the condition or process of: *The nurse was* **on** *duty.* **6.** About; concerning: *a book* **on** *art.* **7.** During the time, course or occasion of: *We left* **on** *Wednesday.* **8.** Connected or associated with as a member: *I am* **on** *the committee that is planning the spring dance.* **9.** For the purpose of: *They went to the city* **on** *business. Preposition.* ○ **1.** In or into contact with something: *I'm putting some water* **on** *to boil.* **2.** Forward in time or space; onward: *Please move* **on** *so that others can pass by.* **3.** In, to, or into action, operation, or movement: *Switch the light* **on.** *The riders*

urged their horses **on.** *Adverb.* ○ **1.** In operation or use: *Why is the TV* **on** *?* **2.** Taking place; happening: *The war is still* **on.** *Adjective.*

 • **on and off.** Stopping and starting; not continuously: *He's been writing a novel* **on and off** *for ten years.*

 • **on and on.** Without stopping: *The speaker talked* **on and on** *for two hours.*

on (ôn *or* on) *preposition; adverb; adjective.*

ON Postal abbreviation for **Ontario.**

once 1. One time: *I have a piano lesson* **once** *a week.* **2.** In a time now past; before: *Parents were* **once** *children. Adverb.* ○ One single time: *May I borrow your bicycle just this* **once?** *Noun.* ○ As soon as; when: *The game is easy,* **once** *you learn the rules. Conjunction.*

 • **at once. 1.** Without any delay; now: *Come here* **at once**! **2.** At the same time: *Everyone in class tried to talk* **at once.**

 • **once and for all.** Finally and definitely: *Let's settle this argument* **once and for all.**

 • **once in a while.** Not often; occasionally: *We visit our cousins only* **once in a while.**

 • **once upon a time.** At some time in the past; long ago: *Once upon a time there were knights in armor.*

once (wuns) *adverb; noun; conjunction.*

oncoming Approaching; coming nearer: *The* **oncoming** *car had its lights off.* **on·com·ing** (ôn′kum′ing *or* on′kum′ing) *adjective.*

one 1. The first and lowest number; **2.** A single person, thing, or unit: *Someone's been eating the cherries; there's only* **one** *left. Noun.* ○ **1.** Being a single person or thing: *I have only* **one** *pencil.* **2.** Being a particular person, thing, or group: *The squirrel ran from* **one** *side of the yard to the other.* **3.** Some: *Your jokes will get you into trouble* **one** *day. Adjective.* ○ **1.** A particular person or thing: **One** *of the paintings won an award.* **2.** Any person: **One** *can see snow in the mountains. Pronoun.* Another word that sounds like this is **won.**

 • **one and all.** Everyone: *He said good-bye* **to** *one and all.*

 • **one another.** Each other: *The two sisters hugged* **one another.**

 • **one by one.** One after another; each following the preceding one: *We entered the bus* **one by one.**

one (wun) *noun, plural* **ones;** *adjective; pronoun.*

oneself One's own self: *Seeing* **oneself** *on television would be exciting.* **one·self** (wun self′) *pronoun.*

one-sided 1. For or showing only one side; unfair; partial: *Your story of the argument is* **one-sided.** 2. Not even or equal: *The basketball game was very* **one-sided,** *with our team losing by forty points.* **one-sid·ed** (wun′sī′did) *adjective.*

one-way Moving or allowing movement in one direction only: *a* **one-way** *street.* **one-way** (wun′wā′) *adjective.*

ongoing Continuing or progressing: *We have an* **ongoing** *discussion about chores at our house.* **on·go·ing** (on′gō′ing) *adjective.*

onion The round or oval bulb of a plant that is also known as an onion. Onions have a strong, sharp taste and smell. **on·ion** (un′yən) *noun, plural* **onions.**

online *or* **on-line** Having or offering a connection to a network of computers: *We subscribe to an* **online** *service so that we can use e-mail. Our company recently went* **online.** **on·line** (on′līn′) *adjective; adverb.*

Onions **are eaten as a vegetable either raw or cooked.**

only 1. Alone of its kind; solitary: *My friend is an* **only** *child. This is the* **only** *hat I own.* 2. Best of all: *You are the* **only** *singer for the role. Adjective.*
○ 1. No more than: *I have* **only** *two dollars.* 2. No one or nothing other than: **Only** *you remembered my birthday.* 3. No time or no place except: *My dog comes indoors* **only** *at night. Adverb.*
○ Except that; but: *I would have gone to the park,* **only** *it was raining. Conjunction.*
• **only child.** A person with no sisters or brothers.

on·ly (ōn′lē) *adjective; adverb; conjunction.*

onset 1. The beginning of something: *At the* **onset** *of summer, we move to the seashore.* 2. An attack; assault: *the* **onset** *of the hurricane.* **on·set** (ôn′set′ *or* on′set′) *noun, plural* **onsets.**

Ont. An abbreviation for Ontario.

Ontario A province in central Canada. Its capital is Toronto. **On·tar·i·o** (on târ′ē ō) *noun.*

onto To a position on: *The door opens* **onto** *the porch. The actor walked* **onto** *the stage.* **on·to** (ôn′tü *or* on′tü) *preposition.*

LANGUAGE NOTE

Do not confuse onto **and** on to**. *Onto* is a preposition, and it is written as one word. *On to* is a combination of the adverb *on* and the preposition *to* and so is written as two words: After looking at the lions, we walked *on to* the next exhibit at the zoo. The cat jumped *onto* the back of the chair.**

onward Toward the front: *They climbed* **onward** *to the top of the hill. Adverb.*
○ Moving or directed toward a point in front; forward: *It was impossible to stop the* **onward** *flow of the flood. Adjective.*
on·ward (ôn′wərd *or* on′wərd) *adverb; adjective.*

ooze To leak or pass out slowly through small holes or openings; seep: *The mud* **oozed** *between my toes.* **ooze** (üz) *verb,* **oozed, oozing.** **ooze,** *noun.*

opal A mineral used as a gem. Opals are white, blue, yellow, or black. **o·pal** (ō′pəl) *noun, plural* **opals.**

Opals **change color slightly when moved in the light.**

opaque 1. Not letting light through; not transparent: *Opaque curtains keep sunlight out of the room.* 2. Not shining; dull: *The table was painted*

PRONUNCIATION KEY:

| at | āpe | fär | câre | end | mē | it | īce | pierce | hot | ōld | sông | fôrk |
| oil | out | up | ūse | rüle | pull | tûrn | chin | sing | shop | thin | this | |

hw in white; zh in treasure. The symbol ə stands for the unstressed vowel sound in about, taken, pencil, lemon, and circus.

525

an opaque black. **o·paque** (ō pāk′) *adjective.*

open 1. Allowing movement in, out, or through: *The bird flew in through the open window.* 2. Not having its lid, door, or other covering closed: *There is an open box of tissues on the self.* 3. Not closed in or covered; having no barriers: *The horses ran across the open meadow.* 4. Spread out or unfolded: *The open umbrella blew away in the wind.* 5. Free to be used, taken, entered, or attended; available: *The job of school secretary is still open. The meeting of the city council is open to the public.* 6. Able or ready to take in new ideas, facts, or beliefs: *Our teacher is always open to suggestions.* 7. Honest; frank: *I am open with my friends about my problems.* 8. Ready to do business: *a store open every day but Sunday.* 9. Having spaces, holes, or gaps between the parts: a *net with an open weave. Adjective.*

○ 1. To make or become open: *Open the envelope and read the letter. The door creaked as it opened.* 2. To have an opening: *The room opens onto a porch.* 3. To spread out; unfold: *The petals of the flower opened.* 4. To set up or become available: *The pool opens in June.* 5. To begin; start: *The governor opened the speech with a joke. Verb.*

○ Any space or area that is not closed in or hidden: *The party was held in the open. Noun.* **o·pen** (ō′pən) *adjective; verb,* **opened, opening;** *noun.*

opener 1. A tool that is used to open closed or sealed containers, such as cans or bottles. 2. The first thing or part in a series: *We won the opener of the baseball season.* **o·pen·er** (ō′pə nər) *noun,* plural **openers.**

opening 1. An empty or clear space: *We squeezed through an opening in the fence.* 2. The first part; beginning: *The opening of the book was boring.* 3. A job that is not filled: *an opening for a clerk at the store.* 4. The first time something is performed or open for business: *the opening of a new movie.* 5. The act of becoming open or being made open: *The real opening of the West took place when the railroads were built.* **o·pen·ing** (ō′pə ning) *noun,* plural **openings.**

openly Freely and honestly: *He spoke openly about his troubles in school.* **open·ly** (ō′pən lē) *adverb.*

open-minded Willing to consider different opin-ions and new ideas: *The principal tried to be open-minded when the teachers suggested changes in school policies.* **o·pen-mind·ed** (ō′pən mīn′dəd) *adjective.*

opera A play in which all or most of the words are sung. Operas include costumes, scenery, act-ing, and music. **op·er·a** (op′ər ə *or* op′rə) *noun,* plural **operas.**

operate 1. To go or run; work; function: *The car's motor operates well.* 2. To cause to work or con-trol the working of: *How do you operate the ele-vator? I know how to operate a computer.* 3. To perform surgery on the body of a person or ani-mal: *The doctors operated on the patient.* **op·er·ate** (op′ə rāt′) *verb,* **operated, operating.**

SYNONYMS

operate, handle, run, work
Do you know how to operate this machine? The principal handled that problem very well. The programmer showed us how to run the new soft-ware. Can you work the VCR?

---

operation 1. The act or way of working or direct-ing. *The operation of the business took up a lot of the owner's time. I would like to learn about the operation of car engines.* 2. The condition of being at work: *The machine is in operation.* 3. Treatment that is performed on the body of a sick or hurt person or animal by surgery: *I had an operation to remove my tonsils.* **op·er·a·tion** (op′ə rāsh′ən) *noun,* plural **operations.**

operator A person who operates a machine or other device: *a telephone operator.* **op·er·a·tor** (op′ə rā′tər) *noun,* plural **operators.**

operetta A short opera that is light and amusing. An operetta includes music and songs combined with spoken parts and dancing. **op·er·et·ta** (op′ə ret′ə) *noun,* plural **operettas.**

ophthalmologist A doctor who specializes in diseases of the eye. **oph·thal·mol·o·gist** (of′thəl mol′ə jist) *noun,* plural **ophthalmologists.** —**ophthalmology** *noun.*

opinion 1. A belief that is based on what a person thinks rather than what is proved or known to be true: *It is my opinion that our team will win the race. What is your opinion of that movie?* 2. A formal statement or decision made by an expert: *My parents wanted to get a lawyer's opinion* *before they signed the contract.* **o•pin•ion** (ə pin′yən) *noun, plural* **opinions**.

opossum A furry American animal that lives in trees. Female opossums carry their young in a pouch as kangaroos do. This animal is also called a *possum.* **o•pos•sum** (ə pos′əm) *noun, plural* **opossums**.

opponent A person or group that is against anoth-

When frightened, an opossum
lies still as if dead.

er in a fight, contest, or discussion: *The soccer team beat its* **opponent.** **op•po•nent** (ə pō′nənt) *noun, plural* **opponents**.

opportunity A good chance; favorable time: *When the pond froze, we had an* **opportunity** *to go ice skating.* **op•por•tu•ni•ty** (op′ər tü′ni tē *or* op′ər tū′ni tē) *noun, plural* **opportunities**.

oppose 1. To be against; resist: *Most voters* **opposed** *the tax increase.* 2. To be the opposite of; contrast: *Good is* **opposed** *to evil.* **op•pose** (ə pōz′) *verb,* **opposed, opposing**.

opposite 1. On the other side of or across from another person or thing; facing: *They live on the* **opposite** *side of the street from me. That student sits* **opposite** *me.* 2. Turned or moving the other way: *We passed a car going in the* **opposite** *direction.* 3. Completely different: *Hot is* **opposite** *to cold. Adjective.*
○ A person or thing that is completely different from another: *Summer and winter are* **opposites**. *Noun.*
○ Across from: *Stand* **opposite** *me. Preposition.* **op•po•site** (op′ə zit) *adjective; noun, plural* **opposites**; *preposition.*

opposition 1. Disagreement with or action against: *My* **opposition** *to the plan surprised my friends.* 2. A political party that is opposed to the party in power. **op•po•si•tion** (op′ə zish′ən) *noun, plural* **oppositions**.

oppress 1. To control or rule by cruel and unjust means: *The dictator's army* **oppressed** *the people of the country.* 2. To be a burden to; trouble or depress: *The loss* **oppressed** *the team's spirits.* **op•press** (ə pres′) *verb,* **oppressed, oppressing.** —**oppressive** *adjective.*

opt To make a choice or decision: *We* **opted** *not to go bowling with them.*
• **to opt out.** To choose not to participate: *I* **opted out** *of tryouts for the chorus.* **opt** (opt) *verb,* **opted, opting**.

optical 1. Relating to the sense of sight: *A mirage is an* **optical** *illusion.* 2. Designed to help one see: *Microscopes and eyeglasses are* **optical** *devices.* **op•ti•cal** (op′ti kəl) *adjective.*

optician A person who makes and sells glasses and contact lenses. **op•ti•cian** (op tish′ən) *noun, plural* **opticians**.

optimistic Tending to look on the favorable side of things and believe that everything will turn out for the best: *The students were* **optimistic** *about getting good grades.* **op•ti•mis•tic** (op′tə mis′tik) *adjective.* —**optimism** *noun.*

option A choice; alternative: *You must go to school; staying home is not an* **option.** **op•tion** (op′shən) *noun, plural* **options**.

optional Left to one's choice; not required: *Going to the class party is* **optional.** **op•tion•al** (op′shə nəl) *adjective.*

optometrist A person who is trained and licensed to examine people's eyes and prescribe glasses or contact lenses. **op•tom•e•trist** (op tom′ə trist) *noun, plural* **optometrists.** —**optometry** *noun.*

or 1. A word that is used to connect words, phrases, and clauses that represent choices: *Is the water warm* **or** *cold? Eat lunch* **or** *you will be hungry later.* 2. A word that is used to introduce the second of two choices when the first is introduced by either or whether: *Either write* **or** *phone me. We didn't know whether to stay* **or** *leave.* 3. A word that is used to introduce a word or phrase that means the same as something already mentioned: *We saw a cougar,* **or** *mountain lion, at the zoo.* Other words that sound like this are **oar** and **ore**.

PRONUNCIATION KEY:

| at | āpe | fär | câre | end | mē | it | īce | pîerce | hot | ōld | sông | fôrk |
| oil | out | up | ūse | rüle | pull | tûrn | chin | sing | shop | thin | this | |

hw in white; zh in treasure. The symbol ə stands for the unstressed vowel sound in about, taken, pencil, lemon, and circus.

527

or (ôr) *conjunction.*

-or A suffix that means a person or thing that does something: *Inventor means a person who invents. Generator means a machine that produces or generates something.* The suffix -er sometimes has the same meaning. Look up -er¹ for more information.

OR Postal abbreviation for Oregon.

oral 1. Not written; using speech; spoken: *Each student must give an oral book report.* 2. Having to do with the mouth: *Brush your teeth for good oral hygiene.* **o•ral** (ôr′əl) *adjective.* **orally,** *adverb.*

orange 1. A round citrus fruit that has a thick orange or yellow skin and a sweet juice. Oranges grow on evergreen trees in warm climates. 2. A reddish yellow color. *Noun.*
○ Having the color orange; reddish yellow. *Adjective.*
or•ange (ôr′inj *or* or′inj) *noun, plural* **oranges;** *adjective.*

Oranges **are a good source of vitamin C.**

orangeade A drink made of orange juice and water and sweetened with sugar. **orangeade** (ôr′in jād′ *or* or′in jād′) *noun, plural* **orangeades.**

orangutan A large ape that lives in trees in certain parts of Asia. Orangutans have very long, strong arms, a shaggy coat of reddish brown hair, and no tail. **o•rang•u•tan** (ô rang′ù tan′) *noun, plural* **orangutans.**

orbit 1. The path that a planet or other heavenly body follows as it moves in a circle around another heavenly body: *The orbit of the earth around the sun takes about 365 days.* 2. One complete trip of a spacecraft along such a path: *The scientists sent a satellite into orbit around the earth. Noun.*
○ To move in an orbit around a heavenly body: *The earth orbits the sun. Verb.*
or•bit (ôr′bit) *noun, plural* **orbits;** *verb,* **orbited, orbiting.**

orchard An area of land where fruit trees are grown. **or•chard** (ôr′chərd) *noun, plural* **orchards.**

orchestra 1. A group of musicians playing together on various instruments. 2. The violins, horns, drums, and other instruments played by

such a group. 3. The main floor of a theater. 4. The area just in front of a stage in which the orchestra plays. **or•ches•tra** (ôr′kə strə) *noun, plural* **orchestras.**

An orchestra **can have as many as 100 or more musicians playing in it.**

orchid A tropical plant with flowers that grow in various shapes and colors. **or•chid** (ôr′kid) *noun, plural* **orchids.**

ordain 1. To decide or order by law or authority: *The law ordains the punishment that a criminal receives.* 2. To admit formally to the clergy or other religious office: *My cousin was ordained a minister.* **or•dain** (ôr dān′) *verb,* **ordained, ordaining.**

There are least 15,000 species of orchids.

ordeal A very hard or painful experience or test: *Living through the earthquake was quite an ordeal.* **or•deal** (ôr dēl′) *noun, plural* **ordeals.**

order 1. A command to do something: *The soldier obeyed orders.* 2. The way in which things are arranged; position in a series: *The teacher called the students' names in alphabetical order.* 3. A condition in which laws or rules are obeyed: *The*

police restored **order** after the riot. **4.** Clean, neat, or proper condition: *Please keep your room in order.* **5.** A request for goods: *I called the store and gave them our order.* **6.** Goods that have been requested or supplied: *The waiter delivered their order.* **7.** A group of people who live under the same rules or belong to the same organization: *Nuns and monks belong to religious orders.* **8.** A related group of animals, plants, or other living things. Each order is made up of several families: *Mice and squirrels are both in the rodent order. Noun.*
○ **1.** To tell to do something; give an order to; command: *The police officer ordered the driver to stop.* **2.** To place an order for; ask for: *We ordered tickets to the show by phone.* **3.** To put into proper order; arrange neatly or properly: *I ordered the books on my shelves. Verb.*

• **in order to.** So as to be able to: *The child stood on a chair in order to see better.*

• **out of order.** Not working in the proper way: *The broken telephone had been out of order for a week.*

or•der (ôr′dər) *noun, plural* **orders**; *verb,* **ordered, ordering.**

orderly **1.** Arranged in a certain way or order; having order: *The children marched in an orderly line. I keep my room orderly.* **2.** Not causing or making trouble or noise: *An orderly crowd of people waited outside of the White House for the president to come out. Adjective.*
○ **1.** A worker in a hospital who cleans and does other jobs. **2.** A soldier assigned to an officer or group of officers. An orderly carries messages and does other tasks. *Noun.*

or•der•ly (ôr′dər lē) *adjective; noun, plural* **orderlies.**

ordinal number A number that shows position in a series. First, second, and third are ordinal numbers. **or•di•nal number** (ôr′də nəl)

ordinarily In normal conditions or circumstances; usually: *Ordinarily, the museum is open on Sundays.* **or•di•nar•i•ly** (ôr′də ner′ə lē) *adverb.*

ordinary **1.** Commonly used; regular; usual: *My ordinary tone of voice is soft.* **2.** Not different in any way from others; average: *I thought the movie was very ordinary.* **or•di•nar•y** (ôr′də ner′ē) *adjective.*

SYNONYMS

Ordinary, average, common, commonplace
I'm just an ordinary citizen. She's about average height and weight for her age. It's common to find rabbits in the forest. Polar bears are almost commonplace where my aunt and uncle live in Alaska.

ore A mineral or rock that is mined for the metal or other substance it contains. Other words that sound like this are **oar** and **or.** **ore** (ôr) *noun, plural* **ores.**

Ore. *or* **Oreg.** An abbreviation for Oregon.

Oregon A state in the northwestern United States on the Pacific. Its capital is Salem. **Or•e•gon** (ôr′i gon *or* ôr′i gən) *noun.*

WORD HISTORY

The origin of the name **Oregon** is not definitely known. Somehow, the Native American name for the Wisconsin River was written incorrectly on a map. When explorers in the Northwest found the Columbia River, they thought it was the river on the map. The river's name was later changed to the Columbia River, but the name Oregon was kept as the name of the state that lies south of this river.

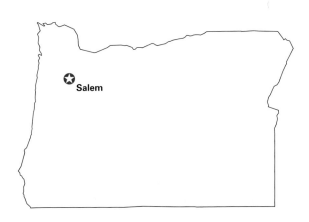

Oregon
U. S. Postal Abbreviation: **OR**
Capital: **Salem**
Population: **2,724,000**
Area: **96,981 sq. mi./251,180 sq. km**
State Nickname: **Beaver State**
State Bird: **Western Meadowlark**
State Flower: **Oregon Grape**

PRONUNCIATION KEY:

| at | āpe | fär | câre | end | mē | it | īce | pierce | hot | ōld | sông | fôrk |
| oil | out | up | ūse | rüle | pull | tûrn | chin | sing | shop | thin | this | |

hw in white; zh in treasure. The symbol ə stands for the unstressed vowel sound in about, taken, pencil, lemon, and circus.

529

organ 1. A musical instrument made up of pipes of different lengths which are sounded by air blown from a bellows. The organ is played by means of one or more keyboards. 2. A similar musical instrument that has no pipes and uses electricity and loudspeakers to produce sound. 3. A part of an animal or plant that is made up of several kinds of tissues and that does a particular job: *The heart, liver, and eyes are* **organs** *of the body. Leaves and flowers are plant* **organs.** **or·gan** (ôr′gən) *noun, plural* **organs.**

organic 1. Having to do with or coming from living things: *Decaying leaves and other* **organic** *matter can be used to make soil fertile.* 2. Using or grown by farming or gardening methods in which manufactured chemicals are not used: *organic vegetables.* **or·gan·ic** (ôr gan′ik) *adjective.*

organism A living thing. Animals, plants, amebas, and bacteria are all organisms. **or·gan·ism** (ôr′gə niz′əm) *noun, plural* **organisms.**

organization 1. The act of organizing: *Who is responsible for the* **organization** *of the school dance?* 2. The condition or way of being organized: *In our library, the* **organization** *of books is by subject.* 3. A group of people joined together for a particular purpose: *The Red Cross is an international* **organization.** **or·gan·i·za·tion** (ôr′gə nə zā′shən) *noun, plural* **organizations.**

organize 1. To arrange or put together in an orderly way: *I* **organize** *my stamp collection by countries. Who is in charge of* **organizing** *the trip to the zoo?* 2. To cause to join together in a labor union or other organization. **or·gan·ize** (ôr′gə nīz′) *verb,* **organized, organizing. —organizer** *noun.*

Orient The countries of Asia: *China and Japan are countries of the* **Orient.** **O·ri·ent** (ôr′ē ənt) *noun.*

Oriental Having to do with or belonging to the Orient. *Adjective.*
○ A member of one of the peoples living in the Orient. *Noun.*
Oriental (ôr′ē en′təl) *adjective; noun, plural* **Orientals.**

orientation Preparation or instruction for a new situation: *A two-day* **orientation** *prepares new students for life at college.* **o·ri·en·ta·tion** (ôr′ē ən tā′shən) *noun.*

origami The Japanese art of paper folding. **o·ri·ga·mi** (ôr ə gä′mē) *noun.*

origin 1. The cause or source of something; what something begins or comes from: *The* **origin** *of the fire was in the basement.* 2. Parents; ancestors: *My family is of Irish* **origin.** **or·i·gin** (ôr′i jin *or* or′i jin) *noun, plural* **origins.**

original 1. Made, done, thought of, or used for the first time; new: *The idea for my story is* **original.** 2. Able to do, make, or think of something new or different: *An inventor must be an* **original** *thinker.* 3. Relating to or belonging to the origin or beginning of something; first: *The* **original** *owner of the house still lives there. Adjective.*
○ Something that is original; not a copy, imitation, or translation: *That painting is an* **original** *by a famous artist. Noun.* **o·rig·i·nal** (ə rij′ə nəl) *adjective; noun, plural* **originals.**

originality 1. The quality of being new or unusual: *The* **originality** *of this painting fascinates me.* 2. The ability to do, make, or think of something new or unusual: *That sculptor shows great* **originality.** **o·rig·i·nal·i·ty** (ə rij′ə nal′i tē) *noun.*

originally At or from the start: *Basketball was* **originally** *played in the United States.* **o·rig·i·nal·ly** (ə rij′ə nə lē) *adverb.*

originate 1. To bring into being; start: *Who* **originated** *the design for this new airplane?* 2. To come into being; begin: *The fire* **originated** *in the kitchen.* **o·rig·i·nate** (ə rij′ə nāt′) *verb,* **originated, originating.**

oriole Any of various brightly colored songbirds that are found in most parts of the world. **o·ri·ole** (ôr′ē ōl′) *noun, plural* **orioles.**

The male oriole is usually bright orange or yellow with black markings.

ornament Something that is used as a decoration: *The Christmas tree* **ornaments** *were painted bright colors. Noun.*
○ To decorate with ornaments. *Verb.* **ornament** (ôr′nə mənt *for noun;* ôr′nə ment′ *for verb) noun, plural* **or·na·ments;** *verb,* **ornamented, ornamenting. —ornamental** *adjective.*

ornate Having much decoration: *The palace was filled with* **ornate** *furniture.* **or·nate** (ô rnāt′) *adjective.*

ornery Bad-tempered and stubborn: *Watch out - that ornery mule kicks!* **or·ner·y** (ôr nə rē) *adjective.*

ornithology The study of birds. **or·ni·thol·o·gy** (ôr nə thol′ə jē) *noun.*

orphan A child whose parents are dead. *Noun.*
○ To make an orphan of: *The war orphaned hundreds of children. Verb.*
or·phan (ôr′fən) *noun, plural* **orphans**; *verb,* **orphaned, orphaning.**

orphanage A place that takes in and cares for orphans. **or·phan·age** (ôr′fə nij) *noun, plural* **orphanages.**

orthodontist A dentist whose work is straightening the teeth. **or·tho·don·tist** (ôr′thə don′tist) *noun, plural* **orthodontists.**

orthodox 1. The same or almost the same as what most people believe or accept: *orthodox opinions on politics.* 2. Holding or following widely accepted or traditional beliefs or practices: *That family is very orthodox in their religious beliefs.* **or·tho·dox** (ôr′thə doks′) *adjective.*

osmosis The process by which a fluid passes from one solution through a membrane and into a more concentrated solution until there is an equal concentration of solutions on both sides. **os·mo·sis** (os mō′sis) *noun.*

ostrich A large bird that has a long neck, long, strong legs, and a small, flat head. The ostrich is the largest of all living birds. It cannot fly, but it can run very fast. **os·trich** (ôs′trich or os′trich) *noun, plural* **ostriches.**

Ostriches are found in Africa.

other 1. Different from the one or ones already mentioned: *If you can't help me, maybe some other person can.* 2. Remaining: *The other guests haven't arrived yet.* 3. More, extra, or further: *I have no other gloves.* 4. Not very long ago: *just the other day. Adjective.*
○ 1. A different or additional person or thing: *If you don't like that hat we have others.* 2. The remaining one: *I didn't know the others at the party. Pronoun.*
○ In a different way; otherwise: *I could not feel other than surprised. Adverb.*
oth·er (u<u>th</u>′ər) *adjective; pronoun, plural* **others**; *adverb.*

otherwise 1. In other respects besides that: *It rained a little , but otherwise the picnic was a success.* 2. If the circumstances were different: *We were lucky to have an umbrella; we would have gotten wet otherwise.* 3. In a different way or in any other way: *I'm sure our team will win; I cannot believe otherwise. Adverb.*
○ Different; other: *The spy's story sounds true, but the facts are otherwise. Adjective.*
○ Because if not; or else: *The roof must be fixed; otherwise, it'll leak if it rains. Conjunction.*
oth·er·wise (u<u>th</u>′ər wīz′) *adverb; adjective; conjunction.*

otter A water animal that looks like a weasel. Otters have webbed feet, long, slightly flattened tails, and brown, shiny fur. **ot·ter** (ot′ər) *noun, plural* **otters** *or* **otter.**

Some otters can swim at speeds up to 6 miles per hour.

ouch A word used to express sudden pain: *Ouch! I burned my finger on the stove!* **ouch** (ouch) *interjection.*

ought An auxiliary *verb* that is used in the following ways: 1. To express an obligation or responsibility: *You ought to obey the law.* 2. To express what is expected or likely: *I put in new batteries,*

PRONUNCIATION KEY:

| at | āpe | fär | câre | end | mē | it | īce | pierce | hot | ōld | sông | fôrk |
| oil | out | up | ūse | rüle | pu̇ll | tûrn | chin | sing | shop | thin | <u>th</u>is | |

hw in white; zh in treasure. The symbol ə stands for the unstressed vowel sound in about, taken, pencil, lemon, and circus.

531

so the radio **ought** to work. **3.** To offer advice: *You* **ought** *to wear a warmer coat.* **ought** (ôt) *verb.*

ounce **1.** A unit of weight equal to 1/16 of a pound. Sixteen ounces equal one pound. **2.** A unit of measure for liquids. Thirty-two ounces equal one quart. **3.** A small bit: *By the end of the race, the runners didn't have an* **ounce** *of energy left.* **ounce** (ouns) *noun, plural* **ounces.**

our Of, belonging to, or relating to us: *Our house is on Oak Street.*
Another word that sounds like this is **hour.**
our (our) *adjective.*

ours The one or ones that belong or relate to us: *Their dog is larger than* **ours.** *The error was* **ours.** **ours** (ourz) *pronoun.*

ourselves **1.** Our own selves: *We hurt* **ourselves** *in the game. We cooked for* **ourselves** *when our parents were away.* **2.** Our usual, normal, or true self: *We're not feeling* **ourselves** *in this hot, humid weather.* **our•selves** (our selvz′) *pronoun.*

-ous A suffix that means having or full of: *Envious means having envy;* **dangerous** *means full of danger.*

oust To force out; drive out; expel: *The player was* **ousted** *from the game for arguing with the umpire.* **oust** (oust) *verb,* **ousted, ousting.**

out **1.** Away from the center or from inside: *I turned on the faucet, and water gushed* **out.** *The children went* **out** *to play.* **2.** Away from one's home or business: *My parents went* **out** *to a movie.* **3.** So as to be no longer active or available: *Our supplies will soon run* **out.** **4.** Into view or to the attention of the public: *The sun just came* **out.** *The book came* **out** *last month. Adverb.*
○ **1.** Not active, being used, or in proper condition: *The road is* **out** *because of the flood.* **2.** Not successful in reaching a base in a baseball game. **3.** Away or outside: *I was* **out** *when you phoned. Adjective.*
○ Through: *I looked* **out** *the window. Preposition.* **out** (out) *adverb; adjective; preposition.*

out- A prefix that means: **1.** Forth; away: *Outburst means a bursting forth.* **2.** More than; longer than; better than: *Outnumber means to number more than. Outdo means to do better than.* **3.** Away from; outside: *Outlying means lying outside. Outpost means a post away from the main post.*

outboard motor A motor attached to the outside of the stern of a small boat. **out•board motor** (out′bôrd′).

outbreak A breaking out of something: *There was an* **outbreak** *of flu last winter.* **out•break** (out′brāk′) *noun, plural* **outbreaks.**

outburst A bursting forth of something: *We were surprised by your* **outburst** *of anger.* **out•burst** (out′bûrst′) *noun, plural* **outbursts.**

outcast A person rejected by and driven out of a group: *When Dad refused to quit smoking, the family made him feel like an* **outcast.** **outcast** (out′kast′) *noun, plural* **outcasts.**

outcome A result; end: *waiting to hear the* **outcome** *of the election.* **out•come** (out′kum′) *noun, plural* **outcomes.**

outcry **1.** A strong objection or protest: *There was an immediate* **outcry** *when they announced the concert was canceled.* **2.** A cry; shout: *a loud* **outcry** *from the yard.* **out•cry** (out′krī′) *noun, plural* **outcries.**

outdated No longer used or fashionable; out-of-date: *That kind of hat is* **outdated.** **out•dat•ed** (out′dā′tid) *adjective.*

outdid Past tense of outdo: *You* **outdid** *everyone in the spelling bee.* **out•did** (out′did′) *verb.*

outdo To do better than: *I tried to* **outdo** *the rest of the class in geography.* **out•do** (out′dü′) *verb,* **outdid, outdone, outdoing.**

outdone Past participle of outdo: *You won't be* **outdone** *in class if you study very hard.* **out•done** (out′dun′) *verb.*

outdoor Used or done out in the open instead of inside a house or other building: *Baseball is an* **outdoor** *game.* **out•door** (out′dôr′) *adjective.*

In mild weather, outdoor concerts are very popular.

outdoors Not in a house or other building; out under the sky: *We ate* **outdoors.** *Adverb.*
○ The world that is outside houses or other buildings: *We took a walk in the* **outdoors.** *Noun.* **out•doors** (out′dôrz′) *adverb; noun.*

outer On the outside: *We wear warm outer clothes in the winter.* **out·er** (ou′tər) *adjective.*

outer space The space beyond the earth's atmosphere. *The planets and stars are in outer space.*

outfield The part of a baseball field beyond the infield and between the foul lines. **out·field** (out′fēld′) *noun.*

outfit 1. All the articles or pieces of equipment needed for doing something: *the football team's outfits.* 2. A set of clothes: *a new outfit for the first day of school.* 3. A group of people who work or belong together: *What army outfit did that general lead during the war? Noun.*
○ To provide with articles or equipment needed for doing something: *The store outfitted the campers. Verb.*
out·fit (out′fit′) *noun, plural* **outfits;** *verb,* **outfitted, outfitting.**

outgoing 1. Friendly and liking to talk: *An outgoing person makes friends easily.* 2. Going out or departing: *The outgoing governor lost the last election. When is the first outgoing bus tomorrow?* **out·go·ing** (out′gō′ing) *adjective.*

outgrew Past tense of **outgrow:** *The baby soon outgrew her bonnets.* **out·grew** (out′grü′) *verb.*

outgrow 1. To grow too big for: *The baby will soon outgrow these clothes.* 2. To leave behind or lose as one grows older: *I outgrew my fear of the dark.* 3. To grow bigger than: *I have outgrown everyone in the class.* **out·grow** (out′grō′) *verb,* **outgrew, outgrown, outgrowing.**

outgrown Past participle of **outgrow:** *Haven't you outgrown that silly behavior yet?* **out·grown** (out′grōn′) *verb.*

outhouse A small building used as a toilet, common in the days before people had indoor plumbing. **out·house** (out′hous′) *noun, plural* **outhouses.**

outing A short trip for pleasure: *All the students enjoyed the school outing to the park.* **out·ing** (ou′ting) *noun, plural* **outings.**

outlaw A person who constantly breaks the law; criminal: *The sheriff searched for the outlaws. Noun.*
○ To make illegal; prohibit: *The state outlawed the sale of fireworks. Verb.*
out·law (out′lô′) *noun, plural* **outlaws;** *verb,* **outlawed, outlawing.**

outlet 1. A place at which something comes out: *Dead leaves clogged the outlets of the gutters.* 2. A means of expressing or getting rid of something: *Playing tennis is a good outlet for a person's energy.* 3. A place in an electric wiring system where appliances are plugged in. 4. A store that usually sells the goods of only one manufacturing company: *a clothing outlet with low prices.* **out·let** (out′let′) *noun, plural* **outlets.**

outline 1. The shape of an object formed by following along its outer edges: *We drew the outlines of the states on our U.S. maps.* 2. A summary of a story, speech, or other writing: *Make an outline of your report before you write it. Noun.*
○ 1. To give a summary of: *The general outlined the plan for the attack.* 2. To draw the outline of: *Each student outlined oak and maple leaves on paper. Verb.*
out·line (out′līn′) *noun, plural* **outlines;** *verb,* **outlined, outlining.**

outlook 1. A view into the future; situation that is expected: *The weather outlook for tomorrow is not good.* 2. A way of looking at or thinking about something: *I try to have a positive outlook.* **out·look** (out′lùk′) *noun, plural* **outlooks.**

outlying Located far from the center of something: *an outlying district of the city.* **out·ly·ing** (out′lī′ing) *adjective.*

outnumber To be greater in number than: *The sheriff's posse outnumbered and surrounded the gang.* **out·num·ber** (out′num′bər) *verb,* **outnumbered, outnumbering.**

out-of-date No longer in style or use; old-fashioned: *out-of-date clothes from our grandparents' attic.* **out-of-date** (out′əv dāt′) *adjective.*

outpatient A person who gets treatment at a hospital but does not stay there overnight. **out·pa·tient** (out′pā′shənt) *noun, plural* **outpatients.**

outpost A small military station that controls an area and guards against attack. **out·post** (out′pōst′) *noun, plural* **outposts.**

output 1. The amount of something produced: *The employees increased their output by working extra hours.* 2. Information that a computer displays on its screen or prints on paper. **out·put** (out′pùt′) *noun.*

PRONUNCIATION KEY:
at ape fär câre end mē it īce pierce hot ōld sông fôrk
oil out up ūse rüle pull tûrn chin sing shop thin this
hw in white; zh in treasure. The symbol ə stands for the unstressed vowel sound in about, taken, pencil, lemon, and circus.
533

outrage 1. An act of great violence or cruelty: *The dictator committed many* **outrages** *against the people of the country.* 2. Great anger: *Everyone felt* **outrage** *at the crime.* Noun. ○ To cause to feel great anger: *The unprovoked attack against the small country* **outraged** *many people.* Verb. **out·rage** (out′rāj′) *noun, plural* **outrages**; *verb,* **outraged, outraging.**

outrageous Shocking: *Insulting people in public is an* **outrageous** *thing to do.* **out·ra·geous** (out rā′jəs) *adjective.* —**outrageously** *adverb* —**outrageousness** *noun.*

outran Past tense of outrun: *The winner of the race* **outran** *fifteen other athletes.* **out·ran** (out′ran′) *verb.*

outrigger A frame that is attached to the outside of a canoe. It keeps the canoe from turning over. **out·rig·ger** (out′rig′ər) *noun, plural* **outriggers.**

outright Complete; total: *We caught him in an* **outright** *lie.* Adjective. ○ 1. In a direct or honest way; openly: *Please say* **outright** *what you think.* 2. Completely and all at once: *We paid for the bicycle* **outright.** Adverb. **out·right** (out′rīt′) *adjective; adverb.*

outrun To run faster or farther than: *That horse* **outran** *all the others in the race.* **out·run** (out′run′) *verb,* **outran, outrun, outrunning.**

outset The beginning or start: *We knew from the* **outset** *it would be a tough game.* **out·set** (out′set′) *noun.*

outside The outer side, surface, or part: *Paint the* **outside** *of the house.* Noun. ○ 1. On the outside; outer: *a waterproof* **outside** *layer of clothing.* 2. Extremely slight; not likely: *There is only an* **outside** *chance that we will be able to go.* Adjective. ○ On or to the outside; outdoors: *We played* **outside** *all day.* Adverb. ○ Beyond the limits or range of: *They live just* **outside** *Philadelphia.* Preposition. **out·side** (out′sīd′ *or* out′sīd′ *or* out′sīd′) *noun, plural* **outsides**; *adjective; adverb; preposition.*

outsider A person who is not considered a member of a group: *It's a small town that doesn't welcome* **outsiders.** **out·sid·er** (out′sī′dər) *noun, plural* **outsiders.**

outskirts The region or area that is outside or at the edge of a town or city: *a house on the* **outskirts** *of town.* **out·skirts** (out′skûrts′) *plural noun.*

outsmart To get the better of; be cleverer than: *I sometimes* **outsmart** *my parents at chess.* **out·smart** (out′smärt′) *verb,* **outsmarted, outsmarting.**

outspoken Honest or open: *Reviewers were* **outspoken** *in their criticism of the film.* **out·spo·ken** (out′spō′kən *or* out′spō′kən) *adjective.* —**outspokenly** *adverb* —**outspokenness** *noun.*

outstanding 1. So good as to stand out from others of its kind: *famous as an* **outstanding** *athlete. The student wrote an* **outstanding** *book report.* 2. Not paid or settled: *The business has an* **outstanding** *debt of $1,000.* **out·stand·ing** (out′stan′ding) *adjective.*

outward To or toward the outside: *The gate opens* **outward.** *This word is also spelled* **outwards.** Adverb. ○ 1. Toward or on the outside: *a fishing boat's* **outward** *journey.* 2. Capable of being seen from the outside: *There was no* **outward** *sign of anyone's being at home.* Adjective. **out·ward** (out′wərd) *adverb; adjective.*

outwards Another spelling for the *adverb* outward: *The eyes on many kinds of fish look* **outwards.** **outwards** (out′wərdz) *adverb.*

outwit To get the better of; be more clever than: *The cat* **outwitted** *the dog chasing it.* **out·wit** (out′wit′) *verb,* outwitted, outwitting.

oval Shaped like an egg or an ellipse: *The turkey was on an* **oval** *platter.* Adjective. ○ Something shaped like an egg or an ellipse. Noun. **o·val** (ō′vəl) *adjective; noun, plural* **ovals.**

oval

ovary 1. The part of a female animal that produces eggs. 2. The part of a flowering plant in which seeds are formed. **o·va·ry** (ō′və rē) *noun, plural* **ovaries.**

oven An enclosed space that is used to heat, bake, or roast food that is placed inside. A kitchen stove usually has an oven. **ov·en** (uv′ən) *noun, plural* **ovens.**

**The moon is over
the mountain.**

over 1. In a place or position higher than; above: *Birds flew **over** our heads.* 2. Upon so as to cover: *The nurse put a blanket **over** the patient. I spread wax **over** the floor.* 3. From one side or end to the other; across or along: *The horse jumped **over** the fence.* 4. During the time of; throughout: *School is closed **over** the holidays.* 5. More than: *We spent **over** twenty dollars to buy groceries.* 6. Concerning; about: *Are you upset **over** your grades ? Preposition.*
○ 1. In a higher place or position; above: *We could see a plane flying **over**.* 2. Above and beyond the top or edge: *The water in the pot boiled **over**.* 3. Across a distance or space; from another place: *Come **over** to my house for dinner.* 4. From an upright or erect position: *The cat knocked the vase **over**.* 5. Once more; again: *If you make a mistake, start **over**. Adverb.*
○ At an end; finished: *The game is **over**. Adjective.*
   • **over and above.** Besides; in addition to: *The teacher assigned book reports to do **over and above** the regular homework.*
   • **over and over.** Many times; repeatedly: *I tried **over and over** to reach him, but his phone was always busy.*
o•ver (ō′vər) *preposition; adverb; adjective.*

over- A prefix that means: 1. Too much: *Overwork means to work too much.* 2. Above; across; beyond: *Overhead means above the head; Overseas means across the sea. Overflow means to flow beyond normal bounds.* 3. From one point past another point: *Overthrow means to throw beyond.*

overalls Loose-fitting trousers. Overalls usually have a piece that covers the chest with suspenders attached. **o•ver•alls** (ō′vər ôlz′) *plural noun.*

overboard Over the side of a ship into the water: *The sailor slipped and fell **overboard**.* **o•ver•board** (ō′vər bôrd′) *adverb.*

overcame Past tense of overcome: *I **overcame** my fear of the water and learned to swim.* **o•ver•came** (ō′vər kām′) *verb.*

overcast Covered with clouds; cloudy: *The rain stopped at noon, but the sky was still **overcast**.* **o•ver•cast** (ō′vər kast′) *adjective.*

overcoat A heavy outer coat worn over other clothing for warmth. **o•ver•coat** (ō′vər kōt′) *noun, plural* **overcoats.**

overcome 1. To get the better of; beat or conquer: *The tired runner couldn't **overcome** the others in the race. Our soldiers **overcame** the enemy.* 2. To get over or deal with: *I **overcame** my fear of small spaces to explore the cave.* 3. To make tired or helpless: *People were **overcome** by the heat and smoke from the fire. I was **overcome** with emotion while watching the play.* **o•ver•come** (ō′vər kum′) *verb,* **overcame, overcome, overcoming.**

overdid Past tense of overdo: *I'm still stiff from when I **overdid** my exercises.* **o•ver•did** (ō′vər did′) *verb.*

overdo 1. To do or use too much; carry too far: *The other politicians gave the mayor so much praise that they **overdid** it.* 2. To cook food too much: *Be careful not to **overdo** the steak.* Another word that sounds like this is **overdue.** **o•ver•do** (ō′vər dü′) *verb,* **overdid, overdone, overdoing.**

overdone Past participle of overdo: *The steak was **overdone**. It's hard to laugh when a person has **overdone** a joke.* **o•ver•done** (ō′vər dun′) *verb.*

overdose Too large an amount of a medicine or drug: *Follow directions on bottles of medicine to avoid taking an **overdose**.* **o•ver•dose** (ō′vər dōs′) *noun, plural* **overdoses.**

PRONUNCIATION KEY:

| at | āpe | fär | câre | end | mē | it | īce | pîerce | hot | ōld | sông | fôrk |
| oil | out | up | ūse | rüle | pull | tûrn | chin | sing | shop | thin | this | |

hw in white; zh in treasure. The symbol ə stands for the unstressed vowel sound in about, taken, pencil, lemon, and circus.

535

overdress To dress in clothes that are too formal or too warm for the occasion: *Don't overdress; this will be a very casual party.* **o·ver·dress** (ō'vər dres') *verb*, **overdressed, overdressing.**

overdue 1. Not paid even though the date when payment is due has passed: *The rent is overdue.* 2. Not on time; late: *The plane from New York is twenty minutes overdue.*
Another word that sounds like this is overdo.
o·ver·due (ō'vər dü' *or* ō'vər dū') *adjective*.

overeat To eat too much: *I overate at dinner.* **o·ver·eat** (ō'vər ēt') *verb*, **overate** (ō'vər āt'), **overeaten** (ō'vər ē'tən), **overeating.**

overflow 1. To flow beyond the usual limits: *Water from the sink overflowed onto the floor.* 2. To be so full that the contents flow over: *The bathtub overflowed.* 3. To flow over the top edge of: *Milk overflowed the glass.* 4. To flow or spread over; flood: *The dam burst and water overflowed the town. Verb.*
○ Something that flows over: *We mopped up the overflow of water from the bathtub. Noun.*
o·ver·flow (ō'vər flō' *for verb;* ō'vər flō' *for noun*) *verb*, **overflowed, overflowed, overflowing;** *noun*.

overgrew Past tense of overgrow: *The weeds overgrew the flowers in the garden.* **o·ver·grew** (ōvərgrü) *verb*.

overgrow To grow over: *The gardeners pulled up the weeds that were overgrowing the park.* **o·ver·grow** (ōvərgrō) *verb*, **overgrew, overgrown, overgrowing.**

overgrown Past participle of overgrow: *The hedge around the old house was overgrown with poison ivy.* **o·ver·grown** (ō'vər grōn') *verb*.

overhand Done with the hand raised above the elbow or the arm raised above the shoulders: *Throw the ball with an overhand pitch. Adjective.*
○ With an overhand style or motion: *That pitcher throws overhand. Adverb*
o·ver·hand (ō'vər hand') *adjective; adverb.*

overhaul 1. To examine completely and make needed repairs or changes: *The mechanic overhauled the car's engine.* 2. To catch up with: *The large motorboat quickly overhauled the small sailboat. Verb.*
○ The act of overhauling: *The car's engine needs an overhaul. Noun.*
o·ver·haul (ō'vər hôl' *or* ō'vər hôl' *for verb;* ō'vər hôl' *for noun*) *verb*, **overhauled, overhauling;** *noun, plural* **overhauls.**

overhead Above one's head: *Birds flew overhead. The light was on overhead. Adverb.*
○ The general expenses of running a business: *Money spent for rent, taxes, heating, and lighting is part of the overhead. Noun.*
○ Located above one's head: *Please turn on the overhead lights. Adjective.*
o·ver·head (ō'vər hed' *for adverb;* ō'vər hed' *for noun and adjective*) *adverb; noun, plural* **overheads;** *adjective.*

overhear To hear something one is not supposed to: *Did you overhear the conversation of the men behind us on the train?* **o·ver·hear** (ō'vər hîr') *verb*, **overheard, overhearing.**

overheard Past tense and past participle of overhear: *I overheard my parents talking about a surprise party.* **o·ver·heard** (ō'vər hûrd') *verb*.

overjoyed Extremely happy: *We were overjoyed when our team won.* **o·ver·joyed** (ō'vər joid') *adjective.*

overlap To rest on top of something and partly cover it: *The magazines on the table were arranged so that one overlapped the other.* **o·ver·lap** (ō'vər lap') *verb*, **overlapped, overlapping.**

overload To put too much of something in or on: *We overloaded our car with suitcases. We can't make a phone call because all of the circuits are overloaded with calls.* **o·ver·load** (ō'vər lōd') *verb*, **overloaded, overloading.**

overlook 1. To not see, notice, or think of: *I overlooked the possibility that it might rain.* 2. To think of as never having happened; ignore: *I overlooked your rudeness because I knew you were upset.* 3. To have a view of from a place above: *a house overlooking a river.* **o·ver·look** (ō'vər lük') *verb*, **overlooked, overlooking.**

overnight 1. During or through the night: *A storm struck the farm overnight.* 2. Very quickly; suddenly: *His success seemed to come overnight. Adverb.*
○ 1. For one night: *an overnight guest.* 2. Lasting through or happening during the night: *an overnight flight from California to New York.* 3. Used or made for short trips: *I packed an overnight bag for my weekend visit. Adjective.*
o·ver·night (ō'vər nīt' *or* ō'vər nīt' *for adverb;* ō'vər nīt' *for adjective*) *adverb; adjective.*

overpass A bridge or road that crosses above another road or a railroad. **o•ver•pass** (ō′vər pas′) *noun, plural* **overpasses**.

Overpasses **help to make the highway systems work.**

overpower 1. To beat or conquer by greater strength or power: *The prisoner overpowered the guard and escaped.* 2. To make helpless: *overpowered by sadness.* **o•ver•pow•er** (ō′vər pou′ər) *verb,* **overpowered, overpowering**.

overran Past tense of overrun: *Poison ivy overran the shrubs around the empty house.* **o•ver•ran** (ō′vər ran′) *verb*.

overrule 1. To rule against by higher authority: *The Supreme Court overruled the decision of a lower court.* 2. To decide against: *I wanted to leave Friday, but the others overruled me, and we left Saturday.* **o•ver•rule** (ō′vər rül′) *verb,* **overruled, overruling**.

overrun 1. To spread or swarm over or throughout: *Weeds have overrun the flower garden. The enemy had overrun the fort.* 2. To flow over: *The river overran its banks.* 3. To run beyond: *That baseball player always overruns second base.* **o•ver•run** (ō′vər run′) *verb,* **overran, overrun, overrunning**.

overseas Over, across, or beyond the sea; abroad: *We plan to travel overseas this summer, visiting France and Italy. Adverb.*
   ○ 1. Working, located, or serving overseas: *That company has an overseas office.* 2. Relating to countries across the sea; foreign: *Many farmers depend on our nation's overseas trade. Adjective.* **o•ver•seas** (ō′vər sēz′) *adverb; adjective*.

overshoe A shoe or boot that is worn over an ordinary shoe to protect against cold, snow, water, or mud. Overshoes are usually made of rubber. **overshoe** (ōvərshü) *noun, plural* **overshoes**.

oversight 1. A careless mistake that was not made on purpose: *Leaving your name off the guest list for the party was an oversight.* 2. The act or process of watching over with care and guiding: *That committee is in charge of the oversight of the state's hospitals.* **o•ver•sight** (ō′vər sīt′) *noun, plural* **oversights**.

oversleep To sleep longer than one meant to: *I overslept and was late for school.* **o•ver•sleep** (ō′vər slēp′) *verb,* **overslept, oversleeping**.

overslept Past tense and past participle of oversleep: *I overslept and missed the school bus.* **o•ver•slept** (ō′vər slēpt′) *verb*.

overtake 1. To move from being behind to being beside or ahead of; catch up with or pass: *The police car tried to overtake the speeding car.* 2. To come upon in a sudden or unexpected way: *The rain overtook the campers as they hiked in the woods.* **o•ver•take** (ō′vər tāk′) *verb,* **overtook, overtaken, overtaking**.

overtaken Past participle of overtake: *That runner has overtaken the others in the race and might win.* **o•ver•tak•en** (ō′vər tā′kən) *verb*.

overthrew Past tense of overthrow: *The citizens rose up and overthrew the tyrant.* **o•ver•threw** (ō′vər thrü′) *verb*.

overthrow To cause to lose power; defeat, as by force or a struggle: *After years of suffering, the people overthrew the dictator. Verb.*
   ○ The loss of power; defeat: *Huge crowds celebrated the overthrow of the tyrant. Noun.* **o•ver•throw** (ō′vər thrō′ *for verb;* ō′vər thrō′ *for noun*) *verb,* **overthrew, overthrown, overthrowing;** *noun*.

overthrown Past participle of overthrow: *The country's political leaders were overthrown in a popular election.* **o•ver•thrown** (ō′vər thrōn′) *verb*.

overtime Time worked beyond the regular working hours: *You will be paid extra for any overtime you work. Noun.*

PRONUNCIATION KEY:

| at | āpe | fär | câre | end | mē | it | īce | pierce | hot | old | sông | fôrk |
| oil | out | up | ūse | rüle | pull | tûrn | chin | sing | shop | thin | this | |

hw in white; zh in treasure. The symbol ə stands for the unstressed vowel sound in about, taken, pencil, lemon, and circus.

537

○ Beyond the hours one is usually expected to work: *My family worked* **overtime** *to get ready for the wedding. Adverb.*

○ Of or for overtime: *Do you get* **overtime** *pay at your job? Adjective.*

o·ver·time (ō′vər tīm′) *noun; adverb; adjective.*

overtook Past tense of **overtake**: *The brown horse* **overtook** *the black one to win the race.* **o·ver·took** (ō′vər tŭk′) *verb.*

overture 1. A musical composition played by an orchestra to introduce an opera, ballet, or other large musical work. 2. An offer to begin something; suggestion or proposal: *overtures of friendship to a new neighbor.* **o·ver·ture** (ō′vər chər) *noun, plural* **overtures.**

overturn 1. To turn or throw over; capsize; upset: *I* **overturned** *my chair when I jumped up. The canoe* **overturned.** 2. To reverse a decision made by someone else: *A higher court* **overturned** *the judge's ruling.* **o·ver·turn** (ō′vər tûrn′) *verb,* **overturned, overturning.**

overweight Having more than the normal or needed weight: *I dieted because the doctor said I was* **overweight.** **o·ver·weight** (ō′vər wāt′) *adjective.*

overwhelm 1. To overcome completely; overpower or make helpless: *The enemy* **overwhelmed** *our soldiers.* 2. To cover or bury completely: *The waves* **overwhelmed** *the small island during the storm.* **o·ver·whelm** (ō′vər hwelmor′ ō′vər welm′) *verb,* **overwhelmed, overwhelming.**

overwork To cause to work too much: *The farmer* **overworked** *the mule. Verb.*

○ Too much work: *Overwork was the cause of your illness. Noun.*

o·ver·work (ō′vər wûrk′ *for verb;* ō′vər wûrk′ *for noun) verb,* **overworked, overworking;** *noun.*

owe 1. To have to pay: *I* **owe** *my parents money for the bicycle they helped me buy.* 2. To have to give: *I* **owe** *you an apology for being so late.* 3. To be obliged for: *I* **owe** *a great deal to my brother and sister for all the help they gave me with my report.* Another word that sounds like this is **oh.** **owe** (ō) *verb,* **owed, owing.**

owl A bird that has a round head with large, staring eyes and a hooked bill, a short square tail, and soft feathers. Owls eat mice, frogs, snakes, and insects and usually hunt for them at night. **owl** (oul) *noun, plural* **owls.**

Owls hunt at night using their keen sense of hearing.

own Of, relating to, or belonging to oneself or itself: *I use my* **own** *baseball bat even though our school has them. The accident was your* **own** *fault. Adjective.*

○ Something that belongs to one: *That bicycle is my* **own.** *When I get older I will have a room of my very* **own.** *Noun.*

○ 1. To have as belonging to one; possess: *That farmer* **owns** *all the land between here and the river.* 2. To admit doing something; confess; acknowledge: *The children* **owned** *that they had broken the window by accident. Verb.*

• **on one's own.** Relying or dependent only on oneself or one's own efforts, as for support or success: *I know exactly what to do when I'm* **on my own** *in the woods.*

• **to hold one's own.** To do well, as against opposition or competition: *I was able to* **hold my own** *in the debate.*

own (ōn) *adjective; noun; verb,* **owned, owning.**

owner A person who owns something: *Who is the* **owner** *of the blue car?* **own·er** (ōn′ər) *noun, plural* **owners.**

ox 1. The adult male of domestic cattle. It is used as a work animal or for beef. An ox cannot father young. 2. Any of various animals related to the ox. Buffaloes, bison, and yaks are also called *oxen.* **ox** (oks) *noun, plural* **oxen.**

oxbow A U-shaped piece of wood that is placed around and under the neck of an ox or other similar animal. It supports a yoke. Look up **yoke** for more information. **ox·bow** (oks′bō′) *noun, plural* **oxbows.**

oxcart A cart pulled by an ox or oxen. **oxcart** (oks′kärt) *noun, plural* **oxcarts.**

oxen Plural of ox: *Two* ***oxen*** *were pulling the cart.* **ox·en** (ok′sən) *plural noun.*

oxeye daisy A daisy whose flower has a yellow center and white petals. **ox·eye daisy** (oks′ī′).

oxford A shoe that is laced over the top of the foot. **ox·ford** (oks′fərd) *noun, plural* **oxfords.**

oxide A compound of oxygen and one or more chemical elements. **ox·ide** (ok′sīd) *noun, plural* **oxides.**

oxidize To combine a chemical substance with oxygen. **ox·i·dize** (ok′si dīz′) *verb,* **oxidized, oxidizing.**

oxygen A gas that has no color or smell. Oxygen makes up about one fifth of the air. Living things need oxygen to live, and fires need it to burn. Oxygen is a chemical element. **ox·y·gen** (ok′si jən) *noun.*

oyster An animal that has a soft body and a rough, hinged shell. Oysters are found in shallow waters along coasts. Some kinds of oysters are used for food, while other kinds are raised for the pearls they produce. **oys·ter** (ois′tər) *noun, plural* **oysters.**

oyster catcher A bird that lives near water and has a long, wedge-shaped bill. It has black and white plumage and feeds on mollusks, such as oysters and clams.

oz. An abbreviation for **ounce** or **ounces.**

ozone A form of oxygen. It is formed by lightning or other electricity in the air. Ozone is used to kill germs and freshen the air. **o·zone** (ō′zōn′) *noun.*

WORD HISTORY

Ozone goes back to the Greek word meaning "smelling." The gas ozone was named for its sharp odor.

ozone hole A part of the ozone layer in which the ozone has become very thin.

ozone layer A layer of ozone high in the earth's atmosphere that protects living things from the harmful rays of the sun.

PRONUNCIATION KEY:
at   āpe   fär   câre   end   mē   it   īce   pîerce   hot   ōld   sông   fôrk
oil   out   up   ūse   rüle   pull   tûrn   chin   sing   shop   thin   this
hw in white; zh in treasure. The symbol ə stands for the unstressed vowel sound in about, taken, pencil, lemon, and circus.

539

Pp

ozone layer

p, P The sixteenth letter of the alphabet. **p, P** (pē) *noun, plural* **p's, P's.**

p. An abbreviation for **page.**

Pa. An abbreviation for **Pennsylvania.**

PA Postal abbreviation for **Pennsylvania.**

pace 1. A single step: *Take two **paces** forward.* 2. The length of a single step. 3. The rate of speed in walking, running, or moving: *a fast **pace**.* 4. A way of stepping or moving; gait: *The trot is one of the **paces** of a horse. Noun.*
○ 1. To walk back and forth across: *The tiger **paced** its cage.* 2. To measure a distance by taking paces. *Verb.*
pace (pās) *noun, plural* **paces;** *verb,* **paced, pacing.**

pacemaker A small electronic device put under the skin of a person's body, used to help regulate a person's heartbeat. **pace·mak·er** (pās′mā′kər) *noun, plural* **pacemakers.**

Pacific The ocean that separates North America and South America from Asia and Australia. This is also called the Pacific Ocean. *Noun.*
○ Of the Pacific. *Adjective.*
Pa·cif·ic (pə sif′ik) *noun; adjective.*

WORD HISTORY

The name Pacific comes from a Latin word meaning "peaceful." The explorer Magellan named this ocean "pacific" because it seemed calm compared to the Atlantic.

SPELLING HINTS

The letter P has one sound in English. That sound can be made by:
  p in words such as pail and put;
  pp in dipper and happy.

The combination pp usually appears in the middle of a word.

pacify To make calm or quiet. **pac·i·fy** (pas′ə fī) *verb,* **pacified, pacifying.**

pack 1. A group of things wrapped or tied together for carrying; bundle: *I strapped the books together to form a secure **pack**.* 2. A sturdy bag for carrying things on the back of a person or animal. 3. A set or group of things that are alike: *a **pack** of wolves.* 4. A big number or amount; a lot: *a **pack** of lies; a **pack** of trouble. Noun.*
○ 1. To place in something for storing or carrying: *Pack the dishes in boxes.* 2. To fill up with things: *Pack your suitcase.* 3. To press together tightly: *Pack snow into a ball.* 4. To fill by crowding together: *The church was **packed**. Verb.*
pack (pak) *noun, plural* **packs;** *verb,* **packed, packing.**

package 1. A thing or group of things packed, wrapped up, or tied together; bundle: *I got a big **package** on my birthday.* 2. A box, case, or other container in which something is packed: *Follow the directions on the **package** to make the soup. Noun.*
○ To make or put into a package: *My favorite cereal is **packaged** in a red box. Verb.*
pack·age (pak′ij) *noun, plural* **packages;** *verb,* **packaged, packaging.**

packet A small package or parcel. **pack·et** (pak′it) *noun, plural* **packets.**

pact An agreement between persons or countries; treaty: *The two nations signed a peace **pact**. The friends made a secret **pact**. **pact** (pakt) *noun, plural* **pacts.**

pad 1. A soft piece of thick material used as stuffing or for protection or comfort: *shoulder **pads** for football.* 2. A number of sheets of paper glued together along one edge: *We leave a **pad** and pencil by the telephone.* 3. A part like a small, soft cushion on the bottom of the feet of dogs, foxes, and other animals. 4. A block of cloth soaked

with ink and used with a rubber stamp. *Noun.*
○ **1.** To cover, stuff, or line with a pad: *The chair was **padded** so that it would be more comfortable.* **2.** To make longer by adding unnecessary material: *The report was too short, so the writer **padded** it with extra statistics. Verb.*
pad (pad) *noun, plural* **pads**; *verb,* **padded, padding.**

paddle **1.** A short oar with a flat, wide blade. A paddle is used to move and steer a canoe or other small boat. **2.** A small, broad board with a short handle, used to hit the ball in some games. **3.** A flat, wooden tool used for beating, mixing, or stirring. *Noun.*
○ **1.** To move a canoe or other boat with a paddle or paddles: *You can **paddle** across the lake in fifteen minutes.* **2.** To hit with a paddle or with the hand; spank. *Verb.*
pad·dle (pad′əl) *noun, plural* **paddles**; *verb,* **paddled, paddling.**

paddle wheel A big wheel with broad boards, or paddles, fixed around it.

A paddle wheel can be used to move
a steamship through water.

paddock **1.** A small field or area that is fenced in. Animals can graze or exercise in a paddock. **2.** A small, fenced area near a racetrack. **pad·dock** (pad′ək) *noun, plural* **paddocks.**

paddy A field where rice is grown. **pad·dy** (pad′ē) *noun, plural* **paddies.**

padlock A lock with a U-shaped bar that is hinged on one end. Padlocks can be opened with a key or a dial. *Noun.*
○ To fasten or lock with a padlock. *Verb.*
pad·lock (pad′lok′) *noun, plural* **padlocks**; *verb,* **padlocked, padlocking.**

pagan A person who is not a Christian, Jew, or Muslim. Some pagans believe in many gods or no god at all. **pa·gan** (pā′gən) *noun, plural* **pagans.**

page¹ One side of a sheet of paper in a book, newspaper, or magazine. **page** (pāj) *noun, plural* **pages.**

page² **1.** A young person who runs errands and carries messages. **2.** Long ago, a boy working as a servant or helper for an important person. *Noun.*
○ To try to find someone by calling out his or her name: *They **paged** the doctor over the loudspeaker in the hospital. Verb.*
page (pāj) *noun, plural* **pages**; *verb,* **paged, paging.**

pageant **1.** A kind of play about events in history or legend. **2.** A colorful parade or ceremony for an important event. **pag·eant** (paj′ənt) *noun, plural* **pageants.**

pagoda A temple or tower that is many stories high. The roof of each story usually curves upward. **pa·go·da** (pə gō′də) *noun, plural* **pagodas.**

paid Past tense and past participle of **pay**. **paid** (pād) *verb.*

pail A round, open container with a flat bottom and a curved handle; bucket.
Another word that sounds like this is **pale**.
pail (pāl) *noun, plural* **pails.**

pain **1.** A feeling of being hurt; suffering. **2. pains.** Care or effort: *I took **pains** to put the model airplane together neatly. Noun.*
○ To cause pain to: *It **pains** me to hear people quarreling. Verb.*
Another word that sounds like this is **pane**.
pain (pān) *noun, plural* **pains**; *verb,* **pained, paining.** —**painful** *adjective* —**painless** *adjective.*

paint A mixture of pigments and water, oil, or other liquid, spread on a surface to color it or protect it. *Noun.*
○ **1.** To cover with paint. **2.** To make a picture or design of something by using paint: *Paint a mountain scene. Verb.*
paint (pānt) *noun, plural* **paints**; *verb,* **painted, painting.**

painter **1.** A person who paints pictures. **2.** A person whose work is painting things like walls and houses. **paint·er** (pān′tər) *noun, plural* **painters.**

PRONUNCIATION KEY:

| at | āpe | fär | câre | end | mē | it | īce | pîerce | hot | ōld | sông | fôrk |
| oil | out | up | ūse | rüle | půll | tûrn | chin | sing | shop | thin | this | |

hw in white; zh in treasure. The symbol ə stands for the unstressed vowel sound in about, taken, pencil, lemon, and circus.

541

painting 1. Something painted; picture: *A painting of the family hangs over the sofa.* 2. The act or art of using paints: *I hope to study drawing and painting.* **paint·ing** (pān'ting) *noun, plural* **paintings**.

pair 1. A set of two things meant to be used together: *a pair of shoes.* 2. A single thing made up of two parts: *You will find a pair of scissors in the top drawer.* 3. Two persons or animals that are alike or that go together; couple: *A pair of black horses were pulling the wagon. Noun.*

Artists create paintings **with oils, water colors, and other materials.**

○ To join or match in a pair: *They paired the two tallest band members to lead the march. Verb.*

• **to pair off** To form into pairs: *The whole class paired off for the square dance.*

Other words that sound like this are **pare** and **pear**. **pair** (pâr) *noun, plural* **pairs** or **pair**; *verb,* **paired, pairing**.

pajamas A set of clothes to sleep in, usually made up of a shirt and trousers. **pa·ja·mas** (pə jä'məz *or* pə jam'əz) *plural noun.*

Pakistan A country in south-central Asia. **Pak·i·stan** (pak'ə stan' *or* pä'kə stän') *noun.*

pal A close friend: *I play softball with my pals every day after school.* **pal** (pal) *noun, plural* **pals**.

palace A big fancy building where a king, queen, or other ruler lives. **pal·ace** (pal'is) *noun, plural* **palaces**.

WORD HISTORY

The word palace goes back to the Latin word for the *Palatine*. The Palatine is a hill in Rome where the first Roman emperor, Augustus, built his palace.

---

palate 1. The roof of the mouth. The bony part in the front is called the **hard palate**, and the fleshy part in the back is called the **soft palate**. 2. The sense of taste: *Ripe peaches please my palate.*

Other words that sound like this are **palette** and **pallet**. **pal·ate** (pal'it) *noun, plural* **palates**.

pale 1. Having skin color that is light or lighter than usual: *The sick child looked weak and pale.* 2. Not bright in color. *The lake glimmered in the pale moonlight. Adjective.*

○ To turn pale: *Their faces paled when they saw the accident. Verb.*

Another word that sounds like this is **pail**. **pale** (pāl) *adjective,* **paler, palest**; *verb,* **paled, paling**.

paleontology The science that deals with fossils of prehistoric animal and plant life. **pa·le·on·tol·o·gy** (pā'lē ən tol'ə jē) *noun.* —**paleontologist** *noun.*

Paleozoic Belonging to or having to do with the era in the earth's early history from about 570 million years ago to about 230 million years ago. During this time, fish, insects, and reptiles began to appear. **Pa·le·o·zo·ic** (pā'lē ə zō'ik) *adjective.*

Palestine A region in southwest Asia. In biblical times, Palestine was the land of the Jews. The area is now occupied by Israel and Jordan. **Pal·es·tine** (pal'ə stīn) *noun.*

palette A thin, oval board with a hole for the thumb at one end. Artists place and mix their paints on palettes.

Other words that sound like this are **palate** and **pallet**. **pal·ette** (pal'it) *noun, plural* **palettes**.

palisades A line of steep cliffs that rise along a river. **pal·i·sades** (pal'ə sādz') *plural noun.*

pallet 1. A bed or mattress made of straw. 2. A small, hard, or temporary bed: *During the flood, we slept on pallets at the emergency shelter.*

Other words that sound like this are **palate** and palette. **pal·let** (pal'it) *noun, plural* **pallets**.

palm¹ The inside surface of the hand between the wrist and the fingers. *Noun.*

○ 1. To hold or hide in the hand: *The magician palmed the cards so we would think they had disappeared.* 2. To get rid of by fooling someone: *The crook palmed off the cheap stone as a diamond. Verb.*

palm (päm) *noun, plural* **palms**; *verb,* **palmed, palming**.

palm² Any of a number of trees, shrubs, or vines of warm climates. **palm** (päm) *noun, plural* **palms.**

palmetto A kind of palm of the southern United States and some other warm areas. It has leaves shaped like fans. **pal·met·to** (pal met′ō) *noun, plural* **palmettos** *or* **palmettoes.**

Palm **trees have large leaves like feathers or fans that grow at the top of the trunk.**

palomino A light tan or golden horse having a white or yellowish white mane and tail. **pal·o·mi·no** (pal′ə mē′nō) *noun, plural* **palominos.**

pamper To treat too well; spoil: *They pamper their baby.* **pam·per** (pam′pər) *verb,* **pampered, pampering.**

pamphlet A small book that has a paper cover: *The board game came with a pamphlet of playing instructions.* **pam·phlet** (pam′flit) *noun, plural* **pamphlets.**

pan 1. A metal dish used for cooking or baking. Pans are usually broad and shallow and do not have a cover. 2. A shallow container that is like a cooking pan. Pans are used to wash gold ore from gravel. *Noun.*
○ To wash soil or gravel in a pan to separate the gold in it: *The prospectors panned for gold. Verb.* **pan** (pan) *noun, plural* **pans;** *verb,* **panned, panning.**

Panama A country in Central America. **Pan·a·ma** (pan′ə mä′) *noun.*

pancake A flat, thin cake made of batter, cooked in a pan or on a griddle. **pan·cake** (pan′kāk′) *noun, plural* **pancakes.**

pancreas A gland near the stomach that makes digestive juices and hormones such as insulin. **pan·cre·as** (pan′krē əs) *noun, plural* **pancreases.**

pancreas

panda 1. A big animal that looks like a bear. It has thick, black and white fur and lives in western China. It is also called the giant panda. 2. A reddish brown animal that looks like a raccoon. It has short legs, a long bushy tail marked with darker rings, and a white face. It is also called the lesser panda. **pan·da** (pan′də) *noun, plural* **pandas.**

The main food for a giant panda **is bamboo.**

pane A sheet of glass in a window or door. Another word that sounds like this is **pain.** **pane** (pān) *noun, plural* **panes.**

panel 1. A part or section of something that is different in some way from what is around it because it is raised, sunken, or bordered. A panel may be in a door or a wall, part of a piece of furniture, or a section of a garment. 2. A group of persons gathered together to talk about or judge something: *A panel of judges for the baking contest awarded the prizes.* 3. A board containing the dials, instruments, and controls for running something: *My electric train has a control panel. Noun.*
○ To arrange in panels; decorate with panels: *The walls of the living room are paneled in pine. Verb.* **pan·el** (pan′əl) *noun, plural* **panels;** *verb,* **paneled, paneling.**

pang A sudden, sharp feeling: *I get pangs of hunger just before lunch. The thief began to feel pangs of guilt.* **pang** (pang) *noun, plural* **pangs.**

panic A strong feeling of fear that makes a person lose self-control and want to run away: *When the theater caught fire, panic spread through the crowd. Noun.*
○ To fill with or have a feeling of great fear. *Verb.* **pan·ic** (pan′ik) *noun, plural* **panics;** *verb,* **panicked, panicking.**

panorama A wide or complete view of an area: *You can see a panorama of the whole valley from*

PRONUNCIATION KEY:
at   āpe   fär   câre   end   mē   it   īce   pierce   hot   ōld   sông   fôrk
oil   out   up   ūse   rüle   púll   tûrn   chin   sing   shop   thin   this
hw in white; zh in treasure. The symbol ə stands for the unstressed vowel sound in about, taken, pencil, lemon, and circus.

543

the top of the mountain. **pan•o•ram•a** (pan′ə ra′mə or pan′ə rä′mə) *noun*, *plural* **panoramas**.

pansy A plant with flowers that have five flat petals overlapping each other. **pan•sy** (pan′zē) *noun*, *plural* **pansies**.

Pansies have flowers of
many colors.

pant 1. To breathe quickly and hard; gasp for breath: *After the race, the runners stood panting at the finish line.* 2. To say while gasping for breath: *"Help me," the stranger panted.* **pant** (pant) *verb*, **panted, panting**.

panther A leopard that is so dark that it looks almost black. **pan•ther** (pan′thər) *noun*, *plural* **panthers** or **panther**.

pantomime 1. The telling of a story without talking, through the use of gestures, body movements, and facial expressions. 2. A play acted in this way: *The class put on a pantomime of the first Thanksgiving. Noun.*
○ To act or show in pantomime: *The clown pantomimed riding on a subway. Verb.*
pan•to•mime (pan′tə mīm′) *noun*, *plural* **pantomimes**; *verb*, **pantomimed, pantomiming**.

pantry A small room for storing food, dishes, or silverware. **pan•try** (pan′trē) *noun*, *plural* **pantries**.

pants A garment for the part of the body below the waist. Pants are divided so that they cover each leg separately. **pants** (pants) *plural noun*.

papaya A yellowish orange fruit that grows on a tropical American tree. It looks like a melon and has a sweet taste. **pa•pa•ya** (pə pä′yə) *noun*, *plural* **papayas**.

paper 1. A material used for writing and printing, wrapping things, covering walls, and many other

purposes. Paper is made from ground wood, rags, or certain grasses. It is usually made in thin pieces called sheets. 2. A piece or sheet of paper: *Write your name at the top of the paper.* 3. A piece of paper with writing or printing on it; document: *These papers prove that we own the house.* 4. A written report or essay for school: *My history paper is finished.* 5. A newspaper: *We buy the evening paper. Noun.*
○ To cover with wallpaper: *The workers papered the hall. Verb.*
pa•per (pā′pər) *noun*, *plural* **papers**; *verb*, **papered, papering**.

WORD HISTORY

The earliest writing material that was like the paper we use today was made from the papyrus plant. The word *paper* goes back to the Greek word meaning "papyrus."

---

paperback A book that has a soft paper cover. **pa•per•back** (pā′pər bak′) *noun*, *plural* **paperbacks**.

paper clip A small piece of bent wire that is used to hold sheets of paper together.

papoose A North American Indian baby or small child. **pa•poose** (pa püs′) *noun*, *plural* **papooses**.

paprika A reddish orange powder used as a spice and to add color to food. It is made from sweet red peppers. **pap•ri•ka** (pa prē′kə or pap′ri kə) *noun*, *plural* **paprikas**.

Papua New Guinea An island country in southeastern Asia. **Pap•u•a New Guinea** (pap′ū ə or pä′pü ä′).

papyrus 1. A tall plant that grows in swamps and along rivers in parts of Africa and Europe. 2. A material like paper made from this plant. The ancient Egyptians used this material to write on. **pa•py•rus** (pə pī′rəs) *noun*, *plural* **papyri** (pə pī′rī).

par 1. An average or normal amount, condition, or degree: *Their work is above par.* 2. An equal level: *The skills of the two athletes are not on a par.* **par** (pär) *noun*, *plural* **pars**.

parachute A device that allows a person or object attached to it to be dropped slowly and safely from an airplane or other high place. Parachutes are made of fabric and open out like an umbrella when unfolded. *Noun.*
○ To come or send down by parachute: *The pilot parachuted from the burning plane. The air force*

parachuted supplies to the soldiers who were surrounded by the enemy. Verb.
par•a•chute (par′ə shüt′) *noun, plural* **parachutes;** *verb,* **parachuted, parachuting.**

WORD HISTORY

The word parachute comes from a French word that originally meant "guarding against a fall."

---

parade A march or procession in honor of a person or event: *a Fourth of July parade. Noun.*
○ **1.** To march in a parade. **2.** To make a great show of; show off: *Some people like to parade their knowledge before everyone they meet. Verb.*
pa•rade (pə rād′)

Parades celebrate special occasions.

noun, plural **parades;** *verb,* **paraded, parading.**

paradise **1.** Heaven. **2.** A place or state of great happiness: *The island where they spent their vacation was a paradise of peace and beauty.*
par•a•dise (par′ə dīs′) *noun.*

paraffin A white substance like wax, used for making candles and waxed paper and for sealing jars. **par•af•fin** (par′ə fin) *noun.*

paragraph A part of something written, made up of one or more sentences about a particular subject or idea. It begins on a new line, usually indented from the rest of the lines. **par•a•graph** (par′ə graf′) *noun, plural* **paragraphs.**

WORD HISTORY

The word paragraph goes back to a Greek word that means "to write beside." The Greeks used this word for a symbol drawn beside a piece of writing to mark the beginning of a new idea or topic. This was also the first meaning of *paragraph* in English. Later the word came to mean a section of writing containing a single topic or idea.

Paraguay A country in central South America.
Par•a•guay (par′ə gwī′ *or* par′ə gwā′) *noun.*

parakeet A small parrot with a slender body, a long, pointed tail, and brightly colored feathers. Parakeets are often kept as pets. **par•a•keet** (par′ə kēt′) *noun, plural* **parakeets.**

parallel **1.** Being the same distance apart at all points. If lines are parallel, they never meet or cross each other: *The rails of a railroad track are parallel.* **2.** Alike in some way; similar: *These children live in different cities but have parallel experiences. Adjective.*
○ **1.** A parallel line or surface: *The teacher drew a line and then drew a parallel.* **2.** A being alike; similarity: *There are many parallels in the lives of pioneers.* **3.** Any of the imaginary lines that circle the earth in the same direction as the equator. They are used to mark latitude. *Noun.*
○ **1.** To be or lie in the same direction and always the same distance apart: *The railroad parallels the road.* **2.** To be similar to: *The growth of the small town paralleled that of the city nearby. Verb.*
○ Always the same distance apart: *The road runs parallel to the river. Adverb.*
par•al•lel (par′ə lel′) *adjective; noun, plural* **parallels;** *verb,* **paralleled, paralleling;** *adverb.*

parallelogram A flat figure with four sides. The opposite sides of a parallelogram are both equal in length and parallel.
par•al•lel•o•gram (par′ə lel′ə gram′) *noun, plural* **parallelograms.**

parallelogram

paralysis A loss of the power to move or feel in a part of the body. **pa•ral•y•sis** (pə ral′ə sis) *noun, plural* **paralyses** (pa ral′ə sēz).

paralyze **1.** To take away the power to move or feel in a part of the body: *After the accident, my right arm was paralyzed.* **2.** To make unable to move or act; make helpless: *The bus strike paralyzed the city.* **par•a•lyze** (par′ə līz′) *verb,* **paralyzed, paralyzing.**

paramecium A tiny living thing that has only one cell and lives in fresh water. It can be seen only through a microscope. **par•a•me•ci•um** (par′ə mē′shē əm *or* par′ə mē′sē əm) *noun, plural* **paramecia** (par′ə mē′shē ə *or* par′ə mē′sē ə).

PRONUNCIATION KEY:

| at | āpe | fär | câre | end | mē | it | īce | pierce | hot | ōld | sông | fôrk |
| oil | out | up | ūse | rüle | pull | tûrn | chin | sing | shop | thin | this | |

hw in white; zh in treasure. The symbol ə stands for the unstressed vowel sound in about, taken, pencil, lemon, and circus.

545

paramount Above all others, as in influence or importance; greatest; highest: *a matter of paramount importance.* **par·a·mount** (par′ə mount′) *adjective.*

parasite An animal or plant that lives on or in another animal or plant, called a host. A parasite gets food or shelter from its host. Fleas and tapeworms are parasites on animals. Mistletoe is a parasite on trees. **par·a·site** (par′ə sīt′) *noun, plural* **parasites.**

parasol A small, light umbrella used as a protection against the sun. **par·a·sol** (par′ə sôl′) *noun, plural* **parasols.**

paratrooper A soldier trained to parachute from an airplane into an area of battle. **par·a·troop·er** (par′ə trü′pər) *noun, plural* **paratroopers.**

parcel 1. A bundle or package: *I received three heavy parcels in the mail.* 2. A piece or section. *Noun.*
○ To divide into sections; give out in parts: *The coach parceled equipment. Verb.*
par·cel (pär′səl) *noun, plural* **parcels;** *verb,* **parceled, parceling.**

parch 1. To make very dry: *The summer drought parched the fields.* 2. To make very hot and thirsty: *Hiking parched us.* **parch** (pärch) *verb,* **parched, parching.**

parchment The skin of sheep, goats, or other animals prepared so that it can be written on, or paper made to look like this skin. **parch·ment** (pärch′mənt) *noun, plural* **parchments.**

pardon 1. To free a person from punishment: *The governor pardoned the prisoner.* 2. To not have hard feelings about; not want to blame or punish. *Verb.*
○ 1. A freeing from punishment: *The prisoner got a pardon from the governor.* 2. The act of refusing to blame or punish; forgiveness: *I beg your pardon if I hurt you. Noun.*
par·don (pär′dən) *verb,* **pardoned, pardoning;** *noun, plural* **pardons.**

pare 1. To cut or peel off the outer part of something: *Pare an apple with a knife.* 2. To make less little by little; cut down: *The family pared expenses.* Other words that sound like this are **pair** and **pear.**
pare (pâr) *verb,* **pared, paring.**

parent 1. A father or mother. 2. A living thing, as an animal or plant, that has produced offspring. **par·ent** (pâr′ənt) *noun, plural* **parents.**

parenthesis Either one of two curved lines, ( ), that are used to enclose and set apart a word or group of words in a sentence. Parentheses are also used to enclose numbers and mathematical symbols. **pa·ren·the·sis** (pə ren′thə sis) *noun, plural* **parentheses** (pə ren′thə sēz).

parish 1. An area that has its own church and minister or priest. 2. The people who belong to this church. **par·ish** (par′ish) *noun, plural* **parishes.**

park 1. A piece of land, often having benches, trees, paths, and playgrounds, used by people for enjoyment and recreation. 2. A large area of land left in its natural state by the government. *Noun.*
○ To leave an automobile or other vehicle in a place for a time: *We parked the car next to the supermarket and went in. Verb.*
park (pärk) *noun, plural* **parks;** *verb,* **parked, parking.**

parka A warm fur or cloth jacket with a hood. **par·ka** (pär′kə) *noun, plural* **parkas.**

parkway A highway or wide road with trees, bushes, or grass planted along it. **park·way** (pärk′wā′) *noun, plural* **parkways.**

parliament 1. A group of people who make the laws of a country. A parliament also chooses the leaders of a government. 2. Parliament. A group like this in Great Britain or Canada. **par·lia·ment** (pär′lə mənt) *noun, plural* **parliaments.**

parlor 1. A room in a house used for entertaining. 2. A room or rooms used as a shop: *an ice cream parlor.* **par·lor** (pär′lər) *noun, plural* **parlors.**

parochial Of or run by a church or parish: *Our neighborhood has a public school and parochial school.* **pa·ro·chi·al** (pə rō′kē əl) *adjective.*

parole The release of a person from prison before his or her full sentence has been served. People are usually put on parole for good behavior, and they must then obey certain rules for a time. *Noun.*
○ To release a person from prison before his or her full sentence is served: *The burglar was paroled after four years in prison. Verb.*
pa·role (pə rōl′) *noun, plural* **paroles;** *verb,* **paroled, paroling.**

parrot A bird with a wide, curved bill, a long, pointed tail, and glossy, brightly colored feathers. Some parrots can imitate speech and other sounds. *Noun.*
○ To repeat or imitate what someone else has said

without thinking about it or understanding it: *The little child **parroted** everything the older children said. Verb.*

par·rot (par′ət) *noun, plural* **parrots**; *verb,* **parroted, parroting.**

parsley A small herb with leaves used to flavor and decorate food. **pars·ley** (pär′slē) *noun, plural* **parsleys.**

parsnip The thick, white root of a plant related to the carrot. This root is cooked and eaten as a vegetable. **pars·nip** (pär′snip) *noun, plural* **parsnips.**

parson A member of the Protestant clergy in charge of a church; minister. **par·son** (pär′sən) *noun, plural* **parsons.**

part **1.** Something less than the whole: *We liked the last **part** of the movie the best. I ate only **part** of my dinner.* **2.** A piece that helps make up a machine or device: *The technician replaced the broken **part** in the computer.* **3.** A share: *They all did their **part** to make the picnic a success.* **4.** One of the sides in an argument or contest: *When the disagreement started, I took my friend's **part**.* **5.** A line made to divide one's hair when combing it: *I used a comb to make my **part** straight.* **6.** A character or role in a movie or play: *You can play the **part** of the lawyer. Noun.*

○ **1.** To separate by coming between; force or hold apart: *The referee **parted** the two boxers.* **2.** To go in different directions; separate: *They shook hands and **parted**.* **3.** To comb the hair to make it fall on either side of a line: *I **part** my hair in the middle. Verb.*

○ In some degree; partly: *The sled is **part** mine and **part** yours. Adverb.*

○ Not full or complete; partial: *Each of the partners is **part** owner of the store. Adjective.*

• **to part with.** To give away; give up: *I refused to **part** with the stray kitten.*

A macaw is the largest type of parrot.

• **to take part.** To join with others, as in an activity.

part (pärt) *noun, plural* **parts**; *verb,* **parted, parting**; *adverb; adjective.*

partial **1.** Not complete; not total: *We have a partial list of club members.* **2.** Showing more favor than is fair to one side, person, or group: *The umpire should not be **partial** to the home team.* **3.** Having a strong liking; fond: *I'm **partial** to plums.* **par·tial** (pär′shəl) *adjective.*

participate To join with others; take part: *Everyone **participated** in the rally.* **par·tic·i·pate** (pär tis′ə pāt′) *verb,* **participated, participating.** —**participation** *noun.*

participle The form that a verb has when it is used with a helping verb to form certain tenses. A participle also can act as a noun or adjective. In the sentence "I am going to the movies now that my homework is finished," the words "going" and "finished" are participles. **par·ti·ci·ple** (pär′tə sip′əl) *noun, plural* **participles.**

particle A very small bit or piece of something: *A **particle** of dirt flew into my eye.* **par·ti·cle** (pär′ti kəl) *noun, plural* **particles.**

particular **1.** Taken by itself; apart from others: *This **particular** suitcase is too small for me.* **2.** Having to do with some one person or thing: *This artist's **particular** talent is drawing plants.* **3.** Unusual in some way; special: *That book should be of **particular** interest to you.* **4.** Very careful about details; hard to please: *I'm **particular** about keeping my room neat. Adjective.*

○ A single and separate fact or part; detail: *All the **particulars** of the robbery were in the morning paper. Noun.*

par·tic·u·lar (pər tik′yə lər) *adjective; noun, plural* **particulars.** —**particularly** *adverb.*

partition A wall or panel that divides space: *We use a movable **partition** to make two separate areas in our classroom. Noun.*

○ **1.** To divide into parts: *The farm was **partitioned** into small lots for houses.* **2.** To separate by a wall or panel: *We **partitioned** off a small room in the basement for the washer and dryer. Verb.*

par·ti·tion (pär tish′ən) *noun, plural* **partitions**; *verb,* **partitioned, partitioning.**

PRONUNCIATION KEY:

| at | āpe | fär | câre | end | mē | it | īce | pierce | hot | ōld | sông | fôrk |
| oil | out | up | ūse | rüle | pull | tûrn | chin | sing | shop | thin | this | |

hw in white; zh in treasure. The symbol ə stands for the unstressed vowel sound in about, taken, pencil, lemon, and circus.

547

partly In some degree; to some extent; in part: *You were **partly** to blame for my being late.* **part·ly** (pärt′lē) *adverb*.

partner 1. A person who runs a business with one or more other persons and who shares the profits and losses of the business: *My mother and my uncle are **partners** in a law firm.* 2. A person who plays with another person on the same side in a game: *My classmate and I were tennis **partners** today.* 3. A person who dances with another: *Choose a **partner** for the first dance.* **part·ner** (pärt′nər) *noun, plural* **partners**.

partnership A business run by two or more persons who share the profits and losses: *The appliance store on the corner is a **partnership** run by three friends.* **part·ner·ship** (pärt′nər ship′) *noun, plural* **partnerships**.

part of speech A class of words that have the same purpose when used in sentences. The eight parts of speech into which the English language is divided are noun, pronoun, adjective, verb, adverb, preposition, conjunction, and interjection. Many words can be used as more than one part of speech.

partridge 1. A plump bird hunted as game. Partridges have gray, brown, and white feathers. 2. Another word for **quail**. Look up **quail** for more information. **par·tridge** (pär′trij) *noun, plural* **partridge** *or* **partridges**.

part-time For only part of the usual working time: *I got a **part-time** job working Saturdays.* *Adjective.*
○ On a part-time schedule: *I work **part-time** after school.* *Adverb.*
part-time (pärt′tīm′) *adjective; adverb*.

party 1. A gathering of people to have a good time: *a birthday **party**.* 2. A group of people doing something together: *a search **party** looking for a lost child.* 3. An organization working to gain political power or control: *a political **party**.* 4. A person who takes part in an action or plan: *I refused to be a **party** to their practical joke.* 5. A person: *The **party** I telephoned was not there.* **par·ty** (pär′tē) *noun, plural* **parties**.

pass 1. To go past; go by: *I **pass** the park on my way to school.* 2. To move: *Many thoughts passed through my mind as I waited.* 3. To hand or move from one person to another: *Please **pass** the salt. The center **passed** the basketball to the*

forward. 4. To complete a test or course of study with success: *To become a lifeguard, you have to **pass** a swimming test.* 5. To come to an end: *The storm raged for an hour and then **passed**.* 6. To use or spend time: *I **passed** time by reading a magazine.* 7. To approve or make into law: *The Senate **passed** the bill quickly.* 8. To happen: *Tell me everything that **passed** at the meeting.* *Verb.*
○ 1. A written permission: *No one can get in without a **pass**.* 2. A free ticket. 3. A gap or passage in a mountain range. 4. A moving or throwing of a ball from one player to another: *The quarterback made a long **pass** to another player on the team.* *Noun.*
• **to pass away** *or* **to pass on**. To die: *My grandparents have **passed** away.*
• **to pass out**. 1. To distribute; give out: *The teacher **passed** out the books.* 2. To lose consciousness; faint: *Several marchers in the parade **passed** out from the heat.*
pass (pas) *verb*, **passed**, **passing**; *noun, plural* **passes**.

passage 1. A short part of a piece of music or writing: *The teacher read a **passage** from a long poem.* 2. A route, path, or other way by which a person or thing can pass: *an underground **passage**.* 3. A trip or voyage: *The ship's **passage** across the Atlantic was rough.* 4. A passing or moving: *The **passage** of time in the play was shown by dimming the lights.* 5. A making into law; approval: *Passage of the bill in Congress seemed certain.* **pas·sage** (pas′ij) *noun, plural* **passages**.

passageway A way along which a person or thing can pass: *an underground **passageway**.* **pas·sage·way** (pas′ij wā′) *noun, plural* **passageways**.

passenger A person who travels in a vehicle. **pas·sen·ger** (pas′ən jər) *noun, plural* **passengers**.

passing 1. Going or moving by: *Many people watched the **passing** parade. The family grew richer with the **passing** years.* 2. Not lasting; brief: *We had a **passing** interest in video games.* 3. Given or done quickly, without pausing: *After a **passing** glance at my identification card, the guard let me in.* 4. Allowing one to pass a test or course of study: *a **passing** grade on the test.* *Adjective.*
○ A going by or past: *the **passing** of summer and the arrival of fall.* *Noun.*
pas·sing (pas′ing) *adjective; noun, plural* **passings**.

passion 1. A very strong feeling. Love, hate, and anger are passions. 2. A very strong liking: *a passion for baseball.* **pas·sion** (pash′ən) *noun, plural* **passions.**

passionate Having, showing, or resulting from passion: *a passionate speech.* **pas·sion·ate** (pash′ə nit) *adjective.* —**passionately** *adverb.*

Passover A Jewish holiday celebrated for seven or eight days in March or April. Passover celebrates the anniversary of the Jews' escape from slavery in Egypt. **Pass·o·ver** (pas′ō′vər) *noun.*

passport A document given to a person to show what country the person is a citizen of. It helps to identify a person traveling in foreign countries. **pass·port** (pas′pôrt′) *noun, plural* **passports.**

password 1. A secret word or phrase that a person must say to be allowed to pass a guard. 2. A string of letters or numbers that must be typed to gain access to a computer system. **pass·word** (pas′wûrd′) *noun, plural* **passwords.**

past 1. Gone by; ended; over: *Past events are described in history books.* 2. Gone by just before the present time; just ended: *I've seen three movies in the past week.* 3. Of time gone by; former: *Our neighbor is a past mayor of the town. Adjective.*
◦ 1. A time gone by: *Dinosaurs lived in the distant past.* 2. Things that have happened; history: *We studied our state's past.* 3. The past tense. Look up **past tense** for more information. *Noun.*
◦ Beyond in place, time, or amount: *My grandparents are past seventy. Preposition.*

In the distant past people sailed the ocean in wooden ships.

◦ So as to pass or go by: *The train rolled past. Adverb.*
past (past) *adjective; noun, plural* **pasts;** *preposition; adverb.*

pasta A food made from flour paste or dough. Macaroni and spaghetti are pasta. **pas·ta** (pä′stə) *noun.*

paste 1. A mixture used to stick things together, usually made of flour and water. 2. Any soft, smooth, very thick mixture: *tomato paste. Noun.*
◦ 1. To stick with paste: *Let's paste the photographs into an album.* 2. To cover with something stuck on with paste: *We pasted the walls of the classroom with travel posters. Verb.*
paste (pāst) *noun, plural* **pastes;** *verb,* **pasted, pasting.**

pastel 1. A crayon that is like chalk. Pastels are used in drawing. 2. A picture drawn with such crayons. 3. A pale, soft shade of a color. *Noun.*
◦ 1. Drawn with pastels. 2. Having a pale, soft shade: *The towel was a pastel blue. Adjective.*
pas·tel (pas tel′) *noun, plural* **pastels;** *adjective.*

pasteurize To heat milk or other liquids to a specific temperature for a given period of time. The heat kills germs that may be living in the milk. **pas·teur·ize** (pas′chə rīz′) *verb,* **pasteurized, pasteurizing.** —**pasteurization** *noun.*

WORD HISTORY

The word **pasteurize** comes from the name of Louis *Pasteur.* Louis Pasteur was a French scientist who lived from 1822 to 1895. He discovered this way of killing certain germs in milk without changing its taste or food value.

---

pastime Something that makes time pass in a pleasant and happy way: *We played word games in the car as a pastime during the long drive.* **pas·time** (pas′tīm′) *noun, plural* **pastimes.**

pastor A minister or priest in charge of a parish or church. **pas·tor** (pas′tər) *noun, plural* **pastors.**

past participle The form of a verb used with the auxiliary verbs *have* or *be* to show that an action or condition is completed. In the sentences "They had already gone," "My uncle was born in 1960," and "I have been sick," "gone," "born," and "been" are past participles.

PRONUNCIATION KEY:

| at | āpe | fär | câre | end | mē | it | īce | pîerce | hot | old | sông | fôrk |
| oil | out | up | ūse | rüle | pull | tûrn | chin | sing | shop | thin | this | |

hw in white; zh in treasure. The symbol ə stands for the unstressed vowel sound in about, taken, pencil, lemon, and circus.

549

pastry 1. Pies, tarts, and other sweet baked goods. 2. Crust made of dough: *The meat pie was topped with a layer of pastry.* **pas•try** (pās′trē) *noun, plural* **pastries.**

Pastries **come in many different sizes and shapes.**

past tense A form of a verb that shows that an action happened or that a condition existed in the past. In the sentence "We drove to the city yesterday," the verb "drove" is in the past tense. In the sentence "I felt sick last night," the verb "felt" is in the past tense. The past tense is also called the **past.**

pasture 1. A piece of land on which animals graze. 2. Grass and other growing plants that animals feed on: *This valley provides excellent pasture for livestock. Noun.*
○ To put animals in a pasture to graze: *The farmer pastured the ponies. Verb.*
pas•ture (pas′chər) *noun, plural* **pastures;** *verb,* **pastured, pasturing.**

pat To tap or stroke gently with the hand. *Verb.*
○ 1. A gentle tap or stroke: *The child finished the mud pie with three pats.* 2. A small, flat slice: *a pat of butter. Noun.*
pat (pat) *verb,* **patted, patting;** *noun, plural* **pats.**

patch 1. A small piece of material. Patches are often used to cover holes or worn spots in clothing. They are also used as decorations, badges, or bandages: *I sewed a patch over the hole in my blue jeans. The pirate captain wore a patch over one eye.* 2. A small area that is different from what is around it: *The car skidded on a patch of ice.* 3. A small piece of ground where something grows: *a strawberry patch. Noun.*
○ 1. To cover or repair with a patch; put a patch

on: *You can patch the hole in the elbow of your sweater.* 2. To fix or put together in a hasty or careless way: *We tried to patch the car's engine so it would run for another month or two. Verb.*
• **to patch up.** To smooth over; settle: *We patched up our quarrel and became friends again.*
patch (pach) *noun, plural* **patches;** *verb,* **patched, patching.**

patchwork Pieces of cloth of different colors and shapes sewed together. **patch•work** (pach′wûrk′) *noun.*

patent A piece of paper issued to a person or company by the government. It gives someone the right to be the only one to make, use, or sell a new invention for a certain number of years: *The engineer took out a patent on the new motor. Noun.*
○ To get a patent for: *The company patented the new machine. Verb.*
pat•ent (pat′ənt) *noun, plural* **patents;** *verb,* **patented, patenting.**

patent leather A leather with a very smooth and shiny surface.

paternal 1. Of or like a father: *The old store-keeper had paternal feelings for the little child.* 2. Related through one's father: *My paternal grandparents come from China.* **pa•ter•nal** (pə tûr′nəl) *adjective.*

path 1. A trail or way for walking: *a path through the snow.* 2. The line along which a person or thing moves: *the path of a comet around the sun.* **path** (path) *noun, plural* **paths.**

This **path** leads down to the ocean.

pathetic Causing pity or sorrow: *The wet, frightened puppy was a pathetic sight.* **pa•thet•ic** (pə thet′ik) *adjective.* —**pathetically** *adverb.*

patience The quality or fact of being able to put up with hardship, pain, trouble, or delay without getting angry or upset: *The crowd showed great patience as they waited in the rain to buy tickets to the movie.* **pa•tience** (pā′shəns) *noun.*

patient Having or showing an ability to put up with hardship, pain, trouble, or delay without getting angry or upset: *I tried to be **patient** while I waited in the line at the post office. The teacher repeated the instructions several times in a **patient** voice. Adjective.*

○ A person under the care or treatment of a doctor. *Noun.*

pa·tient (pā′shənt) *adjective; noun, plural* **patients.**

patio A paved outdoor space for cooking, eating, and relaxing: *Our neighbors have a barbecue on their **patio** every weekend.* **pat·i·o** (pat′ē ō′) *noun, plural* **patios.**

patriarch 1. The father and head of a family or tribe. 2. An old man who is respected and honored: *Many people go to the **patriarch** of the village for advice.* **pa·tri·arch** (pā′trē ärk′) *noun, plural* **patriarchs.**

patriot A person who loves his or her country and defends or supports it. **pa·tri·ot** (pā′trē ət) *noun, plural* **patriots.**

patriotic Characterized by or showing love and loyal support of one's country: *The parade for the Fourth of July was planned by a group of **patriotic** citizens.* **pa·tri·ot·ic** (pā′trē ot′ik) *adjective.*

patriotism Love and loyal support of one's country: *A time of war is a great test of a people's **patriotism**.* **pa·tri·ot·ism** (pā′trē ə tiz′əm) *noun.*

WORD HISTORY

Patriotism goes back to the Greek word for "native land." Someone who has *patriotism* has a sense of pride in the land or country of his or her birth.

patrol To go through or around an area to guard it or make sure that everything is all right: *Police cars **patrol** the neighborhood. Verb.*

○ 1. A going through or around an area to guard it or make sure that everything is all right: *The scouts went on **patrol** to find enemy troops.* 2. A group of people or vehicles that do this: *The night **patrol** of the building is made up of two guards. Noun.*

pa·trol (pə trōl′) *verb,* **patrolled, patrolling;** *noun, plural* **patrols.**

patron 1. A person who regularly shops at a particular store or regularly uses the services of a particular business establishment. 2. A person, especially one who is rich or powerful, who sup-

ports or helps another person, a group, or a cause: *That banker who gave money to build the new concert hall has always been a **patron** of the arts.* **pa·tron** (pā′trən) *noun, plural* **patrons.**

patronize To shop at or use the services of regularly: *We **patronize** the grocery on the corner.* **pa·tron·ize** (pā′trə nīz′) *verb,* **patronized, patronizing.**

pattern 1. The way in which colors, shapes, or lines are arranged or repeated in some order; design: *wallpaper with a flower **pattern**.* 2. A guide or model to be followed when making something: *The kit for sewing a dress included a **pattern**.* 3. A set of actions or qualities that is repeated or that does not change: *The scientist noticed **patterns** in the way the animals in the experiment behaved. Noun.*

○ To make according to a pattern: *I decided to **pattern** my singing style after my favorite singer. Verb.*

pat·tern (pat′ərn) *noun, plural* **patterns;** *verb,* **patterned, patterning.**

patty 1. A small, round, flat piece of chopped or ground food: *We had hamburger **patties** for lunch.* 2. A small, flat piece of candy. **pat·ty** (pat′ē) *noun, plural* **patties.**

pauper A very poor person, especially one supported by charity or welfare. **pau·per** (pô′pər) *noun, plural* **paupers.**

pause To stop for a short time: *The grown-ups **paused** to let the children catch up. Verb.*

○ A short stop or rest: *After a **pause** because of rain, the game continued. Noun.*

pause (pôz) *verb,* **paused, pausing;** *noun, plural* **pauses.**

pave To cover a road or street with a hard surface. **pave** (pāv) *verb,* **paved, paving.**

pavement A hard covering or surface for a street, road, or sidewalk. A pavement is usually made from concrete or asphalt. **pave·ment** (pāv′mənt) *noun, plural* **pavements.**

pavilion 1. A building or other structure used for a show or exhibit, or for recreation. A pavilion often has open sides: *The dance was held at a **pavilion** in the park.* 2. One of a group of buildings, such as those that make up a hospital. **pa·vil·ion** (pə vil′yən) *noun, plural* **pavilions.**

PRONUNCIATION KEY:

| at | āpe | fär | câre | end | mē | it | īce | pierce | hot | ōld | sông | fôrk |
| oil | out | up | ūse | rüle | pûll | tûrn | chin | sing | shop | thin | this | |

hw in white; zh in treasure. The symbol ə stands for the unstressed vowel sound in about, taken, pencil, lemon, and circus.

551

paw The foot of an animal that has four feet and nails or claws. Dogs and cats have paws. *Noun.*
○ **1.** To strike or scrape something with a paw or a hoof: *The angry bull pawed the ground and then charged toward the gate.* **2.** To touch or handle roughly, clumsily, or without care: *The shoppers pawed the fruit on sale. Verb.*
paw (pô) *noun, plural* **paws**; *verb,* **pawed, pawing.**

pawn[1] To leave something valuable with a lender of money in order to get a loan. The lender gets to keep the object if the person who borrowed the money does not pay it back: *I pawned a watch for ten dollars.* **pawn** (pôn) *verb,* **pawned, pawning.**

pawn[2] **1.** One of the pieces used in the game of chess. The pawn is the piece of lowest value used in the game. **2.** A person or thing used by someone to gain some advantage: *The robbers used their hostage as a pawn to bargain for a safe escape.* **pawn** (pôn) *noun, plural* **pawns.**

pay **1.** To give money to someone in return for things or work: *We had to pay fifteen dollars to have the radio fixed. Pay the salesperson for the coat.* **2.** To give money in order to settle: *The driver who was caught speeding had to pay a fine.* **3.** To be worthwhile or good for someone: *It pays to study.* **4.** To give or suffer something in return: *They paid for their bad eating habits by having poor health.* **5.** To make or give: *I paid my cousin a visit. Verb.*
○ Money given in return for things or work: *The workers struck for higher pay. Noun.*
• **to pay back.** To return what one has borrowed; repay: *I want to pay back the money you lent me.*
pay (pā) *verb,* **paid, paying;** *noun.*

payment **1.** The act of paying: *Payment has to be made for the television set when it is delivered.* **2.** Something paid: *I ordered some seeds from the catalog and mailed the payment in.* **pay·ment** (pā′mənt) *noun, plural* **payments.**

payroll **1.** A list of people to be paid and the amount that each one is to receive: *The company added the new employees' names to the payroll as soon as they began working.* **2.** The total amount of money to be paid. **pay·roll** (pā′rōl′) *noun, plural* **payrolls.**

PE Postal abbreviation for Prince Edward Island.

pea A small, round green vegetable. It grows in a pod and is a seed. **pea** (pē) *noun, plural* **peas.**

peace **1.** Freedom from fighting or conflict: *After the war, a period of peace began.* **2.** A lack of noise or disorder; quiet or calm: *We love the peace and quiet of the country.* **3.** Public order and safety: *The police department keeps the peace.* Another word that sounds like this is **piece.**
peace (pēs) *noun.*

peaceful **1.** Free from war or disorder; quiet and calm: *Everyone who visited the peaceful valley never forgot its beauty.* **2.** Liking peace; avoiding fights and disorder: *They are peaceful people and do not keep an army.* **peace·ful** (pēs′fəl) *adjective.*

peace pipe A long pipe smoked by North American Indians as a symbol of peace or friendship.

peach **1.** A round, sweet, juicy fruit with a fuzzy, yellow or reddish skin. **2.** A yellowish pink color. *Noun.*
○ Having a yellowish pink color. *Adjective.*
peach (pēch) *noun, plural* **peaches;** *adjective.*

Peaches grow on a tree that is also called a peach.

peacock A large bird that is related to a pheasant. The male peacock has shiny blue feathers on its head, neck, and body. The peacock's tail has bright green and gold feathers with spots like eyes on them. **pea·cock** (pē′kok′) *noun, plural* **peacocks** *or* **peacock.**

When a peacock raises its tail, its feathers spread out like a fan.

peak **1.** A high mountain, or the pointed top of one. **2.** A sharp or pointed end or top: *If you stand on the peak of our roof, you can see the* *ocean.* **3.** The highest point or greatest level: *Traffic reached its **peak** during the late afternoon.* **4.** The brim or front part of a cap that sticks out. A baseball player's cap has a peak.

Another word that sounds like this is **peek**.

peak (pēk) *noun, plural* **peaks.**

peal A loud, long sound or series of sounds: *A **peal** of bells came from the church tower. **Peals** of laughter greeted the clown. Noun.*
○ To sound or ring out in a peal: *The church bells **pealed** loudly on Sunday morning. Verb.*

Another word that sounds like this is **peel**.

peal (pēl) *noun, plural* **peals;** *verb,* **pealed, pealing.**

peanut A seed like a nut that grows in a pod under the ground. Peanuts are eaten for food and are also used to make peanut butter. The oil from peanuts is used for cooking. **pea·nut** (pē′nut′) *noun, plural* **peanuts.**

peanut butter A soft, creamy food made from ground, roasted peanuts. It is used as a spread on crackers and in sandwiches.

pear A sweet, juicy fruit that grows on trees. Pears are shaped like bells and usually have smooth yellow or brown skins.

Other words that sound like this are **pair** and **pare**.

pear (pâr) *noun, plural* **pears.**

pearl **1.** A small, round gem that is white or cream in color and has a soft, glowing shine. **2.** Something that looks like a pearl: *Pearls of dew covered the flowers.* **pearl** (pûrl) *noun, plural* **pearls.**

peasant A person who works on a farm or owns a small farm. **peas·ant** (pez′ənt) *noun, plural* **peasants.**

peat A kind of soil made up of decayed plants. It is found in wet areas and is used as a fertilizer and as fuel. **peat** (pēt) *noun.*

pebble A small stone that is usually round and smooth. **peb·ble** (peb′əl) *noun, plural* **pebbles.**

pecan A nut that has a sweet taste. **pe·can** (pi kän′ *or* pi kan′) *noun, plural* **pecans.**

A pecan grows on a large tree and has a thin shell.

peck¹ **1.** A unit of measure used for fruits, vegetables, grains, and other dry things. A peck is equal to eight quarts, or one fourth of a bushel. **2.** A lot: *You'll get into a **peck** of trouble if you break a window.* **peck** (pek) *noun, plural* **pecks.**

peck² To strike or pick up something with the beak in a short, quick movement: *The hen **pecked** at the crumbs. Verb.*
○ **1.** A short, quick stroke made with the beak: *The canary gave me a **peck** on the finger.* **2.** A quick kiss: *The parents gave each child a **peck** on the cheek as the children went to bed. Noun.*

peck (pek) *verb,* **pecked, pecking;** *noun, plural* **pecks.**

peculiar **1.** Not usual; strange; queer: *It's **peculiar** that the sky is so dark at noon.* **2.** Belonging to a certain person, group, place, or thing: *The kangaroo is **peculiar** to Australia and New Guinea.* **pe·cul·iar** (pi kūl′yər) *adjective.* —**peculiarly** *adverb.*

peculiarity **1.** Something peculiar: *The **peculiarities** of the old house included a sloping floor and a main entrance in the back.* **2.** The quality of being peculiar. **pe·cu·li·ar·i·ty** (pi kū′lē ar′i tē) *noun, plural* **peculiarities.**

pedal A lever or other device moved by the foot to run or control something. The pedals on a bicycle make it go. The pedals on a piano change the length and loudness of the notes played. *Noun.*
○ To work or use the pedals of something: *I **pedaled** my bicycle hard to catch up with the others. Verb.*

Another word that sounds like this is **peddle**.

ped·al (ped′əl) *noun, plural* **pedals;** *verb,* **pedaled, pedaling.**

peddle To carry goods from place to place and offer them for sale: *I **peddle** newspapers downtown after school.*

Another word that sounds like this is **pedal**.

ped·dle (ped′əl) *verb,* **peddled, peddling.** —**peddler** *noun.*

pedestal **1.** A base on which a column or statue stands. **2.** The base or other part of something that supports it: *The **pedestal** of the lamp was cracked.* **ped·es·tal** (ped′ə stəl) *noun, plural* **pedestals.**

at	āpe	fär	câre	end	mē	it	īce	pîerce	hot	ōld	sông	fôrk
oil	out	up	ūse	rüle	pull	tûrn	chin	sing	shop	thin	this	

PRONUNCIATION KEY:

hw in white; zh in treasure. The symbol ə stands for the unstressed vowel sound in about, taken, pencil, lemon, and circus.

553

pedestrian A person who travels on foot; walker: *Sidewalks are for pedestrians.* **ped·es·tri·an** (pə des′trē ən) *noun, plural* **pedestrians.**

pediatrician A doctor who takes care of and treats babies and children. **pe·di·a·tri·cian** (pē′dē ə trish′ən) *noun, plural* **pediatricians.**

pedigree A line of ancestors; descent: *This dog's pedigree includes many champions.* **ped·i·gree** (ped′i grē′) *noun, plural* **pedigrees.**

peek To look quickly or secretly: *The children peeked into the box holding the present.* Verb.
○ A quick or secret look. *Noun.*
Another word that sounds like this is **peak.**
peek (pēk) *verb,* **peeked, peeking;** *noun, plural* **peeks.**

peel The skin or outer covering of certain fruits and vegetables: *a banana peel. Noun.*
○ **1.** To take off the skin or outer covering of something: *Please peel these potatoes.* **2.** To remove or strip: *Can you peel the label off the jar?* **3.** To come off in pieces or strips: *The paint is peeling.* **4.** To lose or shed an outer covering or layer: *My sunburned back is peeling. Verb.*
Another word that sounds like this is **peal.**
peel (pēl) *noun, plural* **peels;** *verb,* **peeled, peeling.**

peep¹ **1.** To look secretly or quickly through a narrow opening or from a hiding place: *The actors peeped through the curtain to see how big the audience was.* **2.** To come slowly or partly into view; show slightly: *The moon peeped through the clouds. Verb.*
○ A secret or quick look: *The children took a peep at the rabbit through the bushes so they would not frighten it. Noun.*
peep (pēp) *verb,* **peeped, peeping;** *noun, plural* **peeps.**

peep² A short, sharp sound like that made by a young bird or chicken. *Noun.*
○ To make a peep: *The chicks peeped. Verb.*
peep (pēp) *noun, plural* **peeps;** *verb,* **peeped, peeping.**

peer¹ **1.** A person who is the same as another in age, status, or ability; equal: *As a baseball player, our star pitcher has few peers.* **2.** A member of British nobility.
Another word that sounds like this is **pier.**
peer (pîr) *noun, plural* **peers.**

peer² **1.** To look hard or closely, as if trying to see something clearly: *The scientist peered at the slide through a microscope.* **2.** To come slightly into view: *The sun peered over the mountain.*
Another word that sounds like this is **pier.**
peer (pîr) *verb,* **peered, peering.**

peg A piece of wood, metal, or other material that can be fitted or driven into a surface. Pegs are used to fasten parts together, to hang things on, or to mark the score in a game. *Noun.*
○ To fasten with pegs: *We watched the workers peg down the circus tents. Verb.*
peg (peg) *noun, plural* **pegs;** *verb,* **pegged, pegging.**

P.E.I. An abbreviation for **Prince Edward Island.**

Pekingese A small dog with a long, silky coat and a flat, wrinkled face. The Pekingese originated in China. **Pe·king·ese** (pē′kə nēz′ or pē′king ēz′) *noun, plural* **Pekingese.**

A pelican uses its pouch to catch and store fish.

pelican A large bird that lives near the water and has a pouch under its long bill. **pel·i·can** (pel′i kən) *noun, plural* **pelicans.**

pellet A small, hard ball of something: *I put food pellets in the cage for my pet mice. Pellets of ice hit the windshield.* **pel·let** (pel′it) *noun, plural* **pellets.**

pell-mell In a jumbled or confused way: *Clothing had been thrown pell-mell into the closet. The frightened pickpocket ran pell-mell through the crowd.* **pell-mell** (pel′mel′) *adverb.*

pelt¹ To strike over and over with small hard things: *Hail pelted the roof.* **pelt** (pelt) *verb,* **pelted, pelting.**

pelt² The skin of an animal with its fur or hair still on it. Pelts are used to make clothing and rugs. **pelt** (pelt) *noun, plural* **pelts.**

pen¹ A long, thin tool for writing or drawing with ink. **pen** (pen) *noun, plural* **pens.**

pen² 1. A small, fenced yard for cows, pigs, sheep, or other animals. 2. Any small area that is enclosed. *Noun.*
○ To hold or shut up in a pen: *The farmer penned the horses. Verb.*
pen (pen) *noun, plural* **pens;** *verb,* **penned, penning.**

penalize To give a penalty or punishment to: *The referee penalized the football team for taking too much time between plays.* **pe·nal·ize** (pē′nə līz′) *verb,* **penalized, penalizing.**

penalty 1. A punishment: *The penalty for illegal parking in this city is a fine of thirty dollars.* 2. A disadvantage or punishment placed on a player or team for breaking the rules: *The referee called a penalty of five yards against the team.* **pen·al·ty** (pen′əl tē) *noun, plural* **penalties.**

pencil A long, thin tool for writing or drawing, usually made of a stick of graphite in a case of wood. *Noun.*
○ To write, draw, or mark with a pencil: *I penciled in my name on the form. Verb.*
pen·cil (pen′səl) *noun, plural* **pencils;** *verb,* **penciled, penciling.**

pendant An ornament that hangs from something. Jewels or lockets are often worn as pendants. **pend·ant** (pen′dənt) *noun, plural* **pendants.**

pendulum A weight hung from a fixed point in such a way that it can swing back and forth. Pendulums are used in some clocks. **pen·du·lum** (pen′jə ləm) *noun, plural* **pendulums.**

penetrate 1. To go into or pass through: *The sword penetrated the knight's shield. The headlights of the car could not penetrate the thick evening fog.* 2. To find the meaning of; understand: *Science tries to penetrate the mysteries of nature.* **pen·e·trate** (pen′i trāt′) *verb,* **penetrated, penetrating.** —**penetration** *noun.*

penguin A bird whose feathers are black or gray on the back and white on the front. Penguins cannot fly. Their wings look like flippers and are used for swimming. **pen·guin** (pen′gwin *or* peng′gwin) *noun, plural* **penguins.**

penicillin A powerful drug that destroys bacteria and is used to treat many diseases. It is made from a fungus mold. **pen·i·cil·lin** (pen′ə sil′ən) *noun.*

Most penguins **live in or near Antarctica.**

peninsula A piece of land that sticks out into water from a larger body of land. The southern part of Florida is a peninsula. **pen·in·su·la** (pə nin′sə lə *or* pə nin′syə lə) *noun, plural* **peninsulas.**

WORD HISTORY

The word **peninsula** goes back to two Latin words that mean "almost" and "island."

---

penitentiary A prison for people found guilty of serious crimes. **pen·i·ten·tia·ry** (pen′i ten′shə rē) *noun, plural* **penitentiaries.**

penknife A small pocketknife, once used to make and sharpen quill pens. **pen·knife** (pen′nīf′) *noun, plural* **penknives** (pen′nīvz′).

penmanship The art or a style of handwriting. **pen·man·ship** (pen′mən ship′) *noun.*

Penn. or **Penna.** An abbreviation for Pennsylvania.

pen name A made-up name an author uses instead of his or her real name: *The pen name of Samuel Clemens was Mark Twain.*

pennant A long, narrow flag shaped like a triangle. Pennants are used for signaling and as emblems, decorations, and prizes. **pen·nant** (pen′ənt) *noun, plural* **pennants.**

penniless Having no money at all; broke: *After paying all my bills, I was penniless.* **pen·ni·less** (pen′i lis) *adjective.*

PRONUNCIATION KEY:

| at | āpe | fär | câre | end | mē | it | īce | pierce | hot | ōld | sông | fôrk |
| oil | out | up | ūse | rüle | pull | tûrn | chin | sing | shop | thin | this | |

hw in white; zh in treasure. The symbol ə stands for the unstressed vowel sound in about, taken, pencil, lemon, and circus.

555

Pennsylvania A state in the eastern United States. Its capital is Harrisburg. **Penn·syl·va·nia** (pen′səl vān′yə) *noun.*

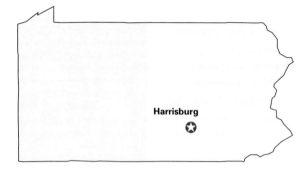

Pennsylvania
U. S. Postal Abbreviation: **PA**
Capital: **Harrisburg**
Population: **11,936,000**
Area: **45,333 sq. mi./117,412 sq. km**
State Nickname: **Keystone State**
State Bird: **Ruffed Grouse**
State Flower: **Mountain Laurel**

WORD HISTORY

The word Pennsylvania comes from the last name of William *Penn* and a Latin word meaning "woods." King Charles II of England named this colony when he gave it to William Penn.

---

penny 1. A coin worth one cent, used in the United States and Canada. One hundred pennies equal one dollar. 2. A British coin. One hundred pennies equal one pound. **pen·ny** (pen′ē) *noun, plural* **pennies.**

pension Money paid regularly to a retired or disabled person. **pen·sion** (pen′shən) *noun, plural* **pensions.**

pentagon A figure that has five sides. **pen·ta·gon** (pen′tə gon′) *noun, plural* **pentagons.**

penthouse An apartment or house built on the roof of a building. **pent·house** (pent′hous′) *noun, plural* **penthouses** (pent′houz′iz).

peony A garden plant with big pink, red, or white flowers. **pe·o·ny** (pē′ə nē) *noun, plural* **peonies.**

people 1. Men, women, and children; persons: *This theater can seat 500 people.* 2. All of the persons making up a nation, race, tribe, or group: *The museum exhibit shows the crafts of African peoples.* 3. The public; persons in general: *This country was founded on a belief in government by the people.* 4. Family; relatives: *My teacher's people came from Cuba. Noun.*
○ To fill with people; inhabit: *A great number of human beings people the earth. Verb.*
peo·ple (pē′pəl) *noun, plural* **people** *or* **peoples** *(for definition 2); verb,* **peopled, peopling.**

pep A lively, vital quality; activity; spirit: *After the brisk walk outside, I was full of pep. Noun.*
○ To make lively or energetic: *Whenever I need to be pepped up I do some exercises. Verb.*
pep (pep) *noun; verb,* **pepped, pepping.**

pepper 1. A spice used to flavor foods. Black pepper is ground from the whole dried berries of a tropical plant. White pepper comes from the seeds inside these berries. 2. The hollow green, red, or yellow fruit of any of a group of plants. The fruit of some plants can be eaten and may be sweet or hot. *Noun.*
○ 1. To flavor with pepper: *I salted and peppered the fried eggs.* 2. To cover or sprinkle: *The gardener peppered the ground with grass seed. Verb.*
pep·per (pep′ər) *noun, plural* **peppers**; *verb,* **peppered, peppering.**

peppermint 1. A kind of mint plant. The oil from peppermint leaves is used in medicine and to flavor candy, chewing gum, and toothpaste. 2. A candy flavored with peppermint oil. **pep·per·mint** (pep′ər mint′) *noun, plural* **peppermints.**

per For each: *My summer job paid sixty dollars per week.* **per** (pûr *or unstressed* pər) *preposition.*

perceive 1. To become aware of through seeing, hearing, tasting, smelling, or feeling: *I perceived a faint knocking at the door.* 2. To understand; comprehend: *The teacher soon perceived that the students did not understand.* **per·ceive** (pər sēv′) *verb,* **perceived, perceiving.**

percent The number of parts in every hundred: *Two percent of fifty is one. Twenty percent of the class was out sick with chicken pox.* The symbol for "percent" when it is written with a number is %. For example, "five percent" is also written "5%." **per·cent** (pər sent′) *noun.*

percentage 1. The proportion of something, expressed as the number of hundredths: *What percentage of the class passed the test?* 2. A part of a whole; portion: *A large percentage of students walk to school.* **per·cent·age** (pər sen′tij) *noun, plural* **percentages.**

perception 1. The act or power of perceiving: *A cat's* **perception** *of colors is poor.* 2. The understanding, comprehension, or knowledge that is the result of perceiving: *The astronauts'* **perception** *of the problems that arose during their flight saved their lives.* **per·cep·tion** (pər sep′shən) *noun, plural* **perceptions.**

perch¹ 1. A bar, branch, or anything else a bird can rest on: *Our pet canary uses a swinging bar in its cage as a* **perch.** 2. Any raised place for sitting or standing: *The lifeguard watched the swimmers from a* **perch** *above the pool. Noun.*
○ To sit or rest on a perch: *The bird* **perched** *on the fence. The cat loved to* **perch** *itself on a window ledge in the sun. Verb.*
perch (pûrch) *noun, plural* **perches**; *verb,* **perched, perching.**

perch² 1. A small fish that is found in fresh water in North America and most parts of Europe. It is used for food. 2. A similar fish that lives in salt water. **perch** (pûrch) *noun, plural* **perch** *or* **perches.**

percussion 1. The striking of one thing against another with force; collision: *Over a long time, the* **percussion** *of shoes on stone wore out the pavement.* 2. The sound or vibration from one thing striking another with force: *We could hear the* **percussion** *of the waves on the rocks.* **per·cus·sion** (pər kush′ən) *noun.*

percussion instrument A musical instrument played by striking one thing against another. The drum, cymbal, and xylophone are percussion instruments.

perennial 1. Lasting or existing through the year or through many years: *The ice in this cave is* **perennial.** 2. Lasting for a long time; enduring: *Peace is a* **perennial** *dream.* 3. Of plants, living more than two years: *Roses are* **perennial** *plants. Adjective.*
○ A plant that lives and produces flowers for more than two years: *This part of the garden is full of* **perennials.** *Noun.*
pe·ren·ni·al (pə ren′ē əl) *adjective; noun, plural* **perennials.** —**perennially** *adverb.*

perfect 1. Without a mistake or fault: *a* **perfect** *day at the beach.* 2. Not missing anything; complete; exact: *You can draw a* **perfect** *circle with a compass. The picture the artist drew was a* **perfect** *likeness of my mother.* 3. Very great: *My father told me that I was making a* **perfect** *nuisance of myself. Adjective.*
○ To make or complete without any mistakes or faults: *I went to Mexico to* **perfect** *my Spanish. Verb.*
per·fect (pûr′fikt *for adjective;* pər fekt′ *for verb*) *adjective; verb,* **perfected, perfecting.**

perfection 1. The condition of being perfect or without fault; excellence: *The diver practiced over and over, striving for* **perfection.** 2. The act or process of making perfect: *The* **perfection** *of a ballet dancer's technique takes many years.* **per·fec·tion** (pər fek′shən) *noun.*

perfectly 1. In an excellent way; without fault: *That suit fits you* **perfectly.** 2. Completely; entirely: *I had a* **perfectly** *wonderful time at the party.* **per·fect·ly** (pûr′fikt lē) *adverb.*

perforate To make a hole or holes through: *We* **perforated** *the box with a pencil so the kitten could breathe more easily. Sheets of stamps are* **perforated** *to make it easy to tear off one or two at a time.* **per·fo·rate** (pûr′fə rāt′) *verb,* **perforated, perforating.** —**perforation** *noun.*

perform 1. To carry out; do: *The surgeon* **performed** *a difficult operation.* 2. To sing, act, or do something in public that requires skill: *Our band* **performed** *at the game.* **per·form** (pər fôrm′) *verb,* **performed, performing.**

performance 1. A public presentation of something entertaining: *The audience enjoyed last night's* **performance** *of the school play.* 2. The act of carrying out an action: *You may watch the factory workers, but don't interfere with the* **performance** *of their jobs.* 3. The way in which something works; operation: *The advertisement said that the* **performance** *of the car had been tested on rough country roads.* **per·form·ance** (pər fôr′məns) *noun, plural* **performances.**

performer A person who sings, acts, or does some form of entertainment in public. Dancers and clowns are performers. **per·form·er** (pər fôrm′ər) *noun, plural* **performers.**

perfume 1. A liquid used to give people or things a pleasant smell. 2. A pleasant smell: *The* **perfume** *from the flowers filled the room. Noun.*

PRONUNCIATION KEY:

| at | āpe | fär | câre | end | mē | it | īce | pîerce | hot | ōld | sông | fôrk |
| oil | out | up | ūse | rüle | pull | tûrn | chin | sing | shop | thin | this | |

hw in white; zh in treasure. The symbol ə stands for the unstressed vowel sound in about, taken, pencil, lemon, and circus.

557

○ To fill with a pleasant smell: *The roses per-fumed the air. Verb.*
per·fume (pûr′fūm *or* pər fūm′ *for noun;* pər fūm′ *for verb*) *noun, plural* **perfumes;** *verb,* **perfumed, perfuming.**

perhaps Maybe; possibly: *Perhaps it will rain tomorrow.* **per·haps** (pər haps′) *adverb.*

peril 1. A chance or risk of harm; danger: *A fire-fighter's life is often in* **peril.** 2. Something danger-ous: *Crocodiles and quicksand were* **perils** *faced by the jungle explorers.* **per·il** (per′əl) *noun, plural* **perils.** —**perilous** *adjective* —**perilously** *adverb.*

perimeter The boundary of a figure or an area: *The* **perimeter** *of a square is equal to four times the length of one side.* **pe·rim·e·ter** (pə rim′i tər) *noun, plural* **perimeters.**

period 1. A portion of time: *A day is a* **period** *of twenty-four hours. Our team made a goal in the second* **period** *of the hockey game.* 2. A punctua-tion mark (.) used at the end of a declarative sen-tence or an imperative sentence or at the end of an abbreviation. **pe·ri·od** (pîr′ē əd) *noun, plural* **periods.**

periodic Happening again and again at regular times: *We make* **periodic** *visits to the dentist.* **pe·ri·od·ic** (pîr′ē od′ik) *adjective.* —**periodically** *adverb.*

periodical A magazine printed at regular times. Most periodicals come out every week, every month, or every three months. **pe·ri·od·i·cal** (pîr′ē od′i kəl) *noun, plural* **periodicals.**

periscope A device that looks like a telescope and sticks out from the top of a submarine. It is used to see ships, land, or other things above the sur-face of the water. **per·i·scope** (per′ə skōp′) *noun, plural* **periscopes.**

perish To be destroyed; die. *Many people perished when the ship sank.* **per·ish** (per′ish) *verb,* **per-ished, perishing.**

perishable Likely to spoil or decay quickly: *Milk and meat are* **perishable** *foods.* **per·ish·a·ble** (per′i shə bəl) *adjective.*

perjury The act or crime of lying after swearing under oath to tell the truth. **per·ju·ry** (pûr′jə rē) *noun, plural* **perjuries.**

permanent Lasting or meant to last; enduring: *After graduating from college, I started looking for a* **permanent** *job.* **per·ma·nent** (pûr′mə nənt) *adjective.* —**permanently** *adverb.*

permission A consent from someone in authori-ty: *You should ask your parents for* **permission** *to stay overnight at my house.* **per·mis·sion** (pər mish′ən) *noun.*

permit To allow or let: *My parents will not* **permit** *me to play outside after dark. Verb.*
○ A written order giving permission to do some-thing: *You need a* **permit** *to fish here. Noun.*
per·mit (pər mit′ *for verb;* pûr′mit *or* pər mit′ *for noun*) *verb,* **permitted, permitting;** *noun, plural* **permits.**

perpendicular 1. Straight up and down; upright: *The expert mountain climber climbed the* **perpen-dicular** *face of the cliff.* 2. At right angles to a given line or surface: *The telephone pole is* **per-pendicular** *to the road.* **per·pen·dic·u·lar** (pûr′pən dik′yə lər) *adjective.* —**perpendicularly** *adverb.*

perpetual 1. Lasting for a very long time or for-ever: *Some mountains are covered by* **perpetual** *snow.* 2. Continuing without stopping: *The* **per-petual** *rise and fall of the tides is influenced by the moon and sun.* **per·pet·u·al** (pər pech′ü əl) *adjective.* —**perpetually** *adverb.*

perpetuate To keep alive or active; preserve: *Holidays* **perpetuate** *important traditions.* **per·pet·u·ate** (pər pech′ü āt′) *verb,* **perpetuated, perpetuating.** —**perpetuation** *noun.*

persecute To treat continually in a cruel and unjust way: *The rebels* **persecuted** *the people who were loyal to the king.* **per·se·cute** (pûr′si kūt′) *verb,* **persecuted, persecuting.**

persecution Continual cruel treatment: *The refugees fled their country after years of* **persecu-tion.** **per·se·cu·tion** (pûr′si kū′shən) *noun, plural* **persecutions.**

Persia 1. An ancient empire of southwestern Asia. 2. The former name of **Iran.** **Per·sia** (pûr′zhə) *noun.*

Persian 1. A person who lived in ancient Persia. 2. The language of ancient Persia or modern Iran. *Noun.*
○ Of or having to do with Persia, its people, or their language. *Adjective.*
Per·sian (pûr′zhən) *noun, plural* **Persians;** *adjective.*

persimmon A round fruit that has thin orange or yellow skin and grows on a tree or shrub. Persimmons are sweet when they are fully ripe.

per·sim·mon (pər sim′ən) *noun*, *plural* **persimmons**.

persist To continue firmly and steadily: *The rainy weather persisted all week.* **per·sist** (pər sist′) *verb*, **persisted, persisting**.

persistent 1. Continuing firmly and steadily: *A persistent person does not give up when faced with trouble.* 2. Lasting a long time: *I had a persistent cough for a month.* **per·sist·ent** (pər sis′tənt) *adjective.* —**persistently** *adverb.*

person 1. A man, woman, or child; human being: *Every ten years, the government takes an official count of every person living in this country.* 2. The body of and clothing worn by a human being: *I usually keep a handkerchief somewhere on my person.* 3. Any of three groups of personal pronouns and verb forms. The words of the *first person* are used for the speaker or speakers. The words of the *second person* are used for the one or ones spoken to. And the words of the *third person* are used for the one or ones spoken of.
• **in person**. Physically present: *The movie star looked better in person.*
per·son (pûr′sən) *noun*, *plural* **persons**.

personal 1. Private; not public: *My diary is personal, so please don't read it.* 2. Done or made in person: *The movie stars made personal appearances at the opening of their movie.* 3. Having to do with a person's body: *personal cleanliness.* **per·son·al** (pûr′sə nəl) *adjective.*

personal computer A small computer for use by one person. Look up **microcomputer** for more information.

personality 1. All of a person's characteristics, habits, behavior, and other qualities. A person's personality makes him or her different from everybody else: *The class chose a student with a friendly personality to greet and guide the foreign visitors.* 2. A well-known person: *television personalities.* **per·son·al·i·ty** (pûr′sə nal′i tē) *noun*, *plural* **personalities**.

personally 1. Without the help of others; by oneself: *The senator answered my letter personally.* 2. As far as oneself is concerned; for oneself: *Personally, I am in favor of going camping.* 3. As a person or individual: *I don't like our neighbor personally.* **per·son·al·ly** (pûr′sə nə lē) *adverb.*

personnel The group of people working for a company or other organization: *The personnel in this company are given two weeks of vacation a year.* **per·son·nel** (pûr′sə nel′) *noun.*

perspective 1. The way in which a picture on a flat surface can show objects that seem to be at a distance. 2. A point of view: *From a child's perspective, the house seemed very large.* 3. The relation of things to one another; relative size or importance: *If you see things in their proper perspective, you won't worry about small matters.* **per·spec·tive** (pər spek′tiv) *noun*, *plural* **perspectives**.

perspiration 1. Moisture that is given off through the pores of the skin; sweat. 2. The process of sweating. When a person's body gets too hot, it cools off through perspiration. **per·spi·ra·tion** (pûr′spə rā′shən) *noun.*

perspire To give off perspiration; sweat: *I perspire when I play tennis.* **per·spire** (pər spīr′) *verb*, **perspired, perspiring**.

persuade To cause to do or believe something by pleading or giving reasons; convince: *They persuaded me to go with them.* **per·suade** (pər swād′) *verb*, **persuaded, persuading**. —**persuasion** *noun.*

pertain 1. To be connected or related: *I have a collection of programs, autographs, and other objects pertaining to professional baseball.* 2. To belong: *Some important duties pertain to that office.* **per·tain** (pər tān′) *verb*, **pertained, pertaining**.

pertinent Having to do with what is being discussed or considered; relevant: *The weather forecast is pertinent because we're planning to have our party in the garden.* **per·ti·nent** (pûr′tə nənt) *adjective.* —**pertinence** *noun.*

Peru A country in western South America. **Pe·ru** (pə rü′) *noun.*

peso A unit of money in Mexico and in several South American countries. **pe·so** (pā′sō) *noun*, *plural* **pesos**.

pessimistic Having a negative attitude about things; expecting the worst: *Since our best player was sick, we were pessimistic about winning the game.* **pes·si·mis·tic** (pes′ə mis′tik) *adjective.* —**pessimism** *noun* —**pessimistically** *adverb.*

pest A person or thing that is troublesome or annoying; nuisance. **pest** (pest) *noun*, *plural* **pests**.

pester To trouble or bother; annoy again and again: *Please don't pester me for any more candy*

PRONUNCIATION KEY:

at	āpe	fär	câre	end	mē	it	īce	pierce	hot	ōld	sông	fôrk
oil	out	up	ūse	rüle	pull	tûrn	chin	sing	shop	thin	this	

hw in white; zh in treasure. The symbol ə stands for the unstressed vowel sound in about, taken, pencil, lemon, and circus.

559

because it's all gone. **pes·ter** (pes′tər) *verb,* **pestered, pestering.**

pesticide A chemical substance used to kill insects, mice, rats, or other animal pests. **pes·ti·cide** (pes′tə sīd′) *noun, plural* **pesticides.**

pestle A tool shaped like a club, used for pounding, grinding, or mixing something in a bowl called a mortar. **pes·tle** (pes′əl *or* pes′təl) *noun, plural* **pestles.**

pet 1. An animal kept in a person's home for fun and companionship. Dogs, cats, and birds are common pets. 2. A person who is treated with special kindness or favor; favorite: *My friend accused me of being the teacher's pet. Noun.*
○ Kept or treated as a pet: *a pet rabbit. Adjective.*
○ To stroke or pat in a gentle or loving way: *The cat purrs whenever we pet it. Verb.*
pet (pet) *noun, plural* **pets;** *adjective; verb,* **petted, petting.**

petal One of the parts of a flower. Petals come in many colors and shapes: *The petals of a daisy are usually white and are arranged in a circle.* **pet·al** (pet′əl) *noun, plural* **petals.**

The petals of most flowers are very fragile.

petition A formal request that is made to a person in authority: *All the people on our street signed a petition asking the city to put a stop sign on the corner. Noun.*
○ To make a formal request to: *The students in our school petitioned the principal to keep the library open on weekends. Verb.*
pe·ti·tion (pi tish′ən) *noun, plural* **petitions;** *verb,* **petitioned, petitioning.**

petrify 1. To turn into stone. Petrified wood forms when water seeps through the dead wood of fallen trees and leaves minerals inside the wood cells. 2. To make helpless with fear: *The sudden bolt of thunder and lightning petrified us.* **pet·ri·fy** (pet′rə fī′) *verb,* **petrified, petrifying.**

The minerals in petrified wood take the place of wood cells when they decay.

petroleum An oily liquid found beneath the surface of the earth and made into gasoline, kerosene, oil for heating buildings, and many other products. **pe·tro·le·um** (pi trō′lē əm) *noun.*

WORD HISTORY

The word petroleum comes from two Greek words meaning "rock" and "oil." Petroleum is oil that comes from the ground instead of from olives or other fruit.

petticoat A skirt that is made to be worn under a dress or outer skirt. **pet·ti·coat** (pet′ē kōt′) *noun, plural* **petticoats.**

petty 1. Not important; insignificant: *petty problems.* 2. Mean or intolerant: *Petty gossip.* **pet·ty** (pet′ē) *adjective,* **pettier, pettiest. —pettiness** *noun.*

petunia A garden plant that has flowers that are shaped like trumpets. The flowers come in many colors. **pe·tu·nia** (pi tün′yə *or* pi tūn′yə) *noun, plural* **petunias.**

pew A long bench in church for people to sit on. Pews have backs and are arranged in rows. **pew** (pū) *noun, plural* **pews.**

pewter A metal made by combining tin, copper, and other metals, used to make plates, pitchers, mugs, and candlesticks. **pew·ter** (pū′tər) *noun.*

pg. An abbreviation for page.

phantom Something that appears to be real but is not. **phan·tom** (fan′təm) *noun, plural* **phantoms.**

Pharaoh The title of the kings of ancient Egypt. **Phar·aoh** (fâr′ō) *noun, plural* **Pharaohs.**

pharmacist A person trained to prepare and dispense drugs and medicines. **phar·ma·cist** (fär′mə sist) *noun, plural* **pharmacists.**

pharmacy A store where drugs and medicines are

sold; drugstore. **phar·ma·cy** (fär′mə sē) *noun,* *plural* **pharmacies.**

phase 1. A stage of development: *Most babies go through a phase when they put everything in their mouths.* 2. A part or side; aspect: *Advertising, accounting, and selling are some of the phases of many businesses.* 3. The appearance and shape of the moon or a planet as it is seen at a particular time, which depends on how much of its lighted side can be seen from the earth. **phase** (fāz) *noun,* *plural* **phases.**

pheasant A large bird with a long tail and brightly colored feathers. Pheasants live on the ground. **pheas·ant** (fez′ənt) *noun,* *plural* **pheasants.**

phenomenon 1. A fact or event that can be seen or sensed: *The strange phenomenon in the sky was a meteor that exploded.* 2. A person or thing that is extraordinary or remarkable. **phe·nom·e·non** (fə nom′ə non′) *noun,* *plural* **phenomena** or **phenomenons.** —**phenomenal** *adjective* —**phenomenally** *adverb.*

Philippines A country that is a group of islands in southeast Asia. **Phil·ip·pines** (fil′ə pēnz′ or fil′ə pēnz′) *plural noun.*

philodendron A tropical American vine. There are many different kinds of philodendrons, and they are often grown indoors. **phil·o·den·dron** (fil′ə den′drən) *noun,* *plural* **philodendrons.**

philosopher A person who studies or specializes in philosophy. Philosophers often try to answer basic questions about reality, matter, knowledge, or life. **phi·los·o·pher** (fə los′ə fər) *noun,* *plural* **philosophers.**

philosophy 1. The study of the basic nature of reality, matter, knowledge, and life. 2. A person's principles and beliefs: *My parents' philosophy is to be kind to others.* **phi·los·o·phy** (fə los′ə fē) *noun,* *plural* **philosophies.** —**philosophical** *adjective* —**philosophically** *adverb.*

phlox A plant that has groups of small white, pink, red, pur-

Phlox is often used to cover ground.

ple, or blue flowers. **phlox** (floks) *noun,* *plural* **phloxes.**

phone A telephone. *Noun.*
○ To call on the telephone: *Will you please phone me tomorrow? Verb.*
phone (fōn) *noun,* *plural* **phones;** *verb,* **phoned, phoning.**

phonetic Having to do with or representing speech sounds: *We use the phonetic symbol ô to show how to pronounce the sound of the letter "o" in "fork."* **pho·net·ic** (fə net′ik) *adjective.* —**phonetically** *adverb.*

phonograph An instrument that reproduces sound from records. The needle of a phonograph picks up the sounds that have been recorded in the grooves of a record as the record turns. It plays them through loudspeakers so they can be heard. **pho·no·graph** (fō′nə graf′) *noun,* *plural* **phonographs.**

phosphorus A substance that looks like white or yellow wax. Phosphorus glows in the dark. Plants and animals need phosphorus. Phosphorus is a chemical element. **phos·pho·rus** (fos′fə rəs) *noun.*

photo A short form of the word "photograph." Look up **photograph** for more information. **pho·to** (fō′tō) *noun,* *plural* **photos.**

photograph A picture that is made with a camera. *Noun.*
○ To take a picture of with a camera: *We photographed the beautiful sunset from the balcony. Verb.*
pho·to·graph (fō′tə graf′) *noun,* *plural* **photographs;** *verb,* **photographed, photographing.**

photographer A person who takes photographs for fun or as a profession. **pho·tog·ra·pher** (fə tog′rə fər) *noun,* *plural* **photographers.**

photography The art or business of taking or making photographs. **pho·tog·ra·phy** (fə tog′rə fē) *noun.*

photosynthesis The process by which green plants use carbon dioxide, water, and sunlight to make their own food. **pho·to·syn·the·sis** (fō′tə sin′thə sis) *noun.*

phrase 1. A group of words that expresses a thought but does not contain both a subject and a predicate. In the sentence "We walked to town," "to town" is a phrase. 2. A short expres-

PRONUNCIATION KEY:

| at | āpe | fär | câre | end | mē | it | īce | pierce | hot | ōld | sông | fôrk |
| oil | out | up | ūse | rüle | pull | tûrn | chin | sing | shop | thin | this | |

hw in white; zh in treasure. The symbol ə stands for the unstressed vowel sound in about, taken, pencil, lemon, and circus.

561

sion: *"Lower taxes!" was the **phrase** that the marchers chanted. Noun.*

○ To express in chosen words: *The teacher **phrased** the questions very carefully. Verb.* **phrase** (frāz) *noun, plural* **phrases**; *verb,* **phrased, phrasing.**

physical 1. Having to do with the body: *An elephant has great **physical** strength.* 2. Having to do with matter and energy: *Chemistry and physics are **physical** sciences.* 3. Having to do with nature or natural objects: *mountains, lakes, and other **physical** features of the country.* **phys·i·cal** (fiz′i kəl) *adjective.* —**physically** *adverb.*

physician A person who is trained and licensed to treat sickness or injury; doctor. **phy·si·cian** (fə zish′ən) *noun, plural* **physicians.**

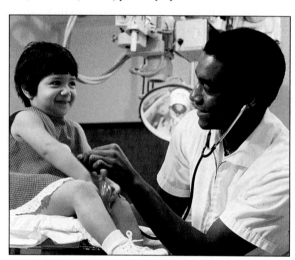

It takes many years of schooling to become a physician.

physicist A person who works or specializes in physics. **phys·i·cist** (fiz′ə sist) *noun, plural* **physicists.**

physics The science that deals with matter and energy and the laws governing them. Physics includes the study of motion, light, heat, sound, and electricity and force. The word "physics" is used with a singular *verb.* **phys·ics** (fiz′iks) *noun.*

pi The symbol π. It represents the ratio of the circumference of a circle to its diameter. Pi is equal to about 3.1416.

Another word that sounds like this is **pie.** **pi** (pī) *noun, plural* **pis.**

pianist A person who plays the piano. **pi·an·ist** (pē an′ist *or* pyan′ist *or* pē′ə nist) *noun, plural* **pianists.**

piano A musical instrument, usually a wooden box shaped like a rectangle or harp with a keyboard. The keys control little hammers inside the box that strike metal strings to produce tones. **pi·an·o** (pē an′ō *or* pyan′ō) *noun, plural* **pianos.**

piccolo A small flute with a higher pitch than an ordinary flute. **pic·co·lo** (pik′ə lō) *noun, plural* **piccolos.**

pick¹ 1. To take from a number offered; select or choose: *Pick a card from the deck.* 2. To gather with the fingers: *We **picked** blueberries for a pie.* 3. To remove with the fingers or something pointed: *Our dog loves to **pick** the meat off a bone.* 4. To pull at and let go; pluck: *The folk singer **picked** the strings of a guitar.* 5. To cause on purpose: *Are you trying to **pick** a fight?* 6. To steal the contents of: *The thief **picked** the subway rider's pocket.* 7. To open with a wire or something pointed instead of a key: *The burglar **picked** the lock. Verb.*

○ 1. The best one or ones: *That puppy is the **pick** of the litter.* 2. An act of choosing; selection: *Take your **pick** of the books.* 3. A small, thin piece of plastic or other material used to pluck the strings of a guitar or similar instrument. *Noun.*

• **to pick at.** To eat just a little of: *You just **picked** at your dinner so I guess you aren't feeling well.*

• **to pick on.** To treat or tease someone smaller or weaker in a mean way: *Older children sometimes **pick on** younger children.*

• **to pick out.** To choose: *Have you **picked out** a name for the puppy?*

• **to pick up.** 1. To take and lift up: *Pick your clothes **up** off the floor.* 2. To get without much planning or by chance: *I **pick up** extra money by doing odd jobs.* 3. To stop for and take on: *The bus **picked up** two passengers.* 4. To manage to receive or record: *Sometimes my radio **picks up** police conversations.* 5. To get better; improve: *Business is **picking up.*** 6. To learn: *My cousin **picked up** Italian after a few months in Italy.*

pick (pik) *verb,* **picked, picking**; *noun, plural* **picks.**

pick² 1. A tool with a wooden handle and a metal head that is pointed at one end or both. A pick is used for breaking rocks and loosening dirt. It is also called a **pickax.** 2. A pointed tool. An ice pick can be used to break up ice. **pick** (pik) *noun, plural* **picks.**

pickax or **pickaxe** A pick, especially one with a head with a point at one end and a blade like that of a chisel at the other end. Look up **pick**[2] for more information. **pick·ax** or **pick·axe** (pik′aks′) *noun, plural* **pickaxes.**

pickerel A freshwater fish with a thin body and a pointed head. Pickerels are members of the pike family. They live in North America and are used for food. **pick·er·el** (pik′ə rəl) *noun, plural* **pickerel** *or* **pickerels.**

picket 1. A pointed stake driven into the ground to hold something in place or to be part of a fence. 2. A person who stands or walks outside a place to protest or demand something: *The pickets outside the store carried signs asking customers to support an employees' strike by not shopping there. Noun.*
○ To stand in front of or walk about as a picket: *The workers picketed the steel factory. Verb.*
pick·et (pik′it) *noun, plural* **pickets;** *verb,* **picketed, picketing.**

pickle Any food that has been preserved and flavored in salt water or vinegar. Cucumbers are often prepared in this way. *Noun.*
○ To preserve in salt water or vinegar: *We pickle beets every year. Verb.*
pick·le (pik′əl) *noun, plural* **pickles;** *verb,* **pickled, pickling.**

pickpocket A person who steals from other people's pockets or purses. **pick·pock·et** (pik′pok′it) *noun, plural* **pickpockets.**

pickup 1. The act of getting hold of and lifting or taking something: *There is a pickup of mail this afternoon.* 2. A small truck with an open back, used for carrying light loads. **pick·up** (pik′up′) *noun, plural* **pickups.**

picnic A party or trip for which food is taken along and eaten outside: *We made sandwiches and lemonade for a picnic on the beach. Noun.*
○ To go on or have a picnic: *We picnicked in the park. Verb.*
pic·nic (pik′nik) *noun, plural* **picnics;** *verb,* **picnicked, picnicking.**

picture 1. A painting, drawing, or photograph of a person or thing. 2. An image on a television, motion-picture, or computer screen. 3. A description in words: *A student from Germany spoke to our class, giving us a detailed picture of life in that country.* 4. A likeness or perfect example: *That child is the picture of health.* 5. A motion picture; movie. *Noun.*
○ 1. To draw or paint a picture of: *The artist pictured the old couple sitting on a bench.* 2. To give a description of: *The writer pictured the horrors of war.* 3. To imagine: *It is hard for me to picture what our town will be like in ten years. Verb.*
pic·ture (pik′chər) *noun, plural* **pictures;** *verb,* **pictured, picturing.**

picturesque Being a good subject for a picture; pleasant or interesting to look at or imagine: *A cottage by the sea is picturesque.* **pic·tur·esque** (pik′chə resk′) *adjective.*

pie A pastry shell filled with fruit, meat, or other food and baked in an oven.
Another word that sounds like this is **pi.**
pie (pī) *noun, plural* **pies.**

piece 1. A part that has been broken, cut, or torn from something; fragment: *There are pieces of broken glass all over the floor.* 2. One of a group or set of similar things: *We're missing two chess pieces.* 3. A work of art, music, or literature: *I'm learning a new piece of music for the piano.* 4. An example or instance: *What a piece of luck!* 5. A coin: *A dime is a ten-cent piece. Noun.*
○ To join the parts or pieces of: *The police were able to piece together the evidence and solve the crime. Verb.*
Another word that sounds like this is **peace.**
piece (pēs) *noun, plural* **pieces;** *verb,* **pieced, piecing.**

pier 1. A structure built out over the water, used as a landing place for boats or ships. 2. A pillar or other kind of support used to hold up a bridge. Modern bridges have steel piers to support them.
Another word that sounds like this is **peer.**
pier (pîr) *noun, plural* **piers.**

pierce 1. To make a hole through: *A nail pierced the tire of my bicycle.* 2. To pass through; penetrate: *A shrill cry pierced the stillness of the night.* **pierce** (pîrs) *verb,* **pierced, piercing.**

pig 1. An animal that has a stout body, short legs with hooves, a short snout, and a short, curly tail; a young hog. Some pigs are raised for their meat, called pork. 2. A messy or greedy person. **pig** (pig) *noun, plural* **pigs.**

PRONUNCIATION KEY:
at ape fär câre end mē it īce pierce hot ōld sông fôrk
oil out up ūse rüle pull tûrn chin sing shop thin this
hw in white; zh in treasure. The symbol ə stands for the unstressed vowel sound in about, taken, pencil, lemon, and circus.
563

pigeon A bird with a plump body, a small head, and thick, soft feathers; dove. Pigeons live in the wild, but are also found in nearly every city of the world. **pi·geon** (pij′ən) noun, plural **pigeons**.

piggyback On the back or shoulders: *Those children love it when grown-ups give them **piggyback** rides. Adjective.*
○ On the back or shoulders: *The guide had to carry the injured climber piggyback. Adverb.* **pig·gy·back** (pig′ē bak′) adjective; adverb.

The mother is carrying her child piggyback.

pigment 1. A substance that is used for coloring. A pigment is often a powder that is mixed with a liquid to make a paint or dye. 2. A substance in a plant or in animal tissue that gives it color: *Chlorophyll is the green **pigment** in leaves.* **pig·ment** (pig′mənt) noun, plural **pigments**.

pigpen 1. An enclosed place where pigs are kept. This place is also called a **sty** or a **pigsty**. **pig·pen** (pig′pen′) noun, plural **pigpens**.

pigsty A pigpen. **pig·sty** (pig′stī′) noun, plural **pigsties**.

pigtail A braid or fastened bunch of hair hanging from the head. **pig·tail** (pig′tāl′) noun, plural **pigtails**.

pike A large freshwater fish with a long, thin body, a large mouth, and sharp teeth. **pike** (pīk) noun, plural **pikes** or **pike**.

pile¹ 1. A number of things lying one on top of the other; heap: *There is a **pile** of newspapers on the floor.* 2. A large amount: *I have to finish a **pile** of homework. Noun.*
○ 1. To form or put into a heap or mass: *Pile the dishes in the sink.* 2. To cover with a large amount: *The carpenters **piled** their table with lumber and tools. Verb.*
pile (pīl) noun, plural **piles**; verb, **piled**, **piling**.

pile² A heavy, upright post that is driven into the ground to support a bridge or pier. **pile** (pīl) noun, plural **piles**.

pile³ The soft, thick fibers on the surface of a rug or a piece of cloth. Pile is often made of loops of yarn. **pile** (pīl) noun.

pilgrim 1. A person who travels to a sacred place for a religious purpose: *For centuries, Christian **pilgrims** have been going to Palestine to pray and worship in the places where Jesus lived.* 2. Pilgrim. One of a group of English settlers who founded the colony of Plymouth in New England in 1620. **pil·grim** (pil′grəm) noun, plural **pilgrims**.

WORD HISTORY

The word pilgrim comes from a Latin word that means "foreigner." Pilgrims often travel far from home, to places where they are foreigners.

---

pill A small tablet of medicine to be swallowed or chewed. **pill** (pil) noun, plural **pills**.

pillar A column that supports a building or stands alone as a monument: *The roof of the porch is supported by **pillars**.* **pil·lar** (pil′ər) noun, plural **pillars**.

pillory A frame of wood with holes for a person's head and hands. A pillory used to be set up in a public place, and people were put in it as a punishment. **pil·lo·ry** (pil′ə rē) noun, plural **pillories**.

pillow A bag or case filled with feathers or other soft material, and used to support the head when resting or sleeping. **pil·low** (pil′ō) noun, plural **pillows**.

pillowcase A cloth case open at one end, used to cover a pillow. **pil·low·case** (pil′ō kās′) noun, plural **pillowcases**.

pilot 1. A person who operates an aircraft or spacecraft. 2. A person who steers large ships into and out of a harbor or through dangerous waters. *Noun.*
○ To act as a pilot: *The captain **piloted** the airplane safely through the dangerous thunderstorm. Verb.*
pi·lot (pī′lət) noun, plural **pilots**; verb, **piloted**, **piloting**.

An airline pilot **uses instruments to fly a plane.**

pimple A small, red bump on the skin. Pimples are often painful and filled with pus. **pim·ple** (pim′pəl) noun, plural **pimples**.

pin **1.** A short piece of wire with a pointed end, used for holding things together. Some pins are stiff and straight. Others are U-shaped, like pins for the hair. Others can be closed, with the pointed end covered, like safety pins. **2.** An ornament or badge that has a clasp for attaching it to clothing: *I wore a pin in the shape of a butterfly on my collar.* **3.** A short, slender, round piece of wood or other hard material. A pin fits into a hole in each of two parts of something, so that the parts are held together: *The doctors put a metal pin into the badly broken bone.* **4.** One of ten pieces of wood shaped like bottles that are used in bowling. *Noun.*
○ **1.** To hold together or attach with a pin or pins: *Her dress was too long, so she pinned the hem up.* **2.** To hold fast in one position: *In wrestling, you try to pin your opponent to the mat. Verb.*
 • **on pins and needles.** Very nervous or anxious: *I was on pins and needles until I got my job.*
pin (pin) *noun, plural* **pins**; *verb,* **pinned, pinning.**

pinch **1.** To squeeze between the finger and thumb or between other surfaces: *I pinched my finger in the drawer when I closed it.* **2.** To make thin or wrinkled: *The child's face was pinched from the cold weather. Verb.*
○ **1.** A sharp squeeze: *Grandpa gave me a pinch to keep me awake during the movie.* **2.** An amount that can be held between the thumb and a finger: *The recipe said to add a pinch of salt.* **3.** A time of need or emergency: *I can lend you money if you're in a pinch. Noun.*
pinch (pinch) *verb,* **pinched, pinching**; *noun, plural* **pinches.**

pincushion A small, firm cushion into which needles and pins are stuck when they are not being used. **pin·cush·ion** (pin′kùsh′ən) *noun, plural* **pincushions.**

pine An evergreen tree with cones and leaves that look like needles. **pine** (pīn) *noun, plural* **pines.**

pineapple A large, oval fruit. The outside of a pineapple is hard and prickly, but the yellow meat inside is sweet and juicy. Pineapples grow on a tropical plant that has long, stiff leaves. **pine·ap·ple** (pīn′ap′əl) *noun, plural* **pineapples.**

Ping-Pong The trademark for the game of table tennis. Look up **table tennis** for more information. **Ping-Pong** (ping′pong′) *noun.*

pink **1.** A light red color made by mixing red and white. **2.** A garden plant that has pink, red, white, or sometimes yellow flowers with a sweet fragrance. *Noun.*
○ Having the color pink. *Adjective.*
pink (pingk) *noun, plural* **pinks**; *adjective,* **pinker, pinkest.**

pinkeye A disease of the eye that causes the covering on the eyeball and on the inside of the eyelid to become red and sore. **pink·eye** (pingk′ī′) *noun.*

pinpoint To locate or fix exactly: *The rescue team used a helicopter to pinpoint the place where the airplane had crashed.* **pin·point** (pin′point′) *verb,* **pinpointed, pinpointing.**

pint A unit of measurement equal to half a quart. **pint** (pīnt) *noun, plural* **pints.**

pinto A horse or pony with spots or patches of two or more colors. **pin·to** (pin′tō) *noun, plural* **pintos.**

pinwheel A toy made of colored paper or plastic that is pinned to a stick. It spins when the wind blows it. **pin·wheel** (pin′hwēl′ *or* pin′wēl′) *noun, plural* **pinwheels.**

pioneer **1.** A person who is among the first to explore and settle a region: *Pioneers settled the American West.* **2.** A person who is among the first to develop an area of thought or research: *The Wright brothers were pioneers in aviation. Noun.*
○ To be among the first to explore for others: *American scientists pioneered in sending human beings to the moon. Verb.*
pi·o·neer (pī′ə nîr′) *noun, plural* **pioneers**; *verb,* **pioneered, pioneering.**

The wood of the pine is used in building and in making turpentine.

PRONUNCIATION KEY:
at   āpe   fär   câre   end   mē   it   īce   pîerce   hot   ōld   sông   fôrk
oil   out   up   ūse   rūle   pùll   tûrn   chin   sing   shop   thin   <u>th</u>is
hw in white; zh in treasure. The symbol ə stands for the unstressed vowel sound in about, taken, pencil, lemon, and circus.

565

pious **1.** Very religious; devout. **2.** Of or relating to religious devotion: *They studied the **pious** writings of religious leaders.* **pi·ous** (pī′əs) *adjective.* —**piously** *adverb.*

pipe **1.** A tube of metal, glass, or other material used for carrying a gas or liquid: *The water in our house flows through copper **pipes**.* **2.** A tube with a bowl of wood or clay at one end that is used for smoking tobacco. **3.** A musical instrument that is in the shape of a tube. A person plays a pipe by blowing into it at one end. *Noun.*
○ **1.** To carry by means of a pipe or pipes: *The farmer **piped** water to the fields.* **2.** To play on a pipe: *The flutes **piped** a tune during the parade.* *Verb.*
pipe (pīp) *noun, plural* **pipes;** *verb,* **piped, piping.**

pipeline A line of pipes for carrying a liquid or gas over a long distance. **pipe·line** (pīp′līn′) *noun, plural* **pipelines.**

piracy The robbing of ships at sea. **pi·ra·cy** (pī′rə sē) *noun, plural* **piracies.**

pirate A person who robs ships at sea. **pi·rate** (pī′rit) *noun, plural* **pirates.**

pistachio A small, green nut with a tan shell that sometimes is dyed red. **pis·ta·chi·o** (pi stash′ē ō) *noun, plural* **pistachios.**

pistil The tiny stalk in the center of a flower. The pistil is the female part of a flower. Seeds develop in the pistil.
Another word that sounds like this is **pistol**.
pis·til (pis′təl) *noun, plural* **pistils.**

pistol A small gun that is held and fired with one hand.
Another word that sounds like this is **pistil**.
pis·tol (pis′təl) *noun, plural* **pistols.**

piston A cylinder that fits closely inside a tube or hollow cylinder, where it moves back and forth. The movement of the pistons in an automobile engine turns the car wheels. **pis·ton** (pis′tən) *noun, plural* **pistons.**

pit¹ **1.** A hole in the ground that occurs naturally or is dug: *The workers dug a deep **pit** in the backyard for the pool.* **2.** A sunken or indented area on a surface: *Acne sometimes leaves scars that are **pits** on the skin.* *Noun.*
○ **1.** To make pits in; mark with sunken areas: *Pebbles thrown against the window **pitted** the glass. Craters **pit** the surface of the moon.* **2.** To set against each other in a contest: *The World*

Series **pits** the two champion baseball teams against each other. *Verb.*
pit (pit) *noun, plural* **pits;** *verb,* **pitted, pitting.**

pit² The single hard seed in some fruits. Peaches and plums have pits. *Noun.*
○ To remove a pit from: *We **pitted** cherries for a pie.* *Verb.*
pit (pit) *noun, plural* **pits;** *verb,* **pitted, pitting.**

pitch¹ **1.** To throw or toss: *We spent the afternoon trying to **pitch** horseshoes.* **2.** To set up: *The campers **pitched** their tents.* **3.** To fall or plunge forward: *The ship **pitched** and rolled in the rough seas.* *Verb.*
○ **1.** A throw of the ball from the pitcher to a batter in baseball: *The batter struck out on three **pitches**.* **2.** A high point or degree: *We worked ourselves up to a **pitch** of excitement just before the big festival.* **3.** The highness or lowness of a sound in music: *The music director hummed the **pitch** for the chorus before each song.* **4.** A slope: *The roof of the ski lodge had a steep **pitch**.* *Noun.*
pitch (pich) *verb,* **pitched, pitching;** *noun, plural* **pitches.**

pitch² A dark, sticky substance that is made from tar. Pitch is used to make the roof of houses waterproof and to pave streets. **pitch** (pich) *noun.*

pitcher¹ A container with a handle and a lip or spout. A pitcher is used for holding and pouring milk, water, and other liquids. **pitch·er** (pich′ər) *noun, plural* **pitchers.**

pitcher² A baseball player who throws the ball to the batter. The pitcher stands near the middle of the diamond facing home plate. **pitch·er** (pich′ər) *noun, plural* **pitchers.**

pitchfork A tool that looks like a large fork, used to lift and throw hay. **pitch·fork** (pich′fôrk′) *noun, plural* **pitchforks.**

A good pitcher must throw the ball with accuracy.

pith **1.** The soft tissue in the center of the stems of certain plants. The pith is important in storing food. **2.** Any soft tissue that is like this. The pith of an orange is the soft white part that is inside the rind. **pith** (pith) *noun.*

pitiful **1.** Arousing sorrow and sympathy: *The lost puppy looked so **pitiful** that we took it home and kept it as a pet.* **2.** Arousing scorn or contempt: *a **pitiful** excuse.* **pit·i·ful** (pit′i fəl) *adjective.* —**pitifully** *adverb.*

pity **1.** A feeling of sorrow and sympathy for the troubles of another: *We felt **pity** for the family who lost everything when their house burned down.* **2.** A cause for regret: *What a **pity** you have a cold and can't come to the party. Noun.*
○ To feel sorrow and sympathy for someone: *We **pity** the people who lost their homes in the flood. Verb.*
pit·y (pit′ē) *noun, plural* **pities**; *verb,* **pitied, pitying.**

pivot A fixed point, shaft, or pin that something else turns on: *The hands of a clock turn on a **pivot**. Noun.*
○ To turn on a pivot or as if on a pivot: *The gun on that tank can **pivot** and fire in any direction. The basketball player **pivoted** and passed the ball to another player. Verb.*
piv·ot (piv′ət) *noun, plural* **pivots**; *verb,* **pivoted, pivoting.**

pixel The very small shape that is used in combinations to form numbers, letters, and pictures on a computer monitor. **pix·el** (pik′səl) *noun, plural* **pixels.**

pizza An Italian pie made of a flat crust covered with tomato sauce and cheese. Sometimes extra ingredients such as sausage, peppers, and mush-

**Pizza is a popular
American food.**

rooms are added before the pizza is baked. **piz·za** (pēt′sə) *noun, plural* **pizzas.**

pl. An abbreviation for **plural.**

place **1.** A part of space; location; area: *We visited many interesting **places** on our trip. The **place** where I hit my elbow is still sore.* **2.** A home: *My parents have rented a **place** in the country.* **3.** A passage in a book or other writing: *I marked my **place** in the book.* **4.** A space or seat for a person: *Would you save my **place**?* **5.** A position in an order or series; rank: *My poem won third **place** in the contest.* **6.** A proper or usual position: *When we finished cleaning, everything was in its **place**.* **7.** Duty or business: *It is not your **place** to criticize their work. Noun.*
○ **1.** To put or be in a particular spot or location: ***Place** the napkin beside the plate. My friend **placed** third in the swimming race.* **2.** To identify by connecting with the correct time and location: *I know I've seen you, but I can't **place** you. Verb.*
 • **to take place.** To happen: *The band concert took **place** in the park.*
place (plās) *noun, plural* **places**; *verb,* **placed, placing.**

placid Calm and peaceful: *There was no wind, so the lake was **placid**. The **placid** child was seldom excited or disturbed.* **plac·id** (plas′id) *adjective.* —**placidly** *adverb.*

plague **1.** A very serious disease that spreads quickly among the people in an area. A plague often causes death. **2.** Anything that causes great misfortune: *The trees were destroyed by a **plague** of caterpillars. Noun.*
○ To trouble or annoy: *Mosquitoes **plagued** the hikers. Verb.*
plague (plāg) *noun, plural* **plagues**; *verb,* **plagued, plaguing.**

**Casual clothes are
often plaid.**

plaid A pattern of stripes of different colors and widths crossing each other. Cloth with a pattern of plaid is used to make clothing,

PRONUNCIATION KEY:

| at | āpe | fär | câre | end | mē | it | īce | pierce | hot | ōld | sông | fôrk |
| oil | out | up | ūse | rüle | pull | tûrn | chin | sing | shop | thin | this | |

hw in white; zh in treasure. The symbol ə stands for the unstressed vowel sound in about, taken, pencil, lemon, and circus.

567

blankets, and other things. **plaid** (plad) *noun, plural* **plaids**.

plain 1. Clearly seen, heard, or understood: *As the airplane descended for a landing, the people and houses on the ground came into* **plain** *view. My friends made it* **plain** *that they did not agree with me.* 2. Straightforward; direct; frank: *I will be* **plain** *with you and tell you the truth.* 3. Without decoration: *You can wear your* **plain** *black dress with a silver necklace.* 4. Not rich or highly seasoned: *When I was sick I could eat only* **plain** *foods.* 5. Common or ordinary: **Plain** *people as well as famous people have a right to vote.* 6. Not beautiful: *That child has a* **plain** *but sweet face. Adjective.*

○ An area of flat or almost flat land: *Buffaloes used to roam the western* **plains**. *Noun.*

Another word that sounds like this is **plane**.

plain (plān) *adjective,* **plainer, plainest;** *noun, plural* **plains.** —**plainly** *adverb* —**plainness** *noun.*

plan 1. A way of doing something thought out ahead of time: *Our* **plan** *for climbing the mountain is to zigzag up the south slope.* 2. Something a person intends to do: *I have no* **plans** *for this weekend.* 3. A drawing that shows how the parts of something are arranged: *We looked at a* **plan** *of the museum to find out where the dinosaur bones were. Noun.*

○ 1. To think out a way of doing something ahead of time: *We* **planned** *the dinner so that there would be plenty of food for everyone.* 2. To have an intention; intend: *I* **plan** *to go to college.* 3. To make a drawing of: *An architect* **planned** *the new school. Verb.*

plan (plan) *noun, plural* **plans;** *verb,* **planned, planning.**

plane¹ 1. A level or grade: *The book was on such a high* **plane** *that I couldn't understand it.* 2. An aircraft that has an engine and wings that are not movable; airplane. Look up **airplane** for more information. *Noun.*

○ Level or flat: *This highway has a* **plane** *surface. Adjective.*

Another word that sounds like this is **plain**.

plane (plān) *noun, plural* **planes;** *adjective.*

plane² A hand tool with a sharp blade that sticks out from the bottom. A plane is used for smoothing wood. *Noun.*

○ To smooth with a plane: *The carpenter* **planed**

the door down a little so it would fit the door opening exactly. *Verb.*

Another word that sounds like this is **plain**.

plane (plān) *noun, plural* **planes;** *verb,* **planed, planing.**

planet One of nine large heavenly bodies that orbit the sun. The planets in our solar system are Mercury, Venus, Earth, Mars, Jupiter, Saturn, Uranus, Neptune, and Pluto. **plan·et** (plan′it) *noun, plural* **planets.**

WORD HISTORY

The word **planet** goes back to a Greek word meaning "wandering star." People noticed that most stars held the same positions night after night, but that the planets shifted their positions and "wandered" among the other stars.

planetarium A building in which there is a device that shows the movements of the sun, moon, planets, and stars by projecting their images on a curved ceiling. **plan·e·tar·i·um** (plan′i târ′ē əm) *noun, plural* **planetariums** *or* **planetaria** (plan′i târ′ē ə).

plank A long, flat piece of wood thicker than a board. **plank** (plangk) *noun, plural* **planks.**

plankton Very small plants and animals that float in seas and lakes. Many fish and whales feed on plankton. **plank·ton** (plangk′tən) *noun.*

plant 1. A living thing that, unlike animals, stays in one place, makes its own food, and has rigid cell walls. Shrubs, trees, mosses, and most algae

plant

flower bud — flower
— petal
flowers make seeds

leaves collect energy from the sun — leaf
— leaf stalk
— stem

roots anchor the plant and collect water and nutrients from the soil — root
— root hairs
— root cap is the growing end of the root

are plants. **2.** A building or group of buildings containing equipment used in making something: *A power* **plant** *produces electricity. Noun.*

○ **1.** To set or place in the ground so that it will take root and grow: *We* **planted** *our tomato seeds in May.* **2.** To place or set firmly in position: *The donkey* **planted** *its feet on the ground and refused to move. Verb.*

plant (plant) *noun, plural* **plants**; *verb,* **planted, planting.**

plantain A kind of banana. Plantains contain a lot of starch. They are cooked before being eaten. **plan·tain** (plan′tən) *noun, plural* **plantains.**

plantation A large estate or farm worked by laborers who live there: *Before the American Civil War, cotton, tobacco, and rice were grown on* **plantations** *in the South.* **plan·ta·tion** (plan tā′shən) *noun, plural* **plantations.**

plaque **1.** A flat, decorated piece of wood or metal hung on a wall. **2.** A sticky film of bacteria, food, and saliva that forms on the teeth. **plaque** (plak) *noun, plural* **plaques.**

plasma The clear, yellow liquid that forms the watery part of blood. Blood cells, salts, antibodies, and other things carried by the blood are suspended in the plasma. **plas·ma** (plaz′mə) *noun, plural* **plasmas.**

plaster A mixture of lime, sand, and water that becomes hard when dry. Plaster is used for covering walls and ceilings. Artists sometimes use plaster to make statues and molds. *Noun.*

○ **1.** To cover with plaster: *We* **plastered** *the ceiling to repair the damage done by the leak.* **2.** To cover thoroughly: *They* **plastered** *the wall with posters. Verb.*

plas·ter (plas′tər) *noun; verb,* **plastered, plastering.**

plastic Any of a number of artificially made substances that can be molded and shaped into materials or objects. Dishes, furniture, food wrappers, raincoats, film, false teeth, and eyeglasses can all be made of plastic. *Noun.*

○ **1.** Capable of being molded and shaped: *Wax is a* **plastic** *material when it is heated.* **2.** Made of plastic: *The radio has a* **plastic** *case. The* **plastic** *seats in this car are made to look like leather. Adjective.*

plas·tic (plas′tik) *noun, plural* **plastics**; *adjective.*

plate **1.** A flat or shallow dish: *Food is served or eaten from* **plates.** **2.** A flat, thin piece of metal: *Modern warships are covered with* **plates** *of steel. A knight's armor was made of metal* **plates.** **3.** A piece of metal on which something is or can be engraved. In printing, the words or pictures to be printed are copied onto metal plates that fit into a printing press. **4.** Home plate in a baseball game. **5.** One of the huge parts of the earth's crust on which the continents and oceans rest. These plates move very slowly over millions of years and sometimes cause earthquakes. *Noun.*

○ To cover with a coat of silver, gold, or other metal: *The jeweler* **plated** *the steel box with gold. Verb.*

plate (plāt) *noun, plural* **plates**; *verb,* **plated, plating.**

plateau An area of flat land higher than the surrounding country. **pla·teau** (pla tō′) *noun, plural* **plateaus.**

plate tectonics A branch of geology that studies the drift of continents that float on giant plates on the mantle of the earth. There are a lot of volcanoes and earthquakes where the edges of these plates meet. The noun phrase "plate tectonics" is used with a singular verb. **plate tec·ton·ics** (tek ton′iks).

platform **1.** A raised, flat surface: *The speaker stood on a* **platform.** *We waited on the* **platform** *for the train. The huge* **platform** *at sea contained a rig for drilling oil.* **2.** A statement of the principles or beliefs of a group: *The political party adopted a* **platform** *that called for lowering the voting age.* **plat·form** (plat′fôrm′) *noun, plural* **platforms.**

This oil rig stands on a strong platform.

platinum A soft, heavy metal that looks like silver. Platinum does not tarnish and is used in

PRONUNCIATION KEY:
at   āpe   fär   câre   end   mē   it   ice   pierce   hot   ōld   sông   fôrk
oil   out   up   ūse   rüle   pull   tûrn   chin   sing   shop   thin   this
hw in white; zh in treasure. The symbol ə stands for the unstressed vowel sound in about, taken, pencil, lemon, and circus.

569

jewelry and alloys. Platinum is a chemical element. **plat·i·num** (plat′ə nəm) *noun*.

platoon A military unit that includes two or more squads: *A platoon is usually commanded by a lieutenant.* **pla·toon** (plə tün′) *noun, plural* **platoons**.

platter A large shallow dish used for serving food. **plat·ter** (plat′ər) *noun, plural* **platters**.

platypus An animal that has a wide flat bill, webbed feet, and soft brown fur. The platypus is one of the only mammals that lay eggs. It lives near streams in Australia. **plat·y·pus** (plat′ə pəs) *noun, plural* **platypuses**.

play 1. Activity that is done for fun or pleasure; sport: *Children were at play in the playground.* 2. A move or turn in a game: *The quarterback made a great play.* 3. A story written to be acted out on stage: *We saw a play about the American Revolution.* 4. Action or operation: *The engine was in full play.* 5. A quick flickering movement: *The painter tried to capture the play of light on the water. Noun.*

○ 1. To do something for fun or pleasure: *The children played all morning.* 2. To be in or have a game: *Let's play tag. Some members of the basketball team never got a chance to play.* 3. To compete against in a game: *We played them last year.* 4. To act carelessly with something: *Don't play with matches.* 5. To act the part of: *The star of the movie played an old sailor.* 6. To make or cause to make music or other sounds: *I'm learning how to play the piano.* 7. To act or behave: *An honest person plays fair with everyone. Verb.* **play** (plā) *noun, plural* **plays**; *verb,* **played, playing**. **—player** *noun*.

playful 1. Wanting or liking to play; lively: *a playful kitten.* 2. Meant to amuse or tease; humorous: *The speaker made some playful remarks before discussing serious matters.* **play·ful** (plā′fəl) *adjective*. **—playfully** *adverb* **—playfulness** *noun*.

playground An outdoor area for children to play in. Playgrounds often have slides, swings, and sandboxes. **play·ground** (plā′ground′) *noun, plural* **playgrounds**.

playing card A card used in a card game. The most common group of playing cards has fifty-two cards and is divided into four suits called clubs, diamonds, hearts, and spades.

playmate A child who plays with another child. **play·mate** (plā′māt′) *noun, plural* **playmates**.

playpen A small pen that folds up easily. It is used for a baby or small child to play in. **play·pen** (plā′pen′) *noun, plural* **playpens**.

plaything A thing to play with; toy. **play·thing** (plā′thing′) *noun, plural* **playthings**.

playwright A person who writes plays: *William Shakespeare was a very famous English playwright.* **play·wright** (plā′rīt′) *noun, plural* **playwrights**.

plaza A public square or open space in a city or town: *There is a plaza with benches and a large fountain at the center of town.* **pla·za** (plä′zə or plaz′ə) *noun, plural* **plazas**.

Plazas are often popular gathering places.

plea 1. A sincere request: *a plea for money to aid flood victims.* 2. An answer given to a charge in a court of law: *a plea of not guilty.* **plea** (plē) *noun, plural* **pleas**.

plead 1. To make a sincere request; beg: *I pleaded with my friend not to swim near the rocks.* 2. To give as an excuse: *I pleaded illness when they asked me why I was not coming to the party.* 3. To speak in defense of someone in a court of law: *The lawyer agreed to plead the accused person's case.* 4. To give as an answer to a charge in a court of law: *The prisoner will plead guilty.* **plead** (plēd) *verb,* **pleaded** *or* **pled, pleading**.

pleasant 1. Giving pleasure: *a pleasant summer day.* 2. Behaving in a pleasing way; friendly: *The bus driver was pleasant to all the passengers.* **pleas·ant** (plez′ənt) *adjective,* **pleasanter, pleasantest**. **—pleasantly** *adverb* **—pleasantness** *noun*.

please 1. To give pleasure to: *My shiny new bicycle pleases me.* 2. To want or prefer: *The children may buy whatever they please. Verb.*

○ To be so kind as to: *Please give me some more beans. Close the door, please. Adverb.* **please** (plēz) *verb,* **pleased, pleasing**; *adverb*.

pleasure **1.** A feeling of enjoyment or happiness: *The clowns gave* **pleasure** *to the children. A good nurse takes* **pleasure** *in helping others.* **2.** Something that gives a feeling of enjoyment or happiness: *It was a* **pleasure** *to see you again.* **pleas·ure** (plezh′ər) *noun, plural* **pleasures**.

pleat A flat fold made by doubling cloth upon itself and fastening or pressing it into place. Skirts often have pleats. *Noun.*
　○ To make pleats in: *I decided to* **pleat** *the skirt I was making. Verb.*
　pleat (plēt) *noun, plural* **pleats**; *verb*, **pleated**, **pleating**.

pled A past tense and a past participle of **plead**: *The prisoner* **pled** *not guilty.* **pled** (pled) *verb.*

pledge **1.** A serious promise: *The children made a* **pledge** *to keep the secret. My parents made a* **pledge** *to give money to the hospital.* **2.** Something given to another person for a time, as part of an agreement: *I gave the storekeeper my watch as a* **pledge** *that I would come back and pay what I owed. Noun.*
　○ **1.** To promise: *The children* **pledge** *allegiance to the flag each morning.* **2.** To give something as a pledge: *I* **pledged** *my violin for the loan. Verb.*
　pledge (plej) *noun, plural* **pledges**; *verb*, **pledged**, **pledging**.

plentiful More than enough; abundant: *a* **plentiful** *supply of firewood.* **plen·ti·ful** (plen′ti fəl) *adjective.*

plenty A large amount; more than enough of something: *There is* **plenty** *of milk left.* **plen·ty** (plen′tē) *noun.*

plesiosaur A huge dinosaur with a long neck and legs shaped like paddles. It lived in the sea millions of years ago. This dinosaur is also called plesiosaurus. **ple·si·o·saur** (plē′sē ə sôr′) *noun, plural* **plesiosaurs**.

pliers A tool that has a pair of jaws for gripping or bending things. Some pliers can also cut wire. **pli·ers** (plī′ərz) *plural noun.*

plod **1.** To move in a slow, heavy way: *plodding through deep snow.* **2.** To work in a slow, steady way: *I* **plodded** *through all my homework.* **plod** (plod) *verb,* **plodded**, **plodding**.

plot **1.** A secret plan: *a* **plot** *to rob a bank.* **2.** The main story in a novel, play, or movie. **3.** A small piece of ground: *We had our picnic on a grassy* **plot** *in the shade. The gardener prepared the* **plot** *for vegetables. Noun.*
　○ **1.** To make a secret plan: *They* **plotted** *to take over the government.* **2.** To make a chart or map of: *plotting a ship's course. Verb.*
　plot (plot) *noun, plural* **plots**; *verb*, **plotted**, **plotting**.

plover A bird with a short bill and long, pointed wings. Plovers run along shores and beaches in search of food. **plo·ver** (pluv′ər *or* plō′vər) *noun, plural* **plovers**.

plow **1.** A heavy farm tool for cutting through and turning over soil. A farmer uses a plow to prepare soil for planting seeds. A plow can be drawn by a tractor or by animals. **2.** A device for clearing away or pushing aside matter in its path. A snowplow is a plow for removing snow from roads and sidewalks. *Noun.*
　○ **1.** To cut through and turn over with a plow: *The farmer* **plowed** *the field for planting corn.* **2.** To move ahead in a steady, strong way, as a plow does: *The ship* **plowed** *through the waves. Verb.*
　plow (plou) *noun, plural* **plows**; *verb*, **plowed**, **plowing**.

Modern plows can turn over a large area of soil at one time.

pluck **1.** To pull off; pick: *The butcher* **plucked** *the feathers from the chicken. I* **plucked** *a rose from the rose bush.* **2.** To pull off hair or feathers from: *We* **plucked** *the chicken.* **3.** To pull at and quickly let go: *The player* **plucked** *the banjo strings.* **4.** To give a quick, short pull; tug: *The child* **plucked** *at the grown-up's coat to get her attention. Verb.*

PRONUNCIATION KEY:
| at | āpe | fär | câre | end | mē | it | īce | pîerce | hot | ōld | sông | fôrk |
| oil | out | up | ūse | rüle | pull | tûrn | chin | sing | shop | thin | this | |

hw in white; zh in treasure. The symbol ə stands for the unstressed vowel sound in about, taken, pencil, lemon, and circus.

571

○ **1.** A quick, short pull; tug: *The musician gave a **pluck** to the strings of the guitar.* **2.** Courage: *It takes **pluck** to stand up to a bully.* *Noun.*
pluck (pluk) *verb*, **plucked, plucking**; *noun, plural* **plucks.**

plug **1.** A piece of rubber, wood, or some other thing used to stop up a hole: *Don't forget to pull out the **plug** to let the water out of the bathtub.* **2.** A device with prongs, placed on the end of a cord or wire. It is put into an electrical outlet to make a connection with a source of electricity. *Noun.*
○ **1.** To stop up: *I **plugged** the big bottle of cider with a stopper. Grease **plugged** the kitchen drain.* **2.** To put the electrical plug of a machine, appliance, or cord into an outlet: ***Plug** in the radio.* **3.** To work in a slow, steady way: *We **plugged** away at the jigsaw puzzle.* *Verb.*
plug (plug) *noun, plural* **plugs**; *verb,* **plugged, plugging.**

plum A soft, juicy fruit with smooth red or purple skin and a pit. It grows on a tree that has oval leaves and small white or pink flowers. Dried plums are called prunes.
Another word that sounds like this is **plumb**.
plum (plum) *noun, plural* **plums.**

plumage The feathers of a bird: *The male cardinal has bright red **plumage**.* **plum·age** (plü′mij) *noun.*

plumb A weight at the end of a line marked with units of length. It is used to test whether something is straight up and down, or to measure how deep something is. *Noun.*
○ To measure with a plumb: ***Plumb** the well to see how deep the water is.* *Verb.*
Another word that sounds like this is **plum**.
plumb (plum) *noun, plural* **plumbs**; *verb,* **plumbed, plumbing.**

plumber A person who puts in and repairs water and sewage pipes in buildings. **plumb·er** (plum′ər) *noun, plural* **plumbers.**

plumbing The pipes for bringing water in and taking water and sewage out of a building. **plumb·ing** (plum′ing) *noun.*

plume A big fluffy feather: *Ostriches have long **plumes** on their tails and wings.* **plume** (plüm) *noun, plural* **plumes.**

plump Full and round; nicely fat: *a baby with **plump**, rosy cheeks.* **plump** (plump) *adjective,* **plumper, plumpest.** —**plumpness** *noun.*

Ostrich **plumes** were once used on clothing.

plunder To steal from; rob: *Soldiers **plundered** the town.* *Verb.*
○ Something stolen: *The outlaws hid their **plunder** in an old shed.* *Noun.*
plun·der (plun′dər) *verb,* **plundered, plundering**; *noun.*

plunge **1.** To put in suddenly: *I **plunged** my hand into the water to catch the fish.* **2.** To dive or fall suddenly: *The swimmer **plunged** into the pool. The kite **plunged** to the ground.* *Verb.*
○ The act of plunging: *an early morning **plunge** in the lake.* *Noun.*
plunge (plunj) *verb,* **plunged, plunging**; *noun, plural* **plunges.**

plural Of or having to do with a form of a word that names or refers to more than one person or more than one thing. "Chairs" and "oxen" are plural nouns. "Chair" and "ox" are singular nouns. *Adjective.*
○ The form of a word that names or refers to more than one person or more than one thing. The nouns "chickens" and "baskets" are in the plural. The nouns "chicken" and "basket" are in the singular. *Noun.*
plu·ral (plür′əl) *adjective; noun, plural* **plurals.**

plus With the addition of: *Two plus two is four. They each ordered dinner plus dessert.* Preposition.
○ Somewhat higher than: *a grade of B plus.* Adjective.
○ A sign (+) showing that something is to be added. *Noun.*
plus (plus) *preposition; adjective; noun, plural* **pluses.**

Pluto The smallest planet in our solar system. It is the planet farthest from the sun. Pluto can be seen from earth only with the aid of a telescope. **Plu·to** (plü′tō) *noun.*

Pluto
Usually the farthest planet from the Sun, but until 1999, its orbit carries it inside the orbit of Neptune. Pluto is the least-known planet. Its moon, Charon, is more than half Pluto's size, making the pair seem like a double-planet. The view from Charon might look like this illustration.
Average distance from sun: **3,676,200,000 miles**
Diameter: **1,430 miles**
Length of Day: **6 days, 9 hours, 18 minutes**
Length of Year: **248.5 years**
Average Temperature: **-419°F**
Mass compared to Earth: **2**
Weight of 100 pounds: **5**
Atmosphere: **Nitrogen, Methane**
Number of rings: **0**
Number of satellites: **1**

plutonium A silver-colored radioactive metal. Plutonium is a rare chemical element. It is not found in nature but is made in nuclear reactors. **plu·to·ni·um** (plü tō′nē əm) *noun.*

plywood A strong board made of thin layers of wood glued together. **ply·wood** (plī′wu̇d′) *noun.*

p.m. or **P.M.** An abbreviation meaning the time of day between noon and midnight.

pneumonia A disease in which the lungs become inflamed and fill with thick fluid. Pneumonia is caused by a virus. A person who has pneumonia might cough or have a hard time breathing. **pneu·mo·nia** (nü mōn′yə *or* nū mōn′yə) *noun.*

P.O. An abbreviation for **post office.**

pocket 1. A small bag or pouch that is sewn on or into a garment, suitcase, or purse. Pockets are for holding coins, papers, keys, and other small things. 2. A place in the earth that contains ore: *The miners found a pocket of iron ore. Noun.*
○ Small enough to be carried in the pocket: *a pocket watch. Adjective.*
○ To put in a pocket: *The customer pocketed the coins. Verb.*
pock·et (pok′it) *noun, plural* **pockets;** *adjective;* *verb,* **pocketed, pocketing.**

pocketbook A bag for carrying money, keys, and other small things; handbag; purse. **pock·et·book** (pok′it bu̇k′) *noun, plural* **pocketbooks.**

pocketknife A small knife with one or more blades that fold into the handle. **pock·et·knife** (pok′it nīf′) *noun, plural* **pocketknives.** (pok′it nīvz′).

pod A part of a plant that holds a number of seeds as they grow. A pod splits open along the side when it is ripe. Beans and peas grow in pods. **pod** (pod) *noun, plural* **pods.**

poem A form of writing that expresses imaginative thought or strong feeling. A poem is usually written with a rhythmic arrangement of words and often with rhyme. **po·em** (pō′əm) *noun, plural* **poems.**

poet A person who composes poetry. **po·et** (pō′it) *noun, plural* **poets.**

poetic Of or like poetry: *Poetic language is chosen for its sound as well as its meaning.* **po·et·ic** (pō et′ik) *adjective.* **—poetically** *adverb.*

poetry 1. Poems: *I like to read poetry.* 2. The art of creating poems: *Some writers are skilled in both poetry and prose.* **po·et·ry** (pō′i trē) *noun.*

PRONUNCIATION KEY:
at   āpe   fär   câre   end   mē   it   īce   pierce hot   ōld   sông   fôrk
oil   out   up   ūse   rüle   pu̇ll   tûrn   chin   sing   shop   thin   this
hw in white; zh in treasure. The symbol ə stands for the unstressed vowel sound in about, taken, pencil, lemon, and circus.

573

poinsettia A plant with small flowers and big, bright red, pink, or white leaves that look like flower petals. Poinsettias are used for decoration during the Christmas season. **poin·set·ti·a** (poin set′ē ə *or* poin set′ə) *noun, plural* **poinsettias.**

Poinsettias are commonly displayed at Christmas.

point 1. A fine, sharp end: *The knife has a point. You write with the point of your pencil.* 2. A piece of land with a sharp end sticking out into the water: *A lighthouse was built on the point.* 3. A dot; mark: *We use a point to separate dollars and cents when we write $3.50.* 4. A place, position, step, or degree: *Tourists visit the points of interest in our town. The chapter ended at an exciting point in the story.* 5. A particular time; moment: *At that point, everyone left the room.* 6. The main part, idea, or purpose: *What is the point of that joke?* 7. A special quality; trait: *Honesty is one of my friend's good points.* 8. A score in a game: *Our football team is ahead by six points.* 9. One of the thirty-two marks that show direction on a compass. *Noun.*
○ 1. To show where something is by aiming a finger or other thing at it: *I pointed at the bicycle I liked best. The road sign points in the direction of town.* 2. To aim; direct: *I pointed the telescope at the moon. Verb.*
　• **beside the point.** Not related to a subject; not changing a fact or judgment: *It is illegal to go through a red light; whether you are driving a car or riding a bicycle is beside the point.*
　• **to point out.** To show; indicate: *The teacher read our tests and pointed out our mistakes to us.*
　• **to the point.** Related to the subject; relevant: *The speech was brief and to the point.*
point (point) *noun, plural* **points;** *verb,* **pointed, pointing.**

pointer 1. A long stick or other object for pointing out things. 2. A hunting dog with a short coat and long ears. A pointer will stand very still and point its body toward any game it senses. 3. A piece of advice; hint: *Can you give me some pointers on fishing?* **point·er** (poin′tər) *noun, plural* **pointers.**

point of view A way of looking at or thinking about something: *From my point of view, reading a good book is much more interesting than watching television.*

Pointers are highly trained hunting dogs.

poise 1. Calmness and confidence: *The child spoke in front of the class with poise.* 2. Balance: *The acrobat walked across the tightrope with perfect poise. Noun.*
○ To be or keep in balance: *The dancer poised on one foot. Verb.*
poise (poiz) *noun; verb,* **poised, poising.**

poison A drug or other substance that harms or kills by chemical action. *Noun.*
○ 1. To give poison to: *The farmer poisoned the insect pests.* 2. To put poison in something: *The villain poisoned the victim's food.* 3. To have a bad effect on: *They poisoned the minds of others with lies. Verb.*
poi·son (poi′zən) *noun, plural* **poisons;** *verb,* **poisoned, poisoning.** —**poisonous** *adjective.*

poison ivy A plant that has shiny leaves with three leaflets. It may grow along the ground, as a shrub, or as a vine. It causes a rash that itches if you touch the leaves.

poke 1. To push with something pointed; jab: *I poked the frog gently with a stick to make it jump.* 2. To stick out quickly; thrust: *The woodchuck poked its head out of the burrow.* 3. To move slowly: *The little children poked along behind us. Verb.*
○ A push with something pointed; jab: *A friend gave me a poke to wake me up. Noun.*
poke (pōk) *verb,* **poked, poking;** *noun, plural* **pokes.**

poker[1] A metal rod for stirring a fire. **pok·er** (pō′kər) *noun, plural* **pokers.**

poker[2] A card game in which the players bet on cards that they hold. **pok·er** (pō′kər) *noun.*

Poland A country in east-central Europe. **Po·land** (pō′lənd) *noun.*

polar Of or having to do with the North Pole or the South Pole: *That explorer has led many polar expeditions.* **po·lar** (pō′lər) *adjective.*

polar bear A big bear that lives in the Arctic. Polar bears have thick, white fur.

Polar bears **have thick white fur and are strong animals**.

pole¹ A long, thin piece of wood, metal, or other hard material.
Other words that sound like this are **Pole** and **poll**.
pole (pōl) *noun, plural* **poles.**

pole² **1.** Either end of the earth's axis. The North Pole is opposite the South Pole. **2.** Either end of a magnet or battery where the force is strongest.
Other words that sound like this are **Pole** and **poll**.
pole (pōl) *noun, plural* **poles.**

Pole A person who was born in or is a citizen of Poland.
Other words that sound like this are **pole** and **poll**.
Pole (pōl) *noun, plural* **Poles.**

polecat **1.** A European animal that belongs to the weasel family. The polecat gives off a strong-smelling spray similar to that of a skunk. **2.** The skunk of North America. **pole·cat** (pōl′kat′) *noun, plural* **polecats.**

pole vault A contest in which a person uses a long pole to leap over a very high bar.

police A group of persons given power by a government to keep order and to enforce the law.

The word "police" may be used with a singular or plural verb: *The state police patrols the highways. Noun.*
○ To keep order in: *Guards policed the city streets. Verb.*
po·lice (pə lēs′) *noun; verb,* **policed, policing.**

policeman A man who is a member of the police. **po·lice·man** (pə lēs′mən) *noun, plural* **policemen** (pə lēs′mən).

police officer A member of the police; policeman or policewoman.

policewoman A woman who is a member of the police. **po·lice·wom·an** (pə lēs′wum′ən) *noun, plural* **policewomen** (pə lēs′wim′ən).

policy¹ A guiding belief or plan that people use to help them make decisions: *What is the school's policy about pets in class?* **pol·i·cy** (pol′ə sē) *noun, plural* **policies.**

policy² A written contract that is an agreement between an insurance company and the person being insured. **pol·i·cy** (pol′ə sē) *noun, plural* **policies.**

polio A short form of the word **poliomyelitis**. **po·li·o** (pō′lē ō) *noun.*

poliomyelitis A disease that can cause paralysis by attacking the spinal cord. It is caused by a virus and affects mainly children. There are two vaccines that help to prevent the disease. This disease is also called polio. **po·li·o·my·e·li·tis** (pō′lē ō mī′ə lī′tis) *noun.*

polish **1.** The smoothness or shine of a surface: *The waxed floor had a bright polish.* **2.** A substance used to give a shine to something: *shoe polish. Noun.*
○ To shine: *We waxed and polished the wooden table. Verb.*
pol·ish (pol′ish) *noun, plural* **polishes;** *verb,* **polished, polishing.**

Polish The language of Poland. *Noun.*
○ Of or having to do with Poland, the Poles, or their language. *Adjective.*
Po·lish (pō′lish) *noun; adjective.*

polite Having good manners; showing consideration for others; courteous: *It is polite to say "thank you" and "please."* **po·lite** (pə līt′) *adjective,* **politer, politest.** —**politely** *adverb* —**politeness** *noun.*

PRONUNCIATION KEY:
at āpe fär câre end mē it īce pierce hot ōld sông fôrk
oil out up ūse rüle pull tûrn chin sing shop thin this
hw in white; zh in treasure. The symbol ə stands for the unstressed vowel sound in about, taken, pencil, lemon, and circus.

575

political Of or having to do with politics, politicians, or government: *Democracy is one kind of political system. A political party helps people to get elected or appointed to government offices.* **po·lit·i·cal** (pə lit′i kəl) *adjective*.

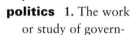
Political posters have long been used by candidates for office.

politician A person who holds or seeks a government office. **pol·i·ti·cian** (pol′i tish′ən) *noun*, *plural* **politicians**.

politics 1. The work or study of government; the management of public affairs: *The young person went into politics and ran for Congress.* 2. The activities of political leaders, candidates, and parties: *Around election time, politics is always in the news.* 3. Opinions or beliefs about government: *My parents' politics are conservative.* The word "politics" is used with a singular verb in definitions 1 and 2, and with a plural verb in definition 3. **pol·i·tics** (pol′i tiks) *noun*.

polka A lively dance that originated in central Europe. **pol·ka** (pōl′kə *or* pō′kə) *noun*, *plural* **polkas**.

polka dot One of many round dots spaced evenly to form a pattern on cloth or other material. This pattern is used on scarves, ties, blouses, and other clothing.

poll 1. A collecting of votes or opinions. A public opinion poll is the collecting of answers to questions about important issues or happenings. 2. **polls**. A place where votes are cast and recorded. *Noun.*
○ 1. To receive votes: *The winner of the election polled twice as many votes as the loser.* 2. To question a group of people to get their opinions: *The newspaper polled the town to find out what people thought about the president's decision.* *Verb.*
Other words that sound like this are **pole** and **Pole**.
poll (pōl) *noun*, *plural* **polls**; *verb*, **polled**, **polling**.

WORD HISTORY

The word **poll** comes from a Middle English word meaning "head" or "top of the head." In a crowd of people, someone could determine the number of people present by counting heads or "taking a poll." Since this count could also indicate the number of people in favor of something or against it, the word later came to mean "counting votes."

pollen A yellowish powder made in the anthers of flowers. Pollen is made up of the male cells of flowering plants. **pol·len** (pol′ən) *noun*.

pollination The transfer of pollen from the stamen to the pistil of the same flower or another flower. After pollen reaches the pistil, the plant can form seeds. The wind and some insects, birds, and animals help with pollination. **pol·li·na·tion** (pol′ə nā′shən) *noun*.

Pollen fertilizes a flower's female cells so they form seeds.

pollute To make dirty or impure: *Automobile exhaust pollutes the air.* **pol·lute** (pə lüt′) *verb*, **polluted, polluting**.

pollution 1. Harmful materials such as certain gases, chemicals, and wastes that pollute the air, water, or soil: *Pollution in the pond killed the reeds that once grew there.* 2. The act or process of polluting. **pol·lu·tion** (pə lü′shən) *noun*.

polo A game played on horseback with mallets that have long handles. **po·lo** (pō′lō) *noun*.

The object of polo is to hit a wooden ball through the other team's goal posts.

polygon A figure that has three or more straight sides. A square is a polygon. **pol·y·gon** (pol′ē gon′) *noun, plural* **polygons**.

polyp A small sea animal that has a tube-shaped body. The polyp's mouth has tentacles around it that catch food. Corals are polyps that live close together in big colonies. **pol·yp** (pol′ip) *noun, plural* **polyps**.

pomegranate A round reddish yellow fruit that has a tough skin, a juicy red pulp, and a lot of seeds. The pomegranate grows on a tree in warm areas. **pome·gran·ate** (pom′gran′it) *noun, plural* **pomegranates**.

pomp Stately and splendid display; magnificence; splendor: *The foreign rulers were greeted with great pomp.* **pomp** (pomp) *noun.*

poncho A cloak made of one piece of cloth or other material. It has a hole in the middle for the head. **pon·cho** (ponch′ō) *noun, plural* **ponchos**.

pond A body of water surrounded by land. **pond** (pond) *noun, plural* **ponds**.

ponder To think about something carefully: *They pondered what to do next.* **pon·der** (pon′dər) *verb,* **pondered, pondering**.

pony A small kind of horse. **po·ny** (pō′nē) *noun, plural* **ponies**.

A pond is smaller than a lake.

pony express A postal service in which relays of riders on horseback carried mail across the western United States. The pony express ran from 1860 to 1861.

ponytail A way of wearing one's hair. The hair is pulled back and fastened behind the head, where it hangs down like a pony's tail. **po·ny·tail** (pō′nē tāl′) *noun, plural* **ponytails**.

poodle A dog with thick curly hair. Poodles vary in size from large to very small. A poodle's hair is sometimes cut in a fancy way. **poo·dle** (pü′dəl) *noun, plural* **poodles**.

pool¹ 1. A tank of water to swim in, either indoors or outdoors. 2. A small body of still water. 3. A small amount of any liquid: *A pool of spilled gravy was on the table.* **pool** (pül) *noun, plural* **pools**.

pool² 1. A game played with hard balls and a long stick called a cue. Pool is played on a large table that has six pockets. The object of the game is to hit the balls into the pockets by striking one ball against another with the cue. 2. An arrangement in which a number of people share something: *There is a typing pool at that office.* Noun.
○ To put into a common fund or group effort: *The children pooled their money to buy a present for their teacher.* Verb.
pool (pül) *noun, plural* **pools**; *verb,* **pooled, pooling**.

poor 1. Having little money: *a poor neighborhood that can't afford new streetlights.* 2. Below standard; bad: *The farmer had a poor wheat crop.* 3. Unfortunate: *The poor child was crying over the lost dog.* **poor** (pùr) *adjective,* **poorer, poorest**.

pop 1. To make or cause to make a short, sharp sound: *The cork popped as it came out of the bottle.* 2. To move or appear quickly or without being expected: *Our neighbor popped in to see us. The dog popped its head out of the car window.* Verb.
○ 1. A short, sharp sound: *The firecracker exploded with a loud pop.* 2. A soft drink: *a bottle of pop.* Noun.
pop (pop) *verb,* **popped, popping**; *noun, plural* **pops**.

popcorn A kind of corn having kernels that burst open with a pop when heated. The kernels become white and fluffy, and are a popular snack. **pop·corn** (pop′kôrn′) *noun.*

pope The head of the Roman Catholic Church. **pope** (pōp) *noun, plural* **popes**.

poplar A tall tree that grows rapidly and has wide leaves. The wood of the poplar is used to make pulp for paper and cardboard. **pop·lar** (pop′lər) *noun, plural* **poplars**.

poppy A garden plant with round red, yellow, or white flowers. **pop·py** (pop′ē) *noun, plural* **poppies**.

popular 1. Liked or accepted by many people: *The beach is a popular place on summer afternoons. It is a popular belief that a four-leaf clover brings good luck.* 2. Having many friends: *That popular actor is in a lot of movies.* 3. Of or

PRONUNCIATION KEY:

| at | āpe | fär | câre | end | mē | it | īce | pîerce | hot | ōld | sông | fôrk |
| oil | out | up | ūse | rüle | püll | tûrn | chin | sing | shop | thin | this | |

hw in white; zh in treasure. The symbol ə stands for the unstressed vowel sound in about, taken, pencil, lemon, and circus.

577

for the people: *Since 1913, United States senators have been elected by popular vote.* **pop·u·lar** (pop'yə lər) *adjective.* —**popularly** *adverb.*

popularity The condition of being popular: *You could tell the popularity of the library book by how worn its cover was.* **pop·u·lar·i·ty** (pop'yə lar'i tē) *noun.*

population 1. The number of people who live in a place: *What is the population of your city?* 2. The people or animals living in a place; inhabitants: *The entire population was forced to leave the town because of the flood.* **pop·u·la·tion** (pop'yə lā'shən) *noun, plural* **populations.**

populous Having a lot of people: *New York is a populous city. China and India are populous countries.* **pop·u·lous** (pop'yə ləs) *adjective.*

porcelain A kind of hard, fine pottery. It is thin enough to see through when held to the light. Cups, plates, and other dishes are sometimes made of porcelain. **por·ce·lain** (pôr'sə lin) *noun.*

Fine decorative pieces are often made of porcelain.

porch An area with a roof that is built onto the outside of a house by a door: *We play on our front porch in the summer. I left my galoshes on the porch before going in.* **porch** (pôrch) *noun, plural* **porches.**

A porch is a good place to relax.

porcupine A forest animal whose body is covered with sharp quills. **por·cu·pine** (pôr'kyə pīn') *noun, plural* **porcupines.**

pore¹ A very small opening in the skin or other surface: *Perspiration passes through the pores in our skin.*
Another word that sounds like this is **pour.**
pore (pôr) *noun, plural* **pores.**

pore² To read or study carefully: *I pored over my notes the night before the test.*
Another word that sounds like this is **pour.**
pore (pôr) *verb,* **pored, poring.**

pork The meat of a pig used as food. **pork** (pôrk) *noun.*

porous Having or full of pores: *Water seeped through the porous rock.* **po·rous** (pôr'əs) *adjective.*

porpoise A mammal that lives in the sea. It is related to the dolphin and whale. It looks like a dolphin but has a rounded head and a short snout. **por·poise** (pôr'pəs) *noun, plural* **porpoises** *or* **porpoise.**

porridge A soft food made by boiling ground grains in water or milk. **por·ridge** (pôr'ij) *noun, plural* **porridges.**

port 1. A place where boats and ships can dock or anchor safely; harbor. 2. A city with a harbor. **port** (pôrt) *noun, plural* **ports.**

portable Easy to carry from place to place: *a portable computer.* **port·a·ble** (pôr'tə bəl) *adjective.*

porter 1. A person who carries baggage: *The porter at the hotel carried our suitcases to our room.* 2. A person who waits on the passengers on a train. **por·ter** (pôr'tər) *noun, plural* **porters.**

porthole A small round window in the side of a boat or ship. It lets in both air and light. **port·hole** (pôrt'hōl') *noun, plural* **portholes.**

portico A porch or covered walk. A portico usually has columns supporting its roof. Some churches, courthouses, and large homes have porticoes at the entrance. **por·ti·co** (pôr'ti kō') *noun, plural* **porticoes** *or* **porticos.**

portion 1. A part or share of something: *I spent a portion of the day running errands.* 2. An amount of food served to one person: *Each of us had a portion of potatoes. Noun.*
○ To divide and give out in parts; distribute: *We portioned out the cheese so that each camper had some. Verb.*
por·tion (pôr'shən) *noun, plural* **portions;** *verb,* **portioned, portioning.**

portrait A picture of someone: *The artist painted a portrait of the famous explorer.* **por·trait** (pôr′trit *or* pôr′trāt) *noun, plural* **portraits.**

portray 1. To make a picture of someone or something: *The artist portrayed the family in a painting.* 2. To picture in words; describe: *The book portrays life in a small town.* 3. To play the part of: *The star portrays a sheriff in the movie.* **por·tray** (pôr trā′) *verb,* **portrayed, portraying.**

Portugal A country in southwestern Europe. **Por·tu·gal** (pôr′chə gəl) *noun.*

Portuguese 1. A person who was born in or is a citizen of Portugal. 2. The language of Portugal and Brazil. *Noun.*
◦ Of or having to do with Portugal, its people, their language, or their culture. *Adjective.*
Por·tu·guese (pôr′chə gēz′ *or* pôr′chə gēs′) *noun, plural* **Portuguese;** *adjective.*

pose 1. A position of the body: *I took a sitting pose for the photograph.* 2. A way of behaving or looking that hides the truth: *The new student adopted a pose of self-confidence.* *Noun.*
◦ 1. To hold a position, such as for a painting, photograph, or sculpture: *We all posed for the class photograph.* 2. To take on a false manner or appearance: *The thief posed as a plumber to get into the house.* *Verb.*
pose (pōz) *noun, plural* **poses;** *verb,* **posed, posing.**

position 1. The place where a person or thing is: *From my position at the window, I could see the whole parade.* 2. A way of being placed: *The teacher was seated in a comfortable position.* 3. A way of thinking about something; point of view: *What is the senator's position on the proposal to increase taxes?* 4. Rank; standing: *a person of high position.* 5. A job: *My cousin has held the same position with a company for many years.* **po·si·tion** (pə zish′ən) *noun, plural* **positions.**

positive 1. Certain; sure: *I am positive that I locked the door.* 2. Helpful or favorable: *The teacher made positive comments about my work.* 3. Saying or meaning yes; consenting: *Their answer to our invitation was positive.* 4. More than zero: *Five is a positive number.* 5. Having one of two opposite kinds of electric charge: *Magnets have a positive pole at one end and a negative pole at the other.* **pos·i·tive** (poz′i tiv) *adjective.* —**positively** *adverb.*

posse A group of people gathered by a sheriff to help capture a criminal. **pos·se** (pos′ē) *noun, plural* **posses.**

possess 1. To have or own: *That singer possesses a fine voice. The family possesses great wealth.* 2. To have an influence over: *A desire for ice cream possessed me, and I ordered a sundae.* **pos·sess** (pə zes′) *verb,* **possessed, possessing.**

possession 1. The act or condition of possessing something: *The two prospectors fought for possession of the gold.* 2. Something owned: *The family lost all their possessions in the fire.* 3. A place under the control of a foreign country: *The Philippine Islands were once a possession of the United States.* **pos·ses·sion** (pə zesh′ən) *noun, plural* **possessions.**

possessive 1. The form of a word that shows possession. In the sentence "The child's hat blew off," the noun "child's" is in the possessive. 2. A word in the form that shows possession. In the sentence "The books are theirs," the pronoun "theirs" is a possessive. *Noun.*
◦ Having to do with or showing possession. *My* is the possessive form of the pronoun *I. Cousin's* is the possessive form of the noun *cousin. Adjective.*
pos·ses·sive (pə zes′iv) *noun, plural* **possessives;** *adjective.*

possibility 1. The fact of being possible: *The possibility that you might come to visit made me clean up my room.* 2. Something that may happen: *The weather report says that snow is a possibility on Monday.* **pos·si·bil·i·ty** (pos′ə bil′i tē) *noun, plural* **possibilities.**

possible 1. Capable of being, being done, or happening: *It is not possible to be in two places at the same time.* 2. Capable of being used or con-

PRONUNCIATION KEY:

at	āpe	fär	câre	end	mē	it	īce	pierce	hot	ōld	sông	fôrk
oil	out	up	ūse	rüle	pull	tûrn	chin	sing	shop	thin	this	

hw in white; zh in treasure. The symbol ə stands for the unstressed vowel sound in about, taken, pencil, lemon, and circus.

579

sidered: *The park is a **possible** place for our picnic.* **pos·si·ble** (pos′ə bəl) *adjective.*

possibly **1.** In any way possible: *I can't **possibly** get to your house before noon.* **2.** Perhaps; maybe: *I'll see you tonight, or **possibly** tomorrow.* **pos·si·bly** (pos′ə blē) *adverb.*

possum A small, furry animal; opossum. Look up opossum for more information. **pos·sum** (pos′əm) *noun, plural* **possums.**

post- A prefix that means "after": *Postwar means after a war.*

post¹ A piece of wood or other hard material set firmly upright to support or mark something: *We started building the fence by digging holes for the posts. Posts supported the roof of the cabin. Noun.* ○ To put up a notice of something: *The teacher posted the names of the winners. Verb.* **post** (pōst) *noun, plural* **posts;** *verb,* **posted, posting.**

post² **1.** A place where a soldier, police officer, or guard must be to do his or her duty: *A guard was assigned to the **post** in front of police headquarters.* **2.** A place where soldiers work or are trained: *There is an army **post** near our town.* **3.** A job; position: *The diplomat was named to the **post** of ambassador. Noun.* ○ To assign to a post: *The police **posted** a guard near the valuable painting. Verb.* **post** (pōst) *noun, plural* **posts;** *verb,* **posted, posting.**

post³ **1.** A system for picking up and delivering mail: *I will send the letter by **post**.* **2.** A delivery of mail: *The package came in today's **post**. Noun.* ○ **1.** To put in a mailbox: *I will **post** the package right away.* **2.** To let know; inform of news: *Please keep me **posted**. Verb.* **post** (pōst) *noun, plural* **posts;** *verb,* **posted, posting.**

postage The amount of money charged for sending something by mail. **post·age** (pōs′tij) *noun.*

postage stamp A small printed piece of paper issued by a government. It is placed on mail to show that postage has been paid.

postal Of or having to do with mail: *A letter carrier is a **postal** worker.* **post·al** (pōs′təl) *adjective.*

postcard A card that can be sent through the mail without an envelope. **post·card** (pōst′kärd′) *noun, plural* **postcards.**

poster A big printed sign that often has a picture. A poster usually has a notice or advertisement for the public to see. **post·er** (pōs′tər) *noun, plural* **posters.**

postman A person who delivers mail; letter carrier. **post·man** (pōst′mən) *noun, plural* **postmen** (pōst′mən).

postmark An official mark stamped on mail. A postmark cancels the postage stamp and shows the place and date of mailing. **post·mark** (pōst′märk′) *noun, plural* **postmarks.**

postmaster The person in charge of a post office. **post·mas·ter** (pōst′mas′tər) *noun, plural* **postmasters.**

postmistress The woman in charge of a post office. **post·mis·tress** (pōst′mis′tris) *noun, plural* **postmistresses.**

post office **1.** A department of a government in charge of handling mail. **2.** A place where mail is brought and made ready for delivery and stamps are sold.

postpone To put off until later: *We **postponed** the baseball game until next Sunday because of rain.* **post·pone** (pōst pōn′) *verb,* **postponed, postponing.** —**postponement** *noun.*

postscript A message or note added to a letter after the writer's signature: *In a **postscript**, I put the time of my train's arrival.* **post·script** (pōst′skript′) *noun, plural* **postscripts.**

posture The way a person holds the body when sitting, standing, or walking: *Your **posture** is good, because your back is straight and your shoulders are relaxed.* **pos·ture** (pos′chər) *noun, plural* **postures.**

postwar Having to do with the period after a war: *Foods that were scarce during the war were easier to get in the **postwar** period.* **post·war** (pōst′wôr′) *adjective.*

pot A deep, round container for cooking or for holding things. Pots are made of baked clay, metal, glass, or other hard material. **pot** (pot) *noun, plural* **pots.**

potassium A soft, silver-colored metal. Potassium is a chemical element. Compounds that contain potassium are used to make soap, fertilizers, and explosives. **po·tas·si·um** (pə tas′ē əm) *noun.*

potato The thick, rounded underground stem of a leafy plant. Potatoes are eaten as a vegetable. **po·ta·to** (pə tā′tō) *noun, plural* **potatoes.**

potential Capable of becoming something; possible but not yet actual: *A board with rusty nails sticking out is a potential danger.* **po·ten·tial** (pə ten′shəl) *adjective.* —**potentially** *adverb.*

potter A person who makes pottery. **pot·ter** (pot′ər) *noun, plural* **potters.**

This **potter** is using a wheel
to shape a pot.

pottery Pots, bowls, dishes, and other things made from clay. **pot·ter·y** (pot′ə rē) *noun.*

pouch 1. A bag; sack: *The mail carrier took the letters out of a pouch.* 2. A pocket of skin in some animals. Kangaroos and opossums carry their young in pouches. Chipmunks carry nuts in the pouches of their cheeks. **pouch** (pouch) *noun, plural* **pouches.**

poultry Chickens, turkeys, geese, and other birds raised for their eggs or meat. **poul·try** (pōl′trē) *noun.*

pounce To come down suddenly and take hold of; leap or swoop suddenly: *The kitten pounced on the rubber ball. Verb.*
○ The act of pouncing on something. *Noun.*
pounce (pouns) *verb,* **pounced, pouncing;** *noun, plural* **pounces.**

pound¹ 1. A unit of weight equal to 16 ounces. One kilogram is equal to 2.2 pounds. 2. A unit of money in Great Britain and other countries. **pound** (pound) *noun, plural* **pounds** or **pound.**

pound² 1. To hit with heavy blows: *I pounded the nails in with a hammer. The waves pounded against the rocks during the storm.* 2. To beat heavily: *My heart was pounding with fright.* **pound** (pound) *verb,* **pounded, pounding.**

pound³ A place where stray dogs and other animals are kept. **pound** (pound) *noun, plural* **pounds.**

pour 1. To flow or cause to flow: *The cook poured a cup of rice into the boiling water. The crowd poured out of the theater.* 2. To rain hard: *It poured all day.*
Another word that sounds like this is **pore.**
pour (pôr) *verb,* **poured, pouring.**

pout To thrust out the lips to show displeasure: *The children pouted when they were scolded.* **pout** (pout) *verb,* **pouted, pouting.**

poverty 1. A lack of money; the condition of being poor: *That family lives in poverty.* 2. The lack of what is needed: *The poverty of the soil caused the farmer to give up the farm.* **pov·er·ty** (pov′ər tē) *noun.*

powder 1. Fine bits made by grinding, crushing, or crumbling something: *When I rubbed the plaster, a white powder came off on my hand.* 2. Anything in the form of small dry particles: *I put some powder on my hot, tired feet to soothe them: We washed our clothes with soap powder. Noun.*
○ 1. To make or turn into fine bits: *We powdered the dried herbs by grinding them.* 2. To cover with fine bits: *I powdered my face after I finished putting on my makeup for the play. The baker powdered the rolling pin with flour. Verb.*
pow·der (pou′dər) *noun, plural* **powders;** *verb,* **powdered, powdering.**

power 1. The ability to do or bring about something; strength: *I used all my power to lift the heavy box. Human beings have the power of speech.* 2. The right to do something; authority: *Congress has the power to declare war.* 3. A person, thing, or nation that has strength or influence: *The world powers signed a trade agreement.* 4. Energy that can do work: *Toasters, irons, and other household appliances are run by electric power.* 5. The product of a number that is multiplied by itself a given

PRONUNCIATION KEY:

at	āpe	fär	câre	end	mē	it	īce	pierce	hot	ōld	sông	fôrk
oil	out	up	ūse	rüle	pull	tûrn	chin	sing	shop	thin	this	

hw in white; zh in treasure. The symbol ə stands for the unstressed vowel sound in about, taken, pencil, lemon, and circus.

581

number of times: *5 to the second **power** is 25.* *Noun.*

○ To provide with power: *That lawn mower is **powered** by a gasoline motor.* *Verb.*
pow·er (pou′ər) *noun, plural* **powers**; *verb,* **powered, powering.**

powerful Having great power: *The Speaker of the House of Representatives is one of the most **powerful** members of Congress. This big truck has a **powerful** engine.* **pow·er·ful** (pou′ər fəl) *adjective.*

pp. An abbreviation for **pages.**

PQ Postal abbreviation for **Province of Quebec.**

PR Postal abbreviation for **Puerto Rico.**

P.R. An abbreviation for **Puerto Rico.**

practical **1.** Having to do with real life; coming from experience: *I gained much **practical** knowledge of farming by working on a farm last summer.* **2.** Easy to use, do, or put into effect: *Heavy clothes are not **practical** for a hike on a hot day.* **3.** Having or showing good sense; sensible: *A **practical** person sets goals that can be achieved.* **prac·ti·cal** (prak′ti kəl) *adjective.*

practical joke A prank or trick. Putting salt in the sugar bowl is a practical joke.

practically **1.** Nearly; almost: *I'm **practically** finished.* **2.** In a practical way; sensibly: *When you travel, dress **practically**.* **prac·ti·cal·ly** (prak′ti kə lē or prak′ti klē) *adverb.*

practice **1.** The doing of some action over and over again to gain skill: *You need more **practice** before you can be a good tennis player. **Practice** will help you to learn to speak Spanish.* **2.** The usual way of doing something; habit: *Don't make a **practice** of skipping breakfast.* **3.** Actual use or performance: *The idea seemed good, but it did not work in **practice**.* **4.** The business of a doctor or other professional: *a law **practice**.* *Noun.*

○ **1.** To do some action over and over again to gain skill: *I **practice** the violin every day.* **2.** To do as a habit: ***Practice** doing good deeds instead of just talking about it.* **3.** To work at a profession: *I hope to **practice** medicine.* *Verb.*
prac·tice (prak′tis) *noun, plural* **practices**; *verb,* **practiced, practicing.**

prairie Flat or rolling land covered with grass. A prairie has few or no trees. **prai·rie** (prâr′ē) *noun, plural* **prairies.**

prairie dog An animal that is related to the squirrel, living in underground dens in the prairies of the western United States. The prairie dog is a small, plump animal with a short tail and a grayish brown coat.

Prairie dogs can be pests to farmers.

prairie schooner A covered wagon used by American pioneers to cross the prairies.

praise Words that show high regard and approval: *Good work deserves **praise**.* *Noun.*

○ **1.** To express high regard and approval of: *The teacher **praised** the student's fine drawing.* **2.** To worship: *The minister **praised** God in the sermon.* *Verb.*
praise (prāz) *noun, plural* **praises**; *verb,* **praised, praising.**

prance **1.** To move in a proud, happy way: *The children **pranced** around the house in their fancy costumes.* **2.** To spring forward on the hind legs: *The colt **pranced** and leaped about the field.* **prance** (prans) *verb,* **pranced, prancing.**

prank A playful or mischievous act meant to trick or tease someone: *As a **prank**, I hid my friend's notebook.* **prank** (prangk) *noun, plural* **pranks.**

pray **1.** To speak to God to give thanks: *Many people **pray** before dinner.* **2.** To ask earnestly from God: *We **prayed** for the safe return of the lost child.* **3.** To be so kind as to; please. ***Pray** be quiet.*
Another word that sounds like this is **prey.**
pray (prā) *verb,* **prayed, praying.**

prayer **1.** The act of praying to God. **2.** The words said when praying. **3.** Something prayed for: *The*

farmer's **prayer** *was that rain would come soon.*
prayer (prâr) *noun, plural* **prayers.**

The praying mantis **uses its front legs to capture smaller insects.**

praying mantis An insect related to the grasshopper. **praying man·tis** (man′tis) *noun, plural* **mantises** *or* **mantes** (man′tēz).

WORD HISTORY

This insect is called a praying mantis **because it holds its front legs in a way that looks like hands folded in prayer.** *Mantis comes from a Greek word that means "religious teacher" or "prophet."*

pre- A prefix that means "before" or "ahead of time": *Prehistoric means before history was written down. Prepaid means paid for ahead of time.*

preach 1. To give a talk on a religious subject; give a sermon: *The minister* **preaches** *each Sunday.* 2. To give advice; urge: *My parents always* **preach** *about saving money.* **preach** (prēch) *verb,* **preached, preaching.**

preacher A person who preaches, especially a Protestant minister. **preach·er** (prē′chər) *noun, plural* **preachers.**

precaution Something done beforehand to prevent harm or danger: *Looking both ways is a good* **precaution** *to take before crossing the street.* **pre·cau·tion** (pri kô′shən) *noun, plural* **precautions.**

precede To come or go before: *The number 3* **precedes** *the number 7. Lightning* **precedes** *thunder.* **pre·cede** (pri sēd′) *verb,* **preceded, preceding.**

precedent An action or decision that may serve as an example to be followed in the future: *The deci-*

sion of the court set a **precedent** *for how similar cases would be settled.* **prec·e·dent** (pres′i dənt) *noun, plural* **precedents.**

precinct A part of a town or city: *Each* **precinct** *in our city has a police station.* **pre·cinct** (prē′singkt) *noun, plural* **precincts.**

precious 1. Having great value: *Gold is a* **precious** *metal.* 2. Dear; beloved: *The stray dog became a* **precious** *pet in our family.* **pre·cious** (presh′əs) *adjective.*

precipitate 1. To make something happen suddenly; bring on: *The unkind remark* **precipitated** *an argument.* 2. To change from vapor in the air into rain, sleet, hail, or snow. **pre·cip·i·tate** (pri sip′i tāt′) *verb,* **precipitated, precipitating.**

precipitation The falling of water in the form of rain, sleet, hail, or snow: *The weather forecast warned of some* **precipitation** *during the day.* **pre·cip·i·ta·tion** (pri sip′i tā′shən) *noun.*

precise 1. Definite; exact: *"8:03 a.m." is a* **precise** *time; "about eight o'clock" is not.* 2. Strict or careful: *The teacher speaks in a clear and* **precise** *way.* **pre·cise** (pri sīs′) *adjective.* —**precisely** *adverb.*

precision Accuracy; exactness: *This watch keeps time with great* **precision.** **pre·ci·sion** (pri sizh′ən) *noun.*

precocious Having more skill, talent, or knowledge than is usual at an early age: *The* **precocious** *child read books at age three.* **pre·co·cious** (pri kō′shəs) *adjective.* —**precociously** *adverb.*

predator An animal that lives by hunting other animals for food. Lions, wolves, sharks, and owls are predators. **pred·a·tor** (pred′ə tər) *noun, plural* **predators.**

predecessor A person who held an office or position before another person: *President Dwight Eisenhower was President John Kennedy's* **predecessor** *in the White House.* **pred·e·ces·sor** (pred′ə ses′ər) *noun, plural* **predecessors.**

predicament An unpleasant or difficult situation; fix: *Look at the* **predicament** *you're in because you accepted two invitations for the same evening!* **pre·dic·a·ment** (pri dik′ə mənt) *noun, plural* **predicaments.**

predicate A word or group of words in a sentence that tells what the subject does or what is done to the subject. The predicate may also give some

PRONUNCIATION KEY:

at	āpe	fär	câre	end	mē	it	īce	pierce	hot	ōld	sông	fôrk
oil	out	up	ūse	rüle	pull	tûrn	chin	sing	shop	thin	this	

hw in white; zh in treasure. The symbol ə stands for the unstressed vowel sound in about, taken, pencil, lemon, and circus.

583

descriptive information about the subject. In the sentence "Because of the rain our car skidded," the verb "skidded" is the predicate. **pred·i·cate** (pred′i kit) *noun, plural* **predicates.**

predict To tell beforehand: *Tomorrow's weather report predicts rain.* **pre·dict** (pri dikt′) *verb,* **predicted, predicting.**

prediction 1. The act of predicting something: *The weather forecaster's job is the prediction of the weather.* 2. Something predicted: *My prediction that our team would win has come true.* **pre·dic·tion** (pri dik′shən) *noun, plural* **predictions.**

preface An introduction to a book or speech: *Our spelling book has a short preface written by the author.* **pref·ace** (pref′is) *noun, plural* **prefaces.**

prefer To like better: *Which sport do you prefer, tennis or basketball?* **pre·fer** (pri fûr′) *verb,* **preferred, preferring.**

preference Something liked better; first choice: *My preference is to go to the seashore rather than to the mountains this summer.* **pref·er·ence** (pref′ər əns) *noun, plural* **preferences.**

prefix A syllable or group of syllables that is added to the beginning of a word or root to change the meaning and form a new word. The word *dislike* is made up of the prefix *dis-* and the word *like.* **pre·fix** (prē′fiks) *noun, plural* **prefixes.**

LANGUAGE NOTE

Many words that begin with prefixes are not listed in this dictionary. To find out the meaning of most of these words, first look up the meaning of the word or root that the prefix is attached to. Then look up the meaning of the prefix. Put the prefix meaning and the meaning of the word or root together. The word *reestablish* is formed from the prefix *re-* and the word *establish. Establish* means to set something up or prove something true. The prefix *re-* means again. Therefore *reestablish* means to set something up again or prove something true again.

---

pregnant Having one or more unborn young developing within the body. A woman is pregnant for about nine months before she gives birth to a baby. **preg·nant** (preg′nənt) *adjective.* —**pregnancy** *noun.*

prehistoric Belonging to a time before people started writing history: *Mammoths and dinosaurs were prehistoric animals.* **pre·his·tor·ic** (prē′his tôr′ik) *adjective.*

This prehistoric animal was known as a muttaburrasaurus.

prejudice 1. An opinion that has been formed beforehand or before all the facts are known; bias: *A judge must patiently hear a whole case without prejudice.* 2. Hatred or unfair treatment of a particular group, such as members of a race or religion: *Because of prejudice, the owners of the company only hired workers of their own religion. Noun.*
○ To cause to have prejudice: *Being hurt once by a dentist prejudiced me against all dentists. Verb.* **prej·u·dice** (prej′ə dis) *noun, plural* **prejudices;** *verb,* **prejudiced, prejudicing.**

preliminary Coming before the main part: *We bought food and made other preliminary arrangements for the party.* **pre·lim·i·nar·y** (pri lim′ə ner′ē) *adjective.*

premature Arriving, happening, existing, or done before the usual or proper time; too early or too soon: *Don't you think shopping for Christmas presents in July is premature?* **pre·ma·ture** (prē′mə chủr′ *or* prē′mə tủr′) *adjective.* —**prematurely** *adverb.*

premier The chief minister in a government; prime minister. **pre·mier** (pri mîr′) *noun, plural* **premiers.**

premise 1. A statement accepted as true without needing proof. A premise is used as a starting point for a line of reasoning or argument. 2. **premises.** Land and the buildings on it: *The owner of the warehouse hired someone* to guard the *premises*. **prem·ise** (prem′is) *noun*, *plural* **premises**.

preparation 1. The act of preparing something, or the condition of being prepared: *The cook was busy with the preparation of dinner.* 2. An action needed to make something ready: *Putting on costumes and makeup are some of the preparations for going on stage.* 3. Something put together for a purpose: *That medicine is a preparation to help stop coughing.* **prep·a·ra·tion** (prep′ə rā′shən) *noun*, *plural* **preparations**.

prepare To make or get ready: *We prepared for the race by doing some exercises.* **pre·pare** (pri pâr′) *verb*, **prepared**, **preparing**.

preposition A word that shows the relation between another word and a noun or pronoun. In the sentence "The neighbors across the street never argue with us," the words "across" and "with" are prepositions. **pre·po·si·tion** (prep′ə zish′ən) *noun*, *plural* **prepositions**. —**prepositional** *adjective*.

prescribe To order for use as a medical treatment: *The doctor prescribed an ointment for my rash.* **pre·scribe** (pri skrīb′) *verb*, **prescribed**, **prescribing**.

prescription 1. An order written by a doctor to a pharmacist for medicine: *The doctor gave me a prescription for cough medicine.* 2. Medicine ordered by a prescription. **pre·scrip·tion** (pri skrip′shən) *noun*, *plural* **prescriptions**.

presence 1. The fact of being in a place at a certain time: *The presence of the growling dog at the door made me nervous.* 2. The area around or near a person: *The document was signed in the presence of a witness.* **pres·ence** (prez′əns) *noun*.

present¹ 1. In a place at a certain time: *I was present at the graduation ceremony.* 2. Going on at this time; being or happening now: *Do you know the present mayor of your town? Adjective.* ○ 1. The time that is going on now: *At present, there are two supermarkets in town.* 2. The present tense. Look up **present tense** for more information. *Noun.* **pres·ent** (prez′ənt) *adjective*; *noun*.

present² 1. To introduce a person to another person: *I presented my new friend to my parents.*

2. To bring or place before another person or group: *The two candidates for mayor presented themselves at the town meeting.* 3. To give in a formal way: *The principal presented the awards to the students with the highest marks.* 4. To put before an audience; display; show: *The class presented a puppet show. Verb.* ○ Something given; gift: *I made a necklace and gave it to my friend as a present. Noun.* **pre·sent** (pri zent′) *verb*, **presented**, **presenting**; **pres·ent** (prez′ənt) *noun*, *plural* **presents**.

Presents are usually attractively wrapped.

presentation The act of presenting something: *The whole school attended the ceremony for the presentation of scholastic awards.* **pres·en·ta·tion** (prez′ən tā′shən or prē′zən tā′shən) *noun*, *plural* **presentations**.

presently 1. In a little while; soon: *The doctor will see you presently.* 2. At the present time; now: *Our geography class is presently studying Mexico.* **pres·ent·ly** (prez′ənt lē) *adverb*.

present participle A form of a verb ending in -ing and used with the auxiliary verb to show that an action is taking place at the time of speaking or writing, is continuing, or will happen in the future. In the sentences "Your mother's calling you," "She was rapping on the window," and "She's coming out to get you in a minute," "calling," "rapping," and "coming" are present participles.

present tense A form of a verb that shows that an action is happening or that a condition exists at the present time. In the sentence "I like this book," the verb "like" is in the present tense. The present tense is also called the **present**.

preservation Protection from loss, damage, or decay: *Freezing is a method of food preservation.*

PRONUNCIATION KEY:

| at | āpe | fär | câre | end | mē | it | īce | pîerce | hot | ōld | sông | fôrk |
| oil | out | up | ūse | rüle | pull | tûrn | chin | sing | shop | thin | <u>th</u>is | |

hw in white; zh in treasure. The symbol ə stands for the unstressed vowel sound in about, taken, pencil, lemon, and circus.

585

p preservative ▸ pretend

*We encourage the **preservation** of our country's forests.* **pres·er·va·tion** (prez′ər vā′shən) *noun*.

preservative A substance that keeps something from spoiling or being damaged: *Salt is used as a **preservative** for meat.* **pre·serv·a·tive** (pri zûr′və tiv) *noun, plural* **preservatives**.

preserve 1. To keep from being lost, damaged, or decayed; protect: *You can **preserve** the wood of the old table by waxing it. It is important that we **preserve** our freedoms in this country.* 2. To fix food so that it won't spoil. *Verb.*
○ 1. An area set aside for the protection of plants and animals: *Rare birds and mammals breed in that nature **preserve**.* 2. **preserves.** Fruit that has been boiled with sugar and then put in glass jars for later use: *strawberry **preserves**. Noun.* **pre·serve** (pri zûrv′) *verb,* **preserved, preserving;** *noun, plural* **preserves**.

preside 1. To run things, as at a meeting: *The mayor **presides** at town meetings.* 2. To exert authority: *The mayor **presides** over the town's affairs.* **pre·side** (pri zīd′) *verb,* **presided, presiding.**

presidency 1. The office of president: *The young manager hoped someday to gain the **presidency** of the company.* 2. The time during which a president is in office: *The Civil War took place during the **presidency** of Abraham Lincoln.* **pres·i·den·cy** (prez′i dən sē) *noun, plural* **presidencies.**

president 1. A person who is head of the government of a republic, such as the United States. The word "president" is often capitalized when it means the president of the United States: *The **President** answered questions at a news conference yesterday.* 2. The person in charge of a company, a college or university, or other organization. **pres·i·dent** (prez′i dənt) *noun, plural* **presidents.**

WORD HISTORY

The word president comes from an old French word meaning "one appointed to rule." The French word goes back to two Latin words meaning "in front of" and "to sit." The ruler or leader of a group would sit at a place of honor in front of the people.

president-elect A person who has been elected president, but has not yet been inaugurated. **pres·i·dent-e·lect** (prez′i dənt i lekt′) *noun, plural* **presidents-elect.**

Presidents' Day A holiday observed in most of the United States on the third Monday in February to celebrate the birthdays of George Washington and Abraham Lincoln.

press 1. To use force on something; push: *Press this button to start the machine.* 2. To push forward; go on: *We **pressed** through the crowd of people.* 3. To squeeze: *I **pressed** juice from the grapefruit.* 4. To iron: *I **press** my own pants.* 5. To hold close; hug: *I **pressed** the kitten to my chest.* 6. To try to persuade; urge: *We **pressed** our guests to stay. Verb.*
○ 1. A pushing on something: *A **press** of the button started the elevator.* 2. A tool or machine for pressing: *We put the apples into a **press** to squeeze out the juice.* 3. A machine for printing things; printing press. 4. Newspapers and magazines and the people who write them: *The president's speech was described in the **press**. Noun.* **press** (pres) *verb,* **pressed, pressing;** *noun, plural* **presses.**

pressure 1. Force caused by one thing pushing against another thing: *The **pressure** of the driver's foot on the gas pedal made the car go faster.* 2. Strong influence or persuasion: *The parents put **pressure** on their children to do well in school.* 3. A burden; strain: *They went camping to get away from the **pressure** of city life. Noun.*
○ To urge strongly: *The salesperson tried to **pressure** people into buying things they didn't need. Verb.* **pres·sure** (presh′ər) *noun, plural* **pressures;** *verb,* **pressured, pressuring.**

prestige Respect from others; high regard: *The scientists' discovery brought them **prestige** and also brought **prestige** to their laboratory.* **pres·tige** (pre stēzh′ *or* pre stēj′) *noun.*

presume 1. To believe to be true without question; take for granted; assume: *I **presumed** you would want to go to the game, so I bought you a ticket.* 2. To attempt without permission or authority; dare: *Don't **presume** to tell me how to run my own business.* **pre·sume** (pri züm′) *verb,* **presumed, presuming.** —**presumption** *noun.*

pretend 1. To claim: *I like to play chess, but I don't **pretend** to be an expert at it.* 2. To give a false show: *The children **pretended** to be asleep.* 3. To make believe: *We **pretended** we were pirates.* **pre·tend** (pri tend′) *verb,* **pretended, pretending.**

pretty Sweetly pleasing; attractive; charming: *Your cousin is very pretty. They sang a pretty tune. Adjective.*
◦ Fairly; quite: *It is raining pretty hard. Adverb.* **pret·ty** (prit′ē) *adjective*, **prettier, prettiest**; *adverb*.

pretzel A crisp food baked in the shape of a knot or stick and salted on the outside. **pret·zel** (pret′səl) *noun*, *plural* **pretzels**.

prevent 1. To keep something from happening: *Putting out campfires helps prevent forest fires.* 2. To keep someone from doing something; hinder: *The noise outside our window prevented us from sleeping.* **pre·vent** (pri vent′) *verb*, **prevented, preventing. —prevention** *noun*.

preventive Helping to prevent something: *preventive medicine. Adjective.*
◦ Something that prevents, as a drug: *A vaccine is a preventive against a disease. Noun.* **pre·ven·tive** (pri ven′tiv) *adjective*; *noun*.

preview A showing of something ahead of time: *a preview of a movie.* **pre·view** (prē′vū) *noun*, *plural* **previews**.

previous Coming before; earlier: *We were introduced at the previous meeting.* **pre·vi·ous** (prē′vē əs) *adjective*. **—previously** *adverb*.

prey 1. An animal that is hunted by another animal for food: *Rabbits, birds, and snakes are the prey of foxes.* 2. The habit of hunting animals for food: *A tiger is a beast of prey.* 3. A person who is the object of an attack; victim: *The customer was the prey of a dishonest salesperson. Noun.*
◦ 1. To hunt for food: *Owls prey on small animals.* 2. To take advantage of: *The bully preyed upon the smaller children.* 3. To trouble; distress: *Worry about failing the test preyed on the student's mind. Verb.*
Another word that sounds like this is **pray**. **prey** (prā) *noun*, *plural* **preys**; *verb*, **preyed, preying**.

price 1. The amount of money for which something is sold or offered for sale: *What is the price of that radio?* 2. The cost at which something is gained: *The country won the war, but paid a great price in lives lost. Noun.*
◦ 1. To set a price on: *The bicycle is priced at $99.* 2. To find out the price of: *We priced the coats on display in the window. Verb.*

price (prīs) *noun*, *plural* **prices**; *verb*, **priced, pricing**.

priceless So valuable that it cannot be measured by a price: *The priceless ancient statue is always guarded.* **price·less** (prīs′lis) *adjective*.

prick To make a small hole with a sharp point: *I pricked my finger on a pin. Verb.*
◦ A small hole in something: *Make several pricks on the top of the pie crust. Noun.* **prick** (prik) *verb*, **pricked, pricking**; *noun*, *plural* **pricks**.

prickly 1. Having small, sharp thorns or points: *The rose bushes are prickly.* 2. Stinging or tingling: *Do you ever get a prickly sensation in your foot?* **prick·ly** (prik′lē) *adjective*, **pricklier, prickliest**.

prickly pear A cactus that has yellow flowers and pear-shaped fruit.

These athletes are showing off their Olympic medals with pride.

pride 1. A feeling that one has worth and importance; self-respect: *It is important to keep your pride even during difficult times.* 2. Too high an opinion of oneself: *They knew they were wrong, but their foolish pride kept them from apologizing.* 3. Pleasure or satisfaction in something that one does or is connected with: *The mechanics in this shop take pride in their work. Noun.*
• **to pride oneself.** To feel pride; be proud: *I pride myself on always being on time. Verb.* Other words that sound like this are **pried**[1] and **pried**[2]. **pride** (prīd) *noun*; *verb*, **prided, priding**.

pried[1] Past tense and past participle of **pry**[1]. Another word that sounds like this is **pride**. **pried** (prīd) *verb*.

PRONUNCIATION KEY:

| at | āpe | fär | câre | end | mē | it | īce | pierce | hot | old | sông | fôrk |
| oil | out | up | ūse | rüle | pull | tûrn | chin | sing | shop | thin | this | |

hw in white; zh in treasure. The symbol ə stands for the unstressed vowel sound in about, taken, pencil, lemon, and circus.

587

pried² Past tense and past participle of **pry²**. Another word that sounds like this is **pride**. **pried** (prīd) *verb*.

priest In certain religions, a member of the clergy. **priest** (prēst) *noun*, *plural* **priests**.

primary **1.** First or greatest in importance; main: *The travelers' **primary** concern was finding a place to stay for the night.* **2.** First in order or in time: *Digging a foundation is one of the **primary** stages of building a house. Adjective.*
○ An election in which members of the same political party run against one another. The winner becomes the party's candidate for an office in a later, general election. *Noun.*
pri·ma·ry (prī′mer ē) *adjective*; *noun*, *plural* **primaries**.

primary color One of the basic colors from which all other colors can be made. In mixing paint, red, yellow, and blue are the primary colors.

primary school A school that includes the first three or four grades of elementary school. It sometimes includes kindergarten.

primate A group of mammals that includes humans, apes, and monkeys. All primates have large brains, eyes that look forward, and fingers and thumbs that can grasp things. **pri·mate** (prī′māt) *noun*, *plural* **primates**.

prime **1.** First or greatest in importance or value; main: *My **prime** concern was getting home safely.* **2.** Of the best quality; excellent: *They serve **prime** beef at that restaurant. Adjective.*
○ The best stage or condition: *This bouquet is past its **prime**. Noun.*
○ To get ready by putting something in or on: *You should **prime** the woodwork before painting it. Verb.*
prime (prīm) *adjective*; *noun*, *plural* **primes**; *verb*, **primed**, **priming**.

prime minister The leader of a governing group of ministers. Both Great Britain and Canada have prime ministers.

prime number A number that can be divided evenly only by itself and the number 1. The number 13 is a prime number.

primitive **1.** Having to do with an early or first stage of development: *A worm is a **primitive** form of life.* **2.** Very simple or crude: *A stone ax is a **primitive** tool.* **prim·i·tive** (prim′i tiv) *adjective*.

primrose A small garden plant with brightly col-ored flowers. It grows in moist, shady areas. **prim·rose** (prim′rōz′) *noun*, *plural* **primroses**.

prince **1.** A man or boy of a royal family other than a king. **2.** A nobleman of very high rank. **prince** (prins) *noun*, *plural* **princes**.

Prince Edward Island An island province in eastern Canada. Its capital is Charlottetown. **Prince Ed·ward Island** (ed′wərd).

princess **1.** A woman or girl of a royal family other than a queen. **2.** The wife of a prince. **3.** A noblewoman of very high rank. **prin·cess** (prin′sis or prin′ses) *noun*, *plural* **princesses**.

principal Greatest or first in importance; chief: *Our **principal** task this weekend is to weed the garden. Adjective.*
○ **1.** The person who is the head of a school. **2.** A person who leads or plays an important role in some activity: *After the **performance**, the principals in the play came out for a special bow. Noun.*
Another word that sounds like this is **principle**. **prin·ci·pal** (prin′sə pəl) *adjective*; *noun*, *plural* **principals**.

principle **1.** A basic truth, law, or belief: *Our legal system is based on the **principle** that a person is innocent until proven guilty.* **2.** A rule of behavior that a person chooses to live by: *I make it a **principle** to answer all my mail promptly.* Another word that sounds like this is **principal**. **prin·ci·ple** (prin′sə pəl) *noun*, *plural* **principles**.

print **1.** To put letters, words, or pictures on a surface by pressing, stamping, or photographing: *Machines **print** words and pictures on paper for books and magazines.* **2.** To make something appear in a book, magazine, or newspaper; publish: *Our town newspaper **printed** my poem.* **3.** To write in separated letters like the letters in books: *We **print** our names before we learn to write them in script. Verb.*
○ **1.** Letters made by printing: *That book has large **print**.* **2.** A mark made by pressing into something: *There were **prints** in the snow where the dog had walked.* **3.** A picture made by pressing paper against an engraved or raised surface covered with ink. **4.** A photograph made from a negative. **5.** Cloth with a design on it: *a cotton **print** of black and white checks. Noun.*
print (print) *verb*, **printed**, **printing**; *noun*, *plural* **prints**.

printer 1. A person or company whose business is printing. 2. An instrument that can be connected to a computer to produce a printed copy of a file that is stored on a disk. **print·er** (prin′tər) *noun*, *plural* **printers**.

printing 1. The business or process of making books, magazines, and other printed material. 2. Writing in which the letters are separated like the letters in books. **print·ing** (prin′ting) *noun*.

printing press A machine that prints letters or words on paper.

printout A printed paper copy of the output from a computer. **print·out** (print′out′) *noun*, *plural* **printouts**.

prism A solid object that is transparent. A prism can be made of glass or crystal and can break up a ray of light into the colors of the rainbow. A prism has three sides shaped like rectangles that are equal in area and two triangular ends that are parallel to one another. **prism** (priz′əm) *noun*, *plural* **prisms**.

prison A building or other place where people accused or convicted of crimes are forced to stay. **pris·on** (priz′ən) *noun*, *plural* **prisons**.

prisoner 1. A person kept in a prison. 2. Any person who is captured by someone else; captive: *The kidnapers kept the hostage a prisoner in the basement of the old house.* **pris·on·er** (priz′ə nər) *noun*, *plural* **prisoners**.

privacy The condition of being alone or private: *The writer went to a cabin in the mountains in order to have privacy to finish a novel.* **pri·va·cy** (prī′və sē) *noun*.

private 1. Belonging to a particular person or group: *That is a private driveway, not a town road.* 2. Not meant to be shared with others; not public: *Our telephone conversation was private.* 3. Not holding a public office: *The senator retired and became a private citizen. Adjective.*
○ A soldier of the lowest rank. A private is next below a corporal. *Noun.*
• **in private.** Without other people being present: *May I speak to you in private?*
pri·vate (prī′vit) *adjective*; *noun*, *plural* **privates**.

privilege A special right given to a person or group: *had the privilege of staying up late.* **priv·i·lege** (priv′ə lij) *noun*, *plural* **privileges**.
—**privileged** *adjective*.

prize¹ Something that is won in a contest or game: *The blue ribbon was the top prize in the dog show. Noun.*
○ Having won or good enough to win a prize: *The children raised a prize calf for the state fair. Adjective.*
prize (prīz) *noun*, *plural* **prizes**; *adjective*.

prize² To think very highly of: *I prize this fossil because I found it on my birthday.* **prize** (prīz) *verb*, **prized**, **prizing**.

Winners of contests usually receive prizes.

pro A person who is a professional, not an amateur: *A tennis pro gives lessons at the town tennis courts.* **pro** (prō) *noun*, *plural* **pros**.

probability 1. The chances of something happening; likelihood: *Bad weather increases the probability of accidents on the roads.* 2. Something that is likely to happen: *Rain today is a strong probability.* **prob·a·bil·i·ty** (prob′ə bil′i tē) *noun*, *plural* **probabilities**.

probable Likely to happen or be true: *Our team is far ahead, so it is probable that we will win the game.* **prob·a·ble** (prob′ə bəl) *adjective*.

probably Almost surely; most likely: *It'll probably rain. We are about the same size, so my coat will probably fit you. We will probably need to buy some groceries before the weekend.* **prob·a·bly** (prob′ə blē) *adverb*.

probation A period of time for testing a person's ability, behavior, or qualifications: *After a month of probation, the new worker was accepted as a permanent employee.* **pro·ba·tion** (prō bā′shən) *noun*, *plural* **probations**.

probe 1. A thorough investigation of something: *The newspaper report led to a probe of prison conditions.* 2. A tool or device used to test or explore: *A doctor might use a probe to look into an injured ear. A space probe is a spacecraft used to gather information about outer space. Noun.*

PRONUNCIATION KEY:
at   āpe   fär   câre   end   mē   it   īce   pierce   hot   ōld   sông   fôrk
oil   out   up   ūse   rüle   pull   tûrn   chin   sing   shop   thin   this
hw in white; zh in treasure. The symbol ə stands for the unstressed vowel sound in about, taken, pencil, lemon, and circus.

589

○ To investigate or explore thoroughly: *The police probed the details of the bank's dishonest practices. Verb.*
probe (prōb) *noun, plural* **probes**; *verb,* **probed, probing.**

problem 1. A question to be thought about and answered: *There were ten problems on the arithmetic test.* 2. A condition or fact that causes trouble and must be dealt with: *Being nearsighted can be a problem.* **prob•lem** (prob′ləm) *noun, plural* **problems.**

procedure A proper way of doing something, usually by a series of steps: *When the alarm rang, we followed the procedure for leaving the building in an emergency.* **pro•ce•dure** (prə sē′jər) *noun, plural* **procedures.**

proceed To move on or continue, especially after a stop: *The speaker waited for the applause to stop and then proceeded.* **pro•ceed** (prə sēd′) *verb,* **proceeded, proceeding.**

proceeds Money raised for a special purpose by selling something: *The proceeds from the cake sale will pay for the class trip.* **pro•ceeds** (prō′sēdz) *plural noun.*

process A series of actions performed in making or doing something: *The process of making bread is simple but takes time. Noun.*
○ To treat or change something by a special series of steps: *That factory processes cheese and other foods. Verb.*
proc•ess (pros′es) *noun, plural* **processes**; *verb,* **processed, processing.**

procession 1. A continuous forward movement of something or someone: *We followed the procession of the parade along the avenue.* 2. A group of persons moving forward in a line or in a certain order: *The wedding procession started down the aisle.* **pro•ces•sion** (prə sesh′ən) *noun, plural* **processions.**

proclaim To announce publicly: *The mayor proclaimed a town holiday.* **pro•claim** (prə klām′) *verb,* **proclaimed, proclaiming.**

proclamation An official announcement of something: *Abraham Lincoln made a proclamation in 1863 that freed slaves in many states.* **proc•la•ma•tion** (prok′lə mā′shən) *noun, plural* **proclamations.**

prod 1. To push with something sharp or pointed; jab or poke: *My friend prodded me with a pencil to get my attention.* 2. To make do something; urge: *I prodded the guests into singing a song. Verb.*
○ 1. A push or jab. 2. Something pointed: *The shepherds used prods to keep the sheep moving through the gates. Noun.*
prod (prod) *verb,* **prodded, prodding**; *noun, plural* **prods.**

This market sells a variety of produce.

produce 1. To make or create something: *That factory produces automobiles. A cow produces milk.* 2. To bring forth; show: *The lawyer produced new evidence at the trial.* 3. To prepare a play or movie and present it to the public: *The partners produced a movie based on the book. Verb.*
○ Something made or yielded: *The market sells lettuce, tomatoes, carrots, and other garden produce. Noun.*
pro•duce (prə düs′ *or* prə dūs′ *for verb;* prod′üs *or* prod′ūs *or* prō′düs *or* prō′dūs *for noun*) *verb,* **produced, producing**; *noun.*

producer A person, company, or thing that makes or creates something: *That company is a leading producer of automobiles. The producer hired actors for a new film.* **pro•duc•er** (prə dü′sər *or* prə dū′sər) *noun, plural* **producers.**

product 1. Anything that is made or created: *Milk, butter, and yogurt are dairy products. A made-up story is a product of the imagination.* 2. A number that is gotten by multiplying two other numbers: *When you multiply 3 times 4, the product is 12.* **prod•uct** (prod′əkt) *noun, plural* **products.**

$$\text{In } 3 \times 6 = \mathbf{18} \text{ or } \begin{array}{r} 3 \\ \times 6 \\ \hline 18 \end{array}$$

18 is the product.

production 1. The act of making or creating something: *The production of steel is an important industry in that town.* 2. Something that is made or created: *The opera was an elaborate production.* **pro·duc·tion** (prə duk′shən) *noun, plural* **productions**.

productive 1. Making or yielding large amounts of something: *fertile and productive land that yields rich harvests.* 2. Having good results: *The talks were productive and an agreement was reached.* **pro·duc·tive** (prə duk′tiv) *adjective.*

profess 1. To make known; declare: *They professed their love for each other.* 2. To say that something is true when it isn't; pretend: *They professed to be interested in the show, but they were really bored.* **pro·fess** (prə fes′) *verb,* **professed, professing.**

profession 1. An occupation that requires special education and training: *Medicine is a profession that requires years of study.* 2. The act of declaring something: *The knight made a profession of loyalty to the king.* **pro·fes·sion** (prə fesh′ən) *noun, plural* **professions.**

A lawyer is a highly trained professional.

professional 1. Having to do with an occupation that requires special education: *An architect is a professional person.* 2. Making money by doing something that other people do for fun: *a professional athlete. Adjective.*

○ 1. A person who has an occupation that requires special education: *Engineers and architects are professionals.* 2. A person who works for money doing something that other people do for fun: *After years of being an amateur golfer,* my cousin became a **professional.** *Noun.* **pro·fes·sion·al** (prə fesh′ə nəl) *adjective; noun, plural* **professionals.**

professor A teacher having a high rank in a college or university. **pro·fes·sor** (prə fes′ər) *noun, plural* **professors.**

profile 1. A side view or outline of a person's head or of something else: *There is a profile of George Washington on a quarter.* 2. A short description of someone or something: *The newspaper printed a profile of the new mayor.* **pro·file** (prō′fīl) *noun, plural* **profiles.**

profit 1. The amount of money left after all the costs of running a business have been paid: *We bought the old boat for $100, spent $50 fixing it, and sold it for $200, which gave us a profit of $50.* 2. Anything gained by doing something; advantage; benefit: *It will be to our profit to study hard for the test. Noun.*

○ To gain or benefit in some way: *It will profit you to go to summer school because you will be better prepared for next year. A wise person profits from past mistakes. Verb.*

Another word that sounds like this is **prophet.** **prof·it** (prof′it) *noun, plural* **profits;** *verb,* **profited, profiting.**

profitable Giving a profit: *That coffee shop is a very profitable business.* **prof·it·a·ble** (prof′it ə bəl) *adjective.* —**profitably** *adverb.*

profound 1. Showing great understanding or knowledge: *The professor is a profound thinker. That book contains a profound analysis of ancient ideas about life.* 2. Very great or deep: *There was a profound silence following the explosion. We felt profound sorrow when we heard of our friend's death.* **pro·found** (prə found′) *adjective.*

profuse 1. Very abundant; plentiful: *In spring, the flowers in the meadow are profuse.* 2. Given or giving in a generous way; lavish: *We gave profuse thanks for all the help we'd received. Our dinner guests were profuse in their compliments.* **pro·fuse** (prə fūs′) *adjective.* —**profusely** *adverb.*

program 1. A list telling what will be done and who will do it in a play, concert, or other presentation: *Photographs of the players on the baseball team appeared in the program sold at the stadium.* 2. A play or other presentation or performance:

PRONUNCIATION KEY:
| at | āpe | fär | câre | end | mē | it | īce | pierce | hot | ōld | sông | fôrk |
| oil | out | up | ūse | rüle | pull | tûrn | chin | sing | shop | thin | this | |

hw in white; zh in treasure. The symbol ə stands for the unstressed vowel sound in about, taken, pencil, lemon, and circus.

591

*The class planned an interesting **program** for their parents. What is your favorite television **program**?* **3.** A plan of what will be done: *We have a new **program** to fight crime in our city.* **4.** A series of instructions that a computer follows in order to perform some task. **pro·gram** (prō′gram) *noun, plural* **programs.**

programmer A person who writes programs for computers. **pro·gram·mer** (prō′gram ər) *noun, plural* **programmers.**

progress A forward movement: *A storm slowed the ship's progress across the ocean. Are you making any **progress** with your book report? Noun.*
○ To move forward: *The building of the new house **progressed** rapidly. Verb.*
prog·ress (prog′res) *noun;* **pro·gress** (prə gres′) *verb,* **progressed, progressing.**

progressive **1.** Moving forward; developing: *Some diseases cause **progressive** deterioration of health.* **2.** In favor of reform or improvement: *The new senator had many **progressive** ideas for protecting the environment. Adjective.*
○ A person who favors improvement or reform in politics or some other area. *Noun.*
pro·gres·sive (prə gres′iv) *adjective; noun, plural* **progressives.**

prohibit To not allow; forbid or prevent: *Smoking is **prohibited** in the bus.* **pro·hib·it** (prō hib′it) *verb,* **prohibited, prohibiting.** —**prohibition** *noun.*

project **1.** A plan or activity to be done: *Our **project** for science class was to raise a baby chicken.* **2.** A group of apartment buildings designed as a unit: *That is the new housing **project**. Noun.*
○ **1.** To throw or propel: *A slingshot **projects** stones into the air.* **2.** To cause light, a shadow, or an image to fall on a surface: *The movie was **projected** on a screen.* **3.** To imagine or predict what will happen: *The newspapers took polls to **project** the winner of the election.* **4.** To stick out; protrude: *Fine hairs **project** from the sides of some kinds of caterpillars. Verb.*
proj·ect (proj′ekt) *noun, plural* **projects;** **pro·ject** (prə jekt′) *verb,* **projected, projecting.**

projectile Any object that can be thrown or shot through the air. A bullet is a projectile. **pro·jec·tile** (prə jek′tīl) *noun, plural* **projectiles.**

projection **1.** The act of throwing something forward: *The **projection** of objects onto the rink is*

forbidden. **2.** The picture or other image that is projected onto a screen or other surface: *The **projection** of the slide was so clear that we could see every detail.* **3.** A prediction that is based on certain information: *The network announced its **projection** of who would win the election.* **4.** Something that sticks out or projects: *The surface of the moon has many rocky **projections**.* **pro·jec·tion** (prə jek′shən) *noun, plural* **projections.**

prolong To make longer, especially in time; extend: *New medical treatments can **prolong** people's lives.* **pro·long** (prə lông′) *verb,* **prolonged, prolonging.** —**prolongation** *noun.*

prominent **1.** Well-known or important: *The town council was made up of five **prominent** citizens.* **2.** Very easy to see because it stands out in some way; noticeable: *The lone tree was **prominent** in the open field.* **prom·i·nent** (prom′ə nənt) *adjective.* —**prominently** *adverb.*

promise **1.** A statement made by a person, saying that something will or will not be done or happen: *I gave a **promise** that I would clean my room.* **2.** Something that gives a reason for expecting success or progress in the future: *You show **promise** as a writer. Noun.*
○ **1.** To give one's word that something will or will not be done or happen: *I **promise** to be home by 5:30.* **2.** To give reason to expect something: *The beautiful red sunset **promises** a sunny day for tomorrow. Verb.*
prom·ise (prom′is) *noun, plural* **promises;** *verb,* **promised, promising.**

promontory A high piece of land that sticks out into a body of water: *There was an old lighthouse on the promontory.* **prom·on·to·ry** (prom′ən tôr′ē) *noun, plural* **promontories.**

The boats are sailing between two promontories.

promote 1. To give a higher rank or importance to: *Everyone in the class was* **promoted** *from third to fourth grade.* 2. To help in doing or contribute to something: *Eating too much sugar* **promotes** *tooth decay.* **pro•mote** (prə mōt′) *verb,* **promoted, promoting.**

promotion 1. A change to a higher rank, position, or grade: *She received a* **promotion** *from lieutenant to captain.* 2. The act of promoting: *The candidate needed a great deal of money for the* **promotion** *of the campaign.* **pro•mo•tion** (prə mō′shən) *noun, plural* **promotions.**

prompt Quick or on time: *The restaurant gave very* **prompt** *service. Adjective.*
○ 1. To cause someone to do something: *The sound of thunder* **prompted** *me to close the windows.* 2. To remind an actor or speaker of what to say if he or she forgets: *Your job is to* **prompt** *the actors and keep the play moving forward. Verb.* **prompt** (prompt) *adjective,* **prompter, promptest;** *verb,* **prompted, prompting.** —**promptly** *adverb* —**promptness** *noun.*

prone 1. Lying flat with the face downward: *I stretched out* **prone** *on the floor.* 2. Having the wish or tendency to do something: *Some people are* **prone** *to eat too much.* **prone** (prōn) *adjective.*

prong One of the pointed ends of an antler or of a fork or other tool. **prong** (prông *or* prong) *noun, plural* **prongs.**

pronoun A word that takes the place of one or more nouns or noun phrases. In the sentence "We gave it to them yesterday," "We," "it," and "them" are pronouns. **pro•noun** (prō′noun′) *noun, plural* **pronouns.**

pronounce 1. To make the sound of a letter or word: *People from different parts of the country* **pronounce** *certain words differently. If you look up the word "adult," you will see that there are two ways to* **pronounce** *this word, and both ways are correct.* 2. To say or declare: *The judge* **pronounced** *the prisoner not guilty.* **pro•nounce** (prə nouns′) *verb,* **pronounced, pronouncing.**

pronunciation A way of making the sound of a letter, a word, or words: *In this dictionary,* **pronunciations** *are shown between parentheses.* **pro•nun•ci•a•tion** (prə nun′sē ā′shən) *noun, plural* **pronunciations.**

proof Facts or evidence showing that something is true: *The lawyer had* **proof** *of her client's innocence.* **proof** (prüf) *noun, plural* **proofs.**

proofread To read written or printed material to find and correct mistakes: **Proofread** *your report before you give it to the teacher.* **proof•read** (prüf′rēd′) *verb,* **proofread** (prüf′red′), **proofreading.**

prop To hold up or hold in place by putting something under or against; support: *We* **propped** *up the sagging roof with some pieces of lumber. Verb.*
○ A thing used to hold something in a position: *They used a small rock as a* **prop** *to keep the door open. Noun.* **prop** (prop) *verb,* **propped, propping;** *noun, plural* **props.**

propaganda Information or ideas that are deliberately spread to try to influence the thinking of other people. Often propaganda is not completely true or fair: *That government publishes* **propaganda** *criticizing the way of life in other countries.* **prop•a•gan•da** (prop′ə gan′də) *noun.*

propel To cause to move forward or onward: *This plane is* **propelled** *by jet engines.* **pro•pel** (prə pel′) *verb,* **propelled, propelling.**

Before jet engines were invented, airplanes were driven by propellers.

propeller A device made up of blades mounted on a hub. When a propeller turns, it moves air or water and provides the force to drive a boat or aircraft forward. **pro•pel•ler** (prə pel′ər) *noun, plural* **propellers.**

proper 1. Correct or suitable for a certain purpose or occasion: *A carpenter must have the* **proper** *tools to do good work. Proper attire should be*

PRONUNCIATION KEY:

| at | āpe | fär | câre | end | mē | it | īce | pierce | hot | ōld | sông | fôrk |
| oil | out | up | ūse | rüle | pull | tûrn | chin | sing | shop | thin | this | |

hw in white; zh in treasure. The symbol ə stands for the unstressed vowel sound in about, taken, pencil, lemon, and circus.

593

worn at the wedding. **2.** Thought of in a strict sense: *The village we live in is not part of the city proper.* **prop·er** (prop′ər) *adjective.*

properly **1.** In a correct or suitable way: *The dentist showed us how to brush properly.* **2.** In a strict sense: *Properly speaking, that book is not a novel; it is a biography.* **prop·er·ly** (prop′ər lē) *adverb.*

proper noun A noun that names a particular person, place, or thing. A proper noun is always capitalized. In the sentence "George Washington was born in Virginia," "George Washington" and "Virginia" are proper nouns.

property **1.** Anything owned by a person or organization: *The school building was town property. That coat is my property.* **2.** A piece of land: *We bought some property near the ocean.* **3.** A characteristic of something: *Heat is a property of fire.* **prop·er·ty** (prop′ər tē) *noun, plural* **properties.**

prophecy **1.** Something that a person says will happen in the future; prediction: *They believe a prophecy that there will be a great flood in ten years.* **2.** The act of predicting. **proph·e·cy** (prof′ə sē) *noun, plural* **prophecies.** —**prophesy** *verb.*

prophet **1.** A person who tells others a message that is believed to be from God. **2.** A person who tells what will happen in the future. Another word that sounds like this is **profit.** **proph·et** (prof′it) *noun, plural* **prophets.**

proportion **1.** The relation of one thing to another with regard to size, number, or amount: *The proportion of boys to girls in the class is two to one.* **2.** proportions. The size or dimensions of something: *We measured the proportions of the room.* **pro·por·tion** (prə pôr′shən) *noun, plural* **proportions.**

proposal **1.** A plan or suggestion that is presented to others for consideration: *The committee wrote a proposal to change some of the rules of the school.* **2.** An offer of marriage. **pro·pos·al** (prə pō′zəl) *noun, plural* **proposals.**

propose **1.** To suggest something or someone to other people for their consideration: *The governor proposed increased taxes for next year. Several of the students have proposed you for class president.* **2.** To intend or plan to do something: *My friend proposes to study to be a doctor.* **3.** To

make an offer of marriage. **pro·pose** (prə pōz′) *verb,* **proposed, proposing.**

proposition **1.** Something that is suggested for consideration: *They accepted our proposition to mow their lawn in exchange for the use of their swimming pool.* **2.** A statement or subject to be discussed: *The proposition is whether taxes should be increased.* **pro·po·si·tion** (prop′ə zish′ən) *noun, plural* **propositions.**

propulsion The force that moves something forward or onward: *The spacecraft was launched by means of rocket propulsion.* **pro·pul·sion** (prə pul′shən) *noun.*

prose Written or spoken language that is like normal speech, rather than like poetry. **prose** (prōz) *noun.*

prosecute To investigate or examine a person accused of a crime in a court of law: *They prosecuted two people for the theft.* **pros·e·cute** (pros′i kūt′) *verb,* **prosecuted, prosecuting.** —**prosecution** *noun.*

prospect Something looked forward to or expected: *I was excited at the prospect of owning a bike.* **2.** A person who will probably do something that is expected: *The salesperson thought I was a good prospect for buying the vacuum cleaner.* Noun. ○ To search or explore: *Many went prospecting for gold in Alaska.* Verb. **pros·pect** (pros′pekt) *noun, plural* **prospects;** *verb,* **prospected, prospecting.**

prospector A person who explores for gold or other minerals. **pros·pec·tor** (pros′pek tər) *noun, plural* **prospectors.**

prosper To be successful; do very well: *The town prospered when several companies moved their offices there.* **pros·per** (pros′pər) *verb,* **prospered, prospering.**

prosperity Success, wealth, or good fortune in life: *Many people benefit in times of prosperity.* **pros·per·i·ty** (pros per′i tē) *noun.*

prosperous Having success, wealth, or good fortune: *The prosperous family tried to help others less fortunate.* **pros·per·ous** (pros′pər əs) *adjective.*

protect To keep from harm; defend: *That law protects our right to vote.* **pro·tect** (prə tekt′) *verb,* **protected, protecting.**

protection **1.** The keeping of someone or something from harm: *Our state has game preserves* *for the protection of wild animals.* **2.** A person or thing that protects: *I put lotion on my skin as a* **protection** *against sunburn.* **pro·tec·tion** (prə tek′shən) *noun.*

protective Keeping from harm; protecting: *A turtle has a* **protective** *shell. We put a* **protective** *coating of wax on the floors.* **pro·tec·tive** (prə tek′tiv) *adjective.*

protein A substance found in all living cells of animals and plants. It is necessary for growth and life. Meat, eggs, and milk contain protein. **pro·tein** (prō′tēn) *noun, plural* **proteins.**

protest An objection or complaint against something: *The people of the town made a* **protest** *against the building of the new highway. The parents ignored the child's* **protests** *about going to bed early. Noun.*
○ To make a protest; object to: *The students* **protested** *against closing the library. Verb.* **pro·test** (prō′test *for noun;* prə test′ *for verb) noun, plural* **protests;** *verb,* **protested, protesting.**

Protestant A member of any Christian church other than the Roman Catholic Church or the Orthodox Church. **Prot·es·tant** (prot′ə stənt) *noun, plural* **Protestants.**

proton A tiny particle found in the nucleus of an atom. A proton has a positive electrical charge. **pro·ton** (prō′ton) *noun, plural* **protons.**

protoplasm A substance that is like a jelly and is the living matter of all cells. **pro·to·plasm** (prō′tə plaz′əm) *noun.*

protozoan A cell that captures its food. Protozoans are so small that they can be seen only through a microscope. An ameba is one kind of protozoan. **pro·to·zo·an** (prō′tə zō′ən) *noun, plural* **protozoans** *or* **protozoa** (prō′tə zō′ə).

protrude To stick out: *Rocks* **protruded** *from the surface of the sea.* **pro·trude** (prō trüd′) *verb,* **protruded, protruding.**

proud **1.** Having a strong sense of satisfaction in a person or thing: *I am* **proud** *of the bookcase I made.* **2.** Having self-respect: *They were too* **proud** *to ask for money even though they needed it.* **proud** (proud) *adjective,* **prouder, proudest.**

prove **1.** To show that something is what it is supposed to be, or does what it is supposed to do: *They asked the salesperson to* **prove** *that the soap* would really get clothes cleaner. The lawyer **proved** the innocence of the prisoner. **2.** To have a certain result: *The new play* **proved** *to be a great success.* **prove** (prüv) *verb,* **proved, proved** *or* **proven, proving.**

proven Past participle of prove: *You have* **proven** *that you are a loyal friend.* **prov·en** (prü′vən) *verb.*

proverb A short saying that expresses something that many people believe to be true. "Haste makes waste" is a proverb. **prov·erb** (prov′ərb) *noun, plural* **proverbs.**

provide **1.** To give what is needed or wanted; supply: *The art teacher* **provided** *paper, brushes, and paint. Trees* **provide** *shade from the sun.* **2.** To set as a rule or condition: *The law* **provides** *that a person is innocent until proven guilty.* **3.** To take care of a present or future need: *They* **provide** *for their family by working.* **pro·vide** (prə vīd′) *verb,* **provided, providing.**

provided On the condition that; if: *I'll lend you my bicycle,* **provided** *you return it tomorrow.* **pro·vid·ed** (prə vī′did) *conjunction.*

province **1.** One of the divisions of some countries. Canada is made up of ten provinces. **2.** An area of activity or authority: *Representing a person in a court of law is within the* **province** *of a lawyer.* **3.** the provinces. The regions of a country away from the main cities. **prov·ince** (prov′ins) *noun, plural* **provinces.**

provincial **1.** Of or having to do with a province: *They are running for office in the* **provincial** *government.* **2.** Belonging to or characteristic of a certain province: *On holidays the people of the village wear* **provincial** *costumes.* **pro·vin·cial** (prə vin′shəl) *adjective.*

provision **1.** The act of giving something needed: *The coach was responsible for the* **provision** *of equipment to the team.* **2.** The act of planning ahead for a future need: *Has any* **provision** *been made for the party if it rains?* **3.** A condition or requirement: *A* **provision** *for voting is being a citizen.* **4.** provisions. A supply of food: *The ship has* **provisions** *for one month.* **pro·vi·sion** (prə vizh′ən) *noun, plural* **provisions.**

provoke **1.** To make angry: *Their rudeness* **provoked** *me.* **2.** To stir; excite: *Unfair laws* **provoked** *the people to riot.* **3.** To bring out; arouse: *The*

PRONUNCIATION KEY:

at	āpe	fär	câre	end	mē	it	īce	pierce	hot	ōld	sông	fôrk
oil	out	up	ūse	rüle	pull	tûrn	chin	sing	shop	thin	this	

hw in white; zh in treasure. The symbol ə stands for the unstressed vowel sound in about, taken, pencil, lemon, and circus.

595

newspaper article **provoked** *a lot of discussion.*
pro•voke (prə vōk′) *verb,* **provoked, provoking.**

prow The front part of a boat or ship; bow. **prow**
(prou) *noun, plural* **prows.**

**The prow of this ocean liner rises more than
thirty feet above the water.**

prowl To move or roam quietly or secretly:
The tiger **prowled** *through the forest. The thief*
prowled *the streets at night.* **prowl** (proul) *verb,*
prowled, prowling.

prudence Good judgment and caution: *You show*
prudence *in saving half your allowance each*
week. **pru•dence** (prü′dəns) *noun.*

prudent Having or showing prudence: *It is* **pru-**
dent *to have the car checked before starting on*
a long trip. **pru•dent** (prü′dənt) *adjective.* —**pru-**
dently *adverb.*

prune¹ A plum that has been dried. **prune** (prün)
noun, plural **prunes.**

prune² To cut off or cut out parts from something:
We **pruned** *dead branches from the tree.* **prune**
(prün) *verb,* **pruned, pruning.**

pry¹ To look or inquire too closely or curiously:
They don't want to discuss the matter, so please
don't **pry.** **pry** (prī) *verb,* **pried, prying.**

pry² 1. To move or raise by force: *Pry the top off*
the crate with a crowbar. 2. To get with much
effort: *The reporter tried to* **pry** *information*
about the accident from the victims. **pry** (prī)
verb, **pried, prying.**

P.S. An abbreviation for **postscript** or **public**
school.

psalm A sacred song or poem: *There is a collec-*
tion of **psalms** *in the Bible.* **psalm** (säm) *noun,*
plural **psalms.**

psychiatrist A doctor who treats emotional
and mental illness. **psy•chi•a•trist** (si kī′ə trist
or sī kī′ə trist) *noun, plural* **psychiatrists.**

psychiatry A branch of medicine that deals
with emotional and mental illness. **psy•chi•a•try**
(si kī′ə trē *or* sī kī′ə trē) *noun.*

psychological 1. Having to do with the study of
the mind and the way people behave. 2. Having
to do with the mind or the way people behave:
Scientists study the **psychological** *effects of noise on*
people. **psy•cho•log•i•cal** (sī′kə loj′i kəl) *adjective.*

psychologist A person who works or specializes
in psychology. **psy•chol•o•gist** (sī kol′ə jist) *noun,*
plural **psychologists.**

psychology The study of the mind and of the
way people or animals behave. **psy•chol•o•gy**
(sī kol′ə jē) *noun.*

pt. An abbreviation for **pint** or **pints.**

pterodactyl A flying reptile that lived in prehistoric times. The pterodactyl's wings were membranes that stretched from the sides of its body
and arms to its fourth fingers. **pter•o•dac•tyl**
(ter′ə dak′təl) *noun, plural* **pterodactyls.**

public 1. Having to do with or for all the people:
The mayor made a **public** *announcement over the*
radio. A **public** *beach is for anybody to use.*
2. Working for the government of a town, city, or
country: *A judge is a* **public** *official. Adjective.*
○ All the people of a town, city, or country: *The*
museum is open to the **public** *every day. Noun.*
  • **in public.** In a place where other people are
  present, sometimes a lot of them: *The singer*
  has talent but rarely performs **in public.**
pub•lic (pub′lik) *adjective; noun.* —**publicly**
adverb.

publication A magazine, newspaper, book, or
other printed material that is published: *We sub-*
scribe to several **publications** *about nature.*
pub•li•ca•tion (pub′li kā′shən) *noun, plural*
publications.

publicity 1. Information given out to bring a person or thing to the attention of the public: *The*
publicity *about the band brought a large crowd*
to hear it perform. 2. The attention of the public:
Most politicians like **publicity.** **pub•lic•i•ty**
(pu blis′i tē) *noun.*

public school A free school that is supported by
people's taxes.

publish To print a newspaper, magazine, book, or
other material and offer it for sale. **pub•lish**
(pub′lish) *verb,* **published, publishing.** —**publisher**
noun.

puck A thick, black disk made of hard rubber. A puck is used in playing ice hockey. **puck** (puk) *noun, plural* **pucks.**

pudding A sweet, soft dessert that is cooked. **pud·ding** (pŭd′ĭng) *noun, plural* **puddings.**

puddle A small pool of water or other liquid that is not very deep: *There were **puddles** in the road after the rain. There was a **puddle** of spilled milk on the floor.* **pud·dle** (pŭd′əl) *noun, plural* **puddles.**

pueblo 1. An American Indian village consisting of adobe and stone houses joined together. Pueblo are built by certain Native American tribes in the southwest United States. 2. **Pueblo.** A member of a Native American tribe of New Mexico and Arizona. **pueb·lo** (pwĕb′lō) *noun, plural* **pueblo** *for definition 1;* **Pueblo** *or* **Pueblos** *for definition 2.*

Puerto Rican A person who was born or is living in Puerto Rico. *Noun.*

○ Having to do with Puerto Rico or its people. *Adjective.*

Puer·to Ri·can (pwĕr′tō rē′kən *or* pôr′tə rē′kən) *noun, plural* **Puerto Ricans;** *adjective.*

Puerto Rico An island in the Caribbean Sea. It is a territory of the United States. **Puer·to Ri·co** (pwĕr′tō rē′kō *or* pôr′tə rē′kō).

Puerto Rico
Visited by Columbus in 1493, Puerto Rico became a possession of the United States after the Spanish-American War in 1898. It is self-governing and has a primarily Hispanic culture.
U.S. Postal Abbreviation: **PR**
Capital: **San Juan**
Population: **3,801,977**
Area: **3,508 sq. mi./13,541 sq. km**
Commonwealth Bird: **Reinita**
Commonwealth Flower: **Maga**

puff 1. A short, gentle burst of air, breath, smoke, or something similar: *A **puff** of smoke came out of the chimney.* 2. Anything soft, round, and fluffy: *The chicks were **puffs** of yellow down. Noun.*

○ 1. To blow or breathe in a puff or puffs: *The engine **puffed** smoke. We **puffed** from climbing the stairs.* 2. To swell up or out: *My finger **puffed** up from the bee sting. The little bird **puffed** out its feathers. Verb.*

puff (pŭf) *noun, plural* **puffs;** *verb,* **puffed, puffing.**

puffin A bird that lives in Arctic waters and coastal regions. Puffins have black and white feathers, a plump body, and a large, brightly colored bill. **puf·fin** (pŭf′ĭn) *noun, plural* **puffins.**

pull 1. To grab or hold something and move it forward or toward oneself: *Two horses **pulled** the wagon. I **pulled** the door open.* 2. To remove or tear out something: *The dentist had to **pull** my tooth.* 3. To go or move: *The ferry **pulled** away from the dock. Verb.*

○ 1. The work done or the force used in moving something by pulling it: *It was a long, hard **pull** to the top of the hill with the supplies on the sled. The strong **pull** of the magnet attracted the nails.* 2. The act of pulling something: *Give a **pull** on the rope and the bell will ring. Noun.*

• **to pull through.** To manage to exist through a difficult or dangerous situation: *The puppies were very sick with distemper, but they all **pulled through.***

• **to pull up.** To stop: *A car **pulled up** in front of the house.*

pull (pŭl) *verb,* **pulled, pulling;** *noun, plural* **pulls.**

pulley A wheel with a groove around it that a rope or chain can be pulled over. Pulleys are used to lift heavy weights. **pul·ley** (pŭl′ē) *noun, plural* **pulleys.**

pulp 1. The soft, juicy part of fruits and vegetables. 2. Any soft, wet mass of material. Wood pulp is used to make paper. 3. The soft inner part of a tooth. **pulp** (pŭlp) *noun, plural* **pulps.**

pulpit A platform in a church from which sermons are given. **pul·pit** (pŭl′pĭt *or* pul′pĭt) *noun, plural* **pulpits.**

pulse 1. The rhythmic beat of the arteries caused by the beating of the heart: *I felt my **pulse** by resting my fingers on blood vessels in my wrist.* 2. Any regular, rhythmic beat: *We heard the steady **pulse** of the train engine.* **pulse** (pŭls) *noun, plural* **pulses.**

puma A wild cat of North America and South America. This animal is usually called a **cougar.**

PRONUNCIATION KEY:

| at | āpe | fär | câre | end | mē | it | īce | pierce | hot | ōld | sông | fôrk |
| oil | out | up | ūse | rüle | pull | tûrn | chin | sing | shop | thin | this | |

hw in white; zh in treasure. The symbol ə stands for the unstressed vowel sound in about, taken, pencil, lemon, and circus.

597

Look up **cougar** for more information. **pu·ma** (pū′mə *or* pü′mə) *noun, plural* **pumas.**

pump A machine used to move water or other liquids or a gas from one place to another: *a gasoline* **pump.** *Noun.*

○ **1.** To move a liquid or gas from one place to another with a pump: *We* **pumped** *water into the swimming pool. My cousin* **pumps** *gas at the gas station on weekends.* **2.** To fill with air or other gas: *I* **pumped** *up the flat tire.* **3.** To get or try to get information from by questioning closely: *The police* **pumped** *the suspects about their associates. Verb.*

pump (pump) *noun, plural* **pumps;** *verb,* **pumped, pumping.**

pumpkin A large, yellowish orange fruit with a hard outer rind and a soft pulp inside. **pump·kin** (pump′kin *or* pung′kin) *noun, plural* **pumpkins.**

pun A joke in which something can have two meanings. A pun can contain two different meanings of one word or two words that sound the same but have different meanings. For example, "The colt couldn't speak because he was a little hoarse (horse)." **pun** (pun) *noun, plural* **puns.**

Pumpkins grow on vines.

punch¹ **1.** To hit a person or thing with the fist or part of the hand: *The boxers* **punched** *each other. I* **punched** *the elevator button for the eighth floor.* **2.** To herd or drive: *The cowhands* **punched** *cattle in the fall. Verb.*

○ A blow with the fist or part of the hand: *The detective knocked out the thief with one powerful* **punch.** *Noun.*

punch (punch) *verb,* **punched, punching;** *noun, plural* **punches.**

punch² A tool for making holes in or putting a design on a surface: *One kind of* **punch** *can fix plain paper so that it will fit into a loose-leaf notebook. Noun.*

○ To make holes in or press a design on with a punch: *I* **punched** *another hole in the belt so I could tighten it. Verb.*

punch (punch) *noun, plural* **punches;** *verb,* **punched, punching.**

punch³ A drink made by mixing different fruit juices, sodas, or other ingredients. **punch** (punch) *noun, plural* **punches.**

punctual On time; prompt: *I always try to be* **punctual** *for appointments.* **punc·tu·al** (pungk′chü əl) *adjective.* —**punctuality** *noun* —**punctually** *adverb.*

punctuate To mark written material with punctuation marks. **punc·tu·ate** (pungk′chü āt′) *verb,* **punctuated, punctuating.**

WORD HISTORY

The word **punctuate** comes from a Latin word meaning "point." Latin writing was marked by dots and other "points" to show where sentences began or ended and to give other information.

punctuation **1.** The use of periods, commas, and other punctuation marks to make the meaning of written material clear: *Your spelling is excellent, but you are poor at* **punctuation.** **2.** One or more punctuation marks: *The* **punctuation** *of the poem will help you read it correctly.* **punc·tu·a·tion** (pungk′chü ā′shən) *noun.*

punctuation mark Any of a group of marks used to make the meaning of written material clear. Periods, commas, semicolons, hyphens, quotation marks, and question marks are punctuation marks.

puncture To make a hole in something with a sharp object: *I* **punctured** *the balloon with a pin. Verb.*

○ A hole made by a sharp object: *a* **puncture** *in a tire. Noun.*

punc·ture (pungk′chər) *verb,* **punctured, puncturing;** *noun, plural* **punctures.**

pungent Sharp or strong to the taste or smell: *I like a* **pungent** *mustard on frankfurters. Ammonia has an unpleasant,* **pungent** *odor.* **pun·gent** (pun′jənt) *adjective.* —**pungently** *adverb.*

punish **1.** To make a person suffer for a wrong he or she has done: *The law* **punishes** *criminals.* **2.** To treat or handle roughly: *The bumpy dirt road* **punished** *our old car.* **pun·ish** (pun′ish) *verb,* **punished, punishing.**

punishment **1.** The act of punishing: *The* **punishment** *of criminals is left to the courts.* **2.** The penalty for a crime or wrong: *Their punishment was five years in prison.* **pun·ish·ment** (pun'ish mənt) *noun*, *plural* **punishments.**

pup 1. A young dog; puppy. 2. One of the young of certain other animals. The young of foxes, wolves, and seals are called pups. **pup** (pup) *noun*, *plural* **pups.**

pupa An insect at the stage after it is a larva and before it is an adult. A caterpillar in its cocoon is a pupa. **pu·pa** (pū'pə) *noun*, *plural* **pupas.**

pupil¹ A person who is studying in school or with a teacher; student. **pu·pil** (pū'pəl) *noun*, *plural* **pupils.**

pupil² The opening in the center of the iris of the eye. Light enters the eye through the pupil. The pupil gets smaller in bright light and larger in darkness. **pu·pil** (pū'pəl) *noun*, *plural* **pupils.**

puppet A doll that looks like a person or animal and has parts that can be moved. Some puppets fit over a person's hand and are made to move by the fingers. Other puppets have strings attached to parts of their bodies and are moved by pulling the strings. **pup·pet** (pup'it) *noun*, *plural* **puppets.**

People all over the world are entertained by puppets.

puppy A young dog. **pup·py** (pup'ē) *noun*, *plural* **puppies.**

purchase To get something by paying money; buy: *We purchased our plane tickets at the airport. Verb.*

○ 1. The act of purchasing: *I saved for the purchase of a new bike.* 2. Something that is gotten by being paid for: *They piled their purchases on the table. Noun.*

pur·chase (pûr'chəs) *verb*, **purchased, purchasing**; *noun*, *plural* **purchases.**

pure 1. Not mixed with anything else: *I bought a scarf of pure silk.* 2. Not dirty or polluted; clean: *We drank pure water from a spring.* 3. Nothing but: *It was pure luck that we won.* 4. Free from evil or guilt; innocent: *a pure mind.* **pure** (pyŭr) *adjective*, **purer, purest.** —**purely** *adverb.*

purebred Having ancestors that are all the same breed or kind of animal: *a purebred Irish setter.* **pure·bred** (pyŭr'bred') *adjective.*

purify To make pure or clean: *The filter will purify the water.* **pu·ri·fy** (pyŭr'ə fī') *verb*, **purified, purifying.** —**purification** *noun.*

Puritan A member of a group of Protestants in England during the 1500s and 1600s. The Puritans wanted simpler forms of worship and stricter morals than those of the national church of England. Some Puritans fled England and settled in America. **Pu·ri·tan** (pyŭr'i tən) *noun*, *plural* **Puritans.**

purple The color made by mixing red and blue. *Noun.*

○ Having the color purple. *Adjective.*

pur·ple (pûr'pəl) *noun*, *plural* **purples**; *adjective.*

purpose The reason for which something is made or done: *What is the purpose of that hook on the wall?*

• **on purpose.** Not by accident; deliberately: *Did you do that that on purpose or by mistake?*

pur·pose (pûr'pəs) *noun*, *plural* **purposes.**

purposeful 1. Having a purpose or meaning. 2. Having determination: *They made a purposeful effort to learn French.* **pur·pose·ful** (pûr'pəs fəl) *adjective.*

purposely On purpose; deliberately: *We purposely left the radio on when we went out.* **pur·pose·ly** (pûr'pəs lē) *adverb.*

purr A soft, murmuring sound like the one made by a cat when it's happy: *the purr of a new car's engine. Noun.*

○ To make a soft, murmuring sound: *The kitten purred when I petted it. Verb.*

purr (pûr) *noun*, *plural* **purrs**; *verb*, **purred, purring.**

purse 1. A pocketbook or handbag. 2. A small bag or case used to carry money. *Noun.*

PRONUNCIATION KEY:

| at | āpe | fär | câre | end | mē | it | īce | pierce | hot | ōld | sông | fôrk |
| oil | out | up | ūse | rüle | pull | tûrn | chin | sing | shop | thin | this | |

hw in white; zh in treasure. The symbol ə stands for the unstressed vowel sound in about, taken, pencil, lemon, and circus.

599

○ To draw together: *The babysitter's lips were pursed in anger. Verb.*
purse (pûrs) *noun, plural* **purses;** *verb,* **pursed, pursing.**

pursue 1. To follow in order to catch up to or capture: *The police **pursued** the thief down the street.* 2. To follow or carry out: *I see that you **pursue** your hobby very seriously.* **pur•sue** (pər sü′) *verb,* **pursued, pursuing.**

pursuit 1. The act of pursuing: *The police were in **pursuit** of the speeding car.* 2. A hobby or other interest a person has: *Making model cars is one of my **pursuits**.* **pur•suit** (pər süt′) *noun, plural* **pursuits.**

pus A yellowish fluid that collects in an infection. Pus is made up of dead germs and white blood cells. **pus** (pus) *noun.*

push 1. To press on something in order to move it: *I **pushed** the shopping cart through the market. You have to **push** hard against that door to open it.* 2. To move forward with effort: *We had to **push** through the crowd.* 3. To work hard to do or sell something: *The senator **pushed** for the passage of tax reform. The store is **pushing** canned soup this week. Verb.*
○ A shove or strong effort to move forward or accomplish something: *They made a big **push** to finish the work by five o'clock. Noun.*
push (push) *verb,* **pushed, pushing;** *noun, plural* **pushes.**

push-up An exercise in which a person lies face down and raises and lowers the body by straightening and bending the arms while keeping the rest of the body straight. **push-up** (push′up′) *noun, plural* **push-ups.**

pussy willow A shrub that has silver-colored, furry flowers that grow on long straight branches. **pus•sy willow** (pus′ē).

put 1. To cause a thing or a person to be in a certain place, condition, or position; place; set: *Put the box on the table. Your warm smile **put** them at ease.* 2. To cause to undergo or experience: *You **put** them to a lot of trouble by being late.* 3. To apply: *We **put** our knowledge of machinery to use in repairing the engine.* 4. To state or express: *Put your question clearly.* 5. To impose;

levy: *The government **puts** a tax on cigarettes.*
• **to put off.** To delay or postpone: *Don't **put** off going to the dentist.*
• **to put on.** To present or perform: *The class **put on** a Christmas play.*
• **to put up with.** To bear patiently; endure: *My parents do not **put up with** yelling in the house.*
put (put) *verb,* **put, putting.**

putty A soft material that is like clay and that is used to fill cracks in wood or plaster, or to fasten panes of glass to window frames. **put•ty** (put′ē) *noun.*

puzzle 1. Something that confuses: *It is a **puzzle** to me how you got here so fast.* 2. A toy, game, or other object that presents a problem to solve: *We tried to fit together the pieces of the **puzzle**. Noun.*
○ 1. To confuse or be hard to understand: *The arithmetic problem **puzzled** me. The twins' strange behavior **puzzled** their friends.* 2. To think hard in order to answer or solve something: *I **puzzled** over the last question. Verb.*
puz•zle (puz′əl) *noun, plural* **puzzles;** *verb,* **puzzled, puzzling.**

The pyramids of Egypt are among the marvels of the world.

pyramid 1. An object that has triangular sides that meet at a point at the top. Its base is usually square. 2. **the Pyramids.** Huge stone structures that are in the shape of a pyramid. The Pyramids were built in ancient Egypt as royal tombs. **pyr•a•mid** (pir′ə mid′) *noun, plural* **pyramids.**

python A large snake that coils around its prey and suffocates it. **py•thon** (pī′thon) *noun, plural* **pythons.**

The letter Q often sounds like K, as in liquid and unique.

Notice that Q almost never appears in English without being followed by u or ue.

q, Q The seventeenth letter of the alphabet. **q, Q** (kū) *noun, plural* **q's, Q's.**

qt. An abbreviation for **quart** or **quarts.**

quack¹ The harsh, flat sound that a duck makes. *Noun.*

○ To make the sound that a duck makes. *Verb.* **quack** (kwak) *noun, plural* **quacks;** *verb,* **quacked, quacking.**

quack² A dishonest person pretending to be a doctor or an expert: *The quack claimed that the tonic of sugar and water would cure the flu. Noun.*

○ Relating to or like a quack: *Don't follow quack advice on how to invest your money. Adjective.* **quack** (kwak) *noun, plural* **quacks;** *adjective.*

quadrilateral A design or figure having four sides and four angles. A square and a rectangle are quadrilaterals. **quad·ri·lat·er·al** (kwod′rə lat′ər əl) *noun, plural* **quadrilaterals.**

quadruped An animal that has four feet. **quad·ru·ped** (kwod′rə ped′) *noun, plural* **quadrupeds.**

quadruple To make or become four times as great: *The population of the city quadrupled in just ten years. We plan to quadruple the size of our garden.* **quad·ru·ple** (kwo drü′pəl) *verb,* **quadrupled, quadrupling.**

quadruplet 1. One of four children or animals born at the same time to the same mother. 2. A group of four. **quad·ru·plet** (kwo drü′plit) *noun, plural* **quadruplets.**

quahog A round clam that has a thick shell. It lives in shallow waters along the Atlantic coast of North America and is used for food. **qua·hog** (kwô′hôg′ or kwô′hog′) *noun, plural* **quahogs.**

A quail is a very shy bird.

quail A bird that has a plump body and brown or gray feathers often dotted with white. **quail** (kwāl) *noun, plural* **quail** or **quails.**

quaint Pleasant or attractive in an old-fashioned or amusing way: *the narrow streets of a quaint old village.* **quaint** (kwānt) *adjective,* **quainter, quaintest.** —**quaintly** *adverb* —**quaintness** *noun.*

A quake can cause serious damage to roads.

quake To shake or tremble: *The kitten quaked with terror when it first went outside. The thunder made the house quake. Verb.*

○ 1. A trembling or shaking: *We felt a quake as the train went by.* 2. A shaking or trembling of

601

the ground; earthquake: *There was a small quake last night.* Look up **earthquake** for more information. *Noun.*

quake (kwāk) *verb,* **quaked, quaking;** *noun,* *plural* **quakes.**

Quaker A member of a Christian religion founded by George Fox in England around 1650. **Quak·er** (kwā′kər) *noun, plural* **Quakers.**

qualification 1. Something that makes a person or thing fit for a job: *The ability to swim well is one of the qualifications for the job of lifeguard.* 2. Something that limits or restricts: *You are, without qualification, the best tennis player I know.* **qual·i·fi·ca·tion** (kwol′ə fi kā′shən) *noun, plural* **qualifications.**

qualified 1. Meeting the requirements; fit: *a well-qualified candidate for the job.* 2. Limited; restricted: *The teacher gave qualified approval to the plan for a class party.* **qual·i·fied** (kwol′ə fīd) *adjective.*

qualify 1. To make or be fit for something: *Their years of experience qualify them to go on the difficult hike.* 2. To limit or restrict: *I qualified my statement that children like the circus with the word "usually."* 3. To limit the meaning of; modify: *Adjectives can qualify nouns, and adverbs can qualify verbs, adjectives, and other adverbs.* **qual·i·fy** (kwol′ə fī′) *verb,* **qualified, qualifying.**

quality 1. Something that makes a person or thing what it is: *You have all the qualities needed for success. The most obvious quality of water is wetness.* 2. Degree of excellence: *meat of the highest quality.* **qual·i·ty** (kwol′i tē) *noun, plural* **qualities.**

qualm 1. A feeling that something is bad or wrong: *The suspect had no qualms about lying to the police.* 2. A sudden feeling of doubt or uneasiness: *I had qualms about being away from home for the first time.* **qualm** (kwäm) *noun, plural* **qualms.**

quantity 1. A number or amount: *The recipe calls for a small quantity of milk.* 2. A large number or amount: *Restaurants buy food in quantity.* **quan·ti·ty** (kwon′ti tē) *noun, plural* **quantities.**

quarantine The keeping of a person, animal, or thing away from others to stop the spreading of a disease: *The camper with chicken pox was put in quarantine to keep the disease from spreading to anyone else. Noun.*

○ To put a person or thing in quarantine: *During the cruise, the passengers with measles were quarantined. Verb.*

quar·an·tine (kwôr′ən tēn′) *noun, plural* **quarantines;** *verb,* **quarantined, quarantining.**

quarrel An angry argument or disagreement: *The children had a quarrel about whose turn it was to wash the dishes. Noun.*

○ 1. To have an angry argument or disagreement: *We quarreled about who would ride the bicycle first.* 2. To find fault: *I won't quarrel with your decision. Verb.*

quar·rel (kwôr′əl) *noun, plural* **quarrels;** *verb,* **quarreled, quarreling.**

quarry A place where stone is cut or blasted out. **quar·ry** (kwôr′ē) *noun, plural* **quarries.**

quart A unit of measure that equals 2 pints, or 1/4 of a gallon. A quart is slightly less than a liter. **quart** (kwôrt) *noun, plural* **quarts.**

quarter 1. One of four equal parts: *We divided the pie into quarters. Three months is a quarter of a year.* 2. A coin of the United

Quarries **supply stone for use in building.**

States and Canada equal to twenty-five cents or 1/4 of a dollar. **3.** The moment at the end of each fourth of an hour: *I left the house at **quarter** after seven.* **4.** One of four periods of about seven days each that together make up the time it takes for the moon to revolve around the earth; phase. **5.** One of the four equal time periods into which certain games are divided. **6.** A section or district: *Their house was in the old **quarter** of the city.* **7.** **quarters.** A place to live or stay: *The soldiers' **quarters** were at the edge of the base. Noun.*
○ **1.** To divide into four equal units: *I **quartered** the pie.* **2.** To give a place to live: *The soldiers are **quartered** in tents. Verb.*
quar·ter (kwôr′tər) *noun, plural* **quarters**; *verb,* **quartered, quartering.**

quarterback The football player who leads the team when they are trying to score. A quarterback usually throws the passes. **quar·ter·back** (kwôr′tər bak′) *noun, plural* **quarterbacks.**

quarterly Happening or done once every three months: *The bank pays **quarterly** interest on my savings account. Adjective.*
○ Once every three months: *That magazine is published **quarterly**. Adverb.*
quar·ter·ly (kwôr′tər lē) *adjective; adverb.*

quartet **1.** A musical piece written for four singers or musicians. **2.** A group of four singers or musicians performing together. **3.** Any group of four people or things. **quar·tet** (kwôr tet′) *noun, plural* **quartets.**

quartz A kind of clear, hard rock. It is the main ingredient of sand. **quartz** (kwôrts) *noun.*

Quartz is the most common mineral.

quasar A heavenly body similar to a star. Quasars send out huge quantities of light or of very powerful radio waves. **qua·sar** (kwā′zär *or* kwā′sär) *noun, plural* **quasars.**

quay A landing place for boats or ships, usually made of stone.
Another word that sounds like this is **key.**

quay (kē) *noun, plural* **quays.**

queasy **1.** Feeling sick to one's stomach: *I felt **queasy** after the roller coaster ride.* **2.** Feeling uneasy or worried: *I was **queasy** about the math test.* **quea·sy** (kwē′zy) *adjective,* **queasier, queasiest.** —**queasily** *adverb* —**queasiness** *noun.*

Que. An abbreviation for **Quebec.**

Quebec A province in eastern Canada. Its capital is also called Quebec. **Que·bec** (kwi bek′) *noun.*

queen **1.** The wife or widow of a king. **2.** A woman who rules a kingdom. A woman usually becomes queen because she is related to the ruler before her and usually rules until she dies. **3.** A woman who is beautiful or outstanding: *People call that singer the **queen** of jazz.* **4.** A female bee or other insect that lays eggs. **5.** A playing card that has a picture of a queen. **6.** The most powerful piece in the game of chess. **queen** (kwēn) *noun, plural* **queens.**

Queen Elizabeth II reigns over the United Kingdom.

queer Different from what is normal or usual; strange; peculiar: *My classmate has some **queer** ideas about studying.* **queer** (kwir) *adjective,* **queerer, queerest.** —**queerly** *adverb* — **queerness** *noun.*

quench **1.** To put an end to by satisfying: *I **quenched** my thirst with iced tea.* **2.** To make something stop burning; put out; extinguish: *I **quenched** the fire.* **quench** (kwench) *verb,* **quenched, quenching.**

query A question: *Any **queries** from the audience may be put to the speaker after the speech is over. Noun.*
○ **1.** To ask about: *They **queried** my reasons for quitting.* **2.** To express doubt about: *The teacher **queried** the facts in my report. Verb.*
que·ry (kwir′ē) *noun, plural* **queries**; *verb,* **queried, querying.**

quest A search or pursuit: *The explorers went in **quest** of gold.* **quest** (kwest) *noun, plural* **quests.**

PRONUNCIATION KEY:

| at | āpe | fär | câre | end | mē | it | īce | pierce | hot | ōld | sông | fôrk |
| oil | out | up | ūse | rüle | pull | tûrn | chin | sing | shop | thin | this | |

hw in white; zh in treasure. The symbol ə stands for the unstressed vowel sound in about, taken, pencil, lemon, and circus.

603

question 1. Something asked to get an answer or find out something: *The tourist asked us questions about our town.* 2. A matter to be talked over: *The meeting dealt with the question of who would be the next president of the club.* 3. Doubt; uncertainty: *My friend is, without question, the best student in the class.* Noun.
○ 1. To ask questions of or about: *The police questioned the witness to the robbery.* 2. To express doubt about: *I question the truth of your story.* Verb.
ques·tion (kwes′chən) *noun, plural* **questions**; *verb,* **questioned, questioning.**

question mark A punctuation mark (?) that is used at the end of a question or at the end of an interrogative sentence.

questionnaire A printed list of questions used for gathering information from people or for finding out their opinions. **ques·tion·naire** (kwes chə nâr′) *noun, plural* **questionnaires.**

quetzal A bird of Central America that has a bright red breast and a shiny green head, back, and long, drooping tail. **quet·zal** (ket säl′) *noun, plural* **quetzals.**

quick 1. Done or happening in a short time; fast: *a quick trip to the store.* 2. Thinking, learning, or reacting easily and rapidly: *a quick mind.* **quick** (kwik) *adjective,* **quicker, quickest.** —**quickly** *adverb* —**quickness** *noun.*

SYNONYMS

quick, fast, rapid
We had time for only a quick visit. Both sisters are fast runners. The students made rapid progress in learning to use the computers.

quicksand Very deep, wet sand. A person or thing that moves or stands on quicksand will sink into it. **quick·sand** (kwik′sand′) *noun.*

quiet 1. Making little or no noise; without noise: *It is always very quiet in the library.* 2. With little or no disturbance or motion; not busy; peaceful: *Our family spent a quiet weekend at home.* *Adjective.*
○ The condition of being quiet: *I enjoy the peace and quiet of my own room.* Noun.
○ To make or become quiet: *The baby-sitter quieted the crying baby.* Verb.
qui·et (kwī′it) *adjective,* **quieter, quietest**; *noun*;

verb, **quieted, quieting.** —**quietly** *adverb* —**quietness** *noun.*

quill 1. A large, stiff feather. 2. A pen made from the hollow stem of a feather. 3. One of the sharp spines of a porcupine or other animal. **quill** (kwil) *noun, plural* **quills.**

quilt A bed covering made of two pieces of cloth and stuffed with soft material. The two pieces of cloth are held together by lines of stitching sewn all over the surface of the cloth. *Noun.*
○ 1. To make a quilt or quilts. 2. To stitch together with a soft lining. *Verb.*
quilt (kwilt) *noun, plural* **quilts**; *verb,* **quilted, quilting.** —**quilted** *adjective* —**quilting** *noun.*

Making quilts is an American folk art.

quintuplet 1. One of five children or animals born at the same time to the same mother. 2. A group of five. **quin·tu·plet** (kwin tup′lit) *noun, plural* **quintuplets.**

quit 1. To stop doing something: *I quit reading to go for a walk.* 2. To go away from; leave: *I quit my job for a new one.* 3. To give up or stop trying: *You refused to quit, even though you knew you couldn't win the race.* **quit** (kwit) *verb,* **quit** or **quitted, quitting.**

quite 1. Very much or completely: *The sign made it quite clear which road to take.* 2. Really; actually: *Climbing the mountain was quite an achievement.* **quite** (kwīt) *adverb.*

quiver¹ To shake slightly; shiver: *The leaves quivered in the breeze.* Verb.
○ The act or motion of quivering: *There was a quiver in my voice before I started to cry.* Noun.

quiv·er (kwiv′ər) *verb*, **quivered, quivering**; *noun*, *plural* **quivers**.

quiver² A case for holding arrows. **quiv·er** (kwiv′ər) *noun*, *plural* **quivers**.

quiz A short or informal test: *The teacher gave us a spelling quiz today. Noun.*
○ To question: *The class was quizzed on last week's work. Verb.*
quiz (kwiz) *noun*, *plural* **quizzes**; *verb*, **quizzed, quizzing**.

quota A certain share or amount due to or from a person, group, or organization: *Each soldier received a daily quota of rations.* **quo·ta** (kwō′tə) *noun*, *plural* **quotas**.

quotation 1. A person's words repeated exactly by another person: *The book began with a quotation from the Bible.* 2. The act of quoting. **quo·ta·tion** (kwō tā′shən) *noun*, *plural* **quotations**.

quotation mark One of a pair of punctuation marks (" ") used mainly to indicate the beginning and end of a quotation.

quote To repeat the exact words of: *The newspaper quoted the mayor's speech. Verb.*
○ A quotation. *Noun.*
quote (kwōt) *verb*, **quoted, quoting**; *noun*, *plural* **quotes**.

quotient A number obtained by dividing one number by another: *If you divide 12 by 4, the quotient is 3.* **quo·tient** (kwō′shənt) *noun*, *plural* **quotients**.

In 12 ÷ 6 = **2** or 6/$\frac{2}{12}$
2 is the **quotient**.
In 9 ÷ 3 = **3** or 3/$\frac{3}{9}$
3 is the **quotient**.

PRONUNCIATION KEY:
at ape far care end rule me it ice pierce hot old song fork
oil out up use rule pull turn chin sing shop thin this
hw in white; zh in treasure. The symbol ə stands for the unstressed vowel sound in about, taken, pencil, lemon, and circus.

605

r, R The eighteenth letter of the alphabet.
• **the three R's.** Reading, writing, and arithmetic. The idiom *the three R's* originated in the humorous spelling reading, 'riting, and 'rithmetic. **r, R** (är) *noun, plural* **r's, R's.**

rabbi A teacher of the Jewish religion and usually the leader of a Jewish congregation. **rab·bi** (rab′ī) *noun, plural* **rabbis.**

WORD HISTORY

The word rabbi comes from a Hebrew word meaning "my master." The word was used as a term of respect for the leader of a synagogue.

rabbit 1. A small animal that has long ears, a short tail, and soft fur. Rabbits live in burrows that they dig in the ground. 2. A hare. 3. The fur of the rabbit. **rab·bit** (rab′it) *noun, plural* **rabbits.**

rabies A disease that is caused by a virus and can affect people, dogs, bats, and all other warm-blooded animals. People get rabies if they are bitten by an animal that already has the disease and almost always die of it if they are not treated. **ra·bies** (rā′bēz) *noun.*

raccoon A small animal with brownish gray fur. It has a pointed face with black markings that look like a mask and a long, bushy tail marked with black rings. Raccoons live in wooded areas near water and feed at night on plants, fish, and other foods. **rac·coon** (ra kün′) *noun, plural* **raccoons.**

SPELLING HINTS

The letter R has only one sound in English, but it can be spelled in several different ways. R in words such as red, river, parent, more, and wear;

> rr in berry and merry;
> rh in rhyme;
> wr in wrong.

The letter R also combines with other vowels to make special sounds. These can be found at the Spelling hints for A, E, I, O, and U.

race¹ 1. A contest to find out who is fastest: *Our horse won the race.* 2. Any contest: *There are three candidates in the race for governor.* Noun.
∘ 1. To take part in a contest of speed; be in a race against: *The two children raced each other to school.* 2. To move or go very fast: *I raced down the stairs to the door.* 3. To cause to move or go too fast: *The driver raced the engine of the car.* Verb.
race (rās) *noun, plural* **races;** *verb,* **raced, racing.**

race² A very large group of people having certain physical characteristics in common. These characteristics are passed on from one generation to another. **race** (rās) *noun, plural* **races.**

racer 1. A person, animal, or vehicle that competes in races: *That horse is a fine racer.* 2. Any of a group of American snakes that moves very quickly. **rac·er** (rā′sər) *noun, plural* **racers.**

racetrack An area used for racing. **race·track** (rās′trak′) *noun, plural* **racetracks.**

racial Of or relating to a race of human beings: *Racial prejudice is prejudice against people because of their race.* **ra·cial** (rā′shəl) *adjective.*
—**racially** *adverb.*

racism Thought, words, or action based on the belief that one human race is better or worse than another race; racial prejudice. **rac·ism** (rā′siz əm) *noun.* —**racist** *noun, adjective.*

rack A frame or stand for hanging, storing, or showing things: *The store had many racks of suits.* Noun.
∘ To cause great pain or suffering to: *The injured victim was racked with pain.* Verb.
rack (rak) *noun, plural* **racks;** *verb,* **racked, racking.**

racket¹ 1. A loud or confusing noise: *I could hardly hear what you were saying because of the racket in the bus.* 2. A dishonest plan or way to get money from someone. **rack·et** (rak′it) *noun, plural* **rackets**.

racket² A round or oval frame with a network of strings and a thin handle. Rackets are usually made of wood or metal and are used to hit the ball in tennis and other games. **rack·et** (rak′it) *noun, plural* **rackets**.

racquetball A game in which two or four players use short rackets to hit a small ball off the floor, walls, and ceiling of an enclosed court. **rac·quet·ball** (rak′it bôl′) *noun.*

radar A device used to find and track objects such as aircraft and automobiles. It uses reflected radio waves. **ra·dar** (rā′där) *noun.*

WORD HISTORY

The word **radar** is short for *radio detecting and ranging.* It is made up of the first two letters of radio and the beginning letter of each of the other three words.

radiant 1. Shining brightly; beaming: *We shielded our eyes from the radiant summer sun. The child's face was radiant from the excitement.* 2. Given off in waves or made up of waves: *The warmth we get from the sun is radiant heat.* **ra·di·ant** (rā′dē ənt) *adjective.* —**radiantly** *adverb.*

radiate 1. To give off rays: *The lamp radiated light through the room.* 2. To be given off in rays: *Heat and light radiate from the sun.* 3. To move or branch outward from a center: *Many spokes radiated from the hub of the bicycle wheel.* 4. To show: *Your face radiates happiness.* **ra·di·ate** (rā′dē āt′) *verb,* **radiated, radiating.**

radiation Energy given off in the form of waves or very tiny particles; radiant energy. **ra·di·a·tion** (rā′dē ā′shən) *noun.*

radiator 1. A device for heating a room, made up of a series of pipes through which steam or hot water passes. 2. A device for cooling something. The radiator in a car's engine holds and cools a liquid that is passed through the engine. **ra·di·a·tor** (rā′dē ā′tər) *noun, plural* **radiators.**

radical 1. Involving or affecting the most important part; basic: *Moving from the country to the city caused a radical change in my life.* 2. Favoring extreme changes or reforms: *radical political beliefs. Adjective.*
○ A person who favors extreme changes or reforms. *Noun.*
rad·i·cal (rad′i kəl) *adjective; noun, plural* **radicals.** —**radically** *adverb.*

WORD HISTORY

The word **radical** comes from a Latin word meaning "root" or "origin." Something that is radical affects even the roots of a problem or situation.

radii A plural of radius: *Measure the radii of these two circles.* **ra·di·i** (rā′dē ī′) *plural noun.*

radio 1. A way of sending messages, programs, or music through the air without wires. 2. A device for receiving or sending such sounds. *Noun.*
○ To send a message to or report by radio: *The pilot radioed the airport for permission to land. Verb.*
ra·di·o (rā′dē ō′) *noun, plural* **radios;** *verb,* **radioed, radioing.**

radioactive Of, caused by, or having radioactivity: *Uranium is radioactive.* **ra·di·o·ac·tive** (rā′dē ō ak′tiv) *adjective.* —**radioactively** *adverb.*

radioactivity The giving off of energy in the form of rays. The rays are given off during a process in which atoms of one element split apart. **ra·di·o·ac·tiv·i·ty** (rā′dē ō ak tiv′i tē) *noun.*

radish The small, thick, red or white root of a plant. Radishes have a strong, sharp taste and are usually eaten raw in salads. **rad·ish** (rad′ish) *noun, plural* **radishes.**

radium A white metal that is highly radioactive. Radium is a chemical element. **ra·di·um** (rā′dē əm) *noun.*

radius 1. A line going from the center to the outside of a circle or sphere. 2. A circular area measured by the length of its radius: *There are no houses within a three mile radius of the farm.* **ra·di·us** (rā′dē əs) *noun, plural* **radii** or **radiuses.**

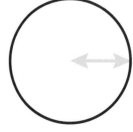

radius

PRONUNCIATION KEY:

| at | āpe | fär | câre | end | mē | it | īce | pierce | hot | ōld | sông | fôrk |
| oil | out | up | ūse | rüle | pull | tûrn | chin | sing | shop | thin | this | |

hw in white; zh in treasure. The symbol ə stands for the unstressed vowel sound in about, taken, pencil, lemon, and circus.

607

radon A heavy, radioactive gas found in soil and rocks and produced by the element radium. Doctors use radon to treat cancer. Radon is a chemical element. **ra·don** (rā′don) *noun*.

raft A kind of flat boat made of logs or boards fastened together. **raft** (raft) *noun, plural* **rafts**.

rag **1.** A small piece of cloth usually made of worn or torn material. **2. rags.** Old clothing that is torn or worn out. **rag** (rag) *noun, plural* **rags**.

rage 1. Violent anger: *Those spoiled children go into a rage if they can't have what they want.* **2.** A fad; fashion: *Floppy hats were the rage last year. Noun.*
○ To talk or act in a violent way: *The storm raged along the coast. Verb.*
rage (rāj) *noun, plural* **rages**; *verb*, **raged, raging**.

ragged 1. Worn or torn into rags: *a stained and ragged jacket.* **2.** Wearing torn or worn out clothing: *a ragged beggar.* **3.** Rough and uneven: *Ragged cliffs rose over the beach.* —**rag·ged** (rag′id) *adjective.* —**raggedly** *adverb.*

ragweed A common weed whose pollen is a cause of hay fever. **rag·weed** (rag′wēd′) *noun, plural* **ragweeds**.

raid A sudden, surprise attack: *The soldiers left quietly at dawn to go on a raid. Noun.*
○ To make a raid on: *Enemy troops raided the village during the night. Verb.*
raid (rād) *noun, plural* **raids**; *verb*, **raided, raiding**.

rail 1. A long, narrow bar of wood or metal, used as a guard or support. The long metal bars on which a train rides are rails. **2.** A railroad: *My parents prefer traveling by rail to driving a car.* **rail** (rāl) *noun, plural* **rails**.

railing A fence or barrier made of a rail or rails: *Hold onto the railing when you go down the stairs.* **rail·ing** (rā′ling) *noun, plural* **railings**.

railroad 1. The metal tracks on which a train runs: *The railroad runs near our house.* **2.** All the tracks, stations, and cars that are part of a system of transportation by rail: *That railroad has been in operation since 1872.* Another word for this is railway. **rail·road** (rāl′rōd′) *noun, plural* **railroads**.

railway 1. A railroad. **2.** The tracks on which a train runs. **rail·way** (rāl′wā′) *noun, plural* **railways**.

rain 1. Water that falls in drops from clouds to the earth. **2.** A falling of rain; storm or shower: *Don't go out in the rain without an umbrella.* **3.** A heavy or rapid fall of anything: *A rain of rice hit the*

bride and groom as they left the church. *Noun.*
○ **1.** To fall in drops of water: *We put off our picnic because it rained.* **2.** To fall or pour like rain: *Bullets rained on the soldiers. Verb.*
Other words sounding like this are **reign** and **rein.**
   • **to rain out.** To cancel or postpone because of rain: *The game was rained out.*
rain (rān) *noun, plural* **rains**; *verb*, **rained, raining**.

The moisture supplied by rain
helps flowers grow.

rainbow A curve of colored light seen in the sky, caused by the sun's shining through tiny drops of water in the air. **rain·bow** (rān′bō′) *noun, plural* **rainbows**.

raincoat A waterproof coat that keeps a person dry when it is raining. **rain·coat** (rān′kōt′) *noun, plural* **raincoats**.

raindrop A drop of rain. **rain·drop** (rān′drop′) *noun, plural* **raindrops**.

A rainbow is made up
of seven colors.

rainfall The amount of rain, snow, sleet, or hail that falls on an area in a certain period of time: *The yearly rainfall here is 30 inches.* **rain·fall** (rān′fôl′) *noun, plural* **rainfalls**.

rain forest A dense forest that receives a large amount of rain during the year.

rainy Having much rain: *It is important to drive carefully in* **rainy** *weather.* **rain•y** (rā′nē) *adjective,* **rainier, rainiest.**

raise **1.** To move or cause to move to a higher position, place, degree, or amount: *I* **raised** *my arm above my head. My parents* **raised** *my allowance.* **2.** To cause to rise or appear: *The bee-sting* **raised** *a bump on the child's arm.* **3.** To gather together; collect: *The town* **raised** *the money for a new school.* **4.** To take care of and help to grow: *They* **raise** *cattle on their ranch.* **5.** To ask or bring up: *He* **raised** *an interesting question.* **6.** To build: *A new house was* **raised** *on that empty lot.* **7.** To stir up; bring about: *Someone was* **raising** *a commotion in the hall. Verb.*

○ An increase in amount: *a pay* **raise** *of twenty dollars a week. Noun.*

raise (rāz) *verb,* **raised, raising;** *noun, plural* **raises.**

raisin A sweet, dried grape. **rai•sin** (rā′zin) *noun, plural* **raisins.**

rake A tool that has a long handle with teeth or prongs attached at one end. It is used to gather leaves or hay together or to smooth down earth. *Noun.*

○ **1.** To gather or smooth with a rake: *We* **raked** *the fallen leaves.* **2.** To search carefully: *I* **raked** *through my desk for a pen. Verb.*

rake (rāk) *noun, plural* **rakes;** *verb,* **raked, raking.**

rally **1.** To bring or come together for a purpose: *The farmers* **rallied** *to rebuild the burned barn.* **2.** To come to the aid or support of a person or thing: *My friends* **rallied** *behind me when I was teased.* **3.** To recover strength, energy, or health: *With the doctor's help, the patient began to* **rally.** *Verb.*

○ A meeting for a purpose: *a political* **rally.** *Noun.*

ral•ly (ral′ē) *verb,* **rallied, rallying;** *noun, plural* **rallies.**

ram **1.** A male sheep. **2.** A device used to batter, crush, or force something: *The firefighters used a* **ram** *to break down the door. Noun.*

○ **1.** To strike or strike against with great force: *In the train wreck one train* **rammed** *into another.* **2.** To force or drive down or into something: *The*

worker **rammed** *the post into the ground. Verb.* **ram** (ram) *noun, plural* **rams;** *verb,* **rammed, ramming.**

A ram **has long, curved horns.**

RAM Memory in a computer that can be added to or changed by the person using the computer. The computer uses this memory to store and retrieve information quickly. RAM stands for *random-access memory.* **RAM** (ram) *noun.*

Ramadan The ninth month of the Muslim calendar. During Ramadan, people fast daily between dawn and sunset. **Ra•ma•dan** (rom′ə don) *noun.*

ramble **1.** To wander about; roam: *We* **rambled** *through the fields.* **2.** To talk or write in a confused way: *The speaker* **rambled** *on and never came to the point. Verb.*

○ A pleasant stroll or walk. *Noun.*

ram•ble (ram′bəl) *verb,* **rambled, rambling;** *noun, plural* **rambles.**

ramp A sloping platform or passageway connecting two different levels. **ramp** (ramp) *noun, plural* **ramps.**

ramrod **1.** A rod used to ram the gunpowder down the barrel of a gun that is loaded through the muzzle. **2.** A rod used to clean the barrel of a gun. **ram•rod** (ram′rod′) *noun, plural* **ramrods.**

ran Past tense of **run:** *We were so late that we* **ran** *all the way to school.* **ran** (ran) *verb.*

ranch A large farm on which large herds of cattle, sheep, and horses are raised. *Noun.*

PRONUNCIATION KEY:

at   āpe   fär   câre   end   mē   it   īce   pîerce   hot   ōld   sông   fôrk
oil   out   up   ūse   rüle   pull   tûrn   chin   sing   shop   thin   this
hw in white; zh in treasure. The symbol ə stands for the unstressed vowel sound in about, taken, pencil, lemon, and circus.

609

To manage or work on a ranch. *Verb.*
ranch (ranch) *noun, plural* **ranches;** *verb,*
ranched, ranching.

WORD HISTORY

The word **ranch** comes from a Spanish word that
means "a camp" or "a small farm." Today a ranch is
often a very large estate.

---

random   Made or done with no clear pattern; made
or done by chance: *The teacher made a* **random**
choice of three students to pass out the books.
   • **at random.** With no pattern or method: *I
picked up a magazine* **at random** *from the pile.*
ran·dom (ran′dəm) *adjective.* —**randomly**
adverb.

rang   Past tense of **ring:** *The mail carrier* **rang**
the doorbell twice, but no one was home. **rang**
(rang) *verb.*

range   1. The distance or extent between certain
limits: *There is a* **range** *in ticket prices from $7
to $20.* 2. The distance or area over which some-
thing can travel or extend: *Our* **range** *of vision
was limited by the fog.* 3. A place set aside for
shooting practice or for testing rockets: *The
police officers practiced shooting on the pistol*
range. 4. A large area of land on which livestock
roam and graze: *The cowhands rounded up the
cattle on the open* **range.** 5. A row or series of
mountains: *A* **range** *of mountains rises from the
coastline.* 6. A large stove having burners and an
oven. 7. The extent of the tones that can be produced by a particular singing voice or musical
instrument. *Noun.*
   ○ 1. To go between certain limits: *The prices for
those bicycles* **range** *from one hundred to two
hundred dollars.* 2. To wander or roam: *Cattle*
ranged *over the prairie.* 3. To stretch out or
extend in some direction: *The hills* **range** *west
from the shore. Verb.*
range (rānj) *noun, plural* **ranges;** *verb,* **ranged,
ranging.**

ranger   1. A person whose work is looking after
and guarding a forest or other natural area.
2. A member of a group of armed people who
go through an area to keep law and order.
ran·ger (rān′jər) *noun, plural* **rangers.**

rank¹   1. A position or grade: *The soldier was promoted to the* **rank** *of sergeant. I have a high rank*
in my class. 2. High position or grade: *The governor is a person of* **rank.** 3. **ranks.** The common
soldiers of an army. *Noun.*
   ○ 1. To put in or have a certain position or grade:
The students were **ranked** *according to their
grades.* 2. To arrange in a row or rows: *The students were* **ranked** *for the fire drill. Verb.*
rank (rangk) *noun, plural* **ranks;** *verb,* **ranked,
ranking.**

rank²   1. Having a strong, bad smell or taste: *The
cheese became* **rank** *after a week.* 2. Complete;
extreme: *a* **rank** *coward.* **rank** (rangk) *adjective,*
ranker, rankest.

ransom   1. The release of a captive in return for
payment of money: *The ambassador was kidnapped and was being held for* **ransom.** 2. The
amount of money paid or demanded before a
captive is set free. *Noun.*
   ○ To pay money for a captive to be set free. *Verb.*
ran·som (ran′səm) *noun, plural* **ransoms;** *verb,*
ransomed, ransoming.

rap¹   A quick, sharp knock or tap: *We heard a* **rap**
on the window. Noun.
   ○ To knock or tap sharply: *I* **rapped** *on the door
but there was no answer. Verb.*
Another word that sounds like this is **wrap.**
rap (rap) *noun, plural* **raps;** *verb,* **rapped,
rapping.**

rap²   A kind of music in which words are spoken,
often in verses that rhyme, to the rhythm of background music with a strong beat.
Another word that sounds like this is **wrap.**
rap (rap) *noun.* —**rapper** *noun.*

rapid   Very quick; fast: *The train went at a* **rapid**
pace. Adjective.
   ○ **rapids.** A part of a river where the water flows
very fast: *It was dangerous to go over the* **rapids**
in a canoe. Noun.
rap·id (rap′id) *adjective; plural noun.* —**rapidity**
noun —**rapidly** *adverb.*

rapture   Great happiness, delight, or joy; ecstasy:
We stared in **rapture** *at the beautiful scenery.*
rap·ture (rap′chər) *noun.*

rare¹   1. Not often happening, seen, or found:
Thunderstorms are **rare** *at this time of year.*
2. Unusually fine; excellent: *The cliffs have a*
rare *beauty.* 3. Not dense; thin: *The air is* **rare**
at high altitudes. **rare** (râr) *adjective,* **rarer,
rarest.** —**rarity** *noun.*

rare² Cooked for only a short time: *rare hamburgers*. **rare** (râr) *adjective*, **rarer**, **rarest**.

rarely Not often; seldom: *We rarely go to the movies*. **rarely** (râr′lē) *adverb*.

rascal 1. A mischievous person: *That pup is a real rascal*. 2. A dishonest person; rogue. **ras•cal** (ras′kəl) *noun*, *plural* **rascals**.

rash¹ Too hasty; not careful: *a rash decision*. **rash** (rash) *adjective*, **rasher**, **rashest**. —**rashly** *adverb* —**rashness** *noun*.

rash² A condition in which red spots appear on the skin: *Poison ivy causes a rash*. **rash** (rash) *noun*, *plural* **rashes**.

rasp To make a harsh, grating sound: *The iron gate rasped on the rusty hinges*. *Verb*.
○ A harsh, grating sound: *I spoke with a rasp because I had a sore throat*. *Noun*.
rasp (rasp) *verb*, **rasped**, **rasping**; *noun*, *plural* **rasps**.

raspberry A small, sweet fruit of a prickly plant. Raspberries are usually red or black. **rasp•ber•ry** (raz′ber′ē) *noun*, *plural* **raspberries**.

rat 1. A rodent that looks like a large mouse. A rat has a long nose, round ears, and a long, thin tail. 2. A mean or dishonest person. **rat** (rat) *noun*, *plural* **rats**.

rate 1. An amount or number measured against the amount or number of something else: *The car was going at a rate of 60 miles per hour*. 2. The price or charge for something: *Telephone rates went up last year*. 3. A rank or class: *Your school work has always been of the first rate*. *Noun*.
○ 1. To consider; regard: *My friend rated the movie as very good*. 2. To place in or have a certain class or rank: *Our team is rated first in its league*. *Verb*.
rate (rāt) *noun*, *plural* **rates**; *verb*, **rated**, **rating**.

rather 1. More willingly: *I would rather stay home than go out tonight*. 2. More properly; instead: *Our team rather than theirs deserved to win*. 3. More correctly: *The airplane is landing at noon or, rather, at 12:10 P.M.* 4. Somewhat: *It is rather cold today*. **rath•er** (rath′ər) *adverb*.

ratify To agree to officially; approve: *Congress ratified the trade agreement*. **rat•i•fy** (rat′ə fī′) *verb*, **ratified**, **ratifying**. —**ratification** *noun*.

ratio A comparison in number or quantity between two things. The ratio is the number or times the second thing can be divided into the first thing: *If there are 12 girls and 6 boys in a class, the ratio of girls to boys is 2 to 1*. **ra•ti•o** (rā′shē ō′) *noun*, *plural* **ratios**.

ration A fixed portion or share, especially of food: *The mountain climber carried rations in a pack*. *Noun*.
○ 1. To give out in portions: *Supplies were rationed to victims of the flood*. 2. To limit to fixed portions: *The government rationed meat during the war*. *Verb*.
ra•tion (rash′ən *or* rā′shən) *noun*, *plural* **rations**; *verb*, **rationed**, **rationing**.

rational 1. Based on reason or logic; sensible: *rational arguments*. 2. Able to think or think clearly: *Humans are rational animals*. **ra•tion•al** (rash′ə nəl) *adjective*. —**rationally** *adverb*.

rattle 1. To make or cause to make a series of short, sharp sounds: *The windows rattled from the wind*. 2. To talk or say quickly: *My classmate rattled off the names of all the states*. 3. To confuse or embarrass: *I was rattled by the question*. *Verb*.
○ 1. A series of short, sharp sounds: *We could tell by the rattle of the doorknob that someone was trying to get into the room*. 2. A baby's toy or other thing that makes a rattling noise when it is shaken. *Noun*.
rat•tle (rat′əl) *verb*, **rattled**, **rattling**; *noun*, *plural* **rattles**.

rattlesnake A poisonous American snake. A rattlesnake has a number of horny rings at the end of its tail that rattle when shaken by the snake. **rat•tle•snake** (rat′əl snāk′) *noun*, *plural* **rattlesnakes**.

rave 1. To talk in a wild or crazy way: *A high fever caused the patient to rave*. 2. To talk with much or too much enthusiasm:

**A rattlesnake rattles its
tail as a warning.**

PRONUNCIATION KEY:
at āpe fär câre end mē it īce pierce hot ōld sông fôrk
oil out up ūse rüle pull tûrn chin sing shop thin this
hw in white; zh in treasure. The symbol ə stands for the unstressed vowel sound in about, taken, pencil, lemon, and circus.

611

They **raved** about their new car. **rave** (rāv) verb, **raved, raving.**

ravel To separate into loose threads; fray: Pulling the piece of yarn made my sweater **ravel.** **rav•el** (rav′əl) verb, **raveled, raveling.**

raven A bird that looks like a large crow. Noun. ○ Shiny and black: **raven** hair. Adjective. **ra•ven** (rā′vən) noun, plural **ravens;** adjective.

ravenous Very hungry. **rav•e•nous** (rav′ə nəs) adjective. —**ravenously** adverb.

ravine A deep, narrow valley. **ra•vine** (rə vēn′) noun, plural **ravines.**

ravioli Little packets of pasta filled with meat, cheese, or spinach, boiled and served with sauce. **rav•i•o•li** (rav ē ō′lē) plural noun.

raw 1. Not cooked: **raw** carrots. 2. Not treated or processed; natural: Milk before it is pasteurized is **raw.** 3. Not trained or experienced: **raw** recruits. 4. Having the skin rubbed off: My heel was **raw** from my new shoe. 5. Damp and cold: **raw** weather. **raw** (rô) adjective, **rawer, rawest.**

rawhide The hide of cattle that has not been tanned: boots made of **rawhide.** **raw•hide** (rô′hīd′) noun.

ray¹ 1. A narrow beam of light or other radiant energy: The sun's **rays** shone brightly. 2. One of a group of lines or parts coming from a center: The arms of a starfish are **rays.** 3. A very small amount: There was only a **ray** of hope for the lost sailors. **ray** (rā) noun, plural **rays.**

ray² A fish that has a broad, flat body, broad fins, and a skeleton made of cartilage. **ray** (rā) noun, plural **rays.**

rayon A fiber or cloth made from cellulose. **ray•on** (rā′on) noun.

razor A device with a sharp blade used for shaving or for cutting hair. **ra•zor** (rā′zər) noun, plural **razors.**

re- A prefix that means: 1. Again: **Reelect** means to elect again. 2. Back: **Recall** means to call back.

LANGUAGE NOTE

A word formed with **re-** is written with a hyphen if it is spelled the same way as another word with a different meaning. For example, the word **re-cover** means to cover again, but **recover** means to get something back again. The hyphen helps to tell the words apart.

reach 1. To arrive at; come to: We finally **reached** the cabin after walking for two miles through the woods. 2. To touch or grasp: I can't **reach** the top shelf. 3. To stretch or extend: The draperies **reached** from the ceiling to the floor. 4. To stretch the arm or hand out: I **reached** across the table for the salt. 5. To try to grasp something: I **reached** into my pocket for my keys. 6. To get in touch with; contact: I tried to **reach** you by phone. Verb. ○ 1. The distance covered in reaching: Someone with a long **reach** can get that box off the closet shelf. 2. As much as a person can do or understand: Victory was within our **reach.** 3. The act of reaching: With a **reach** of my arm I pulled the apple from the tree. 4. A stretch of something; extent: vast **reaches** of desert. Noun. **reach** (rēch) verb, **reached, reaching;** noun, plural **reaches.**

SYNONYMS

reach, achieve, gain, attain
Our class **reached** its goal of reading 300 books. She **achieved** her ambition of becoming an astronaut. You can **gain** valuable experience as a volunteer. He **attained** his diploma through hard work.

react To act because something has happened; respond: My friend **reacted** to the good news by smiling. **re•act** (rē akt′) verb, **reacted, reacting.**

reaction An action in response to something that has happened or has been done: What was your parents' **reaction** when they saw your report card? **re•ac•tion** (rē ak′shən) noun, plural **reactions.**

reactor A device that produces atomic energy for making electricity. It splits atoms without causing an atomic explosion. **re•ac•tor** (rē ak′tər) noun, plural **reactors.**

read 1. To look at and understand the meaning of something written: I learned to **read** in first grade. 2. To say aloud something written: The teacher **read** a story to the class. 3. To learn by reading: Do you like to **read** about horses? 4. To get the meaning of; understand: My parents seem to be able to **read** my thoughts. 5. To give or show; register: The thermometer **read** 70 degrees.
Another word that sounds like this is **reed.**
read (rēd) verb, **read** (red), **reading.**

The word **read** goes back to Old English and originally meant "to think or consider." Later it came to mean "to figure out the meaning of." This use of read led to the meaning "to discover the meaning of something written" and finally to our modern use of read.

readily 1. In a prompt and willing way: *I readily followed my parents' advice.* 2. Without difficulty; easily: *The story was readily understood by everyone in the class.* **read·i·ly** (red′ə lē) *adverb.*

reading 1. The act of looking at and understanding something written: *I prefer reading to sports.* 2. The act of saying aloud something written: *The writer gave a reading of a new poem.* 3. Something read or to be read: *This book is interesting reading.* 4. The information shown on a meter: *The gas company took a reading from our meter.* **read·ing** (rē′ding) *noun, plural* **readings.**

ready 1. Prepared for use or action: *When I finish packing I'll be ready for the trip.* 2. Willing: *I am ready to work hard.* 3. Likely to do something: *The dynamite was ready to explode.* 4. Quick; prompt: *They had a ready answer for the question.* 5. Easy to get at: *ready cash for an emergency. Adjective.*
○ To make ready; prepare: *The mechanics ready the plane before it can take off. Verb.*
read·y (red′ē) *adjective,* **readier, readiest;** *verb,* **readied, readying.**

real 1. Actual or true; not imagined: *Our adventures were real; we did not make them up.* 2. Genuine; not imitation: *These flowers are real, not plastic.* **re·al** (rē′əl *or* rēl) *adjective.*

Real is an adjective, so it modifies a noun or pronoun: Is that a *real* arrowhead? Ghosts are not *real*. **Really** is an adverb, so it modifies a verb, an adjective, or another adverb: Did you *really* go to the beach? I was *really* tired. The plane traveled *really* fast.

real estate Land together with the buildings, trees, water, and other things on it.

realistic 1. Showing people, things, or events as they appear in everyday life: *a realistic painting.* 2. Tending to see and accept things as they are; practical: *You need to be realistic about your chances of winning.* **re·al·is·tic** (rē′ə lis′tik) *adjective.* —**realistically** *adverb* —**realism** *noun.*

reality 1. The state or quality of being real: *Some people doubted the reality of the story.* 2. Something real: *Their dream of owning a house became a reality.* **re·al·i·ty** (rē al′i tē) *noun, plural* **realities.**

realization 1. The act of understanding completely: *The realization that we were lost made us anxious.* 2. Something made real: *Buying their own house was the realization of their dreams.* **re·al·i·za·tion** (rē′ə lə zā′shən) *noun, plural* **realizations.**

realize 1. To understand completely: *I didn't realize how late it was.* 2. To make real: *Years of saving money helped us to realize our dream of owning a house.* **re·al·ize** (rē′ə līz′) *verb,* **realized, realizing.**

really 1. In fact; actually: *Although we argue, we are really good friends.* 2. Truly; very: *We spent a really pleasant afternoon.* See Language Note at *real.* **real·ly** (rē′ə lē *or* rē′lē) *adverb.*

realm 1. A kingdom. 2. An area or field of interest, knowledge, or power: *I enjoy almost everything in the realm of science.* **realm** (relm) *noun, plural* **realms.**

reap 1. To cut down and gather; harvest: *The workers used sickles to reap the grain.* 2. To cut down or harvest a crop from: *The farmer reaped the fields.* 3. To get as a reward: *The child's good behavior reaped high praise.* **reap** (rēp) *verb,* **reaped, reaping.**

reappear To come into sight again; be seen again: *It stopped raining and the sun reappeared.* **re·ap·pear** (rē′ə pîr′) *verb,* **reappeared, reappearing.** —**reappearance** *noun.*

rear[1] 1. The part behind or in the back: *I sat in the rear of the car.* 2. The part of a military force farthest from the fighting area. *Noun.*
○ At or in the back: *the rear door. Adjective.*
rear (rîr) *noun, plural* **rears;** *adjective.*

rear[2] 1. To take care of and help to grow up: *My grandparents reared three children.* 2. To go up on the back legs: *The frightened horse reared.* 3. To lift up: *The lion reared its head.* **rear** (rîr) *verb,* **reared, rearing.**

rearrange To arrange again, especially in a different way. **re·ar·range** (rē′ə rānj′) *verb,* **rearranged, rearranging.** —**rearrangement** *noun.*

PRONUNCIATION KEY:
at   āpe   fär   câre   end   mē   it   īce   pierce   hot   ōld   sông   fôrk
oil   out   up   ūse   rüle   pùll   tûrn   chin   sing   shop   thin   this
hw in white; zh in treasure. The symbol ə stands for the unstressed vowel sound in about, taken, pencil, lemon, and circus.

613

reason **1.** A cause or motive: *I have no reason to doubt you.* **2.** A statement that explains something; excuse: *I could give no reason for being late.* **3.** The ability to think clearly: *The shock made me lose all reason. Noun.*
○ **1.** To think or think about clearly: *I reasoned out the answer to the arithmetic problem.* **2.** To try to change a person's mind: *It is useless to reason with them. Verb.*
rea•son (rē′zən) *noun, plural* **reasons**; *verb,* **reasoned, reasoning.**

reasonable **1.** Showing or using good sense and thinking; not foolish: *Reasonable people listen to both sides of an argument.* **2.** Not asking too much; fair: *a reasonable request.* **3.** Not too expensive: *The price was reasonable.*
rea•son•a•ble (rē′zə nə bəl *or* rēz′nə bəl) *adjective.*
—reasonably *adverb.*

reasoning **1.** The process of drawing conclusions from facts; clear and sensible thinking: *To do well in mathematics, you must be good at reasoning.* **2.** Reasons or arguments: *I don't agree with your reasoning.* **rea•son•ing** (rē′zə ning *or* rēz′ning) *noun.*

reassure To restore confidence or courage in: *Before the curtain rose, the director reassured the actors.* **re•as•sure** (rē′ə shùr′) *verb,* **reassured, reassuring. —reassurance** *noun.*

rebate A return of part of an amount paid: *The company is offering a $50 rebate to customers who buy their computers.* **re•bate** (re′bāt) *noun, plural* **rebates.**

rebel **1.** A person who fights against or will not obey authority: *The rebels attacked the palace.* **2.** Rebel. A soldier who fought against the North in the Civil War. *Noun.*
○ **1.** To fight against authority: *The teenagers rebelled at being ordered around.* **2.** To feel or show great dislike: *The sick child rebelled against taking the medicine because it tasted bad. Verb.*
reb•el (reb′əl *for noun;* ri bel′ *for verb) noun, plural* **rebels**; *verb,* **rebelled, rebelling.**

WORD HISTORY

The word **rebel** goes back to a Latin word that means "to make war again." The word was used to talk about people who had been conquered in war and started another war against the people who had beaten them.

rebellion **1.** An armed fight against one's government: *The American Revolution was a rebellion by the colonists against the British.* **2.** A struggle against any authority. **re•bel•lion** (ri bel′yən) *noun, plural* **rebellions. —rebellious** *adjective.* **—rebelliously** *adverb.*

recall **1.** To bring back to mind; remember: *Her face is familiar, but I don't recall her name.* **2.** To take or order back: *The auto manufacturer recalled the defective cars. Verb.*
○ The act of recalling: *I have little recall of the book because I read it so long ago. Noun.*
re•call (ri kôl′ *for verb;* ri kôl′ *or* rē′kôl′ *for noun) verb,* **recalled, recalling**; *noun, plural* **recalls.**

recapture **1.** To catch or capture again: *The police recaptured the escaped prisoner.* **2.** To bring back to mind; recall: *They tried to recapture their childhood by visiting their birthplace.* **re•cap•ture** (rē kap′shər) *verb,* **recaptured, recapturing.**

recede To move back or away: *The waves receded from the shore.* **re•cede** (ri sēd′) *verb,* **receded, receding.**

receipt **1.** A written statement showing that a package, mail, or money has been received: *The clerk gave me a receipt for my purchase.* **2.** receipts. The amount of money received: *The store's receipts for the week were over $1,000.* **3.** A receiving or being received: *We thanked them on receipt of their gift.* **re•ceipt** (ri sēt′) *noun, plural* **receipts.**

receive **1.** To take or get: *I received a watch for my birthday.* **2.** To greet or welcome: *The host received the guests at the door.* **re•ceive** (ri sēv′) *verb,* **received, receiving.**

receiver **1.** A person or thing that receives. **2.** A device that changes electrical impulses or radio waves into pictures or sounds. The part of a telephone that you hold to your ear is a receiver. **re•ceiv•er** (ri sē′vər) *noun, plural* **receivers.**

recent Done, made, or happening not long ago: *the most recent news.* **re•cent** (rē′sənt) *adjective.* **—recently** *adverb.*

receptacle An object used to hold something; container: *We use a large metal can as a receptacle for garbage.* **re•cep•ta•cle** (ri sep′tə kəl) *noun, plural* **receptacles.**

reception **1.** The act or way of receiving: *The play got a warm reception from the audience.* **2.** A party or gathering where guests are received.

3. The quality of the sound of a radio or the sound and picture of a television: *The new antenna improved our television's reception.* **re·cep·tion** (ri sep′shən) *noun, plural* **receptions**.

recess 1. A time during which work or other activity stops: *We played baseball during recess at school.* 2. A part of a wall set back from the rest; niche. 3. A hidden place or part: *Many thoughts are buried in the recesses of our minds. Noun.*
○ To stop work or other activity for a time: *The trial started again after the court had recessed for lunch. Verb.*
re·cess (rē′ses *for noun* ri ses′ *for verb*) *noun, plural* **recesses**; *verb,* **recessed, recessing**.

recipe A list of ingredients and instructions for making something to eat or drink. **rec·i·pe** (res′ə pē′) *noun, plural* **recipes**.

WORD HISTORY

The word **recipe** comes from a Latin word that means "Take!" Doctors wrote this word in prescriptions to tell a druggist to "take" certain drugs and combine them to make the medicine.

---

recital 1. A performance or concert of music or dance: *a piano recital.* 2. A story or account: *Your recital of your experiences in Africa was interesting.* **re·cit·al** (ri sī′təl) *noun, plural* **recitals**.

These members of a dance class are giving a recital.

recite 1. To repeat something from memory: *Can you recite the names of all the fifty states?* 2. To tell the story of: *I recited my adventures at camp to the class.* 3. To repeat a lesson or answer ques-

tions in class: *The teacher asked me to recite.* **re·cite** (ri sīt′) *verb,* **recited, reciting**.

reckless Not careful: *It was reckless of them to have skated out onto the thin ice.* **reck·less** (rek′lis) *adjective.* —**recklessly** *adverb* —**recklessness** *noun.*

reckon 1. To count or calculate: *Income tax is reckoned according to the amount of money a person makes.* 2. To think or consider: *I reckon my best friend to be the smartest student in the class.* **reck·on** (rek′ən) *verb,* **reckoned, reckoning**. —**reckoning** *noun.*

recline To lean back; lie down: *I reclined on the sofa.* **re·cline** (ri klīn′) *verb,* **reclined, reclining**.

recognition 1. A recognizing or being recognized. 2. An accepting of something as being true, right, or valid: *They demanded recognition of their rights as citizens.* 3. Favorable attention or notice: *That band has gained recognition.* **rec·og·ni·tion** (rek′əg nish′ən) *noun.*

recognize 1. To know and remember from before; identify: *I didn't recognize you at first.* 2. To understand and accept as being true, right, or valid: *We recognized our duty to report the crime to the police.* **rec·og·nize** (rek′əg nīz′) *verb,* **recognized, recognizing**.

recollect To remember; recall: *I cannot recollect their address at the moment.* **re·col·lect** (rek′ə lekt′) *verb,* **recollected, recollecting**.

recommend 1. To speak in favor of: *The librarian recommended this book.* 2. To advise; suggest: *The nurse recommended that I stay home until my cold was better.* 3. To make acceptable or pleasing: *Your excellent skills recommend you for this job.* **rec·om·mend** (rek′ə mend′) *verb,* **recommended, recommending**. —**recommendation** *noun.*

record 1. A written account of something: *The school keeps a record of each student's attendance.* 2. All the facts about what a person, group, or thing has done: *Your school record is excellent.* 3. A performance or act that is better than all others: *The runner set a new record for the event.* 4. A disk on which recorded music or other sounds is played back on a phonograph. *Noun.*
○ 1. To set down in writing: *I recorded my thoughts in my diary.* 2. To indicate or show: *This thermometer records temperatures up to 120*

PRONUNCIATION KEY:

| at | āpe | fär | câre | end | mē | it | īce | pierce | hot | ōld | sông | fôrk |
| oil | out | up | ūse | rüle | pull | tûrn | chin | sing | shop | thin | this | |

hw in white; zh in treasure. The symbol ə stands for the unstressed vowel sound in about, taken, pencil, lemon, and circus.

615

degrees. **3.** To put music or other sounds on a phonograph record or a magnetic tape. *Verb.* **rec·ord** (rek′ərd) *noun, plural* records; **re·cord** (ri kôrd′) *verb,* **recorded, recording.**

recorder **1.** A person whose job is taking notes and keeping records. **2.** A machine that records sound on magnetic tape. **3.** A musical instrument similar to a flute, usually made of wood or hard plastic. **re·cord·er** (ri kôr′dər) *noun, plural* **recorders.**

recording **1.** A CD, phonograph record, or magnetic tape: *I have a new recording of that song.* **2.** The sound recorded on a CD, phonograph record, or magnetic tape: *The quality of the recording is poor.* **re·cord·ing** (ri kôr′ding) *noun, plural* **recordings.**

recover **1.** To get back: *The police recovered the two missing bicycles.* **2.** To make up for: *We took the short route to recover lost time.* **3.** To return to a normal condition or position: *My friend is recovering from the measles.* **re·cov·er** (ri kuv′ər) *verb,* **recovered, recovering.**

re-cover To cover again: *After the chair's cover was worn out, we re-covered it.* **re-cov·er** (rē kuv′ər) *verb,* **re-covered, re-covering.**

recovery The act of recovering: *I was given a reward for my recovery of the lost wallet. The patient made a speedy recovery.* **re·cov·er·y** (ri kuv′ə rē) *noun, plural* **recoveries.**

recreation Something done for amusement or relaxation, such as sports, games, and hobbies. **rec·re·a·tion** (rek′rē ā′shən) *noun, plural* **recreations.** **—recreational** *adjective.*

recruit **1.** A newly enlisted soldier or sailor. **2.** A new member of a group or organization. *Noun.*
○ To get to join: *The coach recruited players for the baseball team. Verb.* **re·cruit** (ri krüt′) *noun, plural* **recruits;** *verb,* **recruited, recruiting.**

rectangle A figure with four sides that

This was a popular recruiting poster during World War I.

has four right angles. A square is a rectangle whose four sides are equal. **rec·tan·gle** (rek′tang′gəl) *noun, plural* **rectangles.** **—rectangular** *adjective.*

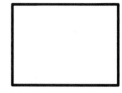

rectangle

recuperate To get better after being sick: *It took me weeks to recuperate from pneumonia.* **re·cu·per·ate** (ri kü′pə rāt′ *or* ri kū′pə rāt′) *verb,* **recuperated, recuperating. —recuperation** *noun.*

recur To happen or appear again: *The pain recurs every time I lift something heavy.* **re·cur** (ri kûr′) *verb,* **recurred, recurring. —recurrence** *noun* **—recurrent** *adjective.*

recycle To make fit to be used again: *Our city recycles cans and bottles.* **re·cy·cle** (rē sī′kəl) *verb,* **recycled, recycling.**

red **1.** The color of blood. **2.** Something having this color: *They used a bright red to paint the fire engine. Noun.*
○ **1.** Having the color red. **2.** Blushing: *red with embarrassment. Adjective.*
A word sounding like this is the past tense verb **read.**
 • **in the red.** Losing or owing money: *Our business was not a success, and we found ourselves in the red.*
 • **to see red.** To be or become very angry: *Those people were so nasty that I saw red.*
red (red) *noun, plural* **reds;** *adjective,* **redder, reddest.**

red blood cell A cell in the blood that picks up oxygen in the lungs and carries it to the cells and tissues of the body.

redcoat A British soldier during the American Revolution and other wars of that period. At those times, a red coat was part of the British military uniform. **red·coat** (red′kōt′) *noun, plural* **redcoats.**

Red Cross An international organization whose main purpose is to take care of victims of war and of floods, fires, earthquakes, and other disasters.

redeem **1.** To exchange something for money, a prize, or merchandise: *I redeemed the coupon for free French fries.* **2.** To make up for; save: *The team redeemed the poor first half of the season by winning the rest of their games.* **re·deem** (ri dēm′) *verb,* **redeemed, redeeming.**

—**redemption** *noun*.

red-handed In the act of doing something wrong: *The police caught them red-handed.* **red-hand·ed** (red′hand′id) *adjective*.

reduce **1.** To make or become less or smaller in size, number, or degree: *The store reduced its prices.* **2.** To bring to a lesser form, condition, or position: *The forest was reduced to ashes by the fire.* **re·duce** (ri düs′ *or* ri dūs′) *verb*, **reduced, reducing**.

reduction **1.** The act of reducing or the state of being reduced: *The reduction of the speed limit resulted in fewer traffic accidents.* **2.** The amount by which something is reduced: *The store is offering a 10-percent reduction on summer clothes.* **re·duc·tion** (ri duk′shən) *noun*, *plural* **reductions**.

redwood One of the largest trees in the world. It is evergreen and has thick reddish brown bark. Its wood is used as timber. Redwoods grow along the western coast of North America. **red·wood** (red′wŭd′) *noun*, *plural* **redwoods**.

reed **1.** A tall grass having long, narrow leaves and jointed stems. Reeds usually grow in marshes. **2.** A thin piece of wood, reed, metal, or plastic used in some musical instruments. A reed makes a sound when air passes over it and makes it vibrate. Reeds are found in wind instruments. Another word that sounds like this is **read**. **reed** (rēd) *noun*, *plural* **reeds**.

reef A ridge of sand, rock, or coral at or near the surface of the ocean. **reef** (rēf) *noun*, *plural* **reefs**.

reek A strong, bad smell: *the reek of cigarette smoke.* Another word that sounds like this is **wreak**. **reek** (rēk) *noun*, *plural* **reeks**. —**reek** *verb*.

reel¹ **1.** A spool or similar device on which something is wound. **2.** The amount of film or other material wound on a reel. *There are two reels of film left.* *Noun*.

Fishing line, motion picture film, and magnetic tape are wound on reels.

○ **1.** To wind on a reel: *The sailor reeled the rope.* **2.** To pull by winding a line on a reel: *My friend reeled in a huge swordfish.* *Verb*.

• **to reel off**. To say or write quickly and easily: *I reeled off all the answers.*

reel (rēl) *noun*, *plural* **reels**; *verb*, **reeled, reeling**.

reel² **1.** To be thrown off balance; stagger: *I reeled when someone ran into me.* **2.** To turn or seem to turn around and around: *The merry-go-round ride made my head reel.* **reel** (rēl) *verb*, **reeled, reeling**.

reel³ A lively folk dance performed by two or more couples who form two lines facing each other. **reel** (rēl) *noun*, *plural* **reels**.

reelect To elect again: *The president was reelected for four more years.* **re·e·lect** (rē′i lekt′) *verb*, **reelected, reelecting**. —**reelection** *noun*.

reentry **1.** An entering again. **2.** The return of a spacecraft or missile from space into the earth's atmosphere. **re·en·try** (rē en′trē) *noun*, *plural* **reentries**.

ref A short form of **referee**. **ref** (ref) *noun*, *plural* **refs**.

refer **1.** To send or direct to someone or something: *The doctor referred me to a specialist.* **2.** To turn to for help or information: *The speaker referred to written notes.* **3.** To call or direct attention: *The speaker referred to a movie I had not seen.* **4.** To turn over to someone else: *The teacher will refer the problem to the principal.* **re·fer** (ri fûr′) *verb*, **referred, referring**.

referee An official in certain sports and games who enforces the rules. *Noun*.

○ To act as a referee in: *Our teacher refereed the hockey game.* *Verb*.

ref·er·ee (ref′ə rē′) *noun*, *plural* **referees**; *verb*, **refereed, refereeing**.

reference **1.** A statement that calls or directs attention to something: *The authors made a reference to their other book.* **2.** A person or thing referred to; source of information: *The encyclopedia was the reference for my report.* **3.** A statement about a person's ability or character: *I have good references from the people I worked for.* **4.** Connection; relation: *I am writing to you in reference to your letter of last week.* **ref·er·ence** (ref′ər əns *or* ref′rəns) *noun*, *plural* **references**.

PRONUNCIATION KEY:

| at | āpe | fär | câre | end | mē | it | īce | pierce | hot | ōld | sông | fôrk |
| oil | out | up | ūse | rüle | pŭll | tûrn | chin | sing | shop | thin | this | |

hw in white; zh in treasure. The symbol ə stands for the unstressed vowel sound in about, taken, pencil, lemon, and circus.

617

reference book A book that has information arranged in an orderly, convenient way. Dictionaries, encyclopedias, atlases, and almanacs are reference books.

refill To fill again: *The hiker refilled the canteen with water. Verb.*
○ Something that replaces the material that first filled a container: *I had to buy a refill for my pen when it ran out of ink. Noun.*
re•fill (rē fil′ *for verb;* rē′fil′ *for noun*) *verb,* **refilled, refilling;** *noun, plural* **refills.**

refine To make fine and pure: *Crude oil is refined before it can be used for gasoline.* **re•fine** (ri fīn′) *verb,* **refined, refining.**

reflect 1. To turn or throw back: *Sand reflects light and heat from the sun.* 2. To give back an image of something: *I saw myself reflected in the pond.* 3. To think seriously or carefully: *I often reflect on what I have done.* 4. To bring blame or discredit: *Your actions reflect on your character.* 5. To bring or give back as a result: *Their brave acts reflected honor upon their families.* 6. To show or express: *Your clothes reflect your good taste.* **re•flect** (ri flekt′) *verb,* **reflected, reflecting.**

Sometimes it is hard to tell which is the reflection and which is the real thing.

reflection 1. An image given back by a reflecting surface: *I looked at my reflection in the mirror.* 2. Something that is reflected: *The reflection of the sun on the car windshield made the driver squint.* 3. Serious or careful thinking: *Upon reflection, I decided to take the job.* 4. A statement or idea that results from careful thinking: *What are your reflections on the problem?* 5. Something that shows or expresses something else: *My smile was a reflection of my happiness.*

6. Something that causes blame or discredit: *My parents think my behavior is a reflection on them.* **re•flec•tion** (ri flek′shən) *noun, plural* **reflections.**

reflector A device or surface that throws back light, heat, or sound: *My bicycle is easy to see at night because it has reflectors.* **re•flec•tor** (ri flek′tər) *noun, plural* **reflectors.**

reforest To plant trees on land that was once a forest to replace those that have been cut down or destroyed by fire. **re•for•est** (rē fôr′ist *or* rē for′ist) *verb,* **reforested, reforesting.**

reform 1. To make a change for the better in; correct; improve: *The government tried to reform the prison system.* 2. To become better: *The criminal promised to reform and live an honest life. Verb.*
○ A change for the better: *The town planned several reforms in the schools. Noun.*
re•form (ri fôrm′) *verb,* **reformed, reforming;** *noun, plural* **reforms.**

refrain A part of a song or poem that is repeated several times. **re•frain** (ri frān′) *noun, plural* **refrains.**

refresh To make fresh again; revive: *The cold drink refreshed us after the hike. I have to read my notes to refresh my memory.* **re•fresh** (ri fresh′) *verb,* **refreshed, refreshing.**

refreshment 1. Food or drink: *What refreshments will you serve at the party?* 2. A refreshing or being refreshed: *I needed refreshment after working all day.* **re•fresh•ment** (ri fresh′mənt) *noun, plural* **refreshments.**

refrigerate To make or keep cool or cold: *Refrigerate the meat to keep it from spoiling.* **re•frig•er•ate** (ri frij′ə rāt′) *verb,* **refrigerated, refrigerating. —refrigeration** *noun.*

refrigerator An appliance, box, or room with a cooling system, used to keep food from spoiling. **re•frig•er•a•tor** (ri frij′ə rā′tər) *noun, plural* **refrigerators.**

refuge 1. Shelter or protection from danger or trouble: *The frightened puppy took refuge under the bed.* 2. A place that gives shelter or protection: *a wildlife refuge.* **ref•uge** (ref′ūj) *noun, plural* **refuges.**

refugee A person who flees from a place to find safety or protection: *The refugees left their homeland for another country.* **ref•u•gee** (ref′yū jē′) *noun, plural* **refugees.**

refund To give or pay back. *The store refunded my money. Verb.*
○ **1.** The return of money that has been given or paid: *I returned my pants to the store for a refund.* **2.** The amount of money returned: *I got a refund of five dollars. Noun.*
re·fund (ri fund′ *for verb;* rē′fund′ *for noun*) *verb,* **refunded, refunding;** *noun, plural* **refunds.**

refuse¹ **1.** To say no to; reject: *I refused their offer of help.* **2.** To be unwilling to do, give, or allow something: *My parents refused to let me go.* **re·fuse** (ri fūz′) *verb,* **refused, refusing.** —**refusal** *noun.*

refuse² Anything thrown away as useless or worthless; trash or rubbish. **ref·use** (ref′ūs) *noun.*

regain **1.** To get back again; recover: *The dog regained its health.* **2.** To get back to: *We regained the highway after a detour.* **re·gain** (rē gān′) *verb,* **regained, regaining.**

regard **1.** To think of; consider: *I regard you as my best friend.* **2.** To look at closely: *The stranger regarded us with suspicion.* **3.** To respect or consider: *Always regard other people's feelings.* **4.** To relate to; concern: *The speech regarded plans for the new year.* **5.** To pay attention to: *We regarded our parents' warnings. Verb.*
○ **1.** Careful thought, attention, or consideration: *Have regard for others.* **2.** Respect or affection: *I hold you in high regard.* **3. regards.** Best wishes: *Give my regards to your family. Noun.*
re·gard (ri gärd′) *verb,* **regarded, regarding;** *noun, plural* **regards.**

regarding Relating to; concerning; about: *I wrote a letter to the company regarding their new product.* **re·gard·ing** (ri gär′ding) *preposition.*

regardless In spite of everything; nevertheless: *The book's expensive, but I'm going to buy it, regardless.*
• **regardless of.** In spite of: *Let's do this play, regardless of the work it will take.*
re·gard·less (ri gärd′lis) *adverb.*

regime A system of government: *The people suffered under the regime of the dictator.* **re·gime** (rə zhēm′ *or* rā zhēm′) *noun, plural* **regimes.**

regiment A military unit made up of several battalions. **reg·i·ment** (rej′ə mənt) *noun, plural* **regiments.**

region Any large area or territory: *desert regions.* **re·gion** (rē′jən) *noun, plural* **regions.** —**regional** *adjective.*

register **1.** An official list or record or a book used for this: *a guest register.* **2.** A machine that automatically records and counts: *a cash register.* **3.** An opening or a similar device that controls the passage of air in a heating or ventilating system. **4.** The range of a voice or musical instrument. *Noun.*
○ **1.** To write in a list or record: *The teacher registered the names of absent students.* **2.** To have one's name placed on a list or record: *Voters must register before they can vote.* **3.** To show or express: *Your face registered your surprise.* **4.** To show or record, as on a scale or meter: *The temperature registered 50 degrees.* **5.** To have officially recorded at the post office by paying a fee: *This mail is registered. Verb.*
reg·is·ter (rej′ə stər) *noun, plural* **registers;** *verb,* **registered, registering.**

registered nurse A nurse who has a license from a state government to practice nursing.

regret To feel sorry about: *I regret having said unkind things to my friends. Verb.*
○ **1.** A feeling of sadness or sorrow: *They felt no regret about moving.* **2. regrets.** A polite apology for turning down an invitation: *I couldn't go to the party, so I sent my regrets to the host and hostess. Noun.*
re·gret (ri gret′) *verb,* **regretted, regretting;** *noun, plural* **regrets.**

regular **1.** Normal; usual: *Our regular teacher is absent.* **2.** Happening again and again at the same time: *the regular ticking of a clock.* **3.** According to habit or usual behavior: *a regular customer.* **4.** Evenly shaped, spaced, or arranged: *The dentist said I have regular teeth.* **5.** Following a rule: *The regular ending for a plural noun is "-s" or "-es."* **reg·u·lar** (reg′yə lər) *adjective.* —**regularly** *adverb* —**regularity** *noun.*

regulate **1.** To control, manage, or set: *Valves regulate the flow of blood through your heart.* **2.** To put or keep in good working order: *The jeweler regulated my watch to make it keep better time.* **reg·u·late** (reg′yə lāt′) *verb,* **regulated, regulating.**

PRONUNCIATION KEY:

| at | āpe | fär | câre | end | mē | it | īce | pierce | hot | ōld | sông | fôrk |
| oil | out | up | ūse | rüle | pull | tûrn | chin | sing | shop | thin | this | |

hw in white; zh in treasure. The symbol ə stands for the unstressed vowel sound in about, taken, pencil, lemon, and circus.

619

The word **regulate** comes from a Latin word meaning "a rule" or "a standard." When you *regulate* something, you put it in order according to rules or standards.

regulation 1. A law, rule, or order: *Smoking is against school regulations.* 2. The act of regulating or the state of being regulated: *A thermostat controls the regulation of heat in the building.* **reg·u·la·tion** (reg′yə lā′shən) *noun, plural* **regulations.**

rehearsal A practicing in order to prepare for a performance: *The actors had many rehearsals before the play opened.* **re·hears·al** (ri hûr′səl) *noun, plural* **rehearsals.**

rehearse To practice or train for a performance: *The dancers rehearsed the ballet. The director rehearsed the actors until they knew all their lines.* **re·hearse** (ri hûrs′) *verb,* **rehearsed, rehearsing.**

reign 1. The period of time that a monarch rules: *during Queen Victoria's reign.* 2. The power or rule of a monarch: *The people lived in peace under the reign of the new king. Noun.*
○ 1. To hold or have the power of a monarch: *The queen reigned for nearly sixty years.* 2. To be widespread; exist everywhere: *Peace reigned for many years. Verb.*
Other words that sound like this are **rain** and **rein.** **reign** (rān) *noun, plural* **reigns;** *verb,* **reigned, reigning.**

rein 1. One of two or more narrow straps attached to a bridle or bit, used to guide and control a horse. 2. Any means of control: *I kept a tight rein on my temper. Noun.*
○ To guide, control, or hold back: *The rider reined the galloping horse. Verb.*
Other words sounding like this are **rain** and **reign.** **rein** (rān) *noun, plural* **reins;** *verb,* **reined, reining.**

reindeer A large deer with a white, gray, or brown coat and branching antlers. It is found in northern regions. In some parts of the world reindeer have been tamed and used to pull sleds or are raised for their milk and meat. **rein·deer** (rān′dîr′) *noun, plural* **reindeer.**

reinforce To give more strength to by adding new or extra parts, materials, or people: *They reinforced the dam with bags of sand.* **re·in·force** (rē′in fôrs′) *verb,* **reinforced, reinforcing.** —**reinforcement** *noun.*

reject To refuse to accept, allow, or approve: *The voters rejected the tax plan.* **re·ject** (ri jekt′) *verb,* **rejected, rejecting.** —**rejection** *noun.*

rejoice To show or feel great joy: *We rejoiced at the good news.* **re·joice** (ri jois′) *verb,* **rejoiced, rejoicing.**

relapse A slipping back into a former condition: *Just when I thought I was over the flu, I had a relapse.* **re·lapse** (rē′laps′) *noun, plural* **relapses.**

relate 1. To tell the story of: *The witness related how the accident occurred.* 2. To connect or be connected in thought or meaning: *The teacher related my improved grades to better study habits. My question relates to the homework assignment.* **re·late** (ri lāt′) *verb,* **related, relating.**

related 1. Belonging to the same family: *You and your sisters, brothers, cousins, aunts, uncles, and grandparents are all related.* 2. Having some connection: *problems related to school.* **re·lat·ed** (ri lā′tid) *adjective.*

relation 1. A connection in thought, meaning, action, or condition between two or more things: *the relation between a good diet and good health.* 2. A connection or dealings between one person or thing and another: *The two countries improved their relations.* 3. A person of the same family as someone else; relative: *The young couple sent wedding invitations to all their close relations.* **re·la·tion** (ri lā′shən) *noun, plural* **relations.**

relationship The condition of being related; connection: *There was a relationship between the amount of time we rehearsed and how well we performed.* **re·la·tion·ship** (ri lā′shən ship′) *noun, plural* **relationships.**

relative Having meaning only in relation or comparison to something else: *The words "right" and "left" are relative because their meaning depends on which way a person looks at something. Adjective.*
○ A person who

The child, her parents, and grandparents are all relatives.

belongs to the same family as someone else. *Noun.*

rel•a•tive (rel′ə tiv) *adjective*; *noun, plural* **rela-tives.** —**relatively** *adverb.*

relax 1. To make or become less tense: *A hot bath helps to relax me. I like to relax by reading.* 2. To make less strict: *The principal relaxed the dress code.* **re•lax** (ri laks′) *verb,* **relaxed, relaxing.** —**relaxation**

relay A fresh set, team, or supply that replaces or relieves another: *The stagecoaches that carried mail across the plains used several relays of horses. Noun.*
  ○ To pass along: *If I'm not home, my parents will relay your message. Verb.*
  re•lay (rē′lā *for noun;* rē′lā *or* ri lā′ *for verb*) *noun, plural* **relays;** *verb,* **relayed, relaying.**

relay race A race between two or more teams. Each team member goes a certain distance and then is replaced by another team member.

release 1. To set free; let go: *The hostage was released after being held prisoner for ten days.* 2. To allow to be seen, published, or broadcast: *The film was released today. Verb.*
  ○ The act of releasing or the state of being released: *a criminal's release from prison. Noun.*
  re•lease (ri lēs′) *verb,* **released, releasing;** *noun, plural* **releases.**

relent To become less strict or harsh; to be more lenient: *My teacher relented and gave me a later deadline.* **re•lent** (ri lent′) *verb,* **relented, relenting.**

relevant Relating to what is being discussed or considered; pertinent: *Your question was relevant to our discussion.* **rel•e•vant** (rel′ə vənt) *adjective.* —**relevance** *noun.*

reliable Able to be depended on and trusted: *a reliable worker.* **re•li•a•ble** (ri lī′ə bəl) *adjective.* —**reliably** *adverb* —**reliability** *noun.*

SYNONYMS

reliable, dependable, responsible, trustworthy
This dictionary is a reliable source of information. They leave their children with a dependable baby-sitter. We need to elect a responsible person as class president. A trustworthy neighbor will look after her dog while she is away.

---

relic 1. A thing from the past: *We found arrow-heads and other Indian relics.* 2. An object belonging to a holy person. **rel•ic** (rel′ik) *noun, plural* **relics.**

relief¹ 1. The freeing from discomfort or pain; comfort: *The medicine gave me relief from my headache. It was a relief when our lost dog came home.* 2. Freedom from a job or duty: *The guard got relief at seven o'clock.* **re•lief** (ri lēf′) *noun, plural* **reliefs.**

relief² A figure or design that stands out from a flat background. **re•lief** (ri lēf′) *noun, plural* **reliefs.**

It takes great skill to carve a relief.

relief map A map that shows how high or low all the places in a certain area are.

relieve 1. To free from discomfort or pain; comfort: *The doctor gave me medicine to relieve my cough.* 2. To free from a job or duty: *The life-guards stayed on duty until they were relieved.* **re•lieve** (ri lēv′) *verb,* **relieved, relieving.**

religion 1. Belief in or worship of God, or a god or gods. 2. A particular system of belief and worship. Judaism, Christianity, Islam, and Hinduism are some of the world's major religions. **re•li•gion** (ri lij′ən) *noun, plural* **religions.**

religious 1. Showing devotion to a religion: *Are you from a religious family?* 2. Of or relating to religion: *My friend's religious beliefs are not the same as mine.* 3. Very careful and exact; strict: *The artist paid religious attention to details.* **re•li•gious** (ri lij′əs) *adjective.* —**religiously** *adverb.*

relish 1. A mixture of spices, pickles, olives, and chopped vegetables, used as a side dish and to flavor food. 2. Interest or pleasure; enjoyment: *The child opened the presents with relish. Noun.*

PRONUNCIATION KEY:

| at | āpe | fär | câre | end | mē | it | īce | pierce | hot | ōld | sông | fôrk |
| oil | out | up | ūse | rüle | pull | tûrn | chin | sing | shop | thin | this | |

hw in white; zh in treasure. The symbol ə stands for the unstressed vowel sound in about, taken, pencil, lemon, and circus.

621

○ To take pleasure in; enjoy: *We all relished the delicious holiday meal. Verb.*
rel·ish (re′lish) *noun, plural* **relishes;** *verb,* **relished, relishing.**

reluctant Unwilling: *I am reluctant to lend you the book because you seldom return what you borrow.* **re·luc·tant** (ri luk′tənt) *adjective.* —**reluctantly** *adverb* —**reluctance** *noun.*

rely To trust; depend: *You can rely on friends for help.* **re·ly** (ri lī′) *verb,* **relied, relying.** —**reliance** *noun.*

remain 1. To stay behind or in the same place: *I remained at home while my family went out.* 2. To go on being: *We remained friends for years.* 3. To be left: *All that remains of the ancient city is ruins.* **re·main** (ri mān′) *verb,* **remained, remaining.**

remainder 1. A remaining part: *I gave my friend the remainder of my sandwich.* 2. The number found when one number is subtracted from another: *If you subtract 3 from 10, the remainder is 7.* 3. The number left over when a number cannot be divided evenly: *If you divide 3 into 10, the answer is 3 with a remainder of 1.* **re·main·der** (ri mān′dər) *noun, plural* **remainders.**

remains 1. Things that are left: *The explorers found the remains of an ancient city.* 2. A dead body: *The victim's remains were buried in a local cemetery.* **re·mains** (ri mānz′) *plural noun.*

remark A short statement or comment: *The farmer made a few remarks about the weather. Noun.*
○ 1. To say briefly; comment; mention: *Our teacher remarked that we had all done well on the test.* 2. To notice; observe: *I remarked that two classmates were absent yesterday. Verb.* **re·mark** (ri märk′) *noun, plural* **remarks;** *verb,* **remarked, remarking.**

remarkable Worthy of being noticed; unusual: *Your science project is remarkable.* **re·mark·a·ble** (ri mär′kə bəl) *adjective.* —**remarkably** *adverb.*

remedy Something that heals or improves a bad condition: *The scientists hoped to discover a remedy for the common cold. Noun.*
○ To heal, improve, or get rid of: *The city government hoped to remedy the air pollution in the town. Verb.* **rem·e·dy** (rem′i dē) *noun, plural* **remedies;** *verb,* **remedied, remedying.**

remember 1. To bring back to mind; recall: *Do you remember where you left your jacket?* 2. To keep in mind carefully: *Remember to see the dentist today.* 3. To reward or present with a gift: *My parents remember all their charities once a year.* 4. To send greetings from: *Remember me to your family.* **re·mem·ber** (ri mem′bər) *verb,* **remembered, remembering.**

remind To make think of someone or something; cause to remember: *The note reminded me of her birthday.* **re·mind** (ri mīnd′) *verb,* **reminded, reminding.** —**reminder** *noun.*

remission A temporary end to the pain or other symptoms of a disease. **re·mis·sion** (ri mish′ən) *noun, plural* **remissions.**

remodel To change the design, structure, or purpose of: *The architect remodeled the store.* **re·mod·el** (rē mod′əl) *verb,* **remodeled, remodeling.**

This carpenter is helping remodel a house.

remote 1. Not near; far away: *The explorer traveled to remote regions.* 2. Far from cities or towns: *a remote mountain village.* 3. Small; slight: *There was only a remote possibility that our team would win.* **re·mote** (ri mōt′) *adjective,* **remoter, remotest.** —**remotely** *adverb* —**remoteness** *noun.*

remote control 1. The controlling of a machine or device from a distance: *Some assembly line machines are run by remote control.* 2. A device used to control a machine from a distance: *I used the remote control to change TV channels.*

removal The act of removing or the condition of being removed: *Removal of the books from the shelf took a few minutes.* **re·mov·al** (ri mü′vəl) *noun, plural* **removals.**

remove 1. To take or move away or off: *I removed my sweater because the room was warm.* 2. To do away with; get rid of: *The pilot's calm words removed our fear.* 3. To dismiss from an office or position: *The mayor was removed from office.* **re·move** (ri müv′) *verb,* **removed, removing.**

renaissance 1. A renewal or revival of something, especially in learning, art, and literature.

2. Renaissance. The revival in learning, art, and literature that began in Italy in the fourteenth century and was based on classical Latin and Greek. **ren·ais·sance** (ren′ə säns′) *noun*.

render **1.** To cause to be or become; make: *The surprise gift rendered me speechless.* **2.** To give or present; deliver: *The jury rendered a verdict of not guilty.* **ren·der** (ren′dər) *verb*, **rendered, rendering.**

rendezvous **1.** An appointment to meet at a certain place at a certain time: *The scouts made a rendezvous to meet at the camp at noon.* **2.** A place for meeting or gathering: *Our favorite rendezvous is the playground.* **ren·dez·vous** (rän′də vü′) *noun*, *plural* **rendezvous.**

renew **1.** To make new or as if new again: *The carpenter renewed the finish on the table.* **2.** To begin again: *They renewed their friendship years later.* **3.** To cause to continue for a period of time: *I renewed my subscription to the magazine.* **re·new** (ri nü′ *or* ri nū′) *verb*, **renewed, renewing. renewable** *adjective* —**renewal** *noun*.

renovate To make like new; restore: *The landlord renovated the entire building.* **ren·o·vate** (ren′ə vāt′) *verb*, **renovated, renovating.** —**renovation** *noun*.

renowned Known and honored by many people; famous: *The doctors were renowned for their successes in heart surgery.* **re·nowned** (ri nound′) *adjective*.

rent A payment for the use of something: *My parents pay the rent for our apartment. Noun.*
○ **1.** To get the right to use in return for paying rent: *We rented a car for the weekend.* **2.** To give the right to use in return for the paying of rent: *The store rents out bicycles.* **3.** To be available for renting: *The apartment rents for $500 a month. Verb.*
• **for rent.** Available for use in return for the payment of rent: *Is that apartment for rent?*
rent (rent) *noun*, *plural* **rents**; *verb*, **rented, renting.**

repair To put into good condition again; fix: *We repaired the broken lamp. Verb.*
○ **1.** The act of repairing: *The chair was beyond repair.* **2.** The condition that something is in: *a bicycle in good repair. Noun.*
re·pair (ri pâr′) *verb*, **repaired, repairing**; *noun*, *plural* **repairs.**

repay **1.** To pay or give back: *The family repaid the loan quickly.* **2.** To pay or give something back to: *You forgot to repay me for the money you borrowed.* **3.** To give, make, or do in return: *I will repay your kindness someday.* **re·pay** (ri pā′) *verb*, **repaid, repaying.** —**repayment** *noun*.

repeal To do away with officially: *Congress voted to repeal the law. Verb.*
○ The act of repealing: *The president supported the repeal of the law. Noun.*
re·peal (ri pēl′) *verb*, **repealed, repealing**; *noun*, *plural* **repeals.**

repeat To say, do, or make again: *The teacher repeated the question to the class. I am careful not to repeat my mistakes. Verb.*
○ Something that is repeated: *That television show is a repeat from last season. Noun.*
re·peat (ri pēt′) *verb*, **repeated, repeating**; *noun*, *plural* **repeats.**

repel **1.** To drive back or away: *The soldiers repelled the enemy attack.* **2.** To cause to feel dislike or disgust. **3.** To keep off or out: *This raincoat repels water.* **re·pel** (ri pel′) *verb*, **repelled, repelling.**

repellent Driving back or away; repelling: *A repellent odor drove them from the building. Adjective.*
○ Something that drives away: *an insect repellent. Noun.*
re·pel·lent (ri pel′ənt) *adjective*; *noun*, *plural* **repellents.**

repetition The act of repeating: *Repetition of numbers helps me to remember them.* **rep·e·ti·tion** (rep′i tish′ən) *noun*, *plural* **repetitions.**

replace **1.** To take or fill the place of: *Who will replace you as captain?* **2.** To get or give something similar in place of: *We replaced the broken toy.* **3.** To put back: *I replaced the book on the shelf.* **re·place** (ri plās′) *verb*, **replaced, replacing.** —**replacement** *noun*.

replay To play something back or again, especially a tape, in order to see or hear it again. *Verb.*
○ A second contest or game when the first one ended in a tie. *Noun.*
re·play (rē plā′ *for verb*, rē′plā′ *for noun*) *verb*, **replayed, replaying**; *noun*, *plural* **replays.**

PRONUNCIATION KEY:

| at | āpe | fär | câre | end | mē | it | īce | pierce | hot | ōld | sông | fôrk |
| oil | out | up | ūse | rüle | pull | tûrn | chin | sing | shop | thin | this | |

hw in white; zh in treasure. The symbol ə stands for the unstressed vowel sound in about, taken, pencil, lemon, and circus.

623

replica A scale model of something: *a replica of Christopher Columbus's ship the Niña.* **rep·li·ca** (rep′li kə) *noun, plural* **replicas.**

reply To answer in speech, writing, or action: *The mayor replied to my letter. I replied that I enjoyed the movie. Verb.*
○ Something said, written, or done in answer: *the correct reply to the question. Noun.*
re·ply (ri plī′) *verb,* **replied, replying;** *noun, plural* **replies.**

report An account, statement, or announcement, often prepared for the public: *I wrote a book report. The principal prepared a report for the school board. Noun.*
○ 1. To make or give a report of: *My neighbor reported the crime to the police.* 2. To present oneself: *Two students were asked to report to the principal. Verb.*
re·port (ri pôrt′) *noun, plural* **reports;** *verb,* **reported, reporting.**

report card A written report of a student's grades and behavior.

reporter A person whose job is to gather and report news for a newspaper, magazine, or television or radio show. **re·port·er** (ri pôr′tər) *noun, plural* **reporters.**

represent 1. To be a symbol of; stand for: *The letters of the alphabet represent sounds.* 2. To speak or act for: *Two senators represent the citizens of each state.* 3. To give a picture of: *This painting represents the artist's grandparents.* **rep·re·sent** (rep′ri zent′) *verb,* **represented, representing.**

representative 1. A person chosen to speak or act for others: *The members of Congress are our elected representatives.* 2. A person or thing characteristic of a group or kind: *The lion is a representative of the cat family. Noun.*
○ 1. Characteristic of a group or kind: *The museum has a representative collection of modern art.* 2. Made up of or based on representatives: *Congress is a representative body. Adjective.* **rep·re·sent·a·tive** (rep′ri zen′tə tiv) *noun, plural* **representatives;** *adjective.*

reproduce 1. To produce, form, or bring about again: *The tape recorder reproduced my voice.* 2. To produce offspring: *Most plants reproduce by means of seeds.* **re·pro·duce** (rē′prə düs′ or rē′prə dūs′) *verb,* **reproduced, reproducing.**

reproduction 1. The process by which living things produce offspring or others like themselves. 2. Something that is reproduced: *That picture is a reproduction of a famous painting.* **re·pro·duc·tion** (rē′prə duk′shən) *noun, plural* **reproductions.**

reptile One of a class of cold-blooded animals with a backbone. Reptiles have dry, scaly skin and move by crawling on their stomachs or creeping on short legs. Most reptiles reproduce by laying eggs. Lizards, snakes, alligators, and turtles are reptiles. **rep·tile** (rep′təl or rep′tīl) *noun, plural* **reptiles.**

republic 1. A form of government in which the authority belongs to the people. The people elect representatives to manage the government: *A republic is usually headed by a president, rather than a royal ruler.* 2. A country with such a government: *The United States is a republic.* **re·pub·lic** (ri pub′lik) *noun, plural* **republics.**

republican Of or like a republic: *The rebels overthrew the tyrant and set up a republican government. Adjective.*
○ 1. A person who believes in or supports a republic as a form of government. 2. Republican. A member of the Republican Party. *Noun.* **re·pub·li·can** (ri pub′li kən) *adjective; noun, plural* **republicans.**

Republican Party One of the two main political parties of the United States.

reputation What most people think of a person or thing: *The judge has a reputation for honesty.* **rep·u·ta·tion** (rep′yə tā′shən) *noun, plural* **reputations.**

request To ask or ask for: *I requested permission to leave early. Verb.*
○ 1. The act of asking for something: *The teacher's request for attention made the class quiet down.* 2. Something asked for: *People can call the radio station with song requests. Noun.* **re·quest** (ri kwest′) *verb,* **requested, requesting;** *noun, plural* **requests.**

require 1. To have a need of: *We all require food and sleep.* 2. To force, order, or demand: *The law requires drivers to stop at a red light.* **re·quire** (ri kwīr′) *verb,* **required, requiring.**

requirement Something that is necessary; demand or need: *Eating properly is a requirement for good health.* **re·quire·ment** (ri kwīr′mənt) *noun, plural* **requirements.**

rerun **1.** To run again: *We had to **rerun** the race.* **2.** To play again: *We **reran** the tape to hear our favorite song again. Verb.*
○ **1.** The replaying of a movie or TV show. **2.** The movie or TV show replayed.
re•run (rē run′ *for verb,* rē′run′ *for noun, verb* **reran**, **rerunning**; *noun, plural* **reruns**.

rescue To save or free: *The lifeguard **rescued** the drowning child. Verb.*
○ The act of rescuing: *a daring **rescue**. Noun.*
res•cue (res′kū) *verb,* **rescued**, **rescuing**; *noun, plural* **rescues**.

research A careful study to find and learn facts: *I did **research** in the library for my report. Noun.*
○ To do research on or for: *I **researched** my speech by reading many books on the subject. Verb.*
re•search (ri sûrch′ *or* rē′sûrch) *noun, plural* **researches**; *verb,* **researched**, **researching**.

resemblance A likeness in appearance: *There is a close **resemblance** between the two sisters.*
re•sem•blance (ri zem′bləns) *noun, plural* **resemblances**.

resemble To be like or similar to: *That hat **resembles** mine.* **re•sem•ble** (ri zem′bəl) *verb,* **resembled**, **resembling**.

resent To feel anger or bitterness at or toward: *I **resent** your unkind remark.* **re•sent** (ri zent′) *verb,* **resented**, **resenting**. —**resentful** *adjective.*

resentment A feeling of anger or bitterness: *He thinks he was treated unfairly and is filled with **resentment**.* **re•sent•ment** (ri zent′mənt) *noun, plural* **resentments**.

reservation **1.** An arrangement to have something kept for a particular person or persons: *We called the restaurant to make dinner **reservations**.* **2.** Land set aside by the government for a special purpose. Reservations have been set aside for Native American tribes to live on. Places where wild animals can live without danger of being killed are also called reservations. **3.** Something that limits or causes doubt: *I had some **reservations** about walking home alone at night.*
res•er•va•tion (rez′ər vā′shən) *noun, plural* **reservations**.

reserve **1.** To arrange to have something kept for someone or something: *My parents **reserved** rooms in a hotel.* **2.** To save or keep for a future or special purpose: *My neighbors **reserve** their weekends for gardening.* **3.** To keep for oneself: *I **reserve** the right to make up my own mind. Verb.*
○ **1.** Something saved or available for future use; supply: *The squirrel had a **reserve** of nuts for the winter.* **2.** Land used for a special purpose: *a wildlife **reserve**.* **3.** The habit of keeping one's feelings or thoughts to oneself: *My **reserve** makes it hard for me to make friends quickly.* **4.** **reserves.** The part of the armed forces kept ready for service in an emergency. *Noun.*
re•serve (ri zûrv′) *verb,* **reserved**, **reserving**; *noun, plural* **reserves**.

reserved **1.** Set apart for a person or purpose: *a **reserved** seat in the theater.* **2.** Keeping one's thoughts and feelings to oneself: *a quiet and **reserved** man.* **re•served** (ri zûrvd′) *adjective.*

The water system in many towns and cities uses water from reservoirs.

reservoir A place where water is stored.
res•er•voir (rez′ər vwär′) *noun, plural* **reservoirs**.

reside To make one's home for a long period of time: *My family **resides** in Florida.* **re•side** (ri zīd′) *verb,* **resided**, **residing**.

residence **1.** A place where a person lives: *You enter his **residence** from a side door.* **2.** A period of time spent living in a place: *After ten years' **residence** in the city, my family moved.*
res•i•dence (rez′i dəns) *noun, plural* **residences**.

resident A person who lives in a particular place: *I am a **resident** of this town.* **res•i•dent** (rez′i dənt) *noun, plural* **residents**.

PRONUNCIATION KEY:

| at | āpe | fär | câre | end | mē | it | īce | pierce | hot | ōld | sông | fôrk |
| oil | out | up | ūse | rüle | pull | tûrn | chin | sing | shop | thin | this | |

hw in white; zh in treasure. The symbol ə stands for the unstressed vowel sound in about, taken, pencil, lemon, and circus.

625

residential Relating to or suitable for residences: *A residential neighborhood does not have factories or office buildings.* **res•i•den•tial** (rez′i den′shəl) *adjective.*

resign To give up a job, position, or office: *I resigned as team captain.* **re•sign** (ri zīn′) *verb,* **resigned, resigning.**

resignation **1.** The act of resigning: *We were surprised by the treasurer's resignation.* **2.** A formal notice that a person is resigning: *I handed my resignation to my boss.* **3.** A giving in to something without complaint: *We accepted the defeat with resignation.* **res•ig•na•tion** (rez′ig nā′shən) *noun, plural* **resignations.**

resin A yellow or brown sticky substance that comes from pine and balsam trees, used especially in paints, plastics, glue, and rubber. **res•in** (rez′in) *noun, plural* **resins.**

resist **1.** To keep from giving in to: *My friend can't resist telling me secrets.* **2.** To fight against or overcome: *The country resisted attack.* **3.** To overcome the effect or action of: *This metal resists corrosion.* **re•sist** (ri zist′) *verb,* **resisted, resisting.**

resistance **1.** The act of resisting: *The soldiers put up a lot of resistance to the enemy.* **2.** The ability to overcome something: *I caught a cold because my resistance was low.* **3.** A force that opposes or works against the motion of another: *Race cars are designed to overcome air resistance.* **re•sist•ance** (ri zis′təns) *noun.*

resolution **1.** Something decided upon: *I made a resolution to stop biting my nails.* **2.** The state or quality of being determined: *They approached the difficult task with resolution.* **res•o•lu•tion** (rez′ə lü′shən) *noun, plural* **resolutions.**

resolve **1.** To decide; determine: *I have resolved to go to college.* **2.** To settle, explain, or solve: *I resolved the argument about the baseball player by looking up the statistics.* Verb.
○ Firmness of purpose; determination: *It takes resolve to do well in school.* Noun.
re•solve (ri zolv′) *verb,* **resolved, resolving;** *noun.*

resonant **1.** Able to amplify sounds or make them last longer: *The wood of a guitar is resonant.* **2.** Having a full, rich sound: *a resonant voice.* **res•o•nant** (rez′ə nənt) *adjective.*

resort To use or go to for help or protection: *I resort to my family when I'm in trouble.* Verb.
○ **1.** A place where people go for fun or relaxation: *a ski resort.* **2.** A person or thing used for help: *The dictionary is your best resort when you need information about a word.* Noun.
re•sort (ri zôrt′) *verb,* **resorted, resorting;** *noun, plural* **resorts.**

Many resorts are built along the seashore.

resound **1.** To be filled with sound: *The stadium resounded with cheers.* **2.** To make a loud, long, or echoing sound: *Thunder resounded in the air.* **re•sound** (ri zound′) *verb,* **resounded, resounding.**

resource **1.** Something used for help or support: *The library is a great resource for students.* **2.** **resources.** The wealth of a country or its way of producing wealth: *Oil is one of that country's largest natural resources.* **3.** Skill and cleverness in dealing with situations: *You showed great resource in finding enough wood for a campfire.* **4.** The action or means used in an emergency or a difficult time: *Your only resource may be to ask others for help.* **re•source** (rē′sôrs′ or ri sôrs′ or rē′zôrs′ or ri zôrs′) *noun, plural* **resources.**

respect **1.** High regard or consideration: *You must show respect for the rights of others.* **2.** A favorable opinion; admiration: *The mayor had little respect in the town.* **3.** Affectionate regard, honor, or esteem: *The twins had respect for their elders.* **4.** A special way; particular point: *In some respects, you are a better student than I am.* **5.** Relation; reference: *You show improvement with respect to grades.* **6.** **respects.** Regards or greetings: *Please give my respects to your family.* Noun.

○ To have or show honor or consideration for: *We **respect** our elders. Verb.* **re·spect** (ri spekt′) *noun, plural* respects; *verb,* **respected, respecting.**

respectable **1.** Honest and decent; having a good reputation: *respectable people.* **2.** Better than average; fairly good or large: *respectable grades.* **3.** Fit to be seen or used: *Wear a **respectable** suit to your job interview.* **re·spect·a·ble** (ri spek′tə bəl) *adjective.* —**respectably** *adverb.*

respectful Having or showing respect: *I am always **respectful** when I talk to my teacher.* (ri spekt′ful) *adjective.* —**respectfully** *adverb.*

respective Belonging to each: *The children went to their **respective** homes after school.* **re·spec·tive** (ri spek′tiv) *adjective.*

respectively Regarding each in the order given: *The train and the bus leave at 2:00 P.M. and 3:00 P.M., respectively.* **re·spec·tive·ly** (ri spek′tiv lē) *adverb.*

respiration The act or process of breathing: *Respiration is more difficult at high altitudes because the air has less oxygen.* **res·pi·ra·tion** (res′pə rā′shən) *noun.*

respiratory Relating to respiration or the organs used in respiration: *A disease that affects the lungs is a **respiratory** disease.* **res·pi·ra·to·ry** (res′pər ə tôr′ē) *adjective.*

respiratory system The system in the body made up of the lungs, the diaphragm, the windpipe, and nasal passages.

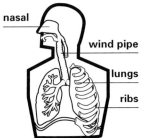

nasal

wind pipe

lungs

ribs

respiratory system

respond **1.** To give an answer: *The witness responded to the lawyer's question.* **2.** To act in return; react: *The patient responded well to the medicine.* **re·spond** (ri spond′) *verb,* **responded, responding.**

response Something said or done in answer: *What is your **response** to my question?* **re·sponse** (ri spons′) *noun, plural* **responses.**

responsibility **1.** The quality or condition of being responsible: *I feel a great deal of **responsibility** for my pet.* **2.** Something for which a person is responsible: *Setting the table is your **responsi-bility.*** **re·spon·si·bil·i·ty** (ri spon′sə bil′i tē) *noun, plural* **responsibilities.**

responsible **1.** Having as a job, duty, or concern: *I am **responsible** for collecting the class dues.* **2.** Able to be trusted; reliable: *a very **responsible** baby-sitter.* **3.** Being the main cause: *Careless driving is **responsible** for many accidents.* **4.** Involving important duties: *Being president of a bank is a **responsible** job.* **re·spon·si·ble** (ri spon′sə bəl) *adjective.* —**responsibly** *adverb.*

rest¹ **1.** A time of relaxation; stopping of activity: *The plumber took a **rest** before finishing the job.* **2.** Freedom from work or anything that disturbs; quiet: *The patient needs two more weeks' **rest** to recover.* **3.** Sleep: *I did not get enough **rest** last night.* **4.** The state of not being in motion: *The butterfly came to **rest** on the flower.* **5.** Something that acts as a support for something else: *This chair has a foot **rest**.* **6.** A silence in music. *Noun.*
○ **1.** To stop work or activity; take a rest: *The children **rested** on the porch after their game.* **2.** To be quiet or at ease: *The parents couldn't **rest** until they knew where their children were.* **3.** To support or be supported: *I **rested** my arm on the table.* **4.** To give rest to: *The rider **rested** the horse after the race.* **5.** To be directed or fixed: *The child's eyes **rested** on the cake.* **6.** To lie in death: *May they **rest** in peace. Verb.*
rest (rest) *noun, plural* **rests;** *verb,* **rested, resting.**

rest² **1.** Something left; remainder: *I ate the **rest** of the cake.* **2.** Those people or things remaining; others: *The **rest** will meet us in the park. Noun.*
○ To continue to be; remain: *The responsibility **rests** with you. Verb.*
rest (rest) *noun; verb,* **rested, resting.**

restaurant A place where food is prepared and served to customers. In some restaurants customers serve themselves. **res·tau·rant** (res′tə rənt or res′tə ränt) *noun, plural* **restaurants.**

WORD HISTORY

The word restaurant comes from a French word meaning "to restore." At a restaurant people can sit down, eat, and feel refreshed, or "restored."

---

restful **1.** Allowing or marked by rest. **2.** Peaceful; quiet. **rest·ful** (rest′fəl) *adjective.*

PRONUNCIATION KEY:
at   āpe   fär   câre   end   mē   it   īce   pîerce   hot   ōld   sông   fôrk
oil   out   up   ūse   rüle   pull   tûrn   chin   sing   shop   thin   this
hw in white; zh in treasure. The symbol ə stands for the unstressed vowel sound in about, taken, pencil, lemon, and circus.

627

restless **1.** Not able to rest: *We got **restless** during the long speech*. **2.** Not giving rest: *The patient spent a **restless** night*. **rest·less** (rest′lis) *adjective.* —**restlessly** *adverb* —**restlessness** *noun.*

restore **1.** To bring back; establish again: *The police **restored** order in the crowd*. **2.** To bring back to a former or original condition: *The old house was **restored** by its new owners*. **3.** To give or put back: *The police **restored** the bicycle to its owner*. **re·store** (ri stôr′) *verb,* **restored, restoring.** —**restoration** *noun.*

This historic document is being carefully restored.

restrain **1.** To hide or keep secret; keep in: *We tried to **restrain** our laughter*. **2.** To keep from doing something; hold back: *We **restrained** the child from running*. **re·strain** (ri strān′) *verb,* **restrained, restraining.** —**restraint** *noun.*

restrict To keep within limits: *Please **restrict** your speech to three minutes*. **re·strict** (ri strikt′) *verb,* **restricted, restricting.**

restriction **1.** Something that restricts: *There are **restrictions** on who can use the pool*. **2.** The act of restricting or the condition of being restricted: *Club membership is open to all without **restriction***. **re·stric·tion** (ri strik′shən) *noun, plural* **restrictions.**

restroom A room with toilets and sinks in a public building. **rest·room** (rest′rüm′ or rest′rüm′) *noun, plural* **restrooms.**

result Something that happens because of something else: *The accident was a **result** of carelessness. Noun.*
○ **1.** To be a result: *High grades **result** from good study habits*. **2.** To have as a result: *The lack of rain **resulted** in a poor crop. Verb.*
re·sult (ri zult′) *noun, plural* **results;** *verb,* **result-ed, resulting.**

resume **1.** To go on again after stopping: *I **resumed** talking after taking a drink*. **2.** To take again: *We **resumed** our places after recess*. **re·sume** (ri züm′) *verb,* **resumed, resuming.**

retail The sale of goods in small amounts directly to customers. *Noun.*
○ Relating to the selling of goods directly to customers: *a **retail** clothing store. Adjective.*
re·tail (rē′tāl) *noun; adjective.*

retain **1.** To continue to have or hold; keep: *The cracked jar would not **retain** water*. **2.** To keep in mind; remember: *I **retained** all the important dates of the American Revolution*. **3.** To hire the services of by paying a fee: *The family **retained** a lawyer for legal advice*. **re·tain** (ri tān′) *verb,* **retained, retaining.**

retarded Slow, especially in mental development. A retarded person cannot learn as fast or as much as most other people. **re·tard·ed** (ri tär′did) *adjective.*

retina The lining of the back of the eyeball. It is made up of several layers of cells that are sensitive to the light that enters the eye. These cells send messages to the brain, which translates the messages into pictures. **ret·i·na** (ret′ə nə) *noun, plural* **retinas.**

retire **1.** To take oneself away from a business, job, or office: *My parents plan to **retire** when they are sixty-five*. **2.** To go to bed: *We **retired** early last night*. **3.** To go away to rest or be alone: *They often **retire** to the country on weekends*. **re·tire** (ri tīr′) *verb,* **retired, retiring.**

retirement The act of retiring or the state of being retired: *They took up gardening after their **retirement** from business*. **re·tire·ment** (ri tīr′mənt) *noun, plural* **retirements.**

retreat To draw or move back: *The soldiers **retreated** to their original position. Verb.*
○ **1.** The act of retreating: *The soldiers surrendered after their **retreat***. **2.** A place in which to rest or relax: *a summer **retreat***. **3.** A signal for soldiers to retreat: ***Retreat** was sounded by the bugler. Noun.*
re·treat (ri trēt′) *verb,* **retreated, retreating;** *noun, plural* **retreats.**

retrieve **1.** To get back; recover: *The golfer **retrieved** the ball from the pond*. **2.** To find and bring back dead or wounded game: *Our dog is trained to **retrieve***. **re·trieve** (ri trēv′) *verb,* **retrieved, retrieving.** —**retrieval** *noun.*

retriever A dog trained to retrieve game for a hunter. **re·triev·er** (ri trē′vər) *noun, plural* **retrievers.**

retrorocket A small rocket attached to a larger rocket, a spacecraft, or an aircraft. It is fired in the direction opposite to the one in which the vehicle is traveling and decreases the vehicle's speed. **ret·ro·rock·et** (ret′rō rok′it) *noun.*

return **1.** To come or go back: *I returned home to get the book I had forgotten.* **2.** To happen or take place again: *Winter returns every year.* **3.** To take, bring, send, give, or put back: *I returned the book to the library.* **4.** To give or put back in the same way: *She returned my compliment by saying that my coat was nice.* **5.** To report in an official way: *The jury returned its verdict. Verb.*
○ **1.** The act of returning: *I'll call you after my return.* **2.** An official report: *I mailed my tax return on time.* **3.** An amount of money made as a profit: *The returns from the cake sale were fifty dollars. Noun.*
re·turn (ri tûrn′) *verb,* **returned, returning;** *noun, plural* **returns.**

reunion A coming or bringing together of family, friends, or other groups of people: *My class is holding its tenth reunion this year.* **re·un·ion** (rē ūn′yən) *noun, plural* **reunions.**

Some families hold a reunion every year.

reveal **1.** To make known: *Don't reveal my secret.* **2.** To show; display: *The magician opened the lid to reveal a bunny.* **re·veal** (ri vēl′) *verb,* **revealed, revealing.**

revelation **1.** The act of revealing. **2.** Something revealed, especially something unknown: *The newspaper printed surprising revelations about the candidates.* **rev·e·la·tion** (rev ə lā′shən) *noun, plural* **revelations.**

revenge Injury, harm, or punishment done to pay back a wrong: *The couple swore revenge on their attacker. Noun.*
○ To return or pay back by causing injury, harm, or punishment: *It is often wise not to try to revenge an insult. Verb.*
re·venge (ri venj′) *noun; verb,* **revenged, revenging.**

revenue **1.** Money made from property or investments. **2.** Money made by a government from taxes. **rev·e·nue** (rev′ə nü′ *or* rev′ə nū′) *noun, plural* **revenues.**

reverence A feeling of deep love and respect: *Everyone in the town had reverence for the old doctor.* **rev·er·ence** (rev′ə rəns *or* rev′rəns) *noun.*

reverse **1.** Something directly opposite of something else; contrary: *You did the reverse of what I told you to do.* **2.** The position of gears in a machine that makes them move backwards: *Put the car in reverse to back up.* **3.** The back side of something: *There is an eagle on the reverse of the coin.* **4.** A change of luck from good to bad: *The store had a reverse in the first year of its business. Noun.*
○ Opposite in position or direction: *The driver put the car in reverse gear. Adjective.*
○ **1.** To turn around, upside down, or inside out: *I reversed the sock to mend the hole.* **2.** To change to the opposite: *I reversed my opinion later. Verb.*
re·verse (ri vûrs′) *noun, plural* **reverses;** *adjective; verb,* **reversed, reversing.** —**reversal** *noun.*

review **1.** To study or examine again: *I reviewed my notes.* **2.** To go over in one's mind: *I reviewed the day's events.* **3.** To give a critical account of: *He's a critic who reviews new movies for a newspaper.* **4.** To make a formal or official inspection of: *The general reviewed the troops. Verb.*
○ **1.** A studying, going over, or examining again: *Let's get together for a review of the plans.* **2.** A looking back: *The magazine's review of the past year is in this issue.* **3.** An account of a movie, play, book, or other work given to praise or criticize it: *book reviews in the newspaper.* **4.** A formal or official inspection: *There was a review of*

PRONUNCIATION KEY:

| at | āpe | fär | câre | end | mē | it | īce | pierce | hot | ōld | sông | fôrk |
| oil | out | up | ūse | rüle | pull | tûrn | chin | sing | shop | thin | this | |

hw in white; zh in treasure. The symbol ə stands for the unstressed vowel sound in about, taken, pencil, lemon, and circus.

629

the troops before the parade. Noun.
re•view (ri vū′) *verb,* **reviewed, reviewing**; *noun,*
plural **reviews.**

revise **1.** To change in order to correct or make
better: *The author* **revised** *a confusing paragraph.*
2. To make different: *I* **revised** *my opinion after
I learned more.* **re•vise** (ri vīz′) *verb,* **revised,
revising.** —**revision** *noun.*

revival **1.** The act of reviving or the condition of
being revived: *There has been a* **revival** *of interest
in jazz.* **2.** A showing of an old movie or a new
production of an old play: *Our drama club plans
two* **revivals** *this season.* **3.** A special service to
renew interest in religion: *The preacher held a
revival in our town.* **re•viv•al** (ri vī′vəl) *noun,
plural* **revivals.**

revive **1.** To bring back to consciousness: *The firefighter* **revived** *the unconscious child.* **2.** To bring
back into use, interest, or notice: *The old movie
was* **revived** *with great success.* **3.** To give new
strength or freshness to: *A good meal* **revived** *the
hungry children.* **re•vive** (ri vīv′) *verb,* **revived,
reviving.**

revoke To cancel; make no longer good: *A driver's
license can be* **revoked** *if the driver does not obey
traffic laws.* **re•voke** (ri vōk′) *verb,* **revoked,
revoking.**

revolt An uprising or rebellion against a government or other authority: *The citizens staged a
revolt against the tyrant.* Noun.
○ **1.** To rebel against a government or other
authority: *The prisoners* **revolted.** **2.** To cause to
feel sick or disgusted: *The smell of the garbage
revolted us.* Verb.
re•volt (ri vōlt′) *noun, plural* **revolts**; *verb,* **revolted, revolting.** —**revolting** *adjective.*

revolution **1.** The overthrow of a system of government and the setting up of a new or different
system of government. Revolutions are often carried out through the use of force. **2.** A sudden or
complete change: *Modern machines brought
about a* **revolution** *in industry.* **3.** Movement in a
circle around a central point or object: *The spacecraft made three* **revolutions** *around the moon
before landing.* **rev•o•lu•tion** (rev′ə lü′shən) *noun,
plural* **revolutions.**

revolutionary Relating to or tending to bring
about a revolution: *The* **revolutionary** *leaders
invaded the palace. The steam engine was a*

revolutionary invention. **rev•o•lu•tion•ar•y**
(rev′ə lü′shə ner′ē) *adjective.*

Revolutionary War The war the American
colonies fought to become independent. Look up
American Revolution for more information.

revolve **1.** To move in a circle around a central
point or object: *The planets* **revolve** *around the
sun.* **2.** To spin or turn around a central point:
Wheels **revolve** *when in motion.* **3.** To depend on:
My whole life **revolves** *around school.* **re•volve**
(ri volv′) *verb,* **revolved, revolving.**

**This amusement park ride
revolves very quickly.**

revolver A pistol that can be fired several times
without putting more bullets into it. The bullets
are held in a cylinder that revolves. **re•volv•er**
(ri vol′vər) *noun, plural* **revolvers.**

reward **1.** Something given or received in return
for something done: *The students got extra recess
as a* **reward** *for good behavior.* **2.** Money offered
or given for the return of lost property or the
capture of criminals: *We offered a reward for the
return of our lost dog.* Noun.
○ **1.** To give something, especially money, for
something done: *I* **rewarded** *the children with ten
dollars for finding my watch.* **2.** To give an award
for some quality: *Our country* **rewards** *bravery in
battle.* Verb.
re•ward (ri wôrd′) *noun, plural* **rewards**; *verb,*
rewarded, rewarding.

reword To put into different words: *The teacher
reworded the question because the students did
not understand it.* **re•word** (rē wûrd′) *verb,*
reworded, rewording.

RFD or **R.F.D.** An abbreviation for **rural free
delivery.**

rhinoceros A very large animal having thick skin and one or two horns rising from the snout. **rhi·noc·er·os** (rī nos′ər əs) *noun, plural* **rhinoceroses** *or* **rhinoceros.**

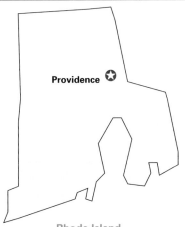

Rhinoceroses live in open, grassy areas of Africa and Asia.

Rhode Island A state in the northeastern United States. It is the smallest state in the country. Its capital is Providence. **Rhode Island** (rōd).

WORD HISTORY

Rhode Island was named after the island of Rhodes in the Aegean Sea. An Italian explorer gave this name to an island near what is now known as Rhode Island because he thought that the island was about the size of Rhodes. This name was later used for the whole colony and then for the state.

Rhode Island
U. S. Postal Abbreviation: **RI**
Capital: **Providence**
Population: **986,000**
Area: **1,214 sq. mi./3,144 sq. km**
State Nickname: **Ocean State**
State Bird: **Rhode Island Red**
State Flower: **Violet**

rhododendron An evergreen shrub with clusters of flowers shaped like bells and shiny leaves. **rho·do·den·dron** (rō′də den′drən) *noun, plural* **rhododendrons.**

rhombus A flat figure with four sides of equal length. The opposite sides of a rhombus are parallel. **rhom·bus** (rom′bəs) *noun, plural* **rhombuses** *or* **rhombi** (rom′bī).

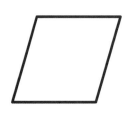

rhombus

rhubarb A plant with green or reddish stalks with a slightly sour taste. The stalks are cooked in pies and sauces. **rhu·barb** (rü′bärb) *noun, plural* **rhubarbs.**

rhyme **1.** The repetition of similar sounds at the ends of lines of verse. For example, in the verse "Humpty Dumpty sat on a wall, Humpty Dumpty had a great fall," there is a rhyme with the words "wall" and "fall." **2.** A word that sounds like or the same as another: *"Mail" is a rhyme for "pail."* **3.** Verse or poetry having sounds at the ends of lines that are alike or the same. *Noun.*
○ To make a rhyme: *"Wide" rhymes with "side."* *Verb.*
rhyme (rīm) *noun, plural* **rhymes;** *verb,* **rhymed, rhyming.**

rhythm A regular or orderly repeating of sounds or movements: *We marched to the rhythm of drums.* **rhythm** (rith′əm) *noun, plural* **rhythms.**

rhythmic or **rhythmical** Relating to or having rhythm: *That poem is rhythmic.* **rhyth·mic** *or* **rhyth·mi·cal** (rith′mik *or* rith′mi kəl) *adjective.* **—rhythmically** *adverb.*

RI *or* **R.I.** An abbreviation for **Rhode Island.**

rib **1.** One of the curved bones that are attached to the backbone and curve around to enclose the chest cavity. The ribs protect the heart and lungs. **2.** Something that looks like or acts as a rib. An umbrella has ribs. **rib** (rib) *noun, plural* **ribs.**

ribbon **1.** A band of cloth used for decoration: *The gift was tied with ribbons.* **2.** A band of material like a ribbon but not used for decoration: *a typewriter ribbon.* **rib·bon** (rib′ən) *noun, plural* **ribbons.**

PRONUNCIATION KEY:
| at | āpe | fär | câre | end | mē | it | īce | pierce | hot | ōld | sŏng | fôrk |
| oil | out | up | ūse | rüle | pull | tûrn | chin | sing | shop | thin | this | |
hw in white; zh in treasure. The symbol ə stands for the unstressed vowel sound in about, taken, pencil, lemon, and circus.

631

rice The grains of a grass plant grown in many warm areas of the world. Rice is an important food crop. **rice** (rīs) *noun.*

rich 1. Having much money, land, or other valuable things. 2. Having a lot of something: *a country rich in natural resources.* 3. Able to produce much; fertile: *rich soil.* 4. Deep and full: *That singer has a rich voice.* 5. Having a heavy, strong taste or having large amounts of butter or other fat, eggs, sugar, or flavoring: *a rich sauce.* **rich** (rich) *adjective,* **richer, richest. —richly** *adverb* **—richness** *noun.*

riches Much money, land, and other valuable things; wealth: *The royal family has great riches.* **rich·es** (rich′iz) *plural noun.*

rickety Likely to fall or break; shaky: *We were afraid to cross the rickety bridge.* **rick·et·y** (rik′i tē) *adjective.*

rid To clear or free of something not wanted: *How do we rid the house of ants?*

• **to get rid of. 1.** To get free from: *It's hard to get rid of a cold.* **2.** To destroy: *Poison got rid of the bugs in the house.*

rid (rid) *verb,* **rid** or **ridded, ridding.**

riddle¹ A question or problem that is hard to figure out or understand. For example: What has two hands but no fingers? Answer: A clock. **rid·dle** (rid′əl) *noun, plural* **riddles.**

riddle² To make many holes in: *The soldier riddled the target with bullets.* **rid·dle** (rid′əl) *verb,* **riddled, riddling.**

ride 1. To sit on a vehicle or animal and make it move in order to be carried by it: *She likes to ride horses.* 2. To travel on or in a car, train, or other vehicle: *We rode through the town on the bus.* 3. To be carried along: *The sailboat rode over the waves. Verb.*

○ 1. A short trip on an animal or in a car, train, or other vehicle: *We took a ride on our bicycles.* 2. A device on which people ride for amusement: *We tried all the rides at the fair. Noun.*

ride (rīd) *verb,* **rode, ridden, riding;** *noun, plural* **rides.**

rider A person who rides: *horseback riders.* **rid·er** (rī′dər) *noun, plural* **riders.**

ridge 1. The long and narrow upper part of something: *The brown cow had a white spot on the ridge of her back.* 2. A raised, narrow strip: *Corduroy has ridges.* 3. A long and narrow chain of hills or mountains. 4. The line where the two slanting sides of a roof come together. **ridge** (rij) *noun, plural* **ridges.**

ridicule To make fun of: *The bully ridicules other children. Verb.*

○ Words or actions that make fun of a person or thing: *His strange way of dressing leaves him open to ridicule. Noun.*

rid·i·cule (rid′i kūl′) *verb,* **ridiculed, ridiculing;** *noun.*

ridiculous Very silly or foolish: *a ridiculous hat with fruit and flowers on it.* **ri·dic·u·lous** (ri dik′yə ləs) *adjective.* **—ridiculously** *adverb.*

rifle A firearm that is meant to be fired from the shoulder. **ri·fle** (rī′fəl) *noun, plural* **rifles.**

rig 1. To fit a boat or ship with masts, sails, and lines: *The workers rigged the boat in two weeks.* 2. To fit out; equip: *We rigged our car with a rack for carrying skis.* 3. To make or build in a hurry or by using odd bits and pieces of material: *We rigged up a radio from used parts. Verb.*

○ 1. An arrangement of masts, sails, and lines on a boat or ship. 2. Equipment used for a special purpose: *The field is filled with oil drilling rigs. Noun.*

rig (rig) *verb,* **rigged, rigging;** *noun, plural* **rigs.**

rigging 1. All the lines of a boat or ship. The rigging includes ropes, chains, and wires. 2. Equipment used for a special purpose: *The workers set up the rigging for drilling the oil well.* **rig·ging** (rig′ing) *noun, plural* **riggings.**

right 1. Correct or true; free from mistakes: *the right answer to an arithmetic problem.* 2. Just, moral, or good: *Telling the truth was the right thing to do.* 3. On or toward the side of the body that is to the east when one is facing north: *He writes with his right hand.* 4. Proper; suitable: *the right person to head the committee.* 5. Healthy; well: *I don't feel right.* 6. Meant to be seen: *Which is the right side of this cloth? Adjective.*

○ 1. Something just, moral, or good: *The parents taught their children to do right.* 2. A just, moral, or lawful claim: *the right to free speech.* 3. The right side or direction: *the house on your right. Noun.*

○ 1. Correctly: *You didn't spell my name right.* 2. According to what is just, moral, or good: *You must do right and return the wallet you found.* 3. In a proper way; suitably: *This tape doesn't* work **right**. **4.** Exactly: *Put the book* **right** *here.* **5.** Without delay; immediately: *Let's leave* **right** *after lunch.* **6.** To or toward the right: *Turn* **right** *at the corner.* **7.** Completely: *The rain soaked* **right** *through.* **8.** In a straight line: *I went* **right** *to the door. Adverb.*

○ **1.** To make good, just, or correct: *I* **righted** *the wrong I had done.* **2.** To put or get back into a proper or normal position: *We* **righted** *the raft after it turned over. Verb.*

Another word that sounds like this is **write**.

• **right away** *or* **right off**. At once; immediately: *I'll be there* **right away**.

right (rīt) *adjective; noun, plural* **rights**; *adverb; verb,* **righted**, **righting**.

right angle An angle of 90 degrees. It is formed by two lines that are perpendicular to each other.

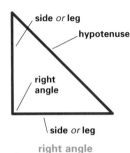

right angle

right-hand **1.** On or toward the right: *the* **right-hand** *side of the street.* **2.** For the right hand: *my* **right-hand** *glove.* **right-hand** (rīt′hand′) *adjective.*

right-handed **1.** Using the right hand more often and more easily than the left hand. **2.** Done with the right hand: *a* **right-handed** *throw.* **right-hand·ed** (rīt′han′did) *adjective.* —**right-hander** *noun.*

right triangle A triangle with a right angle.

rigid **1.** Not bending or giving; stiff: *a* **rigid** *steel beam.* **2.** Not changing; fixed: *a* **rigid** *schedule.* **rig·id** (rij′id) *adjective.* —**rigidly** *adverb* —**rigidity** *noun.*

rile To annoy or irritate: *It* **riles** *me to have to listen to their nonstop chatter.* **rile** (rīl) *verb,* **riled**, **riling**.

rim The outer edge or border of something: *The* **rim** *of the glass is chipped. Noun.*

○ To form a rim around: *The mountains* **rimmed** *the valley. Verb.*

rim (rim) *noun, plural* **rims**; *verb,* **rimmed**, **rimming**.

rind A firm outer covering or skin. Oranges and watermelons have rinds. Some cheeses have rinds. **rind** (rīnd) *noun, plural* **rinds**.

ring[1] **1.** A closed, curved line; circle: *The children sat in a* **ring** *around the teacher.* **2.** A band of metal or other material in the shape of a circle: *I wear a* **ring** *on my finger.* **3.** An enclosed area. Rings are used for circus performances or for sports events. *Noun.*

○ To put or form a ring around: *Trees* **ringed** *the pond. Verb.*

Another word that sounds like this is **wring**.

ring (ring) *noun, plural* **rings**; *verb,* **ringed**, **ringing**.

These are part of the rings that surround the planet Saturn.

ring[2] **1.** To make a clear sound like that of a bell: *Did you hear the telephone* **ring**? **2.** To cause to make a clear sound: *The visitor* **rang** *the doorbell.* **3.** To be full of loud and clear sounds; echo: *Shots* **rang** *out.* **4.** To hear a ringing or buzzing sound: *My ears* **rang** *from the loud music.* **5.** To call or announce by ringing a bell: *I* **rang** *for the hotel clerk.* **6.** To seem to be; sound: *That story* **rings** *true. Verb.*

○ **1.** A clear sound like a bell's: *the* **ring** *of an alarm clock.* **2.** A telephone call: *I'll give you a* **ring**. **3.** A certain impression or quality: *the* **ring** *of sincerity. Noun.*

Another word that sounds like this is **wring**.

ring (ring) *verb,* **rang**, **rung**, **ringing**; *noun, plural* **rings**.

rink A place that has a surface for ice-skating or roller-skating. **rink** (ringk) *noun, plural* **rinks**.

PRONUNCIATION KEY:

| at | ape | far | câre | end | mē | it | īce | pierce | hot | ōld | sông | fôrk |
| oil | out | up | ūse | rüle | pull | tûrn | chin | sing | shop | thin | this | |

hw in white; zh in treasure. The symbol ə stands for the unstressed vowel sound in about, taken, pencil, lemon, and circus.

633

rinse 1. To wash with clear water; take out soap with water: *I **rinsed** the shirt before hanging it up to dry.* 2. To wash lightly: ***Rinse** the glass before you put it in the dishwasher. Verb.*
○ The act of rinsing: *I gave my hair a **rinse** after I got out of the pool. Noun.*
rinse (rins) *verb,* **rinsed, rinsing**; *noun, plural* **rinses.**

riot 1. A noisy and violent disorder caused by a crowd of people. 2. A very funny person or thing. *Noun.*
○ To take part in a noisy and violent disorder: *The prisoners **rioted**. Verb.*
ri•ot (rī′ət) *noun, plural* **riots**; *verb,* **rioted, rioting.**

rip To tear or pull apart: *I **ripped** my pants on the fence. Verb.*
○ A torn place; tear: *You have a **rip** in your shirt. Noun.*
• **rip off.** To steal from or cheat: *The audience at the concert felt they had been **ripped off** when the band played for only an hour.*
rip (rip) *verb,* **ripped, ripping**; *noun, plural* **rips.**

ripe 1. Fully grown and ready to be eaten: *ripe tomatoes.* 2. Ready; well prepared: *Political unrest made the country **ripe** for revolution.*
ripe (rīp) *adjective,* **riper, ripest. —ripeness** *noun.*

**Most of these grapes
are not yet** ripe.

ripen To make or become ripe: *The heat and sun have **ripened** the pears.*
rip•en (rī′pən) *verb,* **ripened, ripening.**

ripple 1. A very small wave: *ripples on the surface of the pond.* 2. Anything like a ripple: *The wind makes **ripples** in the curtains.* 3. A sound like the sound made by the flowing of very small waves: *There was only a **ripple** of applause when the speaker finished. Noun.*
○ To have or cause to have ripples: *The stone I threw **rippled** the water. Verb.*
rip•ple (rip′əl) *noun, plural* **ripples**; *verb,* **rippled, rippling.**

rise 1. To get up from a sitting, kneeling, or lying position; stand up: *Everyone **rose** when the judge entered.* 2. To get out of bed: *We **rise** at 7:00 every morning.* 3. To move from a lower to a higher place; go upward: *Smoke **rose** from the chimney.* 4. To reach up: *The building **rises** above the others.* 5. To become greater, larger, or higher: *Yeast makes bread dough **rise.*** 6. To go up in position, rank, or importance: *The lawyer **rose** to a prominent position.* 7. To start; begin: *The river **rises** in the mountains.* 8. To rebel; revolt: *The people **rose** against the dictator. Verb.*
○ 1. A moving upward. 2. An upward slope: *The campers climbed the **rise** of the hill. Noun.*
rise (rīz) *verb,* **rose, risen, rising**; *noun, plural* **rises.**

risk A chance of loss or harm; danger: *There is great **risk** in skydiving. Noun.*
○ 1. To put in danger of loss or harm: *Firefighters **risk** their lives every day.* 2. To take the risk of: *My parents **risked** losing money when they bought a store. Verb.*
risk (risk) *noun, plural* **risks**; *verb,* **risked, risking.**

ritual 1. A system or fixed form of special ceremonies: *Baptism is part of the **ritual** of many churches.* 2. A procedure or set of actions regularly followed: *A bedtime story is part of the children's nightly **ritual.*** **rit•u•al** (rich′ü əl) *noun, plural* **rituals. —ritually** *adverb.*

rival A person who is, or tries to be, as good as or better than another: *The two students were **rivals** for class president. Noun.*
○ 1. To be the equal of: *Nothing **rivals** the enjoyment I get from fishing.* 2. To try to be as good as or better than. *Verb.*
○ Trying to get the same thing as another; competing: *rival teams. Adjective.*
ri•val (rī′vəl) *noun, plural* **rivals**; *verb,* **rivaled, rivaling**; *adjective.* **—rivalry** *noun.*

river 1. A large natural stream of water that empties into a lake, ocean, or other river. 2. Anything like a river: *A **river** of oil spilled from the truck.*
riv•er (riv′ər) *noun, plural* **rivers.**

rivet A metal bolt that fastens pieces of metal together. *Noun.*

○ **1.** To fasten with a rivet: *The workers **riveted** the steel beams together.* **2.** To hold or fasten firmly: *The children's attention was **riveted** on the puppet show.* Verb.
riv·et (riv′it) *noun, plural* **rivets**; *verb,* **riveted**, **riveting**.

roach A brown or black insect often found as a pest in homes. This insect is also called a cockroach. **roach** (rōch) *noun, plural* **roaches**.

road **1.** A strip of pavement or cleared ground that people or vehicles use to go from one place to another. **2.** A way for going or moving toward something wanted: *Many people helped the actor on the **road** to fame.*
Another word that sounds like this is **rode.**
road (rōd) *noun, plural* **roads**.

road map A map that shows the streets and highways of an area.

Roadrunners **are found in the southwestern United States.**

roadrunner A bird with brownish black streaked feathers, a long tail tipped with white, and a shaggy crest on top of its head. Roadrunners usually run very fast instead of flying. **road·run·ner** (rōd′run′ər) *noun, plural* **roadrunners**.

roadside An area along the side of a road: *We pulled up on the **roadside** to rest.* Noun.
○ Located along the side of the road: *We stopped at a **roadside** stand.* Adjective.
road·side (rōd′sīd′) *noun, plural* **roadsides**; *adjective.*

roam To go or move around without any particular place to go; wander: *We **roamed** through the woods.* **roam** (rōm) *verb,* **roamed**, **roaming**.

roar **1.** To make a loud, deep sound or cry: *The lion **roared**.* **2.** To laugh loudly: *They all **roared** at my jokes.* Verb.
○ A loud, deep sound or cry: *the **roar** of the ocean; an engine's **roar**.* Noun.
roar (rôr) *verb,* **roared**, **roaring**; *noun, plural* **roars**.

roast **1.** To cook in an oven or over an open fire or hot coals: *The children **roasted** marshmallows over the fire.* **2.** To dry and brown by heat: *Coffee beans are **roasted** and ground.* **3.** To be or make too hot: *I'm **roasting** in this coat.* Verb.
○ A piece of meat that has been roasted or is ready to be roasted: *We had a **roast** of pork for dinner.* Noun.
○ Roasted: *My whole family likes **roast** beef.* Adjective.
roast (rōst) *verb,* **roasted**, **roasting**; *noun, plural* **roasts**; *adjective.*

rob To take away from by using force or violence; steal from: *Have the police found the man who **robbed** the jewelry store?* **rob** (rob) *verb,* **robbed**, **robbing**.

robber A person who robs. **robber** (rob′ər) *noun, plural* **robbers**.

robbery The act of robbing; theft: *Did you read about the bank **robbery**?* **rob·ber·y** (rob′ə rē) *noun, plural* **robberies**.

robe **1.** A loose piece of clothing worn as a covering: *I bought a **robe** to wear over my pajamas.* **2.** A piece of clothing worn to show one's office, profession, or rank. *Members of the clergy and judges sometimes wear **robes**.* Noun.
○ To put a robe on: *Servants **robed** the emperor before the ceremony.* Verb.
robe (rōb) *noun, plural* **robes**; *verb,* **robed**, **robing**.

robin A bird that lives in North America and Europe. The robin that lives in North America has a reddish orange breast and a black head and tail. **rob·in** (rob′in) *noun, plural* **robins**.

robot A machine that can do some of the same things that a human being can do. **ro·bot** (rō′bət or rō′bot) *noun, plural* **robots**.

robust Having strength and energy; in good

PRONUNCIATION KEY:
at   āpe   fär   câre   end   mē   it   īce   pîerce   hot   ōld   sông   fôrk
oil   out   up   ūse   rüle   pu̇ll   tûrn   chin   sing   shop   thin   this
hw in white; zh in treasure. The symbol ə stands for the unstressed vowel sound in about, taken, pencil, lemon, and circus.

635

health: *a robust wrestler.* **ro·bust** (rō bust′ or rō′bust) *adjective.* —**robustly** *adverb.*

rock¹ 1. A piece of stone: *The children threw rocks into the lake.* 2. A large mass of stone forming a cliff or peak: *The waves threw the boat against the rocks.* 3. A mass of mineral that is formed naturally and is part of the earth's crust. Granite, limestone, and slate are rocks. 4. Something like a rock in hardness or strength; strong support: *My cousin was our rock during the family crisis.* **rock** (rok) *noun, plural* **rocks.**

rock² 1. To move back and forth or from side to side in a gentle way: *I rocked the baby in my arms.* 2. To move or shake violently: *The explosion rocked the building. Verb.*
   ○ Rock 'n' roll. *Noun.*
   rock (rok) *verb,* **rocked, rocking;** *noun, plural* **rocks.**

rocker 1. A rocking chair. 2. One of the two curved pieces on which a cradle, rocking chair, or other object rocks. **rock·er** (rok′ər) *noun, plural* **rockers.**

The exploration of space has been made possible by rockets.

rocket A device that is driven through the air by a stream of hot gases released from the rear. Rockets are used as fireworks and weapons and to propel spacecraft. *Noun.*

○ To move or rise very quickly: *The price of food is rocketing. Verb.*
rock·et (rok′it) *noun, plural* **rockets;** *verb,* **rocketed, rocketing.**

rocking chair A chair mounted on rockers or springs so that it can rock.

rocking horse A toy horse mounted on rockers and large enough for a child to ride.

rock 'n' roll A kind of popular music with a strong, steady beat. **rock 'n' roll** (rok′ən rōl′).

rocky¹ Full of rocks: *a rocky beach.* **rock·y** (rok′ē) *adjective,* **rockier, rockiest.**

rocky² Likely to fall or sway: *Don't sit on that rocky old stool.* **rock·y** (rok′ē) *adjective,* **rockier, rockiest.**

rod 1. A thin, straight piece of metal, wood, or plastic. 2. A long pole used for fishing. This is also called a fishing rod. 3. A stick or bundle of sticks used to beat or punish. 4. A unit for measuring. It is equal to 5 1/2 yards or 16 1/2 feet. **rod** (rod) *noun, plural* **rods.**

rode Past tense of **ride:** *My friend rode a bicycle.* Another word that sounds like this is **road.** **rode** (rōd) *verb.*

rodent Any of a large group of animals that have a pair of big front teeth used for gnawing. Rats, mice, squirrels, guinea pigs, and beavers are rodents. **ro·dent** (rō′dənt) *noun, plural* **rodents.**

rodeo A show with contests in horseback riding, roping, and other similar skills. **ro·de·o** (rō′dē ō′ or rō dā′ō) *noun, plural* **rodeos.**

roe¹ The eggs of fish.
   Another word that sounds like this is **row.**
   roe (rō) *noun.*

roe² A small deer with a reddish brown coat, found in the forests of Europe and northern Asia. Another word that sounds like this is **row.**
   roe (rō) *noun, plural* **roes** or **roe.**

rogue 1. A dishonest person; cheat. 2. A playful or mischievous person. 3. A vicious animal, especially a male elephant that lives apart from the herd. **rogue** (rōg) *noun, plural* **rogues.**

role 1. A part played by an actor: *I have a role in the play.* 2. A part played by a person or thing;

position: *Our teacher took the **role** of guide on our trip.*

Another word that sounds like this is **roll**.

role (rōl) *noun, plural* **roles**.

roll **1.** To move by turning over and over: *The ball **rolled** away.* **2.** To move or be moved on wheels or rollers: *The wagon **rolled** down the hill. I **rolled** the cart down the street.* **3.** To turn over many times: *The dog **rolled** in the grass.* **4.** To move in an up-and-down motion or from side to side: *The ship **rolled** in the storm.* **5.** To make a deep, continuous sound; rumble: *The drums **rolled**.* **6.** To wrap around on itself or on something else: ***Roll** up the sleeping bag.* **7.** To wrap in a covering: *I **rolled** the fish in paper.* **8.** To spread out or make flat with a roller: *I **rolled** dough for the cookies.* **9.** To pronounce with a trill: *Italians **roll** their r's.* **10.** To pass or go: *The days **rolled** by. Verb.*
○ **1.** Something rolled up: *a **roll** of stamps.* **2.** A list of names of people in a group: *The teacher called the **roll**.* **3.** A piece of baked bread: *a hamburger on a **roll**.* **4.** A rolling or swaying motion: *the **roll** of a boat.* **5.** A quick, continuous series of short sounds, as those made by beating on a drum. *Noun.*

Another word that sounds like this is **role**.

roll (rōl) *verb*, **rolled**, **rolling**; *noun, plural* **rolls**.

roller **1.** A cylinder on which something is rolled or wound up: *A window shade is on a **roller**.* **2.** A cylinder that smoothes, spreads out, flattens, or crushes: *We painted the walls with a roller.* **3.** A small wheel on which something is rolled or moved: *They had to move the piano on **rollers**.* **4.** A long, swelling wave that breaks on the shore. **roll·er** (rō′lər) *noun, plural* **rollers**.

roller coaster A ride in an amusement park or fair. On a roller coaster, people sit in a car that

A roller coaster is one of the most popular of all amusement park rides.

moves very fast over a track having sharp turns and sudden, steep inclines.

roller-skate To skate on roller skates: *The children **roller-skated** down the street.* **roller-skate** (rō′lər skāt′) *verb*, **roller-skated**, **roller-skating**.

roller skate A skate with small wheels on the bottom, used for skating on flat surfaces, such as sidewalks.

rolling pin A smooth cylinder for rolling out dough, often made of wood and having a handle at each end.

ROM A type of memory that is installed in a computer and that cannot be changed. The information stored in ROM is permanent. ROM stands for *read-only memory*. **ROM** (rom) *noun*.

Roman **1.** Of or relating to ancient or modern Rome, its people, or their culture. **2. roman.** Of or relating to the style of type most widely used in printing. The letters of roman type are upright. This sentence is printed in roman type. *Adjective.*
○ **1.** A person born or living in Rome. **2.** A person who lived in ancient Rome. **3. roman.** Roman type or lettering. *Noun.* **Ro·man** (rō′mən) *adjective; noun, plural* **Romans**.

Roman Catholic Church The Christian church that recognizes the pope as its head.

romance **1.** A love affair: *The story of Sleeping Beauty is about a **romance** that she has with a prince.* **2.** A quality of love, excitement, mystery, or adventure: *The dim lights gave a sense of **romance** to the room.* **3.** A story or poem that tells of heroes and their deeds, of adventure, and of love. **ro·mance** (rō mans′ *or* rō′mans) *noun, plural* **romances**.

WORD HISTORY

The word romance comes from an old French word that meant "something written in a Romance language." In the Middle Ages, stories of love and adventure were usually written in one of these Romance languages instead of in Latin, which was used in more serious writings.

Romance language One of the languages that developed from Latin. French, Spanish, Italian, Portuguese, and Romanian are Romance languages.

PRONUNCIATION KEY:

| at | āpe | fär | câre | end | mē | it | īce | pierce | hot | ōld | sông | fôrk |
| oil | out | up | ūse | rüle | pùll | tûrn | chin | sing | shop | thin | <u>th</u>is | |

hw in white; zh in treasure. The symbol ə stands for the unstressed vowel sound in about, taken, pencil, lemon, and circus.

637

Roman numeral Any one of the letters used in a numbering system based on that used by the ancient Romans. In this system I = 1, V = 5, X = 10, L = 50, C = 100, D = 500, and M = 1,000.

romantic 1. Relating to or marked by romance: *My friend's head is full of romantic dreams.* 2. Having thoughts and feelings of love and adventure. 3. Suitable for love or romance: *The candles gave the room a romantic atmosphere.* **ro•man•tic** (rō man′tik) *adjective.* —**romantically** *adverb.*

Rome The capital of Italy, in the central part of the country. In ancient times, Rome was the center of the Roman Empire. **Rome** (rōm) *noun.*

romp To play in a lively and noisy way: *The children romped in the waves. Verb.*
○ Lively and noisy play: *I took my dog along for a romp in the woods. Noun.*
romp (romp) *verb,* **romped, romping;** *noun,* *plural* **romps.**

roof 1. The outer covering of the top of a building: *The workers replaced the shingles on the roof.* 2. Something that is like a roof in position or use: *the roof of the mouth. Noun.*
○ To cover with a roof: *Our new house will be roofed this week. Verb.*
roof (rüf *or* růf) *noun, plural* **roofs;** *verb,* **roofed, roofing.**

rook A piece used in the game of chess. The rook moves any number of spaces across or up and down the board parallel to the sides. **rook** (růk) *noun, plural* **rooks.**

rookie 1. A person who has just joined a group and has no experience: *Those police officers are rookies.* 2. An athlete who has just started playing a professional sport. **rook•ie** (růk′ē) *noun, plural* **rookies.**

room 1. An area that is or may be taken up by something; space: *Is there room for this book in the suitcase?* 2. An area in a building separated or set off by walls: *Our house has seven rooms.* 3. The people in a room: *The whole room was laughing.* 4. A chance or opportunity; possibility: *room for improvement. Noun.*
○ To live in a room or rooms: *They roomed together at college. Verb.*
room (rüm *or* rům) *noun, plural* **rooms;** *verb,* **roomed, rooming.**

roommate A person with whom one shares a room or rooms. **room•mate** (rüm′māt′ *or* rům′māt′) *noun, plural* **roommates.**

roomy Having plenty of room; large: *a roomy old house.* **room•y** (rü′mē *or* rům′ē) *adjective,* **roomier, roomiest.**

roost 1. A perch on which birds rest or sleep. 2. A building or other place for birds to rest or sleep for the night. *Noun.*
○ To rest or sleep on a roost as a bird does. *Verb.*
roost (rüst) *noun, plural* **roosts;** *verb,* **roosted, roosting.**

Many roosters make a loud crowing sound at dawn.

rooster An adult male chicken. **roost•er** (rüs′tər) *noun, plural* **roosters.**

root¹ 1. The part of a plant that grows down into the ground. Roots hold the plant in the soil and take in water and minerals to feed the plant. 2. A part that acts as or looks like a root. Teeth and hair have roots. 3. A part where something begins; origin: *the root of the problem.* 4. A word to which a prefix or suffix is added to make other words: *"Faith" is the root of "faithful," and "bear" is the root of "bearable" and "unbearable." Noun.*
○ 1. To develop roots and begin to grow: *The cuttings will root soon.* 2. To fix or establish firmly: *Fear rooted me to the spot.* 3. To pull, tear, or get rid of completely: *We rooted weeds from the lawn. Verb.* Another word that sounds like this is **route.**
root (rüt *or* růt) *noun, plural* **roots;** *verb,* **rooted, rooting.**

root² 1. To dig in the earth with the snout: *The pig rooted about for food.* 2. To search for something; rummage: *I rooted through the closet for my shoes.* Another word that sounds like this is **route.**
root (rüt *or* růt) *verb,* **rooted, rooting.**

root³ To support a team or a person in a contest: *I* **root** *for the home team.*
Another word that sounds like this is **route**.
root (rüt *or* rût) *verb,* **rooted, rooting.**

rope **1.** A strong cord made of twisted or woven strands of wire, fiber, or nylon. Ropes are used for pulling, lifting, or hanging objects. **2.** A number of things joined together by twisting or stringing: *a* **rope** *of pearls. Noun.*
○ **1.** To tie, bind, or fasten with a rope: *The clerk* **roped** *the boxes together to make them easier to carry.* **2.** To separate or enclose with a rope or ropes: *The police* **roped** *off the area.* **3.** To catch with a lasso or rope: *The cowhand* **roped** *the calf. Verb.*
rope (rōp) *noun, plural* **ropes;** *verb,* **roped, roping.**

Roses are usually red, pink, yellow, or
white and often have a sweet smell.

rose¹ **1.** A flower that grows on a thorny bush or vine. **2.** A pinkish red color. *Noun.*
○ Having the color rose. *Adjective.*
rose (rōz) *noun, plural* **roses;** *adjective.*

rose² Past tense of **rise:** *Everyone* **rose** *when the principal entered the room.* **rose** (rōz) *verb.*

rosebud The bud of a rose. **rose·bud** (rōz′bud′) *noun, plural* **rosebuds.**

Rosh Hashanah A holiday celebrating the first day of the Jewish year, which occurs in September or October. **Rosh Ha·sha·nah** (rōsh′ hə shä′nə).

rosy **1.** Having the color rose; pinkish red: *The baby's cheeks were* **rosy** *from the cold.* **2.** Full of hope; bright; cheerful: *a* **rosy** *outlook on the future.* **ros·y** (rō′zē) *adjective,* **rosier, rosiest.** —**rosiness** *noun.*

rot To make or become rotten; decay: *The apples* **rotted** *on the tree. Verb.*
○ **1.** The process of rotting: **Rot** *ruined the books in the damp basement.* **2.** One of several diseases of plants or animals caused by any of various fungi or bacteria. *Noun.* **rot** (rot) *verb,* **rotted, rotting;** *noun, plural* **rots.**

rotary Having a part or parts that turn or rotate. Some old telephones have a rotary dial. **ro·ta·ry** (rō′tə rē) *adjective.*

rotate **1.** To turn or cause to turn around on an axis: *The earth* **rotates** *from west to east.* **2.** To change in a fixed order; take turns regularly: *The guards will* **rotate** *every four hours. Farmers* **rotate** *their crops to keep the soil fertile.* **ro·tate** (rō′tāt) *verb,* **rotated, rotating.** —**rotation** *noun.*

rotor **1.** The part of a motor that turns or rotates. **2.** A set of large, turning blades that lifts and moves a helicopter or other aircraft. **ro·tor** (rō′tər) *noun, plural* **rotors.**

rotten **1.** Decayed; spoiled: *a* **rotten** *apple.* **2.** Likely to break, crack, or give way; weak: *The wood in this old floor is* **rotten.** **3.** Very bad or unpleasant: *a* **rotten** *movie.* **rot·ten** (rot′ən) *adjective,* **rottener, rottenest.**

rouge A red or pink cosmetic used to color the cheeks. **rouge** (rüzh) *noun, plural* **rouges.**

rough **1.** Having an uneven surface; not smooth or level: *the* **rough** *bark of a tree; a* **rough** *road.* **2.** Marked by or showing force or violence: *Football can be a* **rough** *game.* **3.** Not having or showing gentleness or politeness; rude: **rough** *language.* **4.** Not completely or perfectly finished or made: *a* **rough** *sketch.* **5.** In a natural or unfinished state: **rough** *diamonds.* **6.** Hard or unpleasant: *I had a* **rough** *day. Adjective.*
○ To plan, sketch, or shape in an incomplete way: *The builder* **roughed** *out a plan for the house. Verb.*
Another word that sounds like this is **ruff**.
rough (ruf) *adjective,* **rougher, roughest;** *verb,* **roughed, roughing.** —**roughly** *adverb* —**roughness** *noun.*

PRONUNCIATION KEY:
| at | ape | fär | câre | end | mē | it | īce | pierce | hot | ōld | sông | fôrk |
| oil | out | up | ūse | rüle | pull | tûrn | chin | sing | shop | thin | this |
hw in white; zh in treasure. The symbol ə stands for the unstressed vowel sound in about, taken, pencil, lemon, and circus.

639

round **1.** Shaped like a ball or globe: *A grapefruit is round.* **2.** Shaped like a circle; circular: *Tires are round.* **3.** Having a curved outline or surface: *The chair has a round back. Adjective.*
○ **1.** Something with a round shape: *The cook cut the cookie dough into rounds.* **2.** Movement in a circle or about an axis; revolution: *The spacecraft made two rounds of the moon before it landed.* **3. rounds.** A fixed or regular course or route: *The guards made their rounds every hour.* **4.** A series of happenings or actions: *a round of parties over the holidays.* **5.** A single outburst: *a round of applause.* **6.** A complete game or a section of a game or contest: *a round of golf.* **7.** A short song sung by three or more voices. Each voice begins the song at a different time. "Row, Row, Row Your Boat" is a round. **8.** A single discharge of a gun or the ammunition needed for this: *The police officer fired three rounds at the target. Noun.*
○ **1.** To make or become round: *I rounded the corners of the table I was making.* **2.** To pass or travel to the other side of; go around: *The car rounded the corner. Verb.*
○ Around: *The top spun round and round. The children gathered round the teacher. Adverb, preposition.*
   • **to round off.** To make into a round number: *I rounded off 49.8 to 50.*
   • **to round out.** To make complete: *That coin rounds out my collection.*
   • **to round up.** To drive or gather together: *I rounded up a bunch of my friends.*
round (round) *adjective,* **rounder, roundest;** *noun, plural* **rounds;** *verb,* **rounded, rounding;** *adverb; preposition.*

roundabout Not straight or direct: *We took a roundabout route home.* **round•a•bout** (round'ə bout' *or* round'ə bout') *adjective.*

roundhouse A round building with a turntable inside, used to store or repair locomotives. **round•house** (round'hous') *noun, plural* **round-houses** (round'hou'ziz).

round number A number given in terms of the nearest whole number or in tens, hundreds, thousands, and the like: *The number 500 is the round number for 498.*

round trip A trip to a place and back to the starting point: *a round trip from Florida to New York and back to Florida.*

roundup **1.** The act of driving or gathering scattered cattle together for counting, branding, or selling. **2.** A gathering together of people or things: *The announcer presented a roundup of the latest news items.* **round•up** (round'up') *noun, plural* **roundups.**

rouse **1.** To awaken from sleep or rest: *The loud noise roused us.* **2.** To stir up; excite: *The touchdown roused the crowd.* **rouse** (rouz) *verb,* **roused, rousing.**

rout¹ A complete defeat, or a disorderly retreat following such a defeat: *The surprise attack resulted in a rout of the enemy. Noun.*
○ **1.** To beat completely: *Our team routed theirs by twenty points.* **2.** To force to retreat: *Our soldiers routed the enemy. Verb.*
rout (rout) *noun, plural* **routs;** *verb,* **routed, routing.**

rout² **1.** To find or uncover by searching; discover: *I routed my old shoes from the closet.* **2.** To drive out; make leave: *They routed us from our tents at seven o'clock.* **rout** (rout) *verb,* **routed, routing.**

route **1.** A road or other course used for traveling: *the route to the beach.* **2.** A regular course or territory covered by a person who delivers or sells something: *a newspaper route. Noun.*
○ **1.** To arrange the route for: *The travel agency routed our trip for us.* **2.** To send by a certain route: *The company routes its mail through New York. Verb.*
Another word that sounds like this is **root.**
route (rüt *or* rout) *noun, plural* **routes;** *verb,* **routed, routing.**

routine **1.** A regular way of doing something: *Shopping for groceries is part of my weekly routine.* **2.** Sameness of actions or ways of doing things: *The children became bored with the routine of camp life. Noun.*
○ According to or using routine; regular: *Making my bed is one of my routine chores. Adjective.*
routine (rü tēn') *noun, plural* **routines;** *adjective.* **—routinely** *adverb.*

row¹ **1.** A series of people or things arranged in a line. **2.** A line of chairs or seats: *the last row of the theater.*
Another word that sounds like this is **roe.**
row (rō) *noun, plural* **rows.**

row² **1.** To use oars to make a boat move: *We rowed to shore.* **2.** To carry in a rowboat: *Will you row me across the lake? Verb.*

A trip in a rowboat: *It is a long **row** across the river. Noun.*
Another word that sounds like this is **roe**.
row (rō) *verb,* **rowed, rowing;** *noun, plural* **rows.**

row³ A noisy quarrel or fight: *They had a **row** over who would use the bathroom first.* **row** (rou) *noun, plural* **rows.**

rowboat A boat that is moved by oars. **row‧boat** (rō′bōt′) *noun, plural* **rowboats.**

royal 1. Of or relating to a king or queen or their family: *the **royal** family.* 2. Coming from or by a king or queen or their family: *a **royal** command.* 3. Suitable for or like a king or queen or their family: *a **royal** welcome.* **roy‧al** (roi′əl) *adjective.* —**royally** *adverb.*

England's Queen in a royal appearance.

royalty 1. A royal person or persons. Kings, queens, princes, and princesses are royalty. 2. The position or power of a king or queen or other member of a royal family: *The crown is a symbol of **royalty**.* 3. An amount of money paid to an author, a composer, or an inventor from the sale, performance, or use of his or her work. **roy‧al‧ty** (roi′əl tē) *noun, plural* **royalties.**

R.R. An abbreviation for *railroad.*

Rte. An abbreviation for *route.*

rub 1. To press something back and forth over; move back and forth with pressure: *The nurse **rubbed** my leg to ease the cramp.* 2. To spread by using pressure: *I **rubbed** lotion on my arms.* 3. To move against something else or against each other: *I **rubbed** my hands together to make them warm.* 4. To apply pressure to in order to clean, polish, or make smooth: *I **rubbed** the table with wax.* 5. To take away by applying pressure: *I used my foot to **rub** out what I had written in the sand. Verb.*
  ○ The act of rubbing: *a back **rub**. Noun.*
    • **rub it in.** To keep mentioning something unpleasant, such as a person's mistake.
  rub (rub) *verb,* **rubbed, rubbing;** *noun, plural* **rubs.**

rubber 1. A strong, elastic, waterproof substance that comes from the milky liquid in certain tropical trees. Rubber is used to make tires. 2. A short boot or overshoe that protects shoes from water. **rub‧ber** (rub′ər) *noun, plural* **rubbers.**

WORD HISTORY

The word rubber comes from the word rub. This material was first used to rub out, or erase, pencil marks.

---

rubber band An elastic loop of rubber used to hold things together.

rubbish 1. Useless waste material; trash: *Put all the **rubbish** by the back door.* 2. Worthless talk or thoughts; nonsense: *Those rumors were just **rubbish**.* **rub‧bish** (rub′ish) *noun.*

rubble Rough, broken pieces of stone, rock, or other solid material: *The rescue workers searched through the **rubble** of the bombed building.* **rub‧ble** (rub′əl) *noun.*

ruble A unit of money in Russia. **ru‧ble** (rüb′əl) *noun, plural* **rubles.**

ruby 1. A clear, red precious stone. 2. A deep red color. *Noun.*
  ○ Having the color ruby; deep red. *Adjective.*
  ru‧by (rü′bē) *noun, plural* **rubies;** *adjective.*

rudder 1. A broad, flat, movable piece of wood or metal attached to the rear of a boat or ship. It is used in steering. 2. A piece like the rudder of a boat or ship, attached at the tail of an aircraft. **rud‧der** (rud′ər) *noun, plural* **rudders.**

ruddy Having a healthy redness: *a **ruddy** complexion.* **rud‧dy** (rud′ē) *adjective,* **ruddier, ruddiest.**

rude 1. Having or showing bad manners; not polite: *His sharp reply was very **rude**.* 2. Roughly made or done; primitive: *Cave dwellers used **rude** tools.* **rude** (rüd) *adjective,* **ruder, rudest.** —**rudely** *adverb* —**rudeness** *noun.*

ruff 1. A ring of feathers or hairs growing around the neck of a bird or other animal. 2. A stiff, round frill, worn as a collar by men and women in former times.
Another word that sounds like this is **rough**.
ruff (ruf) *noun, plural* **ruffs.**

ruffle 1. To disturb the smoothness or calmness of: *The bird **ruffled** its feathers.* 2. To disturb or upset: *The noisy crowd didn't*

PRONUNCIATION KEY:

| at | āpe | fär | câre | end | mē | it | īce | pierce | hot | ōld | sông | fôrk |
| oil | out | up | ūse | rüle | pull | tûrn | chin | sing | shop | thin | <u>th</u>is | |

hw in white; zh in treasure. The symbol ə stands for the unstressed vowel sound in about, taken, pencil, lemon, and circus.

641

ruffle the speaker. *Verb.*

○ A strip of ribbon or lace gathered along one edge. It is used for trimming or decoration on clothes, curtains, and bedspreads. *Noun.*
ruf·fle (ruf′əl) *verb,* **ruffled, ruffling;** *noun, plural* **ruffles.**

rug A piece of heavy fabric used to cover part of a floor. **rug** (rug) *noun, plural* **rugs.**

rugged 1. Having a sharp, rough outline or surface; rough and uneven: *The mountain has many rugged peaks.* 2. Very strong and sturdy: *a rugged football team.* 3. Hard to do or put up with; harsh: *Life on the frontier was very rugged.* **rug·ged** (rug′id) *adjective.* —**ruggedly** *adverb.* —**ruggedness** *noun.*

ruin 1. Destruction, damage, or collapse: *financial ruin.* 2. **ruins.** The remains of something destroyed or decayed: *ruins of an ancient city.* 3. Something that causes destruction, damage, or collapse: *Money will be their ruin. Noun.*

○ To bring to ruin; harm or damage greatly: *The earthquake ruined the town. My broken ankle ruined my chance to make the team. Verb.*
ru·in (rü′in) *noun, plural* **ruins;** *verb,* **ruined, ruining.**

SYNONYMS

ruin, wreck, destroy, demolish
Bad weather ruined our plans for the picnic. He had an accident and wrecked his car. The hurricane destroyed houses along the coast. The old building was demolished to make room for a new one.

---

rule 1. A direction that guides behavior or action. Games have rules to play by; clubs have rules for members to follow: *One rule of good manners is not to speak when your mouth is full.* 2. Control or government; reign: *The people were happy under the king's rule.* 3. Something that usually or normally happens or is done: *Getting up early is the rule in our house.* 4. An instrument for measuring; ruler. *Noun.*

1. To have power or control over; govern: *The queen ruled her subjects fairly.* 2. To make a decision with authority: *The court ruled in their favor.* 3. To mark with straight lines: *I write on ruled paper. Verb.*

• **to rule out.** To decide against; exclude from consideration: *The mayor ruled out higher taxes as a way of raising money.*

rule (rül) *noun, plural* **rules;** *verb,* **ruled, ruling.**

ruler 1. A person who rules. 2. A strip of wood, plastic, or metal marked off in measuring units, such as inches. It is used for drawing straight lines and for measuring. **rul·er** (rü′lər) *noun, plural* **rulers.**

rum An alcoholic liquor made from molasses or the juice of sugar cane. **rum** (rum) *noun, plural* **rums.**

rumble 1. To make a heavy, deep, rolling sound: *Thunder rumbled in the distance.* 2. To move with such a sound: *The tanks rumbled down the road. Verb.*

○ A heavy, deep, rolling sound: *We heard the rumble of thunder. Noun.*
rum·ble (rum′bəl) *verb,* **rumbled, rumbling;** *noun, plural* **rumbles.**

rummage To search completely by moving things around: *I rummaged in the closet for my missing shoe.* **rum·mage** (rum′ij) *verb,* **rummaged, rummaging.**

rumor 1. A story or statement passed from one person to another as truth with no proof: *I heard a rumor that the game was canceled.* 2. What people are saying; general talk: *Rumor has it that school will close early. Noun.*

○ To spread or tell by rumor: *It is rumored that our teacher is getting married. Verb.*
ru·mor (rü′mər) *noun, plural* **rumors;** *verb,* **rumored, rumoring.**

rump 1. The part of an animal's body where the back and legs are joined. 2. A cut of meat from this part. **rump** (rump) *noun, plural* **rumps.**

run 1. To go or cause to go quickly; move at a faster pace than a walk: *The child had to run to catch the bus.* 2. To do by or as if by running: *I ran an errand for my parents.* 3. To leave quickly; escape: *run away from home.* 4. To operate; work: *I oiled the lawn mower so it would run better.* 5. To go or travel regularly: *A bus runs by here every hour.* 6. To move or cause to move freely and easily: *I ran my eyes over the page.* 7. To take part in or enter a race or contest: *Who do you think should run for mayor?* 8. To pass into or bring to a particular place or condition: *If you run into any trouble, just call me.* 9. To keep going or happening; continue: *The sale will run for one week. Blond hair runs in my family.* 10. To be in charge of: *Our friend runs the gro-*

cery store. **11.** To spread and mix together when exposed to water: *The colors in this shirt* **ran** *after the first washing.* **12.** To suffer from; have: *The patient was* **running** *a high fever.* **13.** To have the stitches break and come undone: *Her nylon stocking* **ran.** **14.** To get past or through: *The ship* **ran** *the blockade.* **15.** To give out liquid: *My nose is* **running.** **16.** To give to a computer as an instruction: **Run** *that program again.* **17.** To read and follow the instructions in a program: *The computer is* **running** *the new program. Verb.*

○ **1.** The act of running: *I took the dog for a* **run.** **2.** A pace faster than a walk: *The children broke into a* **run.** **3.** A trip: *This train makes four* **runs** *a day.* **4.** The freedom to move about or use: *Our friends gave us the* **run** *of the house.* **5.** A period of time during which something continues to happen: *a* **run** *of hot weather.* **6.** A place where stitches have broken and come undone: *a* **run** *in a stocking.* **7.** In baseball, a score made by touching home plate after touching the three bases. **8.** A sudden demand: *a* **run** *on eggs at the store.* **9.** A steep pathway or track: *a ski* **run.** *Noun.*

• **in the long run.** In the last part of a course of events; at the end; finally: *The project started well, but* **in the long run,** *we abandoned it.*

• **on the run.** **1.** Running: *He caught the ball* **on the run.** **2.** Running away; trying to escape: *The robbers are* **on the run** *from the police.*

• **to run across.** To meet or find by chance: *If you* **run across** *any bargains at the book sale, buy something for me.*

• **to run into.** **1.** To meet or find by chance: *I* **ran into** *my dentist at the library.* **2.** To collide with: *The car* **ran into** *a truck.*

• **to run out of.** To use up the supply of: *We have* **run out of** *eggs.*

run (run) *verb,* **ran, run, running;** *noun, plural* **runs.**

runaway A person or animal that runs away. A horse that has broken away from the rider's control is a runaway. *Noun.*

○ Running away; fleeing; escaping: *a* **runaway** *horse. Adjective.*

run·a·way (run′ə wā′) *noun, plural* **runaways;** *adjective.*

run-down **1.** Having bad health; tired or sick: *I*

felt **run-down** *after working so hard.* **2.** In need of repair; falling apart: *an old,* **run-down** *house.* **run-down** (run′doun′) *adjective.*

rung¹ Past participle of **ring:** *The telephone has* **rung** *three times.* **rung** (rung) *verb.*

rung² **1.** A piece that forms a step of a ladder. **2.** A piece placed between the legs of a chair or forming part of the back of a chair. **rung** (rung) *noun, plural* **rungs.**

Long distance runners need to be in good physical shape.

runner **1.** A person or animal that runs: *The greyhound is a fast* **runner.** **2.** One of the long narrow parts or blades on which a sled or an ice skate moves. **3.** A narrow strip of rug, carpet, or other material: *We have a* **runner** *on the floor in the hall.* **4.** The thin stem of certain plants that trails along the ground and puts down roots to produce new plants: *Strawberry plants have* **runners.** **run·ner** (run′ər) *noun, plural* **runners.**

runner-up A person, group, or team that finishes in second place in a contest. **run·ner-up** (run′ər up′) *noun, plural* **runners-up.**

running mate A candidate for office from the same political party as another. A presidential candidate's running mate is the candidate for vice president.

runny Soft and liquid and beginning to flow or drip. *My ice cream became* **runny** *in the sun.* **run·ny** (run′ē) *adjective,* **runnier, runniest.**

PRONUNCIATION KEY:

| at | āpe | fär | câre | end | mē | it | īce | pierce | hot | ōld | sông | fôrk |
| oil | out | up | ūse | rüle | pull | tûrn | chin | sing | shop | thin | this | |

hw in white; zh in treasure. The symbol ə stands for the unstressed vowel sound in about, taken, pencil, lemon, and circus.

643

runway A long, narrow area where an airplane can take off and land. **run·way** (run′wā′) *noun, plural* **runways**.

rupture **1.** The act of breaking open or bursting: *The **rupture** of the main water pipe caused a flood.* **2.** A break in a friendship between people or nations. *Noun.*

○ To break open or off: *I **ruptured** a tiny blood vessel in my leg. Verb.*

rup·ture (rup′chər) *noun, plural* **ruptures**; *verb,* **ruptured, rupturing**.

rural In, relating to, or like the country: *The farm family lives in a **rural** area.* **ru·ral** (rùr′əl) *adjective.*

Many people are attracted to the uncrowded rural countryside.

rush¹ **1.** To move, go, or come quickly: *Water **rushed** out of the faucet. The police **rushed** the child to the hospital.* **2.** To act or do in a quick or hasty way: *Don't **rush** your work! Verb.*

○ **1.** The act of rushing; sudden, quick movement: *There was a **rush** of water from the broken dam.* **2.** Busy or hurried activity or movement: *There was such a **rush** in the store that I couldn't find a clerk to help me.* **3.** A busy or hurried state: *in a **rush** to leave. Noun.*

○ Needing to be done quickly; urgent: *a **rush** job. Adjective.*

rush (rush) *verb,* **rushed, rushing**; *noun, plural* **rushes**; *adjective.*

rush² A plant that looks like grass. It usually has slender, hollow stems and bunches of small green or brown flowers. **rush** (rush) *noun, plural* **rushes**.

The rushes are also called bulrushes.

Russia **1.** A country in eastern Europe and in Asia. **2.** A former empire in eastern Europe and northern Asia. **Rus·sia** (rush′ə) *noun.*

Russian **1.** A person born in or a citizen of Russia. **2.** The language of Russia. *Noun.*

○ Of or relating to Russia, its people, or their language. *Adjective.*

Rus·sian (rush′ən) *noun, plural* **Russians**; *adjective.*

rust **1.** A reddish brown or orange coating that forms on iron exposed to moisture or air. **2.** A plant disease that causes reddish brown spots to appear on leaves and stems. Rust is caused by a fungus. **3.** A reddish brown or orange color. *Noun.*

○ To become covered with rust: *The hinges on the gate **rusted**. Verb.*

○ Having the color rust. *Adjective.*

rust (rust) *noun, plural* **rusts**; *verb,* **rusted, rusting**; *adjective.*

rustic Of, relating to, or like the country: *The artist is famous for painting **rustic** scenes.* **rus·tic** (rus′tik) *adjective.*

rustle **1.** To make or cause to make soft, fluttering sounds: *The leaves **rustled** in the wind.* **2.** To steal cattle. *Verb.*
○ A soft, fluttering sound of things being rubbed together or stirred about: *We heard the **rustle** of papers in the next room. Noun.*
rus·tle (rus′əl) *verb*, **rustled, rustling;** *noun*, *plural* **rustles.**

rusty **1.** Covered with rust: *Let's **replace** the rusty nails in the fence.* **2.** Made by rust: *There are **rusty** spots on these metal chairs.* **3.** Not as good as it used to be because of not being used: *My piano playing is a bit **rusty** because I haven't practiced for a while.* **rust·y** (rus′tē) *adjective,* **rustier, rustiest.**

rut **1.** A track or groove made in the ground by a wheel or by constant use: *The tractor left **ruts** in the dirt road.* **2.** A fixed way of living, thinking, or acting; boring routine or sameness: *Don't get into a **rut** by doing the same things every day. Noun.*
○ To make ruts in: *The heavy trucks **rutted** the road. Verb.*
rut (rut) *noun, plural* **ruts;** *verb,* **rutted, rutting.**

ruthless Not having pity or mercy: *a **ruthless** dictator.* **ruth·less** (rüth′lis) *adjective.* **—ruthlessly** *adverb* **—ruthlessness** *noun.*

rye A grass plant that has slender stems. The grain of this plant is used as food for animals and in making flour and whiskey.
Another word that sounds like this is **wry.**
rye (rī) *noun, plural* **ryes.**

PRONUNCIATION KEY:
at   āpe   fär   câre   end   mē   it   īce   pierce   hot   ōld   sông   fôrk
oil   out   up   ūse   rüle   pull   tûrn   chin   sing   shop   thin   this
hw in white; zh in treasure. The symbol ə stands for the unstressed vowel sound in about, taken, pencil, lemon, and circus.

645

s, S The nineteenth letter of the alphabet. **s, S** (es) *noun, plural* **s's, S's.**

S or S. An abbreviation for **south** or **southern.**

Sabbath The day of the week that is used for worship. Sunday is the Sabbath for most Christians. Saturday is the Sabbath for Jews. **Sab·bath** (sab′əth) *noun, plural* **Sabbaths.**

saber A heavy sword that has a long, usually curved blade and one cutting edge. **sa·ber** (sā′bər) *noun, plural* **sabers.**

saber-toothed tiger A large animal that lived millions of years ago. It had long, curved teeth in the upper jaw and is closely related to lions, tigers, and other cats. **sa·ber-toothed tiger** (sā′bər tütht′) *noun.*

sable A small animal that looks like a weasel. Its soft, brown fur is very valuable. **sa·ble** (sā′bəl) *noun, plural* **sables.**

sabotage The deliberate damage or destruction of buildings, machinery, or other property, in order to interfere with some activity. Sabotage is used during a time of war against an enemy. *Noun.*
○ To damage, destroy, or interfere with on purpose: *Enemy agents sabotaged our radar. Verb.* **sab·o·tage** (sab′ə täzh) *noun; verb,* **sabotaged, sabotaging.**

sac A part in a plant or animal that is shaped like a bag and usually holds liquid.
Another word that sounds like this is **sack.**
sac (sak) *noun, plural* **sacs.**

646

The letter S has two sounds in English. The first sound can be made by:

s in words such as sit, aside, and pets;

ss in pass, toss, and Mississippi;

sc in science;

c in cent and century;

ps in psychology.

The letter S can also sound like Z in words such as rose and treasure.

saccharine 1. Having to do with sugar or sweetness. 2. Much too nice or sentimental: *a saccharine birthday card.* **sac·cha·rine** (sak′ər in) *adjective.*

sack¹ 1. A large bag that is made of coarse, strong material: *We bought a sack of potatoes at the market.* 2. In baseball, one of the bases, including home plate. *Noun.*
○ To dismiss from a job or position; fire: *Her boss finally sacked her for not doing her job. Verb.*
Another word that sounds like this is **sac.**
sack (sak) *noun, plural* **sacks;** *verb,* **sacked, sacking.**

sack² To steal all the valuable things from a town or city that has been captured in a war: *The army sacked the town. Verb.*
○ The act of sacking. *Noun.*
Another word that sounds like this is **sac.**
sack (sak) *verb,* **sacked, sacking;** *noun, plural* **sacks.**

sacred 1. Belonging to God or a god; having to do with religion: *Our choir sings sacred music.* 2. Regarded as deserving respect: *The memory of the dead hero was sacred to the town.* **sa·cred** (sā′krid) *adjective.*

sacrifice 1. The ceremony of offering something to God or a god as an act of worship: *The sacrifice of animals once was common in many religions.* 2. Something that is offered in an act of worship: *The ancient Greeks often killed a sheep on the altar as a sacrifice to a god.* 3. The giving up of something that is wanted for the sake of someone else or something else: *The parents made many sacrifices in order to send their chil-*

dren to college. **4.** In baseball, a bunt or fly ball that enables a base runner to advance even though the batter is put out. *Noun.*

○ **1.** To offer as a sacrifice to God or a god: *Ancient peoples **sacrificed** animals to their gods.* **2.** To give up for the sake of someone else or something else: *I **sacrificed** a chance to go skiing because I had promised to help my parents. Verb.*

sac·ri·fice (sak′rə fīs) *noun, plural* **sacrifices**; *verb,* **sacrificed, sacrificing.** —**sacrificial** *adjective.*

sad **1.** Unhappy or sorrowful: *I was **sad** when my friend moved to another city.* **2.** Causing unhappiness or sorrow: *The wet and hungry dog was a **sad** sight.* **sad** (sad) *adjective,* **sadder, saddest.**

sadden To make or become sad: *The death of our dog **saddened** us.* **sad·den** (sad′ən) *verb,* **saddened, saddening.**

saddle **1.** A seat for a rider on the back of a horse or similar animal. Saddles are usually made of leather. **2.** Something that is used like or looks like a saddle. The seat of a bicycle is often called a saddle. *Noun.*

○ **1.** To put a saddle on: *The cowhand **saddled** the horse.* **2.** To load or burden: *The club **saddled** me with all the work. Verb.* **sad·dle** (sad′əl) *noun, plural* **saddles**; *verb,* **saddled, saddling.**

His **saddle** was a cowboy's most important possession.

safari A hunting trip: *Many hunters once went on **safaris** in Africa.* **sa·fa·ri** (sə fä′rē) *noun, plural* **safaris.**

safe **1.** Free from or giving protection from harm or danger: *The spy found a **safe** place to hide the secret paper.* **2.** Without a chance of failure or error: *It is a **safe** guess that it will rain today.* **3.** Careful: *My parents are very **safe** drivers.* **4.** Having reached a base in baseball without being put out. *Adjective.*

○ A strong metal box or other container. It is used to store money, jewelry, or other valuable things. *Noun.*

safe (sāf) *adjective,* **safer, safest**; *noun, plural* **safes.** —**safely** *adverb.*

safeguard Something that protects: *We put a screen in front of the fireplace as a **safeguard** against escaping sparks. Noun.*

○ To protect or guard: *The new alarm **safeguards** our house. Verb.*

safe·guard (sāf′gärd′) *noun, plural* **safeguards**; *verb,* **safeguarded, safeguarding.**

safety Freedom from harm or danger: *The police work for the **safety** of us all.* **safe·ty** (sāf′tē) *noun.*

safety belt A strong band of cloth, leather, or other material that is used to hold a person in place or to prevent a person from falling. Window washers use safety belts when working outside on tall buildings.

safety pin A pin that is bent so as to form a spring. It has a guard at one end to cover the point.

sag **1.** To sink or hang down: *The old bed **sagged** in the middle.* **2.** To become less firm or lose strength: *Our spirits **sagged** after we lost four games in a row.* **sag** (sag) *verb,* **sagged, sagging.**

sage A very wise person, usually also old and very respected: *My grandmother is the **sage** in our family. Noun.*

○ Having or showing great wisdom and sound judgment: *My grandparents often give me **sage** advice. Adjective.*

sage (sāj) *noun, plural* **sages**; *adjective,* **sager, sagest.**

sagebrush A plant that has silver-white leaves and small yellow or white flowers. Sagebrush grows on the dry plains of western North America. **sage·brush** (sāj′brush′) *noun.*

sail **1.** A large piece of canvas or other material that is attached to a mast on a boat. When it catches the wind it moves the boat forward in the water. **2.** Something that is like a sail in shape or use. The flat part of the arm of a windmill is called a sail. **3.** A trip or ride in a boat: *go for a **sail**. Noun.*

○ **1.** To move through or travel over the water: *The boat **sailed** to sea.* **2.** To begin a trip by water: *The ship **sails** for Hawaii in two weeks.* **3.** To steer or run a boat: *I am going to learn* *how to sail.* **4.** To move smoothly and without difficulty: *The hawk sailed across the sky. Verb.* Another word that sounds like this is **sale.**

   sail (sāl) *noun, plural* **sails;** *verb,* **sailed, sailing.**

sailboat A boat that is moved by the wind blowing against its sail or sails. **sail•boat** (sāl′bōt′) *noun, plural* **sailboats.**

sailboat

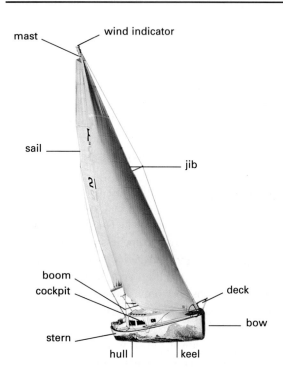

mast — wind indicator
sail —
— jib
boom
cockpit —
— deck
— bow
stern —
hull — keel

sailor A person whose work is sailing or working on a boat. A sailor may work for a steamship company or be in the navy. **sail•or** (sā′lər) *noun, plural* **sailors.**

saint **1.** A very holy person. Some churches publicly honor such holy people after they have died. **2.** A person who is very kind to or patient with other people: *The sick patient thought the helpful nurse was a saint.* **saint** (sānt) *noun, plural* **saints.** —**saintly** *adjective* —**saintliness** *noun.*

sake **1.** Benefit or advantage; good: *Finish school for your own sake.* **2.** Purpose or reason: *Did you take the new job for the sake of making more money?* **sake** (sāk) *noun, plural* **sakes.**

salad A cold dish that is made with lettuce, tomatoes, or other vegetables and often served with a dressing. Meat, fish, eggs, or fruit are also used in salads. **sal•ad** (sal′əd) *noun, plural* **salads.**

salamander An animal that looks like a small lizard. Salamanders are amphibians and are related to frogs and toads. They live in or near fresh water. **sal•a•man•der** (sal′ə man′dər) *noun, plural* **salamanders.**

salami A spicy sausage made out of beef and pork. **sa•la•mi** (sə lä′ mē) *noun, plural* **salamis.**

salary A fixed amount of money that is paid to someone for work done. It is paid at regular times: *That job pays a good salary.* **sal•a•ry** (sal′ə rē) *noun, plural* **salaries.**

WORD HISTORY

The word salary comes from the Latin word for "pay" or "allowance," which originally came from the Latin word for "salt." A Roman soldier's salary was the money he was given to buy salt. Later it came to mean "wages paid for work done."

sale **1.** An exchange of goods or property for money: *A real estate agent arranged for the sale of our house.* **2.** The selling of something for less than it usually costs: *The store is having a sale on bathing suits.*

Another word that sounds like this is **sail.**

   • **for sale.** Available for purchase: *Is that house for sale?*

   • **on sale.** Available for purchase at a price that is lower than usual: *Furniture is on sale at our local department store.*

   sale (sāl) *noun, plural* **sales.**

salesman A man whose job is selling things. **sales•man** (sālz′mən) *noun, plural* **salesmen** (sālz′mən).

salespeople People who sell things for a living: *All the salespeople in that store are friendly and helpful.* **sales•peo•ple** (sālz′pē′pəl) *plural noun.*

salesperson A salesman or saleswoman. **sales•per•son** (sālz′pûr′sən) *noun, plural* **salespersons.**

saleswoman A woman whose job is selling things. **sales•wom•an** (sālz′wùm′ən) *noun, plural* **saleswomen** (sālz′wim′ən).

saliva A clear liquid that is given off into the mouth by glands. It keeps the mouth moist, helps in chewing, and starts digestion. **sa•li•va** (səl ī′və) *noun.*

salmon **1.** A large fish with a silver-colored body. Most salmon live in salt water but swim to fresh water to lay their eggs. **2.** A yellowish pink color. *Noun.*

○ Having the color salmon. *Adjective.* **sal·mon** (sam′ən) *noun, plural* **salmon** *or* **salmons**; *adjective.*

salsa A spicy sauce made of chopped tomatoes, onion, garlic, chili, and other spices, used especially with Mexican food. **salsa** (säl′sə) *noun, plural* **salsas.**

salt **1.** A white substance that is found in sea water and in the earth. Salt is used to season and preserve foods. **2.** A chemical substance that is formed by the reaction of an acid with a base. *Noun.*

○ Containing or preserved with salt: *The ocean is made up of salt water. Adjective.* To season or preserve with salt: *Please don't salt my vegetables. Verb.*

• **with a grain of salt.** With some doubt; not too seriously: *Since they were not reliable, I took their advice with a grain of salt.* **salt** (sôlt) *noun, plural* **salts**; *adjective; verb,* **salted, salting.**

saltwater Of, having to do with, or living in salt water. A shark is a saltwater fish. **salt·wa·ter** (sôlt′wô′tər) *adjective.*

salty Containing or tasting of salt: *The food was too salty to eat.* **salt·y** (sôl′tē) *adjective,* **saltier, saltiest.**

This astronaut is **saluting** the American flag he has placed on the moon.

salute **1.** To show formal respect by raising the right hand to the forehead: *The sailor saluted when the flag was raised.* **2.** To greet with friendly or respectful words or actions: *The audience saluted the speaker with loud applause. Verb.* The act or gesture of saluting: *I gave the sergeant a smart salute. The president was greeted by a* twenty-one gun *salute. Noun.*

salute (sə lüt′) *verb,* **saluted, saluting**; *noun, plural* **salutes.**

WORD HISTORY

The word **salute** comes from a Latin word that means "to wish good health to."

salvage To save from being lost or destroyed: *Our friends were able to salvage some furniture from their burning house. Verb.*

○ The rescue of something from being lost or destroyed: *The tugboats helped in the salvage of the sinking ship. Noun.* **sal·vage** (sal′vij) *verb,* **salvaged, salvaging**; *noun.*

salve A soft, often greasy substance that heals or soothes wounds or sores; ointment: *The nurse put salve on my scraped knee.* **salve** (sav) *noun, plural* **salves.**

same **1.** Like another in every way: *Two people wore the same costume to the party.* **2.** Being the very one; not another; identical: *That is the same person I sat next to on the bus yesterday.* **3.** Not changed: *You are the same kind, friendly person you were a year ago. Adjective.*

○ A person or thing that is alike or identical: *My friend ordered a slice of melon for dessert, and I asked for the same. Noun.* **same** (sām) *adjective; noun.*

sample A small part or piece of anything that shows what the whole is like: *Show me a sample of the carpet you like. Noun.*

○ To test or judge a part of: *The cook sampled the soup to see how it tasted. Verb.* **sam·ple** (sam′pəl) *noun, plural* **samples**; *verb,* **sampled, sampling.**

samurai A Japanese warrior of medieval times. **sam·u·rai** (sam′ü rī′) *noun, plural,* **samurais.**

sanction To give approval: *My parents sanctioned my choice of college. Verb.*

○ **1.** Approval: *Do you need your parent's sanction to play volleyball?* **2. sanctions.** Punishment for failing to observe a law or some other unacceptable action: *impose sanctions against a country for human rights violations. Noun.* **sanc·tion** (sangk′shən′) *noun, plural,* **sanctions**; *verb,* **sanctioned, sanctioning.**

PRONUNCIATION KEY:

| at | āpe | fär | câre | end | mē | it | īce | pierce | hot | ōld | sông | fôrk |
| oil | out | up | ūse | rüle | pu̇ll | tûrn | chin | sing | shop | thin | this | |

hw in white; zh in treasure. The symbol ə stands for the unstressed vowel sound in about, taken, pencil, lemon, and circus.

649

sanctuary **1.** Safety or protection: *The escaped prisoners found* **sanctuary** *in the woods.* **2.** A natural area where birds and animals are protected. **3.** A holy or sacred place. **sanc·tu·ar·y** (sangk′chü er′ē) *noun, plural* **sanctuaries.**

sand Tiny, loose grains of crushed rocks. Sand is found on beaches and in deserts. *Noun.*
○ **1.** To scrape and smooth with sandpaper or sand: *Sand the edges before you paint.* **2.** To sprinkle or cover with sand: *The city* **sanded** *the roads after the snowstorm.* *Verb.*
sand (sand) *noun; verb,* **sanded, sanding.**

Beaches and deserts are made up mainly of sand.

sandal A shoe with a sole that is held to the foot by one or more straps. **san·dal** (san′dəl) *noun, plural* **sandals.**

sandbar A ridge or bank of sand, in a river or bay or along a shore, built up by the action of waves or currents. **sand·bar** (sand′bär′) *noun, plural* **sandbars.**

sandpaper A strong, heavy paper with a rough coating of sand or other material on one side, used to smooth and clean wood and other surfaces. *Noun.*
○ To smooth and clean by rubbing with sandpaper: *The worker* **sandpapered** *the old door until it was smooth.* *Verb.*
sand·pa·per (sand′pāp′ər) *noun; verb,* **sandpapered, sandpapering.**

sandstone A kind of rock that is made up mainly of grains of sand held together by a kind of natural cement. **sand·stone** (sand′stōn′) *noun.*

sandwich Two or more slices of bread with meat, cheese, or some other filling between them. *Noun.*
○ To fit or squeeze in tightly: *The book was* **sandwiched** *between two others on the top shelf.* *Verb.*

sand·wich (sand′wich) *noun, plural* **sandwiches;** *verb,* **sandwiched, sandwiching.**

sandy **1.** Containing or like sand: *The cactus is a plant that grows in* **sandy** *soil.* **2.** Yellowish brown in color: *You have* **sandy** *hair.* **sand·y** (san′dē) *adjective,* **sandier, sandiest.**

sane **1.** Having a healthy mind; not crazy. **2.** Having or showing good sense: *My friend gave me some* **sane** *advice.*
Another word that sounds like this is **seine.**
sane (sān) *adjective,* **saner, sanest.**

sanitation The protection of people's health by keeping living conditions clean. Sanitation includes getting rid of garbage and keeping drinking water clean. **san·i·ta·tion** (san′i tā′shən) *noun.*

sanity A healthy state of mind. **san·it·y** (san′i tē) *noun.*

sap A liquid that flows through a plant. Sap carries water and food from one part of a plant to another: *The* **sap** *of the maple tree is used to make syrup.* **sap** (sap) *noun, plural* **saps.**

sapling A young tree: *The thin trunk of the* **sapling** *bent easily.* **sap·ling** (sap′ling) *noun, plural* **saplings.**

sarcastic Using sharp or bitter words that are meant to hurt or make fun of someone or something: *Your* **sarcastic** *answer hurt my feelings.* **sar·cas·tic** (sär kas′tik) *adjective.* —**sarcastically** *adverb.*

sardine A small fish that lives in salt water and is used for food. Sardines are packed tightly in oil in flat cans: *We had* **sardines** *and crackers for lunch.* **sar·dine** (sär dēn′) *noun, plural* **sardines** *or* **sardine.**

sari A piece of clothing worn by women of India and Pakistan. A sari is one long piece of cloth that is wrapped around the body to form a skirt and cover one shoulder. **sa·ri** (sär′ē) *noun, plural* **saris.**

sash¹ A broad piece of cloth that is worn around the waist or over one shoulder: *This dress has a bright pink* **sash** *instead of a belt.* **sash** (sash) *noun, plural* **sashes.**

sash² The frame that holds the glass in a window or door. **sash** (sash) *noun*, *plural* **sashes**.

Sask. An abbreviation for Saskatchewan.

Saskatchewan A province in central Canada. Its capital is Regina. **Sas·katch·e·wan** (sas kach′ə won′) *noun*.

Sat. An abbreviation for Saturday.

Satan The evil spirit that is thought to rule hell; the Devil. **Sa·tan** (sā′tən) *noun*.

satellite 1. A heavenly body that moves in an orbit around another body larger than itself. The moon is the earth's only natural satellite. 2. A space-craft that moves in an orbit around the earth, the moon, or other bodies in space. Satellites are used to forecast the weather, to connect radio, tele-phone, and television communications, and to provide informa-tion about conditions in space. 3. A country that is dependent on or controlled by another, more powerful country: *Hungary used to be a satellite of the Soviet Union.* **sat·el·lite** (sat′ə līt′) *noun*, *plural* **satellites**.

Many hundreds of satellites are in orbit around the earth.

satin A fabric that has a smooth, shiny surface. It is made of silk or similar materials. **sat·in** (sat′in) *noun*, *plural* **satins**.

satisfaction The condition of being satisfied or the act of satisfying: *Many people get a lot of satisfaction from doing their job well.* **sat·is·fac·tion** (sat′is fak′shən) *noun*.

satisfactory Good enough to meet a need, desire, or standard; giving satisfaction: *Your high grade on the arithmetic test is more than satisfactory.* **sat·is·fac·to·ry** (sat′is fak′tə rē) *adjective*.

satisfy 1. To be or give enough to meet the need, desire, or demand of: *The sandwich will satisfy me until dinner.* 2. To make free from doubt; convince: *The children's explanation of where they had been all afternoon satisfied their parents.* **sat·is·fy** (sat′is fī′) *verb*, **satisfied**, **satisfying**.

saturate To soak or fill completely: *The spilled milk saturated the rug.* **sat·u·rate** (sach′ə rāt′) *verb*, **saturated**, **saturating**.

Saturday The seventh day of the week. **Sat·ur·day** (sat′ər dē *or* sat′ər dā′) *noun*, *plural* **Saturdays**.

Saturn
The second largest planet, Saturn is the first to be known to have rings. They can be seen from Earth through a small telescope. Its moon, Titan, is the largest in the Solar System.
Average distance from sun: **887,100,000 miles**
Diameter: **74,915 miles**
Length of Day: **10 hours, 40 minutes**
Length of Year: **29.5 years**
Average Temperature: **-301°F**
Mass compared to Earth: **95**
Weight of 100 pounds: **108**
Atmosphere: **Hydrogen, Helium**
Number of rings: **Hundreds**
Number of satellites: **18**

Saturn The second largest planet in our solar sys-tem. It is the sixth planet in order of distance

PRONUNCIATION KEY:

| at | āpe | fär | câre | end | mē | it | īce | pierce | hot | ōld | sông | fôrk |
| oil | out | up | ūse | rüle | pull | tûrn | chin | sing | shop | thin | this | |

hw in white; zh in treasure. The symbol ə stands for the unstressed vowel sound in about, taken, pencil, lemon, and circus.

651

from the sun. Saturn is surrounded by large rings and many moons. **Sat•urn** (sat′ərn) *noun*.

sauce **1.** A liquid or creamy mixture that is served with food: *The chef made a lemon* **sauce** *for the fish.* **2.** A food consisting of fruit that has been stewed: *cranberry* **sauce.** **sauce** (sôs) *noun, plural* **sauces.**

saucepan A small pot with a handle, used for cooking. **sauce•pan** (sôs′pan′) *noun, plural* **saucepans.**

saucer A small, shallow dish that is used for holding a cup. **sau•cer** (sô′sər) *noun, plural* **saucers.**

sausage Finely chopped meat that is mixed with spices. It is often stuffed into a thin case like a tube. Frankfurters are sausages. **sau•sage** (sô′sij) *noun, plural* **sausages.**

savage **1.** Cruel or fierce: *There was savage fighting all day on the battlefield.* **2.** Not tamed; wild: *a savage animal.* **3.** Not civilized: *the savage life of the jungle. Adjective.*
○ **1.** A person who is cruel, fierce, or brutal.
2. A person who lives a way that is not thought to be civilized. *Noun.*
sav•age (sav′ij) *adjective; noun, plural* **savages.**

savanna or **savannah** A flat, grassy plain that has only a few trees: *the African savanna.* **sa•van•na** (sə van′ə) *noun,* **savannas.**

save **1.** To free from harm; make safe: *The firefighters saved the child from the burning house.*
2. To set aside money or anything else for use in the future: *I am saving my allowance to buy a baseball mitt.* **3.** To keep from being lost, spent, or damaged: *save time by shopping close to home.*
4. To keep from being needed: *We borrowed a cup of flour and saved a trip to the store.*
5. To avoid expense or waste: *We save on food by buying what is on sale.* **save** (sāv) *verb,* **saved, saving.**

savings Money that is saved: *It will take all of your savings to buy that camera.* **sav•ings** (sā′vingz) *plural noun.*

saw A tool or machine that has a sharp

The man is using a gasoline powered saw.

metal blade with teeth. It is used for cutting wood, metal, or other hard materials. *Noun.*
○ To cut or be cut with a saw: *The lumberjack sawed the log in half. Verb.*
saw (sô) *noun, plural* **saws;** *verb,* **sawed, sawed** or **sawn, sawing.**

sawdust The fine particles that fall from wood as it is being sawed. **saw•dust** (sô′dust′) *noun.*

sawmill A place where machines saw logs into lumber. **saw•mill** (sô′mil′) *noun, plural* **sawmills.**

saxophone A musical instrument that has a curved metal body with keys fitted along it. It is played by blowing into the mouthpiece and pushing down the keys with the fingers. **sax•o•phone** (sak′sə fōn′) *noun, plural* **saxophones. —saxophonist** *noun.*

say **1.** To speak or pronounce words: *What did you say?* **2.** To make known or express in words; declare: *They said that they enjoyed meeting you.* **3.** To estimate or suppose: *How much money would you say that cashier earns?* **4.** To repeat; recite: *The class said the pledge of allegiance to the flag. Verb.*
○ **1.** The right or chance to speak: *You'll have your say.* **2.** The right or power to influence or decide: *have a say in foreign policy. Noun.*
say (sā) *verb,* **said, saying;** *noun.*

saying A familiar statement that contains some truth or common sense; proverb. "A stitch in time saves nine" is a saying. **say•ing** (sā′ing) *noun, plural* **sayings.**

SC Postal abbreviation for **South Carolina.**

S.C. An abbreviation for **South Carolina.**

scab **1.** A crust that forms over a sore or wound to protect it as it heals. **2.** A person who is not a member of a labor union who works for a company while the union is on strike. This is an informal usage. **scab** (skab) *noun, plural* **scabs.**

scabbard A case for the blade of a sword, dagger, or similar weapon; sheath. **scab•bard** (skab′ərd) *noun, plural* **scabbards.**

scaffold A platform that workers stand on as they work on a building. **scaf•fold** (skaf′əld) *noun, plural* **scaffolds.**

scale¹ A device used to find out how heavy something is. It works by balancing the thing to be weighed against another weight or against the force of a spring. **scale** (skāl) *noun, plural* **scales.**

scale² **1.** One of the thin, flat plates that cover the body of fish, snakes, and lizards. **2.** A thin, flat piece of something: *The old paint is coming off the house in scales. Noun.*

○ To take off the scales from: *The clerk in the fish store scaled the fish for us. Verb.*
scale (skāl) *noun, plural* **scales;** *verb,* **scaled, scaling.**

scale³ **1.** A series of marks made along a line at regularly spaced points. A scale is used for measuring: *The scale of that ruler is in inches.* **2.** The size of a plan, map, or model compared with what it represents: *The pay scale for that job is from $200 per week to $300 per week.* **4.** Relative size or extent: *The artist worked on a large scale.* **5.** A series of musical tones that go up or down in pitch: *A scale is usually made up of eight notes. Noun.*

○ **1.** To climb to or over the top of: *The climbers scaled the steep cliff.* **2.** To change by a fixed amount: *The two countries scaled down the building of weapons. Verb.*
scale (skāl) *noun, plural* **scales;** *verb,* **scaled, scaling.**

scalene triangle A triangle with each of its three sides a different length. **sca·lene trian·gle** (skā lēn′)

scalene triangle

scallop **1.** A shellfish enclosed by two shells that protect the soft body inside, and open to let in food and water. The scallop is a mollusk. **2.** One of a series of curves that looks like the edge of a scallop shell: *The dress had scallops along the bottom. Noun.*

○ To shape or make with a series of curves: *The edges of the quilt were scalloped. Verb.*
scal·lop (skol′əp *or* skal′əp) *noun, plural* **scallops;** *verb,* **scalloped, scalloping.**

scalp The skin that covers the head and is usually covered with hair. *Noun.*

○ To cut or tear the scalp from. *Verb.*
scalp (skalp) *noun, plural* **scalps;** *verb,* **scalped, scalping.**

scaly Covered or partly covered with scales: *Fish and snakes are scaly.* **scal·y** (skā′lē) *adjective,* **scalier, scaliest.**

scamper To run or to move quickly: *The rabbit*

scampered into the woods. **scam·per** (skam′pər) *verb,* **scampered, scampering.**

scan **1.** To look at closely and carefully: *The sailor scanned the horizon for land.* **2.** To read quickly or glance over: *We scanned the newspaper headlines. Verb.*

○ The movement of a beam of light over something, such as a page in a book, to copy writing or an image into a computer. *Noun.*
scan (skan) *verb,* **scanned, scanning;** *noun, plural* **scans.** —**scanner** *noun.*

Scandinavia **1.** A part of north-central Europe consisting of Denmark, Norway, and Sweden. Sometimes Finland and Iceland are considered part of Scandinavia. **2.** A large peninsula in north-central Europe. Norway and Sweden are on this peninsula. **Scan·di·na·vi·a** (skan′də nā′vē ə) *noun.*

Scandinavian A person who was born in or is a citizen of a country in Scandinavia. *Noun.*

○ Of or relating to Scandinavia, its peoples, or its languages. *Adjective.* **Scan·di·na·vi·an** (skan′də nā′vē ən) *noun, plural* **Scandinavians;** *adjective.*

scant **1.** Not enough or barely enough: *We brought only scant supplies for the trip.* **2.** A little less than full; not quite full: *The recipe calls for a scant teaspoon of salt.* **scant** (skant) *adjective,* **scanter, scantest.** —**scantily** *adverb* —**scanty** *adjective.*

scar **1.** A mark on the skin left by a cut or burn that has healed: *I have a scar on my knee.* **2.** Any mark that is like this: *The burning cigar left an ugly scar on the table. Noun.*

○ To mark with a scar or scars: *Our dog scarred the door by scratching it. Verb.*
scar (skär) *noun, plural* **scars;** *verb,* **scarred, scarring.**

scarce Difficult to get or find: *Water is scarce in the desert.* **scarce** (skârs) *adjective,* **scarcer, scarcest.** —**scarcity** *noun.*

scarcely **1.** Only just or almost not; barely or hardly. *There was scarcely a person on the street.* **2.** Certainly not: *I would scarcely go back to visit them.* **scarce·ly** (skârs′lē) *adverb.*

scare To frighten or become afraid: *My older cousin doesn't scare easily. Verb.*

○ A sudden fear or fright: *The explosion gave us*

PRONUNCIATION KEY:

at	āpe	fär	câre	end	mē	it	īce	pierce	hot	ōld	sông	fôrk
oil	out	up	ūse	rüle	pull	tûrn	chin	sing	shop	thin	this	

hw in white; zh in treasure. The symbol ə stands for the unstressed vowel sound in about, taken, pencil, lemon, and circus.

653

quite a scare. **2.** A condition of widespread fear or fright; panic: *There was a bomb scare on the plane. Noun.*
scare (skâr) *verb,* **scared, scaring;** *noun, plural* **scares.**

scarecrow A figure of a person used to scare crows and other birds away from crops. A scarecrow is often dressed in old clothes. **scare·crow** (skâr′krō′) *noun, plural* **scarecrows.**

scarf A piece of cloth worn about the neck or head, either for warmth or decoration. **scarf** (skärf) *noun, plural* **scarves** or **scarfs.**

scarlet A bright red color. *Noun.*
○ Having the color scarlet: I *like scarlet roses. Adjective.*
scar·let (skär′lit) *noun, plural* **scarlets;** *adjective.*

These onions are a deep scarlet.

scary Causing alarm or fear; frightening: *It was scary to be all alone in the big old house.* **scary** (skâr′ē) *adjective,* **scarier, scariest.**

scatter **1.** To spread or throw about in various places: *The wind scattered the leaves all over the yard.* **2.** To separate or cause to separate and go in different directions: *The mob scattered when the police arrived.* **scat·ter** (skat′ər) *verb,* **scattered, scattering.**

scavenger **1.** An animal that feeds on carcasses or decaying plant matter. **2.** A person who searches through trash for things that can be used or sold to others. **scav·en·ger** (skav′ən jər) *noun, plural* **scavengers.**

scene **1.** The place where something happens: *The police arrived at the scene of the accident.* **2.** A part of an act in a play or movie. **3.** View; sight: *The scene of the valley from the porch was beautiful.* **4.** A show of strong feeling in front of oth-

ers: *cause a scene in the restaurant.* **scene** (sēn) *noun, plural* **scenes.**

scenery **1.** The general appearance of a place; the sights in an area: *They drove to the mountains to look at the scenery.* **2.** The painted pictures or objects that are used to make the setting of a play or movie: *The scenery looked realistic.* **scen·er·y** (sē′nə rē) *noun, plural* **sceneries.**

scent **1.** A smell: *The scent of lilacs was in the air.* **2.** The trail by which someone or something can be traced or found: *Hunting dogs track foxes by their scent.* **3.** The sense of smell: *Bloodhounds are known for their keen scent.* **4.** A liquid with a pleasant smell; perfume: *What scent is that you're wearing? Noun.*
○ To sense by or as if by the sense of smell: *I scent trouble. Verb.*
scent (sent) *noun, plural* **scents;** *verb,* **scented, scenting.**

scepter A rod or staff that is carried by a king or queen. A scepter is used as a symbol of royal office or power. **scep·ter** (sep′tər) *noun, plural* **scepters.**

schedule **1.** A list of times, events, or things to do: *Check the bus schedule before you go.* **2.** The time at which something is supposed to happen: *The train was running behind schedule because of the weather. Noun.*
○ To put in or on a schedule; plan or arrange for a particular time: *I scheduled an appointment with my dentist for Friday. Verb.*
sched·ule (skej′ül) *noun, plural* **schedules;** *verb,* **scheduled, scheduling.**

scheme **1.** A plan or plot for doing something: *The crooks had a scheme for robbing the bank.* **2.** An orderly arrangement of related things; design: *You can choose the color scheme for your room. Noun.*
○ To plan or plot: *The rebels schemed to capture the king and queen. Verb.*
scheme (skēm) *noun, plural* **schemes;** *verb,* **schemed, scheming.**

scholar **1.** A person who has much knowledge. **2.** A person who attends school. **schol·ar** (skol′ər) *noun, plural* **scholars.**

scholarship **1.** Money that is given to a student to help pay for his or her studies. **2.** Knowledge or learning. **schol·ar·ship** (skol′ər ship′) *noun, plural* **scholarships.**

school¹ **1.** A place for teaching and learning: *They are my classmates at school.* **2.** The students,

teachers, and other people who work at such a place: *The entire school went on the trip.* **3.** A period or time of teaching at a school: *There is no school today.* **4.** The process of being educated at a school: *I found school very difficult when I was your age.* **5.** A department of a college or university for teaching in a particular field: *My cousin attends the university's school of medicine. Noun.*
○ To train or teach: *Doctors must school themselves to handle emergencies. Verb.*
school (skül) *noun, plural* **schools**; *verb,* **schooled, schooling.**

school² A large group of fish or water animals swimming together. **school** (skül) *noun, plural* **schools.**

schoolhouse A building used as a school. **school·house** (skül′hous′) *noun, plural* **school-houses** (skül′hou′ziz).

schooner A ship that has two or more masts and sails that are set lengthwise. **schoon·er** (skü′nər) *noun, plural* **schooners.**

schwa The symbol (ə) used in English for a vowel sound that is spoken without any force. The *a* in *ago* and the *o* in *lemon* are represented by a schwa. **schwa** (shwä) *noun, plural* **schwas.**

science **1.** Knowledge about things in nature and the universe. Science is based on facts that are learned from experiments and careful study. **2.** Any particular branch of such knowledge. Biology, chemistry, and physics are sciences. **sci·ence** (sī′əns) *noun, plural* **sciences.**

scientific Having to do with or used in science: *All of the students in our class had to plan and carry out a scientific experiment.* **sci·en·tif·ic** (sī′ən tif′ik) *adjective.*
—scientifically *adverb.*

scientist A person who works or specializes in a branch of science. Biologists, chemists, and physicists are scientists. **sci·en·tist** (sī′ən tist) *noun, plural* **scientists.**

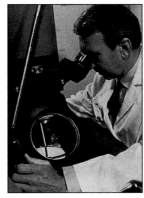
The **scientist** is using a microscope.

scissors A tool used for cutting paper, thread, cardboard, cloth, and many other kinds of material. Scissors have two blades held together in the middle. When the blades are brought together, they form a double cutting edge. **scis·sors** (siz′ərz) *plural noun.*

scold To find fault with; speak sharply to: *The teacher scolded the student. Verb.*
○ A person who scolds. *Noun.*
scold (skōld) *verb,* **scolded, scolding**; *noun, plural* **scolds.**

scoop **1.** A tool shaped like a small shovel, used for taking up flour, sand, or other soft substances. **2.** The large bucket of a steam shovel, used for picking up dirt, sand, or other material from the ground. **3.** A tool shaped like a cup attached to a handle, used to take up portions of food. **4.** The amount any scoop holds: *I only want one scoop of mashed potatoes. Noun.*
○ To take up with a scoop, or as if with a scoop: *The children scooped up their books and ran off to school. Verb.*
scoop (sküp) *noun, plural* **scoops**; *verb,* **scooped, scooping.**

scope The range or extent of an idea, action, or a person's understanding: *The lecture on nuclear energy was beyond my scope.* **scope** (skōp) *noun.*

scorch **1.** To burn slightly on the surface: *I scorched my shirt with the iron.* **2.** To dry up with heat: *The hot sun scorched the grass. Verb.*
○ A slight burn: *A necktie will cover the scorch on the front of that shirt. Noun.*
scorch (skôrch) *verb,* **scorched, scorching**; *noun, plural* **scorches.**

score **1.** The points or a record of the points made in a game or on a test: *The final score was 5 to 4. What was your score on the test?* **2.** A set or group of twenty: *A score of people came to the meeting.* **3.** Written or printed music. A score shows all the parts for instruments and voices. **4. scores,** *plural.* A great many: *Scores of people have seen that movie. Noun.*
○ **1.** To make a point or points in a game or test: *I scored twenty points in the game.* **2.** To keep a record of points made or assign points in a game or test: *The teacher scored our tests right after we finished.* **3.** To achieve or win: *You scored a great*

PRONUNCIATION KEY:

| at | āpe | fär | câre | end | mē | it | īce | pîerce | hot | ōld | sông | fôrk |
| oil | out | up | ūse | rüle | pull | tûrn | chin | sing | shop | thin | this | |

hw in white; zh in treasure. The symbol ə stands for the unstressed vowel sound in about, taken, pencil, lemon, and circus.

655

success by winning all three races. Verb.
score (skôr) *noun, plural* **scores**; *verb,* **scored**, **scoring.**

scorn A feeling of hatred for someone or something thought of as low or bad: *The defeated villain slipped away as the play's hero and heroine looked on with* **scorn.** *Noun.*

○ To treat or reject as low or bad: *The whole town* **scorned** *the idea of turning the playground into a parking lot. Verb.*
scorn (skôrn) *noun; verb,* **scorned**, **scorning.** —**scornful** *adjective.*

scorpion A small animal, related to the spider, that has four pairs of legs and a long tail with a poisonous stinger on the end. **scor·pi·on** (skôr′pē ən) *noun, plural* **scorpions.**

This **scorpion** is carrying its young
on its back.

Scot A person who was born in or is a citizen of Scotland. **Scot** (skot) *noun, plural* **Scots.**

Scotch Of or having to do with Scotland: *I have a skirt made of* **Scotch** *plaid.* This term is usually used only in compound words referring to Scottish things, not people or places. **Scotch** (skoch) *adjective.*

Scotland A section of the United Kingdom. It occupies the northern part of the island of Great Britain. **Scot·land** (skot′lənd) *noun.*

Scottish 1. the Scottish. The people of Scotland. 2. The dialect of English spoken in Scotland. *Noun.*
○ Of or having to do with Scotland, its people, or its language. *Adjective.*
Scot·tish (skot′ish) *noun; adjective.*

scoundrel A wicked or dishonest person; villain; rogue. *The gang was a bunch of* **scoundrels** *who had stolen a lot of money.* **scoundrel** (skoun′drəl) *noun, plural* **scoundrels.**

scour¹ 1. To clean or polish by rubbing hard, as with steel wool or a cleanser: *I* **scoured** *the pots to make them shiny.* 2. To remove by rubbing hard: *I* **scoured** *the grime off the bathtub.* 3. To clean or remove something that clogs, as by flushing: *We have to* **scour** *our kitchen drain.* **scour** (skour) *verb,* **scoured**, **scouring.**

scour² To go through or examine in search of something: *We* **scoured** *the house for signs of termites.* **scour** (skour) *verb,* **scoured**, **scouring.**

scout 1. A soldier, ship, or plane sent to find out and bring back information: *The* **scout** *brought back word that the enemy was camped nearby.* 2. A person who belongs to the Boy Scouts or Girl Scouts. *Noun.*
○ To look at or explore in order to find out and bring back information: *Two campers went ahead to* **scout** *the trail. Planes were sent out to* **scout** *for the enemy. Verb.*
scout (skout) *noun, plural* **scouts**; *verb,* **scouted**, **scouting.**

scoutmaster An adult who leads a troop of Boy Scouts. **scout·mas·ter** (skout′mas′tər) *noun, plural* **scoutmasters.**

scowl An angry frown: *Dad had a* **scowl** *on his face. Noun.*
○ To frown in an angry way: *The mother* **scowled** *at her child's rude behavior. Verb.*
scowl (skoul) *noun, plural* **scowls**; *verb,* **scowled**, **scowling.**

scramble 1. To mix together; mix up: *We* **scrambled** *the pieces of the puzzle.* 2. To cook eggs with the whites and yolks mixed together. 3. To move or climb quickly: *The children* **scrambled** *down the rocks.* 4. To struggle or compete with others: *The players* **scrambled** *for the ball. Verb.*
○ 1. The act of moving or climbing quickly: *The* **scramble** *up the hill left everyone tired.* 2. A struggle or competition: *There was a* **scramble** *for the best seats. Noun.*
scram·ble (skram′bəl) *verb,* **scrambled**, **scrambling**; *noun, plural* **scrambles.**

scrap 1. A small piece or little bit of something: *I wrote a note on a* **scrap** *of paper.* 2. scraps. Bits of leftover food: *We fed* **scraps** *to the dog.* 3. Worn or used material that can be used again in some way: *They sold the car for* **scrap.** *Noun.*
○ 1. To throw away or give up as useless: *We decided to* **scrap** *the idea of going on a picnic.*

2. To break up into scrap: *The navy decided to scrap the old battleship. Verb.*

scrap (skrap) *noun, plural* **scraps**; *verb,* **scrapped, scrapping.**

scrapbook A book with blank pages on which pictures, newspaper clippings, and other items may be mounted and kept. **scrap·book** (skrap′bůk′) *noun, plural* **scrapbooks.**

scrape **1.** To injure or scratch by rubbing against something sharp or rough: *The runner scraped a knee sliding into first base.* **2.** To rub or move with a harsh, grating sound: *I scraped the chalk on the blackboard.* **3.** To clean or smooth by rubbing: *We scraped the food off our plates.* **4.** To get or collect with difficulty: *The cycling club scraped up enough money for a trip. Verb.*
○ **1.** A mark made on a surface by rubbing or scratching against something sharp or rough: *There is a big scrape on the car.* **2.** A harsh, grating sound: *We heard the scrape of sleds on the road.* **3.** A difficult, unpleasant situation: *We got into a scrape. Noun.*

scrape (skrāp) *verb,* **scraped, scraping**; *noun, plural* **scrapes.**

scratch **1.** To scrape or cut with nails, claws, or anything else that is sharp and pointed: *The cat scratched my arm.* **2.** To rub or scrape in order to stop itching. **3.** To rub with a harsh, grating sound: *Is that the puppy scratching at the door?* **4.** To cancel or strike out: *Scratch my name off the list. Verb.*
○ **1.** A mark made by scraping or cutting: *I had scratches on my legs.* **2.** A harsh, grating sound: *The scratch of the branch against the window startled us. Noun.*
• **from scratch.** From the beginning; with no resources: *When their business failed, they had to start again from scratch.*

scratch (skrach) *verb,* **scratched, scratching**; *noun, plural* **scratches.**

scream To make a loud, shrill, piercing cry or sound: *I screamed when the monster appeared in the movie. Verb.*
○ A loud, shrill, piercing cry or sound: *The scream of a train whistle broke the silence of the night. Noun.*

scream (skrēm) *verb,* **screamed, screaming**; *noun, plural* **screams.**

screech To make a shrill, harsh cry or sound: *The car's brakes screeched. Verb.*
○ A shrill, harsh cry or sound: *We heard a screech as the car came to a stop. Noun.*

screech (skrēch) *verb,* **screeched, screeching**; *noun, plural* **screeches.**

screen **1.** Wire mesh or netting in a frame: *We use screens on the windows to keep out the flies.* **2.** A covered frame that is used to hide or divide: *A screen separates the dining area from the kitchen.* **3.** Anything like a screen: *A screen of bushes hides the house.* **4.** A surface that reflects light, on which motion pictures or slides are projected. **5.** The front surface of a television set or computer monitor. *Noun.*
○ To hide or protect with a screen: *A hat will screen your eyes from the sun. Verb.*

screen (skrēn) *noun, plural* **screens**; *verb,* **screened, screening.**

screen saver A computer program that makes a monitor last longer by creating different images on the screen when the computer is turned on but is not being used.

screw A kind of nail with ridges cut around its length and a slot on its head. *Noun.*
○ **1.** To attach or fasten with a screw or screws: *I screwed a lock onto the door.* **2.** To fix in place by twisting or turning: *Screw a new light bulb into the socket. Verb.*

screw (skrü) *noun, plural* **screws**; *verb,* **screwed, screwing.**

screwdriver A tool for turning screws. One end is a handle and the other end fits into the slot on the head of a screw. **screw·driv·er** (skrü′drī′vər) *noun, plural* **screwdrivers.**

scribble To write or draw quickly or carelessly: *I scribbled a note to my friend. Verb.*
○ Writing or drawing that is made by scribbling: *The piece of paper was covered with messy scribbles. Noun.*

scrib·ble (skrib′əl) *verb,* **scribbled, scribbling**; *noun, plural* **scribbles.** —**scribbler** *noun.*

scribe A person who writes down or copies letters, books, or other written materials. **scribe** (skrīb) *noun, plural* **scribes.**

script **1.** Handwriting in which the letters are joined together: *Our teacher taught us how to*

PRONUNCIATION KEY:

| at | āpe | fär | câre | end | mē | it | īce | pierce | hot | ōld | sông | fôrk |
| oil | out | up | ūse | rüle | půll | tûrn | chin | sing | shop | thin | this | |

hw in white; zh in treasure. The symbol ə stands for the unstressed vowel sound in about, taken, pencil, lemon, and circus.

657

write script. **2.** The written text of a play, movie, or television or radio show. **script** (skript) *noun, plural* **scripts.**

scroll A roll of paper, parchment, or other material with writing on it. Each end of a scroll is often rolled around a rod. *Noun.*

○ To move the text on a computer up or down in order to read it. *Verb.*

scroll (skrōl) *noun, plural* **scrolls;** *verb,* **scrolled, scrolling.**

scrub To rub in order to wash or clean: *You'll have to* **scrub** *your hands to get them clean. Verb.*

○ The act of scrubbing: *I gave the kitchen floor a good* **scrub.** *Noun.*

scrub (skrub) *verb,* **scrubbed, scrubbing;** *noun, plural* **scrubs.**

scruple A feeling about what is right and wrong that keeps one from doing something: *I couldn't lie because of my* **scruples. scru•ple** (skrü′pəl) *noun, plural* **scruples.**

scrupulous **1.** Very careful to do what is right or proper; moral: *My neighbor is* **scrupulous** *in dealing with others.* **2.** Very careful about details: *The* **scrupulous** *clerk made sure everything was ready for the sale.* **scru•pu•lous** (skrü′pyə ləs) *adjective.* —**scrupulously** *adverb.*

scrutinize To look at very carefully: *The police officer* **scrutinized** *my driver's license.* **scru•ti•nize** (skrüt′ən īz) *verb,* **scrutinized, scrutinizing.** —**scrutiny** *noun.*

scuba diving Swimming underwater with the help of special breathing equipment. The equipment includes a cylinder of compressed air, which is strapped to the diver's back, and a hose through which the diver can breathe the compressed air. **scu•ba diving** (skü′bə)

scuff To scratch the surface of by scraping or wear: *The child* **scuffed** *the new shoes on the gravel. Verb.*

○ The act or result of scuffing: *There is a* **scuff** *on the new floor. Noun.*

scuff (skuf) *verb,* **scuffed, scuffing;** *noun, plural* **scuffs.**

scuffle A confused struggle or fight: *Two hockey players had a* **scuffle.** *Noun.*

○ To struggle or fight in a confused way: *The two dogs* **scuffled** *on the street. Verb.*

scuf•fle (skuf′əl) *noun, plural* **scuffles;** *verb,* **scuffled, scuffling.**

sculpt To shape or give form to: *She* **sculpted** *a bust of Mozart in marble.* **sculpt** (skulpt) *verb,* **sculpted, sculpting.**

sculptor A person who makes or carves figures in stone, clay, metal, or any other material. **sculp•tor** (skulp′tər) *noun, plural* **sculptors.**

sculpture **1.** The art of carving or making figures or designs that occupy space. Sculpture usually is done by carving stone, wood, or marble, modeling in clay, or casting in bronze or another metal. **2.** The figure or design that is made in this way:

---

scuba diving

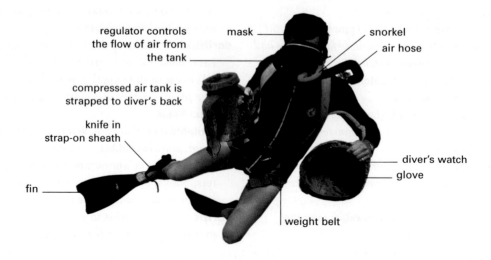

regulator controls the flow of air from the tank

mask

snorkel

air hose

compressed air tank is strapped to diver's back

knife in strap-on sheath

diver's watch

glove

fin

weight belt

That statue is a beautiful piece of **sculpture.** *Noun.*
○ To carve, model, or cast figures or designs: *The artist* **sculptured** *a lion. Verb.*
sculp·ture (skulp′chər) *noun, plural* **sculptures;** *verb,* **sculptured, sculpturing.**

The art of sculpture dates back to the earliest civilizations.

scurry To go or move in a hurry: *The children scurried after their parents.* **scur·ry** (skûr′ē) *verb,* **scurried, scurrying.**

scurvy A disease that is caused by a lack of vitamin C. A person with scurvy feels very weak and has bleeding gums. Scurvy can be prevented by eating vegetables and fruits that contain a large amount of vitamin C. **scur·vy** (skûr′vē) *noun.*

scythe A tool with a long curved blade and a long bent handle that is used to mow or cut grasses and crops by hand. **scythe** (sīth) *noun, plural* **scythes** (sī̱ths).

SD Postal abbreviation for **South Dakota.**

S.D. or **S. Dak.** An abbreviation for **South Dakota.**

SE or **S.E.** An abbreviation for **southeast.**

sea 1. The large body of salt water that covers almost three fourths of the earth's surface; ocean. 2. A large part of this body of salt water, usually partly enclosed by land. 3. The movement of the water of the ocean; wave or waves: *The crew struggled to keep the ship afloat in the rough seas.* 4. An overwhelming amount or number: *A* **sea** *of fans surrounded the rock band.* Another word that sounds like this is **see.**

• **at sea.** 1. Out on the ocean: *We were at sea for a week.* 2. Confused; bewildered: *I was at sea about what to do.*

• **to go to sea.** 1. To become a sailor: *They joined the navy and* **went to sea.** 2. To begin a voyage at sea: *They* **went to sea** *a week ago.* **sea** (sē) *noun, plural* **seas.**

sea anemone A sea animal that is shaped like a tube and that attaches itself to rocks and other objects.

seaboard The land on or near the sea: *California is on the Pacific* **seaboard.** **sea·board** (sē′bôrd′) *noun, plural* **seaboards.**

seacoast Land that is near the sea or bordering the sea. **sea·coast** (sē′kōst′) *noun, plural* **seacoasts.**

seafaring 1. Making a living by working at sea: *The* **seafaring** *merchant visited many lands.* 2. Of or having to do with the sea or sailors: *The sailor told* **seafaring** *tales.* **sea·far·ing** (sē′fâr′ing) *adjective.* —**seafarer** *noun.*

seafood Saltwater fish or shellfish used for food. **sea·food** (sē′füd′) *noun, plural* **seafoods.**

sea gull A white and gray bird with long wings that lives near the sea. Look up **gull** for more information.

sea horse A kind of fish with a head that looks like that of a horse. It has a curling tail that it uses to hold onto underwater plants.

seal¹ A mammal that lives in coastal waters and has flippers instead of feet. Seals spend some of their time on land. **seal** (sēl) *noun, plural* **seals** *or* **seal.**

seal² 1. A design that is stamped on wax, paper, or other soft material or a picture of such a design. A seal is used to show who owns something or that something is genuine. 2. Something that closes tightly and completely: *The* **seal** *of this envelope is a flap with glue on it.* 3. The condition of being closed tightly: *The* **seal** *on the jar was so tight that we had to put the top under hot water to loosen it.* 4. A stamp or sticker. Some kinds of seals are sold to raise money for a cause, and people who buy seals usually put them on letters and packages. *Noun.*
○ 1. To close tightly and completely: *Please* **seal** *the envelope. The worker* **sealed** *the cracks in the wall with plaster before painting.* 2. To settle or decide. *The two neighbors* **sealed** *their agreement by shaking hands.* 3. To place a seal on: *The diplo-*

PRONUNCIATION KEY:

| at | āpe | fär | câre | end | mē | it | īce | pîerce | hot | ōld | sông | fôrk |
| oil | out | up | ūse | rüle | pull | tûrn | chin | sing | shop | thin | <u>th</u>is | |

hw in white; zh in treasure. The symbol ə stands for the unstressed vowel sound in about, taken, pencil, lemon, and circus.

659

*ma was stamped and **sealed** by the college. Verb.*
seal (sēl) *noun, plural* **seals**; *verb,* **sealed, sealing.**

sea level The level of the surface of the sea, between high and low tide, used to measure heights and depths: *The city of Denver is one mile above **sea level**.*

sea lion One of several large seals that are found in the Pacific Ocean.

seam 1. A line formed by sewing together the edges of two or more pieces of cloth, leather, or other material: *One of the **seams** in this coat is coming apart.* 2. Any mark or line like a seam: *Water leaked into the rowboat because the **seams** were no longer sealed.* 3. A layer of a mineral or metal in the earth: *The mining company found a **seam** of coal in the mountain.*
Another word that sounds like this is **seem.**
seam (sēm) *noun, plural* **seams.**

seaplane An airplane with floats attached to its underside enabling it to take off from and land on water. **sea·plane** (sē′plān′) *noun, plural* **seaplanes.**

seaport A port or harbor, or a town or city with a harbor that is used by ships that travel on the sea. **sea·port** (sē′pôrt′) *noun, plural* **seaports.**

search To look, look through, or examine carefully in order to find something: *We've **searched** through the house for your keys. Verb.*
○ The act of searching: *The police led a **search** through the building. Noun.*
search (sûrch) *verb,* **searched, searching**; *noun, plural* **searches.**

searchlight A special lamp that produces a very strong beam of light: *The battleship used a **searchlight** to spot enemy airplanes at night.*
search·light (sûrch′līt′) *noun, plural* **searchlights.**

seashell The shell of an oyster, clam, or other sea animal. **sea·shell** (sē′shel′) *noun, plural* **seashells.**

seashore The land near or on the sea.
sea·shore (sē′shôr′) *noun, plural* **seashores.**

The **seashore** is a particularly popular place in the summer.

seasick Sick and dizzy because of the rolling motion of a boat or ship. **sea·sick** (sē′sik′) *adjective.*

season 1. One of the four parts of the year; spring, summer, fall, or winter. 2. Any special part of the year: *There is almost no rain during the dry **season** in parts of Africa. Noun.*
○ 1. To add seasoning to food in order to bring out the flavor: *I **seasoned** the stew with pepper and other spices.* 2. To make or become right for use: *They let the newly cut logs dry to **season** them for firewood. Verb.*
• **in season.** 1. Available or in the best condition for eating: *Peaches are **in season**.*
2. Legally permitted to be hunted or caught: *Salmon are now **in season**.*
• **out of season.** Not in season: *Are pumpkins **out of season** in the summer?*
sea·son (sē′zən) *noun, plural* **seasons**; *verb,* **seasoned, seasoning.**

seasonal Of, happening at, or influenced by a certain season or seasons: *The blooming of flowers is a **seasonal** event.* **sea·son·al** (sē′zə nəl) *adjective.*

seasoning Something that is used to bring out the flavor of food. Salt, pepper, and herbs are seasonings. **sea·son·ing** (sē′zə ning) *noun, plural* **seasonings.**

seat 1. Something to sit on. A chair, stool, or bench is a seat: *We have enough **seats** for everyone.* 2. A place to sit: *I couldn't get a **seat** on the bus.* 3. The part of a thing that one sits on: *The **seat** of this bicycle is uncomfortable.* 4. The part of the body that one sits on, or the clothes covering it: *Those pants have a rip in the **seat**.* 5. A membership or position: *Our neighbor has a **seat** on the town council.* 6. A center: *A college is a **seat** of learning. Noun.*
○ 1. To place on or lead to a seat: *The barber **seated** the little child in the chair. The usher **seated** us.* 2. To have seats for: *That theater **seats** 500 people. Verb.*

• **to be seated.** To sit down: *Will you please be seated?*

seat (sēt) *noun, plural* **seats;** *verb,* **seated, seating.**

seat belt A strap that is fastened to hold a person in the seat of a car, truck, airplane, or other vehicle in case of a crash, bump, or jolt.

sea urchin A sea animal that has a round shell covered with hard spines. The spines help the sea urchin move and protect itself. **sea ur·chin** (ûr′chin)

seaweed A plant that grows in the sea, especially certain kinds of algae. Seaweeds are green, brown, or red in color. All seaweeds need sunlight to make their own food. **sea·weed** (sē′wēd′) *noun, plural* **seaweeds.**

sec. An abbreviation for **second.**

secede To withdraw from a group or organization: *South Carolina was the first Southern state to secede from the Union before the Civil War.* **se·cede** (si sēd′) *verb,* **seceded, seceding.**

secluded 1. Kept away from others: *a secluded prisoner.* 2. Hidden from sight: *a secluded cabin in the woods.* **se·clud·ed** (si klü′did) *adjective.*

second¹ 1. Next after the first: *I liked the movie better the second time I saw it.* 2. Below the first or best: *He is the second pitcher on the team.* 3. Another: *May I have a second helping of potatoes, please?* 4. Skipping one after each: *We receive that magazine every second month. Adjective.*
○ In second place; after the first: *My friend finished first, and I finished second. Adverb.*
○ 1. A person or thing that is next after the first: *She was the second in line.* 2. Something lower in quality: *The shirts were sold as seconds because some buttons were missing. Noun.*
○ To help or support: *Who will second the motion to end the meeting? Verb.*
sec·ond (sek′ənd) *adjective; adverb; noun, plural* **seconds;** *verb,* **seconded, seconding.**

second² 1. One of the sixty equal parts of a minute. 2. Any very short period of time: *I'll come outside in a second.* **sec·ond** (sek′ənd) *noun, plural* **seconds.**

secondary After the first or main thing; not as important: *The bus took a secondary road during the blizzard because the main road was closed.* **sec·ond·ar·y** (sek′ən der′ē) *adjective.*

secondhand 1. Already used or owned by someone else; gotten from another: *a secondhand car. secondhand knowledge about the accident.* 2. Selling goods that someone else has owned or used: *a secondhand store.* **sec·ond·hand** (sek′ənd hand′) *adjective.*

secrecy 1. The condition of being secret or being kept secret: *The rebels made their plans in secrecy.* 2. The ability or practice of keeping things secret: *Our secrecy about the party helped make it a real surprise.* **se·cre·cy** (sē′krə sē) *noun.*

secret 1. Known only to oneself or a few; hidden: *The pirates buried the treasure in a secret place.* 2. Acting in a hidden way: *The secret agent spied on the enemy. Adjective.*
○ 1. Something that is secret: *I'll tell you a secret.* 2. A hidden reason or cause: *Hard work is the secret of my success. The scientist sought to learn the secrets of nature. Noun.*
• **in secret.** In a private place or in a manner that prevents other people from knowing: *The two old friends discussed their plans in secret.*
se·cret (sē′krit) *adjective; noun, plural* **secrets.**

secretary 1. A person whose work is writing letters and keeping records for another person, a business, or an organization: *I was elected secretary of the stamp club.* 2. A person who is the head of a department of a government: *The Secretary of Defense heads the Defense Department.* 3. A piece of furniture: It has a writing surface, drawers, and sometimes shelves. **sec·re·tar·y** (sek′rə ter′ē) *noun, plural* **secretaries.**

secrete To produce and release a chemical substance into the body: *The thyroid gland secretes a hormone that controls growth.* **se·crete** (si krēt′) *verb,* **secreted, secreting.**

section 1. A part taken from a whole; portion: *They planted vegetables in one section of the garden.* 2. A part of something written: *I always read the sports section of the newspaper.* 3. A part of an area or group: *We visited the old section of the city. The trumpet player plays in the brass section of the orchestra.* 4. A picture or model of something that shows what it would look like if it were cut open: *This lengthwise sec-*

PRONUNCIATION KEY:
| at | āpe | fär | câre | end | mē | it | īce | pierce | hot | ōld | sông | fôrk |
| oil | out | up | ūse | rüle | pùll | tûrn | chin | sing | shop | thin | this | |

hw in white; zh in treasure. The symbol ə stands for the unstressed vowel sound in about, taken, pencil, lemon, and circus.

661

tion of a flower shows all the inner parts. *Noun.*
○ To cut into parts or divide: *Please section the watermelon. Verb.*
sec·tion (sek′shən) *noun, plural* **sections;** *verb,* **sectioned, sectioning.**

secure **1.** Safe from harm or loss: *The basement was a secure place to be during the tornado. The jewels were secure in a safe.* **2.** Firm; steady; sound: *The old ladder is not secure enough to climb.* **3.** Certain or guaranteed: *Our victory seemed secure. Adjective.*
○ **1.** To get: *They secured tickets to the game.* **2.** To fasten firmly: *I secured the lock on the suitcase.* **3.** To make safe: *The guards in the armored truck secured the gold against robbers. Verb.*
se·cure (si kyŭr′) *adjective,* **securer, securest;** *verb,* **secured, securing.**

security **1.** Protection from harm or loss; safety: *I ran to the security of the school during the storm. Having money in the bank gives me a feeling of security.* **2.** Something that gives protection: *A burglar alarm is security against thieves.* **3.** Something that is given to make sure that an agreement will be fulfilled: *The pawnbroker accepted a gold ring as security for the loan.*
se·cu·ri·ty (si kyŭr′i tē) *noun, plural* **securities.**

sedan An automobile with a roof. It has two or four doors, and seats in both the front and the back. **se·dan** (si dan′) *noun, plural* **sedans.**

sediment **1.** Small pieces of matter that settle at the bottom of a liquid: *There was sediment at the bottom of the bottle.* **2.** Rocks, dirt, or other solid matter carried and left by water, glaciers, or wind: *The flood left a layer of sediment on the streets and sidewalks.* **sed·i·ment** (sed′ə mənt) *noun.*

sedimentary Formed from particles of stone or animal remains that have been deposited by water, wind, or ice over millions of years. Sedimentary rocks usually show layers of the materials that formed them. **sed·i·men·ta·ry** (sed′ə men′tə rē) *adjective.*

see **1.** To look or look at with the eyes; view: *Do you want to go see a movie?* **2.** To understand. *I see what you mean.* **3.** To find out: *Please see who is at the door.* **4.** To make sure: *See that you finish your homework.* **5.** To go with; accompany: *I'll see you to the door.* **6.** To visit or meet with: *The dentist will see you now.* **7.** To experience: *Those old shoes have seen much wear.*

Another word that sounds like this is **sea.**
● **to see off.** To go with to a place of departure: *I'll see you off at the airport.*
● **to see through. 1.** To continue with to the end: *This project is difficult, but I'm going to see it through.* **2.** To help or take care of during a period of difficulty: *We saw the dogs through a serious case of distemper.* **3.** To understand the real meaning or nature of: *We saw through their story.*
● **to see to.** To attend to; take care of: *Please see to this task immediately.*
see (sē) *verb,* **saw, seen, seeing.**

seed **1.** The part of a flowering plant from which a new plant will grow. Many seeds are in the form of a small nut or kernel surrounded by a hard shell: *plant seeds for a vegetable garden.* **2.** The source or cause of something: *A lack of sleep was the seed of my bad mood. Noun.*
○ **1.** To plant land with seeds: *We seeded the lawn.* **2.** To take seeds out of: *seed a watermelon. Verb.*
seed (sēd) *noun, plural* **seeds** *or* **seed;** *verb,* **seeded, seeding.**

seedling A young plant grown from a seed. **seed·ling** (sēd′ling) *noun, plural* **seedlings.**

seek **1.** To try to find; go in search of: *The police were seeking a stolen car.* **2.** To try: *Every candidate in the election will seek to win.* **3.** To try to get; ask for: *The victims of the flood sought help.* **seek** (sēk) *verb,* **sought, seeking.**

With proper care, this seedling will grow into a pine tree.

seem **1.** To appear to be: *The dark clouds make it seem later than it really is.* **2.** To appear to oneself: *I seem to have forgotten your name.* Another word that sounds like this is **seam.**
seem (sēm) *verb,* **seemed, seeming.**

seep To flow or spread slowly: *Water seeped into the ground after the rain.* **seep** (sēp) *verb,* **seeped, seeping.**

seethe 1. To boil: *Let the stew seethe for a while.* 2. To be very angry or upset: *My mother was seething because I got home late.* **seethe** (sēth) *verb,* **seethed, seething.**

segment One of the parts into which a whole is or can be divided; section: *You can separate the segments of a grapefruit with your fingers.* **seg·ment** (seg′mənt) *noun, plural* **segments.**

segregation The practice of setting one racial group apart from another: *There are laws against the segregation of black children and white children in the public schools.* **seg·re·ga·tion** (seg′ri gā′shən) *noun.*

seine A fishing net. It has floats on the top edge and weights on the bottom edge. Another word that sounds like this is **sane.** **seine** (sān) *noun, plural* **seines.**

seismograph An instrument used to measure the power of earthquakes. **seis·mo·graph** (sīz′mə graf′) *noun, plural* **seismographs.**

seize 1. To take hold of; grab: *The dog seized the bone.* 2. To get control of; capture: *The soldiers seized the fort.* **seize** (sēz) *verb,* **seized, seizing.**

seizure 1. A sudden attack of an illness; a spasm. 2. The seizing of a person or thing: *the seizure of a drug dealer's property.* **sei·zure** (sē′zhər) *noun, plural* **seizures.**

seldom Not often; rarely: *I seldom see my friend who moved to another city.* **sel·dom** (sel′dəm) *adverb.*

These children have helped select this tree.

select To pick out; choose: *Would you select this red coat or that green one? Select your friends with care. Verb.*
  ○ Picked or chosen because of a special ability or quality: *A select group of athletes will compete in the games. Adjective.*
  se·lect (si lekt′) *verb,* **selected, selecting;** *adjective.*

SYNONYMS

select, choose, elect, pick

*The teachers **selected** the tallest student to carry the flag. The children got to **choose** the color of their bedroom. My sister was **elected** president of her class. I **picked** the shoes I would wear with my graduation cloths.*

---

selection 1. The selecting of something: *The magician had me make a selection of a card from the deck.* 2. A person or thing that is or can be selected: *What are the selections on the menu?* **se·lec·tion** (si lek′shən) *noun, plural* **selections.**

selective Very careful in choosing: *Be selective when you buy fruit.* **se·lec·tive** (si lek′tiv) *adjective.*

self 1. One's own person apart from all other persons: *I know my own self best.* 2. The way that one feels, looks, or acts: *He was very angry and unlike his usual self.* **self** (self) *noun, plural* **selves.**

self- A prefix that means oneself: *Self-respect means respect for oneself.* The prefix *self-* is always followed by a hyphen.

self-confidence Faith in one's own ability or worth: *The pitcher's self-confidence inspired the rest of the softball team.* **self-con·fi·dence** (self′kon′fi dəns) *noun.*

self-control Control over one's own emotions and actions: *When I hurt myself, it took a lot of self-control to keep from crying.* **self-con·trol** (self′kən trōl′) *noun.*

self-esteem Pride in oneself; self-respect. **self-es·teem** (self′i stēm′) *noun.*

self-explanatory Not needing any explanation: *I think her instructions were self-explanatory.* **self-ex·plan·a·to·ry** (self′ik splan′ə tôr′ē) *adjective.*

selfish Thinking only of oneself; not thinking of others. A selfish person is not interested in the wishes and feelings of other people. **self·ish** (sel′fish) *adjective.*

self-respect Proper regard for one's own worth or importance; respect for oneself: *It helped his self-respect in defying that bully.* **self-re·spect** (self′ri spekt′) *noun.*

PRONUNCIATION KEY:

| at | āpe | fär | câre | end | mē | it | īce | pîerce | hot | ōld | sông | fôrk |
| oil | out | up | ūse | rüle | püll | tûrn | chin | sing | shop | thin | this | |

hw in white; zh in treasure. The symbol ə stands for the unstressed vowel sound in about, taken, pencil, lemon, and circus.

663

self-service Set up so that customers serve themselves: *a self-service gas station.* **self-ser·vice** (self′sûr′vis) *adjective.*

self-sufficient Able to take care of oneself without any help from other people; independent. **self-suf·fi·cient** (self′sə fish′ənt) *adjective.*

sell 1. To give something in return for money: *We sold the old bicycle for twenty-five dollars.* 2. To deal in: *That store sells shoes.* 3. To be offered for sale: *This candy sells for twenty-five cents.* Another word that sounds like this is **cell.** **sell** (sel) *verb,* **sold, selling.**

semester One of two terms into which a school or college year may be divided. **se·mes·ter** (si mes′tər) *noun, plural* **semesters.**

semicircle Half a circle: *The children sat in a semicircle around the campfire.* **sem·i·cir·cle** (sem′ē sûr′kəl) *noun, plural* **semicircles.**

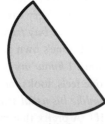

semicircle

semicolon A punctuation mark (;) that is used to separate parts of a sentence. A semicolon marks a greater separation than a comma does. **sem·i·co·lon** (sem′ē kō′lən) *noun, plural* **semicolons.**

semifinal A game or match that comes right before the final one in a series: *Our team made it to the semifinal. Noun.*
○ Coming right before the final game or match in a series: *We played in the semifinal game. Adjective.*
sem·i·fi·nal (sem′ē fī′nəl) *noun, plural* **semifinals;** *adjective.*

seminary A school that trains students to be priests, ministers, or rabbis. **sem·i·nary** (sem′ə ner′ē) *noun, plural* **seminaries.**

Seminole A member of a tribe of Native Americans that settled in Florida. Many of the Seminole now live in Oklahoma. **Sem·i·nole** (sem′ə nōl′) *noun, plural* **Seminole** *or* **Seminoles.**

semitrailer A large trailer for carrying freight. It is attached at its forward end to the truck tractor. **sem·i·trail·er** (sem′i trā′lər *or* sem′ī trā′lər) *noun, plural* **semitrailers.**

senate 1. One of the branches of an assembly that makes laws. The legislatures of most states of the United States have senates. 2. **Senate.** One of the branches of the United States Congress. **sen·ate** (sen′it) *noun, plural* **senates.**

WORD HISTORY

The word **senate** comes from a Latin word that means "old man." In Rome, the government council known as the senate was made up of the heads of noble families, who were old men.

---

senator A member of a senate. **sen·a·tor** (sen′i tər) *noun, plural* **senators.**

send 1. To cause to go from one place to another: *Do you send birthday cards to your friends?* 2. To cause to go, come, or be: *The soft music sent me to sleep.*
• **to send for.** 1. To ask someone to come; summon: *Did you send for the police?* 2. To ask that something be brought or sent: *We sent for a free booklet.*
send (send) *verb,* **sent, sending.**

senior 1. The older of two. "Senior" is used after the name of a father whose son has the same name: *William Lawrence, Senior, is the father of William Lawrence, Junior.* 2. Higher in rank, longer in service, or older in age: *Our senator is a senior member of Congress.* 3. Of or having to do with the last year of high school or college: *Next year I will be a senior in high school. Adjective.*
○ 1. A person who is older than another or higher in rank than another: *My sister is my senior by five years.* 2. A student who is in the last year of high school or college. *Noun.*
sen·ior (sēn′yər) *adjective; noun, plural* **seniors.**

senior citizen An elderly person, especially one who is over 65 years of age and has retired: *My grandparents are senior citizens.*

señor The Spanish title for a man. **se·ñor** (sen′yôr) *noun, plural* **señores.**

señora The Spanish title for a married woman or for a widow. **se·ño·ra** (sen yô′rə) *noun, plural* **señoras.**

señorita The Spanish title for a girl or unmarried woman. **se·ño·ri·ta** (sen′yə rē′tə) *noun, plural* **señoritas.**

sensation 1. The power or ability to see, hear, smell, taste, or touch. 2. A condition of being aware; feeling: *The little children felt a sensation* of fear when they saw the big dog. **3.** Great excitement; strong feeling: *The news caused a sensation.* **4.** A person or thing that causes great excitement or interest: *The new invention was a sensation.* **sen•sa•tion** (sen sā′shən) *noun, plural* **sensations.**

sensational Causing or meant to cause great excitement or strong feeling: *The football player made a sensational catch.* **sen•sa•tion•al** (sen sā′shə nəl) *adjective.*

sense **1.** A power of a living being to know about its surroundings and about changes in its own body. Sight, hearing, smell, taste, and touch are the five senses. **2.** Feeling: *I had a sense of failure after losing the race.* **3.** Understanding or appreciation: *You have a good sense of humor.* **4.** Intelligence; good judgment: *The puppy hasn't sense enough to come in out of the rain.* **5.** Use; reason: *What is the sense of keeping that old radio if it doesn't work?* **6.** Meaning: *The word "run" has many different senses.* *Noun.*
○ To feel; understand: *We could sense that you were glad to be home.* *Verb.*
- **to make sense.** To have a clear meaning; be reasonable, logical, or understandable: *This paragraph doesn't make sense to me.*
sense (sens) *noun, plural* **senses;** *verb,* **sensed, sensing.**

sense organ An organ in the body that takes in information from its surroundings. In humans, the eyes, ears, nose, taste buds, and skin are sense organs.

sensible Having or showing good sense; wise: *It is sensible to look both ways before crossing the street.* **sen•si•ble** (sen′sə bəl) *adjective.*

sensitive **1.** Easily affected or hurt: *A sensitive person can become very upset if criticized.* **2.** Having deep feelings; very aware: *A poet must be a sensitive person.* **3.** Able to react to a certain thing or condition: *The film in a camera is very sensitive to light.* **sen•si•tive** (sen′si tiv) *adjective.*

sensor A device that detects changes in heat, sound, or pressure and sends the information to another instrument that controls it. **sen•sor** (sen′sôr) *noun, plural* **sensors.**

sentence **1.** A group of words that gives a complete thought. A sentence states something or

asks a question. "The dog and cat" is not a sentence. "The dog and cat are fighting" is a sentence. **2.** A punishment for crime set by a court: *The judge gave the thief a sentence of three years in the state prison.* *Noun.*
○ To set the punishment of: *The judge sentenced them to thirty days in jail for refusing to pay their parking fines.* *Verb.*
sen•tence (sen′təns) *noun, plural* **sentences;** *verb,* **sentenced, sentencing.**

sentiment Feeling or emotion: *There is much sentiment in our town against closing the park on Sundays.* **sen•ti•ment** (sen′tə mənt) *noun, plural* **sentiments.**

sentimental Having or showing tender feeling: *The couple in the movie sang a sentimental song.* **sen•ti•men•tal** (sen′tə men′təl) *adjective.*

sentry A person stationed to keep watch and warn others of danger; guard: *A sentry guarded the palace twenty-four hours a day.* **sen•try** (sen′trē) *noun, plural* **sentries.**

sepal One of a ring of usually green parts that are shaped like leaves and lie at the base of a flower. They cover and protect the flower when it is a bud and fold back from the flower when it blooms. **se•pal** (sē′pəl) *noun, plural* **sepals.**

Each of these farm plots is separated **by roads.**

separate **1.** To keep apart; divide: *A fence separates our yard from theirs.* **2.** To set apart; place apart: *We separated the old books from the new ones.* **3.** To go in different directions; part: *The two friends separated and went home for dinner.* *Verb.*

PRONUNCIATION KEY:

at	āpe	fär	câre	end	mē	it	īce	pierce	hot	ōld	sông	fôrk
oil	out	up	ūse	rüle	pùll	tûrn	chin	sing	shop	thin	this	

hw in white; zh in treasure. The symbol ə stands for the unstressed vowel sound in about, taken, pencil, lemon, and circus.

665

○ Set apart; not joined: *The twins have separate rooms. Adjective.*

sep·a·rate (sep′ə rāt′ *for verb*; sep′ər it *or* sep′rit *for adjective*) *verb*, **separated**, **separating**; *adjective*.

separation 1. The act of separating things: *The recipe called for the separation of the egg's white and yolk.* 2. The condition of being separated: *The friends were happy to see each other again after a year's separation.* **sep·a·ra·tion** (sep′ə rā′shən) *noun, plural* **separations**.

Sept. An abbreviation for September.

September The ninth month of the year. September has thirty days. **Sep·tem·ber** (sep tem′bər) *noun*.

WORD HISTORY

September comes from the Latin word for "seven." The early Roman calendar began with March, making September the seventh month.

---

sequel A book or movie that continues the story begun in an earlier work. **se·quel** (sē′kwəl) *noun, plural* **sequels**.

sequence 1. The coming of one thing after another in a fixed order: *Winter, spring, summer, and fall follow each other in sequence.* 2. A series of things that are related in some way: *This sequence of photos shows how the explosion happened.* **se·quence** (sē′kwəns) *noun, plural* **sequences**.

sequoia A huge evergreen tree that grows in California. It has thick, reddish brown bark, sharply pointed leaves, and hard cones that stay on the tree for years. **se·quoi·a** (si kwoi′ə) *noun, plural* **sequoias**.

serene Calm and peaceful; quiet: *The lake was serene after the storm had passed.* **se·rene** (sə rēn′) *adjective*, **serener**, **serenest**.

serf In olden times, a person who was like a slave. Serfs were forced to stay on the land where they lived and were sold along with the land. Another word that sounds like this is **surf**. **serf** (sûrf) *noun, plural* **serfs**.

sergeant 1. An army or marine officer who ranks below a lieutenant but above a corporal. 2. An air force enlisted person who ranks above an airman. **ser·geant** (sär′jənt) *noun, plural* **sergeants**.

serial A long story divided into parts. The parts are presented on television or radio or published in a magazine or newspaper at scheduled times. Another word that sounds like this is **cereal**. **se·ri·al** (sîr′ē əl) *noun, plural* **serials**.

series A number of similar things coming one after another: *The famous explorer gave a series of talks at the school.* **se·ries** (sîr′ēz) *noun, plural* **series**.

serious 1. Having a thoughtful, solemn manner; grave: *The judge is a serious person.* 2. Not joking; sincere: *Were you serious about taking piano lessons?* 3. Important: *Failing in school is a serious matter.* 4. Dangerous: *Cancer is a serious illness.* **se·ri·ous** (sîr′ē əs) *adjective*.

sermon 1. A public talk about religion or morals. A sermon is given by a member of the clergy. 2. Any serious talk: *The parents gave their child a sermon about sharing.* **ser·mon** (sur′mən) *noun, plural* **sermons**.

serpent A snake. **ser·pent** (sûr′pənt) *noun, plural* **serpents**.

serum 1. A thin, clear liquid that separates from blood when a clot forms. 2. The serum of an animal that has already had a disease and is now immune to it. This serum can be taken from the animal and used to protect humans and other animals from getting the disease. **se·rum** (sîr′əm) *noun, plural* **serums**.

servant A person hired to work for the comfort or protection of others. Employees in a household are servants. Mail carriers and mayors are public servants. **ser·vant** (sûr′vənt) *noun, plural* **servants**.

serve 1. To bring food to: *I helped serve dinner.* 2. To supply enough for: *That stew will serve ten people.* 8. To be a servant to; work: *The butler served the family for many years.* 3. To spend time in jail or fulfilling a duty: *The thief had to serve five years in jail.* 5. To be used: *This sofa can serve as a bed.* 4. To be of use or help to: *This airport serves many people.* 6. In some games, to hit a ball in order to begin playing. 7. To give; present: *The driver was served with a summons. Verb.*

○ In some games, the act of hitting a ball in order to begin playing: *The tennis player's serve was good. Noun.*

• **to serve one right.** To be just what one deserves: *It served them right to fail the test since they tried to cheat.*

serve (sûrv) *verb*, **served**, **serving**; *noun, plural* **serves**.

server 1. A person who serves food: *If you will cook the dinner, I will be the server.* 2. A person who serves a ball in a game like tennis: *Of all the players here, he is the strongest server.* 3. A computer that takes care of much of the work in a network of computers.

service 1. A helpful act; useful work: *Our neighbor spends much time in service to the poor. The sick patient needs the services of a doctor.* 2. Employment as a servant: *The maid and butler have been in the service of the family for many years.* 3. Use or help: *"How may I be of service to you?" said the salesperson.* 4. A system or way of giving something needed or requested by a person or people: *Mail service is good in our town. The service in this restaurant is slow today.* 5. A branch of the armed forces: *My cousin spent three years in the service.* 6. A branch or department of a government: *The diplomat works in the foreign service.* 7. A religious ceremony: *The wedding service lasted an hour.* 8. The act of repairing or keeping ready for use: *The old car needed service.* 9. A set of things needed for use while eating: *This china service is for eight people. Noun.*
○ To make or keep ready for use: *The mechanic serviced the car. Verb.*
ser·vice (sûr′vis) *noun, plural* **services**; *verb,* **serviced, servicing.**

service station A place to buy gasoline, oil, and other things necessary for the operation of cars, trucks, and other motor vehicles. Service stations also provide repairs.

serving A helping of food: *May I have another serving of corn?* **serv·ing** (sûr′ving) *noun, plural* **servings.**

session 1. A meeting of a group, such as a court or legislature: *We attended a session of the Supreme Court.* 2. A series of such meetings: *This session of Congress ends today.* 3. A time or period when students attend classes at a school or college.
• **in session.** Meeting: *Classes won't be in session until after the holidays.*
ses·sion (sesh′ən) *noun, plural* **sessions.**

set 1. To place; put: *Set your books on the table. The child set the toy horse on its feet.* 2. To put in a useful or the correct order; arrange; fix: *Please set the table. Set your watch by the clock.*

The doctor set my broken arm. 3. To cause to be or become; put in some condition: *We set our pet mouse free. Set the logs on fire.* 4. To begin; start: *I set to work on my report.* 5. To fix or establish: *Have they set a date for the party?* 6. To achieve or provide: *The runner set a new record.* 7. To go down below the horizon: *The sun will set in an hour.* 8. To become firm or hard: *This glue sets in five minutes. Verb.*
○ 1. Fixed or decided: *Most games have set rules.*
2. Stubborn about changing: *My mind is set.*
3. Ready; prepared: *We are all set to leave. Adjective.*
○ 1. A group of things or persons: *We have a new set of dishes.* 2. A device for sending out or receiving by radio, television, telephone, or telegraph: *The television set broke.* 3. The scenery for a play or motion picture. 4. One group of games in tennis. *Noun.*
• **to set aside.** To keep available or save for a special use or reason: *I set aside an hour each day to practice playing the drums. Set aside a little money each week.*
• **to set forth.** 1. To make known; state; declare: *The speakers set forth their ideas.*
2. To start to go, as on a journey: *The pioneers set forth on their journey.*
• **to set in.** To begin: *Fall set in early.*
• **to set off.** 1. To make more prominent by contrast: *Dark hair sets off a fair complexion.*
2. To start to go or to begin: *We'll set off for the beach in an hour.* 3. To cause to explode: *We set off fireworks.*
• **to set out.** To begin a trip: *The ship set out for Australia yesterday.*
• **to set up.** 1. To assemble, erect, or prepare for use: *The scout set up a tent.* 2. To establish; found: *We set up a car wash.*
set (set) *verb,* **set, setting;** *adjective; noun, plural* **sets.**

settle 1. To agree about something; decide: *The two children could not settle their argument.* 2. To come to rest: *The bird settled on the branch.* 3. To make a home in a place: *We decided to settle in a small town.* 4. To sink: *The pebble settled to the bottom of the pond.* 5. To make calm: *The medicine settled my stomach.*

PRONUNCIATION KEY:

| at | āpe | fär | câre | end | mē | it | īce | pîerce | hot | ōld | sông | fôrk |
| oil | out | up | ūse | rüle | pull | tûrn | chin | sing | shop | thin | this | |

hw in white; zh in treasure. The symbol ə stands for the unstressed vowel sound in about, taken, pencil, lemon, and circus.

667

• **to settle down. 1.** To become calm or quiet: *The class settled down quickly after recess.* **2.** To devote effort and attention: *After dinner I settled down to two hours of studying.* **set·tle** (set′əl) *verb,* **settled, settling.**

settlement 1. The act of settling or the condition of being settled: *The settlement of Jamestown, Virginia, took place in 1607.* **2.** A small village or group of houses: *During the 1800s, pioneers built many settlements in the American West.* **3.** A colony: *Part of Canada was once a French settlement.* **set·tle·ment** (set′əl mənt) *noun, plural* **settlements.**

settler A person who settles in a new land or country: *The first European settlers of Florida were from Spain.* **set·tler** (set′lər) *noun, plural* **settlers.**

seven One more than six; 7. **sev·en** (sev′ən) *noun, plural* **sevens;** *adjective.*

seventeen Seven more than ten; 17. **sev·en·teen** (sev′ən tēn′) *noun, plural* **seventeens;** *adjective.*

seventeenth Next after the sixteenth. *Adjective, noun.*
○ One of seventeen equal parts; 1/17. *Noun.* **sev·en·teenth** (sev′ən tēnth′) *adjective; noun, plural* **seventeenths.**

seventh Next after the sixth. *Adjective, noun.*
○ One of seven equal parts; 1/7. *Noun.* **sev·enth** (sev′ənth) *adjective; noun, plural* **sevenths.**

seventieth Next after the sixty-ninth. *Adjective, noun.*
○ One of seventy equal parts; 1/70. *Noun.* **sev·en·ti·eth** (sev′ən tē ith) *adjective; noun, plural* **seventieths.**

seventy Seven times ten; 70. **sev·en·ty** (sev′ən tē) *noun, plural* **seventies;** *adjective.*

several More than two, but not many: *We saw several of our friends at the parade.* **sev·er·al** (sev′ər əl *or* sev′rəl) *adjective; noun.*

severe 1. Very strict; harsh: *The dictator established many severe laws.* **2.** Dangerous; serious: *The soldier had a severe wound.* **3.** Causing great difficulty or suffering; violent or sharp: *A severe storm is expected.* **se·vere** (sə vîr′) *adjective,* **severer, severest.**

sew To make, fasten, or close things with a needle and thread. A person can sew by hand or with a sewing machine: *Sew the button on your shirt. I sewed the tear closed on my pants.*

Other words that sound like this are **so** and **sow.**

• **to sew up.** To close a hole or tear: *I sewed up the hole in my shirt.*
sew (sō) *verb,* **sewed, sewed** *or* **sewn, sewing.**

sewage Waste that is carried off from sinks, toilets, and other devices in houses and factories by sewers and drains. **sew·age** (sü′ij) *noun.*

sewer A pipe or channel under the ground for carrying off waste from sinks, toilets, and other devices in houses and factories. **sew·er** (sü′ər) *noun, plural* **sewers.**

sewing machine A machine for sewing things. Most sewing machines are run by electric motors.

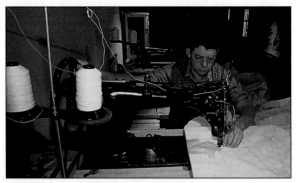

The **sewing machine** made possible the production of large quantities of clothing.

sex 1. One of the two divisions, male and female, that people and most other living things are divided into. **2.** The fact of being male or female. **sex** (seks) *noun, plural* **sexes.**

sexist Treating a person unfairly because of her or his sex: *It is sexist to assume that girls can't be athletes or police officers.* **sex·ist** (sek′sist) *adjective.* —**sexism** *noun.*

shabby 1. Worn-out and faded: *The beggar wore a shabby coat.* **2.** Mean or unfair: *It's cruel and shabby to make fun of other people.* **shab·by** (shab′ē) *adjective,* **shabbier, shabbiest.**

shack A small, roughly built hut or cabin. **shack** (shak) *noun, plural* **shacks.**

shade 1. A place sheltered from the sun; place darker than the area around it: *They rested in the shade of a tree.* **2.** Something that shuts out or reduces light: *Please lower the shades on the living room windows.* **3.** A particular variety of a color: *The pants are a light shade of green.* **4.** A small amount or difference: *The word "run" has many shades of meaning.* **5. shades.** Sunglasses. This is a slang use. *Noun.*

○ **1.** To shelter from heat or light: *The umbrella shaded us from the sun.* **2.** To mark with different amounts of darkness: *The artist shaded the faces in the painting. Verb.*
shade (shād) *noun, plural* **shades**; *verb,* **shaded, shading.**

shadow **1.** A dark area or figure made when rays of light are blocked by a person or thing: *The child cast a shadow.* **2.** A slight amount; suggestion: *There is not a shadow of a doubt that they are lying. Noun.*
○ To follow and watch another person closely and secretly: *The detective shadowed the suspected criminal. Verb.*
shad·ow (shad'ō) *noun, plural* **shadows**; *verb,* **shadowed, shadowing.**

shady **1.** Full of or giving shade: *We sat in a shady part of the yard.* **2.** Not completely honest: *The dishonest manager tried to carry out a shady business deal.* **shad·y** (shā'dē) *adjective,* **shadier, shadiest.**

shaft **1.** A long, thin part connected to the head of an arrow or spear, or the entire arrow or spear. **2.** The long handle of a hammer, golf club, hockey stick, or the like. **3.** A bar in a machine that supports parts or carries motion to other parts. **4.** A ray or beam: *Shafts of light came through the window.* **5.** A deep passage that goes straight down: *An elevator goes up and down an elevator shaft.* **shaft** (shaft) *noun, plural* **shafts.**

shaggy **1.** Covered with long, rough hair or something like hair: *The dog is large and shaggy.* **2.** Long, bushy, and rough: *a shaggy beard.*
shag·gy (shag'ē) *adjective,* **shaggier, shaggiest.**

shake **1.** To move quickly up and down, back and forth, or from side to side: *Shake the bottle to mix the salad dressing.* **2.** To remove or throw by moving up and down or from side to side: *The dog shook the water from its coat.* **3.** To tremble or cause to tremble: *The cold wind made me shake.* **4.** To weaken: *Nothing will shake our friendship.* **5.** To upset: *The news has shaken us. Verb.*
○ The act of shaking: *The child scared the dog away with a shake of a big stick. Noun.*
 • **to shake hands.** To clasp another's hand, as in greeting or agreement.

 • **to shake up.** To disturb mentally or physically; shock: *The argument I had with my best friend shook me up.*
shake (shāk) *verb,* **shook, shaken, shaking**; *noun, plural* **shakes.**

shaky **1.** Trembling; shaking: *The frightened person answered in a shaky voice.* **2.** Not firm; unsound. *The old bridge is shaky and should be rebuilt.* **shak·y** (shā'kē) *adjective,* **shakier, shakiest.**

Shale is found in thin layers.

shale A rock formed from mud that has hardened. Shale is found in thin layers. **shale** (shāl) *noun.*

shall An auxiliary verb that is used in the following ways: **1.** To express future actions and conditions: *I shall be happy to see you.* **2.** To express a requirement: *You shall do as I say.* **3.** To ask a question that extends an invitation or offers a suggestion: *Shall we dance?* **shall** (shal) *verb.*

shallow Not deep: *The water in the pond is shallow. Adjective.*
○ **shallows.** A shallow part of a body of water: *They waded in the shallows of the stream. Noun.* This word can be used with a singular or plural verb.
shal·low (shal'ō) *adjective,* **shallower, shallowest**; *plural noun.*

shame **1.** A painful feeling caused by having done something wrong or foolish: *He felt shame for having cheated.* **2.** Dishonor; disgrace: *Her arrest for robbery brought shame to her family.* **3.** A thing to be sorry for: *It is a shame that our team lost. Noun.*

PRONUNCIATION KEY:

| at | āpe | fär | câre | end | mē | it | īce | pîerce | hot | ōld | sông | fôrk |
| oil | out | up | ūse | rüle | pùll | tûrn | chin | sing | shop | thin | this | |

hw in white; zh in treasure. The symbol ə stands for the unstressed vowel sound in about, taken, pencil, lemon, and circus.

669

○ **1.** To cause to feel shame: *I was **shamed** by my foolish mistake.* **2.** To force by causing shame or the fear of shame: *Did your friends **shame** you into helping them? Verb.*

shame (shām) *noun; verb,* **shamed, shaming.**

SYNONYMS

shame, disgrace, dishonor
The political scandal brought shame to the mayor and the whole city. The theft of the company's funds caused disgrace to the thief. The soldiers brought dishonor upon themselves when they deserted their comrades.

shampoo To wash hair, rugs, or furniture coverings with a special soap: *I **shampoo** my hair twice a week. Verb.*
○ **1.** A special soap used to wash hair, rugs, or furniture coverings. **2.** An act of washing with shampoo: *Give the dog a **shampoo**. Noun.*
sham·poo (sham pü′) *verb,* **shampooed, shampooing;** *noun, plural* **shampoos.**

shamrock A leaf with three parts or leaflets that is an emblem of Ireland. A clover leaf with three leaflets is a shamrock. **sham·rock** (sham′rok′) *noun, plural* **shamrocks.**

shape **1.** Form; figure: *All circles have the same **shape**.* **2.** Condition: *The runner was in bad **shape** after the fall.* **3.** Regular, proper, or good form or condition: *Get your room in **shape**. Noun.*
○ **1.** To give form to; mold: *I **shaped** the wire into the figure of a dog.* **2.** To change the form of: *The tailor can **shape** this jacket to fit you better. Verb.*
shape (shāp) *noun, plural* **shapes;** *verb,* **shaped, shaping.**

share **1.** The part that is given or belongs to one person: *Each of us will do a **share** of the work on this project.* **2.** One of the equal parts into which the ownership of a company or business is divided: *Each partner owns ten **shares** of stock in the company. Noun.*
○ **1.** To use with another or others: *Two of us **shared** a tent.* **2.** To divide into portions and give to others as well as to oneself: *I **shared** my sandwich.* **3.** To have a share; take part: *We all **shared** in the fun. Verb.*
share (shâr) *noun, plural* **shares;** *verb,* **shared, sharing.**

shareware Software that can be used free of charge, but if a person plans to use it a lot, it is considered good manners to pay the author of the software a small fee. **share·ware** (shâr′wâr′) *noun.*

shark **1.** A fish that lives in the sea and has gray scales, a skeleton made of cartilage, and a large mouth with sharp teeth. **2.** A person who cheats other people. **shark** (shärk) *noun, plural* **sharks.**

sharp **1.** Having an edge or point that cuts or pierces easily: *That knife has a **sharp** blade.* **2.** Having a pointed end; not rounded: *This table has **sharp** edges.* **3.** Harsh or biting: *The strong cheese had a **sharp** taste.* **4.** Having a sudden change in direction: *The road ahead has a **sharp** curve.* **5.** Clear: *Your camera takes **sharp** pictures.* **6.** Watchful; alert: *The dog has **sharp** ears.* **7.** Quick and strong: *The falling book gave me a **sharp** blow on the head.* **8.** Very smart; clever: *My sister has a **sharp** mind.* **9.** Fashionable: *a **sharp** jacket.* This is an informal use. *Adjective.*
○ **1.** No earlier or later; exactly: *We must leave at ten o'clock **sharp**.* **2.** In a sharp manner: *Look **sharp** or you will miss the turn. Adverb.*
○ **1.** A tone or note in music that is one half note above its natural pitch. **2.** A symbol (♯) that shows this tone or note. *Noun.*
sharp (shärp) *adjective,* **sharper, sharpest;** *adverb; noun, plural* **sharps.**

sharpen To make or become sharp: *Sharpen the knife. My vision **sharpened** when I got my new glasses.* **shar·pen** (shär′pən) *verb,* **sharpened, sharpening.**

shatter **1.** To break into pieces: *The glass **shattered** when I dropped it.* **2.** To destroy completely or damage very much; ruin: *The storm **shattered** our hopes of going sailing.* **shat·ter** (shat′ər) *verb,* **shattered, shattering.**

shave **1.** To remove hair with a razor: *My cousin **shaves** with an electric razor.* **2.** To cut off in thin strips: *The carpenter **shaved** the board with a plane. Verb.*
○ The removing of hair with a razor: *You can go to the barber for a **shave**. Noun.*
shave (shāv) *verb,* **shaved, shaved** or **shaven, shaving;** *noun, plural* **shaves.**

shaving A thin piece or slice: *The floor of the workshop was covered with wood **shavings**.* **shav·ing** (shā′ving) *noun, plural* **shavings.**

shawl A piece of cloth that is worn over the shoulders or head. **shawl** (shôl) *noun, plural* **shawls.**

she A female person or animal that is being talked about: *Betty told us that she would come to our party. Pronoun.*

○ A female person or animal: *Is the puppy a she or a he? Noun.*

she (shē) *pronoun; noun, plural* **shes.**

Special types of clippers are used to shear wool from sheep.

shear 1. To cut or clip with shears or scissors: *Please shear the hedge.* 2. To cut or cut off; remove: *The farmer sheared wool from the sheep. The side of the building was sheared off by the explosion.*

Another word that sounds like this is **sheer.**

shear (shîr) *verb,* **sheared, sheared** *or* **shorn, shearing.**

shears A cutting instrument like scissors. There are shears for cutting grass and cutting metal. **shears** (shîrz) *plural noun.*

sheath A case for the blade of a sword, dagger, or similar weapon; scabbard. **sheath** (shēth) *noun, plural* **sheaths** (shēthz).

shed¹ A small building used for storing or sheltering things. **shed** (shed) *noun, plural* **sheds.**

shed² 1. To let fall or cause to flow: *I shed a few tears when we moved away.* 2. To lose or drop:

A dog sheds hair. 3. To send out: *The moon shed little light last night because it was just a crescent.* **shed** (shed) *verb,* **shed, shedding.**

sheep 1. An animal with a thick, heavy coat that is raised on farms for its wool and meat. 2. Any of several less common kinds of sheep that live wild in mountain regions. 3. A person who follows the ideas or actions of another person without thinking. **sheep** (shēp) *noun, plural* **sheep.**

sheer 1. So thin that one can see through it; very fine and thin: *The window has sheer curtains.* 2. Total; utter: *This is sheer nonsense!* 3. Steep: *There is a sheer drop of 400 feet from the edge of the cliff.*

Another word that sounds like this is **shear.**

sheer (shîr) *adjective,* **sheerer, sheerest.**

sheet 1. A large piece of cotton, linen, or other cloth. It is used to cover a bed. 2. A thin, broad piece or surface of something: *We bought four sheets of plywood.* **sheet** (shēt) *noun, plural* **sheets.**

sheik A leader or chief of an Arab clan, tribe, or village. **sheik** (shēk *or* shāk) *noun, plural* **sheiks.**

shelf 1. A thin piece of wood, metal, or other material fastened to a wall or frame. It is used to hold books, dishes, and other things. 2. Anything like a shelf: *The ship was stuck on an underwater shelf of sand.* **shelf** (shelf) *noun, plural* **shelves.**

shell 1. A hard outer covering. A shell helps protect what it holds inside. Turtles, snails, eggs, and nuts have shells. 2. Something like a shell: *I filled the pasta shells with cheese.* 3. A case of metal or cardboard filled with explosives or bits of metal. It is fired from a cannon or gun. *Noun.*

○ 1. To take something out of its shell: *Will you help by shelling the peanuts for the party?* 2. To bombard with shells: *The army shelled the city. Verb.*

shell (shel) *noun, plural* **shells;** *verb,* **shelled, shelling.**

shellac A liquid used as a varnish on floors and furniture to protect them and make them shine. *Noun.*

○ To coat with shellac: *I'm going to shellac the table. Verb.*

shel·lac (shə lak′) *noun, plural* **shellacs;** *verb,* **shellacked, shellacking.**

PRONUNCIATION KEY:

| at | āpe | fär | câre | end | mē | it | īce | pierce | hot | ōld | sông | fôrk |
| oil | out | up | ūse | rüle | pull | tûrn | chin | sing | shop | thin | this | |

hw in white; zh in treasure. The symbol ə stands for the unstressed vowel sound in about, taken, pencil, lemon, and circus.

671

shellfish An animal with a shell that lives in water. Shrimps, crabs, and clams are shellfish. Shellfish are not actually fish. **shell·fish** (shel'fish') *noun, plural* **shellfish** *or* **shellfishes.**

shelter 1. Something that covers or protects: *The hikers used an old barn as a **shelter** during the thunderstorm.* 2. The condition of being covered or protected: *An umbrella will give you **shelter** from rain.* 3. A place where a person or an animal who is lost or doesn't have a home can stay: *The victims of the flood slept in the emergency **shelter**. Noun.*
○ To give shelter to: *The tent **sheltered** us from the rain. Verb.*
shel·ter (shelt'ər) *noun, plural* **shelters;** *verb,* **sheltered, sheltering.**

shepherd A person who takes care of sheep. *Noun.*
○ 1. To take care of as a shepherd: *Who **shepherds** this flock of sheep?* 2. To guide or watch over: *The teacher **shepherded** the class through the museum. Verb.*
shep·herd (shep'ərd) *noun, plural* **shepherds;** *verb,* **shepherded, shepherding.**

sherbet A frozen dessert. It is made of fruit juices, water, sugar, and a small amount of egg whites or milk. **sher·bet** (shûr'bit) *noun, plural* **sherbets.**

sheriff The main officer responsible for enforcing the law in a county. The sheriff is also in charge of taking care of the jails. **sher·iff** (sher'if) *noun, plural* **sheriffs.**

Shetland pony A small pony that originally came from the Shetland Islands of Scotland. It has a rough coat and a long mane and tail. **Shet·land po·ny** (shet'lənd).

shield 1. A piece of armor used in olden times. It was carried on the arm to protect the body or head during a battle. 2. A person or thing that defends or protects: *She stood as a **shield** between her little brother and the growling dog.* 3. Something shaped like a shield: *A police officer's badge is called a **shield**. Noun.*
○ To defend or protect: *I **shielded** my eyes from the bright sun with my hand. A face mask **shields** a baseball catcher from injury. Verb.*
shield (shēld) *noun, plural* **shields;** *verb,* **shielded, shielding.**

shift To move or change: *I **shifted** my position in the chair. The driver of the car **shifted** from first gear into second gear. Verb.*
○ 1. A movement or change: *The camper's sudden **shift** in the canoe tipped it over.* 2. A group of workers, or the time that they work: *My cousin works during the day **shift** at the factory.* 3. A device that connects a set of gears to a motor; gearshift. *Noun.*
shift (shift) *verb,* **shifted, shifting;** *noun, plural* **shifts.**

shilling A coin that was once used in Great Britain. Twenty shillings were equal to one pound. **shil·ling** (shil'ing) *noun, plural* **shillings.**

shimmer To shine with a faint, flickering light; glimmer: *The lake **shimmered** in the moonlight.* **shim·mer** (shim'ər) *verb,* **shimmered, shimmering.**

shin The front part of the leg from the knee to the ankle. *Noun.*
○ To climb by using the arms and legs: *I like to **shin** up trees. Verb.*
shin (shin) *noun, plural* **shins;** *verb,* **shinned, shinning.**

shinbone The large bone of the lower part of the leg in a person's skeleton. **shin·bone** (shin'bōn') *noun, plural* **shinbones.**

shine 1. To give or reflect light: *Stars **shine** in the night sky.* 2. To be or make bright: *Their faces **shone** with happiness.* 3. To do very well: *You **shine** in arithmetic at school. Verb.*
○ 1. Light or brightness: *The polished floor has a nice **shine**.* 2. The act of polishing: *Those shoes need a **shine**. Noun.*
• **to take a shine to.** To like very much: *You've really **taken a shine** to my cat.*
shine (shīn) *verb,* **shone** *or* **shined, shining;** *noun, plural* **shines.**

shingle A thin piece of wood or other material. Shingles are placed in overlapping rows to cover the roofs and sometimes the walls of buildings. *Noun.*
○ To cover with shingles: *The workers will **shingle** the roof. Verb.*
shin·gle (shing'gəl) *noun,* **plural** shingles; *verb,* **shingled, shingling.**

Shinto The chief religion of Japan. **Shin·to** (shin'tō) *noun.*

shiny Shining; bright: *We have a **shiny** car.* **shin·y** (shī'nē) *adjective,* **shinier, shiniest.**

ship 1. A large boat that travels across deep water. 2. An airplane, airship, or spacecraft. *Noun.*
○ 1. To send by ship, train, truck, or airplane:

*They will **ship** the bed by truck.* **2.** To go on a ship as a member of the crew: *My cousin **shipped** as a cook. Verb.*
ship (ship) *noun, plural* **ships**; *verb,* **shipped, shipping.**

-ship A suffix that means: **1.** The state or quality of being: ***Friendship** means the state of being a friend.* **2.** The art or skill of: ***Workmanship** means the art or skill of a workman.*

shipment **1.** The shipping of goods: *The farmer's crops were loaded for **shipment** to market.* **2.** Something that is shipped or an amount of something that is shipped: *Several **shipments** of books arrived at the library.* **ship•ment** (ship′mənt) *noun, plural* **shipments.**

shipping **1.** The act or business of sending goods by ship, train, truck, or airplane. **2.** Ships: *That harbor is open to the world's **shipping**.* **ship•ping** (ship′ing) *noun, plural* **shippings.**

shipwreck **1.** The destruction or loss of a ship at sea: *All those aboard survived the **shipwreck**.* **2.** The remains of a wrecked ship: *Divers explored the **shipwreck**. Noun.*
○ **1.** To cause to be destroyed or lost: *The storm **shipwrecked** the boat.* **2.** To cause to experience the destruction or loss of a ship at sea: *The sailor was **shipwrecked** and stranded on an island. Verb.*
ship•wreck (ship′rek′) *noun, plural* **shipwrecks**; *verb,* **shipwrecked, shipwrecking.**

shipyard A place where ships are built or repaired. **ship•yard** (ship′yärd′) *noun, plural* **shipyards.**

shirk To avoid or neglect doing something that should be done: *They **shirked** their chores and went swimming.* **shirk** (shûrk) *verb,* **shirked, shirking.**

shirt A piece of clothing worn on the upper part of the body. One kind of shirt has a collar, sleeves, and buttons down the front. **shirt** (shûrt) *noun, plural* **shirts.**

shiver To shake; tremble: *They **shivered** in the cold room. Verb.*
○ The act or instance of shivering: *The story about ghosts sent **shivers** up my back. Noun.*
shiv•er (shiv′ər) *verb,* **shivered, shivering**; *noun, plural* **shivers.**

shoal A place in a river, lake, or ocean where the water is shallow. **shoal** (shōl) *noun, plural* **shoals.**

shock¹ **1.** A sudden, violent upsetting of the mind or emotions: *The parents never got over the **shock** of their child's death.* **2.** A sudden, violent blow or jolt: *The **shock** caused by the explosion broke windows in nearby buildings.* **3.** A feeling caused by electricity passing through the body: *I felt a **shock** when we shook hands.* **4.** A serious weakening of the body caused by injury, disease, or emotional upset. A person is said to be in shock when too little blood reaches the body's tissues. *Noun.*
○ **1.** To disturb the mind or emotions of:

---

ship (passenger liner)

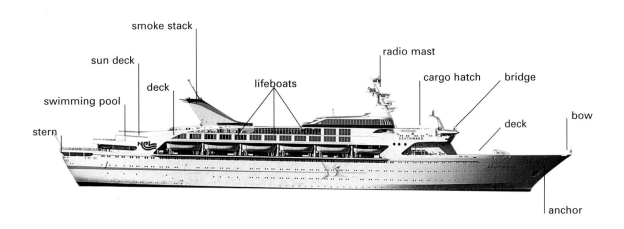

swimming pool · stern · sun deck · deck · smoke stack · lifeboats · radio mast · cargo hatch · bridge · deck · bow · anchor

My friend's rudeness shocked me. **2.** To give an electric shock. *Verb.*
shock (shok) *noun, plural* **shocks;** *verb,* **shocked, shocking.**

shock² **1.** A bundle of wheat, corn, or other grain stalks propped up on end in a field to dry. **shock** (shok) *noun, plural* **shocks.**

shock³ A thick, bushy mass: *We recognized you in the crowd by your shock of blond hair.* **shock** (shok) *noun, plural* **shocks.**

shocking Causing horror, surprise, or disgust: *We heard some shocking news.* **shock·ing** (shok'ing) *adjective.*

shoe **1.** An outer covering for the foot. Shoes are usually made of leather. **2.** A piece of metal curved to fit the shape of a horse's hoof; horseshoe. *Noun.*
○ To provide with a shoe or shoes: *The blacksmith will shoe the horse. Verb.*
shoe (shü) *noun, plural* **shoes;** *verb,* **shod, shoeing.**

shoelace A string or cord used to pull and hold together the sides of a shoe. **shoe·lace** (shü'lās') *noun, plural* **shoelaces.**

shoot **1.** To hit with a bullet, arrow, or the like: *Hunters shoot deer with rifles.* **2.** To send forth from a weapon: *I shot an arrow at the target.* **3.** To cause a weapon to send forth bullets, arrows, or the like; fire: *The sheriff shot at the escaping outlaw.* **4.** To move or cause to move fast: *The snake shot out its tongue.* **5.** To come forth; sprout; grow: *The bean plants are shooting up from the ground.* **6.** To photograph or film: *That movie was shot in Rome. Verb.*
○ A new or young plant or stem; sprout. *Noun.*
Another word that sounds like this is **chute.**
shoot (shüt) *verb,* **shot, shooting;** *noun, plural* **shoots.**

shooting star A mass of metal or stone that burns up as it enters the earth's atmosphere; meteor. Look up **meteor** for more information.

shop **1.** A place where goods are sold: *Can we go to the pet shop?* **2.** A place where a particular kind of work is done: *The broken radio is at the repair shop. Noun.*
○ To visit stores in order to look at and buy goods: *I shopped for a new coat. Verb.*
shop (shop) *noun, plural* **shops;** *verb,* **shopped, shopping.**

shoplift To steal merchandise from a store while pretending to be a shopper there. **shop·lift** (shop'lift') *verb,* **shoplifted, shoplifting.**

shopping center A group of stores and other business establishments. Shopping centers are usually built in suburbs and usually have a lot of space for parking cars.

Some people get their exercise by walking in large indoor shopping centers.

shore **1.** The land along the edge of an ocean, lake, or large river: *We walked along the shore.* **2.** Land: *The sailors were glad to be back on shore after the long voyage.* **shore** (shôr) *noun, plural* **shores.**

short **1.** Not long or tall: *The grass is cut very short. That was a short speech.* **2.** Not having or being enough: *The hikers were short of food.* **3.** Taking less time to pronounce: *The "i" in "bit" is a short vowel. Adjective.*
○ **1.** In a sudden or unexpected way; suddenly: *The horse stopped short, and the rider fell off.* **2.** Not quite up to: *The golf ball stopped short of the hole. Adverb.*
○ **1.** A short circuit. **2. shorts.** Pants that are worn above the knee. **3. shorts.** Short pants worn by men as underwear. *Noun.*
• **for short.** As a shortened or shorter form: *A taxicab is called a cab for short.*
• **short for.** Being a shorter form of: *"Phone" is short for "telephone."*
short (shôrt) *adjective,* **shorter, shortest;** *adverb; noun, plural* **shorts.**

shortage Too small an amount or supply; lack: *There is a shortage of water.* **short·age** (shôr'tij) *noun, plural* **shortages.**

shortcoming A fault, defect, or weakness, as in character or behavior: *The habit of breaking promises is a serious shortcoming.* **short·com·ing** (shôrt'kum'ing) *noun, plural* **shortcomings.**

shortcut **1.** A quicker way of reaching a place: *took a shortcut to school.* **2.** A way of doing something faster: *Don't use any shortcuts in completing your science experiment.* **short·cut** (shôrt'cut') *noun, plural* **shortcuts.**

shorten To make or become short or shorter: *The tailor has to shorten these pants. The days shorten during fall.* **short•en** (shôr′tən) *verb,* **shortened, shortening.**

shortening Any of various fats that are used in cooking. *Butter, lard, and vegetable oil are kinds of shortening.* **short•en•ing** (shôr′tə ning) *noun.*

short-handed Without enough people to do a job. **short-hand•ed** (shôrt′han′did) *adjective.*

shortly In a short time; soon: *The doctor will see you shortly.* **short•ly** (shôrt′lē) *adverb.*

shortsighted **1.** Not thinking about, caring about, or planning for the future: *We were shortsighted in bringing so little food for the long hike.* **2.** Not able to see distant objects clearly; nearsighted. Look up **nearsighted** for more information. **short•sight•ed** (shôrt′sī′tid) *adjective.*

shortstop A baseball or softball player whose position is between second and third base. **short•stop** (shôrt′stop′) *noun, plural* **shortstops.**

shot **1.** The firing of a gun or other weapon: *Did you hear a shot?* **2.** A person who fires a gun or other weapon: *That hunter is a good shot.* **3.** A ball or balls of metal that are fired from a gun or cannon. **4.** The launching of a rocket or missile into space: *We watched the moon shot on television.* **5.** The distance over which something can travel; range: *The soldier didn't fire until the enemy was within rifle shot.* **6.** An injection of medicine: *I had to get a measles shot.* **7.** A throw or stroke in certain games: *I need a few practice shots before we start the game.* **8.** An attempt; try: *Let's give it a shot.* **shot** (shot) *noun, plural* **shots** *or* **shot** (for definition 3).

Great strength is required in throwing the shot put.

shot put An event in track and field in which athletes compete to see who can throw a heavy metal ball the farthest. **shot•put** (shot′pùt′) *noun.* **—shot-putter** *noun* **—shot-putting** *noun.*

should An auxiliary verb that is used in the following ways: **1.** To express obligation or duty: *A judge should know the law.* **2.** To offer advice: *You should see a doctor.* **3.** To say that something is probable or expected: *They should be here soon.* **4.** To express a possible condition or action: *If anyone should call, take a message.* **should** (shùd) *verb.*

shoulder **1.** The area on either side of the body at which an arm, foreleg, or wing joins the trunk. **2. shoulders.** Both shoulders plus the part of the back that lies between them. **3.** The part of a shirt, dress, or other piece of clothing that covers the shoulder: *I ripped my sweater at the shoulder.* **4.** The edge or border on either side of a road or highway: *The driver changed the flat tire on the shoulder of the road.* Noun.
○ To push with the shoulder or shoulders: *I shouldered my way onto the train.* Verb.
shoul•der (shōl′dər) *noun, plural* **shoulders;** *verb,* **shouldered, shouldering.**

shoulder blade One of two flat, triangular bones in the upper corners of the back.

shout To call loudly; yell: *I shouted "Hello!" to the people in the boat.* Verb.
○ A loud call; yell: *I gave a shout when I found the lost puppy.* Noun.
shout (shout) *verb,* **shouted, shouting;** *noun, plural* **shouts.**

shove **1.** To push along or forward from behind: *We shoved the bed closer to the wall.* **2.** To push in a rude or rough way: *The bully shoved the young child.* Verb.
○ A strong push: *You need to give this door a shove to close it.* Noun.
shove (shuv) *verb,* **shoved, shoving;** *noun, plural* **shoves.**

shovel **1.** A tool or machine with a broad scoop. A shovel is used for digging and moving dirt, snow, and other loose material. **2.** The amount a shovel holds: *Throw a few shovels of dirt on the campfire.* Noun.
○ **1.** To move or dig with a shovel: *The worker shoveled dirt into the back of the truck.* **2.** To

PRONUNCIATION KEY:

at	āpe	fär	câre	end	mē	it	īce	pierce	hot	ōld	sông	fôrk
oil	out	up	ūse	rüle	pùll	tûrn	chin	sing	shop	thin	this	

hw in white; zh in treasure. The symbol ə stands for the unstressed vowel sound in about, taken, pencil, lemon, and circus.

675

move or throw in large amounts: *Stop **shoveling** food into your mouth. Verb.*
shov·el (shuv′əl) *noun, plural* **shovels;** *verb,* **shoveled, shoveling.**

show 1. To bring to sight or view; make able to be seen: *The theater **showed** that movie last week.* 2. To be able to be seen; be in sight: *The light **showed** through the curtains.* 3. To make or be made known or clear: *I **showed** my anger by stamping my foot. Your worry **shows** in your face.* 4. To point out or lead: ***Show** us the way to the zoo.* 5. To explain to: *The mechanic **showed** me how to change a tire.* 6. To grant or give: *The judge **showed** mercy in the decision. Verb.*
○ 1. Something that is seen in public; display: *We went to a horse **show**.* 2. Any program or entertainment in the theater or on radio or television: *Did you see that nature **show** last night?* 3. A display meant to attract attention or give a false impression: *The older students made a **show** of their knowledge. Noun.*

 • **to show off.** 1. To display in a proud or showy way: *I **showed off** my new coat to my friends.* 2. To behave in a way that calls attention to oneself: *The twins love to **show off** at parties.*

 • **to show up.** 1. To reveal; expose: *You **showed up** those frauds for what they really are.* 2. To arrive; come: *When do you think they'll **show up**?*
show (shō) *verb,* **showed, shown** *or* **showed, showing;** *noun, plural* **shows.**

shower 1. A brief fall of rain: *The forecast is for **showers** today.* 2. A fall of anything in large numbers: *I saw a **shower** of sparks when the fireworks went off.* 3. A bath in which water is sprayed on a person from overhead. 4. A room or device that is used for such a bath. 5. A party where gifts are given to a future bride or a pregnant woman: Noun.*
○ 1. To fall or make fall in a shower: *It **showered** all day, so I stayed home.* 2. To bathe by taking a shower: *They **showered** and got dressed.* 3. To wet with water or another liquid: *We were **showered** by water from the sprinkler.* 4. To give freely and in large amounts: *The astronauts were **showered** with praise. Verb.*
show·er (shou′ər) *noun, plural* **showers;** *verb,* **showered, showering.**

show-off A person who behaves in a way that gets attention. **show-off** (shō′ôf′) *noun, plural* **show-offs.**

showy 1. Attracting attention by being bright or colorful: *I bought a bunch of **showy** flowers.* 2. Too bright or colorful; gaudy: *I don't like **showy** clothing.* **show·y** (shō′ē) *adjective,* **showier, showiest.**

shred 1. A small piece or narrow strip torn or cut off: *Put **shreds** of paper in the puppies' box.* 2. A small amount; bit: *There is not a **shred** of truth to the story. Noun.*
○ To tear or cut into small pieces or narrow strips: *I **shredded** cabbage for the salad. Verb.*
shred (shred) *noun, plural* **shreds;** *verb,* **shredded** *or* **shred, shredding.**

shrew A small animal that looks like a mouse but has a long, pointed nose. Shrews eat insects and are related to moles and hedgehogs. **shrew** (shrü) *noun, plural* **shrews.**

shrewd Clever and sharp: *The **shrewd** customer found a bargain.* **shrewd** (shrüd) *adjective,* **shrewder, shrewdest.**

shriek A loud, sharp cry or sound: *The child let out a **shriek** of laughter. Noun.*
○ To utter a loud, sharp cry or sound: *We all **shrieked** with laughter at her jokes. Verb.*
shriek (shrēk) *noun, plural* **shrieks;** *verb,* **shrieked, shrieking.**

shrill Having a sharp, high sound: *The officer used a **shrill** whistle to direct traffic.* **shrill** (shril) *adjective,* **shriller, shrillest.**

shrimp A sea animal that is covered with a thin shell and has a long tail. Shrimp are related to lobsters and crabs and are often used for food. **shrimp** (shrimp) *noun, plural* **shrimp** *or* **shrimps.**

shrine 1. A holy place for worship. A shrine often marks the tomb of a saint, contains a holy object, or is in memory of a religious person or event. 2. A place or thing that is honored and visited

It takes a lot of work to catch the **shrimp** that people eat.

because it is connected with something important: *The site of the great victory became a national shrine.* **shrine** (shrīn) *noun, plural* **shrines.**

shrink **1.** To make or become smaller because of heat, cold, or wetness: *That wool sweater will shrink if it's washed in hot water.* **2.** To draw back in fear or horror: *The child shrank from the barking dog. Verb.*
○ A psychologist or psychiatrist. This a slang use. *Noun.*
shrink (shringk) *verb,* **shrank** *or* **shrunk, shrunk** *or* **shrunken, shrinking;** *noun, plural* **shrinks.**

shrivel To shrink, wrinkle, or wither: *The plant shriveled because it was too hot in the room.* **shriv·el** (shriv′əl) *verb,* **shriveled, shriveling.**

shrub A woody plant that is smaller than a tree. A shrub has many stems that branch out at or near the ground. **shrub** (shrub) *noun, plural* **shrubs.**

shrug To raise or draw up the shoulders to show doubt or lack of interest. *Verb.*
○ The act of shrugging: *Please don't answer my question with a shrug. Noun.*
shrug (shrug) *verb,* **shrugged, shrugging;** *noun, plural* **shrugs.**

shudder To tremble suddenly from fear or cold: *Strange sounds make me shudder. Verb.*
○ The act of trembling suddenly from fear or cold: *The child awoke from the nightmare with a shudder. Noun.*
shud·der (shud′ər) *verb,* **shuddered, shuddering;** *noun, plural* **shudders.**

shuffle **1.** To drag the feet while walking: *Don't shuffle your feet when you walk.* **2.** To mix playing cards to change the order: *When you play cards, you should shuffle them after each game.* **3.** To move from one place to another: *The customer shuffled the books on the display. Verb.*
○ An act of shuffling: *They walked with a shuffle. Give the cards a shuffle. Noun.*
shuf·fle (shuf′əl) *verb,* **shuffled, shuffling;** *noun, plural* **shuffles.**

shun To keep away from deliberately; avoid on purpose: *That family shuns the city.* **shun** (shun) *verb,* **shunned, shunning.**

shut **1.** To move something so as to block or cover up an entrance or opening; close: *We shut the win-* *dow because it was cold.* **2.** To become closed: *The door shut behind me.* **3.** To make or force to stay; confine: *The dog was shut inside.*
 • **to shut down.** To stop operating or cause to stop operating, usually for a short time: *The factory had to shut down because of the strike.*
 • **to shut off.** To stop the flow, passage or operation of: *Shut the water off.*
 • **to shut out.** **1.** To keep from entering; exclude: *That building next door shuts out sunlight.* **2.** To prevent the opposing team from scoring in a contest: *We shut out our rival football team in the Thanksgiving Day game.*
 • **to shut up.** To stop talking or cause to stop talking: *Please shut up!*
shut (shut) *verb,* **shut, shutting.**

shutter **1.** A movable cover for a window, usually attached to the frame by hinges. Shutters are used to shut out light and to keep people from looking in. **2.** The part of a camera that snaps open and shuts quickly to let light onto the film when a picture is taken. **shut·ter** (shut′ər) *noun, plural* **shutters.**

shuttle **1.** A device on a loom during weaving. It carries yarn back and forth through the yarn strung on the loom. **2.** A train, airplane, or bus that makes short trips back and forth between two places. **3. The space shuttle.** Look up **space shuttle** for more information. *Noun.*
○ To move back and forth: *That bus shuttles guests from the hotel to the airport. The doctor shuttled between the two hospitals. Verb.*
shut·tle (shut′əl) *noun, plural* **shuttles;** *verb,* **shuttled, shuttling.**

shy **1.** Not comfortable around other people; bashful: *The shy little child wouldn't come into the room.* **2.** Easily frightened; timid: *Animals that live in the woods are usually too shy to get close to people.* **3.** Being or having less than a certain amount or not having enough; short: *We are three cents shy of five dollars. Adjective.*
○ To move back or aside suddenly in fear: *The horse shied at the loud noise. Verb.*
shy (shī) *adjective,* **shyer** *or* **shier, shyest** *or* **shiest;** *verb,* **shied, shying.**

Siamese cat A breed of cat that has a long, narrow body and short hair. A Siamese cat's ears,

PRONUNCIATION KEY:

| at | āpe | fär | câre | end | mē | it | īce | pierce | hot | ōld | sông | fôrk |
| oil | out | up | ūse | rüle | pull | tûrn | chin | sing | shop | thin | this | |

hw in white; zh in treasure. The symbol ə stands for the unstressed vowel sound in about, taken, pencil, lemon, and circus.

677

paws, and tail are often a darker color than the rest of its body. **Si•a•mese** (sī′ə mēz′ *or* sī′ə mēs′)

sick 1. Suffering from a disease or having poor health; ill: *My friend was sick with the flu for a week.* 2. Having to do with sickness or illness: *When several children were ill at camp, two rooms were set up as sick rooms.* 3. Feeling nausea: *The carnival ride made me sick.* 4. Upset; disturbed: *We were sick at having to miss the party.* 5. Tired or disgusted: *I bought new curtains because I was sick of the old ones.* **sick** (sik) *adjective,* **sicker, sickest.**

sickle A tool having a sharp, curved blade that is attached to a short handle. A sickle is used for cutting grass or grain by hand. **sick•le** (sik′əl) *noun, plural* **sickles.**

sickly 1. Usually or always sick: *The sickly child often missed school.* 2. Caused by or showing sickness: *a pale and sickly complexion.* **sick•ly** (sik′lē) *adjective,* **sicklier, sickliest.**

sickness 1. Illness or poor health: *There has been quite a lot of sickness in our family this year.* 2. A disease or illness: *Chicken pox is usually a childhood sickness.* **sick•ness** (sik′nis) *noun, plural* **sicknesses.**

side 1. A line or surface that encloses or forms something: *A triangle has three sides. The workers painted one side of the house.* 2. One of the two surfaces of a piece of paper or cloth or any other flat object: *One side of the coin is worn.* 3. The place or space away from a central line, point, or thing: *Put the chairs on the left side of the room. We live on the south side of the river.* 4. The right or left part of the body of a person or animal: *I got a pain in my side.* 5. The area next to a person: *Come stand at my side.* 6. One of two opposing groups or persons: *Which side won the game? He was on his friend's side during the argument.* 7. A point of view or position: *I want to hear your side of the story.* 8. A series or group of people that have a common ancestor: *I am a cousin of that senator on my mother's side. Noun.* ○ 1. At or near one side: *Use the side entrance.* 2. Coming from or directed toward one side: *The army surprised the enemy with a side attack.* 3. Less important or not the main: *We will discuss the side issues later. Adjective.*

• **side by side.** Next to each other: *The twins walked down the street side by side.*

• **to side with.** To agree with or support a person or group that disagrees with or opposes another person or group: *Only one newspaper sided with the mayor in the disagreement with the town council.*

side (sīd) *noun, plural* **sides;** *adjective.*

sideline 1. A line along each side of the playing area in certain sports: *The spectators sat behind the sidelines at the tennis match.* 2. Work done in addition to one's usual job: *The lawyer's sideline is coaching basketball.* **side•line** (sīd′līn′) *noun, plural* **sidelines.**

sideshow A small show that is part of a larger show or entertainment: *I like to see the sideshows at the circus.* **side•show** (sīd′shō′) *noun, plural* **sideshows.**

sidestep 1. To step to one side: *I had to sidestep to get out of the way of the bicycle.* 2. To avoid or delay; dodge: *The candidate cleverly sidestepped the newspaper reporter's questions.* **side•step** (sīd′step′) *verb,* **sidestepped, sidestepping.**

sidewalk A path by a side of a street or road where people can walk. A sidewalk is usually paved. **side•walk** (sīd′wôk′) *noun, plural* **sidewalks.**

sideways 1. Toward or from one side: *I had to move sideways to get through the door.* 2. With one side forward: *Turn that box sideways or we won't be able to fit it through the door. Adverb.* ○ Moving or directed toward one side: *a sideways glance. Adjective.* **side•ways** (sīd′wāz′) *adverb; adjective.*

siege The surrounding of an enemy position for a long time in order to cut off supplies and force surrender. **siege** (sēj) *noun, plural* **sieges.**

sierra A chain of hills or mountains with sharp peaks. There are many sierras in the western part of the United States. **si•er•ra** (sē er′ə) *noun, plural* **sierras.**

WORD HISTORY

Sierra comes from the Spanish word for "saw." Sierra refers to the jagged appearance of the mountain ridges, which look like the teeth of a saw.

---

sieve A utensil that has a bottom with many holes in it. A sieve is used for sifting or draining. **sieve** (siv) *noun, plural* **sieves.**

sift 1. To separate large pieces from small pieces by using a sieve. 2. To put through a sieve to take out lumps or make finer. **3.** To fall loosely as if through a sieve: *Snow **sifted** through the cracks in the roof.* **sift** (sift) *verb,* **sifted, sifting.**

sigh **1.** To make a long, deep breathing sound because of sadness, tiredness, or relief: *I **sighed** with relief when I found my lost watch.* **2.** To make a sound like this: *The wind **sighed** through the trees. Verb.*
○ The act or sound of sighing: *I uttered a **sigh** of relief. Noun.*
sigh (sī) *verb,* **sighed, sighing;** *noun, plural* **sighs.**

sight **1.** The power or ability to see. **2.** The act of seeing: *I recognized you at first **sight**.* **3.** The range or distance a person can see: *Keep out of **sight**.* **4.** The presence of something in the range that a person can see: *The **sight** of the strangers frightened the baby.* **5.** Something that is seen or is worth seeing: *The sunset was a beautiful **sight**.* **6.** Something that is unpleasant, funny, or odd to look at: *You're a **sight** in that hat.* **7.** Something on a gun or other object that helps in aiming or seeing: *Line up the target in the **sight**. Noun.*
○ To see with the eyes: *The group finally **sighted** the cabin. Verb.*

Other words that sound like this are **cite** and **site.**
sight (sīt) *noun, plural* **sights;** *verb,* **sighted, sighting.**

sightless Not able to see; blind: *Kangaroos are sightless at birth.* **sight·less** (sīt′lis) *adjective.*

sightseeing The act of visiting places of interest: *We went **sightseeing** in Washington, D.C. Noun.*
○ Visiting or used for visiting places of interest: *The **sightseeing** bus was late. Adjective.*
sight·see·ing (sīt′sē′ing) *noun; adjective.*

sign **1.** Something that stands for, shows, or suggests something else: *÷ is a **sign** for division. A fever is a **sign** of illness.* **2.** A notice or board with writing on it that gives information: *The **sign** said "Closed on Sundays."* **3.** Something that warns or points out what is to come: *Some people believe that breaking a mirror is a **sign** of bad luck.* **4.** A trace: *There was no **sign** of our pet cat.* **5.** One of the twelve parts of the zodiac. **6. Sign language.** Look up **sign language** for more information. *Noun.*
○ **1.** To write one's name on: *I **signed** my name at the bottom of the letter.* **2.** To communicate using sign language. *Verb.*

SIGNS AND SYMBOLS

The words you speak or see on this page can also be spoken or written with other signs. Morse code is one kind of sign language used for radio and the telegraph. Two others are in wide use today. Braille is a system of raised dots on a page that can be read by people with poor eyesight through touch. American Sign Language is designed for the hearing impaired. They can talk as rapidly as you can, only they do it with their hands.

Braille

A	B	C	D	E	F	G	H	I	J	K	L	M

N	O	P	Q	R	S	T	U	V	W	X	Y	Z

Manual Alphabet

A	B	C	D	E	F	G	H	I	J	K	L	M

N	O	P	Q	R	S	T	U	V	W	X	Y	Z

• **to sign off**. To announce the end of broadcasting and to stop broadcasting: *This radio station signs off at midnight.*

• **to sign up**. To sign a written agreement in order to join an organization or group or in order to obtain something: *My friend and I signed up for a pottery class.*

sign (sīn) *noun, plural* **signs**; *verb,* **signed, signing.**

SYNONYMS

sign, evidence, indication, mark, symptom, token
There was no sign that carelessness caused the accident. New evidence shows that the suspect is actually innocent. The flashing warning light is an indication that there is something wrong with the engine. Paying attention to details is a mark of good craftsmanship. A severe headache and aching muscles are two of the symptoms of the flu. My grandfather gave this gold pin to my grandmother as a token of his love.

---

signal Something that warns, directs, or informs: *The red light on the dashboard is a signal that the car needs oil. A gun was fired as the signal for the race to begin.* Noun.
○ **1.** To make a signal to: *The people on the sinking ship signaled for help.* **2.** To make known by a signal or signals: *A bell signals the end of the school day.* Verb.
○ Used as a signal: *The signal light showed that a train was coming.* Adjective.
sig·nal (sig′nəl) *noun, plural* **signals**; *verb,* **signaled, signaling**; *adjective.*

Railroad signals warn of oncoming trains.

signature **1.** The name of a person written in his or her own handwriting: *We need your signature on this petition.* **2.** A sign or signs at the beginning of each section of music. The signature shows the pitch, key, and time of a piece of music.
sig·na·ture (sig′nə chər) *noun, plural* **signatures.**

significance Special value or meaning; importance: *The election of a new president is an event of great significance. What was the significance of that remark?* **sig·nif·i·cance** (sig nif′i kəns) *noun.* —**significant** *adjective.*

sign language A way of communicating in which gestures, especially hand motions, are used instead of speech. Sign language is used especially by the deaf.

silence **1.** A lack of sound; complete quiet: *There was silence in the deep cave.* **2.** The condition of being or keeping quiet or silent: *Does your silence mean you agree with me?* Noun.
○ To make or keep silent: *The judge banged a gavel to silence the noisy spectators.* Verb.
si·lence (sī′ləns) *noun, plural* **silences**; *verb,* **silenced, silencing.**

silent **1.** Completely quiet; still: *She crept through the silent house.* **2.** Not speaking, or saying little: *The children remained silent during the play.* **3.** Not spoken or expressed; not said out loud: *The "k" in "know" is silent. A silent fear filled my heart when the alarm sounded.*
si·lent (sī′lənt) *adjective.*

silhouette **1.** A picture or drawing showing the outline of a figure or object and filled in with black or another solid color. **2.** A dark outline seen against a lighter background: *From our window at dusk, you can see the silhouette of the mountains against the sky.* Noun.
○ To show as a dark outline against a lighter background: *The horse standing on the hill was silhouetted against the sky.* Verb.
sil·hou·ette (sil′ü et′) *noun, plural* **silhouettes**; *verb,* **silhouetted, silhouetting.**

silicon A chemical element found in rocks and sand. Silicon is used in making glass, transistors, and computer chips. **sil·i·con** (sil′i kən *or* sil′i kon′) *noun.*

silk **1.** A soft, shiny cloth that is made from threads that are spun by silkworms. Silk is used to make scarves, ties, blouses, and many other pieces of clothing. **2.** Anything that is like silk. The tassels on an ear of corn are called silk. Noun.
○ Made of or like silk: *The silk blouse was very expensive.* Adjective.
silk (silk) *noun, plural* **silks**; *adjective.*

silkworm A caterpillar that makes silk thread to spin its cocoon, originally found in China. They are raised on farms, and their silk is gathered and

used to make silk cloth. **silk•worm** (silk′wûrm′)
noun, plural **silkworms**.

silky Like silk in the way it looks and feels; shiny
and soft: *The horse's mane was long and silky.*
silk•y (sil′kē) *adjective*, **silkier**, **silkiest**.

sill The piece of wood, stone, or other material at
the bottom of a door or window.
sill (sil) *noun, plural* **sills**.

silly Without judgment or common sense; foolish:
*Before the airplane was invented, some people
thought that flying was a silly idea.* **sil•ly** (sil′ē)
adjective, **sillier**, **silliest**.

**A large farm may need
a number of silos.**

silo 1. A tall, round tower that is used to store
food for farm animals. Silos are made out of
metal, concrete, or other material. 2. An underground structure in which missiles are stored.
si•lo (sī′lō) *noun, plural* **silos**.

silt Fine particles of sand, clay, dirt, and other
material. Silt is carried by flowing water, as in a
river, and eventually it settles to the bottom.
silt (silt) *noun*.

silver 1. A shiny white metal that is soft and easily
shaped. It is used to make coins, jewelry, spoons,
forks, and knives. Silver is a chemical element.
2. Coins that are made from silver; change.
3. Spoons, forks, or other things made of or coated with silver. 4. The color of silver. *Noun.*
○ 1. Made of, coated with, or containing silver:
You haven't polished the silver tray. 2. Having
the color of silver. *Adjective.*
○ To coat with silver or a metal like silver: *Take
the old bowl to a jeweler to have it silvered. Verb.*

sil•ver (sil′vər) *noun, plural* **silvers**; *adjective*;
verb, **silvered**, **silvering**.

silversmith A person who makes or repairs
objects of silver. **sil•ver•smith** (sil′vər smith′)
noun, plural **silversmiths**.

silverware 1. Spoons, forks, dishes, or anything
else for the table that is made of or coated with
silver. 2. Spoons, forks, or knives: *I'll bring the
plates and napkins for the picnic if you'll bring
the silverware.* **sil•ver•ware** (sil′vər wâr′) *noun.*

similar Having many but not all qualities the
same; alike: *Our dresses are similar.* **sim•i•lar**
(sim′ə lər) *adjective.*

similarity 1. The quality or condition of being
similar; likeness: *There is a similarity between
you and your brother.* 2. A way in which things
are similar or alike: *There are several similarities
between those two houses.* **sim•i•lar•i•ty**
(sim′ə lar′i tē) *noun, plural* **similarities**.

simmer To cook at or just below the boiling
point: *Simmer the soup for two hours.* **sim•mer**
(sim′ər) *verb*, **simmered**, **simmering**.

simple 1. Easy to understand or do: *Learning to
ride a bicycle is not so simple.* 2. Without anything added or any ornament; plain: *A simple
"yes" or "no" will do.* 3. Natural and honest:
Our neighbor is a simple soul. 4. Foolish.
sim•ple (sim′pəl) *adjective*, **simpler**, **simplest**.

simple sentence A sentence that expresses only
one complete thought. A simple sentence cannot
be divided into shorter sentences. "Our dog is
still a puppy" is a simple sentence.

simplicity 1. The condition or quality of being simple or plain: *The instructions that came with the
toy were written with simplicity.* 2. The quality of
being natural and sincere; honesty: *The young children charmed us with their simplicity.*
sim•plic•i•ty (sim plis′i tē) *noun, plural* **simplicities**.

simplify To make easier: *The teacher simplified
the arithmetic problem.* **sim•pli•fy** (sim′plə fī′)
verb, **simplified**, **simplifying**.

simply 1. In a clear or natural way: *The lecturer
spoke simply.* 2. Without decoration; plainly.
I dressed simply. 3. Merely; only: *If you need
help, it is simply a matter of asking.* 4. To the
greatest degree; absolutely: *That picture is simply
beautiful.* **sim•ply** (sim′plē) *adverb.*

PRONUNCIATION KEY:

| at | āpe | fär | câre | end | mē | it | īce | pîerce | hot | ōld | sông | fôrk |
| oil | out | up | ūse | rüle | pull | tûrn | chin | sing | shop | thin | this | |

hw in white; zh in treasure. The symbol ə stands for the unstressed vowel sound in about, taken, pencil, lemon, and circus.

681

simultaneous Done, existing, or happening at the same time: *Three acrobats performed simultaneous somersaults.* **si·mul·ta·ne·ous** (sī′məl tā′nē əs) *adjective.*

sin **1.** An act that goes against a religious law: *In many religions, murder is a sin.* **2.** Any wrong or bad act: *It's a sin to be cruel to animals. Noun.* ○ To go against a religious law: *They asked to be forgiven for having sinned. Verb.* **sin** (sin) *noun, plural* **sins;** *verb,* **sinned, sinning.**

since **1.** From a particular time in the past until now: *My cousin left last week and has been away ever since.* **2.** At some time between a particular time in the past and now: *I was sick last month but have since recovered.* **3.** Before now; ago: *Our neighbors have long since moved away. Adverb.* ○ During the time after: *There have been many changes in American life since 1945. Preposition.* ○ **1.** During the period after: *I haven't seen the twins since they graduated.* **2.** For the reason that; because: *Since the car isn't working, we'll have to take the bus. Conjunction.* **since** (sints) *adverb; preposition; conjunction.*

sincere Not false or pretended; honest and true: *We gave them our sincere thanks.* **sin·cere** (sin sîr′) *adjective,* **sincerer, sincerest.**

sinew A strong cord or band of tissue that joins a muscle to a bone; a tendon. The sinews make it possible for the muscles to move an arm, leg, or other part of the body. **sin·ew** (sin′ū) *noun, plural* **sinews.**

sing **1.** To utter words or make sounds with musical tones: *The school choir sings beautifully.* **2.** To make a whistling or humming sound: *The tea kettle sang when the water boiled.* **sing** (sing) *verb,* **sang** *or* **sung, sung, singing.**

singer A person or bird that sings: *I am one of the singers in the school chorus.* **sing·er** (sing′ər) *noun, plural* **singers.**

single **1.** Only one: *There was a single flower in the vase.* **2.** To be used by one person only: *The traveler asked for a single room at the hotel.* **3.** Not married: *My older cousin is single. Adjective.* ○ A hit in baseball or softball that allows the batter to reach first base safely. *Noun.* ○ **1.** To pick or choose from others: *They singled out the orange cat as their favorite.* **2.** To hit a

single in a baseball or softball game: *I singled my first time at bat. Verb.* **sin·gle** (sing′gəl) *adjective; noun, plural* **singles;** *verb,* **singled, singling.**

single-handed Without the help or support of anyone: *The firefighter's single-handed rescue of the baby won great praise.* **sin·gle-hand·ed** (sing′gəl han′did) *adjective.* —**single-handedly** *adverb.*

single-minded Having only one purpose in mind; focused: *She is single-minded in her determination to be a good soccer player.* **sin·gle-mind·ed** (sing′gəl mīn′did) *adjective.* —**single-mindedly** *adverb.*

singular Of or having to do with a form of a word that names or refers to one person or thing. Child and tree are singular nouns. Children and trees are plural nouns. *Adjective.* ○ The form of a word that names or refers to one person or thing. The nouns neighbor and box are in the singular. The nouns neighbors and boxes are in the plural. *Noun.* **sin·gu·lar** (sing′gyə lər) *adjective; noun, plural* **singulars.**

sinister Evil or suggesting evil: *The dark old house looked sinister at night.* **sin·is·ter** (sin′ə stər) *adjective.*

sink **1.** To go down or cause to go down partly or completely below a surface: *The car sank into the mud. The canoe could sink if it has a hole. The ship hit an iceberg and sank.* **2.** To become less: *Our voices sank to a whisper.* **3.** To fall into a certain state: *I sank into a deep sleep as soon as I got into bed.* **4.** To dig: *We sunk a well in the yard.* **5.** To go or cause to go through or into deeply: *The rain sank into the soil. Sink your teeth into this. Verb.* ○ A basin of metal, porcelain, or other material that is used to hold water for washing. A sink has faucets to turn water on and off and a drain to take water away. *Noun.* **sink** (singk) *verb,* **sank** *or* **sunk, sunk** *or* **sunken, sinking;** *noun, plural* **sinks.**

sinus A hollow space in the bones of the face. There are sinuses above the eyes and on each side of the nose. **si·nus** (sī′nəs) *noun, plural* **sinuses.**

Sioux A member of a group of Native American tribes of the North American plains; Dakota. **Sioux** (sü) *noun, plural* **Sioux.**

sip To drink little by little: *I sipped the cold water. Verb.*
○ **1.** A small amount to drink: *Can I have a sip of your juice?* **2.** The act of sipping: *Have a short sip of water. Noun.*
sip (sip) *verb*, **sipped**, **sipping**; *noun, plural* **sips**.

siphon A bent tube with one side longer than the other. A siphon is used to move a liquid from one container to another. The liquid is moved by air pressure. **si·phon** (sī′fən) *noun, plural* **siphons**.

sir **1.** A title used in place of a man's name: *I said to the man, "May I help you, sir?"* **2.** Sir. A title used before a knight's name: *Sir Lancelot was a brave knight.* **sir** (sûr) *noun, plural* **sirs**.

siren A device that makes a loud, shrill sound. It is used as a signal or warning. Ambulances and police cars have sirens. **si·ren** (sī′rən) *noun, plural* **sirens**.

sister **1.** A girl or woman with the same mother and father as another person. **2.** A woman who belongs to a religious order; nun. **3.** A woman who has the same interest or is a member of the same organization as another person. **sis·ter** (sis′tər) *noun, plural* **sisters**.

sisterhood **1.** The close feeling between sisters or women. **2.** A group of women who are united by a common interest or aim. **sis·ter·hood** (sis′tər hùd′) *noun, plural* **sisterhoods**.

sister-in-law **1.** The sister of one's husband or wife. **2.** The wife of one's brother. **sis·ter-in-law** (sis′tər in lô′) *noun, plural* **sisters-in-law**.

sit **1.** To be in a position in which the weight of the body rests on the lower back part and not the feet: *Sit in a chair.* **2.** To cause to sit; seat: *We sat the children around the table.* **3.** To rest on a perch; roost: *The bird sat on a branch.* **4.** To take care of a child or children while the parents are away for a time; babysit: *Can you sit for us tonight?* **5.** To cover eggs in order to hatch them: *Hens sit on their eggs.* **6.** To be placed or be kept: *The cabin sits in the woods.* **7.** To hold a position for an artist or photographer: *The governor sat for a portrait.* **8.** To be a member of a group of officials: *My cousin sits in the state assembly.* **9.** To hold a session or meeting: *This court will sit next week.*
• **to sit down.** To lower oneself so that one is in a sitting position: *When everyone sat down, the meeting began.*
• **to sit up.** **1.** To raise oneself so that one is in a sitting position: *The patient had to sit up when lunch was served.* **2.** To sit with the upper part of the body in an upright position: *Sit up straight!* **3.** To stay up; not go to bed: *My parents and their guest sat up for half the night.*
sit (sit) *verb*, **sat**, **sitting**.

LANGUAGE NOTE

The verbs *sit* and *set* each have many different meanings. Their most common meanings, however, are sometimes confused. Remember that *set* means to put or place something in a certain position. *Please set the books over there.* *Sit* means to be in or take a certain position. *We were sitting on the couch in the living room. Please sit down.*

---

site The position or location of something: *Our house is in a mountain site with a beautiful view. That town is the site of a major battle in the Civil War.*
Other words sounding like this are cite and sight. **site** (sīt) *noun, plural* **sites**.

situate To give a position to; place: *A large garden was situated alongside the house.* **sit·u·ate** (sich′ü āt′) *verb*, **situated**, **situating**.

situation **1.** A condition or state of affairs; circumstance: *We found ourselves in a difficult situation when our car broke down.* **2.** The work one is hired and paid to do; job: *What is your situation with that company?* **sit·u·a·tion** (sich′ü ā′shən) *noun, plural* **situations**.

sit-up A kind of exercise in which a person lying with the back flat on the floor rises to a sitting position without lifting the feet and then returns to the original position. **sit-up** (sit′up′) *noun, plural* **sit-ups**.

six One more than five; 6. **six** (siks) *noun, plural* **sixes**; *adjective*.

sixteen Six more than ten; 16. **six·teen** (sik′stēn′) *noun, plural* **sixteens**; *adjective*.

sixteenth Next after the fifteenth. *Adjective, noun.*
○ One of sixteen equal parts; ¹/₁₆. *Noun.*
six·teenth (sik′stēnth′) *adjective*; *noun, plural* **sixteenths**.

PRONUNCIATION KEY:
at   āpe   fär   câre   end   mē   it   īce   pierce   hot   ōld   sông   fôrk
oil   out   up   ūse   rüle   pùll   tûrn   chin   sing   shop   thin   this
hw in white; zh in treasure. The symbol ə stands for the unstressed vowel sound in about, taken, pencil, lemon, and circus.

683

sixth Next after the fifth. *Adjective, noun.*
○ One of six equal parts; ⅙. *Noun.*
sixth (siksth) *adjective; noun, plural* **sixths.**

sixtieth Next after the fifty-ninth. *Adjective, noun.*
○ One of sixty equal parts; ⅟₆₀. *Noun.*
six·ti·eth (siks′tē ith) *adjective; noun, plural*
sixtieths.

sixty Six times ten; 60. **six·ty** (siks′tē) *noun, plural*
sixties; *adjective.*

sizable or **sizeable** Quite large: *A sizable*
amount of my salary is spent on rent. **siz·a·ble**
(sīz′ə bəl) *adjective.*

size 1. The amount of space something takes up;
the length, width, and height of something: *Your*
room is the same size as mine. 2. Amount or
number: *Did you ask your parents to increase*
the size of your allowance? 3. One of a series of
measurements used for shoes, clothing, and other
things sold in stores: *What size shirt do you*
wear? **size** (sīz) *noun, plural* **sizes.**

SIZE

Animals come in all sizes, from the microscopic
to the giant. The smallest is hard to choose
because there are numerous one-celled animals.
The records for the largest living animals are:

Largest animal: the blue whale with a length
of 110 feet and a weight of 209 tons.
Largest land animal: the African elephant
which weighs 8 tons.
Largest reptile: the saltwater crocodile at
16 feet long and 1,150 pounds.
Largest fish: the whale shark at 41 feet long.
Largest bird: the ostrich which is 9 feet tall and
weighs 345 pounds.
Largest insect: the stick insect which is 15
inches long.

---

sizzle To make a hissing or sputtering sound:
The bacon sizzled as it cooked in the frying pan.
siz·zle (siz′əl) *verb,* **sizzled, sizzling.**

SK Postal abbreviation for Saskatchewan.

skate¹ 1. A special shoe with a metal runner
attached to the sole; ice skate. It is used for moving over ice. 2. A special shoe with small wheels
attached to the sole; roller skate. It is used for
moving over a flat surface, like a sidewalk. *Noun.*
○ To glide or move along on skates: *The children*

can skate when the ice on the pond is thicker. Verb.
skate (skāt) *noun, plural* **skates;** *verb,* **skated,**
skating.

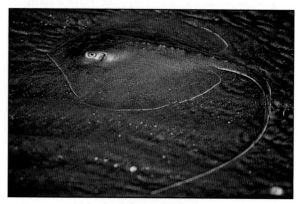

A skate is related to
sharks and rays.

skate² A broad, flat fish that lives in salt water off
the Pacific coast of the United States. **skate** (skāt)
noun, plural **skates** or **skate.**

skateboard A low, flat board that has wheels
on the bottom, used for riding. **skate·board**
(skāt′bôrd′) *noun, plural* **skateboards.**

skeleton 1. A framework that supports and protects the body of an animal. Birds, fish, and
humans have skeletons made up of bones or cartilage. 2. Any framework or structure used as a
support: *The workers built the steel skeleton of*
the building first. **skel·e·ton** (skel′i tən) *noun,*
plural **skeletons.**

skeptical Having or showing doubt or disbelief:
My classmates were skeptical of my plan to get
the governor to visit our class. **skep·ti·cal**
(skep′ti kəl) *adjective.*

sketch 1. A rough, quick drawing: *The artist*
made several sketches of the model before start-
ing the painting. 2. A short piece of writing; essay
or story: *This sketch describes a room in a run-*
down hotel. Noun.
○ 1. To make a sketch of: *I sketched an old barn*
for my art class. 2. To make a sketch or sketches:
I want to learn to sketch. Verb.
sketch (skech) *noun, plural* **sketches;** *verb,*
sketched, sketching.

sketchy 1. Done without detail; rough: *The sketchy*
drawing showed only a few outlines of the build-
ings. 2. Incomplete; lacking much detail: *The police*
got only a sketchy description of the suspect.
sketch·y (skech′ē) *adjective,* **sketchier, sketchiest.**

ski 1. One of a pair of long, narrow strips of wood, metal, or plastic that curve upward at the front. Skis are made to be attached to boots and are used for gliding over snow. 2. One of a pair of similar strips that are used for gliding over water; water ski. *Noun.*
○ To glide on skis: *We skied down the mountain. Verb.*
ski (skē) *noun, plural* **skis**; *verb,* **skied, skiing.**

skid To slide or slip out of control or sideways: *The car skidded out of control. Verb.*
○ The act of skidding: *The car went into a skid on the wet road. Noun.*
skid (skid) *verb,* **skidded, skidding**; *noun, plural* **skids.**

skill The power or ability to do something. Skill comes from practice, study, or experience: *My neighbor works with children who have poor reading skills.* **skill** (skil) *noun, plural* **skills.**

skilled 1. Having or showing skill and ability: *That skilled mechanic repairs old cars.* 2. Requiring special ability or training: *The factory is hiring workers for skilled jobs.* **skilled** (skild) *adjective.*

skillet A shallow pan with a handle. A skillet is used for frying. **skil·let** (skil′it) *noun, plural* **skillets.**

skillful Having or showing skill; expert: *That is a skillful portrait.* **skill·ful** (skil′fəl) *adjective.*

skim 1. To remove something that is floating from the surface of a liquid: *The cook skimmed the fat from the soup.* 2. To read quickly: *Skim the newspaper for the baseball scores.* 3. To move or move over lightly and swiftly: *The sailboat skimmed easily across the lake.* 4. To throw so as to bounce lightly across a surface: *Let's see who can skim a stone the farthest across the pond.*
skim (skim) *verb,* **skimmed, skimming.**

skim milk or **skimmed milk** Milk from which the cream has been removed.

skin 1. The outer covering of the body of a person or other animal with a backbone. The skin protects the organs inside the body and is the sense organ for touch, temperature, and pain. 2. The outer covering or hide that is removed from a dead animal. The skins of such animals as calves and snakes are used to make shoes, handbags,

and clothing. 3. Anything that is like skin: *This apple has a bright red skin. Noun.*
○ To take off the skin from: *I skinned my knees when I fell off my bicycle. Verb.*
• **by the skin of one's teeth.** By a very narrow margin; only just; barely: *I passed the test by the skin of my teeth.*
skin (skin) *noun, plural* **skins**; *verb,* **skinned, skinning.**

skin diving Swimming underwater for long periods of time. A face mask and flippers, and sometimes an oxygen tank or a snorkel, are used in skin diving.

skinny Very thin: *You were very skinny when you were sick.* **skin·ny** (skin′ē) *adjective,* **skinnier, skinniest.**

skip 1. To spring or bound along, hopping lightly on one foot and then on the other: *The children skipped down the path.* 2. To jump or leap over: *We skipped rope in the playground.* 3. To pass by or leave out: *Skip the arithmetic problems you can't do.* 4. To bounce or cause to bounce across a surface: *Let's skip stones across the pond.* 5. To not go to or attend: *They skipped the meeting last night.* 6. To be promoted to the next higher grade: *The bright student skipped fifth grade. Verb.*
○ A light springing or jumping step: *I took a skip to avoid the puddle. Noun.*
skip (skip) *verb,* **skipped, skipping**; *noun, plural* **skips.**

skirt 1. A piece of clothing that is worn by women or girls. It hangs down from the waist. Skirts are worn with a blouse, sweater, or other garment on top. 2. The part of a dress or similar piece of clothing that hangs down from the waist. *Noun.*
○ To move or lie along the border or edge of: *The highway skirts the town. Verb.*
skirt (skûrt) *noun, plural* **skirts**; *verb,* **skirted, skirting.**

skit A short, usually funny play: *Our class wrote a skit to perform for Thanksgiving.* **skit** (skit) *noun, plural* **skits.**

skull The bony framework of the head in animals that have a backbone. The skull protects the brain. **skull** (skul) *noun, plural* **skulls.**

skunk 1. An animal of the weasel family that has a bushy tail and black fur with white stripes

PRONUNCIATION KEY:

| at | āpe | fär | câre | end | mē | it | īce | pierce | hot | ōld | sòng | fôrk |
| oil | out | up | ūse | rüle | pull | tûrn | chin | sing | shop | thin | this | |

hw in white; zh in treasure. The symbol ə stands for the unstressed vowel sound in about, taken, pencil, lemon, and circus.

685

along its back. Skunks can spray a strong, bad-smelling liquid when frightened or attacked. They are found only in North and South America. **2.** A mean person who is worthy of contempt. **skunk** (skungk) *noun, plural* **skunks**.

sky The space or air above the earth: *On clear days, the sky has a light blue color.* **sky** (skī) *noun, plural* **skies**.

skydiving The act or sport of jumping from an airplane and falling as far as is safe before opening a parachute. **sky·div·ing** (skī′dī′ving) *noun*.

skylight A window in a ceiling or roof. Some skylights can be opened and closed. **sky·light** (skī′līt′) *noun, plural* **skylights**.

skyline **1.** The outline of buildings, mountains, or other objects as seen against the sky: *We saw the city's skyline as we drove over the bridge.* **2.** The line at which the earth and sky seem to come together; horizon: *The sunset turned the skyline red and orange.* **sky·line** (skī′līn′) *noun, plural* **skylines**.

skyrocket A kind of firecracker that explodes high in the air and produces a shower of colored sparks. *Noun.*
○ To rise suddenly and quickly: *The cost of food skyrocketed last year.* *Verb.*
sky·rock·et (skī′rok′it) *noun, plural* **skyrockets**; *verb*, **skyrocketed**, **skyrocketing**.

skyscraper A very tall building: *Big cities often have many skyscrapers.* **sky·scrap·er** (skī′skrā′pər) *noun, plural* **skyscrapers**.

slab A broad, flat, thick piece or slice of stone, bread, or other material: *The workers had to remove the concrete slabs.* **slab** (slab) *noun, plural* **slabs**.

slack **1.** Not tight or firm; loose: *Tighten the slack rope.* **2.** Slow and not rushed: *We walked at a slack pace. Adjective.*

Most skyscrapers contain scores of offices and businesses.

○ A part that hangs loose: *Pull the rope tight to remove the slack.* *Noun.*
slack (slak) *adjective*, **slacker**, **slackest**; *noun, plural* **slacks**.

slacks Long pants for casual wear. **slacks** (slaks) *plural noun*.

slam **1.** To close with force and a loud noise: *Please don't slam the door.* **2.** To throw, move, or put with force and a loud noise: *I'm sorry I slammed the phone down.* **3.** To strike or hit with force and a loud noise: *The batter slammed the ball. Verb.*
○ A forceful and noisy closing or striking: *The door closed with a slam. Noun.*
slam (slam) *verb*, **slammed**, **slamming**; *noun, plural* **slams**.

slander A false statement made to damage a person's reputation: *The slander kept the senator from being reelected. Noun.*
○ To utter false and damaging statements about a person: *The mayor said the governor had slandered the city officials Verb.*
sland·er (slan′dər) *noun; verb* **slandered**, **slandering**.

slang An informal kind of language used in everyday conversation. Slang uses new words and new and different meanings for old words. The use of slang helps to keep language lively and interesting. **slang** (slang) *noun*.

LANGUAGE NOTE

Most slang is used for only a short time, and then it disappears from the language. Some slang words and phrases that people once said but we no longer use today are *skiddoo,* meaning "go away," and *the cat's pajamas,* meaning "wonderful." There are other words, however, that were slang at first and are now part of our standard language. *Kidnap, skyscraper,* and *jazz* were all considered slang at one time. Slang words do make our language interesting, but in most cases you should use slang only in everyday conversation, not in writing and formal speaking.

---

slant To run or slope away from a straight line: *The roof slants toward the ground. Verb.*
○ A sloping direction, line, or surface: *Hang the picture straight, not on a slant. Noun.*
slant (slant) *verb*, **slanted**, **slanting**; *noun, plural* **slants**.

slap A sharp, quick blow with the open hand or

something flat: *He greeted his friend with a slap on the back. Noun.*
○ **1.** To hit with a sharp, quick blow: *She slapped the fly with an old magazine.* **2.** To put or throw with noise and force: *Don't slap your books down on the desk. Verb.*
slap (slap) *noun, plural* **slaps**; *verb,* **slapped, slapping.**

slapdash Not done with care; careless: *The teacher refused to accept such a slapdash piece of homework.* **slap·dash** (slap′dash′) *adjective.*

slash **1.** To cut or try to cut with a sweeping stroke of a knife or another sharp object: *The vandals slashed the tires of our car.* **2.** To lower or decrease greatly: *The store slashed its prices. Verb.*
○ **1.** A sweeping stroke with great force: *The slash of the whip made a sound like a crack.* **2.** A long cut or wound: *The patient had a slash on the leg.* **3.** A great lowering or decrease: *The store advertised a slash in the prices of all its clothing. Noun.*
slash (slash) *verb,* **slashed, slashing**; *noun, plural* **slashes.**

slat A thin, flat strip of wood, metal, or other material: *The slats on the back of the chair are coming loose.* **slat** (slat) *noun, plural* **slats.**

slate **1.** A bluish gray rock that splits easily into thin layers. Slate is used to make blackboards and garden walks, and to cover roofs. **2.** A piece of this rock that has been cut for some use: *The roof had many broken slates.* **3.** A dark, bluish gray color. **slate** (slāt) *noun, plural* **slates.**

slaughter **1.** The act of killing an animal or animals for use as food. **2.** A brutal killing; massacre. *Noun.*
○ **1.** To kill for use as food. **2.** To kill in a brutal way; massacre. *Verb.*
slaugh·ter (slô′tər) *noun, plural* **slaughters**; *verb,* **slaughtered, slaughtering.**

slave **1.** A person who is owned by another person. **2.** A person who is controlled by another person, a habit, or other influence: *When I do my math homework, I try not to be a slave to my calculator.* **3.** A person who works or is made to work hard and long. *Noun.*
○ To work hard and long: *The writer slaved at the assignment for hours. Verb.*

slave (slāv) *noun, plural* **slaves**; *verb,* **slaved, slaving.**

WORD HISTORY
The word slave comes from a Latin word meaning "Slav." The Slavs are a group of people who live in eastern and central Europe. In the Middle Ages, many Slavs had been conquered and made to work as slaves.

slavery **1.** The practice of owning slaves. **2.** The condition of being a slave. **slav·er·y** (slā′və rē) *noun.*

slay To kill in a violent way: *In this story, a brave knight slays a large, frightening dragon.* Another word that sounds like this is **sleigh.**
slay (slā) *verb,* **slew, slain, slaying.**

sled A wooden framework mounted on runners. A sled is used to carry people or loads over the snow. *Noun.*
○ To ride on a sled: *The children sledded down the hill. Verb.*
sled (sled) *noun, plural* **sleds**; *verb,* **sledded, sledding.**

sledgehammer A heavy hammer that has a long handle that is held with both hands. **sledge·ham·mer** (slej′ham′ər) *noun, plural* **sledgehammers.**

sleek **1.** Smooth and shiny: *That cat has sleek black fur.* **2.** Looking healthy and well cared for: *A sleek horse won the race.* **sleek** (slēk) *adjective,* **sleeker, sleekest.**

sleep **1.** A time or condition of rest that occurs naturally and regularly in humans and other animals. During sleep, a person becomes unaware of most things, and the body regains its strength and energy. **2.** A condition that resembles sleep. The hibernation of a bear is sometimes called *sleep. Noun.*
○ **1.** To be in a state of sleep; be asleep: *A baby sleeps a large part of the day.* **2.** To be in a state that resembles sleep. *Verb.*
sleep (slēp) *noun*; *verb,* **slept, sleeping.**

sleeping bag A long bag that is lined or padded to keep a person warm. It is often used for sleeping outdoors.

sleepy **1.** Ready for or needing sleep: *I feel sleepy.* **2.** Dull or quiet: *We live in a sleepy little town.* **sleep·y** (slē′pē) *adjective,* **sleepier, sleepiest.**

PRONUNCIATION KEY:
at ape fär câre end mē it īce pierce hot ōld sông fôrk
oil out up ūse rüle pull tûrn chin sing shop thin this
hw in white; zh in treasure. The symbol ə stands for the unstressed vowel sound in about, taken, pencil, lemon, and circus. **687**

sleet Frozen or partly frozen rain. *Noun.*
  ○ To shower sleet: *The roads were very slippery because it had sleeted all day. Verb.*
  sleet (slēt) *noun; verb,* **sleeted, sleeting.**

sleeve The part of a piece of clothing that covers all or part of the arm. **sleeve** (slēv) *noun, plural* **sleeves.**

sleigh A carriage on runners that is drawn by a horse. A sleigh is used for traveling over snow or ice.
  Another word that sounds like this is **slay.**
  sleigh (slā) *noun, plural* **sleighs.**

slender 1. Not big around; thin: *The new dining room chairs have slender legs.* 2. Small in size or amount: *The candidate won the election by only a slender margin.* **slen·der** (slen′dər) *adjective,* **slenderer, slenderest.**

slice A thin, flat piece cut from something larger: *May I have a slice of bread? Noun.*
  ○ 1. To cut into a thin, flat piece or pieces: *I sliced the bread.* 2. To move or cut through like a knife: *The shark's fin sliced the water. Verb.*
  slice (slīs) *noun, plural* **slices;** *verb,* **sliced, slicing.**

slick 1. Smooth and shiny: *The horse had a slick brown coat.* 2. Smooth and slippery: *A newly waxed floor is slick. Adjective.*
  ○ A smooth or slippery place on a surface: *The boat left a slick of oil on the water. Noun.*
  slick (slik) *adjective,* **slicker, slickest;** *noun, plural* **slicks.**

slide 1. To move or cause to move smoothly, easily, or quietly: *The wet bar of soap slid across the floor.* 2. To fall or move suddenly from a position: *The truck slid off the icy road into a ditch. Verb.*

○ 1. The act of sliding: *Let's take a slide down the hill on our sleds.* 2. A smooth surface for sliding: *I like the slide in the playground.* 3. A small sheet of glass or plastic. Objects are put on a glass slide and looked at under a microscope. Slides with pictures on them are put in a projector and shown on a screen. 4. The fall of a mass of rock, snow, or other material down a slope: *The road was closed because of rock slides. Noun.*
  slide (slīd) *verb,* **slid, slid, sliding;** *noun, plural* **slides.**

slight 1. Not much or not important; small: *There is a slight chance of rain.* 2. Not big around; thin: *My older cousin is very slight and weighs only 100 pounds. Adjective.*
  ○ To treat as unimportant; not pay enough attention to: *I felt I had been slighted when I was not invited to your picnic. Verb.*
  ○ The act of treating someone or something as unimportant: *They weren't invited to the party, and they resented the slight. Noun.*
  slight (slīt) *adjective,* **slighter, slightest;** *verb,* **slighted, slighting;** *noun, plural* **slights.**

slim 1. Small in thickness; thin: *The fashion model had a very slim figure.* 2. Small in amount; slight: *The team felt it had only a slim chance of winning the championship game. Adjective.*
  ○ To become slim: *You can slim down by exercising more. Verb.*
  slim (slim) *adjective,* **slimmer, slimmest;** *verb,* **slimmed, slimming.**

slime 1. Wet, soft, sticky mud. 2. A thin, sticky substance given off by some animals, such as snails. **slime** (slīm) *noun.*

slimy Of, covered with, or like slime; disgusting: *Don't go in the slimy pond.* **slim·y** (slī′mē) *adjective,* **slimier, slimiest.**

sling 1. A device for throwing stones. A sling is usually made of a piece of leather with a string fastened to each end. 2. A device that loops around the neck to support an injured arm or hand: *When I broke my arm, I had to wear a sling. Noun.*
  ○ 1. To hang with a sling or strap: *The workers slung bags of potatoes over their shoulders.* 2. To hang or throw loosely: *The campers slung the hammock between two trees. Verb.*
  sling (sling) *noun, plural* **slings;** *verb,* **slung, slinging.**

slingshot A Y-shaped piece of wood, metal, or

This water slide provides
many thrills.

other material with an elastic band fastened to the tips of the two upper ends. A slingshot is used to shoot stones or other small objects. **sling·shot** (sling′shot′) *noun, plural* **slingshots.**

slip¹ **1.** To move suddenly from a position or out of control; slide: *The man slipped on the icy sidewalk.* **2.** To move or go quietly: *The thief slipped out of the house.* **3.** To move or cause to move smoothly and easily: *A little oil will help the ring to slip off your finger.* **4.** To put or give quietly and quickly: *Don't slip each other notes during class.* **5.** To fail to be noticed or remembered: *I know you, but your name slips my mind.* **6.** To put on or take off clothing quickly and easily: *He slipped into his pajamas.* **7.** To make a mistake: *She only slipped once during the test.* **8.** To become worse or lower: *Your score slipped on this test. Verb.*

○ **1.** The act of slipping: *I fell as a result of a slip on the icy sidewalk.* **2.** A piece of clothing worn under a woman's or girl's dress or skirt. A slip is made out of a light material like cotton or nylon. **3.** A mistake or error: *One little slip gave the thieves' hiding place away. Noun.*

• **to slip up.** To make a mistake: *I slipped up on the first question of the test.*

slip (slip) *verb,* **slipped, slipping;** *noun, plural* **slips.**

slip² **1.** A small piece of paper, cloth, or any other material: *I wrote my friend's telephone number on a slip of paper.* **2.** A small shoot or twig cut from a plant. **slip** (slip) *noun, plural* **slips.**

slipper A light, low shoe that is easily slipped on or off the foot. Slippers are worn indoors. **slip·per** (slip′ər) *noun, plural* **slippers.**

slippery **1.** Causing or likely to cause slipping or sliding: *Rain made the roads slippery.* **2.** Slipping or sliding away easily: *The wet fish was slippery.* **3.** Not trustworthy: *The villain was a slippery character.* **slip·pery** (slip′ə rē) *adjective,* **slipperier, slipperiest.**

slipshod Not carefully done; careless: *Your homework is too slipshod to get a good grade.* **slip·shod** (slip′shod′) *adjective.*

slit A long, narrow cut or opening: *I opened the door a little and looked through the slit. Cut two slits in the paper. Noun.*

○ To cut or make a slit or slits in: *Slit open the envelope with a dull knife. Verb.*

slit (slit) *noun, plural* **slits;** *verb,* **slitted, slitting.**

slither To slide or glide like a snake: *The snake slithered across the hot sand.* **slith·er** (slith′ər) *verb,* **slithered, slithering.**

sliver A thin, often pointed piece that has been broken, cut, or torn off; splinter: *I got a sliver of wood in my toe.* **sliv·er** (sliv′ər) *noun, plural* **slivers.**

slogan A phrase or motto. Slogans are used by a person, a group, or a business: *"No taxation without representation" was a slogan used by American colonists.* **slo·gan** (slō′gən) *noun, plural* **slogans.**

WORD HISTORY

The word slogan comes from a word meaning "battle cry" in the language spoken in the highlands of Scotland.

---

sloop A sailboat with one mast and sails that run from front to rear. **sloop** (slüp) *noun, plural* **sloops.**

slope To lie or cause to lie at an angle between flat and upright: *The road slopes toward the river. Verb.*

○ **1.** A line, piece of ground, or any surface that is not flat or level: *The house was built on a slope.* **2.** The amount that something slopes or slants: *The river bank has a steep slope at this point. Noun.*

slope (slōp) *verb,* **sloped, sloping;** *noun, plural* **slopes.**

A sloop is one of the fastest sailboats.

sloppy **1.** Not neat; messy: *Your clothes looked very sloppy after you had slept overnight in them.* **2.** Careless: *Sloppy addition gave you the wrong answer.* **3.** Very wet or covered with mud or slush: *The roads are sloppy from the snow and*

PRONUNCIATION KEY:

| at | āpe | fär | câre | end | mē | it | īce | pierce | hot | ōld | sông | fôrk |
| oil | out | up | ūse | rüle | pull | tûrn | chin | sing | shop | thin | this | |

hw in white; zh in treasure. The symbol ə stands for the unstressed vowel sound in about, taken, pencil, lemon, and circus.

689

rain today. **slop·py** (slop'ē) *adjective,* **sloppier, sloppiest.**

slot A narrow, straight opening or groove: *Put the coin in the slot.* **slot** (slot) *noun, plural* **slots.**

sloth 1. A slow-moving animal that lives in the forests of South America. Sloths use their long arms and legs and their curved claws to hang upside down from trees. 2. Laziness. **sloth** (slôth *or* slōth) *noun, plural* **sloths.**

slouch 1. To sit, stand, or walk in a loose, drooping way: *Sit up and don't slouch.* 2. To hang or bend down: *Don't slouch your shoulders. Verb.*
○ 1. A drooping of the head and shoulders while sitting, standing, or walking: *The tired hikers walked with a slouch.* 2. An awkward, lazy, or sloppy person: *Do your share of the work; don't be a slouch. Noun.*
slouch (slouch) *verb,* **slouched, slouching**; *noun, plural* **slouches.**

slovenly Untidy or careless, especially in dress or appearance: *It's important not to look slovenly at work.* **slov·en·ly** (sluv'ən lē) *adjective,* **slovenlier, slovenliest.**

slow 1. Acting, moving, or happening with little speed; not fast or quick: *It was a slow climb up the mountain.* 2. Behind the correct time: *Your watch is slow.* 3. Not quick to learn or understand: *I am slow in arithmetic.* 4. Not easily excited or moved: *I'm slow to anger.* 5. Not busy or interesting; dull: *It was a slow day at work. Adjective.*
○ In a slow manner: *Drive slow. Adverb.*
○ To make or become slow or slower: *The car slowed to a halt. Verb.*
slow (slō) *adjective,* **slower, slowest**; *adverb*; *verb,* **slowed, slowing.**

slug¹ 1. An animal that looks like a snail, but either has a very small shell or none at all. Some slugs eat plants and can become harmful pests in gardens. 2. A piece of lead or other metal that is fired from a gun. 3. A round, flat piece of metal. A slug is used in place of a coin in a vending machine or other device that requires coins. It is against the law to use slugs. **slug** (slug) *noun, plural* **slugs.**

slug² To strike or hit hard: *The batter slugged the ball over the fence. Verb.*
○ A hard or heavy strike or hit: *Give that nail a good slug with the hammer. Noun.*
slug (slug) *verb,* **slugged, slugging**; *noun, plural* **slugs.**

sluggish 1. Not energetic or alert: *I feel sluggish today because I did not get enough sleep.* 2. Slow in movement or action: *Sales are usually sluggish right after Christmas.* **slug·gish** (slug'ish) *adjective.*

sluice 1. An artificially made channel for water that has a gate or valve for controlling the amount of flow. 2. The gate or valve of such a channel. 3. A long, sloping trough through which water is run. A sluice is often used for separating gold ore from dirt. **sluice** (slüs) *noun, plural* **sluices.**

slum A poor, crowded section of a city. Bad housing and dirty living conditions are some of the problems in slums. **slum** (slum) *noun, plural* **slums.**

slumber 1. To sleep or spend in sleeping: *The baby slumbered peacefully.* 2. To be quiet or calm: *The town slumbered. Verb.*
○ A period of sleep: *In the fairy tale, the prince woke the princess from her long slumber. Noun.*
slum·ber (slum'bər) *verb,* **slumbered, slumbering**; *noun.*

slump To fall or sink suddenly or heavily: *I slumped in my favorite chair. Verb.*
○ A sharp, sudden fall or decline: *This store has had a slump in sales every summer. The baseball team was in a slump and had lost six of its last seven games. Noun.*
slump (slump) *verb,* **slumped, slumping**; *noun, plural* **slumps.**

slurp To drink noisily: *The dog slurps his water.* **slurp** (slûrp) *verb,* **slurped, slurping.**

sly 1. Clever and shrewd; crafty: *The sly fox stole a chicken.* 2. Mischievous in a playful way: *One child gave me a sly glance.*
• **on the sly.** In a secret or crafty way: *The treasurer was stealing part of the club's funds on the sly.*
sly (slī) *adjective,* **slier** *or* **slyer, sliest** *or* **slyest.**

smack 1. To press together and open quickly so as to make a sharp sound: *The boy smacked his lips when he saw the food.* 2. To strike or hit sharply: *The car smacked into the fence.* 3. To kiss loudly: *I smacked my mother on the cheek. Verb.*
○ 1. A loud slap: *The dog got a smack for chewing on the furniture.* 2. A loud kiss: *The boy got a smack on his cheek from his sister for the gift he had given her. Noun.*
○ Directly or squarely: *The child rode the bicycle smack into a tree. Adverb.*
smack (smak) *verb,* **smacked, smacking**; *noun, plural* **smacks**; *adverb.*

small 1. Not large; little: *A mouse is a small animal.* 2. Not important: *We had a small problem trying to decide who should give the speech.* 3. Soft or weak: *The shy student replied in a small voice.* 4. Buying and selling goods or doing some other activity in a limited way: *Each of these shops is a small business. Adjective.*
○ A small or narrow part: *Be careful you don't strain the small of your back when you lift that heavy carton. Noun.*
small (smôl) *adjective*, **smaller**, **smallest**; *noun.*

small intestine A part of the digestive system that forms a long, coiled tube which connects the stomach and the large intestine. As food passes through the small intestine it is broken down into materials the body can use, and these materials are absorbed into the bloodstream.

small letter A letter that is not a capital letter: The letter "a" is a small letter, and "A" is a capital letter.

smart 1. Clever or intelligent; bright: *It was very smart of him to figure out the answer.* 2. Amusing and clever in a way that fails to show respect: *My parents told me not to act so smart.* 3. Neat and trim: *You look very smart.* 4. Stylish or fashionable: *That store is selling smart new dresses.* 5. Quick or brisk; lively: *The soldiers marched at a smart pace. Adjective.*
○ 1. To cause or feel a sharp, stinging pain: *Our faces smarted from the icy cold wind.* 2. To feel hurt: *The twins smarted from the scolding their parents gave them. Verb.*
smart (smärt) *adjective*, **smarter**, **smartest**; *verb*, **smarted**, **smarting**.

smash 1. To break violently into pieces: *The plate fell and smashed on the floor.* 2. To hit with a hard blow: *The car smashed into a tree.* 3. To destroy, crush, or defeat completely: *The soldiers smashed the enemy. Verb.*
○ The act or sound of breaking violently: *We heard the smash of glass from the next room. Noun.*
smash (smash) *verb*, **smashed**, **smashing**; *noun*, *plural* **smashes**.

smear 1. To cover or make dirty with something wet, sticky, or greasy: *The girl had smeared her dress with mud.* 2. To spread something wet, sticky, or greasy on something else: *He smeared paint all over his hands.* 3. To become or cause to become blurred or messy: *The wet paint smeared when I touched it.* 4. To harm a person's reputation: *One candidate for governor smeared the others by saying that they were crooks. Verb.*
○ A mark or stain made by smearing: *There was a smear of dirt on the cat's fur. Noun.*
smear (smîr) *verb*, **smeared**, **smearing**; *noun*, *plural* **smears**.

smell 1. To sense an odor by using the nose: *Do you smell gas?* 2. To test or sample by smelling; sniff: *The dog smells everyone that comes into the house.* 3. To have or give off an odor: *The kitchen smelled of fish.* 4. To have or give off an unpleasant odor: *The spoiled milk smelled. Verb.*
○ 1. The sense by which odors are recognized: *Taste and smell are often affected by colds.* 2. An odor or scent: *I love the smell of the sea.* 3. The act of smelling: *Won't you have a smell of this rose? Noun.*
smell (smel) *verb*, **smelled** *or* **smelt**, **smelling**; *noun*, *plural* **smells**.

smelt¹ A small, thin, silver-colored fish found in cold waters of the Northern Hemisphere. It is caught for food. **smelt** (smelt) *noun*, *plural* **smelts** *or* **smelt**.

smelt² To melt ore in order to separate the metal from it: *The first step in making steel is to smelt iron ore.* **smelt** (smelt) *verb*, **smelted**, **smelting**.

People are often encouraged to smile **while having their picture taken.**

smile An expression of the face that is made by turning up the corners of the mouth. A smile can show that a person is happy, amused, or being friendly. *Noun.*

PRONUNCIATION KEY:
at   āpe   fär   cāre   end   mē   it   ice   pierce   hot   ōld   sông   fôrk
oil   out   up   ūse   rūle   pull   tûrn   chin   sing   shop   thin   this
hw in white; zh in treasure. The symbol ə stands for the unstressed vowel sound in about, taken, pencil, lemon, and circus.

691

○ To have or give a smile: *The children smiled when they saw the clown. Verb.*
smile (smīl) *noun, plural* **smiles;** *verb,* **smiled, smiling.**

smock A loose garment that looks like a long shirt. A smock is worn over other clothing to protect it. **smock** (smok) *noun, plural* **smocks.**

smog A combination of smoke and fog in the air. Smog is found especially over cities where there are factories and many cars. **smog** (smog) *noun.*

WORD HISTORY

The word smog was made using the first two letters of smoke and the last two letters of fog.

smoke 1. A gas given off by something that is burning. The carbon particles in smoke give it a gray color. 2. The act of drawing in and breathing out smoke from burning tobacco. *Noun.*
○ 1. To send out or produce smoke: *We could see a chimney smoking in the distance.* 2. To draw in and breathe out smoke from burning tobacco. 3. To preserve food by exposing it to smoke: *This company smokes ham and sausage. Verb.*
smoke (smōk) *noun, plural* **smokes;** *verb,* **smoked, smoking.**

smoke detector A device that gives a loud signal to warn people of smoke or fire.

smokestack A tall chimney or pipe from which smoke is released. **smoke·stack** (smōk′stak′) *noun, plural* **smokestacks.**

smoky 1. Giving off or filled with smoke: *We moved away from the smoky campfire.* 2. Like the color or taste of smoke: *They own a beautiful smoky gray cat.* **smok·y** (smō′kē) *adjective,* **smokier, smokiest.**

Smokestacks **are used by factories and big ships.**

smolder 1. To burn and smoke with few or no flames: *When I awoke, the campfire was still smoldering.* 2. To exist or continue in a hidden condition: *Anger against the dictator smoldered*

in the minds of the people. **smol·der** (smōl′dər) *verb,* **smoldered, smoldering.**

smooth 1. Having a surface that is not uneven or rough: *The baby has such smooth skin.* 2. Even or gentle in movement: *The pilot made a smooth landing.* 3. Free from difficulties or trouble: *We are making smooth progress in our plans to start a gardening club.* 4. Able and skillful: *That smooth skater made difficult turns appear easy. Adjective.*
○ 1. To make even or level or remove what is keeping something from being smooth: *We smoothed the dirt around the shrubs we had planted.* 2. To free from difficulty; make easy: *The club president smoothed the way for the vice-president to become president next year. Verb.*
smooth (smū<u>th</u>) *adjective,* **smoother, smoothest;** *verb,* **smoothed, smoothing.**

smother 1. To keep from or kill by keeping from breathing air: *The avalanche smothered several climbers.* 2. To be kept from breathing air: *The cat will smother in that small box.* 3. To put out or cause to burn less by covering: *We used dirt to smother our campfire.* 4. To cover thickly: *The cook smothered the steak with onions.* 5. To hide or hold back: *I smothered a yawn.* **smoth·er** (smu<u>th</u>′ər) *verb,* **smothered, smothering.**

smudge To make or become dirty or smeared: *My dirty hands smudged the white towel. Verb.*
○ A dirty mark or stain: *Someone's dirty hand left a smudge on the wall. Noun.*
smudge (smuj) *verb,* **smudged, smudging;** *noun, plural* **smudges.**

smug So certain or pleased about one's own worth that one annoys other people: *The contest winners were so smug that no one else would talk to them.* **smug** (smug) *adjective,* **smugger, smuggest.**

smuggle 1. To take in or out of a country secretly and against the law: *The thief tried to smuggle the jewels out of the country.* 2. To take or carry secretly: *Who smuggled a gun to one of the prisoners?* **smug·gle** (smug′əl) *verb,* **smuggled, smuggling.**

snack A small amount of food or drink eaten between regular meals. *Noun.*
○ To eat a little bit: *We snacked on popcorn during the movie.*
snack (snak) *noun, plural* **snacks.**

snail 1. An animal that has a soft body protected by a shell shaped like a spiral. Snails are mollusks and are found in water and on land. **2.** A person who moves very slowly: **snail** (snāl) *noun, plural* **snails.**

snake **1.** A kind of animal that has a long body covered with scales and no legs, arms, or wings. Snakes are reptiles that move by curving and then straightening out their bodies. Some snakes have a poisonous bite. **2.** A person who is sly or evil or cannot be trusted. **snake** (snāk) *noun, plural* **snakes.**

A snake **should only be handled with proper supervision.**

snap **1.** To make or cause to make a sudden, sharp sound: *The dry wood snapped as it burned.* **2.** To break suddenly and sharply: *The twig snapped when I stepped on it.* **3.** To move, act, or speak quickly and sharply: *The soldiers snapped to attention as the general walked by.* **4.** To open, close, or move into a position with a sudden, sharp sound: *We closed the door and the lock snapped shut.* **5.** To seize or snatch suddenly or eagerly: *The fish snapped at the bait.* **6.** To take a photograph: *I snapped a picture of my cousin. Verb.*
○ **1.** A sudden, sharp or breaking sound or action: *The stem of the glass broke with a snap.* **2.** A fastener or clasp that makes a snapping sound: *My jacket has snaps.* **3.** A sudden bite or snatch: *The dog took a snap at the mail carrier.* **4.** A short period of cold weather. **5.** A thin, crisp cookie: *The bakery sells lemon and ginger snaps.* **6.** Something that is easy to do: *That spelling test was a snap. Noun.*
○ Made or done quickly and with little thought: *You think about things for a while and never*

make a snap decision. Adjective.
snap (snap) *verb,* **snapped, snapping;** *noun, plural* **snaps;** *adjective.*

snapshot An informal photograph that is taken with a small, often inexpensive camera.
snap·shot (snap′shot′) *noun, plural* **snapshots.**

snare A trap for catching small animals. A snare has a noose that jerks tight around the animal when the trap is set off. *Noun.*
○ To catch with or as if with a snare: *The hunter snared a rabbit. Verb.*
snare (snâr) *noun, plural* **snares;** *verb,* **snared, snaring.**

snare drum A small drum with wires or strings stretched across the bottom part. When the top of the drum is struck, the wires vibrate and give the drum a rattling sound.

snarl¹ **1.** To growl while showing the teeth: *The dog snarled at the stranger.* **2.** To speak in an angry, growling way: *The plumber snarled at the leaking pipe. Verb.*
○ An angry growl. *Noun.*
snarl (snärl) *verb,* **snarled, snarling;** *noun, plural* **snarls.**

snarl² **1.** A tangled or knotted mass: *Please help me brush the snarls out of my hair.* **2.** A confused condition: *The accident caused a traffic snarl on the highway. Noun.*
○**1.** To make or become tangled or knotted: *The wind and rain snarled your hair. The kite's string snarled in the tree.* **2.** To make or become confused: *The snowstorm snarled the highways. Verb.*
snarl (snärl) *noun, plural* **snarls;** *verb,* **snarled, snarling.**

snatch To seize or grab suddenly or quickly: *I was scolded for snatching grapes from the counter. Verb.*
○ **1.** The act of seizing or grabbing suddenly and quickly. **2.** A small amount: *We could hear snatches of the conversation at the next table. Noun.*
snatch (snach) *verb,* **snatched, snatching;** *noun, plural* **snatches.**

sneak To move, act, or take secretly or slyly: *Did you sneak an orange from the kitchen? Verb.*
○ A sly, dishonest person: *They are such sneaks that I don't trust them to tell the truth. Noun.*
○ Done, planned, or acting secretly or slyly: *a sneak attack. Adjective.*

PRONUNCIATION KEY:

| at | āpe | fär | câre | end | mē | it | īce | pîerce | hot | ōld | sông | fôrk |
| oil | out | up | ūse | rüle | pùll | tûrn | chin | sing | shop | thin | this | |

hw in white; zh in treasure. The symbol ə stands for the unstressed vowel sound in about, taken, pencil, lemon, and circus.

693

sneak (snēk) *verb,* **sneaked** *or* **snuck, sneaking;** *noun, plural* **sneaks;** *adjective.* —**sneaky** *adjective.*

sneaker A shoe made of canvas or other material with a rubber sole. **sneak•er** (snēk′ər) *noun, plural* **sneakers.**

sneer An expression of the face or a remark that shows hatred or scorn: *The rude child answered with a sneer. Noun.*
○To show or say with a sneer: *The thief sneered at the police. Verb.*
sneer (snîr) *noun, plural* **sneers;** *verb,* **sneered, sneering.**

sneeze To put forth air from the nose and mouth in a sudden, violent way: *Ever since I caught this cold I have been sneezing. Verb.*
○The act of sneezing: *I found my handkerchief just in time to cover my sneeze. Noun.*
sneeze (snēz) *verb,* **sneezed, sneezing;** *noun, plural* **sneezes.**

sniff **1.** To take in air through the nose in a short, quick breath: *The kitten sniffed at its food.* **2.** To take in through the nose: *We sniffed the clean mountain air.* **3.** To smell by sniffing: *Sniff this flower. Verb.*
○The act or sound of sniffing. *Noun.*
sniff (snif) *verb,* **sniffed, sniffing;** *noun, plural* **sniffs.**

sniffle To sniff again and again because of a cold or to keep from crying: *The unhappy child sat in the corner and sniffled. Verb.*
○ **the sniffles:** A condition that causes sniffing, such as a cold: *My sniffles didn't prevent me from going to the game. Plural noun.*
snif•fle (snif′əl) *verb,* **sniffled, sniffling;** *plural noun.*

snip To cut with scissors in short, quick strokes: *Snip those loose threads off the dress. Verb.*
○ **1.** The act of snipping: *The barber made a few last snips.* **2.** A small piece snipped off: *We took a snip of fabric to see if we could match it. Noun.*

snip (snip) *verb,* **snipped, snipping;** *noun, plural* **snips.**

snob **1.** A person who places great value on wealth and social position. **2.** A person who feels he or she is better than others. **snob** (snob) *noun, plural* **snobs.** —**snobby** *adjective.*

snooze To sleep for a short time; nap; doze: *I snoozed during the movie. Verb.*
○A short sleep; nap. *Noun.*
snooze (snüz) *verb,* **snoozed, snoozing;** *noun, plural* **snoozes.**

snore To make harsh, rattling breathing sounds while sleeping: *My old dog snores loudly. Verb.*
○ A harsh, rattling breathing sound made while sleeping. *Noun.*
snore (snôr) *verb,* **snored, snoring;** *noun, plural* **snores.**

snorkel A tube through which a person can breathe while swimming with the face held underwater: *We used masks with snorkels to look at the fish around the reef.* **snor•kel** (snôr′kəl) *noun, plural* **snorkels.**

snout The front part of an animal's head, including the nose, mouth, and jaws. **snout** (snout) *noun, plural* **snouts.**

When water vapor freezes in the air, snow is formed.

snow **1.** Soft, white crystals of ice that fall to earth. **2.** A fall of snow. *Noun.*
○ To fall as snow. *Verb.*
 • **to snow in.** To cover or surround with so much snow that a person cannot leave a place: *After the blizzard, we were snowed in for two days.* **snow** (snō) *noun, plural* **snows;** *verb,* **snowed, snowing.** —**snowy** *adjective.*

snowball A ball made of snow packed together. **snow·ball** (snō'bôl') *noun, plural* **snowballs**.

snowflake One of the small ice crystals that fall as snow. **snow·flake** (snō'flāk') *noun, plural* **snowflakes**.

snowman A figure of a person made by shaping a mass of snow. **snow·man** (snō'man') *noun, plural* **snowmen** (snō'men').

snowmobile A vehicle for travel on the snow. It has a motor and runners or skis. **snow·mo·bile** (snō'mō bēl') *noun, plural* **snowmobiles**.

snowplow A wide, curved metal blade used to push snow off a road or other surface, or a vehicle having such a blade. **snow·plow** (snō'plou') *noun, plural* **snowplows**.

snowshoe A flat, webbed frame attached to boots and used for walking over deep snow without sinking. **snow·shoe** (snō'shü') *noun, plural* **snowshoes**.

snowstorm A storm with strong winds and much snow. **snow·storm** (snō'stôrm') *noun, plural* **snowstorms**.

snub To treat someone coldly or with contempt, especially by ignoring the person: *Do you know why my friend snubbed me and didn't come to my party? Verb.*
○ Treatment that is cold, full of contempt, or lacking in respect. *Noun.*
snub (snub) *verb,* **snubbed, snubbing;** *noun, plural* **snubs.**

snug 1. Comfortable, warm, and cozy: *It is nice to get into a snug bed on a cold night.* 2. Fitting very closely or tightly: *The sweater is a bit snug, but I can still wear it.* **snug** (snug) *adjective,* **snugger, snuggest.** —**snugly** *adverb* —**snugness** *noun.*

snuggle To lie close to or hold closely for warmth or protection, or to show love: *The wolf cubs snuggled against their parents.* **snug·gle** (snug'əl) *verb,* **snuggled, snuggling.**

so 1. To this or that extent or degree: *It was so cold that we stayed indoors.* 2. Very: *I am so glad.* 3. Very much: *They love their parents so.* 4. For this or that reason; therefore: *We were tired, and so we went home early.* 5. Too; also: *I sing, and so does my friend.* 6. In this or that way: *Hold the tennis racket so. Adverb.*

○ True: *I found out that what they say is so. Adjective.*
○ For the purpose that: *Please turn off the light so I can go to sleep. Conjunction.*
○ 1. More or less: *We will be away for a month or so.* 2. The same: *That is a lazy dog and will always be so. Pronoun.*
○ The word so is also used to express or to introduce another thought: *So! You decided to come after all. Interjection.*
Other words sounding like this are **sew** and **sow**.
• **so as** or **so that**. With the purpose or result: *We divided the food carefully so as to have enough for everyone.*
so (sō) *adverb; adjective; conjunction; pronoun; interjection.*

soak 1. To make very wet: *We were soaked by the thunderstorm.* 2. To take in; absorb: *The sponge soaked up the spilled juice.* 3. To let something stay in water or other liquid: *We let the dirty clothes soak overnight. Verb.*
○ The act or process of soaking: *Give those dirty clothes a soak. Noun.*
soak (sōk) *verb,* **soaked, soaking;** *noun, plural* **soaks.**

soap A substance used for washing and cleaning, made with fats and lye. Soaps are made in the form of bars, powders, and liquids. *Noun.*
○ To rub or cover with soap: *Did you soap your hands well? Verb.*
soap (sōp) *noun, plural* **soaps;** *verb,* **soaped, soaping.**

soapy 1. Containing soap: *Wash the dishes in hot, soapy water.* 2. Covered with soap: *The soapy toy slipped out of the child's hands.* 3. Like soap: *The drink tasted soapy.* **soap·y** (sō'pē) *adjective.*

soar 1. To fly high in the air: *The birds soared in the sky.* 2. To go very high: *Food prices soared this year.*
Another word that sounds like this is **sore**.
soar (sôr) *verb,* **soared, soaring.**

sob To cry with short gasps of breath: *The little boy sobbed because he couldn't go with his friends. Verb.*
○ The act or sound of crying with short gasps of breath. *Noun.*
sob (sob) *verb,* **sobbed, sobbing;** *noun, plural* **sobs.**

PRONUNCIATION KEY:

| at | āpe | fär | câre | end | mē | it | īce | pierce | hot | ōld | sông | fôrk |
| oil | out | up | ūse | rüle | pull | tûrn | chin | sing | shop | thin | this | |

hw in white; zh in treasure. The symbol ə stands for the unstressed vowel sound in about, taken, pencil, lemon, and circus.

695

sober 1. Not drunk: *A driver of a car should be sober.* 2. Serious and solemn: *The room was decorated in a sober way, with no bright colors.* *Adjective.*

○ To make or become sober: *The sad news sobered the people at the party.* *Verb.*

so·ber (sō′bər) *adjective*, **soberer**, **soberest**; *verb*, **sobered**, **sobering**. —**soberly** *adverb*.

Soccer **is played by two teams of eleven players each.**

soccer A game in which the players try to move a round ball into a goal by kicking it or striking it with any part of their bodies except the hands and arms. **soc·cer** (sok′ər) *noun*.

social 1. Having to do with people as a group: *A family is a social unit. Geography and history are social studies.* 2. Having to do with people being together in a friendly way: *We paid a social visit to our neighbor.* 3. Liking to be with other people; friendly; sociable: *They're very social and like to have visitors.* 4. Having to do with the part of society that is wealthy or that sets or follows current fashions. 5. Living together in organized communities: *A bee is a social insect.* *Adjective.*

○ A party or other friendly gathering: *We are going to a social tonight.* *Noun.*

so·cial (sō′shəl) *adjective*; *noun*, *plural* **socials**.

socialism An economic system in which the major businesses, factories, farms, and other means of producing and distributing goods are owned and run by the government or by the people as a whole, rather than by individuals. **so·cial·ism** (sō′shə liz′əm) *noun*.

socialist A person who favors or supports socialism. **so·cial·ist** (sō′shə list) *noun*, *plural* **socialists**.

social studies In an elementary school or a secondary school, a course of study that includes geography, history, and civics.

society 1. Human beings as a group; all people: *Having enough food may become one of society's biggest problems.* 2. A club or other group of people who join together because of an interest they all share: *My father is the head of our town's historical society.* 3. The people who are wealthy or who set or follow current fashions in a group or community. 4. Companionship; company: *We enjoy our neighbors' society and invite them to dinner often.* **so·ci·e·ty** (sə sī′i tē) *noun*, *plural* **societies**.

sock A knitted or woven cloth covering for the foot and the lower leg. **sock** (sok) *noun*, *plural* **socks**.

socket An opening into which something fits: *We screwed the light bulb into the socket. Our eyes are set in sockets.* **sock·et** (sok′it) *noun*, *plural* **sockets**.

sod The top layer of soil that has grass growing on it. People who do not want to plant grass seed to start a lawn buy pieces of sod. *Noun.*

○ To plant with sod. *Verb.*

sod (sod) *noun*; *verb*, **sodded**, **sodding**.

soda 1. A sweet drink made with soda water and flavoring, and sometimes ice cream. 2. A white powder made with sodium, used in cooking, medicine, and in making soaps and other cleaners; baking soda. 3. A soft drink. 4. Soda water. **so·da** (sō′də) *noun*, *plural* **sodas**.

soda water A drink with bubbles, made of water mixed with carbon dioxide gas.

sodium A soft, silver-colored metal. Salt is a compound that contains sodium. Sodium is a chemical element. **so·di·um** (sō′dē əm) *noun*.

sofa A long upholstered seat with a back and arms; couch. A sofa has room for two or more people. **so·fa** (sō′fə) *noun*, *plural* **sofas**.

soft 1. Easy to shape; not hard: *The soft clay was easy to mold. I like to rest my head on a soft pillow.* 2. Smooth to the touch; not rough: *A baby has very soft skin.* 3. Gentle or light; not harsh or sharp: *The police officer's soft voice calmed the lost child. The soft spring breeze felt warm.* 4. Kind or easily influenced by emotions: *a soft heart.* 5. Weak: *Her muscles were soft after her* *broken leg mended.* **soft** (sôft) *adjective*, **softer**, **softest**. —**softly** *adverb* —**softness** *noun*.

SYNONYMS

soft, lenient, subdued, tender
My grandmother had a soft Welsh accent. The principal was lenient with the pupils who had been fighting. The tone of the policeman's voice was firm but subdued. The girls spoke in a very tender voice to her baby brother.

---

softball **1.** A game like baseball, but played on a smaller field and with a larger, softer ball. **2.** The ball used in this game. **soft·ball** (sôft′bôl′) *noun*, *plural* **softballs**.

In **softball**, a pitcher throws the ball underhand.

soften To make or become soft or softer: *You can soften your skin with a lotion. Butter will soften in a warm room.* **soft·en** (sô′fən) *verb*, **softened**, **softening**.

software Programs that a computer uses to perform tasks. Software is put on a storage device, such as a diskette. **soft·ware** (sôft′wâr′) *noun*.

soggy Very wet or damp; soaked: *The ground was soggy after the rain.* **sog·gy** (sog′ē) *adjective*, **soggier**, **soggiest**. —**sogginess** *noun*.

soil¹ **1.** The top part of the ground in which plants grow; dirt; earth: *There is sandy soil near the coast.* **2.** A country or land: *The United States has fought in many wars on foreign soil.* **soil** (soil) *noun*, *plural* **soils**.

soil² To make or become dirty: *I soiled my jacket when I dropped it. White clothes soil easily.* **soil** (soil) *verb*, **soiled**, **soiling**.

solar **1.** Having to do with or coming from the sun: *This solar telescope will be used for studying the sun. Solar energy is sometimes used to heat homes.* **2.** Using or powered by the energy of the sun: *This solar car uses sunshine for energy.* **so·lar** (sō′lər) *adjective*.

solar system The sun and all the planets, satellites, asteroids, and comets that revolve around it.

sold Past tense and past participle of **sell**. Look up sell for more information. **sold** (sōld) *verb*.

solder Any metal that can be melted and used to join two other metal surfaces together. A mixture of tin and lead is often used as solder. *Noun.*
○ To join, fasten, or fix with solder. *Verb.*
sol·der (sod′ər) *noun*, *plural* **solders**; *verb*, **soldered**, **soldering**.

soldier A person who is a member of an army. **sol·dier** (sōl′jər) *noun*, *plural* **soldiers**.

sole¹ The bottom part of the foot or of a boot, shoe, or sock: *The skin on the soles of your feet gets tougher when you walk barefoot. Noun.*
○ To put a sole on a shoe or other foot covering. *Verb.*
Another word that sounds like this is **soul**.
sole (sōl) *noun*, *plural* **soles**; *verb*, **soled**, **soling**.

sole² **1.** Being the only one or ones; only: *Those two people were the sole survivors of the fire.* **2.** Belonging to a single person or group: *The company has sole rights to make that machine.*
Another word that sounds like this is **soul**.
sole (sōl) *adjective*. —**sole·ly** *adverb*.

sole³ A kind of flatfish used as food.
Another word that sounds like this is **soul**.
sole (sōl) *noun*, *plural* **soles** or **sole**.

solid **1.** Having shape and hardness; not liquid or gaseous: *Melted wax becomes solid when it cools. Water in its solid form is ice.* **2.** Of one material, color, or kind; not mixed or hollow: *Those rabbits are solid chocolate. The carpet is solid green.* **3.** Not interrupted or broken: *I slept for twelve solid hours.* **4.** Very strong or hard; not weak or loose: *The foundation of a house must be solid.* **5.** Having a good character; reliable: *Our neighbors are all solid citizens.* **6.** Having length, width, and thickness: *A cube is a solid figure. Adjective.*

PRONUNCIATION KEY:

| at | āpe | fär | câre | end | mē | it | īce | pîerce | hot | ōld | sông | fôrk |
| oil | out | up | ūse | rüle | p̈ull | tûrn | chin | sing | shop | thin | this | |

hw in white; zh in treasure. The symbol ə stands for the unstressed vowel sound in about, taken, pencil, lemon, and circus.

697

○ **1.** A form of matter that has shape and hardness. A solid is not a liquid or a gas. **2.** An object in geometry that has length, width, and thickness. A cube, sphere, and pyramid are solids. *Noun.*
sol·id (sol'id) *adjective; noun, plural* **solids**; —**solidly,** *adverb.*

solitary 1. Alone: *We saw a solitary hiker on the trail.* **2.** Single: *Not a solitary customer came into the store.* **3.** Made, done, or spent alone: *a solitary life in a cabin in the mountains.*
sol·i·tar·y (sol'i ter'ē) *adjective.*

solo Music that only one person sings or plays on an instrument: *The drummer had a solo. Noun.*
○ **1.** Played by one instrument or sung by one person alone: *There are three solo parts in the concert.* **2.** Made or done by one person alone: *a solo airplane flight. Adjective.*
○ By oneself; alone: *He sang solo. Adverb.*
so·lo (sō'lō) *noun, plural* **solos;** *adjective; adverb.*

This man is singing a solo at a sporting event.

WORD HISTORY

The word solo comes from an Italian word that means "alone." This Italian word came from a Latin word meaning "only" or "the only one."

solution 1. The answer to a problem: *We tried to find the solution to the puzzle.* **2.** The act, process, or method of finding an answer to a problem: *The detectives worked on the solution of the crime for a year.* **3.** A mixture formed by a substance dissolved in a liquid. Salt in water forms a solution. **so·lu·tion** (sə lü'shən) *noun, plural* **solutions.**

solve To find the answer to: *I solved all the arithmetic problems correctly.* **solve** (solv) *verb,* **solved, solving.**

somber Dark or gloomy: *The sky became gray and somber before the thunderstorm. Why are you in such a somber mood?* **som·ber** (som'bər) *adjective.* —**somberly** *adverb* —**somberness** *noun.*

sombrero A hat with a broad brim worn in Mexico and the southwestern United States. **som·brer·o** (som brâr'ō) *noun, plural* **sombreros.**

some 1. Being one or ones not named or known: *Some birds cannot fly. Some friends of mine invited me to a party.* **2.** Being of a number or amount not stated: *We met some weeks ago. Have some dessert. Adjective.*
○ A number or amount not stated: *Some of my friends want to start a football team. Please eat some of the salad. Pronoun.*
○ Approximately; about: *The club has some forty members. Adverb.*
Another word that sounds like this is **sum.**
some (sum) *adjective; pronoun; adverb.*

somebody A person not named or known; someone: *Somebody took my hat. Pronoun.*
○ An important or famous person: *Some of the guests at the party were real somebodies. Noun.*
some·bod·y (sum'bod'ē) *pronoun; noun, plural* **somebodies.**

someday At some future time: *Someday I'm going to Europe.* **some·day** (sum'dā') *adverb.*

somehow In a way not known or stated: *Don't worry, we'll do it somehow.* **some·how** (sum'hou') *adverb.*

someone A person not named or known; somebody: *Someone is at the door.* **some·one** (sum'wun') *pronoun.*

somersault To roll the body by turning the heels over the head: *The acrobat somersaulted ten times without stopping. Verb.*
○ A roll of the body done by turning the heels over the head. *Noun.*
som·er·sault (sum'ər sôlt') *verb,* **somersaulted, somersaulting;** *noun, plural* **somersaults.**

WORD HISTORY

The word somersault comes from an old French word meaning "leap." This French word comes from two Latin words meaning "over" and "to jump."

something A thing not known or stated: *Something is wrong with our car. I brought something for you. Pronoun.*
○ To some extent; somewhat: *Your house looks something like ours. Adverb.*
some·thing (sum'thing') *pronoun; adverb.*

sometime At a time not known or stated: *I saw that movie **sometime** last year.* **some·time** (sum'tīm') *adverb*.

sometimes At some times; on certain occasions: *Sometimes we spend a weekend in the country.* **some·times** (sum'tīmz') *adverb*.

somewhat To some extent; rather: *You look somewhat upset. Adverb.*
○ Some part, amount, or degree: *That party was somewhat of a surprise. Noun.*
some·what (sum'hwut' *or* sum'hwot' *or* sum'wut' *or* sum'wot') *adverb; noun*.

somewhere 1. In, at, or to some place not known or stated: *We'll stop for lunch somewhere along the highway.* 2. At some point, as in time, space, or amount: *Be there somewhere between noon and one. Adverb.*
○ A place not known or stated: *We will find somewhere to stay when we get to the lake. Noun.*
some·where (sum'hwâr' *or* sum'wâr') *adverb; noun*.

son A male child. A man or a boy is the son of his mother and father.
Another word that sounds like this is **sun**.
son (sun) *noun, plural* **sons**.

sonar An instrument that sends out radio waves to discover and locate objects under the water. **so·nar** (sō'när) *noun, plural* **sonars**.

song 1. A piece of music that has words set to it. 2. The musical call of a bird, whale, or other animal. **song** (sông) *noun, plural* **songs**.

songbird A bird that has a musical call. The canary and the lark are songbirds. **song·bird** (sông'bûrd') *noun, plural* **songbirds**.

sonnet A poem that has 14 lines and a fixed pattern of rhymes. **son·net** (son'it) *noun, plural* **sonnets**.

soon 1. In a short time: *Come to visit us again soon.* 2. Before

A finch is one of the most common songbirds.

the expected time; early: *The guests arrived too soon, and we weren't ready.* 3. Without a delay; quickly: *I'll be there as soon as I can.* 4. Readily: *I would just as soon do it now as later.* **soon** (sün) *adverb*.

soot A black, greasy powder that forms when such fuels as wood, coal, and oil are burned. **soot** (sút *or* süt) *noun*.

soothe To quiet, calm, or ease: *The nurse soothed the crying child with a lullaby. The ointment soothed my sunburn.* **soothe** (sü<u>th</u>) *verb*, **soothed, soothing**.

sophisticated Having or showing much knowledge and experience of the world. **so·phis·ti·cat·ed** (sə fis'ti kā'tid) *adjective*. **—sophistication** *noun*.

sophomore A student in the second year of a four-year high school or college. **soph·o·more** (sof'ə môr') *noun, plural* **sophomores**.

soprano 1. The highest singing voice of women and boys. 2. A singer who has such a voice. **so·pra·no** (sə pran'ō) *noun, plural* **sopranos**.

WORD HISTORY

The word soprano comes from an Italian word meaning "above." The soprano part is written "above" the other voices, because a soprano has a higher voice than other singers.

---

sore 1. Painful; hurting: *My back was sore from lifting heavy boxes.* 2. Feeling anger; annoyed: *Don't be sore just because your team lost.* 3. Causing misery or distress: *My report card was a sore subject. Adjective.*
○A place on the body that has been hurt: *There was a sore on my arm from the blister. Noun.*
Another word that sounds like this is **soar**.
sore (sôr) *adjective*, **sorer, sorest**; *noun, plural* **sores**.

sorrow 1. A strong feeling of loss and being unhappy; sadness or grief. People feel sorrow when someone they love dies. 2. A cause of sadness or grief: *The fire that destroyed many homes was a sorrow to the town.* **sor·row** (sor'ō) *noun, plural* **sorrows**. **—sorrowful** *adjective*.

sorry 1. Feeling sadness, sympathy, or regret: *I am sorry to hear that you are sick.* 2. Not very good;

PRONUNCIATION KEY:

| at | āpe | fär | câre | end | mē | it | īce | pierce | hot | ōld | sông | fôrk |
| oil | out | up | üse | rüle | púll | tûrn | chin | sing | shop | thin | <u>th</u>is | |

hw in white; zh in treasure. The symbol ə stands for the unstressed vowel sound in about, taken, pencil, lemon, and circus.

699

poor: *The old car was a sorry sight.* **sor•ry** (sor′ē) *adjective,* **sorrier, sorriest.**

sort A group of people or things alike in some way; kind; type: *This sort of plant grows best in the shade. Noun.*

○ To place or separate according to kind or type: *We sorted the socks by color and size. Verb.*

sort (sôrt) *noun, plural* **sorts;** *verb,* **sorted, sorting.**

SOS A call or signal for help: *The ship sent an SOS when the engines broke down.* **SOS** (es′ō′es′).

The workers are sorting shrimp according to size.

sought Past tense and past participle of **seek.** *I sought help from the librarian.* **sought** (sôt) *verb.*

soul 1. The part of a person thought to control what he or she thinks, feels, and does; spirit. 2. A person: *Don't tell another soul what I told you.* 3. A person's ability and desire to do things; energy and emotion: *I put all my soul into my project.* 4. A person who leads or inspires: *That captain is the soul of this ship and its crew.* Another word that sounds like this is **sole.** **soul** (sōl) *noun, plural* **souls.**

sound¹ 1. What can be heard. Sounds are vibrations that move through the air and produce sensation in the ear. 2. One of the noises that make up human speech: *The word "cat" begins with a "k" sound.* 3. The distance a sound can be heard: *The house was within the sound of the stream. Noun.*

○ 1. To make or cause to make a noise that can be heard: *The bell sounded at nine.* 2. To pronounce or be pronounced: *"Doe" and "dough" sound alike.* 3. To seem to be: *Your excuse sounds reasonable.* 4. To announce by means of a sound: *The trumpets sounded the arrival of the royal couple. Verb.*

sound (sound) *noun, plural* **sounds;** *verb,* **sounded, sounding.**

sound² 1. Strong and healthy: *The doctor said my arm had healed and was perfectly sound.* 2. Free from any damage, flaw, decay, or weakness: *The house was built on a sound foundation.* 3. Based on facts, truth, or good sense; sensible: *sound advice.* 4. Deep and not interrupted: *a sound sleep. Adjective.*

○ Deeply and completely: *The baby is sound asleep. Adverb.*

sound (sound) *adjective,* **sounder, soundest;** *adverb.*

sound³ 1. To measure the depth of water: *One way to sound water is to drop a line or rope with a weight on the end until it touches bottom.* 2. To dive deeply and quickly: *Whales sound when they sense danger.* **sound** (sound) *verb,* **sounded, sounding.**

sound⁴ 1. A long, narrow passage of water between two larger bodies of water or between the mainland and an island. 2. A long inlet or arm of the sea. **sound** (sound) *noun, plural* **sounds.**

sound bite A short statement or part of a speech recorded on tape and later played on a news broadcast or political advertisement.

soup A liquid food made by boiling meat, fish, or vegetables in water. **soup** (süp) *noun, plural* **soups.**

sour 1. Having a sharp taste: *Lemons are sour.* 2. Bad or unpleasant: *a sour look. Adjective.*

○ To get or cause to get a sharp taste: *The milk soured because it wasn't kept cold. Verb.*

sour (sour *or* sou′ər) *adjective,* **sourer, sourest;** *verb,* **soured, souring.**

source The person, place, or thing from which something comes or begins: *Who was the source of that news? A mountain lake is the source of this river.* **source** (sôrs) *noun, plural* **sources.**

south 1. The direction to your left as you watch the sun set in the evening. South is one of the four main points of the compass and located opposite north. 2. **South.** Any region or place in this direction. 3. **the South.** The region of the United States south of Pennsylvania, the Ohio River, and Missouri, especially those states that fought as the Confederacy in the Civil War. *Noun.*

○ 1. Toward or in the south: *The south side of our house gets a lot of sunlight.* 2. Coming from the south: *a south wind. Adjective.*

○ Toward the south: *Many birds travel south in the winter. Adverb.*

south (south) *noun; adjective; adverb.*

South Africa A country in southern Africa.

South America A continent in the Western Hemisphere. It is southeast of North America. It is the fourth largest continent.

South Carolina A state in the southeastern United States. Its capital is Columbia. **South Car·o·li·na** (kar′ə lī′nə).

South Carolina
U. S. Postal Abbreviation: **SC**
Capital: **Columbia**
Population: **3,425,000**
Area: **31,055 sq. mi./80,432 sq. km**
State Nickname: **Palmetto State**
State Bird: **Carolina Wren**
State Flower: **Yellow Jessamine**

South Dakota A state in the north-central United States. Its capital is Pierre. **South Da·ko·ta** (də kō′tə).

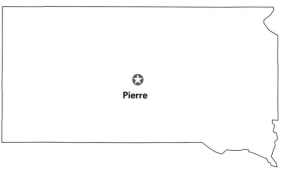

South Dakota
U. S. Postal Abbreviation: **SD**
Capital: **Pierre**
Population: **709,000**
Area: **77,047 sq. mi./199,551 sq. km**
State Nicknames: **Sunshine State; Coyote State**
State Bird: **Ring-Necked Pheasant**
State Flower: **Pasqueflower**

southeast 1. The direction halfway between south and east. 2. The point of the compass showing this direction. 3. A region or place in this direction. 4. **the Southeast.** The region in the south and east of the United States. *Noun.*
○ 1. Toward or in the southeast: *The bus stops at the* ***southeast*** *corner of the street.* 2. Coming from the southeast: *a* ***southeast*** *wind. Adjective.*
○ Toward the southeast: *The plane was traveling* ***southeast.*** *Adverb.*
south·east (south′ēst′) *noun; adjective; adverb.*

southern 1. In or toward the south: *Australia is a* ***southern*** *continent.* 2. Coming from the south: *a* ***southern*** *breeze.* 3. Of or in the part of the United States in the South. **southern** (su<u>th</u>′ərn) *adjective.*

southerner 1. A person born or living in the southern part of a country or region. 2. **Southerner.** A person born or living in the southern part of the United States. **south·ern·er** (su<u>th</u>′ər nər) *noun, plural* **southerners.**

Southern Hemisphere The half of the earth located south of the equator. Australia, most of South America, and parts of Africa and Asia are located in the Southern Hemisphere.

South Pole The point on the earth that is farthest south. The South Pole is the southern end of the earth's axis.

southward Toward the south: *We traveled south-ward along the rim of the hill. Adverb.*
○ Toward or in the south: *We skied on the south-*

ward slope of the mountain. Adjective.
south·ward (south′wərd) *adverb; adjective.*

southwards Another spelling of the adverb southward: *They drove* **southwards.** **south·wards** (south′wərdz) *adverb.*

southwest **1.** The direction halfway between south and west. **2.** The point of the compass showing this direction. **3.** A region or place in this direction. **4.** the Southwest. The region in the south and west of the United States. *Noun.*
○ **1.** Toward or in the southwest: *the southwest corner of the street.* **2.** Coming from the southwest: *a southwest wind. Adjective.*
○ Toward the southwest: *The ship sailed southwest. Adverb.*
south·west (south′west′) *noun; adjective; adverb.*

souvenir Something kept because it reminds one of a person, place, or event: *I bought a pennant as a* **souvenir** *of the baseball game.* **sou·ve·nir** (sü′və nîr′ *or* sü′və nîr′) *noun, plural* **souvenirs.**

sovereign A king or queen. *Noun.*
○ **1.** Having the greatest power or highest rank or authority: *The king and queen were the* **sovereign** *rulers of the country.* **2.** Not controlled by others; independent: *Mexico is a* **sovereign** *nation. Adjective.*
sov·er·eign (sov′ər ən *or* sov′rən) *noun, plural* **sovereigns;** *adjective.*

Soviet Union Formerly, a large country in eastern Europe and northern Asia. It was composed of 15 republics and was also called the U.S.S.R. The largest and most important of the 15 republics was Russia.

sow¹ **1.** To scatter seeds over the ground; plant: *The farmer will* **sow** *corn in this field.* **2.** To spread or scatter: *The clown* **sowed** *happiness among the children.*
Other words that sound like this are **sew** and **so.**
sow (sō) *verb,* **sowed, sown** *or* **sowed, sowing.**

sow² An adult female pig. **sow** (sou) *noun, plural* **sows.**

soybean A seed rich in oil and protein and used as food. Soybeans grow in pods on bushy plants. **soy·bean** (soi′bēn′) *noun, plural* **soybeans.**

space **1.** The area in which the whole universe exists. It has no limits. The planet earth is in space. **2.** The region beyond the earth's atmosphere; outer space: *The rocket was launched into space.* **3.** A distance or area between things: *There is not much* **space** *between our house and theirs.* **4.** An area reserved or available for some purpose: *a parking* **space.** **5.** A period of time: *Both jets landed in the* **space** *of ten minutes. Noun.*
○ To put space in between: *The architect* **spaced** *the houses far apart. Verb.*
space (spās) *noun, plural* **spaces;** *verb,* **spaced, spacing.**

spacecraft A vehicle used for flight in outer space. This is also called a spaceship. **space·craft** (spās′kraft′) *noun, plural* **spacecraft.**

space shuttle A spacecraft that carries a crew into space and returns to land on earth. The same

---

space shuttle

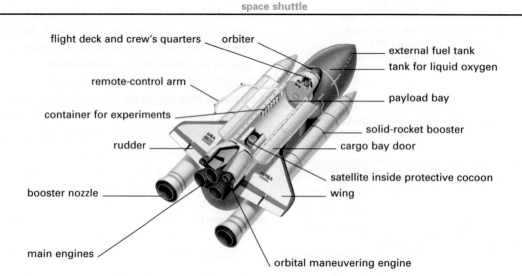

flight deck and crew's quarters — orbiter
external fuel tank
tank for liquid oxygen
remote-control arm
payload bay
container for experiments
solid-rocket booster
rudder
cargo bay door
satellite inside protective cocoon
booster nozzle
wing
main engines
orbital maneuvering engine

space shuttle can be used again. A space shuttle is also called a shuttle.

space station A spaceship that orbits around the earth like a satellite and on which a crew can live for long periods of time.

spacesuit Special clothing worn by an astronaut in space. A spacesuit covers an astronaut's entire body and has equipment to help the astronaut breathe. **space·suit** (spās'süt') *noun, plural* **spacesuits.**

Astronauts take spacewalks **to repair satellites and vehicles.**

spacewalk A period of activity during which an astronaut in space is outside a spacecraft. **space·walk** (spās'wôk') *noun, plural* **spacewalks.**

spacious Having a lot of space or room; roomy; large. —**spa·cious** *adjective* —**spaciousness** *noun.*

spade¹ A tool used for digging. It has a long handle and a flat blade that can be pressed into the ground with the foot. *Noun.*
○ To dig with a spade: *We spaded the garden and then raked it. Verb.*
spade (spād) *noun, plural* **spades;** *verb,* **spaded, spading.**

spade² **1.** A playing card marked with one or more figures shaped like this. **2. spades.** The suit of cards marked with this figure. **spade** (spād) *noun, plural* **spades.**

spaghetti A kind of pasta that looks like long, thin strings. It is made of a mixture of flour and water. **spa·ghet·ti** (spə get'ē) *noun.*

WORD HISTORY

The word spaghetti comes from an Italian word meaning "strings" or "little cords." Spaghetti looks a bit like strings.

Spain A country in southwest Europe. **Spain** (spān) *noun.*

spamming The sending of the same message to large numbers of e-mail addresses or to many newsgroups at the same time. Spamming is often thought of as impolite behavior on the Internet. **spam·ming** (spa'ming) *noun.*

span **1.** The distance or part between two supports: *The span of that bridge is very long.* **2.** The full reach or length of anything: *Some people accomplish a great deal in the span of their lives. Noun.*
○ To extend over or across. *Verb.*
span (span) *noun, plural* **spans;** *verb,* **spanned, spanning.**

This bridge spans **a wide river.**

spaniel Any of various dogs of small to medium size with long, drooping ears, a silky, wavy coat, and short legs. The larger types are used in hunting. **span·iel** (span'yəl) *noun, plural* **spaniels.**

Spanish **1.** The people of Spain. The word *Spanish* in this sense is used with a plural verb. **2.** The language spoken in Spain. It is also spoken in many countries south of the United States as well as in parts of the U.S. *Noun.*
○ Of or having to do with Spain, its people, or the Spanish language. *Adjective.*
Span·ish (span'ish) *noun; adjective.*

PRONUNCIATION KEY:

| at | āpe | fär | câre | end | mē | it | īce | pierce | hot | ōld | sông | fôrk |
| oil | out | up | ūse | rüle | pull | tûrn | chin | sing | shop | thin | this | |

hw in white; zh in treasure. The symbol ə stands for the unstressed vowel sound in about, taken, pencil, lemon, and circus.

703

spank To hit with the open hand or something flat as punishment. **spank** (spangk) *verb*, **spanked, spanking.**

spare 1. To not hurt or injure; show mercy to: *They spared my feelings by not telling me what a poor job I had done.* 2. To give or get along without: *Can you spare a dollar?* 3. To free from the need to make, do, or take; save: *Your hard work spared us much trouble.* 4. To have remaining as extra or not used: *There's no room to spare in the closet.* 5. To fail to use or spend; use or spend only in small amounts: *Don't spare any effort to do your best. Verb.*
○ 1. More than needed; extra: *a spare tire in the trunk.* 2. Small in amount or quantity: *I had to eat spare meals when I dieted.* 3. Not fat; thin: *That skinny child is too spare. Adjective.*
○ 1. One or an amount of something extra: *In case you get a flat, it is wise to always carry a spare.* 2. The knocking down of all the pins in bowling with two rolls of the ball: *I bowled eight spares in that game. Noun.*
spare (spâr) *verb*, **spared, sparing**; *adjective*, **sparer, sparest**; *noun, plural* **spares.**

spark 1. A small bit of burning or glowing material. Sparks fly off burning wood. 2. A flash of light. One kind of spark is the small flash caused by electricity passing through the air. 3. A small amount; trace: *The student didn't show a spark of interest. Noun.*
○ 1. To send out sparks: *The burning logs hissed and sparked.* 2. To be the force or influence that causes or arouses: *The question sparked a lively discussion. Verb.*
spark (spärk) *noun, plural* **sparks**; *verb*, **sparked, sparking.**

sparkle 1. To shine in quick, bright flashes; glitter: *The diamonds sparkled. Their eyes sparkled with laughter.* 2. To bubble like soda water: *Soft drinks sparkle.* 3. To be brilliant and lively: *Your conversation sparkled and delighted our guests. Verb.*
○ A bright, glittering look: *the sparkle of the sun on water. Noun.*
spar·kle (spärk'əl) *verb*, **sparkled, sparkling**; *noun, plural* **sparkles.**

sparrow A common, small bird with brown, white, and gray feathers. The sparrow has a short bill shaped for eating seeds. **spar·row** (spar'ō) *noun, plural* **sparrows.**

sparse Not living or growing close together: *The vegetation in the desert was sparse.* **sparse** (spärs) *adjective*, **sparser, sparsest.** **—sparsely** *adverb.*

spat¹ A short, unimportant argument or disagreement: *The sisters had a spat about what to watch on TV.* **spat** (spat) *noun, plural* **spats.**

spat² A past tense and past participle of **spit.** Look up **spit** for more information. **spat** (spat) *verb.*

spatula A small tool with a flat blade, used to lift and turn over foods, and also to spread thick, soft foods. **spat·u·la** (spach'ə lə) *noun, plural* **spatulas.**

spawn The eggs of fish, frogs, and other animals that live in water. *Noun.*
○ To produce eggs. *Verb.*
spawn (spôn) *noun; verb*, **spawned, spawning.**

speak 1. To use or utter words; talk: *The baby cannot speak yet.* 2. To make known or express an idea, fact, or feeling: *Did you speak to him about going fishing? She always speaks the truth.* 3. To make a speech: *The senator spoke at our graduation.* 4. To use or be able to use in speaking: *You speak French very well.* 5. To have a conversation: *We spoke with our cousins yesterday.* **speak** (spēk) *verb*, **spoke, spoken, speaking.**

speaker 1. A person who speaks. People who give speeches are called speakers. 2. **Speaker.** The person who heads a meeting of a legislature. 3. A device that changes electrical signals into sounds, as in a stereo system; loudspeaker. **speak·er** (spēk'ər) *noun, plural* **speakers.**

spear 1. A weapon with a sharp, pointed head attached to a long shaft. 2. A long, thin stalk, blade, or sprout of a plant. Asparagus grows in spears. *Noun.*
○ To stab with something sharp. *Verb.*
spear (spîr) *noun, plural* **spears**; *verb*, **speared, spearing.**

spearmint A kind of mint. The leaves of this plant are used to flavor candy and foods. **spear·mint** (spîr'mint') *noun, plural* **spearmints.**

special Different from others in a certain way; not ordinary; unusual: *The sports fan had a special interest in hockey. My birthday is a special day for me. An electrician must have special training.* **spe·cial** (spesh'əl) *adjective.* **—specially** *adverb.*

specialist A person who knows a great deal about something: *A veterinarian is a specialist in the treatment and care of animals.* **spe·cial·ist** (spesh'ə list) *noun, plural* **specialists.**

specialty 1. A special thing that a person knows a great deal about: *This mechanic's* ***specialty*** *is repairing old motorcycles.* 2. A special product or service: *Italian food is the* ***specialty*** *of this restaurant.* **spe·cial·ty** (spesh′əl tē) *noun, plural* **specialties.**

species A group of animals or plants that have many characteristics in common. Members of the same species can mate and have offspring. Poodles and beagles belong to the same species. Beagles and wolves belong to different species. **spe·cies** (spē′shēz) *noun, plural* **species.**

SPECIES

Scientists estimate that the Earth has more than 5 million species. Rain forests and coral reefs are home to the largest variety of species, but animal life can be found almost everywhere, from volcanic vents in the ocean floor to glaciers at the South Pole. The number of species for each kind of animal varies widely. Some examples are:

Beetles	290,000 species
Ants	20,000 species
Flowering plants	250,000 species
Birds	9,040 species
Humans	1 species

---

specific 1. Exact; particular: *Nine hundred dollars is the* ***specific*** *amount of money you need to buy this used car.* 2. Stated in a way that is easily understood; clear: *Please make your questions as* ***specific*** *as you can.* **spe·cif·ic** (spi sif′ik) *adjective.* —**specifically** *adverb.*

specimen A single person or thing that shows what the whole group is like; sample: *I collect* ***specimens*** *of different kinds of butterflies.* **spec·i·men** (spes′ə mən) *noun, plural* **specimens.**

speck A very small bit, spot, or mark: *The messy sandwich dripped on my shirt and left greasy* ***specks*** *all over it.* **speck** (spek) *noun, plural* **specks.**

spectacle 1. An unusual sight or show: *The sunrise was a magnificent* ***spectacle.*** 2. **spectacles.** A pair of lenses in a frame that help a person see better; eyeglasses. **spec·ta·cle** (spek′tə kəl) *noun, plural* **spectacles.**

spectacular Very unusual or impressive a spectacular view from the mountain. **spec·tac·u·lar** (spek tak′yə lər) *adjective.* —**spectacularly** *adverb.*

spectator A person who watches something but does not take part; observer: *There were many* ***spectators*** *at the game.* **spec·ta·tor** (spek′tā tər) *noun, plural* **spectators.**

The scenery in this area provides a spectacular sight.

spectrum 1. A band of colors into which white light is separated by being passed through a prism or by other means. A rainbow is a spectrum caused by sunlight passing through raindrops. The colors of the spectrum are red, orange, yellow, green, blue, indigo, and violet. 2. The whole range of colors that exist in nature, including those that cannot be seen by human eyes. **spec·trum** (spek′trəm) *noun, plural* **spectrums.**

speculate 1. To think of reasons or answers for something: *The children* ***speculated*** *about what was in the boxes.* 2. To risk losses in an attempt to make a profit: *They lost money when they* ***speculated*** *in real estate.* **spec·u·late** (spek′yə lāt′) *verb,* **speculated, speculating.** —**speculation** *noun.*

speech 1. The ability to use spoken words to express ideas, thoughts, and feelings. Animals do not have the power of speech. 2. Something spoken; talk: *The president's* ***speech*** *was broadcast on television.* 3. A way in which someone speaks: *Your* ***speech*** *shows no trace of an accent.* **speech** (spēch) *noun, plural* **speeches.**

speed 1. Quick or fast motion: *She ran with great* ***speed.*** 2. The rate of motion: *He drove at a* ***speed*** *of forty miles per hour.* Noun.
○ 1. To go or cause to go quickly or rapidly: *We* ***sped*** *down the hill on our sleds.* 2. To drive faster than is lawful: *They were arrested because they were* ***speeding.*** Verb.

PRONUNCIATION KEY:

| at | āpe | fär | câre | end | mē | it | īce | pîerce | hot | ōld | sông | fôrk |
| oil | out | up | ūse | rüle | pull | tûrn | chin | sing | shop | thin | this | |

hw in white; zh in treasure. The symbol ə stands for the unstressed vowel sound in about, taken, pencil, lemon, and circus.

705

speed (spēd) *noun, plural* **speeds;** *verb,* **sped** *or* **speeded, speeding.**

SPEED

Fastest Animals: In the animal world, speed is sometimes very useful, both for capturing prey and escaping.

Fastest animal: a swift, a bird that hunts insects and can fly up to 200 miles per hour in a dive.

Fastest swimmer: the sailfish at 68 miles per hour.

Fastest land animal: the cheetah at 60 miles per hour.

Fastest insect: the dragonfly at 36 miles per hour.

Fastest human: the world record for running is about 28 miles per hour, but only for short distances.

Slowest Animals: Some animals get along just fine by moving slowly, the **tortoise** travels at .17 miles per hour. A **snail** is even slower, moving at .03 miles per hour.

---

spell¹ 1. To write or say the letters of a word in the right order: *You spell "speak" s-p-e-a-k. We are learning how to spell.* 2. To be the letters that form: *D-o-g spells "dog."* 3. To mean: *The player's injury spelled defeat for the team.*
 • **to spell out.** To explain clearly and completely: *The official spelled out the rules for sailing in the harbor to us.*
spell (spel) *verb,* **spelled, spelling.**

spell² 1. A word or words supposed to have magic power: *The magician cast a spell that put everyone in the kingdom to sleep.* 2. The power to attract or delight greatly: *It was hard to resist the spell of the beautiful music.* **spell** (spel) *noun, plural* **spells.**

spell³ 1. A period of time: *Sit and rest for a short spell.* 2. A period of a certain kind of weather: *The unusual cold spell destroyed the crops.* 3. An attack of something: *a spell of nausea left me weak and dizzy. Noun.*
 ○ To take a person's place at doing something for a time: *If you're tired, I'll spell you at mowing the lawn for a while. Verb.*
spell (spel) *noun, plural* **spells;** *verb,* **spelled** *or* **spelt, spelling.**

speller 1. A person who spells words: *Who is the best speller in your class?* 2. A book used to teach spelling. **spell·er** (spel′ər) *noun, plural* **spellers.**

spelling 1. The way words are spelled: *We have to study spelling.* 2. The writing or saying of the letters of a word in the right order: *K-e-t-c-h-u-p and c-a-t-s-u-p are two spellings of the same word.* **spell·ing** (spel′ing) *noun, plural* **spellings.**

spend 1. To pay money: *You spent too much for your bike.* 2. To pass: *We spent the weekend in the country.* 3. To use up: *The mechanic spent a lot of time on the car.* **spend** (spend) *verb,* **spent, spending.**

sperm A special male cell that, if it is joined with a female egg, can develop into offspring. **sperm** (spûrm) *noun, plural* **sperm** *or* **sperms.**

sperm whale A large whale with a square head. Sperm whales produce a valuable oil called sperm oil.

sphere 1. A round body like a ball. All the points on the surface of a sphere are the same distance from its center. 2. An area of interest, knowledge, or activity: *Chemistry is outside my sphere of knowledge.* **sphere** (sfîr) *noun, plural* **spheres.**

sphinx 1. A mythical creature having a human head and a lion's body. 2. **the Sphinx.** A large statue of this creature in Egypt. **sphinx** (sfingks) *noun, plural* **sphinxes.**

The Sphinx is one of the world's greatest wonders.

spice 1. The seeds or other parts of certain plants used to flavor food. Pepper, cloves, and cinnamon are spices. 2. Something that adds interest or excitement: *The speaker called variety "the spice of life." Noun.*
 ○ 1. To flavor with a spice or spices: *I spiced the hamburgers with pepper.* 2. To add interest or excitement to: *A good speaker often spices a speech with funny stories. Verb.*
spice (spīs) *noun, plural* **spices;** *verb,* **spiced, spicing.** —**spicy** *adjective.*

spider A small animal with four pairs of legs, a body divided into two parts, and no wings. Most spiders spin webs to catch insects for food. **spi·der** (spī′dər) *noun, plural* **spiders.**

spike **1.** A large, heavy nail used to hold rails to railroad ties. **2.** Any sharp, pointed object or part that sticks out: *Baseball shoes have spikes on the soles.* **spike** (spīk) *noun, plural* **spikes.**

Most spiders **spin webs so they can catch insects for food.**

spill **1.** To make or let something fall, run out, or flow: *The child spilled milk on the tablecloth.* **2.** To fall or flow out: *Water spilled onto the floor.* **3.** To cause to tumble or fall out or off: *The canoe tipped and spilled us into the stream.* **4.** To make known; reveal: *I didn't mean to spill the secret. Verb.*
○ **1.** An act or instance of spilling or the amount spilled: *an oil spill.* **2.** A tumble or fall: *The jockey was hurt in a spill from a horse. Noun.*
spill (spil) *verb,* **spilled** *or* **spilt, spilling;** *noun, plural* **spills.**

spin **1.** To turn around quickly: *The car's wheels spun in the mud. The child spun the top.* **2.** To make thin fibers into thread. **3.** To make a web or cocoon by giving off a sticky substance that hardens into thread: *Spiders spin webs.* **4.** To tell: *Our counselor at camp was good at spinning ghost stories.* **5.** To feel dizzy: *The sun made my head spin. Verb.*
○ **1.** A quick turning motion: *Give the wheel a spin.* **2.** A quick ride: *I took a spin on my bicycle. Noun.*
spin (spin) *verb,* **spun, spinning;** *noun, plural* **spins.**

spinach The dark green leaves of a garden plant. eaten as a vegetable. **spin·ach** (spin′ich) *noun.*

spinal column The column of bones in the back; backbone. Look up **backbone** for more information. **spi·nal column** (spī′nəl).

spinal cord A thick cord of nerve tissue running through the center of the backbone. The spinal cord links the brain to the rest of the nerves in the body.

spindle A stick or rod on or around which something is turned. Fibers of cotton are spun into thread from a spindle. **spin·dle** (spin′dəl) *noun, plural* **spindles.**

spine **1.** The column of bones in the back; backbone. Look up backbone for more information. **2.** A sharp, pointed growth on a plant or animal. *The quills of a porcupine are spines.* **spine** (spīn) *noun, plural* **spines.**

spiral A curve that keeps winding. A spiral may wind inward and outward or downward and upward. Some springs are spirals. *Noun.*
○ To move in or take the shape of a spiral. *Verb.*
○ Having the shape or form of a spiral: *a spiral staircase. Adjective.*
spi·ral (spī′rəl) *noun, plural* **spirals;** *verb,* **spiraled, spiraling;** *adjective.*

This building is built in the shape of a spiral.

spire A tall, narrow structure that tapers to a point at the top. Spires are built on top of towers. **spire** (spīr) *noun, plural* **spires.**

spirit **1.** The part of a person thought to control what he or she thinks, feels, and does; soul. **2.** A supernatural being; ghost. **3.** Enthusiasm and pep: *They danced with spirit.* **4.** spirits. The way a person thinks or feels: *I was in good spirits after the test.* **5.** The real meaning or intent: *The spirit of a law is more than what is written down.* **spir·it** (spir′it) *noun, plural* **spirits.**

spiritual **1.** Of or having to do with the spirit. **2.** Of or having to do with religion: *Priests, ministers, and rabbis are spiritual leaders. Adjective.*
○ A religious folk song. Spirituals were originally sung by the blacks of the southern United States. *Noun.*
spir·i·tu·al (spir′i chü əl) *adjective; noun, plural* **spirituals.**

PRONUNCIATION KEY:

| at | āpe | fär | câre | end | mē | it | īce | pierce | hot | ōld | sông | fôrk |
| oil | out | up | ūse | rüle | pull | tûrn | chin | sing | shop | thin | this | |

hw in white; zh in treasure. The symbol ə stands for the unstressed vowel sound in about, taken, pencil, lemon, and circus.

707

spit¹ To force out saliva or another substance from the mouth: *The cat spit at the dog.* Verb.
○ A clear liquid given off into the mouth; saliva. *Noun.*
spit (spit) *verb,* **spit** or **spat, spitting;** *noun.*

spit² 1. A slender, pointed rod on which meat is roasted over a fire. 2. A narrow piece of land extending into a body of water. **spit** (spit) *noun,* *plural* **spits.**

spite A feeling of ill will toward another. *Noun.*
○ To show ill will toward someone. *Verb.*
• **in spite of.** Without being hindered or prevented by; despite; regardless of: *We went on the hike in spite of the rain.*
spite (spīt) *noun; verb,* **spited, spiting.**

splash 1. To throw water or other liquid about: *The children had fun splashing in the pool. The passing car splashed mud on my coat.* 2. To fall, strike, or move with the throwing about of water: *The diver splashed into the pool. Verb.*
○ 1. The act or sound of throwing water about: *When you dove, you hit the water with a loud splash.* 2. A spot of water or other liquid, or a spot of color: *The black horse had a splash of white on its nose. Noun.*
splash (splash) *verb,* **splashed, splashing;** *noun,* *plural* **splashes.**

splendid 1. Very beautiful or magnificent: *A peacock's tail has a splendid display of colors.* 2. Very good; excellent: *Having a party was a splendid idea.* **splen·did** (splen′did) *adjective.* —**splendidly** *adverb.*

splint A piece of wood or other material used to hold a broken bone in place. A splint is often used until a cast can be put on. **splint** (splint) *noun,* *plural* **splints.**

splinter A thin, sharp piece broken off from something hard or brittle: *I got a splinter in my hand from the wooden board. Noun.*
○ To break into thin, sharp pieces: *The glass splintered when the brick hit it. Verb.*
splin·ter (splin′tər) *noun,* *plural* **splinters;** *verb,* **splintered, splintering.**

split To break apart or divide into parts or layers: *The jacket split at the seam. The search party split into two groups. Split these logs for firewood. Verb.*
○ 1. A break or division in something: *The heavy wind made a split in the sail. There was a split in*

the political party over the tax issue. 2. A movement in which a person's body slides to the floor with the legs spread out in opposite directions. This movement is also called **the splits.** *Noun.*
split (split) *verb,* **split, splitting;** *noun,* *plural* **splits.**

spoil 1. To damage or hurt in some way: *Too much salt spoiled the taste of the soup.* 2. To raise poorly so that a child is not guided to form a good character: *You spoil children if you always give them whatever they want.* 3. To become so bad it cannot be eaten: *The meat spoiled because we forgot to put it back in the refrigerator. Verb.*
○ **spoils.** Property seized by force: *The soldiers carried away jewels and other spoils from the conquered city. Noun.*
spoil (spoil) *verb,* **spoiled** or **spoilt, spoiling;** *plural noun.*

spoke One of the rods or bars that connect the rim of a wheel to the hub. **spoke** (spōk) *noun,* *plural* **spokes.**

spoken Said in speech; oral: *People communicate by the spoken word.* **spok·en** (spō′kən) *adjective.*

sponge 1. A simple water animal that has a body that is full of holes and absorbs water easily. Many sponges live in large colonies attached to rocks. The dried skeletons of some sponge colonies are used for cleaning and washing. 2. A cleaning pad that looks like the skeleton of a sponge colony. *Noun.*
○ To clean with a sponge: *We sponged and dried the dirty walls. Verb.*
sponge (spunj) *noun,* *plural* **sponges;** *verb,* **sponged, sponging.**

sponsor 1. A person responsible in some way for another person or a thing: *That senator is the sponsor of the bill. The sponsors of that television program paid the costs of making the program.* 2. A person who attends the baptism of a child and agrees to help with the child's religious training; godparent. *Noun.*
○ To act as a sponsor for: *The school sponsored the fair to raise money. Verb.*
spon·sor (spon′sər) *noun,* *plural* **sponsors;** *verb,* **sponsored, sponsoring.**

spontaneous 1. Not planned or forced: *There was a spontaneous burst of applause when the batter hit a home run.* 2. Happening without any apparent outside cause: *There was a spontaneous*

explosion at the factory. **spon•ta•ne•ous**
(spon tā′nē əs) *adjective.* —**spontaneously** *adverb.*

spool A piece of wood or other material shaped
like a cylinder. Wire, thread, and tape are wound
around spools. **spool** (spül) *noun, plural* **spools.**

**Storing thread on a spool keeps it
from getting tangled.**

spoon A utensil with a small, shallow bowl at
one end of a handle. *A spoon is used for eating,
measuring, or stirring. Noun.*
○ To lift up or move with a spoon: *I spooned the
food into the baby's mouth. Verb.*
spoon (spün) *noun, plural* **spoons;** *verb,*
spooned, spooning.

sport **1.** A game in which a person is physically
active and often is competing with someone else.
Baseball, bowling, and swimming are sports.
2. Amusement; fun: *They collect butterflies for
sport.* **3.** A person who has a definite attitude and
behavior in games, contests, and sports: *They
were good sports to congratulate us when we
beat them. Noun.*
○ To amuse oneself; play: *We watched the colts
sporting in the field. Verb.*
sport (spôrt) *noun, plural* **sports;** *verb,* **sported,
sporting.**

sportsmanship **1.** Conduct or behavior in playing
a sport: *You got a low grade in gym because of
poor sportsmanship.* **2.** Good conduct in playing a
sport; fair play: *Both athletes are admired for their
sportsmanship.* **sports•man•ship** (spôrts′mən ship′)
noun.

spot **1.** A mark or stain left by dirt, food, or other
matter: *There is a spot of gravy on your necktie.*

2. A mark or area on something different from
the rest: *a white dog with black spots.* **3.** A
place: *a pleasant spot for a picnic. Noun.*
1. To mark or be marked with a stain or blot:
The paint spotted the floor. **2.** To see; recognize:
I spotted you in the crowd. Verb.
 • **on the spot. 1.** At the place referred to:
 *We had the good luck to be on the spot when
 the movie star arrived at the hotel.* **2.** Without
 delay; immediately; at once: *The manager
 refunded my money on the spot.* **3.** In a difficult or embarrassing condition or situation:
 I was on the spot when I didn't have bus fare.
spot (spot) *noun, plural* **spots;** *verb,* **spotted,
spotting.**

spout **1.** To force out water or other liquid
through a narrow opening: *The elephant spouted
water from its trunk.* **2.** To flow with force from
an opening: *Water spouted from the hydrant.
Verb.*
○ A narrow opening through which a liquid flows
or is poured: *a teakettle with a curved spout. At a
water fountain, the water comes up out of a
spout. Noun.*
spout (spout) *verb,* **spouted, spouting;** *noun,
plural* **spouts.**

sprain To injure a joint or muscle of the body by
twisting or straining it: *I sprained my ankle.
Verb.*
○ An injury to a joint or muscle caused by twisting or straining: *A bad sprain kept our best pitcher from playing. Noun.*
sprain (sprān) *verb,* **sprained, spraining;** *noun,
plural* **sprains.**

sprawl **1.** To lie or sit with the body stretched out
in an awkward or careless manner: *I sprawled in
the chair with one leg hooked over the arm.* **2.** To
spread out in a way that is not regular or organized: *New houses sprawl across the countryside.*
sprawl (sprôl) *verb,* **sprawled, sprawling.**

spray **1.** Water or other liquid in tiny drops: *The
spray from the ocean waves felt cool.* **2.** A device
used to produce a spray or the substance put out
by such a device: *We used a spray to kill the mosquitoes in the tent. Noun.*
○ To put on or send out in a spray: *The workers
sprayed paint on the wall. Verb.*

PRONUNCIATION KEY:
| at | āpe | fär | câre | end | mē | it | īce | pîerce | hot | ōld | sông | fôrk |
| oil | out | up | ūse | rüle | pu̇ll | tûrn | chin | sing | shop | thin | this | |

hw in white; zh in treasure. The symbol ə stands for the unstressed vowel sound in about, taken, pencil, lemon, and circus.

709

spray (sprā) *noun, plural* **sprays;** *verb,* **sprayed, spraying.**

spread **1.** To open wide or stretch out: *We spread the blanket on the sand. The bird spread its wings and flew away.* **2.** To put or make a thin layer or covering on: *I spread peanut butter on my toast.* **3.** To scatter or reach out over an area; extend: *The farmer spread fertilizer over the fields. The fire spread through the house.* **4.** To make or become known by more people: *Who spread the rumor that school would be closed tomorrow? News of the accident spread quickly. Verb.*
○ **1.** The act of spreading: *Medicines can stop the spread of disease.* **2.** The amount or extent to which something opens wide: *The spread of the robin's wings was 15 inches from the tip of one wing to the other.* **3.** A cloth covering for a bed. **4.** Food soft enough to be spread: *We had sandwiches made with chicken spread. Noun.*
spread (spred) *verb,* **spread, spreading;** *noun, plural* **spreads.**

spring **1.** To move forward or jump up quickly; leap: *The dog had to spring out of the way of the bicycle.* **2.** To move or snap quickly: *The door sprang shut behind me.* **3.** To come or appear suddenly: *The words sprang from my lips. After the rain, weeds sprang up on our lawn.* **4.** To make known or cause to happen suddenly: *They heard the good news yesterday, but they didn't spring it on us until tonight. Verb.*
○ **1.** A jump or leap: *The acrobat made a beautiful spring from one trapeze to the next.* **2.** An elastic device that can be stretched or bent and will move back to its original shape when it is released: *This bed has metal springs shaped like spirals inside it.* **3.** A place where underground water comes out of the earth. **4.** The season of the year that comes between winter and summer. *Noun.*
spring (spring) *verb,* **sprang** or **sprung, sprung, springing;** *noun, plural* **springs.**

sprinkle **1.** To scatter something in small drops or bits: *We sprinkled sugar on the cookies.* **2.** To rain gently: *It sprinkled for a few minutes, and then the sun came out.* **sprin•kle** (spring′kəl) *verb,* **sprinkled, sprinkling.**

sprint To run fast for a short distance: *We sprinted across the football field. Verb.*
○ A short, fast run or race: *The 50-yard dash is a sprint. Noun.*

sprint (sprint) *verb,* **sprinted, sprinting;** *noun, plural* **sprints.**

It takes great effort to run a sprint.

sprout To begin to grow: *The seeds I planted have sprouted. Verb.*
○ A young shoot from a seed or plant: *The sprouts grew into new leaves. Noun.*
sprout (sprout) *verb,* **sprouted, sprouting;** *noun, plural* **sprouts.**

spruce An evergreen tree with drooping cones and short leaves shaped like needles. Its wood is used in making pulp for paper. **spruce** (sprüs) *noun, plural* **spruces.**

spur A sharp metal piece worn on the heel of a horse rider's boot. A horse is pricked with a spur to make it go faster. *Noun.*
○ **1.** To prick a horse with a spur or spurs: *The rider spurred the horse so it would run faster.* **2.** To urge on: *The crowd's cheers spurred the team to victory. Verb.*
spur (spûr) *noun, plural* **spurs;** *verb,* **spurred, spurring.**

spurt To pour out suddenly in a stream: *Water spurted from the broken pipe. Verb.*
○ A sudden pouring out or bursting forth: *A spurt of water came out of the hose. Noun.*
spurt (spûrt) *verb,* **spurted, spurting;** *noun, plural* **spurts.**

A spur **fits tightly on the heel of a boot.**

sputter **1.** To make popping or spitting noises: *The hot oil sputtered when I put the onions in it.* **2.** To speak quickly in a confused way: *The child sputtered with anger.* **3.** To throw out saliva or small bits of food when speaking in a quick or excited way: *The baby sputtered when trying to speak.* *Verb.*
○ The act or sound of sputtering. *Noun.*
sput·ter (sput′ər) *verb*, **sputtered**, **sputtering**; *noun*, *plural* **sputters**.

spy A person who watches others secretly. A person is sometimes hired as a spy by a government to discover secret information about another government. *Noun.*
○ **1.** To watch others secretly; act as a spy: *The submarine was sent to spy on enemy ships.* **2.** To catch sight of; spot: *The sailor spied a ship on the horizon.* *Verb.*
spy (spī) *noun*, *plural* **spies**; *verb*, **spied**, **spying**.

sq. An abbreviation for **square**.

squad **1.** A small group of soldiers who train, work, or fight together. **2.** A small group of people working together: *The counselor picked a squad to clean our cabin.* **squad** (skwod) *noun*, *plural* **squads**.

squall A strong gust of wind that arises very suddenly. Squalls often bring rain, snow, or sleet. **squall** (skwôl) *noun*, *plural* **squalls**.

square 1. A figure having four sides all the same length and four right angles. **2.** Something having the shape of a square: *A checkerboard is covered with light and dark squares.* **3.** An open space in a city or town that has streets on all sides. *Squares are often planted with grass, trees, or flowers and used as parks.* **4.** An instrument shaped like an L or a T, used to draw or measure right angles: *The architect used a square to draw the design.* **5.** The number obtained when a number is multiplied by itself: *The square of 4 is 16 because 4 x 4 = 16.* **6.** A person uninterested in new fashions or trends: *Don't be such a square—you might enjoy this music. Noun.*

square

○ **1.** Having four sides that are all the same length and four right angles: *Is this sheet of paper square or triangular?* **2.** Shaped somewhat like a cube: *The hat came in a square box.* **3.** Forming a right angle: *This desk has square corners.* **4.** Being a square or squares with each side equal to one unit of the named length, used for measuring area: *Our back yard is 50 feet wide and 100 feet long, so its total area is 5,000 square feet.* **5.** Fair or just; honest: *That car dealer promises to give all customers a square deal.* **6.** Conservative or not interested in new fashions or trends; old-fashioned. *Adjective.*
○ **1.** To make into the form of a right angle; make look like part of a square: *The carpenter squared the door frame so the door would close easily.* **2.** To mark in a square or squares: *The children squared off part of the playing field for their game.* **3.** To fit or match with something else; agree: *The witness's story doesn't square with the facts.* **4.** To multiply a number by itself: *Two squared equals four because 2 x 2 = 4. Verb.*
○ Directly and firmly: *The truck hit the car square on its fender. Adverb.*
square (skwâr) *noun*, *plural* **squares**; *adjective*, **squarer**, **squarest**; *verb*, **squared**, **squaring**; *adverb*.

square root A number that, when multiplied by itself, will produce a certain number. The square root of 36 is 6 because 6 x 6 = 36.

squash¹ **1.** To squeeze or press into a soft or flat mass; crush: *I squashed the flower when I accidentally stepped on it.* **2.** To force or squeeze into a small area: *We squashed our clothes into a small suitcase. Verb.*
○ A game somewhat like tennis and handball. It is played by two or four people with rackets and a rubber ball in a court with walls. *Noun.*
squash (skwosh) *verb*, **squashed**, **squashing**; *noun*.

squash² Any of several vegetables of various shapes that grow

A squash is usually yellow or green in color.

PRONUNCIATION KEY:

| at | āpe | fär | câre | end | mē | it | īce | pîerce | hot | ōld | sông | fôrk |
| oil | out | up | ūse | rüle | pull | tûrn | chin | sing | shop | thin | this | |

hw in white; zh in treasure. The symbol ə stands for the unstressed vowel sound in about, taken, pencil, lemon, and circus.

711

on vines. Squashes are usually yellow or green in color. **squash** (skwosh) *noun, plural* **squashes**.

squat To crouch or sit with the knees bent and drawn close to the body: *I squatted to pet the cat. Verb.*
○ Short and thick; low and broad: *That squat vase was a present. Adjective.*
squat (skwot) *verb,* **squatted** *or* **squat, squatting;** *adjective,* **sqatter, squattest.**

squeak A short, thin, high sound or cry: *the squeak of the rusty hinges. Noun.*
○ To make such a sound: *The mouse squeaked and ran. Verb.*
squeak (skwēk) *noun, plural* **squeaks;** *verb,* **squeaked, squeaking.**

squeal To make a loud, shrill cry or sound. *Verb.*
○ A loud, shrill cry or sound: *The squeal of brakes. Noun.*
squeal (skwēl) *verb,* **squealed, squealing;** *noun, plural* **squeals.**

squeeze 1. To press hard: *Squeeze the tube of toothpaste from the bottom.* 2. To get by squeezing or by putting on pressure: *I squeezed the juice from an orange.* 3. To hug or clasp in affection: *The mother squeezed the child in her arms.* 4. To force by pushing or shoving: *squeezed through the opening in the fence. Verb.*
○ The act of squeezing: *a squeeze of the hand. Noun.*
squeeze (skwēz) *verb,* **squeezed, squeezing;** *noun, plural* **squeezes.**

squid A sea animal that looks something like an octopus. A squid has ten arms and a body shaped like a tube. **squid** (skwid) *noun, plural* **squids** *or* **squid.**

squint To partly close the eyes. *The sunlight made me squint. Verb.*
○ The act or an example of looking at something in this way. *Noun.*
squint (skwint) *verb,* **squinted, squinting;** *noun, plural* **squints.**

squirm 1. To turn or twist the body; wriggle: *I was bored and began to squirm in my seat.* 2. To feel uncomfortable or nervous: *The lawyer's questions made the witness squirm. Verb.*
○ A turn or twist of the body: *With a squirm, the puppy jumped out of my arms. Noun.*
squirm (skwûrm) *verb,* **squirmed, squirming;** *noun, plural* **squirms.**

squirrel A small animal with a long, bushy tail. **squir·rel** (skwûr′əl) *noun, plural* **squirrels.**

squirt 1. To force out liquid in a thin stream through a narrow opening: *The worker squirted oil on the rusty hinge.* 2. To come out in a thin stream: *Ink squirted from the fountain pen. Verb.*
○ The act of squirting or the amount squirted. *Noun.*
squirt (skwûrt) *verb,* **squirted, squirting;** *noun, plural* **squirts.**

A **squirrel** lives in a tree and feeds mainly on nuts.

Sr. An abbreviation for **Senior.**

St. An abbreviation for **Street** used in a written address and for **Saint.**

stab 1. To wound or make a hole with a pointed weapon. 2. To stick or drive something pointed into something: *I stabbed a fork into the steak. Verb.*
○ 1. A blow or thrust made with or as if with a pointed weapon. 2. A sharp but brief feeling; pang: *You'll feel a stab of pain if you try to move your sprained ankle.* 3. An attempt; try: *I'll take a stab at skiing. Noun.*
stab (stab) *verb,* **stabbed, stabbing;** *noun, plural* **stabs.**

stable¹ A building where horses or cattle are kept and fed. *Noun.*
○ To put or keep in a stable. *Verb.*
sta·ble (stā′bəl) *noun, plural* **stables;** *verb,* **stabled, stabling. —stability** *noun.*

stable² Not easily moved, shaken, or changed: *The wooden bridge over the river is stable and can support a lot of weight. That new country does not have a stable government.* **sta·ble** (stā′bəl) *adjective,* **stabler, stablest.**

stack 1. A large, neat pile of hay, straw, or grain: *We saw the hay arranged in stacks all over the field.* 2. A number of things piled up one on top of the other; pile: *a stack of pancakes. Noun.*
○ To pile or arrange in a stack: *Please stack the dishes in the cabinet. Verb.*
stack (stak) *noun, plural* **stacks;** *verb,* **stacked, stacking.**

People watch sporting events and concerts in stadiums.

stadium A structure made up of rows of seats built around an open field. **sta·di·um** (stā′dē əm) *noun, plural* **stadiums.**

staff 1. A stick, rod, or pole: *The shepherd held a staff.* 2. A pole for flying a flag; flagpole. 3. A group of people who work for an institution, company, or person: *A hospital staff includes doctors and nurses.* 4. The lines and spaces on which music is written. *Noun.*
○ To provide with workers: *The new library won't open until it is staffed. Verb.*
staff (staf) *noun, plural* **staves** (stāvz) *(for definitions 1 and 4)* or **staffs** *(for definitions 2 and 3); verb,* **staffed, staffing.**

stag A fully grown male deer. **stag** (stag) *noun, plural* **stags.**

stage 1. A raised platform on which actors, dancers, singers, or other entertainers perform. 2. A place where something important takes place: *Europe was the principal stage of World War I.* 3. A single step, period, or degree in a process or development: *During the last stage of their journey, the explorers had very little food left.* 4. A short form of the word *stagecoach.* Look up **stagecoach** for more information. 5. A section of a rocket that has its own engine and fuel. It is usually separated from the rest of the rocket when its fuel is used up. *Noun.*
○ To plan, put on, or present: *The children staged a play for Thanksgiving. Verb.*
stage (stāj) *noun, plural* **stages;** *verb,* **staged, staging.**

stagecoach A large, closed coach pulled by horses, once used for carrying passengers, mail, and baggage. **stage·coach** (stāj′kōch′) *noun, plural* **stagecoaches.**

stagger 1. To move or cause to move with a swaying motion: *You staggered because you were dizzy from spinning around.* 2. To stun; shock: *The nation was staggered by the news of war.* 3. To arrange by scheduling at different times: *The school staggered lunch hours so that the cafeteria would be less crowded. Verb.*
○ An unsteady or swaying motion: *I walked with a stagger after the boat ride. Noun.*
stag·ger (stag′ər) *verb,* **staggered, staggering;** *noun, plural* **staggers.**

stain 1. A mark or spot: *The ink left a stain on the rug.* 2. A cause of shame or dishonor: *They vowed to wipe out the stain on their family's reputation.* 3. A dye or other substance used to color something: *I put a brown stain on the bookcase. Noun.*
○ 1. To spot or soil: *They stained the towels with their greasy hands.* 2. To color with a dye or something like a dye: *They stained the bookcase brown.* 3. To bring shame or dishonor to: *The dishonesty of one person stained the reputation of the group. Verb.*
stain (stān) *noun, plural* **stains;** *verb,* **stained, staining.**

stair 1. stairs. A set of steps for going from one level or floor to another. 2. A step in such a set. Another word that sounds like this is **stare.**
stair (stâr) *noun, plural* **stairs.**

staircase A set of stairs with the railing and framework that support it. This is also called a stairway. **stair·case** (stâr′kās′) *noun, plural* **staircases.**

A staircase can be simple or very grand like this one.

PRONUNCIATION KEY:

| at | āpe | fär | câre | end | mē | it | īce | pîerce | hot | ōld | sông | fôrk |
| oil | out | up | ūse | rüle | pull | tûrn | chin | sing | shop | thin | this | |

hw in white; zh in treasure. The symbol ə stands for the unstressed vowel sound in about, taken, pencil, lemon, and circus.

713

stake 1. A stick or post pointed at one end so that it can be driven into the ground: *The campers drove stakes into the ground and tied the corners of the tent to them.* 2. An amount of money or anything else risked in a bet or gamble. 3. An interest or share in something: *My folks have a large stake in the business.* Noun.
1. To fasten or hold up with a stake: *The gardener staked the beans.* 2. To mark the boundaries of a piece of land; claim: *Each of the prospectors staked a claim.* Verb.
Another word that sounds like this is **steak.**
stake (stāk) *noun, plural* **stakes;** *verb,* **staked, staking.**

stalactite A piece of stone that looks like an icicle and hangs from the roof of a cave. A stalactite is formed by drips of water that contain lime.
sta·lac·tite (stə lak′tīt) *noun, plural* **stalactites.**

stalagmite A piece of stone shaped like a cone, built up from the floor of a cave. A stalagmite is formed by drips of water that contain lime.
sta·lag·mite (stə lag′mīt) *noun, plural* **stalagmites.**

Stalagmites **and** stalactites **are formed by lime-filled drips of water.**

stale 1. Not fresh: *stale bread.* 2. Not new or interesting: *The audience grew bored with the comic's stale jokes.* **stale** (stāl) *adjective,* **staler, stalest.**

stalk¹ 1. The main stem of a plant or part of a plant. *The flower and leaves of a rose grow on the stalk.* 2. Something shaped like a plant's stalk. *In some crabs, each eye is located at the end of a short stalk.* **stalk** (stôk) *noun, plural* **stalks.**

stalk² 1. To follow someone or something quietly and carefully in order to catch it: *The lion stalked the antelope.* 2. To walk in a stiff, proud manner: *I was so angry that I stalked out of the room.* **stalk** (stôk) *verb,* **stalked, stalking.**

stall¹ 1. A place in a barn or stable for an animal. 2. A counter or booth where things are shown for sale. *Noun.*
○ To stop running: *The engine of our car stalls on cold days.* Verb.
stall (stôl) *noun, plural* **stalls;** *verb,* **stalled, stalling.**

stall² To delay or prevent: *The neighborhood wants a traffic light installed at this corner, but the city has been stalling.* Verb.
○ Something used to delay or prevent: *Complaints about the new chairperson were a stall to keep us from voting.* Noun.
stall (stôl) *verb,* **stalled, stalling;** *noun, plural* **stalls.**

stallion An adult male horse. **stal·lion** (stal′yən) *noun, plural* **stallions.**

stamen The part of a flower that produces pollen. A stamen consists of a long stalk with a pollen sac at the end. **sta·men** (stā′mən) *noun, plural* **stamens.**

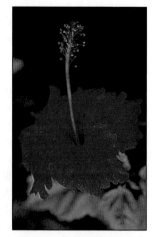

The stamens **of a flower are usually surrounded by the petals.**

stammer To speak or say with difficulty. A person who stammers might repeat the same sound several times when trying to say a word: *I sometimes stammer when I'm nervous.* Verb.
○ The act of stammering: *I sometimes speak with a stammer when I'm nervous.* Noun.
stam·mer (stam′ər) *verb,* **stammered, stammering;** *noun, plural* **stammers.**

stamp 1. A small piece of paper stuck on letters or packages to show that a mailing fee has been paid; postage stamp. Look up **postage stamp** for more information. 2. A tool for cutting, shaping, or pressing a design, numbers, or letters on paper, wax, metal, or other material: *The librarian used a rubber stamp to put the date on the library card.* 3. A bringing down of one's foot with force: *With a stamp of the foot, the child refused to go to bed.* Noun.
○ 1. To bring down one's foot or feet with force: *The spoiled children stamped their feet in anger.*

2. To mark with a tool that makes or prints a design, numbers, or letters: *The salesperson stamped the bill to show it had been paid.* **3.** To put a postage stamp on: *I sealed the envelope and stamped it. Verb.*

• **to stamp out.** To put out, stop, or do away with: *Citizens of our town are doing their best to stamp out pollution.*

stamp (stamp) *noun, plural* **stamps**; *verb,* **stamped, stamping.**

stampede **1.** A sudden, wild running of a frightened herd of animals: *The thunderstorm frightened the cattle and caused a stampede.* **2.** A sudden, wild rush of many people: *There was a stampede toward the exit when the fire broke out in the theater. Noun.*

○ To make a sudden, wild rush: *The wild horses stampeded when they heard the helicopter overhead. Verb.*

stam·pede (stam pēd′) *noun, plural* **stampedes**; *verb,* **stampeded, stampeding.**

stand **1.** To be upright on one's feet: *We had to stand because there were no more seats.* **2.** To get up on one's feet: *The crowd stood to sing the national anthem.* **3.** To be or put upright: *A ladder stood against the side of the barn. We stood the barrel on its end.* **4.** To be in a particular place, condition, or situation: *The village stands at the foot of the hill. The door at the end of the hall stood open.* **5.** To stay the same; be unchanged: *The rule against chewing gum in class still stands.* **6.** To be patient about; bear: *I can't stand all this noise.* **7.** To have an opinion or point of view: *How does the mayor stand on that issue? Verb.*

○ **1.** A position or opinion: *What is the candidate's stand on taxes?* **2.** A stop or halt for battle: *The troops made a stand by the river.* **3.** A place where someone or something should be or usually is: *I took my stand at the door.* **4.** A rack or something like it to put things on or in: *an umbrella stand.* **5.** A booth, counter, or other small place where things are sold: *You can get a newspaper at the stand on the corner.* **6.** A raised place where people can sit or stand: *The mayor watched the parade from the reviewing stand. We sat in the stands at the baseball game. Noun.*

• **to stand by. 1.** To support or defend: *My friends stood by me when I was in trouble.* **2.** To be or become ready; wait in preparation: *The TV announcer said to stand by for an important message.*

• **to stand for. 1.** To mean, represent, or symbolize: *What does the contraction "can't" stand for?* **2.** To allow or endure; put up with: *This is terrible, and I won't stand for it.*

• **to stand out.** To be easy to see; stick out: *Your red hair makes you stand out in this picture.*

stand (stand) *verb,* **stood, standing**; *noun, plural* **stands.**

standard **1.** Anything used to set an example or serve as something to be copied: *New cars must meet strict safety standards.* **2.** A flag or emblem: *I carried my school's standard in the parade. Noun.*

○ **1.** Used as a standard: *A pound is a standard measure of weight.* **2.** Widely used or usual: *It's our standard practice to send bills on the first day of the month.* **3.** Thought of as excellent or as an authority: *This is the standard book on gardening. Adjective.*

stand·ard (stan′dərd) *noun, plural* **standards**; *adjective.*

stanza A group of lines in poetry arranged in a particular pattern. A stanza forms one of the parts of a poem or song. **stan·za** (stan′zə) *noun, plural* **stanzas.**

staple¹ A piece of wire bent into the shape of a U, used to hold papers, fabrics, and other materials together. *Noun.*

○ To hold together or attach with a staple: *I stapled the pages of my book report. Verb.*

sta·ple (stā′pəl) *noun, plural* **staples**; *verb,* **stapled, stapling.** —**stapler** *noun.*

staple² **1.** A very important product that everyone needs or uses. Flour, salt, and sugar are staples. **2.** A very important crop or product of a country or region. **sta·ple** (stā′pəl) *noun, plural* **staples.**

star **1.** A heavenly body that shines by its own light, which comes from burning gases. Our sun is the nearest star to earth. Other stars are so far away that they look like tiny points of light in the night sky. **2.** A figure that has five or more points: *A starfish has the shape of a star.* **3.** A person very good or outstanding in some field: *They are the stars of our school's basketball*

PRONUNCIATION KEY:

| at | āpe | fär | câre | end | mē | it | īce | pîerce | hot | ōld | sông | fôrk |
| oil | out | up | ūse | rüle | pull | tûrn | chin | sing | shop | thin | this | |

hw in white; zh in treasure. The symbol ə stands for the unstressed vowel sound in about, taken, pencil, lemon, and circus.

715

team. **4.** An actor who plays a leading role in a play, movie, or television show. *Noun.*

○ **1.** To mark with a star: *I **starred** the words that I need to study.* **2.** To play a leading role in a play, movie, or television show. *Verb.*

○ Leading; best: *You are the **star** speller in our class. Adjective.*

star (stär) *noun, plural* **stars**; *verb,* **starred,** **starring**; *adjective.* —**starry** *adjective.*

starboard The right side of a boat, ship, or aircraft when a person standing on deck faces forward. *Noun.*

○ On the right side of a boat, ship, or aircraft: *The tugboat moved toward the **starboard** side of the ship. Adjective.*

star·board (stär′bərd) *noun; adjective.*

starch **1.** A white food substance made and stored in most plants. It has no taste or smell. Potatoes, wheat, corn, and rice contain starch. **2.** A substance used to make clothes or cloth stiffer or stiff. *Noun.*

○ To make stiffer or stiff by using starch: *The laundry **starched** your shirts. Verb.*

starch (stärch) *noun, plural* **starches**; *verb,* **starched,** **starching.**

stare To look very hard or very long with the eyes wide open: *We **stared** at the watches in the store window. Verb.*

○ A long, fixed look with the eyes wide open. *Noun.*

Another word that sounds like this is **stair.**

stare (stâr) *verb,* **stared,** **staring**; *noun, plural* **stares.**

starfish A sea animal that has a flat body shaped like a star. A starfish is not a fish. **star·fish** (stär′fish′) *noun, plural* **starfish** or **starfishes.**

Stars and Stripes The flag of the United States.

start **1.** To begin to act, move, or happen: *If everyone is ready, we can **start.** The car **started** easily when it got warmer. What time does the game **start?*** **2.** To make something act, move, or happen: *You turn the key to **start** the car's engine. My cousin has **started** a new business in town.* **3.** To move suddenly from surprise or fear: *The kitten **started** when I tapped it on the back. Verb.*

○ **1.** The act of starting; beginning: *We got an early **start** and reached the lake before noon.* **2.** A sudden movement: *I woke with a **start** when the phone rang. Noun.*

start (stärt) *verb,* **started,** **starting**; *noun, plural* **starts.**

startle **1.** To excite or cause to move suddenly, as with surprise or fright: *A spider dropped from the ceiling and **startled** me.* **2.** To become excited or move suddenly, as with surprise or fright: *Deer **startle** easily.* **star·tle** (stär′təl) *verb,* **startled,** **startling.**

starve **1.** To suffer from or die of hunger. **2.** To be very hungry: *It's time for lunch, and I'm **starving.*** **3.** To need or want very much: *The lost puppy was **starving** for attention.* **starve** (stärv) *verb,* **starved,** **starving.**

state **1.** The condition of a person or thing: *They were upset after the accident and were in no **state** to see anyone.* **2.** A group of people living under one government; nation: *Africa has many newly independent **states.*** **3.** A group of people living in a political unit that is part of a larger government: *Hawaii is a **state** of the United States.* **4.** The area where the people of a state live. **5. the States.** The United States. *Noun.*

○ To show or explain in words; express: *The test question asked us to **state** the causes of the Civil War. Verb.*

○ **1.** Having to do with a state: *a **state** highway system.* **2.** Having to do with an official ceremony; formal: *A **state** dinner was held for the visiting diplomat. Adjective.*

state (stāt) *noun, plural* **states**; *verb,* **stated,** **stating**; *adjective.*

statement **1.** Something stated: *The police took a **statement** from the witness.* **2.** A report of financial matters. **state·ment** (stāt′mənt) *noun, plural* **statements.**

statesman A person who has shown skill or wisdom in politics or government: *Benjamin Franklin was an American **statesman.*** **states·man** (stāts′mən) *noun, plural* **statesmen** (stāts′mən).

static Showing little or no growth, change, or movement; staying the same: *The town's population has remained **static.** Adjective.*

○ Electrical charges in the air. Static causes the crackling or hissing sounds that may interfere with radio broadcasts. *Noun.*

stat·ic (stat′ik) *adjective; noun.*

station **1.** A regular stopping place along a route: *There are **stations** along bus routes where passengers can get on or off.* **2.** A building or place used

by a business or other organization: *a gas **station**.* **3.** The place or position in which a person or thing is supposed to stand: *The guards could not leave their **stations**.* **4.** A place where radio or television programs are recorded or transmitted. *Noun.*
○ To place in a post or position: *We **stationed** ourselves by the door. Verb.*
sta·tion (stā′shən) *noun, plural* **stations**; *verb,* **stationed, stationing.**

stationary **1.** Standing still; not moving: *Traffic leaving the beach was nearly **stationary**.* **2.** Not able to be moved: *The old desks in the classroom were **stationary** because they were bolted to the floor.* **3.** Staying the same; not changing: *The price of eggs has been **stationary** for months.*
Another word that sounds like this is **stationery**.
sta·tion·ar·y (stā′shə ner′ē) *adjective.*

stationery Paper, envelopes, and other materials used for writing.
Another word that sounds like this is **stationary**.
sta·tion·er·y (stā′shə ner′ē) *noun.*

statistics Numbers, facts, and other data collected about a particular subject. **sta·tis·tics** (stə tis′tiks) *plural noun.*

statue A likeness of a person or animal, made out of stone, bronze, or clay. **stat·ue** (stach′ü) *noun, plural* **statues.**

status **1.** The position or rank of someone compared with other people: *Did your status change with your new job?* **2.** The condition or situation of a person or thing; state: *Where the form asked for job **status**, I wrote "employed."*
sta·tus (stā′təs *or* stat′əs) *noun.*

stay¹ **1.** To wait in one place; not leave; remain: *Stay where you are so that you don't get lost.* **2.** To continue being: *We **stayed** friends for years.* **3.** To live for a short time: *Did you **stay** at a hotel during your vacation? Verb.*

This is a statue of the singer and songwriter Buddy Holly.

○ A visit or stop: *After a brief **stay** at the seashore, they returned home. Noun.*
stay (stā) *verb,* **stayed, staying**; *noun, plural* **stays.**

stay² **1.** A strong rope or wire used to support the mast of a ship. **2.** Something used as a support.
stay (stā) *noun, plural* **stays.**

steady **1.** Firm in movement or position; not shaky: *a **steady** ladder.* **2.** Going at an even rate: *We walked at a **steady** pace.* **3.** Not changing; regular: ***steady** customers.* **4.** Not easily upset; calm: *When the fire started, the students showed **steady** nerves. Adjective.*
○ To make or become steady: *I **steadied** myself on the end of the diving board. Verb.*
stead·y (sted′ē) *adjective,* **steadier, steadiest**; *verb,* **steadied, steadying. —steadily** *adverb* **—steadiness** *noun.*

steak A thick piece of meat or fish for broiling or frying.
Another word that sounds like this is **stake**.
steak (stāk) *noun, plural* **steaks.**

steal **1.** To take something that does not belong to one: *No one **stole** my bicycle.* **2.** To take in a secret or tricky way: *We **stole** a glance behind the curtain.* **3.** To get, take, or win by surprise or charm: *The kitten **stole** my heart.* **4.** To move or pass secretly, quietly, or without being noticed: *They **stole** past the guard and into the stadium.* **5.** To get to the next base in baseball without the help of a hit or error: *The catcher **stole** second base. Verb.*
○ **1.** The act of stealing a base in baseball. **2.** Something bought at a low price; bargain. *Noun.*
Another word that sounds like this is **steel**.
steal (stēl) *verb,* **stole, stolen, stealing**; *noun, plural* **steals.**

steam **1.** Water in the form of a gas. Water turns into steam when it is heated to the boiling point. Steam is often used to heat buildings and to run engines. **2.** Power; energy: *By the end of the game, we had run out of **steam**. Noun.*
○ **1.** To cook with steam or apply steam to: *I **steamed** the wrinkles out of my shirt.* **2.** To give off steam: *The boiling water **steamed**.* **3.** To be covered with steam or mist: *My eyeglasses*

PRONUNCIATION KEY:

at	āpe	fär	câre	end	mē	it	īce	pierce	hot	ōld	sông	fôrk
oil	out	up	ūse	rüle	pull	tûrn	chin	sing	shop	thin	this	

hw in white; zh in treasure. The symbol ə stands for the unstressed vowel sound in about, taken, pencil, lemon, and circus.

717

steamed up when I came into the warm building.
4. To move by means of steam power: *The boat steamed into port. Verb.*
steam (stēm) *noun; verb,* **steamed, steaming.**

steamboat A boat powered by steam.
steam·boat (stēm′bōt′) *noun, plural* **steamboats.**

steam engine An engine run by steam.

steamroller A large engine on wide, heavy rollers, powered by steam and used to press and smooth the material used in making roads. **steam·roll·er** (stēm′rō′lər) *noun, plural* **steamrollers.**

steamship A large ship powered by steam.
steam·ship (stēmship) *noun, plural* **steamships.**

steed A horse. **steed** (stēd) *noun, plural* **steeds.**

steel A hard, strong metal made of iron, carbon, and other materials. Steel is used to make machines, tools, automobiles, and many other things. *Noun.*
○ Made of steel: *a steel blade. Adjective.*
○ To make hard or strong like steel: *We steeled ourselves for the bad news. Verb.*
Another word that sounds like this is **steal.**
steel (stēl) *noun; adjective; verb,* **steeled, steeling.**

The drums this man is playing are made of steel.

steep¹ Having a very sharp slope: *a steep hill.*
steep (stēp) *adjective,* **steeper, steepest. —**
steeply *adverb.*

steep² **1.** To soak in water: *I steeped tea leaves in hot water.* **2.** To be full of something: *The disappearance of the painting was steeped in mystery.*
steep (stēp) *verb,* **steeped, steeping.**

steeple A high tower that narrows to a point and is built on a roof. Many churches have steeples.
stee·ple (stē′pəl) *noun, plural* **steeples.**

steer¹ **1.** To guide the course of: *We steered our*

bicycles around the hole. **2.** To be guided: *A large truck does not steer as easily as a car.* **3.** To follow or direct one's course: *The sailboat steered a course for the dock.* **steer** (stîr) *verb,* **steered, steering.**

steer² A young bull raised to produce meat rather than to produce young. **steer** (stîr) *noun, plural* **steers.**

stegosaurus A dinosaur that had bony plates sticking up along its backbone. It ate only plants and walked on all four feet. **steg·o·sau·rus** (steg′ə sôr′əs) *noun, plural* **stegosauri** (steg′ə sôr′ī).

stem **1.** The main part of a plant that supports the leaves and flowers. **2.** Anything like the stem of a plant in shape or purpose: *The stem of the wine glass broke. Noun.*
○ **1.** To remove the stem of: *We stemmed the cherries before serving them.* **2.** To originate; begin: *The air pollution in our town stems from the refinery. Verb.*
stem (stem) *noun, plural* **stems;** *verb,* **stemmed, stemming.**

stencil **1.** A thin sheet of paper, metal, or plastic, with a pattern or letters cut out. When a stencil is placed on a surface and ink or paint is spread on it, the pattern or letters appear on the surface. **2.** The pattern or letters produced by using a stencil. *Noun.*
○ To mark or paint with a stencil: *We stenciled our names on the boxes. Verb.*
sten·cil (sten′səl) *noun, plural* **stencils;** *verb,* **stenciled, stenciling.**

step **1.** The movement of lifting the foot and putting it down again in a new position: *I took two steps across the porch.* **2.** The distance walked with a step: *The store is only a few steps from our house.* **3.** Any place to put the foot in going up or coming down. *A stair or the rung of a ladder is a step.* **4.** **steps.** A set or flight of steps; stairs: *We climbed the steps to the second floor.* **5.** An action or stage in a series: *Learning to float is the first step in learning to swim.* **6.** The sound made by putting the foot down: *Our dog starts barking when it hears steps in the hall.* **7.** A pattern or rhythm of walking or dancing: *Can you teach me the new step? Noun.*
○ **1.** To move by taking a step or steps: *The driver asked everyone to step to the rear of the bus.*

2. To put or press the foot: *Don't* **step** *on the broken glass. Verb.*

• **in step.** With the feet or body moving in a certain pattern or rhythm: *The soldiers marched* **in step** *with each other.*

• **out of step.** With the feet or body not moving in a certain pattern or rhythm: *The dancers were* **out of step** *with the music.*

• **step by step.** Gradually and steadily, advancing from one stage to the next: *We learned to make pottery* **step by step***.*

• **to step up.** To increase or accelerate: *The company had* **to step up** *production to fill all its orders.*

step (step) *noun, plural* **steps;** *verb,* **stepped, stepping.**

stepfather A man who has married a person's mother after the death or divorce of the natural father. **step·fa·ther** (step′fä′thər) *noun, plural* **stepfathers.**

stepmother A woman who has married a person's father after the death or divorce of the natural mother. **step·moth·er** (step′muth′ər) *noun, plural* **stepmothers.**

stereo An electronic system for producing sound through two or more sets of speakers. **ster·e·o** (ster′ē ō′ *or* stîr′ē ō′) *noun, plural* **stereos.**

sterling **1.** A metal made of 92.5 percent silver. It is also called sterling silver. **2.** The British system of money. *Noun.*
○ **1.** Made of sterling silver: *We use the* **sterling** *tea set on special occasions.* **2.** Of very fine quality; excellent: *That senator has a* **sterling** *character. Adjective.*
ster·ling (stûr′ling) *noun; adjective.*

stern¹ **1.** Harsh or strict: *Our parents became* **stern** *when they realized that we had lied to them.* **2.** Not wavering or giving in; firm; hard: *The* **stern** *determination of the settlers helped them bear the icy winter.* **stern** (stûrn) *adjective,* **sterner, sternest.** —**sternly** *adverb.*

stern² The rear part of a boat or ship. **stern** (stûrn) *noun, plural* **sterns.**

stethoscope An instrument used by doctors and nurses to listen to heartbeats and other sounds in the body. **steth·o·scope** (steth′ə skōp′) *noun, plural* **stethoscopes.**

WORD HISTORY

The word **stethoscope** comes from two Greek words that mean "chest" and "to examine."

---

stew A dish made of pieces of meat or fish and vegetables cooked together in a liquid. *Noun.*
○ To cook food slowly in a liquid: *The chef let the prunes* **stew** *on the stove. Verb.*
stew (stü *or* stū) *noun, plural* **stews;** *verb,* **stewed, stewing.**

stick¹ **1.** A long, thin piece of wood. **2.** Something shaped like a stick: *a peppermint* **stick***.*
stick (stik) *noun, plural* **sticks.**

stick² **1.** To push something pointed or sharp into something else; pierce; stab: *I* **stuck** *my finger with the needle.* **2.** To make something stay on something else; fasten; attach: **Stick** *a stamp on the envelope.* **3.** To hold fast or close: *The wet shirt* **stuck** *to my back.* **4.** To be or become set or fixed in place: *The thorn* **stuck** *in the dog's paw.* **5.** To put in a place or position: *I* **stuck** *my hand in the water to check the temperature.* **6.** To keep from moving: stuck in traffic. **7.** To continue something; keep on: *I had better* **stick** *to practicing if I want to play in the recital.*

• **to stick out.** **1.** To project or extend out from something else: *A nail* **stuck out** *from the board.* **2.** To be easy to see; stand out: *The family in the red hats* **sticks out** *from the rest of the spectators.*

• **to stick up for.** To support or defend; stand up for: *I* **stick up for** *my friends.*
stick (stik) *verb,* **stuck, sticking.**

sticker A piece of paper, plastic, or other material that has glue on one side: *I covered my notebook with stickers.* **stick·er** (stik′ər) *noun, plural* **stickers.**

sticky **1.** Tending to stick to anything it touches: *sticky glue.* **2.** Covered with something sticky: *My hands were* **sticky** *after I ate the jelly sandwich.* **stick·y** (stik′ē) *adjective,* **stickier, stickiest.** —**stick·i·ness** *noun.*

stiff **1.** Not easily bent: *The new leather belt was* **stiff***.* **2.** Not able to move or flow easily: *The glue in the open jar became* **stiff***.* **3.** Not natural or easy in manner; formal: *The guard made a* **stiff** *bow to the king and queen.* **4.** Hard to deal with;

PRONUNCIATION KEY:

at	āpe	fär	câre	end	mē	it	īce	pierce	hot	ōld	sông	fôrk
oil	out	up	ūse	rüle	pull	tûrn	chin	sing	shop	thin	this	

hw in white; zh in treasure. The symbol ə stands for the unstressed vowel sound in about, taken, pencil, lemon, and circus.

719

severe: *stiff competition.* **5.** Greater than usual: *They're asking a stiff price. Adjective.*

○ Completely; extremely: *I was bored stiff. Adverb.*

stiff (stif) *adjective,* **stiffer, stiffest;** *adverb.* —**stiffly** *adverb* —**stiffness** *noun.*

still **1.** Without motion: *The pond was still.* **2.** Without sound; silent: *The house was still after everyone went to bed. Adjective.*

○ To make or become quiet or calm: *I held the kitten to still its shivering. Verb.*

○ Quiet and calm; silence: *the still of the night. Noun.*

○ **1.** Without motion; not moving: *I sat still.* **2.** Up to this or that time; as before: *They still live on the same street.* **3.** Beyond this; even; yet: *After I fell off the bicycle, I tried still harder to learn to ride it.* **4.** Nevertheless: *You're the shortest player on the basketball team, but you're still the best. Adverb.*

○ In spite of that: *The children were tired; still they wanted to wait up for their parents to come home. Conjunction.*

still (stil) *adjective,* **stiller, stillest;** *verb,* **stilled, stilling;** *noun; adverb.*

stilt **1.** One of a pair of long sticks with a small block on which the foot can rest. By using stilts, a person can stand or walk several feet above the ground. **2.** One of the posts that holds a building or other structure above ground or water. **stilt** (stilt) *noun, plural* **stilts.**

stimulate To make more active or excited: *The fantastic book stimulated my imagination.* **stim·u·late** (stim′yə lāt′) *verb,* **stimulated, stimulating.** —**stimulation** *noun.*

sting **1.** To prick or wound with a small, sharp point. *A bee is an insect that stings.* **2.** To have or cause to have sharp, burning pain or hurt: *My finger stings where I scraped it. Verb.*

○ **1.** A sharp, pointed part of an insect or animal; stinger. **2.** A wound made by a stinger: *The bee sting on my arm is red and swollen.* **3.** A sharp, burning pain: *This lotion will ease the sting of your sunburn. Noun.*

sting (sting) *verb,* **stung, stinging;** *noun, plural* **stings.**

stinger A sharp, pointed part of an insect or animal, used to prick or wound. **sting·er** (sting′ər) *noun, plural* **stingers.**

stingy **1.** Not willing to give or share; not generous: *You were stingy when you wouldn't share your peanuts.* **2.** Too small in amount: *We were hungry after a stingy lunch.* **stin·gy** (stin′jē) *adjective,* **stingier, stingiest.** —**stinginess** *noun.*

stink A strong, bad smell. *Noun.*

○ To give off or have a strong, bad smell: *Those rotten eggs stink. Verb.*

stink (stingk) *noun, plural* **stinks;** *verb,* **stank** or **stunk, stunk, stinking.**

stir **1.** To mix something by moving it around with a spoon or stick: *I stirred the milk into my tea.* **2.** To move or cause to move about: *The wind stirred the leaves.* **3.** To affect; move the feelings of: *The speaker stirred the audience.* **4.** To excite; awake: *The stories stirred my desire to travel. Verb.*

○ **1.** A burst of activity or excitement: *The arrival of the star caused a stir.* **2.** The act of stirring: *Give the soup a stir. Noun.*

stir (stûr) *verb,* **stirred, stirring;** *noun, plural* **stirs.**

stirrup One of a pair of metal or leather loops that hang from either side of a saddle and hold a rider's foot. **stir·rup** (stûr′əp) *noun, plural* **stirrups.**

A stirrup can help a rider control a horse

stitch **1.** One complete movement made with a needle and thread. Stitches are made in sewing and in closing up wounds or cuts. **2.** A similar movement made with a needle and thread or yarn in knitting, crocheting, and embroidering. *Noun.*

○ To make, fasten, or mend with stitches; sew: *I stitched up the tear in my shirt. Verb.*

stitch (stich) *noun, plural* **stitches;** *verb,* **stitched, stitching.**

stock **1.** A supply of things kept to be sold or used: *This store has a large stock of fishing rods.* **2.** Cattle, sheep, and other animals raised on a farm or ranch; livestock. **3.** Family or race;

descent: *My grandparents come from German stock.* **4.** Shares in the owning of a company or business: *My cousin owns stock in an automobile company.* **5. stocks.** A wooden frame with holes for a person's ankles and, sometimes, hands. *People used to be put in stocks as a punishment for minor crimes.* **6.** A liquid in which meat, poultry, or fish has been cooked, often used in making soup or gravy. **7.** The part of something used as a handle or support: *Place the stock of the rifle against your shoulder and then aim. Noun.*
○ **1.** To fill or supply something with a stock: *They stocked the cabin with enough food for a week.* **2.** To put in, have, or keep a stock or supply of something: *The hardware store stocks all kinds of tools. Verb.*
stock (stok) *noun, plural* **stocks;** *verb,* **stocked, stocking.**

stockade **1.** An area closed off by a fence made of strong upright posts. A stockade serves as a barrier against an attack. **2.** A jail for military personnel.
stock·ade (sto kād′) *noun, plural* **stockades.**

stocky Having a solid, sturdy form or build: *You are tall and thin, but your friend is short and stocky.* **stock·y** (stok′ē) *adjective,* **stockier, stockiest.**

stockyard A place with pens and sheds where livestock are kept before being shipped or slaughtered.
stock·yard (stok′yärd′) *noun, plural* **stockyards.**

Large stockyards like this one hold thousands of head of livestock.

stoke To tend or feed fuel to a fire or furnace: *The workers stoked the furnace all through the night.* **stoke** (stōk) *verb,* **stoked, stoking.**
—**stoker** *noun.*

stomach **1.** In humans and other animals with backbones, a large muscular pouch that receives food and helps to break it down. The stomach lies between the esophagus and the small intestine. It is part of the digestive system. **2.** The part of

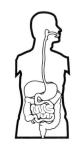

stomach

the body containing the stomach; belly. *Noun.*
○ To be patient about; bear: *I just can't stomach the way you tease people. Verb.*
stom·ach (stum′ək) *noun, plural* **stomachs;** *verb,* **stomached, stomaching.**

stomp **1.** To walk heavily or violently on the floor: *The angry child stomped out of the room.* **2.** To bring down the foot or feet heavily and with force; stamp: *I was so angry that I stomped my feet.*
stomp (stomp) *verb,* **stomped, stomping.**

stone **1.** The hard material that rocks are made of. Stone is used for building. **2.** A piece of this material: *They threw small stones into the pond.* **3.** A valuable jewel; gem: *The stones in the necklace are diamonds.* **4.** The hard pit of cherries, peaches and other fruits. *Noun.*
○ Made of stone: *a stone wall. Adjective.*
○ To throw stones at. *Verb.*
stone (stōn) *noun, plural* **stones;** *adjective; verb,* **stoned, stoning.**

Stone Age The earliest period of human culture. During the Stone Age, people developed stone tools and weapons.

stool **1.** A seat without a back or arms: *We sat on stools at the counter.* **2.** A low bench used to rest the feet on. **stool** (stül) *noun, plural* **stools.**

stoop **1.** To bend forward and downward: *I stooped to pick up the pencil.* **2.** To stand or walk with the head and shoulders bent forward: *I stoop when I walk because my back hurts.* **3.** To lower or degrade oneself to do something: *I would never stoop to cheating. Verb.*

PRONUNCIATION KEY:

| at | āpe | fär | câre | end | mē | it | īce | pierce | hot | ōld | sông | fôrk |
| oil | out | up | ūse | rüle | pull | tûrn | chin | sing | shop | thin | this | |

hw in white; zh in treasure. The symbol ə stands for the unstressed vowel sound in about, taken, pencil, lemon, and circus.

721

○ A bending forward of the head and shoulders. *Noun.*

stoop (stüp) *verb*, **stooped, stooping;** *noun, plural* **stoops.**

stop 1. To keep from moving or doing something: *The driver stopped the car.* 2. To keep from continuing; end: *The firefighters stopped the spread of the fire.* 3. To come to an end or halt: *The snow stopped.* 4. To close up: *I used a cork to stop the bottle. Verb.*

○ 1. The act of stopping or the state of being stopped: *Make a stop at the traffic light.* 2. A place where a stop is made: *a bus stop. Noun.*

stop (stop) *verb*, **stopped, stopping;** *noun, plural* **stops.**

stopper Something used to stop the opening of a bottle or other container. **stop·per** (stop′ər) *noun, plural* **stoppers.**

stopwatch A watch used to time races or contests. It has a button that can be pressed to stop or start a hand instantly so that the exact time can be measured. **stop·watch** (stop′woch′) *noun, plural* **stopwatches.**

storage 1. The act of storing things or the condition of being stored: *The furniture was picked up for storage today.* 2. A place for storing things: *The chest is used as a storage for our toys.* 3. A place in a computer system for keeping information until it is needed. Memory and disks are two different kinds of storage. **stor·age** (stôr′ij) *noun.*

store 1. A place where goods are sold: *a book store.* 2. A supply of things put away for future use: *a store of firewood. Noun.*

○ To put away for future use: *The farmer stored supplies for the winter. Verb.*

• **in store.** Set aside; waiting: *There is a surprise in store for you when you get home.*

store (stôr) *noun, plural* **stores;** *verb*, **stored, storing.**

stork A wading bird with long legs, a long neck, and a long,

A stork lives in marshes and grasslands.

pointed bill. **stork** (stôrk) *noun, plural* **storks** *or* **stork.**

storm 1. A strong wind with heavy rain, hail, sleet, or snow. Storms may also have thunder and lightning. 2. A sudden, strong outburst: *The baby's storm of tears made us worry.* 3. A sudden, violent attack: *The soldiers took the town by storm. Noun.*

○ 1. To blow hard with rain, hail, sleet, or snow: *It stormed all day.* 2. To rush with violence and anger: *After our argument, I stormed out of the house.* 3. To attack violently: *Troops stormed the fort. Verb.*

storm (stôrm) *noun, plural* **storms;** *verb*, **stormed, storming.** —**stormy** *adjective.*

story[1] 1. An account of something that happened: *The newspaper has a story about the circus.* 2. An account made up to entertain people: *We told scary stories.* 3. A lie: *They told a story about why they were late.* **sto·ry** (stôr′ē) *noun, plural* **stories.**

story[2] A level or floor of a building: *That office building has twenty-five stories.* **sto·ry** (stôr′ē) *noun, plural* **stories.**

stout 1. Thick and heavy; fat: *The stout dog found it hard to climb our stairs.* 2. Having courage; brave: *The stout soldier wasn't afraid.* 3. Having strength; strong: *Stout beams held up the roof.* **stout** (stout) *adjective*, **stouter, stoutest.** —**stoutly** *adverb* —**stoutness** *noun.*

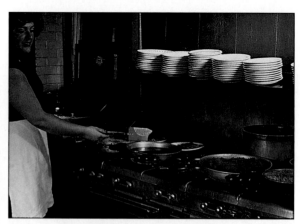

Stoves burn wood, coal, or gas or work by electricity.

stove An object made of metal, used for cooking or heating. **stove** (stōv) *noun, plural* **stoves.**

stow To put away or load; store or pack: *We stowed the suitcase in the trunk of the car.* **stow** (stō) *verb*, **stowed, stowing.**

straggle To wander or stray: *The tired hikers straggled back to camp.* **strag·gle** (strag'əl) *verb,* **straggled, straggling.**

straight 1. Not bent, curved, or crooked: *a straight line.* 2. In proper order: *Please keep your closet straight.* 3. Direct and truthful; honest; upright: *a straight answer. Adjective.*
○ 1. In a straight way: *Stand up straight.*
2. Without delay; immediately: *We went straight home from school. Adverb.*
Another word that sounds like this is **strait.**
straight (strāt) *adjective,* **straighter, straightest;** *adverb.*

straighten 1. To make or become straight: *The picture on the wall slanted to the left, so I straightened it.* 2. To put into proper order: *Straighten your room.* **straight·en** (strā'tən) *verb,* **straightened, straightening.**

strain 1. To draw or pull tight; pull with force: *The dog strained at the leash.* 2. To hurt or weaken by using too much or stretching too far: *I strained my eyes reading in dim light.* 3. To use or drive to the utmost: *The porter strained every muscle to lift the heavy trunk.* 4. To press or pour through a strainer: *We always strain the fresh orange juice we make. Verb.*
○ 1. Great force or weight: *The strain on the wire made it snap.* 2. A hurt; injury: *a muscle strain.* 3. Harmful pressure caused by worry or too much work; stress; tension: *The coach's headache was caused by nervous strain. Noun.*
strain (strān) *verb,* **strained, straining;** *noun,* *plural* **strains.**

strainer A utensil, such as a sieve, used to separate liquids from solids. **strain·er** (strā'nər) *noun,* *plural* **strainers.**

strait 1. A narrow channel between two larger bodies of water. 2. **straits.** Distress or difficulty: *The family was in terrible straits after their house burned down.*
Another word that sounds like this is **straight.**
strait (strāt) *noun,* *plural* **straits.**

strand¹ To leave in a helpless position: *We were stranded when our car broke down.* **strand** (strand) *verb,* **stranded, stranding.**

strand² 1. One of the threads or wires twisted together to form a rope, cord, or cable.

2. Something similar to a thread: *Strands of hair fell across the baby's face.* **strand** (strand) *noun,* *plural* **strands.**

strange 1. Odd or unusual: *She painted a picture of a strange animal with green hair.* 2. Not familiar: *a strange voice.* 3. Ill at ease; uncomfortable: *I felt strange when I was first at camp.* **strange** (strānj) *adjective,* **stranger, strangest.** —**strangely** *adverb* —**strangeness** *noun.*

stranger 1. A person whom one does not know: *A stranger rang our doorbell.* 2. A person from another place or country. **stran·ger** (strān'jər) *noun,* *plural* **strangers.**

strangle 1. To kill by squeezing the throat to stop the breath. 2. To choke. **stran·gle** (strang'gəl) *verb,* **strangled, strangling.** —**strangler** *noun.*

strap A long strip of leather or cloth used to hold things together or in place: *This bag hangs by a strap from the shoulder. Noun.*
○ To fasten or hold with a strap: *Strap your knapsack to your back for the hike. Verb.*
strap (strap) *noun,* *plural* **straps;** *verb,* **strapped, strapping.**

strategy 1. The planning and directing of the movements of troops and ships during a war. 2. A plan for achieving a goal: *What is the team's strategy for winning the game?* **strat·e·gy** (strat'i jē) *noun,* *plural* **strategies.**

stratosphere The layer of the earth's atmosphere that begins about 8 miles (13 kilometers) above the earth and ends about 30 miles (50 kilometers) above the earth. The air in the stratosphere is very thin and cold. **strat·o·sphere** (strat'ə sfir) *noun.*

straw 1. A tube used to suck up a liquid. 2. The dry stalks of rye, oats, wheat, or other grains after they have been cut and threshed. **straw** (strô) *noun,* *plural* **straws.**

strawberry The sweet red fruit of a plant that grows close to the ground. **straw·ber·ry** (strô'ber'ē) *noun,* *plural* **strawberries.**

stray To wander away: *The kitten strayed from the yard. Please don't stray from the point of your story. Verb.*
○ 1. Wandering or lost: *a stray dog.* 2. Found here and there; scattered: *A few stray flowers grew in the yard. Adjective.*
○ A lost or homeless animal. *Noun.*

PRONUNCIATION KEY:
at āpe fär câre end mē it īce pîerce hot ōld sông fôrk
oil out up ūse rüle pull tûrn chin sing shop thin this
hw in white; zh in treasure. The symbol ə stands for the unstressed vowel sound in about, taken, pencil, lemon, and circus.

723

stray (strā) *verb*, **strayed, straying**; *adjective*; *noun*, *plural* **strays**.

streak 1. A long, thin mark: *Streaks of lightning flashed across the sky.* 2. A trace of anything: *That bully has a mean streak.* 3. A short period of time or brief series: *Our winning streak ended last night. Noun.*
○ 1. To mark with streaks: *The soccer player's face was streaked with dirt.* 2. To move at great speed. *Verb.*
streak (strēk) *noun*, *plural* **streaks**; *verb*, **streaked, streaking.**

The water in some streams
moves very quickly.

stream 1. A body of flowing water. 2. A steady flow or movement: *A stream of people came out of the theater. Noun.*
○ 1. To move steadily; flow: *Light streamed into the room.* 2. To wave or float: *Banners streamed in the wind. Verb.*
stream (strēm) *noun*, *plural* **streams**; *verb*, **streamed, streaming.**

street A public way in a town or city, often with sidewalks and buildings on both sides. **street** (strēt) *noun*, *plural* **streets**.

streetwise Being aware of the things that might make the streets of a city dangerous. **street·wise** (strēt′wīz′) *adjective*.

strength 1. The quali-

ty of being strong; power or force: *I lift weights to develop my strength.*
2. The ability to take much strain; firmness: *We tested the strength of the rope.* 3. The degree of power or force; intensity: *What is the strength of this medicine?* **strength** (strengkth *or* strength) *noun*, *plural* **strengths**.

strengthen To make or become strong: *I strengthened my muscles by lifting weights.*
strength·en (strengk′thən *or* streng′thən) *verb*, **strengthened, strengthening.**

stress 1. The force, pressure, or strain put on one thing by another: *A rocket withstands great stress.* 2. A special importance: *Our baby-sitter puts much stress on courtesy.* 3. A stronger tone of voice given to a word or syllable of a word; accent: *In the word "table," the stress is on the first syllable.* 4. Harmful pressure caused by worry or too much work; strain; tension. *Noun.*
○ 1. To give special importance to: *The teacher stressed the need for good study habits.* 2. To pronounce a word or syllable of a word with stress: *When you say the word "begin," you stress the second syllable. Verb.*
stress (stres) *noun*, *plural* **stresses**; *verb*, **stressed, stressing.**

stretch 1. To spread out one's arms, legs, or body to full length: *I got up and stretched.* 2. To reach; extend: *The elephant stretched its trunk for the nut.* 3. To spread out when pulled: *Rubber stretches easily. Verb.*
○ 1. An unbroken space or area: *The campers canoed along a stretch of the river.* 2. The act of stretching: *I can touch the ceiling with a stretch of my arms. Noun.*
stretch (strech) *verb*, **stretched, stretching**; *noun*, *plural* **stretches**.

strict 1. Following or enforcing a rule in a careful, exact way: *The teacher is strict about spelling.*
2. To be followed in a careful, exact way; carefully enforced: *That school has strict rules.* 3. Complete; absolute: *We kept the secret in strict confidence.*
strict (strikt) *adjective*, **stricter, strictest.** —**strictly** *adverb* —**strictness** *noun*.

stride 1. To walk with long steps: *We watched the models stride in their fancy clothes.* 2. To pass over with a long step: *I strode across the mud puddle. Verb.*
○ 1. A long step. 2. Progress or improvement:

Wind surfing takes
strength **and balance.**

*Science has made **strides** in fighting disease. Noun.* **stride** (strīd) *verb,* **strode, stridden, striding;** *noun, plural* **strides.**

strike **1.** To give a blow to; hit: *The car **struck** the tree.* **2.** To make an impression on: *What they said **struck** me as funny.* **3.** To find or discover suddenly: *The prospectors **struck** oil.* **4.** To set on fire by rubbing or hitting: *We **struck** a match.* **5.** To give the time by sounding: *The clock **struck** twelve.* **6.** To stop work in order to get higher pay, better working conditions, or other improvement or benefit. *Verb.*
○ **1.** The stopping of work: *The workers went on **strike**.* **2.** A sudden discovery: *The gold **strike** made them rich.* **3.** In baseball, a pitched ball that the batter swings at and misses or hits foul, or a pitched ball that passes through the strike zone. *Noun.* **strike** (strīk) *verb,* **struck, struck** *or* **stricken, striking;** *noun, plural* **strikes.**

This girl is playing a game with a string.

string **1.** A thin line of twisted threads or wire: *I held the kite by a **string**.* **2.** Something like a string: *The violinist needs new **strings** for the violin.* **3.** A series or row of persons, things, or events. **4. strings.** Musical instruments with strings, played with a bow or plucked. *Noun.*
○ **1.** To put on a string: *My cousin likes to **string** beads.* **2.** To provide with strings: *I **strung** my guitar.* **3.** To stretch from one place to another: *Our neighbors **strung** a wire from their television to the antenna.* **4.** To arrange in a row or series. *Verb.* **string** (string) *noun, plural* **strings;** *verb,* **strung, stringing.**

string bean A long, green bean pod eaten as a vegetable.

strip¹ **1.** To take off the clothing or covering; undress. **2.** To pull off: *I **stripped** the bark from the log.* **strip** (strip) *verb,* **stripped, stripping.**

strip² A long, narrow piece of something: *They tore the paper into **strips**.* **strip** (strip) *noun, plural* **strips.**

stripe A long, narrow band: *Zebras have **stripes**. Noun.*
○ To mark with a stripe or stripes: *The work table was **striped** with spilled paint. Verb.* **stripe** (strīp) *noun, plural* **stripes;** *verb,* **striped, striping.**

strive To make a great effort; try hard: *I always **strive** to win in sports.* **strive** (strīv) *verb,* **strove** *or* **strived, striven** *or* **strived, striving.**

stroke¹ **1.** The act of striking: *That lumberjack can split a log with one **stroke** of an ax.* **2.** An unexpected event: *a **stroke** of good luck.* **3.** A mark made by a pen, pencil, or brush: *The student finished the drawing with a few **strokes** of the crayon.* **4.** A sudden weakness or sickness caused by the breaking or blocking of a blood vessel in the brain. **5.** A combination of arm and leg movements used in swimming: *I learned a new **stroke** at the swimming pool today.* **stroke** (strōk) *noun, plural* **strokes.**

stroke² To rub gently: *I **stroked** the puppy.* **stroke** (strōk) *verb,* **stroked, stroking.**

stroll To walk in a slow, relaxed way: *We **strolled** through the park. Verb.*
○ A slow, relaxed walk. *Noun.* **stroll** (strōl) *verb,* **strolled, strolling;** *noun, plural* **strolls.**

strong **1.** Having much power, force, or energy; full of strength: *Are you **strong** enough to move the table?* **2.** Able to resist; firm: *You are **strong** in your beliefs.* **strong** (strông) *adjective,* **stronger, strongest.**

structure **1.** Anything built: *A house, office building, or bridge is a **structure**.* **2.** An arrangement of parts, or the way parts are arranged: *We saw the **structure** of a plant cell through a microscope.* **struc·ture** (struk′chər) *noun, plural* **structures.**

struggle **1.** To make a great effort: *The children **struggled** through the snow.* **2.** To fight; battle:

PRONUNCIATION KEY:
at āpe fär câre end mē it īce pierce hot ōld sông fôrk
oil out up ūse rüle pull tûrn chin sing shop thin this
hw in white; zh in treasure. The symbol ə stands for the unstressed vowel sound in about, taken, pencil, lemon, and circus.

725

*The soldiers **struggled** with the enemy. Verb.*
○ **1.** A great effort: *It was a **struggle** to learn French.* **2.** A fight, battle, or war. *Noun.*
strug·gle (strug′əl) *verb,* **struggled, struggling;** *noun, plural* **struggles.**

strum To play in an easy, relaxed, or unskilled way: *I like to **strum** on my guitar.* **strum** (strum) *verb,* **strummed, strumming.**

strut To walk in such a manner as to attract attention to oneself or show off: *Our pitcher **strutted** around after striking out 12 batters in a row. Verb.*
○ A manner of walking to attract attention to oneself or show off. *Noun.*
strut (strut) *verb,* **strutted, strutting;** *noun, plural* **struts.**

stub A short part that remains after the rest has been used, broken off: *a pencil **stub**. Noun.*
○ To strike one's toe or foot against something: *What did you **stub** your toe on? Verb.*
stub (stub) *noun, plural* **stubs;** *verb,* **stubbed, stubbing.**

stubborn **1.** Not yielding: *The **stubborn** children would not admit that they were wrong.* **2.** Hard to overcome or deal with: *My **stubborn** cold lasted a month.* **stub·born** (stub′ərn) *adjective.*
—**stubbornly** *adverb* —**stubbornness** *noun.*

student **1.** A person who goes to a school: *The fourth grade has thirty **students**.* **2.** A person who studies something: *That scientist is a **student** of animal behavior.* **stu·dent** (stü′dənt *or* stū′dənt) *noun, plural* **students.**

studio **1.** A place where an artist or craftsperson works: *a photographer's **studio**.* **2.** A place where motion pictures are filmed. **3.** A place where radio or television programs are broadcast or recorded. **stu·di·o** (stü′dē ō *or* stū′dē ō) *noun, plural* **studios.**

study **1.** To learn by reading about, thinking about, or looking carefully at something: *Our class **studied** the solar system.* **2.** To look at closely; examine: *I **studied** the face in the picture. Verb.*
○ **1.** The act of studying: *A lot of **study** is needed to learn French well.* **2.** A close look at something; examination: *Make a careful **study** of the photograph to see if you know anyone in it.* **3.** A thing studied; subject: *How are your **studies** going?* **4.** A room used for studying: *We use the extra bedroom as a **study**. Noun.*
stud·y (stud′ē) *verb,* **studied, studying;** *noun, plural* **studies.**

stuff **1.** Material used to make something: *What kind of **stuff** did you use to make that sheep costume?* **2.** Useless matter or things: *The box was full of **stuff** to be thrown away.* **3.** Things of any sort: *What sort of **stuff** do you keep in your scrapbook? Noun.*
○ **1.** To pack full: *We **stuffed** the suitcase with clothes.* **2.** To force in: *I **stuffed** the papers into the drawer.* **3.** To fill: *I **stuffed** myself at dinner.* **4.** To fill the skin of a dead animal in order to make it look natural or alive. **5.** To put stuffing into a food to be cooked. *Verb.*
stuff (stuf) *noun; verb,* **stuffed, stuffing.**

stuffing Something used to fill or pack another thing: *A mixture of bread crumbs and other food is used as **stuffing** for turkey. Feathers are used as **stuffing** for pillows.* **stuff·ing** (stuf′ing) *noun, plural* **stuffings.**

stuffy **1.** Without fresh air; close: *The room is **stuffy**; please open a window.* **2.** Dull and uninteresting; boring: *The professor's **stuffy** talk almost put the students asleep.* **stuff·y** (stuf′ē) *adjective,* **stuffier, stuffiest.**

stumble **1.** To lose one's balance; trip: *I **stumbled** over the rake.* **2.** To move or speak in a clumsy way: *We **stumbled** around in the dark.* **3.** To discover by chance: *The detective **stumbled** on a clue.* **stum·ble** (stum′bəl) *verb,* **stumbled, stumbling.**

It often requires heavy machinery to remove stumps.

stump **1.** The lower part of a tree trunk left when the tree has been cut down. **2.** The part of anything left after the main part is gone: *The artist drew with a **stump** of chalk. Noun.*

○ To puzzle; confuse: *This arithmetic problem has stumped me. Verb.*

stump (stump) *noun, plural* **stumps;** *verb,* **stumped, stumping.**

stun **1.** To make unconscious: *The robin was stunned when it flew into the window.* **2.** To shock: *We were stunned by the news.* **stun** (stun) *verb,* **stunned, stunning.**

stunt¹ To slow or hinder growth: *Lack of light stunted the plant.* **stunt** (stunt) *verb,* **stunted, stunting.**

stunt² An act of skill or strength: *The acrobat performed stunts on the high trapeze.* **stunt** (stunt) *noun, plural* **stunts.**

stupid Lacking common sense or intelligence: *It would be stupid to drive in this blizzard.* **stu·pid** (stü′pid *or* stū′pid) *adjective.* —**stupidity** *noun* —**stupidly** *adverb.*

sturdy **1.** Strong; hardy: *Heavy trucks can drive on the sturdy bridge.* **2.** Hard to overcome: *Their football team put up a sturdy defense, but we won.* **stur·dy** (stûr′dē) *adjective,* **sturdier, sturdiest.** —**sturdily** *adverb* —**sturdiness** *noun.*

stutter To repeat sounds when speaking. Many people who stutter often repeat sounds at the beginning of a word. *Verb.*

○ The act or condition of stuttering. *Noun.* **stut·ter** (stut′ər) *verb,* **stuttered, stuttering;** *noun.*

sty¹ A pen or enclosed yard where pigs are kept; pigpen. **sty** (stī) *noun, plural* **sties.**

sty² A small, sore, white or red bump on the eyelid, caused by an infection. **sty** (stī) *noun, plural* **sties.**

style **1.** A particular way of saying or doing something: *a writer with a clear and simple style.* **2.** Fashion: *Models wear clothes in the latest style.* **3.** A beautiful or excellent quality or manner: *That skater really has style.* **style** (stīl) *noun, plural* **styles.** —**stylish** *adjective.*

sub **1.** An abbreviation for **submarine.** **2.** An abbreviation for **substitute.**

subdivide **1.** To divide into smaller parts something already divided. **2.** To divide a tract of land into lots for sale: *The property was subdivided and many houses were built on it.* **sub·di·vide** (sub′di vīd′ *or* sub′di vīd′) *verb,* **subdivided, subdividing.** —**subdivision** *noun.*

subdue **1.** To defeat; conquer: *The soldiers sub-dued the enemy.* **2.** To control or overcome: *I subdued my anger.* **3.** To reduce the intensity or strength of: *The drapes subdued the light.* **sub·due** (səb dü′ *or* səb dū′) *verb,* **subdued, subduing.**

subject **1.** Something thought or talked about: *The subject of the student's report was birds' nests.* **2.** A course or field studied: *Math is my favorite subject.* **3.** A person or thing that experiences something: *We used mice as subjects in our experiment.* **4.** A person under the control of another: *loyal subjects of the queen.* **5.** A word or group of words in a sentence that tells whom or what the sentence is about. In the sentence "Astronauts get a lot of training," "Astronauts" is the subject. *Noun.*

○ **1.** Under the control of a person or organization: *The members are subject to the club's rules.* **2.** Likely to be affected; liable to have: *Some people are subject to colds.* **3.** Depending on: *You may go on the trip, subject to your parents' approval. Adjective.*

○ **1.** To bring under control: *The dictator subjected the people to tyranny.* **2.** To cause to experience: *If you wear those clothes, you will subject yourself to teasing. Verb.*

sub·ject (sub′jikt *for noun and adjective;* səb jekt′ *for verb) noun, plural* **subjects;** *adjective; verb,* **subjected, subjecting.**

submarine **1.** A ship that can travel under water. **2.** A sandwich made with one long loaf of bread. *Noun.*

○ Growing or lying underwater: *Seaweed is a submarine plant. Adjective.*

sub·mar·ine (sub′mə rēn′ *for noun;* sub′mə rēn′ *for adjective) noun, plural* **submarines;** *adjective.*

submerge **1.** To cover with a liquid: *The dock was*

This woman is fully
submerged.

PRONUNCIATION KEY:

| at | āpe | fär | câre | end | mē | it | īce | pierce | hot | ōld | sông | fôrk |
| oil | out | up | ūse | rüle | pùll | tûrn | chin | sing | shop | thin | <u>th</u>is | |

hw in white; zh in treasure. The symbol ə stands for the unstressed vowel sound in about, taken, pencil, lemon, and circus.

727

submerged during the flood. **2.** To go beneath the surface of water or another liquid: *The diver submerged to look for the sunken ship.* **sub·merge** (səb mûrj′) *verb,* **submerged, submerging.**

submit **1.** To yield to power or authority: *The children submitted to their parents' wishes.* **2.** To present: *Submit your book reports on Monday.* **sub·mit** (səb mit′) *verb,* **submitted, submitting.**

subordinate Lower in rank or importance: *Colonels are subordinate to generals. Adjective.*
○ A person or thing lower in rank or importance: *The president of that company listens to her subordinates. Noun.*
○ To make lower in rank or importance. *Verb.* **sub·or·di·nate** (sə bôr′də nit) *adjective; noun, plural* **subordinates;** *verb,* **subordinated, subordinating.**

subscribe **1.** To agree to receive and pay for: *We subscribe to the local newspaper.* **2.** To give or show one's agreement or approval: *They subscribe to the belief that world peace is possible.* **sub·scribe** (səb skrīb′) *verb,* **subscribed, subscribing.**

subscription An arrangement by which one agrees to receive and pay for something: *I have a subscription to a newspaper.* **sub·scrip·tion** (səb skrip′shən) *noun, plural* **subscriptions.**

subset A set whose members are all members of another set. The set of even whole numbers, for example, is a subset of the set of whole numbers. **sub·set** (sub′set′) *noun, plural* **subsets.**

subside **1.** To sink to a lower level: *It took a week for the flood waters to subside.* **2.** To become less: *My anger subsided after my friend apologized.* **sub·side** (səb sīd′) *verb,* **subsided, subsiding.**

substance **1.** The material that something is made of: *Wood is the main substance in paper.* **2.** Material of a certain kind: *The floor was covered with a greasy substance.* **3.** The important part of something; meaning: *The substance of the letter was that they were homesick.* **sub·stance** (sub′stəns) *noun, plural* **substances.**

substitute A person who does something in place of another; a thing used instead of another: *The baker used margarine as a substitute for butter. Noun.*
○ **1.** To put in place of another. The coach substituted a new player for the pitcher. **2.** To take the place of another: *The principal substituted for our regular teacher. Verb.* **sub·sti·tute** (sub′sti tüt′ *or* sub′sti tūt′) *noun, plural* **substitutes;** *verb,* **substituted, substituting.**

subtract To take away from: *If you subtract 3 from 7, you get 4.* **sub·tract** (səb trakt′) *verb,* **subtracted, subtracting.**

subtraction The subtracting of one number from another number to find the difference. $5 - 2 = 3$ is an example of subtraction. **subtraction.** (səb trak′shən) *noun, plural* **subtractions.**

subtrahend The number to be subtracted from another number. When you subtract 4 from 11, the number 4 is the subtrahend. **sub·tra·hend** (sub′trə hend′) *noun, plural* **subtrahends.**

suburb An area with homes and stores next to or near a city: *We live in the suburbs, and my parents drive to work in the city.* **sub·urb** (sub′ûrb) *noun, plural* **suburbs.** **—suburban** *adjective.*

Subways carry thousands of passengers every day.

subway An electric railroad in a city that runs under the ground. **sub·way** (sub′wā′) *noun, plural* **subways.**

succeed **1.** To have a good result; manage; do well: *The team succeeded in winning the award.* **2.** To come after and take the place of: *If the president dies, the vice-president succeeds to the office of president.* **suc·ceed** (sək sēd′) *verb,* **succeeded, succeeding.**

success **1.** A result hoped for; favorable end: *The coach was pleased with the success of the team.* **2.** A person or thing that does or goes well: *The party was a big success.* **suc·cess** (sək ses′) *noun, plural* **successes.** **—successful** *adjective.*

succession **1.** A group of persons or things following one after another: *The debating team had* *a succession of victories.* **2.** The coming of one person or thing after another: *The claps of thunder came in quick succession.* **suc·ces·sion** (sək sesh′ən) *noun, plural* **successions.**

successive Following one after another: *Our team has had three successive defeats.* **suc·ces·sive** (sək ses′iv) *adjective.* —**successively** *adverb.*

successor A person or thing that comes next after or takes the place of another: *The retiring senators wished their successors luck.*
suc·ces·sor (sək ses′ər) *noun, plural* **successors.**

such **1.** Of the same kind; of that kind: *I have never seen such weather.* **2.** Similar; like: *We bought tomatoes, lettuce, and other such vegetables for a salad.* **3.** So much of: *It is such a surprise to see you! Adjective.*
○ A person or thing of that kind: *We need paper plates and such for the picnic. Pronoun.*
such (such) *adjective; pronoun.*

suck **1.** To draw something into the mouth: *I sucked the juice through a straw.* **2.** To draw liquid from something with the mouth: *The baby sucked a bottle.* **3.** To hold in the mouth and lick: *I sucked on a piece of ice.* **4.** To draw in: *A vacuum cleaner sucks in dust.* **suck** (suk) *verb,* **sucked, sucking.**

suction The pulling of a gas or liquid into a space from which part or all of the air has been removed. *A vacuum cleaner works by suction.* **suc·tion** (suk′shən) *noun.*

sudden **1.** Happening without warning; not expected: *A sudden storm caught me outside.* **2.** Hasty; quick: *A sudden decision may not be the best one.* **sud·den** (sud′ən) *adjective.* —**suddenly** *adverb*

suds Soapy water with foam or bubbles. **suds** (sudz) *plural noun.*

sue To start a case against in a court of law. **sue** (sü) *verb,* **sued, suing.**

suffer **1.** To have pain or sorrow: *I suffered from a sore throat.* **2.** To have or feel: *Are you suffering pain from your broken leg?* **3.** To be harmed or damaged: *My grades suffer if I don't study.* **suf·fer** (suf′ər) *verb,* **suffered, suffering.**

suffix A syllable or group of syllables added to the end of a word or root to change its meaning. The word *painter* is made up of the word *paint* and the suffix *-er.* **suf·fix** (suf′iks) *noun, plural* **suffixes.**

LANGUAGE NOTE

Many words that end with a suffix are not listed in this dictionary. To find out the meaning of most of these words, first look up the meaning of the root. Then look up the meaning of the suffix. Put the meaning of the root and the suffix together. For example, the word *properly* is formed from the root *proper* and the suffix *-ly. Proper* means correct or suitable. The suffix *-ly* means in a certain way or manner. Therefore, *properly* means "in a correct or suitable way." The spelling of a root may change when a suffix is added. This often happens when the root ends in the letter *y.* For example, *philosopher* is formed from *philosophy* and *-er.* When *-er* is added, the *y* at the end of *philosophy* is dropped. *Merciless* is formed from *mercy* and *-less.* When *-less* is added, the *y* at the end of *mercy* becomes *i.*

---

suffocate **1.** To kill by keeping from breathing. **2.** To die from a lack of air: *A pet can suffocate in a box that has no holes for air.* **3.** To keep or be kept from breathing easily: *I was suffocating in the hot room.* **suf·fo·cate** (suf′ə kāt′) *verb,* **suffocated, suffocating.** —**suffocation** *noun.*

suffrage The right to vote. **suf·frage** (suf′rij) *noun.*

sugar A white or brown sweet substance. **sug·ar** (shùg′ər) *noun, plural* **sugars.**

sugarcane A tall grass with a woody stem. The juice in its stem is a source of sugar. **sug·ar·cane** (shùg′ər kān′) *noun.*

Sugar comes mainly from sugar beets and sugarcane.

suggest **1.** To offer as something to think about: *Who suggested that we play baseball?* **2.** To come or bring into the mind: *The color red suggests warmth.* **3.** To hint: *Your smile suggests that you are happy.* **sug·gest** (səg′jest′ or sə jest′) *verb,* **suggested, suggesting.** —**suggestion** *noun.*

suicide **1.** The killing of oneself on purpose. **2.** A person who has committed suicide. **su·i·cide** (sü′ə sīd) *noun, plural* **suicides.**

PRONUNCIATION KEY:

| at | āpe | fär | câre | end | mē | it | īce | pîerce | hot | ōld | sông | fôrk |
| oil | out | up | ūse | rüle | pùll | tûrn | chin | sing | shop | thin | this | |

hw in white; zh in treasure. The symbol ə stands for the unstressed vowel sound in about, taken, pencil, lemon, and circus.

729

suit 1. A set of clothes to be worn together. A suit has trousers or a skirt, a jacket, and sometimes a vest. 2. A case brought to a court of law. 3. Any of the four sets of playing cards in a deck: *The suits are spades, hearts, diamonds, and clubs. Noun.*
○ 1. To meet the needs of; be right for: *The lively music suits my happy mood.* 2. To be convenient to; please; satisfy: *Stay as long as it suits you.* 3. To be becoming to: *The yellow jacket suits you perfectly. Verb.*
suit (süt) *noun, plural* **suits;** *verb,* **suited, suiting.** —**suitable** *adverb.*

suitcase A flat bag for carrying clothes when traveling. **suit·case** (süt′kās′) *noun, plural* **suitcases.**

suite 1. A group of connected rooms: *a suite in the hotel.* 2. A set of matching or similar things: *Mom and Dad bought a suite of furniture for the dining room.*
Another word that sounds like this is **sweet.**
suite (swēt) *noun, plural* **suites.**

sulfur or **sulphur** A yellow substance used to make matches, fertilizers, and explosives. Sulfur is a chemical element. **sul·fur** (sul′fər) *noun.*

sulk To be angry and silent: *The children sulked because their party was canceled. Verb.*
○ A silent, angry mood: *I was in a sulk because I was unjustly punished. Noun.*
sulk (sulk) *verb,* **sulked, sulking;** *noun, plural* **sulks.** —**sulky** *adjective.*

sullen 1. Gloomy and silent from anger: *The child was sullen after being scolded.* 2. Gloomy; dismal. **sul·len** (sul′ən) *adjective.*

sultan The king of certain Muslim countries. *Turkey was once ruled by a sultan.* **sul·tan** (sul′tən) *noun, plural* **sultans.**

sum 1. The number that results from adding two or more numbers together: *The sum of 6 plus 8 is 14.* 2. An amount of money: *I was paid the sum of ten dollars for mowing their lawn.*
Another word that sounds like this is **some.**
sum (sum) *noun, plural* **sums.**

sumac A tree or shrub with pointed leaves and clusters of flowers and berries. One kind of sumac can cause a rash that itches. **su·mac** (shü′mak *or* sü′mak) *noun, plural* **sumacs.**

summary A brief account that contains the main points of something: *The radio announcer gave a summary of the day's news.* **sum·ma·ry** (sum′ə rē) *noun, plural* **summaries.**

summer The season of the year between spring and autumn. *Noun.*
○ To spend the summer: *We summer in the mountains. Verb.*
sum·mer (sum′ər) *noun, plural* **summers;** *verb,* **summered, summering.**

summit The highest point: *the summit of the mountain.* **sum·mit** (sum′it) *noun, plural* **summits.**

summon 1. To ask to come: *We summoned the police to the accident.* 2. To stir up; arouse: *I summoned my courage and dived off the high diving board.* **sum·mon** (sum′ən) *verb,* **summoned, summoning.**

summons An official notice or command to appear somewhere or do something: *a summons to appear in court.* **sum·mons** (sum′ənz) *noun, plural* **summonses.**

sun 1. The star around which the earth and other planets revolve. The sun gives light and heat. 2. Light and heat from the sun: *The plants need plenty of sun. Noun.*
○ To be in the light and heat of the sun: *We sunned ourselves on the beach. Verb.*
Another word that sounds like this is **son.**
sun (sun) *noun; verb,* **sunned, sunning.**

Sun. An abbreviation for Sunday.

sunbathe To lie in the sun: *Our neighbors sunbathe in their backyard.* **sun·bathe** (sun′bāth′) *verb,* **sunbathed, sunbathing.**

sunburn A redness or burn on the skin caused by the sun. *Noun.*
○ To burn the skin by exposure to the sun. *Verb.*
sun·burn (sun′bûrn′) *noun, plural* **sunburns;** *verb,* **sunburned** or **sunburnt, sunburning.**

sundae Ice cream served with syrup, fruit, or nuts on top. **sun·dae** (sun′dē *or* sun′dā) *noun, plural* **sundaes.**

Sunday The first day of the week. **Sun·day** (sun′dē *or* sun′dā) *noun, plural* **Sundays.**

WORD HISTORY

The ancient Romans dedicated the first day of their week to the sun. The Latin name was translated into an Old English word meaning "sun's day," which became Sunday.

sundial A device that consists of a plate with numbers and a pointer that casts a shadow. It shows the time of day by the movement of the shadow across the numbers. **sun·di·al** (sun′dī′əl) *noun, plural* **sundials.**

sunflower A large flower that grows on a tall plant. A sunflower has a brown center and yellow petals. **sun·flow·er** (sun′flou′ər) *noun, plural* **sunflowers.**

sunglasses Dark eyeglasses that help to protect the eyes from the glare of the sun. **sun·glass·es** (sun′glas′iz) *plural noun.*

sunlight The light of the sun. **sun·light** (sun′līt′) *noun.*

sunny 1. Full of sunlight; warmed by sunlight: *a sunny porch.* 2. Cheerful; happy: *a sunny smile.* **sun·ny** (sun′ē) *adjective,* **sunnier, sunniest.**

sunrise The rising of the sun. **sun·rise** (sun′rīz′) *noun, plural* **sunrises.**

sunscreen A lotion or cream that has a chemical that protects the skin from the harmful rays of the sun. **sun·screen** (sun′skrēn′) *noun.*

sunset The setting of the sun. **sun·set** (sun′set′) *noun, plural* **sunsets.**

sunshine The light that comes from the sun. **sun·shine** (sun′shīn′) *noun.*

suntan A dark coloring of the skin that comes from exposure to the sun. **sun·tan** (sun′tan′) *noun, plural* **suntans.**

superb Very fine; excellent: *The actor gave a superb performance.* **su·perb** (sü pûrb′) *adjective.* —**superbly** *noun.*

superintendent 1. A person who directs or manages something: *The superintendent of police is the head of the police department.* 2. The janitor or custodian of a large building such as a school or an apartment house. **su·per·in·ten·dent** (sü′pər in ten′dənt) *noun, plural* **superintendents.**

superior 1. Higher, greater, or better: *The champion baseball team has superior players.* 2. Proud; haughty: *Those children have a superior attitude because their parents are famous. Adjective.*
○ A person in a higher position: *The principal of a school is the teachers' superior. Noun.* **su·pe·ri·or** (sə pîr′ē ər) *adjective; noun, plural* **superiors.**

superiority The state or quality of being superior: *The chess team showed its superiority by winning the state championship.* **su·pe·ri·or·i·ty** (sə pîr′ē ôr′i tē) *noun.*

superlative Of the highest sort; above all others: *Landing astronauts on the moon was a superlative achievement. Adjective.*
○ The form of an adjective or adverb that shows the greatest degree of whatever is expressed by the basic form. For example, *darkest* is the superlative of *dark. Noun.* **su·per·la·tive** (sə pûr′lə tiv) *adjective; noun, plural* **superlatives.** —**superlatively** *adverb.*

supermarket A large store that sells food and household goods. **su·per·mar·ket** (sü′pər mär′kit) *noun, plural* **supermarkets.**

supernatural Having an existence not limited by the laws of nature: *Ghosts and demons are supernatural creatures.* **su·per·nat·u·ral** (sü′pər nach′ər əl) *adjective.* —**supernaturally** *adverb.*

superstition A belief based on ignorance and fear. **su·per·sti·tion** (sü′pər stish′ən) *noun, plural* **superstitions.** —**superstitious** *adjective.*

supervise To watch over and direct: *The manager supervised workers at the plant.* **su·per·vise** (sü′pər vīz′) **supervised, supervising.** —**supervision** *noun* —**supervisor** *noun.*

supper The last meal of the day. **sup·per** (sup′ər) *noun, plural* **suppers.**

supple 1. Easy to bend; not stiff: *I used supple branches to weave the basket.* 2. Able to adapt to changes or new things: *A person with a supple mind learns easily.* **sup·ple** (sup′əl) *adjective,* **suppler, supplest.**

supply To provide with something needed or wanted: *Rain supplies water. Verb.*
○ A quantity of something needed or ready for use: *We have supplies for our camping trip. Noun.* **sup·ply** (sə plī′) *verb,* **supplied, supplying;** *noun, plural* **supplies.**

support 1. To hold up: *The columns support the roof.* 2. To provide for: *Our parents support our family by working.* 3. To help or back: *Many people support that candidate for mayor.* 4. To give strength or comfort to: *The family supported each other during a difficult time.* 5. To show to be true: *The facts support your story. Verb.*
○ 1. The supporting of something or someone: *My friends gave me support when I ran for club president.* 2. A person or thing that supports: *The*

PRONUNCIATION KEY:

| at | āpe | fär | câre | end | mē | it | īce | pîerce | hot | ōld | sông | fôrk |
| oil | out | up | ūse | rüle | pull | tûrn | chin | sing | shop | thin | this | |

hw in white; zh in treasure. The symbol ə stands for the unstressed vowel sound in about, taken, pencil, lemon, and circus.

731

*center pole is the main **support** of the tent. Noun.* **sup·port** (sə pôrt′) *verb,* **supported, supporting;** *noun, plural* **supports.**

suppose 1. To imagine to be possible: *Suppose we were able to fly by flapping our arms.* 2. To believe; guess: *I **suppose** I'll be finished with my work soon.* 3. To expect or require: *My friend is **supposed** to be here by now.* **sup·pose** (sə pōz′) *verb,* **supposed, supposing.**

supreme 1. Greatest in power or authority; most important: *The dictator was **supreme** in that country.* 2. Highest; utmost: *We made a **supreme** effort to lift the box.* **su·preme** (sə prēm′) *adjective.* —**supremely** *adverb.*

sure 1. Having no doubt; confident: *I am **sure** that you are right.* 2. Certain to be; dependable: *Our team is a **sure** winner.* 3. Steady; firm: *Keep a **sure** grip on the bat when you swing it. Adjective.* ○ Surely; certainly: *Sure, I'm going. Adverb.* **sure** (shür) *adjective,* **surer, surest;** *adverb.*

surely Without any doubt; truly: *I will **surely** be there.* **sure·ly** (shür′lē) *adverb.*

surf The rise and splash of the waves of the sea on the shore. *Noun.* ○ To ride on a wave with a surfboard: *My cousin **surfs** where the waves are big. Verb.* Another word that sounds like this is **serf.** **surf** (sûrf) *noun; verb,* **surfed, surfing.**

surface 1. The outside of a thing: *The astronauts explored the **surface** of the moon.* 2. Outer look or appearance: *The problem seemed simple on the **surface**. Noun.* ○ Of or having to do with a surface; on a surface: *We scraped off the **surface** rust from the metal. Adjective.* ○ 1. To come or rise to the surface: *The submarine **surfaced**.* 2. To cover the surface of: *Our driveway is **surfaced** with tar. Verb.* **sur·face** (sûr′fis) *noun, plural* **surfaces;** *adjective; verb,* **surfaced, surfacing.**

surfboard A long, flat board used to ride on the crest of a wave.

surf·board (sûrf′bôrd′) *noun, plural* **surfboards.**

surge To swell and move with force like a wave: *The crowd **surged** forward. Verb.* ○ 1. A swelling movement: *The **surge** of the waves tossed the ship.* 2. A sudden rise: *There was a **surge** in food prices. Noun.* **surge** (sûrj) *verb,* **surged, surging;** *noun, plural* **surges.**

surgeon A doctor who performs surgery. **sur·geon** (sûr′jən) *noun, plural* **surgeons.**

surgery 1. The branch of medicine that deals with the removal and repair of diseased or damaged parts of the body. 2. An operation performed by a surgeon. **sur·ger·y** (sûr′jə rē) *noun, plural* **surgeries.**

surname A last name; family name: *My **surname** is Banks.* **sur·name** (sûr′nām′) *noun, plural* **surnames.**

surpass 1. To be better, greater, or stronger than: *I am a good runner, but two of my friends **surpass** me.* 2. To be beyond the power or reach of; exceed: *A few problems on the math test **surpassed** my ability.* **sur·pass** (sər pas′) *verb,* **surpassed, surpassing.**

surplus An amount greater than what is used or needed; quantity remaining: *We have a **surplus** of furniture in the attic. Noun.* ○ Greater than what is needed: *The farmer gave the **surplus** fruit to a charity. Adjective.* **sur·plus** (sûr plus′) *noun; adjective.*

surprise 1. To cause to feel sudden wonder or amazement: *You **surprised** us with all the gifts you brought.* 2. To find suddenly and unexpectedly: *One morning we **surprised** two deer in our backyard. Verb.*

Riding a surfboard has become a popular sport.

○ 1. A feeling of wonder or amazement caused by something unexpected: *Winning the contest filled me with **surprise**.* 2. Something that causes surprise: *Was the party a **surprise** to you?* 3. The act of coming upon someone suddenly and unexpectedly: *We caught them by **surprise**. Noun.* **sur·prise** (sər prīz′) *verb,* **surprised, surprising;** *noun, plural* **surprises.**

surrender To yield: *The outlaw **surrendered** to the sheriff. Verb.*
  ○ The act of surrendering. *Noun.*
  sur·ren·der (sə ren′dər) *verb,* **surrendered, surrendering;** *noun, plural* **surrenders.**

surround To be on all sides of; form a circle around: *A fence **surrounds** our yard.* **sur·round** (sə round′) *verb,* **surrounded, surrounding.**

surroundings The things or conditions that surround a person: *We moved to the country for the quiet **surroundings**.* **sur·round·ings** (sə roun′dingz) *plural noun.*

survey 1. To look at or study in detail: *The mayor **surveyed** the damage to the city after the storm.* 2. To measure land to fix or find out its boundaries: *They **surveyed** the property before it was divided into lots. Verb.*
  ○ 1. A detailed study: *The company made a **survey** to find out who might buy its products.* 2. A measuring of land: *That family had a **survey** made of their property. Noun.*
  sur·vey (sər vā′ *for verb;* sûr′vā *or* sər vā′ *for noun*) *verb,* **surveyed, surveying;** *noun, plural* **surveys. —surveyor** *noun.*

survival 1. The act of surviving: *The **survival** of all the bus passengers in the accident seemed a miracle.* 2. A thing that survives: *The custom of throwing rice at a bride and groom is a **survival** from the past.* **sur·viv·al** (sər vī′vəl) *noun.*

survive 1. To live through: *The passengers **survived** the plane crash.* 2. To continue to exist: *These plants need water to **survive**.* **sur·vive** (sər vīv′) *verb,* **survived, surviving. —survivors** *noun.*

suspect 1. To think that something is possible or true: *I **suspect** that they have already gone.* 2. To think without proof that someone is guilty: *The sheriff **suspected** the stranger of the crime.* 3. To not believe or trust; doubt: *We **suspected** their honesty. Verb.*
  ○ A person suspected of committing a crime. *Noun.*
  sus·pect (səs pekt′ *for verb;* sus′pekt′ *for noun*) *verb,* **suspected, suspecting;** *noun, plural* **suspects.**

suspend 1. To attach so as to hang down: *We **suspended** the swing from a tree branch.* 2. To support while allowing movement: *Bits of lemon were **suspended** in the lemonade.* 3. To stop or cause to stop for a time: *Why did you **suspend** payments on your car?* 4. To take away the privilege of using or attending: *The principal **suspended** the student from school for breaking the rules.* **sus·pend** (sə spend′) *verb,* **suspended, suspending. —suspension** *noun.*

suspense The condition of being in doubt and worried about what will happen: *The book kept me in **suspense**.* **sus·pense** (sə spens′) *noun.*

suspicion 1. The act or instance of suspecting: *My **suspicion** that the apple was rotten was correct.* 2. The condition of being suspected: *The gang was under **suspicion** for the crime.* **sus·pi·cion** (sə spish′ən) *noun, plural* **suspicions.**

suspicious 1. Causing suspicion: *The person outside the bank acted in a **suspicious** manner.* 2. Feeling or showing suspicion: *My dog is **suspicious** of strangers.* **sus·pi·cious** (sə spish′əs) *adjective.* **—suspiciously** *adverb.*

SW or **S.W.** An abbreviation for **southwest.**

swallow¹ 1. To cause food to pass from the mouth to the stomach. 2. To take in and cover: *The sea **swallowed** the ship.* 3. To take or keep back: *I **swallowed** my pride.* 4. To believe something without questioning whether it makes sense or is true: *That story is just too fantastic to **swallow**. Verb.*
  ○ 1. The act of swallowing. 2. The amount that can be swallowed at a time: *I took a **swallow** of water before I dashed out. Noun.*
  swal·low (swol′ō) *verb,* **swallowed, swallowing;** *noun, plural* **swallows.**

swallow² A small bird with long wings. Swallows are very good fliers. **swal·low** (swol′ō) *noun, plural* **swallows.**

swamp An area of wet land. Swamps may have trees and shrubs growing in them. *Noun.*
  ○ To fill with water: *The high waves **swamped** the boat and made it sink. Verb.*
  swamp (swomp) *noun, plural* **swamps;** *verb,* **swamped, swamping.**

swan A large water bird that has a long, graceful neck and

A swan belongs to the same family as ducks and geese.

PRONUNCIATION KEY:

| at | āpe | fär | câre | end | mē | it | īce | pierce | hot | ōld | sŏng | fôrk |
| oil | out | up | ūse | rüle | pull | tûrn | chin | sing | shop | thin | this | |

hw in white; zh in treasure. The symbol ə stands for the unstressed vowel sound in about, taken, pencil, lemon, and circus.

733

webbed feet. **swan** (swon) *noun, plural* **swans**.

swap To exchange or trade: *My brother and I swapped bicycles. Verb.*
○ An exchange or trade. *Noun.*
swap (swop) *verb,* **swapped, swapping;** *noun, plural* **swaps**.

swarm **1.** A group of bees that leave their hive to start a new colony. **2.** A large group of people or animals: *Swarms of tourists visited the beach. Noun.*
○ **1.** To leave a hive together to start a new colony: *The bees swarmed.* **2.** To move in a large group: *People swarmed out of the theater.* **3.** To be filled: *The river swarmed with alligators. Verb.*
swarm (swôrm) *noun, plural* **swarms;** *verb,* **swarmed, swarming.**

sway **1.** To move or cause to move back and forth: *The dancers swayed to the music.* **2.** To change the thinking of; influence: *Can I sway you from quitting your job? Verb.*
○ **1.** The act of swaying. **2.** Influence or control. *Noun.*
sway (swā) *verb,* **swayed, swaying;** *noun, plural* **sways.**

swear **1.** To make a solemn statement, often by calling on God or another sacred being or thing: *The witness swore on a Bible to tell the truth.* **2.** To promise in a solemn way: *I swear I'm telling the truth.* **3.** To say words that show hatred and anger; curse. **swear** (swâr) *verb,* **swore, sworn, swearing.**

sweat **1.** A salty fluid given off through the skin. *Sweat helps to keep the body cool.* **2.** Moisture formed in drops on a surface: *Sweat formed on the glass of cold water.* **3.** The condition of sweating: *I broke into a sweat. Noun.*
○ **1.** To give off sweat: *The horse sweated in the hot sun.* **2.** To gather moisture in drops from the surrounding air: *The glass of cold lemonade sweated in the warm room. Verb.*
sweat (swet) *noun; verb,* **sweated, sweating.**

sweater A warm, knitted piece of cloth-

This colorful sweater **is made of the wool of sheep.**

ing worn over the upper part of the body.
sweat·er (swet′ər) *noun, plural* **sweaters.**

sweatshirt A heavy, knitted shirt that usually has long sleeves and no collar. **sweat·shirt** (swet′shûrt′) *noun, plural* **sweatshirts.**

sweep **1.** To clean with a broom or brush. **2.** To clear away or take up: *We swept the crumbs from the floor.* **3.** To move or carry quickly and with force: *The fire swept through the barn.* **4.** To pass over with a quick, steady motion: *The sailor's eyes swept the horizon. Verb.*
○ Any quick, sweeping motion. *Noun.*
sweep (swēp) *verb,* **swept, sweeping;** *noun, plural* **sweeps.**

sweet **1.** Having a taste like that of sugar or honey. **2.** Pleasing to the smell: *A rose has a sweet odor.* **3.** Not sour; fresh: *Store the cream in the refrigerator to keep it sweet.* **4.** Not salted: *The baker uses only sweet butter.* **5.** Pleasing and kindly; good-natured: *a sweet person. Adjective.*
○ Something that tastes sweet: *That store sells cookies, candy, and other sweets. Noun.*
Another word that sounds like this is **suite**.
sweet (swēt) *adjective,* **sweeter, sweetest;** *noun, plural* **sweets.**

sweeten To make or become sweet or sweeter: *The cook sweetened the lemonade with sugar.*
sweeten (swē′tən) *verb,* **sweetened, sweetening.** —**sweetener** *noun.*

swell **1.** To grow or cause to grow in size: *The sprain swelled my wrist.* **2.** To rise above the normal level: *This symphony swells to a loud ending. Verb.*
○ A wave or series of waves: *The boat rose and fell on the ocean swells. Noun.*
○ Fine; excellent: *You look swell in your new clothes. Adjective.* This meaning is used mostly in everyday conversation.
swell (swel) *verb,* **swelled, swollen** or **swelled, swelling;** *noun, plural* **swells;** *adjective,* **sweller, swellest.**

swelling A swollen part: *I had a swelling on my leg where the baseball hit me.* **swell·ing** (swel′ing) *noun, plural* **swellings.**

swerve To turn aside suddenly: *The driver swerved to avoid hitting a dog. Verb.*
○ The act of swerving. *Noun.*
swerve (swûrv) *verb,* **swerved, swerving;** *noun, plural* **swerves.**

swift 1. Moving or able to move very quickly: *a swift horse*. 2. Happening quickly; quick: *The frog made a swift leap into the pond*. *Adjective.*
○ A bird with narrow wings and dark gray, brown, or bluish feathers. *Noun.*
swift (swift) *adjective*, **swifter**, **swiftest**; *noun*, *plural* **swifts**. —**swiftly** *adverb* —**swiftness** *noun*.

swim 1. To move in the water by using the arms and legs or the fins and tail. 2. To move across something in this way: *How fast can you swim across the pool?* 3. To be in a liquid or be covered with a liquid: *The child's eyes swam with tears*. 4. To have a dizzy feeling: *The rocking of the boat made my head swim*. *Verb.*
○ The act, time, or distance of swimming: *Let's take a quick swim*. *Noun.*
swim (swim) *verb*, **swam**, **swum**, **swimming**; *noun*, *plural* **swims**.

swimmer A person or animal that swims.
swim·mer (swim′ər) *noun*, *plural* **swimmers**.

swindle To take someone's money or property dishonestly; cheat: *The dealer swindled me and never delivered the goods*. *Verb.*
○ The act of swindling. *Noun.*
swin·dle (swin′dəl) *verb*, **swindled**, **swindling**; *noun*, *plural* **swindles**. —**swin·dler** *noun*.

swine A member of the pig family; pig or hog.
swine (swīn) *noun*, *plural* **swine**.

This swing was made from a tire.

swing 1. To move back and forth: *We like to swing on the tire that hangs from the tree*. 2. To move or turn in a curved motion: *The player swung the bat*. *Verb.*
○ 1. The swinging of something: *A swing of the golf club sent the ball flying*. 2. A seat hung by chains or ropes in which a person can sit and swing: *We play on the swings at the playground*. *Noun.*
swing (swing) *verb*, **swung**, **swinging**; *noun*, *plural* **swings**.

swirl To move around and around: *The wind swirled the dry leaves*. *Verb.*
○ 1. A spinning or twisting motion: *The breeze made the smoke of the campfire rise with a swirl*. 2. Something shaped like a curl: *My signature ends in a swirl*. *Noun.*
swirl (swûrl) *verb*, **swirled**, **swirling**; *noun*, *plural* **swirls**.

switch 1. A long, thin stick or rod used for whipping. 2. A stroke or lash: *The cow brushed flies off with a switch of its tail*. 3. A change: *The coach made a switch to a new pitcher in the ninth inning*. 4. A device used to open or close an electric circuit: *a light switch*. 5. A device by which a train can change from one track to another. *Noun.*
○ 1. To strike with a switch. 2. To move or swing with a quick motion: *The cat switched its tail nervously back and forth*. 3. To change: *Let's switch seats*. 4. To turn on or off by means of an electrical switch. 5. To move a train from one track to another. *Verb.*
switch (swich) *noun*, *plural* **switches**; *verb*, **switched**, **switching**.

swivel A device that allows parts attached to it to move freely: *My lamp has a swivel that lets me raise or lower it*. *Noun.*
○ To turn on a swivel. *Verb.*
swiv·el (swiv′əl) *noun*, *plural* **swivels**; *verb*, **swiveled**, **swiveling**.

swollen Made larger by swelling: *I can't get my ring on my swollen finger*. **swol·len** (swō′lən) *adjective*.

swoop To rush down suddenly: *The hawk swooped on the rabbit*. *Verb.*
○ The act of swooping. *Noun.*
swoop (swüp) *verb*, **swooped**, **swooping**; *noun*, *plural* **swoops**.

sword A weapon that has a long, sharp blade set in a handle. **sword** (sôrd) *noun*, *plural* **swords**.

swordfish A large saltwater fish with a long, flat, bony part like a sword that sticks out from the

PRONUNCIATION KEY:

| at | āpe | fär | câre | end | mē | it | īce | pîerce | hot | ōld | sông | fôrk |
| oil | out | up | ūse | rüle | pull | tûrn | chin | sing | shop | thin | this | |

hw in white; zh in treasure. The symbol ə stands for the unstressed vowel sound in about, taken, pencil, lemon, and circus.

735

upper jaw. **sword·fish** (sôrd′fish′) *noun*, *plural* **swordfish** *or* **swordfishes**.

syllable **1.** A spoken sound without interruption that forms a word or part of a word. The word "break" has one syllable. The word "important" has three syllables. **2.** A letter or group of letters that form a syllable. **syl·la·ble** (sil′ə bəl) *noun*, *plural* **syllables**.

symbol Something that represents something else: *The dove is a symbol of peace.*
Another word that sounds like this is **cymbal**.
sym·bol (sim′bəl) *noun*, *plural* **symbols**.

A starfish has
symmetry.

symmetry A balanced grouping of parts on either side of a line or around a center. **sym·me·try** (sim′i trē) *noun*, *plural* **symmetries**.
—symmetrical *adjective*.

sympathetic **1.** Feeling or showing sympathy: *A sympathetic neighbor brought flowers to me when I was sick.* **2.** In agreement: *The counselor is sympathetic to our plans for a picnic.* **sym·pa·thet·ic** (sim′pə thet′ik) *adjective*.

sympathize **1.** To feel sympathy; have or show compassion: *I sympathized with my neighbors when their cat ran away.* **2.** To be in agreement: *My parents sympathize with my plan to be an actor.* **sym·pa·thize** (sim′pə thīz′) *verb*, **sympathized, sympathizing**.

sympathy **1.** The ability to feel and understand the sorrow or troubles of others: *I had sympathy for the hurt dog.* **2.** Agreement: *The teacher is in*

sympathy with us. **sym·pa·thy** (sim′pə thē) *noun*, *plural* **sympathies**.

symphony **1.** A long musical work written for an orchestra. **2.** A large orchestra. **sym·pho·ny** (sim′fə nē) *noun*, *plural* **symphonies**.

symptom A sign of something: *A sore throat often is a symptom of a cold.* **symp·tom** (simp′təm) *noun*, *plural* **symptoms**.

synagogue A building used by Jews for worship and religious instruction. **syn·a·gogue** (sin′ə gog′ *or* sin′ə gôg′) *noun*, *plural* **synagogues**.

syndrome A group of at least three signs that occur together and characterize a disease. **syn·drome** (sin′drōm) *noun*, *plural* **syndromes**.

synonym A word with the same or almost the same meaning as another word: *"Large" is a synonym for "big."* **syn·o·nym** (sin′ə nim) *noun*, *plural* **synonyms**.

LANGUAGE NOTE

A *synonym* is a word that can be used instead of another word. Synonyms help us make our writing clearer and more interesting. Some words are so close in meaning that they can replace each other in a sentence. For example, the synonyms *gift* and *present* can be used in the same sentence: I received four gifts (presents) for my birthday. Some synonyms, such as *make, form,* and *manufacture,* are not close enough in meaning to be substituted for one another. The meaning of these synonyms must be understood before they can be used properly in a sentence.

synonymous Having the same or almost the same meaning: *The words "leap" and "jump" are synonymous.* **syn·on·y·mous** (si non′ə məs) *adjective*.

syntax The rules of grammar by which words are arranged in phrases, clauses, and sentences. **syn·tax** (sin′taks) *noun*.

synthetic Artificial. *Plastic is synthetic.* **syn·thet·ic** (sin thet′ik) *adjective*.

syrup A thick, sweet liquid. Some syrups are made by boiling sugar and water or juice. **syr·up** (sir′əp *or* sûr′əp) *noun*, *plural* **syrups**.

system **1.** A group of things that form a whole. **2.** A group of laws, beliefs, or facts. **3.** An orderly method. **sys·tem** (sis′təm) *noun*, *plural* **systems**.

The letter T has one sound in English which can be made by:

t in words such as tag, top, and sit;

th in Thomas;

tt in better and button;

ght in bought and taught;

ed in dressed and looked.

The letter T also combines with H to give two slightly different sounds:

th in words such as thin, panther, and both;

and th in words such as this, mother, and smooth.

t, T The twentieth letter of the alphabet.
t, T (tē) *noun, plural* **t's, T's.**

t or **tsp.** An abbreviation for *teaspoon.*

T or **tbs.** or **tbsp.** An abbreviation for *tablespoon.*

tab A small flap that sticks out from something: *The **tab** on the file folder was marked with the name of a customer.*
tab (tab) *noun, plural* **tabs.**

table 1. A piece of furniture with a flat top supported by one or more legs: *We eat at the dining room **table**.* 2. The people seated at a table: *The **table** next to us was very noisy.* 3. A list of facts or information: *A **table** in my history book lists all the states and their capitals.*
ta·ble (tā′bəl) *noun, plural* **tables.**

tablecloth A cloth used to cover a table.
ta·ble·cloth (tā′bəl klôth′) *noun, plural* **tablecloths.**

tablespoon A large spoon that is used to serve and measure food: *A **tablespoon** holds the same amount as three teaspoons.* **ta·ble·spoon** (tā′bəl spün′) *noun, plural* **tablespoons.**

tablet 1. A number of sheets of paper glued together at one edge; pad: *a **tablet** of writing paper.* 2. A small, flat piece of medicine or candy: *Those red **tablets** will help your cold.* 3. A thin, flat slab of wood or stone that has writing on it.
tab·let (tab′lit) *noun, plural* **tablets.**

table tennis A game played on a table with a low net stretched across it. Players use paddles to hit a small ball back and forth.

taboo A custom or social rule that forbids something.
ta·boo (tə bü′ *or* ta bü′) *noun, plural* **taboos;** *adjective.*

tack 1. A short nail that has a sharp point and a broad, flat head. 2. A course of action: *We weren't succeeding, so we tried a new **tack**.*
tack (tak) *noun, plural* **tacks.**

tackle 1. The equipment used for some activity or sport: *The store sold rods, hooks, nets, and other fishing **tackle**.* 2. A system of ropes and pulleys used for raising and lowering heavy loads: *Tackle is used for raising and lowering the sails on a ship.* 3. The act of stopping and bringing to the ground: *The football player made a good **tackle** of the ball carrier. Noun.*
○ To stop and bring to the ground: *The farmer **tackled** the fleeing pig. Verb.*
tack·le (tak′əl) *noun, plural* **tackles;** *verb,* **tackled, tackling.**

taco A tortilla wrapped around a filling, such as cheese, ground beef, or chicken. **ta·co** (täk′ō) *noun, plural* **tacos.**

WORD HISTORY

Taco is a word from Mexico. In Spanish, taco can mean "a little wad" and is the word often used for "a snack."

---

tact The ability to say or do the right thing when dealing with people or difficult situations. **tact** (takt) *noun.* —**tact·ful** *adjective.*

tactics Methods planned and used to win a competition or achieve a goal: *The general's clever* *tactics led to victory for his army.* **tac·tics** (tak′tiks) *plural noun.*

tadpole A very young frog or toad when it still lives under water and has gills, a tail, and no legs. **tad·pole** (tad′pōl) *noun, plural* **tadpoles.**

taffy A chewy candy made of brown sugar or molasses mixed with butter. **taf·fy** (taf′ē) *noun, plural* **taffies.**

tag¹ A piece of paper or other material that is attached to something: *a price tag.* **tag** (tag) *noun, plural* **tags.**

tag² A game in which one player chases the other players until he or she touches one. The player who is touched must then chase the others. *Noun.* ○ **1.** To touch or tap in the game of tag: *I tagged you, so now you chase us.* **2.** To put a runner out in baseball by touching the runner with the ball. *Verb.*
tag (tag) *noun; verb,* **tagged, tagging.**

tail **1.** A slender, flexible part of an animal's body that sticks out from the back end: *Our dog wags her tail when she sees us coming home.* **2.** Anything that is shaped like a tail: *the tail of a comet.* **3.** The end or rear part of anything: *the tail of an airplane.* **4. tails.** The reverse side of a coin. *Noun.* ○ To follow closely and secretly. *Verb.*
Another word that sounds like this is **tale.**
tail (tāl) *noun, plural* **tails;** *verb,* **tailed, tailing.**

taillight A red warning light attached to the rear end of a vehicle. **tail·light** (tāl′līt′) *noun, plural* **taillights.**

tailor A person who makes, alters, or repairs clothing. **tai·lor** (tā′lər) *noun, plural* **tailors.**

take **1.** To get a hold of; grasp: *I took the child's hand before crossing the street.* **2.** To capture or win by using force or skill: *My painting has taken first prize!* **3.** To obtain; get: *The nurse took my temperature.* **4.** To carry with one; bring: *You can take only two suitcases on the trip.* **5.** To make use of: *Let's take the bus home.* **6.** To move or remove: *If you take 3 from 5, you get 2.* **7.** To lead or conduct: *I took the dog for a walk.* **8.** To receive or accept: *Take my advice and get a good night's sleep.* **9.** To make or do: *I took a photograph.* **10.** To need or require: *It takes practice to learn how to play the guitar.* **11.** To have a sense of; feel: *Some collectors take great pride in their rare coins.* **12.** To put up with; tolerate; endure: *Our teacher won't take rude behavior.*

• **to take after.** To look like or be like: *I don't take after either of my parents.*
• **to take off.** **1.** To remove: *Take off your hat.* **2.** To rise up in flight: *The airplane took off.* **3.** To leave: *It's time for us to take off and go home.*
• **to take over.** To take charge of: *A substitute teacher will take over the class.*
• **to take up.** **1.** To begin, as a hobby or a course of instruction: *I'm going to take up tennis.* **2.** To consume or fill; occupy. *That truck takes up a lot of space.* **3.** To gather or collect. *We took up a collection for our friend.*
take (tāk) *verb,* **took, taken, taking.**

SYNONYMS

take, grasp, seize, hold
Let's take a lunch with us to the beach. Grasp my hand while we are crossing the street. The hawk seized the snake in its talons. You must hold the dog's leash so it doesn't run away.

---

takeoff The act of leaving the ground: *The space shuttle takeoff is set for noon.* **take·off** (tāk′ôf′) *noun, plural* **takeoffs.**

An airplane travels at great speed during its takeoff.

takeout Food bought from a restaurant to eat somewhere else. **take·out** (tāk′out) *noun.* —**take-out** *adjective.*

talc A mineral that is ground up for use in face powder, plastics, and paints. **talc** (talk) *noun.*

tale **1.** A story: *What a good tale about life at sea!* **2.** A story that is not true; falsehood: *Stop telling tales and give us the truth.*
Another word that sounds like this is **tail.**
tale (tāl) *noun, plural* **tales.**

talent **1.** A natural ability or skill: *a talent for playing the piano.* **2.** A person or persons who have talent: *We need more **talent** for our play.* **tal·ent** (tal′ənt) *noun, plural* **talents.** —**talented** *adjective.*

talk **1.** To say words; speak: *The baby cannot **talk** yet.* **2.** To discuss: ***Talk** with the doctor about the pain in your back.* **3.** To bring or persuade by speech: *The salesperson **talked** me into buying two pairs of shoes. Verb.*
○ **1.** An exchange of spoken words; conversation: *The two friends had a long **talk**.* **2.** An informal speech or lecture. *Noun.*
talk (tôk) *verb,* **talked, talking;** *noun, plural* **talks.**

talk show A television or radio program on which a host interviews and talks with guests and may take questions from callers or audience members.

tall **1.** Higher than average; not short or low: ***tall** basketball players; **tall** buildings.* **2.** Measured from the bottom to the top; having a certain height: *I am four feet **tall**.* **3.** Made-up or exaggerated: *I think stories about ghosts are **tall** tales.* **tall** (tôl) *adjective,* **taller, tallest.**

tallow The fat from cattle and sheep. Tallow is used in making candles and soap. **tal·low** (tal′ō) *noun.*

tally An account or a record: *Keep a **tally** of your expenses. Noun.*
○ **1.** To count up; add: *The waitress **tallied** our bill.* **2.** To match; agree: *The two drivers' descriptions of the accident did not **tally**. Verb.*
tal·ly (tal′ē) *noun, plural* **tallies;** *verb,* **tallied, tallying.**

Talmud The collection of writings that form the basis for Jewish civil and religious law. **Tal·mud** (tal′mùd *or* tol′mùd) *noun.*

talon The strong, sharp claw of an eagle, hawk, or other bird of prey. **tal·on** (talən) *noun, plural* **talons.**

tamale A Mexican dish made from chopped meat and peppers, rolled in cornmeal dough, and steamed in corn husks. **ta·ma·le** (tamä′lē) *noun, plural* **tamales.**

tambourine A small drum that has metal disks attached loosely around the rim. **tam·bou·rine** (tambərēn) *noun, plural* **tambourines.**

tame **1.** Taken from a wild or natural state by human beings and made gentle or obedient: ***tame** elephants at the circus.* **2.** Not fearful or shy: *The*

goat was **tame** enough to let us feed it. Adjective.
○ To take from a wild or natural state and make gentle or obedient. *Verb.*
tame (tām) *adjective,* **tamer, tamest;** *verb,* **tamed, taming.** —**tamely** *adverb.*

tamper To interfere in an improper manner: *If you **tamper** with this recipe, the bread won't rise.* **tam·per** (tam′pər) *verb,* **tampered, tampering.**

tan **1.** To make into leather by soaking in a special solution. **2.** To make or become brown by exposure to the sun: *Sunlight **tanned** the climber's face. Verb.*
○ **1.** A yellowish brown color. **2.** The brown color given to a person's skin by exposure to the sun. *Noun.*
tan (tan) *verb,* **tanned, tanning;** *noun, plural* **tans.**

tang A sharp or strong taste, flavor, or odor. **tang** (tang) *noun, plural* **tangs.**

tangerine A small, sweet, juicy fruit that is like an orange. A tangerine has a reddish orange skin that peels easily. **tan·ge·rine** (tan′jərēn′) *noun, plural* **tangerines.**

tangle To twist together in a confused mass; snarl: *The strong wind **tangled** my hair. Verb.*
○ A twisted, confused mass. *Noun.*
tan·gle (tang′gəl) *verb,* **tangled, tangling;** *noun, plural* **tangles.**

tangram A Chinese puzzle that consists of a square that is cut into different pieces. The pieces can be combined in different ways to make other shapes, such as triangles and parallelograms. **tan·gram** (tan′grəm *or* tang′grəm) *noun, plural* **tangrams.**

tank **1.** A large container for holding liquid or gas: *the gas **tank** of a car.* **2.** An enclosed, armored vehicle used in combat. It has machine guns and a cannon and moves on two continuous belts. **tank** (tangk) *noun, plural* **tanks.**

tantrum An outburst of temper or anger. **tan·trum** (tan′trəm) *noun, plural* **tantrums.**

tap¹ **1.** To hit or strike lightly: *The teacher **tapped** on the desk with a ruler for attention.* **2.** To make or do by striking or hitting lightly again and again: *I **tapped** out the beat of the music with my foot. Verb.*
○ **1.** A light or gentle blow: *I felt a gentle **tap** on my shoulder.* **2.** A metal plate attached to the sole

PRONUNCIATION KEY:

| at | āpe | fär | câre | end | mē | it | īce | pîerce | hot | ōld | sông | fôrk |
| oil | out | up | ūse | rüle | pùll | tûrn | chin | sing | shop | thin | this | |

hw in white; zh in treasure. The symbol ə stands for the unstressed vowel sound in about, taken, pencil, lemon, and circus.

739

of a shoe for tap dancing. *Noun.*

tap (tap) *verb,* **tapped, tapping;** *noun, plural* **taps.**

tap² A device for starting or stopping the flow of water or another liquid from a pipe, sink, or container; faucet: *Our kitchen sink has two taps. Noun.*
○ 1. To put a hole in to draw liquid from: *People tap sugar maple trees to collect sap for making syrup.* 2. To make a hidden connection in order to listen to someone's conversations: *The spy tapped the enemy's telephone lines. Verb.*

tap (tap) *noun, plural* **taps;** *verb,* **tapped, tapping.**

Maple trees are tapped in the spring.

tap dance A dance in which the dancer creates a rhythm of sharp clicking sounds with metal taps on the toes and heels of the shoes.

tape 1. A long narrow strip of cloth, paper, plastic, or some other material: *The runner broke the tape as he crossed the finish line.* 2. A specially treated plastic band that is used to record and play sounds or images: *music tapes and CDs. Noun.*
○ 1. To fasten with a tape: *Tape the two pieces of paper together.* 2. To record on a specially treated plastic tape. *Verb.*

tape (tāp) *noun, plural* **tapes;** *verb,* **taped, taping.**

tape measure A long strip of cloth, plastic, or steel marked off in units for measuring.

taper 1. To make or become gradually smaller at one end: *The tailor tapered the legs of the slacks.* 2. To become less and less: *The rain finally tapered off.*
Another word that sounds like this is **tapir.**

ta·per (tā′pər) *verb,* **tapered, tapering.**

tape recorder A machine that records and plays sound on a kind of plastic tape.

tapestry A cloth that has designs and pictures woven into it. **tap·es·try** (tap′ə strē) *noun, plural* **tapestries.**

tapir An animal that looks like a large pig but is related to horses and rhinoceroses. Tapirs live in Central and South America and Asia.

Another word that sounds like this is **taper.**

ta·pir (tā′pər) *noun, plural* **tapirs.**

taps A bugle call that is played at the end of the day in military camps as a signal that all lights must be put out. **taps** (taps) *noun.*

tar A dark, sticky substance that is made from coal or wood. Tar is used to pave roads and to waterproof roofs and sheds. *Noun.*
○ To cover or coat with tar. *Verb.*

tar (tär) *noun; verb,* **tarred, tarring.**

tarantula A hairy spider that is found in warm areas. It has a painful bite. **ta·ran·tu·la** (tə ran′chə lə) *noun, plural* **tarantulas.**

tardy Arriving or happening after the appointed time; late: *students tardy for class.* **tar·dy** (tär′dē) *adjective,* **tardier, tardiest.**

target 1. A mark or object that is aimed at. 2. A person or thing that is made fun of or criticized: *I was the target for teasing after I struck out.* **tar·get** (tär′git) *noun, plural* **targets.**

tariff A charge or tax that a government puts on goods coming into a country. **tar·iff** (tar′if) *noun, plural* **tariffs.**

tarnish 1. To dull the shine or color of: *Sulfur in the air can tarnish silver.* 2. To lose shine or color: *The old candlesticks have tarnished. Verb.*
○ A surface coating that results from tarnishing. *Noun.*

tar·nish (tär′nish) *verb,* **tarnished, tarnishing;** *noun.*

tart¹ Sharp in taste; not sweet: *a tart green apple.* **tart** (tärt) *adjective,* **tarter, tartest.**

tart² A pastry crust containing a custard, fruit, or other filling. **tart** (tärt) *noun, plural* **tarts.**

tartan A woolen cloth with a plaid pattern. Each Scottish clan has its own special tartan. **tar·tan** (tär′tən) *noun, plural* **tartans.**

tartar A yellowish substance that forms on teeth and becomes hard if not removed. **tar·tar** (tär′tər) *noun.*

task A piece of work to be done. **task** (task) *noun, plural* **tasks.**

tassel 1. A hanging group of threads or cords that are tied together at one end. 2. Anything that is like this in shape: *An ear of corn has a silky tassel at one end.* **tas·sel** (tas′əl) *noun, plural* **tassels.**

taste 1. The sense by which the flavor of something in the mouth is noticed. 2. A particular flavor of something taken into the mouth. The four

basic tastes are sweet, bitter, sour, and salty. **3.** A small amount; sample: *May I have a **taste** of your fish?* **4.** A liking or preference: *I found a shirt to my **taste**.* **5.** A feeling of appreciation for what is good or beautiful: *good **taste** in music. Noun.*
◦ **1.** To recognize the flavor of something by means of the sense of taste: *I can **taste** the garlic in this stew.* **2.** To have a particular flavor: *The sauce **tastes** too sweet.* **3.** To find out the flavor of something by taking a little of it into the mouth: ***Taste** the soup to see if it needs pepper. Verb.*
taste (tāst) *noun, plural* **tastes;** *verb,* **tasted, tasting.**

taste bud One of the small rounded structures on the tongue that sense flavors.

tasteless **1.** Having little or no flavor: *The soup was **tasteless**, so I added some pepper.* **2.** Having or showing little sense of what is good or appropriate. **taste·less** (tāst′lis) *adjective.*

tasty Pleasing to the sense of taste: *a **tasty** dessert.* **tast·y** (tās′tē) *adjective,* **tastier, tastiest.**

tattle To tell secrets about someone: *Speak softly, or someone might hear and **tattle** on us.* **tat·tle** (tat′əl) *verb,* **tattled, tattling.**

tattletale A person who tells the secrets of others. **tat·tle·tale** (tat′əl tāl′) *noun, plural* **tattletales.**

tattoo A colored figure or design made on the skin with needles that have been dipped in colors: *The sailor had **tattoos** of ships on each arm. Noun.*
◦ To mark with tattoos. *Verb.*
tat·too (ta′tü) *noun, plural* **tattoos.** —**tat·too** *verb,* **tattooed, tattooing.**

taunt To tease or make fun of in an insulting way: *The taller kids held the ball out of my reach and **taunted** me. Verb.*
◦ A teasing and scornful remark. *Noun.*
taunt (tônt *or* tont) *verb,* **taunted, taunting;** *noun, plural* **taunts.**

taut Tightly drawn or stretched; not loose: *Make sure the ropes on the tent are **taut**.* Another word that sounds like this is **taught.** **taut** (tôt) *adjective,* **tauter, tautest.**

tavern A place where travelers stay overnight; inn. **tav·ern** (tav′ərn) *noun, plural* **taverns.**

tawny Having a light yellowish-brown color: *a lion's **tawny** coat.* **taw·ny** (tônē *or* ton′ē) *adjective.*

tax **1.** Money that people or businesses must pay the government for its support. **2.** A heavy bur-

den or demand; strain: *The delay was a **tax** on our patience. Noun.*
◦ **1.** To put a tax on: *Our state **taxes** gasoline and uses the money to build highways.* **2.** To make a heavy demand on; strain: *The problem **taxed** my brain. Verb.*
tax (taks) *noun, plural* **taxes;** *verb,* **taxed, taxing.**

taxation The practice or system of taxing: *Taxation gives the government money to provide schools, clean water, and many other services.* **tax·a·tion** (tak sā′shən) *noun.*

taxi A taxicab. *Noun.*
◦ To move slowly along the ground or over the surface of the water. *Verb.*
tax·i (tak′sē) *noun, plural* **taxis;** *verb,* **taxied, taxiing** *or* **taxying.**

taxicab An automobile that can be hired to carry passengers where they want to go. A taxicab usually has a meter that records the fare to be paid. **tax·i·cab** (tak′sē kab′) *noun, plural* **taxicabs.**

tbs. or **tbsp.** An abbreviation for **tablespoon.**

T cell A type of white blood cell that helps protect the body against disease.

tea **1.** A drink that is made by pouring boiling water over the dried leaves of a shrub that is grown in China, Japan, and India. **2.** This shrub or its dried and crumbled leaves. **3.** A drink prepared in the same way from other dried leaves: *herbal **tea**.* **4.** A light meal or gathering held in the late afternoon, during which tea is served. **tea** (tē) *noun, plural* **teas.**

teach To help a person to learn; show how: *My neighbor **teaches** swimming in a camp and **taught** me to swim last summer.* **teach** (tēch) *verb,* **taught, teaching.** —**teacher** *noun.*

teal **1.** A small duck with a short neck. **2.** A medium to dark greenish-blue color. **teal** (tēl) *noun, plural* **teal** *or* **teals.**

team **1.** A group that plays, acts, or works together: *A **team** of scientists discovered a cure for the disease.* **2.** Two or more horses or other animals that are harnessed together to do work:

A team of horses is used to pull a heavy load.

PRONUNCIATION KEY:

| at | āpe | fär | câre | end | mē | it | īce | pîerce | hot | ōld | sông | fôrk |
| oil | out | up | ūse | rüle | pull | tûrn | chin | sing | shop | thin | this | |

hw in white; zh in treasure. The symbol ə stands for the unstressed vowel sound in about, taken, pencil, lemon, and circus.

741

A **team** of oxen pulled the plow. *Noun.*
○ To work together; form a team: *The children teamed up to carry the boxes of books. Verb.* Another word that sounds like this is **teem.**
team (tēm) *noun, plural* **teams;** *verb,* **teamed, teaming.**

teammate A person who is a member of the same team: *We're basketball teammates.* **team•mate** (tēmˈmāt) *noun, plural* **teammates.**

tear¹ 1. To pull or become pulled apart by force: *I tore the envelope open.* 2. To make a hole or cut into by force; rip: *I tore my shirt when I caught it on a nail.* 3. To move very quickly; rush: *When the door was opened, the dog tore out of the house. Verb.*
○ A torn part or place. *Noun.*
tear (târ) *verb,* **tore, torn, tearing;** *noun, plural* **tears.**

tear² 1. A drop of clear, salty liquid that comes from the eye. Tears help keep the eye clean. 2. **tears.** The act of crying. Another word that sounds like this is **tier.**
tear (tîr) *noun, plural* **tears.**

tease To annoy or make fun of in a playful way: *Don't tease the cat or it will scratch you. Verb.*
○ A person who annoys or makes fun of people. *Noun.*
tease (tēz) *verb,* **teased, teasing;** *noun, plural* **teases.**

teaspoon A spoon that is used to eat with and to measure food. Three teaspoons hold the same amount as one tablespoon. **tea•spoon** (tēˈspün′) *noun, plural* **teaspoons.**

technical 1. Relating to the special skills, facts, or terms that belong to a science, art, or profession: *The judge explained the case in the technical language of the law.* 2. Relating to engineering or any of the mechanical or industrial arts: *You can learn to be an electrician at a technical school.* **tech•ni•cal** (tekˈni kəl) *adjective.*

technician A person who is trained in the techniques of a certain job or science: *The dental technician cleaned the patient's teeth.* **tech•ni•cian** (tek nishˈən) *noun, plural* **technicians.**

technique A method or way of bringing about a desired result in a science, art, sport, or profession: *Techniques for growing crops are taught at agricultural schools.* **tech•nique** (tek nēkˈ) *noun,*

plural **techniques.**

technology 1. The use of science for practical purposes, especially in engineering and industry. 2. Methods, machines, and devices that are used in doing things in a science or profession: *X rays were an important advance in medical technology.* **tech•nol•o•gy** (tek nolˈəj ē) *noun.*

teddy bear A toy bear stuffed and covered with soft material. **teddy bear** (tedˈē).

teem To be full; swarm: *The creek near our house teems with fish.* Another word that sounds like this is **team.**
teem (tēm) *verb,* **teemed, teeming.**

teenager A person who is between the ages of thirteen and nineteen. **teen•ag•er** (tēnˈāˈjər) *noun, plural* **teenagers.**

teens The years of a person's life between thirteen and nineteen. **teens** (tēnz) *plural noun.*

teepee Another spelling for tepee. **tee•pee** (tēˈpē) *noun, plural* **teepees.**

teeth Plural of **tooth.** **teeth** (tēth) *plural noun.*

teethe To grow teeth: *Many babies chew on rubber rings when they are teething.* **teethe** (tēth) *verb,* **teethed, teething.**

telecast To broadcast for television: *That network will telecast the Olympics. Verb.*
○ A program broadcast by television. *Noun.*
tel•e•cast (telˈi kast′) *verb,* **telecasted, telecasting;** *noun, plural* **telecasts.**

Molar Bicuspids Canine

teeth

telecommunications The science and technology of sending messages over long distances by electronic means, such as radio, telephone, or satellite. **tel•e•com•mu•ni•ca•tions** (telˈə kə mūˈni kāˈshənz) *noun.*

telecommute To work at home and communicate with one's office by electronic means, such as a computer with a modem. **tel•e•com•mute** (telˈə kə mūt′) *verb,* **telecommuted, telecommuting.**

telegram A message sent by telegraph. **tel•e•gram** (telˈi gram′) *noun, plural* **telegrams.**

telegraph A system or equipment used for sending messages by wire over a long distance. The message is sent in code over wires by means of electricity. **tel·e·graph** (tel′i graf′) *noun, plural* **telegraphs.**

telephone **1.** A system for sending sound or other information by wire or radio waves over a long distance. **2.** An instrument used to send sound or other information over a long distance. A telephone includes a part for speaking into and a part for listening. It can also be used to send messages between computers. *Noun.*

○ **1.** To talk with someone by telephone: *I will telephone you tomorrow.* **2.** To send by telephone: *Grandma telephoned her love. Verb.* **tel·e·phone** (tel′ə fōn′) *noun, plural* **telephones;** *verb,* **telephoned, telephoning.**

WORD HISTORY

The word telephone comes from two Greek words that mean "far away" and "sound or voice." A telephone lets someone hear sounds from far away.

---

telescope An instrument that makes distant objects seem larger and nearer. Telescopes are very useful for studying the stars and other heavenly bodies. **tel·e·scope** (tel′ə skōp′) *noun, plural* **telescopes.**

televise To send by television: *All the major stations televised the president's speech.* **tel·e·vise** (tel′ə vīz′) *verb,* **televised, televising.**

**Many baseball games
are televised.**

television **1.** A system for sending and receiving pictures and sound over long distances by means of electricity. **2.** A set or device on which these pictures are seen and the sound is heard. **tel·e·vi·sion** (tel′ə vizh′ən) *noun, plural* **televisions.**

tell **1.** To put in words; say: *Tell us a story.* **2.** To give an order to; command: *The librarian told us to quiet down.* **3.** To reveal something secret: *I know who did it, but I won't tell.* **4.** To recognize; identify: *Can you tell the twins apart?*

• **tell off.** To scold or criticize harshly: *I told him off for taking my bike without asking.*

• **tell on.** To report the wrongdoing of; tattle on: *The boy threatened to tell on his sister if she didn't stop teasing him.*

tell (tel) *verb,* **told, telling.**

---

reflecting telescope

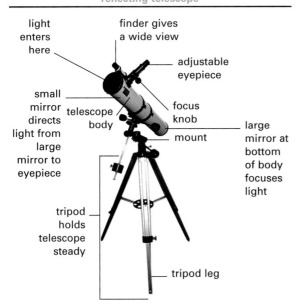

light enters here

finder gives a wide view

adjustable eyepiece

small mirror directs light from large mirror to eyepiece

telescope body

focus knob

mount

large mirror at bottom of body focuses light

tripod holds telescope steady

tripod leg

---

refracting telescope

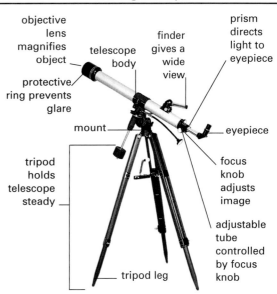

objective lens magnifies object

protective ring prevents glare

telescope body

finder gives a wide view

prism directs light to eyepiece

mount

eyepiece

tripod holds telescope steady

focus knob adjusts image

adjustable tube controlled by focus knob

tripod leg

teller 1. A person who tells or relates: *a teller of tall tales*. 2. A person who works in a bank giving out and receiving money. **tell·er** (tel′ər) *noun*, *plural* **tellers**.

temper 1. A tendency to become angry or irritated: *I have quite a temper when someone insults me.* 2. A usual state of mind; disposition: *She has an even temper, and few things upset her.* 3. Control over the emotions: *I lost my temper and yelled. Noun.*
○ To lessen the harshness of; soften: *The teacher tempered her criticism with a smile. Verb.* **tem·per** (tem′pər) *noun*, *plural* **tempers**; *verb*, **tempered**, **tempering**.

temperate Not too hot and not too cold: *a temperate climate.* **tem·per·ate** (tem′pərit) *adjective*.

temperature The degree of heat or cold. Temperature is often measured with a thermometer: *The nurse sent me home from school today with a high temperature. The temperature outside is going down.* **tem·per·a·ture** (tem′pər əchər′) *noun*, *plural* **temperatures**.

template 1. A tool that serves as a pattern for making things with the same shape, as on paper or in metal: *I used a template to draw a triangle.* 2. A computer document used to create other documents that follow the same pattern: *Our school newspaper staff created a template for the paper's front page so it always looks the same.* **tem·plate** (tem′plit) *noun*, *plural* **templates**.

temple[1] A building that is used for the worship of a god or gods: *In Greece, we saw the ruins of the ancient temples. People of the Jewish religion worship in temples.* **tem·ple** (tem′pəl) *noun*, *plural* **temples**.

temple[2] The flattened part on either side of the forehead. The temple is above the cheek and in front of the ear. **tem·ple** (tem′pəl) *noun*, *plural* **temples**.

tempo The rate of speed of a piece of music: *The band played at a fast tempo.* **tem·po** (tem′pō) *noun*, *plural* **tempos**.

temporary Lasting or used for a short time only: *Some students try to find temporary jobs for the summer.* **tem·po·rar·y** (tem′pə rer ′ē) *adjective*.

tempt 1. To give someone thoughts of doing something wrong or foolish: *Don't tempt me with chocolate; I'm allergic to it.* 2. To appeal strongly to; attract: *The clothing in that store tempts me.*

tempt (tempt) *verb*, **tempted**, **tempting**. —**temptation** *noun*

ten One more than nine; 10. **ten** (ten) *noun*, *plural* tens; *adjective*.

tenant A person who pays money to use a house, apartment, office, or land that belongs to someone else. **ten·ant** (ten′ənt) *noun*, *plural* **tenants**.

tend[1] To be likely or apt: *Some people tend to gain weight easily.* **tend** (tend) *verb*, **tended**, **tending**.

tend[2] To take care of; look after: *tend a garden.* **tend** (tend) *verb*, **tended**, **tending**.

tendency A likelihood of behaving or thinking in a certain way; inclination: *The chain on this old bike has a tendency to slip.* **tend·en·cy** (ten′dən sē) *noun*, *plural* **tendencies**.

tender 1. Not tough or hard; soft: *a tender steak.* 2. Not strong; delicate: *the tender leaves of a young plant.* 3. Kind or loving: *Both parents were especially tender toward their new baby.* 4. Very sensitive; painful: *My thumb was still tender after the cut had healed.* **ten·der** (ten′dər) *adjective*.

tendon A strong cord or band of tissue that attaches a muscle to a bone or other part of the body. **ten·don** (ten′dən) *noun*, *plural* **tendons**.

Tenn. An abbreviation for Tennessee.

Tennessee A state in the southeastern United States. Its capital is Nashville. **Ten·nes·see** (ten′ə sē′) *noun*.

WORD HISTORY

Tennessee comes from the name that the Cherokee had for their ancient capital. The name was given to a stream near the city, and later the river into which the stream flows was also called Tennessee. The name of the state came from the Tennessee River.

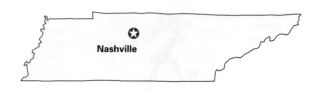

Tennessee
U.S. Postal Abbreviation: **TN**
Capital: **Nashville**
Population: **4,855,000**
Area: **42,244 sq. mi./109,411 sq. km**
State Nickname: **Volunteer State**
State Bird: **Mockingbird**
State Flower: **Iris**

tennis A game in which two or four players hit a small ball over a net with a racket. Tennis is played on grass, clay, concrete, or other courts. **ten·nis** (ten′is) *noun*.

tenor **1.** A man's singing voice that is higher than a baritone or a bass. **2.** A singer who has such a voice. **3.** A musical instrument that has the range of a tenor voice. **ten·or** (ten′ər) *noun, plural* **tenors**.

tense¹ **1.** Stretched or drawn tight; strained: *When you lift something heavy, your arm muscles become tense.* **2.** Showing or causing strain or suspense: *Our argument made me feel tense. Adjective.*
○ To make or become tense: *Tense your leg muscle. Verb.*
tense (tents) *adjective,* **tenser, tensest;** *verb,* **tensed, tensing.**

tense² A form of a verb that shows the time of the action or condition that the verb expresses. In the sentence "I am taller than you," the verb "am" is in the present tense. In the sentence "I ran home," the verb "ran" is in the past tense. **tense** (tents) *noun, plural* **tenses.**

tension **1.** The force that affects objects that are pulled or stretched: *That rope will break if you apply more tension.* **2.** A harmful feeling of pressure caused by worry or too much work. **ten·sion** (ten′shən) *noun, plural* **tensions.**

Some tents are large and can hold many people.

tent A portable shelter that is usually made out of canvas or nylon. A tent is held up by one or more poles or flexible rods. **tent** (tent) *noun, plural* **tents.**

tentacle A long, thin body part of certain animals. Tentacles are used to feel, grasp, and move: *An octopus has eight tentacles.* **ten·ta·cle** (tentə kəl) *noun, plural* **tentacles.**

tenth Next after the ninth. *Adjective; noun.*
○ One of ten equal parts; ¹/₁₀. *Noun.*
tenth (tenth) *adjective; noun, plural* **tenths.**

tepee A tent shaped like a cone. A tepee is made from animal skins stretched over poles. Native Americans who lived on the plains used tepees. **te·pee** (tē′pē′) *noun, plural* **tepees.**

WORD HISTORY

Tepee comes from a Native American word for this kind of tent. This word came from two other words that meant "to be used for living."

tepid Slightly warm: *By the time the child finished her bath, the water was tepid.* **tep·id** (tep′id) *adjective.*

term **1.** A word or group of words that has a specific meaning: *"Serve," "set," and "racket" are terms used in tennis.* **2.** A definite or limited period of time: *The term of office for the president of the United States is four years.* **3.** **terms.** A relationship between people: *We are on good terms with our neighbors.* **4.** A condition that is part of an agreement or a legal document: *The terms of the peace treaty called for an immediate end to the fighting. Noun.*
○ To call or name: *Hurricanes in the western Pacific Ocean are termed "typhoons." Verb.*
term (tûrm) *noun, plural* **terms;** *verb,* **termed, terming.**

terminal **1.** A station at either end of a railroad, bus, air, or other transportation line. **2.** A keyboard and a monitor that can be connected to a computer. *Noun.*
○ Fatal: *a terminal illness. Adjective.*
ter·mi·nal (tûr′mə nəl) *noun, plural* **terminals;** *adjective.*

termite An insect that has a white body. Termites live in large groups and eat wood, paper, and other similar material. **ter·mite** (tûr′mīt) *noun, plural* **termites.**

terrace **1.** A paved outdoor space next to a house: *Let's have tea on the terrace.* **2.** A balcony of an apartment house. **3.** A raised bank of earth with a flat top and sloping sides. Farmers often build terraces on hillsides to make a level area for growing crops. **ter·race** (ter′is) *noun, plural* **terraces.**

PRONUNCIATION KEY:

| at | āpe | fär | câre | end | mē | it | īce | pîerce | hot | ōld | sông | fôrk |
| oil | out | up | ūse | rüle | pull | tûrn | chin | sing | shop | thin | this | |

hw in white; zh in treasure. The symbol ə stands for the unstressed vowel sound in about, taken, pencil, lemon, and circus.

745

terrain Ground or land: *The hikers moved slowly over the rough terrain.* **ter·rain** (tə rān') *noun.*

terrapin A North American turtle that lives in or near fresh water or along the seashore. **ter·ra·pin** (ter'ə pin) *noun, plural* **terrapins.**

terrarium A container that is used for growing small plants or raising small animals. It is usually made of glass. **ter·rar·i·um** (tə râr'ē əm) *noun, plural* **terrariums** *or* **terraria** (tə râr'ē ə).

terrestrial 1. Of or relating to the earth or its inhabitants. 2. Of or relating to land instead of water or air: *Elephants are terrestrial creatures; fish are not.* **ter·res·tri·al** (tə res'trē əl) *adjective.*

terrible 1. Causing fear or terror; awful: *The volcano erupted with a terrible roar.* 2. Very bad: *terrible weather.* **ter·ri·ble** (ter'ə bəl) *adjective.*

terrier One of various lively, small dogs that can have either a smooth or curly coat. **ter·ri·er** (ter'ē ər) *noun, plural* **terriers.**

terrific 1. Unusually great or severe: *Today's terrific heat melted the tar on our roof.* 2. Causing terror; frightening: *a terrific storm.* 3. Extremely good; wonderful: *That's a terrific idea!* **ter·ri·fic** (tə rif'ik) *adjective.*

terrify To fill with terror; frighten greatly: *The child was terrified by the bad dream.* **ter·ri·fy** (ter'ə fī) *verb,* **terrified, terrifying.**

territory 1. Any large area of land; region: *The plane was shot down over enemy territory.* 2. Land that is under the control of a distant government. A territory does not have the full rights of a state or province: *Hawaii was a territory of the United States before it became a state in 1959.* **ter·ri·to·ry** (ter'i tôr'ē) *noun, plural* **territories.**

terror 1. Great fear: *That horror movie filled me with terror.* 2. A person or thing that causes great fear: *That vicious dog is a terror to the whole neighborhood.* **ter·ror** (ter'ər) *noun, plural* **terrors.**

terrorism The use of violence and threats to get people to obey, often to gain a political goal. **ter·ror·ism** (ter'ə riz'əm) *noun.* —**terrorist** *noun, plural* **terrorists.**

terrorize To fill with great fear: *The pirates terrorized the ship's passengers.* **ter·ror·ize** (ter'ə rīz') *verb,* **terrorized, terrorizing.**

test 1. A set of problems or tasks; examination. A test is used to determine a person's knowledge or skill: *a spelling test.* 2. Any method of finding out the nature or quality of something: *The doctor gave me several tests to find out why I felt sick. Noun.*
○ To give a test to or check: *The baker opened the oven and tested the bread. Verb.*
test (test) *noun, plural* **tests;** *verb,* **tested, testing.**

Testament Either of two main divisions of the Bible, the Old Testament or the New Testament. **Tes·ta·ment** (tes'tə mənt) *noun, plural* **Testaments.**

testimony 1. A statement made under oath by a witness in a court of law: *The jury heard the testimony of each witness.* 2. Proof or evidence: *Your good report card is testimony to your hard work.* **tes·ti·mo·ny** (tes'tə mō'nē) *noun, plural* **testimonies.**

test tube A narrow glass tube that is closed at one end. A test tube is used in laboratory tests and experiments.

tetanus A serious disease that is caused by a germ that enters the body through a deep, narrow wound. Tetanus causes extreme stiffness of some muscles, especially those that control the jaw. This disease is also called **lockjaw.** **tet·a·nus** (tet'ə nəs) *noun.*

tether A rope or chain tied to an animal to keep it within a small area. *Noun.*
○ To tie with a tether: *The cowboy tethered his horse. Verb.*
teth·er (teth'ər) *noun, plural* **tethers;** *verb,* **tethered, tethering.**

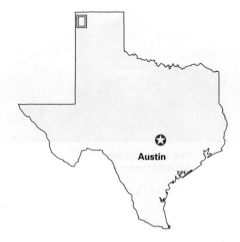

Texas
U.S. Postal Abbreviation: **TX**
Capital: **Austin**
Population: **16,789,000**
Area: **267,338 sq. mi./692,402 sq. km**
State Nickname: **Lone Star State**
State Bird: **Mockingbird**
State Flower: **Bluebonnet**

Texas A state in the south-central United States. Its capital is Austin. **Tex·as** (tek′səs) *noun.*

text 1. The main body of reading matter in a book: *The text in each chapter of our history book is followed by questions.* 2. The actual words of a writer or speaker: *The newspaper printed the full text of the president's speech.* 3. A textbook: *Please bring your texts to class tomorrow.* **text** (tekst) *noun, plural* **texts.**

textbook A book that is used in school for the study of a particular subject: *a history textbook.* **text·book** (tekst′bŭk′) *noun, plural* **textbooks.**

textile A fabric that is made by weaving or knitting. *Noun.*
 ○ Relating to textiles or their manufacture: *a textile factory where cloth is made. Adjective.* **tex·tile** (teks′tīl *or* teks′təl) *noun, plural* **textiles**; *adjective.*

texture The look and feel of something: *Sandpaper has a rough texture.* **tex·ture** (teks′chər) *noun, plural* **textures.**

than 1. In comparison with: *My cousin is older than I am.* 2. Except; but; besides: *Haven't you any fruit other than apples?* **than** (<u>th</u>an *or un-stressed* <u>th</u>ən) *conjunction.*

thank 1. To say that one is grateful to: *I thanked him for his help.* 2. To hold responsible; blame: *I have you to thank for getting us into this mess.* **thank** (thangk) *verb,* **thanked, thanking.**

thankful Feeling or expressing thanks; grateful: *The thirsty traveler was thankful for the water that I offered.* **thank·ful** (thangk′fəl) *adjective.*

thanks I thank you: *Thanks for the help. Interjection.*
 ○ An expression or feeling of gratitude: *The family gave thanks that no one had been hurt in the fire. Noun.*
thanks (thangks) *interjection; plural noun.*

Thanksgiving 1. A holiday in the United States observed on the fourth Thursday in November to celebrate the anniversary of the Pilgrims' first harvest feast, held in 1621. 2. A similar Canadian holiday celebrated on the second Monday in October. **Thanks·giv·ing** (thangksgiving) *noun, plural* **Thanksgivings.**

that 1. Used to indicate a person or thing being looked at or already mentioned: *Who wrote that book?* 2. Used to indicate something more distant than or contrasted with another thing: *That mountain is higher than this one. Adjective.*
 ○ 1. The person or thing being looked at or already mentioned: *That is my best friend.* 2. Something more distant than or contrasted with another thing: *This is a nice color, but that is my favorite.* 3. Who, whom, or which: *The people that live next door are my neighbors. Pronoun.*
 ○ 1. Used to introduce a clause in a sentence: *I think that I will accept the job.* 2. Used to show reason or cause: *I'm sorry that you can't come.* 3. Used to show result: *We ate so much for lunch that we couldn't eat dinner. Conjunction.*
 ○ To that extent; so: *Was it really that cold yesterday? Adverb.*
that (<u>th</u>at) *adjective; pronoun, plural* **those**; *conjunction; adverb.*

thatch Straw, reeds, or similar material that is used to cover a roof. *Noun.*
 ○ To cover with thatch: *The farmer thatched the roof of the house with straw. Verb.*
thatch (thach) *noun; verb,* **thatched, thatching.**

thaw 1. To free or become free of frost or ice; melt: *The sun thawed the snow on the roof.* 2. To become warm: *The ice skaters thawed out in front of a large fire.* 3. To become friendlier: *The unfriendly relations between the two countries began to thaw. Verb.*
 ○ Weather that is warm enough to melt ice and snow: *a spring thaw. Noun.*
thaw (thô) *verb,* **thawed, thawing**; *noun, plural* **thaws.**

the¹ Used before a noun that stands for a particular person, thing, or group: *The president made a speech. Close the door.* **the** (<u>th</u>ə before a consonant *or* <u>th</u>ē *before a vowel*) *definite article.*

PRONUNCIATION KEY:

at	āpe	fär	câre	end	mē	it	īce	pierce	hot	ōld	sông	fôrk
oil	out	up	ūse	rüle	pŭll	tûrn	chin	sing	shop	thin	<u>th</u>is	

hw in white; zh in treasure. The symbol ə stands for the unstressed vowel sound in about, taken, pencil, lemon, and circus.

747

the² To that degree; by that much: *The harder you work, the sooner you'll finish.* **the** (<u>th</u>ə before a consonant or <u>th</u>ē before a vowel) *adverb.*

theater 1. A building or other place where plays or movies are presented. 2. The writing and performing of plays: *a book on the history of the theater.* This word is sometimes spelled **theatre**. **the·a·ter** (thē′ə tər) *noun, plural* **theaters**.

thee An old form of the word "you." **thee** (<u>th</u>ē) *pronoun.*

theft The act of stealing. **theft** (theft) *noun, plural* **thefts**.

their Of, belonging to, or relating to them: *Our house is smaller than their house.* Other sound alike words are **there** and **they're**. **their** (<u>th</u>âr) *adjective.*

theirs The one or ones that belong to or relate to them: *Our car is new; theirs is old.* **theirs** (<u>th</u>ârz) *pronoun.*

them The persons or things being talked about: *I ran to my parents and hugged them. Carrots are good for you; eat them up!* **them** (<u>th</u>em or unstressed <u>th</u>əm) *pronoun.*

theme 1. The main subject or idea of something: *The theme of the book was the loyalty of a dog to its master.* 2. The main melody in a piece of music. 3. A short piece of writing on one subject; essay. **theme** (thēm) *noun, plural* **themes**.

themselves 1. Their own selves: *The dinner guests seated themselves.* 2. Their usual, normal, or true selves: *The players on the losing team were not themselves today.* **them·selves** (<u>th</u>em selvz′ or <u>th</u>əm selvz′) *pronoun.*

then 1. At that time: *That was five years ago; I was the only child then.* 2. After that; next: *I ate a sandwich and then an apple.* 3. In that case; if that is so: *If you want to come, then get ready. Adverb.*
○ Acting or serving at that time: *The then governor of our state decided to run for president. Adjective.*
○ That time: *The deadline is Friday; we must finish before then. Noun.*
then (then) *adverb; adjective; noun.*

theory 1. A group of ideas or principles that explain why or how something happens: *The theory of gravity explains why a leaf falls to the ground when it drops off a tree.* 2. An opinion based on some evidence but not proved: *The fire department has a theory about how the fire started.* **the·o·ry** (thē′ə rē) *noun, plural* theories.

therapy Treatment for a disability, injury, psychological problem, or illness. **ther·a·py** (the′rə pē) *noun, plural* **therapies**.

there 1. At, in, or to that place: *Put the box down there.* 2. Used to introduce a sentence in which a linking verb such as "be" comes before the subject: *There is some milk in the refrigerator. Adverb.*
○ That place: *Do you know the way home from there? Noun.*
○ A word used to express satisfaction or sympathy: *There! I did it! There, there, don't cry. Interjection.*
Other sound alike words are **their** and **they're**. **there** (<u>th</u>âr) *adverb; noun; interjection.*

thereafter From that time on; after that: *The sun shone the first day of our vacation, but it rained every day thereafter.* **there·af·ter** (<u>th</u>âr af′tər) *adverb.*

thereby By that means; in that way: *I cut the straw in half, thereby forming two short straws.* **there·by** (<u>th</u>âr bī′) *adverb.*

therefore For that reason; as a result: *The runner was hurt and therefore could not run.* **there·fore** (<u>th</u>âr′fôr′) *adverb.*

thermal Relating to or holding in heat: *thermal underwear.* **ther·mal** (thû′rməl) *adjective.*

thermometer A device for measuring temperature. Some thermometers are glass tubes containing mercury or alcohol that moves as the temperature changes. Other thermometers show the temperature in other ways.

Many thermometers show both Fahrenheit and Celsius.

ther·mom·e·ter (thər momi′t ər) *noun, plural* **thermometers**.

thermos bottle A container made to keep liquids hot or cold for many hours. **ther·mos bottle** (thûr′məs).

thermostat A device that automatically controls temperature, as in furnaces, ovens, cars, and refrigerators. **ther·mo·stat** (thûr′mə stat′) *noun, plural* **thermostats**.

thesaurus A book or list of synonyms and antonyms. **the·sau·rus** (thəsôrəs) *noun, plural* **thesauri** (thə sôr′ī) *or* **thesauruses**.

Thesaurus comes from a Greek word meaning "storehouse for treasure" or just "treasure." A thesaurus is a kind of treasure chest of words.

---

these Plural of this. *Do you prefer* **these** *flowers or the ones over there?* Look up **this** for more information. **these** (<u>th</u>ēz) *adjective; plural pronoun.*

they 1. The persons or things being talked about: *The travelers were late because* **they** *missed the bus.* 2. Some people: **They** *say that cats have nine lives.* **they** (<u>th</u>ā) *plural pronoun.*

they're Shortened form of "they are." Other sound alike words are **their** and **there**. **they're** (<u>th</u>âr) *contraction.*

thick 1. Having much space between one side or surface and the other; not thin: *The walls of this fort are very* **thick**. 2. Measured from one side or surface to the other: *That stone wall is two feet* **thick**. 3. Not flowing or pouring easily: *The* **thick** *pea soup was very filling.* 4. Growing or being close together; dense: *It was difficult to make our way through the* **thick** *forest. Adjective.*
○ So as to be thick: *The butcher always cuts the steaks* **thick**. *Adverb.*
○ The part or place of greatest activity or danger: *The brave soldier was in the* **thick** *of the fight. Noun.*
thick (thik) *adjective,* **thicker**, **thickest**; *adverb; noun.*

thicken To make or become thick or thicker: *The cook* **thickened** *the gravy. The fog* **thickened**. **thick·en** (thik′ən) *verb,* **thickened**, **thickening**.

thicket A thick growth of shrubs or bushes. **thick·et** (thik′it) *noun, plural* **thickets**.

thickness 1. The quality of being thick: *The* **thickness** *of the walls makes the house quiet.* 2. The distance between two sides or surfaces of something; the measurement other than the length or width: *The* **thickness** *of this board is 1 inch.* **thick·ness** (thik′nis) *noun, plural* **thicknesses**.

thief A person who steals: *The* **thief** *broke into the house and stole the television.* **thief** (thēf) *noun, plural* **thieves**.

thigh The part of the leg between the hip and the knee. **thigh** (thī) *noun, plural* **thighs**.

thighbone The large bone that goes from the hip

to the knee in a person's skeleton. **thigh·bone** (thī′bōn′) *noun, plural* **thighbones**.

thimble A small plastic or metal cap that is worn on the finger to protect it when pushing the needle through material in sewing. **thim·ble** (thim′bəl) *noun, plural* **thimbles**.

thin 1. Having little space between one side or surface and the other; not thick: *The* **thin** *wrapping paper did not hide the title of the book.* 2. Not fat; slender or lean: *Horses have* **thin**, *long faces.* 3. Flowing or pouring easily; watery: *The patient drank some* **thin** *broth.* 4. Easily seen through; flimsy: *Light came through the* **thin** *curtains. That's a* **thin** *excuse for being late to class.* 5. Not dense: **thin** *air in the mountains.* 6. Having a faint, shrill sound; weak: *The old man spoke in a* **thin** *voice. Adjective.*
○ So as to be thin: *roast beef sliced* **thin**. *Adverb.*
○ To make or become thin: *You can* **thin** *the soup with water. Dad's hair is* **thinning**. *Verb.*
thin (thin) *adjective,* **thinner**, **thinnest**; *adverb; verb,* **thinned**, **thinning**.

thing 1. Whatever is spoken of, thought of, or done: *That was an unkind* **thing** *to say.* 2. Something that can be touched, seen, heard, smelled, or tasted but is not a human being. *A book, a tree, and the moon are all things.* 3. A person or animal: *A kitten is a soft little* **thing**. 4. Affair; matter: *I have to settle this* **thing** *before I can leave.* 5. **things.** The general state of affairs: *How are* **things** *at school?* 6. **things.** Belongings: *I packed my* **things** *for the trip.* **thing** (thing) *noun, plural* **things**.

think 1. To use the mind to form ideas or to make decisions: **Think** *carefully before you answer.* 2. To have or form in the mind as an opinion, belief, or idea: *It's getting dark; I* **think** *we should go home.* 3. To call to mind or remember: *I often* **think** *of last summer.* 4. To have care or consideration: *A selfish person seldom* **thinks** *of others.* **think** (thingk) *verb,* **thought**, **thinking**.

third Next after the second. *Adjective; noun.*
○ One of three equal parts; ⅓. *Noun.*
third (thûrd) *adjective; noun, plural* **thirds**.

Third World The poorer, developing nations of the world.

PRONUNCIATION KEY:
at   āpe   fär   câre   end   mē   it   īce   pîerce   hot   ōld   sông   fôrk
oil   out   up   ūse   rüle   pull   tûrn   chin   sing   shop   thin   <u>th</u>is
hw in white; zh in treasure. The symbol ə stands for the unstressed vowel sound in about, taken, pencil, lemon, and circus.

749

thirst 1. An uncomfortable feeling of dryness in the mouth and throat. Thirst is caused by the need to drink water. 2. The desire or need for something to drink: *This juice should satisfy your thirst.* 3. A strong desire for something: *a thirst for adventure.* **thirst** (thûrst) *noun, plural* **thirsts.** —**thirsty** *adjective.*

thirteen Three more than ten; 13. **thir·teen** (thûr'tēn') *noun, plural* **thirteens;** *adjective.*

thirteenth Next after the twelfth. *Adjective; noun.* ◦ One of thirteen equal parts; ¹/₁₃. *Noun.* **thir·teenth** (thûr'tēnth') *adjective; noun, plural* **thirteenths.**

thirtieth Next after the twenty-ninth. *Adjective; noun.* ◦ One of thirty equal parts; ¹/₃₀. *Noun.* **thir·ti·eth** (thûr'tē ith) *adjective; noun, plural* **thirtieths.**

thirty Three times ten; 30. **thir·ty** (thûr'tē) *noun, plural* **thirties;** *adjective.*

this 1. Used to indicate a person or thing that is present, nearby, or just mentioned: *This house is ten years old.* 2. Used to indicate something that is nearer than or contrasted with another thing: *This house is larger than the one across the street. Adjective.* ◦ 1. The person or thing that is present, nearby, or just mentioned: *Is this your coat?* 2. Something that is nearer than or contrasted with another thing: *This is mine; that is yours.* 3. Something about to be said or explained: *This is what I mean. Pronoun.* ◦ To this extent or degree: *Is it this hot here every day? Adverb.* **this** (this) *adjective; pronoun, plural* **these;** *adverb.*

thistle A prickly plant with white, yellow, red, or purple flowers. **this·tle** (this'əl) *noun, plural* **thistles.**

thong 1. A narrow strip of leather or other material that is used for fastening.

The thistle is the national emblem of Scotland.

2. A sandal that is held on the foot by a small strap that fits between the first two toes. **thong** (thông *or* thong) *noun, plural* **thongs.**

thorax 1. The part of the body between the neck and the abdomen, including the heart, lungs, and ribs. 2. The part of an insect's body that is between the head and the abdomen. The thorax includes the wings and legs. **tho·rax** (thôr'aks) *noun, plural* **thoraxes.**

thorn 1. A sharp point on a branch or stem. Roses and various other plants have thorns. 2. A tree or shrub that has thorns. **thorn** (thôrn) *noun, plural* **thorns.** —**thorny** *adjective.*

thorough Leaving nothing out; careful and complete: *I made a thorough search for the missing key.* **thor·ough** (thûr'ō) *adjective.*

thoroughfare A main road. **thor·ough·fare** (thûr'ə fâr') *noun, plural* **thoroughfares.**

those Plural of that: *Do you prefer those shirts or the ones here on the shelf?* Look up **that** for more information. **those** (thōz) *adjective; plural pronoun.*

thou An old form of the word "you." **thou** (thou) *pronoun.*

though 1. In spite of the fact that: *I was late for school, though I got up early.* 2. But; yet; however: *The movie was good, though it could have been better. Conjunction.* ◦ Nevertheless; however: *The salad was not very fresh; the dressing was good, though. Adverb.* • **as though.** In the way it would be if: *You look as though you need to take a nap.* **though** (thō) *conjunction; adverb.*

thought Past tense and past participle of **think:** *I thought about the movie as I walked home. Verb.* ◦ 1. The act of thinking: *My friend sat alone, deep in thought.* 2. A product of thinking; an idea or opinion: *What are your thoughts on this problem?* 3. Careful attention or consideration: *Give some thought to the questions before writing the answers. Noun.* **thought** (thôt) *verb; noun, plural* **thoughts.**

thousand Ten times a hundred; 1,000. **thou·sand** (thou'zənd) *noun, plural* **thousands;** *adjective.*

thousandth Next after the 999th. *Adjective; noun.* ◦ One of a thousand equal parts; ¹/₁₀₀₀. *Noun.* **thou·sandth** (thou'zəndth) *adjective; noun, plural* **thousandths.**

thrash 1. To give a beating to: *The farmer threatened to thrash any child caught stealing cherries.* 2. To make wild movements; toss violently: *The animal thrashed about in its cage.* **thrash** (thrash) *verb,* **thrashed, thrashing.**

thread 1. A very thin cord that is used in sewing and in weaving cloth. 2. Anything that is thin and long like a thread: *Threads of paint dripped from the brush.* 3. The main idea or thought that connects the parts of a story or speech: *I couldn't follow the* **thread** *of the confusing story.* 4. A curved ridge that twists around a screw or nut. The threads of a screw make it hold tightly to whatever it is inserted or driven into. *Noun.*
○ 1. To pass a thread through: *Please* **thread** *this needle for me.* 2. To put on a thread; string: *I* **threaded** *beads for a necklace.* 3. To make one's way through a narrow or obstructed place: *I* **threaded** *my way through the crowd to the front. Verb.*
thread (thred) *noun, plural* **threads;** *verb,* **threaded, threading.**

threat 1. A statement of something that will be done to hurt or punish: *The hunters heeded our* **threat** *to call the sheriff if they trespassed.* 2. A person or thing that might cause harm; danger: *The outbreak of flu was a* **threat** *to everyone in the community.* 3. A sign or possibility of some danger or harm that might happen: *The* **threat** *of rain made us cancel our picnic.* **threat** (thret) *noun, plural* **threats.**

threaten 1. To say what will be done to hurt or punish; make a threat of or against: *The teacher* **threatened** *punishment if we kept making noise.* 2. To be the cause of danger or harm: *The forest fire* **threatened** *the town.* 3. To be a sign or possibility of: *The dark clouds* **threatened** *rain.* **threat·en** (thre′tən) *verb,* **threatened, threatening.**

three One more than two; 3. **three** (thrē) *noun, plural* **threes;** *adjective.*

thresh To separate the grain or the seeds from a cereal plant or grass. Farmers today use machines to thresh their crops. **thresh** (thresh) *verb,* **threshed, threshing.**

threshold 1. A piece of wood, stone, or metal that forms the bottom of a door frame. 2. A point of entering or beginning: *on the* **threshold** *of an important discovery.* **thresh·old** (thresh′hōld) *noun, plural* **thresholds.**

thrift Careful management of money or of anything valuable; lack of waste: *If you practice* **thrift,** *you can save enough for that bicycle.* **thrift** (thrift) *noun.* —**thrifty** *adjective.*

thrill 1. A sudden feeling of pleasure or excitement: *Seeing the ocean for the first time gave me a great* **thrill.** 2. Something that gives such a sudden feeling of pleasure or excitement: *It was a* **thrill** *to see the famous athlete in person. Noun.*
○ To fill with pleasure or excitement: *The home team's victory* **thrilled** *the crowd. Verb.*
thrill (thril) *noun, plural* **thrills;** *verb,* **thrilled, thrilling.**

WORD HISTORY

The word **thrill** comes from an Old English word meaning "to pierce or pass through quickly." At first, *thrill* was only used to refer to objects. For example, "A spear *thrilled* through the shield." Later this word was used to describe how an emotion sharply affects a person.

thrive To be successful; do well: *This plant* **thrives** *in the sun.* **thrive** (thrīv) *verb,* **thrived** *or* **throve, thrived** *or* **thriven, thriving.**

throat 1. The passage in the body between the mouth and the esophagus. Food and air pass through the throat. 2. The front of the neck: *a shirt left open at the* **throat.** 3. A narrow opening that is like the throat: *I held the bottle by the* **throat.** **throat** (thrōt) *noun, plural* **throats.**

throb To beat or pound heavily and fast: *My heart* **throbbed** *with excitement. Verb.*
○ A heavy, fast beat or sensation: *A* **throb** *of pain shot through my ankle as I fell. Noun.*
throb (throb) *verb,* **throbbed, throbbing;** *noun, plural* **throbs.**

This **throng** of bicycle riders is awaiting the start of a race.

throne 1. The chair that a king or queen sits on during ceremonies and other special occasions. 2. The power or authority of a king or queen. Another word that sounds like this is **thrown.** **throne** (thrōn) *noun, plural* **thrones.**

throng A large number of people; crowd: *A* **throng** *of people watched the parade. Noun.*

PRONUNCIATION KEY:

| at | āpe | fär | câre | end | mē | it | īce | pïerce | hot | ōld | sông | fôrk |
| oil | out | up | ūse | rüle | pull | tûrn | chin | sing | shop | thin | this | |

hw in white; zh in treasure. The symbol ə stands for the unstressed vowel sound in about, taken, pencil, lemon, and circus.

751

○ To move in a large group; crowd: *People from all over **thronged** to the state fair. Verb.*
throng (thrông *or* throng) *noun, plural* **throngs**; *verb,* **thronged, thronging.**

through **1.** From the beginning to the end of: *I read **through** the book in one day.* **2.** In one side and out the other side of: *We drove **through** Ohio on our way west.* **3.** In or to various places in: *We plan to travel **through** New England this summer.* **4.** In the midst of; among: *We strolled **through** the cherry trees.* **5.** Because of: *My cousin got a promotion **through** hard work.* **6.** By means of: *We heard the news **through** a friend.* **7.** Finished with; at the end of: *When will you be **through** high school? Preposition.*
○ **1.** From one side or end to the other side or end: *I opened the door and the cat went **through.*** **2.** Completely; totally: *My clothes got soaked **through** in the storm. Adverb.*
○ **1.** Allowing passage from one place to another with no obstruction: *Is this a **through** street or a dead end?* **2.** Having reached a point of completion; finished: *Are you **through** with your work yet? Adjective.*
Another word that sounds like this is **threw.**
through (thrü) *preposition; adverb; adjective.*

throughout **1.** In every part of; everywhere in: *The senator is famous **throughout** the state.* **2.** During the whole time or course of: *They visited us frequently **throughout** the summer. Preposition.*
○ In, to, or through every part; everywhere: *The color of the walls of the apartment is the same **throughout.** Adverb.*
through·out (thrü out′) *preposition; adverb.*

throw **1.** To send up into or through the air: *The two players **threw** a ball back and forth.* **2.** To make fall to the ground: *The horse **threw** its rider.* **3.** To put quickly and carelessly: *I **threw** a coat on and ran outside.* **4.** To put or place suddenly in a certain position or condition: *The fire alarm **threw** the crowd into a panic. Verb.*
○ The act of throwing; toss: *The shortstop made the **throw** to third base. Noun.*
• **to throw up.** To vomit.
throw (thrō) *verb,* **threw, thrown, throwing**; *noun, plural* **throws.**

thrush One of a number of birds that are known for their song. The robin, the bluebird, and the nightingale are thrushes. **thrush** (thrush) *noun,* plural **thrushes.**

thrust To push or shove suddenly or with force: *He **thrust** the note into his pocket. Verb.*
○ A sudden, strong drive or push: *The army made a **thrust** into enemy territory. Noun.*
thrust (thrust) *verb,* **thrust, thrusting**; *noun, plural* **thrusts.**

thruway A wide highway with several lanes used for rapid, long-distance travel. This word is also spelled throughway. **thru·way** (thrü′wā) *noun, plural* **thruways.**

thug A rough and violent criminal. **thug** (thug) *noun, plural* **thugs.**

thumb **1.** The short, thick finger on the hand. The thumb makes it easier to pick things up and grip things. **2.** The part of a glove or mitten that covers the thumb. *Noun.*
○ To turn and look through pages quickly: *I **thumbed** through a magazine while I waited. Verb.*
• **all thumbs.** Clumsy; awkward: *Dad tried to braid my sister's hair, but he was **all thumbs.***
• **thumbs up** or **thumbs down.** A sign of approval or disapproval: *The boss gave **thumbs up** to the plan for an office party.*
thumb (thum) *noun, plural* **thumbs**; *verb,* **thumbed, thumbing.**

thumbtack A tack with a flat, round head that can be pressed into a wall or board with the thumb. Notices are often posted on bulletin boards with thumbtacks. **thumb·tack** (thum′tak′) *noun, plural* **thumbtacks.**

thump A dull, heavy sound: *The heavy suitcase dropped with a **thump.** Noun.*
○ **1.** To beat or hit so as to make a dull, heavy sound: *The speaker **thumped** the table with a fist to get our attention.* **2.** To beat rapidly: *My heart **thumped** as I stepped up to the microphone. Verb.*
thump (thump) *noun, plural* **thumps**; *verb,* **thumped, thumping.**

thunder **1.** A loud rumbling or cracking sound that follows lightning. **2.** A noise that is like thunder: *the **thunder** of cannons in the distance. Noun.*
○ To make thunder or a noise that is like thunder:

*The express train **thundered** through the station. Verb.*

thun·der (thun′dər) *noun; verb,* **thundered, thundering.**

thundercloud A dark cloud of great height that produces thunder and lightning. **thun·der·cloud** (thun′dər kloud′) *noun, plural* **thunderclouds.**

thunderstorm A storm that has thunder and lightning. **thun·der·storm** (thun′dər stôrm′) *noun, plural* **thunderstorms.**

Thurs. An abbreviation for *Thursday.*

Thursday The fifth day of the week. **Thurs·day** (thûrz′dē *or* thûrz′dā) *noun, plural* **Thursdays.**

WORD HISTORY

Thursday comes from the Old English word meaning "Thor's day." Thor was the pagan English god of thunder.

thus 1. In this way: *The dance teacher said, "The waltz is done **thus**," and then demonstrated the steps.* 2. As a result; therefore: *You did not study and, **thus**, you failed the test.* 3. To this extent; so: *We have not heard from them **thus** far.* **thus** (<u>th</u>us) *adverb.*

thy An old form of the word "your." **thy** (<u>th</u>ī) *pronoun.*

thyme A low plant with fragrant leaves that are used to flavor foods.
Another word that sounds like this is **time.**
thyme (tīm) *noun, plural* **thymes.**

tick¹ A light, clicking sound. Many clocks mark time with a tick. *Noun.*
○ 1. To make a light, clicking sound: *The clock stopped **ticking**.* 2. To pass: *The minutes **ticked** away.* 3. To mark with a dot, slash, or other mark; check: *They **ticked** off each item on the grocery list. Verb.*
tick (tik) *noun, plural* **ticks;** *verb,* **ticked, ticking.**

tick² A tiny animal that looks like a spider. Ticks attach themselves to the skin of humans and other animals to suck their blood. **tick** (tik) *noun, plural* **ticks.**

ticket 1. A card or piece of paper that gives the person who holds it the right to be admitted or to get a service: *You need a **ticket** to ride the train.* 2. A tag or label that is attached to something to show its price or give other information. 3. A notice that orders a person to pay a fine or come to court: *a parking **ticket**. Noun.*
○ 1. To attach a tag or label to: *The clerk at the airport **ticketed** our suitcases for the flight to Washington.* 2. To give a traffic ticket to: *The police officer **ticketed** the driver for speeding. Verb.*
tick·et (tik′it) *noun, plural* **tickets;** *verb,* **ticketed, ticketing.**

tickle 1. To touch the body in a way that causes a tingling feeling: *It makes me laugh whenever someone **tickles** my feet.* 2. To have a tingling feeling: *The dust in the air made my nose **tickle**.* 3. To please or delight: *The children were **tickled** by the sight of the clowns. Verb.*
○ A tingling feeling: *The **tickle** in my throat made me cough. Noun.*
tick·le (tik′əl) *verb,* **tickled, tickling;** *noun, plural* **tickles.**

ticklish 1. Sensitive to tickling: *My feet are very **ticklish**.* 2. Needing skillful handling or sensitive treatment: *a **ticklish** situation.* **tick·lish** (tik′lish *or* tik′ə lish) *adjective.*

tic-tac-toe A game played on a block of nine squares arranged in three rows of three squares. Two players take turns putting an X or O into an empty square. The first player to get three X's or O's in a row wins. **tic-tac-toe** (tik tak tō′) *noun.*

tidal Relating to, caused by, or having tides: *This shore has suffered a great amount of **tidal** erosion.* **ti·dal** (tī′dəl) *adjective.*

tide 1. The regular rise and fall of the water level of the oceans and other large bodies of water that is caused by the pull of the moon and sun on the earth. High tide and low tide each occur about twice a day. 2. A movement or tendency that is hard to resist: *The **tide** of the battle turned against the invading army.* **tide** (tīd) *noun, plural* **tides.**

tidings News; information: *We hoped for good **tidings** from the travelers.* **tid·ings** (tī′dingz) *plural noun.*

tidy Clean and neat: *My closet is not very **tidy**. Adjective.*
○ To make clean and neat: *Please **tidy** up your room. Verb.*
ti·dy (tī′dē) *adjective,* **tidier, tidiest;** *verb,* **tidied, tidying.**

PRONUNCIATION KEY:

| at | āpe | fär | câre | end | mē | it | īce | pierce | hot | ōld | sông | fôrk |
| oil | out | up | ūse | rüle | pùll | tûrn | chin | sing | shop | thin | <u>th</u>is | |

hw in white; zh in treasure. The symbol ə stands for the unstressed vowel sound in about, taken, pencil, lemon, and circus.

753

tie 1. To fasten or attach with a bow or knot: *The child is learning to tie his shoes.* 2. To draw together or join closely: *A common interest in football tied the two friends together.* 3. To equal the score or total of: *The two teams were tied at 5–5. Verb.* ○ 1. A cord, string, or line that is used to fasten things together: *This apron has a tie in back.* 2. A strip of cloth that is worn around the neck; necktie. 3. A feeling or relationship that holds people together; bond: *family ties.* 4. An equal score: *The game ended in a tie.* 5. A timber or rod that holds together and strengthens other parts. The rails of a railroad track are attached to wooden ties. *Noun.*
tie (tī) *verb*, **tied, tying**; *noun, plural* **ties.**

tier One of a series of layers or rows that are arranged one above another: *The football stadium has tiers of seats for the spectators.* Another word that sounds like this is **tear.**
tier (tîr) *noun, plural* **tiers.**

tiger A large animal that is a member of the cat family. Most tigers have an orange or yellow coat with black or brown stripes. **ti•ger** (tī′gər) *noun, plural* **tigers.**

Tigers live in Asia.

tight 1. Held firmly; secure: *Make a tight knot so the string won't come loose.* 2. Made so that the parts are close together: *This sweater has a tight knit.* 3. Fitting the body closely: *My belt was tight after I ate that big dinner.* 4. Having little time or space to spare: *I'll try to fit that into my tight schedule.* 5. Hard to deal with; difficult: *The question put me in a tight spot.* 6. Not generous; stingy: *The customer was too tight to leave a tip.* 7. Evenly matched; close: *The race is very tight;*

it's hard to tell who will win. Adjective. ○ Firmly; securely: *Be sure to twist the lid tight on the jar. Adverb.*
tight (tīt) *adjective; adverb,* **tighter, tightest.**

tighten To make or become tight or tighter: *Tighten that knot. The leash tightened when the dog tried to walk faster.* **tight•en** (tīt′ən) *verb,* **tightened, tightening.**

tightrope A wire or rope that is stretched taut and placed high above the ground. Acrobats perform on a tightrope. **tight•rope** (tīt′rōp′) *noun, plural* **tightropes.**

tights A closely fitting covering for the lower part of the body and the legs. Tights are worn by dancers. **tights** (tīts) *plural noun.*

tile A thin, flat piece of hard material used for covering roofs, floors, or walls. Most tiles are made of baked clay. *Noun.* **tile** (tīl) *noun, plural* **tiles.**

till¹ 1. Up to the time of; until: *Wait till tomorrow before deciding.* 2. Before; until: *They won't arrive till Sunday. Preposition.* ○ 1. Up to the time when or that; until: *Wait till you hear from me before writing.* 2. Before; until: *Don't leave till you finish doing the dishes. Conjunction.*
till (til) *preposition; conjunction.*

till² To prepare and use land for growing crops: *Farmers use a plow to till the soil.* **till** (til) *verb,* **tilled, tilling.**

till³ A drawer where money is kept: *The cashier put the money in the till.* **till** (til) *noun, plural* **tills.**

tiller A bar or handle used to turn the rudder of a boat. **till•er** (til′ər) *noun, plural* **tillers.**

tilt To raise one end or side of; tip: *Don't tilt your chair back or you may fall over. Verb.* ○ A sloping or slanting position: *The tilt of her head suggested she was listening carefully. Noun.*
tilt (tilt) *verb,* **tilted, tilting**; *noun, plural* **tilts.**

timber 1. Wood that is used in building things; lumber. 2. A large, heavy piece of wood; beam. 3. Trees; forest: *New England was mostly covered with timber when European settlers first came to America.* **tim•ber** (tim′bər) *noun, plural* **timbers.**

time 1. The period during which all events, conditions, and actions happen or continue: *The changing of summer into fall shows the passing of time.* 2. An exact point in time: *It's time for lunch.* 3. A portion of time available or taken for some purpose: *The runner's time for the mile was four min-*

utes. **4.** A portion of time in history: *colonial times.* **5.** A person's experience: *We had a great time at the game.* **6.** One of a number of repeated actions or happenings: *We saw that movie four times.* **7.** The beat or rhythm of a piece of music: *music written in waltz time. Noun.*

○ **1.** To arrange or set according to time: *The alarm clock was **timed** to go off at seven o'clock.* **2.** To measure the time or rate of: *The coach **timed** the runners. Verb.*

Another word that sounds like this is **thyme.**

• **ahead of time.** Before the time when one is due or expected; early: *There was little traffic, so we arrived **ahead of time.***

• **at times.** Sometimes; periodically: *My best friend gets grouchy **at times.***

• **behind the times.** Out dated; old-fashioned: *They should get a computer for their business; they're **behind the times.***

• **in no time.** Quickly: *Don't worry about being late; we'll be there **in no time.***

• **in time. 1.** Before it is too late: *Please come **in time** for lunch.* **2.** In the correct beat or rhythm: *We all clapped our hands **in time** with the music.*

• **on time.** At the correct time; according to schedule: *Did you get to the concert **on time?***

• **times.** Multiplied by: *Two **times** two equals four.*

time (tīm) *noun, plural* **times;** *verb,* **timed, timing.**

timely Happening at a good time: *The **timely** arrival of the police prevented the bank robbers' escape.* **time•ly** (tīm′lē) *adjective,* **timelier, timeliest.**

timer 1. A person or thing that measures time: *Several volunteers served as **timers** for the race.* **2.** A device that can start or stop another mechanism at set times: *When we go away on vacation, we set **timers** to control the lights in our house.* **tim•er** (tī′mər) *noun, plural* **timers.**

timetable A schedule that shows at what time certain events are to take place. Timetables are used to show arrivals and departures of buses and trains. **time•table** (tīm′tā′bəl) *noun, plural* **timetables.**

time zone A region in which all the clocks are set to the same time. There are seven time zones in the United States and Canada, including those for Alaska and Hawaii.

timid Easily frightened; lacking courage or boldness; shy: *The **timid** child was afraid to speak up in class.* **tim•id** (tim′id) *adjective.*

tin 1. A soft, silver-white metal that does not rust easily. It is used to coat steel cans. Tin is a chemical element. **2.** A can or other container that is made of a metal coated with tin. *Noun.*

○ Made out of tin or a metal coated with tin: *Food is preserved in **tin** cans. Adjective.*

tin (tin) *noun, plural* **tins;** *adjective.*

tinfoil A very thin, flexible sheet of tin or aluminum that is used as a wrapping. **tin•foil** (tin′foil′) *noun.*

tinge A small amount, as of a color or quality: *blue with a **tinge** of green; a **tinge** of sadness in her voice. Noun.*

○ **1.** To color slightly: *cheeks **tinged** pink from the cold.* **2.** To affect slightly: *His words seemed **tinged** with jealousy. Verb.*

tinge (tinj) *noun, plural* **tinges;** *verb,* **tinged, tingeing** or **tinging.**

tingle To have a slight stinging feeling: *The skater's face **tingled** from the cold. Verb.*

○ A slight stinging feeling: *a **tingle** of excitement. Noun.*

tin•gle (ting′gəl) *verb,* **tingled, tingling;** *noun, plural* **tingles.**

tinkle To make a light, ringing sound: *The chimes **tinkled** in the wind. Verb.*

○ A light, ringing sound: *We heard the **tinkle** of sleigh bells in the distance. Noun.*

tin•kle (ting′kəl) *verb,* **tinkled, tinkling;** *noun, plural* **tinkles.**

tint A shade of a color: *We added a little red to white paint to get a pink **tint.** Noun.*

○ To give a slight color to: *The windows on our new car are **tinted.** Verb.*

tint (tint) *noun, plural* **tints;** *verb,* **tinted, tinting.**

tiny Very small: *Babies' hands are **tiny.** ti•ny** (tī′nē) *adjective,* **tinier, tiniest.**

tip¹ The end part or point: *the **tips** of the fingers; the **tip** of an iceberg.* **tip** (tip) *noun, plural* **tips.**

tip² 1. To raise one end or side of; tilt: *I **tipped** the bowl slightly to get out the last few drops of soup.* **2.** To knock or turn over: *My aunt accidentally **tipped** over her glass.* **3.** To raise or touch as a greeting: *Grandfather **tips** his hat to friends he meets on the street.* **tip** (tip) *verb,* **tipped, tipping.**

PRONUNCIATION KEY:

| at | āpe | fär | câre | end | mē | it | īce | pîerce | hot | ōld | sông | fôrk |
| oil | out | up | ūse | rüle | pull | tûrn | chin | sing | shop | thin | this | |

hw in white; zh in treasure. The symbol ə stands for the unstressed vowel sound in about, taken, pencil, lemon, and circus.

755

tip³ **1.** An extra sum of money that is given as a way of thanking someone for good service: *We gave our newspaper carrier a tip.* **2.** A piece of useful information: *The mechanic gave us a tip about the care of our new car. Noun.*

○ **1.** To give an extra sum of money as a way of thanking someone for good service: *We paid our bill, tipped the waiter, and left the restaurant.* **2.** To give a piece of useful information to: *Someone tipped off the police about the gang's plan. Verb.*

tip (tip) *noun, plural* **tips;** *verb,* **tipped, tipping.**

tiptoe To walk quietly on or as if on the tips of one's toes: *I tiptoed out of the room so I wouldn't wake the baby.* **tip·toe** (tip′tō′) *verb,* **tiptoed, tiptoeing.**

tire¹ **1.** To make or become weak from too much work or use: *The long walk tired us. Sick people tire easily.* **2.** To lose or cause to lose interest; bore or become bored: *The long lecture tired the audience.* **tire** (tīr) *verb,* **tired, tiring.**

tire² A band of rubber that fits around a wheel of a vehicle, such as a car or bicycle. Most tires are filled with air. **tire** (tīr) *noun, plural* **tires.**

Some tires are enormous.

tissue **1.** A group of cells in a plant or animal that are similar in form and in function. The bark that protects a tree is a kind of plant tissue. In animals, the nervous tissue sends messages from the brain to other parts of the body. **2.** A soft, thin paper. **tis·sue** (tish′ü) *noun, plural* **tissues.**

tissue paper A very thin paper that is used for wrapping or packing.

title **1.** The name of a book, painting, song, or other work of art. **2.** A word or group of words used to show a person's status, rank, or occupation: "Miss," "vice president," and "doctor" are titles. **3.** A championship: *Our school soccer team won the state title.* **ti·tle** (tīt′əl) *noun, plural* **titles.**

TN An abbreviation for *Tennessee.*

TNT A powerful explosive. **TNT** (te′en tē′) *noun.*

to **1.** In the direction of; toward: *Turn to the left.* **2.** On, upon, or against: *The stamp stuck to the envelope.* **3.** Into a condition of; into: *The glass was smashed to bits.* **4.** For the purpose of; for: *The police came to our aid.* **5.** Until: *The store is open from nine to six.* **6.** Earlier than; before: *It's five minutes to three.* **7.** As compared with: *Our team won by a score of three to one.* **8.** About; concerning; regarding: *What did you say to that?* **9.** A word that is used to show who receives the action of a verb: *I gave the letter to them.* **10.** A word that is used before a verb to form an infinitive: *We started to leave.*

Other words that sound like this are **too** and **two.**

to (tü *or unstressed* tü *or* tə) *preposition.*

toad An animal that looks something like a frog. A toad has rough, dry skin and spends most of its time on land rather than in water. Toads are amphibians. **toad** (tōd) *noun, plural* **toads.**

toadstool **1.** A mushroom. Many people use the word "toadstool" to mean a poisonous mushroom. **toad·stool** (tōd′stül′) *noun, plural* **toadstools.**

toast¹ Sliced bread that has been browned by heat. *Noun.*

○ **1.** To brown by heating: *We toasted marshmallows over the campfire.* **2.** To warm thoroughly: *Our guests toasted their cold feet next to the radiator. Verb.*

toast (tōst) *noun; verb,* **toasted, toasting.**

toast² The act of drinking in honor of or to the health of a person or thing: *There were several toasts to the bride and groom at the reception. Noun.*

○ To drink in honor of or to the health of: *Mother toasted Grandfather on his ninetieth birthday. Verb.*

toast (tōst) *noun, plural* **toasts;** *verb,* **toasted, toasting.**

toaster An appliance that toasts bread. **toast·er** (tōs′tər) *noun, plural* **toasters.**

tobacco A tall plant whose broad leaves are dried, chopped up, and used for chewing and for making cigarettes and cigars. **to·bac·co** (tə bak′ō) *noun, plural* **tobaccos.**

toboggan A long, flat sled without runners. A toboggan has a front end that is curled upward. It is used to travel over snow. *Noun.*

○ To ride on a toboggan: *The children*

tobogganed down the hill. Verb.
to·bog·gan (tə bog′ən) *noun, plural* **toboggans;**
verb, **tobogganed, tobogganing.**

The word **toboggan** comes from a Native American
name for this kind of sled.

today The present day or time: *Have you seen
today's newspaper? Noun.*
  ○ **1.** On or during the present day: *Do you want
to go ice skating today?* **2.** At the present time:
*Today most homes in this country have electrici-
ty. Adverb.*
to·day (tə dā′) *noun; adverb.*

toddler A child who has just learned to walk.
tod·dler (tod′lər) *noun, plural* **toddlers.**

toe **1.** One of the slender parts that stick out from
a foot. People have five toes on each foot. **2.** The
part of a sock, shoe, or stocking that covers the
toes: *The toe of my sock has a big hole in it.*
Another word that sounds like this is **tow.**
toe (tō) *noun, plural* **toes.**

tofu A soft white food made from soybeans.
Tofu is used in salads and in cooked foods.
to·fu (tō′fü) *noun.*

An orangutan mother and child stay
together while the child is young.

together **1.** With one another: *The friends walked
to school together.* **2.** Into one gathering or mass:
Mix the butter and sugar together. **3.** In agreement or cooperation: *Let's work together to solve
this problem.* **4.** Considered as a whole: *Alaska is
larger than Texas, California, and Montana
together.* **to·geth·er** (tə ge<u>th</u>′ər) *adverb.*

toil Hard and exhausting work or effort: *Planting
the vegetables was easy, but soon the toil of
weeding began. Noun.*
  ○ **1.** To do hard and exhausting work: *We toiled
for hours to clear the snow.* **2.** To move with difficulty, weariness, or pain: *The old horse toiled
up the hill. Verb.*
toil (toil) *noun; verb,* **toiled, toiling.**

toilet **1.** A bowl or box with a seat on it, used
for getting rid of body wastes. Most toilets are
filled with water that can be flushed away down
a sewer. **2.** A bathroom. **toi·let** (toi′lit) *noun,
plural* **toilets.**

token **1.** Something that is a sign of something
else; symbol: *Please accept this small gift as a
token of our appreciation.* **2.** A piece of metal
that looks like a coin and is used in place of
money: *a subway token.*
to·ken (tō′kən) *noun, plural* **tokens.**

tolerance **1.** Willingness to respect the customs,
ideas, or beliefs of others; lack of prejudice: *They
showed tolerance even though they did not agree
with me.* **2.** The ability to put up with something;
endurance: *I have a great tolerance for cold.*
tol·er·ance (tol′ər əns) *noun.*

tolerant Willing to respect or try to understand
customs, ideas, or beliefs that are different from
one's own. **tolerant** (tol′ər ənt) *adjective.*

tolerate To put up with; endure; stand: *I can't tolerate people who talk during a movie.* **tol·er·ate**
(tol′ə rāt) *verb,* **tolerated, tolerating.**

toll¹ To sound with slow, regular strokes: *Bells in
the town hall toll at noon. Verb.*
  ○ The stroke or sound of a bell tolling: *the faint
toll of distant bells. Noun.*
toll (tōl) *verb,* **tolled, tolling;** *noun, plural* **tolls.**

toll² **1.** A tax or fee paid for the right to do or use
something: *Some highways, bridges, and tunnels
charge a toll to drivers.* **2.** An amount of damage
done or lives lost: *The earthquake took a heavy
toll.* **toll** (tōl) *noun, plural* **tolls.**

tomahawk A small ax. It was once used as a tool
or weapon by certain Native Americans. It is now
used in ceremonies. **tom·a·hawk** (tom′ə hôk′)
noun, plural **tomahawks.**

tomato **1.** The round, juicy fruit of a plant. The
fruit is usually red when it is ripe and is eaten

PRONUNCIATION KEY:
at   āpe   fär   câre   end   mē   it   īce   pierce   hot   ōld   sông   fôrk
oil   out   up   ūse   rüle   pull   tûrn   chin   sing   shop   thin   <u>th</u>is
hw in white; zh in treasure. The symbol ə stands for the unstressed vowel sound in about, taken, pencil, lemon, and circus.
757

either raw or cooked. **2.** The plant that produces this fruit. **to•ma•to** (tə mā′tō *or* tə mä′tō) *noun, plural* **tomatoes.**

Many different kinds of sauces are made from tomatoes.

tomb A grave or building in which a dead body is placed. **tomb** (tüm) *noun, plural* **tombs.**

tombstone A stone that marks a grave. Tombstones often show the dead person's name and dates of birth and death. **tomb•stone** (tüm′stōn′) *noun, plural* **tombstones.**

tomorrow **1.** The day after today: *If today is Saturday, then tomorrow is Sunday.* **2.** The future: *I wonder if people will live in outer space in the world of tomorrow. Noun.*
○ On the day after today: *We are going on a trip tomorrow. Adverb.*
to•mor•row (tə môr′ō *or* tə mor′ō) *noun; adverb.*

tom-tom A small drum. Tom-toms are usually played by being beaten with the hands. **tom-tom** (tom′tom′) *noun, plural* **tom-toms.**

ton A measure of weight equal to 2,000 pounds in the United States and Canada, and 2,240 pounds in Great Britain. **ton** (tun) *noun, plural* **tons.**

tone **1.** A single sound, thought of in terms of its quality, length, pitch, or loudness: *The musician produced soft tones on the violin.* **2.** The difference in pitch between two musical notes: *The notes C and D are one tone apart.* **3.** A way of speaking or writing that shows a person's feelings or attitude: *an angry tone of voice.* **4.** The main style or character of something: *The tone of the essay was serious.* **5.** A shade of a color: *The artist used several tones of red.* **tone** (tōn) *noun, plural* **tones.**

tongs A tool used to pick up things. It usually has two movable arms. **tongs** (tongz *or* tôngz) *plural noun.*

tongue **1.** A movable piece of flesh in the mouth. It is used for tasting and swallowing. People also use their tongues to speak. **2.** An animal's tongue cooked and used as food. **3.** A language: *My mother is from Puerto Rico, and Spanish is her native tongue.* **4.** The ability to speak: *Dad was so shocked that he lost his tongue for a moment.* **5.** Something that is shaped like a tongue, such as the piece of material under the laces of a shoe.
• **hold one's tongue.** To keep quiet: *I wanted to argue but I held my tongue.*
tongue (tung) *noun, plural* **tongues.**

tonic Something that acts like a medicine to improve one's health or level of energy: *A day off was just the tonic I needed.* **ton•ic** (ton′ik) *noun, plural* **tonics.**

tonight The night of this day: *The rain should stop by tonight. Noun.*
○ On or during this night: *I am going to go to sleep early tonight. Adverb.*
to•night (tə nī′t) *noun; adverb.*

tonsil Either of two small, oval pieces of flesh in the throat at the back of the mouth. **ton•sil** (ton′səl) *noun, plural* **tonsils.**

tonsillitis An illness in which the tonsils become red, sore, and swollen. **ton•sil•li•tis** (ton′səl ī′tis) *noun.*

too **1.** In addition; also: *I love to read, but I like movies, too.* **2.** More than is needed or wanted: *That toy costs too much.* **3.** Very: *I'm not too pleased with my drawing.*
Other words that sound like this are **to** and **two.**
too (tü) *adverb.*

tool **1.** An object that is specially made to help people do work. Tools are usually held in the hand. A hammer, a saw, and a screwdriver are tools. **2.** A person or thing that is used to help someone accomplish things: *A good memory is a useful tool for learning. Noun.*
○ To work, shape, or mark with a tool or tools: *You can tool designs on leather. Verb.*
tool (tül) *noun, plural* **tools;** *verb,* **tooled, tooling.**

toolbox A box for storing or carrying tools. **tool•box** (tül′boks′) *noun, plural* **toolboxes.**

toot The short, quick noise that a horn or whistle makes. *Noun.*
○ To make or cause to make a short, quick blast of sound: *The bus driver tooted the horn. Verb.*
toot (tüt) *noun, plural* **toots;** *verb,* **tooted, tooting.**

tooth 1. One of the hard, white, bony parts in the mouth. Teeth are used for biting and chewing food and also in speaking. 2. One of a row of pointed parts that stick out from something, as on a comb or saw. **tooth** (tüth) *noun, plural* **teeth.**

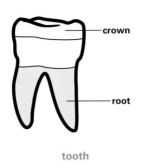

crown

root

tooth

toothache A pain in a tooth or teeth. **tooth·ache** (tüth′āk′) *noun, plural* **toothaches.**

toothbrush A small, narrow brush with a handle. It is used to clean the teeth. **tooth·brush** (tüth′brush′) *noun, plural* **toothbrushes.**

toothpaste A paste for cleaning the teeth. **tooth·paste** (tüth′pāst′) *noun, plural* **toothpastes.**

toothpick A small, narrow piece of wood or other material that is used to remove food from between the teeth. **tooth·pick** (tüth′pik′) *noun, plural* **toothpicks.**

top¹ 1. The highest or upper part of something: *A bird built a nest near the top of the tree.* 2. The highest position or rank: *That student is at the top of the class.* 3. A cover or lid: *Put the top on the bottle.* 4. A piece of clothing for the upper half of the body: *a blue skirt and a white top.* 5. The highest pitch or degree: *I shouted for help at the top of my voice. Noun.*
○ 1. Of or at the top: *the top drawer.* 2. Highest or greatest: *The drivers raced around the track at top speed. Adjective.*
top (top) *noun, plural* **tops;** *adjective.*

top² A child's toy shaped like a cone that can be made to spin on its pointed end. **top** (top) *noun, plural* **tops.**

topic What a speech, discussion, or piece of writing is about; subject: *The senator spoke on the topic of forest conservation.* **top·ic** (top′ik) *noun, plural* **topics.**

topography The shapes and forms of the land in a particular region. The topography of a region includes mountains, valleys, plains, lakes, rivers, and other features. **to·pog·ra·phy** (tə pog′rə fē) *noun, plural* **topographies.**

topple To fall or make fall forward: *The bookcase toppled over with a loud crash.* **top·ple** (top′əl) *verb,* **toppled, toppling.**

topsy-turvy 1. Upside down: *I hung topsy-turvy from the bar.* 2. In or into complete confusion or disorder: *My life turned topsy-turvy when I moved to a new city. Adverb.*
○ 1. Turned upside down: *Did you notice the topsy-turvy picture in the newspaper?* 2. Completely confused or disordered: *The store was topsy-turvy after the sale. Adjective.*
top·sy-tur·vy (top′sē tûr′vē) *adverb; adjective.*

Torah 1. In Judaism, the first five books of the Bible. 2. A scroll on which these books are written in Hebrew. **Tor·ah** (tôr′a) *noun.*

torch 1. A flaming light that can be carried in the hand. 2. A tool that has a hot flame, used to burn through or soften metal. **torch** (tôrch) *noun, plural* **torches.**

torment To cause someone great pain or suffering: *Mosquitoes tormented us all night. Verb.*
○ Great pain or suffering: *Bad burns can cause torment. Noun.*
tor·ment (tôr ment′ *for verb;* tôr′ment *for noun*) *verb,* **tormented, tormenting;** *noun, plural* **torments.**

tornado A powerful storm with winds that whirl in a dark cloud shaped like a funnel. It can cause great destruction. **tor·na·do** (tôr nā′dō) *noun, plural* **tornadoes** *or* **tornados.**

torpedo A large metal shell shaped like a cigar. It moves underwater and explodes when it hits something. *Noun.*
○ To hit with a torpedo: *The submarine torpedoed the enemy battleship. Verb.*
tor·pe·do (tôr pē′dō) *noun, plural* **torpedoes;** *verb,* **torpedoed, torpedoing.**

torrent A fast, heavy stream of water or other liquid: *When the dam broke, torrents of water flowed over the land.* **tor·rent** (tôr′ənt) *noun, plural* **torrents.**

torso The part of the human body between the neck and the legs, not including the arms. **tor·so** (tôr′sō) *noun, plural* **torsos.**

tortilla A thin, round, flat bread made from water and cornmeal. **tor·til·la** (tôr tē′yə) *noun, plural* **tortillas.**

PRONUNCIATION KEY:

at	āpe	fär	câre	end	mē	it	īce	pîerce	hot	ōld	sông	fôrk
oil	out	up	ūse	rüle	púll	tûrn	chin	sing	shop	thin	this	

hw in white; zh in treasure. The symbol ə stands for the unstressed vowel sound in about, taken, pencil, lemon, and circus.

759

WORD HISTORY

The word tortilla comes from Mexico. In Spanish, the word *tortilla* means "little round cake."

tortoise A turtle that lives on land. **tor·toise** (tôr′tǝs) *noun, plural* **tortoises.**

torture To cause severe pain or suffering to: *Nightmares of the accident* ***tortured*** *the survivors. Verb.*
○ **1.** The act of causing severe pain, especially as a punishment or as a way of forcing someone to do something. **2.** A cause of great pain or suffering: *Wearing the tight shoes was* ***torture***. *Noun.*
tor·ture (tôr′chǝr) *verb,* **tortured, torturing;** *noun.*

toss **1.** To throw lightly into or through the air: *Please* ***toss*** *me a towel.* **2.** To move back and forth: *The waves* ***tossed*** *the little boat.* **3.** To throw a coin into the air in order to decide something depending on which side lands face up: *Neither of us wanted to wash the dishes, so we* ***tossed*** *for it. Verb.*
○ A throw: *We decided which team was going to bat first by a* ***toss*** *of a coin. Noun.*
toss (tôs) *verb,* **tossed, tossing;** *noun, plural* **tosses.**

SYNONYMS

toss, throw, hurl, pitch
*She casually **tossed** the paper into the wastebasket. The campers **threw** water on the fire to put it out. The rocket **hurled** the satellite into space. Players were in the park, **pitching** the ball back and forth to each other.*

tot A young child. **tot** (tot) *noun, plural* **tots.**

total **1.** Being all there is; making up the whole; entire: *the* ***total*** *amount of the bill.* **2.** Complete; utter: *a* ***total*** *failure. Adjective.*
○ The whole amount: *My expenses came to a* ***total*** *of seventy dollars. Noun.*
○ **1.** To find the sum of; add up: *I* ***totaled*** *the long column of numbers.* **2.** To amount to: *The bill* ***totaled*** *ten dollars. Verb.*
to·tal (tō′tǝl) *adjective; noun, plural* **totals;** *verb,* **totaled, totaling.**

totally Completely; entirely: *No one can see anything in a* ***totally*** *dark room.* **to·tal·ly** (tō′tǝ lē) *adverb.*

tote To carry or haul: *shoppers* ***toting*** *their packages home.* **tote** (tōt) *verb,* **toted, toting.**

totem An animal, plant, or object that is the symbol of a family or a clan. Certain Native American peoples carved these symbols on poles that stood outside their homes. **to·tem** (tō′tǝm) *noun, plural* **totems.**

totem pole A pole carved or painted with symbols that are called totems.

totter **1.** To rock or sway as if about to fall: *The child's tower of blocks* ***tottered*** *and fell.* **2.** To walk unsteadily: *Children* ***totter*** *when they first learn to walk.* **tot·ter** (tô′tǝr) *verb,* **tottered, tottering.**

toucan A bird that has a heavy body, a very large beak, and colorful feathers. Toucans are found in tropical America. **tou·can** (tü′kan) *noun, plural* **toucans.**

Toucans use their beaks to eat fruits.

touch **1.** To put a hand or other part of the body on or against something: *I* ***touched*** *the hot stove and burned my finger.* **2.** To bring something against something else: *I* ***touched*** *a match to the candle.* **3.** To come or be in contact: *Our hands* ***touched***. **4.** To affect a person's feelings or emotions; move: *I was* ***touched*** *by his kind words. Verb.*
○ **1.** The sense by which a person becomes aware of things by putting a part of the body on or against them: *People can often recognize objects by* ***touch***, *even without seeing them.* **2.** The act of touching: *The balloon burst at the* ***touch*** *of a pin.* **3.** A small amount; little bit: *The salad needs a* ***touch*** *of pepper.* **4.** Communication between people: *My best friend and I keep in* ***touch*** *by telephone. Noun.*
touch (tuch) *verb,* **touched, touching;** *noun, plural* **touches.**

touchdown 1. A score made in football by carrying the ball across the other team's goal line. 2. The act or moment of landing an aircraft or spacecraft. **touch·down** (tuch′doun′) *noun, plural* **touchdowns.**

touchy Easily annoyed or offended: *She's touchy about her bad spelling, so be careful what you say.* **touch·y** (tüch′ē) *adjective,* **touchier, touchiest.**

tough 1. Not easy to break, cut, or damage; strong: *Canvas is a tough cloth.* 2. Able to put up with difficulty, strain, or hardship: *The pioneers had to be tough.* 3. Rough; violent: *a tough gang.* 4. Hard to deal with or do; demanding: *a tough job.* 5. Not giving in easily; stubborn: *This cleaning fluid removes the toughest stains.* **tough** (tuf) *adjective,* **tougher, toughest.**

tour A trip or journey in which many places are visited or many things are seen. *Noun.*
○ To travel in or through a place. *Verb.*
tour (tùr) *noun, plural* **tours;** *verb,* **toured, touring.**

tourist A person who is traveling for pleasure or to learn about other places. **tour·ist** (tùr′ist) *noun, plural* **tourists.**

tournament A series of contests between two or more people or teams: *a chess tournament.* **tour·na·ment** (tùr′nə mənt *or* tôr′nə mənt) *noun, plural* **tournaments.**

tow To pull or drag behind: *The tugboat towed the barge up the river.*
Another word that sounds like this is **toe.**
tow (tō) *verb,* **towed, towing.**

toward or **towards** 1. In the direction of: *I ran toward the house.* 2. In regard to; concerning; about: *kindness towards other people.* 3. Near in time; shortly before: *The snow stopped toward morning.* **to·ward** or **to·wards** (tə wôrd′ *or* tôrd; tə wôrdz′ *or* tôrdz) *preposition.*

towel A piece of paper or cloth that is used for wiping or drying something. *Noun.*
○ To wipe or dry with a towel: *The swimmers toweled off quickly. Verb.*
tow·el (touə′l) *noun, plural* **towels;** *verb,* **toweled, toweling.**

tower A tall, narrow building or structure: *a fire tower. Noun.*
○ To rise high up in the air: *The skyscraper tow-ered above the city. Verb.*
tow·er (tou′ər) *noun, plural* **towers;** *verb,* **towered, towering.**

town An area with buildings where people live and work. It is usually larger than a village but smaller than a city. **town** (toun) *noun, plural* **towns.**

A tower often adds to the beauty of a building.

toxic Relating to or caused by a poison; poisonous: *Those factories no longer dump toxic wastes in the river.* **tox·ic** (tok′sik) *adjective.*

toy Something for a person to play with. A doll, a kite, and a ball are toys. *Noun.*
○ To handle in a careless way: *I was nervous and toyed with the button on my jacket. Verb.*
toy (toi) *noun, plural* **toys;** *verb* **toyed, toying.**

trace A small bit or sign left behind showing that something was there: *Archaeologists dug up traces of an old village. Noun.*
○ 1. To follow the trail, course, or path of: *The explorers traced the river to its source.* 2. To copy by following lines seen through a piece of thin paper: *I traced the map so that my copy would be exact.* 3. To study or describe thoroughly, step by step: *The book traces the history of science. Verb.*
trace (trās) *noun, plural* **traces;** *verb,* **traced, tracing.**

track 1. A mark or marks left by a person, animal, or object as it moves over a surface: *deer tracks in the snow; tire tracks on the road.* 2. A path, race course, or other trail: *The horses raced around the track.* 3. A group of sports events held at a running track; track and field. 4. A set of rails on which trains move. *Noun.*
○ 1. To follow the marks, path, or course of: *The

Huge screens are used to show the track of a space flight.

PRONUNCIATION KEY:
| at | āpe | fär | câre | end | mē | it | īce | pîerce | hot | ōld | sông | fôrk |
| oil | out | up | ūse | rüle | pùll | tûrn | chin | sing | shop | thin | <u>th</u>is | |

hw in white; zh in treasure. The symbol ə stands for the unstressed vowel sound in about, taken, pencil, lemon, and circus.

761

dogs *tracked* the fox. *The scientists **tracked** the flight of the missile on their radar screens.* **2.** To make marks on something: *I **tracked** mud on the carpet. Verb.*

track (trak) *noun, plural* **tracks;** *verb,* **tracked, tracking.**

track and field A group of sports events that includes running, jumping, and throwing contests.

tract **1.** A piece of land; area: *a **tract** of wooded land for sale.* **2.** A group of parts or organs in the body that work together: *The stomach and the intestines are part of the digestive **tract**.* **tract** (trakt) *noun, plural* **tracts.**

traction The grip that a moving object has on a surface. Traction keeps a car wheel or a rock climber's shoe from slipping. **trac·tion** (trak'shən) *noun.*

tractor A vehicle with heavy tires or tracks. Tractors are used to pull heavy loads over rough ground. **trac·tor** (trak'tər) *noun, plural* **tractors.**

A **tractor** is one of the most useful pieces of farm machinery.

trade **1.** The business of buying and selling goods; commerce: *foreign **trade**.* **2.** The giving of one thing in return for something else: *The farmers made a **trade** of milk for eggs.* **3.** A kind of job or work: *I hope to work in the building **trade**. Noun.*
○ **1.** To buy or sell as a business: *At the stock exchange, people **trade** in stocks and bonds.* **2.** To give one thing in return for something else: *I'll **trade** you these three baseball cards for those two of yours. Verb.*

trade (trād) *noun, plural* **trades;** *verb,* **traded, trading.**

trademark A picture, word, or mark that a manufacturing company uses on its product. Only a trademark's owner may use it legally. **trade·mark** (trād'märk') *noun, plural* **trademarks.**

trader A person who buys and sells things as a business. **trad·er** (trā'dər) *noun, plural* **traders.**

trading post A store set up in a frontier region where people get food and supplies in exchange for things like hides or furs.

tradition **1.** The practice of passing down customs, beliefs, or other knowledge from parents to their children. **2.** A custom or belief that is passed on in this way. **tra·di·tion** (trə dish'ən) *noun, plural* **traditions.** —**traditional** *adjective.*

traffic **1.** Automobiles, airplanes, ships, or people moving along a route: *heavy rush hour **traffic**.* **2.** A buying and selling of goods; trade: *The police work to stop **traffic** in illegal guns. Noun.*
○ To buy or sell; deal: ***trafficking** in stolen goods. Verb.*

traf·fic (tra'fik) *noun; verb,* **trafficked, trafficking.**

tragedy **1.** A serious story or play about great misfortunes, usually with a sad ending. **2.** A sad or dreadful event; disaster: *The explosion in the coal mine was a great **tragedy**.* **trag·e·dy** (traj'i dē) *noun, plural* **tragedies.**

tragic **1.** Relating to serious stories about great misfortunes: *A **tragic** hero is a great person who fails or dies in a noble way.* **2.** Very sad or dreadful: *a **tragic** accident.* **trag·ic** (traj'ik) *adjective.*

trail **1.** A path through an area that is wild or not lived in: *a **trail** through the woods.* **2.** A mark, scent, or path made by a person or animal: *The hunters followed the bear's **trail**.* **3.** Something that follows along behind: *The jet left a **trail** of smoke in the sky. Noun.*
○ **1.** To follow behind: *The children **trailed** the parade.* **2.** To follow the scent or path of: *The photographer **trailed** the deer.* **3.** To drag or be dragged behind: *My long robe **trailed** along the floor.* **4.** To be behind or losing in a game or contest: *Our team **trailed** by ten points. Verb.*

trail (trāl) *noun, plural* **trails;** *verb,* **trailed, trailing.**

trailer A vehicle that is pulled by a car or a truck. Some trailers are used to carry goods, and some are made for people to live in. **trail·er** (trā'lər) *noun, plural* **trailers.**

train **1.** A line of railroad cars connected together. Some trains carry passengers; other trains carry only freight. **2.** A group of people, animals, or vehicles traveling together in a long line: *A **train** of mules carried supplies.* **3.** A connected series of events, ideas, or parts:

a writer's **train** *of thought.* **4.** A part of a dress or robe that trails on the ground behind the person who wears it: *The bride's gown had a long* **train.** *Noun.*

○ **1.** To teach to behave, think, or grow up in a certain way; bring up: *She* **trained** *her children to respect others.* **2.** To teach how to do something; instruct: **train** *a dog.* **3.** To get ready for something by practicing, exercising, or learning how: *Boxers have to* **train.** **4.** To make something grow or go a certain way: *We* **trained** *the vine to cover the fence. Verb.*

train (trān) *noun, plural* **trains;** *verb,* **trained, training.**

trainer 1. A person who trains, as one who trains a pet to behave. **2.** A person who helps athletes train to compete. **train·er** (trā′nər) *noun, plural* **trainers.**

This animal trainer **is teaching dolphins to do tricks.**

trait A quality of a person or animal; characteristic: *Bravery is a necessary* **trait** *for a firefighter.* **trait** (trāt) *noun, plural* **traits.**

traitor A person who does something to harm his or her own country or friends; one who betrays a group or cause: *The* **traitors** *gave secrets to the enemy.* **trai·tor** (trā′tər) *noun, plural* **traitors.**

tramp **1.** To walk or step heavily: *Don't* **tramp** *on the flowers!* **2.** To travel on foot; walk or hike: *hikers* **tramping** *through the woods. Verb.*

○ **1.** A person who wanders from place to place and has no home or job. **2.** The sound of a heavy

step: *the* **tramp** *of soldiers marching. Noun.* **tramp** (tramp) *verb,* **tramped, tramping;** *noun, plural* **tramps.**

trampoline A piece of canvas attached by springs to a metal frame. People do tumbling exercises on trampolines. **tram·po·line** (tram′pə lēn′ *or* tram′pə lēn′) *noun, plural* **trampolines.**

trance A condition during which a person is conscious but is not aware what is going on in the immediate surroundings. A trance can be brought

Gymnasts practice their moves on trampolines.

about by hypnosis, shock, or drugs. **trance** (trans) *noun,* **trances.**

tranquil Free from noise or disturbance; calm; peaceful: *a* **tranquil** *pond.* **tran·quil** (trang′kwəl) *adjective.*

trans- A prefix that means across, beyond, or through: **Transatlantic** *means across or beyond the Atlantic.*

transaction The act of carrying out a business exchange: *I have several* **transactions** *to make at the bank.* **trans·ac·tion** (tran zak′shən) *noun, plural* **transactions.**

transatlantic **1.** On or from the other side of the Atlantic Ocean: *the company's* **transatlantic** *customers.* **2.** Crossing the Atlantic Ocean: *a* **transatlantic** *flight.* **trans·at·lan·tic** (tran′zət lan′tik) *adjective.*

transcontinental Crossing a continent: *a* **transcontinental** *phone call.* **trans·con·ti·nen·tal** (tranz′kon tə nen′təl) *adjective.*

transfer To move from one person or place to another: *Next year we have to* **transfer** *to a new school. Verb.*

○ **1.** A move from one person or place to another: *The secretary got a* **transfer** *to the company's main office.* **2.** A ticket that lets a person change from one bus, train, or plane to another without

PRONUNCIATION KEY:
at   āpe   fär   câre   end   mē   it   īce   pierce   hot   ōld   sông   fôrk
oil   out   up   ūse   rüle   pu̇ll   tûrn   chin   sing   shop   thin   this
hw in white; zh in treasure. The symbol ə stands for the unstressed vowel sound in about, taken, pencil, lemon, and circus.

763

paying more money. *Noun.*

trans·fer (trans fûʹ *or* transʹfər *for verb;* tranʹsfər *for noun*) *verb,* **transferred, transferring;** *noun,* *plural* **transfers.**

transfusion The transfer of one person's blood to another person. **trans·fu·sion** (trans fūʹzhən) *noun, plural* **transfusions.**

transistor A very small electronic device that controls the electric current in television sets, radios, computers, and other equipment. **tran·sis·tor** (tranz isʹtər) *noun, plural* **transistors.**

transit 1. The act of passing across or through; movement from one place to another: *the sun's transit across the sky.* 2. The act of carrying things from one place to another: *damaged in transit.* 3. A system for carrying passengers on subways, buses, and other public vehicles. **trans·it** (tranʹsit *or* tranʹzit) *noun, plural* **transits.**

transitive verb A verb that has a direct object. In the sentence "I put jam on the bread," "put" is a transitive verb and "jam" is its direct object. **tran·si·tive verb** (transʹit iv *or* tranʹzi tiv)

translate To say in or change into another language: *translate a story from English to French.* **trans·late** (trans lātʹ) *verb,* **translated, translating.**

translation A changing of a speech or piece of writing into another language. **trans·la·tion** (trans lāʹshən) *noun, plural* **translations.**

translucent Allowing some light to pass through: *The frosted glass is translucent.* **trans·lu·cent** (trans lüʹsənt) *adjective.*

transmission 1. The act of sending or passing from one person or place to another: *Insects cause the transmission of some diseases.* 2. The broadcasting of radio or television waves. 3. A series of gears in an automobile that causes power to be transferred from the engine to the wheels. **trans·mis·sion** (trans mishʹən) *noun, plural* **transmissions.**

transmit 1. To send, pass, or cause to go from one person or place to another: *A telegraph system transmits messages across long distances.* 2. To send out signals by radio or television: *That station transmits the news twenty-four hours a day.* **trans·mit** (trans mitʹ) *verb,* **transmitted, transmitting.**

transmitter A device that sends out radio or television signals. **trans·mit·ter** (trans mitʹər) *noun, plural* **transmitters.**

transom A small window above a door or another window. **tran·som** (tranʹsəm) *noun, plural* **transoms.**

transparent 1. Allowing light to pass through so that things on the other side can be clearly seen: *The lenses in eyeglasses are transparent.* 2. Easy to understand; obvious: *That excuse is a transparent lie.* **trans·par·ent** (trans pârʹənt *or* trans parʹənt) *adjective.*

transpiration The passage of water through a plant from the roots to the atmosphere. **trans·pir·a·tion** (trants pə rā shən) *noun.*

transplant 1. To take from one place and put in another: *transplant a bush.* 2. To transfer skin or an organ from one person or animal to another. *Verb.*
○ The act of transplanting: *The surgeon performed a heart transplant. Noun.*
trans·plant (trans plantʹ *for verb;* transʹplantʹ *for noun*) *verb,* **transplanted, transplanting;** *noun,* *plural* **transplants.**

transport To bring or carry from one place to another: *The new cars were transported by ship. Verb.*
○ 1. The act of transporting: *the transport of vegetables from farms to markets.* 2. A ship or airplane used to carry people or freight. *Noun.*
trans·port (trans pôrtʹ *for verb;* trans pôrtʹ *for noun*) *verb,* **transported, transporting;** *noun,* *plural* **transports.**

transportation The act or means of carrying or moving something from one place to another: *A bicycle provides my transportation to school.* **trans·por·ta·tion** (transʹpər tāʹshən) *noun.*

In San Francisco special vehicles called cable cars are used for transportation.

trap 1. A device that catches animals that step into or on it. 2. A trick used to catch a person or get a person to do something not intended: *The lawyer's question was a trap for the witness. Noun.*
○ To catch in a trap: *The hunter trapped the tiger. Verb.*

trap (trap) *noun, plural* **traps**; *verb*, **trapped**, **trapping**.

trapdoor A door in a ceiling or floor. **trap·door** (trap′dôr′) *noun, plural* **trapdoors**.

trapeze A short bar hung between two ropes, used by acrobats. **tra·peze** (tra pēz′) *noun, plural* **trapezes**.

trapezoid A flat figure with four sides. Only two of the sides are parallel. **trap·e·zoid** (trap′ə zoid) *noun, plural* **trapezoids**.

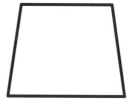

trapezoid

trapper A person who traps wild animals for their fur. **trap·per** (trap′ər) *noun, plural* **trappers**.

trash Unwanted things that are to be thrown away: *We took our **trash** to the dump.* **trash** (trash) *noun.*

traumatic Deeply upsetting; shocking: *His car accident was a **traumatic** experience.* **trau·mat·ic** (trə ma′tik *or* trô ma′tik) *adjective.*

travel **1.** To go from one place to another; make a trip: *We **traveled** through England.* **2.** To pass or move from one point to another: *Sound **travels** in waves.* *Verb.*
◦ **1.** The act of traveling: *Camels are used for desert **travel**.* **2.** **travels.** A long trip or series of trips; journeys. *Noun.*
trav·el (trav′əl) *verb,* **traveled, traveling**; *noun, plural* **travels.** —**traveler** *noun.*

WORD HISTORY

The word **travel** comes from a similar English word that means "to work hard or labor." This word came from an old French word meaning both "to labor" and "to journey." The meaning of *travel* became limited to the work of getting from one place to another.

---

trawl A strong net that is shaped like a bag. Trawls are dragged slowly over the ocean bottom to catch fish. *Noun.*
◦ To fish with a trawl. *Verb.*
trawl (trôl) *noun, plural* **trawls**; *verb*, **trawled, trawling.**

tray A flat, open container with a low rim, used to carry or display things: *Waiters often carry food on large **trays**.* **tray** (trā) *noun, plural* **trays**.

treacherous **1.** Betraying one's country or friends; disloyal: *The **treacherous** soldier gave secrets to the enemy.* **2.** Full of danger; hazardous: *treacherous waters for ships.* **treach·er·ous** (trech′ə rəs) *adjective.*

treachery A breaking or betraying of trust; disloyal behavior. **treach·er·y** (trech′ə rē) *noun, plural* **treacheries.**

tread **1.** To go on foot; walk: *It felt good to **tread** the sand barefoot.* **2.** To step heavily; trample: *The dog **trod** on the flowers and broke their stems.* *Verb.*
◦ **1.** The way or sound of walking; footstep: *I heard your **tread** on the stairs.* **2.** The outer, grooved surface of a tire. **3.** The horizontal part of a step in a staircase. *Noun.*
• **tread water.** To stay upright in deep water with one's head above the surface by moving the legs as if walking.
tread (tred) *verb*, **trod, trodden** *or* **trod, treading**; *noun, plural* **treads.**

treadmill A device turned by animals or persons walking on moving steps or on a belt formed into a loop. Some treadmills produce motion to run machines; others are used for exercise. **tread·mill** (tred′mil′) *noun, plural* **treadmills.**

treason The betraying of one's country by helping an enemy: *Giving the army's battle plans to the enemy was an act of **treason**.* **trea·son** (trē′zən) *noun.*

treasure Money, jewels, or other things that are valuable: *pirate **treasure**. Noun.*
◦ To think of as being of great value or importance; cherish: *We **treasure** the memory of our grandparents. Verb.*
treas·ure (trezh′ər) *noun, plural* **treasures**; *verb*, **treasured, treasuring.**

treasurer A person responsible for taking care of the money of a club or business. **treas·ur·er** (trezhərər) *noun, plural* **treasurers.**

treasury **1.** The money or other funds of a business, government, or other group: *The club paid for a party out of its **treasury**.* **2.** Treasury. A department of the government in charge of the

PRONUNCIATION KEY:
| at | āpe | fär | câre | end | mē | it | īce | pierce | hot | ōld | sông | fôrk |
| oil | out | up | ūse | rūle | pull | tûrn | chin | sing | shop | thin | this | |

hw in white; zh in treasure. The symbol ə stands for the unstressed vowel sound in about, taken, pencil, lemon, and circus.

765

country's finances. **treas·ur·y** (trezh'ə rē) *noun, plural* **treasuries.**

treat **1.** To behave toward or deal with in a certain way: *The principal* **treated** *the student fairly.* **2.** To talk or write about; consider or discuss: *The newspaper* **treated** *the story in detail.* **3.** To give medical care to: *The doctor* **treated** *my burned hand.* **4.** To subject to a process: *You can* **treat** *cloth with a chemical to make it waterproof.* **5.** To pay for the entertainment of another person: *I will* **treat** *you to the movie. Verb.*
○ Something that is a special pleasure: *Going to the circus was a* **treat.** *Noun.*
treat (trēt) *verb,* **treated, treating;** *noun, plural* **treats.**

treatment **1.** The way something or someone is treated: *A fragile package needs careful* **treatment.** **2.** The care or medicine used to help cure a sick or injured person: *Rest was the recommended* **treatment.** **treat·ment** (trē'tmənt) *noun, plural* **treatments.**

treaty A formal agreement between countries: *A* **treaty** *was signed to end the war.* **trea·ty** (trē'tē) *noun, plural* **treaties.**

tree A plant with a single main stem or trunk that is made up of solid, woody tissue. Trees have branches and leaves at a distance above the ground. *Noun.*
○ To chase up a tree: *The dog* **treed** *the cat. Verb.*
tree (trē) *noun, plural* **trees;** *verb,* **treed, treeing.**

trek To make a long, slow journey, especially on foot: *The explorers* **trekked** *through the mountains. Verb.*
○ A long and difficult journey: *a* **trek** *across the desert. Noun.*
trek (trek) *verb,* **trekked, trekking;** *noun, plural* **treks.**

tremble **1.** To shake with cold, fear, weakness, or anger: *The wet kitten* **trembled.** **2.** To move or vibrate: *The building* **trembled** *from the explosion.* **trem·ble** (trem'bəl) *verb,* **trembled, trembling.**

tremendous Very large or great; enormous: *A* **tremendous** *clap of thunder shook the house.* **tre·men·dous** (tri men'dəs) *adjective.*

tremor A shaking or trembling: *Earthquakes cause* **tremors** *in the earth.* **trem·or** (trem'ər) *noun, plural* **tremors.**

trench A long, narrow ditch: *The soldiers fought*

from *trenches in the battlefield.* **trench** (trench) *noun, plural* **trenches.**

trend A direction or course that seems to be followed; tendency: *a* **trend** *toward higher prices.* **trend** (trend) *noun, plural* **trends.**

trespass To go on another person's property without permission. *Verb.*
○ A sin. *Noun.*
tres·pass (tres'pəs *or* tres'pas') *verb,* **trespassed, trespassing;** *noun, plural* **trespasses.**

trestle A framework used to hold up a railroad bridge or other raised structure. **tres·tle** (tres'əl) *noun, plural* **trestles.**

Most trestles **are built of iron or steel.**

tri- A prefix that means having or involving three: *A* **triangle** *is a figure with three sides.*

trial **1.** The examination of a person accused of a crime in a court of law. **2.** A trying or testing of something. **3.** A test of someone's strength, patience, or faith; hardship: *The cold winter was a* **trial** *for the Pilgrims.* **tri·al** (trī'əl) *noun, plural* **trials.**

triangle **1.** A figure or object with three sides and three angles. **2.** A musical instrument made of a metal bar bent in the shape of a triangle. A triangle sounds like a bell when it is hit. **tri·an·gle** (trī'ang'gəl) *noun, plural* **triangles.**

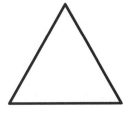

triangle

triangular Relating to or like a triangle: *The tent had a triangular shape.* **tri·an·gu·lar** (trī ang′yəl ər) *adjective.*

tribal Relating to a tribe: *tribal customs.* **trib·al** (trī′bəl) *adjective.*

tribe A group of people who have the same ancestors, social customs, and other characteristics: *There are many Native American tribes.* **tribe** (trīb) *noun, plural* **tribes.**

tributary A river or stream that flows into a larger river: *The Tennessee River is a main tributary of the Ohio River.* **trib·u·tar·y** (trib′yə terē′) *noun, plural* **tributaries.**

tribute Something done or given to show thanks or respect: *The statue was a tribute to the soldiers who had died in the war.* **trib·ute** (trib′ūt) *noun, plural* **tributes.**

triceratops A dinosaur that had a long horn over each eye, a short horn on its snout, and a bony collar over the back of its head. **tri·cer·a·tops** (trī ser′ə tops′) *noun, plural* **triceratopses.**

trick 1. An action done to fool or cheat someone: *A deliberate lie is a dirty trick.* 2. A clever or skillful act: *The magician pulled a rabbit out of a hat and did many other tricks.* 3. A joke or prank: *The boy hid to play a trick on his sister.* *Noun.*
○ To fool or cheat with a trick: *We tried to trick the teacher into letting us leave early.* *Verb.*
trick (trik) *noun, plural* **tricks;** *verb,* **tricked, tricking.**

trickle To flow or fall drop by drop or in a thin stream: *The rain trickled down the window.* *Verb.*
○ A small flow or thin stream: *a trickle of milk down the side of the carton.* *Noun.*
trick·le (trik′əl) *verb,* **trickled, trickling;** *noun, plural* **trickles.**

tricky 1. Using or marked by tricks: *The magician could do some tricky things with cards.* 2. Hard in an unexpected way; needing careful handling: *a tricky question on a test.* **trick·y** (trik′ē) *adjective,* **trickier, trickiest.**

tricycle A vehicle with two wheels in the back and one in front. It is moved by pedaling and steered with handlebars. **tri·cy·cle** (trīs′i kəl) *noun, plural* **tricycles.**

trifle Something that is small in amount or impor-

tance: *One twin is just a trifle taller than the other.* *Noun.*
○ To treat something in a careless way: *Don't trifle with the camera.* *Verb.*
tri·fle (trī′fəl) *noun, plural* **trifles;** *verb,* **trifled, trifling.**

trigger A small lever that is pulled or pressed to shoot a gun. *Noun.*
○ To start or cause something: *A spark from a campfire triggered the forest fire.* *Verb.*
trig·ger (trig′ər) *noun, plural* **triggers;** *verb,* **triggered, triggering.**

trillion One thousand times one billion; 1,000,000,000,000. **tril·lion** (tril′yən) *noun, plural* **trillions;** *adjective.*

trim 1. To cut away or remove parts to make something neat and orderly: *The man trimmed his mustache.* 2. To add ornaments or decorations to: *trim a Christmas tree.* *Verb.*
○ 1. A slight cutting to make neat: *The barber gave my hair a trim.* 2. Something that decorates or ornaments: *curtains with white lace trim.* 2. A good, fit condition: *You should exercise to keep in trim.* *Noun.*
○ Neat, tidy, or in good order: *a trim sailboat.* *Adjective.*
trim (trim) *verb,* **trimmed, trimming;** *noun, plural* **trims;** *adjective,* **trimmer, trimmest.**

trio 1. A group of three persons or things. 2. A musical piece written for three singers or musicians. **tri·o** (trē′ō) *noun, plural* **trios.**

trip The act of traveling or going from one place to another: *The bus ride was a long, slow trip.* *Noun.*
○ 1. To catch one's foot on something and stumble or fall: *I tripped on the edge of the rug.* 2. To cause someone to stumble or fall: *The wire on the floor might trip someone.* 3. To make or cause to make a mistake: *I tripped up on the third question of the test.* *Verb.*
trip (trip) *noun, plural* **trips;** *verb,* **tripped, tripping.**

triple 1. Made up of three parts: *Three movies were shown in a special triple feature.* 2. Three times as much or as many: *The capital is triple the size of our town.* *Adjective.*
○ To make or become three times as much or as many: *The population of our state tripled in ten years.* *Verb.*

PRONUNCIATION KEY:

at	āpe	fär	câre	end	mē	it	īce	pierce	hot	ōld	sông	fôrk
oil	out	up	ūse	rüle	pull	tûrn	chin	sing	shop	thin	this	

hw in white; zh in treasure. The symbol ə stands for the unstressed vowel sound in about, taken, pencil, lemon, and circus.

767

tri·ple (trip'əl) *adjective*; *verb*, **tripled, tripling.**

triplet One of three children or animals born at the same time to the same mother. **tri·plet** (trip'lit) *noun, plural* **triplets.**

tripod A stand with three legs used to hold up a telescope, camera, or some other instrument. **tri·pod** (trī'pod') *noun, plural* **tripods.**

triumph 1. A great success or victory: *The discovery of a polio vaccine was a medical triumph.* 2. Great happiness caused by success or victory: *The winners shouted in triumph. Noun.*
○ To succeed or win: *triumph over an enemy. Verb.* **tri·umph** (trī'umf) *noun, plural* **triumphs**; *verb,* **triumphed, triumphing. —triumphant** *adjective.*

trivial Of little or no importance: *trivial details.* **triv·i·al** (triv'ē əl) *adjective.*

troll¹ To fish with a line that is moving, usually by dragging it behind a moving boat. **troll** (trōl) *verb,* **trolled, trolling.**

troll² A dwarf or giant in stories who lives underground or in a cave. **troll** (trōl) *noun, plural* **trolls.**

trolley 1. A small wheel that moves along an overhead wire and picks up electricity to run a streetcar, train, or bus. 2. A streetcar that runs on tracks and gets its power from an electric wire overhead. **trol·ley** (trol'ē) *noun, plural* **trolleys.**

trombone A brass musical instrument. A trombone is made up of two long, U-shaped tubes. The pitch is changed by sliding one of the tubes back and forth. **trom·bone** (trom bōn' or trom'bōn) *noun, plural* **trombones.**

troop 1. A group of persons doing something together: *A troop of ten volunteers cleaned the park.* 2. troops. Soldiers: *The enemy troops surrendered. Noun.*
○ To walk or march in a group: *The students trooped into the classroom. Verb.* **troop** (trüp) *noun, plural* **troops**; *verb,* **trooped, trooping.**

trooper A police officer: *The state trooper patrolled the highway.* **troop·er** (trüp'ər) *noun, plural* **troopers.**

trophy A cup, small statue, or other prize given to someone for winning a contest or race or doing something outstanding. **tro·phy** (trō'fē) *noun, plural* **trophies.**

tropical Relating to or found in the tropics. **trop·i·cal** (trop'i kəl) *adjective.*

tropics A region of the earth that is near the equator. It is always warm in the tropics. **trop·ics** (trop'iks) *plural noun.*

trot 1. The gait of an animal that is faster than a walk: *In a graceful trot, the horse circled the ring.* 2. A slow run; jog: *I headed for school at a trot. Noun.*
○ 1. To move or ride at a trot: *The horse trotted toward the stable.* 2. To run slowly; jog: *The little children trotted after the grown-ups. Verb.* **trot** (trot) *noun, plural* **trots**; *verb,* **trotted, trotting.**

trouble 1. A difficult or dangerous situation: *The town will be in trouble if the dam breaks.* 2. Extra work or effort: *They went to a lot of trouble to make a fine dinner.* 3. A cause of difficulty: *The trouble with your plan is that it costs too much. Noun.*
○ 1. To disturb or make uncomfortable: *Does your headache still trouble you?* 2. To cause someone to make an extra effort: *May I trouble you for a glass of water? Verb.* **trou·ble** (trub'əl) *noun, plural* **troubles**; *verb,* **troubled, troubling.**

trousers A piece of clothing that reaches from the waist to the ankles and covers each leg separately; pants. **trou·sers** (trouzərz) *plural noun.*

trout A fish that lives in fresh water. Some trout have speckles on their bodies. **trout** (trout) *noun, plural* **trout** or **trouts.**

trowel 1. A tool with a flat blade that is used for spreading and smoothing wet plaster, cement, or a similar substance. 2. A tool that is shaped like a small scoop. It is used for digging. **trow·el** (trou'əl) *noun, plural* **trowels.**

truant A student who is absent from school without permission. **tru·ant** (trü'ənt) *noun, plural* **truants.**

truce A short stop in fighting. A truce is agreed to by both sides, who then sometimes try to reach a peace agreement. **truce** (trüs) *noun, plural* **truces.**

WORD HISTORY

The word **truce** comes from a Middle English word meaning "agreement." The Middle English word comes from an Old English word meaning "true" or "faithful." In a truce, both sides must be faithful to their agreement.

---

truck A large motor vehicle that is made to carry heavy loads. Some trucks are open in the back and some are closed. *Noun.*

○ To move something by truck: *A moving company* **trucked** *our furniture to our new house. Verb.*
truck (truk) *noun, plural* **trucks**; *verb,* **trucked**, **trucking**.

trudge To walk slowly and with effort: *The tired hikers* **trudged** *up the hill. Verb.*

○ A slow, tiring walk: *The campers had a long* **trudge** *back to their camp. Noun.*
trudge (truj) *verb,* **trudged**, **trudging**; *noun, plural* **trudges**.

true **1.** Agreeing with the facts; not false, wrong, or made-up: *The movie was based on a true story.* **2.** Faithful to someone or something; loyal: *a* **true** *friend.* **3.** Genuine; real: *The koala is not a* **true** *bear.* **true** (trü) *adjective,* **truer**, **truest**.

trumpet **1.** A brass musical instrument. A trumpet is made up of a long tube coiled into a loop with a flared end. **2.** A sound like the sound made with a trumpet: *The cry of an elephant is called a* **trumpet**. *Noun.*

○ To make a sound like a trumpet: *The elephant* **trumpeted** *loudly. Verb.*
trum·pet (trumpit) *noun, plural* **trumpets**; *verb,* **trumpeted**, **trumpeting**.

trunk **1.** The main stem of a tree. The branches grow out from the trunk. **2.** A large, sturdy box used for carrying and storing things. **3.** The covered space in an automobile where things are stored and carried. **4.** The long snout of an elephant. **5.** trunks. Short pants: *men's swim* **trunks**. **6.** The main part of the human body, apart from the legs, arms, and head; torso. **trunk** (trungk) *noun, plural* **trunks**.

trust **1.** To believe to be true, honest, or reliable: *We should not have* **trusted** *the weather report.* **2.** To feel sure; hope or expect confidently: *I* **trust** *that you will enjoy this movie. Verb.*

○ **1.** A belief that someone or something is true, honest, or reliable; confidence: *I have complete* **trust** *in your abilities.* **2.** The care or keeping of someone or something: *He left his dog in my* **trust** *for the week. Noun.* **trust** (trust) *verb,* **trusted**, **trusting**; *noun.*

trustworthy Able to be trusted; reliable: *I told*

my secret to a **trustworthy** *friend.* **trust·wor·thy** (trust'wûr'thē) *adjective.*

truth **1.** Something that is true: *You must tell the* **truth**. **2.** The quality of being true, honest, or sincere: *There was* **truth** *in my friend's criticism of me.* **truth** (trüth) *noun, plural* **truths**.

truthful Telling the truth: *a* **truthful** *answer.* **truth·ful** (trüth'fəl) *adjective.*

try **1.** To make an effort to do something; attempt: *Please* **try** *not to be late.* **2.** To make a test of: **Try** *the bicycle's brakes before you start down the hill.* **3.** To examine a person accused of a crime in a court of law: *The man was* **tried** *for robbery and found guilty.* **4.** To put a strain on; tax: *The long wait* **tried** *my patience. Verb.*

○ An effort or attempt: *I hit the target with an arrow on my third* **try**. *Noun.*

  • **to try on.** To put on to test the fit or appearance: **try on** *shoes in a store.*

  • **to try out.** **1.** To demonstrate one's skill or ability in order to show that one is suitable or fit: *Are you going* **to try out** *for the basketball team?* **2.** To test: *My parents* **tried** *out the new car before they bought it.*
try (trī) *verb,* **tried**, **trying**; *noun, plural* **tries**.

T-shirt A light, knit undershirt or outer shirt with short sleeves and no collar. This word is sometimes spelled tee shirt. **T-shirt** (tē'shûrt') *noun, plural* **T-shirts**.

tsp. An abbreviation for *teaspoon.*

tub **1.** A large open container used for taking a bath; bathtub. **2.** A round container used to hold butter, honey, or other foods. **tub** (tub) *noun, plural* **tubs**.

tuba A very large brass musical instrument that has a deep, mellow tone. **tu·ba** (tü'bə *or* tū'bə) *noun, plural* **tubas**.

tube **1.** A hollow piece of glass, rubber, plastic, or metal in the shape of a long or curved pipe, used especially to carry liquids or gases.

Rubber tubes are often used for floating.

PRONUNCIATION KEY:

| at | āpe | fär | câre | end | mē | it | īce | pierce | hot | ōld | sông | fôrk |
| oil | out | up | ūse | rüle | püll | tûrn | chin | sing | shop | thin | this | |

hw in white; zh in treasure. The symbol ə stands for the unstressed vowel sound in about, taken, pencil, lemon, and circus.

769

2. Something that is like a tube in shape or use. A tunnel is a tube. **3.** A container of soft metal or plastic from which the contents are removed by squeezing: *a **tube** of toothpaste.* **tube** (tüb *or* tūb) *noun, plural* **tubes.**

tuber A thick underground stem of a plant, such as a potato. **tu·ber** (tü′bər) *noun, plural* **tubers.**

tuck **1.** To push or fold the edge or ends of something in place: *I **tucked** my shirt in.* **2.** To put into a hidden, safe, or covered space: *There is a wasp's nest **tucked** under the eaves.* *Verb.*
○ A fold sewed in a piece of clothing to make it fit better or to decorate it: *Let's make a **tuck** in the waist of the coat.* *Noun.*
tuck (tuk) *verb,* **tucked, tucking;** *noun, plural* **tucks.**

Tues. An abbreviation for *Tuesday.*

Tuesday The third day of the week. **Tues·day** (tüz′dē *or* tüz′dā *or* tūz′dē *or* tūz′dā) *noun, plural* **Tuesdays.**

WORD HISTORY

Tuesday comes from the Old English word meaning "Tiw's day." Tiw was the pagan English god of war.

---

tuft A bunch of hair, grass, threads, or other things that grows or is fastened together at one end and is loose at the other: *The bird had a **tuft** of feathers on its head.* **tuft** (tuft) *noun, plural* **tufts.**

tug To give a pull on something: *The little child **tugged** at my sleeve to get my attention.* *Verb.*
○ A hard pull: *Suddenly I felt a **tug** on the fishing line.* *Noun.*
tug (tug) *verb,* **tugged, tugging;** *noun, plural* **tugs.**

tugboat A small, powerful boat that is used to push or pull barges and other boats: *The **tugboat** guided the ocean liner into its berth.* **tug·boat** (tug′bōt′) *noun, plural* **tugboats.**

tulip A flower that is shaped like a cup. The plant that it grows on is also called a tulip. **tu·lip** (tü′lip *or* tū′lip) *noun, plural* **tulips.**

Tulips grow from bulbs.

tumble **1.** To fall in a helpless or clumsy way: *When our sled tipped over, we **tumbled** down the icy hill.* **2.** To roll or toss about: *We could hear the pail **tumbling** around in the trunk of the car.* **3.** To do somersaults, handsprings, or similar feats. *Verb.*
○ A fall: *The skater slipped on the ice and took a **tumble**.* *Noun.*
tum·ble (tum′bəl) *verb,* **tumbled, tumbling;** *noun, plural* **tumbles.**

tumbleweed A bushy plant that grows in the deserts and plains of western North America. In the autumn, the tumbleweed breaks off from its roots and is blown about by the wind. **tum·ble·weed** (tum′bəl wēd′) *noun, plural* **tumbleweeds.**

tumor A group of cells in the body that grow much faster than normal cells. **tu·mor** (tü′mər *or* tū′mər) *noun, plural* **tumors.**

tuna A large fish found in warm seas all over the world. It is used for food. **tu·na** (tü′nə) *noun, plural* **tuna** *or* **tunas.**

tundra A huge plain with no trees that lies in arctic regions. **tun·dra** (tun′drə) *noun, plural* **tundras.**

tune **1.** A series of musical tones that form a pleasing, easily remembered unit; melody: *We hummed the **tune** when we couldn't remember the words.* **2.** A song: *The band played popular **tunes**.* **3.** The right pitch or key: *The old piano was out of **tune**.* **4.** Agreement or harmony: *The speaker's opinions were not in **tune** with modern ideas.* *Noun.*
○ To adjust a musical instrument so that it plays notes of the right pitch: *I learned how to **tune** my guitar.* *Verb.*
tune (tün *or* tūn) *noun, plural* **tunes;** *verb,* **tuned, tuning.**

tunic **1.** A piece of clothing that looks like a shirt and reaches to the knees. **2.** A short jacket that fits closely. Tunics are often worn as part of a military or police uniform. **tu·nic** (tü′nik *or* tū′nik) *noun, plural* **tunics.**

tunnel A long passage built underneath the ground or water or through a mountain: *a traffic **tunnel** under the river.* *Noun.*
○ To make a tunnel under or through something: *The dog **tunneled** under the fence.* *Verb.*
tun·nel (tun′əl) *noun, plural* **tunnels;** *verb,* **tunneled, tunneling.**

turban A long scarf that is wound around the

head and worn like a hat. **tur·ban** (tûr′bən) *noun,* *plural* **turbans.**

turf The surface layer of the soil, including the tangled plant roots that make it like a mat. **turf** (tûrf) *noun.*

turkey A large North American bird with black and brown feathers and a tail shaped like a fan. **tur·key** (tûr′kē) *noun, plural* **turkeys.**

A turkey can fly short distances.

Turkey A country partly in western Asia and partly in southeastern Europe. **Tur·key** (tûr′kē) *noun.*

Turkish The language of Turkey. *Noun.*
○ Relating to Turkey, its people, or their language. *Adjective.*
Turk·ish (tûr′kish) *noun; adjective.*

turmoil Great confusion or disorder: *The airport was in turmoil during the snowstorm.* **tur·moil** (tûr′moil) *noun.*

turn **1.** To move or cause to move around in a circle or part of a circle; rotate or revolve: *The earth turns. I turned the key in the lock. Power from the car engine turns the wheels.* **2.** To go or make go a certain or different way: *Turn left at the corner. Turn the pancakes over. Let's turn to the next question.* **3.** To change or cause to change in nature or condition: *Leaves turn brown in the fall. In the fairy tale, the frog turned into a prince.* **4.** To have or cause to have different feelings: *Our neighbors turned against us when our dog kept chasing their cat.* **5.** To make or become sick: *My stomach turned when the roller coaster went down the big hill. Verb.*

○ **1.** A movement around in a circle or part of a circle: *I had to make a quick turn to catch the ball.* **2.** A change in position or direction: *Make a left turn. There is a sharp turn in the road ahead.* **3.** A time, occasion, or chance at something: *It's the pitcher's turn at bat. Noun.*

• **to turn in**. **1.** To turn and go in; enter: *Turn in at the next driveway.* **2.** To give or return: *We turned in our homework.* **3.** To go to bed: *I think I'll turn in early tonight.*

• **to turn off**. To cause to stop flowing or operating: *Please turn off the water.*

• **to turn on**. To cause to flow or to operate: *Turn on the lamp .*

• **to turn out**. **1.** To produce: *The machine turns out fifty copies per minute.* **2.** To come; assemble; show up: *A large crowd turned out for the game.* **3.** To end or result: *How did the movie turn out?* **4.** To cause to stop operating: *Turn out the lights before you leave.*

turn (tûrn) *verb,* **turned, turning**; *noun, plural* **turns.**

turnip A round, white or yellow vegetable that is the root of a certain plant. **tur·nip** (tûr′nip) *noun, plural* **turnips.**

turnpike A highway with more than two lanes and no intersections or stoplights. Turnpikes are used for fast travel between cities. **turn·pike** (tûrn′pīk′) *noun, plural* **turnpikes.**

turnstile A revolving gate or movable bar at an exit or entrance. People pass through a turnstile one at a time. **turn·stile** (tûrn′stīl′) *noun, plural* **turnstiles.**

turntable A round platform that turns things around. Phonographs have turntables that turn the records. **turn·table** (tûrn′tābəl′) *noun, plural* **turntables.**

turpentine A liquid that is mixed with paints and other substances to make them thinner. **tur·pen·tine** (tûr′pən tīn′) *noun.*

turquoise **1.** A greenish blue mineral used as a gem. **2.** A greenish blue color. *Noun.*
○ Having the color turquoise. *Adjective.*
tur·quoise (tûr′kwoiz or tûr′koiz) *noun, plural* **turquoises**; *adjective.*

turret **1.** A small tower on a building: *Some castles have turrets at each corner.* **2.** A structure on

PRONUNCIATION KEY:
| at | āpe | fär | câre | end | mē | it | īce | pierce | hot | ōld | sông | fôrk |
| oil | out | up | ūse | rüle | pùll | tûrn | chin | sing | shop | thin | this | |
hw in white; zh in treasure. The symbol ə stands for the unstressed vowel sound in about, taken, pencil, lemon, and circus.

771

top of a military tank or ship that holds guns or cannons. **tur·ret** (tûr′it) *noun, plural* **turrets**.

turtle **1.** An animal with a low, wide body covered by a hard, rounded shell. A turtle can pull its head, legs, and tail into its shell for protection. Turtles are reptiles. **2.** A small triangle that appears on a computer monitor when the computer language LOGO is used. **tur·tle** (tûr′təl) *noun, plural* **turtles**.

Turtles live on land and in water.

turtleneck A sweater or other garment with a high collar that fits snugly around the neck and is usually worn turned down. **tur·tle·neck** (tûr′təl nek′) *noun, plural* **turtlenecks**.

tusk A long, pointed tooth that sticks out of each side of the mouth in certain animals. Elephants and walruses have tusks. **tusk** (tusk) *noun, plural* **tusks**.

tutor A teacher who gives private lessons to a pupil: *When I was sick for three months, I had a tutor at home. Noun.*
○ To teach privately; act as a tutor: *The college student made money by tutoring French. Verb.*
tu·tor (tü′tər *or* tū′tər) *noun, plural* **tutors**; *verb*, **tutored, tutoring**.

WORD HISTORY

The word **tutor** comes from a Latin word meaning "defender" or "guardian." Later, in some English universities, the word tutor was used for a graduate responsible for a younger student. From this meaning came the sense of "a private teacher."

---

tutu A short many-layered skirt worn by a ballerina. **tu·tu** (tü′tü) *noun, plural* **tutus**.

TV Television: *We watched TV for an hour.* **TV** (tē′vē′) *noun, plural* **TVs**.

tweed A rough, wool cloth woven with two or more colors of yarn. **tweed** (twēd) *noun, plural* **tweeds**.

tweezers A small instrument with two prongs. It is used for plucking out hairs or for picking up tiny objects. **tweez·ers** (twē′zərz) *plural noun*.

twelfth Next after the eleventh. *Adjective; noun.*
○ One of twelve equal parts; 1/12. *Noun.*
twelfth (twelfth) *adjective; noun, plural* **twelfths**.

twelve Two more than ten; 12. **twelve** (twelv) *noun, plural* **twelves**; *adjective*.

twentieth Next after the nineteenth. *Adjective; noun.*
○ One of twenty equal parts; 1/20. *Noun.*
twen·ti·eth (twen′tē ith) *adjective; noun, plural* **twentieths**.

twenty Two times ten; 20. **twen·ty** (twen′tē) *noun, plural* **twenties**; *adjective*.

twice Two times: *I rang the doorbell twice.* Twenty is twice as much as ten. **twice** (twīs) *adverb*.

twig A small branch of a tree or other woody plant: *We gathered dry twigs to start a campfire.* **twig** (twig) *noun, plural* **twigs**.

twilight The time just after sunset or just before sunrise when there is a soft, hazy light. **twi·light** (twī′līt′) *noun*.

twin One of two children or animals born at the same time to the same mother. Some twins look exactly alike. *Noun.*
○ **1.** Being a twin: *Those two are twin sisters. Twin lambs were born to our sheep.* **2.** Being identical or very much alike: *twin mountain peaks. Adjective.*
twin (twin) *noun, plural* **twins**; *adjective*.

twine A strong string made of two or more strands twisted together. *Noun.*
○ To wind or coil one thing around another: *Ivy twined around the gate post. A ribbon was twined through the lace. Verb.*
twine (twīn) *noun, plural* **twines**; *verb*, **twined, twining**.

twinge A sudden, sharp pain: *I felt a twinge in my sore ankle when I stood up.* **twinge** (twinj) *noun, plural* **twinges**.

twinkle To shine with flashes of light: *Stars seem to twinkle in the sky at night. The child's eyes twinkled with laughter. Verb.*

○ A flash of light or brightness: *the **twinkle** of distant city lights. Noun.*
twin·kle (twing'kəl) *verb,* **twinkled, twinkling;** *noun, plural* **twinkles.**

twirl To spin around quickly: *A drum majorette **twirled** a baton at the head of the parade. The dancers **twirled** around the floor.* **twirl** (twûrl) *verb,* **twirled, twirling.**

twist 1. To wind or turn around something: *The dog's chain was **twisted** around the tree. The road **twisted** around the mountain.* 2. To change the natural or usual shape of: *Anger **twisted** the child's face.* 3. To change the meaning of; distort: *Don't **twist** my words.* 4. To hurt a part of the body by turning it suddenly or too far: *I **twisted** my ankle when I slipped off the ladder. Verb.*
○ A turn or bend in something: *I can't straighten this **twist** in the wire. Noun.*
twist (twist) *verb,* **twisted, twisting;** *noun, plural* **twists.**

twister A dark, whirling column of wind; tornado. **twist·er** (twis'tər) *noun, plural* **twisters.**

twitch To move or pull with a sudden jerk or tug: *The rabbit's nose **twitched**.* **twitch** (twich) *verb,* **twitched, twitching.**

twitter 1. A series of short, light, chirping sounds made by a bird or birds. 2. A nervous or excited state: *Everyone was in a **twitter** on the last day of school. Noun.*
○ To make short, light, chirping sounds: *Birds **twittered** in the trees. Verb.*
twit·ter (twit'ər) *noun, plural* **twitters;** *verb,* **twittered, twittering.**

two One more than one; 2.
Other words that sound like this are to and too.
two (tü) *noun, plural* **twos;** *adjective.*

TX An abbreviation for Texas.

tycoon A wealthy, powerful businessman or businesswoman. **ty·coon** (tī kü'n) *noun, plural* **tycoons.**

type 1. A group of things that are alike or have the same qualities; kind: *A collie is a **type** of dog.* 2. Small pieces of metal with raised letters or numbers on their surfaces. Type is coated with ink and pressed onto paper in printing. 3. Printed or typewritten letters or numbers: *The small **type** was hard to read. Noun.*
○ To write with a typewriter: *I **typed** a letter. Verb.*
type (tīp) *noun, plural* **types;** *verb,* **typed, typing.**

SYNONYMS

type, kind, sort
This is a different type of tree from the one on your property. A new kind of television is being developed for the future. There were candies of every sort in the glass case.

---

typewriter A machine with keys for each letter of the alphabet, for numbers, and for punctuation marks. When you press a key, the letter is printed on a piece of paper. **type·writ·er** (tīp'rī'tər) *noun, plural* **typewriters.**

typhoon A tropical storm with violent winds. Typhoons occur in the western Pacific Ocean. **ty·phoon** (tī fün') *noun, plural* **typhoons.**

WORD HISTORY

The word typhoon is derived from two words in the Chinese language that mean "great wind."

---

typical Showing the qualities or characteristics of a certain type: *A **typical** movie lasts about ninety minutes.* **typ·i·cal** (tip'i kəl) *adjective.*

tyrannosaur A huge dinosaur that lived in North America in prehistoric times. It walked upright on its hind feet. This dinosaur is also called tyrannosaurus. **ty·ran·no·saur** (ti ran'ə sôr'əs) *noun, plural* **tyrannosaurs.**

tyranny The unjust use of power; harsh or cruel government: *The people rose up against the dictator's **tyranny**.* **tyr·an·ny** (tir'ə nē) *noun, plural* **tyrannies.**

tyrant A person who uses power in a cruel or unjust way: *The king was a **tyrant** who put anyone who disagreed with him in prison.* **ty·rant** (tī'rənt) *noun, plural* **tyrants.**

PRONUNCIATION KEY:

| at | āpe | fär | câre | end | mē | it | īce | pierce | hot | ōld | sông | fôrk |
| oil | out | up | ūse | rüle | pùll | tûrn | chin | sing | shop | thin | this | |

hw in white; zh in treasure. The symbol ə stands for the unstressed vowel sound in about, taken, pencil, lemon, and circus.

773

Uu

The letter U has several sounds in English and each of these sounds can be made in several different ways.

The sound of u in up, mud, and summer is made by:

o in words such as above or son;
ou in double and cousin;
oe in does; oo in flood.

The sound of u in use and mule can also be made by:

ue in words such as cue and value;
ew in few and threw;
eu in feud;
ie in view; ough in through.

The sound of u in rule can also be made by:

o in words such as move;
oo in food and tool; ou in soup;
ue in blue and true; ui in fruit;
oe in words such as shoe.

The sound of u in push and put can be made by:

oo in words such as wood;
ou in should;
o as in woman.

In words such as circus the sound of the letter u is represented in the pronunciations in this dictionary by a ə.

---

u, U The twenty-first letter of the alphabet. **u, U** (ū) *noun, plural* **u's, U's**.

udder A sac that hangs from the underside of certain female animals, especially cows, goats, ewes, and mares. It contains the glands that make milk. Each gland is connected to a nipple where a baby animal can nurse. **ud·der** (ud′ər) *noun, plural*.

UFO An object seen or believed to be seen flying in the sky, especially one thought to be a spacecraft from another planet. UFO stands for unidentified flying object.

ugly 1. Not nice or pleasing to look at: *an ugly painting*. 2. Unpleasant; offensive: *an ugly rumor*. 3. Likely to cause trouble or harm: *An ugly storm is on the way*. 4. Bad-tempered; cross: *an ugly mood*. **ug·ly** (ug′lē) *adjective*, **uglier, ugliest**.

Ukraine A country in southeastern Europe. **U·kraine** (ū krān′) *noun*.

ulcer A painful sore on the skin or the lining of the stomach. **ul·cer** (ul′sər) *noun, plural* **ulcers**.

ultra- A prefix that means beyond the limit or the usual degree of: *Ultrasonic means relating to sounds beyond what the human ear can hear; ultraconservative means extremely conservative.*

ultraviolet light Light that is invisible to the human eye. It lies beyond the violet end of the light spectrum. It helps to form Vitamin D and causes the skin to darken after exposure to the sun.

umbilical cord The cord that connects an unborn baby to its mother and through which pass food and oxygen for the baby. **um·bil·i·cal cord** (um bil′i kəl)

umbrella A circular piece of often colored cloth or plastic stretched on a framework that can be folded up when not in use. **um·brel·la** (um brel′ə) *noun, plural* **umbrellas**.

An umbrella is used to give protection from the rain and sun.

WORD HISTORY

The word **umbrella** comes from the Italian word for this device. The Italian word came from a Latin word meaning "shade" or "shadow."

umpire A person who rules on plays in baseball or certain other sports. *Noun.*
○ To act as an umpire of: *Who will **umpire** our softball game on Saturday? Verb.*
um·pire (um′pīr) *noun, plural* **umpires**; *verb,* **umpired, umpiring.**

un- A prefix that means: **1.** The opposite of; not: *Unexpected means not expected. Unemployment means the opposite of employment.* **2.** To do the opposite of: *Unlock means to do the opposite of lock.*

UN An abbreviation for **United Nations.**

unable Not having the power or skill to do something; not able: *I was **unable** to reach the top shelf.* **un·a·ble** (un ā′bəl) *adjective.*

unanimous In or showing total agreement: *My friend was elected club president by a **unanimous** vote.* **u·nan·i·mous** (ū nan′ə məs) *adjective.*

unaware Not knowing or realizing; not aware: *We were **unaware** that the road ahead was closed.* **un·a·ware** (un′ə wâr′) *adjective.*

unawares By surprise; unexpectedly: *The cat caught its prey **unawares**.* **un·a·wares** (un′ə wârz′) *adverb.*

unbecoming **1.** Not flattering or attractive; not becoming: *an **unbecoming** hat.* **2.** Not suitable or proper: *Such childish behavior is **unbecoming** for someone of your age!* **un·be·com·ing** (un′bi kum′ing) *adjective.*

unbelievable **1.** Hard to believe: *The child told an **unbelievable** story about seeing a ghost.* **2.** Remarkable; amazing: *The circus acrobats did **unbelievable** tricks.* **un·be·liev·a·ble** (un′bi lē′və bəl) *adjective.*

unbreakable Not able to be broken or not easily broken: *unbreakable plastic plates.* **un·break·a·ble** (un brā′kə bəl) *adjective.*

uncanny **1.** Strange and mysterious: *uncanny sounds coming from a deserted house.* **2.** Remarkable; extraordinary: *an **uncanny** ability to know what others are thinking.* **un·can·ny** (un kan′ē) *adjective.*

uncertain **1.** Not known for sure; not certain: *It is still **uncertain** whether our team will win the game.* **2.** Not dependable; changing: *The weather was **uncertain**, so we canceled the picnic.* **un·cer·tain** (un sûr′tən) *adjective.*

uncle **1.** The brother of one's mother or father. **2.** The husband of one's aunt. **un·cle** (ung′kəl) *noun, plural* **uncles.**

Uncle Sam The U.S. government or the people of the United States, represented as a tall, thin man with a white beard and a top hat who is dressed in red, white, and blue.

uncomfortable **1.** Causing discomfort or uneasiness: *a hard and **uncomfortable** chair. An awkward and **uncomfortable** situation arose when unexpected guests arrived at dinnertime.* **2.** Feeling discomfort: *I am **uncomfortable** in these tight shoes.* **un·com·fort·a·ble** (un kum′fər tə bəl *or* un kumf′tə bəl) *adjective.*

uncommon Unusual; rare: *That bird is **uncommon** in this part of the country.* **un·com·mon** (un kom′ən) *adjective.*

unconscious **1.** Not conscious: *I was knocked **unconscious** when I fell and hit my head.* **2.** Not knowing; not aware: *They were **unconscious** of how sloppy they looked.* **3.** Not done on purpose: *I made an **unconscious** mistake when I called you by the wrong name.* **un·con·scious** (un kon′shəs) *adjective.*

unconstitutional Not in keeping with the constitution of a state or country: *The Supreme Court declared the new state law **unconstitutional**.* **un·con·sti·tu·tion·al** (un′kon sti tü′shə nəl *or* un′kon sti tū′shə nəl) *adjective.*

uncooperative Unwilling to cooperate or help: *The dentist can't do her job if her patient is **uncooperative**.* **un·co·op·er·a·tive** (un′kō op′ər ə tiv) *adjective.*

uncover **1.** To take away the cover from: *The cook **uncovered** the pan.* **2.** To discover; make known: *The detective **uncovered** some new clues.* **un·cov·er** (un kuv′ər) *verb,* **uncovered, uncovering.**

undecided **1.** Not having one's mind made up: *I am **undecided** about what to wear.* **2.** Not yet settled: *The result of the election is still **undecided**.* **un·de·cid·ed** (un′di sī′did) *adjective.*

PRONUNCIATION KEY:

| at | āpe | fär | câre | end | mē | it | īce | pierce | hot | ōld | sông | fôrk |
| oil | out | up | ūse | rüle | pull | tûrn | chin | sing | shop | thin | this | |

hw in white; zh in treasure. The symbol ə stands for the unstressed vowel sound in about, taken, pencil, lemon, and circus.

775

under 1. In or to a place lower than; beneath; below: *I found the paper* **under** *a pile of books.* 2. Less than: *The book cost* **under** *five dollars.* 3. Subject to or affected by the authority or guidance of: *My cousin studied painting in Paris* **under** *a famous artist.* 4. According to: ***Under** the new rules, the pool is open five nights a week.* 5. During the reign or rule of: ***Under** the last king, the country grew rich and powerful. Preposition.*

○ In or into a position lower than something: *We passed* **under** *the bridge in our canoe. Adverb.* **un·der** (un′dər) *preposition; adverb.*

Some of these roads go under other roads.

under- A prefix that means: 1. Below or beneath in position: *An* **undershirt** *is worn beneath a shirt.* 2. Less than is normal or right; too little: ***Underfed** means fed too little.*

underdog A person or group that is thought most likely to lose, as in a contest or game: *Our school team started the tournament as the* **underdog** *but won the championship.* **un·der·dog** (un′dər dôg) *noun, plural* **underdogs.**

undergo To go through; experience: *The street will* **undergo** *repairs this summer. The early settlers of America had to* **undergo** *many hardships.* **un·der·go** (un′dər gō′) *verb,* **underwent, undergone, undergoing.**

underground 1. Below the earth's surface: *an* **underground** *passage for the subway.* 2. Secret; hidden: *The spies belonged to an* **underground** *organization. Adjective.*

○ 1. A place below the earth's surface. 2. A group working in secret: *The* **underground** *continued to fight against the government. Noun.*

○ 1. Below the earth's surface: *Moles live under-*

ground. 2. In or into hiding: *The outlaws went* **underground** *to escape the police. Adverb.* **un·der·ground** (un′dər ground′ *for adjective and adverb;* un′dər ground′ *for noun) adjective; noun, plural* **undergrounds;** *adverb.*

undergrowth Small plants growing under large trees in a forest; underbrush. **un·der·growth** (un′dər grōth′) *noun.*

It is often difficult to walk through underground.

underhand Thrown or done with the hand brought forward and up from below the shoulder: *an* **underhand** *pitch.* **un·der·hand** (un′dər hand′) *adjective.*

underline To draw a line under: *The teacher* **underlined** *the words that I had spelled wrong on the test.* **un·der·line** (un′dər līn′) *verb,* **underlined, underlining.**

underneath In or to a place or position lower than; under; beneath: *The ball rolled* **underneath** *the chair. Preposition.*

○ In a place or position below: *a jacket with a sweater* **underneath.** *Adverb.* **un·der·neath** (un′dər nēth′) *preposition; adverb.*

underpants Short pants worn as underwear. **un·der·pants** (un′dər pants′) *plural noun.*

underpass A section of road that goes under a bridge or another road. **un·der·pass** (un′dər pas′) *noun, plural* **underpasses.**

undersea Lying, done, or used below the surface of the sea: ***undersea** explorations for sunken ships.* **un·der·sea** (un′dər sē′ *or* un′dər sē′) *adjective.*

underside The bottom side or surface of something: *The bird had brown wings and a red* **underside.** **un·der·side** (un′dər sīd′) *noun, plural* **undersides.**

understand 1. To get the meaning of; comprehend: *I didn't* **understand** *the teacher's question.* 2. To know very well: *My parents* **understand** *French because they lived for a time in France.* 3. To be in sympathy or agreement with: *The two friends* **understand** *each other.* 4. To be told; hear; learn: *I* **understand** *that you hope to go to college.* 5. To take as a fact; assume: *I* **understand** *that I can get my money back if I return the CD unopened.* **un•der•stand** (un′dər stand′) *verb,* **understood, understanding.**

understanding 1. A grasping of the meaning of something; knowledge: *a good* **understanding** *of arithmetic.* 2. Opinion; belief; conclusion: *It was my* **understanding** *that we would meet at three o'clock.* 3. Sympathy or agreement: *My parents always show* **understanding** *when I bring them my problems. The two friends reached an* **understanding** *that ended their quarrel. Noun.*
○ Feeling or showing sympathy: *an* **understanding** *look. Adjective.*
un•der•stand•ing (un′dər stand′ing) *noun, plural* **understandings;** *adjective.*

undertake 1. To try to do; start: *The explorers planned to* **undertake** *a journey.* 2. To agree to do; accept as a duty: *He* **undertook** *the care of his sick parents.* **un•der•take** (un′dər tāk′) *verb,* **undertook, undertaken, undertaking.**

undertaker A person whose job is arranging funerals and preparing dead people for burial. **un•der•tak•er** (un′dər tā′kər) *noun, plural* **undertakers.**

undertow A strong current just below the surface of a body of water, such as a river or the ocean. It usually moves in a different direction than the surface current moves, and it can pull swimmers away from shore or safe swimming areas. **un•der•tow** (un′dər tō′) *noun, plural* **undertows.**

underwater Lying, used, or done below the surface of the water: *an* **underwater** *tunnel. Adjective.*
○ Below the surface of the water: *I like to swim* **underwater.** *Adverb.*
un•der•wa•ter (un′dər wô′tər) *adjective; adverb.*

underwear Clothing worn under a person's outer clothing; underclothes. **un•der•wear** (un′dər wâr′) *noun.*

underweight Having less than the normal or needed weight: *The child was a little* **underweight** *after being sick.* **un•der•weight** (un′dər wāt′) *adjective.*

underworld 1. The people involved in organized crime. 2. In Greek and Roman mythology, the place where the spirits of dead people go. **un•der•world** (un′dər wûrld′) *noun.*

undo 1. To loosen something that is fastened or tied: *This is a hard knot to* **undo.** *Let me help you* **undo** *the package.* 2. To do away with; wipe out: *The storm* **undid** *the farmer's hard work.* 3. To bring to ruin; destroy: *Nasty rumors finally* **undid** *the politician.* 4. To reverse the effect or result of: *She can't* **undo** *the damage she's caused.*
Another word that sounds like this is **undue.**
un•do (un dü′) *verb,* **undid, undone, undoing.**

undress To take clothes off: *The tired child* **undressed** *and went to bed.* **un•dress** (un dres′) *verb,* **undressed, undressing.**

undue Beyond what is right or proper; too much: *The newspaper suggested the police used* **undue** *force in arresting the man.*
Another word that sounds like this is **undo.**
un•due (un dü′) *adjective.*

unearth 1. To dig up out of the earth: *The dog* **unearthed** *a bone it had buried.* 2. To search for and find; discover: *My mother* **unearthed** *some old family photographs.* **un•earth** (un ûrth′) *verb,* **unearthed, unearthing.**

uneasy 1. Worried; nervous; restless: *I finally dropped off into an* **uneasy** *sleep.* 2. Embarrassed or awkward: *The speaker's rude remark was followed by an* **uneasy** *silence in the group.* **un•eas•y** (un ē′zē) *adjective,* **uneasier, uneasiest.**

unemployed Not having a job; out of work: *The closing of the factory left many people* **unemployed.** **un•em•ployed** (un′em ploid′) *adjective.*
—**unemployment** *noun.*

unequal 1. Not the same; uneven: *We complained that the cake was divided into* **unequal** *pieces. The sleeves of the sweater are of* **unequal** *length.* 2. Not well matched; unfair: *When the older children played the younger children in football, it was an* **unequal** *contest.* **un•e•qual** (un ē′kwəl) *adjective.*

PRONUNCIATION KEY:

| at | āpe | fär | câre | end | mē | it | īce | pîerce | hot | ōld | sông | fôrk |
| oil | out | up | ūse | rüle | pull | tûrn | chin | sing | shop | thin | this | |

hw in white; zh in treasure. The symbol ə stands for the unstressed vowel sound in about, taken, pencil, lemon, and circus.

777

uneven 1. Not straight, smooth, or regular: *The car bounced along the uneven road.* 2. Being an odd number: *1, 3, and 5 are uneven.* 3. Not well matched; unfair: *There was no way our team could win the uneven contest.* 4. Not always the same; changing: *uneven in quality.* **un·e·ven** (un ē′vən) *adjective.*

Hills can make some roads very uneven.

unfair Not fair or just: *The bigger child had an unfair advantage over the smaller child in the fight.* **un·fair** (un fâr′) *adjective.*

unfamiliar 1. Not well known or easily recognized; strange: *The handwriting on the envelope is unfamiliar to me.* 2. Not acquainted: *The librarian was unfamiliar with the book I wanted.* **un·fa·mil·iar** (un′fə mil′yər) *adjective.*

unfold 1. To open or spread out something folded: *Please unfold the tablecloth.* 2. To make or become known gradually: *unfold a plan; listen as a story unfolds.* 3. To become open: *The flower petals unfolded.* **un·fold** (un fōld′) *verb,* **unfolded, unfolding.**

unfortunate 1. Not fortunate; unlucky: *It was very unfortunate that their luggage was stolen.* 2. Not proper or suitable: *An unfortunate joke offended his listeners.* **un·for·tu·nate** (un fôr′chə nit) *adjective.*

unfriendly 1. Feeling or showing dislike; not friendly: *unfriendly neighbors.* 2. Not pleasant or favorable: *a cold, unfriendly climate.* **un·friend·ly** (un frend′lē) *adjective,* **unfriendlier, unfriendliest.**

unhappy 1. Without happiness or joy; sad: *My cousin is unhappy about having to move to a different town.* 2. Not suitable: *Red and green was an unhappy choice of colors for the living room.* **un·hap·py** (un hap′ē) *adjective,* **unhappier, unhappiest.**

unhealthy Not having, showing, or giving good health; not healthy: *His skin was an unhealthy color from staying indoors all the time. Lack of exercise is unhealthy.* **un·heal·thy** (un hel′thē) *adjective,* **unhealthier, unhealthiest.**

unheard-of Not known or happening before; unknown: *Before jet planes, travel across the Atlantic in six hours was unheard-of.* **un·heard-of** (un hûrd′uv′ *or* un hûrd′ov′) *adjective.*

uni- A prefix that means one or single: *Unicycle means a vehicle that has one wheel.*

unicorn An imaginary animal that looks like a white horse with a long pointed horn in the middle of its forehead. **u·ni·corn** (ū′ni kôrn′) *noun, plural* **unicorns.**

uniform 1. Always the same; not changing: *The cake needs to bake at a uniform temperature.* 2. Showing little or no difference; all alike: *houses of uniform design. Adjective.* ○ The special or official clothes that the members of a particular group wear. Soldiers, police officers, and students at some schools wear uniforms. *Noun.* **u·ni·form** (ū′nə fôrm′) *adjective; noun, plural* **uniforms.**

Band members wear uniforms.

unify To cause to be or feel like one thing; bring or join together; unite: *Fear of invasion unified the people of the small country.* **u·ni·fy** (ū′nə fī′) *verb,* **unified, unifying.**

unimportant Of no special value, meaning, or interest; not important: *The newspaper didn't bother to print a story on the unimportant incident. It is unimportant what color the car is as long as it runs well.* **un·im·por·tant** (un′im pôr′tənt) *adjective.*

uninhabited Not lived in: *an uninhabited wilderness.* **un·in·hab·it·ed** (un′in hab′i tid) *adjective.*

uninterested Not interested: *The students seemed tired and **uninterested** in schoolwork.* **un·in·ter·est·ed** (un in′tər ə stid) *adjective*.

union 1. A joining together of two or more people or things: *a town formed by the **union** of three small villages.* 2. Something formed by a joining together; confederation: *The three countries formed a **union** to increase trade among them.* 3. the Union: a. The United States of America. b. The states that stayed loyal to the federal government during the Civil War. 4. A group of workers joined together to protect their interests and improve their working conditions: *a labor **union.*** **un·ion** (ūn′yən) *noun, plural* **unions**.

unique Not having an equal; being the only one of its kind: *Being the first person to set foot on the moon was a **unique** achievement.* **u·nique** (ū nēk′) *adjective*.

unison In unison. Making the same sounds or movements at the same time: *The students recited the poem in **unison.*** **u·ni·son** (ū′nə sən or ū′nə zən) *noun*.

unit 1. A single person, thing, or group that is part of a larger group: *That apartment building contains fifty **units.*** 2. A fixed quantity or amount that is used as a standard of measurement: *An hour is a **unit** of time.* 3. A piece of equipment having a special purpose: *an air conditioning **unit.*** 4. The smallest whole number; one. **u·nit** (ū′nit) *noun, plural* **units**.

unite To bring or join together; make or become one: *The couple was **united** in marriage.* **u·nite** (ū nīt′) *verb*, **united, uniting**.

United Kingdom The country that includes England, Scotland, Wales, and Northern Ireland. It is also called **Great Britain**.

United Nations An international organization that includes most of the countries of the world as its members. It was founded in 1945 to help keep world peace. Its headquarters are in New York City.

United States A country that has forty-nine states in North America and the state of Hawaii in the Pacific Ocean. Its capital is Washington, D. C. This country is also called the *United States of America*.

unity The condition of being one: *The candidates expressed **unity** on foreign trade.* **u·ni·ty** (ū′ni tē) *noun, plural* **unities**.

universal 1. Of, for, or shared by all: *universal joy at the end of the war.* 2. Being everywhere; affecting everything: *Disease is **universal.*** **u·ni·ver·sal** (ū′nə vûr′səl) *adjective*.

universe Everything that exists, including the earth, the planets, the stars, and all of space. **u·ni·verse** (ū′nə vûrs′) *noun, plural* **universes**.

WORD HISTORY

The word universe comes from a Latin word that means "the whole world."

university A school that is made up of one or more colleges. It also may have special schools that give training in many professions. **u·ni·ver·si·ty** (ū′nə vûr′si tē) *noun, plural* **universities**.

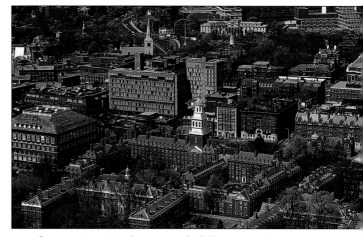

Some universities have many buildings spread over a large area of land.

unkind Not kind; cruel: *Your **unkind** remark hurt my feelings.* **un·kind** (un kīnd′) *adjective*, **unkinder, unkindest**.

unless Except on the condition that: ***Unless** you return the library books you have borrowed, you cannot borrow any more.* **un·less** (un les′) *conjunction*.

unlike 1. Different from: ***Unlike** most of my friends, I enjoy dancing.* 2. Not usual for: *It is **unlike** you to be rude. Preposition.* ○ Not the same; different: *The two sisters are quite **unlike.** Adjective.*

PRONUNCIATION KEY:

| at | āpe | fär | câre | end | mē | it | īce | pierce | hot | ōld | sông | fôrk |
| oil | out | up | ūse | rüle | pull | tûrn | chin | sing | shop | thin | this | |

hw in white; zh in treasure. The symbol ə stands for the unstressed vowel sound in about, taken, pencil, lemon, and circus.

779

un·like (un līk´) *preposition; adjective.*

unlimited Without any limits: *This card gives you **unlimited** use of the library.* **un·lim·it·ed** (un lim´i tid) *adjective.*

unload 1. To take off or remove from a vehicle: *unload cargo from a ship.* 2. To remove a load from: *We **unloaded** the car when we got home.* 3. To remove ammunition from: *unload a gun.* **un·load** (un lōd´) *verb,* **unloaded, unloading.**

unlock 1. To open the lock of: *This key will **unlock** the front door.* 2. To make known: *The detective **unlocked** the mystery of the missing car.* **un·lock** (un lok´) *verb,* **unlocked, unlocking.**

unlucky 1. Not having good luck: *The **unlucky** travelers were stranded when their car broke down.* 2. Causing bad luck: *Some people call thirteen an **unlucky** number.* **un·luck·y** (un luk´ē) *adjective,* **unluckier, unluckiest.**

SYNONYMS

unlucky, unfortunate

*Monday seems like an **unlucky** day for me because something always goes wrong. It is **unfortunate** that you can't join us for the holidays.*

---

unmanned Without a human crew: *an **unmanned** spacecraft.* **un·manned** (un mand´) *adjective.*

unnatural Going against or different from what is usual or normal in nature; not natural: *The tree grew to an **unnatural** size. We all have **unnatural** smiles in the class photograph.* **un·nat·u·ral** (un nach´ər əl) *adjective.*

unnecessary Not necessary; needless: *It was **unnecessary** for you to repeat your question, because I heard it the first time.* **un·nec·es·sar·y** (un nes´ə ser´ē) *adjective.*

unpack 1. To open and take things out of: *I **unpacked** my suitcase when I got home.* 2. To take out from a container or package: *We **unpacked** glasses from the box.* **un·pack** (un pak´) *verb,* **unpacked, unpacking.**

unpleasant Not pleasing; disagreeable: *an **unpleasant** odor from the sewer.* **un·pleas·ant** (un plez´ənt) *adjective.*

unpopular Not generally liked or accepted: *I am afraid I might be **unpopular** at my new school. The politician had a number of ideas that were **unpopular** with the voters.* **un·pop·u·lar** (un pop´yə lər) *adjective.*

unravel 1. To separate the threads of something knitted, woven, or tangled: *I **unraveled** the scarf I was knitting and started over.* 2. To come apart: *an old sweater starting to **unravel** at the neck.* **un·rav·el** (un rav´əl) *verb,* **unraveled, unraveling.**

unreliable Not to be trusted: *That car is **unreliable** because it won't always start.* **un·re·li·a·ble** (un´ri lī´ə bəl) *adjective.*

unrest A disturbed or discontented condition: *political **unrest**.* **un·rest** (un rest´) *noun.*

unruly Hard to control or manage: *The police tried to control the **unruly** mob. After I wash my hair, it is **unruly** and hard to comb.* **un·ru·ly** (un rü´lē) *adjective,* **unrulier, unruliest.**

unsatisfactory Not good enough to meet a need, desire, or hope; not satisfactory: *I won't hire those painters again because their work was **unsatisfactory**.* **un·sa·tis·fac·to·ry** (un´sat is fak´tə rē) *adjective.*

unseen Not seen or noticed: *Some flowers were left at the door by an **unseen** visitor.* **un·seen** (un sēn´) *adjective.*

unsettled 1. Not peaceful, calm, or orderly: *There were **unsettled** conditions in the country after the war.* 2. Not decided or determined: *The question of how much the club should charge new members for dues is still **unsettled**.* 3. Not paid: *unsettled medical bills.* 4. Not being lived in; not inhabited: *Many areas of Alaska are still **unsettled**.* 5. Changing; uncertain: *We called off our trip to the beach because of the **unsettled** weather.* **un·set·tled** (un set´əld) *adjective.*

unsightly Not pleasant to look at; ugly: *The park was covered with **unsightly** litter after the big picnic.* **un·sight·ly** (un sīt´lē) *adjective,* **unsightlier, unsightliest.**

unstable 1. Not firmly fixed; easily moved: *The chair is **unstable** because one leg is broken.* 2. Likely to change: *A group of army officers tried to overthrow the **unstable** government of that country.* **un·sta·ble** (un stā´bəl) *adjective.*

unsteady Not firm; shaky: *This ladder is **unsteady** because it is not standing on level ground. I fought back my tears and answered in an **unsteady** voice.* **un·stead·y** (un sted´ē) *adjective,* **unsteadier, unsteadiest.**

unsuitable Not right or proper: *Laughing is **unsuitable** behavior for a serious occasion.* **un·suit·a·ble** (un sü´tə bəl) *adjective.*

untangle 1. To remove knots or tangles from: *untangle a fishing line.* 2. To straighten out; clear up; resolve: *untangle a problem.* **un•tan•gle** (un tang′gəl) *verb,* **untangled, untangling.**

untie To loosen or undo; set free: *I untied the ribbon on my birthday gift. They untied the dog as soon as they got home.* **un•tie** (un tī′) *verb,* **untied, untying.**

until 1. Up to the time of: *Wait until eight o'clock before you call.* 2. Before: *Tickets are not available until Monday. Preposition.*
  ○ 1. Up to the time when: *Wait here until I get back.* 2. Before: *We can't leave until we finish our chores. Conjunction.*
  un•til (un til′) *preposition; conjunction.*

untrue 1. Not true; false: *The rumor was untrue.* 2. Not faithful; disloyal: *He was untrue to his friends.* **un•true** (un trü′) *adjective.*

unusual Not usual, common, or ordinary; rare: *It is unusual for them not to call.* **un•u•su•al** (un ū′zhü əl) *adjective.*

SYNONYMS

unusual, rare, uncommon
It is unusual for her to be late for dinner. Diamonds are expensive because they are so rare. Sea lions are an uncommon sight along this coastline.

---

unwell Sick; ill: *He's feeling unwell and can't come to the party.* **un•well** (un wel′) *adjective.*

unwind 1. To unroll: *Unwind the thread from the spool.* 2. To become relaxed: *Watching TV helps me unwind.* **un•wind** (un wīnd′) *verb,* **unwound, unwinding.**

up 1. From a lower to a higher place or position: *I climbed up to the top of the ladder.* 2. In, on, or at a higher place: *They're camping up in the mountains.* 3. To a higher point or degree: *The price went up.* 4. In or to an upright position: *He helped me up when I fell.* 5. Out of bed: *When did you get up this morning?* 6. Entirely; completely: *We used up all our money. Adverb.*
  ○ 1. At a higher point or degree: *The price of food was up again this month.* 2. Above the horizon: *The sun is up.* 3. Out of bed: *They get up at six o'clock.* 4. At an end; finished: *Your turn to play is up.* 5. Working and ready for use: *How*

soon will the computers be *up* again? *Adjective.*
  ○ 1. To or at a point further along or higher on: *Their house is up the block.* 2. To or toward the source, interior, or upper part of: *paddle up a river. Preposition.*
  • **up against.** Faced with: *Our team is up against tough competition in the league.*
  • **ups and downs.** Periods of good and bad luck or high and low spirits: *Life has its ups and downs.*
  • **up to.** 1. Doing or about to do: *What are you up to?* 2. Having the skill, training, power, or other qualities necessary for: *Do you think he's up to handling this job?* 3. Depending on; being the responsibility of: *The decision is up to the governor.*
  up (up) *adverb; adjective; preposition.*

upbringing The care and training received by a child growing up: *My grandparents had a big influence on my upbringing.* **up•bring•ing** (up′ bring′ing) *noun.*

upgrade To raise to a higher standard; improve: *I need to upgrade my computer; it's not powerful enough anymore. Verb.*
  ○ 1. Something that upgrades: *a software upgrade.* 2. An upward slope: *The truck slowed on the upgrade. Noun.*
  up•grade (up′grād′) *verb,* **upgraded, upgrading;** *noun, plural* **upgrades.**

upheaval 1. A sudden and violent change or disturbance: *The blizzard caused an upheaval in everyone's plans.* 2. A forceful upward movement of the earth's crust: *The earthquake brought a series of upheavals.* **up•heav•al** (up hē′vəl) *noun, plural* **upheavals.**

uphill 1. Going up a hill: *an uphill path.* 2. Requiring great effort; difficult: *It was an uphill effort to persuade him to come.* **up•hill** (up′hil′) *adjective.*

uphold 1. To support or defend: *All public officials must promise to uphold the laws. Duels were once fought to uphold a family's honor.* 2. To keep from falling; hold up: *Columns uphold the roof.* **up•hold** (up hōld′) *verb,* **upheld, upholding.**

upholstery Material used to cover furniture: *The couch was covered with soft, comfortable upholstery.* **up•hol•ster•y** (up hōl′stə rē) *noun.*

PRONUNCIATION KEY:
| at | āpe | fär | câre | end | mē | it | īce | pierce | hot | ōld | sông | fôrk |
| oil | out | up | ūse | rüle | půll | tûrn | chin | sing | shop | thin | this | |

hw in white; zh in treasure. The symbol ə stands for the unstressed vowel sound in about, taken, pencil, lemon, and circus.

781

upload To send files from one computer to another: *I will upload all my letters and transmit them to you this afternoon.* **up·load** (up′ lōd′) *verb*, **uploaded, uploading.**

upon In a position above and supported by; atop; on: *The queen sat upon her throne.* **up·on** (ə pôn′ or ə pon′) *preposition*.

upper Higher in position or rank: *the upper stories of a tall building.* **up·per** (up′ər) *adjective*.

upper case Letters that are capitals; capital letters. The letters A, B, C, and D are upper case; a, b, c, and d are lower case.

uppermost 1. Farthest up; highest: *I can't reach the uppermost shelf.* 2. Having the most importance; foremost: *Food was uppermost in their thoughts. Adjective.*
○ In the highest or most important place, position, or rank: *This problem is uppermost on our list of things to do. Adverb.*
up·per·most (up′ər mōst) *adjective; adverb*.

upright 1. Straight up and down; vertical: *Only a few trees remained upright after the storm.* 2. Good; honest: *An upright person would never lie or cheat. Adjective.*
○ In a straight up and down position: *I placed the chair upright after the dog knocked it over. Adverb.*
○ Something that stands straight up. *Noun.*
up·right (up′rīt′) *adjective; adverb; noun, plural* **uprights.**

uprising A revolt against a government or other authority; rebellion: *The dictator used troops to put down the people's uprising.* **up·ris·ing** (up′rī′zing) *noun, plural* **uprisings.**

uproar 1. A noisy and excited disturbance: *The crowd was in an uproar when the player hit a home run.* 2. A loud, confused noise: *I can't sleep because of the uproar in the street.* **up·roar** (up′rôr′) *noun, plural* **uproars.**

uproot 1. To tear or pull up by the roots: *The bulldozers uprooted bushes and trees.* 2. To cause to leave; displace: *The flood uprooted many families from their homes.* **up·root** (up rüt′ or up rút′) *verb*, **uprooted, uprooting.**

upset 1. To turn or knock over: *I accidentally upset the glass of milk.* 2. To interfere with; throw into confusion: *The rain upset our plans for a picnic.* 3. To make nervous and worried; disturb: *The bad news upset me.* 4. To make sick: *Eating too quickly will upset your stomach.* 5. To defeat unexpectedly: *The young tennis player upset the champion. Verb.*
○ 1. Turned or knocked over: *The upset glass of milk spilled all over me.* 2. Nervous and worried: *They were upset about missing their plane.* 3. Sick: *an upset stomach. Adjective.*
○ An unexpected defeat of a team or player. *Noun.*
up·set (up set′ *for verb and adjective*; up′set′ *for noun*) *verb*, **upset, upsetting;** *adjective; noun, plural* **upsets.**

upside down 1. So that the top side or part becomes the bottom side or part: *You're holding the book upside down.* 2. In or into complete disorder or confusion: *I turned my room upside down looking for my keys.* **up·side down** (up′sīd′) *adverb*.

upstairs 1. Up the stairs: *I ran upstairs to my room.* 2. On or to an upper floor: *My parents are watching TV upstairs. Adverb.*
○ On an upper floor: *an upstairs apartment. Adjective.*
up·stairs (up′stârz′) *adverb; adjective; noun*.

up-to-date Using or showing the latest developments or style; modern: *An up-to-date map will show the new highway. The fashion model always wore the most up-to-date clothes.* **up-to-date** (up′tə dāt′) *adjective*.

upward From a lower to a higher place or level: *The people on the street looked upward to see the blimp fly overhead. The cost of food has climbed steadily upward. Adverb.*
○ Moving from a lower to a higher place or level: *The road we were on had a long upward slope. Adjective.*
up·ward (up′wərd) *adverb; adjective*.

upwards Another spelling of the adverb **upward**: *The balloon sailed upwards into the cloudless sky.* **up·wards** (up′wərdz) *adverb*.

uranium A silver-colored metal that is radioactive. It is used as a source of nuclear energy. Uranium is a chemical element. **u·ra·ni·um** (yu̇ rā′nē əm) *noun*.

WORD HISTORY

Scientists named uranium after the planet Uranus, which had just recently been discovered. Both the planet Uranus and the metal uranium were named after Uranus, a god of the sky in Roman and Greek mythology.

Uranus The third largest planet in our solar system. It is the seventh planet in distance from the sun. Uranus is surrounded by rings. **U•ra•nus** (yùr′ə nəs *or* yù rā′nəs) *noun.*

Uranus
Discovered by William Herschel in 1781, Uranus has winds in its atmosphere that have been measured up to 375 miles per hour!
Average distance from sun: **1,783.800,000 miles**
Diameter: **32,490 miles**
Length of Day: **17 hours, 14 minutes**
Length of Year: **84 years**
Average Temperature: **-373˚F**
Mass compared to Earth: **14.5**
Weight of 100 pounds: **91**
Atmosphere: **Hydrogen, Helium, Methane**
Number of rings: **At least 11**
Number of satellites: **15**

urban In, relating to, or like a city or city life: *urban transportation including buses and subways.* **ur•ban** (ûr′bən) *adjective.*

Urban areas contain many people and buildings.

urge **1.** To try to convince or persuade: *They urged their friend to try out for the team.* **2.** To drive or force on: *The rider urged the horse on to win the race.* **3.** To speak or argue strongly for: *The group of citizens urged passage of the law.* Verb.

○ A strong desire or impulse: *I had a sudden urge for a hamburger. Noun.*

urge (ûrj) *verb,* **urged, urging;** *noun, plural* **urges.**

urgent Needing or demanding immediate action or attention: *My boss left the country on urgent business. The hospital made an urgent request for people to give blood.* **ur•gent** (ûr′jənt) *adjective.*

urine A clear, yellow liquid made up of water and wastes taken out of the blood by the kidneys. Urine is stored in the bladder. From time to time the bladder empties and urine flows out of the body. **u•rine** (yùr′in) *noun.*

Urns date back to ancient times.

urn **1.** A vase set on a base. Urns are used for decoration or to hold plants. **2.** A container with a faucet that is used to serve coffee or tea.

Another word that sounds like this is **earn.**

urn (ûrn) *noun, plural* **urns.**

us The persons who are speaking or writing: *The neighbors invited us to a barbecue. Please write to us as soon as you can.* **us** (us *or unstressed* əs) *pronoun.*

U.S. An abbreviation for United States.

U.S.A. An abbreviation for United States of America.

usable or **useable** Fit, suitable, or ready for use: *This old cup is chipped but still usable.* **us•a•ble** (ū′zə bəl) *adjective.*

usage **1.** A way of using or handling something. **2.** The usual way in which people use words in speaking or writing: *This dictionary gives many examples of English usage.* **us•age** (ū′sij *or* ū′zij) *noun, plural* **usages.**

use To put into service for a particular purpose: *May I use your scissors? We use a dictionary to*

PRONUNCIATION KEY:
at   āpe   fär   câre   end   mē   it   īce   pierce   hot   old   sông   fôrk
oil   out   up   ūse   rüle   pùll   tûrn   chin   sing   shop   thin   this
hw in white; zh in treasure. The symbol ə stands for the unstressed vowel sound in about, taken, pencil, lemon, and circus.

783

find out the meanings of words. *Verb.*
○ **1.** The act of using or the state of being used: *We made the bookcase with the* **use** *of a saw and a hammer and nails. The auditorium is in* **use** *until later this afternoon.* **2.** The quality of being useful or helpful: *There's no* **use** *worrying about things you can't change.* **3.** A need or purpose for which something is used: *Do you have any* **use** *for these empty bottles? This tool has many* **uses.** **4.** The right or ability to use something: *They offered us the* **use** *of their car.* **5.** The way of using something: *My neighbor taught me the proper* **use** *of a hammer. Noun.*

> • **used to. 1.** Did at a time in the past: *I* **used** *to ride a tricycle, but now I ride a bicycle.* **2.** Familiar with: *They live on a farm and are not* **used to** *the city.*

> • **used up.** To use all of: *We've* **used up** *the ketchup, so we'll have to buy more before the barbeque.*

use (ūz *for verb*; ūs *for noun*) *verb,* **used, using;** *noun, plural* **uses.**

useable Another spelling of usable. **use•a•ble** (ū′zə bəd) *adjective.*

used That has been used by someone else; not new: *a* **used** *car.* **used** (ūzd) *adjective.*

useful Serving a good use or purpose; helpful: *A pocketknife is a* **useful** *tool.* **use•ful** (ūs′fəl) *adjective.*

useless Serving no use; worthless: *An unreliable clock is* **useless.** **use•less** (ūs′lis) *adjective.*

user-friendly Easy to learn or use: *The software is* **user-friendly,** *so you'll have no trouble understanding it.* **us•er-friend•ly** (ū′zər frend′lē) *adjective.*

usher A person who leads people to their seats in a church, theater, stadium, or other place. *Noun.*
○ To act as an usher; lead: *The waiter* **ushered** *us to a table by the window. Verb.*
ush•er (ush′ər) *noun, plural* **ushers;** *verb,* **ushered, ushering.**

usual Common or expected; customary: *Hot weather is* **usual** *in this part of the country for July and August.* **u•su•al** (ū′zhü əl) *adjective.*
—**usually** *adverb.*

UT An abbreviation for **Utah.**

Utah A state in the western United States. Its capi-

tal is Salt Lake City. **Utah** (ū′tô *or* ū′tä) *noun.*

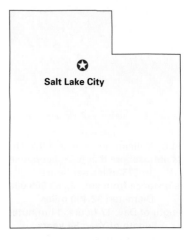

Utah
U. S. Postal Abbreviation: **UT**
Capital: **Salt Lake City**
Population: **1,680,000**
Area: **84,899 sq. mi./219,889 sq. km**
State Nickname: **Beehive State**
State Bird: **Sea Gull**
State Flower: **Sego Lily**

utensil An object or tool that is useful or necessary in doing or making something: *I keep all my cooking* **utensils** *in a drawer.* **u•ten•sil** (ū ten′səl) *noun, plural* **utensils.**

utmost Greatest or highest: *Everyone in school has the* **utmost** *respect for our principal. Adjective.*
○ The most or greatest possible: *I did my* **utmost** *to help our team win the game. Noun.*
ut•most (ut′mōst) *adjective; noun.*

utter¹ To give voice to; express out loud: *I* **uttered** *a sigh of relief.* **ut•ter** (ut′ər) *verb,* **uttered, uttering.**

utter² Complete or perfect; total: *in* **utter** *darkness.* **ut•ter** (ut′ər) *adjective.*

The letter V has one sound in English which is commonly made by:

v in words such as vat, very, save, and victory;

and much less commonly by:

f as in of;
lv as in salve.

v, V The twenty-second letter of the alphabet. **v, V** (vē) *noun, plural* **v's, V's**.

Va. or **VA** An abbreviation for **Virginia**.

vacant 1. Not having anyone or anything in it; empty: *You can sit in the vacant chair*. 2. Lacking or seeming to lack intelligence or awareness: *The dazed child had a vacant stare*. **va·cant** (vā′kənt) *adjective*. —**vacancy** *noun*.

vacation A period of rest or freedom from school, business, or other activity. *Noun*.
○ To take or spend a vacation. *Verb*. **va·ca·tion** (vā kā′shən) *noun, plural* **vacations**; *verb*, **vacationed, vacationing**.

vaccinate To give a vaccine to. **vac·ci·nate** (vak′sə nāt′) *verb*, **vaccinated, vaccinating**. —**vaccination**

vaccine A liquid that contains the dead or weakened germs of a certain disease. This liquid is swallowed or injected into the body, where it helps the body protect itself against this disease. **vac·cine** (vak sēn′ *or* vak′sēn) *noun, plural* **vaccines**.

WORD HISTORY

The word vaccine comes from the Latin word meaning "of a cow." The first vaccine was made from cowpox, a mild disease that people catch from cattle, and was used to vaccinate people against the disease smallpox.

vacuum 1. A space that is completely empty of matter. Scientists have not been able to make a perfect vacuum. Therefore, the word vacuum usually refers to a space with most but not all of the matter removed. 2. A vacuum cleaner. *Noun*.
○ To clean with a vacuum cleaner. *Verb*. **vac·u·um** (vak′ū əm *or* vak′ūm) *noun, plural* **vacuums**; *verb*, **vacuumed, vacuuming**.

vacuum cleaner A machine that is used for cleaning carpets, floors, and other objects and spaces. A vacuum cleaner works by sucking dirt into its tank or bag.

vain 1. Too proud of one's looks, abilities, or accomplishments; conceited: *She is vain and spends a lot of time looking at herself in the mirror*. 2. Not successful: *The mechanic made a vain effort to fix our car*.
Other words sounding like this are **vane** and **vein**. **vain** (vān) *adjective*, **vainer, vainest**.

valentine 1. A greeting card sent on Valentine's Day to one's sweetheart or another person. 2. A sweetheart chosen on Valentine's Day. **val·en·tine** (val′ən tīn′) *noun, plural* **valentines**.

Valentine's Day The day, February 14, named in honor of Saint Valentine, an early Christian saint. It is celebrated by the sending of valentines.

valid 1. Soundly based on facts or evidence; true: *The experiment proved that the scientist's theory was valid*. 2. Acceptable under the law or rules: *Your library card is not valid unless you sign it*. **val·id** (val′id) *adjective*.

valley 1. An area of low land between hills or mountains. Valleys often have rivers flowing through them. 2. An area drained by a river system: *The state of Louisiana is in the Mississippi Valley*. **val·ley** (val′ē) *noun, plural* **valleys**.

valuable 1. Worth much money: *The museum has a very valuable coin collection*. 2. Having great

use or importance: *a valuable experience.*
Adjective.
○ **valuables** Things of value. *Noun.*
val·u·a·ble (val′ū ə bəl *or* val′yə bəl) *adjective;*
plural noun.

value 1. The worth, usefulness, or importance of
something: *He places great value on her friend-*
ship. 2. The worth of something in money or
exchange: *The value of land in this area has gone*
up. 3. A number, amount, or quantity: *What is*
the value of x if x + 5 = 8? Noun.
○ 1. To think of as being worth an amount in
money or exchange; set a price for: *The jeweler*
valued the necklace at three thousand dollars.
2. Think highly of: *I value your advice. Verb.*
val·ue (val′ū) *noun, plural* **values;** *verb,* **valued,**
valuing.

valve A device that controls the flow of liquid or
gases through a pipe or other container: *The*
valves of the heart control the flow of blood into
and out of the heart. **valve** (valv) *noun, plural*
valves.

vampire 1. In horror stories and folk tales, a dead
person who rises from the grave at night to suck
the blood from sleeping people. 2. A tropical
American bat that feeds on the blood of mammals
and birds; a vampire bat. **vam·pire** (vam′pīər)
noun, plural **vampires.**

van 1. A large, covered truck that is used to move
furniture, animals, or other large items. 2. A
small, covered truck with two or more seats
inside. **van** (van) *noun, plural* **vans.**

vandal A person who damages or destroys public
or private property on purpose. **van·dal** (van′dəl)
noun, plural **vandals.** —**vandalism** *noun* —**van-**
dalize *verb.*

vane A flat or curved blade that is made of wood,
metal, or another material.
Other words sounding like this are **vain** and **vein.**
vane (vān) *noun, plural* **vanes.**

vanilla A flavoring that is used in candies, ice
cream, cookies, and other foods. Vanilla comes
from the seed pods of a tropical plant that is a
type of orchid. **va·nil·la** (və nil′ə) *noun.*

vanish To go out of sight or existence; disappear:
The airplane vanished above the clouds.
van·ish (van′ish) *verb,* **vanished, vanishing.**

vanity Too much pride in one's looks, abilities, or
accomplishments; conceit. **van·i·ty** (van′i tē) *noun.*

vapor Small particles
of mist, steam, or
smoke that can be
seen in the air: *When*
water boils in a pot,
you can see the vapor
rising into the air.
va·por (vā′pər) *noun.*

variable Likely to
change: *variable*
weather. Adjective.
○ Something that
changes or is likely to
change. *Noun.*
var·i·a·ble (vâr′ē ə
bəl) *adjective; noun,*
plural **variables.**

Space vehicles leave a
large **vapor** trail.

variety 1. Change or
difference; lack of sameness: *A job that has no*
variety can become boring.
2. A number of different things: *We bought a*
variety of foods. 3. A different kind or form of
something: *This is a new variety of umbrella,*
unlike any I have seen. **va·ri·e·ty** (və rī′i tē) *noun,*
plural **varieties.**

various Different from one another; of different
kinds: *Students of various backgrounds and*
nationalities go to our school. **var·i·ous** (vâr′ē əs)
adjective.

varnish A liquid that gives a hard, clear coating to
wood, metal, or other materials it is spread on. *Noun.*
○ To put varnish on; cover with varnish: *The*
workers varnished the wood floor. Verb.
var·nish (vär′nish) *noun, plural* **varnishes;** *verb,*
varnished, varnishing.

vary 1. To make or become different; change: *The*
store varies its merchandise from season to sea-
son. The color of the stone varies as you move it
around in the light. 2. To be different; differ: *The*
flowers in our garden vary widely in color. **var·y**
(vâr′ē) *verb,* **varied, varying.** —**variation,** *noun.*

vase A container that is usually higher than it is
wide. **vase** (vās *or* vāz *or* väz) *noun, plural* **vases.**

vassal A person in the Middle Ages who received
land and protection from a lord in return for loyalty and service. **vas·sal** (vas′əl) *noun, plural* **vassals.**

vast Very great in extent, size, or amount: *That*
ranch covers a vast area. **vast** (vast) *adjective,*
vaster, vastest.

vat A large tank or container used for holding liquids. **vat** (vat) *noun*, *plural* **vats**.

vault 1. An arched structure serving as a roof or ceiling: *The vault of the tunnel curved up into darkness.* 2. A safe room or compartment that is used especially to store money or other things of value. **vault** (vôlt) *noun*, *plural* **vaults**.

VCR The abbreviation for **videocassette recorder**.

veal The meat of a calf. **veal** (vēl) *noun*.

veer To change direction; turn: *The driver veered suddenly to avoid a pothole.* **veer** (vēr) *verb*, **veered**, **veering**.

vegetable A plant whose roots, leaves, or other parts are used as food: *Carrots, potatoes, lettuce, and beans are vegetables. Noun.*
○ Relating to or made from vegetables or other plants: *a vegetable stand; vegetable soup. Adjective.*
veg·e·ta·ble (vej′i tə bəl *or* vej′tə bəl) *noun*, *plural* **vegetables**.

vegetarian A person who eats only plants and their products and no meat, fish, or poultry. **veg·e·tar·i·an** (vej′i târ′ē ən) *noun*, *plural* **vegetarians**; *adjective*.

vegetation Plant life: *Jungles have very thick vegetation.* **veg·e·ta·tion** (vej′i tā′shən) *noun*.

vehicle 1. A means of carrying or transporting people or goods. Automobiles, ships, and airplanes are vehicles. 2. A means of expressing, communicating, or achieving something: *Some writers use poetry as a vehicle for their ideas.* **ve·hi·cle** (vē′i kəl) *noun*, *plural* **vehicles**.

veil 1. A piece of very thin material that is worn over the head and shoulders or to conceal the face. 2. Something that hides: *A veil of secrecy surrounded the army's plans. Noun.*
○ To cover or hide with a veil or something like a veil: *He tried to veil his anger with a smile. Verb.*
veil (vāl) *noun*, *plural* **veils**; *verb*, **veiled**, **veiling**.

vein 1. One of the blood vessels that carry blood from all parts of the body to the heart. 2. One of the stiff tubes that form the framework of a leaf or an insect's wing. The veins in a leaf carry food and water to the cells in the leaf. The veins in an insect's wing make the wing strong and firm. 3. A band of a mineral deposited in a rock: *a vein of silver in a mine.* Other words sounding like this are **vain** and **vane**. **vein** (vān) *noun*, *plural* **veins**.

Velcro A trademark for a fastener that consists of two pieces of fabric or tape. One is covered with tiny hooks which attach to tiny loops covering the other piece. **Vel·cro** (vel′krō) *noun*.

velocity The rate of motion; speed: *Light has a velocity of about 186,000 miles per second.* **ve·loc·i·ty** (və los′i tē) *noun*, *plural* **velocities**.

velvet A fabric with a soft, thick pile. Velvet can be made out of silk, nylon, or other materials. **vel·vet** (vel′vit) *noun*.

vending machine A machine that is worked by putting coins into a slot. Vending machines are used to sell candy, soft drinks, and many other small items. **vend·ing machine** (ven′ding).

Venetian blind A blind used at a window to keep out light. It has a series of horizontal wooden, metal, or plastic slats that can be opened or closed. The blind can be raised or lowered by using cords that are attached to the side. **Ve·ne·tian blind** (və nē′shən).

WORD HISTORY

This kind of shade may be called a Venetian blind because it was first made and used in the Italian city of Venice.

venom The poison of some snakes, spiders, and other animals. The venom can be passed to prey or an enemy by a bite or sting. **ven·om** (ven′əm) *noun*, *plural* **venoms**. —**venomous** *adjective*.

vent 1. A hole or other opening through which a gas or liquid passes: *A vent above the stove lets air out of the kitchen.* 2. A means of letting something out: *They used exercise as a vent for their tension. Noun.*
○ To let out: *The children vented their anger by kicking the door. Verb.*
vent (vent) *noun*, *plural* **vents**; *verb*, **vented**, **venting**.

The veins in this insect's wings can be clearly seen.

PRONUNCIATION KEY:

| at | āpe | fär | câre | end | mē | it | īce | pîerce | hot | ōld | sông | fôrk |
| oil | out | up | ūse | rüle | pull | tûrn | chin | sing | shop | thin | this | |

hw in white; zh in treasure. The symbol ə stands for the unstressed vowel sound in about, taken, pencil, lemon, and circus.

787

ventilation   The circulation or change of air. **ven•ti•la•tion** (ven′tə lā′shən) *noun.*

ventricle   Either of the two lower chambers of the heart. The ventricles receive blood from the auricles and pump it through the arteries to the lungs and the rest of the body. **ven•tri•cle** (ven′tri kəl) *noun, plural* **ventricles.**

ventricle

ventriloquism   The art of projecting one's voice without moving the lips so that it seems to come from some other source, such as a puppet or dummy. **ven•tril•o•quism** (ven tril′ə kwiz′əm) *noun.* —**ventriloquist** *noun.*

venture   A task or undertaking that involves risk or danger: *The partners invested in a new business venture. Noun.*

○ 1. To put in danger; risk: *The firefighters ventured their lives by entering the burning building.* 2. To go despite risk or danger: *The sailors ventured into the storm. Verb.*

ven•ture (ven′chər) *noun, plural* **ventures;** *verb,* **ventured, venturing.**

Venus

After the Moon, Venus is the brightest object in the night sky. It is completely covered by clouds which reflect sunlight. Venus has the hottest surface of all the planets, hot enough to melt most metals.
Average distance from sun: **67,300,000 miles**
Diameter: **7,520 miles**
Length of Day: **243 days, 14 minutes**
Length of Year: **224.5 days**
Average Temperature: **900˚F**
Mass compared to Earth: **.8**
Weight of 100 pounds: **91**
Atmosphere: **carbon dioxide**
Number of rings: **0**
Number of satellites: **0**

Venus   The sixth largest planet in our solar system. It is the second planet in order of distance from the sun and the one nearest earth. **Ve•nus** (vē′nəs) *noun.*

veranda or **verandah**   An open porch that runs along one or more sides of a building. **ve•ran•da** (və ran′də) *noun, plural* **verandas.**

verb   A word that is used to express an action or condition: *Run, buy, be, build, feel,* and *seem* are verbs. **verb** (vûrb) *noun, plural* **verbs.**

verbal   Expressed in words; spoken: *I gave the police officer a verbal description of the stolen car.* **ver•bal** (vûr′bəl) *adjective.*

verdict   1. The decision of a jury in a trial: *The jurors agreed on a verdict of "guilty."* 2. A decision or conclusion: *The audience's verdict was that the play was worth seeing.* **ver•dict** (vûr′dikt) *noun, plural* **verdicts.**

verge   The extreme edge or border. —**verge** (vûrj) *noun, plural* **verges.**

verify   To prove the truth of. **ver•i•fy** (ver′ə fī′) *verb,* **verified, verifying.**

vermin   Insects or small animals that cause trouble or harm to people. Cockroaches and rats are vermin. This word is used with a plural verb. **ver•min** (vûr′min) *plural noun.*

Montpelier

Vermont
U. S. Postal Abbreviation: **VT**
Capital: **Montpelier**
Population: **548,000**
Area: **9,609 sq. mi./24,887 sq. km**
State Nickname: **Green Mountain State**
State Bird: **Hermit Thrush**
State Flower: **Red Clover**

Vermont   A state in the northeastern United States. Its capital is Montpelier. **Ver•mont** (vər mont′) *noun.*

WORD HISTORY

The area now known as **Vermont** was once known by English settlers as "Green Mountains." The name Vermont probably comes from the French words for "green mountain." This name became popular and was chosen as the official name after the area declared itself independent in 1777.

versatile Able to do many different things well: *a versatile athlete.* **ver·sa·tile** (vûr′sə təl) *adjective.*

verse **1.** Words that are written in a particular rhythmic pattern and often in rhyme; poetry. **2.** A section of a poem or song; stanza: *I know only the first verse of that song.* **3.** One of the short parts into which the chapters of the Bible are divided. **verse** (vûrs) *noun, plural* **verses.**

version **1.** An account given in a particular way or from a particular point of view: *There were different versions of who had started the fight.* **ver·sion** (vûr′zhən) *noun, plural* **versions.**

versus **1.** Against: *We had boys versus girls in the soccer game.* **ver·sus** (vûr′səs) *preposition.*

vertebra One of the small bones that make up the backbone. **ver·te·bra** (vûr′tə brə) *noun, plural* **vertebrae** (vûr′tə brē) *or* **vertebras.**

vertebrate An animal that has a backbone. Fish, amphibians, reptiles, birds, and mammals are vertebrates. *Noun.*
○ Having a backbone: *vertebrate animals.* *Adjective.* **ver·te·brate** (vûr′tə brāt′ *or* vûr′tə brit) *noun, plural* **vertebrates;** *adjective.*

vertex **1.** The highest point of something; summit: *the vertex of a mountain.* **2.** The point at which the sides of an angle meet. **ver·tex** (vûr′teks′) *noun, plural* **vertexes** *or* **vertices** (vû′tə sēz).

vertical Straight up and down; upright. Look up horizontal for a picture of this. **ver·ti·cal** (vûr′ti kəl) *adjective.*

very **1.** To a high degree; to a great extent: *I am very sorry that you are not feeling well.* **2.** Truly; absolutely; exactly: *That is the very best movie I have ever seen.* *Adverb.*
○ **1.** Mere; by itself: *The very idea of having to get up so early makes me groan.* **2.** Exact; precise: *Your gift was the very thing I needed.* **3.** Absolute; utter: *the very top of a hill.* *Adjective.* **ver·y** (ver′ē) *adverb; adjective.*

vessel **1.** A ship or large boat: *Both passenger ships and vessels carrying freight were docked at the pier.* **2.** A hollow container or holder. Vases, cups, and bowls are vessels. **3.** A duct in the body for carrying blood or other fluids. Arteries and veins are vessels. **ves·sel** (ves′əl) *noun, plural* **vessels.**

vest A short, sleeveless piece of clothing that is worn over a shirt or blouse. *Noun.*
○ To give authority or power to: *The new president was vested with all the rights and powers of the office. Verb.* **vest** (vest) *noun, plural* **vests;** *verb,* **vested, vesting.**

veteran **1.** A person who has had a lot of experience: *The actor was a veteran of the stage.* **2.** A person who has been in the armed forces: *The police chief is an army veteran. Noun.*
○ Having had a lot of experience: *The newspaper sent a veteran reporter to cover the important story. Adjective.* **vet·er·an** (vet′ər ən) *noun, plural* **veterans;** *adjective.*

Veterans Day A holiday in the United States that is celebrated on November 11. It honors the people who have served in the armed forces and have fought in wars for the United States.

veterinarian A doctor who treats animals. **vet·er·i·nar·i·an** (vet′ər ə nâr′ē ən) *noun, plural* **veterinarians.**

veto The power of a president, governor, or official group to keep an act or measure from taking effect. *Noun.*
○ To refuse to approve; stop or prevent by a veto. *The president vetoed the bill. Verb.* **ve·to** (vē′tō) *noun, plural* **vetoes;** *verb,* **vetoed, vetoing.**

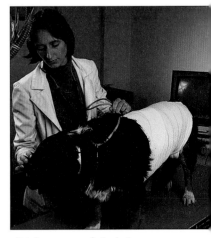

It takes years of study to become a **veterinarian.**

WORD HISTORY

The word **veto** comes from a Latin word that means "I forbid."

PRONUNCIATION KEY:
at　　ape　　fär　　câre　　end　　mē　　it　　īce　　pierce　　hot　　old　　sông　　fôrk
oil　　out　　up　　ūse　　rule　　pull　　tûrn　　chin　　sing　　shop　　thin　　this
hw in white; zh in treasure. The symbol ə stands for the unstressed vowel sound in about, taken, pencil, lemon, and circus.

789

vibrate To move or cause to move rapidly back and forth or up and down: *The strings of a guitar vibrate when they are plucked.* **vi·brate** (vī′brāt) *verb*, **vibrated, vibrating. —vibration** *noun.*

vice **1.** Evil or immoral behavior: *Drug addiction can lead a person into a life of vice.* **2.** A bad habit: *Her chief vice is a tendency to boss people around.* **vice** (vīs) *noun, plural* **vices.**

vice president An officer who ranks second to a president. A vice president takes the place of a president when necessary. **vice pres·i·dent** (vīs′ prez′i dənt) *noun, plural* **vice presidents.**

vice versa The opposite in order; the other way around: *My brother helps me with my homework, and vice versa.* **vi·ce ver·sa** (vī′sə vûr′sə) *adverb.*

vicinity The area near or surrounding a particular place; neighborhood: *There are several parks in the vicinity of our house.* **vi·cin·i·ty** (və sin′i tē) *noun, plural* **vicinities.**

vicious **1.** Wicked; evil: *The kidnappers planned a vicious crime.* **2.** Fierce or dangerous: *a vicious dog.* **vi·cious** (vish′əs) *adjective.*

victim **1.** A person who is injured, killed, or ruined: *victim of an automobile accident.* **2** A person who is cheated or tricked: *The victims of the scheme lost hundred of dollars of their savings.* **vic·tim** (vik′təm) *noun, plural* **victims.**

victor The winner of a struggle, battle, or contest: *A prize will go to the victor.* **vic·tor** (vik′tər) *noun, plural* **victors.**

victorious Having won a victory: *The victorious army was welcomed home.* **vic·to·ri·ous** (vik tôr′ē əs) *adjective.*

victory The defeat of an enemy or opponent: *Our team gained a victory in yesterday's game.* **vic·to·ry** (vik′tə rē) *noun, plural* **victories.**

video **1.** The picture part of television: *The video was fuzzy but the sound was fine.* **2.** A videocassette: *We rented a video to watch Saturday night.* **3.** Videotape: *Is the movie available on video?* **4.** A videotaped performance: *That TV channel shows music videos.* **vid·e·o** (vid′ē ō) *noun, plural* **videos.**

videocassette A videotape in a cassette. It can be recorded on and played by a videocassette recorder. **vid·e·o·cas·sette** (vid′ē ō kə set′) *noun, plural* **videocassettes.**

videocassette recorder An electronic device that records on and plays videotapes.

video display terminal A keyboard and monitor for a computer. A video display terminal can be used to type information to be put into the computer and to retrieve information from the computer for display on the monitor.

video game A game that is played on a television or computer screen. A player can move images on the screen with the help of special controls.

videotape **1.** A strip of magnetic tape on which pictures as well as sound can be recorded. **2.** A recording made on this kind of tape. *Noun.*
○ To make record something on videotape. *Verb.*
vid·e·o·tape (vid′ē ō tāp′) *noun, plural* **videotapes;** *verb*, **videotaped, videotaping.**

Vietnam A country in southeastern Asia. **Vi·et·nam** (vē′et näm′) *noun.* **—Vietnamese** *noun; adjective.*

This view presents a broad panorama of the countryside.

view **1.** The act of looking or seeing; sight: *The sailors got their first view of land after many weeks at sea.* **2.** The range or extent of seeing: *The airplane suddenly came into view.* **3.** Something that is seen or can be seen: *a lovely view of the lake.* **4.** A particular way of thinking about something; opinion: *What's your view on who would make the best class president? Noun.*
○ **1.** To look at or see: *Many people viewed the exhibit at the museum.* **2.** To think about; consider: *Most students viewed the plan for the playground with approval. Verb.*
view (vū) *noun, plural* **views;** *verb*, **viewed, viewing.**

viewpoint An attitude or a way of thinking; point of view. **view·point** (vū′point′) *noun, plural* **viewpoints.**

vigilant Alert and watchful for possible danger. **vig·i·lant** (vij′ə lənt) *adjective*.

vigor 1. Active power or force; strength: *The mayor opposed the state highway plan with vigor.* 2. Healthy strength: *Even though my grandparents are both over eighty, they are still full of vigor.* **vig·or** (vig′ər) *noun.* —**vigorous** *adjective*.

Viking A member of a people who lived in Norway, Sweden, Denmark, and Iceland. The Vikings built ships, raided the coasts of Europe, and voyaged to North America during the eighth to eleventh centuries. **Vi·king** (vī′king) *noun, plural* **Vikings**.

villa A large, luxurious house in the country. **vil·la** (vil′ə) *noun, plural* **villas**.

village 1. A small group of houses. A village is usually smaller than a town: *The countryside was dotted with villages.* 2. The people who live in a village: *The whole village came to the wedding.* **vil·lage** (vil′ij) *noun, plural* **villages**.

villain A wicked or evil person: *In the story, the villains tried to trick the child into going away with them.* **vil·lain** (vil′ən) *noun, plural* **villains**.

vine A plant with a long, thin stem that grows along the ground or climbs on trees, fences, or other supports: *Grapes, melons, and squash grow on vines.* **vine** (vīn) *noun, plural* **vines**.

vinegar A sour liquid that is made by fermenting cider, wine, or juice. Vinegar is used in salad dressing and to flavor and preserve food. **vin·e·gar** (vin′i gər) *noun, plural* **vinegars**.

WORD HISTORY

The word **vinegar** comes from two old French words meaning "wine" and "sour."

vineyard An area where grapes are grown. **vine·yard** (vin′yərd) *noun, plural* **vineyards**.

vinyl A flexible, shiny plastic used to make floor tiles, car upholstery, phonograph records, and other products. **vi·nyl** (vī′nəl) *noun, plural* **vinyls**.

violate 1. To fail to obey or keep; break: *The driver violated the law by going through a red light.* 2. To break in on; disrupt: *The quiet of the afternoon was violated by the loud radio.* **vi·o·late** (vī′ə lāt′) *verb,* **violated, violating**.

violence 1. Strong physical force used to harm: *The robbers threatened to use violence if the banker did not open the vault.* 2. Great or destructive force or action: *the violence of a hurricane.* **vi·o·lence** (vī′ə ləns) *noun.* —**violent** *adjective*.

violet A small purple, white, or pink flower that grows on a low plant. Many violets grow wild, while others are grown in gardens and indoors. **vi·o·let** (vī′ə lit) *noun, plural* **violets**.

violin A musical instrument that has four strings and is played with a bow. **vi·o·lin** (vī′ə lin′) *noun, plural* **violins**. —**violinist** *noun*.

viper A kind of poisonous snake. **vi·per** (vī′pər) *noun, plural* **vipers**.

virgin Not yet used or touched: *We made footprints in the virgin snow.* **vir·gin** (vûr′jin) *adjective*.

Virginia A state in the eastern United States. Its capital is Richmond. **Vir·gin·ia** (vûr jin′yə) *noun*.

WORD HISTORY

Virginia takes its name from a poetic title, "the Virgin Queen," that was given to the English queen Elizabeth I. The colony of Virginia was founded during the reign of Queen Elizabeth and named in her honor.

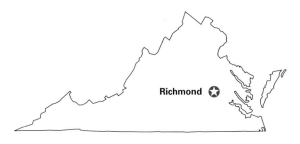

Virginia
U. S. Postal Abbreviation: **VA**
Capital: **Richmond**
Population: **5,904,000**
Area: **40,817 sq. mi./105,716 sq. km.**
State Nickname: **Old Dominion**
State Bird: **Cardinal**
State Flower: **Dogwood**

Virgin Islands A group of islands in the Caribbean Sea. Some of them belong to the United States, and the others belong to the United Kingdom.

PRONUNCIATION KEY:
at   āpe   fär   câre   end   mē   it   īce   pierce   hot   ōld   sông   fôrk
oil   out   up   ūse   rüle   pull   tûrn   chin   sing   shop   thin   this
hw in white; zh in treasure. The symbol ə stands for the unstressed vowel sound in about, taken, pencil, lemon, and circus.

791

virtual reality The effect of computer-generated images, sounds, and sensations that seem to a person like real life. **vir·tu·al reality** (vûr′chü əl).

virtue 1. Moral goodness in one's thinking and behavior: *Their virtue is shown in the thoughtful things they do.* 2. A particular type of moral goodness: *Honesty is a virtue.* 3. Any good quality or characteristic: *This small car has the virtue of fitting into tiny parking spaces.* **vir·tue** (vûr′chü) *noun, plural* **virtues.**

virus 1. A very tiny particle that can reproduce only when it is inside a living cell. Viruses cause many diseases, such as polio, measles, and the common cold. 2. A disease caused by a virus. 3. A computer program designed to hide within another program and cause damage or confusion. **vi·rus** (vī′rəs) *noun, plural* **viruses.**

vise A device with two jaws that are opened and closed with a screw or lever. A vise is used to hold an object firmly in place while it is being worked on. **vise** (vīs) *noun, plural* **vises.**

visible 1. Able to be seen: *Their house is visible from the road.* 2. Easily seen or understood: *There has been no visible improvement in the city government since the election.* **vis·i·ble** (viz′ə bəl) *adjective.* —**visibility** *noun.*

vision 1. The act or power of seeing; sense of sight: *Your vision can weaken as you grow older.* 2. Something that is or has been seen. A vision is usually something beautiful: *The bride was a vision in white.* 3. The ability to plan ahead; foresight: *Designing a new constitution calls for vision.* 4. Something that is imagined or dreamed: *visions of success and fame.* **vi·sion** (vizh′ən) *noun, plural* **visions.**

visit 1. To go or come to see: *We visited my grandparents in Florida.* 2. To stay with as a guest: *Friends from out of town visited us for the weekend.* 3. To go to for pleasure: *visit a museum.* *Verb.*
○ A short stay or call: *We paid a visit to my old friend last night.* *Noun.*
vis·it (viz′it) *verb,* **visited, visiting;** *noun, plural* **visits.** —**visitors** *noun.*

visor A brim that sticks out on the front of a cap. A visor is made to shade the eyes from the sun. **vi·sor** (vī′zər) *noun, plural* **visors.**

vista A distant view, as one seen from a window. **vis·ta** (vis′tə) *noun, plural* **vistas.**

SYNONYMS

vista, scene, view
The vista of a green valley spread out before them as they stood on the balcony. The castle on the hillside made a handsome scene. You'll get the best view of the performers from the front row.

---

visual 1. Relating to or used in seeing: *Eyeglasses are used to correct visual defects.* 2. Able to be seen; visible: *The teacher used charts, slides, and other visual aids to help explain how the heart works.* **vis·u·al** (vizh′ü əl) *adjective.*

visualize To form a mental image of; imagine: *The runner visualized herself winning the race.* **vi·su·al·ize** (vizh′ü ə līz′) *verb,* **visualized, visualizing.**

vital 1. Relating to life: *The victim's heartbeat and other vital signs began to weaken.* 2. Necessary to or supporting life: *The lungs are vital organs.* 3. Full of life and energy. 4. Very important or necessary: *Proper clothing is vital for our camping trip.* **vi·tal** (vī′təl) *adjective.* —**vitality** *noun.*

vitamin One of a group of substances that are needed in small amounts for the health and the normal working of the body. We get most of the vitamins we need from eating the right kinds of food. **vi·ta·min** (vī′tə min) *noun, plural* **vitamins.**

WORD HISTORY

The word **vitamin** comes from a Latin word meaning "life." Vitamins are essential to life.

---

vocabulary All the words used or understood by a person or group. English has one of the largest vocabularies of any language: *Doctors use a special vocabulary when they talk to each other about medical matters.* **vo·cab·u·lar·y** (vō kab′yə ler′ē) *noun, plural* **vocabularies.**

vocal 1. Relating to or expressed by the voice: *Babies produce vocal sounds before they learn how to talk.* 2. Performed by or composed for the voice: *vocal music.* **vo·cal** (vō′kəl) *adjective.*

vocal cords Two folds of skin found in the part of the throat called the larynx. There are two pairs of vocal cords in the larynx. Air from the lungs passes through the lower pair and causes them to vibrate. This makes the sound of the voice.

vocation A profession, occupation, or career: *These students plan on vocations in the building* *trades.* **vo•ca•tion** (vō kā′shən) *noun, plural* **vocations**.

vogue The general fashion, practice, or style: *My grandfather wears clothes that were in* ***vogue*** *forty years ago.* **vogue** (vōg) *noun.*

voice **1.** The sound that is produced through the mouth by speaking, singing, or shouting. **2.** The ability to produce sound through the mouth; speech. **3.** The right to express a view, opinion, or choice: *Citizens must have a* ***voice*** *in their government.* **voice** (vois) *noun, plural* **voices**.

voice mail A system that allows people to leave or play back messages recorded over the telephone.

void An empty space: *The whole group fell silent, leaving an awkward* ***void*** *in the conversation. Noun.*
○ **1.** Completely lacking: *The skier raced toward the jump* ***void*** *of any fear.* **2.** Having no legal force; not valid: *After the investigation, the election results were declared* ***void***. **void** (void) *noun, plural* **voids**; *adjective.*

volcano An opening in the surface of the earth through which lava, gases, and ashes are forced out. Volcanoes often have craters at or near the peak. **vol•ca•no** (vol kā′nō) *noun, plural* **volcanoes** *or* **volcanos**.

WORD HISTORY

The English word **volcano** comes from the Italian word for Vulcan, the Roman god of fire.

volley **1.** The firing of a number of bullets or other missiles at the same time. **2.** An outburst of many things together: *a* ***volley*** *of protests.* **3.** In some sports, the return of a ball before it touches the ground. *Noun.*
○ To return a ball as a volley. *Verb.*
vol•ley (vol′ē) *noun, plural* **volleys**; *verb,* **volleyed, volleying.**

volleyball **1.** A game in which two teams stand on either side of a high net and hit a ball back and forth with their hands. Each side tries not to let the ball touch the ground. **2.** The ball that is used in this game. **vol•ley•ball** (vol′ē bôl′) *noun, plural* **volleyballs**.

volt A unit for measuring the force of an electric current. **volt** (vōlt) *noun, plural* **volts**.

WORD HISTORY

The word **volt** comes from the name of Alessandro Volta, an Italian scientist who invented the first electric battery.

voltage The force of an electric current measured in volts. **vol•tage** (vōl′tij) *noun, plural* **voltages**.

volume **1.** A book. **2.** One of a set or series of related books, newspapers, or magazines. **3.** The amount of space occupied: *Find the* ***volume*** *of a room by multiplying its height by its length by its width.* **4.** The amount of sound: *Please turn down the* ***volume*** *on the radio.* **vol•ume** (vol′ūm) *noun, plural* **volumes**.

volcano

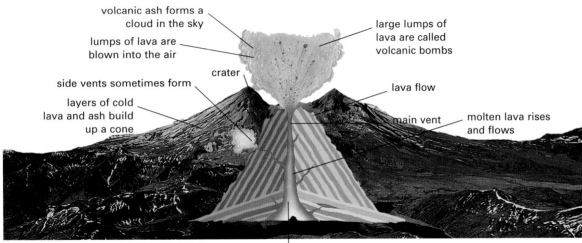

volcanic ash forms a cloud in the sky
lumps of lava are blown into the air
side vents sometimes form
crater
layers of cold lava and ash build up a cone
large lumps of lava are called volcanic bombs
lava flow
main vent
molten lava rises and flows
magma (molten rock) rises from beneath the earth

voluntary 1. Done, made, or acting of one's own free will; not forced: *The robber made a voluntary confession to the police.* 2. Doing something freely; volunteering: *There are many voluntary workers in that hospital.* 3. Controlled by the will: *Raising an arm is done by voluntary muscles, but digesting food in the stomach is not.* **vol·un·tar·y** (vol′ən ter′ē) *adjective.*

volunteer A person who offers to help or does something by choice and often without pay: *The teacher asked for volunteers for the decorating committee. Noun.*
○ 1. To offer to help or do something of one's own free will: *My father volunteered to coach the baseball team.* 2. To give or offer readily: *I volunteered an answer to the teacher's question. Verb.*
○ Relating to or serving as a volunteer: *a volunteer firefighter. Adjective.*
vol·un·teer (vol′ən tîr′) *noun, plural* **volunteers;** *verb,* **volunteered, volunteering;** *adjective.*

vomit To bring up food and other substances from the stomach and expel them through the mouth. **vom·it** (vom′it) *verb,* **vomited, vomiting.**

vote 1. The formal expression of a wish or choice. A vote can be taken by ballot, by voice, or by a show of hands. 2. A decision made by such means. 3. The right of expressing such a wish or choice: *In the United States, women got the vote in 1920.* 4. The number of votes cast: *The vote for the proposal was 250 to 150. Noun.*
○ To express one's wish or choice by a vote. *Verb.*
vote (vōt) *noun, plural* **votes;** *verb,* **voted, voting.**

vouch To give or serve as a guarantee: *Are there any witnesses to vouch for the defendant's innocence?* **vouch** (vouch) *verb,* **vouched, vouching.**

vow A solemn promise or pledge: *The soldiers took a vow of loyalty to the government. Noun.*
○ To promise or pledge solemnly. *Verb.*
vow (vou) *noun, plural* **vows;** *verb,* **vowed, vowing.**

vowel 1. A speech sound made by not blocking the flow of air through the mouth. 2. A letter that represents such a sound. *A, e, i, o, u,* and sometimes *y* are vowels. **vow·el** (vou′əl) *noun, plural* **vowels.**

voyage A journey by water or through space. 2. A long journey. *Noun.*
○ To journey by water or through space. *Verb.*
voy·age (voi′ij) *noun, plural* **voyages;** *verb,* **voyaged, voyaging.**

vs. An abbreviation for **versus.**

Vt. or **VT** An abbreviation for Vermont.

vulgar 1. Showing or marked by a lack of good manners or taste. 2. Offensive in words: *a vulgar joke.* **vul·gar** (vul′gər) *adjective.*

vulnerable 1. Able to be hurt, physically or emotionally: *Newborn animals are often weak and vulnerable.* 2. Open to danger or attack: *The town was in a vulnerable position between the two armies.* **vul·ner·a·ble** (vul′nər ə bəl) *adjective.*

vulture A large bird that has dark, dull feathers and a bald head and neck. Vultures are related to hawks and eagles. They feed on the meat of dead animals. **vul·ture** (vul′chər) *noun, plural* **vultures.**

The letter W has one sound in English which is commonly made by:

w in words such as wet, weathered, and reward;

wh as in while;

and less commonly made by:

o as in choir;

u as in quiet.

w, W The twenty-third letter of the alphabet. **w, W** (dub′əl ū′) *noun, plural* **w's, W's.**

W or **W.** An abbreviation for **west** or **western.**

WA An abbreviation for **Washington.**

wacky Weird or odd in a silly, amusing way: *This computer game has a lot of wacky characters in it.* **wack•y** (wak′ē) *adjective,* **wackier, wackiest.**

wad **1.** A small, tightly packed lump of soft material: *The nurse cleaned my cut with a wad of cotton. I stepped on a wad of chewing gum.* **2.** A tight roll of paper: *The man in line in front of me at the cash register took out a large wad of dollar bills. Noun.*
○ To roll, press, or pack into a wad: *I wadded up the letter and threw it away. Verb.*
wad (wod) *noun, plural* **wads;** *verb,* **wadded, wadding.**

waddle To walk or move with short steps, swaying the body from side to side: *The duck waddled across the yard. Verb.*
○ A swaying or rocking walk: *The audience laughed at the clown's waddle. Noun.*
wad•dle (wod′əl) *verb,* **waddled, waddling;** *noun, plural* **waddles.**

wade **1.** To walk in or through water or mud: *We waded in the shallow pool.* **2.** To move or make one's way slowly and with difficulty: *The secretary had to wade through a pile of papers to find the missing letter.* **wade** (wād) *verb,* **waded, wading.**

waffle A crisp cake made of batter. Waffles have crisscross markings on them that are made by the utensil they are cooked in. *Noun.*
○ **1.** To avoid answering a direct question: *The senator waffled when reporters asked if he would support efforts to clean up our environment.*

2. To change one's opinions or thinking often; be undecided: *You can't keep waffling about which movie we're going to see. Verb.*
waf•fle (wof′əl) *noun, plural* **waffles;** *verb,* **waffled, waffling.**

wag¹ To move quickly from side to side or up and down: *The friendly dog wagged its tail when the visitors arrived. Verb.*
○ The act of wagging; wagging motion: *The puppy greeted us with a wag of its tail. Noun.*
wag (wag) *verb,* **wagged, wagging;** *noun, plural* **wags.**

wag² A witty person. **wag** (wag) *noun, plural* **wags.**

wage Payment for work done: *The factory pays a wage of $6.50 per hour to the workers. Noun.*
○ To carry on or take part in: *The rebels are waging a war against the government. Verb.*
wage (wāj) *noun, plural* **wages;** *verb,* **waged, waging.**

wagon **1.** A vehicle that has four wheels. It is used for carrying heavy loads. Wagons are usually drawn by a horse or horses. **2.** A low vehicle with four wheels that is pulled by a long handle. **wag•on** (wag′ən) *noun, plural* **wagons.**

waif A homeless, lost, or abandoned person or animal, especially a young child: *I saw a sad story on the television news about waifs made orphans by the war.* **waif** (wāf) *noun, plural* **waifs.**

waist 1. The part of the human body between the ribs and the hips. 2. A piece of clothing or part of a piece of clothing that covers this part of the body: *The dress had a high **waist**.* Another word that sounds like this is **waste**. **waist** (wāst) *noun, plural* **waists.**

wait 1. To stay in a place until someone comes or something happens: *"**Wait** for me!" called my friend. **Wait** until it stops raining before you leave.* 2. To be put off or delayed: *The job of cleaning out the garage can **wait** until next week. Verb.*
○ The act of waiting or the amount of time spent waiting: *There will be a two-hour **wait** before the next plane. Noun.*
Another word that sounds like this is **weight**.
• **to wait on.** 1. To serve or help: *A nice salesperson **waited on** us at the grocery store.* 2. To wait for: *She got tired of **waiting on** us and left.* **wait** (wāt) *verb,* **waited, waiting;** *noun, plural* **waits.**

waiter A man whose job is serving food or drink in a restaurant or other place. **wait•er** (wā′tər) *noun, plural* **waiters.**

waitress A woman whose job is serving food or drink in a restaurant or other place. **wait•ress** (wā′tris) *noun, plural* **waitresses.**

wake¹ To stop or cause to stop sleeping: *I **waked** at nine o'clock this morning. Be quiet or you will **wake** the baby. Verb.*
○ A vigil kept over the body of a dead person before burial. *Noun.*
• **to wake up.** To stop or cause to stop sleeping: *I usually **wake up** at 7 A.M. A fire engine's siren **woke** us **up** last night.* **wake** (wāk) *verb,* **waked** *or* **woke, waked** *or* **woken, waking;** *noun, plural* **wakes.**

wake² The track of waves or foam left by a boat, ship, or other thing moving through water. **wake** (wāk) *noun, plural* **wakes.**

waken 1. To stop or cause to stop sleeping; wake: *Do you need an alarm clock, or will you **waken** by yourself? If you're not quiet, you will **waken** the dogs.* 2. To make active; stir up: *Visiting the art museum **wakened** my interest in learning how to paint.* **wak•en** (wā′kən) *verb,* **wakened, wakening.**

Wales A section of the United Kingdom. It is in the southwestern part of the island of Great Britain. **Wales** (wālz) *noun.*

walk 1. To move or travel on foot at a normal, slow pace. A person walks by placing one foot on the ground before lifting the other. 2. To move through, over, or across on foot: *Let's **walk** the beach after we swim.* 3. To go with on foot: *I'll **walk** you to the corner.* 4. To make or help to walk: *We **walk** the dog twice a day.* 5. To go or allow a batter to go to first base in baseball because four balls have been pitched. *Verb.*
○ 1. The act of walking: *We took a **walk** around the park.* 2. A distance covered or a time spent walking: *It's a long **walk** to your house.* 3. A path or area set apart for walking: *There is a shady **walk** along the lake.* 4. A particular social position or occupation: *People from all **walks** of life live in this neighborhood. Noun.* **walk** (wôk) *verb,* **walked, walking;** *noun, plural* **walks.**

wall 1. A solid structure that forms a side of a building, room, or space: *That school building has brick **walls**. The **walls** of my room are decorated with pictures.* 2. Something hard to get over that blocks the way; barrier: *A **wall** of fire kept the firefighters from getting near the burning house. Noun.*
○ To divide, surround, or block with a wall or walls: *The workers **walled** up the old entrance to the building. Verb.*
• **off the wall.** Strange; weird: *She's very creative, but some of her ideas are really **off the wall**.* This is an informal use.
wall (wôl) *noun, plural* **walls;** *verb,* **walled, walling.**

Stone walls are often all that is left of ancient buildings.

wallet A flat, folding case for holding money, cards, or photographs. **wal·let** (wol′it *or* wô′lit) *noun, plural* **wallets**.

wallow To toss or roll about in something: *Pigs wallow in mud in order to stay cool.* **wal·low** (wol′ō) *verb,* **wallowed, wallowing;** *noun, plural* **wallows**.

wallpaper Paper that is pasted on the walls of a room to decorate them. Wallpaper is usually colored or has designs or patterns printed on it. *Noun.*

○ To put wallpaper on the walls of: *The roommates wallpapered their room. Verb.* **wall·pa·per** (wôl′pā′pər) *noun, plural* **wallpapers;** *verb,* **wallpapered, wallpapering.**

walnut A sweet, oily nut that has a hard shell. Walnuts grow on tall trees. The wood of the walnut tree is used to make furniture. **wal·nut** (wôl′nut′) *noun, plural* **walnuts.**

walrus A large animal that lives in water in Arctic regions. Walruses have flippers like seals but are larger and have a pair of long ivory tusks and a tough hide. **wal·rus** (wôl′rəs *or* wol′rəs) *noun, plural* **walruses** *or* **walrus.**

WORD HISTORY

The word walrus comes from the Dutch name for this animal. The Dutch word means "whale horse."

waltz 1. A whirling, gliding dance that is performed by a couple. 2. The music for this dance. *Noun.*

○ To dance a waltz. *Verb.* **waltz** (wôlts) *noun, plural* **waltzes;** *verb,* **waltzed, waltzing.**

wampum Small, polished beads made from shells and strung together or woven into belts, collars, and necklaces. Wampum was used by some Native Americans as money. **wam·pum** (wom′pəm *or* wôm′pəm) *noun.*

WAN A shortened form of **wide area network.** **WAN** (wan) *noun, plural* **WANs.**

wand A thin rod or stick: *The magician waved a wand over the hat and flowers appeared.* **wand** (wond) *noun, plural* **wands.**

wander 1. To go or move about with no particular place to go: *We wandered through the woods looking for flowers.* 2. To lose one's way; stray: *They wandered off the trail and got lost.* 3. To stray from a subject: *My mind wandered during the play.* **wan·der** (won′dər) *verb,* **wandered, wandering.**

wane 1. To lose strength; become smaller or less in size or importance: *Interest in the problems caused by pollution hasn't waned.* 2. To appear to become smaller: *A full moon wanes as the days pass.* **wane** (wān) *verb,* **waned, waning.**

wannabe A person who wants to be someone special, such as a famous musician or movie star: *The theater was filled with celebrities and wannabes.* **wan·na·be** (won′ə bē′ *or* wô′nə bē′) *noun, plural* **wannabes.**

WORD HISTORY

The word wannabe comes from the way the phrase "want to be" sounds when it is said rapidly.

want 1. To feel an impulse to have or do something; wish for; desire: *My neighbor wanted a new bicycle. I want to go home.* 2. To have need of; lack: *Those curtains want washing. Verb.*

○ 1. An impulse to have or do something; desire: *They live simply, and their wants are few.* 2. A need; lack: *For want of wood, the first settlers on the prairie built their houses of sod.* 3. Lack of money and necessary things; poverty: *The homeless people lived in great want. Noun.* **want** (wont *or* wônt) *verb,* **wanted, wanting;** *noun, plural* **wants.**

war 1. A state or time of armed fighting between countries or different groups within a country: *The two nations could not settle their disagreements peacefully, and war broke out.* 2. A long struggle or fight: *Many millions of dollars are spent each year in the war against cancer. Noun.*

○ To carry on a war; fight: *The two countries warred for many years before a peace treaty was finally signed. Verb.*

Another word that sounds like this is **wore.**

war (wôr) *noun, plural* **wars;** *verb,* **warred, warring.**

warbler Any of a number of small, lively American songbirds. Most warblers have bright feathers. **war·bler** (wôr′blər) *noun, plural* **warblers.**

PRONUNCIATION KEY:

| at | āpe | fär | câre | end | mē | it | īce | pierce | hot | ōld | sông | fôrk |
| oil | out | up | ūse | rüle | pull | tûrn | chin | sing | shop | thin | this | |

hw in white; zh in treasure. The symbol ə stands for the unstressed vowel sound in about, taken, pencil, lemon, and circus.

797

ward 1. A large room or area of a hospital: *A number of patients are taken care of in a ward. The children's ward has one hundred beds.* 2. A person who is under the care or control of a court or another person acting as guardian. 3. A division of a city or town: *Cities and towns are divided into wards for purposes of local government. Noun.*
• **to ward off.** To keep or force away: *Our soldiers warded off the enemy attack.*
ward (wôrd) *noun, plural* **wards**; *verb,* **warded, warding.**

warden 1. A person who is in charge of a prison. 2. An official who patrols an area and sees that certain laws are obeyed there: *The game warden reminded us that we could only catch three trout in the lake.* **ward•en** (wôr′dən) *noun, plural* **wardens.**

wardrobe 1. A collection of clothing: *That opera company has a large wardrobe of costumes.* 2. A piece of furniture or a closet for keeping clothes: *Instead of a closet, the hotel room had a large wooden wardrobe.* **ward•robe** (wôr′drōb) *noun.*

WORD HISTORY

The word **wardrobe** comes from an old French word used for a place to keep clothes. The French word was made up of two words that mean "to guard" and "a piece of clothing."

ware 1. Things for sale: *The street vendors put their wares on display in the public square.* 2. Dishes, pots, and other things used for cooking or eating: *We bought a new piece of ceramic ware at the fair.*
Another word that sounds like this is **wear**.
ware (wâr) *noun, plural* **wares.**

Many stores sell a wide variety of wares.

warehouse A building where merchandise is stored: *The new sofa we ordered will be sent from the warehouse.* **ware•house** (wâr′hous′) *noun, plural* **warehouses** (wâr′hou′zīz).

warfare Armed fighting between countries or groups; war. **war•fare** (wôr′fâr′) *noun.*

warm 1. Somewhat hot; not cold: *The fire made the room warm. I'm going to take a warm bath.* 2. Having a feeling of heat in or on the body: *My hands were warm inside my mittens.* 3. Giving off heat: *The warm fire made the autumn night less chilly.* 4. Holding in heat: *We all wore warm clothing on the camping trip.* 5. Full of or showing strong, usually friendly feelings: *A hug is a warm greeting. I was grateful for my teacher's warm, encouraging words. Adjective.*
○ 1. To make or become warm or heated: *Please warm the milk for the baby. The soup will warm quickly on the stove.* 2. To fill or be filled with strong, usually friendly feelings: *The sight of home warmed their hearts. The family warmed to the little puppy. Verb.*
• **to warm up.** 1. To make warm: *Please warm up the rolls in the oven.* 2. To get ready by practicing or exercising: *The team warmed up before the game.*
• **to warm up to.** To become more friendly or enthusiastic about something: *I didn't like using the computer at first, but now I've warmed up to it.*
warm (wôrm) *adjective,* **warmer, warmest;** *verb,* **warmed, warming.** —**warmly** *adverb* —**warmness** *noun.*

warm-blooded Having a body temperature that stays the same even when the temperature of the air or of other surroundings changes. Mammals and birds are warm-blooded. Snakes and turtles are cold-blooded. **warm-blood•ed** (wôrm′blud′id) *adjective.*

warmth The state or quality of being warm: *We felt the warmth of the sun on our faces. The actor was pleased by the warmth of the audience's applause.* **warmth** (wôrmth) *noun.*

warn 1. To tell beforehand about something that may happen; put on guard; alert: *The news on the radio warned us of the coming storm. The flashing yellow light warned of danger ahead.* 2. To give advice to: *Dentists warn us not to eat too much candy.*

Another word that sounds like this **worn**.

warn (wôrn) *verb*, **warned, warning, warning**.

warning Notice or advice given beforehand of a danger or a possible bad result: *The warning on the label said the bottle contained poison.* **warn·ing** (wôr′ning) *noun, plural* **warnings**.

warp To bend out of shape; distort: *The rainy weather warped the boards.* **warp** (wôrp) *verb*, **warped, warping**.

warrior A person who fights or is experienced in fighting battles. **war·ri·or** (wôr′ē ər *or* wor′ē ər) *noun, plural* **warriors**.

warship A ship built and armed for use in war. **war·ship** (wôr′ship′) *noun, plural* **warships**.

wart 1. A small, hard lump that grows on the skin. A wart is caused by a virus. 2. A small lump that grows on part of a plant. **wart** (wôrt) *noun, plural* **warts**. —**warty** *adjective*.

wary Watching carefully; alert; cautious: *Always be wary when crossing a busy street.* **war·y** (wâr′ē) *adjective*, **warier, wariest**. —**warily** *adverb*.

was A form of the past tense of **be** that is used with I, he, she, it, or the name of a person, place, or thing: *I was at home yesterday. The robin was building a nest.* Look up **be** for more information. **was** (wuz *or* woz *or unstressed* wəz) *verb*.

wash 1. To make free of dirt, germs, or the like by using water or soap and water: *I washed my face.* 2. To take out or away by using water or soap and water: *I washed the gravy stain out of the tablecloth.* 3. To clean oneself. 4. To carry away, wear away, or destroy by flowing water: *The rain washed away the fertilizer on the lawn.* Verb. ○ 1. The act of washing: *I gave my hands a quick wash.* 2. The amount of clothes or other things washed at one time: *I hung the wash on the line to dry.* 3. A flow or rush of water, or the sound made by this: *We could hear the wash of the waves on the beach.* 4. A special liquid that is used for bathing, rinsing, or cleansing: *The doctor gave me a wash for my infected eye.* Noun.
•**wash up**. 1. To become deposited by the action of the waves of the ocean: *Sometimes treasure from old shipwrecks is washed up on the shore.* 2. To wash the face and hands: *Go wash up before we sit down to dinner.*

wash (wôsh *or* wosh) *verb*, **washed, washing**; *noun, plural* **washes**.

Wash. An abbreviation for **Washington**.

washable Suitable or safe for being washed: *This jacket has to be dry-cleaned because it isn't washable.* **wash·a·ble** (wosh′ə bəl *or* wô′shə bəl) *adjective*.

washer 1. A person who washes. 2. A machine for washing. 3. A flat ring of metal, rubber, or other material. It is placed between a nut and a bolt to give a tighter fit: *The leaking faucet needs a new washer.* **wash·er** (wô′shər *or* wosh′ər) *noun, plural* **washers**.

washing machine A machine for washing clothes and other things.

Washington 1. A state in the northwestern United States. Its capital is Olympia. 2. The capital of the United States. It lies between Maryland and northern Virginia, and includes all of the District of Columbia. It is also called *Washington, D.C.* **Wash·ing·ton** (wô′shing tən *or* wosh′ing tən) *noun*.

WORD HISTORY

Washington was named after George Washington. It is the only state that is named for a president.

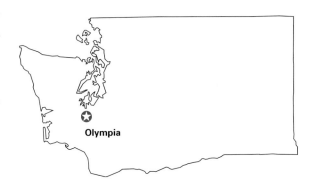

Washington
U. S. Postal Abbreviation: **WA**
Capital: **Olympia**
Population: **4,538,000**
Area: **68,192 sq. mi./176,616 sq. km**
State Nickname: **Evergreen State**
State Bird: **Willow Goldfinch**
State Flower: **Rhododendron**

Washington's Birthday A holiday that used to be observed on February 22 to celebrate George

PRONUNCIATION KEY:

| at | āpe | fär | câre | end | mē | it | īce | pierce | hot | ōld | sòng | fôrk |
| oil | out | up | ūse | rüle | pûll | tûrn | chin | sing | shop | thin | this | |

hw in white; zh in treasure. The symbol ə stands for the unstressed vowel sound in about, taken, pencil, lemon, and circus.

799

Washington's birthday. It is now observed on the third Monday in February. This holiday is also called **Presidents' Day.**

wasn't Shortened form of "was not": *My friend **wasn't** home when I called. I **wasn't** planning to get up early, but the sunlight woke me.* **was·n't** (wuz′ənt *or* woz′ənt) *contraction.*

wasp An insect that has wings and a thin body with a narrow waist. Female wasps can give a painful sting. **wasp** (wosp) *noun, plural* **wasps.**

waste 1. To use or spend in a careless or useless way: *You **wasted** your money when you bought that old bicycle. I **wasted** the whole afternoon daydreaming.* 2. To use up, wear away, or exhaust: *The long sickness **wasted** the old dog's strength.* 3. To destroy; ruin: *The forest fire **wasted** everything in its path.* 4. To lose energy, strength, or health slowly but steadily: *The homeless kitten was **wasting** away from lack of food when we found it. Verb.*
○ 1. The act of wasting or the condition of being wasted: *It's a **waste** of time trying to mend that sock. Avoid the **waste** of water.* 2. Material that has been thrown away or is left over; refuse: *There was a lot of **waste** floating in the dirty river.* 3. Material that has not been digested and is eliminated from the body. *Noun.*
○ Left over or worthless: *Some of the products sold in the lumber store are made from **waste** materials that have been recycled. Adjective.*
  • **to go to waste.** To be unused or used in the wrong way: *After the party, we froze all of the leftovers so they wouldn't **go to waste.***
Another word that sounds like this is **waist.**
waste (wāst) *verb,* **wasted, wasting;** *noun, plural* **wastes;** *adjective.*

wastebasket A basket or other open container used for scraps of paper or other things to be thrown away. **waste·bas·ket** (wāst′bas′kit) *noun, plural* **wastebaskets.**

wasteland A piece of land or an area where there are few or no living things. A desert is a wasteland. **waste·land** (wāst′land′) *noun, plural* **wastelands.**

watch 1. To look at a person or thing carefully: *If you **watch** the magician's tricks a few times, you may learn how they're done.* 2. To guard; take care of: *Please **watch** my dog while I'm in the store.* 3. To wait and look in a careful, alert way: *The prisoner **watched** for a chance to escape. Verb.*
○ 1. The act of looking carefully or guarding: *Please keep **watch** for the bus while I get a newspaper.* 2. One or more persons whose work is guarding something: *My cousin is part of the night **watch** at the museum.* 3. The period of time when a person or persons guard something: *The sailor's **watch** lasted for eight hours.* 4. A small device that measures and shows the time. Watches are usually worn on the wrist or carried in the pocket. *Noun.*
  • **to watch it** *or* **watch out.** To be careful; use caution: *Watch it when you cross that street because there's a lot of traffic.*
watch (woch) *verb,* **watched, watching;** *noun, plural* **watches.**

WORD HISTORY

The word **watch** goes back to an Old English word meaning "to be awake." Sometimes people would stay awake deliberately, or watch, as a religious duty or to tend a sick person. This led to the meaning of staying awake on purpose to look out for something. From this meaning *watch* came to mean "to look at with attention."

---

watchdog A dog that is kept to guard a house or property. *Noun.*
○ Trusted with the job of overseeing a task or group: *a **watchdog** committee of safety experts.* **watch·dog** (woch′dôg′) *noun, plural* **watchdogs.**

watchful Watching carefully; alert: *The babies played while their **watchful** parents sat nearby.* **watch·ful** (woch′fəl) *adjective.* —**watchfully** *adverb* —**watchfulness** *noun*

watchman A person whose work is guarding a building or property. A watchman usually works during the night when a place is empty. **watch·man** (woch′mən) *noun, plural* **watchmen** (woch′mən).

water 1. The liquid that falls as rain and forms the earth's oceans, rivers, lakes, and ponds. Water has no color, smell, or taste in its pure form. We use water for washing and drinking. 2. A body of water: *We swam in the warm Florida **waters**.* The word "water" in this sense is usually used in the plural form. *Noun.*
○ 1. To put water into or on: *I **water** the plants every day.* 2. To give water to for drinking: *We stopped to **water** the horses.* 3. To give forth

water from the body: *The smoke made my eyes water. Verb.*

wa·ter (wô′tər) *noun, plural* **waters**; *verb,* **watered, watering.**

water buffalo A black buffalo of Asia that has long horns that curve backward. The water buffalo is used for carrying or pulling heavy loads.

watercolor **1.** A paint that is made by mixing pigment with water. **2.** The art of painting with watercolors. **3.** A picture or design made with watercolors. **wa·ter·col·or** (wô′tər kul′ər) *noun, plural* **watercolors.**

watercress A plant that grows in running water or wet soil. Its leaves have a sharp taste and are used in salads. **wa·ter·cress** (wô′tər kres′) *noun, plural* **watercresses.**

waterfall A natural stream of water falling from a high place. **wa·ter·fall** (wô′tər fôl′) *noun, plural* **waterfalls.**

water lily A plant that grows in freshwater ponds and lakes. Water lilies have large, showy flowers and leaves that float on the water.

waterlogged Soaked or filled up with water: *After walking in the rain, my shoes were waterlogged.* **wa·ter·logged** (wô′tər lôgd′) *adjective.*

watermelon A large, juicy fruit that usually has a thick green rind, a watery pulp that is pink, red, or yellow, and many seeds. Watermelons grow on vines. **wa·ter·mel·on** (wô′tər mel′ən) *noun, plural* **watermelons.**

water moccasin A kind of poisonous snake; cottonmouth. Look up **cottonmouth** for more information.

waterproof Not letting water pass through: *Our roof is covered with waterproof shingles. Adjective.*

○ To make waterproof: *My boots have been waterproofed with a rubber coating. Verb.* **wa·ter·proof** (wô′tər prüf′) *adjective; verb,* **waterproofed, waterproofing.**

watershed **1.** A ridge or other high land area that separates two different river basins. **2.** The total land area from which water drains into a river or lake: *Nebraska is part of the watershed of the Mississippi River.* **wa·ter·shed** (wô′tər shed′) *noun, plural* **watersheds.**

water-ski To glide over the surface of the water on water skis while being pulled by a rope attached to a boat. **wa·ter-ski** (wô′tər skē′) *verb,* **water-skied, water-skiing.**

It takes strength and balance to water-ski.

water ski One of a pair of short, wide skis used when water-skiing.

watertight Constructed so that water cannot leak into, leak out of, or move through something: *Submarines must be completely watertight.* **wa·ter·tight** (wô′tər tīt′) *adjective.*

waterway A river, canal, or other body of water that is used as a route for ships. **wa·ter·way** (wô′tər wā′) *noun, plural* **waterways.**

waterwheel A wheel that is turned by the weight or pressure of water falling on it or flowing under it. Waterwheels are used to provide power. **wa·ter·wheel** (wô′tər hwēl′ *or* wô′tər wēl′) *noun, plural* **waterwheels.**

Almost all of America's early factories were powered by waterwheels.

PRONUNCIATION KEY:

| at | āpe | fär | câre | end | mē | it | īce | pierce | hot | ōld | sông | fôrk |
| oil | out | up | ūse | rüle | pull | tûrn | chin | sing | shop | thin | this | |

hw in white; zh in treasure. The symbol ə stands for the unstressed vowel sound in about, taken, pencil, lemon, and circus.

801

waterworks 1. The entire system for supplying water to a city or town. Reservoirs, machinery, pipes, and buildings are part of a waterworks. 2. A building in which the machinery for pumping water to a city or town is located. **wa·ter·works** (wô′tər wûrks′) *plural noun*.

watery 1. Covered with or containing water: *My eyes get **watery** when I go out in the cold. The ground is still **watery** from yesterday's heavy rains.* 2. Too much like water; too liquid: *This gravy is **watery**.* **wa·ter·y** (wô′tə rē) *adjective*, **waterier, wateriest.** —**wateriness** *noun*.

watt A unit for measuring electric power. **watt** (wot) *noun, plural* **watts.**

WORD HISTORY

The word watt comes from the name of James Watt. He was a Scottish engineer and inventor.

---

wave 1. To move freely back and forth or up and down; move with a swaying motion: *The stalks of wheat **waved** in the wind. The children **waved** their flags as the parade passed by.* 2. To show or signal by raising and moving the hand or something held in the hand: *Our friends **waved** goodbye to us as the train pulled out. The guard **waved** for us to stop.* 3. To have or give a curving form or appearance to: *I'm tired of having straight hair, so I'm going to **wave** it. Verb.*
○ 1. A long, moving ridge of water on the surface of a body of water: *The ship rode gently over the **waves**.* 2. A motion that transmits energy through matter or space, moving somewhat like a water wave: *Sound, heat, and light move in **waves**.* 3. The act of waving with the hand or with something held in the hand: *The garage attendant signaled for us to come in with a **wave** of the hand.* 4. A sudden rush or increase: *We had a heat **wave** last week and temperatures rose into the high nineties.* 5. A curve or series of curves. *Noun.*
wave (wāv) *verb,* **waved, waving;** *noun, plural* **waves.**

wavy Having a curving movement or shape; full of waves: *My friend has **wavy** hair.* **wav·y** (wā′vē) *adjective,* **wavier, waviest.** —**waviness** *noun.*

wax¹ 1. Any of various substances that are like fat and come from plants or animals. Bees make a wax called beeswax that is used in making their honeycombs. Wax also forms inside the human ear. 2. A substance that is like or contains wax. Wax is used to polish furniture and cars, and to make candles. *Noun.*
○ To cover or polish with wax: *We **waxed** the floors this afternoon. Verb.*
wax (waks) *noun, plural* **waxes;** *verb,* **waxed, waxing.** —**waxiness** *noun* —**waxy** *adjective.*

wax² 1. To become larger in size, brightness, or strength: *The moon **waxes** as it gets nearer to the full moon.* 2. To become: *They **waxed** enthusiastic when they spoke about plans for the camping trip.* **wax** (waks) *verb,* **waxed, waxing.**

way 1. A course of action for doing or getting something; method: *One **way** to paint the ceiling is to stand on a stool. Being kind to others is a good **way** to make friends.* 2. How something is done; manner: *The visitor said "hello" in a friendly **way**.* 3. A road or path that leads from one place to another: *That road is the quickest **way** to town.* 4. A direction: *The storm is heading this **way**.* 5. A moving along a particular route or in a particular direction: *I bought bread on my **way** home from school.* 6. Distance: *They walked a long **way** before finding the right house.* 7. Something that a person wants to have or do; wish: *Some people become angry if they cannot have their **way**.* 8. A particular detail or feature: *In many **ways**, the plan is a good one.* 9. Space for passing; room: *The cars pulled over to make **way** for the fire engine. Noun.*
○ At or to a distance; far: *The water from the breaking waves came **way** up on the beach. Adverb.*
Another word that sounds like this is **weigh**.
• **by the way.** An expression used to introduce a topic that is new but usually related to the one that is being discussed: *By the **way**, we're leaving at four o'clock.*
• **in** *or* **out of the way.** In or out of a position that blocks someone or something from passing: *You'll have to move your bike; it's **in the way**.*
• **to get** *or* **have one's own way.** To get or have what one wants: *It's hard having him on our team because he always expects **to get his own way**.*
• **to give way.** 1. To withdraw or retreat: *The rebels **gave way** after a long battle with govern-*

ment troops. **2.** To collapse: *The bridge* **gave way** *under the heavy load.*

• **under way.** Moving, happening, or being carried out: *The plane was* **under way** *after a delay of an hour. Plans for the party are* **under way.**

way (wā) *noun, plural* **ways**; *adverb.*

we The persons who are speaking: *We won the baseball game.*

Another word that sounds like this is **wee.**

we (wē) *plural pronoun.*

weak 1. Likely to fall or give way: *The legs of the old chair are* **weak. 2.** Not having strength, force, or power: *Lack of food made the lost hikers* **weak.** *The light is too* **weak** *to read by.*

Another word that sounds like this is **week.**

weak (wēk) *adjective,* **weaker, weakest.**

weaken To make or become weak or weaker: *I* **weakened** *the tea by adding water. The runner* **weakened** *near the finish line.* **weak·en** (wē′kən) *verb,* **weakened, weakening.**

weakling A person who lacks physical or moral strength: *A* **weakling** *wouldn't be able to lift that rock. Stand up for your friends and don't be a* **weakling.** **weak·ling** (wēk′ling) *noun, plural* **weaklings.**

weakness 1. The state or quality of being weak: *Weakness from the illness kept the child in bed.* **2.** A weak point; flaw: *My biggest character* **weakness** *is being lazy.* **3.** A special liking; fondness: *My cousin has a* **weakness** *for fancy clothing.* **weak·ness** (wēk′nis) *noun, plural* **weaknesses.**

wealth 1. A great amount of money or valuable things; riches: *That big house belongs to a family of great* **wealth. 2.** A great amount of anything: *The class came up with a* **wealth** *of ideas for the science project.* **wealth** (welth) *noun.*

wealthy Having wealth; rich: *Some* **wealthy** *people founded this museum.* **wealth·y** (wel′thē) *adjective,* **wealthier, wealthiest.**

weapon 1. Something that is used in fighting to attack or defend. Guns and knives are weapons. **2.** Any means used to attack or defend: *The dictator used the threat of prison as a* **weapon** *against opponents.* **weap·on** (wep′ən) *noun, plural* **weapons.**

wear 1. To carry or have on the body: *We* **wear** warm clothes in the winter. **2.** To have or show: *She* **wears** *her hair long. He* **wore** *a big smile.* **3.** To damage or reduce by long use or exposure: *The ocean* **wore** *the rocks until they were smooth.* **4.** To cause or make by rubbing or scraping: *You'll* **wear** *holes in your socks if you don't wear slippers.* **5.** To last or hold out: *These trousers did not* **wear** *well. Verb.*

○ **1.** The act of wearing or the state of being worn: *This suit has had five years of* **wear.** **2.** Clothing: *This store sells both women's* **wear** *and men's* **wear. 3.** Damage caused by use or age. *Noun.*

Another word that sounds like this is **ware.**

• **to wear off.** To lose effect: *When the medicine* **wore off,** *I started coughing again.*

• **to wear out. 1.** To use until no longer fit or able to be used: *The runner* **wore out** *the soles of the shoes after only two months.* **2.** To make tired; exhaust: *We were* **worn out** *from the long hike.*

wear (wâr) *verb,* **wore, worn, wearing**; *noun.*

weary Very tired: *The carpenter was* **weary** *after the day's hard work. Adjective.*

○ To make or become weary; tire: *The long walk* **wearied** *the children. I* **weary** *of watching the same television shows. Verb.*

wea·ry (wîr′ē) *adjective,* **wearier, weariest**; *verb,* **wearied, wearying.** —**wearily** *adverb* —**weariness** *noun.*

weasel A small animal that has a slender body, short legs, a long neck, and soft, thick, brownish fur. Weasels eat rabbits and other small animals, snakes, and small birds. **wea·sel** (wē′zəl) *noun, plural* **weasels** *or* **weasel.**

weather The condition of the air or atmosphere at a particular time and place: *The* **weather** *has been cold and rainy for the past week. Noun.*

○ **1.** To cause to be dried, bleached, or aged by the weather: *The salt air and sun* **weathered** *the houses at the beach.* **2.** To come safely through: *The little boat* **weathered** *the storm. Verb.*

weath·er (weth′ər) *noun; verb,* **weathered, weathering.**

weatherman A person who studies and forecasts the weather. **weath·er·man** (weth′ər man′) *noun, plural* **weathermen** (weth′ər men).

PRONUNCIATION KEY:

| at | āpe | fär | câre | end | mē | it | īce | pierce | hot | ōld | sông | fôrk |
| oil | out | up | ūse | rüle | pull | tûrn | chin | sing | shop | thin | this | |

hw in white; zh in treasure. The symbol ə stands for the unstressed vowel sound in about, taken, pencil, lemon, and circus.

803

weather vane A device that is moved by the wind and is usually placed on the top of a roof.

A **weather vane** shows the direction in which the wind is blowing.

weave 1. To make something by passing strands or lengths of material over and under one another: *This machine weaves yarn into cloth. I wove a basket out of straw.* 2. To spin a web or cocoon: *Spiders weave webs.* 3. To move or make by turning and twisting: *The police had to weave their way through the crowd to reach the accident. Verb.*

○ A way or kind of weaving: *The rug has a tight weave. Noun.*

Another word that sounds like this is **we've**. **weave** (wēv) *verb*, **wove** or (for definition 3) **weaved, woven** or (for definition 3) **weaved, weaving**; *noun, plural* **weaves**.

web 1. A network of fine threads that are spun by a spider; cobweb. 2. A crisscross pattern; network: *We got lost in the web of streets in the old part of town.* 3. The skin between the toes of ducks, frogs, and other animals that swim. **web** (web) *noun, plural* **webs**.

Web The Web. A shortened way of describing the World Wide Web.

webbed Having or joined by a web: *A duck has webbed feet.* **webbed** (webd) *adjective.*

Web browser A program that allows a person to explore and view documents on the World Wide Web.

web-footed Having the toes joined by a web: *Ducks and geese are web-footed.* **web-foot·ed** (web'fŭt'id) *adjective.*

Web page A document belonging to a Web site on the World Wide Web.

Web site A location on the World Wide Web containing a home page and often other documents.

Webzine A magazine that is published on the World Wide Web. It can be read on the computer screen or printed out. **Web·zine** (web'zēn') *noun, plural* **Webzines**.

wed 1. To become husband and wife: *The engaged couple will wed next Saturday.* 2. To join as husband and wife: *Did a judge or a member of the clergy wed your parents? The prince and princess will wed in the palace chapel.* **wed** (wed) *verb,* **wedded, wedded** or **wed, wedding.**

we'd 1. Shortened form of "we would": *We'd be happy to drive you home.* 2. Shortened form of "we had": *We'd just left when the rain began.* 3. Shortened form of "we should": *The postal clerk said we'd get the package tomorrow.* Another word that sounds like this is **weed**. **we'd** (wēd) *contraction.*

Wed. An abbreviation for Wednesday.

wedding 1. A marriage ceremony: *We are going to my cousin's wedding today.* 2. The anniversary of a marriage: *A golden wedding is a celebration of fifty years of marriage.* **wed·ding** (wed'ing) *noun, plural* **weddings**.

wedge 1. A piece of wood, metal, or plastic that is thick at one end and narrow at the other. A wedge is pounded into logs to split them. It is also used to fill a space tightly or to hold a door open. 2. Something that has the shape of a wedge: *We served a wedge of cheese with some crackers. Noun.*

○ 1. To separate or split by driving a wedge into: *The workers wedged the floor boards apart.* 2. To fasten or fix in place with a wedge: *The door was wedged open with a piece of wood.* 3. To drive, push, or crowd: *I wedged the book into place on the crowded shelf. Verb.*

wedge (wej) *noun, plural* **wedges**; *verb,* **wedged, wedging.**

Wednesday The fourth day of the week. **Wednes·day** (wenz'dē or wenz'dā) *noun, plural* **Wednesdays**.

WORD HISTORY

The word **Wednesday** comes from the Old English word meaning "Woden's day." Woden was the king of the English gods.

---

wee 1. Very small; tiny: *The wee baby was asleep in the cradle.* 2. Early: *We stayed awake until the wee hours of the morning.* Another word that sounds like this is **we**. **wee** (wē) *adjective,* **weer, weest.**

weed A plant that is useless or harmful or grows where it is not wanted: *We pulled the weeds out of our vegetable garden. Noun.*

○ **1.** To take out the weeds from: *The gardener used a hoe to* **weed** *the garden.* **2.** To take out what is harmful or not wanted: *The coach* **weeded** *out the worst players from the baseball team. Verb.*
Another word that sounds like this is **we'd.**
weed (wēd) *noun, plural* **weeds**; *verb,* **weeded, weeding.** —**weedy** *adjective.*

week **1.** A period of seven days. A week is usually thought of as starting with Sunday. **2.** The part of a seven-day period during which a person works or goes to school: *Many companies require their employees to work a forty-hour* **week.** *Our school* **week** *begins Monday morning.*
Another word that sounds like this is **weak.**
week (wēk) *noun, plural* **weeks.**

weekday Any day of the week except Saturday and Sunday. **week•day** (wēk′dā′) *noun, plural* **weekdays.**

weekend The period of time from Friday night or Saturday morning until Sunday night or Monday morning: *We went to the country for the* **weekend.** **week•end** (wēk′end′) *noun, plural* **weekends.**

weekly **1.** For or relating to a week or weekdays: *Our family has a* **weekly** *grocery budget.* **2.** Done, happening, or published once a week: *The* **weekly** *newspaper comes out every Thursday. Adjective.*
○ A newspaper or magazine published once a week. *Noun.*
○ Once each week; every week: *I go to dance class* **weekly.** *Adverb.*
week•ly (wēk′lē) *adjective; noun, plural* **weeklies;** *adverb.*

weep To show sorrow, joy, or other strong emotion by crying: *The sad story made us* **weep.** **weep** (wēp) *verb,* **wept, weeping.**

weigh **1.** To find out the weight or heaviness of a person or thing: *The grocer* **weighed** *the tomatoes on a scale.* **2.** To have, amount to, or be equal to a named weight: *The car* **weighs** *3,744 pounds. How much do you* **weigh?** **3.** To think about or examine carefully: *They* **weighed** *their chances of winning the game. You should* **weigh** *your words before answering.* **4.** To lie heavily on; burden: *The heavy snow* **weighed** *down the branches of the trees. Guilt about having lied* **weighed** *on my conscience.*

Another word that sounds like this is **way.**
weigh (wā) *verb,* **weighed, weighing.**

weight **1.** The amount of heaviness of a person or thing: *My* **weight** *is 70 pounds.* **2.** The quality of a thing that comes from the pull of gravity upon it. Weight tends to pull things toward the center of the earth: *The* **weight** *of helium is less than the* **weight** *of air, so a balloon filled with helium will rise in the air.* **3.** A unit or system of units for expressing weight: *The pound and the kilogram are different* **weights.** **4.** A heavy object that is used to hold down things or to keep something steady: *We put rocks as* **weights** *at the corners of the beach towel.* **5.** An object whose weight is known: *Lifting* **weights** *will help you build your muscles.* **6.** A burden or load: *The* **weight** *of all this homework is discouraging.* **7.** Strong influence; importance: *The old chief's advice carried much* **weight** *with the tribe.*
Another word that sounds like this is **wait.**
weight (wāt) *noun, plural* **weights.** —**weighty** *adjective.*

Astronauts often conduct experiments while they are weightless **in space.**

weightless **1.** Having little or no weight: *A feather is practically* **weightless.** **2.** Not influenced by the pull of gravity: *The spacecraft was* **weightless** *when it was in space.* **weight•less** (wāt′lis) *adjective.* —**weightlessness** *noun.*

weird Strange or mysterious; odd: *Weird sounds came from the deserted old house.* **weird** (wîrd)

PRONUNCIATION KEY:

at	āpe	fär	câre	end	mē	it	īce	pîerce	hot	ōld	sông	fôrk
oil	out	up	ūse	rüle	pull	tûrn	chin	sing	shop	thin	this	

hw in white; zh in treasure. The symbol ə stands for the unstressed vowel sound in about, taken, pencil, lemon, and circus.

805

adjective, **weirder**, **weirdest**. —**weirdly** *adverb*
—**weirdness** *noun*.

welcome **1.** To greet someone in a pleasant and friendly way: *My father* **welcomed** *the guests when they arrived at the party.* **2.** To receive or accept with pleasure or gladness: *My mother works so hard that she* **welcomes** *a summer vacation. Verb.*

○ A glad and friendly greeting: *We received a warm* **welcome** *at our grandparents' house. Noun.*

○ **1.** Received kindly and with pleasure: *You are always a* **welcome** *visitor to our house.* **2.** Free to use, have, or enjoy: *Anyone is* **welcome** *to the newspaper after I've finished reading it.* **3.** Welcome is used in the phrase "You are welcome," a polite answer to someone who has thanked you. *Adjective.*

wel·come (wel′kəm) *verb*, **welcomed**, **welcoming**; *noun, plural* **welcomes**; *adjective.*

weld To join pieces of metal or plastic by heating until soft enough to be hammered or pressed together: *The plumber* **welded** *the broken pieces of pipe together.* **weld** (weld) *verb*, **welded**, **welding.**

welfare **1.** The condition of being happy and healthy; well-being: *The parents were concerned about their children's* **welfare**, *so they fed and raised them well.* **2.** Money or other aid given by the government to people who are in need. **wel·fare** (wel′fâr′) *noun.*

we'll Shortened form of "we will" or "we shall": *We'll see you at the party. We'll go to the picnic if it doesn't rain.* **we'll** (wēl) *contraction.*

well¹ **1.** In a good or satisfactory way: *Everything went* **well** *at the rehearsal of the play.* **2.** In a complete way; thoroughly: *Be sure to mix the flour and salt* **well**. **3.** To a considerable degree; much: *The piano weighs* **well** *over 300 pounds.* **4.** In a close or personal way: *Do you know your neighbors* **well***? Adverb.*

○ **1.** In good health; healthy: *The doctor examined me and said I was* **well**. *After resting, I felt* **well** *again.* **2.** Good; fortunate: *It is* **well** *that you called now because we were just leaving. Adjective.*

○ A word used to show surprise or to bring in another idea or thought: **Well***! How nice to see you.* **Well**, *I think that it's time to leave now. Interjection.*

• **as well.** In addition; also: *I play the flute and the guitar* **as well.**

• **as well as.** In addition to; besides: *The twins,* **as well as** *their parents, came to visit us.*
well (wel) *adverb*, **better**, **best**; *adjective; interjection.*

well² **1.** A deep hole that is made in the ground to get water, oil, or natural gas. **2.** A natural spring or fountain. **3.** Something that is like a well in shape or use: *The old desk has a* **well** *for ink. An encyclopedia is a* **well** *of information. Noun.*

○ To rise or fill: *Tears* **welled** *in the lost child's eyes. Verb.*

well (wel) *noun, plural* **wells**; *verb*, **welled**, **welling.**

well-balanced Evenly balanced: *A* **well-balanced** *meal includes a variety of healthful foods.* **well-bal·anced** (wel′bal′ənst) *adjective.*

well-behaved Having or showing good conduct or manners: *The* **well-behaved** *children played quietly.* **well-be·haved** (wel′bi hāvd′) *adjective.*

well-being Health and happiness; welfare: *Lots of exercise is good for the* **well-being** *of a dog.* **well-be·ing** (wel′bē′ing) *noun.*

well-known Known to many people; generally or widely known: *The* **well-known** *movie actor attracted a crowd.* **well-known** (wel′nōn′) *adjective.*

well-mannered Having or showing good manners; polite: *The* **well-mannered** *child thanked the hosts of the birthday party.* **well-man·nered** (wel′man′ərd) *adjective.*

well-off Rich; wealthy: *If I won the lottery I'd be* **well-off.** **well-off** (wel′ôf′) *adjective.*

well-read Having read books about many subjects: *An educated person needs to be* **well-read.** **well-read** (wel′red′) *adjective.*

well-rounded **1.** Properly balanced in its elements: *a* **well-rounded** *study plan.* **2.** Showing skill or ability in different areas: *a* **well-rounded** *student who likes sports and theater and gets good grades.* **well-round·ed** (wel′roun′did) *adjective.*

Welsh **1.** the Welsh. The people of Wales. **2.** The original language of the Welsh. The English language is now more common in Wales. *Noun.*

○ Of or relating to Wales, its people, or their original language. *Adjective.*

Welsh (welsh) *noun; adjective.*

went Past tense of **go**: *I went to bed early last night.* **went** (went) *verb.*

wept Past tense and past participle of **weep**: *Some of our players wept when we lost the championship game.* **wept** (wept) *verb.*

were A form of the past tense of **be** that is used with you, we, they, or the plural form of a noun: *We were at home all day. They were glad to see the puppy. Were you there?* **were** (wûr) *verb.*

we're Shortened form of "we are": *We're going home now.* **we're** (wîr) *contraction.*

weren't Shortened form of "were not": *They weren't home this afternoon.* **weren't** (wûrnt *or* wûr′ənt) *contraction.*

west 1. The direction you face when you watch the sun set in the evening. West is one of the four main points of the compass. It is located directly opposite east. 2. **West.** Any region or place that is in this direction. 3. **the West.** The region of the United States that is west of the Mississippi River. *Noun.*
○ Toward or in the west: *The grocery store is on the west side of the street.* 2. Coming from the west: *A west wind picked up in the afternoon. Adjective.*
○ Toward the west: *Christopher Columbus sailed west from Europe to cross the Atlantic Ocean. Adverb.*
west (west) *noun; adjective; adverb.*

western 1. In or toward the west: *California is a western state.* 2. Coming from the west. 3. **Western.** Of or in the part of the United States that is west of the Mississippi river. *Adjective.*
○ A story, book, or movie about frontier life in the western United States. *Noun.*
west·ern (wes′tərn) *adjective; noun, plural* **westerns.**

westerner 1. A person who was born or is living in the western part of a country or region. 2. **Westerner.** A person living in the western part of the United States. **west·ern·er** (wes′tər nər) *noun, plural* **westerners.**

Western Hemisphere The half of the earth that includes North America and South America.

West Germany After World War II and until 1990 when it was reunited with East Germany, a country in north-central Europe.

West Indies A group of islands in the Caribbean Sea. **West In·dies** (in′dēz).

West Virginia A state in the eastern United States. Its capital is Charleston.

WORD HISTORY

Like Virginia, West Virginia takes its name from a title given to the English queen Elizabeth I. Since she never married, she was called "the Virgin Queen." The colony of Virginia, founded under Queen Elizabeth, included what is now West Virginia. But when Virginia seceded from the Union at the start of the Civil War, the people of the western part of that state decided to remain with the Union. This area became the state of West Virginia.

West Virginia
U. S. Postal Abbreviation: **WV**
Capital: **Charleston**
Population: **1,897,000**
Area: **24,181 sq. mi./62,628 sq. km**
State Nickname: **Mountain State**
State Bird: **Cardinal**
State Flower: **Rhododendron**

westward Toward the west: *The airplane flew westward into the sunset. Adverb.*
○ Toward or in the west: *The pioneers began their westward journey. Adjective.*
west•ward (west′wərd) *adverb; adjective.*

wet 1. Covered, soaked, or moist with water or other liquid: *My bathing suit is still wet from my swim.* 2. Not yet hardened: *A footprint was made in the wet cement.* 3. Having rainfall; rainy. *Adjective.*
○ To make wet: *The directions said to wet the ground before planting the seeds. Verb.*

PRONUNCIATION KEY:
| at | āpe | fär | câre | end | mē | it | īce | pierce | hot | ōld | sông | fôrk |
| oil | out | up | ūse | rüle | pull | tûrn | chin | sing | shop | thin | this | |

hw in white; zh in treasure. The symbol ə stands for the unstressed vowel sound in about, taken, pencil, lemon, and circus.

807

wet (wet) *adjective*, **wetter**, **wettest**; *verb*, **wet** *or* **wetted**, **wetting**. —**wetness** *noun*.

whack **1.** A sharp, hard slap. **2.** An effort; try: *Take a whack at this arithmetic problem.* This is an informal use. *Noun.*
○ To hit sharply: *I really whacked the ball in yesterday's game. Verb.*
• **out of whack**. Not working properly: *This door is out of whack and I can't close it tightly.* **whack** (hwak *or* wak) *noun, plural* **whacks**; *verb,* **whacked, whacking.**

whale A large animal that has a body like a fish. Whales are mammals found in all oceans and in certain fresh waters. **whale** (hwāl *or* wāl) *noun, plural* **whales** *or* **whale.**

whaling The act or work of hunting and killing whales for their oil, meat, and bone. **whal·ing** (hwā′ling *or* wā′ling) *noun.*

wharf A structure built along a shore as a landing place for boats and ships; dock. **wharf** (hworf *or* wôrf) *noun, plural* **wharves** *or* **wharfs.**

what **1.** Used to ask questions about persons or things: *What is today's date?* **2.** The thing that: *They knew what I was thinking.* **3.** Anything that; whatever: *Choose what you want for dinner. Pronoun.*
○ **1.** Which one or ones: *What books are missing from the shelf?* **2.** Any that; whatever: *Take what snacks you need for the trip. Adjective.*
○ In which way; how much; how: *What does it matter? Adverb.*
○ Used to show surprise, disbelief, anger, or other feeling: *What! That's not possible! Interjection.* **what** (hwut *or* hwot *or* wut *or* wot) *pronoun; adjective; adverb; interjection.*

whatever **1.** Anything that: *Take whatever you want to eat from the refrigerator.* **2.** No matter what: *Whatever you say, I still think I'm right. Pronoun.*
○ **1.** Any that: *Buy whatever supplies you need for the hike.* **2.** Of any kind: *He'll let nothing whatever stop him from winning. Adjective.*

what·ev·er (hwət ev′ər *or* wət ev′ər) *pronoun; adjective.*

what's **1.** Shortened form of "what is": *What's the difference?* **2.** Shortened form of "what has": *What's happened?* **what's** (hwuts *or* hwots *or* wuts *or* wots) *contraction.*

Wheat is an important crop in the United States and Canada.

wheat A kind of grass whose seeds are used to make flour and other foods. Wheat is a very important food for human beings and animals. **wheat** (hwēt *or* wēt) *noun.*

wheel **1.** A round frame or solid object. Some wheels have a middle part that is connected to its outside rim by spokes. A wheel turns on its center and is used on cars, wagons, and other vehicles and as a machine part. **2.** Any machine or other thing that has or uses a wheel: *A spinning wheel is used for making thread. Noun.*

Wheels are used to steer large vessels.

○ **1.** To turn quickly: *My friend wheeled around when I called out.* **2.** To move or roll on wheels: *I wheeled the cart around the grocery store. Verb.*
• **at the wheel**. Doing the steering or driving. **wheel** (hwēl *or* wēl) *noun, plural* **wheels**; *verb,* **wheeled, wheeling.**

wheelbarrow A small cart with one or two wheels at the front end and two handles at the back for pushing. Wheelbarrows are used to move small loads for short distances. **wheel·bar·row** (hwēl′bar′ō *or* wēl′bar′ō) *noun, plural* **wheelbarrows.**

wheelchair A chair on wheels that is used by someone who cannot walk to get from one place to another. **wheel·chair** (hwēl′châr′ or wēl′châr′) *noun, plural* **wheelchairs.**

wheeze To breathe with a hoarse, whistling sound: *People with a bad cold or asthma sometimes* **wheeze.** **wheeze** (hwēz or wēz) *verb,* **wheezed, wheezing.**

whelk A large snail that lives in salt water. Whelks have spiral shells. **whelk** (hwelk or welk) *noun, plural* **whelks.**

when At what or which time: *When did they arrive? Adverb.*
○ **1.** At the time that: *I'll come* **when** *you call me.* **2.** At any time that; whenever: *When I am embarrassed, my face turns red.* **3.** And then; at which time: *The children played until noon,* **when** *they had lunch.* **4.** Although; but: *I wore a light sweater* **when** *I should have worn a heavy coat.* **5.** Considering that: *How can we go to the party* **when** *we haven't been invited? Conjunction.* **when** (hwen) *adverb; conjunction.*

whenever At whatever time: *We can eat dinner* **whenever** *you're hungry.* **when·ev·er** (hwen ev′ər or wen ev′ər) *conjunction.*

where In, at, to, or from what place: *Where did they go? Where did you buy that book? Adverb.*
○ **1.** In, at, or to the place in which, at which, or to which: *The keys are* **where** *you left them last night. Why can't I go* **where** *you're going?* **2.** In or at which place: *Let's go inside* **where** *we can sit. Conjunction.*
○ What place: *Where did those people come from? Pronoun.* **where** (hwâr or wâr) *adverb; conjunction; pronoun.*

whereabouts In or near what place; where: *Whereabouts did you last see the lost dog? Adverb.*
○ The place where something or someone is; location: *The* **whereabouts** *of the treasure is a secret. The suspect's* **whereabouts** *are unknown. Noun.* The noun form of the word "whereabouts" may be used with a singular or a plural verb. **where·a·bouts** (hwâr′ə bouts′ or wâr′ə bouts′) *adverb; noun.*

whereas On the other hand: *When the weather is nice, my family usually eats on the patio,* **whereas,** *if it's raining, we eat inside.* **where·as** (hwâr az′ or wâr az′) *conjunction.*

whereupon At which time; after which; and then: *Finally my friends finished their work,* **whereupon** *we all went to the concert.* **where·up·on** (hwâr′ə pôn′ or hwâr′ ə pon′ or wâr′ə pôn′ or wâr′ə pon′) *conjunction.*

wherever In, at, or to whatever place: *Wherever were you all afternoon? I'll go* **wherever** *you go.* **where·ev·er** (hwâr ev′ər or wâr ev′ər) *adverb; conjunction.*

whether **1.** A word that is used to introduce a choice between things: *You must decide* **whether** *to take the train or to go by plane.* **2.** If: *Let me know* **whether** *you can come to my party.* **wheth·er** (hweth′ər or weth′ər) *conjunction.*

whey The watery part of milk that separates from the curd when milk turns sour or thickens. **whey** (hwā or wā) *noun.*

which **1.** What one or ones: *Which of the players did you think was best?* **2.** Any one or ones that; whichever: *Choose* **which** *of the CDs you want to hear.* **3.** Used to introduce a clause that refers to a thing or things mentioned before: *That jacket,* **which** *I bought last year, is my favorite. Pronoun.*
○ What one or ones: *Which skates are yours? Which highway is the most direct route to the mountains? Adjective.* **which** (hwich or wich) *pronoun; adjective.*

whichever **1.** Any one that: *Buy* **whichever** *you like best.* **2.** No matter which: *Whichever you choose is fine. Pronoun.*
○ **1.** Any one that: *You can have* **whichever** *picture you like best.* **2.** No matter which: *Whichever road you follow, you'll arrive at the train station in ten minutes. Adjective.* **which·ev·er** (hwich ev′ər or wich ev′ər) *pronoun; adjective.*

whiff A sudden light puff, breath, or smell: *A* **whiff** *of smoke rose from the fire. The* **whiff** *of bacon made me hungry.* **whiff** (hwif or wif) *noun, plural* **whiffs.**

while A period of time: *We stopped walking and rested for a* **while.** *Noun.*
○ **1.** During or in the time that: *Did anyone call* **while** *I was away?* **2.** In spite of the fact that;

PRONUNCIATION KEY:

| at | āpe | fär | câre | end | mē | it | īce | pierce | hot | ōld | sông | fôrk |
| oil | out | up | ūse | rüle | pull | tûrn | chin | sing | shop | thin | this | |

hw in white; zh in treasure. The symbol ə stands for the unstressed vowel sound in about, taken, pencil, lemon, and circus.

809

although: *While they are our neighbors, we don't know them well. Conjunction.*

○ To pass or spend time in a relaxed, pleasant way: *We whiled away the afternoon listening to music. Verb.*

while (hwīl *or* wīl) *noun; conjunction; verb,* **whiled, whiling.**

whim A sudden idea or wish to do something: *I went to the movie on a whim.* **whim** (hwim *or* wim) *noun, plural* **whims.**

whimper To cry with weak, broken sounds: *The puppy whimpered for its mother. Verb.*

○ A weak, crying sound: *The hungry child let out a whimper. Noun.*

whim·per (hwim′pər *or* wim′pər) *verb,* **whim-pered, whimpering;** *noun, plural* **whimpers.**

whine To cry in a soft, high, complaining voice: *The tired child whined in the back seat of the car.*

whine (hwīn *or* wīn) *verb,* **whined, whining.**

—whiny *adjective.*

whinny To neigh in a low, gentle way: *My horse whinnied when he saw me. Verb.*

○ A soft neigh: *We heard the whinnies of the horses. Noun.*

whin·ny (hwin′ē *or* win′ē) *verb,* **whinnied, whin-nying;** *noun, plural* **whinnies.**

whip 1. To hit with a strap, rod, or something similar: *The driver of the carriage whipped the horses to make them go faster.* 2. To beat egg whites, cream, or the like until thick and foamy: *The baker whipped cream for the cake.* 3. To move, take, or throw suddenly: *We whipped the clean clothes from the line just as the storm began. Verb.*

○ A rod or strap that bends easily and has a handle. Whips are used for driving horses and other animals. *Noun.*

whip (hwip *or* wip) *verb,* **whipped, whipping;** *noun, plural* **whips.**

whippoorwill A plump bird with feathers spotted with brown, gray, and black. The whippoorwill lives in eastern North America. Its call sounds like its name. **whip·poor·will** (hwip′ər wil′ *or* wip′ər wil′) *noun, plural* **whippoorwills.**

whir To move or turn with a whizzing or buzzing sound: *The helicopter whirred overhead. Verb.*

○ A whizzing or buzzing sound. *Noun.*

whir (hwûr *or* wûr) *verb,* **whirred, whirring;** *noun, plural* **whirs.**

whirl 1. To turn or cause to turn quickly in a circle: *The blades of the fan whirled. The breeze whirled the bits of paper around in the air.* 2. To move or turn around suddenly or quickly: *The guards whirled when they heard the noise. Verb.*

○ 1. A quick turn in a circle; a whirling movement: *We watched the skaters make graceful leaps and whirls on the ice.* 2. A confused or dizzy condition: *My head was in a whirl after I was hit by the ball. Noun.*

whirl (hwûrl *or* wûrl) *verb,* **whirled, whirling;** *noun, plural* **whirls.**

whirlpool A current of water that moves quickly in a circle. **whirl·pool** (hwûrl′pül′ *or* wûrl′pül′) *noun, plural* **whirlpools.**

whirlwind 1. A whirling current of air that moves forward with great force. 2. A person who acts with great energy and speed: *She's a whirlwind in the office. Noun.*

○ Very rapid and active: *They gave the visitors a whirlwind tour of the city. Adjective.*

whirl·wind (hwûrl′wind *or* wûrl′wind) *noun, plural* **whirlwinds;** *adjective.*

whisk 1. To brush lightly: *The waiter whisked the crumbs off the table with a napkin.* 2. To move or carry quickly: *The taxi whisked us to the air-port.* **whisk** (hwisk *or* wisk) *verb,* **whisked, whisking.**

whisker 1. whiskers. The hair growing on a man's face; a beard or part of a beard. 2. A stiff hair that grows on the face: *cat whiskers.* **whisk·er** (hwis′kər *or* wis′kər) *noun, plural* **whiskers.**

whiskey A strong alcoholic drink made from rye, corn, or other grains. **whis·key** (hwis′kē *or* wis′kē) *noun, plural* **whiskeys.**

WORD HISTORY

The word whiskey comes from a word in a language that was once spoken by people in Scotland and Ireland. In this language, the word meant "water of life."

whisper To speak or say very softly: *My friend whispered a secret to me. Verb.*

○ A very soft way of speaking, or something said in this way: *The teacher heard whispers from the back of the room. Noun.*

whis·per (hwis′pər *or* wis′pər) *verb,* **whispered, whispering;** *noun, plural* **whispers.**

whistle 1. To make a clear, sharp sound by forcing air out through or as if through rounded lips or through the teeth. 2. To make or move with a sound like this: *The kettle whistled when the water boiled.* 3. To call or signal by whistling: *The police officer whistled for us to stop. Verb.*
○ 1. A device that makes a clear, sharp sound when air is blown through it: *The lifeguard blew a whistle to warn the swimmers.* 2. A whistling sound: *The dog came when it heard my whistle. Noun.*
whis•tle (hwis′əl *or* wis′əl) *verb*, **whistled**, **whistling**; *noun*, *plural* **whistles**.

white 1. Having the lightest of all colors; having the color of fresh snow: *A white cloud floated by.* 2. Light in color: *I like the white meat of turkey better than the dark. The man's face was white with fear.* 3. Pale gray: *My grandparents have white hair.* 4. Belonging to a race of people having pinkish skin: *Both white and black people live on our block.* 5. Not harmful: *I told a white lie about my age.* 6. Snowy: *Let's hope for a white Christmas. Adjective.*
○ 1. The lightest of all colors; the opposite of black. White is the color of fresh snow. 2. Something that is white or light-colored: *The recipe called for the whites of four eggs.* 3. A member of a race of people that has pinkish skin. *Noun.*
white (hwīt *or* wīt) *adjective*, **whiter**, **whitest**; *noun*, *plural* **whites**.

white blood cell A colorless cell found in the blood. White blood cells protect the body against infection by destroying germs that carry disease. They are a part of the immune system.

White House 1. The official home of the president of the United States. The White House is in Washington, D.C. 2. The office of the president of the United States: *The White House announced the president's decision.*

whiten To make or become white: *Bleach whitens clothes. Our faces must have whitened in fear when the door began to open.* **whit•en** (hwī′tən *or* wī′tən) *verb*, **whitened**, **whitening**.

whitewash A watery, white paint used on walls, wood fences, and other surfaces. **white•wash** (hwīt′wôsh′ *or* hwīt′wosh′ *or* wīt′wôsh′ *or* wīt′wosh′) *noun*.

whittle 1. To cut small bits or pieces from wood or soap with a knife: *We whittled the wood into interesting shapes.* 2. To make or shape by cutting away small bits with a knife: *I whittled a dog from a bar of soap.* **whit•tle** (hwit′əl *or* wit′əl) *verb*, **whittled**, **whittling**. —**whittler** *noun*.

whiz To make a buzzing sound while moving quickly: *The plane whizzed over the tops of the trees.* **whiz** (hwiz *or* wiz) *verb*, **whizzed**, **whizzing**.

who 1. What or which person or persons: *Who gave you that pen?* 2. That: *The student who wrote that story has a good sense of humor.* **who** (hü) *pronoun*.

whoa A word used as a command to stop: *"Whoa," the rider said to the horse.* **whoa** (hwō *or* wō) *interjection*.

who'd 1. Shortened form of "who would": *Who'd say such a thing about you?* 2. Shortened form of "who had": *Our guide knew someone who'd climbed that mountain.* **who'd** (hüd) *contraction*.

whoever 1. Any person who; whatever person: *Whoever wants to come along is welcome.* 2. No matter who: *Whoever those strangers are, I like them.* 3. What or which person: *Whoever told you such a story?* **who•ev•er** (hü ev′ər) *pronoun*.

whole Having all its parts; entire; complete: *Have you read the whole book already? Fifty-two cards make a whole deck. Is this whole milk or skim milk? Adjective.*
○ All the parts that make up a thing: *I spent the whole of my allowance on the present. Two halves make a whole. Noun.*
Another word that sounds like this is **hole**.
• **on the whole.** Considering everything: *On the whole, I thought the party was a success.*
whole (hōl) *adjective*; *noun*.

whole number A number that tells how many complete things there are. 0, 1, 2, and 21 are whole numbers; ³⁄₄, ⁷⁄₈, and other fractions are not whole numbers.

wholesome 1. Good for the health: *Exercise and a proper diet are wholesome. This polluted air is not wholesome.* 2. Having habits and attitudes that give good health: *Wholesome people don't smoke cigarettes.* **whole•some** (hōl′səm) *adjective*. —**wholesomely** *adverb* —**wholesomeness** *noun*.

PRONUNCIATION KEY:

| at | āpe | fär | câre | end | mē | it | īce | pierce | hot | ōld | sông | fôrk |
| oil | out | up | ūse | rüle | půll | tûrn | chin | sing | shop | thin | this | |

hw in white; zh in treasure. The symbol ə stands for the unstressed vowel sound in about, taken, pencil, lemon, and circus.

811

who'll Shortened form of "who will" or "who shall": *Who'll bake the cake?* **who'll** (hül) *contraction.*

wholly To the whole amount or extent; entirely; completely: *I am **wholly** to blame for what happened.*
Another word that sounds like this is **holy.**
whol·ly (hō′lē) *adverb.*

whom What or which person or persons: ***Whom** do you suspect? I don't know **whom** I liked best in the play.* **whom** (hüm) *pronoun.*

whomever Any person whom; whatever person: *Ask **whomever** you like to come to the party.* **whom·ev·er** (hüm ev′ər) *pronoun.*

whoop A loud cry or shout: *You gave a **whoop** when you caught the fish. Noun.*
○ To give a loud cry or shout: *We **whooped** with laughter when we saw the comedian's funny act. Verb.*
Another word that sounds like this is **hoop.**
whoop (hüp *or* hwüp *or* wüp) *noun, plural* **whoops;** *verb,* **whooped, whooping.**

whooping cough A very infectious disease of babies and children that causes severe coughing.

whooping crane A crane that has a white body, wings with black tips, and a red face. It is four feet high and the tallest of all North American birds.

The **whooping crane is nearly extinct.**

who's 1. Shortened form of "who is": ***Who's** going to be at the meeting this morning?*
2. Shortened form of "who has": ***Who's** been eating my porridge?*
Another word that sounds like this is **whose.**
who's (hüz) *contraction.*

whose Of or belonging to whom or which: ***Whose** house is that? We tried to help the neighbor **whose** dog had run away. Adjective.*

○ The one or ones belonging to what person or persons: ***Whose** are those books? Pronoun.*
Another word that sounds like this is **who's.**
whose (hüz) *adjective; pronoun.*

why For what reason or purpose: ***Why** are you laughing? **Why** do you want to go swimming today? Adverb.*
○ The reason or purpose for which: *I know **why** they didn't come to the party. Conjunction.*
○ A word used to show mild surprise or other feelings: ***Why,** look who's here! Interjection.*
why (hwī *or* wī) *adverb; conjunction; interjection.*

WI Postal abbreviation for **Wisconsin.**

wick A cord in an oil lamp, candle, or cigarette lighter that soaks up the fuel and burns when it is lit. **wick** (wik) *noun, plural* **wicks.**

wicked Evil, mean, and very bad: *The villain in the story was a **wicked** person who liked to harm other people.* **wick·ed** (wik′id) *adjective.*
—**wickedly** *adverb* —**wickedness** *noun.*

wide 1. Made up of or covering a large area from side to side: *There is a **wide** porch across the back of the house.* 2. Having a certain distance from side to side: *The room is 12 feet **wide.*** 3. Fully opened: *The child's eyes were **wide** with excitement.* 4. Including many different things: *This store carries a **wide** selection of furniture.* 5. Far away from a specific place: *My arrow was **wide** of the target. Adjective.*
○ 1. Over a large area: *The writer traveled far and **wide** to learn about different countries.*
2. To a large or full extent: *The hippopotamus opened its mouth **wide** and yawned. Please open the window **wide.** Adverb.*
wide (wīd) *adjective,* **wider, widest;** *adverb.*
—**widely** *adverb* —**wideness** *noun.*

wide area network A network of computers that spans a large area, such as parts of a city or a country.

widen To make or become wide or wider: *If we get a bigger car, we'll have to **widen** the driveway. The road **widens** just ahead.* **wid·en** (wī′dən) *verb,* **widened, widening.**

widespread 1. Happening over a large area or to many people: *The flu epidemic was **widespread** in the country.* 2. Fully open: *They greeted us with **widespread** arms.* **wide·spread** (wīd′spred′) *adjective.*

widow A woman whose husband is dead and who

has not married again. **wid·ow** (wid′ō) *noun,* *plural* **widows**.

widower A man whose wife is dead and who has not married again. **wid·ow·er** (wid′ō ər) *noun,* *plural* **widowers**.

width The distance from one side of something to the other side: *The **width** of a football field is 52 ¹/₃ yards.* **width** (width) *noun, plural* **widths**.

wife A married woman. **wife** (wīf) *noun, plural* **wives**.

WORD HISTORY

The word wife comes from Old English. It used to mean "a woman," whether she was married or not.

wig A covering for the head made of real or artificial hair. **wig** (wig) *noun, plural* **wigs**.

wiggle To move from side to side in short, sudden movements: *I **wiggled** my loose tooth with my finger. Verb.*
○ A wiggling movement: *You'll need to give the key a **wiggle** to get it to work in the lock.*
wig·gle (wig′əl) *verb,* **wiggled, wiggling;** *noun, plural* **wiggles**.

wigwam A hut made of poles covered with bark, leaves, or hides. Some Native American tribes built wigwams to live in.
wig·wam (wig′wom *or* wig′wôm) *noun, plural* **wigwams**.

wild 1. Not controlled by people; living or growing naturally: *There are **wild** ponies on that island. The forest is full of **wild** plants.* 2. Not disciplined or orderly: *Those **wild** children often play rough games and hurt themselves.* 3. Crazy or fantastic: *I have a **wild** idea for a Halloween costume. Adjective.*
○ Not under the control of people; naturally: *Blueberries grow **wild** in that field. Adverb.*
• **to be wild about.** To like very much or be enthusiastic about: *Everyone **is wild about** the new movie.*
wild (wīld) *adjective,* **wilder, wildest;** *adverb.*
—**wildly** *adverb* —**wildness** *noun.*

wildcat A bobcat, lynx, or other small cat that is not tamed. A wildcat is larger than a domestic cat but smaller than a lion. **wild·cat** (wīld′kat′) *noun, plural* **wildcats**.

wilderness A natural place where no people live. In a wilderness there may be a dense forest and many wild animals. **wil·der·ness** (wil′dər nis) *noun, plural* **wildernesses**.

wildflower Any flower of a wild plant. **wild·flow·er** (wīld′flou′ər) *noun, plural* **wildflowers**.

Wildflowers **come in many shapes and colors.**

wildlife Wild animals that live naturally in an area. **wild·life** (wīld′līf′) *noun.*

will¹ 1. An auxiliary verb that is used to express future actions and states: *I **will** be ten years old next month. The team **will** play here tomorrow.* 2. To have the intention to: *I **will** help with the dishes.* 3. To be required to; have to; must: *You **will** be on time from now on.* 4. To be able to; can: *That chair **will** not support your weight. This camera **will** not work.* **will** (wil) *verb.*

will² 1. The power to decide what to do and to keep wanting and trying to do it: *A person with a strong **will** tries to achieve goals in spite of all obstacles.* 2. Firm purpose; determination: *The athlete had a **will** to win.* 3. A wish; desire: *"What is your **will**?" the servant asked.* 4. A legal document that states what a person wants done with everything he or she owns after the person dies. *Noun.*
○ 1. To use the power of the mind to decide what to do: *The runner **willed** herself to keep going even though her leg hurt badly.* 2. To give away what one owns by a will: *The rich man **willed** all his money to charity. Verb.*
will (wil) *noun, plural* **wills;** *verb,* **willed, willing.**

PRONUNCIATION KEY:

| at | āpe | fär | câre | end | mē | it | īce | pierce | hot | ōld | sông | fôrk |
| oil | out | up | ūse | rūle | pùll | tûrn | chin | sing | shop | thin | this | |

hw in white; zh in treasure. The symbol ə stands for the unstressed vowel sound in about, taken, pencil, lemon, and circus.

813

willful **1.** Done on purpose; deliberate: *willful disobedience.* **2.** Determined; stubborn: *She's a willful person who won't listen to reason.* **will·ful** (wil′fəl) *adjective.* —**willfully** *adverb* —**willfulness** *noun.*

willing Wanting or ready to do something: *Are you willing to help us? To be hypnotized, you have to be a willing subject.* **will·ing** (wil′ing) *adjective.* —**willingly** *adverb* —**willingness** *noun.*

willow A tree or bush that has long, thin branches that bend easily and narrow leaves. Willows usually grow in wet areas. **wil·low** (wil′ō) *noun, plural* **willows.**

wilt To become limp; droop: *The flowers wilted soon after they were cut.* **wilt** (wilt) *verb,* **wilted, wilting.**

wimp A weak person or one who gives in easily to others: *Don't be such a wimp; stand up to that bully!* This is an informal use. **wimp** (wimp) *noun, plural* **wimps.** —**wimpy** *adjective.*

win **1.** To do better than any other in a race or contest; gain a victory: *The home team won the hockey game. We flipped a coin, and I won.* **2.** To get as a prize: *The winner of the baking contest will win a set of bread pans.* **3.** To get by effort; gain: *The explorer is winning new fame as an author. Verb.*
◦ A victory or success: *The team had six wins and five losses this season. Noun.*
win (win) *verb,* **won, winning;** *noun, plural* **wins.**

wince To draw back slightly from something painful, dangerous, or unpleasant: *The child winced when the doctor gave the injection.* **wince** (wins) *verb,* **winced, wincing.**

winch A machine for lifting or pulling things. A winch is made up of a large spool or pulley with a rope or chain around it. Ships' anchors are hoisted on a winch. **winch** (winch) *noun, plural* **winches.**

wind¹ **1.** Air that is moving over the earth: *The wind blew my hat off. The strong winds made the trees bend and sway.* **2.** The power to breathe; breath: *The hard blow knocked the wind out of me. Noun.*
◦ To cause someone to be out of breath: *Climbing the long flight of stairs winded us. Verb.*
• **to get wind of.** To receive information or hints about: *If my cousin gets wind of the*

party, *the surprise will be ruined.*
wind (wind) *noun, plural* **winds;** *verb,* **winded, winding.**

wind² **1.** To wrap something around on itself or on something else: *Please wind this loose yarn into a ball. The vine wound around the pole.* **2.** To move or cause to move in one direction and then another: *The road winds through the mountains. I wound through the traffic on my bicycle.* **3.** To give a machine power by tightening its spring: *The boy wound the key in the little car and then it raced across the floor. Don't forget to wind your alarm clock. Verb.*
• **to wind up.** **1.** To end; finish; conclude: *Let's wind up the work today. The meeting wound up at six o'clock.* **2.** To arrive in a certain place or situation: *My parents changed jobs, so we wound up having to move.* **3.** To make movements with the arms and body before pitching a ball: *The batter watched carefully while the pitcher wound up.*
wind (wīnd) *verb,* **wound, winding.**

windfall **1.** Fruit that has fallen or been blown off a tree. **2.** An unexpected piece of good luck, often in the form of money: *The windfall of a thousand dollars enabled her to take a vacation.* **wind·fall** (wind′fôl) *noun, plural* **windfalls.**

wind instrument A musical instrument that is played by blowing into it. Trumpets and flutes are wind instruments. **wind instrument** (wind).

Windmills **are used to pump water, grind grain, or generate electricity.**

windmill A machine that uses the power of the wind to turn vanes or sails at the top of a tower. **wind·mill** (wind′mil′) *noun, plural* **windmills.**

window An opening in a wall or roof that lets in air and light. Panes of glass fill the openings of most windows. **win·dow** (win′dō) *noun, plural* **windows.**

WORD HISTORY

The word window comes from two Scandinavian words meaning "wind" and "eye." A window was thought of as an opening, or "eye," in a wall to let the wind through.

window-shop To look at things for sale in store windows without any intention of buying. **win·dow-shop** (win′dō shop′) *verb,* **window-shopped, window-shopping.**

windowsill A horizontal piece of wood, stone, or metal that forms the bottom part of a window frame. **win·dow·sill** (win′dō sil′) *noun, plural* **windowsills.**

windpipe The tube in the body that carries air from the throat to the lungs. **wind·pipe** (wind′pīp′) *noun, plural* **windpipes.**

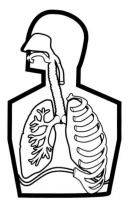

windpipe

windshield A glass or plastic screen attached near the front of an automobile, motorcycle, or other vehicle. A windshield protects the driver and riders from the wind. **wind·shield** (wind′shēld′) *noun, plural* **windshields.**

windsurfing A sailing sport in which a person stands upright on a sailboard and steers it by moving a curved bar to which the sail is attached. **wind·surf·ing** (wind′sûr′fing) *noun.* —**wind-surf** *verb.*

windswept Exposed to and swept by winds: *the windswept*

Windsurfing has become a popular water sport.

prairie. **wind·swept** (wind′swept′) *adjective.*

windy Having or swept by strong winds: *We need a windy day for flying our kites.* **wind·y** (win′dē) *adjective,* **windier, windiest.** —**windiness** *noun.*

wine An alcoholic drink made from the fermented juice of grapes or other fruits. **wine** (wīn) *noun, plural* **wines.**

wing 1. A movable part of the body that is used in flying. Birds, insects, and bats have wings. 2. A structure that sticks out from the side of an airplane. Wings are shaped to help a moving airplane rise and fly. 3. A part that is attached to and sticks out from the main part of a structure: *We added a new wing with two bedrooms to our house.* 4. The part on either side of a stage that is not seen by the audience: *The actors waited in the wings. Noun.*
○ To fly: *Many birds wing their way south in the fall. Verb.*
wing (wing) *noun, plural* **wings;** *verb,* **winged, winging.**

winged Having wings: *Bats are winged animals.* **winged** (wingd *or* wing′id) *adjective.*

wingspan or **wingspread** The distance between the tip of one wing and the tip of another on an airplane or a bird, bat, or insect when it opens its wings wide: *The wingspan of that airplane is 40 feet. Some eagles have a wingspread of 7 feet.* **wing·span** *or* **wing·spread** (wing′span′ *or* wing′spred′) *noun, plural* **wingspans** *or* **wingspreads.**

wink To close and open one or both eyes quickly. People usually wink with one eye as a signal: *Mother winked at me to let me know she knew the secret. Verb.*
○ 1. A quick closing and opening of one or both eyes: *Dad gave me a wink to show that he was just joking.* 2. A very short time: *I didn't get a wink of sleep last night. Noun.*
wink (wingk) *verb,* **winked, winking;** *noun, plural* **winks.**

winner 1. A person or thing that wins: *My friend was the winner of the spelling bee.* 2. An idea, plan, project, or person that seems likely to succeed: *Your idea for advertising the school dance sounds like a winner.* **win·ner** (win′ər) *noun, plural* **winners.**

PRONUNCIATION KEY:
at   āpe   fär   câre   end   mē   it   īce   pierce   hot   ōld   sŏng   fôrk
oil   out   up   ūse   rüle   pu̇ll   tûrn   chin   sing   shop   thin   this   hw in white; zh in treasure. The symbol ə stands for the unstressed vowel sound in about, taken, pencil, lemon, and circus.

815

winning 1. Victorious or successful: *The winning team received a trophy. Who scored the winning goal?* 2. Charming or attractive: *The salesperson had a very winning smile. Adjective.*
○ **winnings.** Something that is won: *My family plays cards for pennies and we get to keep our winnings. Noun.*
win·ning (win′ing) *adjective; plural noun.*

winter The season of the year between fall and spring. *Noun.*
○ To spend the winter: *My grandparents winter in Florida. Verb.*
win·ter (win′tər) *noun, plural* **winters;** *verb,* **wintered, wintering.**

wintergreen A low evergreen plant with white flowers and red berries. Oil from the wintergreen is used in medicine or for flavoring.
win·ter·green (win′tər grēn′) *noun, plural* **wintergreens.**

wintry Relating to or like winter: *It was a cold, wintry day with gray skies overhead.* **win·try** (win′trē) *adjective,* **wintrier, wintriest.**

wipe 1. To clean or dry by rubbing with or on something: *If you wash the dishes, I will wipe them dry. Please wipe your shoes on the mat before coming into the house.* 2. To take away by cleaning or drying: *Please wipe the mud off your shoes.*
• **to wipe out.** To destroy totally: *The epidemic wiped out the population of the village.*
wipe (wīp) *verb,* **wiped, wiping. —wiper** *noun.*

wire 1. A thin metal thread or a bunch of metal threads. Wire is used for fastening, for making such things as fences and screens, and for carrying electricity. 2. A telegram. *Noun.*
○ Made of wire: *We put the eggs into a wire basket. Adjective.*
○ 1. To put in wires for electricity: *The new house was wired but the plumbing was not in yet.* 2. To fasten with a wire: *I wired the broken gate together.* 3. To send a telegram. *Verb.*
wire (wīr) *noun, plural* **wires;** *adjective; verb,* **wired, wiring.**

wireless Sending messages or signals without using wires. Radio is a form of wireless communication. *Adjective.*
○ A radio. *Noun.*
wire·less (wīr′lis) *adjective; noun, plural* **wirelesses.**

wiring A system of wires that carry electric current: *The wiring in our house is connected to a fuse box.* **wir·ing** (wīr′ing) *noun.*

wiry 1. Like wire; thin and stiff: *Some dogs have wiry hair.* 2. Tough and strong: *That athlete has a wiry build.* **wir·y** (wiər′ē) *adjective,* **wirier, wiriest.**

Wis. or **Wisc.** An abbreviation for **Wisconsin.**

Wisconsin A state in the north-central United States. Its capital is Madison. **Wis·con·sin** (wis kon′sən) *noun.*

WORD HISTORY

Wisconsin was named after the Wisconsin River, which is the main river in the state. This name is the English form of an earlier French name. The French name probably came from a Native American word that means "at the big river" or "the place where the waters come together."

Wisconsin
U. S. Postal Abbreviation: **WI**
Capital: **Madison**
Population: **4,807,000**
Area: **56,154 sq. mi./145,438 sq. km**
State Nickname: **Badger State**
State Bird: **Robin**
State Flower: **Wood Violet**

wisdom Good judgment and intelligence in knowing what is right, good, and true: *We grow in wisdom as we gain more experience and knowledge.* **wis·dom** (wiz′dəm) *noun.*

wisdom tooth The last tooth in the back on both sides of each jaw in human beings. The wisdom teeth usually appear when a person is an adult.

wise Having or showing good judgment and intelligence: *The wise counselor gave sound advice. It's wise to stay away from fighting dogs.* **wise** (wīz) *adjective,* **wiser, wisest.** —**wisely** *adverb.*

wish 1. A feeling of wanting something; a strong desire: *My wish to be a firefighter gets stronger every day.* 2. An expression of what a person wants: *Make a wish and blow out the candles.* 3. A thing that a person wants: *I hoped for a compass for my birthday, and I got my wish.* *Noun.*
○ 1. To want something very much; have a wish: *I wish that summer would last longer.* 2. To think of or express a wish: *I wish you good luck and a safe journey.* *Verb.*
wish (wish) *noun, plural* **wishes;** *verb,* **wished, wishing.**

wishbone A forked bone in front of the breastbone of chickens and other birds. Some people make wishes on wishbones. One person holds one end, another person holds the other end, and they pull to break the bone. The person who gets the longer piece is supposed to have a wish come true. **wish•bone** (wish′bōn′) *noun, plural* **wishbones.**

wisp A small bit or piece of something: *The farmer's shirt was covered with wisps of hay. Wisps of smoke drifted up from the chimney.* **wisp** (wisp) *noun, plural* **wisps.** —**wispy** *adjective.*

Wisteria **is native to the eastern United States and eastern Asia.**

wisteria A vine with a woody stem that has long, drooping clusters of white, pink, blue, or purple flowers. **wis•te•ri•a** (wi stîr′ē ə) *noun.*

wit 1. The ability to make clever, amusing, and unusual comments: *The speaker's wit delighted the audience.* 2. A person who has this ability: *We asked the class wit to think of something funny to write on the birthday card.* 3. The ability to think and reason; understanding: *If a fire ever starts, try to keep your wits about you.* The word "wit" in this sense is usually used in the plural. **wit** (wit) *noun, plural* **wits.**

witch A person who is thought to have magic powers. In old fairy tales and legends, a witch is usually a woman who does evil things. **witch** (wich) *noun, plural* **witches.**

with 1. In the company or keeping of: *We went to the movie with friends. We left our keys with a neighbor when we went on vacation.* 2. Having or possessing: *We need someone with good skills for this job.* 3. By means of; by using: *We work with a very powerful microscope in biology class.* 4. In a way that shows: *The skaters glided across the ice with the grace of dancers.* 5. As an accompaniment to; in addition to: *We had fruit with our cereal.* 6. In regard to: *Are you pleased with your gift?* 7. In an association that involves: *I talked on the phone with my friend in California. How often do you correspond with your cousins?* 8. In opposition to; against: *I seldom argue with my friends.* 9. In support of; on the side of: *Are you with us or against us?* **with** (with *or* with) *preposition.*

withdraw 1. To take away; remove: *The captain withdrew the troops from the battle. He will have to withdraw money from the bank to pay for the gifts.* 2. To take back: *She withdrew her offer to buy the house.* 3. To leave a place; go away: *A servant brought food on a tray and then withdrew.* **with•draw** (with drô′ *or* with drô′) *verb,* **withdrew, withdrawn, withdrawing.**

withdrew Past tense of withdraw: *Yesterday I withdrew five dollars from my savings account.* **with•drew** (with drü′ *or* with drü′) *verb.*

wither To dry up or shrivel: *The flowers withered soon after they were cut. The hot sun withered the crops.* **with•er** (with′ər) *verb,* **withered, withering.**

withheld Past tense and past participle of withhold: *Have you withheld any information from us?* **with•held** (with held′) *verb.*

withhold 1. To keep back; hold back: *You*

PRONUNCIATION KEY:
at āpe fär câre end mē it īce pierce hot ōld sông fôrk
oil out up ūse rüle pull tûrn chin sing shop thin this
hw in white; zh in treasure. The symbol ə stands for the unstressed vowel sound in about, taken, pencil, lemon, and circus.

817

shouldn't **withhold** *the truth from your friends.*
2. To refuse to give: *My parents might* **withhold** *their permission for me to go on the field trip.* **with·hold** (with hōld' *or* with hōld') *verb,* **withheld, withholding.**

within 1. In or into the inner part or parts of: *The troops camped* **within** *the walls of the fort.*
2. Not beyond the limits or extent of: *I promise to return* **within** *an hour. It is* **within** *their power to help us. Preposition.*
○ In or into the inner part or parts of: *I heard a noise* **within** *that sounded like an explosion. Adverb.*
with·in (with in' *or* with in') *preposition; adverb.*

without 1. Not having; lacking: *We were exhausted after a night* **without** *sleep.* 2. Not accompanied by: *They went to the movie* **without** *you.*
3. In a way that neglects or avoids: *They slipped out* **without** *saying good-bye.*
  ·to do *or* **go without.** To manage or survive without something needed: *We have no more milk, so we'll have* **to do without.**
with·out (with out' *or* with out') *preposition.*

withstand To resist the effects of; hold out against: *Our roses* **withstood** *the storm.* **with·stand** (with stand' *or* with stand') *verb,* **withstood, withstanding.**

withstood Past tense and past participle of **withstand:** *The strong table* **withstood** *the weight of the heavy sculpture.* **with·stood** (with stood' *or* with stood') *verb.*

witness A person who has seen or heard something, and so can answer questions about what happened: *She was a* **witness** *to the accident and had to testify in court. Noun.*
○ To be present to see or hear something: *Who* **witnessed** *the fight? Two friends of the old man* **witnessed** *the signing of his will. Verb.*
wit·ness (wit'nis) *noun, plural* **witnesses;** *verb,* **witnessed, witnessing.**

witty Clever and amusing; having wit: *We all laughed at the* **witty** *remark.* **wit·ty** (wit'ē) *adjective,* **wittier, wittiest.**

wives Plural of **wife:** *The husbands and* **wives** *of the teachers are invited to the school celebration.* **wives** (wīvz) *plural noun.*

wizard 1. A person who is thought to have magic powers. In old fairy tales and legends, a wizard is usually a man. 2. A person who is very clever and

skillful: *My cousin is a* **wizard** *at arithmetic.* **wiz·ard** (wiz'ərd) *noun, plural* **wizards.**

wk. An abbreviation for **week.**

wobble To move from side to side in an unsteady or shaky way: *The old chair* **wobbled** *because the legs were loose.* **wob·ble** (wob'əl) *verb,* **wobbled, wobbling.** —**wobbly** *adjective.*

woe Great sadness or suffering: *The story told of the hunger, sickness, and other* **woes** *of the settlers of the frontier.* **woe** (wō) *noun, plural* **woes.**

wok A pan that is shaped like a bowl and is used to cook Chinese food. **wok** (wok) *noun, plural* **woks.**

woken A past participle of **wake:** *I was* **woken** *by the barking dog.* **wo·ken** (wō'kən) *verb.*

wolf A wild animal that looks like a dog. Wolves have thick fur, a pointed muzzle, and a bushy tail. They live and hunt in packs. *Noun.*
○ To eat very quickly and hungrily: *The children* **wolfed** *down their lunch. Verb.*
wolf (wŭlf) *noun, plural* **wolves;** *verb,* **wolfed, wolfing.**

wolverine A stout, meat-eating animal that is related to the weasel. It has dark brown fur and a long, bushy tail. Wolverines now live in northern Canada and Alaska. **wol·ver·ine** (wŭl'və rēn') *noun, plural* **wolverines.**

wolves Plural of **wolf:** *Wolves sometimes howl at night.* **wolves** (wŭlvz) *plural noun.*

woman 1. An adult female person. 2. Adult female people as a group. **wom·an** (wŭm'ən) *noun, plural* **women.**

womanhood The condition or the time of being an adult female person: *The girl had not yet reached* **womanhood.** **wom·an·hood** (wŭm'ən hŭd') *noun.*

wombat A stout animal that has coarse fur, short legs, and a large head with small eyes and pointed ears. The female wombat has a pouch in which she carries her young. Wombats are found in Australia. **wom·bat** (wom'bat) *noun, plural* **wombats.**

women Plural of **woman:** *Two* **women** *run the store.* **wom·en** (wim'ən) *plural noun.*

won Past tense and past participle of **win:** *Who* **won** *the first prize? We've* **won** *more games than we've lost.*
Another word that sounds like this is **one.**
won (wun) *verb.*

wonder 1. An unusual, surprising, or very impressive thing: *This huge waterfall is a natural wonder. That tightrope walker is a wonder to behold.* 2. The feeling caused by something unusual, surprising, or very impressive: *I watched with wonder as the artist sketched the scene with just a few strokes of a pencil.* Noun.
1. To want to know or learn; be curious about: *I wonder why the sky is blue.* 2. To feel or be surprised or impressed: *The child wondered at the giraffe's long neck.* Verb.
won·der (wun′dər) *noun, plural* **wonders;** *verb,* **wondered, wondering.**

wonderful 1. Causing wonder; remarkable: *The kangaroo is a strange and wonderful animal.* 2. Very good; fine: *Our friends cooked a wonderful dinner for us.* **won·der·ful** (wun′dər fəl) *adjective.* —**wonderfully** *adverb.*

won't Shortened form of "will not": *The painters won't be able to finish the work today.* **won't** (wōnt) *contraction.*

wood 1. The hard material that makes up the trunk and branches of a tree or bush. Wood is cut and prepared for use as building material and fuel. 2. An area of trees growing naturally; forest. The word "wood" in this sense is often used in the plural form. *Noun.*
○ Made of or consisting of wood; wooden: *We have wood furniture on our porch.* Adjective.
Another word that sounds like this is **would.**
wood (wŭd) *noun, plural* **woods;** *adjective.*

Many things are made from wood, including this bridge.

woodchuck A stout animal with short legs that has coarse, brown fur. Woodchucks live underground in holes that they dig. They eat leaves and grass. This

---

WONDERS

The Seven Wonders of the Ancient World were ancient structures that were considered the greatest in size and splendor. Although some writers disagree about which structures to include, the following are usually listed:

The Pyramids of Egypt Built from 2700 B.C. to 2500 B.C., these are the only surviving ancient wonders. Located near the modern city of Cairo, the pyramids were built as tombs for ancient kings of Egypt known as pharaohs. The largest is the Pyramid of Khufu (Cheops) which covers more than 13 acres.
The Hanging Gardens of Babylon: Probably built by King Nebuchadnezzar II about 600 B.C., these gardens were laid on a brick terrace about 400 feet square. Water was lifted from the river below to irrigate the trees and flowers.
The Statue of Zeus (Jupiter) at Olympia: Made of ivory and gold, this statue was said to be 40 feet tall. It was made about 457 B.C. and showed Zeus sitting on his throne. Olympia was the town where the ancient Olympics were held.
The Colossus of Rhodes: Located overlooking the harbor on the island of Rhodes, this was a bronze statue of the sun god Helios. It was supposed to be 120 feet tall.
The Temple of Artemis (Diana) at Ephesus: The largest temple built in ancient times, it was made of marble and covered with a wooden roof. Ephesus is located in modern Turkey.
The Mausoleum at Halicarnassus: This tomb was built by Artimisia for her husband Mausolus in about 353 B.C. This is the source of our word mausoleum.
The Pharos of Alexandria: Built in Egypt in about 270 B.C., this was a lighthouse for the harbor at Alexandria. It was destroyed by an earthquake in the 13th century.

Numerous other structures have been nominated as one of the Seven Wonders. Some of these are:
The Great Wall of China, Stonehenge, the **Colosseum** in Rome, and the **Mosque of Hagia Sophia** in Istanbul, Turkey.

animal is also called a groundhog. **wood•chuck** (wŭd′chuk′) *noun, plural* **woodchucks.**

wooded Having trees or woods: *We had a picnic in a **wooded** area near our house.* **wood•ed** (wŭd′id) *adjective.*

wooden Made of wood: *I keep my clothes in a **wooden** chest of drawers.* **wood•en** (wŭd′ən) *adjective.*

woodland An area of land that is covered by trees; a forest: *Deer live in the **woodland** near our farm.* **wood•land** (wŭd′land′) *noun, plural* **woodlands.**

woodpecker Any of a number of birds that have strong, pointed bills. Woodpeckers use their bills to make holes in trees in order to get insects to eat. **wood•peck•er** (wŭd′pek′ər) *noun, plural* **woodpeckers.**

Woodpeckers live in forests throughout the world.

woodwind A wind instrument that was originally made of wood, but that is now often made of metal or plastic. Flutes, oboes, clarinets, and saxophones are woodwinds. **wood•wind** (wŭd′wind′) *noun, plural* **woodwinds.**

woodwork Parts or things that are made out of wood. Window and door frames are parts of the woodwork of a house. **wood•work** (wŭd′wûrk′) *noun.*

woody 1. Containing wood: *Woody plants have wood trunks and branches rather than soft green stems.* 2. Having many trees: *We sailed to one of the small, **woody** islands in the bay.* **wood•y** (wŭd′ē) *adjective,* **woodier, woodiest.**

wool 1. The soft, thick, curly hair of sheep and some other animals such as the llama and alpaca. Wool is spun into yarn which is made into cloth. 2. Cloth or yarn made of wool. 3. Any substance made of a thick mass of fibers: *We used steel **wool** to smooth my bike's fender before we painted it. Noun.*

○ Made of wool: *I wear a **wool** coat in the winter. Adjective.*

wool (wŭl) *noun, plural* **wools;** *adjective.* —**woolly** *adjective.*

woolen Made of wool: *I have a red **woolen** jacket.* **wool•en** (wŭl′ən) *adjective.*

word 1. A sound or group of sounds having meaning and forming a unit of a language. 2. A written or printed letter or group of letters standing for such a sound: *The **word** "house" has five letters.* 3. A short conversation or statement: *I'd like a **word** with you.* 4. A promise or vow: *Give me your **word** that you won't tell a soul.* 5. A message or news: *We received **word** of our team's victory. Noun.*

○ To put into words: ***Word** your question so that we can understand. Verb.*

• **word for word.** In exactly the same words: *Copy this message **word for word.***

word (wûrd) *noun, plural* **words;** *verb,* **worded, wording.**

wording The way of saying or writing something in words: *Which **wording** do you think is better: "Wanted, Buyer for Bike" or "Bicycle for Sale"?* **word•ing** (wûr′ding) *noun, plural* **wordings.**

word processing The creating, changing, storing, and printing of words by means of a computer.

wordy Using too many words: *The **wordy** speaker went on and on.* **word•y** (wûr′dē) *adjective,* **wordier, wordiest.**

wore Past tense of **wear:** *I **wore** my new coat.* Another word that sounds like this is **war.** **wore** (wôr) *verb.*

work 1. The use of a person's energy or ability to do something; effort. Work can be done by the mind, as in writing a paper, or by the body, as in chopping wood. 2. What a person does to earn money; a job or occupation: *What kind of **work** does your cousin do?* 3. Something that is done or is to be done; task: *We finished our **work** early.* 4. Something that has been made or done: *The painting was a beautiful **work** of art.* 5. **works.** The moving parts of a machine, watch, or other device. *Noun.*

○ 1. To use one's energy or ability in order to do or get something: *If we **work** hard, we'll finish the job today.* 2. To have a job: *My cousin **works** in a business office.* 3. To act or make act properly; operate: *Can you **work** the tape recorder? Did the medicine **work**?* 4. To make happen; bring about: *We'll have to **work** a miracle to finish on* *time.* **5.** To shape, as by pressing and rolling; mold: *Work the clay in your hands until it becomes soft. Verb.*

   • **out of work.** Without a job; unemployed: *My father lost his job last month and has been **out of work** ever since.*

   • **to work out. 1.** To develop or improve: *Work out your ideas before you begin to write the essay.* **2.** To solve: *Can you **work out** the problem yourself?* **3.** To end or result; turn out: *Did your suggestions **work out** in the way that you hoped?* **4.** To train or do exercises: *I **work out** at the gym every day.*

work (wûrk) *noun, plural* **works;** *verb,* **worked, working.**

Working **together on a project can be a rewarding experience.**

workbench A strong table used for working. Carpenters use workbenches. **work·bench** (wûrk′bench′) *noun, plural* **workbenches.**

workbook A book that has questions and exercises to be answered or done by a student. **work·book** (wûrk′bŭk′) *noun, plural* **workbooks.**

worker 1. A person who works: *There were over one hundred **workers** in the factory.* **2.** A female bee, ant, termite, or other insect that does most of the work in a colony. **work·er** (wûr′kər) *noun, plural* **workers.**

workman A person who works with his or her hands or with machines: *Many **workmen** have been hired to build the new school.* **work·man** (wûrk′mən) *noun, plural* **workmen** (wûrk′mən).

workmanship The skill with which a thing is made: *The beautifully carved cabinet showed excellent **workmanship**.* **work·man·ship** (wûrk′mən ship′) *noun.*

workshop 1. A room or building in which work is done by hand or with machines: *We keep our tools in a **workshop** in the basement. The garage has a **workshop** where cars are repaired.* **2.** A group of people who are studying or working together on a special subject: *The school has a **workshop** in child care this summer.* **work·shop** (wûrk′shop′) *noun, plural* **workshops.**

workstation 1. A work area, as in an office, especially one equipped with a computer. **2.** A powerful microcomputer. **work·sta·tion** (wûrk′stā′shən) *noun, plural* **workstations.**

world 1. The earth: *Old whaling ships sometimes sailed around the **world**.* **2.** A part of the earth: *The United States is in the western **world**.* **3.** All

---

WORLD

The world is filled with natural wonders, but some landmarks are record holders. A few of the best known are listed here.

Tallest Mountain: Mt. Everest in Tibet and Nepal at 29,028 feet.

Lowest Point on Land: The bottom of the Bentley Subglacial Trench in Antarctica is estimated at 8,327 feet below sea level, but it is covered with ice. The Dead Sea in Israel and Jordan is 1,312 feet below sea level.

Deepest Point in the Ocean: The Mariana Trench in the Pacific reaches a depth of 35,840 feet.

Longest River: The Nile in Egypt and Sudan is 4,160 miles long.

Highest Waterfall: Angel Falls in Venezuela is 3,212 feet high.

Largest Lake: The Caspian Sea, bordered by Russia, Azerbaijan, Iran, Turkmenistan, and Kazakhstan covers an area of 143,244 square miles.

Deepest Lake: Lake Baikal in Russia is 4,315 feet deep.

Largest Desert: The Sahara in North Africa covers 3,500,000 square miles.

Largest Island: Greenland has an area of 840,000 square miles.

the people who live on the earth: *The **world** marveled at the appearance of the comet.* **4.** A field of activity, interest, or life: *We studied the **world** of fish and the sea. Many people who work are part of the business **world**.* **5.** A large amount; great deal: *The rain did the corn crop a **world** of good.* **world** (wûrld) *noun, plural* **worlds**.

worldly **1.** Relating to the affairs of the world; not spiritual: *The minister spoke about such **worldly** matters as the need for a new church roof.* **2.** Wise in the ways of the world; sophisticated: *It was a surprisingly **worldly** comment from such a young girl.* **world·ly** (wûrld′lē) *adjective.*

worldwide All over the world: *That movie star has won **worldwide** fame.* **world·wide** (wûrld′wīd′) *adjective.*

World Wide Web A system of Internet computers that support documents written in HTML. It is necessary to have a Web browser in order to use the World Wide Web. A person can then jump from one Web page or site to another by clicking a mouse button on links embedded in them.

worm **1.** A long, thin animal with a soft body, no legs, and no backbone. Worms crawl or creep. **2. worms.** A disease caused by certain worms that live as parasites inside another animal. *Noun.* ○ **1.** To move by wiggling or creeping like a worm: *It took me ten minutes to **worm** my way through the crowd to the door.* **2.** To get by a sly method: *They tried to **worm** the secret out of us.* **3.** To get rid of worms that live inside an animal: *We **wormed** our dog by giving it medicine every morning.* *Verb.*
worm (wûrm) *noun, plural* **worms**; *verb,* **wormed, worming.** —**wormy** *adjective.*

worn-out **1.** Used or worn so much that it should not or cannot be used any more: *It's time to replace those **worn-out** shoes.* **2.** Very tired: *The **worn-out** hikers finally reached the camp.* **worn-out** (wôrn′out′) *adjective.*

worry **1.** To feel or cause to feel uneasy or troubled: *The parents **worried** when the sick child's fever would not go down. That leak in the ceiling **worries** me.* **2.** To pull or bite at something with the teeth: *The puppy **worried** at the rug.* *Verb.* ○ Something that causes an uneasy or troubled feeling: *Their biggest **worry** was that it might rain on the day of the picnic.* *Noun.*

wor·ry (wûr′ē) *verb,* **worried, worrying**; *noun, plural* **worries**.

worse **1.** More inferior; less good: *I am a bad speller, but my friend is **worse**.* **2.** More unfavorable: *The weather was **worse** yesterday than it is today.* **3.** In poorer health; less well: *The doctor said that the patient was **worse**.* *Adjective.* ○ In a worse way: *Our team seems to play **worse** during practice.* *Adverb.* ○ Something that is worse: *The soup was pretty bad, but I have tasted **worse**.* *Noun.*
worse (wûrs) *adjective; adverb; noun.*

worship Prayer, religious services, and other acts done in honor of God or a god: *Churches, temples, and mosques are places of **worship**.* *Noun.* ○ **1.** To pay honor to God or a god. **2.** To give great love or devotion to: *That little girl **worships** her older brother.* *Verb.*
wor·ship (wûr′ship) *noun; verb,* **worshiped** or **worshipped, worshiping** or **worshipping**.

worst **1.** Most inferior; least good: *Throwing water on a grease fire is the **worst** thing you can do.* **2.** Most unfavorable: *That's the **worst** news I've heard all week.* **3.** Most harmful or severe: *The **worst** storm we had last year knocked over our big walnut tree.* *Adjective.* ○ In the worst way: *My sore throat hurts **worst** in the morning.* *Adverb.* ○ Something that is worst: *None of these photographs is good, but this one is the **worst**.* *Noun.*
worst (wûrst) *adjective; adverb; noun.*

worth **1.** Good enough for; deserving of: *That movie was **worth** seeing.* **2.** Having the same value as: *This old coin is **worth** thirty dollars today.* **3.** Having wealth that amounts to: *That banker is **worth** millions of dollars.* *Preposition.* ○ **1.** The quality that makes a person or thing good or useful; excellence: *My raincoat proved its **worth** by keeping me dry during the storm.* **2.** The amount of money that something can be exchanged for; value in money: *That diamond's **worth** is said to be $50,000.* **3.** The amount that a certain sum of money will buy: *The customer asked for a dollar's **worth** of cherries.* *Noun.*
worth (wûrth) *preposition; noun.*

worthless Not good or useful; without value: *This pot is **worthless** because it has a hole in the bottom.* **worth·less** (wûrth′lis) *adjective.*
—**worthlessly** *adverb* —**worthlessness** *noun.*

worthwhile Good enough or important enough to spend time, effort, or money on: *Doing volunteer work at the hospital is a worthwhile activity.* **worth·while** (wûrth′hwīl′ or wûrth′wīl′) *adjective.*

worthy **1.** Having value; good or worthwhile: *The prize should go to a worthy person.* **2.** Having enough value; deserving: *The idea is at least worthy of consideration.* **wor·thy** (wûr′thē) *adjective,* **worthier, worthiest.**

would An auxiliary verb that is used in the following ways: **1.** To express something that might have happened if something else had happened first: *We would be cooler if we had opened the windows.* **2.** To express something that might happen later: *We sat on the platform, wondering if the train would be on time.* **3.** To express something that was planned or intended: *The scouts promised that they would return soon.* **4.** To express something that happened often or commonly: *During the summer we would sit by the lake and talk for hours.* **5.** To express a request: *Would you please turn off the radio?* Another word that sounds like this is **wood.** **would** (wŭd) *verb.*

wouldn't Shortened form of "would not": *I wouldn't do that if I were you.* **wouldn't** (wŭd′ənt) *contraction.*

wound¹ **1.** A cut or other injury to a part of the body. **2.** A hurt to a person's feelings: *It took a long time to recover from the wound of that insult. Noun.*
◦ **1.** To hurt or injure by cutting, piercing, or tearing the skin: *The soldier was wounded during the war.* **2.** To hurt a person's feelings: *The singer's pride was wounded when the leading role went to someone else. Their thoughtlessness wounded me. Verb.*
wound (wŭnd) *noun, plural* **wounds;** *verb,* **wounded, wounding.**

wound² Past tense of **wind²**: *I wound the bandage around my wrist.* **wound** (wound) *verb.*

wove A past tense of **weave**: *Yesterday we wove baskets out of reeds.* **wove** (wōv) *verb.*

woven A past participle of **weave**: *The robin had woven twigs together to make a nest.* **wo·ven** (wō′vən) *verb.*

wrangle **1.** To argue or struggle over: *I'm tired of wrangling about which restaurant to go to.* **2.** To herd horses or cattle: *Cowboys wrangle for a living.* **wran·gle** (rang′gəl) *verb,* **wrangled, wrangling.** —**wrangler** *noun.*

wrap **1.** To cover by putting something around: *We wrapped the presents in colored tissue paper.* **2.** To fold or wind as a covering: *The nurse wrapped a blanket around the baby.* **3.** To hide by covering: *The top of the mountain was wrapped in fog.* **4.** To clasp or fold: *The monkey wrapped its arms around the animal trainer.* Another word that sounds like this is **rap.** **wrap** (rap) *verb,* **wrapped, wrapping.**

These vines have wrapped themselves around the pole.

wrapper A piece of paper or other covering for something: *Be sure to put food wrappers in the wastebasket.* **2.** A person who wraps packages in a store. Another word that sounds like this is **rapper.** **wrap·per** (rap′ər) *noun, plural* **wrappers.**

wrapping Paper or other covering for something: *We burned the wrappings from the birthday presents in the fireplace.* **wrap·ping** (rap′ing) *noun, plural* **wrappings.**

wrath Very great anger: *In the story, the wizard's tricks aroused the wrath of the monster.* **wrath** (rath) *noun.*

wreak To create or cause: *The flu wreaked havoc with my schedule.* Another word that sounds like this is **reek.** **wreak** (rēk) *verb,* **wreaked, wreaking.**

wreath A circle of leaves or flowers woven together: *We hung a holiday wreath on the front door.* **wreath** (rēth) *noun, plural* **wreaths** (rēthz or rēths).

PRONUNCIATION KEY:
at āpe fär câre end mē it īce pierce hot ōld sông fôrk
oil out up ūse rüle pull tûrn chin sing shop thin this
hw in white; zh in treasure. The symbol ə stands for the unstressed vowel sound in about, taken, pencil, lemon, and circus.

823

wreck To destroy or ruin: *The builders **wrecked** the old house to clear the land. The dishonest behavior of the store owners **wrecked** their business. Verb.*
○ What is left of something that has been ruined or damaged: *There are many automobile **wrecks** in the junkyard. Noun.*
wreck (rek) *verb,* **wrecked, wrecking**; *noun, plural* **wrecks.**

wreckage What is left of something that has been ruined or destroyed: *We went to look at the **wreckage** after the building burned down.* **wreck•age** (rek′ij) *noun.*

wren A small songbird with brown feathers, a narrow bill, and a short tail that often sticks upward. **wren** (ren) *noun, plural* **wrens.**

There are many different types of wrens.

wrench 1. A very hard, sharp twist or pull: *I gave the doorknob a **wrench** but the door was stuck.* 2. A tool with jaws that is used to grip and turn a nut or bolt. *Noun.*
○ To twist or pull with a hard, sharp motion: *We had to **wrench** the heavy door open. Verb.*
wrench (rench) *noun, plural* **wrenches**; *verb,* **wrenched, wrenching.**

wrest To take away by force: *The rebels **wrested** control of the government from the military.* Another word that sounds like this is **rest.**
wrest (rest) *verb,* **wrested, wresting.**

wrestle 1. To struggle by grasping and trying to force and hold one's opponent to the ground, without punching: *The children **wrestled** on the lawn.* 2. To force by grasping: *The champion **wrestled** his opponent to the mat.* 3. To struggle very hard: *She **wrestled** with the last problem on the arithmetic test.* **wres•tle** (res′əl) *verb,* **wrestled, wrestling.**

wrestling A sport in which two people struggle by grasping each other. Each person tries to force and hold the other to the ground. Punching is not allowed in wrestling. **wres•tling** (res′ling) *noun.*

wretched 1. Very unhappy, poor, or uncomfortable: *My fever made me feel **wretched**.* 2. Very

bad or evil: *The cruel soldiers were **wretched** people.* **wretch•ed** (rech′id) *adjective.* —**wretchedly** *adverb.*

wriggle 1. To twist or turn from side to side with short, quick moves; squirm: *The bored children **wriggled** in their seats. The snake **wriggled** through the grass.* 2. To get into or out of a position by tricky means: *You always try to **wriggle** out of having to wash the dishes.* **wrig•gle** (rig′əl) *verb,* **wriggled, wriggling.** —**wriggler** *noun.*

wring 1. To squeeze or twist so that liquid is forced out: *You must **wring** the wet clothes before hanging them up to dry.* 2. To force out liquid by squeezing or twisting: *I **wrung** the water from my bathing suit.* 3. To get by force: *The soldiers said they would **wring** the truth out of the spy.* 4. To hold tightly and press or twist: *Some of the people waiting in the dentist's office were **wringing** their hands nervously.* Another word that sounds like this is **ring.**
wring (ring) *verb,* **wrung, wringing.**

wrinkle A small fold, ridge, or line in a smooth surface: *He ironed the **wrinkles** out of his shirt. She had small **wrinkles** at the corners of her eyes. Noun.*
○ To make or have a fold, ridge, or line in a smooth surface: *Some people **wrinkle** their foreheads when they frown. Silk clothing **wrinkles** easily. Verb.*
wrin•kle (ring′kəl) *noun, plural* **wrinkles**; *verb,* **wrinkled, wrinkling.**

wrist The joint between the hand and the arm. **wrist** (rist) *noun, plural* **wrists.**

wristwatch A watch that is worn on a strap around the wrist. **wrist•watch** (rist′woch′) *noun, plural* **wristwatches.**

write 1. To form letters, words, or symbols on paper or some other surface: *The teacher **wrote** his name on the blackboard.* 2. To be the author of: *My aunt **writes** children's stories.* 3. To send a letter: *Please **write** to us when you are on vacation.* Another word that sounds like this is **right.**
write (rīt) *verb,* **wrote, written, writing.**

writer A person who writes stories, poems, or articles; author. **writ•er** (rī′tər) *noun, plural* **writers.**

writing 1. Letters, words, or symbols that are written by hand: *Do you know whose **writing** this is?* 2. A book, play, or other thing that has been written: *We study the **writings** of many* authors in English class. **writ·ing** (rī′ting) *noun, plural* **writings**.

written   Past participle of **write**: *Has your friend **written** you a letter yet?* **writ·ten** (rit′ən) *verb*.

wrong   1. Not correct or true: *Some of your answers were right, and some were **wrong**.* 2. Not moral or good; bad: *It is **wrong** to steal.* 3. Not proper; not suitable: *A heavy sweater is the **wrong** thing to wear on a hot day.* 4. Out of order; not working: *Something is **wrong** with my watch. Adjective.*
  ○ Something that is not moral or good: *Injustice is a great **wrong**. Noun.*
  ○ In a way that is not right; incorrectly: *I spelled several words **wrong** in my report. Adverb.*
  ○ To treat in an unjust or bad way: *The salesperson **wronged** us by accusing us of stealing. Verb.*
  wrong (rông) *adjective; noun, plural* **wrongs**; *adverb; verb*, **wronged**, **wronging**.

wrote   Past tense of **write**: *We all **wrote** down what the teacher said.* **wrote** (rōt) *verb*.

wrought iron   A kind of iron that is somewhat soft and can be formed into various shapes: *outdoor furniture made from curved **wrought iron**.* **wrought iron** (rôt).

wrung   Past tense and past participle of **wring**: *I **wrung** out the wet shirt and hung it up to dry.* Another word that sounds like this is **rung**. **wrung** (rung) *verb*.

wt.   An abbreviation for **weight**.

WV or **W. Va.**   An abbreviation for **West Virginia**.

WY   An abbreviation for **Wyoming**.

Wyo.   An abbreviation for **Wyoming**.

Wyoming   A state in the western United States. Its capital is Cheyenne. **Wy·o·ming** (wī ō′ming) *noun*.

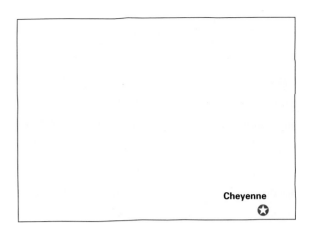

Cheyenne ★

Wyoming
U. S. Postal Abbreviation: **WY**
Capital: **Cheyenne**
Population: **490,000**
Area: **97,914 sq. mi./253,596 sq. km**
State Nickname: **Equality State**
State Bird: **Meadowlark**
State Flower: **Indian Paintbrush**

WORD HISTORY

The name Wyoming comes from a word used by eastern Native Americans to mean "flat area between mountains." They used this name for a valley in Pennsylvania. Congress later gave this name to a new territory in the western plains. The name Wyoming was kept when the territory became a state.

WYSIWYG   Of or relating to a computer-screen display that shows a document exactly as it will appear when it is printed out: *a **WYSIWYG** display of the questionnaire.* The letters of WYSIWYG stand for *What You See Is What You Get*. **WYS·I·WYG** (wiz′ē wig′) *adjective*.

PRONUNCIATION KEY:
at   āpe   fär   câre   end   mē   it   īce   pierce   hot   ōld   sông   fôrk
oil   out   up   ūse   rüle   pull   tûrn   chin   sing   shop   thin   this
hw in white; zh in treasure. The symbol ə stands for the unstressed vowel sound in about, taken, pencil, lemon, and circus.

825

SPELLING HINTS

The letter X has two sounds in English. The first appears in words like x-ray. The second sound of x is like z in words such as xylophone.

X-ray or **x-ray** To examine, photograph, or treat with X rays: *The doctor X-rayed my arm to see if any bones had been broken.* **X-ray** (eks′rā′) *verb,* **X-rayed, X-raying.**

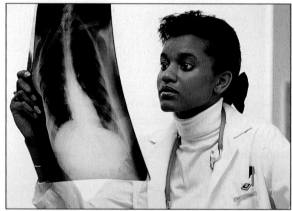

An x ray is one of a doctor's most important tools.

x, X The twenty-fourth letter of the alphabet. **x, X** (eks) *noun, plural* **x's, X's.**

xenophilia A liking for foreign people or foreign things. **xen•o•phil•i•a** (zen′ə fil′ē ə) *noun.*

xenophobia A fear of foreign people or of foreign things. **xen•o•pho•bi•a** (zen′ə fō′bē ə) *noun.*

Xerox A trademark for a process or machine for making photographic copies of written or printed materials. *Noun.*
○ To make a copy of something written or printed by using a Xerox machine: *I Xeroxed the schedule of events and distributed it to the class.* Verb. **Xe•rox** (zîr′oks) *noun; verb,* **Xeroxed, Xeroxing.**

Xhosa 1. A member of a people of South Africa. 2. The language of the Xhosa people. **Xho•sa** (kō′sə) *noun, plural* **Xhosa** or **Xhosas.**

Xmas Christmas. Look up **Christmas** for more information. **Xmas** (kris′məs *or* eks′məs) *noun, plural* **Xmases.**

X ray 1. A kind of radiation that can pass through substances that ordinary rays of light cannot pass through. Doctors use X rays to take pictures of parts inside the body that cannot be seen from outside. X rays can be used to see if a bone has been broken or to see if there is a cavity in a hidden part of a tooth. 2. A photograph made with X rays: *The doctor looked at the X ray of the dog's injured leg.*

xylophone A musical instrument that is made up of one or two rows of wooden bars. The bars are of different lengths, and they are sounded by hitting them with small wooden hammers. **xy•lo•phone** (zī′lə fōn′) *noun, plural* **xylophones.**

WORD HISTORY

The word **Xmas** is made up of the letter "X" and the ending *mas* from the word Christmas. "X" was the first letter of the ancient Greek word meaning "Christ" and this letter was used as a symbol for Jesus Christ.

WORD HISTORY

The word **xylophone** comes from two Greek words meaning "wood" and "sound" or "voice."

The letter Y has two sounds in English. The first can be made by:

y in words such as yes and yellow;

i in onion.

The second sound of y is like e in words such as happy and lucky.

y, Y The twenty-fifth letter of the alphabet. **y, Y** (wī) *noun, plural* **y's, Y's.**

-y A suffix that is often added to a noun to form an adjective and that means: **1.** Full of; having: *Dirty means full of dirt.* **2.** Like: *Wintry means like winter.* **3.** Tending to: *Sticky means tending to stick.*

yacht A large boat or small ship used for pleasure trips. **yacht** (yot) *noun, plural* **yachts.**

Yachts are usually large enough to travel on the ocean.

yak An ox that has long hair and is found in Asia. Yaks are raised for their meat and milk. They are also used to carry heavy loads. There are very few wild yaks left. **yak** (yak) *noun, plural* **yaks.**

yam **1.** The root of a trailing tropical vine. It is ground into flour or eaten baked or broiled. **2.** A kind of sweet potato. Look up **sweet potato** for more information. **yam** (yam) *noun, plural* **yams.**

yank To pull something in a sharp, sudden way; jerk; tug: *The selfish child yanked the toy truck away from the baby. Verb.*

○ A sharp, sudden pull: *With one yank on the ribbon, I untied the bow on my birthday present. Noun.*

yank (yangk) *verb,* **yanked, yanking;** *noun, plural* **yanks.**

Yankee **1.** A person who was born or is living in a state in New England or another Northern state. **2.** A person who fought for the Union during the Civil War. **3.** A person who was born in or is a citizen of the United States; American. **Yan·kee** (yang′kē) *noun, plural* **Yankees.**

yap A sharp barking sound that a dog makes. *Noun.*

○ **1.** To give a sharp bark as a dog does. **2.** To talk at length or in a foolish way: *Stop yapping and wash the dishes. Verb.*

yap (yap) *noun, plural* **yaps;** *verb,* **yapped, yapping.** —**yappy** *adjective.*

yard¹ **1.** An area of ground next to or surrounding a house, school, or other building: *We have a vegetable garden in our yard. We play games in the yard behind the school.* **2.** An enclosed area used for carrying on some work or business: *Wood for building can be bought at a lumber yard. A train yard is where trains are stored and switched.* **yard** (yärd) *noun, plural* **yards.**

yard² **1.** A measure of length equal to 36 inches, or 3 feet. A yard is slightly shorter than a meter. **2.** A long rod fastened across the mast of a ship to support a sail. **yard** (yärd) *noun, plural* **yards.**

yardstick 1. A flat strip of wood, plastic, or metal one yard long and marked with units of length. It is used in measuring. 2. Any standard used in making a judgment or comparison: *One **yardstick** of the quality of a car is the number of miles it can travel using a gallon of gas.* **yard·stick** (yärd′stik′) *noun, plural* **yardsticks.**

yarn 1. Fibers that have been twisted into long strands. Yarn is used in knitting or weaving. It is made from cotton, wool, silk, nylon, or other fiber. 2. A long story; tale: *The old sailors liked to tell **yarns** about their sea voyages.* **yarn** (yärn) *noun, plural* **yarns.**

Seeing an animal or person yawn can make you
want to yawn too.

yawn 1. To open the mouth wide and take a deep breath. People yawn because their brains need more oxygen or because they are tired or bored. 2. To be wide open: *The entrance to the huge cave **yawned** in front of them.* Verb.
○ The act of opening the mouth wide and taking a deep breath: *The tired secretary tried to hide a **yawn** as her boss talked on and on. Noun.*
yawn (yôn) *verb,* **yawned, yawning;** *noun, plural* **yawns.**

yd. An abbreviation for **yard.**

ye You. This word was common in the past, but it is not often used today. **ye** (yē) *pronoun.*

year 1. A period of time made up of the twelve months from January 1 to December 31. A year contains 365 days. There are 366 days in a leap year. 2. Any period of twelve months: *We moved to this house two **years** ago.* 3. A part of a year spent in a particular activity: *During the school **year** I get up at 7:30 in the morning.* **year** (yîr) *noun, plural* **years.**

yearly 1. Happening or returning once a year: *We make a **yearly** trip to my grandparents' house at Thanksgiving.* 2. Measured by the year: *The **yearly** average rainfall in our city is about 42 inches.* **year·ly** (yîr′lē) *adjective.*

year-round Throughout the year: *The athletes follow a **year-round** routine of exercises and special diets. This hotel is open **year-round**.* **year-round** (yîr′round′) *adjective; adverb.*

yeast A substance that is used in baking to make dough rise. It is made up of tiny cells of fungus plants. **yeast** (yēst) *noun, plural* **yeasts.**

yell To call loudly; shout; cry: *My sister got mad and **yelled** at me for taking her bicycle. "Watch out!" he **yelled**. Verb.*
○ A loud call; shout; cry: *Give a **yell** if you need any help. Noun.*
yell (yel) *verb,* **yelled, yelling;** *noun, plural* **yells.**

yellow 1. The color of gold, butter, or ripe lemons. 2. The yolk of an egg: *The cook separated the egg whites from the **yellows**. Noun.*
○ Having the color yellow: *A daisy has a **yellow** center. Adjective.*
○ To make or become yellow: *The old newspaper had **yellowed** with age. Verb.*
yel·low (yel′ō) *noun, plural* **yellows;** *adjective,* **yellower, yellowest;** *verb,* **yellowed, yellowing.**

yellow jacket A kind of wasp that has black and bright yellow markings.

yelp A short, sharp cry such as that made by a dog that is hurt. *Noun.*
○ To give a short, sharp cry like that of a dog in pain. *Verb.*
yelp (yelp) *noun, plural* **yelps;** *verb,* **yelped, yelping.**

yen[1] A unit of money in Japan. **yen** (yen) *noun, plural* **yen.**

yen² A strong desire, longing: *I have a yen to travel to sunny places.* **yen** (yen) *noun, plural* **yens.**

SYNONYMS

yen, longing, itch

I have a yen for fresh orange juice when I'm thirsty. Some folks feel a longing to return to scenes of their childhood. They get an itch to move on after staying in the same place for a while.

---

yes A word used to show agreement or acceptance: *Yes, you are right. Yes, you may borrow my calculator. Adverb.*

○ 1. An answer that shows agreement or acceptance: *Six people said yes to our party invitation.* 2. A vote in favor of something: *The hikers voted on whether to stop for lunch, and there were three yeses and one no. Noun.*

yes (yes) *adverb; noun, plural* **yeses.**

yesterday The day before today: *Yesterday was sunny, but by this morning it had begun to rain. Noun.*

○ On the day before today: *I started to read the book yesterday and finished it this afternoon. Adverb.*

yes·ter·day (yes′tər dē *or* yes′tər dā′) *noun, plural* **yesterdays;** *adverb.*

yet 1. At the present time; now: *I'm not yet old enough to drive a car.* 2. Up to the present time; so far: *They have never yet been late for a meeting.* 3. Continuously up to this or that time; still: *The farmers went to the fields early and are working yet.* 4. At some future time; eventually: *The mystery will be solved yet.* 5. In addition: *There are three days yet to go until our vacation. Adverb.*

○ Nevertheless; however; but: *I thought I knew the way, yet I soon got lost. Conjunction.*

• **as yet.** Up to the present time; so far: *We have not as yet received the package you sent us.*

yet (yet) *adverb; conjunction.*

yew An evergreen tree that has reddish brown bark, flat, needle-shaped leaves, and a seed with a red, fleshy covering. It is native to Europe and Asia. The wood of this tree is used to make bows for archery.

Other words that sound like this are **ewe** and **you.** **yew** (ū) *noun, plural* **yews.**

yield 1. To produce: *The field yielded a large crop of wheat.* 2. To give control or possession of to another: *The defeated army yielded the town to the enemy.* 3. To stop fighting or disagreeing: *We yielded in the argument when we realized that we were wrong.* 4. To give way to force or pressure: *The lock on the door of the old house yielded when we pushed against it. Verb.*

○ An amount produced: *The farm's yield of corn was greater this year than last year. Noun.*

yield (yēld) *verb,* **yielded, yielding;** *noun, plural* **yields.**

This field has yielded a bountiful crop for the season.

YMCA An abbreviation for **Young Men's Christian Association.**

yodel To sing in a voice that goes from low sounds to high sounds very quickly. **yo·del** (yōd′əl) *verb,* **yodeled** *or* **yodelled, yodeling** *or* **yodelling. —yodeler** *or* **yodeller** *noun.*

yoga A method of exercising and meditating that came originally from Hindu religious teachings. **yo·ga** (yō′gə) *noun.*

yogurt A thick, soft food that is made by adding certain bacteria to milk. Yogurt is often sweetened and flavored with fruit. **yo·gurt** (yō′gərt) *noun, plural* **yogurts.**

WORD HISTORY

The word yogurt comes from the Turkish name for this food.

PRONUNCIATION KEY:
at   āpe   fär   câre   end   mē   it   īce   pierce   hot   ōld   sông   fôrk
oil   out   up   ūse   rüle   půll   tûrn   chin   sing   shop   thin   this
hw in white; zh in treasure. The symbol ə stands for the unstressed vowel sound in about, taken, pencil, lemon, and circus.

829

yoke **1.** A wooden frame used to join together two work animals. **2.** A pair of animals joined by a yoke: *The wagon was pulled by a yoke of oxen.* **3.** The part of a shirt, dress, or other piece of clothing that fits around the shoulders and neck: *The yoke on that dress is trimmed with lace.* Noun. ○ To join with a yoke or harness: *The farmer yoked the oxen to the plow.* Verb. Another word that sounds like this is **yolk**. **yoke** (yōk) *noun, plural* **yokes** *(for definitions 1 and 3) or* **yoke** *(for definition 2); verb,* **yoked**, **yoking**.

yolk The yellow part of an egg. The yolk provides food for the young chick or other animal until it hatches: *The recipe calls for three egg yolks.* Another word that sounds like this is **yoke**. **yolk** (yōk) *noun, plural* **yolks**.

Yom Kippur A Jewish holiday that occurs ten days after Rosh Hashanah, which is the first day of the Jewish year. Yom Kippur is a day of fasting and prayer. It is the holiest Jewish holiday. **Yom Kip·pur** (yom kip′ər *or* yōm′kē pür′) *noun*.

yonder In that place; over there: *Yonder stands the castle of the king and queen of this land.* **yon·der** (yon′dər) *adverb*.

Yoruba **1.** A member of a West African people living mostly in southwest Nigeria. **2.** The language of this people. **Yo·ru·ba** (yôr′ə bə) *noun, plural* **Yoruba** *or* **Yorubas**.

you **1.** The person or persons that are spoken or written to: *I'll meet you on the corner at six o'clock. We'll go with you to the concert.* **2.** A person; anyone: *You have to be at least eighteen years old to be able to vote.* Other words that sound like this are **ewe** and **yew**. **you** (ū *or unstressed* yə) *pronoun*.

young **1.** In the early part of life or growth: *These picture books are for young readers. A lamb is a young sheep. The age of space travel is still young.* **2.** Having the look or qualities of a young person: *My grandmother is a very active woman and is quite young for her age.* **3.** Of or belonging to the early part of life: *Our neighbor spent his younger years in England.* Adjective. ○ Young offspring: *The lions caught an antelope to feed their young.* Noun. **young** (yung) *adjective,* **younger**, **youngest**; *noun, plural* **young**.

youngster A young person: *Many of the youngsters in the neighborhood helped to clean up the vacant lot.* **young·ster** (yung′stər) *noun, plural* **youngsters**.

your Of or belonging to you: *Let's meet tomorrow at your house. Is this your coat?* **your** (yùr *or* yôr *or unstressed* yər) *adjective*.

yours The one or ones that belong to or relate to you: *If this hat is mine, the other must be yours. Their plan is good, but yours is even better.* **yours** (yùrz *or* yôrz) *pronoun*.

yourself **1.** Your own self: *You yourself know that what you did was wrong. Be careful of the fire or you will burn yourself.* **2.** Your usual, normal, or true self: *After a good night's sleep you will feel like yourself again.* **your·self** (yùr self′ *or* yôr self′ *or* yər self′) *pronoun, plural* **yourselves**.

youth **1.** The condition or quality of being young: *The new player has youth but lacks experience. Many older people keep the fresh outlook and attitudes of youth.* **2.** The time of life after childhood and before becoming an adult: *In his youth, my father wanted to be a soldier.* **3.** The beginning or early stage of something: *Aviation was still in its youth when my grandmother first flew.* **4.** A young person: *The car was driven by a youth of about eighteen years of age.* **youth** (ūth) *noun, plural* **youths** *or* **youth**.

yowl To make a long, mournful cry. *Verb.* ○ A long, mournful cry. *Noun.* **yowl** (youl) *verb,* **yowled**, **yowling**; *noun, plural* **yowls**.

yo-yo A toy that has two disks attached at their centers with a peg. A yo-yo goes up and down on a string that is attached to the peg. **yo-yo** (yō′yō) *noun, plural* **yo-yos**.

yr. An abbreviation for **year**.

YT An abbreviation for **Yukon Territory**.

Yugoslavia A former country in southeastern Europe. Its capital was Belgrade. **Yu·go·sla·vi·a** (ū′gō slä′vē ə) *noun*.

Yukon Territory A territory in northwestern Canada. Its capital is Whitehorse. **Yu·kon Territory** (ū′kon) *noun*.

Yule Christmas. **yule** (ūl) *noun, plural* **yules**.

Yuletide Christmastime. **Yule·tide** (ūl′tīd′) *noun, plural* **Yuletides**.

The letter Z has two sounds in English. The first sound can be made by:

z in words such as zipper and zoo;

zz at the end of words such as jazz;

s as in rose, dogs, and houses.

ss in scissors;

x in xylophone.

The second sound of Z can be made by:

z in words such as azure;

s in words such as treasure;

si in words such as vision.

z, Z The twenty-sixth and last letter of the alphabet. **z, Z** (zē) *noun, plural* **z's, Z's.**

Zaire A country in central Africa, now known as the Democratic Republic of Congo. **Za·ire** (zä îr′) *noun.*

Zambia A country in south-central Africa. **Zam·bi·a** (zam′bē ə) *noun.*

zap 1. To strike, stun, or kill with great speed and force: *The frog zapped the fly.* 2. To cook in a microwave oven. 3. To use a remote control to change channels very quickly on a television set. This is an informal word. **zap** (zap) *verb,* **zapped, zapping.**

zeal Great enthusiasm or commitment: *The students began to work the arithmetic problems with zeal.* **zeal** (zēl) *noun.* —**zealous** *adjective* —**zealously** *adverb.*

zebra A wild animal that looks like a horse with a black-and-white striped coat. **ze·bra** (zē′brə) *noun, plural* **zebras** or **zebra.**

zenith 1. The point in the sky directly above the place where a person stands. 2. The highest or greatest point: *The musician's recent concert was the zenith of a great career.* **ze·nith** (zē′nith) *noun, plural* **zeniths.**

Zebras are found in southern and eastern Africa.

zero 1. The number 0, which means no quantity or amount at all. When you add zero to any number or subtract zero from any number, the number remains the same. 2. A point on a thermometer or other scale at which numbering or measurement begins: *The temperature outside is ten degrees above zero Fahrenheit.* 3. Nothing: *The business did not lose money, but its profit was zero. Noun.*

○ 1. Of, being, or at zero: *The temperature dropped to zero degrees Fahrenheit last night.* 2. None at all; not any: *The team had zero victories last season. Adjective.*

ze·ro (zîr′ō) *noun, plural* **zeros** or **zeroes;** *adjective.*

zest Exciting or lively quality: *A brisk walk adds zest to my day.* **zest** (zest) *noun.*

zigzag A line, pattern, or course that moves in or has a series of short, sharp turns from one side to the other: *The clown wore a big bright tie with zigzags of different colors. Noun.*
○ To move in or form a zigzag: *The dog zigzagged down the street. Verb.*
zig·zag (zig′zag′) *noun, plural* **zigzags;** *verb,* **zigzagged, zigzagging.**

zilch Nothing; zero: *I looked in the refrigerator for something good to eat but found zilch.* This is an informal word. **zilch** (zilch) *noun.*

Zimbabwe A country in south-central Africa. **Zim·bab·we** (zim bäb′wē) *noun.*

zinc A grayish white metal. It is used to make alloys and in electric batteries. Zinc is a chemical element. **zinc** (zingk) *noun.*

zinnia A garden plant that has rounded, brightly colored flowers. **zin·ni·a** (zin′ē ə) *noun, plural* **zinnias.**

zip To fasten or close with a zipper: *It was cold, so I zipped up my coat.* **zip** (zip) *verb,* **zipped, zipping.**

zip code or **ZIP Code** A number that identifies a postal delivery area in the United States. The zip code is written after the state in an address on a letter, package, or other piece of mail.

zipper A fastener made up of two rows of teeth that fit into each other. The teeth can be joined or separated by pulling a sliding device up or down. Zippers are used on clothing, suitcases, and other articles. **zip·per** (zip′ər) *noun, plural* **zippers.**

zit A pimple. This is an informal word. **zit** (zit) *noun, plural* **zits.**

zither A musical instrument made up of a shallow, wooden box with thirty to forty-five strings stretched across it. It is played by plucking the strings. **zith·er** (zith′ər *or* zi<u>th</u>′ər) *noun, plural* **zithers.**

zodiac An imaginary belt in the heavens. The sun, moon, and most of the planets seem to travel on paths through the zodiac during the year. The zodiac is divided into twelve parts, and each part is named for a constellation. **zo·di·ac** (zō′dē ak′) *noun.*

zone 1. A region or area that has some special quality, condition, or use: *Cars are not allowed to go more than 15 miles per hour in the school zone. The area at the end of a football field is called the end zone.* 2. Any of the five regions of the earth's surface divided according to the climate found there. There is a torrid zone, two temperate zones, and two frigid zones. *Noun.*
○ To divide into zones: *The city government zones the city, so that certain areas are only for private homes, and other areas are only for stores and businesses. Verb.*
zone (zōn) *noun, plural* **zones;** *verb,* **zoned, zoning.**

zoo A park or other public place where wild animals are kept for people to see. **zoo** (zü) *noun, plural* **zoos.**

zoology The science that deals with the study of animals. **zo·ol·o·gy** (zō ol′ə jē) *noun.*

zoom To move or climb suddenly and quickly: *The airplane zoomed into the clouds. A police officer zoomed past on a motorcycle.*
• **zoom in.** To move a camera lens forward quickly: *The cameraman zoomed in on the actor for a close-up.*
zoom (züm) *verb,* **zoomed, zooming.**

zucchini A long, narrow kind of squash that has a green skin. **zuc·chi·ni** (zü kē′nē) *noun, plural* **zucchini.**

Zucchini is among the hardiest of all vegetables.

REFERENCE
SECTION

Table of Contents

PRESIDENTS
of the UNITED STATES

George Washington
Lived from: 1732 to 1799
In Office: 1789 to 1797
Vice President: John Adams
First Lady: Martha Dandridge
   Washington

John Adams
Lived from: 1735 to 1826
In Office: 1797 to 1801
Vice President: Thomas Jefferson
First Lady: Abigail Smith Adams

Thomas Jefferson
Lived from: 1743 to 1826
In Office: 1801 to 1809
Vice Presidents: Aaron Burr (1801-
   1805). George Clinton (1805-1809)
No First Lady

James Madison
Lived from: 1751 to 1836
In Office: 1809 to 1817
Vice Presidents: George Clinton
   (1809-1812). Elbridge Gerry (1813-1814)
First Lady: Dolley Payne Madison

James Monroe
Lived from: 1758 to 1831
In Office: 1817 to 1825
Vice President: Daniel Tompkins
First Lady: Elizabeth Kortright Monro

John Quincy Adams
Lived from: 1767 to 1848
In Office: 1825 to 1829
Vice President: John C. Calhoun
First Lady: Louisa Johnson Adams

Andrew Jackson
Lived from: 1767 to 1845
In Office: 1829 to 1837
Vice Presidents: John C. Calhoun
   (1829-1832). Martin Van Buren
   (1833-1837)
No First Lady

Martin Van Buren
Lived from: 1782 to 1862
In Office: 1837 to 1841
Vice President: Richard M. Johnson
No First Lady

William Henry Harrison
Lived from: 1773 to 1841
Served for one month in 1841
Vice President: John Tyler
First Lady: Anna Symmes Harrison

John Tyler
Lived from: 1790 to 1862
In Office: 1841 to 1845
No Vice President
First Ladies: Letitia Christian Tyler
   (1841-1842) *and* Julia Gardiner
   Tyler (1844-1845)

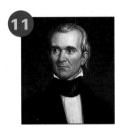

James K. Polk
Lived from: 1795 to 1849
In Office: 1845 to 1849
Vice President: George M. Dallas
First Lady: Sarah Childress Polk

Zachary Taylor
Lived from: 1784 to 1850
In Office: 1849 to 1850
Vice President: Millard Fillmore
First Lady: Margaret Smith Taylor

Millard Fillmore
Lived from: 1800 to 1874
In Office: 1850 to 1853
No Vice President
First Lady: Abigail Powers Fillmore

Franklin Pierce
Lived from: 1804 to 1869
In Office: 1853 to 1857
Vice President: William R. King
 (died in 1853)
First Lady: Jane Appleton Pierce

James Buchanan
Lived from: 1791 to 1868
In Office: 1857 to 1861
Vice President: John C. Breckinridge
No First Lady

Abraham Lincoln
Lived from: 1809 to 1865
In Office: 1861 to 1865
Vice Presidents: Hannibal Hamlin
 (1861-1865). Andrew Johnson (1865)
First Lady: Mary Todd Lincoln

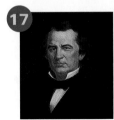

Andrew Johnson
Lived from: 1808 to 1875
In Office: 1865 to 1869
No Vice President
First Lady: Eliza McCardle Johnson

Ulysses S. Grant
Lived from: 1822 to 1885
In Office: 1869 to 1877
Vice Presidents: Schuyler Colfax (1869-
 1873). Henry Wilson (1873-1875)
First Lady: Julia Dent Grant

Rutherford B. Hayes
Lived from: 1822 to 1893
In Office: 1877 to 1881
Vice President: William A. Wheeler
First Lady: Lucy Webb Hayes

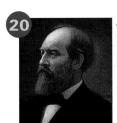

James A. Garfield
Lived from: 1831 to 1881
Served in 1881
Vice President: Chester A. Arthur
First Lady: Lucretia Rudolph Garfield

Chester A. Arthur
Lived from: 1829 to 1886
In Office: 1881 to 1885
No Vice President
No First Lady

Grover Cleveland
Lived from: 1837 to 1908
In Office: 1885 to 1889
Vice President: Thomas A. Hendricks
 (1885)
First Lady: Frances Folsom Cleveland

PRESIDENTS of the UNITED STATES

Benjamin Harrison
Lived from: 1833 to 1901
In Office: 1889 to 1893
Vice President: Levi P. Morton
First Lady: Caroline Scott Harrison

Grover Cleveland
Lived from: 1837 to 1908
In Office: 1893 to 1897
Vice President: Adlai E. Stevenson
First Lady: Frances Folsom Cleveland

William McKinley
Lived from: 1843 to 1901
In Office: 1897 to 1901
Vice Presidents: Garret A. Hobart
 (1897-1899). Theodore Roosevelt
 (1901)
First Lady: Ida Saxon McKinley

Theodore Roosevelt
Lived from: 1858 to 1919
In Office: 1901 to 1909
Vice President: Charles W. Fairbanks
 (1905-1909)
First Lady: Edith Carow Roosevelt

William Howard Taft
Lived from: 1857 to 1930
In Office: 1909 to 1913
Vice President: James S. Sherman
 (1909-1912)
First Lady: Helen Herron Taft

Woodrow Wilson
Lived from: 1856 to 1924
In Office: 1913 to 1921
Vice President: Thomas R. Marshall
First Ladies: Ellen Louise Wilson
 (1913-1914) *and* Edith Bolling
 Wilson (1915-1921)

Warren G. Harding
Lived from: 1865 to 1923
In Office: 1921 to 1923
Vice President: Calvin Coolidge
First Lady: Florence Kling Harding

Calvin Coolidge
Lived from: 1872 to 1933
In Office: 1923 to 1929
Vice President: Charles G. Dawes
First Lady: Grace Goodhue Coolidge

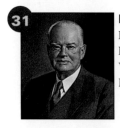

Herbert Hoover
Lived from: 1874 to 1964
In Office: 1929 to 1933
Vice President: Charles Curtis
First Lady: Lou Henry Hoover

Franklin Delano Roosevelt
Lived from: 1882 to 1945
In Office: 1933 to 1945
Vice Presidents: John N. Garner
 (1933-1941). Henry A. Wallace
 (1941-1945). Harry S. Truman (1945)
First Lady: Anna Eleanor Roosevelt

Harry S. Truman
Lived from: 1884 to 1972
In Office: 1945 to 1953
Vice President: Alben W. Barkley
 (1949-1953)
First Lady: Elizabeth (Bess) W. Truman

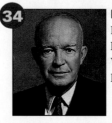

Dwight D. Eisenhower
Lived from: 1890 to 1969
In Office: 1953 to 1961
Vice President: Richard M. Nixon
First Lady: Marie (Mamie) Doud
 Eisenhower

35 John F. Kennedy
Lived from: 1917 to 1963
In Office: 1961 to 1963
Vice President: Lyndon B. Johnson
(1961-1963)
First Lady: Jacqueline Bouvier
Kennedy

36 Lyndon Baines Johnson
Lived from: 1908 to 1973
In Office: 1963 to 1969
Vice President: Hubert H. Humphrey
(1965-1969)
First Lady: Claudia (Lady Bird)
Taylor Johnson

37 Richard M. Nixon
Lived from: 1913 to 1994
In Office: 1969 to 1974
Vice Presidents: Spiro T. Agnew
(1969-1973). Gerald R. Ford
(appointed) (1973-1974)
First Lady: Patricia (Pat) Ryan Nixon

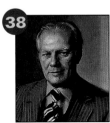

38 Gerald R. Ford
Born: 1913
In Office: 1974 to 1977
Vice President: Nelson A. Rockefeller
(appointed)(1974-1977)
First Lady: Elizabeth (Betty) B. Ford

39 James Earl Carter
Born: 1924
In Office: 1977 to 1981
Vice President: Walter F. Mondale
First Lady: Rosalynn Smith Carter

40 Ronald W. Reagan
Lived from: 1911 to 2004
In Office: 1981 to 1989
Vice President: George Bush
First Lady: Nancy Davis Reagan

41 George Bush
Born: 1924
In Office: 1989 to 1993
Vice President: James Danforth Quayle
First Lady: Barbara Pierce Bush

42 William J. Clinton
Born: 1946
In Office: 1993 to 2001
Vice President: Albert Gore
First Lady: Hillary Rodham Clinton

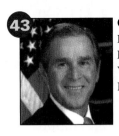

43 George W. Bush
Born: 1946
In Office: elected 2001
Vice President: Richard Cheney
First Lady: Laura Welsh Bush

STATES
of the
UNITED STATES

Additional information on each state can be found at the alphabetical entry for that state in the entry list. The population figures listed here are updated from those stated in the entry list and are the most accurate available

State Name	U. S. Postal Abbreviation	Capital	Population
Alabama	AL	Montgomery	4,486,500
Alaska	AK	Juneau	626,900
Arizona	AZ	Phoenix	5,130,600
Arkansas	AR	Little Rock	2,673,400
California	CA	Sacramento	33,871,600
Colorado	CO	Denver	4,301,300
Connecticut	CT	Hartford	3,405,600
Delaware	DE	Dover	783,600
Florida	FL	Tallahassee	15,982,400
Georgia	GA	Atlanta	8,186,500
Hawaii	HI	Honolulu	1,211,500
Idaho	ID	Boise	1,294,000
Illinois	IL	Springfield	12,419,300
Indiana	IN	Indianapolis	6,080,500
Iowa	IA	Des Moines	2,926,300
Kansas	KS	Topeka	2,688,400
Kentucky	KY	Frankfort	4,041,800
Louisiana	LA	Baton Rouge	4,469,000
Maine	ME	Augusta	1,274,900
Maryland	MD	Annapolis	5,296,500

Massachusetts	MA	Boston	6,349,100
Michigan	MI	Lansing	9,938,400
Minnesota	MN	St. Paul	4,919,500
Mississippi	MS	Jackson	2,844,700
Missouri	MO	Jefferson City	5,595,200
Montana	MT	Helena	902,200
Nebraska	NE	Lincoln	1,711,300
Nevada	NV	Carson City	1,998,300
New Hampshire	NH	Concord	1,235,800
New Jersey	NJ	Trenton	8,414,300
New Mexico	NM	Santa Fe	1,819,000
New York	NY	Albany	18,976,500
North Carolina	NC	Raleigh	8,049,300
North Dakota	ND	Bismarck	642,200
Ohio	OH	Columbus	11,353,100
Oklahoma	OK	Oklahoma City	3,450,700
Oregon	OR	Salem	3,421,400
Pennsylvania	PA	Harrisburg	12,281,100
Rhode Island	RI	Providence	1,048,300
South Carolina	SC	Columbia	4,012,000
South Dakota	SD	Pierre	754,800
Tennessee	TN	Nashville	5,689,300
Texas	TX	Austin	20,851,800
Utah	UT	Salt Lake City	2,233,200
Vermont	VT	Montpelier	608,800
Virginia	VA	Richmond	7,078,500
Washington	WA	Olympia	5,894,100
West Virginia	WV	Charleston	1,808,300
Wisconsin	WI	Madison	5,363,700
Wyoming	WY	Cheyenne	493,800

COUNTRIES
of the WORLD

Afghanistan

Capital: Kabul
Population: 22,664,136
Area: 251,825 sq. mi.
Money: Afghani

Albania

Capital: Tiranë
Population: 3,249,136
Area: 11,100 sq. mi.
Money: Lek

Algeria

Capital: Algiers
Population: 29,183,032
Area: 919,595 sq. mi.
Money: Dinar

Andorra

Capital: Andorra la Vella
Population: 72,766
Area: 181 sq. mi.
Money: French franc,
Spanish peseta

Angola

Capital: Luanda
Population: 10,342,899
Area: 481,354 sq. mi.
Money: Kwanza

Antigua and Barbuda

Capital: St. John's
Population: 65,647
Area: 171 sq. mi.
Money: East Caribbean
dollar

Argentina

Capital: Buenos Aires
Population: 34,672,997
Area: 1,073,518 sq. mi.
Money: Peso

Armenia

Capital: Yerevan
Population: 3,463,574
Area: 11,500 sq. mi.
Money: Dram

Australia

Capital: Canberra
Population: 18,260,863
Area: 2,966,200 sq. mi.
Money: Australian dollar

Austria

Capital: Vienna
Population: 8,023,244
Area: 32,378 sq. mi.
Money: Schilling

Azerbaijan

Capital: Baku
Population: 7,676,953
Area: 33,400 sq. mi.
Money: Manat

Bahamas, The

Capital: Nassau
Population: 259,367
Area: 5,382 sq. mi.
Money: Bahamian dollar

Bahrain

Capital: Manama
Population: 590,042
Area: 268 sq. mi.
Money: Bahrain dinar

Bangladesh

Capital: Dhaka
Population: 123,062,800
Area: 56,977 sq. mi.
Money: Taka

Barbados

Capital: Bridgetown
Population: 257,030
Area: 166 sq. mi.
Money: Barbados dollar

Belarus

Capital: Minsk
Population: 10,415,973
Area: 80,153 sq. mi.
Money: Belarusian rubel

Belgium

Capital: Brussels
Population: 10,170,241
Area: 11,787 sq. mi.
Money: Belgian franc

Belize

Capital: Belmopan
Population: 219,296
Area: 8,867 sq. mi.
Money: Belize dollar

Benin

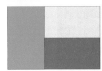

Capital: Porto-Novo
Population: 5,709,529
Area: 43,500 sq. mi.
Money: CFA franc

Bhutan

Capital: Thimphu
Population: 1,822,625
Area: 18,150 sq. mi.
Money: Ngultrum

Bolivia

Capital: Sucre (judicial),
  La Paz (administrative)
Population: 7,165,257
Area: 424,164 sq. mi.
Money: Boliviano

Bosnia & Herzegovina

Capital: Sarajevo
Population: 2,656,240
Area: 19,741 sq. mi.
Money: Yugoslav New
  Dinar

Botswana

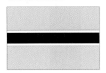

Capital: Gaborone
Population: 1,477,630
Area: 224,607 sq. mi.
Money: Pula

Brazil

Capital: Brasília
Population: 162,661,214
Area: 3,300,171 sq. mi.
Money: Real

Brunei

Capital: Bandar Seri
  Begawan
Population: 299,939
Area: 2,226 sq. mi.
Money: Brunei dollar

Bulgaria

Capital: Sofia
Population: 8,612,757
Area: 42,855 sq. mi.
Money: Lev

Burkina Faso

Capital: Ouagadougou
Population: 10,623,323
Area: 105,946 sq. mi.
Money: CFA franc

Burundi

Capital: Bujumbura
Population: 5,943,057
Area: 10,740 sq. mi.
Money: Burundi franc

Cambodia

Capital: Phnom Penh
Population: 10,861,218
Area: 70,238 sq. mi.
Money: Riel

Cameroon

Capital: Yaoundé
Population: 14,261,557
Area: 183,569 sq. mi.
Money: CFA franc

Canada

Capital: Ottawa, Ontario
Population: 28,820,671
Area: 3,849,674 sq. mi.
Money: Canadian dollar

Cape Verde

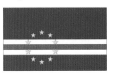

Capital: Praia
Population: 449,066
Area: 1,557 sq. mi.
Money: Cape Verdean
  escudo

Central African Republic

Capital: Bangui
Population: 3,274,426
Area: 240,324 sq. mi.
Money: CFA franc

Chad

Capital: N'Djamena
Population: 6,976,845
Area: 495,755 sq. mi.
Money: CFA franc

Chile

Capital: Santiago
Population: 14,333,258
Area: 292,135 sq. mi.
Money: Peso

China, **People's Republic of**

Capital: Beijing
Population: 1,210,004,956
Area: 3,696,100 sq. mi.
Money: Yuan

Colombia

Capital: Bogotá
Population: 36,813,161
Area: 440,762 sq. mi.
Money: Peso

Comoros

Capital: Moroni
Population: 569,237
Area: 719 sq. mi.
Money: CFA franc

Congo, Democratic Republic of

Capital: Kinshasa
Population: 46,498,539
Area: 905,354 sq. mi.
Money: New Zaire
(formerly Zaire)

Congo, Republic of

Capital: Brazzaville
Population: 2,527,841
Area: 132,047 sq. mi.
Money: CFA franc

Costa Rica

Capital: San José
Population: 3,463,083
Area: 19,730 sq. mi.
Money: Colón

Côte D'Ivoire (Ivory Coast)

Capital: Yamoussoukro
Population: 14,762,445
Area: 124,504 sq. mi.
Money: CFA franc

Croatia

Capital: Zagreb
Population: 5,004,112
Area: 21,889 sq. mi.
Money: Kuna

Cuba

Capital: Havana
Population: 10,951,334
Area: 42,804 sq. mi.
Money: Peso

Cyprus

Capital: Nicosia
Population: 744,609
Area: 3,572 sq. mi.
Money: Cyprus pound

Czech Republic

Capital: Prague
Population: 10,321,120
Area: 30,450 sq. mi.
Money: Koruna

Denmark

Capital: Copenhagen
Population: 5,249,632
Area: 16,639 sq. mi.
Money: Krone

Djibouti

Capital: Djibouti
Population: 427,642
Area: 8,950 sq. mi.
Money: Djibouti franc

Dominica

Capital: Roseau
Population: 82,926
Area: 290 sq. mi.
Money: East Caribbean
dollar

Dominican Republic

Capital: Santo Domingo
Population: 8,088,881
Area: 18,704 sq. mi.
Money: Peso

Ecuador

Capital: Quito
Population: 11,466,291
Area: 105,037 sq. mi.
Money: Sucre

Egypt

Capital: Cairo
Population: 63,575,107
Area: 385,229 sq. mi.
Money: Egyptian pound

El Salvador

Capital: San Salvador
Population: 5,828,987
Area: 8,124 sq. mi.
Money: Colón

Equatorial Guinea

Capital: Malabo
Population: 431,282
Area: 10,831 sq. mi.
Money: CFA franc

Eritrea

Capital: Asmara
Population: 3,909,628
Area: 45,300 sq. mi.
Money: Ethiopian Birr

Estonia

Capital: Tallinn
Population: 1,459,428
Area: 17,462 sq. mi.
Money: Kroon

Ethiopia

Capital: Addis Ababa
Population: 57,171,662
Area: 437,794 sq. mi.
Money: Birr

Fiji

Capital: Suva
Population: 782,381
Area: 7,055 sq. mi.
Money: Fiji dollar

Finland

Capital: Helsinki
Population: 5,105,230
Area: 130,559 sq. mi.
Money: Markka

France

Capital: Paris
Population: 58,040,230
Area: 210,026 sq. mi.
Money: French franc

Gabon

Capital: Libreville
Population: 1,102,798
Area: 103,347 sq. mi.
Money: CFA franc

Gambia, The

Capital: Banjul
Population: 1,204,984
Area: 4,127 sq. mi.
Money: Dalasi

Georgia

Capital: Tbilisi
Population: 5,219,810
Area: 26,831 sq. mi.
Money: Lari

Germany

Capital: Berlin
Population: 83,536,115
Area: 137,828 sq. mi.
Money: Deutsche mark

Ghana

Capital: Accra
Population: 17,698,271
Area: 92,098 sq. mi.
Money: Cedi

Greece

Capital: Athens
Population: 10,538,594
Area: 50,949 sq. mi.
Money: Drachma

Grenada

Capital: St. George's
Population: 94,961
Area: 133 sq. mi.
Money: East Caribbean
dollar

Guatemala

Capital: Guatemala City
Population: 11,277,614
Area: 42,042 sq. mi.
Money: Quetzal

Guinea

Capital: Conakry
Population: 7,411,981
Area: 94,926 sq. mi.
Money: Guinean franc

Guinea-Bissau

Capital: Bissau
Population: 1,151,330
Area: 13,948 sq. mi.
Money: Guinea-Bissau peso

Guyana

Capital: Georgetown
Population: 712,091
Area: 83,044 sq. mi.
Money: Guyana dollar

Haiti

Capital: Port-au-Prince
Population: 6,731,539
Area: 10,695 sq. mi.
Money: Gourde

Honduras

Capital: Tegucigalpa
Population: 5,605,193
Area: 43,433 sq. mi.
Money: Lempira

Hungary

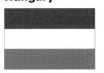

Capital: Budapest
Population: 10,002,541
Area: 35,919 sq. mi.
Money: Forint

Iceland

Capital: Reykjavik
Population: 270,292
Area: 39,699 sq. mi.
Money: Króna

India

Capital: New Delhi
Population: 952,107,694
Area: 1,222,243 sq. mi.
Money: Rupee

Indonesia

Capital: Jakarta
Population: 206,611,600
Area: 741,052 sq. mi.
Money: Rupiah

Iran

Capital: Teheran
Population: 66,094,264
Area: 632,457 sq. mi.
Money: Rial

Iraq

Capital: Baghdad
Population: 21,422,292
Area: 167,975 sq. mi.
Money: Iraqi dinar

Ireland

Capital: Dublin
Population: 3,566,833
Area: 27,137 sq. mi.
Money: Punt (Irish pound)

Israel

Capital: Jerusalem
Population: 5,421,995
Area: 7,876 sq. mi.
Money: Shekel

Italy

Capital: Rome
Population: 57,460,274
Area: 116,336 sq. mi.
Money: Lira

Jamaica

Capital: Kingston
Population: 2,595,275
Area: 4,244 sq. mi.
Money: Jamaican dollar

Japan

Capital: Tokyo
Population: 125,449,703
Area: 145,850 sq. mi.
Money: Yen

Jordan

Capital: Amman
Population: 4,212,152
Area: 34,342 sq. mi.
Money: Jordanian dinar

Kazakhstan

Capital: Almaty
Population: 16,916,463
Area: 1,049,000 sq. mi.
Money: Tenge

Kenya

Capital: Nairobi
Population: 28,176,686
Area: 224,961 sq. mi.
Money: Kenyan shilling

Kiribati

Capital: Tarawa
Population: 80,919
Area: 280 sq. mi.
Money: Australian dollar

Korea, North (Democratic People's Republic of Korea)

Capital: Pyongyang
Population: 23,904,124
Area: 47,399 sq. mi.
Money: Won

Korea, South (Republic of Korea)

Capital: Seoul
Population: 45,482,291
Area: 38,375 sq. mi.
Money: Won

Kuwait

Capital: Kuwait
Population: 1,950,047
Area: 6,880 sq. mi.
Money: Kuwaiti dinar

Kyrgyzstan

Capital: Bishkek
Population: 4,529,648
Area: 76,600 sq. mi.
Money: Som

Laos

Capital: Vientiane
Population: 4,975,772
Area: 91,429 sq. mi.
Money: Kip

Latvia

Capital: Riga
Population: 2,468,982
Area: 24,946 sq. mi.
Money: Lat

Lebanon

Capital: Beirut
Population: 3,776,317
Area: 3,950 sq. mi.
Money: Lebanese pound

Lesotho

Capital: Maseru
Population: 1,970,781
Area: 11,720 sq. mi.
Money: Loti

Liberia

Capital: Monrovia
Population: 2,109,789
Area: 38,250 sq. mi.
Money: Liberian dollar

Libya

Capital: Tripoli
Population: 5,445,436
Area: 678,400 sq. mi.
Money: Libyan dinar

Liechtenstein

Capital: Vaduz
Population: 31,122
Area: 62 sq. mi.
Money: Swiss franc

Lithuania

Capital: Vilnius
Population: 3,646,041
Area: 25,213 sq. mi.
Money: Litas

Luxembourg

Capital: Luxembourg
Population: 415,870
Area: 999 sq. mi.
Money: Luxembourg franc

Macedonia

Capital: Skopje
Population: 2,104,035
Area: 9,928 sq. mi.
Money: Denar

Madagascar

Capital: Antananarivo
Population: 13,670,507
Area: 226,658 sq. mi.
Money: Malagasy franc

Malawi

Capital: Lilongwe
Population: 9,452,844
Area: 45,747 sq. mi.
Money: Kwacha

Malaysia

Capital: Kuala Lumpur
Population: 19,962,893
Area: 127,584 sq. mi.
Money: Ringgit

Maldives

Capital: Malé
Population: 270,758
Area: 115 sq. mi.
Money: Maldivian rufiyaa

Mali

Capital: Bamako
Population: 9,653,261
Area: 482,077 sq. mi.
Money: CFA franc

Malta

Capital: Valletta
Population: 375,576
Area: 122 sq. mi.
Money: Maltese lira

Marshall Islands

Capital: Majuro
Population: 58,363
Area: 70 sq. mi.
Money: U.S. dollar

Mauritania

Capital: Nouakchott
Population: 2,336,048
Area: 398,00 sq. mi.
Money: Ouguiya

Mauritius

Capital: Port Louis
Population: 1,140,256
Area: 786 sq. mi.
Money: Mauritian rupee

Mexico

Capital: Mexico City
Population: 95,772,462
Area: 756,066 sq. mi.
Money: Peso

Micronesia

Capital: Palikir
Population: 125,377
Area: 271 sq. mi.
Money: U.S. dollar

Moldova

Capital: Chisinau
Population: 4,463,847
Area: 13,012 sq. mi.
Money: Leu

Monaco

Capital: Monaco
Population: 31,719
Area: 0.75 sq. mi.
Money: French franc

Mongolia

Capital: Ulaanbaatar
Population: 2,496,617
Area: 604,800 sq. mi.
Money: Tugrik

845

Morocco

Capital: Rabat
Population: 29,779,156
Area: 177,117 sq. mi.
Money: Dirham

Mozambique

Capital: Maputo
Population: 17,877,927
Area: 313,661 sq. mi.
Money: Metical

Myanmar

Capital: Yangôn (Rangoon)
Population: 45,975,625
Area: 261,228 sq. mi.
Money: Kyat

Namibia

Capital: Windhoek
Population: 1,677,243
Area: 318,580 sq. mi.
Money: Dollar

Nauru

Capital: Yaren
Population: 10,273
Area: 8.2 sq. mi.
Money: Australian dollar

Nepal

Capital: Kathmandu
Population: 22,094,033
Area: 56,827 sq. mi.
Money: Nepalese rupee

Netherlands, The

Capital: Amsterdam
Population: 15,568,034
Area: 16,033 sq. mi.
Money: Guilder

New Zealand

Capital: Wellington
Population: 3,547,983
Area: 104,454 sq. mi.
Money: New Zealand
dollar

Nicaragua

Capital: Managua
Population: 4,272,352
Area: 50,838 sq. mi.
Money: Gold Cordoba

Niger

Capital: Niamey
Population: 9,113,001
Area: 496,900 sq. mi.
Money: CFA franc

Nigeria

Capital: Abuja
Population: 103,912,489
Area: 356,669 sq. mi.
Money: Naira

Norway

Capital: Oslo
Population: 4,383,807
Area: 125,050 sq. mi.
Money: Krone

Oman

Capital: Muscat
Population: 2,186,548
Area: 118,150 sq. mi.
Money: Rial Omani

Pakistan

Capital: Islamabad
Population: 129,275,660
Area: 339,697 sq. mi.
Money: Pakistan rupee

Palau, Republic of

Capital: Koror
Population: 16,952
Area: 188 sq. mi.
Money: U.S. dollar

Panama

Capital: Panama City
Population: 2,655,094
Area: 29,157 sq. mi.
Money: Balboa

Papua New Guinea

Capital: Port Moresby
Population: 4,394,537
Area: 178,704 sq. mi.
Money: Kina

Paraguay

Capital: Asunción
Population: 5,504,146
Area: 157,048 sq. mi.
Money: Guarani

Peru

Capital: Lima
Population: 24,523,408
Area: 496,225 sq. mi.
Money: Nuevo sol

Philippines

Capital: Manila
Population: 74,480,848
Area: 115,860 sq. mi.
Money: Peso

Poland

Capital: Warsaw
Population: 38,642,565
Area: 120,728 sq. mi.
Money: Zloty

Portugal

Capital: Lisbon
Population: 9,865,114
Area: 35,575 sq. mi.
Money: Escudo

Qatar

Capital: Doha
Population: 547,761
Area: 4,412 sq. mi.
Money: Qatari riyal

Romania

Capital: Bucharest
Population: 21,657,162
Area: 91,699 sq. mi.
Money: Lei

Russia

Capital: Moscow
Population: 148,178,487
Area: 6,592,800 sq. mi.
Money: Ruble

Rwanda

Capital: Kigali
Population: 6,853,359
Area: 10,169 sq. mi.
Money: Rwanda franc

St. Kitts and Nevis

Capital: Basseterre
Population: 41,369
Area: St. Kitts 65 sq. mi.
and Nevis 35 sq. mi.
Money: East Caribbean
dollar

St. Lucia

Capital: Castries
Population: 157,862
Area: 238 sq. mi.
Money: East Caribbean
dollar

St. Vincent and the Grenadines

Capital: Kingstown
Population: 118,344
Area: 150 sq. mi.
Money: East Caribbean
dollar

San Marino

Capital: San Marino
Population: 24,521
Area: 24 sq. mi.
Money: Italian lira

São Tomé and Príncipe

Capital: São Tomé
Population: 144,128
Area: 386 sq. mi.
Money: Dobra

Saudi Arabia

Capital: Riyadh
Population: 19,409,058
Area: 865,000 sq. mi.
Money: Riyal

Senegal

Capital: Dakar
Population: 9,092,749
Area: 75,951 sq. mi.
Money: CFA franc

Seychelles

Capital: Victoria
Population: 77,575
Area: 176 sq. mi.
Money: Seychelles rupee

Sierra Leone

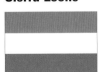

Capital: Freetown
Population: 4,793,121
Area: 27,699 sq. mi.
Money: Leone

Singapore

Capital: Singapore
Population: 3,396,924
Area: 247 sq. mi.
Money: Singapore dollar

Slovakia

Capital: Bratislava
Population: 5,374,362
Area: 18,933 sq. mi.
Money: Koruna

Slovenia

Capital: Ljubljana
Population: 1,951,443
Area: 7,821 sq. mi.
Money: Slovenian tolar

Solomon Islands

Capital: Honiara
Population: 412,902
Area: 10,954 sq. mi.
Money: Solomon Islands
dollar

Somalia

Capital: Mogadishu
Population: 9,639,151
Area: 246,000 sq. mi.
Money: Somali shilling

South Africa

Capitals: Pretoria (legislative), Cape Town (judicial)
Population: 41,743,459
Area: 470,689 sq. mi.
Money: Rand

Spain

Capital: Madrid
Population: 39,181,114
Area: 194,898 sq. mi.
Money: Peseta

Sri Lanka

Capital: Colombo
Population: 18,553,074
Area: 25,332 sq. mi.
Money: Sri Lanka rupee

Sudan

Capital: Khartoum
Population: 31,065,229
Area: 966,757 sq. mi.
Money: Sudanese pound

Suriname

Capital: Paramaribo
Population: 436,418
Area: 63,251 sq. mi.
Money: Suriname guilder

Swaziland

Capital: Mbabane
Population: 998,730
Area: 6,704 sq. mi.
Money: Lilangeni

Sweden

Capital: Stockholm
Population: 8,900,954
Area: 173,732 sq. mi.
Money: Krona

Switzerland

Capitals: Bern (administrative), Lausanne (judical)
Population: 7,207,060
Area: 15,940 sq. mi.
Money: Swiss franc

Syria

Capital: Damascus
Population: 15,608,648
Area: 71,498 sq. mi.
Money: Syrian pound

Togo

Capital: Lomé
Population: 4,570,530
Area: 21,925 sq. mi.
Money: CFA franc

Tajikistan

Capital: Dushanbe
Population: 5,916,373
Area: 55,300 sq. mi.
Money: Tajik ruble

Tanzania

Capital: Dar es Salaam
Population: 29,058,470
Area: 364,017 sq. mi.
Money: Tanzanian shilling

Thailand

Capital: Bangkok
Population: 58,851,357
Area: 198,115 sq. mi.
Money: Baht

Turkey

Capital: Ankara
Population: 62,484,478
Area: 300,948 sq. mi.
Money: Turkish lira

Tonga

Capital: Nuku'alofa
Population: 106,466
Area: 290 sq. mi.
Money: Pa´anga

Trinidad and Tobago

Capital: Port-of-Spain
Population: 1,272,385
Area: 1,980 sq. mi.
Money: Trinidad and Tobago dollar

Tunisia

Capital: Tunis
Population: 9,019,687
Area: 63,378 sq. mi.
Money: Tunisian dinar

Tuvalu

Capital: Funafuti
Population: 10,146
Area: 9.4 sq. mi.
Money: Tuvalua dollar, Australian dollar

Turkmenistan

Capital: Ashgabat
Population: 4,149,283
Area: 188,500 sq. mi.
Money: Manat

Uganda

Capital: Kampala
Population: 20,158,176
Area: 93,070 sq. mi.
Money: Ugandan shilling

Ukraine

Capital: Kiev
Population: 50,864,009
Area: 233,000 sq. mi.
Money: Hryvna

United Arab Emirates

Capital: Abu Dhabi
Population: 3,057,337
Area: 32,280 sq. mi.
Money: U.A.E. dirham

United Kingdom

Capital: London
Population: 58,489,975
Area: 94,251 sq. mi.
Money: Pound sterling

United States

Capital: Washington, D.C.
Population: 265,562,845
Area: 3,536,278 sq. mi.
Money: Dollar

Uruguay

Capital: Montevideo
Population: 3,238,952
Area: 68,037 sq. mi.
Money: Peso

Uzbekistan

Capital: Tashkent
Population: 23,418,381
Area: 172,700 sq. mi.
Money: Sum

Vanuatu

Capital: Port-Vila
Population: 177,504
Area: 4,707 sq. mi.
Money: Vatu

Vatican City (The Holy See)

Capital: Vatican City
Population: 811
Area: 0.17 sq. mi.
Money: Vatican Lira

Venezuela

Capital: Caracas
Population: 21,983,188
Area: 352,144 sq. mi.
Money: Bolivar

Vietnam

Capital: Hanoi
Population: 73,976,973
Area: 127,816 sq. mi.
Money: Dong

Western Samoa

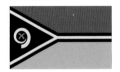

Capital: Apia
Population: 214,384
Area: 1,093 sq. mi.
Money: Tala

Yemen, Republic of

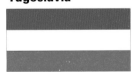

Capital: Sanaá
Population: 13,483,178
Area: 205,356 sq. mi.
Money: Rial

Yugoslavia

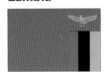

Capital: Belgrade
Population: 10,614,558
Area: 39,449 sq. mi.
Money: New dinar

Zambia

Capital: Lusaka
Population: 9,159,072
Area: 290,586 sq. mi.
Money: Kwacha

Zimbabwe

Capital: Harare
Population: 11,271,314
Area: 150,872 sq. mi.
Money: Zimbabwean
dollar

ARCTIC

GREENLAND
(KALAALLIT NUNAAT)
(Den.)

ALASKA
(U.S.)

Arctic Circle

ICELAND

CANADA

NORTH

UNITED
KINGDOM

IRELAND

AMERICA

AZORES
(Port.)

SPAIN

UNITED STATES

PORTUGAL

ATLANTIC

MADEIRA
IS. (Port.)

MOROCCO

BERMUDA
(U.K.)

OCEAN

CANARY IS.
(Sp.)

Gulf of
Mexico

HAWAIIAN IS.
(U.S.)

BAHAMAS

Tropic of Cancer

WESTERN
SAHARA
(Occ. by Mor.)

CUBA

MEXICO

DOMINICAN
REP.

MAURITANIA

JAMAICA HAITI

PUERTO RICO (U.S.)

BELIZE

ST. KITTS
& NEVIS

ANTIGUA & BARBUDA

CAPE VERDE

SENEGAL

MALI

GUATEMALA HONDURAS

DOMINICA

ST. LUCIA

GAMBIA

BURKINA
FASO

Caribbean Sea

ST. VINCENT
& GREN.

BARBADOS

GUINEA-BISSAU

GUINEA

EL SALVADOR NICARAGUA

GRENADA

SIERRA LEONE

CÔTE
D'IVOIRE

COSTA RICA

TRINIDAD & TOBAGO

VENEZUELA GUYANA

LIBERIA

PANAMA

SURINAME

EQU. GUINEA

COLOMBIA

FR. GUIANA
(Fr.)

PACIFIC

GALAPAGOS IS.
(Ecuador)

ECUADOR

Equator

OCEAN

KIRIBATI

SOUTH

TOKELAU
(N.Z.)

PERU

BRAZIL

W.
SAMOA

AMERICAN
SAMOA
(U.S.)

AMERICA

SAMOA

COOK
ISLANDS
(N.Z.)

BOLIVIA

NIUE
(N.Z.)

FRENCH
POLYNESIA
(Fr.)

PARAGUAY

ATLANTIC

TONGA

Tropic of Capricorn

OCEAN

North

CHILE

URUGUAY

ARGENTINA

FALKLAND IS.
(U.K.)

SOUTH
GEORGIA
(U.K.)

Antarctic Circle

SIBERIA

ASIA

Sea of
Okhotsk

Arctic Circle

TAYMYR
PENINSULA

NOVAYA
ZEMLYA

EUROPE

KAMCHATKA
PEN.

NEW
SIBERIAN IS.

SEVERNAYA
ZEMLYA

FRANZ
JOSEF
LAND

Barents
Sea

SCANDINAVIA

East
Siberian
Sea

ARCTIC OCEAN

SVALBARD

Norwegian
Sea

North
Sea

CHUKCHI
PENINSULA

WRANGEL I.

North Pole

Prime Meridian

BRITISH
ISLES

Bering Sea

Bering Strait

Greenland
Sea

BROOKS
RANGE

North
Magnetic
Pole

GREENLAND

ICELAND

Beaufort
Sea

QUEEN
ELIZABETH
IS.

Baffin
Bay

ATLANTIC
OCEAN

Baffin I.

0   300   600 Miles

0   300 600 Kilometers

NORTH AMERICA

BAFFIN I.

Arctic Circle

CAPE
FAREWELL

© GEOSYSTEMS GLOBAL CORP.

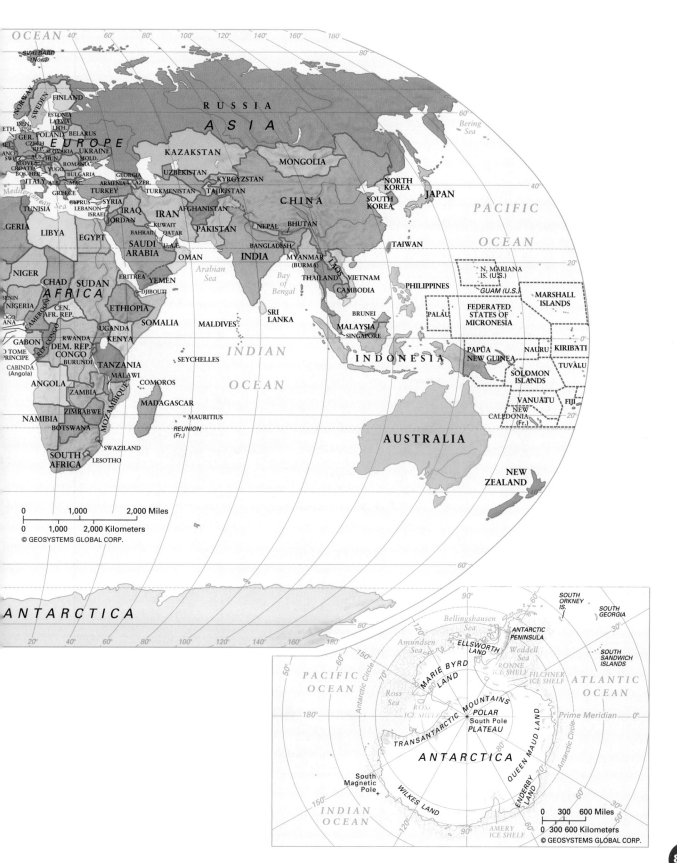

OCEAN

40° 60° 80° 100° 120° 140° 160° 180°

SVALBARD
(Nor.)

80°

NORWAY
SWEDEN
FINLAND
DEN.
ESTONIA
LATVIA
LITH.
GER.
POLAND
BELARUS

RUSSIA

ASIA

60°

Bering
Sea

ETH.
BEL.
CZECH
REP.
FRANCE
SWITZ.
SLOVAKIA
UKRAINE
KAZAKSTAN
MONGOLIA
AUS. HUN.
SLOVE.
CROATIA
YUGO.
ROMANIA
MOLD.
BOS. HER.
ITALY
ALB.
MAC.
BULGARIA
GEORGIA
UZBEKISTAN
KYRGYZSTAN
NORTH
KOREA
JAPAN

PACIFIC

40°

GREECE
TURKEY
ARMENIA
AZER.
TURKMENISTAN
TAJIKISTAN
SOUTH
KOREA

EUROPE

CYPRUS
SYRIA
LEBANON
ISRAEL
IRAQ
IRAN
AFGHANISTAN
CHINA
TAIWAN

OCEAN

Mediterranean Sea

TUNISIA
JORDAN
KUWAIT
BAHRAIN
QATAR
PAKISTAN
NEPAL
BHUTAN

ALGERIA
LIBYA
EGYPT
SAUDI
ARABIA
U.A.E.
OMAN
INDIA
BANGLADESH
MYANMAR
(BURMA)

20°

NIGER
CHAD
SUDAN
ERITREA
YEMEN
Arabian
Sea
Bay
of
Bengal
THAILAND
VIETNAM
LAOS
PHILIPPINES
N. MARIANA
IS. (U.S.)

BENIN
NIGERIA
AFRICA
CEN.
AFR. REP.
ETHIOPIA
DJIBOUTI
CAMBODIA
GUAM (U.S.)

MARSHALL
ISLANDS

GABON
CAMEROON
UGANDA
SOMALIA
MALDIVES
SRI
LANKA
BRUNEI
PALAU
FEDERATED
STATES OF
MICRONESIA

SAO TOME
PRINCIPE
RP. CONGO
DEM. REP.
CONGO
RWANDA
KENYA
MALAYSIA
Singapore

0°

CABINDA
(Angola)
BURUNDI
TANZANIA
SEYCHELLES
INDONESIA
PAPUA
NEW GUINEA
NAURU
KIRIBATI

ANGOLA
ZAMBIA
MALAWI
COMOROS
INDIAN
TUVALU

NAMIBIA
ZIMBABWE
MOZAMBIQUE
MADAGASCAR
OCEAN
SOLOMON
ISLANDS

BOTSWANA
MAURITIUS
VANUATU
FIJI
20°

SOUTH
AFRICA
SWAZILAND
LESOTHO
REUNION
(Fr.)
AUSTRALIA
NEW
CALEDONIA
(Fr.)

0   1,000   2,000 Miles

0   1,000   2,000 Kilometers

© GEOSYSTEMS GLOBAL CORP.

NEW
ZEALAND

60°

ANTARCTICA

20° 40° 60° 80° 100° 120° 140° 160° 180°

SOUTH
ORKNEY
IS.
SOUTH
GEORGIA

90°

Bellingshausen
Sea
ANTARCTIC
PENINSULA

PACIFIC

OCEAN

Amundsen
Sea
ELLSWORTH
LAND
Weddell
Sea

ATLANTIC

60°

Antarctic Circle
MARIE BYRD
LAND
RONNE
ICE SHELF
FILCHNER
ICE SHELF
OCEAN

70°

Ross
Sea

180°
ROSS
ICE SHELF
TRANSANTARCTIC MOUNTAINS
POLAR
South Pole
PLATEAU
QUEEN MAUD LAND
Prime Meridian
0°

ANTARCTICA
Antarctic Circle

80°
70°

South
Magnetic
Pole

WILKES LAND
ENDERBY
LAND
60°

150°
0   300   600 Miles

INDIAN
OCEAN
90°
AMERY
ICE SHELF
0   300 600 Kilometers
© GEOSYSTEMS GLOBAL CORP.

120°
50°
30°

851

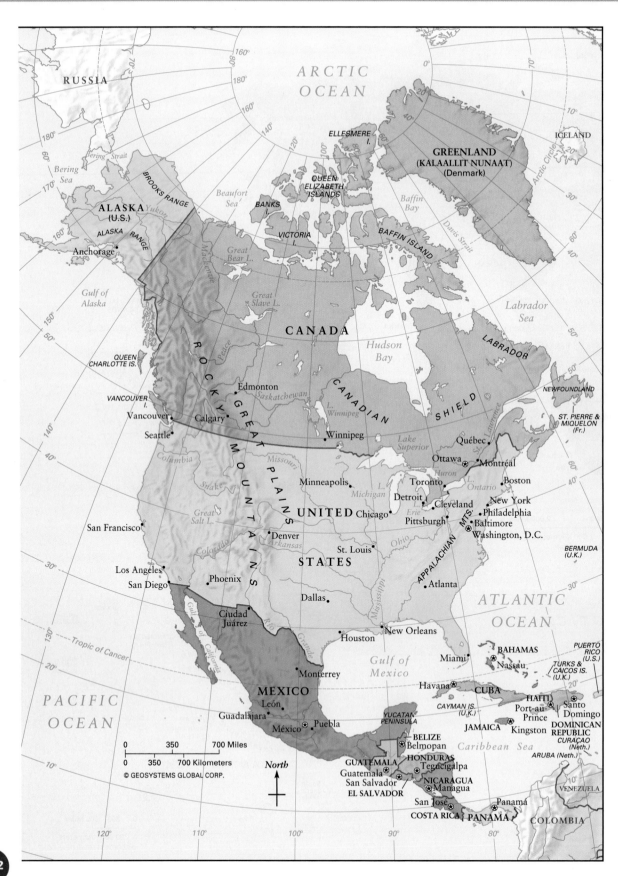

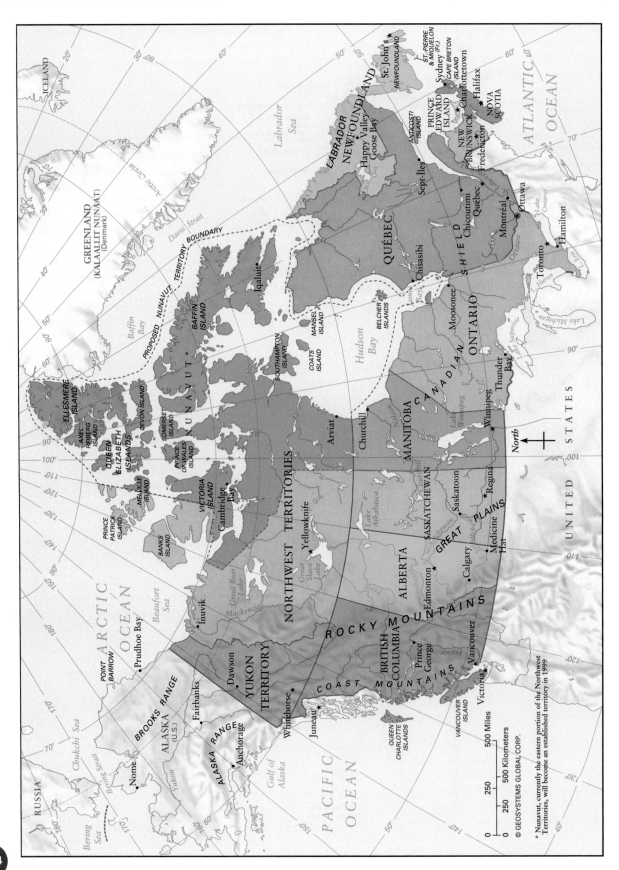

ICELAND

GREENLAND
(KALAALLIT NUNAAT)
(Denmark)

Arctic Circle

Davis Strait

Baffin Bay

PROPOSED NUNAVUT TERRITORY BOUNDARY

ELLESMERE ISLAND

AXEL HEIBERG ISLAND

QUEEN ELIZABETH ISLANDS

DEVON ISLAND

PRINCE PATRICK ISLAND

MELVILLE ISLAND

BANKS ISLAND

BAFFIN ISLAND

Iqaluit

SOMERSET ISLAND

PRINCE OF WALES ISLAND

SOUTHAMPTON ISLAND

COATS ISLAND

VICTORIA ISLAND

Cambridge Bay

N U N A V U T *

MANSEL ISLAND

Hudson Bay

BELCHER ISLANDS

LABRADOR
NEWFOUNDLAND

Happy Valley
Goose Bay

ANTICOSTI ISLAND

Sept-Îles

St. John's
NEWFOUNDLAND

ST-PIERRE
& MIQUELON (Fr.)
Sydney CAPE BRETON ISLAND
PRINCE EDWARD ISLAND Charlottetown
NEW BRUNSWICK Fredericton Halifax
NOVA SCOTIA

QUÉBEC

Chisasibi

James Bay

CANADIAN SHIELD

Chicoutimi
Québec
Montréal
Ottawa

Moosonee

ONTARIO

Thunder Bay

Hamilton
Toronto

Lake Ontario
Ottawa
L. Erie
L. Huron
Lake Superior
Lake Michigan

ATLANTIC OCEAN

Labrador Sea

Arviat

Churchill

MANITOBA

Lake Winnipeg

Winnipeg

Nelson

Yellowknife

NORTHWEST TERRITORIES

Great Slave Lake

Great Bear Lake

Inuvik

Mackenzie

Prudhoe Bay
POINT BARROW

Beaufort Sea

ARCTIC OCEAN

Nome

Chukchi Sea
Bering Sea
Bering Strait

RUSSIA

Fairbanks
BROOKS RANGE
ALASKA (U.S.)
ALASKA RANGE
Anchorage
Yukon

Dawson

YUKON TERRITORY

Whitehorse

Juneau

Gulf of Alaska

PACIFIC OCEAN

COAST MOUNTAINS

QUEEN CHARLOTTE ISLANDS

Prince George

BRITISH COLUMBIA

Fraser

ROCKY MOUNTAINS

ALBERTA

Edmonton

Calgary

Medicine Hat

Lake Athabasca
Churchill

SASKATCHEWAN

Saskatoon

Regina

GREAT PLAINS

VANCOUVER ISLAND

Vancouver
Victoria

North

UNITED STATES

500 Miles
500 Kilometers
250
250
0

© GEOSYSTEMS GLOBAL CORP.

* Nunavut, currently the eastern portion of the Northwest Territories, will become an established territory in 1999

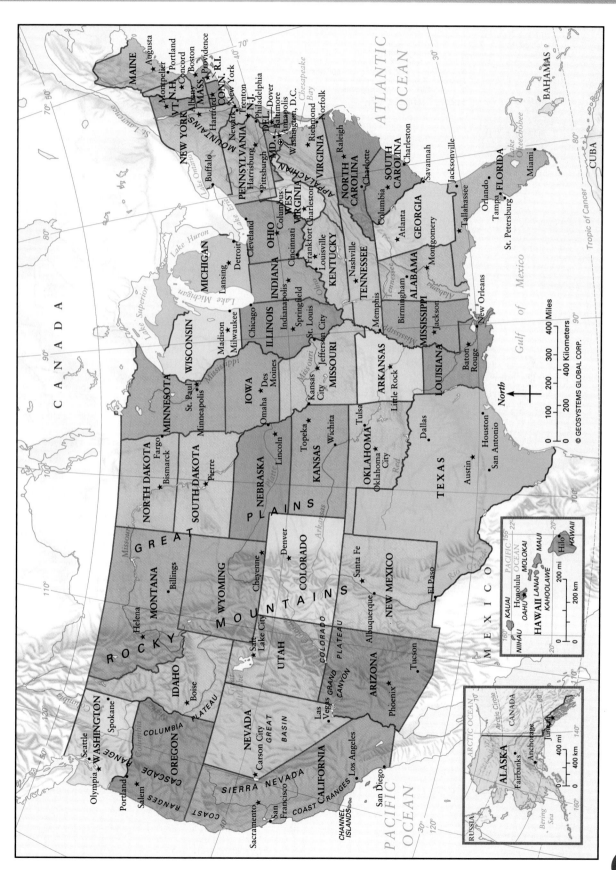

GREENLAND
(KALAALLIT NUNAAT)
(Denmark)

JAN
MAYEN
(Nor.)

*Barents
Sea*

0   250   500 Miles

0   250   500 Kilometers

© GEOSYSTEMS GLOBAL CORP.

North

*L.
Onega*

*White
Sea*

• Murmansk

• Arkhangelsk

LAPLAND

ICELAND
• Reykjavík

Arctic Circle

Norwegian Sea

FINLAND

*L.
Ladoga*

FAROE
ISLANDS
(Den.)

SHETLAND
ISLANDS
(U.K.)

ATLANTIC

OCEAN

Trondheim •

SWEDEN

• Tampere

Gulf of Bothnia

• Turku

Helsinki •

• St. Petersburg

NORWAY

Bergen •

Oslo ⊛

ALAND
IS.
(Fin.)

⊛ Tallinn

RUSSIA

Stockholm ⊛

ESTONIA

Göteborg •

GOTLAND
(Swe.)

• Riga
LATVIA

Scotland

Glasgow •
Edinburgh •

*North
Sea*

Copenhagen ⊛ • Malmö

LITHUANIA
• Vilnius

• Minsk

Northern
Ireland

Belfast •
Newcastle •

BORNHOLM
(Den.)

RUSSIA
Kaliningrad •

BELARUS

• Homyel

Dublin •
UNITED
KINGDOM

• Leeds

DENMARK

Gdansk •

Warsaw ⊛

IRELAND

Liverpool •
Birmingham •

• Manchester

Hamburg •

Elbe

Berlin •

Oder

POLAND

• Kiev

Wales

England

NETHERLANDS
Amsterdam •

Rotterdam •

• Lodz

UKRAINE

Cardiff •

London •

Essen •
Brussels •

Cologne • Leipzig •

GERMANY

Dresden •

Katowice •

• Lviv

MOLDOVA

English Channel

BELGIUM

Bonn •
Frankfurt •

Prague •

Krakow •

• Chisinau

CHANNEL IS.
(U.K.)

LUXEMBOURG
Luxembourg •

CZECH REP.

Ostrava •

CARPATHIAN MOUNTAINS

Odesa •

Paris •

Seine

Strasbourg •

Rhine

Stuttgart •

Vienna •

SLOVAKIA

Bratislava ⊛

Budapest ⊛

Nantes •

Loire

Munich •

AUSTRIA

FRANCE

Bern ⊛
SWITZERLAND

Zürich •
LIECHTENSTEIN

HUNGARY

ROMANIA

Bucharest ⊛

• Constanta

*Bay
of
Biscay*

Lyon •

Rhône

ALPS

Milan •
Po

Ljubljana •
SLOVENIA
CROATIA

Zagreb •

Danube

• Varna

Bordeaux •

Turin •

Venice •

BOSNIA &
HERZEGOVINA

Belgrade •

BULGARIA

*Black
Sea*

Bilbao •

PYRENEES

Toulouse •
Marseille •

Genoa •
Nice •

APENNINES

Florence •

SAN
MARINO

Sarajevo •

Serbia
YUGOSLAVIA
Montenegro

Sofia •

Istanbul •

Porto •

MONACO

Tiber

F.Y.R. MAC.*

Zaragoza •

CORSICA
(Fr.)

VATICAN CITY

Rome •

Skopje •

PORTUGAL

Madrid ⊛

ANDORRA

Barcelona •

ITALY

Tiranë •

• Thessaloniki

ALBANIA

TURKEY

Lisbon •

SPAIN

Valencia •

Ebro

Naples •

GREECE

Tagus

Sevilla •

BALEARIC ISLANDS
(Sp.)

SARDINIA
(It.)

*Tyrrhenian
Sea*

Adriatic Sea

*Ionian
Sea*

Athens ⊛

Aegean Sea

Málaga •

*Strait of
Gibraltar*

Palermo •

SICILY
(It.)

• Catania

PELOPONNESUS

CRETE
(Gr.)

RHODES

MOROCCO

ALGERIA

TUNISIA

MALTA • Valletta

*Mediterranean
Sea*

LIBYA

*F.Y.R. MAC. - The Former Yugoslav Republic of Macedonia

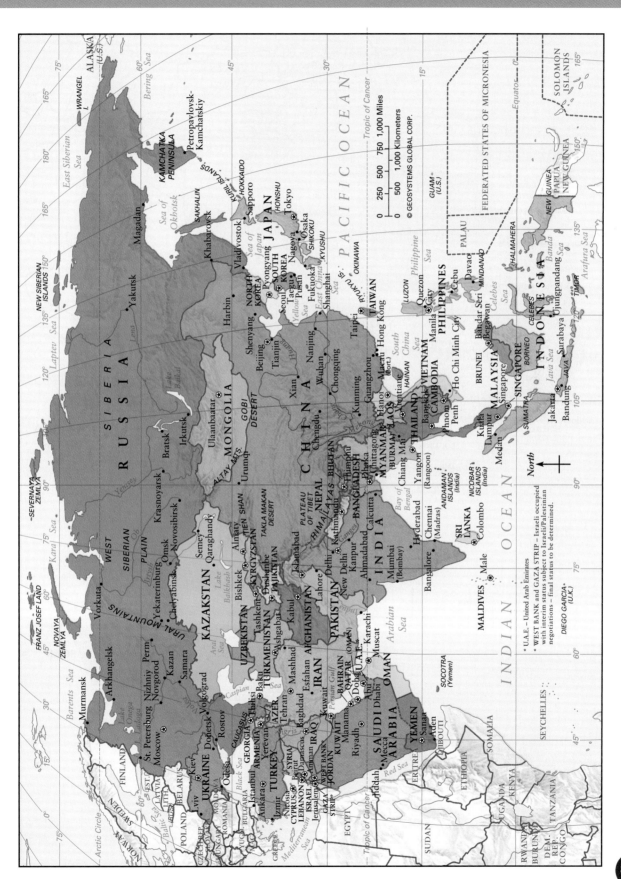

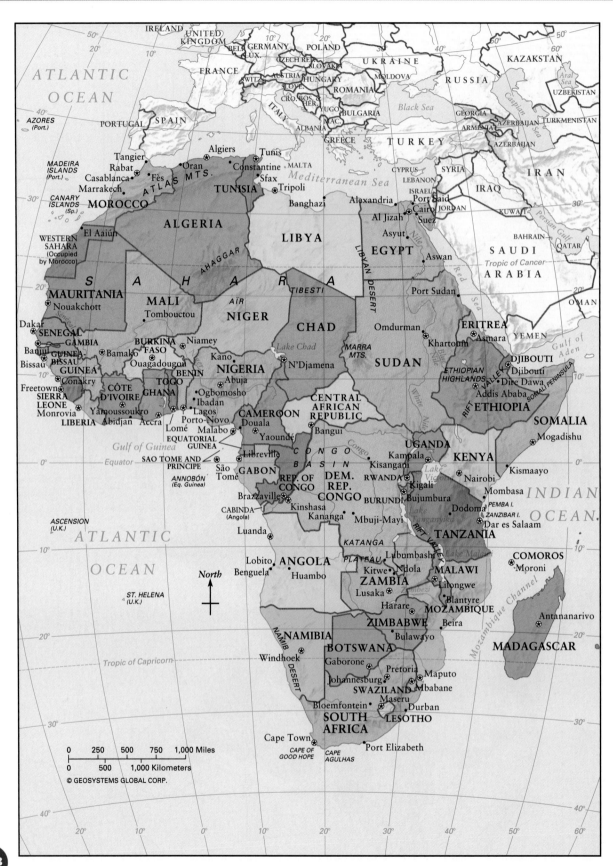

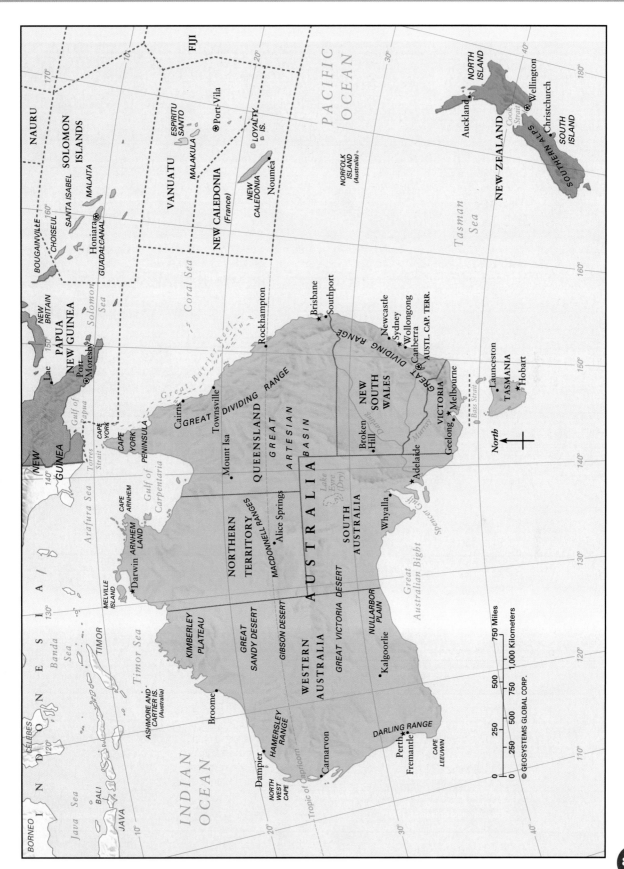

SUN

Mercury

Venus

Earth

Jupiter

Mars

Asteroid belt

Saturn

Uranus

Titan

Rhea

Tethys

Mimas

Dione

Saturn

Jupiter

Miranda

Triton

Nereid

Pluto

Neptune

Uranus

Ganymede

Note: Only major satellites are shown.

Sources: *The World Book Encyclopedia, 1993; The World Almanac, 1995;*
The New American Desk Encyclopedia, 1993;
Encyclopaedia Britannica, 1993.

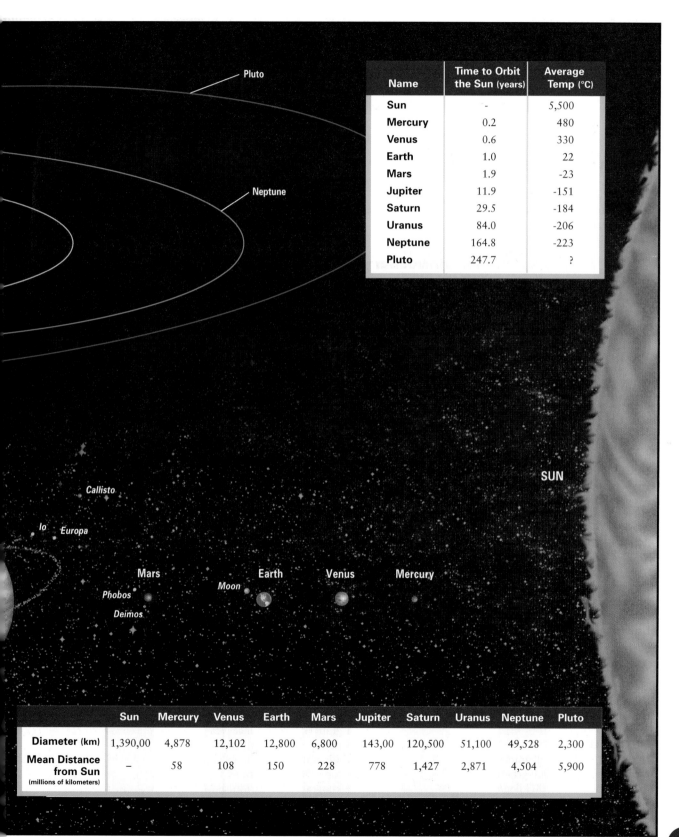

Name	Time to Orbit the Sun (years)	Average Temp (°C)
Sun	-	5,500
Mercury	0.2	480
Venus	0.6	330
Earth	1.0	22
Mars	1.9	-23
Jupiter	11.9	-151
Saturn	29.5	-184
Uranus	84.0	-206
Neptune	164.8	-223
Pluto	247.7	?

Pluto

Neptune

Callisto

Io Europa

Mars

Phobos

Deimos

Moon

Earth

Venus

Mercury

SUN

	Sun	Mercury	Venus	Earth	Mars	Jupiter	Saturn	Uranus	Neptune	Pluto
Diameter (km)	1,390,00	4,878	12,102	12,800	6,800	143,00	120,500	51,100	49,528	2,300
Mean Distance from Sun (millions of kilometers)	–	58	108	150	228	778	1,427	2,871	4,504	5,900

Tables of Weights and Measures and Conversion Tables

UNITS FOR MEASURING LENGTH, WIDTH, HEIGHT, DEPTH, AND DISTANCE

ENGLISH UNITS
1 foot (ft.) = 12 inches (in.)
1 yard (yd.) = 3 feet
1 mile (mi.) = 1,760 yards = 5,280 feet

METRIC UNITS
1 centimeter (cm) = 10 millimeters (mm)
1 decimeter (dm) = 10 centimeters
1 meter (m) = 100 centimeters
1 dekameter (dam) = 10 meters
1 hectometer (hm) = 100 meters
1 kilometer (km) = 1,000 meters

CONVERSION TABLE

Unit	Conversion Number
1 inch = 2.54 centimeters	
1 centimeter = 0.3937 inch	
1 foot = 0.3048 meter	
1 meter = 3.2808 feet	

Unit	Conversion Number
1 yard = 0.914 meter	
1 meter = 1.0936 yards	
1 mile = 1.609 kilometers	
1 kilometer = 0.621 mile	

CONVERSION FORMULA

To convert English units to metric units or metric units to English units, use the following formulas:

English to Metric: English Unit X *Conversion Number = Metric Unit
Example: 6 centimeters X 0.3937 (conversion number) = 2.36
6 centimeters = 2.36 inches
Metric to English: Metric Unit X *Conversion Number = English Unit
Example: 12 inches X 2.54 (conversion number) = 30.48
12 inches = 30.48 centimeters

*See Conversion Tables

UNITS FOR MEASURING AREA

ENGLISH UNITS
1 square foot (ft.^{2}) = 144 square inches (in.^{2})
1 square yard (yd.^{2}) = 9 square feet
1 acre (a.) = 43,560 square feet = 4,840 square yards

METRIC UNITS
1 square meter (m^2) = 10,000 square centimeters (cm^2)

CONVERSION TABLE

Unit	Conversion Number
1 square inch = 6.45 square centimeters	
1 square centimeter = 0.155 square inch	
1 square foot = 0.093 square meter	
1 square meter = 10.76 square feet	
1 square yard = 0.836 square meter	

Unit	Conversion Number
1 square meter = 1.196 square yards	
1 square mile = 2.59 square kilometers	
1 square kilometer = 0.386 square mile	

UNITS FOR MEASURING MASS OR WEIGHT

ENGLISH UNITS
1 pound (lb.) = 16 ounces (oz.)
1 ton (tn.) = 2,000 pounds

METRIC UNITS
1 gram (g) = 1,000 milligrams (mg)
1 kilogram (kg) = 1,000 grams
1 metric ton (t) = 1,000 kilograms

CONVERSION TABLE

Unit	Conversion Number
1 ounce = 28.35 grams	
1 gram = 0.0353 ounce	
1 pound = 0.4536 kilogram	
1 kilogram = 2.2 pounds	
1 ton = 907.2 kilograms	
1 kilogram = 0.001 ton	

ENGLISH UNITS
1 cubic foot (ft.³) = 1,728 cubic inches
1 cubic yard (yd.³) = 27 cubic feet

METRIC UNITS
1 cubic meter (m³) = 1,000,000 cubic centimeters (cm³)

CONVERSION TABLE

Unit	Conversion Number
1 cubic inch	= 16.387 cubic centimeters
1 cubic centimeter	= 0.061 cubic inch
1 cubic yard	= 0.765 cubic meter
1 cubic meter	= 1.31 cubic yards
1 cubic foot	= 0.028 cubic meter
1 cubic meter	= 35.315 cubic feet

ENGLISH UNITS

Liquid Measure
1 cup (c.) = 8 fluid ounces (oz.)
1 pint (pt.) = 2 cups
1 quart (qt.) = 2 pints
1 gallon (gal.) = 4 quarts

Dry Measure
2 pints = 1 quart
8 quarts = 1 peck (pk.)
4 pecks = 1 bushel (bu.)

METRIC UNITS
1 liter (L) = 1,000 milliliters (mL)
1 kiloliter (kL) = 1,000 liters

LIQUID VOLUME CONVERSION TABLE

Unit	Conversion Number
1 fluid ounce	= 29.57 milliliters
1 milliliter	= 0.0338 fluid ounce
1 quart	= 0.946 liter
1 liter	= 1.057 quarts
1 gallon	= 3.785 liters
1 liter	= 0.264 gallon

DRY MEASURE CONVERSION TABLE

Unit	Conversion Number
1 dry quart	= 1.101 liters
1 liter	= 0.908 dry quart
1 peck	= 8.810 liters
1 liter	= 0.114 peck
1 bushel	= 35.24 liters
1 liter	= 0.028 bushel

ENGLISH UNITS
Fahrenheit (F.)
Freezing Point of Water = 32°F.
Boiling Point of Water = 212°F.
Normal Body Temperature = 98.6°F.

METRIC UNITS
Celsius (C)
Freezing Point of Water = 0°C
Boiling Point of Water = 100°C
Normal Body Temperature = 37°C

CONVERSION FORMULA

To convert Fahrenheit to Celsius or Celsius to Fahrenheit, use the following formula:

Fahrenheit to Celsius:
Fahrenheit unit −32; then divide by 1.8.
Example: 80° − 32 = 48 ÷ 1.8 = 26.6°
80°F. = 26.6°C

Celsius to Fahrenheit:
Celsius unit × 1.8; then add 32.
Example: 20° × 1.8 = 36 + 32 = 68°
20° C = 68°F.

PHOTO CREDITS